D1716816

Principles of Sociology: Societal Issues & Behavior

Principles of Sociology: Societal Issues & Behavior

Kimberly Ortiz-Hartman, Psy.D., LMFT

SALEM PRESS

A Division of EBSCO Information Services, Inc.
Ipswich, Massachusetts

GREY HOUSE PUBLISHING

Cover photo: iStock/patpitchaya

For information contact Grey House Publishing/Salem Press, 4919 Route 22, PO Box 56, Amenia, NY 12501.

Principles of Sociology: Societal Issues & Behavior, published by Grey House Publishing, Inc., Amenia, NY, under exclusive license from EBSCO Information Services, Inc.

∞ The paper used in these volumes conforms to the American National Standard for Permanence of Paper for Printed Library Materials, Z39.48 1992 (R2009).

Publisher's Cataloging-In-Publication Data
(Prepared by The Donohue Group, Inc.)

Names: Ortiz-Hartman, Kimberly, editor.
Title: Principles of sociology. Societal issues & behavior / editor, Kimberly Ortiz-Hartman, Psy.D., LMFT.
Other Titles: Societal issues & behavior | Societal issues and behavior
Description: [First edition]. | Ipswich, Massachusetts : Salem Press, a division of EBSCO Information Services, Inc. ; [Amenia, New York] : Grey House Publishing, [2018] | Series: Principles of | Includes bibliographical references and index.
Identifiers: ISBN 9781642651133
Subjects: LCSH: Social problems. | Social interaction. | Sociology.
Classification: LCC HN18.3 .P753 2018 | DDC 306—dc23

Contents

Publisher's Note

Principles of Sociology: Societal Issues & Behavior is the third title in Salem's *Principles of Sociology* series. *Personal Relationships & Behavior* and *Group Relationships & Behavior,* were published by Salem Press this year. This series is intended to introduce students and researchers to the fundamentals of important and far-reaching topics in sociology using easy-to-understand language.

The field of sociology is vital in the world we live in today, and relevant in many social groupings and behaviors. This work includes categories such as "Deviance & Social Control," "Race & Ethnicity," "Sex, Gender & Sexuality," "Society & Technology," and "Sociology of Health & Medicine."

The entries in this volume are arranged in five major sections, and then A to Z within each, making it easy to find the topic of interest. Each entry includes the following:

- *Abstract* giving a brief introduction to the topic;
- *Overview* that presents key terms and concepts;
- Clear, concise *presentation of the topic,* including a discussion of applications and issues;
- Definitions of key *Terms & Concepts*;
- *Bibliography* for further reading.

The back matter in *Principles of Sociology: Societal Issues & Behavior* contains a thorough and valuable index.

Salem Press thanks the contributors, whose names are listed with each essay. Their diverse backgrounds include graduate degrees in a wide field of expertise and experience that allows them to offer information in language that is often more accessible than that of sociology specialists, whose explanations may be narrowly focused. A list of contributors' names follows this Publisher's Note.

The essays in this volume are written for a varied audience. Our goals include attention to clarity and avoidance of unnecessary jargon. For those readers who desire more specific information on any one topic, each essay includes a list of entries for further reading.

Principles of Sociology: Societal Issues & Behavior is, as are all Salem Press titles, available in print, as an e-book and on https://online.salempress.com.

Introduction

Welcome to volume three in the *Principles of Sociology* series. In this volume you will find topics that relate to society and behavior. It includes the following major sections: Deviance & Social Control, Race & Ethnicity, Society of Technology, Sociology of Health & Medicine, and Sex, Gender, & Sexuality. The articles in these categories explore how these topics affect American culture collectively on a widespread level.

The first section, Deviance & Social Control, contains articles exploring societal behavior that goes against the cultural norms, rules and/or laws. Deviant behavior has been seen since the beginning of time when people started coming together to live in a community. Although most people do follow the laws of the culture they belong to, there is always a group of outliers who go against the grain. These articles look to understanding why certain people do this, what the personal, social or economic gain is and why some take this further to engage in aggression and violence. Deviant behavior can be thought of as going against the norm, such as a person getting tattoos or piercing, which may be upsetting for family members but is not against any laws. Deviant behavior can be lying on your taxes or speeding. Deviant behavior can be joining a gang, known to be involved with selling drugs and violence toward others. Aggression, such as a bar fight, and violence such as kidnapping, rape or murder, are also categorized as deviant behavior. Therefore, deviant behavior has a broad range, with very different implications and impacts for those involved.

In this section you will see a breakdown of these different levels of deviant behavior with articles exploring each of them. Sociology theories look at deviant behavior and have attempted to explain the *why* of this behavior. These theories take into account biological, psychological, and social impacts and influences to find the breakdown of why some people fall into this category. There is a long-standing debate throughout these theories between nature and nurture. For example, if a young boy grows up where his entire family belongs to a gang, will this cause him to also join in this behavior? What if this same boy was adopted when he was two years old by a law-abiding family but still chooses to engage in deviant behavior? When we see people acting out when it seems to be against their environment, we start to look at more psychological variables. An example of this is a young man involved in a mass killing who appears to have come from a non-deviant family; the media seems to immediately question his mental health and his possible psychological issues. However, if a teenager from an oppressed group and community kills someone, generally his race and socioeconomic status tend to be highlighted and blamed for his behavior.

This section also explores how deviant behavior is dealt with in American society and the punishments in place to attempt to deter this behavior. Laws, police, court systems and the prison system are all explored in this section. Other important topics include gender differences, victim blaming, gang membership, racial impact on deviance and reactions, and the struggle of deviant behavior to be rehabilitated.

The second section is Race & Ethnicity. This section explores the sociological understanding of race as a socially constructed term to classify people. In American culture, race is often thought of in relation to oppression, violence and prejudice. The beginning of racial oppression and segregation in American culture starts with slavery. Slavery represented hundreds of years of the horrific treatment of black people, including violence and no chance for opportunity. Other races and ethnicities in American history have also experienced violence and extreme prejudice, such as Native Americans, people of Jewish ethnicity/ religion and in more current times, Muslim and Middle Eastern groups.

Following the end of slavery, oppression and subjugation continued in our culture with racial segregation, prejudice of different groups and inequality. Based on this historical mistreatment of certain groups, our modern-day culture continues to see inequalities in the treatment, acceptance, and social opportunities of these populations. This mistreatment ranges in impact and influence for different groups including internalized racism, institutional prejudice, racial profiling, segregation, income inequality, hate crimes and genocide. In this section theories explore the nature of prejudice and racism, such as the *Scapegoat Theory,* where racial minorities are blamed for negativity that they are not responsible for. An example of this would be politicians talking publicly about how immigrants are having a negative impact on citizens struggling to get jobs, when economists disagree with the truth of these statements.

The third section in this volume explores Society & Technology, which is a topic that continues to evolve. The technology in our society has exploded in recent times, expanding exponentially compared to decades before. With the birth of the world wide web in the 1990s we have seen advancements in all areas of societal communication, transportation, knowledge and opportunity. We are seeing this advancement causing a *digital divide,* where societies and people who can afford to move forward with technology are leaving behind those who are unable to keep up with technology. A child growing up in a technologically advanced culture has the ability for far more social, educational, and economic success in their lives as compared to someone growing up in a third world country in a rural farming community with no access to technology. This divide created by the digital boom is developing a much larger gap between cultures and societies than ever before.

The fourth section, Sociology of Health & Medicine, explores public health issues that are impacting a large population in American culture. A physical or mental health concern can be classified as a public health issue when it affects many people, it is studied for patterns and causes, and is researched for solutions. Issues such as obesity, suicide and substance abuse qualify as such public health concerns. In this section you will find articles that explore the public health issues themselves, the impact of these and societal reactions to them. For example, religion has a role in how health and medicine are utilized by people and how health issues are understood. Some religions believe that illnesses are punishments from God, while other religions do not condone utilizing certain medical treatments. Religion also gives us information about our mortality, which helps in making medical and end of life decisions. Other topics in this section include legal and ethical issues of life and death, and doctor-patient communication. These articles represent how as a society we are attempting to work together to remedy these problems and the complexities and challenges we are facing. Due to the power of the medical profession, people either choose to blindly follow all recommendations or find themselves rebelling and feeling a lack of trust for their medical professionals when the research they do themselves provides different information and they feel unheard, rushed, or dismissed by their medical professional. Unfortunately for American society, our overburdened, medical field often lacks time to provide comprehensive and compassionate care for all patients. This dynamic may push people towards more mistrust and finding other options for their medical care, such as seeking out *holistic providers.*

The last section in this volume is Sex, Gender & Sexuality. Although these concepts are naturally grouped together, it is important to understand the differences. *Sex* is the biological concept of having male or female chromosomes. The male or female sex is assigned at birth and is the first way we are identified in the world. *Gender* is known as the range of qualities including personality and behavior which is heavily influenced by society on the masculine/feminine continuum. Gender is thought of as being "performed" by people through our actions and behaviors. When our labeled sex differs from how we perform our gender people often struggle with support or acceptance. Men are thought of as having to behave in a traditionally masculine way, which may include acting strong, fixing things around the house, getting angry when upset instead of sad, or wanting to watch sports and drink beer. If a man engages in traditionally feminine behavior such as being unable to use tools to fix things, crying when upset and hating sports, he may experience negative feedback from others around him. When people perform their gender in opposition to their sex they may experience harassment, bullying, or even assault and violence. Men who engage in stereotypically feminine seeming behavior may experience a higher rate of disapproval than women who engage in more masculine behavior. Often these men are questioned about their sexuality, however gender and sexuality are not necessarily correlated with each other. In this section you will find also articles exploring gender in terms of domestic responsibilities, economic inequality, sexual orientation and societal treatment.

Sexuality is the attraction we feel towards others. Sex and performance of gender do not always give us information about someone's sexuality. Sexual orientation is decided based on self-identification, since it is an internalized feeling of attraction. Sexual orientation labels include heterosexual (attraction to the opposite sex), and LGBTQIA (Lesbian, Gay, Bisexual, Transgender, Queer/Questioning, Intersex, and

Biological & Psychological Theories of Deviance

ABSTRACT

Many psychological theories of deviance are inextricably linked to biological conditions of the human body and mind. Characteristics of deviants, such as poor self-control, impulsivity, aggression, lack of empathy, thrill-seeking, and poor reasoning and verbal skills, all may have a biological component that predisposes an individual to antisocial behavior. New scientific methodologies, such as magnetic resonance imaging (MRI), provide additional insights into the relationship between biology, psychology, and learning as they relate to deviance and criminality. Regardless of causation, poor parenting skills, child abuse, parental criminal history, and lower verbal IQ scores, all are important elements in the development of deviant and delinquent behaviors.

OVERVIEW

The debate of nature versus nurture is a central theme in any review of psychological theories of deviance. Is a person born bad, or is it by interacting with others that an individual fails to learn acceptable social behavior? In part, the answer to that question depends upon the focus one brings to the issue. Experts in genetics, neurology, and related biological sciences tend to develop perspectives based upon more innate physical qualities that impact human behavior. Social scientists and psychologists tend to focus on human interactions as a basis of social development. Some individual scholars view one factor as causal in terms of deviance and criminality, while others seek a more integrated theoretical analysis that looks at several factors. For example, although a detailed analysis of the causes of sexual offending is beyond the scope of this article, Ward and Beecher (2008) provide a useful integrated theory that includes genetic predisposition; adverse developmental experiences (such as child abuse, rejection); psychological dispositions/trait factors (interpersonal problems, mental disorders); social and cultural structures and process (sexism, masculinity, and other learned behaviors); and contextual factors (such as stress or intoxication). While their theoretical framework is related to sexual offending exclusively, it could also be helpful in the development of theories of violent crime in general. Thus, although the balance of this article looks at the various factors individually, it is important to appreciate the complexity and interconnectedness of biological and psychological theories of deviance and criminality.

Because so many factors pertaining to our physical existence impact our brains and emotional responses, some biological theories of deviance and criminality deserve mention in this look at psychological theories. Biochemical theories of deviance might consider how allergies, vitamin deficiencies, lead poisoning, hypoglycemia, low brain serotonin, alcohol consumption, or responses to drugs like Prozac, for example, could affect an individual's propensity toward deviant or criminal behavior. For example, studies on animals relate high levels of dopamine and norepinephrine to impulsive or reactive acts of aggression (Raine, 1995). It may be the case, then, that no one cause or condition explains criminal deviance.

FURTHER INSIGHTS

Biological Factors in Deviance

The Frontal Cortex

Studies of brain conditions and development also provide some compelling research on the development of antisocial behavior. Raine (1995) and her colleagues surveyed the literature and set forth two areas of the brain that may relate to antisocial behavior: the frontal cortex and the left hemisphere. The frontal cortex regulates aggression, self-control, social judgment, concentration, and intellectual flexibility, while the left hemisphere of the brain governs "functions of language, verbal comprehension, and expressive speech" (p. 53). Studies of adults and delinquent youth show lower verbal IQ scores, suggesting that they may have a left hemisphere dysfunction. Based on magnetic resonance imaging (MRI) studies, scientists believe that the brain of a juvenile is less developed than that of an adult, especially in the front lobe, which is responsible for executive, high order functioning, such as memory, planning, and inhibition. Bower and others suggested that this condition presents some juveniles with difficulties in "regulating aggression, long-range planning, mental flexibility, abstract thinking, the capacity to hold in mind related pieces of information, and perhaps moral judgment" (2004). In addition to the recent findings on children's apparently inherent diminished brain functioning capacity, MRI research suggests that exposure to violent video games and television might negatively impact frontal lobe development and function ("Playing With," 2003; Phillips, 2004). Because of these findings, advocates within the juvenile justice field, such as the Human Rights Watch, are pressuring politicians and judicial leaders to reconsider harsh, punitive measures when sentencing juvenile violent offenders.

Neurology

Neurology, the study of the nervous system, also may provide some insights into the psychological aspects of deviance and criminality. In their review of this literature, Raine and her colleagues point to two major areas of consideration based upon studies of psychopaths, defined as people who exhibit aggressive, violent thoughts and actions and who lack empathy (1995). "Arousal theory" suggests that "antisocial individuals are pathologically under-aroused physiologically, as indicated by low heart rate, low skin conductance, excessive slow-wave electroencephalographic (EEG) activity" (Raine, 1995, p. 52). Individuals with this condition are "less sensitive to the subtle cues required for learning prosocial behavior" and the condition may "impair the classic conditioning of emotional responses thought to be important in conscience formation and avoidance learning" (Raine, 1995, p. 52-53). Arguably, then, the violent behavior might be a mechanism for seeking stimulation or, in the alternative, the individual may not experience violence or stress as something negative and to be avoided. Similar arguments can be made in relation to the second theoretical framework discussed by Raine, "impulse/motivational systems analysis" (p. 51-52). Briefly stated, this theoretical framework argues that psychopaths have a heightened desire for rewards, along with a reduced perception of the risks of punishment. Arguably, this hyper-focus on "reward may also interfere with learning the cues that lead to punishment" (p. 52). Conversely, by being unable to feel anxiety and stress as it relates to punishment, these individuals have an increased likelihood of acting in antisocial or criminal ways.

Extraversion & Neuroticism

Another important look at the interplay between psychological and physiological causes of deviance was set forth by Eysenck in the late 1940s. Eysenck employed statistical analysis to personality studies and determined that high and low levels of two factors were at play in a person's likelihood of exhibiting deviant behavior: "extraversion," which was related to a person's ability to enjoy positive social events; and "neuroticism," which referred to a tendency to experience negative emotions. According to Eysenck's analysis, the neurotic extraverts were the most likely individuals to develop into criminals since they would have difficulty socializing with other children and, as a consequence, not learn acceptable social conduct or be able to adhere to it. Although counterintuitive, Eysenck argued that because the introverts' brain arousal was more active, they sought less stimulation from social or criminal conduct, while extroverts needed the stimulation of highly social or dangerous behaviors. In the 1970s, Eysenck added levels of "psychoticism" to his scale, arguing that psychotics exhibit aggressive, cold, and impersonal behavior that can lead to interpersonal conflicts and criminal conduct (Eysenck, 1989). Gottfredson and Hirschi (1990) criticized Eysenck's work, arguing that his personality dimensions overlapped conceptually and that they could not be measured independently from the behavior that they were meant to describe. Like so many other personality scales developed during the twentieth century, Eysenck and his colleagues had apparently included questions about criminal conduct and violence in their questionnaires, and they concluded that whichever traits the criminal respondents exhibited were proof of criminal tendencies.

Other Personality Traits

Another major contribution on personality traits was by Wilson and Herrnstein (1985). They concluded that individuals with criminal and violent personalities exhibited the following characteristics: assertiveness, fearlessness, aggressiveness, unconventionality, extroversion, poor socialization, psychopathy, schizophrenia, hypomania, hyperactivity, impulsiveness, and left-handedness. Other scales include lower empathy, risk taking, and an external locus of control as additional personality traits that evidence criminality (Gottfredson & Hirschi, 1990). Since questions on these scales related to past criminality and acts of violence, however, these studies fall into the same methodological problems of labeling individuals with criminal pasts as having criminal personality traits.

In their general theory of criminality, Gottfredson and Hirschi argued that self-control factors are the most powerful predictors of deviance and crime (1990). Committing a crime is easy, exciting, and offers immediate gratification. Similarly, it takes little or no planning and does not require any long term commitment or ongoing interpersonal negotiations. Finally, since criminals exhibit little empathy with or consideration for the needs of their victims, the resulting harm to the victim does not disrupt the perpetrator's criminal urges. Gottfredson and Hirschi suggested that two factors are related to an individual's inability to control their behavior: ineffective parenting and biology. Similarly, Hardwick has argued that although parental supervision plays an important role in the development of self-control, biological factors appear to play the most significant role in the relationship between deviance and self-control (2007).

In the theoretical frameworks discussed above, biological factors either exacerbated or diminished cues in such a manner as to cause antisocial or deviant behavior. In some ways, Freud's psychoanalytic theory of personality development describes a similar internal process, possibly because he was a neurophysiologist. According to Freud, human nature is inherently antisocial and lacks feelings of guilt, with sexual desire serving as the motivational force of the psyche. Freud labeled this psychological essence as the id. Through interactions with other human beings, a well-developed child forms a superego, or a moral conscience that helps him or her learn the parameters of acceptable social behavior. If the superego should become overdeveloped, according to Freud's theoretical framework, the individual exhibits an unhealthy desire for punishment. On the other hand, an underdeveloped superego fails to regulate the strong antisocial urges of the id. Negotiating between the id and the superego is the rational ego, which regulates the demands for instant gratification of the id with acceptable behavior (Vito, Maahs, & Holmes, 2006). Freud was focused on the internal process of psyche development, while the balance of the psychological theories of deviance discussed below focus on the interactions of the individual with others. In other words, the focus is turning to "nurture," or the lack thereof, as a cause of deviant behavior.

Psychological Disorders & Deviance

Numerous psychological disorders can lead to deviance and criminality. Passive aggressive disorder, for example, occurs when an individual buries feelings of resentment of an authority figure and then channels those feelings into other behaviors, such as procrastination, forgetfulness, or harmfulness that seems accidental ("Passive Aggressive," 2008). Impulse control disorders involve strong, sudden urges that the individual cannot control. These disorders may lead to pyromania (fire-setting), kleptomania (stealing), or aggressive and violent outbursts (intermittent explosive disorder) (Impulse Control Disorder, 2007). Borderline personality disorder involves extreme mood swings and difficulty controlling emotions and impulses. Individuals suffering a borderline episode may change their careers, friends, and lifestyle suddenly and act violently if he or she feels abandoned or betrayed (Borderline Personality Disorder, 2006). Cognitive disorders involve the mental processing of information. Individuals suffering from cognitive disorders may be confused, forgetful, and exhibit impaired awareness, reasoning, and judgment (Cognitive Disorders, 2006). Dissociative disorders "occur when people frequently escape reality by suppressing their memories or taking on other identities (Dissociative Disorders , 2008, p. 1). It is believed to be a coping mechanism when stress or trauma is unbearable. In rare instances, individuals develop dissociative identity disorder, which was formerly known as multiple personality disorder. In these instances, the individual has two or more distinct identities that control their thoughts and behaviors at different times. This condition is most frequently associated with extreme childhood trauma, such as sexual, emotional, or physical abuse.

People with antisocial personality disorder (APD) formerly were called sociopaths or psychopaths. Adolescents who have these same characteristics are labeled as having a conduct disorder. APD appears to occur in about 3 perent of the general population, and between 20 percent and 25 percent of the prison population. The personality characteristics of APD include a failure to conform to social norms, lying, cheating, stealing, exploiting and manipulating others, lack of remorse, absence of anxiety, self-centeredness, recklessness and impulsivity, and aggressiveness (Vito, 2006). These individuals can be superficially charming, but they have an inconsistent work history, poor judgment, and are financially irresponsible, sexually promiscuous, and irresponsible parents. Punishment does not seem to be effective as they cannot learn from past experiences and continuously exhibit poor judgment (Vito, 2006). Schizophrenia, attention deficit disorder, and some forms of psychosis, such as having hallucinations or delusions, may also play a role in deviance. All of the psychological disorders discussed above may have some biological component as well, such as a head injury, sleep deprivation, substance abuse, brain injury, or dementia.

Learning Theories of Crime

Although biological aspects play an important role in psychological theories of deviance, learning theories of crime have dominated the professional literature as well. The most prominent theoretical framework has been social learning theory. It holds that children can learn inappropriate or deviant forms of behavior, either through the modeling of negative behavior or through repeated reinforcement of negative behavior that thus increases its frequency. Consequently, many studies focus on parenting aspects of child rearing and criminality. Gottfredson and Hirschi offered that "all of the characteristics associated with low self-control tend to show themselves in the absence of nurturance, discipline, or training" (1990, p. 95). At a minimum, they argued, in order to teach self-control, a parent must be able to: "(1) monitor a child's behavior; (2) recognize deviant behavior when it occurs; and (3) punish such behavior" (p. 97). Unfortunately, many parents are not able to perform these responsibilities, possibly in part because they lack self-control themselves. One of the most telling aspects of this parenting research, for example, is that "the parents of delinquents are unusually likely to have criminal records themselves" (p. 97). Many of the interventions to reduce juvenile criminal rates, therefore, focus on teaching parenting skills in high-risk families and communities.

Similarly, Glueck and Glueck (1950) have argued that harsh and inconsistent parenting can lead to child delinquency. More specifically, if parents ignore inappropriate behavior, are inconsistent with punishment when it occurs (or threaten punishment but do not follow through with it), their children are more likely to engage in delinquent behavior as they grew older. Patterson argued that if parents effectively monitored, punished, and reinforced behaviors, their children would not become delinquent (1996). Wilson's study of delinquency in Birmingham, England, for example, concluded that when parents exercised "chaperonage" they significantly lowered the risk of their children becoming delinquent (1980). *Chaperonage* was defined as parents keeping a close watch on their children and sheltering them from negative aspects of neighborhood life. This was accomplished by escorting children to and from school and forbidding them to play with troublemakers. In her analysis, however, Judith Rich Harris argued that peer influences rather than parental behavior affect a child's long-term development toward delinquency (Gladwell, 1998).

From her studies of abused and neglected children, Widom concluded "that childhood victimization increases the likelihood of delinquency, adult criminality, and violent criminal behavior" (1992, p. 254). Widom followed child abuse victims for twenty years, along with a matched control group of individuals, and concluded that "being abused or neglected as a child increases a person's risk for an arrest as a juvenile by 53 percent, as an adult by 38 percent, and for a violent crime by 38 percent" (p. 255). Similarly, although males in general have a higher rate of criminal behavior than women, abused or neglected women in Widom's study faced a 77 percent greater risk of adult arrest than the women in the control group who did not face abuse or neglect (p. 256). In addition to being much more likely to commit violent offenses toward others, Widom's findings concluded that victims of childhood abuse and neglect were at a much greater risk of harming themselves as well. Surveying the role of neglect on language development, psychosocial development, empathic responsiveness, attention deficits, and poorer emotional stability, Widom also concluded that neglect—defined as intentionally failing to provide the material, medical, emotional, psychological, and educational resources necessary to a child's development—can have as significant a negative impact on a child as actual physical violence in terms of subsequent criminality.

Theoretically speaking, several explanations can be offered for a child learning antisocial behavior. In his theory of differential association, Edwin Sutherland argued that criminal behavior is learned through interactions with others. Just like any other learning process, the individual, through observation and training within intimate personal groups, learns the techniques, motivations, rationalizations, and attitudes of a criminal. The greater the frequency, duration, and intensity of the deviant contact, the greater the likelihood that an individual will engage in criminal conduct as an adult. Since young boys are more likely than young girls to be in gangs that engage in delinquent behavior, Sutherland's theory would explain why more men engage in criminal conduct than women. Although empirical studies of Sutherland's theory demonstrate its credibility as an explanation for some criminal behavior, it does not explain criminal conduct by individuals whose childhoods did not contain criminal influences.

VIEWPOINTS

Other Theories of Deviance

Another theory of deviance is called social control theory (Curran & Renzitti, 1994). It argues that strong attachments to social institutions such as the family, a church, or a school prevent the development of criminal delinquency. Unfortunately, close attachments to youth peers, especially for boys, may enhance the likelihood of deviant conduct.

Operant theory argues that behavior is learned by the consequences that it produces. Thus, criminal behavior is learned through a process of desirable consequences and infrequent punishment. The individual is conditioned to engage in repeated criminal conduct because it offers monetary reward, enhanced reputation, masculine credibility, and group identity reinforcement as some of its many reinforcing assets. If punishment is not seen as likely, swift, effective, and harsh, the learning or conditioning process fails to deter deviant behavior.

Cognitive psychological theories of deviance deal with the thought processes that influence behavior, and these too can be learned. Often criminals rationalize their conduct by arguing that they are not hurting anyone or that the victim "was asking for it." Through cognitive-behavioral programs, criminals are taught to develop empathy, moral reasoning, anger management, and self control (Vito, Maahs, & Holmes, 2006).

Theories of moral development are also associated with deviance. Kohlberg, who based is work on Piaget's, is the most prominent theoretician pertaining to moral development (1981). Kohlberg argued that ideal moral development occurred in six stages:

- At Stage 1, the individual blindly obeys authority figures in order to avoid punishment. At this level, the interests of others are not a consideration.
- Stage 2 involves furthering one's own interests and considering the interests of others only as a means to one's own ends.
- Stage 3 moral development involves moral reasoning and caring about others.
- Stage 4 has an even more developed sense of right versus wrong and a commitment to social institutions like family and community.
- Stage 5 moral decisions are driven by social contract as one weighs one's own concerns with legal principles and the common good.
- Stage 6 moral development bases decisions on universal, ethical principles, such as justice and human dignity, that span specific legal principles and cultural contexts.

Individuals' morality can develop throughout their lifetimes, according to Kohlberg, and not all individuals reach the later stages of development. Kohlberg has been criticized most effectively by Gilligan, who argued that his framework's focus on justice is a male-centered concern and does not take into account a female developmental focus on the ethics of caring about others (1977).

The intelligence scales used since the early 1990s are another prominent aspect of the psychology of deviance. Gottfredson and Hirschi provided an excellent review of the strengths and weaknesses of this discipline (1990). Early studies by Goddard found that criminals scored high on feeblemindedness, but when the tests were used on World War I draftees, the draftees also scored dismally. Ongoing criticisms have alleged that the tests contain age, class, gender, and ethnicity biases. One aspect of the testing that does seem to have some credibility is that criminals score lower on verbal IQ measurements. This finding is consistent with the brain imaging studies that evidence left hemisphere brain dysfunction in people with records of deviance, as mentioned above. It suggests that criminals may use less internal speech to analyze and plan their conduct. Having a higher verbal IQ helps one understand the consequences of one's actions and provides one with better reasoning skills. It also could be the case, however, that individuals with lower IQ scores are just not smart enough to avoid being caught, resulting in prison populations that test lower for verbal IQ than the general population. Individuals with learning disabilities, especially in reading, also may account for a higher percentage of the prison population, since they perform poorly in school, drop out, and may then become delinquent and eventually criminal.

CONCLUSION

Clearly, psychological theories of deviance and criminality are a complex mixture of biology and learning issues. With advances in scientific research techniques, such as MRIs, new explanations for deviant behavior are emerging in the literature. Professionals working in this realm have emphasized measurements, scales, testing, and other empirical methodologies since the early 1900s when psychological theories of deviance first emerged from the sociological and criminological literature. This trend is likely to continue.

TERMS & CONCEPTS

Delinquency: Unlawful or antisocial acts performed by individuals under the age of 18.

Empirical: Research based upon observation and measurement.

Neurology: The study of the nervous system.

Operant Theory: Operant theory argues that behavior is learned by the consequences that it produces. Thus, criminal behavior is learned through a process of desirable consequences and infrequent punishment.

Predisposition: A tendency or inclination toward a particular behavior or attitude.

Psychopathy: A severe personality disorder entailing antisocial thoughts and behavior.

Social Control Theory: Social control theory argues that strong attachments to social institutions such as the family, a church, or a school prevent the development of criminal delinquency. Unfortunately, close attachments to youth peers, especially for boys, may enhance the likelihood of deviant conduct.

Social Learning Theory: Social learning theory holds that children can learn inappropriate or deviant forms of behavior, either through the modeling of negative behavior or through repeated reinforcement of negative behavior that thus increases its frequency.

Bibliography

Akers, R., & Silverman, A. (2004). "Toward a social learning model of violence and terrorism." In M. Zahn, H.

Brownstein, & S. Jackson. (Eds.), *Violence: From theory to research.* Cincinnati, OH: Anderson.

"Borderline personality disorder." (2006). ivillage: http://yourtotalhealth.ivillage.com/borderline-personality-disorder.html

Bower, B. (2004, May 8). "Teen brains on trial: The science of neural development tangles with the juvenile death penalty." *Science News,* 165(19), 299-301.

"Cognitive disorders." (2006). ivillage: http://yourtotalhealth.ivillage.com/cognitivedisorders. html

Collins, R. (2008). *Violence: A micro-sociological theory.* Princeton, NJ: Princeton University Press.

Curran, D., & Renzitti, C. (1994). *Crime.* Boston, MA: Allyn and Bacon.

"Dissociative disorders." (2008). ivillage: http://your totalhealth.ivillage.com/dissociative-disorders. html

"Dissociative identity disorder." (2008). ivillage: http://yourtotalhealth.ivillage.com/ dissociative-identity-disorder.html

Eysenck, H. (1989). "Personality & criminality: A dispositional analysis." In, Laufer, W. and Adler, F., *Advances in Criminological Theory,* vol. 1. 89-110. New Brunswick, NJ: Transaction.

Gilligan, C. (1977). "In a different voice: Women's conception of self and morality." *Harvard Educational Review,* 47(4), 481-517.

Gladwell, M. (1998, August 17). "Do parents matter?" *The New Yorker,* 74 (24), 54-64. Gladwell.com: http://www.gladwell.com/pdf/parents. pdf

Glueck, S., & Glueck, E. (1950). *Unraveling juvenile delinquency.* Cambridge, MA: Harvard University Press.

Gottfredson, M., & Hirschi, T. (1990). *A general theory of crime.* Stanford, CA: Stanford University Press.

Hardwick, K. (2007). "Determining the source(s) of self control: Social and biological factors." Paper presented at the 2007 annual meeting of the American Society of Criminology, Atlanta, GA.: http://www.allacademic.com/meta/

Human Rights Watch. (2005). "The rest of their lives: Life without parole for child offender in the United States." http://www.hrw.org/en/reports/2005/10/11/rest-their-lives

"Impulse control disorders." (2007). ivillage: http://yourtotalhealth.ivillage.com/impulsecontrol-disorders.html.

Ingoldsby, E., Shaw, D., Windslow, E., Schonberg, M., Gilliom, M., & Criss, M. (2006, June). "Neighborhood disadvantage, parent-child conflict, neighborhood peer relationships, and early antisocial behavior problem trajectories." *Journal of Abnormal Child Psychology,* 34, 293-309.

Kohlberg, L. (1981). *Essays on moral development: The philosophy of moral development* (Vol. 1). New York: Harper & Row.

"Passive Aggressive." (2008). ivillage: http://yourtotal health.ivillage.com/passiveaggressive. html

Pals, H., & Kaplan, H. (2013). "Long-term effects of adolescent negative self-feelings on adult deviance: Moderated by neighborhood disadvantage, mediated by expectations." *American Journal of Criminal Justice, 38*(3), 348- 368.

Parnaby, P. F., & Buffone, S. (2013). "Darwin Meets the King: Blending Sociology and Evolutionary Psychology to Explain Police Deviance." *Canadian Review Of Sociology,* 50(4), 412-429.

Patterson, G. (1996). "Some characteristics of a developmental theory for early onset delinquency." In M. Lenzenweger & J. Haugaard (Eds.), *Frontiers of developmental psychopathology* (pp. 81-124). New York: Oxford University Press.

Phillips, H. (2004). "Mind-altering media." *New Scientist,* 194 (2600), 33-37.

"Playing with kids' minds?" (2003, Spring). *Medicine.* Indiana University School of Medicine http://www.medicine.indiana.edu/iu%5fmedicine/03%5fspring/articles/ kidsMinds.html

Posick, C., Farrell, A., & Swatt, M. L. (2013). *Do boys fight and girls cut? A general strain theory approach to gender and deviance. deviant behavior, 34*(9), 685-705.

Raine, A., Lencz, T., & Scerbo, A. (1995). "Antisocial behavior: Neuroimaging, neuropsychology, neurochemistry, and psychophysiology." In J. Ratey (Ed.), *Neuropsychiatry of personality disorders* (pp. 50-71). Oxford, UK: Blackwell.

Vito, G., Maahs, J., & Holmes, R. (2006). *Criminology: Theory, research, and practice* (2nd ed.). Sudbury, MA: Jones and Bartlett.

Ward, T., & Beech, A. (2008). "An integrated theory of sexual offending." In D. Laws, & W. O'Donohue (Eds.), *Sexual deviance: Theory, assessment and treatment* (2nd ed.) (pp. 21-36). New York: Guilford.

Widom, C. S. (1992). *The cycle of violence.* Washington, DC: The National Institute of Justice.

Widom, C. S. (2000). "Childhood victimization: Early adversity, later psychopathology." *National Institute of Justice Journal,* 242, 3-9. Washington, D. C.: The National Institute of Justice. Education Resources Information Center: http://eric. ed.gov/ERICWebPortal/custom/portlets/recordDetails/

Wilson, J.(1975). *Thinking about crime.* New York, NY: Basic.

Wilson, J., & Herrnstein, R. (1985). *Crime and Human Nature.* New York: Simon and Schuster.

Suggested Reading

Bartol, C., & Bartol, A. (2005). *Criminal behavior: A psychosocial approach.* Upper Saddle River, NJ: Pearson Education.

Blackburn, R. (1995). *The psychology of criminal conduct: Theory, research and practice* (2nd ed.). New York: John Wiley and Sons.

Blair, J., Mitchell, D., & Blair, K. (2005). *The psychopath: Emotion and the brain.* Oxford, UK: Blackwell.

Burke, P. (Ed.). (2006). *Contemporary social psychological theories.* Palo Alto, CA: Stanford University Press.

Canter, D., & Alison, L. (Eds.). (2000). *The social psychology of crime: Groups, teams, and networks.* Hampshire, UK: Ashgate.

De Block, A., & Adriaens, P. R. (2013). "Pathologizing sexual deviance: A history." *Journal of Sex Research, 50*(3/4), 276-298.

Feldman, P. (1993). *The psychology of crime: A social science textbook.* Cambridge, UK: Cambridge University Press.

Hollin, C. (1989). *Psychology and crime: Introduction to criminological psychology.* New York: Routledge.

Kaplan, H., & Johnson, R. (2001). *Social deviance: Testing a general theory.* New York: Springer.
McGuire, J. (2004). *Understanding psychology and crime: Perspectives on theory and action.* Berkshire, UK: Open University Press.
Pakes, F., & Winstone, J. (2007). *Psychology and crime: Understanding and tackling offending behavior.* Devon, UK: Willan.
Patrick, C. (Ed.). (2006). *Handbook of psychopathy.* New York: Guilford.
Prus, R. (2011). "Morality, deviance, and regulation: pragmatist motifs in Plato's republic and laws." *Qualitative Sociology Review,* 7(2), 1-44.
Ratey, J. (Ed.). (1995). *Neuropsychiatry of personality disorders.* Cambridge, UK: Blackwell.
Roeckelein, J. (Ed.). (2006). *Elsevier's dictionary of psychological theories.* Amsterdam: Elsevier.

Karen M. Harbeck, Ph.D., J.D.

CONFLICT THEORY & DEVIANCE

ABSTRACT

Deviance, the violation of dominant societal norms, is defined from a sociological perspective. The major theorists associated with conflict theory, including Karl Marx and Max Weber, are discussed. Class is established as the major element in deviance from a conflict perspective. How systems work to legitimate those in power is discussed, as well as the dominant norms members are expected to follow. White-collar crime is discussed, as is the prison-industrial complex. The article explores those who control the media, and looks at studies that negate the idea that class and wealth distribution is the source of deviance. A brief look at the major sociological perspective of structural functionalism and its arguments for the causes of deviance in societies is also included.

OVERVIEW

Defining Deviance

Deviance, according to sociologists, is defined as behavior or appearance that violates, or goes against, the norms of society. In every society, there are unwritten rules, called norms, and those who break those rules are considered deviant. But just being different is not what it is to be deviant. There are rare positions in societies, like being a famous baseball player, for instance, and it is not considered deviant to occupy these roles. Also, some very common behaviors are seen as deviant, like cheating on one's spouse. Deviance is not always criminal; one can be socially deviant by breaking the informal rules of a society. For example, a woman who doesn't shave her legs is considered deviant, but for such "odd" behaviors, people are often informally stigmatized in societies, rather than formally punished.

The dominant norms in American society can be directly traced to those who first established the United States: white Anglo-Saxon Protestant men. Consequently, the history of America has been a battle between the dominant norms of a relative few and the norms of various groups that challenge them. In any society, when minority groups start to accept the norms and values of the dominant group, it is called assimilation, or acculturation. All societies expect new members to take on the existing norms. Still, one of the ways societies change is for the dominant structure to adopt some parts of minority cultures. This has occurred in America regularly and is seen in our acceptance of music generally associated with African American culture, like rock and roll, which came out of the American South in the 1950s.

Sociologists recognize that it is very difficult, without training and awareness, to see these rules that define a society. So, one of the ways to see them more clearly is to notice them in relationship to another culture's norms. When you go on vacation or move to another country, it is then that your own norms become clearer. It is also possible to be trained to see these norms. One of the ways sociologists understand norms is to do norm breaching experiments. A researcher will go out into a social setting and intentionally break the rules and record the reaction of others (Garfinkel, 1967). Sociologists are looking for how others react to the norm breaching, attempting to judge what rules apply and how people are sanctioned, or rewarded or punished, for engaging in various behaviors.

Conflict Theory & Deviance

Conflict theorists see the social world as defined by those who have power in any society. The term "**conflict**" is used in this theory not because there is necessarily literal conflict between those who are in power and those who are not. Rather, this term is used to express a conflict of interest between the two groups; that is to say, what is beneficial for one group is not good for the other. For example, for a business owner who has wage laborers, it is *not* in his interest to raise wages. In fact, it is in his interest to keep wages as low as possible. But, naturally, it is in the interest of the worker to have higher wages. So, by definition, these two groups have a conflict of interest.

For the conflict theorist, those who have power, whether it is economic, political, or social, are the ones who define the norms of a society. Karl Marx is the sociological theorist who first identified the idea that those who have control over the production of goods and services, mainly in the form of wealth and ownership of property, have control over all information, and therefore, how those in the society think. For Marx, the capitalist economic system creates wider and wider disparities, or differences, between the rich and the poor. To fully understand Marx, one must see that one of the central tenets, or rules, in capitalism is to achieve wealth, ideally through profit. Marx tried to show that this tenet, and many others that define capitalism, were the most powerful in society; he believed the economic form of a society takes precedence over all other social institutions.

Karl Marx believed that the ideologies of a society, the belief systems upon which we depend in order to make sense of the world, were produced by the wealthy because they owned the means to communicate (Marx & Engels, 1976). Conflict theorists contend that those who hold wealth and power have an interest in insuring that the masses hold particular beliefs, like individualism and competition, because believing they could somehow achieve wealth and power keep those who are not in power from rebelling against the system of oppression. His earliest work focused on how those who hold wealth have the means to form and maintain our ideologies, or our core beliefs, and one of the most important aspects of this control of ideas is that people are not aware that it is happening to them. In order to make sure people don't rebel against the system of dominance, the ruling class is made legitimate by creating and sustaining ways of thinking that seem fair. An Italian Marxist, Antonio Gramsci, called this type of domination "cultural hegemony" (1971). An example of this might be that most Americans—even those who own very little property—believe ideas like competition or private property are simply the way things should be. Speaking out publicly in the United States against, say, private property, is being deviant. This type of social system is very successful because those who are not necessarily benefiting from it support it. Marx called this false consciousness.

Class & Crime

Most conflict theorists argue that inequalities based in class struggles are the reason for crime and deviance. In other words, capitalism creates a stratified, or layered, system because it requires inequality to insure there are workers willing to work for wages and produce goods and services. Owners do not work for wages, but co-opt a portion of the profit that workers create by making the product. Capitalism also produces a level of poverty and, therefore, powerlessness. In capitalism, members are driven to desire wealth, even though it is impossible for everyone to have wealth. This puts most of the members in a very precarious situation since not all members have access to wealth, but most members believe if they work hard enough they can achieve it. In order to access the labor market, or get a job, certain dominant norms must be followed. These norms are created and perpetuated by the owners, not the workers.

Max Weber, also a conflict theorist, did not agree with Marx that the economy was the most powerful social institution. For Weber, it is the systems of power and organization that define societies, adding that those who have power over others, defined as the ability to control others (Weber, 1947) are the source of inequality. Power may or maybe not exist because of unequal distributions of wealth. Economics is one source of inequality, with others being power and status. Weber, then, did not see economics as more important than other major social institutions like religion or politics.

Weber's position on deviance is not as clear as some of the other theorists, although he wrote briefly on the topic of anomie (Orru, 1989), which is a term that describes societies and individuals in a state of social disorder in which the norms are unclear, making it easier for people to be deviant. He did, however, see deviance as a path to social change. Weber's excellent study on religion and its power to effect social change, *The Protestant Ethic and the Spirit of Capitalism,* shows how Martin Luther's famous act of deviance against the Catholic Church in 1517 not only altered the direction of Western religions, it also created a landscape of possibility that was necessary for capitalism to thrive three centuries later.

Critical Theory

Sociologists are careful to note that crime is not the only form of deviance. A branch of conflict theory called critical theory concerns itself more directly with the enormous amount of social control that goes into keeping people from being, not just criminally deviant, but socially deviant. For these thinkers, those of us living in Western democratic systems are duped into believing we are free; however, most aspects of our lives are mechanized to the point of dehumanization. Critical theory holds that there is an elite group that defines the society and perpetuates the myth that we are a democratic structure. Under these circumstances, those who criticize the system must be controlled. Since we technically have freedoms such as speech and assembly, those who attempt to reveal the true system of power and oppression must be termed deviant. This is particularly true for anyone who questions the systems of authority. There are also subtle messages to those who are "odd" in behavior or thinking.

An example of this is atheism in the United States. A 2006 study showed that Americans fear atheists more than they fear Muslims; Americans are more likely to vote for a Muslim than an atheist (Edgell, Gerteis, & Hartmann,2006). About 10 percent of Americans are either atheist or agnostic. Europeans are much more likely to be atheist, with France reporting 40 percent atheism (Higgins, 2007). Critical theorists see religion as a powerful form of social control that is perpetuated by a system that benefits from limiting ideologies through insuring that beliefs that are not mainstream are considered dangerous and deviant.

Ideological State Apparatus

Marxist theorist Louis Althusser contended that the norms that benefit those in power are conveyed to people through ordinary life; in schools, at work, through mass media which encourages loyalty to the state, called ideological state apparatus. At its most oppressive, the state uses the police, the prison and judicial systems, the military to insure conformity to the system. But the ideal is to use the lesser system, because people are less aware of it and less likely to rebel against it. The objective for the dominant group is to maintain positions of power, and by having the ability to define norms in both everyday life as well as on a structural level insures they are able to define deviance.

White-collar Crime

The American sociologist Edwin Sutherland developed the term "criminology" in the 1930s to describe the study of deviance. His pioneering theory of deviance, Differential Association theory, argues that people learn to be deviant through the groups with which they associate, whether it is an urban street gang or a corporate banker. Sutherland's theory that deviance is learned was in reaction to the theories of the past that said deviance is psychological or pathological. Sutherland also developed the term 'white collar-crime' to describe the type of crime that is only possible because of the person's social and employment status. Sociologists have long argued that these crimes, committed almost entirely by the middle and upper classes, are not punishable to the same extent as what is called "street crime" or "garden crime," because the social structure and the way crime is defined is through the lens of the powerful. The United States Uniform Crime Report, the FBI's official database of reported crime, lists no white collar crimes, only violent and non-violent street crime. The losses in the United States in street crime are approximately $4 billion per year; the losses in white collar crime are more staggering. The saving and loan crisis of the 1980s is estimated at $300 to 500 billion, health care fraud is estimated at $100 to $400 annually, auto repair about $40 billion, securities fraud, $15 billion (Leap, 2007). White-collar crime is perceived as non-violent and committed by wayward, though still upstanding citizens.

Culture & Deviance

One of the most interesting sociologists to look at how capitalism works to keep out certain members is the French thinker Pierre Bourdieu. Bourdieu claims that in all societies, there are cultural norms that dominate. In order to gain status in any society, or any organization for that matter, people have to seem like they are one of the crowd. This includes all types of behavior: how to dress, how to speak, what music is important, which table utensils to use. To act like those who are members of the dominant group is to be able to "get your foot in the door," and Bourdieu calls this acquiring "cultural capital." Those who either refuse to behave or are not capable of behaving in these ways are considered deviant. Bourdieu's theory is in many ways based in Marx's, but he is different in a couple of significant ways. First, he believes that culture is the way societies, and therefore deviance, are defined. Marx believed that economics was the dominant factor in all societies to date. Bourdieu also holds that there are various types of capital (economic, social, symbolic) in any given social situation which can be accessed or denied. Marx believed that only wealth mattered.

Strain Theory

The American structural functionalist Robert Merton differed with Emile Durkheim about why certain groups tend to be deviant more than others. Where Durkheim claimed that deviance comes out of a lack of social order that is the result of a lack of cohesion, or common social bonds, Merton took ideas from conflict theory to create a theory that allows for deviance in the context of certain economic forms, in this case capitalism. Merton said that because the norms of capitalism include acquiring wealth, but all members don't have equal access to the workplace, some members are forced to deviate in order to fulfill this social expectation. Merton (1938) observed that the goals for those accumulating wealth and achieving status are the same for the majority of members, but not everyone has the same ability to achieve these goals legitimately. So, the means used to acquire wealth and status are what differs between groups. For example, people who are raised in poverty stricken neighborhoods in America do not get the same quality of public education as those who grow up in middle class or upper class neighborhoods. This means those in the lower classes don't have the skills to get into college or access the job market, but there is still the desire to have wealth and status. So, the result is to, for example, sell illegal drugs, which allows a certain level of status and wealth. For Merton, using deviant means to fulfill goals that are otherwise inaccessible to the members is what causes a certain type of deviance in capitalist societies he calls "non-conformists."

APPLICATIONS

Media Power

In 2008, six major corporations own more the 95 percent of all media in the United States, according to the public interest group the Center for Public Integrity (http://projects.publicintegrity.org/). These corporations have other economic interests that keep them from being self-critical; for example, NBC, the largest media conglomerate in the world, also owns General Electric which manufactures appliances. But General Electric also makes jet engines for fighter planes and in the early 1990s was found guilty of defrauding the U.S. Department of Defense and later corruption charges were brought against the company in relation to jet engines sold to Israel. Conflict theorists point out that it is not in the interest of NBC or GE to publicly discuss their role in defense contracts or our country's foreign policy and will actively discourage people from questioning the possible relationship. One way of doing this is to label those who are opposed to foreign policy, particularly in regards to defense, deviants.

This was done quite successfully in the 1960s, when large groups of students protested American foreign policy. To emphasize the deviant nature of the student's behavior, the media often paired students who were opposed to the war in Viet Nam with extremely radical groups like the Black Panthers, a group developed to bring public awareness to the institutional oppression of African Americans in general, and specifically point out the level of police brutality against blacks. By creating the possibility that a relationship could exist between students voicing their freedom speech peacefully and the quasi-militant group that was working to alleviate oppression among blacks in a much more radical way, many who might have been willing to publicly oppose the war were coerced into being quiet.

The Prison-Industrial Complex

Another way of using the lens of the conflict theorist to understand deviance in society is to look at who goes to prison and why. The prison system in the United States has grown to over 2 million over the past two decades. Each day, 138 people are added to the system in some way. A surprisingly high percentage, between 30 and 55 percent, depending on the state, are black men (Leach & Cheney, 2002). A conflict perspective sees this disproportionate number of men of color incarcerated as more evidence that some members of society are deviant simply by being of a particular ethnicity and unwilling to assimilate. Dominated groups are expected to assimilate, or buy into the dominant society, and when they don't they are penalized.

A 1998 report on the problem of soaring prison population is Eric Schlosser's "The Prison-Industrial Complex." The work looks at the idea that the public supports legislation that allows an increase in mandatory sentencing because most Americans fear males of color. Mandatory minimum sentencing puts thousands in prison for crimes who would never have been sent there under earlier laws. This is coupled with the privatization of some prisons across the country, run by the rules of capitalism, and operating solely for profit. So, the inmates produce goods in private prisons, but the prisons are not required to pay inmates minimum wage (LeBaron, 2008). The implication is that it benefits the owners of the prisons to have more prisoners. Legislators are seduced by lobbyists for the private prisons, and they all benefit from the incarceration of thousands of minority group members and poor people.

The description of the prison system as the "prison-industrial complex" comes from the phrase "military-industrial complex," coined by President Dwight D. Eisenhower to describe the powerful relationship between corporations, the government, and the military. The three entities had become, after World War II, so intertwined and dependent on one another that their interests had all become the same: to promote fear among Americans (in the case of the late 1950s of the Soviet Union) in order to continue public support of increased armaments and a larger defense budget. Eric Schlosser's (1998) work on the prison-industrial complex takes the same notions of fear and the interconnectedness of legitimated leaders and critiques the penal system in America.

VIEWPOINTS

Structural Functionalism

There are several responses to the conflict perspective's claim that deviance lies in class and power relationships. From a structural-functionalist perspective, the best explanation for deviance is a lack of social bonds, or cohesion, among members. That is, some groups are less likely to buy into the dominant normative structure, or assimilate, and so they don't have the sense of unity that is necessary to insure that they don't violate others in the society. Structural functionalists look to the social order, or how harmonious social relationships are and how well the social institutions, like the family or religion, are working in society. While deviance is part of all healthy, normal societies, when levels of deviance grow too great, it is a sign of anomie. This is often attributed to the complex societal states that come from industrialized societies; levels of deviance are much lower in preindustrial cultures. The main theorist to look at deviance from this perspective is Emile Durkheim.

There are also several studies that show class is not the explanation for deviance. A 1980 study showed there was no relationship between class and delinquency among high school youths. Krohn, et. al. (1980) looked at upper, middle, and working class schools and found no support for the idea that class is a predictor of deviance among youth. Still another study looked at the relationship between class and deviance across three states and found no relationship between class and deviance. Tittle and Villemez (1977) contend that the dominant theories in the field of deviance that are bound to the idea that class is the source of deviance must be reconsidered.

CONCLUSION

Deviance, from a conflict perspective, can be best explained by looking at the systems of wealth, power, and domination. It is not only that those who have control over wealth are in positions of power to determine who is deviant. They also are in positions to define what deviance is, both criminally and socially. Reactions against these definitions of deviance are then met with further accusations of being deviant. In this way, the systems of power in any society can be maintained and those who occupy the prestigious positions are legitimated.

TERMS & CONCEPTS

Anomie: A social condition in which norms and values are not clearly defined, thus producing higher rates of deviance.

Assimilation: Members not already part of the dominant cultural group, either immigrants or oppressed groups within the society, take on the norms or the dominant group.

Criminology: A term coined by Edwin Sutherland in the 1930s, it is the study of deviance.

Cultural Capital: The benefits that come from understanding and adhering to the dominant norms and values in any society or organization.

Differential Association: A theory of deviance developed by Edwin Sutherland in which one learns to be deviant because of one'marxs associates.

Hegemony: The control of ideas through the legitimation of a group of elites who benefit from these ideas.

Ideological State Apparatus: The use of a legitimate government as the means of insuring that those in power maintain their status; this occurs in everyday life ideally, but under the worst circumstances, will be implemented by force.

False Consciousness: To support a system of domination, while being exploited by it.

Prison-industrial complex: An explanation for the enormous rise in the prison population in America; it assumes there is a relationship between legislators and private prisons owners, who both benefit from large numbers of people incarcerated.

Stratification: The unequal hierarchy of classes into which groups of people are categorized based on socioeconomic status, race, gender or education.

Uniform Crime Report: The FBI's annual official crime report.

Bibliography

Agnew, R. (2013). "When criminal coping is likely: An extension of general strain theory." *Deviant Behavior, 34*(8), 653–670.

Center for Public Integrity. *Well connected: Tracking the players in telecommunications, media and technology.* http://projects.publicintegrity.org/

Edgell, P., Gerteis, J., & Hartmann, D. (2006). "Atheists as 'other': Moral boundaries and cultural membership in American society." *American Sociological Review, 71*(2), 211–234.

Garfinkel, H. (1967). *Studies in ethnomethology.* Englewood Cliffs, NY: Prentice-Hall.

Gramsci, A. (1971). *Selections from prison notebooks.* London: New Left Books.

Higgins, A. (2007, April 12). "As religious strife grows, Europe's atheists seize pulpit." *Wall Street Journal - Eastern Edition, 249* (85), A1–A11.

Konty, M. (2006). "Of deviance and deviants." *Sociological Spectrum, 26* (6), 621–631.

Krohn, M., Akers, R., Radosevich, M., & Lanza-Kaduce, L. (1980). "Social status and deviance: Class context of school, social status and delinquent behavior." *Criminology 18* (3), 303–318.

Leach, M. & Cheney, D. (2002). *The prisons handbook.* Hook, England: Waterside Press.

Leap, T. (2007). *Dishonest dollars: The dynamics of white-collar crime.* Ithaca, NY: Cornell University Press.

LeBaron, G. (2008). "Captive labour and the free market: Prisoners and production in the USA." *Capital & Class, Summer* (95), 59–81.

Lombardo, R. M. (2010). "The hegemonic narrative and the social construction of deviance: The case of the Black Hand." *Trends in Organized Crime, 13*(4), 263–282.

Marx, K., & Engels, F. (1976). "The German ideology." In *The collected works of Marx and Engels,* vol. 5. New York: International.

Merton, R. (1938). "Social structure and anomie." *American Sociological Review, 3*(5), 672–682.

Orrü, M. (1989). "Weber on Anomie." *Sociological Forum, 4* (2), 263.

Pearce, F. (2006). "Crimes of the Powerful: A theoretical and empirical elaboration." *Conference Papers—American Society of Criminology*.

Tittle, C., & Villemez, W. (1977). "Social class and criminality." *Social Forces 56* (2), 474–502.

Schlosser, E. (1998). "The prison-industrial complex." *Atlantic Monthly, 282* (6), 51–72.

Weber, M. (1958). *The Protestant ethic and the spirit of capitalism.* New York: Scribner's.

Zembroski, D. (2011). "Sociological theories of crime and delinquency." *Journal of Human Behavior in the Social Environment, 21*(3), 240–254.

Suggested Reading

Antonaccio, O., Tittle, C. R., Botchkovar, E., & Kranidiotis, M. (2010). "The correlates of crime and deviance: Additional evidence." *Journal of Research in Crime & Delinquency, 47*(3), 297–328.

Becker, H. S. (1968). *Outsiders: Studies in the sociology of deviance.* Glenscoe, IL: Free Press.

Huck, J. L., Lee, D. R., Bowen, K. N., Spraitz, J. D., & Bowers, J. H. (2012). "Specifying the dynamic relationships of general strain, coping, and young adult crime." *Western Criminology Review, 13*(2), 25–45.

Lesieur, H. R. (1979). "Book review-essays." *Criminal Justice Review 4* (1), 95–100

Rosenfeld, R. (1989). "Robert Merton's contributions to the sociology of deviance." *Sociological Inquiry, 59* (4), 453–466.

Wright, M. (2008). *Making good: Prisons, punishment and beyond.* Hook, England: Waterside Press.

Heidi Goar, M.A.

Control Theory of Deviance

ABSTRACT

An overview of control theory of deviance is provided beginning with a general review of social control followed by brief explanations of specific theories of social control. The development of social control theory is displayed through the review of Sykes and Matza's techniques of neutralization, Matza's Drift theory, Reckless' Containment theory, Gottfredson and Hirschi's low self control theory and ending with the more popular social bond theory developed earlier by Hirschi. Social implications of social control theory are provided. Social control theory generally assumes that the connection people have to each other and to society prevents people from engaging in deviant behavior. Without the presence of social control, society would not exist as we know it. Social control theories aid in our understanding of why most people do not behave in deviant ways most of the time.

OVERVIEW

Control theory of deviance is important to sociology because it aids in our understanding of deviant human behavior. Control theories generally assume that all members of society are motivated to satisfy their needs and wants by whatever means possible. Thus, most interesting to control theorists is why so many people conform to norms and values of society. Put another way, control theories aim to determine why most members of society follow rules, do what is expected of them, and generally are well behaved. While other theories of deviance may also contribute to our understanding of why deviance occurs, control theories have proven to be reliable predictors of conformity: when people do not commit deviant behavior. Control theories suggest that there is opportunity for people to be deviant but more often than not people choose not to be deviant. Control theories are amotivational. They assume all people desire the excitement and thrill of deviant acts. In this sense control theories suggest that socialization prevents one from committing deviant acts.

Contemporary social control theories developed from the work of early social control theorists such as Reiss (1951), Toby (1957), and Nye (1958). Reiss suggested that belief systems were more important in controlling human behavior than formal norms (laws). Contemporary social control theories build upon Reiss' suggestion. Through the process of socialization, the individual develops a bond with society. Social control theories best account for the patterns we see in juvenile delinquency. Various opportunities to commit deviant acts are created by mere temptations, peers, and other factors. According to control theories, the ready availability of these opportunities is not adequate to explain why people participate in deviant behaviors. The opportunity to commit deviant acts does not provide causation. Control theories suggest that inadequate controlling forces determine whether people behave in deviant behaviors.

Social control theories have developed into either a macro-social perspective or a micro-social perspective. As with other social theories, the macro-social perspective is used to explain patterns occurring in formal social systems such as the criminal justice system, law development and enforcement, nongovernmental organizations, and governmental and economic entities. The micro-social control perspective relies on the informal social system to explain why people refrain from committing deviant acts.

FURTHER INSIGHTS

Related Theories

Several social control theories have been developed since Reiss's work in 1951. Control theory (also known as social bond theory), developed by Travis Hirschi (1969), and low self-control theory, developed by Gottfredson and Hirschi, are the two more popular control theories of deviance: Hirschi's control theory has been used in sociology to describe individuals' conforming behavior tendencies. Gottfredson and Hirschi's low self-control theory is a general theory of crime in which the low self-control is generally due to ineffective parenting. It is important to note that there are many forms of control theory. Before reviewing each of these more popular theories, we will first explain a few lessoften used approaches to control theory of deviance: Sykes and Matza's neutralization theory, Matza's drift theory and Reckless' containment theory.

Neutralization Theory: Sykes & Matza

Gresham Sykes and David Matza (1957) developed the theory of neutralization based upon the arguments and justifications provided by persons known to commit deviant acts. These theorists suggested that delinquents were more similar than dissimilar to nondelinquents, because delinquents comply with social expectations most of the time, as do nondelinquents. They suggested that people who participate in deviant behavior more often than not conform to societal expectations. One can justify participation in deviant behavior by waiving or suspending the rules of society using a technique of neutralization. Techniques of neutralization can take various forms. People can justify their deviant acts by claiming they could not help themselves. They merely deny responsibility. Another technique is to convey an attitude that the deviant act did not result in any harm or injury and thus the behavior is irrelevant. Similarly, people can deny that there was any real victim. Essentially, the argument here is that the target of the deviant behavior got what they deserved. A less similar technique is to basically tell the people judging them or claiming that their behavior was deviant they have no right to criticize. Sykes and Matza refer to this as "condemn the condemners." Another technique explained by Sykes and Matza is where people appeal to higher loyalties. People might claim their moral obligation was to do the act with people important to them or for people who are important to them.

They clarify that when people are in their adolescent and young adult years they are most likely to use the techniques of neutralization. Sykes and Matza highlight that adolescents and young adults do not undergo new socialization in middle adulthood that reduces the use of neutralization techniques; rather, they proffer that even in adolescent and young adult years a foundation of morality exists. As people move into their middle and late adult years they become less likely to use techniques of neutralization.

Drift Theory: Matza

Matza moved on to develop drift theory in 1964. The theory is based upon the pattern people have of shifting between conforming behavior and nonconforming behavior. The theory rests upon the premise that conforming and nonconforming people believe in the moral guidelines in society. Matza concluded that people use the techniques of neutralization to waive the moral guidelines. He founded drift theory based upon the patterns of delinquents to express guilt over deviant acts, to express high regard for conforming people, to have a set of guidelines as to whom they can victimize, and to typically conform to society's moral guidelines.

Containment Theory: Reckless

Walter Reckless developed containment theory in the 1960s. Containment theory explains people's conformity with societal expectations using a complex interplay between inner and outer pulls and pushes to deviate that are counterbalanced by containment. Containment can also derive from inner and outer sources. An internal containment may be related to having a positive self-image and an outer containment could be the awareness that discipline by another person may follow the deviant act. Inner containment generally involves a positive self-concept, goals in line with societal expectations, frustration tolerance, and longterm belief in societal norms. Inner containment may result from socialization within the family and outer containment may result from strong relationships with people who profess generally conventional values and behaviors. The pulls and pushes to deviate also can derive from inner and outer sources. Inner push factors can be related to bad family experiences, hostility, boredom, etc. Outer pull factors could be from peer pressure to deviate or other sources of outside suggestion. Reckless suggested that in order for the continued existence of society, society must have conforming members (Reckless, 1967).

Low Self-Control Theory: Gottfredson & Hirschi

Low self-control theory of deviance was proposed by Gottfredson and Hirschi (1990). As a general theory of crime, it aims to explain most crime in society. They argue that the lower one's level of self-control, the more likely one is to participate in criminal activity. They suggest strongly that the reason for low self-control is ineffective parenting. They explain that effective parenting is focused on concern for the child, recognizing deviant behavior, punishing deviant behavior, and rewarding appropriate behavior. When effective parenting is practiced, children and adults will develop high levels of self-control and thus resist temptations to participate in deviant behavior. Persons with low self-control have characteristics of being overly physical, insensitive, impulsive, and exhibit high risk-taking behaviors. Persons with low self-control emanate such characteristics in all types of activities in which they participate, including criminal and analogous acts.

This theory accounts for the onset of deviant behavior: low self-control. But it does not explain the aging-out of crime because, it says, once the person is deviant with low self-control, that is the way the person will remain over the life course. However, Gottfredson and Hirschi suggest that the low self-control follows a similar pattern to aging out of crime, and thus their theory does explain the aging out of crime.

Gottfredson and Hirschi's low self-control theory has received some criticism from scholars. Akers (1999) assails their work by claiming that key terms are not clearly defined and operationalized. Akers suggests the result is that low self-control and a propensity for deviant behavior are inseparable. In spite of the possible internal inconsistency in the theory, some research has found support for the theory.

Social Bonding Theory: Hirschi

Control theory has two basic levels: internal and external. The internal controls are the most relied upon by society to limit deviant behavior. Control theory indicates that social ties influence our inclinations to partake in deviant behavior (Michener, DeLamater, & Myers, 2004). Travis Hirschi developed social bond theory, which relies upon internal mechanisms of social control. In other words, individuals conform to society's norms when the individual's social bonds are stronger, while delinquent behavior and analogous behaviors occur when social bonds are weak. Hirschi (1969), probably the most influential figure of control theory, describes four components of the social bond: attachment, commitment, involvement, and belief.

Hirschi further describes delinquency in his book *Causes of Delinquency* (1969), while also contrasting control theories, strain theories, and differential association. Hirschi asserts that the more bonded one is to society, the less likely one is to commit criminal/deviant behavior. Bonding theory states that attachment, commitment, involvement, and belief are the determining factors in whether one is constrained from deviant acts. His theory assumes one moral or value code. Delinquents defy these values because their attachments to society are weak. Bond theory suggests that delinquents reject the social norms and beliefs of society.

Social bond theory explains deviant behavior by focusing on peoples' bond to society. The bond could consist of caring about other people, having concern about time invested into goals and projects such as athletic or academic pursuits, buying into the use of control mechanisms such as police/law enforcement and moral convictions, and the degree to which one has concern about the broader community.

Hirschi's Four Components

Hirschi's social bond theory has four primary components:

- Attachment (one's interest in others),
- Commitment (the time, energy, and effort one puts on conventional actions/others),
- Involvement (the amount of activities involving society/civic duties/family, school, etc.), and
- Belief (respect for law, people, institutions).

Hirschi's control theory aimed to explain not only deviance but conformity as well. As stated previously, social bonding theory explains a high amount of juvenile delinquency. However, it is less able to predict adult criminality. There may be methodological reasons for social bonding theory not explaining as much variation in adult deviant behavior. The latent variables of the social bond are not as uniformly defined in research on adult deviant behavior as they are on juvenile delinquency research. For example, in research on adolescent behaviors, the elements of the bond are usually defined as amount of involvement in school activities, hours spent on homework or with parents/ friends, feelings of closeness to parents, and respect for law enforcement officers. The indicators of the latent social bond elements are not so uniformly defined when researchers examine adult criminality. The latent constructs are the same across the life course, but how researchers operationally define the terms varies greatly when adult samples are used. Thus, support for social bond theory is less consistent when adult samples are used in research (Hirschi, 1969).

VIEWPOINTS

Social bond theory has been widely tested by criminologists. The overall results vary, with some scholars finding support for the theory and other scholars failing to find support for social bond theory. Control theory, however, has received support in sociological research. In research on family structure and deviant behavior, Rankin and Kern (1994) concluded that the two-parent family structure resulted in less deviant behavior. Krohn and Massey (1980) concluded that social bonds are more related to minor delinquent acts than more serious delinquency. Kendall (2004) concluded that the probability of crime increases when social bonds are weak. Weaker support of social bond theory was found by Akers and Lee (1998), who concluded that both social bonds and social learning theories mediated the relationship between age and marijuana use. Support of social bond theory is usually found using research samples composed of adolescent research subjects. Other theories are occasionally better predictors of juvenile crime (see Akers & Lee, 1998). The pattern of researchers more often finding support for social bond theory using adolescent research participants may be related to the operationalizaton of the elements of the bond as previously discussed. Researchers have found support for social bond theory using elderly research participants when elements of the bond are operationalized differently (see, for example, Akers, LaGreca, & Sellers, 1988).

Hirschi's methods and techniques have been criticized. Even with that criticism, however, his theory of social control does tend to contribute to our ability to predict delinquency. One critique is that Hirschi does not clarify the mechanisms by which one fails to bond or loses the bond. Another critique is that at some point in life, one is either bonded or not bonded. The theory does not leave much room for social bonding later in life.

Implications of Control Theory of Deviance

The social implications of research on control theory is that early childhood intervention is needed that enhances the individual's bond to society. Socialization is important for the continued existence of society as we know it. Mentoring and activities and programs to help develop participation and buy-in to the values of society could develop from policy informed by social control theory. Additional programs could focus on family empowerment and increased social support for families and incorporate parenting classes, and a third type of program may further investigate issues of chemical or medical intervention.

CONCLUSION

There are several approaches to social control theory. While none have been completely discarded by the discipline, Travis Hirschi's social bond theory has undergone more scholarly tests than other social control theories of deviance. Even after Hirschi and Gottfredson later developed the theory of low self- control, a general theory of crime, the original theory developed by Hirschi still receives more recognition in the field of sociology. The concepts and the assumptions of some of the earliest social control theorists remain fundamental to the more contemporary theories of social control. The elements of social control theory that have proven to be reliable predictors of juvenile delinquency are involvement, commitment, and attachment. While testing social control theories among adult samples has proven more challenging than among juvenile samples, the field of sociology is actively applying social control theories to adult deviant behaviors. Key theorists such as Hirschi, Gottfredson, and others continue to build upon the current applications of control theories of deviance. Social control theories have proven useful in predicting deviant behavior, and it is unclear if other types of theories will consistently provide more insight into deviance. While other types of theories also provide insight into deviant behavior, social control theories are widely known and accepted as plausible explanations of human behavior.

TERMS & CONCEPTS

Attachment: One of four elements of Hirschi's social control theory. It involves the level of an individual's closeness and emotional connectedness to people in their lives. The greater one's attachment, the less likely one is to participate in deviant behavior.

Belief: One of four elements of Hirschi's social control theory. It involves the level of an individual's agreement with the norms, morals, and values of society and the extent to which society has the right to enforce those norms, morals, and values. The greater one's belief, the less likely one is to participate in deviant behavior.

Commitment: One of four elements of Hirschi's social control theory. It involves the level of an individual's participation in the community. It is measured in a variety of ways, including participation in school activities (academic and extracurricular) and other aspects of the community. The greater one's commitment, the less likely one is to participate in deviant behavior.

Deviance: Occurs when an individual violates the norms, values, or laws of society. Most deviant behavior occurs in the adolescent and young adult years. The majority of deviant acts do not involve violation of formal norms (laws). However, most of the research on deviance focuses on juveniles' violations of the law (delinquency). Deviance is studied by a variety of subfields in sociology, including criminology, social psychology, and others.

Involvement: One of four elements of Hirschi's social control theory. It involves the level of an individual's time spent on community activities. The more an individual's time is spent on conventional activities, the less time one has to violate the norms and laws of society. The greater one's involvement, the less likely one is to participate in deviant behavior.

Social Bond: A concept used by Hirschi in the development of social control theory. He proposed that the social bond is comprised of four elements: attachment, involvement, commitment, and belief. He postulated that individuals with higher levels of social bond are restrained from participating in deviant behavior.

Social Control: The effort of society to limit the behaviors of people in the society. Society uses two main approaches to limit the peoples' behaviors. The vast majority of peoples' behaviors are limited by informal techniques such as parents' socialization of children; i.e., parents conveying guidelines for acceptable behavior and motivating children to comply. Society less frequently relies on formal mechanisms to limit peoples' behavior. The behaviors enforced by formal systems of control are considered more serious violations of the norms, values, and beliefs of society including homicide, assault, theft, and other crimes.

Techniques of Neutralization: A concept used by Sykes and Matza in the development of their social control theory of deviance. According to Sykes and Matza, individuals who participate in deviant behavior justify it by providing arguments such as denying there was a victim, condemning the condemners, and asserting just rewards.

Bibliography

Akers, R. L., & Lee, G. (1999) "Age, social learning, and social bonding in adolescent substance use." *Deviant Behavior, 20* (1), 1–25.

Akers, R. L., LaGreca, A. J., & Sellers, C. (1988). "Theoretical perspectives on deviant behavior among the elderly." In B. McCarthy & R. Langworthy (Eds.), *Older Offenders: Perspectives in Criminology & Criminal Justice.* (35–50).

Bouffard, J. A., & Rice, S. K. (2011). "The influence of the social bond on self-control at the moment of decision: Testing Hirschi's redefinition of self-control." *American Journal of Criminal Justice, 36*(2), 138–157.

Fitzgerald, C. S. (2011). "Historical theories of crime and delinquency." *Journal of Human Behavior in the Social Environment, 21*(3), 297–311.

Gottfredson, M., & Hirschi, T. (1990). *A general theory of crime.* Stanford, CA: Stanford University Press.

Hirschi, T. (1969). *Causes of delinquency.* Berkeley: University of California Press.

Kendall, D. (2004). *Sociology in our times* (4th ed.). Belmont, CA: Wadsworth.

Krohn, M. D., & Massey, J. L. (1980). "Social control and delinquent behavior: An examination of the elements of the social bond." *Sociological Quarterly, 21* (4), 529–544.

Marganski, A. (2013). "The criminological scale of affectional attachment: A measure of Hirschi's construct of attachment in a variety of close interpersonal relationships as a source of social control." *Internet Journal of Criminology,* 1–16.

Matza, D. (1964). *Delinquency and drift.* New York: John Wiley & Sons, 1964.

Michener, H., DeLamater, J., & Myers, D. (2004.). *Social psychology* (5th ed.). Belmont, CA: Wadsworth.

Nye, F. I. (1958). *Family relationships and delinquent behavior.* New York: John Wiley.

Rankin, J. H., & Kern, R. (1994). "Parental attachments and delinquency." *Criminology, 32*(4), 495–515.

Reckless, W. (1967). *The crime problem.* New York: Appleton-Century-Crofts.

Reiss, A., Jr. (1951). "Delinquency as the failure of personal and social controls." *American Sociological Review 16,* 196–207.

Sykes, G. M., & Matza, D. (1957). "Techniques of neutralization: A theory of delinquency." *American Sociological Review, 22*(6), 664–670.

Toby, J. (1957). "Social disorganization and stake in conformity: complementary factors in the predatory behavior of hoodlums." *Journal of Criminal Law, Criminology, and Police Science, 48*(1), 12–17.

Suggested Reading

Booth, J., Farrell, A., & Varano, S. (2008). "Social control, serious delinquency, and risky behavior: A gendered analysis." *Crime & Delinquency, 54*(3), 423–456.

Burton, V. S., Cullen, F. T., Evans, T. D., Alarid, L. F., & Dunaway, R. G. (1998). "Gender self-control and crime." *Journal of Research in Crime & Delinquency; 35*(2), 123–148.

Cheung, N., & Cheung, Y. (2008). "Self-control, social factors, and delinquency: A test of the general theory of crime among adolescents in Hong Kong." *Journal of Youth & Adolescence 37*(4), 412–430.

Peguero, A. A., Popp, A., Latimore, T., Shekarkhar, Z., & Koo, D. J. (2011). "Social control theory and school misbehavior: Examining the role of race and ethnicity." *Youth Violence & Juvenile Justice, 9*(3), 259–275.

Preparata, G. (2013). "Suburbia's 'crime experts': The neoconservatism of control theory and the ethos of crime." *Critical Criminology, 21*(1), 73–86.

Qiu, M. (2012). "'It's not her fault!': Miley Cyrus, fan culture and the neutralization of deviance." *Yale Journal of Sociology,* 953–996.

Donna Holland, Ph.D.

CORRECTIONAL THEORIES

ABSTRACT

This paper looks at correctional theories through the sociological lens. These theories look at the institutions and structures of punishment, how they are justified, and how well they accomplish what they claim. There is an initial look at deviance and crime as part of normal, healthy societies, establishing the need for all societies to have a means to impose social control on members who commit crimes. Explanations of deviance and the resulting response are explored historically. Forms of negative sanction, or punishment, used in the United States are considered. Various studies looking at the success of the current system and some criticisms of mainstream approaches to punishment are also discussed.

OVERVIEW

Correctional theory studies how and why we punish people in society. These theories look at the institutions and structures of punishment, how they are justified, and how well they accomplish what they claim. The complexity of how we punish people in societies means that this field is very wide and, ideally, requires a general understanding of deviance, social order, law enforcement strategies, and social control. Correctional theories focus mainly on the means of social control, and in the United States these have included monetary fines, incarceration, capital punishment, and the newly developing alternative sentencing programs, including community service and restorative justice programs. Because this arm of sociology is so broad, the thinkers that have contributed to it also include psychologists, anthropologists, historians, and biologists.

Deviance

For someone to be deviant, there must be a rule to break. Put another way, it is not possible to have deviance in a society if there are no rules (called norms in sociology) to be broken. Structural-functionalist Emile Durkheim, one of the classical theorists in sociology, was careful to point out that all normal, healthy societies have deviance. Norms, and therefore deviance, to a structural-functionalist, have several very important purposes:

- They help us to define what our society is and how to live in it;
- They help us insure sense of cohesion, or common social bonds, because we share certain values and norms; and
- They show us what we should and should not do.

Deviants, those members who break the rules, and the negative sanctions, or punishments, applied to them, have a deterrent effect on the compliant members, reinforcing why they should conform to the dominant norms.

For Durkheim, the level of deviance in a society reflects how cohesive the society is. In complex, industrialized societies, there is often a sense of normlessness and confusion that comes from either unclear rules or members being too individualized or too self-interested to go along with all the rules. Durkheim calls this sense of normlessness "anomie." Many theorists agree with Durkheim that a lack of clear rules contributes to deviance.

Robert Merton, an American functionalist, agreed with Durkheim about the effect unclear rules have on a society and its members. But Merton's ideas differ from Durkheim's in that he recognized that some social structures, in this case capitalism, do not provide the same opportunities for everyone to be successful. Merton points out that in American society, most members value wealth because it is a central element in capitalism, and yet all members don't have the same access to wealth. So, some members engage in deviant behavior in order to fulfill the social expectation of achieving wealth. In other words, the goals are the same for most of the members, but the means to accessing the goals are not equal.

History of Modern Corrections

Every correctional theory makes certain assumptions about why there is deviance in a society, and what to do about. Most current correctional theories hold the assumption that deviants should be punished, but also can be reformed or rehabilitated. This way of punishing people in society is relatively new to the social world, and this is well established by the French historian Michel Foucault (1975) in his groundbreaking book investigating the birth of the modern prison system. In this work, Foucault starts by describing the pre-Enlightenment punishment before the early eighteenth century; often public forms of punishment were designed to shame and terrorize the deviant. There was no attempt to allow the deviant a chance for retribution, or pay back society or the victim, or to rehabilitate or bring the criminal back into society.

The modern prison system, developed in the mid-1700s and fully implemented by the early 1800s, was aimed at creating a more humane system. Its advocates argued that the system of torture and public humiliation that characterized the medieval period was antiquated and did not work, but most importantly, it was cruel and dehumanizing. They wanted to develop a system that reflected new and progressive ideas that were seen in other social institutions, like the enlightened governing bodies, novel ways of thinking about the economy, and the powerful critiques of religion. The American judicial and legal systems are historically embedded in Enlightenment ideals, although recently other influences have been a part of their definitions.

The work of social scientists has, in many ways, been the basis for these systems of negative sanctions applied to criminals. There are, of course, other factors that go into how punishment is meted out, like religion or economics. But, sociological theories have historically dominated, and are still employed, to help determine how to punish whom for what offense.

The earliest modern theories of corrections were determined by the earliest modern explanations for deviance. The classical school in criminology is based in the work of Enlightenment thinkers, mainly, Jeremy Bentham and Cesare Beccaria. Bentham, a philosopher and social reformer who despised the idea of "natural law" because he said it served those in power, said laws were good or bad based on the utilitarian principle of "the greatest good for the greatest number." Rules, he said, should be aimed at making the greatest number of people happy. But individuals want to maximize their own pleasure and minimize pain, so they could deviate if the rewards for doing so outweighed the costs of getting caught. Bentham thought that deviants were people who made poor calculations; they were not immoral. Punishments should be just harsh enough to discourage those who were not rational enough to make a self-interested beneficial calculation, but not harsher than needed to deter crime. Bentham's utilitarian principles were the basis for his famous plans for a penitentiary, called the "panopticon." This was a circular building with spokes coming out from a central guard tower. This meant that the prisoners could not see whether the guard was watching them or not, but would always have the sense of being watched. Only two prisons were built using these plans, one in 1825 in Pittsburgh, and one in the 1920s in Statesville, Illinois (Clear, Cole & Reisig, 2005). The system was not considered further.

Italian philosopher and politician, Cesare Beccaria wrote one of the most powerful and widely utilized critiques of the penal system as it was employed during the eighteenth century. A humanist, he rejected any use of the death penalty because, first, it is not the right of the state to determine who will die, and second, because it is neither useful, nor does it enhance public security. Other aspects of Beccaria's reformist ideas were:

- Punishment should be preventative, not retributive (out of vengeance),
- The punishment should fit the crime,
- Crime prevention is insured by making the punishment a known certainty, not through harshness, and
- Punishment should be prompt (Sitze, 2008).

In the early 1800s, America began erecting institutions of all types, not only prisons, but asylums, orphanages, and reformatories. This was a response to a rapidly growing crime rate explained by the lack of social cohesion, which was due to the huge numbers of immigrants. In other words, so many different types of people had come to the United States so rapidly that there lacked the common bonds that keep people from deviating (Harcourt, 2006). By the mid-twentieth century, the rate of institutionalization (including prison, asylums, reformatories, etc.) was almost 650 per 100,000 (Harcourt, 2006). Bear in mind that the development of institutions to this extent was not considered inhumane, and was an attempt to provide a controlled environment for deviants of different types. Erving Goffman (1961), a Canadian sociologist, defines these places of complete confinement as "total institutions," designed to provide a place to systematically remove certain members and control every aspect of their lives.

Differential Association Theory

In the 1930s, sociologist Edwin Sutherland, who coined the term *riminology* to describe the study of deviance, developed a theory claiming deviance is a learned behavior, not pathological. Sutherland's theory, called differential association, argues that one is not born deviant; rather one learns to be deviant just as one learns anything else, through socialization. Socialization is a process of coming to understand a culture, and internalizing its norms and values. Sutherland's theorydemands a look at the social structure, instead of an individual's personality or genetics. He says that within groups, people learn deviant behavior and this knowledge is used to the extent that there is the opportunity to use it. So, one learns to be a plumber, a lawyer, a bank robber, or an embezzler all in the same way. For example, the best single predictor of drug use is association with friends who use drugs (Spohn & Holleran, 2002). Sutherland also says what motivates the criminal is the same thing that motivates the noncriminal, and in American society that is wealth and status. The strength of Sutherland's theory is found in his work on white-collar crime. Many previous theorists surmised that deviance was due to poverty and that it was rational for those who could not access wealth and status to attempt to do so, even if that meant breaking the rules. But this does not explain white-collar crime, which is crime committed by middle and upper-middle class members, generally through their occupational statuses. Proponents of differential association argue that the best way to discourage deviance is to allow the deviant access to status and wealth and access to a different group association (Gaylord & Galliher, 1988).

Labeling Theory

Related to Sutherland's differential association theory is labeling theory. Howard Becker, an interactionist theorist, developed the theory in the 1960s that our sense of self lies in our interpretation of a collective, social definition of how we define ourselves. Becker said that if a behavior is labeled deviant, those who commit those acts are punished for being deviant, they then see themselves as deviant and, in this way, the greater society has contributed to the creation of deviance. These types of stigmas, or social labels, are applied not only to the criminally deviant, but also to social deviants, such as those defined as mentally ill (Becker, 1997).

Both labeling theorists and proponents of differential association argue that incarceration exacerbates, or makes worse, the problem of deviance. The best way to handle deviance is to make opportunities for conformity to norms available to deviants, as well as allowing them the opportunities to redefine themselves. They advocate for alternative sentencing that keeps the offender from being exposed to other deviants, as well as the greater stigma associated with imprisonment. These were the theories that drove the prison reform movement of the 1960s and 70s, which advocated for rehabilitation and which was supported by local, state, and federal governments through funding for education, mental health programs, drug rehabilitation, and other reforms.

APPLICATIONS

Forms of Punishment

Criminologists call all the programs employed to rehabilitate and reduce recidivism rates, notions of who is deviant and why, and theories of social control, a body of literature called the "What Works" literature (Hubbard, 2006, p. 44). There are four categories of punishment in the United States penal system based on what works:

- Monetary fines,
- Incarceration,
- The death penalty, and
- Community service.

Generally, punishment is determined based on the social perception of how serious the crime is, which is measured by how destructive it is to society. This means that the death penalty is reserved for the worst criminals, incarceration is used for a wide range of deviants, from those who break state-set marijuana laws to those who commit murder, monetary fines are used for white-collar criminals and those offenses that seem less dangerous to the overall society (like speeding), and community service, a relatively innovative program for the American judicial system, is used in efforts to reestablish connections between deviants and the community.

Monetary Fines

Monetary fines are penalties in which payment is made to the court. Most state and federal statutes in the United States provide for the ability of the judge to impose monetary fines. This punishment is not commonly used in punishing street crime (versus white-collar crime) because the offender often doesn't have the means to pay and may, therefore, encourage more crime in order to pay the fine. But fines are a common punishment for minor offenses like violations of traffic laws, and white-collar crime, although public outrage has forced sentencing changes for white-collar crimes in the face of decades of light punishments.

Incarceration

Incarceration is defined as being placed in a federal or state prison, or a local jail. According to the Bureau of Justice Statistics (BJS), in 2006, there were 2,299,116 people incarcerated in the United States, an increase of 1.8% from the year before, but less than the average 2.6% increase over the last six years. Thus, there are 509 people imprisoned in America per 100,000. Per 100,000 black men, there are 4,618; per 100,000 Hispanic men there are 1,747; per 100,000 white men, there are 773 in prison. Violent crimes account for about half of the offenses (U.S. Department of Justice, n.d.a.). The chances of being rearrested, or recidivism, within three years of release is about two-thirds, and the chances of being reconvicted is about 50% (U.S. Department of Justice, 2007).

For 2011, the BJS reports that there were 1,504,104 inmates incarcerated in state or federal correctional facilities in the United States, with 492 people imprisoned per 100,000 (Carson, 2013). The BJS also estimates that the 2011 imprisonment rate per 100,000 black men was 3,023; per 100,000 Hispanic men, 1,238; and per 100,000 white men, 478 (Carson & Sabol, 2012).

Capital Punishment

Capital punishment, or the death penalty, is punishment for the highest crimes (such as murder and treason), which vary from state to state in the United States Capital punishment is not used in every state, with twelve states disallowing it for state crimes. If a federal law is broken, it can be imposed even if the state has made it illegal. According the Bureau of Justice Statistics, 42 people were executed in the United States in 2006, all were men, 28 were white, 14 were black. There are 3,328 people on death row, a decrease of 17 from the previous year. The bureau has statistics for executions since 1930, when 155 people were executed. The number peaked in 1935 with 199, and was made illegal in 1968. It was reinstated in 1976, but numbers of executions did significantly rise until the 1980s, after which it has subsequently deceased (U.S. Department of Justice, n.d.b.). The BJS reports that by the end of 2012, nine states executed 43 inmates. By the end of 2011, there were 3,082 death row inmates, of which 55 percent were white and 42 percent were black; 387 death row inmates were Hispanic (Snell, 2013).

America is an oddity among Western industrialized nations in its acceptance and practice of capital punishment. The European Union will not accept any country if it employs the death penalty. Use of this punishment in the United States has almost no evidence of preventing crime, and yet about 70% of Americans support the death penalty, though this is decreasing. Sidanius, et al. (2006) investigated this paradox. They suggest that instead of people supporting the death penalty because they either believe it is a deterrent to crime, meaning it is preventative, or they believe the criminals should "pay" for their crime, people support it because they think those on death row are inferior to them. Using the social dominance theory, or the idea that a society is made up of hierarchies in which some people are members of the dominant group, some hold that they are superior to the others and can be afforded privileges.

Community Service

Community service has been used for about 40 years. Community service is considered an alternate sentence and is designed to help the offender pay back society, as well as make connections in the community. The offender might work for a local non-profit, serve a community organization, clean parks or other public spaces, assist the elderly, and so on. There are several reasons community service has been popular. First, as the incarceration rate has continued to increase and the cost is becoming prohibitive, it has been considered a cost-saving alternative for nonviolent and young criminals. Second, with the recidivism rate at about two-thirds, alternatives to exposing nonviolent and young criminals to more hardened criminals are being explored. Third, community service has a positive reputation in other countries, particularly in Europe.

One of the reasons community service has gained so much attention is the finding that incarceration is not effective in reducing crime. Using data from 1993, Spohn and Holleran (2002) showed that imprisonment does not reduce the chances that someone convicted of a felony will return to prison. In fact, incarceration increases the chances of reoffending and sooner. Those placed on probation were less likely to reoffend, and, for those convicted of drug crimes, this effect was even more pronounced. This type of research has garnered popular support for community service, with 75% of Americans in support of a combination of community service and paying restitution to make the society safer (Maguire & Pastore, 1997).

While community service has been used since the 1960s in the United States, a 2006 study showed that it may not have the results it claims, particularly in reducing recidivism rates. Community service, in this study, showed more effective only when the offender completed the service. Community service was effective, though, in reducing prison costs and overcrowding (Bouffard & Moftic, 2006).

Using Correctional Theories in the Field

Correctional theories are used to determine who to punish and what form that punishment will take. One of the greatest challenges for the US judicial system has been the preferential sentencing treatment of white-collar criminals; historically white-collar criminals are not punished to the same extent as street criminals. White-collar crimes, by definition, are committed by the relatively privileged; they are crimes that arise out of opportunity, mainly through occupation. Recalling the earlier discussion of how deviance is created through the creation of laws, most white-collar crime laws were passed either in the 1920s (antitrust laws), 1930s (social welfare laws), or in the 1960s (consumer protection laws). The FBI does not have an accurate means to collect data about white-collar crime, with the main claim being that it fails to "keep up with the changing face of crime and criminal activity" (Barnett, n.d., p. 2). Between 1997 and 1999, white-collar crime made up 3.8% of crimes reported to the FBI (Barnett, n.d.), but the Justice Department says it has no accurate way of determining the percent of white collar crime in America.

Another way correctional theories are used is in reconsidering the viability of outdated theories. For example, one cutting edge issue in corrections is research done on genetics that places into question many of the theories that rely on socialization as an explanation for deviance. Work on deviance has become more sophisticated as the science of genetics has become so advanced. The 1930s reaction to the biological determinism of Lombroso may need to be reconsidered in light of some of the latest work on DNA. A Finnish study (Johansson, et al. (2008), using a classic twin pairing to study 938 men found that tendency toward sexual coercion, or rape, was tied to genetics. Most of the literature explaining deviance over the past century has been aimed at negating the earliest claims that genes are factors in deviance. This study found that for those who engage in sexual coercion, 26% of this is found to be genetic, with the other 72% being learned behavior, or environmental.

Restorative Justice

Correctional theories are being used in the revamping of the system that includes employing punishments that insure victims are considered, called restorative justice. As mentioned earlier, our current correctional theories are embedded in the enlightenment ideas of reason, and that emotion should not be used when employing punishment. For some, we must reinvent justice to consider the emotions of the victims of crimes, and allow offenders to be aware of the impact they have had on individuals and on society at large. In this model, the term "emotionally intelligent justice" is used to describe a new paradigm of corrections that uses restorative justice, biomedical mental health treatments for offenders, programs to make justice officials more aware of the emotional impact of their words on citizens, and programs to help justice officials manage their own emotions (Sherman, 2003).

VIEWPOINTS

One of the greatest criticisms of the judicial system is the dramatic rise in the prison population between the late twentieth century and early twenty-first century to over two million incarcerated, and that this rate is fueled by both the privatization of prisons, and the general fear of dark-skinned men in American society (Schlosser, 1998). But one study shows that institutionalization in some type of confinement, was higher in the 1950s than in the mid-2000s. Harcourt (2006) found that, if all total institutions were added to the prison rate, the number of incarcerated was higher in 1955 than it was at the time of the study, at 640 per 100,000 aged over 15. Moreover, this study found that homicide rates ebbed and flowed with the number of those institutionalized (Harcourt). This study found that, if all total institutions were added to the prison rate, the numbers of incarcerated was higher in 1955 than at the time of the study, at 640 per 100,000 aged over 15. Moreover, this study found that homicides rates ebbed and flowed with the number of those institutionalized. Finally, this study showed that the murder and institutionalization rates mirror one another, if all institutions are included in the calculation. In other words, the more people institutionalized, the lower the murder rate and vice versa.

There are several perspectives that suggest that the early twenty-first century approach to corrections is inadequate. First, there are some studies that criticize the assumption that deviants are those who are dramatically disconnected from the social world, and therefore have a sense of worthlessness; some work shows the opposite. For those who have suggested that deviance is the result of a lack of connectedness and this creates a lower sense of self esteem, this study found just the opposite (Hubbard, 2006). In fact, low self-esteem was not an explanation for deviance among African Americans; the opposite was true. That is, for blacks the higher the self-esteem the more likely the person was to be arrested. For whites, the opposite was the case; the higher the self-esteem, the less likely they were to be arrested. The implications for this is quite important in the sense that most Western systems designed to deal with deviance are highly bureaucratized, meaning they do not deal with people on an individual basis. Decades of programs designed to keep people from committing crimes have been based on the assumption that low self esteem is a key factor in deviance. One explanation for this seemingly paradoxical occurrence is that blacks who have higher self esteem may be more likely to be arrested is because they are aware of their powerlessness in society and are reacting to their lack of status in society by rebelling against the power structure, represented by the police specifically, and by mainstream society in general.

CONCLUSION

Theories of corrections have historically been reflected in the larger expectations of American society, as well as the larger movements of social reform. The means used to either punish and/or reform criminals in our society are based in primarily sociological theories of deviance. Still, these theories have not necessarily been successful in identifying the reasons for crime, the ways to prevent it, or how criminals should be treated.

TERMS & CONCEPTS

Anomie: A social condition in which norms and values are not clearly defined, thus producing higher rates of deviance.

Biological Determinism: A theory of deviance developed by Lombroso which says people are "born criminals."

Criminology: A term to describe the study of deviance, coined by Edwin Sutherland in the early 1930s.

Deviance: An act that breaks the dominant rules in a society.

Differential Association: A theory of deviance developed in the 1930s by Sutherland and attributes deviance to being associated with others who engage in deviant behavior; one learns to be deviant like learning anything.

Greatest Good for the Greatest Number: A utilitarian ideal of Bentham, it says that society should be not concerned about morality, a corrections, it should be concerned for what is best for the most people.

Labeling Theory: A theory of deviance developed in the 1950s by Becker, which suggests that as a behavior gets labeled by others as deviant, others behave differently toward the person who exhibits such behavior, and the person begins to act as expected.

Sanctions: Positive (rewards) or negative (punishments) sanctions are used to convey to people whether they are conforming or deviating from social expectations.

Socialization: The process of learning how to behave and think through various institutions, including the family, religious beliefs, the education system, and the media.

Street Crime: Crimes limited to larceny, theft, burglary, assault, murder, rape, and property crimes.

Total Institutions: A term coined by Goffman in the 1960s to describe places of complete confinement designed to provide a place to systematically remove certain members and control every aspect of their lives.

White Collar Crime: Crimes committed by mainly middle and upper-middle class members; they include embezzlement, insider trading, and fraud. These crimes are almost always limited to those who have access to them through their occupations.

Bibliography

Barnett, C. (n.d.). "The measurement of white-collar crime using uniform crime reporting (UCR) data." *NIBRS Publications Series* . U.S. Department of Justice, Federal Bureau of Investigation. http://www.fbi.gov/ucr/whitecollarforweb.pdf

Becker, H. S. (1968). *Outsiders: Studies in the sociology of deviance*. Glenscoe, IL: Free Press.

Bouffard, J., & Muftic, L. (2006). "Program completion and recidivism outcomes among adult offenders ordered to complete a community service sentence." *Journal of Offender Rehabilitation, 43* (2), 1-33.

Carson, E. A. (2013). "Inmates in custody of state or federal correctional facilities, including private prison facilities, December 31, 1999–2011." http://www.bjs.gov/index.cfm?ty=nps

Carson, E. A., & Sabol, W. J. (2012). "Estimated imprisonment rate of sentenced prisoners under state and federal jurisdiction by sex, race, Hispanic origin, and age, December 31, 2011." http://www.bjs.gov/index.cfm?ty=nps

Chibe, R. (2006). "A golden age of white-collar criminal prosecution." *Journal of Criminal Law & Criminology, 96* (2), 389-395.

Clear, T., Cole, G, & Reisig, M. (2005). *American corrections,* 7th ed. Belmont, CA: Wadsworth.

Conlon, B., Harris, S., Nagel, J., Hillman, M., & Hanson, R. (2008). "Education: Don't leave prison without it." *Corrections Today, 70(* 1), 48-52.

Foucault, M. (1975). *Discipline and punish: The birth of the prison.* New York: Random House.

Garland, D. (2007). "The peculiar forms of American capital punishment." *Social Research, 74* (2), 435-464.

Gaylord, M. & Galliher, J. (1988). *Criminology of Edwin Sutherland.* New York: Transaction Publishers.

Goffman, E. (1961). *Asylum.* New York: Anchor Books.

Harcourt, B. (2006). "From the asylum to the prison: Rethinking the incarceration revolution." *Texas Law Review, 84* (7), 1751-1786.

Hubbard, D. (2006). "Should we be targeting self-esteem in treatment for offenders: Do gender and race matter in whether self-esteem matters?" *Journal of Offender Rehabilitation, 44* (1), 39-57.

Jacobi, T. (2008). "Writing for change: Engaging juveniles through alternative literacy education." *Journal of Correctional Education, 59* (2), 71-93.

Johansson, A., Santtila, P., Harlaar, N., von der Pahlen, B., Witting, K., Ålgars, M., et al. (2008). "Genetic effects on male sexual coercion." *Aggressive Behavior, 34* (2), 190-202.

Leap. T. (2007). *Dishonest dollars: The dynamics of white-collar crime*. Ithaca, NY: Cornell University Press.

Maguire, K., & Pastore, A. L. (1997). *Sourcebook of criminal justice statistics* . Washington D.C.: United States Department of Justice.

Marcos, A., Bahr, S., & Johnson, R. (1986). "Test of a bonding/association theory of adolescent drug use." *Social Forces, 65* (1), 135.

McAlinden, A. (2011). "'Transforming justice': Challenges for restorative justice in an era of punishment-based corrections." *Contemporary Justice Review, 14*(4), 383-406.

Podgor, E. (2007). "The challenge of white collar sentencing." *Journal of Criminal Law & Criminology, 97* (3), 731-759.

Rosenfeld, R. (1989). "Robert Merton's contributions to the sociology of deviance." *Sociological Inquiry, 59* (4), 453-466.

Schlosser, E. (1998). "The prison-industrial complex." *Atlantic Monthly, 282* (6), 51-72.

Sherman, L. (2003). "Reason for emotion: Reinventing justice with theories, innovation, and research-The

American Society of Criminology 2002 Presidential Address." *Criminology, 41* (1), 1-37.

Sidanius, J., Mitchell, M., Haley, H., & Navarrete, C. (2006). "Support for harsh criminal sanctions and criminal justice beliefs: A social dominance perspective." *Social Justice Research, 19* (4), 433-449.

Sitze, A. (2008). "No mercy." *South Atlantic Quarterly, 107* (3), 597-608.

Snell, T. L. (2013). "Capital punishment, 2011—statistical tables." http://www.bjs.gov/index.cfm?ty=pbdetail&iid=4697

Spohn, C., & Holleran, D. (2002). "The effect of imprisonment of recidivism rates of felony offenders: A focus on drug offenders." *Criminology, 40* (2), 329.

Toews, B. (2013). "Toward a restorative justice pedagogy: reflections on teaching restorative justice in correctional facilities." *Contemporary Justice Review, 16* (1), 6-27.

U.S. Department of Justice, Office of Justice Programs, Bureau of Justice Statistics. (2007, June). http://www.ojp.usdoj.gov/bjs/prisons.htm

U.S. Department of Justice, Office of Justice Programs, Bureau of Justice Statistics. (n.d.a.). http://www.ojp.usdoj.gov/bjs/reentry/recidivism.htm

U.S. Department of Justice, Office of Justice Programs, Bureau of Justice Statistics. (n.d.b.).: http://www.ojp.usdoj.gov/bjs/reentry/cp.htm

Wright, K. A., Pratt, T. C., Lowenkamp, C. T., & Latessa, E. J. (2012). "The importance of ecological context for correctional rehabilitation programs: Understanding the micro- and macro-level dimensions of successful offender treatment." *JQ: Justice Quarterly, 29* (6), 775-798.

Suggested Reading

Gibson, M. (2002). *Born to crime: Cesare Lombroso and the origins of biological criminology.* Westport, CT: Praeger.

Harcourt, B. (2007). "Post-modern meditations on punishment: On the limits of reason and the virtues of randomization: A polemic and manifesto for the twenty-first century." *Social Research, 74* (2), 307-346.

Livers, M., & Kehoe, C. J. (2012). "Juvenile detention and corrections standards: Looking back and ahead." *Corrections Today, 74*(1), 80-38.

Mead, Lawrence M. (2007). "Toward a mandatory work policy for men." *Future of Children 47(* 2), p. 43-72.

Wetzel, J., Smeal, S., Bucklen, K., & McNaughton, S. (2012). "Optimizing the role of community corrections centers in reentry." *Corrections Today, 74* (2), 56-59.

Heidi Goar, M.A.

Court System

ABSTRACT

This article examines the United States judicial system from a sociological perspective. The author starts by briefly discussing the historic origins of the American legal system and continues with an explanation of the roles that the courts hold in society. This includes explanations of the structure of the court system as well as a brief discussion of the appeals process. The article is concluded with a discussion of the role of the court system in enacting social change.

OVERVIEW

While the overwhelming majority of legal cases cycle through the judicial system by settling out of court, courts remain crucial to the orderly operation of American society (Friedman, 1984). The court system as we know it is not unique to the United States. The American legal system is the result of the synthesis of other legal traditions brought on by early immigration, with elements of Dutch, Spanish, English, French, and even Native American law within the system. Perhaps most definitively, due to English colonial supremacy, the American system to most closely resembles the English legal system (Friedman, 1984).

English Example

From the English legal system, the American court system has inherited several critical concepts.

- First, the principle of due process states that all accused persons must be granted the same fair and accepted procedures and that special treatment (or mistreatment) should not be granted to any individual.

- The second major principle is that of precedent. According to this principle, the law must be based on legal decisions made by previous judiciaries. This shows fairness with how others in the past were treated. In this way, our system of common law arose from actual legal controversies in which precedent was established. In this way, common law is dynamic, allowing change as society changes.
- Finally, the English system gave us the tradition of basing our courts around an adversarial system in which each party has an opportunity to argue for his or her side.

Within our judicial system, there are certain expectations of the way the interested parties behave. The accused are entitled to a trial by their peers for even the most trivial of cases. The judge is to act as a passive and impartial arbiter. His or her sole purpose is to maintain the order of proceedings and the behavior of individuals in the court. Attorneys representing either side are to guide clients through the legal process to the best of their capabilities. If all parties perform their jobs properly, the truth should be clear and justice will be served.

Inquisitorial vs. Adversarial

While we are most familiar with an adversarial system in which the involved parties (with the help of their lawyers) control the case and the judge acts as an arbiter, this is not the only way a judiciary may operate. In contrast to the adversarial system is the inquisitorial system. In this system, the judge builds the case, investigates facts, and tries to get to the bottom of the matter. This system trusts the judge to be fair (Friedman, 1984). To accompany our adversarial system, there is an appellate court system which remains obscure to most lay people, but is critical to the pursuit of justice. As set up in our adversarial system, there are two parties (each of which is typically represented by a lawyer). There is the defendant, who is the individual (or individuals) accused of committing some crime (Mullally, 2000). Opposed to the defendant is the plaintiff who is the party who supposedly suffered at the hands of the defendant (Mullally, 2000) Collective bodies, such as nonprofit organizations, corporations, or even state or federal governments, may play either of these roles.

The Power of American States vs. Federal Jurisdiction

The American court system most drastically varies from the English system based on regional differences between states in the Union. Each state has varying laws based on the history of that state and the culture of its initial inhabitants (Friedman, 1984). Historically, the most dramatic difference between states have centered around issues of race. Until the mid 1800s, these variances were most pronounced in issues surrounding slave ownership between states in the Northeast and Southeast (Friedman, 1984). Until the second half of the 1900s, this north/south divide centered around issues of segregation and voting statutes. Other differences between regions, such as differences in statutes regarding same sex marriage, continue to this day. In other, more subtle ways, the federal legal system makes our legal system quite complex. The degree of sovereignty granted to individual states allows those states to run their state court systems so as to reflect the culture of that state. For this reason, people may be under the jurisdiction of multiple courts at the same time, which can lead to complicated trials and difficulty between law enforcement agencies (Friedman, 1984).

Local County Courts

The vast majority of legal cases that go to trial are handled locally. Lower local and county courts typically handle the least serious offenses such as traffic violations and vandalism. At these lower levels, courts may be highly specialized, dealing in traffic offenses, small claims suits, or drug and alcohol offenses. Proceedings tend to be informal and to the point in order to cope with massive case loads. There has been some discussion among legal scholars over the degree to which justice is hindered by this informality, but this debate has little impact on the actual proceedings of the court (Friedman, 1984). Courts of General Jurisdiction are the basic trial courts of communities that are put aside to deal with more serious criminal offenses or monetary grievances. Even among these cases, only a small percentage of cases go on to full trial.

Appeals Court

In the situation that the accused can make an argument that the verdict was unfair, on the grounds that the trial was tainted in some way, in light of new evidence, or a variety of other reasons, his or her lawyer may file for an appeal. An appeal is an application to continue the legal struggle to the next highest level of the legal hierarchy. If found worthy by legal officials the defendant is granted a new trial at a higher court. These appeal courts are higher courts that only see cases after they have been initially tried. In most cases, several appeals are possible before all legal possibilities are exhausted. The far more common reason for a case to cease seeking appeals is that the defendant simply exhausts his or her financial resources and is forced to give up.

Federal Court System

After the defendant exhausts his or her appeals on the state level, it is possible that the case may move onto the federal level. Cases that are of special interest to federal law enforcement, such as interstate smuggling, terrorism, and certain types of murder, are also tried in these federal courts. Each state has at least one standing federal court. Unlike state courts, there are no small claims or federal justices of the peace in federal courts. The basic federal court is called the District Court. This court is the first step in the federal system. These courts handle primarily cases that are federal offenses. The next highest court in the federal system is the circuit court. This court is confined primarily to appeals from the various regional federal courts. Only after the appeals to these elite circuit courts have been exhausted may the case move on to the United States Supreme Court. The Supreme Court is confined solely to appeals. The judges have a high degree of control over its own docket. The reasoning for this is that the judges are only to take cases that are of the highest importance to constitutional law. On a more micro level, there are several people that play roles in every court that are critical to the day to day function of the court.

Courtroom Staff

There are numerous critical staff involved in the courtroom to assure that the trial proceeds in an orderly manner; the most important among these people is the judge. The overwhelming majority of judges are individuals who have completed law school and have specifically chosen to start a career as a judge. Thus, most judges have vast knowledge of the legal system, but they rarely actually have firsthand experience on the other side of the bench (Friedman, 1984). Most judges have been elected by state law. This not only serves to eliminate bad judges via democratic means, but it also underscores the political nature of this position (Friedman, 1984). It is generally seen that judges should be held accountable to the public. The fact that many judges have been political activists as some point in their lives further stresses the political nature of this profession (Friedman, 1984).

Besides the judge, there are a number of other critical courtroom personnel that serve to maintain the judicial process. The bailiff is responsible for courtroom security and enforcing etiquette and order within the court. This individual usually has law enforcement experience, usually as a police officer with police training (Mullally, 2000).

The clerk of court is responsible for administrative functions of the court; coordinating and processing cases for the region the court resides over (Mullally, 2000). The clerk of court, however, is usually not present in the courtroom due to the sheer volume of cases that must be processed. The courtroom clerk serves as a representative of the clerk of court in the courtroom and is responsible for organizing the cases, and the information associated with those cases, that are assigned to the judge so as to avoid any unneeded confusion. As part of the job, a clerk may keep track of courtroom information such as courtroom minutes, names of parties, procedures, and each party's exhibits (Mullally, 2000). The filing clerk serves the court by performing functions such as stamping documents, basic filing, collecting fees, issuing docket numbers, and routing of property in the court's possession (Mullally, 2000). The court reporter is responsible for making a record of court proceedings by taking extensive notes on the proceedings (Mullally, 2000).

Contrary to public perception, most cases do not involve juries, and not all juries perform the same tasks. While every individual is entitled to a trial by jury by his or her peers, the system as it stands tends to discourage jury trials in minor matters that can be resolved via plea bargaining. If a jury is needed for a case, the Jury Commissioner is responsible for overseeing the compilation of jury lists, monitoring policies, and other functions surrounding jury selection (Mullally, 2000). Juries are broken into two types: Grand juries and trial juries.

- A grand jury is generally bigger and is responsible for determining if there is enough evidence for a trial. It is important to note that grand juries are only used in those situations in which it is questionable as to whether there is enough evidence; they are not required and in most cases they are not even necessary.
- Trial juries are comprised of people from the community and are the type typically thought of when juries are mentioned (Mullally, 2000).

To accompany the courtroom's critical staff, there are also a number of secondary staff that serve important functions as needed, but the court may continue business without them on a day-to-day basis. Court interpreters are used in those situations in which parties or individuals involved in the case do not speak English; they may be hired on an as needed basis. Research attorneys are available upon the request of the judge. The job of these fully licensed attorneys is to provide legal research that may be relevant to the case. Law clerks perform legal research, prepare legal memoranda for the court, and draft proposals of legal decisions; these appointments are typically about a year long and held by individuals freshly out of law school. Law librarians are simply librarians who preside over a library that is dedicated to legal research; they rarely have any legal training to speak of. Probation officers and expert witnesses are commonly called upon by the court to provide their professional opinions of the case. Probation officers are typically responsible for overseeing either newly released felons or those who have avoided jail time but are in need of state supervision. Expert witnesses are individuals with specialized knowledge of some aspect of the case and may include professionals as varied as neurologists, criminologists, ichthyologists, or shoe salespeople. In other words, almost anyone who could be considered an expert could be an expert witness.

Trial Procedure

In order to understand the players discussed above, we must examine the way they interact during a trial. During opening statements for the trial, each side introduces their arguments to the judge and jury. During this phase, each side attempts to set the stage for their arguments. After opening statements, the prosecution begins its direct examination. During this time, the prosecution presents its evidence and witnesses in a logical way so as to build its case. The defense is permitted to cross examine each witness after the prosecution has presented them to the jury. Once the prosecution has rested its case, the defense is allowed to present its argument during the cross examination phase. In this phase, the defense presents its evidence and witnesses so as to present the innocence of the defendant. Much like what happened during direct examination, the prosecutor is allowed to cross examine each witness called by the defense. After the defense has rested its case, each side makes a closing statement during closing arguments. Before the jury is dismissed to render its decision, the judge instructs them on the grounds in which they are to render their decision. Once the jury comes to a decision, the judge decides the severity of punishment. Despite the apparent finality of the process, nearly every case has a chance to appeal the ruling for the purpose of overturning a conviction. After the trial has ended, in the event of an unfavorable verdict, the defense is able to apply to appeal the verdict.

Types of Trials

While the general structure of how trials work is nearly identical based on whether it is criminal or civil, there are many variations that the trial's outcomes and causes may take that make them worth individualized discussion. Civil trials are those in which jail time is not a potential punishment; these crimes tend to be deemed by society as not as serious in nature as criminal offenses would be. We will now discuss a few of the types of trials that involve the average individual. Many civil trials fall into the category of tort law. Tort law generally states that individuals must maintain their property in a way that is not harmful to others. Tort law allows for the prosecution of cases in which personal injury or property damage occurs due to the improper maintenance of property. An example of this type of crime could involve the possession of a dangerous dog or a company's violation of environmental regulations. These cases may involve a dog attacking a mail carrier or gasoline leaking out of a tank of a gas station and contaminating an aquifer. Intentional misconduct involves those acts in which and individual commits an act that a rational individual would recognize as creating the risk of harm form others. These types of acts include assault, false imprisonment, libel, invasion of privacy, trespassing, or fraud. Cases of negligence involve the failure to do what a reasonable person would have done under similar circumstances. These instances include medical malpractice, poor care of children, or not intervening in a situation where someone is a great risk of being harmed. Strict liability cases involve individuals who engage in dangerous activities that pose a great likelihood of harm to others and another individual winds up being injured as a result. These are but a few types of civil suits. Others include contract suits, business suits, intellectual property suits, labor law violation suits, antitrust suits, and various types of property suits.

APPLICATIONS

The Law in Action

Due to the variety of societal ills that often become apparent within the judicial system, the court system is of great interest to sociologists. Areas in which social ills are highlighted include plea bargaining, trial outcomes, the apparent fairness of a trial, which cases go to trial, jury selection, and how long an individual is held before he or she even comes to trial. This section will examine a few of the reasons sociologists study the court system.

As hinted to above, the vast majority of crimes involve a guilty plea on behalf of the defendant. Defendants may do this for a variety of reasons. They may simply want to own up to doing what they did, they may want to simply pay their punishment and get on with their lives, or they may engage in plea bargaining. Plea bargaining is the process through which a deal is struck between the defendant and plaintiff in which the defendant usually receives lesser charges in exchange for the guilty plea.

There are both stated and unstated reasons that most cases do not go to full trial. Due to the overwhelming number of cases that plead guilty, most cases stop before a trial is even necessary. At arraignment, the accused individual is formally informed of the charges against him. At this point, the defendant is asked for a formal plea. If the plea is innocent, the trial date is set; if the plea is guilty, the process ends here. After arraignment, a preliminary hearing is held in which the prosecution presents its witnesses and evidence of the crime. At this point, the defending attorney is allowed to cross examine the witnesses and question the merit of specific pieces of evidence. At the end of the preliminary hearing, the judge decides if evidence is sufficient to warrant further proceedings. While the defense and prosecution may engage in plea bargaining at any time, it most typically occurs after evidence has been presented at the preliminary hearing. At a pretrial conference between the two sides and the judge, pleas are formally presented. If the plea is not accepted by the defense at this time, legal proceedings continue.

Trial Fairness

Plea Bargaining

A more nefarious factor surrounding a trial is the social status of the accused. Going to trial is very expensive and requires the expenditure of considerable resources on behalf of the defendant. At a minimum, the defendant is required to travel to the courthouse and usually miss work. The wise defendant will hire a lawyer; the services of whom do not usually come cheap. In this way, a plea bargain acts as the cheaper (but not always just) alternative. Thus, for the simple reason of money, the rich often are treated much better by the legal system than the poor.

Jury Selection

Another factor that brings into question the fairness of trials is jury selection. During this process, each side selects jurors and attempts to create the "ideal jury" for their case. Obviously there is usually contention between the prosecution and defense as to what constitutes an ideal juror. For example, a poor man accused of stealing a stereo so that he can pay his rent is more likely to seem sympathetic to other poor people. For this reason, his lawyer may attempt to select poor people for the jury while the prosecutor will attempt to select richer people who would never be in such a situation.

Racial & Ethnic Identity

Multiple aspects of both the accused and alleged victim may also impact the outcome of the trial. If the accused actually does go through with his or her right to a trial, there are several issues surrounding fairness with regard to identity. Most familiar in contemporary American culture are the issues surrounding racial and ethnic identity in the court system. Sociologists, journalists, and individual accounts more than document the realness of racial profiling in determining who is picked up and how he or she is subsequently treated by the police. Furthermore, certain racist assumptions held by the judge or jury could be influential in determining the course of the trial.

Class Status

Less familiar to us in American culture are the ways that class can impact the court system. Crimes typically committed by upper class individuals are not seen as nearly as grievous as those committed by the lower classes despite the great damage these crimes do to society. The rich are more likely to commit crimes such as embezzling due to their social position, while the poor are more likely to commit crimes such as purse snatching. Since purse snatching is seen as more violent and harmful to society than embezzling, we are more likely to punish this crime harshly. However, the purse-snatcher is unlikely to get away with more than fifty dollars while the embezzler is capable of stealing millions of dollars from hundreds of people.

Age

Another aspect of identity that has major implications to the trial is the age of the accused. In fact, an entirely separate system exists for those under 18 years of age. This is because our society generally sees minors, those under the age of 18, as not as accountable for their actions as those who are over 18. For this reason, all but the most heinous of crimes committed by minors are tried in juvenile court as opposed to adult court. Juvenile law varies from adult law in two major aspects.

- First, because the minor is not seen as fully responsible for their actions, parents may be found guilty or responsible for the actions of their child.
- Second, because those under 18 are seen as being more capable of reform than adults, they are given less severe punishments and put into rehabilitative programs so that they may reform (Lundman, 2001).

Emotional issues surrounding a crime can also be greatly detrimental to the ability of a defendant to receive a fair trial. Socially taboo or highly emotional crimes such as the rape of a child, serial murder, or torture are often very difficult for those involved with the trial to deal with in a completely objective, unemotional way. Additionally, if either the defendant or the plaintiff is especially likeable or unlikable, this may also impact the ability of those involved in the trial to act objectively and unemotionally.

VIEWPOINTS

Law & Social Change

Researchers have consistently shown that there is a significant relationship between law and social change (Friedman, 1984). This may be surprising to some due to the fact that law is resistant to social change. Legal revolutions generally follow social revolutions. While law's reluctance to adopt social change causes it to lag behind the rest of society, once it does accept social change, that change becomes more concrete and less likely to become undone. In this way, the courts channel social change and determine the role change will play in social life (Friedman, 1984). An excellent example of such change can be found in the transitions of African American status during the 20th century.

In the 20th century, African Americans began to take legal action to better their lives; the National Association of Colored People (NAACP) was responsible for the bulk of these actions. In 1896, a judge ruled in the case of Plessy v Ferguson that racial segregation was constitutional as long as the separated facilities were equal in all aspects. Under this interpretation of the law, there was nothing wrong with separating black students from white students in public schools as long as students in both white and black schools received educations of equal quality. Unfortunately, due to the power and prestige enjoyed by white people during the period, separate facilities were very rarely equal. White schools were consistently better equipped than black schools, and black schools were often in disrepair. The Separate but Equal doctrine was overturned in 1954 in the case of Brown v Board of Education. This case ruled that despite the efforts of elected officials, the educations of black and white students in segregated areas remained grossly unequal. Therefore, segregated schools would have to be shut down and students would have to be integrated. This was highly controversial among whites who feared how this action would impact the quality of education their children would receive, as well as other concerns that were more based in racist assumptions than reality.

Similar struggles for equal rights continue in contemporary American society surrounding the prosecution of homosexual behavior, and, therefore, homosexual and bisexual individuals. Very much in the way major judicial cases were overturned in the case of racial segregation, major cases surrounding the legality of homosexual behavior have been altered. Prior to 2003, several states held laws, known as sodomy laws, that made certain sexual acts illegal. While the lurid details of these laws varied greatly from state to state, they all intended to dictate the private sexual behavior of individuals. While many of the sexual acts prohibited by these laws are common among heterosexuals as well as homosexuals and bisexuals, heterosexuals were very rarely prosecuted for these crimes. In fact, individuals were very rarely solely accused of crimes associated with sodomy laws, but rather they were nearly always added to additional charges.

Much like laws surrounding segregation, sodomy laws were first upheld before they were struck down. The first challenge to these laws came in the 1980s in the case of Bowers v Hardwick in Georgia. In this case, the laws were upheld. It was not until 2003 that sodomy laws were once again brought into question in the case of Lawrence v Texas. In this case, the United States Supreme Court found state sodomy laws unconstitutional and subsequently overturned these laws in all states in which they existed.

The controversy exhibited by sodomy laws is, and still remains to a large degree in our society, that of the individual's right to privacy. Specifically, the cases mentioned above focused on the right of individuals to engage in certain types of sexual behavior in the privacy of their own homes. Beyond issues of sexuality, this remains a major issue of our time. The debate over whether we, as American citizens, have a right to privacy is a major controversy of our time. This same controversy is brought up surrounding the War on Terror and the ability of government to know what citizens read, access on computers, and other activities that go on in their homes. The connection between these two seemingly disjointed issues shows not only the implications of this controversy but also the sweeping power of the court system to institute change.

TERMS & CONCEPTS

Adversary System: A system in which the parties (and their lawyers) control the case. The judge acts as an arbiter. This is the type of court system used in the United States

Bailiff: Responsible for courtroom security and enforcing etiquette and order. This individual usually has law enforcement experience and police training

Courtroom Clerk: This individual is a representative of the clerk's office in the courtroom. The courtroom clerk is in charge of cases that are assigned to the judge. He or she also organizes cases for the judge and generally keeps track of courtroom information such as minutes, names of parties, procedures, and each side's exhibits.

Court Interpreter: Used in the case that parties involved do not speak English; may be hired on an as-needed basis.

Court Reporter: Makes a record of court proceedings by taking extensive notes.

Defendant: The person in the trial who is accused of doing something illegal.

Due Process: The fair and accepted procedures for enforcement of the law.

Expert Witness: Individuals with expert knowledge on a topic pertinent to a case.

Filing Clerk: Stamps, files, collects fees, gives docket numbers, routes filed property, etc.

Grand Jury: This jury is larger than a petit jury and is responsible for deciding if there is enough evidence for a trial prior to the actual trial.

Judge: The individual who, in an adversarial judicial system, acts as a neutral arbiter so that the jury may come to a conclusion.

Jury Commissioner: Oversees the compilation of jury lists, monitoring policies, and other functions surrounding jury selection.

Law Clerk: Performs legal research, prepares legal memoranda and drafts proposed legal decisions; most serve for one year following law school.

Law Librarian: Exactly that; they rarely have legal training.

Petit Jury: The jury we typically think of when we conceptualize a jury. This group of people is responsible for making a decision of guilt or innocence at the conclusion of a trial.

Plaintiff: The person who supposedly has suffered some legal wrongdoing in a trial.

Precedent: The law must be based on previously established principles. This shows fairness with how others in the past were treated.

Research Attorneys: Full time, licensed attorneys who provide research at the request of judges.

BIBLIOGRAPHY

Friedman, L. (1984). *American law.* New York: W.W. Norton and Company.

Lundman, R (2001). *Prevention and control of juvenile delinquency* (3rd Ed). New York: Oxford University Press.

Mullally, D. (2000). *Order in the court: A writer's guide to the legal system.* Cincinnati: Writer's Digest.

Murphy, J. (2011). "Drug court as both a legal and medical authority." *Deviant Behavior,* 32, 257–291.

Reeves, A. R. (2011). "Judicial practical reason: Judges in morally imperfect legal orders." *Law & Philosophy,* 30, 319–352.

Sprott, J. B., Webster, C., & Doob, A. N. (2013). "Punishment severity and confidence in the criminal justice system." *Canadian Journal of Criminology & Criminal Justice,* 55, 279–292.

Weber, M. (1954). *Law in economy and society.* Cambridge: Harvard University Press.

SUGGESTED READING

Brooks, T. (1992). *The Supreme Court and legal change: Abortion and the death penalty.* University of North Carolina Press: Chapel Hill.

Cohen, T.H. (2008). "General civil jury trial litigation in State and Federal Courts: A statistical portrait." *Journal of Empirical Legal Studies,* 5, 593–617.

Espinoza, R. E., & Ek, B. (2011). "An examination of juveniles being tried as adults: Influences of ethnicity, socioeconomic status and age of defendant." *National Social Science Journal,* 37, 30–37.

Mirchandani, R. (2008). "Beyond therapy: Problem-solving courts and the deliberative democratic state." *Law & Social Inquiry,* 33, 853–893.

Mullally, D. (2000). *Order in the court: A writer's guide to the legal system.* Cincinnati: Writer's Digest.

Roach-Anleau, S. (2000). *Law and social change.* London: Sage.

Rose, M.R. & Diamond, S.S. (2008). "Judging bias: Juror confidence and judicial rulings on challenges for cause." *Law & Society Review,* 42, 513–549.

Tiger, R. (2011). "Drug courts and the logic of coerced treatment." *Sociological Forum,* 26, 169–182.

Jeremy Baker, M.A.

CRIME THEORY: ORGANIZED CRIME

ABSTRACT

The term "organized crime" refers to highly structured criminal groups who engage in illegal activities for financial gain. While they can operate on local, regional, and national levels, the greatest challenge for law enforcement organizations is international organized crime. Estimates by the Federal Bureau of Investigations place the costs of organized crime worldwide at $1 trillion per year. Technological advancements in communications and global financial deregulation has resulted in a global boom in organized crime. In order to launder money and exert control over various businesses and industries, organized crime has taken over legitimate enterprises through corruption, intimidation, and extortion. Cooperation from political, judicial, and law enforcement officials is gained in the same manner, allowing organized crime to flourish throughout the world. Numerous terrorist groups worldwide utilize organized crime to generate millions of dollars in capital, which they use to acquire weapons and technology.

OVERVIEW

The Organized Crime Control Act defines organized crime as "The unlawful activities of...a highly organized and disciplined association," usually for the purposes of financial gain (U.S., 1970). It can and does exist on any scale, whether local, state, national, or international. In order to thrive, however, organized crime has to have strong ties into legitimate business entities so that money can be moved throughout the economy. Often, the cooperation of respected members of the business community is gained through bribery, extortion, and blackmail. Added protection for criminal endeavors is achieved by bribing judicial and law enforcement officials. Politically motivated organized crime is referred to as terrorism.

The impact of organized crime is difficult to measure since this type of crime is involved in so many legal and illegal enterprises. The Federal Bureau of Investigation (FBI) estimates that its illegal annual profits globally total about $1 trillion per year (FBI, n.d.b). Glenny estimates that this shadow economy nets about 15% to 20% of global GDP (gross domestic product) annually (2008, p. xv). The illegal enterprises organized crime engages in include drug and weapons trafficking, money laundering, gambling, murder for hire, prostitution, bombings, extortion, kidnapping, fraud, political corruption, loan sharking, blackmail, human smuggling, counterfeiting, illegally dumping toxic waste, and terrorism. Not counted in these statistics, however, are the actual and indirect costs and hardships inflicted upon individuals and communities through the violence, intimidation, and corruption used by organized crime to control their criminal enterprises. One trend in organized crime is the increased ability of these organizations to work with one another around the world to achieve their illegal ends. This has increased the need for the FBI to work with its counterparts in other countries in order to disrupt these costly criminal activities.

The Organized Crime Section at the FBI is divided into various geographical units. It also maintains a Sports Bribery Program aimed at ensuring the integrity of American sporting events by educating sports officials and players about the role of organized crime in gambling, corruption, bribery, and drug trafficking. Additionally, the program investigates and prosecutes offenses related to federal gambling and corruption laws in sports.

Within sociological theory, many of the activities engaged in by organized crime come under the concept of white-collar crime. Analysis of white-collar crime focuses on two types: the individual perpetrator having special knowledge or occupational expertise and access that permits him or her to gain illegal financial advantage over others; and, corporate or organizational perpetrators, including organized and governmental crime. Since white-collar crime is intermingled with legitimate business activities and often involves complex and sophisticated technical actions, detection is very difficult. Although white-collar crime is a $300 billion dollar annual harm to our society, few perpetrators are caught and even fewer receive any sort of punishment.

Technically speaking, when a corporation commits an offense, this is called "corporate crime" or "organizational crime," which is considered one type of white-collar crime. This division of white-collar crime categories into two types, occupational and corporate, was advanced by Clinard and Quinney in the

1960s, and it remains influential to this day (Green, 2006). Another aspect of white-collar crime that can be either individual or organized is governmental or political crime, for instance, lawmakers trading their influence and legislative votes for money and gifts.

In an effort to combat organized crime, in 1970 the federal government passed the Racketeer Influenced and Corrupt Organization (RICO) Act (18 U. S. C. A. § 1961 et seq.) In addition to crimes deemed to be white collar in nature, RICO provides penalties for gambling, extortion, prostitution, narcotics trafficking, loan sharking and murder. Punishment under RICO can be extremely harsh, including fines and up to 20 years in prison. Additionally, the defendant must forfeit any claims to the money or property obtained from the criminal enterprise or obtained from any criminal enterprise barred under RICO (White-collar, 2008).

Despite decades of corporate criminal offenses, it was not until 2002 that Congress enacted legislation that seriously penalized corporate wrongdoing. The Public Company Accounting Reform and Investor Protection Act, also known as the Sarbanes-Oxley Act (Pub.L. 107-204, 116 Stat. 745), increased penalties for mail and wire fraud to 20 years in prison. Those convicted of committing securities fraud faced up to 25 years in prison. Additionally, the act criminalized the falsification of corporate financial reports, with fines of up to $5 million dollars and 10 years in prison (White-collar, n.d.). Also contained within the act was the directive that the Federal U.S. Sentencing Commission increase the penalties for other white-collar crimes. These new regulations have changed the historical landscape of both public and law enforcement attitudes towards white-collar crime.

Critical Criminology

In addition to traditional views on the causes of crime and deviance that focus on an individual's motivation or character, several other theories of crime deserve brief mention in relation to organized crime. "Critical criminology" often has been called the Robin Hood theory of crime in that it argues that deviance is a choice and a political act made in response to the inequities of capitalist societies. Based upon Marxist views of capitalism, Taylor, Walton, and Young argued that oppressed groups, such as the working class, women, and minorities, may take action against the dominant, capitalist culture in order to counteract that culture's social, economic, and political power (1973). The dominant culture then labels these actions as criminal in order to maintain its power. In other words, under critical criminology, what constitutes criminal behavior is contingent upon social and historical context, meaning that the definition of criminal behavior can vary over time in relation to the interests of the dominant group. Critics of critical criminology argue that it romanticizes violent, disruptive, and harmful acts and that it has little interest in the realities of crime.

Left Realism Criminology

Although "left realism criminology" developed out of the theoretical framework of critical criminology, it focuses upon realistic approaches to crime. By studying crime victims, left realists focus on the marginalization or powerlessness of both the victims and the perpetrators of crime. Furthermore, relative to most members of society, these individuals are deprived of financial, social, and political resources. Left realists, therefore, advocate crime interventions that create a more egalitarian relationship between the police and the public. One of left realism's contributions to criminology has been the expansion of the basic traditional triangle view of crime as involving an offender, a victim, and the state, by adding the public or a civil society to create the square of crime. Conceptually, public attitudes and policies are brought into crime analysis in addition to law enforcement agencies.

Right Realism Criminology

"Right realism" criminological theory developed out of the rational choice and social control theories of crime. Its focus is less theoretical and more oriented towards the prevention and control of crime from a conservative "law and order" perspective. Basically, right realism advocates believe that crime is a choice and that the solution to crime is to take steps to prevent situations in which criminal conduct can occur. Through educational programs and sign postings, individuals are forewarned that should they choose to engage in criminal conduct, the consequences will be swift, harsh, and long lasting. Situational crime prevention also advocates for increased police presence, neighborhood watches, improved street lighting, alarm systems, and other measures that make committing a crime and getting away with it more difficult.

APPLICATIONS

The Mafia

Traditional views of organized crime have long centered on the Italian criminal societies known as the Mafia. Formed in Italy as underground resistance groups that fought against invading and exploiting armies, these secret societies offered vigilante justice to protect its members' families and friends. A member was called a "Man of Honor," because he was able to disrupt the invading forces' efforts, steal their assets, and, if necessary, die before informing on his society. Sicilians, in particular, were the most clannish and developed into the Mafia in the mid-1800s to "unify the Sicilian peasants against their enemies" (FBI, n.d.e, ¶ 12). By the mid-20th century, the Mafia had "infiltrated the social and economic fabric of Italy and now affect the world (FBI, n.d.e ¶ 1).

By the 1920s, thousands of Sicilian organized crime members had immigrated to the United States and formed La Cosa Nostra or the American Mafia. They found a criminal haven in America at that time due to the passage of the Volstead Act of 1920, otherwise known as Prohibition, which banned the sale of alcohol in the country. Highly organized bootlegging rings moved alcohol throughout the country through loose criminal alliances. Gangland killings and gang wars were common as the various groups fought for influence and territory. Also common was the prosecution of high-ranking political figures, judges, and law enforcement personnel who aided the Mafia in their criminal enterprises (Organized Crime, 2008).

Prohibition was repealed in 1933 and the Mafia turned to labor racketeering, gambling, prostitution, and narcotics trafficking. Labor racketeering is "the domination, manipulation, and control of a labor movement in order to affect related businesses and industries" (FBI, n.d.e ¶ 63). In the past, the Mafia has engaged in labor racketeering by controlling the major labor unions in the building and service industries around large cities like New York, so that which companies obtain contracts involving cement, building materials, garbage disposal, construction, highway development, electricity, and plumbing are largely determined by the Mafia, which expects payments for its influence. In order to influence the public bidding processes, Mafia bosses need highly placed public officials on their payroll to rig the bids towards the Mafia providers. In addition to the increased labor and materials costs of these projects, the Mafia also controls the billions of dollars in the pension, welfare, and health funds of construction union members.

The FBI estimates that the four Italian Mafia groups currently active in the United States have over 25,000 members and 250,000 associates worldwide. Approximately 3,000 members are working throughout the United States in major urban centers like New York, southern New Jersey, and Philadelphia. The FBI estimates that the Italian Mafia's worldwide profits are $100 billion annually (FBI, n.d.e).

By the early 1950s, federal investigations into organized crime revealed that many of the top Mob officials had taken control of legitimate businesses and seemingly distanced themselves from daily criminal operations. With wealth, political influence and apparent respectability, these Mafia officials gained an even greater hold over American criminal enterprises. In the twenty-first century they are similar to any other multinational corporate structure, with their illegal commodities and services laundered through legitimate businesses. In addition to traditional criminal activities, crimes include the sale of fake telephone cards, identity fraud, stock swindles, and online extortion.

International Organized Crime

Since the 1990s organized crime has taken on new significance internationally and within the United States. One factor has been an increased mobility, both in physical space and cyberspace (Berry, 2003, p. 1). This has permitted criminal organizations from around the world to infiltrate American business interests and to transfer funds electronically before they are detected. The second factor has to do with the loosening of restrictions on the transfer of money internationally.

Up until the late 1980s, governmental restraints restricted the movement of large sums of money internationally. Corporations had lobbied for less regulation, arguing "that they needed to have money around the world faster and in much greater quantities in order to take full advantage of its value as they expanded global operations" (Glenny, 2008, p. 172). In the late 1980s, the governments of Ronald Reagan in the United States and Margaret Thatcher in the United Kingdom, "lifted the bureaucratic barriers that blocked the free movement of capital" and "established only primitive mechanisms to regulate this massive surge in the movement of capital" (Glenny, 2008, p. 172). With the combination of technology and deregulation, organized crime has become a powerful force both internationally and within the United States.

Eurasian Organized Crime

Another factor that influenced organized crime in the United States was the breakdown of the former Soviet Union around 1991. Called "Eurasian crime" by the FBI, it was initially organized to profit from the Soviet prison system. When the Soviet Union collapsed, crime leaders and corrupt government officials combined to take control of the industries and natural resources that were being privatized. With this huge infusion of wealth and the legitimate means of laundering money, Eurasian crime has gained the resources to destabilize emerging political institutions that have access to the former Soviet Union's nuclear weapons caches (FBI, n.d.d). Within the United States, Eurasian organized crime involves healthcare fraud, drug trafficking, auto theft, money laundering, extortion, securities and investment fraud, the interstate transportation of stolen property, and prostitution. Like many of their organized crime counterparts, the Eurasian group is also involved in human trafficking, which pertains to two categories: the "buying and selling of women and children for illegal labor and for the sex trade;" and the "movement of illegal immigrants through or into countries without fulfilling the documentation requirements of those countries" (Berry, 2003, p. 2).

Asian Organized Crime

Since the early 1990s, Asian organized crime has been active in the United States as well. Early Chinese American immigrants started social groups, known as "tongs," which eventually evolved into criminal operations. The FBI states that the most dominant groups have ties to China, Korea, Japan, Thailand, the Philippines, Cambodia, Laos, and Vietnam, although all of them have extensive international influence. Situated in more than 50 large metropolitan areas across the United States, these Asian criminal enterprises also use local businesses and large corporations to hide their criminal activities. In addition to traditional racketeering activities associated with organized crime, the Asian groups also "smuggle aliens; traffic heroin and methamphetamine; commit financial frauds; steal autos and computer chips; counterfeit computer and clothing products; and launder money" (FBI, n.d.c, ¶ 6).

African Organized Crime

Few organized crime groups have benefited more from communication technology and the globalization of world economies than the African criminal enterprises that have been developing since the 1980s. Moving into the world markets, these formerly local and regional crime groups have flourished in countries like Nigeria, Ghana, and Liberia. Nigerian criminal enterprises in particular have committed massive financial fraud throughout the world and the United States. The cost to the United States alone is estimated at between $1 billion and $2 billion annually. Additionally, "large populations of ethnic Nigerians in India, Pakistan, and Thailand have given these enterprises direct access to 90% of the world's heroin production" (FBI, n.d.a, ¶5). As well as typical organized crime activities, the FBI focuses on "insurance fraud involving auto accidents; healthcare billing schemes; life insurance schemes; bank, check, and credit card fraud; advance-fee schemes known as 4-1-9 letters; and document fraud to develop false identities" (FBI, n.d.a, ¶7). Since the development of e-mail, the fax machine, and the Internet, their crimes have become more profitable and more prevalent.

VIEWPOINTS

Since organized crime is a global enterprise, the United States government is interested in countries that are hospitable to these enterprises. Berry and her colleagues argue that there are several common characteristics of such governments that provide favorable conditions for the survival and expansion of organized crime, including, "official corruption, incomplete or weak legislation, poor enforcement of existing laws, non-transparent financial institutions, unfavorable economic conditions, lack of respect for the rule of law in society, and poorly guarded national boundaries" (2003, p. 1). In their report, Berry and her colleagues discuss in detail the various countries around the world in relation to organized crime and the policy issues raised by these situations (2003).

Because of their proximity to the United States, two countries cited by Berry and her colleagues are of significant interest: Mexico and Canada (2003). Both are staging points for bringing illegal narcotics and people into American borders. Canada, in particular, is cited as a troublesome source of terrorist entry into the U.S. (p. 143). While Canada is applauded in the report for its efforts to protect human rights, some of these efforts have added to the difficulties of policing the border between Canada and the United States. According to the authors, Canada serves as a base for terrorist operations and as a transit country because it has a "generous social-welfare system, lax immigration laws, infrequent prosecutions, light sentencing, and long borders and coastlines" (p. 146). After the 9/11 terrorist attacks in New York City, however, the Canadian government enacted the Immigration and Refugee Protection Act to heighten border security with the United States by increasing immigrant screening, instituting new criminal charges and penalties for suspected terrorists, shortening the appeal process, and increasing police arrest powers (p. 146).

Mexican organized crime related to drug trafficking continues to plague the border regions of both the United States and Mexico. The crime has resulted in an sixty to seventy thousand person increase of homicides since 2007 (Shirk, 2015). Perhaps more than any other type of organized crime, that of Mexican gangs has been the hardest for US authorities to quell and promises to continue for the foreseeable future.

Terrorism

Although beyond the scope of this article, it is important to add terrorism to the definition of organized crime. Terrorism is coercion through violence, and often is recognized after a given terrorist event when the perpetrators articulate that they committed the act and give their reasons for doing so. Elements of terrorism include violence executed for a political reason with the intent to maximize psychological fear by deliberating targeting non-combatant civilians. Terrorists often disguise themselves as non-combatants in order to escape initial detection and to increase the likelihood of harm to civilians. Some of the organized crime discussed throughout this article is conducted in order to obtain weapons or funding for terrorist efforts. From the perspective of terrorists, their motivations justify their extreme actions. Others would argue that no political, social, economic, or religious motivation is sufficient to excuse these devastating acts of violence.

TERMS & CONCEPTS

Bribery: Persuading somebody to do something dishonest or illegal in exchange for money or other incentives.

Extortion: The crime of obtaining something such as money or information from somebody through coercion.

Gross Domestic Product (GDP): The total market value of all goods and services produced within a country during a specific period of time, usually annually.

Mafia: Term for Sicilian vigilante groups organized during the middle ages to combat Spanish occupation of the land.

Prohibition: The Volstead Act of 1920 made the sale of alcoholic beverages illegal in the United States until 1933. This period of time is referred to as the Prohibition era.

Racketeering: Criminal activity by a structured group.

Racketeer Influenced & Corrupt Organization Act (RICO): A federal law passed in 1970 that provided stiffer penalties for those convicted of participating in criminal acts as part of an organized crime syndicate.

Bibliography

Berry, L., Curtis, G., Gibbs, J., Hudson, R., Karacan, T., Kollars, N., & Miro, R. (2003). *Nations hospitable to organized crime and terrorism.* Washington, D.C.: The Library of Congress, Federal Research Division. www.loc.gov/

Glenny, M. (2008). *McMafia: A journey through the global criminal world.* New York: Alfred Knopf.

Green, S. P. (2006). "The meaning of white-collar crime." *Lying, cheating, and stealing: A moral theory of white-collar crime.* Oxford: Oxford University Press. www.oup.co.uk/pdf/0-19-926858-4.pdf

Federal Bureau of Investigation. (n.d.a). "Organized crime: African criminal enterprises." http://www.fbi.gov/about-us/investigate/organizedcrime/african

Federal Bureau of Investigation. (n.d.b). "Organized crime." http://www.fbi.gov/about-us/investigate/organizedcrime

Federal Bureau of Investigation. (n.d.c). "Organized crime: Asian criminal enterprises." http://www.fbi.gov/about-us/investigate/organizedcrime/asian

Federal Bureau of Investigation. (n.d.d). "Organized crime: Eurasian criminal enterprises." http://www.fbi.gov/about-us/investigate/organizedcrime/eurasian

Federal Bureau of Investigation. (n.d.e)."Organized crime: Italian organized crime." http://www.fbi.gov/about-us/investigate/organizedcrime/italian5%Fmafia

Federal Bureau of Investigation. (n.d.g). "Organized crime: Sports bribery program." http://www.fbi.gov/about-us/investigate/organizedcrime/sports5%Fbribe

Federal Bureau of Investigation. (1989). *White collar crime: A report to the public.* Washington, D.C.: Government Printing Office.

Harbeck, K. M. (2016). "Violent crime in the U.S." *Research Starters Sociology,* 1-6.

Hopkins, M., Tilley, N., & Gibson, K. (2013). "Homicide and Organized Crime in England." *Homicide Studies, 17,* 291-313.

Lavorgna, A., Lombardo, R., & Sergi, A. (2013). "Organized crime in three regions: comparing the Veneto, Liverpool, and Chicago." *Trends in Organized Crime, 16,* 265-285.

Organized crime. (2008). *The Columbia encyclopedia.* (6th ed.). New York: Columbia University Press.

Ruetschlin, C. M., & Bangura, A. (2012). "Transnational Organized Crime: A Global Concern." *Journal of International Diversity,* 94-102.

Ruggiero, V. (2007). "It's the economy, stupid! Classifying power crimes." *International Journal of Sociology and Law,* 35, 163-177.

Siegel, D. (2014). "Women in transnational organized crime." *Trends in Organized Crime, 17*(1/2), 52–65.

Shirk, D., & Wallman, J. (2015). "Understanding Mexico's drug violence." *Journal of Conflict Resolution, 59*(8), 1348–1376.

Smith, R. G. (2014). "Responding to organized crime through intervention in recruitment pathways." *Trends & Issues in Crime & Criminal Justice,* 1–9.

Spalek, B. (2001). "White-collar crime victims and the issue of trust." *British criminology conference: Selected proceedings.* 4.

White-collar crime. (2008). *West's encyclopedia of American law.* (2nd Ed.). The Gale Group. http://legal-dictionary.thefreedictionary.com/White-collar+crime.

Wong, K. (2005). "From white-collar crime to organizational crime: An intellectual history." *Murdoch University Electronic Journal of Law.* Australia. http://www.austlii.edu.au/au/journals/MurUEJL/2005/14.html

SUGGESTED READING

Abadinsky, H. (2006). *Organized crime.* Florence, KY: Wadsworth.

Combs, C. (2008). *Terrorism in the 21st century.* (5th ed.). Englewood Cliffs, NJ: Prenctice-Hall.

Hoffman, B. (2006). *Inside terrorism.* New York: Columbia University Press.

"International Association for the Study of Organized Crime." (n.d.). www.iasoc.net.

Lampe, K. (2012). "Transnational organized crime challenges for future research." *Crime, Law & Social Change,* 58, 179-194.

Lampe, K. (2014). "Recent publications on organized crime." *Trends in Organized Crime, 17,* 342–344.

Lyman, M., & Potter, G. (2006). *Organized crime.* (4th ed.). Englewood Cliffs, NJ: Prentice-Hall.

Martin, G. (2006). *Understanding terrorism: Challenges, perspectives, and issues.* (2nd ed.). Thousand Oaks, CA: Sage.

Michigan State University Libraries. "Criminal justice resources: Organized crime." www.lib.msu.edu/harris23/crimjust/orgcrime.htm.

"Nathanson Centre on Transnational Human Rights, Crime and Security." (n.d.). www.yorku.ca/nathanson/default.htm.

Siegel, D., & Nelen, H. (Eds.). (2008). *Organized crime: Culture, markets, and policies.* New York: Springer Science+Business Media.

Siegel, D., van de Bunt, H., & Zaitch, D. (Eds.). (2003). *Global organized crime: Trends and developments.* Dordrecht, The Netherlands: Kluwer.

Von Lampe, K. (2015). *Organized crime: Analyzing illegal activities, criminal structures, and extra-legal governance.* Thousand Oaks, CA: SAGE.

White, J. (2008). *Terrorism and homeland security: An introduction.* (6th ed.). Florence, KY: Wadsworth.

Zabyelina, Y. (2013). "The untouchables: transnational organized crime behind diplomatic privileges and immunities." *Trends in Organized Crime,* 16, 343-357.

Karen M. Harbeck, Ph.D., J.D.

Criminal Recidivism

ABSTRACT

Depending on the offense, recidivism rates vary for criminals. Some criminologists consider recidivism to mean any act of re-offending, while other specialists consider committing only the same crime to mean recidivism. Black men are more likely to reoffend according to data included here, with social inequity being blamed for this disparity. Access to education, vital job opportunities, and a healthy social network are some necessary considerations for an offender's successful reentry into the community. Pedophiles are a class of offenders for which treatment may never work; studies show that various interventions can lower a pedophile's ability to assault children but not remove the desire to offend for these and other sexual offenders. Female and juvenile offenders are also discussed, and information regarding programs aimed at reducing recidivism is provided.

OVERVIEW

Recidivism is the act of reoffending or relapsing into criminal behavior for a person who has already been incarcerated. It can mean that an offender commits the same crime for which he was originally incarcerated, or it can mean that he has offended in a different way while in jail, on probation, on parole, or after a period of time once reentering society. For practical use, recidivism here means reoffending in any manner after a period of incarceration. The issues with regard to recidivism are many and cross societal, legal and monetary boundaries.

Many people recidivate because they know no other way of life. In most instances, incarceration is a temporary fix for an immediate problem. Eventually, inmates will return to the societies they have offended. Unfortunately, for many of the inmates sent home, being outside of prison becomes the temporary situation. Most studies report that up to two-thirds of the inmates released will reoffend within three years of walking away from prison life. They will violate parole or probation or they will commit new crimes, being arrested and prosecuted and then placed back into the hands of the United States Department of Corrections.

For a majority of recidivists, incarceration has done nothing to assist them with the transition from convict to everyday citizen. They went in without an education; they came out without an education. The same can be said for job skills, social skills, and socioeconomic status. In 2003 the Serious and Violent Offender Reentry Initiative (SVORI) was started by the federal government to fund nationwide reentry programs focusing on education, employment training, and personal and family counseling. SVORI's $100 million budget was spread out between state and local agencies and then distributed to various civic organizations. Lattimore (2007) points out that there is an inequity in such a distribution: "$100 million represents less than $200 for each of the more than 600,000 individuals released to parole each year. Further, the SVORI funds were spread over three years" (p. 89). Ironically, the SVORI program was not refunded after its three year trial period.

Re-Entry Programs

In a report for the Washington State Institute for Public Policy (WSIPP), Aos, Miller and Drake (2006) analyzed 291 evaluations of offender reentry programs and noted that many weren't successful, despite government funding. While some programs show no difference in reducing recidivism, others were positively correlated with recidivism reduction. For example, adult drug courts have been shown to reduce recidivism by almost 11 percent for those incarcerated for drug offenses. On the other hand, education and cognitive-behavioral treatment has been shown to cause no reduction in recidivism for domestic violence offenders (p. 3). While an 11 percent reduction in recidivism may seem small, that figure equates to less crime, fewer victims, fewer prosecutions, and fewer tax-payer dollars spent on incarceration (Aos, Miller & Drake, 2006).

In addition to the programs listed above, Aos et al. (2006) identify the following programming strategies as reducing recidivism.

Within prison settings

- Cognitive-behavioral drug treatment;
- Correctional industry programs;
- Drug treatment;
- Vocational education programs;
- General and specific cognitive-behavioral programs;
- Cognitive-behavioral treatment for sex offenders (in prison or in the community)

Within the community settings

- Drug treatment;
- Treatment-oriented, intensive community supervision programs;
- Employment training and job assistance in the community (Aos, Miller & Drake, 2006, p. 3)

Again, it should be noted that even though these programs have been shown to decrease recidivism rates, the reductions may be small. For example, employment training and job assistance within the community has shown a 5% decrease in recidivism. That figure may equate to only a handful of offenders not reoffending, but the impact on society is much greater.

FURTHER INSIGHTS

According to Lattimore (2007), offenders as a population face a great deal of challenges that make for a difficult reentry into society. For example, various studies indicate that inmates share the following damaging characteristics.

Little education, few job skills, little job experience likely to lead to good employment, substance and alcohol dependency, and other health problems, including mental health problems. In addition, their family and friends are often involved in crime and substance abuse, and they disproportionately return to neighborhoods with few economic opportunities and few, if any, positive role models. Finally, each must cope with a criminal record that can stand in the way of opportunities following release (Lattimore, 2007, p. 89).

Furthermore, the systems created to support society, have failed most inmates in some way or another. For example, ... many of those who end up incarcerated did poorly in the school systems that provide educational foundations for a successful adulthood. Many offenders have histories of abuse and neglect and may have been referred to, or in the custody of, family and social services. Adult inmates often have histories of juvenile confinement and adult probation that failed to provide the services, programming and support to reform and rehabilitate. And finally, many inmates have received alcohol and drug treatment outside the criminal justice system, but may remain addicted to drugs and alcohol (Lattimore, 2007, p. 89).

Race & Recidivism

Reisig, Bales, Hay, and Xia (2007) note that in the U.S. "recidivism is highest among males, African Americans, and those under the age of 18" (Beck & Shipley, 1989; Langan & Levin, 2002, as cited in Reisig et al., 2007, p. 409). In addition, "African Americans make up nearly half of both the prison population and the offenders reentering society from prison" even though they make up less than 15 percent of the population as a whole (Harrison & Beck 2004, as cited in Reisig et al., 2007, p. 411). Furthermore, of those offenders rearrested within a three year time period of being released from prison, African Americans are 16% more likely to be rearrested than other populations (Langan & Levin, 2002, as cited in Reisig et al., 2007, p. 411).

Reisig et al. (2007) conducted a study to predict the recidivism rates of inmates based on the economic stability of each county in the state of Florida. They based their predictions on the racial inequality (the unequal distribution of economic resources based on race) of various communities where inmates would be released. According to census and economic reports the researchers were able to determine that "reconviction rates for Black males are highest in counties where adverse economic conditions (e.g., income, joblessness, and poverty) disproportionately affect Black families" (Reisig et al, 2007, p. 419).

To be specific, Reisig et al (2008) determined that Saint John's County, Florida has the highest degree of racial inequality in the state. As such, they predicted a 100 % recidivism rate for offenders released into that county. That is, 100% of the African American offenders released into that county will reenter the criminal justice system based on the lack of economic resources within the community (p. 428). With no viable job opportunities, a former offender may view criminal behavior as the only means for supporting himself and/or his family. This pattern was repeated across the state; the counties showing high degrees of racial inequality were predicted to have high rates of recidivism for Black males (p. 419). Conversely, White male recidivism rates were not impacted by racial inequality (Reisig et al., 2007, p. 419).

Women & Recidivism

About one in three women will make a successful return to the community once released from prison (Fortuin, 2007). Reentering society is challenging with few job skills and little education, and as such, recidivism rates for women are high. A program created by the Volunteers of America Northern New England was established to assist women in the transition process from prison to the community. In Maine, the incarceration rate for women doubled from 1994 to 2002, a jump of over 52% (Fortuin, 2007). For those women participating in the Transition, Reunification and Re-entry program, however, recidivism rates have decreased, and women are finding the resources necessary to live successful in society. According to Fortuin (2007), the program includes ... case-management services that attend to housing, employment, education, family reunification and empowerment, birth control, and continuity of care for mental health, physical health and substance abuse ... In the early days, transition planning for a female offender began three months prior to her release. It now begins six months prior to release and extends up to six months after release, providing a more comprehensive transition plan and greater support during the critical days immediately following release (Fortuin, 2007, p. 34).

In addition to the services it provides, this program encourages women to believe in their ability to be successful and responsible once in their communities. And, it isolates—from person to person—the services most necessary for each inmate in preparation for her release. For example, where one woman may need mental health services as a priority, another may need basic literacy skills, and another may need family counseling prior to reuniting with her children. Fortuin (2007) notes that this initiative is replicable in most women's correction centers, since much of the assistance is community based and already provided by civic organizations. With the help of many volunteers, this program simply sees to it that prisoner and services are united and that newly released women are mentored closely immediately following their release.

Another initiative created by the Volunteers of America is Women Building Futures. This program teaches construction skills to women by allowing inmates to assist in the building of modular homes for low-income Maine families. The women participating in the program learn skills offering construction certification and opportunities to continue building homes once they leave the DOC. Representatives of the program boast an 80% success rate in transitioning women from incarceration to society (Koegel, 2008).

Juvenile Recidivism

Recidivism is not only committed by adults. In fact, more juveniles will reoffend than adults will with national recidivism rate percentages running about 80 and 67, respectively (Soering, 2007). About ten percent of the juveniles detained each day are sent to adult prisons and jails (Soering, 2007). "Minors sent to adult facilities are eight times more likely to commit suicide, five times more likely to be sexually assaulted and twice as likely to be beaten by staff as youths confined in juvenile detention centers" (Soering, 2007, p. 30).

As is the case with adult criminals, an inequity of race arrests and convictions exists for juveniles. Soering (2007) points to this nation-wide disparity, noting that 44% of all the juveniles incarcerated are African American. Further, While there is some evidence of higher offense rates among minorities in certain crime categories, both state and federal studies have found that for the same offenses, African American adolescents are more likely to be arrested or detained than white teens. Black children are also sent to detention facilities more frequently than whites–in the case of drug crimes, 48 times as often–and their sentences are 41 percent longer. Why the difference? A study published in the American Sociological Review in 1998 suggested that probation officers preparing pre-sentence reports on juvenile criminals tended to characterize white teens as reformable and redeemable victims of circumstances, while black adolescents were often depicted as intrinsically bad (Soering, 2007, p. 28).

Considering this information, it is not a stretch to think that upon release, a black youth represents a better chance of being arrested again in contrast to a white youth. With a previous record, offenders have less chances for leniency. Disparity aside, it may be that a newly released black youth is expected to reoffend and is watched more closely by law enforcement than his white counterpart.

An alternative to either juvenile or adult prison sentences for youth can be taken from the following example.

Missouri achieves its remarkable 8 percent recidivism rate by housing juvenile criminals in small, residential-style facilities whose staff all have college educations. Instead of spending their days turning keys, these officers are encouraged to form positive, nurturing, one-on-one relationships with the adolescents in their charge. Groups of nine to 12 wards and two staff members stay together throughout the wards' sentences, forming a kind of alternate family unit. And the annual cost of housing one minor in this type of facility is $10,000 to $30,000 less than the cost of punitive incarceration (Soering, 2007, p. 31).

Youth who offend often lack role models who do not offend. As such, there is a disconnect between society's expectations and what the offender has experienced. Programs that work for juvenile offenders are those that focus treatment on building personal relationships between youth and the people who are paid to care for them.

Pedophilia

There is no sexual deviant more despised than the person who preys on children. Most people do not know that while the action of molesting a juvenile is criminal, the basis for the deviancy is psychological in nature (Snyder, 2000; Lanning, 2001; as cited in Hall & Hall, 2007). According to the Diagnostic and Statistical Manual of Mental Disorders (5th ed.) (2013), ... a pedophile is an individual who fantasizes about, is sexually aroused by, or experiences sexual urges toward prepubescent children (generally under 13 years) for a period of at least 6 months. Pedophiles are either severely distressed by these sexual urges, experience interpersonal difficulties because of them, or act on them. Pedophiles usually come to medical or legal attention by committing an act against a child because most do not find their sexual fantasies distressing or ego-dystonic enough to voluntarily seek treatment (as cited in Hall & Hall, 2007, p. 457).

When any of these offenders are incarcerated, they do not have access to their victims like rapists or murderers do. As a jail cell cannot lock up an offender's mind, it is fair to say that no pedophile is "rehabilitated" by the incarceration process alone. In light of the serious nature of pedophilic offenses, reentry interventions are an essential part of promoting safety for society.

Treating pedophiles is not easy, and Stone, Winslade & Klugman (2000) note that no treatment is fool-proof: "Individuals can offend again while in active psychotherapy, while receiving pharmacologic treatment, and even after castration" (as cited in Hall & Hall, 2007, p. 465). Again, this is a psychological—rather than a biological—disorder. Even if an offender is castrated or locked up away from children forever, the desire to have sex with children does not go away simply because the physical act of having sex is impossible. Therefore, "much of the focus of pedophilic treatment is on stopping further offenses against children rather than altering the pedophile's sexual orientation toward children" (Hall & Hall, 2007, p. 465).

The current treatments vary depending on the state and the people overseeing treatment. Hormone therapy to decrease levels of testosterone (known as chemical castration), mandatory reporting and monitoring, the use of Selective Serotonin Reuptake Inhibitors (SSRI), and surgical castration are all forms of current treatment to reduce recidivism rates for pedophiles (Schober et al, 2005; Rosler & Witztum, 1998; as cited in Hall & Hall, 2007, p. 465). Hall & Hall (2007), report that a multiple-strategy approach is the most effective when pedophile recidivism is the goal. "The combination of pharmacologic and behavioral treatment coupled with close legal supervision appears to help reduce the risk of repeated offense" (p. 469).

Drug Use & Driving Under the Influence of Alcohol or Drugs (DUI)

Drug use convictions and incarcerations (possession, trafficking, sales, etc.,) do little to deter offenders from reoffending (Huebner & Cobbina, 2007). In fact, Olson and Lurigio (2000) note that people on probation who have a history of drug use are "twice as likely to violate their probation or have it revoked and 60% more likely to be arrested for a new crime while on probation when compared to individuals without a history of drug abuse" (as cited in Huebner & Cobbina, 2007). Similarly, people arrested for driving under the influence of alcohol or other drugs (DUI) are more likely to recidivate if they have been arrested for a non-drug offense in their lifetime when compared to DUI only offenders (LaBrie, Kidman, Albanese, Peller, & Shaffer, 2007, p. 603).

This is notable data as many post-arrest and release programs are focused on treating the individual through drug and/or alcohol rehabilitation services. In many instances, a successful probation or parole is contingent on completion of such a program. In a study conducted by Huebner & Cobbina (2007), over 3,000 responses to a drug questionnaire were analyzed. The questionnaire had been presented to drug users who were on probation to determine effective support programming in the state of Illinois. According to the analysis, ... most offenders with a history of drug use (71%) received drug treatment while on probation, and most (71%) completed the full course of treatment ...[however], 45% of the sample was rearrested for any offense and 18% were rearrested for a drug-related offense ... within four years following discharge from probation (Huebner & Cobbina, 2007, p. 625).

Similar results were found for DUI offenders in a residential facility in Massachusetts. LaBrie et al, (2007) identified DUI recidivists as those who were reconvicted of a second DUI within a ten-year period (p. 606). Looking at over 1000 offenders, LaBrie et al, (2007) note that of the people convicted of a DUI offense at least twice in their lives, those who also had a history of an additional crime were more likely to recidivate (p. 612). Those who had only been convicted of the DUI offenses were the least likely to recidivate (Labrie et al., 2007, p. 609). Again, as most treatment plans enforce attendance at meetings, counseling sessions, or residential facilities that offer specific programming aimed at addiction/abuse rehabilitation, there is an entire "corrective" piece missing with regard to helping these people not reoffend.

VIEWPOINTS

One of the biggest issues behind preventing recidivism is the lack of evidence that programs actually work. The Aos et al. (2006) study analyzed almost three-hundred program evaluations rather than the programs themselves, as a compilation of data was their goal. The actual evaluation is timely and costly. For this reason, Snyder (2007) notes that for over thirty years DOC administrators were divided into two camps. The first was that society, rather than programming was the issue. The belief was that society encouraged criminal behavior, and that "fixing" society would help the overall problem of offenders. The Reisig et al. (2007) study seems to support this notion, as racial inequality is a clear predictor of criminal behavior.

The second camp was based solely upon a reaction to the lack of evidence regarding reentry interventions. This side of the argument held that nothing was going to work and therefore, criminals simply needed to be off the streets. However, since the 1970's when this argument began, prisons have exceeded capacity across the country, juveniles are housed alongside the worst offenders of society, and the cost of criminal justice (law enforcement, prosecution, incarceration, etc.) has increased placing a large burden on taxpayer dollars to keep society safe (Snyder, 2007).

According to Snyder (2007), the problem with reentry intervention programs is that ... a substantial level of effort is needed to prove that a program reduces recidivism. At a minimum, a program must be replicated in more than one site and evaluated using either random assignment or carefully selected control groups. For multiple sites to implement the same program, the program must be well scripted and documented. New programs are not good candidates for replication because they are likely to change and adapt during the first few years of existence. Thus, it takes a lot of time and money to develop, test and eventually give a program the evidence-based seal of approval (Snyder, 2007, p. 6).

Snyder (2007) also suggests that a combination of funding between states would be a solution. Together they [various states] could select an existing, promising program that might be able to serve one of their unmet needs and then lend their support to an empirically-sound, multiple-site evaluation of it. Funds to support the work could come from state legislatures that are demanding evidence-based treatment programs and from local foundations eager to be part (at relatively low costs) of a large R&D [governmental Research & Development] effort that has the potential to produce a model recidivism-reduction program. If the test proved successful, the field would have a new tool to use; if the program failed to produce the desired effects, the costs to each member of the collaborative would be minimal (Snyder, 2007, p. 28).

In addition to the minimal cost, these states would be taking a proactive stance and at least attempting to provide documentation of a program's success. Recidivism is not just a strange word, it is a strange concept. After being arrested, experiencing the court system, losing—quite possibly—everything he owns, including his family, and being incarcerated for a period of time, who would resort to criminal behavior once released? On the inside, one knows from where his meals are coming. In addition, an offender also knows who his friends and enemies are. Once back in society, it is difficult to distinguish who is friend or foe. Furthermore, with few job skills, little (if any) education, and no family support, it would also be difficult to find the motivation to avoid criminal behavior.

For those who do not recidivate in the first three years of release (approximately 30%), the likelihood that they will reoffend is low (Greenfeld, 1985, as cited in Reisig et al., 2007). This might point to the fact that those not reoffending have figured out how to stay clean on their own. It may also be that transitional programming during or shortly after incarceration has worked for these individuals. With little evidence pointing toward successful programming, it is difficult to tell. As there is proof that some interventions work, there continues to be progress for America's criminal justice field. On the other hand, it is necessary to point out the bigger problem: As most of us are guilty of breaking the rules at some point in our lives, recidivism prevention should be a priority, but clearly is not.

TERMS & CONCEPTS

Department of Corrections (DOC): Federal agency under the supervision of the Department of Justice; oversees correction facilities and regulations in the U.S.

Diagnostic Statistical Manual of Mental Illness (5th ed.) (DSM-5): A reference book published by the American Psychiatric Association; describes mental illnesses and other psychological disorders.

Driving Under the Influence (DUI): A motor vehicle conviction for driving under the influence of alcohol or drugs.

Incarceration: Jail or imprisonment.

Juvenile Offender: A person under the age of 18 who commits a crime.

Pedophilia: A sexual deviancy with a psychological basis; offenders desire sexual relations (and/or relationships) with children and adolescents.

Racial Inequality: An unequal distribution of economic resources that affects certain races and not others.

Recidivism: Reoffending (committing a crime, being arrested, or incarcerated) after being released from prison.

Selective Serotonin Reuptake Inhibitor (SSRI): Antidepressant that blocks serotonin (a chemical that sends messages to the brain about mood) from being absorbed in the body, thus increasing the length of its effect.

Serious and Violent Offender Reentry Initiative (SVORI): A program created to reduce recidivism by offering various transition services to released offenders.

Bibliography

Aos, S., Miller, M. & Drake, E. (2006). "Evidence-based adult corrections programs: What works and what does not." Washington State Institute for Public Policy: Washington. http://www.wsipp.wa.gov/rptfiles/06-01-1201.pdf

Fortuin, B. (2007). "Maine's female offenders are reentering - and succeeding." *Corrections Today, 69,* 34-37.

Hall, R. C. W. & Hall, R. C. W. (2007). "A profile of pedophilia: Definition, characteristics of offenders, recidivism, treatment outcomes, and forensic issues." *Mayo Clinic Proceedings, 82,* 457-471.

Huebner, B. M. & Cobbina, J. (2007). "The effect of drug use, drug treatment participation, and treatment completion on probationer recidivism." *Journal of Drug Issues, 37,* 619-641.

Koegel, J. (2008). *Women building futures* . Volunteers of America Northern New England website, http://72.32.194.107/Default.aspx?tabid=6096

Koschmann, M.A., & Peterson, B.L. (2013). "Rethinking recidivism: A communication approach to prisoner reentry." *Journal of Applied Social Sciences (19367244), 7,* 188–207.

LaBrie, R. A., Kidman, R. C., Albanese, M., Peller, A. J. & Shaffer, H. J. (2007). "Criminality and continued DUI offense: criminal typologies and recidivism among repeat offenders." *Behavioral Sciences & the Law, 25,* 603-614.

Lattimore, P. K. (2007). "The challenges of reentry." *Corrections Today,* 69, 88-91.

National Alert Registry. (2008). http://registeredoffenderslist.org

Reisig, M. D., Bales, W. D., Hay, C. & Xia, W. (2007). "The effect of racial inequality on black male recidivism." *JQ: Justice Quarterly, 24,* 408-434.

Rhodes, W. (2011). "Predicting criminal recidivism: A research note." *Journal of Experimental Criminology, 7,* 57–71.

Snyder, H. N. (2007). "Nothing works, something works - but still few proven programs." *Corrections Today, 69,* 6.

Soering, J. (2007). "Uncorrected." *Christian Century, 124,* 28-31.

SUGGESTED READING

American Psychiatric Association. (2000). *Diagnostic and Statistical Manual of Mental Disorders* . Revised 4th ed. Washington, DC: American Psychiatric Association.

Beerman, K., Smith, M., & Hall, R. (1988). "Predictors of recidivism in DUIs." *Journal of Studies on Alcohol, 49,* 443-449.

Beitel, G., Sharp, M., & Glauz, W. (2000). "Probability of arrest while driving under the influence of alcohol." *Injury Prevention, 6,* 158-161.

Bradizza, C. M., Stasiewicz, P. R., & Paas, N. D. (2006). "Relapse to alcohol and drug use among individuals diagnosed with co-occurring mental health and substance use disorders: A review." *Clinical Psychology Review, 26,* 162-178.

Carter, F. C. (2007). "Meeting the needs of returning offenders through employment." *Corrections Today, 69,* p. 98-99.

De Leon, G. (1988). "Legal pressure in therapeutic communities." *Journal of Drug Issues, 4,* 625- 640.

De Li, S., Priu, H., & MacKenzie, D.L. (2000). "Drug involvement, lifestyles, and criminal activities among probationers." *Journal of Drug Issues, 30,* 593-619.

diZerega, M. & Shapiro, C. (2007). "Asking about family can enhance reentry." *Corrections Today, 69,* 58-61.

Eitle, D., D'Alessio, S.J., & Stolzenberg, L. (2002). "Racial threat and social control: A test of the political, economic, and threat of black crime hypotheses." *Social Forces, 81,* 557-576.

Elliott, D., Wilson, W., Huizinga, D., Sampson, R., Elliott, A., & Rankin, B. (1996). "The effects of neighborhood disadvantage on adolescent development." *Journal of Research in Crime and Delinquency, 33,* 389-426.

Lanning, K. V. (2001). *Child molesters: A behavioral analysis.* (4th ed). Alexandria, Va: National Center for Missing & Exploited Children.

Lowenkamp, C. T., Smith, P. & Bechtel, K. (2007). "Reducing the harm: Identifying appropriate programming for low-risk offenders." *Corrections Today, 69,* p. 50-52.

Lynch, J., & Sabol, W. (2001). *Prisoner reentry in perspective.* Washington, DC: The Urban Institute.

Maltz, M. (1984). *Recidivism.* New York: Academic Press.

Marchuk, S. (2013). *The role of education in reducing inmate recidivism: Strategies and guidance.* New York: Nova Science.

Massey, D., & Denton, N. (1993). *American apartheid: Segregation and the making of the underclass.* Cambridge, MA: Harvard University Press.

McMillion, R. (2007). "Getting out-and staying out." *American Bar Association Journal, 93,* 64.

McNulty, T., & Bellair, P. (2003). "Explaining racial and ethnic differences in serious adolescent violent behavior." *Criminology, 41,* 709-748.

Parks, G. A. & Marlatt, G. A. (2000). "Relapse prevention therapy: A Cognitive-Behavioral approach." *The National Psychologist 9.* http://nationalpsychologist.com/articles/art_v9n5_3.htm

Parks, G. A. (2007). "New approaches to using relapse prevention therapy in the criminal justice system." *Corrections Today, 69,* 46-49.

Rosler A, Witztum E. "Treatment of men with paraphilia with a longacting analogue of gonadotropin-releasing hormone." *New England Journal of Medicine, 338,* 416-422.

Schober, J. M., Kuhn, P. J., Kovacs, P. G., Earle, J. H., Byrne, P. M. & Fries, R. A. (2005) "Leuprolide acetate suppresses pedophilic urges and arousability." *Archives of Sexual Behavior 34,* 691-705.

Snyder, H. N. (2000). *Sexual assault of young children as reported to law enforcement: Victim, incident, and offender characteristics.* Washington, DC: US Department of Justice, Bureau of Justice Statistics.

Stone, T. H., Winslade, W. J. & Klugman, C. M. (2000) "Sex offenders, sentencing laws and pharmaceutical treatment: a prescription for failure." *Behavioral Science Law,* 8, 83-110.

Maureen McMahon, M.S.

Defining Deviance

ABSTRACT

An overview of how deviance is defined is provided, beginning with a general review of historical definitions and the most general definitions currently used by sociologists. The development and changes of the definition of deviance across time and societies are highlighted. Special attention is given to Durkheim's views of deviance and Becker's views of the process of becoming deviant. Various types of commonly studied deviant behaviors are very briefly reviewed. The ongoing debate about positive deviance and the political correctness in defining deviance are addressed.

OVERVIEW

Defining *deviance* is not only a sociological endeavor. Several fields of study such as social work, psychology, criminal justice, and religion aim to understand deviant behavior. There are many sociological perspectives that offer a definition of deviance. While there may be some controversies about defining deviance, there are some general patterns that emerge from the literature. First explored here is the general definition of deviance with some emphasis on historical approaches, followed by a review of various approaches to defining deviance and concluding with specific topics that sociologists typically consider deviant behavior.

Historical & Current Definitions of Deviance

There are many perspectives in sociology that define deviance. Deviance generally refers to the violation of culturally established norms, values, and beliefs. From this definition, it is evident that the actions or attitudes that constitute deviance vary from one culture to another. Most definitions of deviance include behaviors that violate the norms of society. Some sociologists' definitions of deviance also include attitudes that vary from the dominant values and beliefs of society and individual characteristics such as birth defects, and/or individuals with physical disabilities. The definition of deviance may also vary from one *subculture* to another. However, how one defines deviance reflects additional assumptions about how human behavior is evaluated and by whom. Deviance can result from violations of either *prescriptive norms* or *proscriptive norms.* Because deviance is often viewed negatively by laymen, it is important to note that deviant behavior may also include activities that have positive connotations.

Positive Deviance

Deviant behavior that is negatively viewed generally reflects the normative approach to deviance. That is, behaviors that are considered deviant fall outside of behaviors that are considered acceptable or desirable by the majority of the population. *Positive deviance* consists of behaviors or attitudes that reflect the norms or values of a given society but are taken to the extreme of the norms or values. For example, most people in the United States would likely agree that altruistic behavior is favorable and is viewed positively. But when someone demonstrates such altruistic behavior at a much greater rate than most people do, it then takes on the characteristics of being a deviant behavior that is viewed positively. The idea that some people may view the extreme altruistic behavior as odd, unusual, or extreme demonstrates that the behavior is now classified as deviant. Not all sociologists agree that there is such a concept as positive deviance (Goode, 1991; Sagarin, 1985). Some sociologists view the concept of positive deviance as a contradiction in terms, and that only negative behaviors and attitudes constitute deviance.

Early Explanations

Some of the earliest efforts of defining deviance involved superstition and supernatural causes. For example, people who acted outside the realm of normal behavior were sometimes accused of being witches. Others suggested that demonic possession of the body accounts for deviant behavior. While there were several social issues with the previously mentioned approaches to explaining deviance, one major problem with them was that the efforts made to correct the deviant behavior and, in essence curing the individual of these problems, often resulted in the death of the deviant person. One example of an early cure for deviance was bloodletting—literally draining some of the blood from the deviant person in order to rid the person's body of demonic possession. Clearly, many people accused of deviant behavior died in the process.

Other early approaches to defining deviance involved biological explanations of deviance. Lombroso (1896) suggested that he could identify individuals prone to criminality by the number and location of bumps on one's head. His attempt to explain deviant behavior was rooted in *biological determinism;* one was born a criminal. Sheldon (1954) suggested that different body types are associated with elevated risks of criminal and deviant behavior. The three main body types are endomorph, ectomorph, and mesomorph. These *somatotypes* developed by Sheldon (1954) were used to explain deviant behavior. Sheldon concluded that deviant behavior varied by body composition.

While many of the original approaches to explaining deviance have been debunked, modern approaches to explaining deviance may have some general connections to the original efforts to define deviance. For example, some twenty-first century theories of crime and deviance include both social elements and individual characteristics of the deviant person. These approaches are referred to as *biosocial* explanations or *trait theories* of deviant behavior. For example, research found support for a relationship between intelligence (IQ) and crime (Cornell & Wilson, 1992; Moffitt & Silva, 1988; Raine et al., 2005); physiological and biological explanations of crime and deviance (Booth & Osgood, 1993; Raine, 1993); and personality, impulsivity, and low self-control (Glueck & Glueck, 1950; Gottfredson & Hirschi, 1990; Tremblay et al, 1994). So while the historical approaches to deviance today seem highly unacceptable and unethical, the assumptions from which they developed are taken by some modern theorists. The modern day notion that an individual's mental or physical characteristics are somewhat related to biological determinism is related to the early approaches to explaining deviance.

Durkheim: Deviance is Inevitable

Emile Durkheim (1938, 1970), one of the earliest and most famous sociologists, concluded that deviant behavior is the result of lower levels of social integration. One of his popular research projects on individuals' suicidal behavior led him to conclude that controlling people's behavior even on a topic as personal as suicide is also related to variations in levels of one's social integration. He suggested that not every member of society can be socialized to the norms, values, and beliefs of society or that every member of society can be socially integrated throughout the life course. Durkheim was a *functionalist.* He believed that deviance is inevitable and that all societies have members who commit deviant behaviors. Inherent to functional theory, Durkheim suggested that the reason deviance occurs in every society is because it serves a purpose for societies.

Durkheim suggested that deviant behavior serves societies in several ways. First, deviant behavior serves to create solidarity among the members of society. The solidarity develops from the group coming together in agreement that the deviant behavior is unacceptable and therefore the person demonstrating the deviant behavior must be dealt with accordingly.

The idea is that deviant behavior results in verbal reinforcements among members of society about the violation of cultural norms. Also, when society responds to the deviant behavior either through actual punishment or other negative social responses, this action serves as a warning to other members of society that they should not participate in deviant behavior or they too will experience the punishment. This process, according to Durkheim, results in greater group conformity. Another function of deviant behavior is that it clarifies what behaviors and attitudes constitute deviant behaviors. In essence, when people commit deviant acts they serve to remind others of the boundaries of acceptable behavior.

Lastly, Durkheim suggested that deviant behavior may serve societies by initiating social change. Basically, when one pushes the boundaries of norms and values in a society, then the members of society are presented with alternative views that may eventually be considered favorably by a majority of the members of the society. Thus, when the behavior or attitude that once was considered deviant becomes acceptable by the majority, it then fails to be considered deviant and other members of society may practice the same behavior. These four functions of deviance indicate how deviant behaviors are beneficial for societies. On the other hand, Durkheim suggested that excessive deviant patterns in society may result from a lack of moral guidance and result in a state of *anomie* in society.

Labeling

Nonconformity is not always viewed as deviant behavior. For example, *labeling* theorists suggest that there is no act that is inherently deviant. For a behavior to be considered deviant several factors must be considered. Labeling theorists critique theories that focus on a normative approach to defining deviance. Rather, they suggest that behaviors that are considered deviant result from the people in society who have the power to assign a deviant label to people in the society with less power. The emphasis in labeling theory is on the process used to assign a deviant label of less powerful people in the society. The acts themselves are not inherently deviant. The process of assigning a deviant label involves an initial act or behavior by a person or group of people. The reaction of other members of society to the behavior determines if the behavior is considered deviant or not. If it is considered deviant by the other members of society, then members of society label the person or group deviant.

Once *primary deviance* occurs and the person who has been assigned the deviant label self-identifies with the label, then *secondary deviance* occurs. In essence, the application of the deviant label serves as a self-fulfilling prophecy and reinforces the actions deemed deviant by the dominant group. Labeling theorists suggest that mental illness, drug addiction, and other such behaviors are not inherently deviant. Yet, once labeled as such persons experience social stigma resulting in fewer social opportunities and more social sanctions. The social separation due to the label creates social outcasts (Becker, 1963).

Labeling theorists have highlighted that not all members of society are equally able to assign labels of deviance. It is only the people with power in society who have the ability to label others. Thus, the process of identifying some behaviors as deviant is inherently biased against members of society who hold less power in a given society. The bias serves to distract members of society from focusing on the harm committed by people with power and focuses attention on the lesser harm committed by people who have less power in society. The approach taken by labeling theorists to define deviance reflects a change in focus from the culture and social structure to an emphasis on the process of becoming labeled a deviant and the resultant secondary deviance that emerges there from.

Rule-Breaking

The progression sociology has experienced arriving at Becker's theory of deviance has created confusion and debate about what constitutes deviance. The confusion and debate revolve around three key issues:

- Who in society has the right to determine what behaviors or attitudes are deviant,
- Whether defining deviance is more a matter of moral entrepreneurs rather than being a clear boundary of behaviors and attitudes, and
- Whether or not positive deviance is really good.

Goode (2002) highlights the debate about the very existence of deviance and how the death of deviance in sociology may or may not make sense. Within sociology there has been a philosophical move from studying deviance to focusing more on studying rule breaking. The same topics tend to fall under study whether they are referred to as deviance or rule-breaking. Thus, the very concept of deviance and defining deviance has taken on a politically correct characteristic. Although the issue of moral entrepreneurs is less obvious when we assume the rule-breaking perspective of studying behaviors and attitudes, it is still present nevertheless. The rules are established by members of society. Feminists and other conflict theorists and labeling theorists suggest that the rules are set by the powerful and are thus still applied with bias.

APPLICATIONS

Types of Deviant Behaviors

There is a wealth of research on specific types of deviant behavior. Perhaps the most commonly examined deviant behavior is crime. Laws are formal norms that, when broken, also have accompanying social sanctions such as community service, probation, and imprisonment. Laws generally reflect the most important norms of a society. When an individual violates laws and the violation is discovered by persons of authority, the criminal justice system determines the sanctions to be applied. Violations of more important formal norms are accompanied by more severe sanctions such as life in prison or the death penalty. Laws are designed to act as a form of social control of deviant behavior. While it may seem easy to determine when a person has broken the law, it is not. Laws are written formalized norms and as such they are interpretable. When people break laws it is referred to as *criminality.* Criminality is one form of deviance and it is widely accepted as such by sociologists, especially criminologists.

Deviance of the Body

A very different form of deviant behavior revolves around how people in a society treat their own bodies. Societies have guidelines for various issues dealing with the body. For example, selecting what clothes to wear is guided by a set of norms. If a person is going to the prom the rules of society suggest that the person dress in formal attire. If someone opted to wear no clothes or just a swimming suit to prom it would be considered deviant. Other norms exist about the body than what clothes to wear. For example, young people commonly acquire tattoos. The norms regarding tattoos have been cyclical, with tattoos being acceptable in one time period and not acceptable in another time period. Even though a certain number and type of tattoos have generally been acceptable and not considered deviant in the early twenty-first century, some people have practiced tattooing at extreme levels. For example, a minority of individuals seek to have tattoos cover 100% of their bodies. The extreme application of tattoos is considered deviant.

Similar norms exist for other forms of body art such as piercing. Some body piercing is not considered deviant among younger people, but a high number of body piercings is considered deviant. Still other norms exist regarding the human body that pertain to defining deviance, such as those that address the normal body weight of individuals. People who fall outside of this weight range are considered deviant. If someone is extremely obese or extremely thin, then members of society would consider the person to be deviant. In particular, if one pursues these types of weights due to eating disorders, the likelihood is very high that societal members will consider this individual to be deviant. Eating disorders such as anorexia and bulimia are often researched under the umbrella of deviance.

Mental health is another element of the individual body that may be addressed by sociologists. Not all sociologists agree about the definition of mental illness or even that it exists at all, although sociologists often consider mental illness to constitute deviance. Even what one does sexually may be considered deviant. People who are nonsexual or who experience sexual dysfunction may be considered deviant. There are many sexual behaviors that may constitute sexual deviance: group sex, sex with a very high number of partners, bestiality, pedophilia, ephebophilia (sexual attraction to post-pubescent male children), and many others. There are many types of deviance that are not discussed here.

Implications

Deviant behavior is typically defined as behavior or attitudes that are not demonstrated or held by the majority of the population. While this is a general definition of deviance, it is clear that the definition is not accepted by all sociologists. Rather, there are many different approaches to defining deviance. Contemporary sociologists are sensitive to the issues of power and subordination in society and are less willing to accept the general definition of deviance without considering rule makers, power, and subordination. As a result, how they define deviance may fall within a realm of political correctness. Nevertheless, the items generally reviewed under the study of deviance also tend to be covered under the study of rule-breaking, albeit from different sets of assumptions. There are many implications inherent in the definition of deviance. The implications vary by the type of definition adopted. When one adopts the *normative* definition of deviance, generally the person committing the deviant act is held responsible for their actions. However, if one adopts a focus on the process of defining one's behaviors as deviant, the implication is that no sanctions need be applied to correct the behavior because there is nothing inherently wrong with the behavior in the first place. The definitions of deviance adopted by sociologists vary between these two main schools of thought: the normative approach and the *relativist* who may focus on the process of becoming labeled deviant. In conclusion, defining deviance is not uniformly approached by sociologists, and the behaviors that are defined as deviant in one culture or time may not be so in other cultures or eras.

TERMS & CONCEPTS

Anomie: A state of normlessness. Anomie results from excessive deviance in a given society. Emile Durkheim was concerned that a lack of moral guidance in society would result in a state of normlessness and society would no longer exist as we know it.

Nonconformity: Takes place when an individual either chooses to behave or unknowingly behaves in different ways than the majority of the members of the group or society. Nonconformity is generally viewed as deviant behavior. However, some sociologists do not believe nonconformity alone constitutes deviant behavior. Labeling theorists suggest that nonconformity is not considered deviant until other members of society are aware of the behavior and apply a deviant label to the person demonstrating nonconformity.

Norms: Expected standards of behaviors for members of a society. Norms are culturally determined and thus vary from culture to culture. Norms may be prescriptive or proscriptive. That is, norms may tell you what behaviors you are expected to demonstrate and what behaviors you are not allowed to demonstrate. Norms reflect the values and beliefs of the members of society.

Prescriptive Norms: Guide behaviors of members of a society by indicating what behaviors are acceptable. Behavior violating prescriptive norms is considered deviant behavior.

Primary Deviance: Occurs when a person randomly or inconsistently violates the norms of society while not holding an internal view of themselves as deviant. Primary deviance can result from social, psychological, or biological origins. Primary deviance, if discovered by members of society and sanctions result, may eventually develop into secondary deviance.

Proscriptive Norms: Guide behaviors of members of a society by indicating what behaviors are unacceptable. Behavior violating proscriptive norms is considered deviant behavior.

Roles: The expected behaviors attached to a particular status. Roles are determined culturally and therefore vary from culture to culture. For example, the roles of wife and husband may vary from one culture to another.

Secondary Deviance: Results from the application of a deviant label to a person whose behavior is discovered by members of a society. The members of society respond negatively or apply some social sanction. Labeling theorists suggest that it is the application of the label that leads to a person internalizing the deviant label and developing a self-concept as a deviant person. The development of the deviant self-concept leads the person to believe they are expected to act in deviant ways. The deviant behavior that follows the development of the deviant self-concept is secondary deviance. The development of secondary deviance may involve repeated negative responses to primary deviance by members of society.

Subculture: A subculture is set apart from the larger group by its members having different values and beliefs and by the smaller group having different norms than the dominant, usually larger society. Subcultures are considered deviant.

BIBLIOGRAPHY

Becker, H. (1963). *Outsiders: Studies in the sociology of deviance.* New York: Macmillan.

Booth, A. & Osgood, D. W. (1993). "The influence of testosterone on deviance in adulthood: Assessing and explaining the relationship." *Criminology 31* (1), 93–117.

Cornell, D. G. & Wilson, L. A. (1992). "The PIQ>VIQ discrepancy in violent and nonviolent delinquents." *Journal of Clinical Psychology 48* (2): 256–261.

Cross, J. C., & Hernandez, A. (2011). "Place, identity, and deviance: A community-based approach to understanding the relationship between deviance and place." *Deviant Behavior, 32*(6), 503–537

Durkheim, E. (1938). *The rules of sociological method.* New York: The Free Press.

Durkheim, E. (1970). *Suicide: A study in sociology.* London: Routledge and Kegan Paul.

Feinberg, S. L. (2011). "Defining deviance: A comparative review of textbooks in the sociology of deviance." *Teaching Sociology, 39*(4), 382–387.

Glueck, S. & Glueck, E. (1950). Unraveling juvenile delinquency. New York: Commonwealth Fund.

Goode, E. (1991). "Positive deviance: A viable concept?" *Deviant Behavior 12* (3) 289–309.

Goode, E. (2002). "Does the deal of the sociology of deviance claim make sense?" *American Sociologist 33* (3): 107–119.

Gottfredson, M. R. & Hirschi, T. (1990). *A general theory of crime.* Stanford, CA: Stanford University Press.

Lauderdale, P. (2011). "An analysis of deviance, law, and diversity: A nascent theoretical framework." *Conference Papers—American Sociological Association,* 1563.

Lombroso, C. (1896). *The criminal man,* 2nd Edition. Turin: Bocca.

Moffitt, T. & Silva, P. (1988). "IQ and delinquency: A direct test of the differential detection hypothesis." *Journal of Abnormal Psychology 97*: 330–333.

Raine, A. (1993). *The psychopathology of crime: Criminal behavior as a clinical disorder.* San Diego: Academic Press.

Raine, A., Loeber, R., Stouthamer-Loeber, M., Moffitt, T. E., Caspi, A., & Lynam, D. (2005, February). "Neurocognitiive impairments of boys on the life-course persistent antisocial path." *Journal of Abnormal Psychology 114* (1): 38–49.

Sagarin, E. (1985). "Positive deviance: An oxymoron." *Deviant Behavior 6* (2): 169–181.

Sheldon, W. H. (1954). *Atlas of men.* New York: Harper.

Tremblay, R. E., Phil, R. O., Vitaro, F., & Dobkin, P. L. (1994). "Predicting early onset of male antisocial behavior from preschool behavior." *Archive of General Psychiatry 51*: 732–739.

SUGGESTED READING

Denegri-Knott, J., & Taylor, J. (2005). "The labeling game: A conceptual exploration of deviance on the internet." *Social Science Computer Review, 23* (1), 93–107.

Goode, E. (2003). "The macguffin that refuses to die: An investigation into the condition of the sociology of deviance." *Deviant Behavior, 24* (6), 507.

Rembis, M. (2011). *Defining deviance: Sex, science, and delinquent girls, 1890–1960.* Urbana, IL: University of Illinois Press.

Victor, J. (1998). "Moral panics and the social construction of deviant behavior: A theory and application to the..." *Sociological Perspectives, 41* (3), 541–565.

Donna Holland, Ph.D.

DETERRENCE THEORY

ABSTRACT

A prime purpose of punishment has long been to deter future illicit behavior. Deterrence works on two levels. Specific Deterrence occurs when an individual is punished for wrongdoing, and learns the price of misbehavior. General Deterrence affects the population at large who observes the fact that misbehavior leads to punishment. Another possible result of punishment that achieves the opposite effect is labeling, whereby the wrongdoer's life is irreparably damaged by the experience of punishment. Not all individuals or populations respond to Deterrence in the same way. Domestic violence offenders, white collar criminals, juvenile delinquents and capital murderers all present unique ways to consider the validity of the deterrent effect.

OVERVIEW

> Punishment is not inflicted by a rational man for the sake of the crime that has been committed—after all one cannot undo what is past—but for the sake of the future, to prevent either the same man, or by the spectacle of his punishment, someone else, from doing wrong again.
>
> —Plato, Protagoras (in Stolzenberg & D'Alessio, 2004, p. 351)

It has long been a source of speculation: just what effect does punishment have on an individual's behavior? As far back as the end of the 19th century, Durkheim posited that the "pain of punishment" would deter offenders from repeating their behavior, especially when the "punishment is swift, certain and severe" (Sherman & Berk, 1984, p. 261). More recent theorists take the opposite tack: punishment serves to make recidivism more likely, as all aspects of the offender's life are altered, and legal avenues for obtaining employment are shut. Sherman and Berk wisely speculate that there is no one effect of punishment; responses vary by personality, but also by the type of offense. They argue that white collar criminals, juveniles, drug dealers and violent offenders all present very different profiles.

In "Punishment and the Spirit of Democracy," Kateb argues that the justifications for state inflicted pain—whether corporal or not, he sees all punishment as pain—deserves far more serious consideration. The arrest and punishment of criminals has long been considered a core function of the state. He finds this troublesome in a constitutional democracy; no longer should mere sovereignty be an adequate justification for punishment. He believes there should be a reluctance to inflict the pain of punishment in a democracy, with the principle justification being that it can serve as Deterrence. It is not that wrongdoing deserves to be answered with pain, but that the pain serves to deter (Kateb, 2007).

Subjective Utility Theory

Economists have long used the subjective utility theory, which assumes that individuals work toward their own self-interests, and attempt to maximize opportunities. Other social scientists have seen the usefulness of this theory for disciplines beyond economics. It can be applied to the study of Deterrence:

> [I]ndividuals assess the net utility of engaging in a prohibited behavior by weighing the expected gain against the expected punishment, with the latter weighted by the certainty of being caught and discounted by time to receipt of punishment (Schneider & Ervin, 1990, p. 586).

The public at large has "amazing faith" in the idea that criminal behavior will be curtailed if only the law spells out certain and severe consequences (Schneider & Ervin, 1990, p. 586). Schneider and Ervin argue that empirical evidence does not uphold this "faith" as criminals' behavior seems to operate outside what should be their own self-interests.

Types of Deterrence

Generally, Deterrence is understood to operate in two distinct ways. General Deterrence works on the population at large; the punishment of one wrongdoer serves as an example to all of society about the cost of misbehavior. Specific Deterrence is aimed at the individual; once the law has been violated, and the consequence realized, that individual should have a new and enhanced understanding of the personal cost of illegal behavior. In 1993, Stafford and Warr brought these two strands together, combining and redefining them:

- Specific Deterrence—directly experiencing punishment and punishment avoidance
- General Deterrence—experiencing punishment and punishment avoidance indirectly when others are punished (cited in Sitren & Applegate, 2007, p. 31).

In this way, they move beyond the notion that distinct populations experience one or the other form of Deterrence; rather, everyone is encapsulated in both types of Deterrence. Further, they suggest that there has been insufficient focus on punishment avoidance behaviors, suggesting this mindset might do more "to encourage crime than punishment does to discourage criminal behavior" (Sitren & Applegate, 2007, p. 31); as individuals watch others commit crimes and escape punishment, the Durkheim notion of "certain, swift and severe" consequences diminishes.

APPLICATIONS

When considering the purpose of punishment, it is critical to understand what factors lead into criminal behavior. A school of criminologists believes that some portion of the population has a "constant and unchanging criminal propensity." Thus those who have committed crimes at one point in their lives are more likely than non-offenders to repeat the criminal behavior. They have a "population heterogeneity perspective," recognizing that antisocial behavior will manifest early in life, and the pattern will continue to repeat (Bhati & Piquero, 2007, p. 213). If this view is accurate, punishment should be used only as retribution and incapacitation, but not as a deterrent, since the individual has a 'propensity' toward crime. Nagin and Patermoster suggest that there is also a factor of contagion; once the offense has occurred, the offender's life circumstances take such a turn for the worse that future crime becomes more likely. Bhati and Piquero consider the evidence on criminal propensity to be quite persuasive, but see room for the contagion model as well. Nagin and Paternoster argue for additional research on influence incarceration plays on the relationship between past and future crime (Bhati & Piquere, 2007).

Incarceration

Incarceration has been the central strategy in the United States for crime reduction since 1980. In 1980, just fewer than 2 million people were in the criminal justice system—probation, incarcerated, or paroled. By 2004, the number exceeded 7 million; this equaled 2.3% of the population. The theory behind incarceration is that it "takes a slice out of an individual career" (Bhati & Piquero, 2007, p. 208). This high level of incarceration leads to one of three possible outcomes: a criminogenic effect, in which subsequent crime activity increases; a deterrent effect, leading to a decrease in future criminal activity or a null effect. Bhati and Piquero argue that it is critical to understand the impact of various corrections programs to develop strategies "that minimize any criminogenic harm and maximize any deterrent benefits that result from it" (2007, pg. 209). They suggest that the impact of incarceration in the aggregate has received far more study than the impact on the individual.

The "classic perspective" of crime holds that "swift, certain and severe punishment" will serve to dissuade individuals from crime; once the individual errs and is punished, the memory of the sanction will be an effective deterrent. Research on the specific deterrent effect of punishment on "subsequent criminal activity is not conclusive, though [it] tends to suggest that the certainty of punishment exhibits a small but significant deterrent effect" (Bhati & Piquero, 2007, p. 211). An alternative point of view suggests that instead of punishment serving as a deterrent, it instead leads to "labeling," which in turn leads to ongoing criminal behavior. The offender becomes labeled as a delinquent or criminal; this label is internalized, and makes it more difficult for the individual to opt for more acceptable pathways. Bhati and Piquero suggests that like the research on Deterrence, the research on labeling is less than conclusive, although there does seem to be an "indirect labeling effect" (2007, p. 211).

Laub and Sampson completed a longitudinal study on 500 Boston area delinquents, looking at the impact incarceration had on job stability; they found a lack of job stability had a positive correlation with subsequent criminal activity. A key theme that emerged from the interviews with these men was that most found the entire system corrupt and disinterested in helping them find a new pathway. Prison was a place to "toughen up," serving as no Deterrence at all. For some, there may even have been a criminogenic effect, for they spent their time in jail without job training or any other services that may have lead to future employment (Bhati & Piquero, 2007).

Domestic violence offenders are a group that offers a unique chance to study the dispute between the specific Deterrence and labeling understandings of the impact of punishment. By the early 1980s, feminists were pushing police departments across the country to move beyond merely separating violent partners and to use their power to arrest to stop what they clearly saw was criminal behavior. A Police Foundation study in Minnesota showed that in 85% of spousal homicides, the police had been involved at least once in the past two years; often they have intervened five or more times in these families (1976). However, the data was not complete enough to determine if making more arrests would have reduced the homicide rate.

At this time, in Minneapolis, police had three options when confronting a domestic violence suspect. The officers and their colleagues often urged separation, creating short term peace. The training officers generally recommended a form of counseling, trying to get both parties to get to the underlying cause of the "dispute," implying that at some level, both parties were at fault. Women's groups urged protection and law enforcement to deter future violence. An experiment was conducted. As police responded to misdemeanor domestic disputes, they were instructed to implement one of the three options outlined above. Victims were then followed for six months, undergoing extensive interviews with female officers, designed to elicit information about any subsequent violence. Police records for the household were also tracked. The study's authors found many flaws in the execution. Randomness was not always maintained; officers occasionally manipulated the situation to obtain the outcome they saw as most desirable. This was potentially significant since it tended to remove "bad guys" out of the mediation group and into the arrest pool; thus results on Deterrence might be less than fully valid. Still, they felt that they had a pool of 314 untainted cases to consider (Sherman & Berk, 1995).

Of the 314 cases in the Minnesota domestic violence study, 59% had a prior arrest rate, and an 80% prior domestic violence call, so the perpetrators were not strangers to the criminal world. A failure in this experiment was considered a fresh call to the police. Of the 314 cases, the group with the lowest recidivism rate was that of the men who were arrested (19%); mediation and advice resulted in the highest rate at 37%. Sherman and Berk took into account the fact that arrests could lead to incarceration; men in jail aren't apt to be re-arrested for domestic assault. They found that arrests seldom lead to significant jail time. Even when the couple was reunited within hours, in no instances within this study did the violence return in the next 24 hours. It seemed to be the arrest and possibility of incarceration that was enough to serve as a specific Deterrence (Sherman & Berk, 1995). They do acknowledge however that the arrest might have been seen as undesirable by the victim (loss of a day's wages, for example) and thus a subsequent call to the police might have been less likely for this group.

White collar criminals have never received as much scrutiny as their "street" counterparts, largely, Weisburd, et al. argues that because they are seen as one time operators, they see an opportunity, take it, and are not likely to repeat the behavior. However, an investigation of a substantial number of white collar criminals found that almost 40% of the sample had a prior arrest record. They contend that because white collar criminals have more to lose than most street criminals, they make for an excellent case study on the assumptions of specific Deterrence theory (1995).

In a study of 742 convicted white collar criminals, Weisburd, et al. looked at cases from 1976 to 1978, and compared the effect of imprisonment and non-prison sanctions on recidivism over a ten and a half year period. Specific Deterrence theory holds that to be effective, punishment should discourage the criminal from future illegal activity by ensuring that he or she knows the consequences of the action. The focus is on the individual. As these individuals were followed, those that received the more drastic penalty (prison time) were no less likely than those with non-prison sentences to repeat their criminal activity (Weisburd, et al., 1995). Prior to this study, most of the focus has been on the role that general Deterrence played, and frequently, the target was corporate rather than individual actors. General Deterrence theory suggests that those in white collar professions, often with a high stake in society, would be susceptible to the influences of being aware of the consequences of misbehavior.

Criminal Justice System

Another factor to consider when trying understanding why specific Deterrence does not seem to be effective is the role that interaction with the criminal justice system itself might play. After experiencing arrest, prosecution, conviction and incarceration, the offender's opportunities in the field of white collar work might well be quite restricted. Without prestige and status, the cost of recidivism might not seem as high. Thus, the specific Deterrence of prison time instead takes on a labeling function instead (Weisburd, 1995).

In 2005, the United States Supreme Court ruled in *Roper v. Simmons* that juveniles were no longer eligible for the death penalty. The Court referenced international standards and compacts that prohibit the execution of juveniles, but it upheld life in prison without the possibility of parole (LWOP) even though that sentence was equally condemned by the same international compacts (Flynn, 2008). This exception is significant. In 2004, 2225 juveniles in state or federal prisons were serving LWOP sentences. Of these, 354 inmates committed their crime before their sixteenth birthday. Flynn writes that the full impact of Roper on the juvenile system has not yet been felt. Many states still treat serious juvenile offenders as adults; Roper's reasoning raises questions about this. Although some of the most violent juveniles might need a level of increased incapacitation, it is now up to debate whether "unreformable 'superpredator' children really exist" (Flynn, 2008, p. 1052).

In June 2012 the United States Supreme Court ruled that mandatory juvenile life without parole is cruel and unusual punishment. This affected laws in nearly thirty states and affected life terms handed to those under the age of eighteen. The 2012 Miller v. Alabama case found that life sentences without the possibility of parole are unconstitutional for juvenile offenders.

Roper built upon the Court's earlier decision in Thompson v. Oklahoma (1988), a case that overturned the death penalty for a fifteen year old boy. Then the Court stressed that the realities of youth worked to withhold privileges and responsibilities that might "explain why their irresponsible conduct is not as morally reprehensible as that of an adult" (Flynn, 2008, p. 1054). Additionally, they held that their youth made them unable to be deterred by even the harshest punishment since their age made them "fail to engage in 'the kind of cost-benefit analysis that attaches any weight to the possibility of execution'" (Flynn, 2008, p. 1055). Flynn sees this argument as confirming that adolescents lack maturity, and:

> are less likely to foresee the consequences of their actions and process the potential effects of their actions on others. Because they fail to engage in such thought processes, children are more reckless than adults and are also less likely to be deterred by punishment (Flynn, 2008, p. 1055).

Whether or not the death penalty provides a general deterrent effect, even in the adult population, is a matter of great controversy. Bedau argues that the society should only tolerate the least invasive means of controlling an undesirable behavior. Since the lesser punishment of life without parole is equally effective at ensuring that the behavior will not be repeated, no higher form of punishment can be permitted. With the option of life without parole, there is no deterrent value in the higher punishment. Schwarzschild takes issue with that argument, suggesting that all of the evidence on the deterrent value of the death penalty is inconclusive, since no controlled study can be undertaken (2002). Stolzenber and D'Alessio have also reviewed the extensive literature and conclude that there is no irrefutable study that demonstrates for or against the deterrent value of capital punishment (2004). Schwarzschild acknowledges that the state could never argue at trial for the execution of an individual to ensure a general Deterrence in society at large, although this is the basis of much of the public support for the death penalty (2002).

FURTHER INSIGHTS

Punitive Damages

Punitive damages serve as a civil parallel to criminal Deterrence. The idea is that behavior that causes civil liability, and is "reprehensible" in nature can incur damage awards. The punitive award is both a punishment for the behavior, and Deterrence (both specific and general) against future action. In 1989, the United States Supreme Court, in *Browning-Ferris Industries, Inc. v. Kelco,* held that the 8th Amendment's prohibition against cruel punishment is not applicable in civil actions when punitive damages are awarded. Arguments were raised that the deterrent value can be counterproductive, as companies are reluctant to bring new products to the market for fear of suit. Starting in 1991, the Court has stepped back, allowing states to create limits on punitive damages. By 1996, in *BMW, Inc. v. Gore,* the Court rejected a punitive damage award as too large. They articulated a rationale that a company must be able to calculate in advance the damages for which they might be liable (Hall, 2005).

A question that springs from punitive damages deals with the fairness of treating wealthy defendants differently from others who lack equivalent resources. Hylton jokingly suggests that a six figure judgment against a multi-billionaire would have the same Deterrence factor as a parking ticket. He argues that there shouldn't be a class of defendants who can view punitive damages as "parking tickets," or an annoying cost of doing business. Others counter that as long as the full social cost of the egregious behavior is covered, than society has recouped its loss. Another approach is to ensure that if the defendant commits a reprehensible act to obtain a profit, or avoid a cost, as long as the damages negates whatever the act was attempting to gain, again, society has been compensated, regardless of the defendant's wealth (Hylton, 2008).

CONCLUSION

While punishment can serve as retribution, or to ensure that the wrong doer is no longer at large in society to cause harm again, a central purpose of punishment has long been Deterrence. Deterrence operates at two levels: specific Deterrence affects the individual who caused the harm, and now faces the consequences; general Deterrence works on society at large, providing "spectators" to the punishment with a reminder of the price tag of wrongdoing. Looking at specific categories of criminal behavior, such as domestic violence or white collar crimes demonstrates just how complicated it can be to determine if punishment serves to deter crime, or to merely make it more difficult for the offender to ever enter civil society again, once he or she has been labeled as a criminal. Both juvenile justice and the death penalty provoke particularly heated debates about the impact of Deterrence.

TERMS & CONCEPTS

***Browning-Ferris Industries, Inc. v. Kelco*:** An 1989 Supreme Court decision that held that the 8th amendment prohibition against cruel and unusual behavior is not applicable to punitive damage awards.

Criminogenic Effect: The opposite impact of Deterrence, punishment instead leads to increased criminal activity in the future.

General Deterrence: This type of deterrence works on society at large, and is a reaction to the observation that criminal behavior carries a risk too high to assume.

Labeling: "Experiences in the criminal justice system leads to increased criminal behavior because of diminished opportunities for success in ...law-abiding activities, or because of a process of self-identification... in which the individual who is 'labeled' adopt the ... behavior patterns that are characteristic of the label" (Schneider & Ervin, 1990, p. 587).

Punishment Avoidance: When a crime is committed, and no punishment follows, future criminal behavior is encouraged, both for the individual and the population at large.

Punitive Damages: "Are awarded in civil actions to punish defendants for, and deter them from engaging in reprehensible behavior" (Hall, 2005, p. 805).

Recidivism: This measures the likelihood that an offender will repeat illicit behavior.

***Roper v. Simmons*:** A 2005 Supreme Court decision that juveniles were no longer eligible for the death penalty.

Specific Deterrence: Focuses on the individual. The purpose of punishment is to discourage the perpetrator from future criminal behavior by encouraging the understanding of the consequences.

Subjective Utility Theory: Individuals are self-interested, utility maximizers.

Bibliography

Apel, R. (2013). "Sanctions, Perceptions, and Crime: Implications for Criminal Deterrence." *Journal Of Quantitative Criminology*, 29(1), 67-101.

Bhati, A., & Piquero, A. (2007). "Estimating the impact of incarceration on subsequent offending trajectories: Deterrent, criminogenic, or null effect?" *Journal of Criminal Law & Criminology*, 98(1), 207-253.

F.-Benard, S. (2013). "Reputation systems, aggression, and Deterrence in social interaction." *Social Science Research*, 42(1), 230–45.

Flynn, E. (2008). "Dismantling the felony-murder rule: Juvenile Deterrence and retribution post-Roper v. Simmons." *University of Pennsylvania Law Review*, 156(4), 1049-1076.

Hall, K. (2005). *The Oxford Companion to the Supreme Court of the United States*. New York: Oxford University Press.

Hylton, K. (2008). "A theory of wealth and punitive damages." *Widener Law Journal*, 17(3), 927-948.

Kateb, G. (2007). "Punishment and the spirit of Democracy." *Social Research*, 74(2), pp. 269-306.

Lucken, K. (2013). "You Say Regulation, I Say Punishment: The Semantics and Attributes of Punitive Activity." *Critical Criminology*, 21(2), 193–210.

Schneider, A., & Ervin, L. (1990). "Specific Deterrence, rational choice, and decision heuristics: Applications in juvenile justice." *Social Science Quarterly* (University of Texas Press), 71(3), 585-601.

Schwarzschild, M. (2002). "Retribution, Deterrence, and the death penalty: A response to Hugo Bedau." *Criminal Justice Ethics*, 21(2), 9.

Sherman, L., & Berk, R. (1984). "The specific deterrent effects of arrest for domestic assault." *American Sociological Review*, 49(2), 261-272.

Sitren, A., & Applegate, B. (2007). "Testing the deterrent effects of personal and vicarious experience with punishment and punishment avoidance." *Deviant Behavior*, 28(1), 29-55.

Stolzenberg, L., & D'Alessio, S. (2004). "Capital punishment, execution publicity and murder in Houston, Texas." *Journal of Criminal Law & Criminology*, 94(2), 351-380.

Weisburd, D., Waring, E., & Chayet, E. (1995). "Specific Deterrence in a sample of offenders convicted of white-collar crimes." *Criminology*, 33(4), 587-607.

Suggested Reading

Braga A, Weisburd D. "The Effects of Focused Deterrence Strategies on Crime: A Systematic Review and Meta-Analysis of the Empirical Evidence." *Journal Of Research In Crime & Delinquency* [serial online]. August 2012;49(3):323-58.

Luna, E. (2007). "Traces of a libertarian theory of punishment." *Marquette Law Review*, 91(1), 263-294.

McGuire, J. (2002). "Criminal sanctions versus psychologically-based interventions with offenders: A comparative empirical analysis." *Psychology, Crime & Law*, 8(2), 183.

Nagin, D. S. (2013). "Deterrence in the Twenty-First Century." *Crime & Justice*, 42(1), 199-263.

Sherman, L., Smith, D., Schmidt, J., & Rogan, D. (1992). "Crime, punishment, and stake in conformity: Legal and informal control of domestic violence." *American Sociological Review*, 57(5), 680-690.

Cheryl Bourassa, M.A.

Deviance and Gender

ABSTRACT

Early studies on deviance largely ignored the intersections of deviance and gender in society. However, recent researchers have been able to better understand and define deviance by examining the points where deviance and gender converge. Although theories regarding social deviance have been generated for decades, it is only recently that theorists have begun to explore the intersections between deviance, crime and gender. This article describes the tenets of Control Balance Theory, Self Control Theory, Differential Association Theory (as described in Social Learning Theory), and Strain Theory and examines these theories using a gender specific lens.

OVERVIEW

By definition, deviance is any action or activity that differs from accepted social standards or what society deems to be normal (Webster's New World College Dictionary, 2001). Early studies on deviance largely ignored the intersections of deviance and gender in society. However, recent researchers have been able to better understand and define deviance by examining the points where deviance and gender converge.

Upon hearing the phrase "deviant behavior," most people immediately think of criminals. And when speaking of criminals, most people will envision males as the criminals. In fact, males are more often found to be involved in criminal behavior than females. For research purposes, criminality is often divided into various categories, such as violent crimes, substance-abuse crimes, and property crimes, all of which tend to be dominated by males (Baron, 2003). Yet a lot of non-criminal behaviors are also, by definition, deviant, while others were considered deviant in the past and are now considered to be acceptable behavior. Defiant behavior, rebellious behavior, causing harm to oneself, and acting outside of roles assigned by society are all considered to be deviant behavior. Due to its location in social attitudes and practices, the definition of deviance changes as society evolves. For example, women who chose to exert themselves in an effort to preserve their constitutional rights were considered to be social deviants from the inception of the United States until the early twentieth century (Kerber, 2000). As society changed and accepted women's claims to personal rights and freedoms, the definition of deviance slowly began to exclude these women.

Today what is considered to be deviant behavior continues to evolve. Consider how views of homosexuality have changed over the past decades. Once considered deviant behavior by the majority of people and the American Psychological Association (APA), it is now viewed as an innate trait and accepted by many people in society, and the APA has dropped it from its diagnostic manual (Cummings, 2006). The evolving nature of what is considered to be deviant makes deviance a bit difficult to understand from a sociological perspective. However, understanding deviance and its impacts on people within a society helps to inform how people deal with the roles imposed on them by society and how society works to maintain these social roles. Hence, many theories of deviance have been developed, and many researchers have examined the differences in perceived deviance in males and females. Some of the more prevalent theories here discussed are control balance theory, self-control theory, differential association theory, and strain theory,

APPLICATIONS

Control Balance Theory

This theory, devised by Charles Tittle (1995), claims that the types of deviance in which one engages are based on a control ratio (i.e., the amount of control that one is under versus the amount of control one commands). Control is placed along a gradient line, with too little control (i.e., a control deficit) to the left of center and too much control (i.e., a control surplus) to the right. It is only when achieving a balance in the center of this gradient that a person will be motivated to conform to social conventions. Tittle hypothesized that when deviance is examined along lines of gender, most females will be subjected to constraints in their ability to exercise control and will most likely violate social conventions via predation or defiance. Conversely, males will more often experience an excess of control and will most likely violate social conventions via predation or exploitation (Tittle, 1995; Hickman & Piquero, 2001). In other words, because women are relegated to social positions in which they are forced into a role of submission relative to males, they are more likely to violate social conventions by defying the structures that control them or by manipulating the structures to get what they want. Men, who are located in social positions that largely afford them control or dominance, are more likely to manipulate the social structure or engage in the outright exploitation of others to get what they want. Figure 1, below, illustrates this hypothesis.

Control balance theorists believe deviance will occur when all three of the following factors are present:

- The person is motivated toward deviance by virtue of temperament or situational circumstances,
- Constraint (i.e., the risk of being caught or punished) is perceived as low, and
- Opportunity is present.

If one of these factors is absent, the deviance is less likely to occur. This theory clearly reveals the convergence of deviance and gender by taking into account the differences in how females and males are socialized in society. Females are generally socialized to care for others, consider the needs of the group as opposed to the individual, and provide support and maintenance for the social group. Males are generally socialized to occupy a position of dominance and privilege in which competition and acquisition of material goods are valued. Though this position provides greater motivation for males to conform, thus maintaining the status quo, it also moves them to commit acts of deviance that are more often categorized as criminal activity within the society (Beutel & Marini, 1995).

Self-Control Theory

This theory purports to have identified one of the major causes of deviant behavior. Gottfredson and Hirschi (1990) hypothesize that the amount of self-control one has is predictive of how likely one will engage in socially deviant behavior (Gottfredson & Hirschi, 1990). They suggest that people who are "insensitive, physical (as opposed to mental), risk-taking, shortsighted, and nonverbal" (Gottfredson & Hirschi, 1990, p. 90) will have less self-control than other people in the general population. Intuitively, this makes sense. A person with low self-control would seem more likely to break a law or engage in behavior that is exciting or gratifying without a thought of future consequences.

Self-control theorists suggest that propensity for self-control is established during childhood, is correlated to the quality of child rearing practiced by

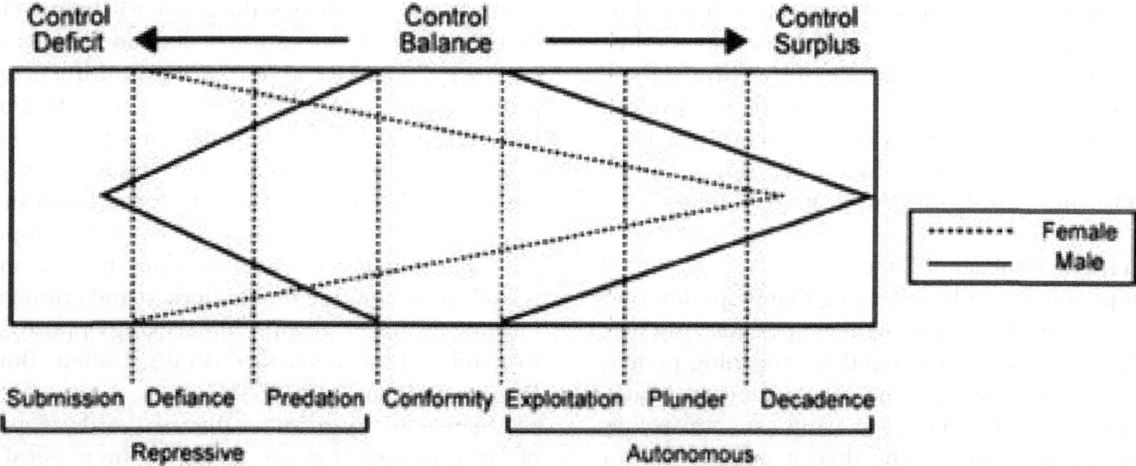

Figure 1: Comparison of levels of control and conformity.

parents, and is unlikely to change much during one's lifetime. They also claim that parents must exert strong influence over a child's level of self-control by setting and adhering to strict behavioral expectations until the child is eight years old (Unnever, Cullen, & Pratt, 2003). An adult with low levels of self-control will have difficulty refraining from temptations that arise when working to create long-term personal or working relationships within a societal structure. People with low self-control will not have the fortitude to pass up opportunities to cheat on spouses, lie for personal gain, steal from work, or execute other breaches of the social contract.

This theory has been challenged and tested several times in the past decades and remains a valid predictor of social deviance (Pratt & Cullen, 2000; Grasmick, Tittle, Bursik, & Arneklev, 1993; Hay, 2001). A few studies have indicated gender to be a significant, indirect factor correlated with criminal and delinquent behavior (Unnever, Cullen, & Pratt, 2003; Tittle, Ward, & Grasmick, 2003). It is suggested that parents are more attentive and controlling of their daughters' behaviors due to their more vulnerable position in society, supporting the finding that females are involved in fewer criminal offenses while manifesting similar levels of self-control as boys (Tittle, Ward, & Grasmick, 2003; Gibbs, Giever, & Martin, 1998; LaGrange & Silverman, 1999). Notably, these studies focused more on criminal behaviors than other types of socially deviant behaviors (e.g., smoking, eating disorders, alternative lifestyles, etc.). It has been noted in the literature that people reporting low self-control tend to form friendship groups with similar people, with whom they tend to engage in deviant behaviors as a group (Gottfredson & Hirschi, 1990). This observation led to the development of the differential association theory, which argues that deviance is a product of socialization (i.e., social learning) and group association.

Differential Association Theory

Older people always have a saying that helps describe what they have learned from life experience, such as "Birds of a feather flock together," meaning people who are similar will hang out with each other. That is the gist of the differential association theory, except in reverse: according to the theory, people tend to adopt the behaviors of the group, rather than deviant people seeking out groups who are deviant. This is more a case of peer influence than one of peer pressure. People who hang out with each other will come to adopt the attitudes and behaviors of those with whom they associate; social deviance is learned from direct and indirect association with one's friends (Akers & Lee, 1996; Sutherland, 1940). In other words, one will adopt the deviant attitudes and behaviors displayed by the majority of one's friends, and this adoption will usually begin with forms of mild experimentation that are rewarded and encouraged by the peer group. Once mild forms of deviance have been noticed by other groups, those groups will come to exclude the person exhibiting the deviance from further membership, leaving that person largely associating with the original group.

Unfortunately, the "learning" referred to in social learning theories, of which differential association is one, often means that the person is being excluded from groups who find the deviant behavior unacceptable. Instead of learning more socially accepted behaviors, the deviant person will be forced to seek out peers who manifest similar behaviors (Akers & Lee, 1996). People will seek out friendship groups whose members generally agree on what is deemed to be fun, acceptable behavior. Good students will join clubs that honor and value good students, while religious students seek out groups that study and value religion. Adventure seekers will locate themselves in a group of friends who skateboard, snowboard, and surf, while emo kids will hang out and listen to their own brand of alternative music while discussing who is into cutting.

Once a person has found a group based on certain interests and proclivities, the group will help socialize that person to the attitudes, beliefs, and behaviors its members believe to be normal or comfortable while providing opportunities to experiment with and refine their participation in those behaviors. It is in this way that a person with tendencies toward deviant behaviors will become involved in a group with similar interests and attributes and will come to adopt the attitude of the group majority. A deviant peer group is likely to encourage similar deviant and criminal behaviors within the group while seeking opportunities to exhibit those behaviors (Evans, Cullen, Burton, Dunaway, & Benson, 1997).

Males tend to gravitate toward the development of large groups that are governed by physical and competitive interactions. Females tend to interact in smaller groups that are organized around cooperation and relationship maintenance. This difference in associative preference tends to provide more opportunity and support for deviant and criminal behavior in males (Broidy & Agnew, 1997). Additionally, females are more likely to adopt the deviant behaviors of their love interests than are males. Some critics of this theory disagree that people with similar attributes and interests will find each other and form a self-supporting social group. They suggest that the groups are actually imposed on people via the social barriers in place within the society. These opponents call this competing theory the strain theory.

Strain Theory: Classic & General

Based on Emile Durkheim's "anomie" and developed by Robert Merton, classic strain theory predicts that people who have high long-term aspirations coupled with low long-term economic expectations will be most likely to engage in criminal and deviant behavior as they attempt to beat the odds society has imposed on them (Merton, 1938). These theorists believe that much of crime and social deviance is directly or indirectly related to social class, more specifically the strain of being a member of a lower social class. However, this theory was not easily validated because many of the people included in strain studies were not manifesting deviant or criminal behaviors and women were dismissively regarded as being insulated against the effects of strain due to their positioning in the social structure (Broidy & Agnew, 1997).

Subsequent theorists realized that strain cannot be simply measured by absolute deprivation (i.e., level of poverty) but must also be examined from the perspective of the person's perception of the gap between expectations and reality and his or her reactions to strain. Studies began to suggest that strain did indeed contribute to criminal and deviant behavior (Pratt & Cullen, 2000). Agnew (2001) revised classic strain theory to create general strain theory, extending the theory to allow researchers to further explore the factors that influence how a person reacts to strain. These new factors add the loss of positive stimuli (jobs, friends, romantic partners, etc.) and the acquisition of negative stimuli (excessive demands, stress, all types of abuse, etc.) to the original strain of failing to achieve aspirations and goals (Broidy & Agnew, 1997).

Once the theory was extended, researchers were better able to identify and measure strain unique to females, such as abortion, sexual abuse, unjust treatment based on gender, burdens associated with private-realm responsibilities, et cetera, and to examine both objective and subjective levels of strain. Evidence suggests that females are subjected to as much or more strain than males, negating the assertion that the level of strain correlates positively with commission of crimes. Related research suggests that the differences between how males and females experience the world will predict whether strain will correlate with deviant/criminal behaviors. Men are more focused on fairness in outcomes, while females are more focused on fairness in the process that results in the outcome (Broidy & Agnew, 1997). Recent research in general strain theory suggests that it is one's emotional response to strain that is the true predictor of criminal behavior.

Anger is the driving emotion that leads to crime; anger lowers inhibitions, moves a person toward action, and increases individual energy (Broidy & Agnew, 1997; Sharp, Brewster, & Love, 2005). Anger is acknowledged to be both situational and trait-based. While situational anger is a robust predictor of shoplifting and assault, trait-based anger only predicts assault. Researchers assert that all people experience similar levels of anger. However, differences between how females and males are socialized account for their different responses to anger (Sharp, Brewster, & Love, 2005). Given this assumption, it follows that criminal acts are more prevalent in males due to their learned responses to strain: they have been taught that it is okay to be angry. Females are taught that their anger is less appropriate, and less effective, than men's. They tend to turn their anger inward, resulting in depression or guilt, thus reducing non-criminal activities but resulting in more covert types of deviant behavior, such as eating disorders, drug abuse, and ignoring or reframing problems (Sharp, Brewster, & Love, 2005; Broidy & Agnew, 1997).

VIEWPOINTS

In 1969, a well-respected psychologist, Lawrence Kohlberg, was deeply involved in research that described moral development. His research suggested that personal morality involves a complex mix of how stringently a person is willing to follow societal conventions and how willing that person is to defy those conventions when faced with a situation in which one must choose between upholding conventions or upholding a personal respect for human life and welfare. Kohlberg's research outcomes suggested that adult females remained morally immature throughout their lives; based on his operationalized definition of morality, only men tended to reach the pinnacle of morality. His lab assistant, Carol Gilligan, criticized his work heavily, noting that based on their place of relative oppression within American society, women were not morally deficit. Indeed, these women developed a morality that was firmly grounded in care for the ongoing needs of society (i.e., sacrificing the good of the individual in favor of society), which differed from Kohlberg's biased analysis. Kohlberg believed the pinnacle of moral behavior was reached when a person was able to value the needs of the individual over the general benefit of society (Gilligan, 1982).

In this debate lies the seed of how females and males may be socialized in ways that differ, creating differing levels of potential deviance. It is also an important example of how personal perspective can introduce bias into research and theories. Studies on deviance and crime often have biases based on gender, race, socioeconomic status, and class. Crime, for instance, is usually regarded as acts for which one is prosecuted and sent to jail. This definition precludes the examination of what is typically referred to as white-collar crime. In reality, crimes are committed by many people in the upper class, but these crimes are prosecuted in civil courts or are handled by administrative boards or commissions (Sutherland, 1940). However, these activities are still crimes and should be carefully considered as such when one is determining whether a theory can be generalized to all types of deviant behavior.

TERMS & CONCEPTS

Control Ratio: The amount of power one has to limit other people's realization of their goals or to escape external limitations of one's own goals versus the extent to which one is subject to real and potential goal limitations by others (Hickman & Piquero, 2001).

Defiance: Deviant acts that reject societal norms in an effort to avoid the infliction of serious harms (e.g., political protest, vandalism, etc.) without providing apparent benefits to the actor (Hickman & Piquero, 2001).

Deviance: Any action or activity that differs from accepted social standards or what society deems to be normal.

Exploitation: The act of using other people or organizations to coerce, manipulate, or extract property from others, creating personal benefit while disregarding the desires or well-being of the exploited (Hickman & Piquero, 2001).

Operationalize: To define abstract concepts in concrete ways so that they can be more easily measured.

Oppression: The empowering or privileging of one group at the expense of another.

Predation: Deviant acts that include direct physical violence, manipulation, or acquisition of property to provide apparent benefits to the actor. Predation includes harm against both self and others (Hickman & Piquero, 2001).

Social Convention: Behaviors and customs generally accepted by a society or conforming to a larger set of rules, whether written or unwritten.

Bibliography

Agnew, R. (1992). "Foundation for a general strain theory of crime and delinquincy." *Criminology*, 30, 47-87.

Akers, R. L., & Lee, G. (1996). "A longitudinal test of social learning theory: Adolescent smoking." *Journal of Drug Issues,* 26.

Augustyn, M., & McGloin, J. (2013). "The risk of informal socializing with peers: Considering gender differences across predatory delinquency and substance use." *JQ: Justice Quarterly,* 30, 117-143

Baron, S. W. (2003). "Self-control, social consequences, and criminal behavior: Street youth and the general theory of crime." *Journal of Research in Crime and Delinquency,* 40 , 403-425.

Beutel, A. M., & Marini, M. M. (1995). "Gender and values." *American Sociological Review,* 60, 436-448.

Broidy, L., & Agnew, R. (1997). "Gender and crime: A general strain theory perspective." *Journal of Research in Crime and Delinquency,* 34, 275-306.

Carstens, L. (2011). "Unbecoming women: Sex reversal in the scientific discourse on female deviance in Britain, 1880-1920." *Journal of The History Of Sexuality*, 20, 62-94.

Cummings, N. A. (2006). *The APA and Psychology Need Reform.* APA Convention. New Orleans.

Evans, T. D., Cullen, F. T., Burton, V. S., Dunaway, G., & Benson, M. L. (1997). "The social consequences of self-control: Testing the general theory of crime." *Criminology*, 35 , 475-501.

Gibbs, J. J., Giever, D., & Martin, J. S. (1998). "Parental management and self-control: An empirical test of Gottfredson and Hirschi's General Theory." *Journal of Research in Crime and Delinquency* , 35, 40-70.

Gilligan, C. (1982). *In a different voice.* Cambridge, MA: Harvard University Press.

Gottfredson, M., & Hirschi, T. (1990). *A general theory of crime.* Stanford, CA: Stanford University Press.

Grasmick, H. C., Tittle, C. R., Bursik, R. J., & Arneklev, B. J. (1993). "Testing the core empirical implications of Gottfredson and Hirschi's general theory of crime." *Journal of Research in Crime and Delinquency*, 30, 5-29.

Hay, C. (2001). "Parenting, self-control, and delinquincy: a test of self control theory." *Criminology*, 39, 707-736.

Hickman, M., & Piquero, A. (2001). "Exploring the relationships between gender, control balance, and deviance." *Deviant Behavior: An Interdisciplinary Journal*, 22, 323-351.

Kerber, L. K. (2000). *No Constitutional right to be ladies* (2nd Edition ed.). New York, NY: Hill and Wang.

LaGrange, T. C., & Silverman, R. A. (1999). "Low self-control and opportunity: Testing the general theory of crime as an explanation for gender differences in delinquency." *Criminology*, 37, 41-72.

Merton, R. (1938). "Social structure and anomie." *American Sociological Review* , 3, 672-682.

Posick, C., Farrell, A., & Swatt, M. L. (2013). "Do boys fight and girls cut? A general strain theory approach to gender and deviance." *Deviant Behavior*, 34, 685-705.

Pratt, T. C., & Cullen, F. T. (2000). "The empirical status of Gottfredson and Hirschi's general theory of crime: A meta-analysis." *Criminology*, 38 , 931-964.

Sharp, S. F., Brewster, D., & Love, S. R. (2005). "Disentangling strain, personal attributes, affective response and deviance: A gendered analysis." *Deviant Behavior* , 26, 133-157.

Sutherland, E. H. (1940). "White-collar criminality." *American Sociological Review* , 5, 1-12.

Tittle, C. R. (1995). *Control balance: Toward a general theory of deviance.* Boulder, CO: Westview.

Tittle, C. R., Ward, D. A., & Grasmick, H. G. (2003). "Gender, age, and crime/deviance: A challenge to self-control theory." *Journal of Research in Crime and Delinquency*, 40, 426-453.

Unnever, J. D., Cullen, F. T., & Pratt, T. C. (2003). "Parental management, ADHD, and delinquent involvement: Reassuring Gottfredson and Hirschi's General Theory." *Justice Quarterly* , 20, 471-500.

Webster's New World College Dictionary (4th Edition ed.). (2001).

Suggested Reading

Alarid, L. F., Burton, V. S., & Cullen, F. T. (2000). "Gender and crime among felony offenders: Assessing the generality of social control and differential association theories." *Journal of Research in Crime and Delinquency*, 37, 171-199.

Hagan, J. & Foster, H. (2003). "S/he's a rebel: Toward a sequential stress theory of delinquency and gendered pathways to disadvantage in emerging adulthood." *Social Forces*, 82, 53-86.

Young, R. L., & Thompson, C. Y. (2011). "Gender, attributions of responsibility, and negotiation of deviant labels in small groups." *Deviant Behavior*, 32, 626-652.

Sherry Thompson, Ph.D.

DIFFERENTIAL ASSOCIATION THEORY

ABSTRACT

Differential association theory suggests that individuals who commit deviant acts are influenced to do so by primary groups and intimate social contacts. The degree of influence one receives from messages favoring deviant behavior varies by intensity, priority, frequency, and duration. An overview of differential association theory of deviance is provided beginning with a general review of the theory, followed by brief explanations of specific assumptions of differential association theory. A brief summary of key research developments are provided. Critiques of differential association are highlighted throughout the report and further developments of the theory are reviewed.

OVERVIEW

Differential Association theory is one of many sociological theories that aims to explain why people commit deviant acts. Differential Association theory was proposed and developed by Edwin Sutherland in the late 1930s and early 1940s, in response to a critique of criminology by Michael and Adler (Laub, 2006). In developing the theory, Sutherland dismissed the notion that individual variants such as age and gender adequately explained criminal involvement. Differential association theory stresses the impact that others have on one's view of deviant behavior and the law. The theory relies on the social context of individuals to explain individual behaviors. Individuals learn deviant behavior through the same mechanisms that they learn other behaviors: through exposure to primary and intimate social contacts. However, he noted that mere exposure to deviant people does not necessarily result in one behaving in a criminal or deviant manner. Rather, he suggested that the mechanisms involved in whether or not deviant behavior or criminal acts take place are more complex. He suggested that even when one is of a mindset to commit a deviant or criminal act, the social context of the situation must be perceived by the individual as an opportunity to commit the deviant or criminal act.

Differential association theory asserts that as one has more definitions favorable to the legal system over definitions unfavorable to the legal system one is less likely to be delinquent. Thus, a person becomes delinquent because of an excess of definitions unfavorable to violation of law over definitions favorable to violation law. Differential association is a theory based on the social environment and its surroundings, individuals and the values those individuals gain from significant others in their social environment. It suggests that these definitions are learned through communications with intimate people or groups from whom the person learns the techniques, motivations, rationalizations, and attitudes. Similarly, it does not suggest that any person who is around criminals necessarily becomes a criminal. Rather, differential association theory posits that those who have a greater ratio of unfavorable to favorable definitions of deviant behavior are more likely to deviate. This implies that one's likelihood of deviating is subject to change, depending upon one's ratio of these definitions. Unlike some other theories of deviance and social control, one's inclination to commit crimes will vary across the life course and is not fixed at any particular stage of development or age. Differential association theory leaves room for criminals to change their ways to become conforming people.

Nine Assumptions of the Theory

Sutherland (1939; 1974) provided the backdrop for how people obtain definitions favorable or unfavorable to violation of the law. While explicating the theory, Sutherland suggested that the following nine assumptions guide how the theory is able to explain criminal behavior. Each assumption is reviewed below:

1. Criminal behaviors, like all other behaviors, are learned. The theory has received criticism due to this first assumption that criminal behavior is learned in no unique way from other behaviors. The main criticism drawn from this assumption is that the theory is overbroad by claiming to explain all behavior.
2. Learning criminal behavior occurs through interaction with people via communication. All forms of communication are viable avenues for one to learn criminal behavior. The means through which one can learn criminal behavior through communication includes

but is not limited to personal face-to-face communication, written communications such as letters and electronic mail, video chat, and telephone conversations.

3. Primary and intimate social groups are responsible for teaching the vast majority of criminal behaviors. The essence of this assumption is that just contact alone with criminals will not result in someone becoming a criminal. If one's father was ever imprisoned or ever participated in criminal behavior, this does not mean that one will become a criminal. But, according to the theory, the primary and intimate social groups would include biological parents, adoptive parents, step-parents, and exstep- parents. It would also include siblings, more distant kin, such as cousins, aunts, and uncles, and other relatives as well. Persons other than family are also considered intimate social groups. Peers are considered a source of learning definitions unfavorable or favorable to law violation. Likewise, school personnel and other more closely tied social groups may also provide definitions favorable or unfavorable to definitions of law violation. As one can tell from this long list of possible sources of learning definitions unfavorable or favorable to criminal acts, differential association theory is complex and may be difficult to model in social science research.
4. Learning criminal behavior requires knowing the techniques necessary to commit the crimes and the reasons, rationalizations, and attitudes involved with committing such criminal acts. There have been reported incidents of parents overtly teaching their children to steal, sell drugs, or commit other criminal acts. While these instances do serve to underscore the way one learns the techniques necessary to commit criminal acts, teaching the reasons and rationalizations and attitudes are not necessarily done in these concrete ways. Take the example of a drug dealing parent of a young adolescent. If the parent is selling drugs to someone there may be a routine the parents follow when the drug purchaser [guest] arrives at the home. Perhaps the father leads the guest to a back bedroom, or a basement, or the garage, and after 10-30 minutes both the father and the guest rejoin the members of the household. The father and the guest tend to do this procedure most of the times the guest visits. Yet, the child may also observe that the father does not do this with all of the guests and that the children are never permitted to follow the father and the guest to the other room. Differential association theory would suggest that by learning this pattern, the adolescent is slowing learning how to be a criminal drug dealer. As the child ages, more learning of the techniques may occur. However, just because the adolescent is exposed to this type of learning does not necessarily mean the child will become a criminal. Differential association does suggest, however, that the risk of criminal behavior may increase as a result of the exposure.
5. The motives and drives to commit criminal acts, whether positive or negative, are derived from one's ratio of favorable to unfavorable definitions of laws. While it is likely that Sutherland intended this assumption to address the onset of criminal behavior, the theory has taken on a large amount of criticism for not providing adequate explanation of why the first person developed definitions favorable to law violations, i.e. differential association theory does not explain the origin of crime. It also has been criticized for not adequately explaining crimes of passion or crimes by a person who otherwise did not appear to have more definitions favorable to law violations than definitions unfavorable to law violations.
6. It is the excess of unfavorable definitions of the law to the number of favorable definitions of the law that raises one's risk of committing delinquent acts. Not all scholars agree about how the concepts "favorable" and "definitions" are defined (Matsueda, 1988). In general, favorable definitions would be communicated when statements favorable or unfavorable to law violations are shared; such as in the case of theft, "if they did not want someone to steal it, they should not have left it unattended," or in the case of assault, "he got his just rewards". These statements, from a differential association perspective, indicate some acceptance of

law violations and thus contribute to the likelihood that persons hearing the comments will adopt definitions favorable to violation of the law. There are a variety of thoughts that can be communicated that suggest law violation is acceptable and perhaps even desirable. Unfavorable definitions could be communicated by saying, "no one wants their son or daughter to be a criminal," or "you are not supposed to steal; it is wrong." The idea of definitions that Sutherland proposed does not necessarily require such clear statements as given in the previous examples. The definitions can be communicated in much more subtle and covert and perhaps even unintentional ways. A recurring critique of differential association theory stems from this assumption. When social scientists conduct research it is imperative that they accurately measure concepts. When the definitions may be learned in such overt and covert ways, it creates difficulty in accurately measuring favorable and unfavorable definitions of law violations.

7. Four aspects of differential association may vary: frequency, duration, priority, and intensity. Determining when and how one develops the definitions favorable or unfavorable to law violations is no simple calculus. The meaning one attaches to statements they are exposed, such as those listed in the previous paragraph, varies depending upon the frequency with which one is exposed to such types of statements and how long of a time period the exposure covers. There is an interplay or interaction among frequency, duration, priority, and intensity. Additionally, Sutherland suggested that priority and intensity also influence the meaning one attaches to the messages that one receives. Priority is generally understood as the amount of influence the speaker has on the person receiving the messages. So, if the speaker has a lot of influence on the listener and the speaker communicates definitions favorable to law violations, the listener would be more likely to adopt some definitions favorable to law violation and thereby add to the excess of definitions favorable to law violations that one held. Intensity is generally considered the amount of prestige that the listen attributes to the speaker. The greater the intensity the more likely one is to adopt the definitions favorable or unfavorable to law violations as the case may be. Thus, one critique of differential association theory is that accurately measuring these items and the inter-relationships between them is complex.
8. All of the mechanisms involved in learning non-crime related behaviors are involved in learning criminal behaviors. Sutherland suggested that there was nothing special about the way people become criminals that was set apart from how people obtain any other status. Rather, he strongly suggested that the mechanisms were the same, regardless of whether it was positive (non-criminal) or negative (criminal). At the time he developed the theory, other popular theories of involved biological explanations of criminal behavior. Thus, the notion that all behavior came about through the same mechanisms was novel. His new approach to explaining crime made him one of the most notable criminologists (Laub, 2006).
9. Criminal behavior and non-criminal behavior are expressions of general needs and values and thus, general needs and values are inadequate to explain criminal behavior. Sutherland refused to distinguish motivations to commit criminal acts differently than non-criminal behavior. The notion that general needs and values motivated deviant and conforming behavior was unique at the time Sutherland developed Differential Association Theory. Sutherland received much criticism for making this assumption.

FURTHER INSIGHTS

Differential Association Research

To this point it may seem that no adequate social science research could be conducted using Differential Association Theory due to the numerous critiques it received concerning measurement and modeling issues. This is not the case however. Many social scientists have conducted research testing Differential Association Theory.

After reviewing the literature Matsueda (1988) concluded that overall, Differential Association Theory does receive support. He suggested that further clarification of measurement of concepts would result in better tests of Differential Association Theory which would allow for a higher degree of prediction of behavior and lead to more explicit policy implications. According to Siegel and Senna (1997) deviant behavior is learned only through social contacts and interactions with persons who have an excess of definitions favorable to crime and law violation. Also finding support for Differential Association Theory, Elliott and Menard (1996) concluded that associations with delinquent peers usually precede delinquent behaviors. Kandel and Davies (1991) concluded that adolescents' associations with delinquent peers lead to delinquency. Similarly, Smith and Brame (1994) found that delinquent peer associations increase the likelihood of one participating in delinquent behaviors and continuing to participate in delinquent behaviors. In other words, they found that delinquent peers were related to the onset and maintenance of delinquent behaviors among adolescents.

The direction of causality has been challenged with some scholars suggesting the opposite; that being a delinquent leads to forming relationships with delinquent peers. However, Warr (1993) indicated that more research shows that having delinquent peer associations lead to delinquency more often than delinquency leads to adolescents developing delinquent peer associations. Tittle, Burke, and Jackson (1986) concluded that although acting indirectly on one learning the motivations to participate in criminal behavior, having criminal associations increases one's likelihood of participating in criminal acts. Skinner and Fream (1997) also find support for Differential Association Theory and suggest that differential associations are at least somewhat responsible for explaining computer crimes.

VIEWPOINTS

Pending Issues & Implications

Differential Association theory has received much criticism (for example see Kornhauser, 1978 and Laub, 2006). Laub highlighted some of the shortcomings of the theory that still remain largely unresolved: the theory does not explain crimes by very young offenders; the pattern of people aging out of crime, i.e. the age-crime curve; or why individual characteristics are related to crime and deviance. Indeed some of the criticisms have not been completely resolved. A thorough understanding of what Sutherland meant by "excess" number of definitions favorable to criminal behavior remains a hot topic of debate. Just exactly what the tipping point is in the ratio of unfavorable definitions of law violation to favorable definitions to law violation necessary to result in one participating in criminal behaviors remains largely unsettled. Although not all of the criticisms of Differential Association Theory are resolved, the theory continues to be developed. DeFleur and Quinney (1966) contribute to researchers' abilities to test Differential Association Theory by more closely aligning the theory with broader sociology and by adding clarity to the roles of primary and secondary groups in teaching definitions favorable or unfavorable to crime and deviant behavior.

Theory integration, a popular movement within sociological theory development, involves transitioning theory building out of pure theory models by merging concepts from two or more existing theories to develop unique theories. Differential association theory has been used in theory integration as well as theory development. Differential association theory is considered a social learning theory.

Cloward and Ohlin (1961) merged elements from Sutherland's

Differential Association Theory with Merton's Anomie theory to form Differential Opportunity theory. Cloward and Ohlin's theory purports that knowledge of illegal means must be learned and that opportunities to learn them are differentially available. Social learning theory is very similar to differential association theory. Both believe the delinquent is socialized or taught how to be delinquent. Akers's theory is build upon Sutherland's differential association theory. Akers developed social learning theory by using concepts from Sutherland's Differential Association theory such as the role of negative relationships and Bandura's learning model such as reinforcement and non-reinforcement of behaviors (Akers, et al, 1979). Social learning theory implies that society plays a role in teaching deviant behavior. Differential association creates the opportunity for people to learn how to commit crime and peer pressure helps to convince them to commit crime.

TERMS & CONCEPTS

Age-Crime Curve: The pattern seen when graphically examining the relationship between age and criminal behavior. The pattern shows a curvilinear relationship having very high rates of crime in the adolescent and young adult years and lower rates in younger and older years. The patterns of the age-crime curve vary by type of crimes, sex of offenders, type of offense, as well as race of offender.

Criminology: The study of crime and criminals and persons who practice criminology are criminologists. Criminology develops and utilizes many theories of crime, such as Differential Association Theory.

Delinquency: A term used to describe a pattern of criminal behavior among persons under the age of majority, usually under 18 years of age. Much research conducted by criminologists focus on delinquency and many criminology theories are dedicated to predicting and explaining delinquency. Some scholars consider delinquency to be a social problem that requires social interventions while others view it as a temporary stage in adolescence.

Deviance: Occurs when an individual violates the norms, values, or laws of society. Most deviant behavior occurs among adolescent and young adult years. The majority of deviant acts do not involve violation of formal norms (laws). However, most of the research on deviance focuses on juveniles violations of the law (delinquency). Deviance is studied by a variety of subfields in sociology including, criminology, social psychology, and others.

Intimate Social Groups: Our closest friends. Intimate social groups interact intimate ways, may be vary in duration, and may have an unlimited number of members that vary across the life course.

Peers: Defined by criminologists as a group of similarly ranked people who hold similar values and adopt similar behaviors. While peer groups can serve pro-social functions, peers are usually studied by criminologists to determine their role in negative or anti-social behaviors, such as delinquency, teen pregnancy, or status offenses.

Primary Groups: Our closest family members. Primary groups interact in intimate ways, are long lasting, and are usually have a limited number of members.

Social Control: The effort of society to limit the behaviors of people in the society. Society uses two main approaches to limit the peoples' behaviors. The vast majority of peoples' behaviors are limited by informal techniques such as parents' socialization of children, parents conveying guidelines for acceptable behavior, and motivating children to comply. Society less frequently relies on formal mechanisms to limit peoples' behavior. The behaviors enforced by formal systems of control are considered more serious violations of the norms, values, and beliefs of society including homicide, assault, and theft, and other behaviors.

Bibliography

Akers, R. A., Krohn, M., Lanza-Kaduce, L. & Rodosevich, M. (1979). "Social learning and deviant behavior: A specific test of a general theory." *American Sociological Review, 44* (4), 636–655.

Cloward, R. & Ohlin, L. (1961). *Delinquency and opportunity*. Glencoe, Ill.: Free Press.

DeFleur, M. L. & Quinney, R. (1966). "A reformulation of Sutherld's differential association theory and a strategy for empirical verification." *Journal of Research in Crime and Delinquency, 3* (1), 1–22.

Elliott, D. S., & Menard, S. (1996). "Delinquent friends and delinquent behavior: Temporal and developmental patterns." In J. D. Hawkin (Ed.), *Delinquency and crime: Current theories* (pp. 28–67). Cambridge, UK: Cambridge University Press.

Kandel, D. & Davies, M. (1991). "Friendship networks, intimacy, and illicit drug use in young adulthood: a comparison of two competing theories." *Criminology, 29* (3): 441–469.

Kornhauser, R. R. (1978). *Social sources of delinquency: An appraisal of analytic models*. Chicago: University of Chicago Press.

Laub, J. H. (2006). "Edwin H Sutherland and the Michael-Adler report: Searching for the soul of

Criminology seventy years later." *Criminology, 44* (2), 235–257.

Matsueda, R. A. (1988). "The current state of differential association theory." *Crime & Delinquency, 34* (3), 277–306.

Poledna, S., Andreica, C., & Gusan, A. (2011). "Social space of criminal vulnerability. a risk factors' perspective." Social Work Review / Revista De Asistenta Sociala, (3), 163–174.

Rebellon, C. J. (2012). "Differential association and substance use: Assessing the roles of discriminant validity, socialization, and selection in traditional empirical tests." *European Journal of Criminology,* 9(1), 73–96.

Siegel, J. J. & Senna, L. J. (1997). *Juvenile delinquency: Theory, practice and law, 6th ed* . St. Paul, MN: West Publishing Co.

Skinner, W. F. & Fream, A. M. (1997). "A social learning theory analysis of computer crime among college student." *Journal of Research in Crime and Delinquency. 34* (4), 495–518.

Smith, D., & Brame, R. (1994). "On the initiation and continuation of delinquency." *Criminology, 32* (4), 607–629.

Sutherland, E. H. (1939). *Principles of criminology.* Philadelphia: J.B. Lippincott Company.

Sutherland, E. H. (1974). *Criminology* . Philadelphia: J.B. Lippincott Company.

Tittle, C., Burke, M., & Jackson, E. (1986). "Modeling Sutherland's theory of differential association: Toward an empirical clarification." *Social Forces, 65* (2), 405.

Vermeersch, H., T'Sjoen, G., Kaufman, J., & Van Houtte, M. (2013). "Social science theories on adolescent risk-taking: The relevance of behavioral inhibition and activation." *Youth & Society,* 45(1), 27–53.

Warr, M. (1993). "Parents, peers, and delinquency." *Social Forces, 72* (1), 247–264.

Suggested Reading

Akers, R. (1996). "Is differential association/social learning cultural deviance theory?" *Criminology, 34* (2), 229–247.

Armstrong, T., & Matusitz, J. (2013). "Hezbollah as a group phenomenon: Differential association theory." *Journal of Human Behavior in the Social Environment,* 23(4), 475– 484.

Costello, R. J. & Vowell, P. R. (1999). "Testing control theory and differential association: a reanalysis of the Richmond youth project." *Criminology, 37* (4), 815–842.

Merton, R. K. (1997). "On the evolving synthesis of differential association and anomie theory: a perspective from the sociology of science." *Criminology, 35* (3), 517–525.

Zaloznaya, M. (2012). "Organizational cultures as agents of differential association: explaining the variation in bribery practices in Ukrainian universities." *Crime, Law & Social Change,* 58(3), 295–320.

Donna Holland, Ph.D.

Durkheim & the Normalization of Deviance

ABSTRACT

This article revolves around Émile Durkheim's (1858-1917) controversial proposal that society necessitates the presence of crime, as criminal activity is both normal and functional, and as Durkheim implies, subjective. Even though different communities possess varying degrees of criminal intensity, acts that are the highest form of malignancy in any particular region (e.g., the vandal in New Hampshire; the gang-banger in Los Angeles) will correspondingly warrant an upper-echelon "criminal" label. Society's reliance upon the existence of crime is confirmed by the fact that it will search for such transgressions, even in the absence of delinquent activity. Likewise, benefits that are acquired by admirable and radical acts of crime, such as those practiced by the revolutionary, help thrust society into that which is ever-evolving. A brief discussion is presented surrounding the pervasive components of crime, which survive the test of time, and exist regardless of regional differences or various forms of punitive retribution. Furthermore, the fact that society isolates unacceptable behavior as a means to shape its values is broached. Anomie, or the absence of structure, rules, and societal organization, and its correlation with crime is introduced, followed by relevant research that intersects Durkheimian theory with deviance. This research includes a detailed account by Liska & Warner (1991), who offer a comparison of different theoretical models on crime, Roshier's (1977) critique of Durkheim's ambiguous inability to properly operationalize pertinent concepts, and Maris' (1971) intriguing Durkheimian twist regarding the view that destructive behavior conducted by females can be viewed in productive terms.

OVERVIEW

Émile Durkheim (LaCapra, 1972; Lukes, 1972; Lukes & Scull, 1983; Mestrovic, 1988) greatly contributed to the field of sociology by expounding upon the nature of suicide ideology (Allett, 1991; Hassan, 1998; Taylor, 1982; Van Poppel & Day, 1996), crime (Cohen & Machalek, 1994; Leavitt, 1990; Schattensberg, 1981), religion (Belier, 1999; Stark, 2003; Tole, 1993), and education (Cladis, 1995; Dill, 2007; Oelkers, 2004). One of his most controversial premises was the notion that criminal activity was a normal, functional element of society, one from which the masses tremendously benefited. Before launching into his ideals that support such a hypothesis, rough elucidation surrounding the nature of crime must first be explored. Although crime appears to be a fairly straightforward concept for which most people have a working definition, theoretical differentiation surrounding deviant classifications exist, such as the debate surrounding whether or nor war involvement is criminal or heroic (Kauzlarich, 2007). Durkheim's definition of criminality recognizes the amount of widespread individuality and uniqueness strewn throughout the world, as demonstrated through varying religions, political beliefs, and personality differences, and which precludes the possibility for uniform customs to exist.

The impossibility of establishing one solid "norm," therefore, lends itself to the existence of several distinct "norms" peppered throughout the realm of human existence, which creates a platform ripe for dissention. Even if a person's behavior is consistently in accordance with mainstream society, his volitions naturally reside outside the periphery of other world-wide ethical frameworks. For example, a person in the United States who adheres to Christian ideology might find comfort in the fact that his ideals are compatible with the larger society, although they might conflict with people inhabiting other regions of the world, including those that are predominately Muslim, Hindu, etc. What is considered acceptable behavior in one location might be viewed unusual in another; hence, a Durkheimian perspective illuminates the unavoidable and subjective nature of values, and therefore the subjectivity of that which constitutes "deviance."

Deviance is Relative

Objectively speaking, it appears indisputable that a villain is a person who breaks conventional boundaries, rules, policies, moral codes and/or ethical expectations. However, the actual tenets comprising a society's moral structure are based on a variety of subjective factors. For example, in a "lawless" society where theft, muggings, and vicious attacks are rampant, a scoundrel might be defined only along extreme conditions, such as rape or murder. On the other hand, districts that hold intolerant views toward social blunders might hastily label a person committing minor crimes as that of a rogue. A case illustrating the latter found notoriety in 1994, when Michael Fay, an American teenager temporarily living in Singapore, an area renowned for punitive directives and low crime rates, was caught vandalizing cars and sentenced to receive both a fierce caning and a jail term (Gill, 1994; Kelley, 1994).

Differentiation can also occur intra-culturally, and the United States currently contains areas that are riddled with crime, as well as safe havens that are idyllic and serene. To highlight such discrepancy, the gang-infested streets of Los Angeles are so dangerous that officials seek community solace by granting immunization to non-violent gangs, and save their retributive energy for those who resort to mayhem and brutality (Living with cockroaches, 2007). On the other side of the spectrum, New Hampshire, deemed untarnished and renowned for its harmless and secure neighborhoods (Northern Safety, 2007), recently attempted to pass legislation surrounding the punishment of vandals via public paddling, which was declined. Though vandalizing is a serious infraction, it is interesting that both areas (i.e., L.A. and New Hampshire) proactively identify, define, and chastise the highest form of corruption infiltrating their streets. Though both actions vary in intensity, the contempt and penalty for both situations are related, and the vandal and the violent gang member render comparable eminence. Durkheim asserts that crime is normal because we search for its existence; even in a "perfect" environment, residents would search for the most "imperfect" behaviors to classify as aberrant, as is alluded to in the following passages:

> Imagine a society of saints, an exemplary and perfect cloister. Crimes in the strict sense would be unknown there. But faults which seem venial to the vulgar would raise the same scandal as ordinary misdemeanors in ordinary consciences. Thus if this society found itself armed with the power to judge and punish, it would qualify these acts as criminal and treat them as such (Durkheim, as cited in Lacapra, 1972, p. 95).

Furthermore,

> ... [society would] denounce more severely acts which it would have judged more leniently: and that, in consequence, criminality, having disappeared under one form, would reappear under another (Durkheim, as cited in Lukes & Scull, 1983, p. 16).

There is an element of high regard that Durkheim extends toward certain types of crime. Whereas law-abiding citizens can descend into the complacent comfort of their safe habitats, renegades that consistently defy norms and established rules are able to test boundaries by encouraging flexibility and change, which reposition society into a broader, more progressive stratosphere. History is brimming with instances that demonstrate the contrary, in which arbitrary, archaic, or stale governing principles have lost their relevancy throughout the course of evolving social mores. A recent example can be seen in "District of Columbia vs. Heller," the Supreme Court's controversial decision to grant Washington DC residents with the ability to bear arms, which some consider a fundamental constitutional privilege (Bravin, Davis, Fields, & Radnofsky, 2008). Others feel that because the constitution was drafted over 200 years ago, its basic doctrine has lost touch with issues that reflect the needs of today's American, and in fact might facilitate combat in an increasingly aggressive society.

In adherence to Durkheim's grounds, those who oppose such legislation should rally against its existence, thus challenging an antiquated constitutional premise. Hence, Durkheim believed that those who retaliate against the regulations with which they contest venture into illicit territory and might be legally reprimanded; however, they ultimately benefit society, who reaps the advanced strides of that which has been stirred up. In this way, the criminal and the idealist are indiscriminately one-andthe- same, rebelliously forging new and innovative pathways on which the members of society can tread. Furthermore, in the process of violating legal guidelines, a person ironically becomes more intimately acquainted with such governing principles. For example, on a small-scale level, a schoolchild who breaks the "no gum-chewing" rule might receive a lecture from the principal and have to attend after-school detention, which more thoroughly acquaints him with the "no gum chewing policy" than his classmates who have remained under the radar of observant faculty members. Similarly, the outlaws of society also relate themselves more intimately to their district's penal code, in ways that the lay public can only theoretically surmise.

Crime is Consistent

Durkheim indicated that another sign suggesting the normalization of crime includes its pervasiveness across several factors, resulting in a civilization that has never been completely devoid of criminal activity. Indeed, this level of consistency proves that deviance is a normal part of social functioning. If one could prove that crime was, say, accidental or random, then one might build a testimonial to the contrary by examining such abnormal fixtures that infrequently disrupt the social order. Durkheim recognizes that there are anomalous, irregular elements of crime, such as those that occur when the crime rate becomes either markedly low or high, and he claims that the former occurs during time of financial or social despondency. However, during "normal" times, crime exists in regulated form and is indiscriminate of chronological timeframes, regional differences, and restitution. For example, historical eras have been interspersed with legal wrongdoings ranging from an insurgence of Ku Klux Klan retaliation following the Civil War (Everitt, 2003) to 20th and 21st century hate crimes targeting the GLBT (i.e., gay, lesbian, bisexual, transsexual) community (Towns, 2006; Tulin, 2006), as well as ethnic minorities (Cuauhtemoc & Hernandez, 2008). From a cross-cultural perspective, crime can be examined internationally through statistics that delineate global aberrant realities, including the 1996 victimization rates in the following countries: U.S., 24%; the Netherlands, 32%; England/Wales, 31%; Switzerland, 27%; Scotland, 26%; France, 25%; Canada, 25%, among others (Mogelonsky, 1998), which suggest regularity despite regional division. Additionally, crime exists regardless of the level of punitive condemnation that a community imparts onto its people, a point validated by New Jersey's recent abolishment of the death penalty, due to its ineffective ability to deter crime rates ("No death penalty," 2008).

Lastly, the delineation of deviance allows populations to sculpt and identify their own tailor-made value systems. The fabric of any given society creates its texture based upon a variety of factors, and in order to fully come to terms with the multicultural dimensions that comprise a group of people, it is necessary to examine their collective preferential leanings, ways of expressing faith, and communication styles. It is simultaneously essential to comprehend acts that are discouraged and liable to be punished including an itemized list of behaviors that are considered vile, taboo, or offensive.

FURTHER INSIGHTS

Anomie

Suicide, in the words of Oppenheim (as cited in Friedman, 1967) is "the negation of the strongest of all human instincts, that of self-preservation..." and was a subject of immense fascination for Durkheim, which inspired his formation of a conceptual framework containing two sets of opposing qualities explicating the reasons why people take their own lives. This framework consists of the following polarities: *egoism,* or extreme self absorption and *altruism,* which entails a lack of individuation; as well as *anomie,* or societal chaos and an absence of structure, and *fatalism,* which is an overbearing amount of control and rigidity (Acevedo, 2005; Bearman, 1991; Dohrenwend, 1959; Johnson, 1965; Pope, 1975).

Durkheim furthered his understanding of these concepts regarding their pertinence to other societal trends, such as crime and deviance. He considered anomie an essential prerequisite for the manifestation of negativity, particularly because humans are so versatile and wide-ranging in both their beliefs and pursuits, and therefore necessitates an organized system of and standards and rules from which to configure their behavior; the absence of such contributes toward a plunge into obliteration. Interestingly, Durkheim believed that a structured and defined set of conventions is ultimately an epitomized ideal, because as society fosters increased levels of industrialization and expansion, anomie has acquiesced into the norm, resulting in augmented rates of delinquency; thus industrialization encourages the normalization of deviance.

Strain Theory

Twentieth-century American sociologist Robert K. Merton furthered Durkheim's conceptualization of anomie and criminality through what he dubbed "strain theory," which revolves around the notion that people naturally aspire to the attainment of dreams and goals, but often lack an organized route by which to achieve such lofty desires (Featherstone & Deflem, 2003; Rosenfield, 1989). The discrepancy between passionate aspirations and nebulous plans of action often render criminality, in which people resort to unscrupulous deeds to produce their targeted objectives. Stephens (1994) discussed the growing envelopment of anomie within the United States based upon a collective, egocentric morale that is instilled into people at very young ages, whereby they are assured that their prospective career paths can entertain any interest that enters their realm of awareness; they can be President of the United States! They can be rich and famous! Moreover, today's media images are inundated with everyday people who instantaneously transform into legendary "reality television" superstars (Setoodeh, 2004), despite an absence of talent or skill, making such a "dream" appear easy and within reach. Unfortunately, such grandiose ambitions are not only unrealistic, but they are typically unaccompanied with specific instructions for proper enactment. This system manufactures a formula for frustration, and eventual crime-laden outcomes.

Hanon and DeFina (2005) integrate the anomie paradigm into their understanding of criminal behavior, with regard to racial demographics and crime rates. In particular, the African American community has been scrutinized for higher levels of legal infractions, which can be explained through an anomie-oriented perspective that suggests the "American Dream" holds appeal to all U.S. residents, although the method for obtaining its magnetic allure is extended more gratuitously toward Caucasians. The harsh and racist obstacles that African Americans face may trounce their abilities to acquire assets through legal means, and they may feel forced to utilize underhanded approaches:

> ...the assimilation of African Americans to mainstream culture patterns, including the American Dream. Black and white Americans disagree on many things, but they are united in their commitment to the core tenets of the dominant successful ideology. (Messner & Rosenfeld, 2001, as cited in Hannon & DeFina, 2005, p. 52)

VIEWPOINTS

Other Crime Theories

Opportunity Theory

Liska and Warner (1991) offer a cross comparison between several disparate theories on the origins of crime (i.e., opportunity theory, routine-activities, traditional functionalist, and fear-of-crime) the second of which exemplifies the tenets of Durkheimian philosophy. *Opportunity theory* postulates that criminality is shrewdly logical in nature, in which the offender proactively places himself in situations that naturally facilitate felonious activity; the "opportunist" therefore lurks in areas that are ripe with attaining his goal of dereliction.

On the other hand, *routine-activity, traditional functionalist,* and *fear-of-crime* models focus on the ways in which people proactively structure their lifestyles in response to amoral deeds, although they examine such phenomena from contradictory standpoints.

Routine-Activity Theory

Routine-activity theory asserts that there are three components necessary for crime to exist: a continual supply of both delinquents and victims, as well as an absence of protective forces that ward off such malevolence (e.g., police officers, security devices), and lifestyle norms that enhance vulnerability to criminal activity, which have incidentally increased in recent decades. These norms include an emergence of single female-headed households, dual-working households that necessitate both parties be absent throughout the course of the day, as well as increased work-travel demands that mandate long-term domestic departure.

Traditional Functionalist Theory

The *traditional functionalist* perspective reflects Durkheim's ideals by emphasizing the societal necessity of crime. This approach postulates that criminal activity ignites a successive chain of events, which in the long run evolves favorably for society. This sequence progressively operates in the following manner:

- The crime is committed
- The public uproariously responds to such a misdeed, including a unanimously endorsed punishment for the perpetrator

- The community assembles together in order to put the pieces back together, as a form of therapeutic alliance and support
- The community creates a sense of solidarity, which serves as a shield to stave off future indiscretions.

In other words, there are meaningful outcomes that result from the most heinous acts of deviance, in that communities can establish close and meaningful emotional bonds, or, from a practical stance, formulate a united front that enforces safety, this banning future chaos from penetrating their residential corridors.

Fear-of-Crime Model

In direct rebuttal to this Durkheimian view, the *fear-of-crime* model refutes the premise outlined by the steps in the above sequence by suggesting that at the offset of misconduct, people relegate themselves to the confines of their own homes in order to enhance their sense of security, thus eliminating opportunities for social solidarity.

Liska and Warner (1991), in an attempt to provide clarity toward the multifaceted origins of criminal activity, examined the existing theories in more detail to unearth precision on these diverse theoretical concepts, which otherwise appear muddled and inconsistent. Their study targeted urban communities where criminal activity is usually quite abundant, and found that living amid such transgressions prompts people to confine themselves to their own personal space. Hence, contrary to Durkheim's premise, this research suggests that crime imparts a sense of detachment and isolation; however, a by-product of such secluded lifestyles serves as a protective barrier from crime. Consequently, although crime does not engender elevated levels of cohesion and camaraderie per se, a positive "final product" (i.e., reduced crime rates) emerges.

Is Crime Necessary?

Roshier (1977) challenges Durkheim's assertion that crime is normal, first by operationalizing the meaning of "normal," which encompasses that which is *both* inevitable and necessary. He feels that Durkheim goes to great length detailing the inevitability of deviance, indicated by specification on its immense societal existence, but feels that he glosses over its necessity by making the following concluding statement "crime is, then, necessary; it is bound up with the fundamental conditions of all social life, and by that very fact it is useful" (Durkheim, as cited in Roshier, 1977 p. 311). Hence, Roshier argues that rather than examining deviance as normal, based on both inevitability and necessity as two separate entities, Durkheim feels that the inevitability of deviance renders it necessary. Further, Roshier acknowledges that Durkheim subsequently addresses the *functionality* of deviance, which he maintains is independent of the notion that it is necessary. In other words, a concept or behavior might be functional, but unnecessary; for example, people might find that partaking in individual interests and hobbies function as cathartic, healthy, and personally gratifying outlets, although such acts might not be a necessary life-sustaining force.

There are several researchers who have touched upon Durkheim's theory, such as Maris (1971), who claims that destructive behavior among females, including deviant sexual acts, substance abuse, and suicide attempts actually act as a barrier from suicide by serving as a survival strategy for life's harsh realities. Certainly, suicide attempts can capitulate into suicide, but if they do not, such attempts, along with other self-injurious patterns should be viewed as an alternate to self-annihilation, perhaps by functioning as a "cry for help" to ensure that some sort of intervention will take place. This assumes a Durkheimian premise by emphasizing that a productive "end" justifies its "means," despite a rocky emotional and physically destructive process.

CONCLUSION

Durkheim's claim that deviance is a natural aspect of society, one that possesses functional properties, can be a jarring premise that does not easily resonate with our logical or intuitive instincts. Indeed, most morally upright citizens go to great lengths to eradicate criminal activity, either by vigilantly guarding their homes or communities à la neighborhood watch techniques, or through the careers that they conscientiously occupy such as police officers and military personnel. However, social scientists have long isolated behavior that, from the layperson's standards seem to defy a sense of shrewd discernment.

For example, there has been an excess of literature specifying the functional and indirect benefits that families obtain when a member is alcoholic. Despite the obvious heartache and despondency that visibly accompanies such a dynamic, there is also often subtle or unconscious remuneration that is derived, such as the distinct roles that become clearly established (e.g., the person who assumes the "caretaker" role, etc.), roles that give people meaning, and are sorely mourned if the alcoholic family member seeks recovery. Similar to this illustration of an illogical yet advantageous derivative that is oftentimes garnered through adverse behavior (e.g., alcoholism), the benefits of endemic crime and deviance, as initiated by Durkheim, are also prolific.

TERMS & CONCEPTS

Altruism: An element of Durkheim's conceptual framework that clarifies the origins of suicide and crime rates, which entails a lack of personal individuation.

Anomie: An element of Durkheim's conceptual framework that clarifies the origins of suicide and crime rates, which involves societal chaos and an absence of structure.

Egoism: An element of Durkheim's conceptual framework that clarifies the origins of suicide and crime rates, which involves extreme self absorption.

Fatalism: An element of Durkheim's conceptual framework that clarifies the origins of suicide and crime rates, which involves an overbearing amount of social control and rigidity.

Strain Theory: Merton's theory, which revolves around the notion that people naturally aspire for the obtainment of dreams and goals, but often lack an organized route by which to achieve such lofty desires. The discrepancy between passionate aspirations and nebulous plans of action often result in criminality.

Traditional Functionalist Theory: A reflection of Durkheim's ideals, which emphasizes the societal necessity of crime. This approach postulates that criminal activity ignites a successive chain of events, which in the long run evolves favorably for society.

BIBLIOGRAPHY

Acevedo, G. A. (2005). "Turning anomie on its head: Fatalism as Durkheim's concealed and multidimensional alienation theory." *Sociological Theory, 23*(1), 75–85.

Allett, J. (1991). "Tono-Bungay: A study of suicide." *University of Toronto Quarterly, 60*(4), 469–475.

Bearman, P. S. (1991). "The social structure of suicide." *Sociological Forum, 6*(3), 501–524.

Belier, W. W. (1999). "Durkheim, Mauss, classical evolutionism and the origin of religion." *Method & Theory in the Study of Religion, 11*(1), 24–46.

Bravin, J., Davis, S., Fields, G., & Radnofsky, L. (2008). "In a first, high court affirms gun rights." *Wall Street Journal, 251*(150), 1–10.

Cladis, M. S. (1995). "Education, virtue and democracy in the work of Emile Durkheim." *Journal of Moral Education, 24* (1), 37–52.

Cohen, L. E. & Machalek, R. (1994). "The normalcy of crime: From Durkheim to evolutionary ecology." *Rationality & Society, 6*(2), 286–308.

Cuauhtemoc, C. & Hernandez, G. (2008). "No human being is illegal." *Monthly Review: An Independent Socialist Magazine, 60*(2), 23–31.

Dill, J. S. (2007). "Durkheim and Dewey and the challenge of contemporary moral education." *Journal of Moral Education, 36*(2), 221–237.

Dohrenwend, B. P. (1959). "Egoism, altruism, anomie, and fatalism: A conceptual analysis of Durkheim's types." *American Sociological Review, 24*(4), 466–473.

Everitt, D. (2003). 1871 "War on terror." *American History, 38*(2), 26–33.

Featherstone, R. & Deflem, M. (2003). "Anomie and strain: Context and consequences of Merton's two theories." *Sociological Inquiry, 73*(4), 471–489.

Fish, J. S. (2013). "Homo duplex revisited: A defence of Émile Durkheim's theory of the moral self." *Journal of Classical Sociology, 13*(3), 338–358.

Friedman, P. (1967). *On suicide.* New York: International Universities Press, Inc.

Gill, R. T. (1994). "The importance of deterrence." *Public Interest, 117,* 51–56.

Hannon, L. & DeFina, R. (2005). "Violent crime in African American and White neighborhoods: Is poverty's detrimental effect race-specific?" *Journal of Poverty, 9*(3), 49–67.

Hassan, R. (1998). "One hundred years of Emile Durkheim's suicide: A study in sociology." *Australian & New Zealand Journal of Psychiatry, 32*(2), 168–171.

Johnson, B. D. (1965). "Durkheim's one cause of suicide." *American Sociological Review, 30*(6), 875–886.

Kauzlarich, D. (2007). "Seeing war as criminal: Peace activist views and critical criminology." *Contemporary Justice Review, 10*(1), 67–85.

Kelley, K. J. (1994). "First discipline, then democracy." *Utne Reader, 64,* 17–18.

LaCapra, D. (1972). *Emile Durkheim, sociologist and philosopher.* Ithaca and London: Cornell University Press.

Leavitt, G. C. (1990). "Relativism and cross-cultural criminology: A critical analysis." *Journal of Research in Crime & Delinquency, 27*(1), 5–29.

Liska, A. E. & Warner, B. D. (1991). "Functions of crime: A paradoxical process." *American Journal of Sociology, 96* (6), 1441–1463.

"Living with cockroaches." (2007). *Economist, 384* (8540), 26–26.

Lukes, S. (1972). *Emile Durkheim: His life and work.* New York: Harper & Row, Publishers.

Lukes, S. & Scull, A. (1983). *Durkheim and the law.* New York: St. Martin's Press.

Maris, R. W. (1971). "Deviance as therapy: The paradox of the self-destructive female." *Journal of Health & Social Behavior, 12*(2), 113–124.

Mestrovic, S. G. (1988). *Emile Durkheim and the reformation of sociology.* USA: Rowman & Littlefield Publishers, Inc.

Mogelonsky, M. (1998). "International crime victims..." *American Demographics, 20*(9), 42.

"No death penalty for Jersey." (2008). *American City & County, 123*(1), 12.

"Northern Safety." (2007). *State Legislatures, 33* (6), 14.

Oelkers, J. (2004). "Nohl, Durkheim, and Mead: Three different types of 'history of education'." *Studies in Philosophy & Education, 23*(5/6), 347–366.

Pope, W. (1975). "Concepts and explanatory structure in Durkheim's theory of suicide." *British Journal of Sociology, 26*(4), 417–434.

Rawls, A. (2012). "Durkheim's theory of modernity: Self-regulating practices as constitutive orders of social and moral facts." *Journal Of Classical Sociology, 12*(3/4), 479–512.

"Robert Merton." (2003). *Economist, 366*(8315), 81.

Roshier, B. (1977). "The function of crime myth." *Sociological Review, 25*(2), 309–323.

Rosenfeld, R. (1989). "Robert Merton's contributions to the sociology of deviance." *Sociological Inquiry, 59*(4), 453– 466.

Schattenberg, G. (1981). "Social control functions of mass media depictions of crime." *Sociological Inquiry, 51*(1), 71–77.

Setoodeh, R. (2004). "Second dish of beefcake." *Newsweek, 144*(12), 59.

Stark, R. (2003). "Why Gods should matter in social science." *Chronicle of Higher Education, 49*(39), 7–9.

Stephens, G. (1994). "The global crime wave." *Futurist, 28*(4), 22–28.

Taylor, S. (1982). *Durkheim and the study of suicide.* New York: St. Martin's Press.

Tole, L. A. (1993). "Durkheim on religion & moral community in modernity." *Sociological Inquiry, 63*(1), 1–29.

Towns, L. (2006). "Ethics and oppression of GLBT citizens: CSWE and NASW involvement." *Journal of Progressive Human Services, 17*(1), 1–4.

Tulin, E. L. (2006). "Where everything old is new again-enduring episodic discrimination against homosexual persons." *Texas Law Review, 84*(6), 1587–1632.

Van Poppel, F. & Day, L. H. (1996). "A test of Durkheim's theory of suicide-without committing the 'ecological fallacy'." *American Sociological Review, 61*(3), 500–507.

SUGGESTED READING

Breathnach, S. (2002). *Emile Durkheim on crime and punishment.* USA: Dissertation.com

Pickering, W. (1994). *Debating Durkheim.* London, USA, and Canada: Routledge, Inc.

Riley, A. T. (2014). *The social thought of Emile Durkheim.* Thousand Oaks, CA: Sage.

Stark, R. (1997). *Religion, deviance, and social control.* New York: Routledge, Inc.

Cynthia Vejar, Ph.D.

Gang Membership

ABSTRACT

For many youth, gang membership is a way of life. Deviance and delinquency, often attributed to gang membership, are a certainty. Most gang members join ranks as young teenagers, and the prevalence of girls in gangs is rising. One study looks at the gang mentality of prison inmates who purposely (and without remorse) attacked law enforcement officials. As part of an attempt to combat gang activity, The U.S. Department of Justice has several commissions to identify gang members and to prevent new members from joining. Law enforcement officials and school administrators are also trained to identify gang tattoos in and outside of school.

OVERVIEW

West Side Story is a tragic love story depicted through a turf-war between two rival gangs—the Jets and the Sharks. Both the film and the Broadway production are based on fictional events starring fictional characters. However, neither Tony nor Maria saw the realistic ending of their romance before it happened; gang activity often involves violence, and violence often results in death. While Tony didn't anticipate his impending demise, school administrators, criminalists, and the federal government do realize the danger of gang membership and try to prevent it whenever they note new affiliates being pursued.

A gang is generally a group of individuals (often adolescents or young adults) who have united as an organized collection in a set territory, often to engage in illegal or deviant behaviors. In most instances, an allegiance forms, and the gang members become loyal to each other and the gang as an entity. Another part is swearing allegiance to the other members of the group, vowing to protect and stand by each of them. This allegiance is what identifies members of the Ku Klux Klan and other cult-like organizations as well. In this vein, gang activity crosses education, racial, socioeconomic, and geographic boundaries.

Juvenile Delinquency

Primarily, though, gangs in America contain male youth, adolescents generally ranging in age from ten to twenty. In many instances, the members of a gang are considered juvenile delinquents, as they tend to behave in ways that are defined as offenses of deviance. A general definition of a juvenile delinquent includes people who are under the age of 18 committing one or more acts that violate the law. Violating the law for a juvenile can include not attending school, running away from home, or drinking alcohol; it can also include many of the same offenses committed by adults, like theft or assault (Smith, 2008).

Smith (2008) also notes that juvenile delinquency has been identified with other youth behavior issues, like antisocial behavior, conduct disorder, and oppositional defiant disorder. Sadly, these disorders are often "seen in combination with other mental health disorders and conditions such as Attention Deficit and Hyperactivity Disorder" (Smith, 2008, p. 4). Young men feeling like they behave differently than their peers may see the community of gang membership as a positive move toward social integration, not to mention a status builder. Peers who never noticed these young men will surely take note when the social misfits become the school drug dealers or the bullies on the playground. What's critical to note here is that most youth will decide to enter a gang by the time they reach the age of fifteen. Any adolescent who violates the law should receive immediate intervention, especially if he's a young teenager.

Youth in Montreal, Canada. In the study, gang members between the ages of 14-16 were evaluated based on self-reported activity as well as court documents. Gatto et al. (2005) focused on the frequency of several behaviors they considered to be delinquent. Drug use, property damage, theft, and violent offenses were the concentration (p. 1178). Of the several hundred youth in the study, those affiliated with a gang were the most likely to act delinquently (p. 1178), so much so that once all of the data was correlated, membership in a gang was noted as an actual predictor for delinquency (p. 1186). This is a circular reference: those who behave delinquently tend to be gang members and gang members—as the study notes—will be delinquent. This is not to say that good kids don't do bad things because they do. However, in this study, those adolescents who used drugs, destroyed property, or behaved violently were members of gangs.

FURTHER INSIGHTS

Gang Mentality

Pinizzotto, Davis & Miller III, (2007), conducted over twenty-years of research interviewing gang members in prison regarding their violent behaviors toward members of law enforcement. During their interviews, Pinizzotto et al. (2007) learned that, ... gang members either attempted to or inflicted injuries of greater severity than appeared warranted under the circumstances. They exhibited no remorse for their actions but, rather, appeared to take pride in attacking sworn law enforcement professionals (p. 3).

For example, attacking a police officer is a high-status endeavor.

What is not surprising is that Pinizotto et al. (2007) noted similarities among the inmates.

- First, all of the gang members they interviewed had no male role models when growing up;
- Second, none of the gang members graduated from high school;
- Third, the average age for the first criminal offense of the interviewees was nine;
- Fourth, all of the inmates interviewed "experienced some form of verbal or physical abuse within the family setting. Outside this unit, all became the victim of at least one physical assault during their early childhoods";
- The fifth similarity involves work; none of the gang members had a non-gang affiliated job when they were arrested;
- Finally, each of the inmates identified their neighborhoods as being an integral part of their lives (Pinizotto et al., 2007 p. 3-6).

Summarizing their findings, the researchers identify a gang mentality that should cause alarm:

The goal of every gang member was to achieve status and respect within their gangs. Respected only when feared, gang members achieved this through repeated acts of physical violence against others ... Once perceived as willing to use violence without conscience, especially when directed toward law enforcement officers, gang members obtained status (p. 7).

Girls in Gangs

According to Wes McBride, a retired L. A. County Sheriff's investigator and an authority on street gangs, "a lot of gang fighting is about girlfriends. It's really a turf dispute. The woman is a man's property, and if she's insulted, he's insulted ... There used to be fistfights, but now shooting the other guy is the only means of problem solving" (as cited in Junod, 2008, p. 100). Someone may wonder why a young woman would join a gang. Eghigian & Kirby (2006) note some possible reasons:

Girls join gangs for the same reason most boys do—multiple factors and circumstances that have existed throughout their lives: financial opportunity, identity and status, peer pressure, family dysfunction and protection. However, some girls readily admit that they join because they are bored and look to gangs for a social life; they are looking for fun and excitement and a means to find parties and meet boys. Regrettably for those who naively join expecting harmless social rewards, they may find out too late about the actual violent nature of street gang existence. Still, others join simply because gangs are there in the neighborhood and are viewed as an everyday way of life (Eghigian & Kirby, 2006, p. 48).

Even if it is a way of life, young women need to endure initiation before gaining member status within a gang. In some gangs the practice of initiation would be dictated, like in a hazing or pledging situation. In other cases, however, the person who will endure the circumstances has the opportunity to choose by what method she is welcomed into the gang (Eghigian & Kirby, 2006). In general, most initiation types fall into one of the following categories.

- "Violated" or "jumped in" refers to a physical beating the candidate must absorb to prove her toughness, loyalty and commitment to the gang;
- The mission method simply requires the girl to commit a criminal act, perhaps ride along on a drive-by shooting or even be dropped off deep in enemy territory and forced to get out alive;
- "Sexed in" is not the most common, but certainly the least respected initiation, in which a female may elect to participate in sex with a gang member. However, both girls and boys alike look down on this initiation, and those who elect this course are usually typecast and have extremely low status; and
- "Walked in" or "blessed in" is reserved only for those girls who have had generations of family as gang members, who have a family member in good gang standing, or who have grown up in

the neighborhood, are well known, respected and have proved their loyalty beyond question (Eghigian & Kirby 2006, p. 49).

One of the roles that young women have within a gang community is to transport contraband like drugs and guns in and outside of a prison. The theory behind this job is that criminalists are less likely to search women. Young women also tend to find employment within the law enforcement system, perhaps in a clerk's office to gather information regarding gang members or witnesses of crimes committed by gang members. Another role is much more dangerous and requires dependability. Some young women act as lures, turning the tables on rival gang members to gather information or to set up the rivals for an ambush. Some young women also sell drugs and participate in other criminal activities in support of the gang. Finally, others take care of the children of gang members and sometimes find steady work to assist in gaining a regular income (Eghigian & Kirby 2006).

In addition to taking on different roles within a gang, young women also take on different positions of power. For example, ... girls range from hardcore members to "groupies" looking for a good time and someplace to hang out. Law enforcement has documented their participation in all forms of violence, and today they are appearing in "girls only" gangs. These gangs form from direct recruits or from the ranks of dissatisfied former members of male gangs looking for more opportunity (Eghigian & Kirby 2006, p. 48).

It is important to note that to build and sustain a "girls only" gang, the power structure would have to be that of any other gang, with people in power calling the shots (i.e., ordering the commission of crimes like drug dealing, theft, and violent offenses). Within these gangs, there would also need to be young women with a lower power status who will commit the crimes as well as youth in the lowest position to keep lookout and recruit new members. What may be shocking is that the delinquent behaviors within the gangs—theft, intimidation, drug dealing, and violent offenses—will be similar regardless of a leader's gender. Indeed, according to the US Centers for Disease Control and Prevention violent crime arrest rates for girls aged 10 to 24 declined from 139.6 arrests per 100,000 in 1995, to 99.7 arrests per 100,000 in 2011. Arrest rates in general, however, were higher for males than for females from during this period.

Getting Out of the Gang

For gang members of either gender, getting out of a gang offers hope for a normal life, free of criminal activity and violence. Leaving a gang can be more difficult than becoming part of one, as gang members are considered the property of the gang itself. Also, it is important to note that as much as parents and school officials want a youth to walk away from the gang life, if the young man or woman doesn't truly want to leave, a half-hearted attempt could be dangerous for the whole family. However, with the careful consideration of the following things, a safe exit is possible if a person truly wants to leave.

- Seeking help from nongang members is crucial to a safe exit. Trusted adults like counselors at school, law enforcement, or clergy can offer assistance in creating an effective exit plan (Eghigian & Kirby 2006).
- It is essential that anyone wanting to leave a gang understands the rules of conduct for the gang. For instance, is there a clear guide to what will happen if someone tries to leave? Understanding these rules can help create a plan for leaving (Eghigian & Kirby 2006).
- Fading away by gradually becoming less active in a gang is a typical method for getting away from the illegal activity of a gang (Preventing Gang Involvement, 2006).
- Creating distance from the gang by being less available for gang activities is a way to fade away. Having a job, participating in supervised and organized recreational programs, or volunteering for a local church are ways to occupy the time that used to be spent with gang members (Preventing Gang Involvement, 2006).
- Finally, relocating the entire family to a community that does not have heavy gang activity may be necessary. This is an extreme way to sever ties with a gang, but in some cases, it is the only way (Preventing Gang Involvement, 2006).

What is important here is that "getting out" is always a possibility as the connection and loyalty felt toward the members of a gang can be redirected toward family and non-deviant friends. However, the reason(s) that youth rejected family and friends in exchange for the community of a gang will still be present once they make the move to reenter their old lives. Going back to the issues and possible conflicts they left will be a difficult adjustment, and the entire family unit should be involved in the transition process, which could be lengthy.

Gang Tattoos

While a lot of people think tattoos are cool and get them to be identified as such, gang members get them as a form of branding, a way to outwardly show the loyalty expected of gang membership. Tattoos are an interesting form of culture with various implications. In some cases, teenagers get tattoos as an act of defiance toward parents or the mainstream culture. In others, getting a tattoo is a sign of loyalty toward a community of people within a gang. In others still, within prisons for instance, tattoos can advertise the crimes committed by those wearing them. The commonality in all of these situations is that the ink on the end of the needle is permanent.

Piley (2006) notes that tattoos are not only representative of gang membership or criminal activity, they represent a mode of communication among and between gang members. For example, gang tattoos can be in the form of numbers, letters, and/or symbols, and the characters mean something different, perhaps a geographical location of the gang's homebase or the numbers of members it has lost to death (Piley, 2006). In any event, one gang member can determine who is friend or foe depending on the tattoo of the person standing next to him.

It should also be noted that "the tattoo is a symbol of membership in the gang and, thus, is 'gang property.' Removal of a gang tattoo may be an outward nonverbal method demonstrating termination of gang membership" (Piley, 2006, p. 46). Furthermore, for criminalists, identifying a tattoo on an offender can help determine if a gang has moved home bases or increased in number, not to mention leaving the offender with no choice but to admit association with the gang whose name is tattooed across his chest.

VIEWPOINTS

What to do with Deviant Youth: Prevention & Treatment Programs

When children misbehave in day care settings, a time-out is rendered; the child is removed from the situation in which he did something wrong and put into a situation where he is isolated from games, fun, and other children. He is not taken from the place where he misbehaved and put into a room with other misbehaving children as a form of punishment. Most people would think that putting two naughty kids together when they can't behave by themselves would do little with respect to helping them behave correctly. However, as Dishion, Dodge, & Lansford (2008) note, many communities respond to youthful offenders in just such a way: the offender is taken out of the community and locked in a facility with other youthful offenders (p. 8).

Warr (1996) identified that much of the illegal/deviant activities of youthful offenders are committed when they are in groups, as peer culture is a priority in their lives (as cited in Dishion et al., 2008, p. 8). Furthermore, Elliot & Menard (1996) have noted that "deviant peer affiliation is a stronger predictor of delinquent behavior than such variables as family, school, and community characteristics" (as cited in Dishion et al., 2008, p. 8). This is a thought-provoking idea in that when defining at-risk youth, family life, attendance in school, and the socioeconomic status of a child's neighborhood are primary tools of identification. However, according to Warr's research, hanging out with the wrong crowd leads to a significant possibility of gang membership. And in turn, when the wrong crowd gets caught behaving badly, they are confined—with little adult supervision—to hanging out with more of the wrong crowd. Dishion et al. (2008) note the irony and effect of this resolution:

> ... when the reason that deviant youth are placed with each other is because they are deviant, their identity and common ground become deviance ... high exposure to deviant peers and minimal adult interaction fail to reduce recidivism and in some cases, may exacerbate it" (pp. 8-9).

Indeed, the 2002 Commission on Deviant Peer Influences studied several programs and means of intervention for youth within a three-year period. Dishion et al. (2008) notes that the Commission discovered specific instances in which deviant peer influences are the strongest on youth (p. 9). Using these criteria, it is important to understand that gang membership and negative influences can be combated by providing meaningful experiences for youth in the following situations:

- First, youth in early adolescence are primary targets for gang affiliation. The Department of Justice (2000) narrows down this time period: "[F]or many children, gang influences begin in elementary school. By the fifth grade, many students are already at the affiliate level, meaning they are making their way into initiation" (as cited in Struyk, 2006, p. 13).
- Second, young people who have perhaps experimented with behavior of a deviant nature but have not yet become delinquent are more at risk to cross over to deviance than youth who have not experimented.
- Third, young people who are exposed to and interact with other youth of a more deviant stature—especially in unsupervised settings are-are also more likely to fall into a deviant lifestyle.
- Finally, substance abuse, violent behaviors, and delinquency are social activities, and at this young age those activities rarely occur in isolation. As such, the activities can be used secondarily to create a social construct of deviance (Dishion et al., 2008, p. 9).

It seems impossible that children this young would consider gang membership to be enticing. However, if they are primarily left alone—before and after school—and if their friends, older siblings, or older neighbors are already affiliated, it would make sense to join the ranks of the only community involvement they may know. If one's friends are making money carrying drugs for an older buddy, carrying drugs may seem like a way to be included, to prove and to feel loyalty. "Gang membership creates a unique bond between its members that is exclusive to all other individuals ... loyalty is to the gang above all else, including family, school, or community" (Struyk, 2006, 11). Furthermore, carrying enough cash to purchase the things poor parents cannot provide is incentive to remain in this community.

Discussion

In February 2006, an initiative to stop gang violence was created by the U.S. Department of Justice. The initiative proposed to "prioritize prevention programs to provide America's youth and offenders ... with opportunities that help them resist gang involvement ... [and also to] ensure robust enforcement policies when gang-related violence does occur" (Department of Justice's Youth Gang Prevention Initiative, n.d.). The initiative was created on the basis of information collected in 2004. According to the data, ... 760,000 gang members and 24,000 gangs were active in more than 2,900 U.S. jurisdictions in 2004, representing all 50 states and all cities with a population over 250,000. As most gang members join between the ages of 12 and 15, prevention is a critical strategy within a comprehensive response to gangs that includes law enforcement, prosecution, and reentry (Department of Justice's Youth Gang Prevention Initiative, n.d.).

Gangs are everywhere and their members do anything from drinking underage to killing police officers to gain respect. Most gang members are in their teenage years when peer pressure and social status are two primary concerns. When lashing out at a person who threatens his friends and community is all that he knows, changing a young man's behavior will not be easy. Put a gun in his hand, and lashing out turns to murder for the sake of turf maintenance. According to the 2004 Teen Gun Survey, "in 2000, 40 percent of teens [surveyed] said they could get a handgun if they needed to" (Vanden Berk, cited in "2004 Teen Gun Survey," 2004). With odds like that, who wants to disagree with anyone?

In 2011 the National Gang Intelligence Center estimated that there were nearly 1.4 million active gang members in cities, prisons, and outdoor motorcycle clubs—making up over 33,000 gangs. Street gangs are often made up of youth and urban criminal organizations. Prison gangs operate within the penal system and prison institutions. Outlaw motorcycle gangs (OMG) are made up of individuals who conduct activities using motorcycle clubs; a subset of OMGs are called "One Percenters," which is a stricter and more formal criminal group. Gangs can also be associated with organized crime, where the term "gangster" originated. In terms of ethnicity, Hispanic gangs are particularly significant as they are closely related to issues of illegal immigration; Hispanics make up nearly 50 percent of gang members in the US.

These varieties of gangs are responsible for a percentage of violent crime that ranges from 48 to 90 percent, depending on the region. Crimes range from violence and drug trafficking to things such as prostitution, white-collar crime, weapons trade, and human trafficking. Gang membership is concentrated most strongly in the northeast and southeast United States with additional high numbers in the West and near the Great Lakes. States with the highest numbers include California, Arizona, and Texas; cities include Detroit, Los Angeles, Chicago, and New York City.

TERMS & CONCEPTS

Aggregation: Putting similar people together as a form of isolation and/or punishment.

Antisocial Behavior: A disorder in which a person's behavior is hostile or indifferent to the needs of those around him/her.

At-risk (youth): A general term meant to identify children who are in danger of failing school, committing criminal acts, or physical violence.

Attention Deficit Hyperactivity Disorder (ADHD): A condition in which the person has difficulty sitting still or focusing on specific tasks (especially while in school).

Conduct Disorder: Refers to a disorder in which a person behaves (conducts himself) inappropriately.

Deviance: Behavior that is different from society's standard.

Gang: A group of people (usually youth) who form a network to work together for some criminal or antisocial purpose.

Juvenile Delinquents: People under the age of 18 committing acts that violate the law

Oppositional Defiant Disorder: Refers to behaviors that are inappropriate at a specific age; behaviors can range from simple irritability to defiance to outward opposition to authority figures.

Recidivism: Generally a criminal term referring to repeating negative behavior or reoffending a crime.

Bibliography

"2004 Teen Gun Survey." (2004, October). *Chicago: Project Safe Neighborhoods: America's Network Against Gun Violence.* http://www.psnchicago.org/news/teen

Cooper, L., Anaf, J. & Bowden, M. (2006). "Contested concepts in violence against women: 'Intimate', 'domestic' or 'torture'?" *Australian Social Work, 59,* pp. 314-327.

"Department of Justice's Youth Gang Prevention Initiative." (n.d.). Washington, D. C.: U.S. Department of Justice, Office of Juvenile Justice and Delinquency Prevention. http://ojjdp.ncjrs.gov/programs/antigang/

Dishion, T. J., Dodge, K. A. & Lansford, J. E. (2008). "Deviant by design: Risks associated with aggregating deviant peers into group prevention and treatment programs." *Prevention Researcher, 15,* pp. 8-11.

Eghigian, M. & Kirby, K. (2006). "Girls in gangs: On the rise in America." *Corrections Today, 68,* pp. 48-50.

Gatti, U., Tremblay, R. E., Vitaro, F. & McDuff, P. (2005). "Youth gangs, delinquency and drug use: A test of the selection, facilitation, and enhancement hypotheses." *Journal of Child Psychology & Psychiatry, 46,* pp. 1178-1190.

Gilman, A. B., Hill, K. G., & Hawkins, J. D. (2014). "Long-term consequences of adolescent gang membership for adult functioning." *American Journal of Public Health, 104,* 938–945.

Junod, T. (2008). "When chivalry is deadly." *Esquire, 149,* p. 100.

Matsuda, K. N., Melde, C., Taylor, T. J., Freng, A., & Esbensen, F. (2013). "Gang membership and adherence to the 'code of the street'". *JQ: Justice Quarterly, 30,* 440–468.

Melde, C., & Esbensen, F. (2013). "Gangs and violence: Disentangling the impact of gang membership on the level and nature of offending." *Journal Of Quantitative Criminology, 29,* 143–166.

Piley, W. (2006). "Interpreting gang tattoos." *Corrections Today, 68,* pp. 46-53.

Pinizzotto, A. J., Davis, E. F. & Miller III, C. E. (2007). "Street-gang mentality." *FBI Law Enforcement Bulletin, 76,* pp. 1-7.

"Preventing Gang Involvement." (2006). Fairfax County, Virginia http://www.fairfaxcounty.gov/gangprevention/preventing.htm

Pyrooz, D. C., Sweeten, G., & Piquero, A. R. (2013). "Continuity and change in gang membership and gang embeddedness." *Journal Of Research In Crime & Delinquency, 50,* 239–271.

Sherman, L.W., Gottfredson, D. C., MacKenzie, D. L., Eck, Reuter, P., & Bushway, S.D. (1998). *Preventing Crime: What Works, What Doesn't, What's Promising.* Washington, D.C.: U.S. Department of Justice, Office of Juvenile Justice and Delinquency Prevention. http://www.ncjrs.gov/works/

Smith, C. A. (2008) "Juvenile delinquency: An introduction." *Prevention Researcher, 15,* pp. 3-7.

Wood, J. L. (2014). "Understanding gang membership: The significance of group processes." *Group Processes & Intergroup Relations, 17,* 710–729.

Suggested Reading

Agnew, R. (2005). *Juvenile delinquency: Causes and control.* Los Angeles, CA: Roxbury.

Braga, A. A., Pierce, G. L., McDevitt, J., Bond, B. J. & Cronin, S. (2008). "The strategic prevention of gun violence among gang-involved offenders." *JQ: Justice Quarterly, 25,* pp. 132-162.

Cooper L., & Bowden, M. (2006). "Working with women associated with bike gangs: Practice Dilemmas." *Australian Social Work, 59,* pp. 309-321.

Decker, S. H. & Curry, D. (2002). "Gangs, gang homicides, and gang loyalty: Organized crimes of disorganized criminals." *Journal of Criminal Justice,* 30, pp. 343-352.

Dishion, T. J. (2000). "Cross-setting consistency in early adolescent psychopathology: Deviant friendships and problem behavior sequelae." *Journal of Personality, 68,* pp. 1,109-1,126.

Dishion, T. J., Andrews, D. W. & Crosby, L. (1995). "Antisocial boys and their friends in early adolescence: Relationship characteristics, quality and interactional process." *Child Development. 66,* pp. 139-151.

Dishion, T. J., McCord, J., & Poulin, F. (1999). "When interventions harm: Peer groups and problem behavior." *American Psychologist. 5,* pp. 755-764.

Dishion, T. J., & Medici Skaggs, N. (2000). "An ecological analysis of monthly 'bursts' in early adolescent substance use." *Applied Developmental Science. 4,* pp. 89-97.

Farmer, A. Y., & Hairston, T. (2013). "Predictors of gang membership: Variations across grade levels." *Journal Of Social Service Research, 39,* 530–544.

"In too deep with the wrong crowd." (2007). *Community Care* (1677), p. 22-23.

Kingsbury, A. (2008). "Dispelling the myths about gangs." *U.S. News & World Report, 144,* p. 14.

Marks, A. (2008). "Key factor in murder trends: youth, gang violence." *Christian Science Monitor, 100,* pp. 1-4.

Moule, R. K., Pyrooz, D. C., & Decker, S. H. (2013). "From 'What the F#@% is a Facebook?' to 'Who doesn't use Facebook?': The role of criminal lifestyles in the adoption and use of the Internet." *Social Science Research, 42,* 1411–1421.

Tapia, M. (2011). "U.S. juvenile arrests: Gang membership, social class, and labeling effects." *Youth & Society, 43,* 1407–1432.

Thornberry, T. P., & Krohn, M. D. (1997a.). "Peers, drug use, and delinquency." In D. M. Stoff, J. Breiling & J. D. Maser (Eds.), *Handbook of Antisocial Behavior* (pp. 218-233). New York: Wiley.

Thornberry, T.P., & Burch, J.H., II. (1997b.). *Gang members and delinquent behavior.* Washington, DC: US Department of Justice, Office of Justice Programs, Office of Juvenile Justice and Delinquency Prevention.

Thornberry, T. P, Krohn, M. D., Lizotte, A. J. & Chard-Wierschem, D. (1993). "The role of juvenile gangs in facilitating delinquent behavior." *Journal of Research in Crime and Delinquency, 30,* pp. 55-87.

Thornberry, T.P, Krohn, M.D., Lizotte, A.J., Smith C.A., & Tobin, K. (2002). *The toll of gang membership: Gangs and delinquency in a developmental perspective.* New York: Cambridge University Press.

Maureen McMahon, M.S.

Informal and Formal Social Control

ABSTRACT

This article focuses on the existence of social control, or the various methods that society employs in order to ensure faithful adherence toward order and restraint. The article launches into two theories that provide clarity toward social control: Labeling theory, which asserts that society creates criminals by branding them with an iniquitous label that subsequently limits their prospective opportunities, and Minority-threat hypothesis, which claims that mainstream America increases punitive admonition toward minorities in order to prevent them from flourishing. Examples of formal demonstrations of social control, or laws and policies that serve as the starting point on which behaviors and attitudes follow, are provided. The refusal to follow such legislation results in legal and illegal punishment (i.e., warnings, fines, threats, persecution, and imprisonment). Outside the dictates of the law, formal social control strategies exist in both educational and workplace institutions. Finally, informal social control influences include nonverbal communication at the micro-level, and on a larger scale, a community's willingness to contest the spread of crime.

OVERVIEW

Labeling Theory

Labeling theory is a framework that most frequently functions as a mechanism for conceptualizing the derivation of deviance and amoral behavior, and was spearheaded by a sociologist named Frank Tannenbaum (Maier, 1974; Davis, 1972; Goode, 1994; Meade, 1974). Understanding Tannenbaum's life story is pertinent to the comprehension of his subsequent theory; his formative years were tumultuous and relationships with parental figures were strained due to his willful opposition toward authority. Also, early in his development, Tannenbaum demonstrated a desire to fight on behalf of the "underdog," and in 1912 at age 19, he organized a rally that encouraged the homeless men of New York City to rally together in contempt of their lifelong plights that had disabled them from meeting basic financial, nutritional, and residential needs. His insurgent methods were highly opposed, and he received a one-year prison sentence. During his detention, he befriended a prison warden who believed in his intellectual abilities and recommended his eventual admission into college, thus spurring his eventual academic route (Maier, 1974).

The basic principles of Labeling theory, as outlined by Tannenbaum, can be captured in the following scenario: Bob and Jon are 15 years of age and neighborhood companions who, as an expression of boredom and adolescent angst, often engage in minor infractions such as throwing bricks through the windows of vacant buildings on forsaken lots or spray-painting profane extractions against the side of bridges and other communal property. Bob has been able to "fly under the radar," and executes such acts of desecration anonymously. Jon, on the other hand, is significantly less circumspect in his exploits and consistently receives verbal reproach from police officials for his unlawful behavior.

Over the course of a year, Bob and Jon continue their illegitimate activities, for which only Jon gets caught, and at the compilation of several warnings he is labeled a criminal and hauled off to jail and sentenced a severe penalty. The future outlook for Jon, according to Labeling Theory, is that he will endure a tattered self-image and will identify with the criminal label with which he had been bequeathed, thus leading him toward lifelong pursuits that are unsavory and illegal in nature. Bob never received any reprimand for his actions, and thus never received a criminal label. Hence, he was able to effortlessly forfeit his immature deeds for that which was more responsible and socially revered, and forged a successful and productive existence. As such, Labeling Theory does not focus on the preemptive, adverse *behavior* that eventually transpires into hardened criminality, for both Bob and Jon participated in identical mishaps. Nor does Labeling Theory discount the fact that criminals are, in many cases, guilty and should be punished accordingly. While such theorists do not disregard faulty actions, they do pinpoint a maladaptive screening process. Goode (1994) describes such shortcomings metaphorically by using the familiar movie line, "*round up the usual suspects* :"

Individuals, or categories of individuals, were being "rounded up" not because they did anything wrong or caused any harm, but simply because they were convenient or acceptable targets of social control. The individuals who were "rounded up": didn't do it; or did it, but so did other individuals; or they did it a little—while others got away—but having gotten caught, they end up doing a lot more; or didn't cause any harm; or they caused some harm, but others caused more. In short, targets of social control didn't *deserve* to become so targeted (p. 92).

The Self-Fulfilling Prophecy

Most importantly, Labeling Theory professes that it is the *system* that creates criminals. In the process of vilifying individuals for their transgressions, immoral traits akin to the "criminal" classification become enmeshed with one's sense of self, and the reinforcement of stereotypes surrounding such a label abound, all of which help the individuals enact their newly developed criminal persona via the self-fulfilling prophecy. Thus, society is at the helm of a corrupt manufacturing system that provides a rigorous training ground for which the "criminal" may cultivate his cunning proclivity for amoralities, and which consequently increases society's overall patterns of delinquency. This process exists when trivial legalities are maximized under the harshest of legal sanctions.

An illustration of this can be seen in the 1997 arrest of four German tourists who were caught defacing the corridors of New York's subway system. These vandals were prosecuted and sentenced to serve a one-week term at the notorious Riker's Island Correctional Institution ("Invasion," 1997) which has a reputation of housing unruly acts of violence between inmates (Lorch, 1996), gang involvement (Purdy, 1994), access to drugs and contraband, and the mistreatment of prisoners by dishonorable guards (Fahim, 2008). Surely the intention for imprisoning the vandals at such an infamous site was to curb their propensity for future acts of property destruction. However, a frightful alternative surrounds the prospect that the aggression and mayhem to which the vandals were exposed desensitized their sense of moral standards, so that their ultimate threshold for wrongdoings actually increased.

Minority-Threat Hypothesis

One might rightfully question society's incentives for proactively sculpting a system that contributes toward the creation of criminals, as the logical assumption would surround a social order that *reigns in* acts of fraudulence and misconduct. The answer to such a query can be found in the *Minority-threat hypothesis* (Jacobs & Tope, 2007; Ruddell & Urbina, 2004; Stults & Baumer, 2007), a theory surrounding the inequitable treatment that is administered to minority groups by the dominant majority presiding within each culture. In particular, the Minority-threat hypothesis claims that society is not only oppressive and discriminatory in its treatment of various ethnic or religious groups, but that the mere presence of non-majority members is daunting and jeopardizes the status quo. As the growth of such minority populations expand, the threat they pose to the larger society increases due to the viable competition they bring to the job market, the fact that they add more entrants who vie for limited resources, as well as that they contend for sacred positions of financial and political power. Thus, as group membership among minorities broadens, intolerance and prejudicial behavior concurrently grows in magnitude.

According to the Minority-threat hypothesis, society utilizes nefarious social-control techniques that diminish the likelihood that promising, up-and-coming minority groups will prevail, including the perpetuation of fear and blame, as well as the dispensation of harsher punitive consequences. The coalition between racial profiling and crime has been extensively documented (Vito & Walsh, 2008; Welch, 2007) and substantiates preexisting stereotypes that people hold. It is difficult for people to shed their biased assumptions that African American and Latin communities are more violent and geared toward dereliction, when every time they open the morning newspaper or turn on the evening news they are infiltrated with images that point to the contrary. Golub, Johnson, & Dunlap (2007) present statistical evidence that compared the penalties Blacks and Hispanics received for smoking marijuana in public with their White counterparts. Cases that were dismissed include the following: 77.8% for both Blacks and Hispanics, whereas 88.9% for White conspirators. Also, 4% of African Americans were incarcerated for such a violation, whereas 3% of Latinos and .9% of Caucasians were detained.

More appalling data is demonstrated through research by Moore & Elkavich (2008) who indicate that while White and Black drug usage is relatively similar (7.2% and 7.4% respectively), 60% of American jails are crowded with African Americans, 62.6% of whom are imprisoned on drug charges. Stuntz (2006) asserts that such biased disproportion is headed by underhanded politicians who operate with prescribed agendas, which causes *and* results in a corroded system filled with "overcriminalization, excessive punishment, racially skewed drug enforcement, overfunding of prisons and underfunding of everything else" (Stuntz, 2006, pp. 781-782).

APPLICATIONS

Formal Demonstrations of Social Control

Legislation

The foundation of formal social control lies within the legislative forces that establish societal guidelines, such as laws and policies, which therefore possess the most significant form of power and behavioral manipulation. Lawfully endorsed injunctions shape many aspects of social conventions such as to whom one may marry, i.e., heterosexual marital unions (Eleveld, 2007), and who has the ability to exercise their right to vote, a political responsibility that women were banned from voicing until 1920 (Wetter, 2008). In examining alcohol consumption, Pittman, Staudenmeier & Kaplan (1991) highlight the fact that governmental decrees determine the following criteria, all of which may vary between regions:

- *Who* may purchase and drink alcohol;
- *What* may be purchased and consumed;
- *Where* it may be purchased and consumed;
- *When* it may be purchased and consumed;
- The *cost* and form of payment;
- The *unacceptable consequences* of drinking (p. 970).

Another way of appreciating the amount of control that is dictated through legislation is by examining international drug and alcohol regulations. For example, the overall manner alcohol is perceived varies significantly between France and Saudi Arabia; likewise, cocaine usage in some countries can be deemed recreational and of no particular concern, whereas it is classified as a "hard" drug among Americans.

If legal doctrines serve as the basis on which people preemptively structure their behavior, there are several provisions targeting those who negligently evade such legal responsibilities. Social control reprisals can be found in the following examples: cautionary warnings, which tend to serve as a deterrent reminder that people have gone astray, and monetary fines, which have undergone scrutiny regarding their level of effectiveness and ability to ignite change ("Doubled fines," 1998). Authority figures venture into immoral territory when their acts of domination and command revolve around unwarranted threats and intimidation ("Shake up," 2006). Illegal ways that people in positions of power demonstrate their clout can be dispensed through acts of insufferable persecution, such as the torture that U.S. military officials imparted onto Iraqi prisoners at Abu Ghraib (Tucker & Triantafyllos, 2008), or the absolute sovereignty that White Americans held over Black slaves until ratification of the Emancipation Proclamation in 1862 (Ewan, 2005).

Imprisonment

Imprisonment is a type of formal social control that serves to retroactively amend problematic behavior. There are several schools of thought circulating around the functionality of prison (Gromet & Darley, 2006; Shoham, Beck, & Kett, 2008; Tewksbury & Mustaine, 2008). Some assert that a jail term is constructive for both the victim and society as a whole, and that the act of sequestering the perpetrator in a secured cell ensures the victim's long awaited sense of safety, while instilling a sense of restoration that will encourage their advancement past the criminal activity. Other theories focus primarily on the convict, by holding the perspective that he or she needs to suffer for his or her wrongdoings retributively; words that encompass this position include "payback" and "vengeance." Yet another angle centering primarily on the criminal is that the prison sentence will serve to rehabilitate his or her reprehensible atrocities. There are several in-house programs that cater to such treatment and moral growth including art therapy (Merriam, 1998), counseling, education, and mentoring (Kupchik, 2007), as well as hands-on job skills such as welding (Conlon, Harris, Nagel, et al., 2008).

Education

Outside of the realm of legal sanctions, additional acts of formal social control are bestowed upon the general public. From a smaller-scale perspective, education operates as a platform for which social control mechanisms are in full function. Lifelong lessons such as self-restraint, punctuality, and adherence to rules (Macionis, 2001) are fundamentally inculcated into the pupil's code of ethics through the structured and meticulous sets of standards, schedules, protocol, and expectations found within public school systems. Moreover, a plethora of data suggests that increased involvement eliminates the likelihood that children and adolescents will entangle themselves within the trenches of indolence or delinquency (Landers & Landers, 1978; Roberts, 2005). Many experts advise involvement in extracurricular activities such as sports, clubs, and other social establishments, although school enrollment itself acts as a barrier against criminal activity (Dalun, Katsiyannis, Barrett, et. al, 2007).

Economic Regulation

School also serves as a preliminary step that prepares for eventual succession into the career force, which demands an equal level of discipline, timeliness, and productivity. Similarly, there is an abundance of literature indicating that unemployment rates correspond significantly with lifestyles rife with crime and other improprieties (Anderson, 2006; Baron & Hartnagel, 1997). Hence, national economic burdens that are placed on residents, including taxation and inflated housing markets, serve as social controls, as they mandate the necessity of employment, thereby diminishing crime rates. A direct social control mechanism that many organizations utilize is regulating the recreational, off-the-clock behavior in which employees engage during their personal time. Such behavior is supervised through the enforcement of workplace drug testing policies (Zimmer & Jacobs, 1992) that measure both the type and amount of chemical agents that employees may have recently ingested.

Informal Social Control

At the micro-level, informal social control can be defined as disapproving communication that is transmitted from person to person, which ultimately influences conformity to standards (Nugier, Niedenthal, Brauer, et al., 2007). For example, Joan and her mother, Mrs. Smith, are shopping for back-to-school clothes. Joan tries on a revealing blouse and examines her mother's facial expression in order to obtain feedback on the risqué garment. Mrs. Smith wrinkles her nose, and says in a forced tone, "Well... it's o.k., I suppose." Based on Mrs. Smith's hesitancy, Joan returns the clothing item to its display shelf for fear of wearing a shameful style that will refute her mother's approval. Professionals and laypersons alike use subtle or apparent forms of nonverbal communication to express their standpoints and exchange directives, which in turn may modify behavior toward a more desirable route. For example, students learn quickly how to discern whether their teacher's tone of voice, physical posturing, and facial expressions function as a form of encouragement or condemnation, and adapt accordingly.

Community Monitoring

Extending outside of the individual self, an example of informal control at the community level can be examined through a study conducted by Silver & Miller (2004), in which they analyzed data on disadvantaged Chicago neighborhoods. In particular, they sought to explain why low-income vicinities tend to impart lower levels of informal social control, manifested by neighbors who were proactive and accountable to their environments. Examples they use to illustrate this notion included, "neighbors taking note and questioning strangers, watching over each other's property, assuming responsibility for the supervision of youth and intervening in local disturbances" (Sampson, 1987, as cited in Silver & Miller, 2004, p. 553). The perplexity held by the researchers was intensified by the fact that underprivileged neighborhoods tend to have strong social networks and a sense of kinship and camaraderie.

Interestingly, the study conducted by Silver & Miller revealed that solidarity and social ties do not necessarily equate with informal social control. Rather, a sense of longevity and investment, as opposed to mobility and fleeting transience practiced within neighborhoods played a pivotal role in imposing social control. Common sense aligns with this premise, in that the more imbedded a person is within his surroundings, the more likely he is to uphold its sense of safety and morale. Another finding that emerged from the Silver & Miller study surrounds the alliance that community members had forged with the police department. Positive affiliation with local police officers yielded citizens who were more apt to implement social control mechanisms, demonstrated by increased reports on suspicious activity, and their overall commitment and attentiveness toward community endeavors.

VIEWPOINTS

Social Control or Censorship?

In contemplating one's values, attitudes, and preferential leanings, it is difficult to discern the separation between that which an individual finds redeemable based on his own psychological underpinnings and belief system, and what he is regurgitating from the influential programming that constantly permeates his everyday life. For example, most television broadcast stations that claim to relay information in unbiased and objective terms tend to lean slightly to the "right" or "left" based on their philosophical predilections, political agendas, and receipt of corporate sponsorship. Hence, the channel that people tune into on a regular basis influences the manner in which they conceptualize the world at large. Or, probably more commonly, people are attuned to such biased reports and pursue the stations that reflect their own convictions, a lackluster process that solely acts to validate their subjective perspectives. Another example of the debilitating effects of social control surrounds a phenomenon that artists have contended with for centuries, in which their retaliation against the norm renders a strict sentence: censorship. Hence, the powers that be, or those who are in charge of disseminating social control mechanisms, have the ability to prompt behavior and attitudes, which elicit robotic and mechanized adherence to prearranged ideologies.

Conversely, social control can be a positive technique used to uphold safety and manage the masses. Seat belt usage, for example, steadily increased between the years 2000 and 2005 from 71% to 82% (Arms, 2005). Initiatives to encourage such a movement, such as stricter laws and scare tactics dispersed throughout the media during that period, which focused on the deadly repercussions of remaining unbuckled, are the likely catalysts that promoted safer lifestyles.

TERMS & CONCEPTS

Formal Social Control: Revolves around laws or policies and serves as the starting point from which widespread norms, behaviors, and attitudes follow.

Informal Social Control: Subtle forms of control that include non-verbal communication or community involvement.

Labeling Theory: Posits that society *creates* criminals by branding them with the criminal label that subsequently limits their prospective opportunities.

Minority-Threat Hypothesis: The theory that mainstream America increases punitive admonition toward minorities in order to prevent them from flourishing.

Recidivism: The rate at which people return to prison after they had been released.

Retribution: The perspective that criminals need to suffer for their wrongdoings; words that encompass this position include "payback" and "vengeance."

Bibliography

Anderson, M. A. (2006). "A spatial analysis of crime in Vancouver, British Columbia: a synthesis of social disorganization and routine activity theory." *Canadian Geographer, 50,* 487–502.

Arms, A. (2005). "National seat belt usage at record 82 percent." *Safety & Health, 172,* 16.

Baron, S. W. & Hartnagel, T. F. (1997). "Attributions, affect, and crime: Street youths' reaction to unemployment." *Criminology, 35,* 409–434.

Conlon, B., Harris, S., Nagel, J., Hillman, M., & Hanson, R. (2008). "Education: Don't leave prison without it." *Corrections Today, 70,* 48–52.

Dalun, Z., Katsiyannis, A., Barrett, D. E., & Wilson, V. (2007). "Truancy offenders in the juvenile justice system." *Remedial & Special Education, 28,* 244–256.

Davis, N. J. (1972). "Labeling theory in deviance research: A critique and reconsideration." *Sociological Quarterly, 13,* 447–474.

Drakulich, K. M., & Crutchfield, R. D. (2013). "The role of perceptions of the police in informal social control: Implications for the racial stratification of crime and control." *Social Problems, 60,* 383–407.

Decker, S. H. (2007). "The relationship between the street and prison." *Criminology & Public Policy, 6* , 183–186.

"Doubled fines don't work." (1998). *Consumer's Research Magazine, 81* , 38.

Drakulich, K. M. (2013). "Perceptions of the local danger posed by crime: Race, disorder, informal control, and the police." *Social Science Research, 42,* 611–632.

Duncan, M. G. (1988). "'Cradled on the sea': Positive images of prison and theories of punishment." *California Law Review, 76,* 1202–1247.

Eleveld, K. (2007). "Republican matters." *Advocate,* 997, 28–31.

Ewan, C. (2005). "The Emancipation Proclamation and British public opinion." *Historian, 67,* 1–19.

Fahim, K. (2008, June 27). "Rikers' guards accused of passing contraband to inmate." *New York Times,* 4.

Georgoulas, S. (2013). "Social control in sports and the CCTV issue: A critical criminological approach." *Sport in Society, 16,* 239–249.

Golub, A., Johnson, B. D., & Dunlap, E. (2007). "The race/ethnicity disparity in misdemeanor marijuana arrests in New York City, 1989-2000." *Criminology & Public Policy, 6,* 131–164.

Goode, E. (1994). "Round up the usual suspects: Crime, deviance, and the limits of constructionism." *American Sociologist, 25,* 90–104.

Gottschalk, M. (2007). "Dollars, sense, and penal reform: Social movements and the future of the carceral state." *Social Research, 74,* 669–694.

Gromet, D. M. & Darley, J. M. (2006). "Restoration and retribution: How including retributive components affects the acceptability of restorative justice procedures." *Social Justice Research, 19,* 395–432.

"Invasion of the Euro-taggers" (1997, January 19). *New York Times Magazine,* 12.

Jacobs, D. & Tope, D. (2007). "The politics of resentment in the post-Civil Rights era: Minority threat, homicide, and ideological voting in congress." *American Journal of Sociology, 112,* 1458–1494.

Kupchik, A. (2007). "The correctional experiences of youth in adult and juvenile prisons." *JQ: Justice Quarterly, 24,* 247–270.

Landers, D. M. & Landers, D. M. (1978). "Socialization via interscholastic athletics: Its effects on delinquency." *Sociology of Education, 51,* 299–303.

Liptak, A. (2008, February 29). "More than 1 in 100 adults are now in prison in U.S." *New York Times,* 14.

Lorch, D. (1996, June 28). "More violence disrupts Rikers Island." *New York Times,* 3.

Macionis, J. J. (2001). *Sociology.* New Jersey, USA: Prentice Hall.

Maier, J. (1974). *Frank Tannenbaum: A biographical essay.* USA: University Seminars.

Meade, A. C. (1974). "The labeling approach to delinquency: State of the theory as a function of the method." *Social Forces, 53,* 83–91.

Merriam, B. (1998). "To find a voice: Art therapy in a women's prison." *Women & Therapy, 21,* 157–172.

Moore, L. D. & Elkavich, A. (2008). "Who's using and who's doing time: Incarceration, the war on drugs, and public health." *American Journal of Public Health, 98,* 782–786.

Nugier, A., Niedenthal, P. M., Brauer, M., & Chekroun, P. (2007). "Moral and angry emotions provoked by informal social control." *Cognition & Emotion, 21,* 1699–1720.

Pittman, D. J., Staudenmeier, W. J., & Kaplan, A. (1991). "Alcohol and other drugs: the response of the political and medical institutions." *British Journal of Addiction, 86,* 967–975.

Purdy, M. (1994, December 21). "Mayor supports correction head despite trouble on Rikers Island." *New York Times,* 4.

Roberts, Y. (2005). "Young people given a sporting chance." *Community Care, 1564,* 21.

Rudell, R. & Urbina, M. G. (2004). "Minority threat and punishment: A cross-national analysis." *JQ: Justice Quarterly, 21,* 903–931.

"Shake up the state police" (2006, December 10). *New York Times,* 15.

Shoham, S. G., Beck, O., & Kett, M. (2008). *International handbook of penology and criminal justice.* Boca Raton, London, New York: CRC Press.

Silver, E. & Miller, L. L. (2004). "Sources of informal social control in Chicago neighborhoods." *Criminology, 42,* 551–583.

Stults, B. J. & Baumer, E. P. (2007). "Racial context and police force size: Evaluating the empirical validity of the minority threat perspective." *American Journal of Sociology, 113,* 507–546.

Stuntz, W. J. (2006). "The political constitution of criminal justice." *Harvard Law Review, 119,* 781–851.

Taggart, W. A., & Winn, R. G. (1993). "Imprisonment in the American States." *Social Sciences Quarterly (University of Texas Press), 74,* 736–749.

Tewksbury, R. & Mustaine, E. E. (2008). "Correctional orientations of prison staff." *Prison Journal, 88,* 207–233.

Tucker, B. & Triantafyllos, S. (2008). "Lynndie England, Abu Ghraib, and the new imperialism." *Canadian Review of American Studies, 38*, 83–100.

Vito, G. F. & Walsh, W. F. (2008). "Suspicion and traffic stops: crime control or racial profiling?" *International Journal of Police Science & Management, 10*, 89–100.

Welch, K. (2007). "Black criminal stereotypes and racial profiling." *Journal of Contemporary Criminal Justice, 23*, 276–288.

Wetter, E. (2008). "Winning the vote: The triumph of the American women suffrage movement." *Bust, 50*, 90–91.

Zimmer, L. & Jacobs, J. B. (1992). "The business of drug testing: Technological innovation and social control." *Contemporary Drug Problems, 19*, 1–25.

SUGGESTED READING

Chriss, J. (2007). *Social control: An introduction.* UK, USA: Polity Publishers.

Garland, D. (2002). *The culture of control: Crime and social order in contemporary society.* USA: University of Chicago Press.

Mustaine, E., & Tewksbury, R. (2011). "Assessing informal social control against the highly stigmatized." *Deviant Behavior, 32*, 944–960.

Pfohl, S. J. (1994). *Images of deviance and Social Control.* USA: McGraw-Hill.

Sargeant, E., Wickes, R., & Mazerolle, L. (2013). "Policing community problems: Exploring the role of formal social control in shaping collective efficacy." *Australian & New Zealand Journal of Criminology, 46*, 70–87.

Cynthia Vejar, Ph.D.

JUVENILE CRIME IN THE U.S.

ABSTRACT

Few social policy issues are as highly emotionally charged as those pertaining to juvenile crime. Opposing views abound concerning the nature and extent of the problem, the causes, theoretical underpinnings, and the best ways to mitigate this tragic trend. Youthful offenders were treated like adult criminals until around 1900, when separate juvenile processing procedures developed with goals of rehabilitation. Facing drastic increases in violent crime during the 1980s, however, the pendulum has swung back to processing many juvenile offenders as adults; possibly being charged with punishments as severe as life in prison and the death penalty. In 2005, the US Supreme Court ruled in *Roper v. Simmons* that the death penalty for those under the age of eighteen was cruel and unusual punishment and was therefore unconstitutional. New research on juvenile brain development and malfunction, made possible by magnetic resonance imaging (MRI), now raises scientific and human rights challenges to many "get tough" social policies.

OVERVIEW

Juvenile crime is defined as illegal acts against people or property committed by individuals under the age of eighteen. It is a complex social concern inextricably linked with issues of race, poverty, gender, child abuse and neglect, family breakdown, educational failure, urban decay, substance abuse, child development, and failed social services and networks. In addition to the science relevant to these issues, however, the debate over juvenile offenders is also governed by the media, public opinion, and personal beliefs. Our own fears and vulnerabilities help shape personal and public policy views toward juvenile criminal offenders and the mechanisms by which crime can be reduced in our cities and towns.

It is clear that most people believe juvenile violent crime to be a national crisis. In January of 2007, for example, the National Council on Crime and Delinquency (NCCD) completed a national poll of US voters and nine out of ten respondents agreed that "youth crime is a major problem in our communities" (Krisberg & Marchionna, 2007). Stories like the following fuel our fears and sense of helplessness: In March of 1998, Andrew Golden, 11, and Mitchell Johnson, 13, were students at the Westside Middle School in Jonesboro, Arkansas. Coming to school dressed in camouflage fatigues and possessing a van full of ammunition, Golden set off the school's fire alarm. While their classmates filed out of the building, the boys opened fire upon them. Fifteen people were injured, five fatally (Ramsland, 2007). In Chicago, an 11-year-old boy murdered a 14-year-old girl in order to impress his fellow gang members (Satterthwaite, 1997, p. 18). In Whitfield County, Georgia, six youths, ages fifteen through seventeen, were arrested and charged with stealing several vehicles and breaking into hundreds of others (Mitchell, 2013).

Many experts in juvenile crime, however, fault the media for what they see as sensationalistic, ratings-driven coverage of a relative few gruesome criminal events. Media reporter Susan Douglas (1993) and others argue that this emphasis on specific incidences of juvenile violent crime is evil in its own right because it fails to consider the institutional violence in our society that fosters juvenile crime, such as poverty, racism, unemployment, lack of gun control, poor educational opportunities, failed drug treatment policies, violent homes and communities, and inadequate social and medical services.

Juvenile Crime Rates

One salient topic concerning juvenile crime, then, is the nature and extent of it in our society. Experts on juvenile crime usually rely on annual data provided by the Federal Bureau of Investigation's (FBI) Uniform Crime Report (UCR), which tracks arrests involving all offenders, and the Office of Juvenile Justice and Delinquency Prevention (OJJDP). Additionally, the National Crime Victimization Survey released by US Department of Justice surveys thousands of households nationwide to gather data on criminal victimization that was not reported to the police. According to the FBI, 8 percent of the people arrested in the United States in 2016 were juveniles (people under age eighteen). The number of juveniles arrested for property crimes in 2016 decreased slightly from the 2015 values (149,774 to 147,350); however, the number of juveniles arrested for murder in 2016 jumped more than 30 percent, from 521 to 682; juvenile violent crime arrests overall jumped 15 percent, from 35,886 to 41,335 (Federal Bureau of Investigation, 2016).

While juvenile crime data raises alarm for some public policy advocates, others argue that juvenile crime rates have not soared over the past four decades, and, in fact, they have declined or remained constant when one considers more detailed and reliable indicators. Since juvenile offenders are more likely to commit crimes with their peers ("co-offend"), for example, the successful arrest of three juveniles for one murder inflates the actual juvenile crime data to suggest that there were three murders, not one. Thus, one major challenge in any analysis of juvenile crime and resulting public policy is one's interpretation of the data available about the nature and extent of juvenile criminal actions annually.

APPLICATIONS

Causes of Youth Violence

Seifert (1999) reports that the Office of Juvenile Justice and Delinquency (OJJDP) identified six risk categories for youth violence that provides a useful way of organizing causal conditions for youthful offenders: Community/society, economic, family, individual, school, and peers.

- "Community/society" entails cultural norms for weapons, violent media and video games, hostile attitudes toward women, easy availability of illegal drugs, and the acquisition of things and power.
- Economic risks pertain to poverty, homelessness, and joblessness.
- Family risks include violence, child abuse and neglect, conflict, and lack of nurturing and support. Additionally, Mocan and Tekin (2006) found that "gun availability at home is positively related to the propensity to commit crime for juveniles." Despite research suggesting that the public believes parents have some responsibility for the crimes of their children, there seems to be little public support for laws making parents liable for those crimes (Brank & Weisz, 2004).

A failed educational experience and failing educational systems reflect the category of "schools" in the OJJDP report. One interesting study on the short-term effect of attending school on juvenile crime is reported by Jacob and Lefgren (2003). During periods of school attendance, juvenile property crime decreased by 14 percent. Unfortunately, during that same period of school attendance, the concentration of youth in schools increased violent crime by 28 percent. School-safety, then, remains a grave educational concern. While policing efforts, such as metal detectors and locker searches remain a necessity, greater attention needs to be paid to the emotional climates of our schools. Anti-bullying programs, conflict resolution measures, diversity, inclusion and gender equity efforts, and other community-building and social service endeavors must become paramount interventions in our goal to make schools safe, just, and compassionate for all youth.

- These efforts, however, are complicated by the pervasive existence of gangs in our culture today, which encompasses of OJJDP category of "peers." While gangs are not new to American society, the vast increase in their numbers, their blanket coverage of our nation throughout urban and rural areas, their subculture of violence, and their enhanced influence in all facets of American life make them a deadly and powerful force in juvenile crime.
- Due to recent scientific inquiry, however, the OJJDP risk category of "individual" is receiving compelling consideration in the debate over juvenile crime. Through magnetic resonance imaging (MRI) studies, scientists know that the brain of a juvenile is less developed than that of an adult, especially in the frontal lobe, which is responsible for executive, high order functioning, such as memory, planning, and inhibition. Bower (2004) and others (Steinberg, 2012) suggest this condition presents some juveniles with difficulties in "regulating aggression, long-range planning, mental flexibility, abstract thinking, the capacity to hold in mind related pieces of information, and perhaps moral judgment." In addition to the findings on inherent diminished brain functioning capacity in children, MRI research also suggests that exposure to violent video games and television might impact frontal lobe development and function negatively (Phillips, 2004; Stukel, 2012). Because of these findings, advocates in juvenile justice, such as the Human Rights Watch, have pressured politicians and judicial leaders to reconsider harsh, punitive measures in sentencing juvenile violent offenders. In September 2013, Massachusetts became the thirty-ninth state, along with the federal government and the District of Columbia, to classify seventeen-year-old defendants as juveniles. Prior to these new laws, seventeen-year-olds were allowed to be tried, arraigned, and sentenced as adults.

While the above risk categories provide some characteristics of juvenile offenders, they do not inevitably lead to crime. Additionally, most of them would be characterized as psychological theories of crime; emphasizing the traits of an individual as the primary factor in criminal causation.

VIEWPOINTS

Child Accountability

Prevailing beliefs about children and criminality can be best viewed as a continuum, with one extreme being the belief that evilness and criminal intent are defined early on, whether by nature (one's biological composition) or nurture (one's upbringing and/or life circumstances). Public policy advocates holding this belief champion imprisonment, and in some cases the death penalty, as the most appropriate mechanism for dealing with the specific offender and sending a message to other potential offenders. The opposing belief system on the continuum would be that children with their brains not fully developed are too immature to be held accountable for their actions to the same degree as adult offenders and that racism, poverty, and other societal ills are also factors in criminality. Improving societal failings and providing services and special rehabilitation experiences for juvenile offenders are more likely to be championed as goals for these public policy advocates. It is clear, however, that reports of violent, multiple murders committed by juvenile offenders, when combined with sensationalized media coverage, shock the public and raise fears about public safety and moral order. Juvenile crime is a complex social problem and competing belief systems and public opinion will continue to be factors in ongoing responses to youthful offenders.

Reform over Punishment

Up until the early nineteenth century, many governments adhered to the traditional belief in Western civilization that there was little difference between an adult and a child, and thus, little difference between an adult criminal and a youthful offender. Those found guilty of a criminal act received the only recognized outcome—punishment. According to Ellen Heath Grinney (1992), children as well as adults faced imprisonment, solitary confinement, branding, fines, whippings, the cutting of ears, and/or death. As ideals of the European Renaissance gained in popularity, new views emerged concerning the innocence of children and their susceptibility to good or bad influences. Judicial and religious leaders began to question the culpability of the youthful offender's parents and community in failing to provide proper guidance, diligence, restraint, and values. Processing children through the adult criminal justice system and punishing them in the adult prisons gradually gave way to beliefs that children should be guided and mentored by judicial agents (probation officers) who would correct the apparent failings of the offender's parents and lead to reform and morality. Rehabilitation, not punishment, was the new goal, and so by the 1850s, reform schools grew in popularity (Grinney, 1992).

Independent Juvenile Court Systems

Since innocence, role modeling, and developmental concerns gained new prominence in social policy, exposing youthful offenders to hardened adult criminals during processing and punishment would provide the worst possible outcomes. By the early 1900s, numerous cities and states had developed separate formal juvenile court systems and intervention processes focusing on second chances, rehabilitation, contrition, and reform (Grinney, 1992). In fact, systems were developed to divert youthful offenders from formal labeling as criminals altogether and to hide the accounts of their misdeeds from scrutiny during their subsequent adulthood. If a young person under the age of eighteen is not tried for murder as an adult, for example, and is found "delinquent" (guilty) under state law, the young person can be held in a juvenile correctional facility or on probation until the age of twenty-one. At that time, then, records are sealed and there is no criminal record following them into adulthood.

Programs for Aiding Re-Entry

Despite decades of focus on the rehabilitation of juvenile offenders, nearly 100,000 youth leave correctional facilities every year and face the daunting task of re-entry into their communities without coordinated social services and public assistance (JustChildren, 2004, p. 5). In an effort to deal with offenders and reduce rates of recidivism, juvenile justice advocates have lobbied Congress to pass federal models of interagency coordination of youth services. The Second Chance Act (P.L. 110-199) was signed into law on April 9, 2008, and was the first federal legislation to authorize grants to government agencies and not-for-profit organizations to provide services and support to reduce the rate of recidivism of young people returning to their communities from jail and juvenile facilities.

The Federal Youth Coordination Act (P.L. 109-365), signed into law in October of 2006, established the Federal Youth Development Council that is empowered to leverage and coordinate the resources of the twelve different federal agencies that currently administer youth programs and fund state-level coordination of services as well (Service, 2006; Federal, 2006). Two attempts were made (September 2008 and June 2009) to introduce a bill to amend the original Federal Youth Coordination Act to create the White House Office of National Youth Policy, which would ensure the coordination and effectiveness of services to youth. Congress rejected the bill each time.

Restorative Justice

One interesting trend in juvenile punishment and rehabilitation is the restorative justice movement. Based upon the principal that a criminal act harms both the victim and the community, restorative justice entails mediated, face-to-face meetings between the victim and the offender that are focused on making the victim as whole as possible, economically, socially, and emotionally, and holding the offender accountable and responsible for their actions. Through this process of repairing the harm, the offender learns the consequences of his or her acts on both the specific victim and the community as a whole. This more personalized rehabilitative process also highlights deficiencies in the life of the offender and provides a means for more direct social service interventions, such as education, job training and employment, mental health and drug treatment.

Punishment over Reform

While much of the framework and belief system of this more lenient view of youthful offenders remains intact in American society, the pendulum has swung back to more rigid beliefs about the innate characteristics of criminality and the necessity of punishment rather than reform. During the mid-1980s, American cities struggled with waves of increased, more violent juvenile crimes that were based in part on the prolific use of crack cocaine and other illegal drugs, the increased availability of guns, and on gang-related violence. In a 1995 article in the *Conservative Weekly*, public policy analyst John DiIulio coined the word "super-predator" to describe what he believed to be a new breed of juvenile criminal. Described as having no conscience and capable of killing at the slightest whim or provocation, DiIulio attributed this development to being raised in "abject moral poverty . . . surrounded by deviant, delinquent, criminal adults in abusive, violence-ridden, fatherless, Godless, and jobless settings" (Satterthwaite, 1997).

Adult Treatment

Left with apparently unsuccessful alternatives and rocked by the tremendous increase in violent crime by juvenile offenders and by sensational, extensive media coverage of those crimes, states began enacting legislation to adjudicate youthful offenders as adults around 1990. During this time, according to Nagin and his colleagues (2006), "in almost every state, youths who [were] 13 or 14 years of age (or less) [could] be tried and punished as adults for a broad range of offenses, including nonviolent crimes." Despite this trend, according to a NCCD national survey at the time, by a margin of 15 to 1, US voters believed that the "decisions to transfer youth to adult court should be made on a case-by-case basis and not be governed by a blanket policy" (Krisberg & Marchionna, 2007).

Once adjudicated to be an adult, the punishments become harsher for youth offenders as well. Nineteen states enacted the death penalty for juvenile offenders before the United States Supreme Court was asked to rule on the legality of that punishment in 2005. In a 5-4 ruling in *Roper v. Simmons*, 543 U.S. 551 (2005), the Court categorically barred the imposition of the death penalty for crimes committed prior to the age of eighteen, finding that such punishment violates the Eighth Amendment of the United State's Constitution prohibition against "cruel and unusual punishments." Seventy-two youthful offenders in twelve states were facing execution at the time of the Court's ruling (Greenhouse, 2005; Lane, 2005; Justices, 2005). Following the Court's ruling, the seventy-two youths were added to the hundreds of other juveniles nationwide that were facing life in prison. According to a 2008 study by Human Rights Watch, for example, there were 227 individuals serving life sentences without the possibility of parole in California prisons who were sentenced as juveniles under the 1990 legislation. Almost half of these people (45 percent) were accessories to murder rather than the actual murderer themselves, meaning that they served as a lookout or in some other facilitative capacity during a criminal act that caused a death (Fuentes, 2008). Arguably, according to Fuentes and others, this less-culpable population of young people would be excellent candidates for rehabilitative efforts instead of spending their lives in prison without proper services and assistance. The Supreme Court agreed, and on June 25, 2012, in a ruling on *Miller v. Alabama*, it was decided that a mandatory sentence of life without parole for juveniles convicted of homicide violated the constitutional ban on cruel and unusual punishment. This decision supported the evolving science that proved that the brains of youths were developmental and fundamentally different than adult brains and that trying and sentencing youths in the same manner as adults was unacceptable.

CONCLUSION

With the debate over juvenile justice moving away from the punitive, "get tough" perspective, Daniel Nagin and his colleagues (2006) have conducted some compelling, sophisticated polling research on public attitudes and our "willingness to pay" (WTP) for incarceration or rehabilitation for serious juvenile offenders. Using cost-benefit analysis, they calculated approximate actual costs and estimates of economic value of juvenile incarceration and various early intervention and rehabilitation programs. Then using "contingent valuation" (CV) methodology, they asked respondents to select their intervention preferences based on these economic projections. Not only were the "reforms that emphasize leniency and rehabilitation . . . justified economically," they were valued by respondents who expressed a willingness to fund them over harsher incarceration options. This view was mirrored in the NCCD national poll in which over 80 percent of respondents believed that "spending on rehabilitative services and treatment for youth will save tax dollars in the long run," and 91 percent believed that such measures would prevent future crime (Krisberg & Marchionna, 2007). Quite possibly the public is expressing a preference for rehabilitative measures except in the face of extreme, violent criminal acts by youthful offenders. Having tested the extreme means to which this country would go to punish juvenile offenders, we are now poised for a more moderate, get tough position in the years to come.

TERMS & CONCEPTS

Adjudicated: A determination made by a judge.

Co-offending: Crime committed jointly by two or more individuals.

Contingent valuation: Survey-based economic technique used to value non-market (no specific actual monetary value) resources such as the preservation of the environment or crime prevention.

Costs/benefit analysis: Attribution of best estimates of actual cost and gain/loss in comparison to each other.

Recidivism: The tendency to relapse into a previously undesirable type of criminal behavior; to commit additional, subsequent criminal acts.

Re-entry: Returning to one's home and/or community from incarceration.

Restorative justice: "Repair" of the personal and economic harm caused by a criminal act through mediated face-to-face meetings between the perpetrator and the victim with the goal of making the victim as "whole" as possible under the circumstances.

Retributive justice: Punishment policies aimed at vengeance or payback.

Bibliography

Barrett, D., & Katsiyannis, A. (2016). "Juvenile offending and crime in early adulthood: A large sample analysis." *Journal of Child & Family Studies, 25*(4), 1086-1097.

Bower, B. (2004, May 8). "Teen brains on trial: The science of neural development tangles with the juvenile death penalty." *Science News Online, 165*, 19.

Brank, E., & Weisz, V. (2004). "Paying for crimes of their children: Public support of parental responsibility." *Journal of Criminal Justice, 32*, 465–475.

Douglas, S. (1997). "Juveniles are unfairly blamed for increasing crime and violence." In A. Sadler (Ed.), *Juvenile crime: Opposing views* (pp. 41–44). San Diego, CA: Greenhaven.

Federal Bureau of Investigation. (2015). *Crime in the United States 2015: Persons arrested.* https://ucr.fbi.gov/crime-in-the-u.s/2015/crime-in-the-u.s.-2015/persons-arrested/persons-arrested

Federal Bureau of Investigation. (2016). *Crime in the United States 2016: Persons arrested.* https://ucr.fbi.gov/crime-in-the-u.s/2016/crime-in-the-u.s.-2016/topic-pages/persons-arrested

Fuentes, A. (2008, Feb. 13). "Give the kids a break." *USA Today.*

Greenhouse, L. (2005, March 2). "The Supreme Court: The overview: Supreme Court, 5-4, Forbids execution in juvenile crime." *New York Times.*

Grinney, H. (1992). *Delinquency and criminal behavior.* Philadelphia, PA: Chelsea House.

Human Rights Watch. (2005). "The difference between youth and adults." www.hrw/reports/2005/us1005/6.htm

Jacob, B., & Lefgren, L. (2003). "Are idle hands the devils workshop? Incapacitation, concentration, and juvenile crime." *American Economic Review, 93*, 1560–1577.

"JustChildren: A summary of best practices in school re-entry for incarcerated youth returning home." (2004). Charlottesville, VA: Legal Aid Justice Center.

"Justices abolish death penalty for juveniles." (2005, March 1). MSNBC. http://www.msnbc.msn.com/id/7051296/

Krisberg, B., & Marchionna, S. (2007, February). "Attitudes of US voters towards youth crime and the justice system." *FOCUS.* Oakland, CA: National Council on Crime and Delinquency.

Kronenberger, W. (2003, Spring). "Playing with kids' minds?" *Medicine* (printed by Indiana University Press). http://www.medicine.indiana.edu/iu%5fmedicine/03%5fspring/articles/kidsMinds.html

Lane, C. (2005, March 2). "5-4, Supreme Court abolishes juvenile executions." *Washington Post,* A01. http://www.washingtonpost.com/wp-dyn/articles/A62584-2005Mar1.html

Lawson, C., & Katz, J. (2004). "Restorative justice: An alternative approach to juvenile crime." *Journal of Socio-Economics, 33,* 175–189.

Mathur, S. R., & Griller Clark, H. (2014). "Community engagement for reentry success of youth from juvenile justice: Challenges and opportunities." *Education & Treatment of Children, 37,* 713–734.

Miller, M. (1996). *Coping with weapons and violence in your schools and on yours streets.* New York, NY: Rosen.

Mitchell, Bill. (2013, September). "Juvenile crime spree broken up." *WDEF News.* http://www.wdef.com/news/story/Juvenile-Crime-Spree-Broken-Up

Mocan, H., & Tekin, E. (2006). "Guns and juvenile crime." *Journal of Law & Economics, 49,* 507–532.

Nagin, D., Piquero, A., Scott, E., & Steinberg, L. (2006). "Public preferences for rehabilitation versus incarceration of juvenile offenders: Evidence from a contingent valuation survey." *University of Virginia Legal Working Paper Series, 5,* 627–652.

National Collaboration for Youth. (2006, October 17). "Federal Youth Coordination Act." *National Juvenile Justice Network.* http://www.youthcoordinationact.org/ncy/documents

Phillips, H. (2007, April 19). "Mind-altering media." *New Scientist.* http://www.newscientist.com/article/mg19426001.900

Prendergast, Alan. (2013, August 30). "A second chance for juveniles serving life." *National Council on Crime and Delinquency.* http://www.nccdglobal.org/blog/a-second-chance-for-juveniles-serving-life

Ramsland, K. (2007). "School killers: The list." truTV Crime Library. www.crimelibrary.com/

Satterthwaite, M. (1997). *Juvenile crime.* Philadelphia, PA: Chelsea House.

Seifert, K. (1999, Fall). "The violent child: Profiles, assessment and treatment." *Paradigm.*

Sells, S., Sullivan, I., & DeVore, D. (2012). "Stopping the madness: A new reentry system for juvenile corrections." *Corrections Today, 74,* 40–45.

Steinberg, Laurence. (2012). "Should the science of adolescent brain development inform public policy?" *Issues in Science and Technology 28,* 67–78.

Stukel, Kayt. (2012, January 9). "Playing video games may make specific changes to the brain." *The Dana Foundation.* http://www.dana.org/news/features/

National Collaboration for Youth, National Juvenile Justice Network. (2006, May). "Service coordination strengthens youth reentry." http://www.youthcoordinationact.org/ncy/documents

U. S. Department of Justice. (2008). "National Criminal Victimization Survey." www.ojp.usdoj.gov/bjs/

"Violence and the brain" (2007). www.crimelibrary.com

SUGGESTED READING

Abrams, L. S., Terry, D., & Franke, T. M. (2011). "Community-based juvenile reentry services: The effects of service dosage on juvenile and adult recidivism." *Journal of Offender Rehabilitation, 50,* 492–510.

Berg, M., Baumer, E., Rosenfeld, R., & Loeber, R. (2016). "Dissecting the prevalence and incidence of offending during the crime drop of the 1990s." *Journal of Quantitative Criminology, 32*(3), 377-396.

Carmichael, J., & Burgos, G. (2012). "Sentencing juvenile offenders to life in prison: The political sociology of juvenile punishment." *American Journal of Criminal Justice, 37,* 602–629.

Chesney-Lind, M., & Sheldon, R. (Eds.) (1998). *Girls, delinquency, and juvenile justice* (2nd ed.). Belmont, CA: Wadsworth.

Feld, B. (1999). *Bad kids: Race and the transformation of the juvenile court.* Oxford: Oxford UP.

Feld, B. (Ed.) (1999). *Readings in juvenile justice administration.* Oxford: Oxford UP.

Finkehor, D. (2008). *Childhood victimization: Violence, crime, and abuse in the lives of young people.* Oxford: Oxford UP.

Flowers, R. (2002). *Kinds who commit adult crimes: Serious criminality by juvenile offenders.* Binghamton, NY: Haworth.

Krisberg, B. (2008). *Juvenile justice: Redeeming our children.* Thousand Oaks, CA: Sage.

Kupchik, A. (2006). *Judging juveniles: Prosecuting adolescents in adult juvenile courts.* New York: New York UP.

Lawrence, R. (1998). *School crime and juvenile justice.* Oxford: Oxford UP.

Muncie, J. and Goldson, B. (Eds.) (2008). *Youth crime and juvenile justice.* Thousand Oaks, CA: Sage.

National Council on Crime and Delinquency. http://www.nccd.crc.org/nccd/

Rhineberger-Dunn, G. M. (2013). "Myth versus reality: Comparing the depiction of juvenile delinquency in metropolitan newspapers with arrest data." *Sociological Inquiry, 83,* 473–497.

Wilson, H. W., Berent, E., Donenberg, G. R., Emerson, E. M., Rodriguez, E. M., & Sandesara, A. (2013). "Trauma history and PTSD symptoms in juvenile offenders on probation." *Victims & Offenders, 8,* 465–477.

Karen M. Harbeck, Ph.D., J.D.

Labeling Theory

ABSTRACT

Labeling theory is a sociological and criminological theory that says that a strong, negative societal reaction to an individual's wrongdoing can lead the individual to become more deviant. Based on the principles of symbolic interactionism, the theory says there are two ways formal Labeling increases deviance. The first is by negatively impacting an individual's self-conception. The second is by blocking access to conventional opportunities. While Labelingtheory was popular in the 1970s, it was difficult to prove and fell out of favor. Recent approaches in criminology are reviving interest in Labeling theory principles.

OVERVIEW

Who we are in the world is often defined by a combination of factors. Our internal selves process our experiences directly and develop an understanding of what it is to touch, feel, see, hear, and smell the physical world. Our internal self interacts with the people around us, processing how they respond to us. The words we use to interact with others help us shape our understanding of the world and of ourselves. We use words to label the objects, people, and ideas that exist outside of us, and we organize our internal states to define who we are amidst all of the other ideas, experiences, and selves that we encounter in daily life. Thus, it is the interaction of self with both world and word that serves to define who we are. Our internal definition helps us to understand our role in society.

This is the understanding of internal processes that serves as the philosophical foundation of Labeling theory. Labeling theory, also known as societal reaction theory, is a sociological and criminological theory that places the concept of deviance in an interactionist framework. Whereas other theories look to the individual in order to understand why some people choose to break a law or act outside the norms of society, Labeling theory says that deviance is the product of the interaction between the individual and society. Unique from a criminological perspective, the theory suggests that the criminal justice system, which is supposed to reduce crime, might actually provide the conditions that create further deviance. Thus, Labeling theory is a theory that supports a less punitive approach to wrongdoing.

Ties to Symbolic Interactionism

The history of Labeling theory is rooted in the early conceptions of sociology that were developed at the University of Chicago's sociology department in the 1920s and 1930s. At that time, scholars at the Chicago School were busy defining the scope of sociology as a discipline. In attempting to understand the world of thieves, prostitutes, and other deviants, they advocated for field observations and analysis of these individuals within their natural environments. These principles developed into the branch of symbolic interactionism, which emphasizes the co-construction of reality and uses ethnographic methods in order to explore human experience (Downes & Rock, 2007).

From a symbolic interactionist perspective, the concept of deviance is a socially constructed one. In order for behavior to be considered deviant, or different from what is expected, someone must first establish the expected behavior. Society as a whole, through its institutions, groups, and individuals, is generally perceived to be both the creator and the enforcer of these expectations. The process by which individuals come to conform to conventional expectations involves a complex interplay between the internal self and the external world. By interacting with others, individuals come to understand who they are and their roles in society. In initial conceptualizations of Labeling theory, sociologists argued that the formal process of enforcement that society was using to deter deviance was backfiring. Instead of encouraging offenders to conform to societal expectations, the criminal justice system was actually pushing offenders toward a life of crime.

Tannenbaum & Lemert

One of the first voices to express this belief was Frank Tannenbaum, who is often credited as the father of Labeling theory. Tannenbaum, like many of his time, believed that criminal behavior was learned as individuals interacted within communities where crime was prevalent. However, one of the most influential learning events the offender experienced, he believed, was that of being apprehended and formally labeled as a criminal by the justice system. This process, he said, was nothing more than a "dramatization of evil" (Tannenbaum, 1938, p. 19–20) that led the individual to develop a negative self-concept and served to position the individual closer to the criminal world. He wrote, "The process of making the criminal, therefore, is a process of tagging, defining, indentifying, segregating, describing, emphasizing, making conscious and self-conscious; it becomes a way of stimulating, suggesting, emphasizing and evoking, the very traits that are complained of" (p. 20).

In 1951, Edwin Lemert offered another important early conception of Labeling theory. Lemert (1951) classified deviance into two types: primary and secondary. Primary deviance, he said, has its roots outside the formal criminal justice system. The factors that cause someone to make a first offense are broad and varied, and the societal reaction the individual receives for such an offense is not likely to impact the individual's identity. Secondary deviance is different, however. In secondary deviance, Lemert said the individual adopts the status of deviant as a primary identity. The difference is between someone who steals once and views the theft as an aberrant action from one's normal behavior and someone who identifies oneself as a thief and views stealing as a normalized and expected outcome of one's identity.

Like Tannenbaum, Lemert blamed the criminal justice system for contributing to the development of secondary deviance. He said that any societal reaction that stigmatized the offender could serve to push the offender away from societal norms and thereby encourage future deviance. However, in general, he did not feel that one instance of severe societal reaction would accomplish this. Rather, he cited a progressive process in which an individual's behavior was met with increasingly severe and stigmatizing societal consequences, begetting even more severely offensive behavior. Ultimately, this process would culminate in the adoption of a deviant identity marked by deviant beliefs, behaviors, and attitudes.

Although Tannenbaum and Lemert explored the role that Labeling and stigmatization played in creating deviance, it was not until the 1960s that the approach was formalized into a unified theory and given its own name. At that time, sociologists had come to view individuals as acting from the perspective of particular identities that were negotiable and grounded in specific situations. The linguistic symbols used to name and define various aspects of the situation and its participants were presumed to be of utmost importance. Transferred to criminology, the Labeling associated with deviance appeared to be a key to understanding how the criminal justice system contributed to the creation of deviant identities.

An influential voice on the topic at this time, Becker (1963) wrote:

Social groups create deviance by making the rules whose infraction constitutes deviance and by applying those rules to particular people and Labeling them as outsiders. From this point of view, deviance is not a quality of the act the person commits, but rather a consequence of the application by others of rules and sanctions to the "offender." The deviant is the one to whom the label has been successfully applied; deviant behavior is behavior people so label. (p. 9)

1960s Labeling theorists focused on the impact formal labels had on an individual's developing self-conceptions. Spurred by a rebirth of symbolic interactionism in the sociological field and a sociopolitical context that invited critiques of state power, Labeling theorists said that the criminal justice system was inducing self-fulfilling prophecies. In other words, by Labeling offenders as criminals, the system was setting in motion the processes that would turn individuals into criminals (Cullen & Agnew, 2006; Downes & Rock, 2007).

APPLICATIONS

Deviance Amplification

There are two mechanisms through which Labeling works. The first, as already noted, is through changes in identity brought on as offenders are faced with the stigmatizing reactions of people around them. As individuals treat the offender as a criminal, the offender is forced to respond and defend his or her actions. In this response, the individual is both utilizing an internal private depiction of self and responding from the stereotypical role that society has about criminals. As the individual negotiates these identities, the role that society imposes may become further internalized. This deviance amplification process is hypothesized to result in permanent changes to self-concept, leading the offender to accept the role and identity of a deviant (Becker, 1963; Cullen & Agnew, 2006; Downes & Rock, 2007; Lemert, 1951).

Blocked Access to Opportunity

The second mechanism by which Labeling is said to work is through initiating the processes that leads to greater social exclusion and blocked access to conventional opportunities. These processes are similar to the ones that other criminology theories tout as the reason for crime. For instance, as in social bond theory, Labeling theorists believe that the weakening of social bonds to conventional relationships play a role in changes in self-concept. When relationships with parents, teachers, or friends are weakened as a result of formal stigmatization, individuals are more likely to seek affiliation with criminal subcultures. By associating more frequently with other deviants, individuals are thought to have a greater opportunity to learn how to be a member of the community of deviants. As they achieve membership in this group, they become rewarded for deviant behavior, and this increases their motivation for such behavior (Bernburg & Krohn, 2003; Cullen & Agnew, 2006; Wellford & Triplett, 1993).

In line with similar views put forth in strain theory, Labeling theorists say blocked educational and employment opportunities resulting from formal processing contribute to future criminal behavior (Cullen & Agnew, 2006). For instance, convicted felons have more difficulty finding conventionally respectable employment (Martinez, 2004). Juveniles who are defined as delinquent may face harsher discipline in school, such as suspension, expulsion, or school transfer. This in turn raises the likelihood that they will drop out of school, limiting their chances for long-term education and career advancement (Bernberg & Krohn, 2003; Sweeten, 2006). When conventional opportunities are blocked as a result of criminal behavior, offenders may find the opportunities of the criminal world, such as easy money or feelings of respect from fellow deviants, to be more appealing. The process again can be said to be one that serves to push individuals out of the conventional world into a world of criminality.

VIEWPOINTS

The influence of Labeling theory was fairly substantial. By the mid-1970s, it was the predominant theory on deviance in the field. Its impact was especially felt in the juvenile justice system, where, in an attempt to eliminate perceived harmful effects of the system, policies of non-intervention took precedence. Under these policies, status offenses were decriminalized, offenders were deviated from legal processing, and many who might have been otherwise incarcerated were not (Downes & Rock, 2007; Horwitz & Wasserman, 1979).

Deterrence Theory

In the 1980s, Labeling theory faded and was supplanted to some extent by deterrence theory, which takes the completely opposite position that harsh societal penalties for crime serve to prevent future misbehavior (Cullen & Agnew, 2006; Horwitz & Wasserman, 1979). Labeling theory's decline is attributed in part to the difficulty of producing empirical support to validate its propositions. Partly, this is because Labeling theory attempts to describe a complex process that was first recognized through qualitative methods. Thus, its complexity is difficult to reduce to a form that can be measured quantitatively. Those who attempted to make this reduction produced studies that sought to identify correlations between offenders who were processed through the justice system and the rates at which they committed second offenses (Bernberg & Krohn, 2003; Horwitz & Wasserman, 1979). A few of these studies showed small but positive results. However, others contended that the results were possibly the result of selection bias, for those who are more likely to commit second crimes are also more likely to be referred to the criminal justice system in the first place (Smith & Paternoster, 1990).

One of the more damaging factors related to Labeling theory's demise was the rise of an interpretation of the theory that viewed Labeling as a sufficient and necessary condition for the production of deviance. In other words, some saw secondary deviance as only the product of Labeling. Furthermore, many disregarded the role that an individual's interpretation of a label had in the Labeling process. Instead, the mere application of the formal label was said to be enough to spur future criminal conduct. Although scholars have criticized these narrow positions as being misinterpretations of the theory, the fact that these perceptions were prevalent impacted the research, and because these ideas were not supported by the research, the entire theory was discounted (Cullen & Agnew, 2006; Downes & Rock, 2007; Wellford & Triplett, 1993).

Labeling Theory Today

Recent approaches to criminology have revived interest in Labeling theory principles. These new theories have broadened the scope of investigation into Labeling; rather than asking simply whether or not Labeling has an effect on offenders, theorists now investigate what kinds of Labeling have an effect and under what conditions.

With regards to the types of Labeling that have an effect, Matsueda (1992) has investigated the role that informal labels, which are labels that parents, teachers, and friends apply to an offender, have in the development of individual self-concept. Focusing on reflected appraisals, which indicate how individuals perceive the way others view them, Matsueda's work draws upon the core interactionist philosophy of Labeling theory. So far, results have indicated that informal labels may be more important than formal labels in the development of self-perceptions.

In seeking to understand the conditions that impact whether labels are effective, several new ideas and theories have been proposed. One approach suggests that labels only have a stigmatizing effect if the offender is considered to be a full member of the society that is applying the label. In other words, a criminal label will be more devastating for someone who holds a respected position in society (e.g., a banker) than someone who is not as socially integrated (e.g., a homeless person) (Wellford & Triplett, 1993). This line of investigation is being used to understand why individuals in certain communities seem to feel less stigmatization from Labeling than others. For instance, Hirshfield (2004) found that in a community where arrests for petty crimes were frequent and the police were perceived by many to make frequent false arrests, youth felt little stigma from being arrested.

Unlike Labeling theory purists, who viewed all formal Labeling as harmful, new theorists suggest that there is a positive role than can be played by formal punishments. Braithwaite (1989) suggests that Labeling processes are a type of societal shaming, and shaming is often an effective means of social control. But certain kinds of shaming, he says, are more effective than others. Shaming that stigmatizes an individual tends to be ineffective because it degrades the offender. The only way for the offender to retain self-respect in such a situation is to reject the rejecter. Braithwaite supports an alternative, reintegrative shaming in which the bonds between shamer and shamed are reinforced rather than broken. Instead of being confronted the problem, the offender is given offers of reintegration and forgiveness.

Defiance Theory

Similar to Braithwaite, Sherman (1993) proposes that the way sanctions are imposed can impact whether individuals are reformed or whether they become repeat offenders. His defiance theory suggests that when rule breakers are punished in a way that they define as unfair or disrespectful, they are more likely to become defensive and deny their feelings of shame for having committed the offense. Thus, the sanction produces more negative consequences than beneficial ones.

In recognizing that Labeling theory, like most criminological theories, cannot explain crime and deviance on its own, Wellford and Triplett (1993) suggest that the time has come to develop an integrated approach to a complex problem. As part of this approach, Labeling theory can offer many contributions, they say. Some of these contributions will be related to new advances in research such as those offered by Matsueda, Braithwaite, and Sherman. They suggest that more research needs to be done to discover upon what factors formal labels are contingent, integrate Labeling theories with other theories, and focus on the effects of different types of labels. They support more longitudinal research to examine the developmental aspect of how individuals interact with systems and are shaped by labels over time. Furthermore, they say that researchers should investigate whether Labeling primarily impacts individuals or the social environment. With this kind of research, Labeling theory, they say, can have a positive role in criminological thought of the future.

TERMS & CONCEPTS

Chicago School: The Chicago School is the school of thought that developed at the University of Chicago Sociological Department in the 1920s and 1930s. It emphasized hands-on observation and analysis of the world.

Defiance Theory: Defiance theory suggests that offenders are more likely to reject their punishers and punishments if they believe that sanctions are applied unfairly or disrespectfully.

Deterrence Theory: Deterrence theory states that individuals try to maximize their benefits from committing crime, and therefore harsh penalties can serve to deter individuals from participating in criminal acts.

Deviance Amplification Process: Deviance amplification process is the process thought to occur when an individual faces formal Labeling in the criminal justice system and as a result becomes more deviant.

Ethnographic Methods: Ethnographic methods are qualitative methods of investigation used in the social sciences that involve close observation and extensive writing about individuals within their environments.

Reintegrative Shaming: Reintegrative shaming is a type of shaming that tries to invite offenders back into the community by offering forgiveness and reconciliation instead of stigmatization.

Self-Fulfilling Prophecies: A self-fulfilling prophecy is when someone's beliefs impact his or her behavior in a way that makes preconceived expectations come true.

Social Bond Theory: Social bond theory is a criminological theory that suggests that the relative strength of an individual's ties to conventional and nonconventional groups in society impacts the extent to which he or she engages in criminal behavior.

Strain Theory: Strain theory is a criminological theory that suggests that societal strains such as unemployment or an abusive situation can serve to pressure individuals into committing criminal acts.

Symbolic Interactionism: Symbolic interactionism views the individual as acting in accordance with how he or she perceives objects and meanings in a society as developed during his or her interactions with members of that society and with his or her internal self.

Bibliography

Ascani, N. (2012). "Labeling theory and the effects of sanctioning on delinquent peer association: A new approach to sentencing juveniles." *Perspectives* (University Of New Hampshire), 80–84.

Becker, H. (1963). *Outsiders: Studies in the sociology of deviance.* New York: The Free Press.

Bernburg, J., & Krohn, M. (2003). "Labeling, life chances, and adult crime: The direct and indirect effects of official intervention in adolescence on crime in early adulthood." *Criminology, 41* (4), 1287-1318.

Braithwaite, J. (1989). *Crime, shame and reintegration.* Cambridge, UK: Cambridge University Press.

Cullen, F.T., & Agnew, R. (2006). *Criminological theory: Past to present.* Los Angeles: Roxbury Publishing Company.

Dellwing, M. (2011). "Truth in Labeling: Are descriptions all we have?" *Deviant Behavior,* 32(7), 653–675.

Downes, D., & Rock, P. (5th ed.). (2007). *Understanding deviance.* Oxford: Oxford University Press.

Hartinger-Saunders, R. M., & Rine, C. M. (2011). "The intersection of social process and social structure theories to address juvenile crime: Toward a collaborative intervention model." *Journal of Human Behavior in the Social Environment,* 21(8), 909–925.

Hirschfield, P. (2004). "Stigmatization or normalization? The declining relevance of Labeling theory in disadvantaged urban communities." *Conference Papers—American Sociological Association.*

Horwitz, A., & Wasserman, M. (1979). "The effect of social control on delinquent behavior: A longitudinal test." *Sociological Focus, 12* (1), 53-70.

Lemert, E. M. (1951). *Social pathology: A systematic approach to the theory of sociopathic behavior.* New York: McGraw-Hill.

Martinez, J. (2004, August 14). "Understanding social factors in hiring decisions involving ex-felons." *Conference Papers—American Sociological Association.*

Matsueda, R. (1992). "Reflected appraisals, parental Labeling, and delinquency: Specifying a symbolic interactionist Theory." *American Journal of Sociology, 97* (6), 1577-1611.

Sherman, L. W. (1993). "Defiance, deterrence, and irrelevance: A theory of the criminal sanction." *Journal of Research in Crime and Delinquency,* 30, 445-473.

Smith, D., & Paternoster, R. (1990). "Formal processing and future delinquency: Deviance amplification as selection artifact." *Law & Society Review, 24* (5), 1109-1131.

Sweeten, G. (2006). "Who will graduate? Disruption of high school education by arrest and court involvement." *JQ: Justice Quarterly, 23* (4), 462-480.

Tannenbaum, F. (1938). *Crime and the community.* New York: Columbia University Press.

Wellford, C., & Triplett, R. (1993). *The future of Labeling Theory: Foundations and promises.* (pp. 1-22). Transaction Publishers.

SUGGESTED READING

Adler, P.A., & Adler, P. (eds.). (1994). *Constructions of deviance: social power, context, and interaction.* Belmont, CA: Wadsworth Publishing Company.

Behravan, H. (2011). "Sociological explanation of prison re-entry." *International Journal of Criminal Justice Sciences,* 6(1/2), 286–296.

Dotter, D. (2004). *Creating deviance: An interactionist approach.* Walnut Creek, CA: Altamira Press.

Mustillo, S. A., Budd, K., & Hendrix, K. (2013). "Obesity, Labeling, and psychological distress in late-childhood and adolescent black and white girls: The distal effects of stigma." *Social Psychology Quarterly,* 76(3), 268–289.

Rubington, E., & Weinberg, M.S. (compilers). (1996). *Deviance: The interactionist perspective.* Boston: Allyn and Bacon.

Noelle Vance, M.A.

MEDIA AND CRIME

ABSTRACT

Some experts argue that the media give greater salience and even sensationalize some types of crime and its perpetrators, while underreporting other kinds of crime and lawbreakers. The media have the power of contributing to fear and prejudice among their audiences, but they also can act as watchdog, in the public interest, of criminal activity by institutions and law compliance for governmental departments. Several main theoretical approaches are commonly used by experts in order to examine the interactions of media, crime representation, and the ways in which audience members use and interpret the information received.

OVERVIEW

The media are crucial producers and vehicles by which information is disseminated to mass audiences. Many societal issues, such as social deviations and law violations, are categorized as crime and processed into public information by the media. The social construction of crime is influenced and shaped by many factors of which the media represent one more, although among the most powerful. For example, information about crime is shaped by the crimes and types of crime the media select to report, the methods by which they gather news and shape the narration, the institutions and agencies they use as their sources, and so on.

A vast variety of studies exist on the ways in which media shape the representation of crime, victims, and lawbreakers, but also on the fear of crime and the appropriate responses to it. Many studies also focus on the ways in which audiences consume and interpret these representations. Although most agree that these representations are broadly influenced by ideology, it is also true that myriad societal and institutional factors are involved, often in conflict with one another. It is also important to bear in mind that there are both similarities and differences in crime representation, as represented in different media, such as serial shows and film, in literature, in print news, and televised news outlets. The representation of crime also varies according to culture and country.

It is not so much that a biased medium shapes news in order to influence the unresisting consciousness of the viewers and readers. In other words, very few experts believe there is an overall conspiracy among the media in how crime is to be represented. Rather, it is that crime news, in general, is susceptible to distortion at different points of the process. To begin with daily crime occurrences are too many to all be featured in news media. This is especially true in very populated metropolitan areas. Moreover, daily crime news may be expanded or shortened, depending upon myriad factors, such as the amount of other news that is considered more newsworthy at a particular time. The population of a region may also affect the ways in which crime is portrayed, such as in less populated areas where there is not much crime to report. So crime may be portrayed differently in different regions nationwide.

In most cases, however, there is an abundance of crime events to report; therefore, journalists and producers must select which will be developed as news. The selection and style of crime reporting varies according to the type of media and institutional interests and views at each. Media consumers also play a role as they select which type of media to consume in line with their own preferences. Other elements add complexity to the representation of crime in the media, which include changes in industry and technology. Examples include the proliferation of cable stations catering to increasingly narrower demographic segments, the growing prevalence of "reality" crime shows and law-and-order serials, the rise of free and paid sources of news in digital media, and the increasing sophistication of news gathering.

Many news outlets now use amateur video and photographic footage captured and sent in by the public. The widespread use of surveillance cameras also provides an array of criminal events caught on tape. Most of the footage, however, is of events that occur in public spaces, so that other types of crime remain underrepresented in the public eye. Crime has enjoyed huge entertainment value in the media starting in the late eighteenth century, with the rise of print periodicals. One of the main consequences of the growing sophistication of media technology has been the ubiquitous featuring of crime in all types of media, including print, radio, broadcast, and film genres.

FURTHER INSIGHTS

Research Findings

Crime reporting in news media has long been a focus of interest for research, particularly driven by the concern that some crimes are given more salience than others. The selective prominence of specific crimes, in turn, inevitably influences the perceptions of media consumers. A long tradition of media studies provides some key findings. For example, the audiences or readerships of media outlets that focus much of their time on crime report the highest levels of fear of crime and mistrust of others. This may occur even in areas where the incidence of crime is low.

Analysis of official crime statistics has shown that official crime data differ from media-reported crime. That is, there are frequent discrepancies between the proportion of crime as portrayed in the media and the actual proportion of crime events in the community. Audience studies reflect that the public believes the proportion of violent crime is much higher than it actually is. In fact, crime has been steadily decreasing. In other studies, crime statistics show that most reported crimes are nonviolent; media coverage, however, suggests the opposite. In most news media, violent crime is overrepresented, while nonviolent crime is underrepresented. Another issue of concern for researchers is the racial bias evidence in much of the media industry as pertains to crime. The relationship between crime and minority groups as portrayed in the media bears little relationship to its actual numbers. News also skews the information between crime and legal control. For example, according to the Federal Bureau of Investigation (FBI), the percentage of crime that clears (is solved) varies significantly according to offense. However, the highest percentage of crime cleared by police authorities is in murder and non-negligent manslaughter, with 61.5 percent of reported crime solved as of 2015 (Federal Bureau of Investigation, 2015). This suggests that close to 40 percent of murder and manslaughter cases remains unsolved. The narrative of news reports and fictional serials, however, make crime control appear to be more effective than the numbers suggest it is. This responds, to a certain extent, to a consideration of crime as entertainment, and the interest in creating a Manichean narrative, in which there are villains and victims, and justice always triumphs at the end. In fact, even television shows that focus on "cold cases"-those that remain unresolved long term-tend to show the crime event resolved at the end.

A wide array of studies shows that news outlets under- and over-represent specific groups as criminals or victims, according to gender, race, ethnicity, and socio-economic status. This provides misleading information about which populations are more prone to commit criminal acts or to be victimized. For example, while media focus on incidents of rape on campus, studies show that women in low-income areas are several times more likely to be victims of rape than college students; and yet, violent crime against low-income women has been underreported. Distorted representations of minorities as more likely to commit crimes fuel the entrenchment of stereotypes. In consequence, such distortions also play a role, some studies suggest, in how targeted populations are treated by the criminal justice system. For example, statistics show that males of color receive much harsher penalties, for the same crime, than their white counterparts. Research also shows that racial minorities in general and African Americans in particular are disproportionately featured as violent crime offenders. It is important to note, however, that many of these studies differ in their findings and have proven ambiguous or inconclusive, nor have they been able to prove direct causal relationships between crime representation and criminal justice practices and policies. Their value often lies in the patterns they uncover.

Theoretical Approaches

Several theories underlie most of the historical as well as contemporary research on media and crime. Broadly speaking, the most prevalent are those that focus either on measuring media effects or identifying hegemonic or dominant ideologies in media industries. These approaches, in turn, have theoretical subsets that are also widely used.

The media effects approach posits that media, especially broadcast, are one of the most influential sources of how people understand the world around them. For example, this approach is important in examining how crime information for news outlets is largely dependent upon daily police reports and, as with any other organization, police departments are guided by their own needs, interests, and priorities. In order not to harm ongoing investigations, for instance, they may have to omit information. There are also political concerns that may have to be taken into consideration.

As pertains to the public, the media effects approach often assumes that individuals receive information unquestioningly. Other studies, however, reveal that people do not receive news uncritically nor are the media their sole sources of information.

Individuals belong to many different groups, formed by kin workplace, and other organizations, in which they also gather and discuss information. Several media effects studies have shown that long-term exposure to a constant stream of alarming news cultivates fear in people not only of crime but of other people as well. It is important to keep in mind that these sentiments also depend on how the news is represented and if these representations are just reinforcing previously held assumptions.

Among the most important theories under this approach is the "agenda setting" theory, developed in the late 1960s. This theory posits that what people know about the world around them—including public affairs—is mediated by mass media. Whatever elements are salient in media productions, those same elements will become prominent for viewers. In this manner, then, the priorities of media producers and managers become priorities for the public. Analysis of crime and media from this standpoint would likely be concerned with how crime and crime perpetrators are portrayed, and who benefits from this. Because this theory also deals with issues of ideology, it can be considered under that approach as well.

Hegemonic approaches deal with ideologies or dominant sets of beliefs in mass media and the cultural industries. In short, the mass media aim to reproduce and disseminate hegemonic culture and ideas and to perpetuate systems of power. Such theories cover a wide range, from content analysis to the different ways in which individuals receive and interpret the products of media. This approach considers that media operate within an ideology and to promote an ideology, which is accepted, to different degrees, by audiences. In other words, media reports are ascribed specific meanings by producers who want to disseminate these ideas, but these are decoded or interpreted differently by different individuals. People do gain knowledge and internalize some meanings from mass media; however, this information is understood from a standpoint of their experiences and assumptions. These approaches are useful to examine how crime is portrayed by media outlets, and how these representations are interpreted by the public. More longitudinal studies may focus on the behaviors or policymaking that individuals or institutions may develop as a consequence.

VIEWPOINTS

Mass media production, encompassing detective novels to news outlets, from reality shows to fictional serials, allots a great deal of effort to crime and police work. News media play a crucial role. Besides covering crime, news media provide many services for police departments, in the form of public service announcements, missing persons alerts, calling for members of the public to inform about crime or eyewitness events and the like. In this manner, news media form relations with police departments and may mediate between them and the public. News about crime is often provided and presented from the point of view of police, and also serves to publicize the work police do. Moreover, often reporters are allowed to ride with police patrols as they make their rounds. Thus, reporters have the type of access to street crime scenes that is, for example, harder to come by in cases of white collar crime, state corruption, and other types of crime. This, many argue, causes a slant on the types of news represented in media, which may not reflect statistical crime data for that society.

Others argue that the type of crime portrayed is what interests most of the audiences. Most police work is routine. Therefore, most of it is not considered newsworthy by the media and would make for tedious stories. Media concentrate on stories with a higher entertainment value, which is what the public prefers. This skews the frequency of the types of crimes represented; however, rather than an ideological bias among producers, it reflects public choice.

Still others argue that rather than becoming allies of police departments, mass media often create problems for these agencies. Media publications and programs often "police the police," or become watchdogs for the public interest. In other words, the media work as a sort of independent mechanism to ensure accountability by the criminal justice system and police compliance with the law. For example, news outlets may focus on specific and local instances of police abuse or corruption and give it national prominence; many police serials portray police departments as bogged down by faulty management and inefficient bureaucracy. To support this argument, experts cite instances in which media coverage has shed light on serious problems, causing embarrassment and leading to institutional changes. This type of coverage, according to some, leads to educating the public about problems faced by city, state, and federal government, such as lack of funds, the need for training, and other matters. However, other experts claim that cases of police problems or mismanagement are underrepresented to the point of being relatively rare in the media, except for a few more conspicuous cases.

Fiction may also play a deleterious role in the representation of anti-crime work. Some experts find that the depiction of police action in film and serials disseminate an image of police work that has little bearing on reality and yet may be problematic. For instance, many fictional accounts portray police officers who, frustrated with the hindrance posed by institutional ineptitude or corruption, must take the law into their own hands, often engaging in illegitimate forms of violence or vigilante justice, which violate civil and constitutional rights. In fact, some such characters have become cultural icons.

Finally, researchers of media and crime argue that an important type of crime which is largely underrepresented in the media is malfeasance in the private sector, also known as corporate or white collar crime. Reporters have limited access to most company headquarters. Moreover, the larger the company, the more the likelihood it has developed powerful connections with public entities, policymakers, and legislators. Companies hire attorneys and also hire or establish public relations departments whose job is to keep them out of the news, except to promote the company's brand. Because of these and other hindrances, prosecution is rare relative to the amount of white collar crime that occurs, according to experts. It is even rarer that it receive widespread coverage, because corporate crime details are often difficult to comprehend. However, news coverage of private sector crime is important because businesses are very concerned about their public images, and much effort is usually invested in upholding it. Coverage and representation of crime is, then, instrumental in effecting transformation, sustaining and establishing standards and compliance, and in driving organizational reform.

TERMS & CONCEPTS

Audience: The people who watch, read, or listen to something.

Crime: An activity that breaks the law. or an omission of a leeally required action. There are many types of crime, such as violent and nonviolent, and these can be catalogued as felonies and misdemeanors. Some crimes are punishable by loss of liberty, others by a fine, others with conditional liberty or community service, or a combination of any of the above.

Hegemony: Influence or control over a group of people.

Media: An aggregate of communication formats used to create, store, and disseminate information to wide audiences. There is a wide array of media types, such as print media, digital media, broadcast, cable, film, and advertising.

News: Events that are reported in a media outlet such as print, television, etc.

Bibliography

Beale, S. (2006). "The news media's influence on criminal justice policy: How market-driven news promotes punitiveness." *William and Mary Law Review, 48*, 397–481.

Bjornstrom, E. S., Kaufman, R. L., Peterson, R. D., Slater, M. D. (2010). "Race and ethnic representations of lawbreakers and victims in crime news: A national study of television coverage." *Social Problems, 57*, 269–293.

Campbell, R., Martin, C, & Fabos, B. (2013). *Media & culture: Mass communication in a digital age.* Boston, MA: Bedford/St. Martin's.

Chagnon, N. (2016). "Reverberate, resonate, reproduce: A reconsideration of ideological influence in crime news production." *Critical Criminology, 23*(1), 105–123.

Dyck, A., Moss, D., & Zingales, L. (2013). "Media versus special interests." *Journal of Law and Economics, 56*, 521–553.

Ericson, R. V. (1991). "Mass media, crime, law, and justice." *The British Journal of Criminology, 31*, 219–249.

Federal Bureau of Investigation. (2015). "2015 crime in the United States: Clearances." *FBI.* https://ucr.fbi.gov/crime-in-the-u.s/2015/crime-in-the-u.s.-2015/offenses-known-to-law-enforcement/clearances/clearances

Moriarty, R (2010). "Framing justice: Media, bias and legal decision-making." *Maryland Law Review, 69*, 849–909.

Muraskin, R. (2006). *Crime and the media: Headlines vs. reality.* Upper Saddle River, NJ: Prentice Hall.

Rennison, C. M. (2014, December 21). "Privilege, among rape victims. Who suffers most from rape and sexual assault in America?" http://www.nytimes.com/2014/12/22/opinion/who-suffers-most-from-rape-and-sexual-assault-in-america.

Robinson, M. B. (2014). *Media coverage of crime and criminal justice.* 2nd edition. Durham, NC: Carolina Academic Press.

Surette, Ray. (2014). *Media, crime and criminal justice: Images, realities and policies.* Boston, MA: Cengage.

Suggested Reading

Beale, S. (2006). "The news media's influence on criminal justice policy: How market-driven news promotes punitiveness." *William and Mary Law Review, 48*, 397–481.

Doyle, A. (2006). "How not to think about crime in the media." *Canadian Journal of Criminology and Criminal Justice, 48.* 867–885.

Farmer, B. (2014). "Does the mainstream media hate blacks?" *New American 30*, 23–28.

Jewkes, Y. (2015). *Media & crime* (3rd ed.). Los Angeles, CA: SAGE.

Rhineberger-Dunn, G.M. (2013). "Myth versus reality: Comparing the depiction of juvenile delinquency in metropolitan newspapers with arrest data." *Sociological Inquiry, 83*, 473–407.

Trudy Mercadal, Ph.D.

Medicalization of Deviance

ABSTRACT

This article examines the medicalization of deviance through a sociological lens. A definition of deviance is offered in terms of behavioral conduct, and indicates potential reasons individuals behave in a deviant manner. Next, a description of the medicalization of deviance is offered that describes ways deviant behaviors have been re-categorized as medical conditions that can be treated through the use of pharmacological interventions. Accompanying applications are offered through the lens of alcohol and substance abuse. Issues are discussed that relate to treatment and conflicting philosophies. Subsequent areas of research for sociologists examining this phenomenon are suggested.

OVERVIEW

From a historical perspective, the study of *deviant behavior* and *social control* began in the late 1960s. Interest emerged in ways categories of deviance are created, how the conflict among interest groups shapes the definition of what is considered deviant, and detailed ways that social policy about deviance develop and change over time (Horwitz, 1981, p. 750). From a reflective perspective, Higgins (1998) observes that "many of us take for granted" that those who engage in deviant behavior "are different kinds of people than we are" (p. 141). This belief is reinforced by stereotypical images of crime and deviance promulgated by the mass media, which often portray offenders as immoral, impulsive, insane, or otherwise unique (Donziger, 1996). From a definitional perspective, Brezina (2000) indicates that deviance and conformity can best be described as "labels or definitions that are differentially applied to various individuals and their behaviors—not in terms of the personal attributes of the individuals, nor in terms of the intrinsic qualities of the behaviors individuals display... Second, sociological theories of deviant involvement are based on the implicit or explicit rejection of explanations focusing on unique personal characteristics, especially abnormal traits of a biological or psychological nature" (p. 72).

Akers (1994) indicates that sociological theorists tend to assume that biological and psychological variations are "more or less within the normal range" and that little or no deviance is directly caused by abnormal physiology or psychology (p. 69). Merton (1938) had previously indicated that strain theorists provide the most forceful argument in this regard by stating that participation in deviant behavior most often represents "the normal reaction, by normal persons, to abnormal conditions" (p. 672). Moreover, Orcutt (1978) indicates that deviance is socially constructed and exists in relation to "interactional processes through which acts and actors are socially defined as deviant" (p. 346). According to researchers, deviant behavior emerged in society after "component elements of the social and cultural structures existed in contradiction, thereby exerting pressure on individuals to engage in forms of illegitimate behaviors (Merton, 1957; Sumner, 1994)." Merton (1995) also indicates that deviant behavior is "more likely to emerge in societies where the emphasis on cultural goals was inconsistent with the available means to achieve them" (Parnaby & Sacco, 2004, p. 3).

Social Learning Theory

From a theoretical perspective, *social learning theory* (Akers, 1985; Burgess & Akers, 1966) posits that people hold definitions of deviance and pro-social behavior that vary according to how they are reinforced:

... the definitions themselves are learned through reinforcement contingencies operating in the socialization process, and they may function less as direct motivators than as facilitative or inhibitory "discriminative stimuli" or cues that signal that certain behavior is appropriate and likely to be rewarded or inappropriate and likely to be punished in a given situation. It is the anticipated reinforcement or punishment that provides motivation for the behavior independently of whatever motivation to engage in or refrain from an act comes from the fact that it conforms to or violates one's beliefs or definitions (Akers, 1996, p. 239).

Akers (1996) further states, "Deviant models are available outside the family and other conventional socializing institutions, in the media, and among peers" (p. 239).

Brezina (2000) indicates that the tendency of individuals to rationalize their deviant involvement can be observed across a wide spectrum of deviant behavior, from academic cheating to interpersonal violence. Moreover, while rationalizations employed by academic cheaters and violent offenders may differ in substance and form, they serve essentially the same function or goal: to justify deviant acts and to neutralize moral prohibitions (p. 77). Stanley Milgram's (1974) classic "obedience" experiments, as described by Higgins (1998), also suggest that ordinary people—not just deranged or disturbed people—have the capacity to deliver harm when circumstances make it doable or justifiable (p. 138–141).

Punishment & Reward

Sykes and Matza (1957) point out that the prohibition of an act and definitions that justify the deviant act may be a product of an embedded *general normative system.* Patterson (1975) notes that, unaware of the system criteria, "parents and other socializers may make inefficient or inconsistent use of rewarding and punishing sanctions with the unintended outcome of reinforcing behavior that is contrary to their own normative standards" (cited in Akers, 1996, p. 239). Moreover, perceived behaviors and rewards play a role in whether individuals violate the general normative system. For example, an individual's "learned normative definitions may be violated because the rewards for the behavior outweigh the normative inhibitions. Individuals may refrain from law violation, despite having learned definitions favorable to violation, because individuals may anticipate more cost than reward attached to a given violation" (Akers, 1996, p. 239).

In attempts to better understand and reframe deviant behavior, theorists began to re-categorize deviance from a medicalized perspective, with one caveat: other trends were present in the study of deviance and societal reactions to deviance, and medicalization is only one way of looking at increased levels of deviance(Horwitz, 1981, p. 751). Many political and economic aspects affected the growth of medicalization within the context of the expanding US welfare state and are perhaps the most important unexplained aspects of the developments considered in the understanding of the medicalization of deviance (Horwitz, 1981).

The Medicalization of Deviance

According to Horwitz (1981), the *medicalization of deviance* "refers to the tendency to define deviance as a manifestation of an underlying sickness, to find the causes of deviance within the individual rather than in the social structure, and to treat deviance through the intervention of medical personnel" (p. 750). Types of deviance that have been viewed through the lens of medicalization include:

- Mental illness;
- Alcoholism;
- Opiate addiction;
- Delinquency;
- Hyperactivity;
- Child abuse;
- Homosexuality; and
- The biological study of crime.

Societal reactions to deviance include deinstitutionalization, normalization, mainstreaming, and the expansion of due process rights, which seem opposed, or at least somewhat related, to medicalization (p. 750). Horwitz (1981) further indicates that "medicalization should not be regarded as the sole, or possibly, even the major trend in deviance definition but rather as one of a number of sometimes conflicting developments in the societal reaction to deviance" (p. 751). He continues, Social policy toward deviants is undergoing dramatic changes. Medicalization requires a substantial resource base and funding for social services is undergoing a drastic decline. For students of social control this situation raises the question of whether medicalization as an explanation of deviant behavior will decline as resources for treatment are withdrawn (p. 752).

Social Constructionism

The medicalization of deviance can be viewed through the lens of *social constructionism,* which defines social problems as created by various political and ideological forces rather than being only a "part of the nature of things" (Berger & Luckman 1967, p. 52). Ajzenstadt and Cavaglion (2005) explain that social constructionism assumes that the meaning of events and human behavior depends on dimensions of cultural and social practices. The construction of a social problem and its cultural categorization (Best, 1995) are a function of the interplay between various interest groups. This interplay subsequently impacts social actions in defining and attempting to resolve problems, while determining the extent of their social and political power, public image, access to the media, and influence on the state apparatus (Pfohl, 1977)—within a specific socio-historical context (Costin, Karger, & Stoesz, 1996; Nelson, 1984). Such individuals can be defined as "claimmakers" (Spector & Kitsuse, 1977), as they utilize a variety of techniques to organize public and official perceptions of the "problem." Claimmakers bring their issue to the public agenda through the influence of power relationships, cultural resources, and professional ideology (Bogard, 2001; Rafter 1992), as well as via a continuous dialogue with their audience, seeking public legitimization in an attempt to make their claims "believable" (Loseke, 1999) (Ajzenstadt & Cavaglion, 2005, p. 256).

More research into this arena is highly suggested, especially the impact of lobbyists on the political arena as a potential manifestation of the definitional process of the medicalization of deviance.

Social Deviance as Disease

Research has suggested that from a political perspective, one means of gaining support in modern Western societies is to frame certain behaviors as a social problem, thereby creating new definitions of social deviance under the heading of a "disease," which could then be scientifically and objectively treated by experts. Framing social problems in terms of a medical model evokes "images of an ongoing condition over which a person has little control and that is amenable to some form of treatment" (Steen, 2001, p. 328). According to this view, when professionals construct a social problem, they cloak themselves in an aura of scientism, objectivity, and "prestige and expert authority" (Freidson, 1973). In this way, individuals can successfully sell an understandable structure of knowledge (Gusfield, 1981). The benefit of creating "ownership of the problem" and new territories of intervention by spreading "scientific" knowledge gives professionals more power and social prestige inside the political system (Cohen, 1985) (Ajzenstadt & Cavaglion, 2005, p. 257).

C. Wright Mills (1943) claimed that social problems, when framed in a positivistic approach, seem to ignore larger social and political "structured wholes" (p. 166). In other words, the medical excuse, by focusing on the individual, silences and denies inherent political strains and social injustices (Halleck, 1971). From past studies on the medicalization of social problems, professionals have demonstrated that categorizing specific behaviors as a disease has an interactive relationship with the existing "hegemonic" moral order (Conrad, 1992; Conrad & Schneider, 1980).

APPLICATIONS

Parsons (1951) indicates that as soon as an individual is labeled as being sick, their label changes their role in society. Categories of "medicalized" deviance include drug abuse, alcoholism, gambling, suicide, sexual addiction, child abuse, hyperactive children, and insanity. In many of these examples, a deviant behavior once viewed as sinful or a criminal behavior has now been characterized as a medical problem. Consequently, a behavior once controlled by a priest or a judge has now become the responsibility of a physician (Rosenberg, 1986). Alcoholism and substance abuse can be examined as applications of the medicalization of deviance (Murphy, 2006).

Alcoholism & Substance Abuse

Drug and alcohol abuse problems are categorized as medicalized deviance. Hospital and other clinical settings offer major treatment and interventions for drug and alcohol problems and medical insurance reimburse costs associated with treatment.

Prescription and the distribution of pharmaceutical substances potentially offer a more "medical" way of treating alcoholism and substance abuse problems. Pharmaceutical innovations also offer the potential of moving the treatment for certain drug problems, like opiate addiction, into the medical realm. As Murphy (2006) notes, after a 1987 Gallup poll indicated that 89% of Americans agreed with the statement that "alcoholism is a disease," additional indicators have supported the widespread notion that alcohol problems are indeed medical problems (Peele, 1989). In a 2001 poll conducted by the Pew Research Center, 52% of Americans indicated that drug addiction should be treated as a disease, while 35% said that it should be treated as a crime. One of the latest psychological Diagnostic and Statistical Manuals (DSMIV) outlines several different diagnoses categories that can be given to alcohol or drug problems, from abuse to dependence, also lends support for the argument that alcohol and drug problems have been medicalized (Murphy, 2006, p. 2).

The "War on Drugs" campaign that started during the 1980s perpetuated an advance of federal dollars spent to support alcohol and drug treatment, especially to law enforcement and prisons. In the late 1980s to the early 1990s statistics indicated a decrease in the numbers of drug users, while the amount of money directed to treatment and intervention programs increased (Akers, 1992). Peele (1989) suggests that increasing amounts spent on treatment programs were due to the treatment industry itself widening the definition of *abuse* to include more individuals with a "problem" (Murphy, 2006, p. 2). Increasing numbers of health insurance companies covering drug and alcohol treatment programs contribute to the increasing numbers of "private hospitals and clinics to treat alcohol and drug problems" (Akers, 2002, as cited in Murphy, 2006, p. 2).

From another perspective, medicalization may not eradicate stigmatization attributed to specific behaviors. Conrad (1992) indicates that certain behaviors may actually be hybrids of medical-moral-legal issues, rather than solely medical problems. The body of research indicated in this realm would specify that responses to a given issue would be different based on a given realm. For example, drug abuse is viewed as a legal category by the courts; religious groups would consider drug abuse to be a moral concern; and substance abuse treatment programs consider abuse to be a medical problem. However, Peyrot (1984) indicates that all of these issues may be integrative. For example, it would be possible for an individual to spend time in jail for purchasing heroin, while still receiving methadone for heroine addiction in a treatment program, which would replace a criminal framework for a medical one and thereby create an integrative definitional category (Murphy, 2006, p. 4).

Moreover, the move toward a more sympathetic and less punitive approach to manage substance abuse issues may have eliminated the negative stigma associated with addictive behaviors. Given the growing number of self-help groups, it seems that the "addict" label is carrying less of a stigma. However, in order for an addiction to be considered as an illness, an individual must first recognize the problem is undesirable and then seek treatment (Parsons, 1951). A caveat for this situation is dependent on whether the treatment is court-mandated, which would also introduce the concept of hybridization (Murphy, 2006, p. 3). Based on these issues, it seems that many issues might complicate the categorization process.

ISSUES

Legal & Moral Considerations

The use of pharmacological treatments for addiction, such as methadone or naltrexone, is one issue that has been debated among medical providers, as well as treatment providers and those in treatment (Volpicelli & Szalavitz, 2000; Rychtarik et. al., 2000). Central to this issue is that pharmaceuticals might replace one addiction with another by attempting to cure a substance abuse issue with another substance. While some of the treatment drugs may not be habit-forming, and regulations around the prescription and distribution of pharmacological treatments are also very extensive, the issue that addiction might be a moral choice factors into the debate (Volpicelli & Szalavitz, 2000). The idea that addiction continues to be perceived as a matter of self-control, or that individuals with addictions might have a "weak moral character or spiritual problem may be a sign that the use of substitute drugs to alleviate cravings or ease withdrawal may seem too easy" (Murphy, 2006, p. 2).

The complicated relationship between the legal and medical aspects of abuse is another issue in the medicalization of deviance. While one individual might be arrested for selling or using drugs and is sent for treatment rather than to jail or released early to a treatment setting, another individual might spend time in jail for drug-related crimes and receive no treatment at all. The unclear boundaries associated with substance abuse make it seem unclear as to whether drug and alcohol abuse should be considered as an illness and medical problem, or whether the problem is legal or moral. Based on the competing definitions, it is difficult to negotiate the competing definitions of alcohol and drug abuse and the most appropriate treatment options (Murphy, 2006, p. 7).

Another issue that should be considered in the medicalization of deviance is the ongoing process of defining and reframing specific social conditions into a medical condition. Medicalization is an ongoing process. Competing interests for defining specific behaviors impact behavioral categorization. Researchers need to be informed regarding the multitude of competing definitional frameworks, characteristics, and potential treatments for different kinds of behaviors. While legal, social, moral, and medical categories are common ways of categorizing behaviors, genetic predisposition is also a framework for describing deviant behaviors (Parnaby & Sacco, 2004).

Child Socialization

Socialization is "the process by which individuals acquire the attitudes, beliefs, values, and skills needed to participate effectively in organized social life" (Dunn, Rouse, & Seff, 1994, p. 375). Socialization can also be described as the process through which a "child or other novice acquires the knowledge, orientations, and practices that enable him or her to participate effectively and appropriately in the social life of a particular community" (Garrett & Baquedano-Lopez, 2002, p. 339). Bragg (1976) further indicates that "the socialization process is the learning process through which an individual acquires the knowledge and skills, the values and attitudes, and the habits and modes of thought of the society to which he belongs" (p. 3). Social commentators have observed and taken note of the growing tendency to rely on medications like Ritalin to "suppress the passion of children and to assist in the correction of perceived behavioral problems" (Gosden, 1997, p. 59). Certainly, all of these ongoing outcomes will continue the ongoing debate surrounding the medicalization of deviance. Additional research into the impacts of the medicalization of deviance would be helpful in determining longitudinal impacts on individuals impacted by the label and subsequent treatments.

Clearly, social policy toward deviance and the potential medicalization of deviance is in the process of undergoing dramatic changes. The medicalization of deviance requires a substantial resource base for treatments and interventions, and funding for social services is undergoing a drastic decline. For researchers analyzing the process of social control, the medicalization of deviance raises the question of whether medicalization as an explanation of deviant behavior will decline as resources for treatment are withdrawn (Horwitz, 1981, p. 752). Moreover, other research seems to indicate that "medicalized" treatments indicate ambiguity and confusion over the label, because of the integration of other categories (Parnaby & Sacco, 2004, p. 13) further exacerbating the definitional categories. The last consideration of the medicalization of deviance is the ongoing impact on the socialization of children.

TERMS & CONCEPTS

Deviance: Deviance can best be described as a label or definition that can be differentially applied to various individuals and their behaviors, which can be viewed through sociological, moral, legal, and "medicalized" lenses.

Medicalization of Deviance: Medicalization of deviance refers to the tendency to define deviance as a manifestation of an underlying sickness, to find the causes of deviance within the individual rather than in the social structure, and to treat deviance through the intervention of medical personnel (Horwitz, 1981).

Social Constructionism Theory: Social constructionism theory defines social problems as problems that are created by various political and ideological forces rather than being only a "part of the nature of things."

Social Learning Theory: Social learning theory indicates that definitions themselves are learned through reinforcement contingencies operating in the socialization process, and they may function less as direct motivators than as facilitative or inhibitory "discriminative stimuli" or cues that signal that certain behavior is appropriate and likely to be rewarded or inappropriate and likely to be punished in a given situation (Akers, 1996, p. 239).

Socialization: Socialization is "the process by which individuals acquire the attitudes, beliefs, values, and skills needed to participate effectively in organized social life" (Dunn, Rouse, & Seff, 1994, p. 375).

Bibliography

Akers, R. L. (1985). *Deviant behavior: A social learning approach.* Belmont, CA: Wadsworth.

Akers, Ronald. (1992). *Drugs, alcohol, and society: Social structure, process, and policy.* Belmont, CA: Wadsworth Publishing.

Akers, R. L. (1994). *Criminological theories.* Los Angeles, CA: Roxbury.

Akers, R. L. (1996). "Is differential association/social learning cultural deviance theory?" *Criminology, 34* (2), 229–247.

Ajzenstadt, M. & Cavaglion, G. (2005). "Stories about child sexual abuse: Textual analysis of instruction manuals in Israel." *Qualitative Sociology, 28* (3), 255–274.

Berger, P. L., & Luckmann, T. L. (1967). *The social construction of reality.* Garden City, NY: Doubleday.

Best, J. (Ed.). (1995). *Images of issues: Typifying contemporary social problems* (2nd ed.). New York: Gruynter.

Bogard, C. (2001). "Claimmakers and contexts in early constructions in homelessness: A comparison of New York City and Washington, DC." *Symbolic Interaction, 24* (4), 425–454.

Brezina, T. (2000). "Are deviants different from the rest of us? Using student accounts of academic cheating to explore a popular myth." *Teaching Sociology, 28*(1), 71–78.

Burgess, R. L. & Akers, R. L. (1966). "A differential association – reinforcement theory of criminal behavior." *Social Problems, 14,* 128–147.

Cohen, S. (1985). *Visions of social control.* Cambridge: Polity Press.

Conrad, P. (1992). "Medicalization and social control." *Annual Review of Sociology, 18,* 209–232.

Conrad, P., & Schneider, J. (1980). *Deviance and medicalization: From badness to sickness.* St. Louis: Mosby.

Costin, L., Karger, H. J., & Stoesz, D. (1996). *The politics of child abuse in America.* New York: Oxford University Press.

Donziger, S. R., (ed). (1996). *The real war on crime.* New York: Harper Perennial.

Dunn, D., Rouse, L., & Seff, M. A. (1994). New faculty socialization in the academic workplace. In J. C. Smart (Ed.), *Higher education: Theory and research, 10,* 374–416. New York: Agathon.

Evans, W. J., & Maines, D. R. (1995). Narrative structures and the analysis of incest. *Symbolic Interaction, 18* (3), 303–322.

Feinberg, S. L. (2011). "Defining deviance: A comparative review of textbooks in the sociology of deviance." *Teaching Sociology, 39*(4), 382–387.

Freidson, E. (1973). *Profession of medicine: A study of the sociology of applied knowledge.* New York: Dodd, Mead.

Garrett, P. & Baquedano-Lopez, P. (2002). "Language socialization: Reproduction and continuity, transformation, and change." *Annual Reviews, 31,* 339–361.

Gosden, R. (1997). "The medicalisation of deviance." *Social Alternatives, 16* (2), 58–60.

Gusfield, J. R. (1981). *The culture of public problems: Drinking, driving and the symbolic order.* Chicago: University of Chicago Press.

Halleck, S. (1971). *The politics of therapy.* New York: Science House.

Higgins, P. (1998). *Thinking about deviance.* Dix Hills, NY: General Hall.

Horwitz, A. V. (1981). "The medicalization of deviance [Book Review]." *Contemporary Sociology, 10* (6), 750–752.

Loseke, D. (1999). *Thinking about social problems.* Hawthorne, NY: Aldine de Gruyter.

McCray, K., Wesely, J. K., & Rasche, C. E. (2011). "Rehab retrospect: Former prostitutes and the (re)construction of deviance." *Deviant Behavior, 32* (8), 743–768.

Merton, R. K. (1938). "Social structure and anomie." *American Sociological Review, 3,* 672–682.

Merton, R. K. (1957). *Social theory and social structure.* Toronto: Collier-Macmillian Canada Ltd.

Merton, R. (1995). "Opportunity structure: The emergence, diffusion, and differentiation of a sociological concept, 1930s–1950s." (p. 3–78). In Freda Adler and William S. Laufer, eds., *The legacy of Anomie Theory.* New Brunswick, NJ: Transaction Publishers.

Mills, C. W. (1943). "The professional ideology of social pathologists." *American Journal of Sociology, 49,* 165–189.

Murphy, J. (2006). "Negotiating the disease concept in the treatment for drug problems." *Conference Papers – American Sociological Association,* 1–16.

Nelson, B. (1984). Making an issue of child abuse: Political agenda setting for social problems. Chicago: University of Chicago Press.

Newberg, E., & Bourne, R. (1978). "The medicalization and legalization of child abuse." *American Journal of Orthopsychiatry, 48,* 593–607.

Orcutt, J. D. (1975). "Deviance as a situated phenomenon: Variations in the social interpretation of marijuana and alcohol use." *Social Problems, 22,* 346–356.

Parnaby, P. F. & Sacco, V. F. (2004). "Fame and strain: The contributions of Mertonian deviance theory to an understanding of the relationship between celebrity and deviant behavior." *Deviant Behavior, 25* (1), 1–26.

Parsons, T. (1951). *The social system.* New York: Free Press.

Peele, S. (1989). *The diseasing of America: Addiction treatment out of control.* Boston: Houghton Mifflin.

Peyrot, M.(1984). "Cycles of social problem development: The case of drug abuse." *Sociological Quarterly, 25,* 83–96.

Pfohl, S. (1977). "The 'discovery' of child abuse." *Social Problems, 24,* 310–323.

Rafter, N. H. (1992). "Claims-making and sociocultural context in the first U.S. eugenics campaign." *Social Problems, 39* (1), 17–34.

Rosenberg, C. (1986). "Disease and social order in America: Perceptions and expectations." *The Milbank Quarterly, 64* (1), 34–55.

Rychtarik, R, Connors, G, Dermen, K. & Stasiewicz, P. (2000). "Alcoholics anonymous and the use of medications to prevent relapse: An anonymous survey of member attitudes." *Journal of Studies on Alcohol, 61,* 134–138.

Scott, S. (2001). "Surviving selves: Feminism and contemporary discourses of child abuse." *Feminist Theory, 2* (3), 349–361.

Sefiha, O. (2012). "Bike racing, neutralization, and the social construction of performance-enhancing drug use." *Contemporary Drug Problems, 39* (2), 213–245.

Spector, M., & Kitsuse, J. I. (1977). *Constructing social problems.* New York: Aldine.

Stanko, E. A. (1997). "Safety talk: Conceptualizing women's risk assessment as a 'technology of the soul'." *Theoretical Criminology, 1* (4), 479–499.

Steen, S. (2001). "Contested portrayals: Medical and legal social control of juvenile sex offenders." *The Sociological Quarterly, 42* (3), 325–350.

Sumner, C. (1994). *The sociology of deviance: An obituary.* New York: The Continuum Publishing Company.

Sykes, G. & Matza, D. (1957). "Techniques of neutralization: A theory of delinquency." *American Journal of Sociology, 22,* 664–670.

Turk, A. (1982). *Political criminality: The defiance and defense of authority.* Beverly Hills: Sage.

Valverde, M. (1998). *Diseases of the will: Alcohol and the dilemmas of freedom.* Cambridge, England: Cambridge University Press.

Volpicelli, J. & Szalavitz, M. (2000). *Recovery options: The complete guide.* New York: John Wiley and Sons, Inc.

Suggested Reading

Adler, P. A., & Adler, P. (2012). *Constructions of deviance: Social power, context, and interaction.* 7th ed. Belmont, CA: Thomson/Wadsworth.

Becker, H. S. (1963). *Outsiders: Studies in the sociology of deviance.* New York: Free Press.

Curra, J. (2014). *The relativity of deviance.* 3rd ed. Thousand Oaks, CA: SAGE Publications.

Fox, R. (1989). *The sociology of medicine: A participant observer's view.* Englewood Cliffs, NJ: Prentice Hall Inc.

Merton, R. K. (1968). *Social theory and social structure.* New York: Free Press.

Miller, K. S. (1980). *The criminal justice and mental health systems: Conflict and collusion.* MA: Oelgeschlager, Gunn & Hain.

Shoham, S. G. & Hoffman, J. (1991). *A primer in the sociology of crime.* New York: Harrow and Heston.

Sharon Link, Ph.D.

Militarization of Police

ABSTRACT

In the wake of rioting and civil unrest in Ferguson, Missouri, and Baltimore, Maryland, as well as several incidents of police killings of unarmed civilians and growing concerns over mass shootings and acts of terrorism on U.S. soil, the subject of police militarization has generated significant public controversy. Criminal justice scholars, law enforcement personnel, and public officials have noted that ever since the late 1960s, state and local police departments nationwide have steadily become more heavily armed with military-grade weaponry, and approaches towards policing have seemed to become more aggressive. This has generated questions about the desirability of these trends.

OVERVIEW

The phrase militarization of police refers to the increased tendency, in recent years, of local police departments and other law enforcement agencies (such as sheriff's offices and state police forces) to become equipped with military-grade weaponry and, subsequently, to become more aggressive in their routine patrolling, apprehension of suspects, and crime-fighting techniques. The term is most commonly used by critics of these developments, although there is a considerable degree support for more aggressive policing and the police acquisition of enhanced weaponry among both the law enforcement community and the general public. However, this subject remains highly controversial and contentious. Riots in 2014 and 2015 in Ferguson, Missouri, and Baltimore, Maryland, respectively, were in response to unarmed young men being killed by police officers, and were met with large assemblages of police officers wearing body armor, carrying assault rifles, and operating armored military vehicles patrolling the streets. More than 1,000 Americans were killed by police in 2015, and an estimated 20 percent were unarmed.

The militarization of police departments nationwide is not an entirely new phenomenon, however; this trend began the late 1960s and has been heavily influenced by two separate developments: the creation of SWAT (Special Weapons and Tactics) units and enactment of the Pentagon's 1033 Program. Furthermore, the launch of the "War on Drugs" in the 1970s and 1980s and the "War on Terror" following the terrorist attacks of September 11, 2001, have contributed to the increasing militarization of America's law enforcement agencies. The militarization of the nation's police departments has garnered significant media attention at a time when, ironically, violent crime rates have actually decreased throughout much of the country.

SWAT Units

SWAT teams are special police units that are highly trained in tactics similar to military commando forces; they have traditionally specialized in hostage crises, standoffs, incidents of domestic terrorism, and other situations considered too "high risk" for conventional police departments to handle. SWAT agents are armed more heavily than traditional police officers and often carry assault rifles and other powerful firearms and wear bullet-resistant body armor. Los Angeles was the first city to form a SWAT unit in the 1960s, but by the mid-1970s nearly five hundred police departments nationwide had their own SWAT teams. Paul Kraska, a professor at Eastern Kentucky University's School of Justice Studies, points out that in the mid-1980s, approximately 13 percent of small American cities (local jurisdictions between 25,000-50,000 residents) had their own SWAT teams, but by 2005, more than 80 percent of small cities had SWAT teams. Kraska also notes than 89 percent of American cities with populations greater than 50,000 now have SWAT teams.

The growing number of SWAT teams nationwide has coincided with a tremendous expansion of duties assigned to SWAT teams. Kraska contends that the number of SWAT raids conducted annually in the United States has exponentially increased over the decades, from a few hundred in the 1970s, to approximately three thousand annually in early the 1980s, to nearly fifty thousand in 2005. Whereas SWAT teams were originally designed to handle relatively rare "high risk" situations, twenty-first century SWAT personnel are increasingly utilized to issue search warrants, conduct drug raids, and patrolling local streets—responsibilities that were formerly assigned to conventional police officers. This has resulted in various incidents that some interpret as a misuse or overreaction of policing. For example, on October 2, 2010, a SWAT team in New Haven, Connecticut, conducted raids on a series of bars suspected of serving alcohol to underage customers. A 2014 report issued by the American Civil Liberties Union stated that 79 percent of SWAT teams were deployed solely to execute search warrants, while only 7 percent of SWAT deployments were for hostage crises or active shooter situations.

1033 Program

Another aspect of the increased militarization of police in American society, which has now generated both criticism and support, is the 1033 Program. Congress established the 1033 Program in 1989 during the height of the "War on Drugs" to assist law enforcement agencies in combating drug trafficking and gang violence in their communities. The 1033 Program, which took effect in 1990, allowed the U.S. Department of Defense (DOD) to provide surplus military equipment to local, county, and state law enforcement agencies at little-to-no cost. In 1996, in the aftermath of the Oklahoma City bombing, which killed 168 people, Congress passed the National Defense Authorization Act that amended the 1033 Program to allow the DOD to supply surplus items to better equip law enforcement agencies for counterterrorism activities.

The role of local and state police in combating terrorist actions took on even greater significance following the attacks on the World Trade Center and Pentagon on September 11, 2001, and the 1033 Program continues to benefit police agencies. The manner in which the 1033 Program operates is relatively straightforward. The Pentagon (the headquarters of the U.S. military) posts its inventory of surplus, unwanted, or discontinued equipment on its Law Enforcement Support Office (LESO) website, and local law enforcement agencies throughout the nation can request this equipment. Coordinators for each of the fifty states at the Defense Logistics Agency either approve or deny these requests. Non-weapon items—such as desks, chairs, computers, office stationery, pickup trucks, all-terrain vehicles, and other non-combat vehicles—are made permanent gifts to law enforcement agencies, but weapons (firearms, explosives, and combat vehicles) are leased to local agencies on a yearly basis; weapons that are provided to law enforcement agencies but go unused are either returned to the Pentagon for reissue or transferred to other police departments.

Between 1997 and 2014, more than $4.3 billion in equipment was transferred from the DOD to local and state police departments, according to an August 2014 report in the *Washington Post.* Since the inception of the 1033 Program in 1990, police agencies have received more than $5.6 million in military equipment. However, weapons account for only 3 percent of all items issued by the Pentagon under the 1033 Program. The U.S. Department of Homeland Security granted $35 billion to local, county, and state police departments between 2002 and 2011 in order to combat terrorism; these funds could be used by agencies to purchase military-grade equipment from sources other than the DOD, such as private corporations that manufacture weapons.

Drug use and violent crime rates have generally declined throughout the 1990s and into the early years of the twenty-first century, causing critics to question the nation's need to more heavily arm its police forces or to permit police to engage in more aggressive tactics. However, the aftermath of the shooting of Michael Brown by police officer Darren Wilson in Ferguson, Missouri, in August 2014 drew national attention to the issue of police militarization. As large crowds protested Brown's death for several days following the shooting in August and again in November 2014 following a grand jury's decision to not indict Wilson for shooting Brown, the Ferguson police department attempted to quell the rioting while wearing military-like gear, carrying assault rifles, and patrolling the streets with Humvees and other armored vehicles.

Images documenting the event were exposed for several weeks on 24-hour cable television networks, Internet websites, and social media, and to some Americans, these visuals appeared to resemble a state of war rather than a Midwestern American city. One of the most controversial and, to some Americans, surprising items seen patrolling the streets of Ferguson during this period of unrest was mine-resistant, armor protected (MRAP) vehicles, which had previously been used by the Army and Marine Corps on the battlefields of Iraq and Afghanistan. President Barack Obama responded to the growing controversy and criticism surrounding the militarization of police by announcing that the White House would review the 1033 Program, and new guidelines for the program were issued in the spring of 2015. Under the new rules implemented by the Obama administration, the Pentagon could no longer transfer certain military weapons to police agencies, including armored track vehicles, grenade launchers, bayonets, guns that are .50-caliber or higher, and aircraft armed with missiles, guns, or other weaponry (known as "weaponized aircraft").

VIEWPOINTS

Much criticism has been raised against the increasing militarization of police departments throughout the United States by elected officials, academics, constitutional and legal experts, private citizens, and even some members of the law enforcement and military communities themselves. One of the most outspoken critics of police militarization has been Rand Paul, a U.S. senator from Kentucky and a candidate for the Republican Party's presidential nomination in the 2016 election. In an August 2014 opinion piece he wrote for *Time* magazine titled "We Must Demilitarize the Police," Paul maintained that the militarization of the nation's police forces threatens to erode Americans' civil liberties by transforming the country into a virtual police state. Senator Paul also claimed that police militarization is ineffective and counterproductive because seeing officers patrolling their neighborhood wearing camouflage and driving armored vehicles, thus suggesting a state of warfare, turns the sentiments of local residents against their cities' police.

Paul also pointed out that the militarization of police has noticeable ramifications tied to racial profiling. The "War on Drugs," which served as one of the original rationales for militarizing police departments, has resulted in disproportionately higher incarceration rates and comparably longer prison sentences for blacks and Latinos arrested for drug-related offenses than for whites. In addition, Paul, a libertarian, has criticized federal policies that provide law enforcement agencies with billions of taxpayers' dollars to purchase equipment from the Pentagon. Paul's candidness on this topic ran against the grain of the Republican Party, which presents itself as tough on crime and strongly supportive of the nation's military personnel and law enforcement agencies. His views, however, were representative of large libertarian wings of both parties.

President Obama also expressed concerns that the proliferation of military equipment in the hands of local and state police agencies can make residents of local communities feel unwelcome and even under siege, thus eroding public trust and a working relationship between residents and police. This perception prompted Obama to review the 1033 Program and issue the new guidelines in May 2015. However, Paul's and Obama's views did not go unchallenged, as both conservative and liberal commentators have expressed criticism.

Rich Lowry, editor of the conservative magazine *National Review*, has challenged the claim that the animosity toward police in certain communities derives from the military fatigues officers may wear while on duty or the armored vehicles officers may drive. Instead, Lowry argues, the resentment residents may feel toward the police stems from police misconduct or excessive use of force, which can result from police in traditional gear as well as from police in military gear. Lowry also contends that media-driven discourses of police militarization have been overblown. On the other hand, some liberal pundits have criticized Obama's revisions to the 1033 Program by asserting that the type of equipment banned under the revised guidelines does not go far enough. For example, police departments can still request MRAP vehicles and several types of military firearms.

Critics note that the next president can simply overturn executive guidelines and revisions to the 1033 Program. Because of this, some lawmakers in the U.S. Congress have attempted to enact longer-lasting or permanent policies to begin demilitarizing police agencies. Congressman Hank Johnson, a Democrat from Georgia, introduced legislation in the U.S House of Representatives in 2014 and 2015 that sought to implement permanent federal guidelines that limited police use of military-grade equipment, although the bill failed to pass and even Johnson himself acknowledged that passage of this bill would be difficult.

Senator Paul's concerns regarding racial profiling by law enforcement in an era of increased police militarization have also been raised by activists within the Black Lives Matter movement. Although originally formed in the summer of 2013, following George Zimmerman's acquittal in the shooting of

Trayvon Martin, the Black Lives Matter movement has since focused most of its attention on highlighting and protesting various instances across the country of the deaths of unarmed African American civilians at the hands of police officers. Some of these high-profile cases include the deaths of Eric Garner in Staten Island, New York, in July 2014; John Crawford III in Beavercreek, Ohio, in August 2014; Tamir Rice in Cleveland in November 2014; Walter Scott in North Charleston, South Carolina, in April 2015; and Freddie Gray in Baltimore, Maryland in April 2015. Black Lives Matter activists point to the disproportionate number of racial minorities killed by police; although African Americans represent 28 percent of all persons arrested in the United States, they account for 35 percent of all persons killed during an arrest, according to the Bureau of Justice Statistics.

At issue in the debate over the militarization of police is a conflicting perception of what, exactly, the public wishes its police officers to be and what the public sees as the ideal role of the police within society. This has led to two very different and mutually opposed visions of police departments. To some, police officers should ideally be armed with overwhelming firepower and military equipment (akin to soliders) to allow them to safely and easily take down any actual or potential threats to themselves or others. Those who subscribe to this view generally do not see police militarization as objectionable. Despite criticisms of the 1033 Program, many local law enforcement agencies—ranging from large metropolitan police departments to small sheriff's departments—maintain that the program is essential for them, as it provides free or low-cost equipment that allows their agencies to preserve their limited finances. On the other hand, some Americans reject the idea of heavy-handed policing in favor of a community policing approach, which is based less on displays of force and more on police officers investing time and engaging with members of the communities they serve in order to gain the public's trust, build respect among the community, and curry favor with local residents to build a working, crime-fighting relationship between the community and the police force. Persons who favor community policing generally express concerns over the militarization of police, and advocates of community policing maintain that public trust and cooperation is necessary for police to obtain tips and information from local residents about criminal behavior and suspicious activities that would allow for more effective policing of communities.

In an era where criminals can gain access to high-powered assault rifles and explosives, as in the mass shooting in San Bernardino, California, in December 2015, that left fourteen people dead and twenty-four injured, it may be understandable why some Americans view arming law enforcement personnel as heavily as the criminals they must confront as not only desirable, but also necessary.

Radley Balko, an investigative journalist who focuses on law enforcement issues, notes that such incidents are extremely rare, as less than 0.00125 percent (one-eighth of one percent) of murders in the United States are committed with military-caliber weapons. The vast majority of murders are committed with simple handguns. Balko, a critic of police militarization for reasons similar to those expressed by Rand Paul, contends that SWAT teams are a vital part of American law enforcement, but that they were intended to be the rare exception to police work, rather than the norm.

TERMS & CONCEPTS

1033 Program: A federal program under which the U.S. Department of Defense can transfer surplus or unwanted military equipment to state and local police departments.

Black Lives Matter: A social movement that originated in 2013 to highlight and protest racial disparities in the criminal justice system; one of its central focuses has been to draw public attention to the mistreatment of African Americans at the hands of police.

Community Policing: An approach to policing based on building community trust and rapport between local residents and police officers; the ultimate objective is for residents to view police as respected members of the community in order to entice residents to assist the police in preventing and fighting crime.

Racial Profiling: A controversial tactic used within policing that is based on suspecting an individual of having committed a crime, or assuming that they are likely to engage in criminal behavior, on the basis of their racial or ethnic heritage.

SWAT Team: An acronym for Special Weapons and Tactics; a specialized and heavily armed police unit that is highly trained in carrying out high-risk, military-like activities, such as search and rescue missions, hostage situations, and active shooter standoffs.

War on Drugs: The metaphorical phrase, particularly popular during the 1980s and 1990s, for the U.S. government's heightened efforts at countering illegal drug trafficking and drug use in American society.

War on Terror: The U.S. government's initiatives, launched in the aftermath of the September 11, 2001, terrorist attacks, to combat terrorism both internationally and domestically through a combination of military, law enforcement, intelligence, and diplomatic activities.

Bibliography

Apuzzo, M. (2014, June 8). "War gear flows to police departments." New York Times. http://www.nytimes.com/2014/06/09/us

Balko, R. (2013, August 7). "Rise of the warrior cop." The Wall Street Journal. http://www.wsj.com/

Cook, L. (2014, August 25). "The 1033 program is actually pretty boring." U.S. News & World Report. http://www.usnews.com/news/blogs/data-mine/2014/08/25/ignore-what-you-see-on-tv-the-1033-program-is-actually-pretty-boring

den Heyer, G. (2014). "Mayberry revisited: A review of the influence of police paramilitary units on policing." *Policing & Society*, 24(3), 346–361.

Economist, T. (2014, March 21). "Why America's police are becoming so militarized." *Business Insider.* http://www.businessinsider.com/why-americas-police-are-becoming-so-militarized-2014-3

Eichenwald, K. (2014, August 18). "Why militarized police departments don't work." *Newsweek.* http://www.newsweek.com/2014/08/29/why-militarized-police-departments-dont-work-265214.html

Ingraham, C. (2014, August 14). "The Pentagon gave nearly half a billion dollars of military gear to local law enforcement last year." *The Washington Post.* https://www.washingtonpost.com/news/wonk/wp/2014/08/14/the-pentagon-gave-nearly-half-a-billion-dollars-of-military-gear-to-local-law-enforcement-last-year/

Kahn, K. B., & Martin, K. D. (2016). "Policing and race: Disparate treatment, perceptions, and policy responses." *Social Issues & Policy Review*, 10(1), 82–121.

Kappeler, V. E., & Kraska, P. B. (2015). "Normalizing police militarization, living in denial." *Policing & Society*, 25(3), 268–275.

Lowry, R. (2014, August 18). "The grossly exaggerated militarization-of-police critique of Ferguson." *National Review.* http://www.nationalreview.com/corner/385656/grossly-exaggerated-militarization-police-critique-ferguson-rich-lowry

Parker, C. (2014, August 27). "Militarized policing is counterproductive, Stanford expert says." *Stanford.edu* http://news.stanford.edu/news/2014/august/police-militarization-sklansky.html

Paul, R. (2014, August 14). "We must demilitarize the police." *Time.* http://time.com/3111474/rand-paul-ferguson-police/

Peralta, E. (2015, May 21). "White House ban on militarized gear for police may mean little." *NPR.* http://www.npr.org/sections/thetwo-way/2015/05/21/407958035/white-house-ban-on-militarized-gear-for-police-may-mean-little

Rezvani, A. et al. (2014, September 3). "MRAPs and bayonets: What we know about the Pentagon's 1033 Program." *NPR.* http://www.npr.org/2014/09/02/342494225/mraps-and-bayonets-what-we-know-about-the-pentagons-1033-program

Rizer, A., & Hartman, J. (2011, November 7). "How the war on terror has militarized the police." *The Atlantic.* http://www.theatlantic.com/national/archive/2011/11/how-the-war-on-terror-has-militarized-the-police/248047/

Swaine, J., Ackerman, S., & Siddiqui, S. (2015, August 11). "Ferguson forced to return Humvees as US military gear still flows to local police." *The Guardian.* http://www.theguardian.com/us-news/2015/aug/11/ferguson-protests-police-militarization-humvees

Swaine, J., & Laughland, O. (2015, November 16). "Number of people killed by US police in 2015 at 1,000 after Oakland shooting." *The Guardian.* http://www.theguardian.com/us-news/2015/nov/16/the-counted-killed-by-police-1000

SUGGESTED READING

Balko, R. (2014). *Rise of the warrior cop: The militarization of America's police forces.* Philadelphia, PA: Public Affairs.

Chumley, C. (2014). *Police state USA: How Orwell's nightmare is becoming our reality.* New York, NY: WorldNetDaily Books.

Spence, G. (2015). *Police state: How America's cops get away with murder.* New York: St. Martin's Press.

Tighe, S., & Brown, W. (2015). "The militarization of law enforcement: Bypassing the Posse Comitatus Act." *Justice Policy Journal,* 12(2), 1–39.

Whitehead, J. (2013). *A government of wolves: The emerging American police state.* New York: Select Books.

Justin D. García, Ph.D.

OVERVIEW OF HATE CRIMES

ABSTRACT

Hate crimes are a specific type of crime committed against individuals or groups because of their race, religion, sexual orientation, gender, age, or ethnicity. Genocide is an extreme form of hate crime, and other examples include cross burnings, physical assault and even threatening text messages. Hate crimes often come about through differences between in groups and out groups, the animosity felt between them, and they are enabled through the behavior of sympathizers and spectators. As an upward law, or a law designed to punish dominant groups in society, rather than a downward law, which is designed to punish subordinate groups, hate crime laws are often under-enforced. Beginning with an historical review of hate crimes, this article moves on to a discussion of the causes of hate crimes, continues with ways in which hate crimes can be prevented, and ends with a debate over the merits of additional hate crime legislation on the federal level.

OVERVIEW

Hate crimes are a specific form of crime in which a person or group is verbally and/or physically attacked because of their gender, sexual orientation, religion, politics, race, ethnicity, disability, or age. Sociologists have identified several ways in which hate can be manifested. These include physical attacks; property damage; bullying tactics; insults; and threatening phone calls, e-mails, text messages, instant messages, or letters.

History of Hate Crimes

While hate crimes have received considerable attention in the late twentieth and early twenty-first centuries, the phenomenon is hardly new. One especially grievous example of hate crimes have been those perpetrated against the Jewish people since even before the time of Jesus, and culminating in the Holocaust during World War II, which is perhaps the greatest hate crime in human history. Other well-known examples of hate crimes include genocides in Armenia, Bosnia, Rwanda, and Sudan; cross burnings, lynchings, and other actions of the Ku Klux Klan against African Americans in the United States; and threats and violence against gay people throughout the world.

In the twenty-first century, as migration patterns are resulting in a world that is more racially, ethnically, culturally, socially, and religiously mixed than it has ever been, hate crimes—crimes against the Other—have attracted considerable public attention. In some ways old hatreds have been given new life. "By 2003, there were more anti-Jewish hate attacks in European countries than at any time since World War II" (Levin, 2007, p. 81).

Researchers have noted that the concept of a hate crime presupposes a community that is morally outraged at prejudice of all kinds, and any particularly prejudicial attitudes and actions toward presumptive victim groups. According to Mason (2007), hate crime has a heavy investment in the capacity of its victim groups to convince the general public that they have been unjustly harmed. The process by which victim status is accorded to a given group is thus far from objective. Rather, it is the product of 'collective definitions that have been developed by watchdog organisations' and 'contested in legal and public arenas' (Jenness & Broad, 1997, p. 173) (Mason, 2007, p. 265).

Hate Crimes in the United States

Hate crimes in the United States have deep roots in American history and culture. As the US Federal Bureau of Investigation (FBI) notes,

> Crimes of hatred and prejudice—from lynchings to cross burnings to vandalism of synagogues—are a sad fact of American history, but the term "hate crime" did not enter the nation's vocabulary until the 1980s, when emerging hate groups like the Skinheads launched a wave of bias-related crime ("Hate Crime," 2008b).

In response to these disturbing trends, forty-five states and the District of Columbia have passed hate crime laws (Smith & Foley, 2010). All these states define a hate crime as a criminal act perpetrated due to the victim's race, religion, and ethnicity, while some also include sexual orientation, gender, and disability as criteria for hate crimes. As of 2016, only Arkansas, Georgia, Indiana, South Carolina, and Wyoming did not have hate crime statutes on their books, though hate crimes in those states are prosecuted under existing statutes covering murder, theft, harassment, and assault.

According to the 2015 FBI Uniform Crime Report Hate Crime Statistics, there were 5,818 "single-bias" criminal hate crime incidents reported involving 7,121 victims (defined as "a person, business, institution, or society as a whole") in 2015 (FBI, 2016).

Apart from the FBI statistics, the US Equal Employment Opportunity Commission (EEOC) reported a 24 percent increase in racial harassment reports between 2006 and 2007. The figure is double what it was in 1991 (Bello, 2008, p. 3a). In fiscal year 2015 there were 9,286 race-based harassment charges filed with the EEOC compared to 6,059 charges in fiscal year 2006 and 7,355 charges in fiscal year 2007 (US EEOC, n.d.)

Hate Crimes against Muslims after September 11, 2001

The attacks of September 11, 2001, sent shockwaves through American society. Coordinated terrorist attacks in New York City and Washington, DC, brought home to many Americans that the United States is not immune to being attacked on its own soil. Because the attacks were carried out exclusively by self-professed Muslims, the attacks also shined a spotlight, perhaps for the first time, on the 2.35 million Muslims then living in the United States (Pew Research Center, 2007, pp. 9-10), as well as on college and university students from Muslim-majority nations studying in the United States.

Researchers have found that the expected spike in anti-Muslim hate crime did occur in the immediate aftermath of the September 11 attacks. As one team of researchers noted, "with over 400 cases of anti-Islamic hate crime occurring nationally in the weeks after 9/11, in-group and out-group social psychology may have been amplified by the terrorist events" (Byers & Jones, 2007, p. 53).

These researchers also found, however, that the anti-Muslim hate crimes followed a specific pattern of intensity: "The time series analysis also showed that the effect of 9/11 largely dissipated within eight days of September 11. That is, the daily reports of anti-Islamic hate crimes began to level off yet did not return, on average, to the lower levels prior to 9/11" (Byers & Jones, 2007, pp. 53-54). Most curiously, given the locations of the terrorist attacks,

Table 1: Overview of Hate Crimes

Motivation	Percentage of incidents	Most impacted group
Racial bias	47.0%	African Americans
Religious bias	18.6%	Jews
Sexual-orientation bias	18.6%	Male homosexuals
Ethnicity/national origins bias	11.9%	Non-Hispanic
Disability bias	1.5%	Mentally disabled

(Source: Hate Crime Statistics, 2014, US Dept. of Justice/FBI, Fall 2015)

"New York City and Washington, DC, anti-Islamic hate crime reports are essentially non-existent (DC did have one report). With the exception of Boston, MA, all other locations on the list of top 10 cities with anti-Islamic hate crime reports in 2001 were some distance from both NYC and DC" (Byers & Jones, 2007, p. 54).

In seeking to explain the spike in anti-Muslim hate crimes more generally, the researchers noted the pivotal role played by political, religious, and community leaders, "Some of this effect may be accounted for by pleas in the media from Islamic and political leaders calling for calm and tolerance" (Byers & Jones, 2007, pp. 53-54).

As for the somewhat counterintuitive finding that anti-Muslim hate crimes were markedly absent from police blotters in New York City and Washington, DC, the research team suggested that this could be accounted for by the leveling of social distinctions as shown by previous researchers (Blocker, Rochford, & Sherkat, 1991; Gonzolas-Garcia & Soriano-Parra, 1989; Neal, 1984; Turkel, 2002). In short, and consistent with the theory of in-group and outgroup differences, such distinctions may have become less important given the collective community level trauma and the "leveling of social distinctions" (Quarantelli & Dynes, 1976) (Byers & Jones, 2007, p. 54).

In other words, the trauma of the attacks drew people in New York and Washington, DC, together rather than driving them apart.

An extensive survey of Muslim Americans conducted by the Pew Research Center five years after the September 11 attacks found that "[a] quarter of Muslim Americans say they have been the victim of discrimination in the United States, while 73% say they have never experienced discrimination while living in this country" (Pew Research Center, 2007, p. 4). A 2011 Pew Research Center for People and the Press report, "A Portrait of Muslim Americans," reported that though there were still significant numbers of Muslim Americans reporting that they experienced prejudice in the United States, these numbers had not changed much since 2007 (Pew Research Center, 2011).

Concern grew that hate crimes against Muslim Americans would increase following terrorist activities connected to the Islamic State of Iraq and Syria (ISIS) beginning in 2014. Such incidents included the coordinated attacks on Paris in November 2015 that left more than one hundred people dead and the shooting perpetrated by a Muslim couple with ties to ISIS at a social services facility in San Bernardino, California, in early December of that year. According to the 2015 FBI Uniform Crime Report Hate Crime Statistics, 22.2 percent of hate crimes motivated by religious bias were anti-Islamic (FBI, 2016). In March 2016, ISIS orchestrated yet another large-scale attack in Europe that involved three suicide bombings of the international airport in Brussels, Belgium, and resulted in the deaths of thirty-two people.

Illegal Immigration & Anti-Hispanic Hate Crimes

One of the most controversial social and political issues in the United States in the early twenty-first century has involved illegal immigrants, also known as undocumented workers. Should they be allowed to stay in the country, and under what conditions? Could they be stopped from coming to America altogether? The vast majority of illegal immigrants come from Mexico and elsewhere in Latin and Central America (Passel, 2005, p. 2), and a considerable portion of the American public believes there are good moral and economic grounds for taking a tougher stand against these migrants. While much of the opposition to illegal immigration is conducted within legal boundaries and does not spill over into hatred and violence, hateful attitudes and actions have emerged.

FBI statistics show that the number of hate crimes perpetrated against Latinos rose 25 percent between 2004 and 2008. Some, such as the Latino civil rights group the National Council of La Raza, attribute the increase to a spike in media coverage of illegal immigration (Ramirez, 2008, p. 14). The Anti-Defamation League (ADL) agrees; Deborah Lauter, its civil rights director adds, "When we saw the rhetoric shift from a legitimate debate to one where immigrants were dehumanized, we believe it inspired extremists and [some] mainstream Americans to act" (as cited in Ramirez, 2008, p. 14).

According to the 2015 FBI Uniform Crime Report Hate Crime Statistics, 9.4 percent of single-bias hate crimes motivated by race/ethnicity/ancestry were classified as anti-Hispanic or Latino bias. One of the issues most prominent in the campaigning for the 2016 presidential election also became immigration. A general sense of increased anti-immigration sentiment subsequently caused concern for several immigrant groups in America, including Muslims and Mexicans. Republican nominee and eventual president-elect Donald Trump's promise of his intention to build a wall at Mexico's expense on the border between Mexico and the United States particularly heightened the debate regarding illegal immigration from Mexico.

FURTHER INSIGHTS

Underreporting of Hate Crimes

The FBI data cited earlier was collected by the FBI in compliance with the 1990 Hate Crime Statistics Act. However, according to hate crimes watchdog organizations such as the Anti-Defamation League, there is evidence that the number of annual hate crimes in the United States may be underreported:

In 2006, 12,620 law enforcement agencies in the United States participated in this data collection effort, compared to 12,417 in 2005. Yet, only 16.7% of participating agencies reported even a single hate crime—and almost 5,000 police departments across the country did not participate in the FBI reporting program at all ("FBI Report Shows," 2007, par. 7).

In 2015 about 14,997 law enforcement agencies participated in the FBI's Uniform Crime Reporting Program (FBI, 2016). Although the number of participating agencies increased between 2006 and 2015, hate crimes remain underreported. The Bureau of Justice Statistics (BJS) published a study in March 2013 based on the National Crime Victimization Survey. The BJS study showed that from 2007 to 2011 the average number of hate crimes occurring each year in the United States was 259,690; however, only about 35 percent of these hate crimes were reported to law enforcement during that time period (SPLC, 2013). In 2014, the BJS reported that out of a total of 293, 800 estimated violent and property hate crimes that occurred in 2012, approximately 60 percent of these incidents were not reported to the police (Wilson, 2014).

Sociologists reviewing the FBI statistics have shown that law enforcement agencies in the Northeast and West have been more forthcoming with hate crime data than their counterparts in the South and Midwest (McVeigh, 2003; cited in King, 2007, pp. 189-190). "Hate crime reporting appears particularly scant in the historic 'Black Belt' states. For example, only one law enforcement agency in Alabama and Mississippi combined submitted a hate crime incident report in 2000 (US Department of Justice 2000: Table 12)" (cited in King, 2007, p.190).

Upward & Downward Law

How can this discrepancy be explained? Scholars note, for example, that when it comes to prosecuting hate crimes perpetrated by white Americans against African Americans, very often the concepts of upward law (law enforced against a higher-ranking person) and downward law (law enforced against a lower-ranking person) apply. According to King (2007),

Disputes that largely entail majority group offenders and minority group victims, such as hate crimes (Messner et al. 2004), constitute "upward law" (Black 1976:21-2) and may thus elicit minimal law enforcement. The present research builds on Black's insight in conjunction with the group threat thesis as advanced in the areas of law enforcement (Jackson 1989), civil rights law (Vines 1964), and prejudice (Taylor 1998; Quillian 1996) to suggest that minority group size increases the use of law that adversely impacts minority groups but decreases the use of law aimed at protecting minorities (King, 2007, p. 190).

Jack Levin, a leading expert on hate crimes, suggests that the police also may not be seeing the distinctive marks of hate crimes:

The low police estimate [of hate crimes] probably reflects their lack of training in recognizing the criteria e.g., slurs and epithets, graffiti, membership in organized hate crime, location where previous hate attacks have occurred, propaganda, hate websites and CDs, and a perpetrator's record of committing hate crimes. Also, police may see hate crimes committed by teenagers as merely childish pranks or hooliganism, deserving of some unofficial reprimand but nothing more. Some youngsters are given a slap on the wrist in the form of probation with no conditions—no community service, victim restitution, or education; others never get into police reports or the courts (Levin, 2007, p. 82).

Reasons for Committing Hate Crimes

Sociologists and others have been interested to learn the reasons underlying the perpetration of hate crimes, and considerable social science research has sought to unravel the mystery.

Several lines of evidence can be brought together. First is data collected by British researchers at the Institute of Education, University of London, indicating that hate crimes were most prevalent in areas with wide disparities in educational achievement, with proportionately few students grouped in the "average" achievement category ("Educational Inequality," 2008).

It is also the case that about 95 percent of hate crimes are committed by individuals and small groups (Levin, 2007, p. 83), and not by organized groups such as the Ku Klux Klan. Levin gives an especially lucid explanation of these individuals and their motivations: But hate comes right from the mainstream of a society. Most hatemongers are dabblers; they commit their offenses on a part-time basis as sort of a hobby. More than half of all hate attacks are perpetrated for the thrill, for the excitement, for bragging rights with friends who think that hate and violence are pretty cool. These thrill hate crimes are typically carried out by teenagers or young adults who go out in groups of 3, 4, 5 or more looking to assault someone who is different. They are bored and idle, they are unsophisticated in terms of hate ideology; but when they bash the enemy, their vulnerable victims, they feel something they never felt before–a sense of their own superiority, a feeling of power, and dominance, and control (Levin, 2007, p. 83).

Others who commit hate crimes do so because they perceive other groups as a threat or because they desire to retaliate against previous hate crimes perpetrated against members of their own group (Levin, 2007, p. 84).

In 2016, one man's horrific attack on a nightclub in Orlando, Florida, sparked debates about whether the attack should be considered both an act of terror and an act of hate as authorities struggled to determine the true motivation behind Omar Mateen's decision to open fire on a large crowd gathered at the popular lesbian, gay, bisexual, and transgender (LGBT) club Pulse. While the LGBT community reacted immediately and fearfully to the attack as one perpetrated specifically against LGBT individuals, authorities remained unsure as to why Mateen chose that location for his attack, which resulted in the deaths of forty-nine people.

Preventing Hate Crimes

No single method has ever been effective against reducing the number of hate crimes. Experts note that it involves the coordinated efforts of law enforcement, the courts, community and religious leaders, educators, and ordinary citizens to stem the tide of hate-inspired criminality. Each group has a role to play:

The Police

- Raise confidence in targeted communities that justice will be served;
- Bring perpetrators of hate crimes to justice;
- Educate young people about the serious costs of committing hate crimes; and
- Protect witnesses in hate crime cases.

The Courts

- Enforce existing statutes against hate crimes; and
- Connect victims of hate crimes to social services.

Community & Religious Leaders

- Drive home the message that hate and violence are never the answer;
- Help develop alternative and positive ways for the disenchanted and disenfranchised–those at risk of committing hate crimes–to connect with the diverse groups in their community; and
- Emphasize religious traditions that put a premium on love and tolerance.

The School System

- Introduces anti-hate, pro-tolerance lessons and curricula in age-appropriate ways;
- Remains vigilant about outbreaks of hate-based activities among students; and
- Works with parents, community groups, and others to provide counseling and positive activities for those students viewed as at-risk for committing hate crimes.

Ordinary Citizens

- Report hate crimes to the police, even anonymously;
- Encourage friends that hate and violence are not the answer to anything; and
- Do not tolerate or encourage hate-filled comments or discussions about various groups. (based on "Hate Crime," 2008a)

Sympathizers & Spectators

Levin notes that two groups in particular enable the spread of hate crimes: sympathizers and spectators. These two groups are: members of society whose behavior gives encouragement and support to those who are willing and able to commit a hate attack. Sympathizers repeat ethnic and racial jokes and epithets. In the process, they teach others, especially children, to hate. Spectators are essentially decent and honorable people. But they lack the courage to stand apart from the masses. They don't hate people who are different, but they do absolutely nothing to discourage hate from being expressed in criminal behavior (Levin, 2007, p. 84).

To address the problem of hate crimes in any sufficient way, these two groups must be re-educated.

For further information on effective ways to educate for tolerance and prevent hate crimes, see the Anti-Defamation League's *How to Combat Bias and Hate Crimes: An ADL Blueprint for Action.*

VIEWPOINTS

Hate Crimes Legislation

There was considerable debate and discussion surrounding the Local Law Enforcement Hate Crime Prevention Act, which was introduced in Congress in 1999, before it was passed a decade later in October 2009. By the time the act was signed into a law, it had become known as the Matthew Shepard and James Byrd Jr. Hate Crimes Prevention Act. The act is named after two victims of hate crimes that occurred in 1998: Matthew Shepard, a college student who was tortured and killed in an acknowledged act of anti-gay hatred; and James Byrd Jr., an African American man who was tortured, dragged behind a truck, and decapitated by white supremacists.

The act expands the scope of federal hate crimes legislation, which has been on the books since 1969, to include crimes against individuals for their sexual orientation, perceived gender, gender identity, and disability. The act gives federal authorities more freedom to intervene in alleged hate crime cases not pursued by state and local authorities; provides additional hate crimes funding to state and local law enforcement agencies; removes the prerequisite that hate crime victims must be engaged in a federally protected activity at the time of the crime, such as attending school or voting; and requires the FBI to track statistics of hate crimes based on gender and gender identity. The act became the first federal law to protect transgender people. According to the Anti-Defamation League (ADL), one of the leading supporters of the legislation,

The Local Law Enforcement Hate Crime Prevention Act is designed to expand the range of assistance federal authorities can provide state and local officials prosecuting hate crimes and, when appropriate, provide authority for federal officials to investigate and prosecute hate crimes in those circumstances where state and local officials cannot or will not act themselves (as cited in, "FBI Report," 2007)

Others argued that federal hate crimes legislation is unnecessary given existing criminal statutes. Daniel Troy of the American Enterprise Institute, in testimony to the House Judiciary Committee in 1999, posited that hate crime legislation is counterproductive:

The way a society gives voice to the need for justice, punishment, and vengeance is through the criminal law. If our criminal laws are not tough enough to satisfy our communal need for justice, by all means let us make them tougher. But we should not give greater legal effect to the grievances of one group over those of another. Crimes should be punished regardless of a victim's immutable characteristics (Troy, 2000, par. 3).

Still others also argued that federal hate crimes legislation "further balkanizes American society along racial and ethnic lines, building walls instead of bridges" and "punishes thought in a manner at odds with the First Amendment" (Troy, 2000). Some religious leaders were concerned that religious statements critical of homosexuality could be construed as hate crimes under the Local Law Enforcement Hate Crime Prevention Act.

In response, the ADL argued that hate crimes are a special category of criminal activity that demand a specific legislative remedy because they threaten the very essence of a multicultural society:

Hate crimes demand a priority response because of their special emotional and psychological impact on the victim and the victim's community. The damage done by hate crimes cannot be measured solely in terms of physical injury or dollars and cents. Hate crimes may effectively intimidate other members of the victim's community, leaving them feeling isolated, vulnerable and unprotected by the law. By making members of minority communities fearful, angry and suspicious of other groups–and of the power structure that is supposed to protect them—these incidents can damage the fabric of our society and fragment communities ("Hate Crimes Laws," 2001, Introduction).

The Matthew Shepard and James Byrd Jr. Hate Crimes Prevention Act went through several sessions of Congress, during which it failed to advance and then was reintroduced a number of times until it reached President Barack Obama's desk, where it was signed into law on October 28, 2009.

When Dylann Roof, a twenty-one-year old accused of espousing racist, white-supremacist views shot and killed nine people at a historically African American church in Charleston, South Carolina, in 2015, he was almost immediately indicted on federal hate crime charges. Within a month of the incident, after authorities had interviewed Roof and examined his computer and social media activities, Attorney General Loretta Lynch announced that the crime was so racially motivated that the federal government was compelled to level hate crime charges against Roof in addition to the several counts of murder charged by state courts.

TERMS & CONCEPTS

Downward Law: A law that involves legal restrictions to defend members of a majority group against members of a minority group.

Genocide: An extreme form of hate crime in which a dominant group engages in mass killing and slaughter of a subordinate group.

Hate Crime: A specific form of crime in which a person or group is verbally and/or physically attacked because of their gender, sexual orientation, religion, politics, race, ethnicity, disability, or age.

In-Group: A social group to which an individual feels like he or she belongs.

Out-Group: A social group to which an individual feels animosity, and, in extreme cases, the desire to fight and destroy.

Spectators: Those who watch hate crimes being committed and do nothing to come to the aid of victims.

Sympathizers: Those who lend tacit, but not active, support to individuals and groups that commit hate crimes. They agree with the motivations behind hate crimes, but often do not perform the hate crimes themselves.

Upward Law: A law that aims to protect disenfranchised groups at the expense of the dominant group.

BIBLIOGRAPHY

Apuzzo, M. (2015, July 22). "Dylann Roof, Charleston shooting suspect, is indicted on federal hate crime charges." *The New York Times.* http://www.nytimes.com/2015/07/23/us/dylann-roof-charleston-shooting-suspect-is-expected-to-face-federal-hate-crime-charges.html

Bello, M. (2007, Nov. 7). "Feds accused of neglecting hate crimes." *USA Today.* http://usatoday30.usatoday.com/printedition/news/20071107/a_hatecrimes07.art.htm

Bello, M. (2008, February 6). "Racial harassment cases rise sharply." *USA Today,* p. 03A.

Blazak, R. (2011). "Isn't every crime a hate crime?: The case for hate crime laws." *Sociology Compass, 5,* 244–255.

Blazak, R. (2011). "Teaching and learning guide for: Isn't every crime a hate crime? The case for hate crime laws." *Sociology Compass, 5,* 392–394.

Bleich, E. (2011). "The rise of hate speech and hate crime laws in liberal democracies." *Journal of Ethnic & Migration Studies, 37,* 917–934.

Byers, B., & Jones, J. (2007). "The impact of the terrorist attacks of 9/11 on anti-Islamic hate crime." *Journal of Ethnicity in Criminal Justice, 5,* 43–56.

"Educational inequality 'may be linked to violent crime.'" (2008, February 28). *Institute of Education, the University of London.*

Federal Bureau of Investigation. (2016). "Incidents and offenses." *2015 Hate Crime Statistics.* https://ucr.fbi.gov/hate-crime/2015/topic-pages/incidentsandoffenses_final

"FBI report shows hate crimes still a major problem; ADL urges approval of legislation to aid law enforcement." (2007, Nov. 19). *Anti-Defamation League.* http://www.adl.org/PresRele/HatCr_51/5180_51.htm.

Haider, S. (2016). "The shooting in Orlando, terrorism or toxic masculinity (or both)?" *Men & Masculinities, 19*(5), 555–565.

"Hate crime" (2008a). British Home Office. http://www.homeoffice. gov.uk/crime-victims/reducing-crime/hate-crime/ Hate crime. (2008b). Federal Bureau of Investigation: http://www.fbi.gov/hq/cid/civilrights/hate.htm

"Hate crimes laws" (2001). *Anti-Defamation League.* http://www.adl.org/99hatecrime/intro.asp.

"Hate crime statistics, 2006." (2007, November). Federal Bureau of Investigation. http://www.fbi.gov/ucr/hc2006/index.html.

"How to combat bias and hate crimes: An ADL blueprint for action (n.d.)." *Anti-Defamation League.* http://www.adl.org/combating_hate/blueprint.asp

King, R. (2007). "The context of minority group threat: Race, institutions, and complying with hate crime law." *Law & Society Review, 41,* 189–224.

Levin, J. (2007). "Hate crimes: Myths and realities." *International Journal of Diversity in Organizations, Communities & Nations, 7,* 81–85.

Lichtblau, E. (2015, Dec. 17). "Crimes against Muslim Americans and Mosques rise sharply." *The New York Times.* http://www.nytimes.com/2015/12/18/us/politics/crimes-against-muslim-americans-and-mosques-rise-sharply.html

Lyons, C. J., & Roberts, A. (2014). "The difference 'hate' makes in clearing crime: an event history analysis of incident factors." *Journal of Contemporary Criminal Justice, 30,* 268–289.

Mason, G. (2007). "Hate crime as a moral category: Lessons from the Snowtown case." *Australian & New Zealand Journal of Criminology, 40,* 249–271.

McVeigh, R., et al. (2003). "Hate crime reporting as successful social movement outcome." *American Sociological Review 68,* pp. 843–867.

Passel, J. S. (2005, June 14). "Unauthorized migrants: Numbers and characteristics: Background briefing prepared for the Task Force on Immigration and America's Future." *Pew Hispanic Center.* http://pewhispanic.org/files/reports/46.pdf.

Perry, B. (2014). "Gendered Islamophobia: hate crime against Muslim women." *Social Identities, 20*(1), 74–89.

Pew Research Center (2007, May 22). "Muslim Americans: Middle class and mostly mainstream." *Pew Research Center.* http://pewresearch.org/pubs/483/muslim-americans.

Pew Research Center (2011, August). :A portrait of Muslim Americans." *Pew Research Center.* http://www.people-press.org/2011/08/30/a-portrait-of-muslim-americans/

Plumm, K., Terrance, C., & Austin, A. (2014). "Not all hate crimes are created equal: an examination of the roles of ambiguity and expectations in perceptions of hate crimes." *Current Psychology, 33,* 321–364.

Ramirez, J. (2008). "When hate becomes hurt." *Newsweek, 151,* 14.

Smith, A. M., & Foley, C. L. (2010). "State statutes governing hate crimes." *Congressional Research Service.* 7–5700; RL33099. http://assets.opencrs.com/rpts/

Southern Poverty Law Center. (2013). DOJ "Study: More Than 250,000 hate crimes a year, most unreported." *Southern Poverty Law Center.* http://www.splcenter.org/blog/2013/03/26/doj-study-more-than-250000-hate-crimes-a-year-a-third-never-reported/

Stacey, M. (2015). "The effect of law on hate crime reporting: The case of racial and ethnic violence." *American Journal of Criminal Justice, 40*(4), 876–900.

Troy, D. E. (2000). "Federal hate crimes legislation. Testimony before the House Judiciary Committee, Washington, DC, August 4, 1999." *American Enterprise Institute.* http://www.aei. org/ publications/pubID.17122,filter.all/pub_detail.asp.

US Equal Employment Opportunity Commission (2013). "Race-based harassment charges: FY1997–FY2013." *US Equal Employment Opportunity Commission.* http://www.eeoc.gov/eeoc/statistics/enforcement/race5%Fharassment.cfm

US Equal Employment Opportunity Commission. (2015). "Charges alleging race and harassment: FY1997–FY2015." *US Equal Employment Opportunity Commission.* https://www.eeoc.gov/eeoc/statistics/enforcement/race_harassment.cfm

Walters, M. (2011). "A general theories of hate crime? Strain, doing difference, and self control." *Critical Criminology, 19,* 313-330.

Wilson, M. M. (2014, February 20). "Hate crime victimization, 2004–2012—Statistical tables." *Bureau of Justice Statistics.* http://www.bjs.gov/index.

Suggested Reading

Gerstenfeld, P. B. (2017). *Hate crimes: Causes, controls, and controversies* (4th ed.). Thousand Oaks, CA: SAGE.

Harlow, C. W. (2005). *Hate crime reported by victims and police* [PDF document]. *Bureau of Justice Statistics.* http://www.bjs.gov/content/pub/pdf/hcrvp.pdf

Hentoff, N. (2007, May 28). "Prosecuting hate crimes." *The Washington Times.* http://www.washingtontimes.com/news/2007

Hodge, J. P. (2011). *Gendered hate: Exploring gender in hate crime law.* Boston, MA: Northeastern University Press.

"Home-grown Nazis." (2007). *Economist, 384,* 58.

Iganski, P., & Levin, J. (2015). *Hate crime: A global perspective.* New York, NY: Routledge.

Knox, G., & Etter, G. (2008). *Hate crimes and extremist gangs.* Peotone, IL: New Chicago School Press.

Kennedy, A. (2007). "The elephant in the room." *Counseling Today, 50,* pp. 1, 24–25.

Levin, J., & McDevitt, J. (1993). *Hate crimes: The rising tide of bigotry and bloodshed.* New York, NY: Plenum.

Levin, J., & McDevitt, J. (2002). *Hate crimes revisited: America's war on those who are different.* Boulder, CO: Westview Press.

Levin, J. & Rabrenovic, G. (2004). *Why we hate.* New York, NY: Prometheus Books.

Levin, J. (2007). *The violence of hate.* Boston, MA: Allyn and Bacon.

Lewis, C. (2012). "Tough-on-crime tolerance: The cultural criminalization of bigotry in the post-civil rights era." *Critical Criminology, 20,* 275–292.

Mason, G. (2014). "The hate threshold: emotion, causation and difference in the construction of prejudice-motivated crime." *Social & Legal Studies, 23,* 293–314.

Page, C. (2007). "Hate crime increase is not what some make it out to be." *Caribbean Business, 35,* 28.

Matt Donnelly, M.Th.

Police

ABSTRACT

This article examines the roles played by police officers in contemporary society. The author first looks at the development of the modern police force. This is followed by an examination of philosophies of policing. The article then details the major social factors facing police in their jobs from day to day. The article is concluded by a discussion of differential treatment of suspects based on race and corruption in police forces.

OVERVIEW

The Role of the Police in Society

Early in the history of every society, its members develop sets of rules of varying degrees of severity that are based on the values held in that society. These rules, or norms, can be classified into two types: folkways and mores. Folkways are those common rules of etiquette. Violating these rules does not result in strong reprisal, but rather in a minor loss of status. Mores are stronger rules that are usually enforced by more severe sanctions. Once an elite, such as a priest class, aristocracy, or group of elected officials, comes to power in society, it will seek to enforce mores in order to ensure social order and the maintenance of the status quo. An elite does this by recording mores as official rules and setting specific punishments for violations of these rules. These set rules with set punishments that are based on mores are known as laws.

Once laws are put into place, law enforcement officers must be recruited. The exact roles of these individuals and their status in society have varied greatly over the ages. One could easily exhaust oneself with the study of law enforcement officers over the ages. For this reason, this paper will focus its energies on the development of and the role played by the police in American society.

As mentioned above, the concept of law enforcement officers is ancient and can be found in the records of the ancient Romans, Egyptians, and Mesopotamians (Barkan, 2001). In pre-modern times, however, the stated purposes of police forces are quite different from those of ancient times. The job of pre-modern law enforcers was to guard influential nobles, protect property, and generally serve society's elites. In the grand scheme of history, the concept of a police force that serves the average citizen is still very new.

The modern model of law enforcement developed in Great Britain in the early 1800s (Barkan, 2001). Early British police, known as watchmen, were charged with security and the enforcement of religiously based morality codes. These watchmen were assigned to specific posts, and the bulk of their function was to keep order in their small farming villages. As the population of Britain became more urbanized, so did police forces (Rubinstein, 1973). During the early Industrial Revolution, England was at the forefront of industrial development and experienced an explosion in the urban population rate. This rapid increase in urban population led to what amounted to urban chaos, and police forces were formed to quell the frequent urban riots (Barkan, 2001).

Just as industrialization spread across the globe, so did urban police forces. Boston and New York were the first cities in the United States to form urban police forces. These early American police forces were notoriously corrupt and ineffective (Barkan, 2001). The departments did not hide the fact that they primarily existed to serve the upper and middle classes; their primary job was to keep poor immigrants and drunkards in check (Adler, 1994). Starting in the early 1900s, police departments across the country experienced a great influx in their numbers. This increase was caused by the use of police to protect the private property rights of wealthy factory owners. Workers of this era frequently went on strike to protest horrible wages and working conditions (Barkan, 2001). The sheer number of strikers forced police departments to greatly expand their departments.

Since the late 1960s, policing has gone through a period of significant innovation. This period was spurred on by the needs of a changing society and social strife. The populations of many cities in the United States were undergoing a crisis in confidence in the ability of the police to do their job, and crime was perceived to be increasing. In response to this crisis of confidence, police forces were compelled to reconsider the fundamental ways in which they served their communities. The traditional model of law enforcement held that police were the sole guardians of law and order; seeking civilian assistance was seen as unprofessional and a waste of time. During this period of crisis, several new models of policing were developed. These models are not so much instruction books for police on how to do their jobs as they are philosophical backdrops upon which policing occurs.

The first innovative model available to police is the community policing model. This model states that the community should play a central role in defining the problems that police commonly address and that these problems should extend beyond conventional law enforcement (Weisburd & Braga, 2006). The broken windows policing model states that there is a link between social disorder and crime. Since unintended behavior tends to break down into the loss of mores and other social controls, under this model behavior such as loitering, drunkenness, and loud parties become a concern of police. The problem oriented policing model requires police to deal with a wide range of behavioral problems in the community, such as a high dropout rate. The pulling levers policing model calls for a comprehensive combination of multiple community problem solving strategies. Through this model, criminal justice intervention, social services, and community resources might all be utilized to resolve a single case. Through the third party policing model resources are expanded to third parties that are believed to offer significant new resources for preventing or controlling crime and disorder.

By using third parties such as civil courts, community organizations, and civil organizations, the police recognize that social control requires and can benefit from institutions other than themselves. Under the hot spots policing model, police are clustered in discrete areas that need the greatest amount of attention. The logic behind this model is that crime clusters itself in certain areas. Therefore, in order for patrols to be effective, they must be more tightly focused on the hot spots. The CompStat policing model, which was developed by the New York City Police Department in direct response to its interdepartmental challenges, states that failures stem from the fact that forces are poorly organized. This system seeks to strengthen the police command structure. Under this model, each level of the command structure, starting with the very top, takes an interest in whether its subordinates are motivated, assessed, and successful. In this way, discipline and hierarchical relationships are maintained. Finally, the evidence-based policing model states that crime control practices should be rooted in the collection of evidence and scientific analysis of that evidence. This model makes the assumption that police cannot be more effective than they already are. Rather, it argues that the reliance on evidence will lead to more effective criminal apprehension and crime prevention (Weisburd & Braga, 2006).

APPLICATIONS

The Day to Day Work of a Police Officer

Police officers are endowed with extraordinary power when compared to the average citizen. They wield powerful physical weapons such as guns, batons, and Tasers, as well as social weapons like the ability to arrest individuals, the state sanctioned ability to use violence, and the power to create an official record of an event (Rubinstein, 1980). However, the modern police officer uses this power sparingly. According to Ericson, police spend relatively little time directly protecting persons and property against criminal threats (1994). In fact, they spend most of their time as knowledge brokers and expert advisors. They give directions, instruct the public on how to prevent bicycle theft, or host antidrug programs such as Drug Abuse Resistance Education (DARE) (Ericson, 1994). Of course, they also do the "real police work" of apprehending suspects, but a single criminal event can result in hours of paperwork. In this way, police spend far more time recording an official version of an event for the public record than they do actually fighting crime (Ericson, 1994). Obviously, different activities are associated with varying amounts of rewards and prestige. Catching a crazed serial killer will merit a plaque, but most other tasks are viewed as simply part of the job (Rubinstein, 1973).

In much the same way that different policing activities are seen as more prestigious than others, so is the pursuit of different crimes. While ideally all crimes would be pursued with equal levels of vigor, in the real world this is not the case. Police departments simply do not have the resources to treat all crimes equally. Because any given force only has so much personnel time per week, low priority crimes will be pursued less vigorously to allow high priority crimes to be pursued more vigorously. More resources may be put into a case if the crime is against a police officer, especially repugnant, or one of high publicity (Rubinstein, 1973).

A large part of crime fighting is the work of rooting out liars. For this reason, officers must often work with little more than suspicions. They may be verbally and physically assaulted by individuals who were cooperative but a minute before. As a result, the average officer comes to deal with this high degree of uncertainly by holding a sense of constant suspicion (Barkan, 2001). For this reason, police officers are forced to view every individual they encounter as potentially dangerous. They are constantly sizing up civilians so that they may be prepared for physical confrontation. According to Rubinstein, becoming a police officer is to accept the risk of assault and injury (1980). For this reason, police must not only learn to accept the fact that they could be seriously injured as part of their job, but they must learn to control this fear so that it does not cause them to act unprofessionally (Rubeinstein, 1980). Skolnick called the set of coping mechanisms developed by police their working personality (1994). He stated that police behave in the ways that they do because of the nature of their work. Kirkham found that due to police officers' tendency to perceive that the general public hates them, they are inclined to believe that all citizens are either out to get them or in some way being covertly uncooperative (1984). When this perception is combined with dangerous situations that require police to think and act quickly, the results can be tragic.

Community Perceptions of the Police

The popularity of police in a community can serve as a gauge of how willing the populace is to accept the state's monopoly on force. If the police are unpopular, then the populace can be interpreted as not being accepting of their monopoly. If they are popular, on the other hand, citizens will accept their power and willingly cooperate with them (Ericson, 1989). In order to maintain control over this monopoly of state sanctioned force, police must actively maintain the persona of the police officer in the public eye. This persona may vary according to the local situation and community needs. Police may encourage the public to view them as people to be feared and respected, people that the public can turn to, or as other personas that may be useful for fighting crime in a particular area (Ericson, 1989).

Another way police manage their identity is through the ways they speak and behave in different settings. Ericson dissected the areas in which police work into three types: secrecy, censorship, and publicity (1989). Areas of secrecy are those to which the police do not give the general public access. They include precinct locker rooms, offices behind closed doors, break rooms, and other areas in which police can converse with each other without worrying about the general public overhearing them. Areas of publicity include public places such as the precinct's front office, the streets, the courtroom, and the media.

In this area the police maintain their public image and work with the public. Areas of censorship act as middle grounds between the two. This region allows police to acknowledge the existence of secret information and take control of otherwise public spaces for the purposes of an investigation (Ericson, 1989).

Police departments use a variety of methods to maintain their persona in the public eye. Not only can media be used to convey vital information to the public, such as the image of a wanted suspect or other information of concern to public safety, but it is also used as an outlet for the maintenance of the public police persona (Ericson, 1989). The relationship between media and police is complex, and at times there are serious disputes between them. However, despite their disagreements, both sides are vested in maintaining the relationship in the long term. In this way, the relationship between law enforcement and media outlets is maintained (Ericson, 1989). Apart from utilizing media outlets, this public persona can be maintained in various ways such as making examples of certain suspects, the way officers conduct themselves in public, and highly ceremonial events like funerals (Ericson, 1989).

VIEWPOINTS

As pointed out by Rubinstein, police wield extraordinary power as compared to the average citizen. However, as is often forgotten, police officers are also human beings with virtues and flaws, and these flaws may be accentuated by the power given to them. As a guardian of the law, an unscrupulous officer is in a unique position to break it. Among the worst problems that have occurred in regard to police in the past century are those relating to corruption and racism.

Racial Profiling

One of the hot button issues in debates over proper law enforcement centers around the legitimacy and effectiveness of racial profiling. Organizations such as the American Civil Liberties Union (ACLU) and National Association for Colored People (NAACP) strongly oppose racial profiling as a racist practice that does little more than encourage police to harass minorities. However, there remains a core of police administrators and officers who support racial profiling, arguing that racial minorities, particularly young, black males, are statistically more likely to commit crimes. From this point of view, it is not the fault of the police that more minority males are arrested, and ultimately imprisoned; it is the fault of the minority males for committing more crime in the first place. To counter this belief, groups such as the NAACP and ACLU argue that minority males are not more likely to commit crimes. Instead, they say, all young males are equally likely to commit crimes, but since police target black males and patrol predominantly black neighborhoods more frequently, black males are caught in their deviant acts more often and, therefore, labeled with the title of criminal more often (Lundman, 2004).

Lundman's research has yielded results that may be surprising to both sides of this controversy. In order to understand the phenomenon of racial profiling, Lundman observed traffic cops in a large midwestern city. His reasoning was that traffic offences are the most common types of legal infractions in American society, and that if there is a difference in how people are treated based on race, it will come through in traffic stops. Findings showed that the primary difference in treatment between racial groups was not in whether the car was pulled over, but the treatment of the suspect after the car was pulled over. Not only were white violators treated qualitatively differently from those of other racial groups, white traffic violators were less likely to have their cars searched than black or Hispanic offenders. Since police cannot find illegal items such as open alcohol containers, drugs, or paraphernalia if they do not search a car, they are less likely to find these contraband items in the cars of whites than the cars of blacks or Hispanics. Women of all races experienced fewer vehicle searches than their male counterparts (Lundman, 2004). Such differential treatment could account for reports of police discrimination against black males.

Two prominent examples that further raised the question of racial profiling within the police force occurred in 2014, sparking lengthy nationwide protests and debate. When a white police officer shot and killed an unarmed black man in Ferguson, Missouri, in August 2014 after a suspected robbery, accusations of racial profiling mounted—especially considering the city's history of maintaining a predominantly white police force that typically arrested twice as many African Americans as whites during traffic stops (Lowery, Leonnig, & Berman, 2014). Earlier that summer, another racially charged case that also highlighted concerns regarding general police brutality involved the death of a black man in New York who had reportedly been placed in a chokehold by a white police officer. Grand juries ultimately decided not to indict either officer, prompting further protests.

Does racial discrimination in law enforcement go beyond official profiling? Could it be that not only police officers, but our entire society is guilty of profiling, and this is the reason for increased police harassment of young, minority males? Lundman argued that the reason for differential treatment by police may reside in the attitudes of lay people (2004). He pointed out that up to three quarters of all encounters police have with citizens are initiated by other citizens who telephoned the police; however, half the time, lay persons do not elect to alert the police to crimes to which they have fallen victim. This is due to the fact that lay persons are generally reluctant to use formal mechanisms of social control, such as the police. The victim's perception of the severity of the crime plays a major role in whether a crime is reported. Thus, the lay person's perception of the perpetrator, and the perpetrator's race, may play an important part in how the situation will play out. (Lundman, 1978)

Corruption

When it comes to police corruption, the bulk of crime committed by police is in relation to money or gifts. This can take the form of both subtle and overt bribes. An overt example would be a police officer accepting a $100 bribe to ignore an obvious case of drunk driving; a subtle case would be a police officer accepting a special "police discount" at a nice restaurant. The Knapp Commission was formed in the 1970s to investigate police corruption in New York City. As part of its investigations, the commission made a number of findings on the nature of police corruption. It found that extreme loyalty within the department was responsible for covering up the majority of corruption. This loyalty was traced to the danger faced by all police officers and their perception that society was hostile to them. Another factor that encouraged cover-ups was the desire of the department to maintain its public image. The admission of large scale corruption would not be beneficial to an institution that is supposed to exemplify law and order.

Conclusion

When considering the police as an institution in society, it is critical to remember that they are human. Like others, they are capable of being corrupted, of acting on prejudices, and of acting rashly when faced with danger. On the other hand, instances of police misconduct have at times become so prevalent that the role of the police has come into question. Considering the prevalence of law enforcement officers in nations around the world, it is unlikely that their presence will be eliminated any time soon. Society must instead seek to improve existing police forces just as their predecessors had been improved.

TERMS & CONCEPTS

Amateur Labelers: Average citizens who initiate the labeling process by reporting to the police an act that they consider deviant

Broken Windows Policing Model: A model of policing that stresses the importance of taking an interest in disruptions in a community that may not be illegal but could lead to or indicate criminal activity.

Censorship Region: The public or private social space that police control and keep secret for the purposes of a criminal investigation.

Community Policing Model: A model of policing that stresses the importance of working with individuals in the community when attempting to solve a criminal case. This is in contrast to the traditional model which views using information from the community as unprofessional and unreliable.

CompStat Policing Model: A model of policing that stresses the importance of maintaining hierarchy and discipline throughout the department.

Corruption: Any crime committed by a police officer. The most common forms of police corruption are those relating to financial benefits such as kickbacks, bribes, material favors, or unsanctioned gifts.

Evidence Based Policing Model: A model of policing that stresses the importance of evidence collection and analysis in solving crimes.

Hot Spots Policing Model: A model of policing that stresses the redistribution of resources toward those areas identified as high risk.

Laws: Social conventions that have been recorded by a society's elite. The violation of these conventions may result in specified punishments.

Problem Oriented Policing Model: A model of policing in which the root causes of a community's problems are identified and police devise solutions for eliminating the causes.

Professional Labelers: Those individuals who are paid to identify individuals as deviant. Police are professional labelers.

Publicity Region: The social space police use to release information to the public and maintain their public persona.

Pulling Levers Policing Model: A model of policing that stresses the use of a variety of resources and solutions to detect criminal activity. Criminal justice intervention, social services, and community resources might all be utilized to resolve a single case.

Racial Profiling: Focusing on individuals of a certain racial group for the purposes of crime detection. This practice is performed under the assumption that members of certain racial groups are more likely to commit crimes than members of other racial groups.

Secrecy Region: The social space that police use to conduct the secret work of policing. This area is maintained so that delicate elements of investigations may be protected and less savory elements of police work may be hidden from public view.

Third Party Policing Model: A model of policing that stresses the expansion of crime prevention to third parties. By using third parties such as civil courts, community organizations, and civil organizations, police recognize that social control requires and can benefit from institutions other than themselves.

Working Personality: The set of social skills and behaviors developed by police officers to deal with the stresses of police work.

Bibliography

Allen, T. T., & Michaux Parker, M. (2013). "Police officers and their perceived relationship with urban communities: Does living in the community influence police decisions?" *Social Development Issues, 35*, 82–95.

Anderson, E. (2000). "The police and the Black male." In P. A. Adler & P. Adler (Eds.), *Constructions of deviance: Social power, context, and interaction* (3rd ed.). Belmont: Wadsworth.

Barkan, S. E. (2001). *Criminology: A sociological understanding* (2nd ed.). New Jersey: Prentice Hall.

Becker, H. S. (2000). "Labeling theory." In P. A. Adler & P. Adler (Eds.), *Constructions of deviance: Social power, context, and interaction* (3rd ed.). Belmont: Wadsworth.

Bittner, E. (1980). "The police charge." In R. J. Lundman (Ed.), *Police behavior: A sociological perspective.* New York: Oxford University Press.

Chambliss, W. J. (2000). "The saints and the roughnecks." In P. A. Adler & P. Adler (Eds.), *Constructions of deviance: Social power, context, and interaction* (3rd ed.). Belmont: Wadsworth.

Davis, M. G., Lundman, R. J. & Martinez, R. (1991). "Private corporate justice: Store police, shoplifters, and civil recovery." *Social Problems, 38*, 395–411.

Ericson, R. V. (1975). "Responsibility, moral relativity, and response ability: Some implications of deviance theory for criminal justice." *The University of Toronto Law Journal, 25*, 23–41.

Ericson, R. V. (1989). "Patrolling the facts: Secrecy and publicity in police work." *The British Journal of Sociology, 40*, 205–226.

Ericson, R. V. (1994). "The division of expert knowledge in policing and security." *The British Journal of Sociology, 45*, 149–175.

Haggerty, K. & Gazso, A. (2005). "Seeing beyond the ruins: Surveillance as a response to terrorist threats." *Canadian Journal of Sociology, 30*, 169–187.

Higgins, G. E., Vito, G. F., Grossi, E. L., & Vito, A. G. (2012). "Searches and traffic stops: Racial profiling and capriciousness." *Journal of Ethnicity in Criminal Justice, 10*, 163–179.

Hirschi, T. (2000). "Control theory of delinquency." In P. A. Adler & P. Adler (Eds.), *Constructions of deviance: Social power, context, and interaction* (3rd ed.). Belmont: Wadsworth.

Knapp Commission. (1980). "Police corruption in New York." In R. J. Lundman (Ed.), *Police behavior:*

A sociological perspective. New York: Oxford University Press.

Long, M. A., Cross, J., Shelley, T., & Kutnjak Ivkovi, S. (2013). "The normative order of reporting police misconduct: Examining the roles of offense seriousness, legitimacy, and fairness." *Social Psychology Quarterly, 76,* 242–267.

Lowery, W., Leonnig, C. D., & Berman, M. (2014, August 13). "Even before Michael Brown's slaying in Ferguson, racial questions hung over police." *Washington Post.* http://www.washingtonpost.com/politics/even-before-teen-michael-browns-slaying-in-mo-racial-questions-have-hung-over-police/2014/08/13

Lundman, R. J. (1974). "Routine police arrest practices: A commonwealth perspective." *Social Problems, 22,* 127–141.

Lundman, R. J. (1978). "Shoplifting and police referral: A reexamination." *The Journal of Criminal Law and Criminology, 69,* 395–401.

Lundman, R. J. (2004). "Driver race, ethnicity, and gender and citizen reports of vehicle searches by police and vehicle search hits: Toward a triangulated scholarly understanding." *The Journal of Criminal Law and Criminology, 94,* 309–350.

Mazerolle, L., Antrobus, E., Bennett, S., & Tyler, T. R. (2013). "Shaping citizen perceptions of police legitimacy: A randomized field trial of procedural justice." *Criminology, 51,* 33–63.

Reinka, M. A., & Leach, C. W. (2017). "Race and reaction: Divergent views of police violence and protest against." *Journal of Social Issues, 73*(4), 768–788.

Reiss, A. J. (1980). "Officer violations of the law." In R. J. Lundman (Ed.), *Police behavior: A sociological perspective*. New York: Oxford University Press.

Reiss, A. J. (1980). "Police brutality." In R. J. Lundman (Ed.), *Police behavior: A sociological perspective.* New York: Oxford University Press.

Rubinstein, J. (1973). *City police.* New York: The Noonday Press.

Rubinstein, J. (1980). "Cop's rules." In R. J. Lundman (Ed.), *Police behavior: A sociological perspective.* New York: Oxford University Press.

Schlosser, M. D. (2013). "Racial attitudes of police recruits in the united states midwest police academy: A quantitative examination." *International Journal of Criminal Justice Sciences, 8,* 215–224.

Skolnick, J. (1994). *Justice without trial* (3rd Ed.). New York: Wiley

Weisburd, D. & Braga A. A. (2006). *Police innovation: Contrasting perspectives.* Cambridge: Cambridge University Press.

Suggested Reading

Beutin, L. P. (2017). "Racialization as a way of seeing: The limits of counter-surveillance and police reform." *Surveillance & Society, 15*(1), 5–20.

Conlon, E. (2004). *Blue blood*. New York: Riverhead Books.

Drakulich, K. M., & Crutchfield, R. D. (2013). "The role of perceptions of the police in informal social control: Implications for the racial stratification of crime and control." *Social Problems, 60,* 383–407.

Kochel, T., Parks, R., & Mastrofski, S. D. (2013). "Examining police effectiveness as a precursor to legitimacy and cooperation with police." *JQ: Justice Quarterly, 30,* 895–925.

Lundman, R.J. (1980). *Police behavior: A sociological perspective.* New York: Oxford University Press.

Rubinstein, J. (1973). *City police.* New York: The Noonday Press.

Wilson, C. P., & Wilson, S. A. (2014). "Are we there yet? Perceptive roles of African American police officers in small agency settings." *Western Journal of Black Studies, 38,* 123–133.

Jeremy Baker, M.A.

Preventing Deviance by Amending Inequality

ABSTRACT

Deviance is any behavior that violates cultural and socially established norms. By investigating Deviance in society, we can better understand the processes that function to maintain social order, and how inequality in society can contribute to deviant activity. Scholarship in this area has taken two divergent paths since the late twentieth century. On the one hand, there are those who argue that Deviance should be studied regardless of criminality or wrongfulness. On the other hand are those who suggest that Deviance is an indicator of criminal activity and attempts should be made by communities and law enforcement to control deviant behavior through various mechanisms of control and sanctions. This paper will look at ways to prevent Deviance by ameliorating inequality and thus, Deviance will be treated as objectively given in society; that is, deviant activities will be described in terms of their social dysfunctions and ability to upset social order. Specific attention is paid to processes by which we can reduce Deviance by reducing inequality.

OVERVIEW

Deviance is any behavior that violates culturally established norms (Rubington & Weinberg, 1996). By investigating Deviance in society, we may better understand the processes that maintain social order and how deviant groups organize their lives and function in society. Stratification, *inequality*, and the social construction of Deviance contribute to the labeling of certain behaviors as deviant and criminal. In order to understand the causes of Deviance and its relationship to inequality we consider a multitude of issues including how Deviance is defined, whether or not it is harmful to society, and how to prevent it by amending social inequalities.

Defining Deviance

The study of Deviance as a social phenomenon relies on widespread agreement among members of society that share similar values and norms that make it easy to identify individuals who breach social norms. Deviant activity evokes a negative reaction by the majority of society. Society applies punishments to deter deviant-minded individuals and other members of society from engaging in activities that challenge the social order (Rubington & Weinberg, 1996).

We can view Deviance as *criminal acts*, violations of formally enacted laws. For example, we might consider those who engage in robbery, theft, rape, murder, and assault, as deviants. We may also view deviant behavior as violations of informal *social norms*, norms that society has not codified into law. Deviant behavior such as this might include various sexual behaviors, alcohol use, and public disorder. These activities are not necessarily criminal but still have the potential to negatively affect society and upset social order.

One example of this is evident in sexual identity. Historically (and to a certain extent today), homosexual behavior has been viewed as deviant. Of course, homosexual behaviors, by most standards, do not cause harm to individuals or society. However, given the marginalization of those who participate in gay activities, subcultures were formed that have developed into social movements that call attention to the inequitable treatment of gays and lesbians in society, initiating social change.

On the other hand, when Deviance causes harm to individuals and society it is important to consider measures to reduce such deviant activity and prevent individuals from harm or harming others. This also suggests a greater understanding of the causes of the harmful deviant behavior. A common explanation for harmful acts of Deviance is rooted in theories of *class conflict*, which asserts that inequality creates hostile conditions that facilitate Deviance and crime.

Because of the varying views on Deviance, scholarship has taken two divergent paths over the past decades. Some scholars argue that research on Deviance should focus on individuals' personal environments without considering the criminality or wrongfulness of their actions (Rubington & Weinberg, 1996). Other scholars suggest that Deviance is an indicator of criminal activity that society must control through various formal and informal social control mechanisms (Hagan, Silva, & Simpson, 1977).

FURTHER INSIGHTS

Symbolic Interactionism

Symbolic interaction theorists suggest that there is nothing inherently wrong with the majority of deviant acts, but rather society has constructed definitions and mechanisms for typifying behavior and actors as deviants in order to maintain the status quo (Becker, 1963). Thus, symbolic interaction theorists define behavior that is considered by society to be deviant as behavior that is labeled deviant (Becker, 1963).

This essay considers a theoretical explanation of Deviance that takes into account variations in access to social and financial resources, reviews empirical examples of the relationship between inequality and Deviance, and addresses the processes through which society can prevent Deviance by ameliorating inequality.

Social Conflict Theory of the Causes of Deviance

Karl Marx developed the *conflict perspective,* a theory renowned for its explanation of class struggles. Marx never actually studied criminality, however, criminologists and sociologists have adapted his theories of *capitalism,* class struggle, and the nature of the relationship between the *bourgeoisie* and the *proletariat* to develop theories of Deviance. These theories of Deviance highlight the consequences of social order and focus on social and structural mechanisms that contribute to inequality in society (Spitzer, 1975).

The conflict perspective provides an explanation of Deviance in which a privileged few determine what actions are deviant and non-deviant. For example, laws in capitalist countries often reflect the norms and values of the privileged or upper classes. Laws related to property ownership tend to favor those with property and disfavor those without property. The power elite use their resources to define Deviance and convince society that it is wrong, thus maintaining class inequality. Consider 2007 headlines regarding the use of deadly force by a man in Texas to protect his neighbor's property. By clearing the man of any charges in 2008, a Texas county court determined that it is acceptable to shoot and kill would-be burglars, thus protecting the rights of property owners at the expense of deviant actors.

The conflict approach asserts that the privileged upper classes are able to avoid a deviant label by changing the definition of Deviance to favor their class. Given their high status in society and access to political power, these groups are able to influence the adoption of social values as expressed by legislative change, or campaign to call attention to undesirable behavior. One example is the changing of legislation regarding loitering and the process by which police respond to homeless people in public. This criminalizes activities that are viewed by a few as deviant, even though these actions are not necessarily harmful to individuals or society. The result is that the masses are much more likely to receive a deviant label and receive punishment due to the inequality among social classes.

Yet another example of how power imbalances relate to Deviance is illustrated in crime reports and corresponding punishments. Privileged members of society who engage in deviant activates are more likely commit white-collar crime. These crimes more often go undetected, receive little police attention, and largely until the late twentieth and early twenty-first centuries, most offenders were unlikely to serve jail time for their actions—even when they resulted in death (as was the case in the Ford Pinto scandal), or in the cheating of thousands of people out of their savings (as in the Enron scandal). Thus, the inequality in society results in additional inequality. Persons of lower classes are more likely to be considered deviant, and when they are considered deviant, they are more likely to suffer greater sanctions.

Response to Crimes

Poor people are more likely to engage in certain types of crimes, such as street crime, robbery, and drug sales. However, the response by police, political officials, and the public is often far greater than would be expected, especially in cases in which the actions are not violent. Individuals who are caught selling drugs can often be subject to lengthy prison terms and other harsh forms of social sanctions.

The process that treats these groups differently has arguably less to do with the nature of their offenses and more to do with the inequality of their class status and social inequality (Turk, 1977). Scholarship that focuses on this disjuncture asserts that the determination of deviant activity and the response by police are functions of one's class status and not a function of their actual propensity toward crime (Reiman, 2007).

Varying Crime Rates Indicate Class Inequality

Those who ascribe to the notion that class conflict and inequality cause Devianceoften point to variations in crime rates as a function of class membership or economic inequality. Much research has attempted to uncover the variation in deviant activity among those from different socioeconomic backgrounds (Krohn, 1976; Tittle, Villemez, & Smith, 1978). The results of this scholarship are mixed. On the one hand, Tittle and his colleagues emphatically disagree with the notion that there is class variation in criminality. Their data suggest that there is no empirical link between inequality and the distribution of social resources and criminal activity. There are differences in arrest rates, convictions, or other indicators that would seemingly highlight the important role social status and inequality plays in assessing the breadth of Deviance in society. It could be the fact that those who are less affluent or privileged are just less likely to be caught. It is evident that even the most well-to-do individuals engage in criminal activity; executives at Ford and Enron both committed crimes, despite having access to social and economic resources. However, their social status (at least in the case of Ford) allowed executives to dodge serious punishment.

In contrast, Krohn (1976) does in fact find a significant variation in criminal activity as a function of inequality. In a cross-national comparison of crime rates, Krohn investigated how variation in inequality within a country relates to homicide rates and property crimes. His findings approach the study of Deviance and inequality from the perspective that Deviance relates specifically to crime, and is characterized as law-violating behavior. Second, he considers the distribution of wealth and access to resources as a central component regarding the likelihood of criminal activity. In order to reduce violence and other criminal responses to economic deprivation, Krohn argues that society must reduce unemployment and other factors contributing to socioeconomic deprivation. Thus, Krohn's work highlights the need to amend inequality in society to reduce or prevent Deviance.

VIEWPOINTS

Amending Inequality

To prevent Deviance by amending inequality we must first consider the notion that Deviance is harmful to society and that Deviance results from differential access to rewards. That is, we may view Deviance and the determination of some behaviors as deviant as a function of one's power and privilege in society to manipulate the definition of what should and should not be considered deviant. Other scholars who study Deviance suggest that it can best be reduced by increasing mechanisms of social control that are often more prevalent in areas with lower rates of inequality. However, this approach does not specifically address how amending inequality can reduce Deviance; it only illustrates that there is a relationship between inequality and Deviance.

Those who assume that Deviance and crime are a reaction to class inequalitywould suggest that the best way to reduce Deviance is through a series of social and economic approaches that focus on the reduction of poverty and unemployment and an increase in access to affordable housing and education. By increasing access to these resources on a universal basis, we would reduce inequality and class conflict, resulting in less Deviance.

A central fact pertaining to the relationship between Deviance and inequality is the notion that inequality produces the normative structures, conditions, and environments that foster the opportunity for a select group in society to determine what is and is not deviant in the first place. By reducing inequality, fewer behaviors would be deviant. This resolution, however, would require a radical change in the organization of society and social structures—one that moves toward the interactionist perspective on deviant activities and is less concerned about how Deviance relates to criminal behavior.

In sum, Deviance is unrelated to crime but rather is a characterization of behavior by elites to indicate what activities are acceptable and what are not. On the other hand, there are those who view Deviance as a pattern of behavior associated with criminal involvement. These two divergent perspectives view the nature of the relationship between inequality and Deviance in vastly different ways. As such, scholars in these two competing camps view the attempt to prevent Deviance by ameliorating inequality differently. The first would argue that ameliorating inequality would only change the definition of what is currently viewed as deviant. The other would suggest that ameliorating inequality would reduce crime and Deviance only as far as it would reduce the need for individuals to use criminal activity as a way to obtain desirable social goods.

These two different views highlight the need for additional scholarship in the area of Deviance and inequality. We have yet to develop a perspective on

Deviance that clearly identifies its relationship to criminal activity and social inequality, thus making it difficult to propose policy and social solutions to decrease deviant behavior through reducing inequality.

TERMS & CONCEPTS

Bourgeoisie: Owners of the means of production in a capitalistic society.

Class Conflict: Conflict within society that arises among individuals or groups with different class positions who compete for scarce resources.

Deviance: The breach of social norms.

Inequality: The inequitable distribution of resources.

Karl Marx: (1818–1883). Philosopher and social theorist who advocated for the implementation of communist ideologies in order to rectify class struggles, which he argued are the cause of social and political inequality.

Proletariat: The working class.

Symbolic Interactionism: The theoretical position that Deviance is not inherently wrong or hurtful but rather an expression of values and ideologies that is in contrast to mainstream views of social order.

Bibliography

Becker, H. 1963. *Outsiders: Studies in the sociology of Deviance.* New York: The Free Press.

Hagan, J. Silva, E., & Simpson, J. (1977). "Conflict and consensus in the designation of Deviance." *Social Forces, 56,* (2), 320–340.

Kelly, D. (1996). *Deviant behavior: A text reader in the sociology of Deviance.* 5th Ed. New York, NY: Worth Publishers.

Krohn, M. (1976). "Inequality, unemployment, and crime: A cross-national analysis." *The Sociological Quarterly, 17* (3), 303–313.

Lauderdale, P. (2011). "An analysis of Deviance, law, and diversity: A nascent theoretical framework." *Conference Papers—American Sociological Association,*1563.

Reiman, J. (2007). *The rich get richer and the poor get prison: Ideology, class, and criminal justice* (8th Ed). Boston, MA: Allyn and Bacon.

Rubington, E. & Weinberg, M. (1999). *Deviance: The interactionist perspective.* 7th Ed. Boston, MA: Allyn and Bacon.

Tittle, C., Villemez, W. & Smith, D. (1978). "The myth of social class and criminality: An empirical assessment of the empirical evidence." *American Sociological Review, 43* (5), 643–656.

Turk, A. (1977). "Class, conflict, and criminalization." *Sociological Focus, 10* (3), 209–236.

Spencer, D. (2011). "Cultural criminology: An invitation... to what?" *Critical Criminology, 19* (3), 197–212.

Williams, D. (2011). "Why revolution ain't easy: Violating norms, re-socializing society." *Contemporary Justice Review, 14* (2), 167–187.

Suggested Reading

Box, S. & Ford, J. (1971). "The facts don't fit: On the relationship between social class and criminal behavior." *Sociological Review, 19* (1) 31–52.

Dixon, J., & Singleton, R. (Eds.) (2013). *Reading social research: Studies in inequality and Deviance.* Thousand Oaks, CA: SAGE Publications.

Georgoulas, S. (Ed.) (2012). *The politics of criminology: Critical studies on Deviance and social control.* Vienna, Austria: Lit. London: Global (distributor).

Humes, E. (1996). *No matter how loud I shout: A year in the life of juvenile court.* New York, NY: Touchstone.

Mann, C. (1993). Unequal justice: A question of color. Bloomington, IN: Indiana University Press.

Jennifer Christian, M.A., and Donna Holland, Ph.D.

Preventing Deviance by Strengthening Social Bonds

ABSTRACT

A definition of deviance and norms in the field of sociology and an overview of deviance from the perspective of the classical sociological perspective structural-functionalism is presented. The social theorist Emile Durkheim's work on deviance as a functional element in normal, health societies is addressed, as well as an understanding of the relationship between the level of social bonds and deviance, particularly as seen by Durkheim, including an explanation for high levels of deviance in a society, which is considered a reflection of a lack of cohesion. The article also presents an overview of Durkheim's classic work "Suicide" and why it is used to understand deviance in general and then addresses the need for members to assimilate into the dominant cultural norms and how this can strengthen social bonds in order to reduce deviance. It also gives an example of immigrants maintaining traditional norms as a means to increase cohesion and reduce deviance.

OVERVIEW

Defining Deviance

Sociologists define *deviance* as behavior or appearance that goes against the dominant rules, or *norms*, of a society. Each society has its own set of norms, and to violate them is to be deviant. Deviance is not just being different from others; there are many instances of this in societies. For example, it is relatively rare to be a celebrity, but it is not deviant. Furthermore, a relatively common behavior, such as smoking marijuana, the most widely used illicit substance in much of the United States, is considered deviant. Deviance is not always criminal; one can be socially deviant by breaking the informal rules of a society; for example, a man wearing a skirt is considered deviant.

In the United States, the dominant norms reflect those of the founders of the country, who were white Anglo-Saxon Protestants. Because of this, many minority groups' norms are considered deviant only because they are different from the mainstream, dominant normative structure. When minority groups begin to take on the dominant norms in a society, it is called *assimilation,* or acculturation, and this is common and expected. There are examples, such as the mainstream acceptance of jazz as a music form, of Americans absorbing minority norms. This is called *pluralism.*

One of the best ways to understand deviance is to think about how important rules are to the smooth operations of a society. However, it is difficult to see these rules when one is immersed in society. This is why it is easier to see norms in another society, because they are different and we are forced to think about our own behavior and ways of thinking. Another way of identifying norms is to engage in *norm-breaching experiments.* Sociologists intentionally break, or breach, norms and record the reactions of others (Garfinkel, 1967). In this way, they can see how rules exist in a society, what the rewards are for following them, and what the punishments are for breaking them.

Norms & Their Functions

Norms have extraordinary power in societies. The purpose of norms is to

- Regulate social behavior,
- Reinforce social boundaries, and
- Help make sense of values, or beliefs the society holds (Durkheim, 1933).

There are three types of norms for behavior in sociology: *folkways, mores* (which include *taboos*), and *laws.* The level of reward for following the rules or, conversely, punishment associated with breaking the rules determines in which categories these rules will fall. Folkways are the hundreds and hundreds of everyday, informal rules we follow that guide us socially. Table manners, how others are addressed, and what to wear to a gathering are all folkways, and breaking these rules renders small irritations like a frown or a sideways look. Mores are the formal rules that are usually, but not always, law. In the mores of any society, you will find the moral imperatives, or the moral structures that inform the society in terms of religion or politics, for example; engaging in adultery or committing murder are breaches of mores. When mores are broken, members are severely punished with social embarrassment or ostracism. Laws are the codified, formally agreed upon rules that are punishable through bureaucratic means, and when these are broken there is a formal structure (the judicial system) that is in place to punish the deviant. Just because a rule is law does not mean it is the norm—for example, someone speeding in an area in which all other drivers are also speeding. In this case, the norm is to speed, yet the law is otherwise.

There are very few norms that are universal, although most social scientists agree that incest is a universal taboo (Levi- Strauss, 1969). Even in the face of massive amounts of evidence that incest is the only norm that every society holds as deviant, aside from a few known ancient practicing cultures, social scientists still look for an explanation for this norm—a *function* of this rule. The most plausible guess is that it extends family ties, strengthening the family, but this is still not a corroborated explanation.

Norms & the Social Bonds of Society

The norms in any society are the glue; they are how we know what to do every day, how to interact with one another, and when and what to do in our lives. Adherents to *structural-functionalism,* one of the classical paradigms or theoretical perspectives in sociology, see norms as one of the most important elements in any society, and the level of adherence to the rules represents how strong the *social bonds* are, or how cohesive the society is. Sociologists are careful to point out that norms are *always* relative (Durkheim, 1933). That means deviance is also always relative, because it is dependent on the rules of the society. One cannot break a rule that does not exist. Put another way, when a rule is created, it is only then, upon its creation, that someone is able to break the rule and be defined as a deviant. In some cases, what one might consider deviant in most cases *is* the norm. For example, if you are a soldier, killing the enemy is not murder and, in fact, you could be required to kill someone or you may be killed.

The relative nature of norms indicates that they are socially constructed, or created, and exist to help the social world remain predictable for its members. If we did not have these rules, we would be easily confused and may feel separated, or alienated from others. Yet, in each society, the members must consider their norms superior to others so that the members agree with and follow these rules.

Structural-Functionalism & Social Bonds

Structural-functionalists see high levels of deviance as a marker of a society's lack of *solidarity,* or lack of strong social bonds. The most well-known structural-functionalist is the French sociologist Émile Durkheim. He argued that rapid social change, or some other abrupt change in the social order, is the source of inordinately high levels of deviance. Durkheim believed that, while it is impossible for a society to be deviance-free, high levels of deviance is a sign that people in the society do not feel connected enough to others, or that the society is in such of state of chaos that its members feel that the rules do not apply. For Durkheim and many other functionalists, deviance is *created* by making more laws. Actions are not inherently right or wrong; they either contribute to the smooth operations of the society or they do not. In other words, all actions are relative to the situation, and, in so far as the rules create and maintain social bonds, they are or are not functional.

Durkheim said that, while deviance is *always* found in normal, healthy societies, when a society has very high levels of deviance it means that the members do not feel connected to the society. When sizable numbers of members in a society break the rules, according to Durkheim, the society is in a state of *anomie* (Durkheim, 1951). Strong social bonds being the basis for a well-balanced society, Durkheim understood that deviance is a reflection of how connected members feel. His concept of anomie was developed to explain one of the four types of suicide that is discussed in his enlightening work *Suicide* (1951).

Suicide as a Deviant Act & the Lack of Social Bonds

Understanding deviance and its relationship to strong social bonds is one of the most important discussions Émile Durkheim took up in his work. In his work on suicide, Durkheim shows that deviance is a sociological phenomenon, not a psychological one. He uses suicide as the example of deviance. He shows that larger social forces are what contribute to whether people deviate from the norms of society, not individual people and the choices they make. Durkheim studied the relationship between *social cohesion,* or social bonds, and *regulation,* or whether people feel compelled to follow the rules, and whether people are more or less likely to deviate from the rules of a society—in this case committing suicide. In this study, Durkheim looked at several factors that might influence whether people would commit suicide, including sex and weather. But he found religion as the most revealing factor. He found that Protestants are the most likely to commit suicide, followed by Catholics and then Jews. Durkheim argues that Protestants have the highest levels of suicide because, as a group, they encourage personal autonomy and individualistic thinking. Catholics are more communal than Protestants and have a higher level of cohesion. Jewish people have the highest level of cohesion or social integration and are the least likely to commit suicide.

Durkheim lists four types of suicide:

- Anomic;
- Altruistic;
- Egoistic; and
- Fatalistic.

Anomic suicide occurs when the social regulation is so weak that members do not feel that the society can fulfill their needs. *Altruistic suicide* occurs when members feel too much social integration and they are willing to sacrifice for the group; while rare, this type of suicide is seen in suicide bombers. *Egoistic suicide* occurs when members do not feel enough integration, making them feel as though no one cares for them; Durkheim argues that this is more likely in highly individualistic societies. *Fatalistic suicide,* dealt with very little in the study, is when regulation is too high, for example when someone is in an abusive prison.

Deviance & the Division of Labor in Society

For Durkheim, the amount of deviance is directly related to whether or not a society is *industrialized.* In preindustrial societies, deviance is much lower, and this is because the people are very similar to one another and they feel very connected to one another. Further, members are allowed very little latitude in small hunting and gathering societies or farming villages; everyone knows one another and any rule broken results in at least public shame. In these societies, when members do break the rules, the punishment is very retributive, or harsh. This is because the deviant is perceived to have violated the entire community. Punishment in these cultures can be vengeful and is often public, including humiliation and even execution (Foucault, 1975).

As societies industrialize and become more complex, deviance becomes more common because members are less likely to know one another. People specialize in their work and we are encouraged to be "individuals" and creative, making deviance more likely. These complex societies develop formal structures to punish deviants in a more objective way, law becomes more regulatory, and deviants are required to do restitution, or pay back society. Punishments in these societies are designed to restore the deviant's status in the society. In Western societies, since the Enlightenment of the eighteenth century, the prison system has been used to rehabilitate deviants in an effort to restore justice (Foucault, 1975). Ideally, the deviant will again feel part of the social fabric and (re) develop social bonds that will deter further deviance.

The Sacred & Profane & Their Roles in Creating Social Bonds

Structural-functionalists believe that the stronger the bond the individual has to the society, the less likely the individual is to be deviant. There are several ways to encourage higher levels of cohesion. One way is to have a shared notion of what is *sacred* and what objects are sacred in a society. The opposite of these sacred objects are called *profane,* which means everyday, or ordinary. Most societies have religious objects that are sacred. For Christians the cross is sacred, as is the Bible. For Muslims the crescent is sacred, as is the Qur'an. For Jewish people the Star of David is sacred, as is the Torah. Durkheim states that, while the idea that these items are actually sacred—and any different from any other objects in society—is socially constructed, societies must have these objects; all societies do. These sacred objects have very important functions in societies. First, they allow the members to collectively agree on some things, in these cases religious objects, and, in this agreement that these objects are more important than other ordinary things, the members find a sense of community, a sense of cohesion, and are less likely to be deviant because they feel connected to others. Second, these objects have an exclusionary value, meaning that if others do not see them as sacred, members can identify those who are not part of the group. This reinforces the social bonds between those who agree on these sacred objects. Sacred objects can also be flags, animals, or even sports trophies.

Assimilation & In-Group vs. Out-Group

One of the major sources of deviance is that members do not agree with the norms of the dominant society. This is particularly the case with minority groups and immigrants. Ideally, these groups assimilate into the culture in which they live. Assimilation is the process of taking on the culture of another, dominant group. This is also sometimes called acculturation. Immigration to another culture generally requires some amount of assimilation. As members become more assimilated, and they display the norms of the dominant culture, social bonds between the immigrant group and the dominant group grow stronger. But if the immigrant group is not willing to take on the dominant group's culture, for whatever reason, the immigrant group's norms are perceived as potentially destructive to the society. The immigrant group's norms are thus seen as deviant to the dominant group. The United States is particularly challenged by this as its history includes waves of immigrants from various parts of the world generally fleeing economic or political strife. Sometimes, particularly when immigrant groups have not chosen to leave their culture, they are not necessarily willing to accept American values of competition or individualism, and may even actively reject them. For this reason, immigrants can be automatically perceived as deviant.

Some American sociologists working in Chicago in the early 1900s began to investigate how immigrants become part of American society. Robert Park, an urban sociologist, developed a theory that in preindustrial societies, social bonds within a group are directly proportional to the group's fear of and animosity against an opposing group (1950). In fact, this *out-group* makes the *in-group* feel a heightened sense of solidarity and accentuates the social bonds between members (Sumner, 1906). This cohesion can perpetuate *ethnocentrism,* or the idea that one's own culture is superior to others and that others should adopt these norms. It is an unintended consequence of cohesion.

Deviance as a Function

For the structural-functionalist, all elements of a society are contributing to the overall balance, and deviance has the role of showing what we should and should not do. Members who deviate are punished, or sanctioned, and others see the result and are then aware of the rule. So, the deviant reinforces the rules of the society. Ultimately, Durkheim believed that deviance has several positive functions in societies, and is a sign of a healthy society. First, it allows the established norms to be challenged, and the bases for laws to be reestablished. Second, it is a source of social cohesion; Durkheim saw it as a means for a society to strengthen social bonds. People form bonds around how destructive they perceive deviants are to the social fabric. Finally, it is a source of social change and terrific creativity. However, inordinately high rates of deviance are a sign that the system is not functioning; according to functionalists, this is a sign that there is not enough social cohesion and that members do not feel connected or meaningful in society.

APPLICATIONS

Social Bonds in the European Union

One way of strengthening social bonds is to provide members with the sense that they share common values. This can be done through a sacred object. As mentioned earlier, this notion of the power of the sacred object as a means for strengthening social bonds extends beyond religion. A national flag communicates a powerful sense of patriotism. Europe has been very successful in developing a sense of cohesion among countries that had, in the recent past, had great animosity for one another. One purpose of the European Union is to insure the sense of nationalism that allowed WWII to develop does not happen again. The social bonds that are developed between nations transcend the old hatred and, in creating other means of common interest (e.g., a common currency), deviance is less likely.

Shared ideas of government and the legitimacy of government can also contribute to more progressive public policy. This idea is explored in a 2007 study that looks at the conditions under which some European countries have a citizenry that support higher taxes. Higher tax morale, meaning the willingness to pay taxes for the greater public good, was found in countries in which political institutions were considered legitimate (Torgler & Schneider, 2007). When the population trusted the government to do the greatest good for the greatest number, the common notion transcended other dissimilar norms among the members.

But European countries have also struggled with the problems of immigration and how to deal with the enormous influx of new cultures into older, firmly defined normative structures. Deviance among minorities in the United Kingdom has been an ongoing problem, and France has experienced rioting in the underprivileged suburbs. In general, many of these problems have been contributed to a lack of common social norms and, therefore, a depleted sense of social cohesion. This is terribly challenging for European countries that have not had historical experience with immigrant groups to the extent that the United States has.

Sports Fans

Sports have long been of interest for sociologists as a form of the sacred and its power to create a sense of belonging among fans. One study looked at how fans not only see themselves as part of the team, but how their fandom transcends the actual event and affects their everyday lives and their very sense of identity (Stone, 2007). These fans carry with them the identity of their team, and these identities allow them to form and maintain social bonds with others they do not know but with whom they feel connected.

However, in some cases, the social bonds that are maintained through the collective appreciation of a sacred object maintain and promote norms that are destructive to the society. In Joshua Newman's study of the force of the Confederate flag flying at sporting events at the University of Mississippi and its effect on the sense of unity among the white students conveys the power of an object to maintain social bonds, even in the face of a good deal of negative press (2007). This work looks at how this symbol of the American South during the American Civil War allows players and fans to maintain social bonds through a collective and assumed notion of what the flag means; in this case, it defines exclusivity, or who is in and who is not.

VIEWPOINTS

Creating Social Bonds & Preventing Deviance

Many criminologists are interested in the means to prevent deviance, or at the very least, to assist a deviant's reintegration into society. Theories of criminology and corrections have moved more and more toward an attempt to understand how to prevent crime and rehabilitate deviants, versus just trying to understand who is deviant and why (Downes & Rock, 1971).

For example, a Canadian study looked at how to reintegrate sex offenders by building a better sense of cohesion between the releasees and the rest of the community (Stacy & Petrunik, 2007). A 2008 study that looked at the relationship between social bonds and African American males in foster care showed that the development of bonds with foster parents, religious organizations, and school dramatically decreased the youths' risk of delinquency. This was in contrast with living with relatives, not feeling stable in the foster family, and being suspended from school (Ryan, 2008).

One interesting study looked at suicide among Hispanic immigrants versus American-born Hispanics. The findings in this study suggest that when immigrants maintain traditional cultural norms and do not assimilate into American society, they have lower suicide rates. So, *not* taking on the dominant norms of American life may keep some people who might otherwise commit suicide from doing so, particularly among Hispanic immigrants, as the norms of the culture are "family honor and the importance of family ties" versus American values of competition and individualism (Wadsworth & Kubrin, 2007).

Another study looked at a shocking increased rate of suicide among young African American men in American society (Poussaint & Alexander, 2001). By the time the study was published, in 2001, suicide had become the third leading cause of death among African American males between the ages of 15 and 24, and among African American men ages 20 to 25—from 5 percent in 1950 to almost 20 percent in 2000. In the past, there had been a strong taboo against suicide in the African American community. This taboo has remained among women; men are five times more likely to commit suicide. This work speculates that the inordinate stress African American males are under, the high rate of single parenthood at 70 percent, high rates of high school dropouts at 50 percent, high incarcerations rates (the surgeon general says incarceration is a high risk factor for suicide), and a high rate of feeling useless and helpless, or what Durkheim called anomie, are what have contributed to this massive increase.

Robert Merton, an American functionalist, saw Durkheim's ideas as valuable, but still not quite accurate. For Merton, deviance is caused not by a lack of social order, but by a lack of access to the goals of the dominant society. In other words, a burglar, for example, has the same goal of achieving wealth as a mainstream member, but does not have the ability to obtain wealth by accepted social norms. So, the goal of the members is the same, but the means are deviant.

Conflict Theory

Sociologists who disagree with the functionalist explanation for deviance are *conflict theorists.* This theory, based on the ideas of Karl Marx and later developed more fully by Max Weber and his followers, takes the position that those who are in control of wealth, property, and power control the rules of society. Therefore, these rules are precisely the rules that keep those who currently have control in control. The rest of the population is not aware they are being controlled and, therefore, support it through following the norms.

A structural-functionalist does not see the role of a social scientist as a critic of society; rather they see themselves as observers and describers of societies. Conflict theorists see themselves as theorists obliged to uncover the power structures of any society. For the conflict theorist, the idea that a society would promote assimilation of a group into the dominant society structure in order to reduce deviance, even if it is done to maintain social order, is inconceivable. For example, the former norm of segregation, commonly known as separate but equal, in the American South kept things "peaceful." To deviate against the system was a breach of mores that one could be killed for.

CONCLUSION

Strong social bonds are crucial to the harmony in any society. While it is important to see the power of social bonds as a means to keep members from regularly deviating from social norms, we must always keep in mind that deviance is normal in a society. As long as there are rules there will be deviance. Further, in order to promote social order and reduce deviance, it is crucial that social structures are flexible enough to make room for new members as they assimilate into the new culture. Finally, one of the most important ways we can prevent deviance in a society is to ensure that members feel part of the group and reduce the potential for the sense of meaninglessness and alienation that comes from pushing those members to the fringe.

TERMS & CONCEPTS

Assimilation: The process of taking on the dominant norms of a culture, also called acculturation. Immigrants are expected to take on the norms of their new culture.

Breaching Experiment: Intentionally breaking rules and recording the reactions of others in an effort to more fully understand what the rules are.

Cohesion: The level to which to members of a society agree on ways of acting (norms) and what to believe (values); it is the strength of the social bonds in a society.

Deviance: Behavior or appearance that violates the dominant rules, or norms, of a society.

Ethnocentrism: The belief that one's own culture is superior to others.

Folkways: William Sumner coined this sociological term that describes the everyday customs and habits of any culture. Punishment for breaking these rules is not severe.

Mores: Almost always reflected by laws, mores are the rules in any society upon which morals lie. Breaking these rules results in severe punishment. A taboo is a type of more.

Laws: These are rules that are codified and enforced through the government.

Norms: Sociologists divide these rules for behavior into three groups: folkways; mores, which includes taboos; and laws.

Taboos: Ritualized rules that can be considered sacred. The only semi-universal taboo is incest, despite several ancient cultures practicing it.

Bibliography

Banks, J. (2012). "Unmasking deviance: The visual construction of asylum seekers and refugees in English national newspapers." *Critical Criminology, 20* (3), 293–310.

Downes, D. & Rock, P. (1971). "Social reaction to deviance and its effects on crime and careers." *British Journal of Society 22* (4), 351.

Durkheim, E. (1933). *The division of labor in society.* New York: Free Press.

Durkheim. E. (1951). *Suicide.* New York: Free Press.

Foucault, M. (1975). *Discipline and punishment.*

Garfinkel, H. (1967). *Studies in ethnomethodology.* Englewood Cliffs, NJ: Prentice-Hall.

Guest, A., Cover, J., Matsueda, R., & Kubrin, C. (2006). "Neighborhood context and neighboring ties." *City & Community, 5* (4), 363–385.

Hannem, S., & Petrunik, M. (2007). "Circles of support and accountability: A community justice initiative for the reintegration of high risk sex offenders." *Contemporary Justice Review, 10* (2), 153–171.

Levi-Strauss, C. (1969). *The elementary structures of kinship.* Boston: Beacon Press.

Newman, J. (2007). "Old times there are not forgotten: Sport, identity, and the Confederate flag in the Dixie South." *Sociology of Sport Journal, 24* (3), 261–282.

Park, R. (1950). *The collected papers of Robert Ezra Park.* Glencoe, IL: Free Press.

Poussaint, A. & Alexander, A. (2001). *Lay my burden down: Suicide and mental health crisis among African Americans.* Boston: Beacon Press.

Pratten, D. (2008). "'The thief eats his shame': Practice and power in Nigerian vigilantism." *Africa, 78* (1), 64–83.

Prus, R. (2011). "Morality, deviance, and regulation: Pragmatist motifs in Plato's republic and laws." *Qualitative Sociology Review, 7* (2), 1–44.

Peacock, J., & Greene, D. (2007). "'I am who I am, and I am who you say I am': Identity salience, commitment, and competing paradigms." *Michigan Sociological Review, 21,* 149–178.

Ryan, J., Testa, M., & Zhai, F. (2008). "African American males in foster care and the risk of delinquency: The value of social bonds and permanence." *Child Welfare, 87* (1), 115–140.

Stone, C. (2007). "The role of football in everyday life." *Soccer & Society, 8* (2/3), 169–184.

Sumner, W. (1906). *Folkways.* Boston: Ginn.

Torgler, B., & Schneider, F. (2007). "What shapes attitudes toward paying taxes? Evidence from multicultural European countries." *Social Science Quarterly (Blackwell Publishing Limited), 88* (2), 443–470.

Victoria, W., Haines, K., & Tucker, J. V. (2011). "Deviance and control in communities with perfect surveillance – The case of Second Life." *Surveillance & Society, 9* (1/2), 31–46.

Wadsworth, T., & Kubrin, C. (2007). "Hispanic suicide in U.S. metropolitan areas: Examining the effects of immigration, assimilation, affluence, and disadvantage." *American Journal of Sociology, 112* (6), 1848–1885.

Suggested Reading

Adler, P. A., & Adler, P. (2012). *Constructions of deviance: Social power, context, and interaction.* 7th ed. Belmont, CA: Thomson/Wadsworth.

Curra, J. (2014). *The relativity of deviance.* 3rd ed. Thousand Oaks, CA: SAGE Publications.

Merton, R. (1968). *Social theory and social structure.* New York: Free Press.

Modood, T. & Werbner, P. (1997). *The politics of multiculturalism in the new Europe.* London: Zed Books.

Park, R. (1967). *On social control and collective behavior.* Chicago: University of Chicago Press.

Heidi Goar, M.A.

Prison System

ABSTRACT

The paper begins by analyzing the demographics of the U.S. prison population and outlining the rise of the prison system as well as policies of expansion in various states. The paper then makes a thorough analysis of the various ways that private business or corporations benefit from the prison system and examines the way in which crime has been politicized to the benefit of politicians and big business. The paper concludes with some suggestions toward prison system reform.

OVERVIEW

Growth of the Prison System

President Richard Nixon began a War on Drugs during his presidency with a formal announcement. Ronald Reagan first developed harsh drug policies at the state level as governor of California, after which he became U.S. president and significantly expanded Nixon's War on Drugs as a federal policy. Smith and Hattery point out that the U.S. government's War on Drugs instituted four major policy changes that directly increased the prison population:

- Longer sentences;
- Mandatory minimums;
- Some drug offenses were moved from the misdemeanor category to the felony category; and
- The institution of the "Three Strikes You're Out" policy [CCL1] (Smith & Hattery, 2007, p. 5).

California demonstrates what became a national trend in the late twentieth and early twenty-first centuries that caused America to far outstrip other countries for incarcerations. California governors of the 1980s and 1990s strongly encouraged more prison construction and helped set a national trend, while the California legislature enacted more than 400 pieces of legislation that increased criminal penalties, and thereby ensured that the state would need even more prisons (Simon, 2007, p. 494). California continued its trend for increasing the number of prisons into the early 2000s. Saskal (2006) reports that Governor Arnold Schwarzenegger in 2008 called for the issuance of $8.7 billion of lease revenue bonds to expand the capacity of California's overfilled prison system. About that time, there were several lawsuits pending over poor and overcrowded conditions in the system, and federal judges were close to intervening (Saskal, 2006, p. 1). By 2006, the number of inmates in California prisons had peaked at 173,942 (Carson & Golinelli, 2013), and Schwarzenegger declared a state of emergency in response ("Schwarzeneggar v. Plata," 2010). Poor health conditions led to lawsuits that eventually went before the Supreme Court, which ruled that they constituted "cruel and unusual punishment," a violation of the Eighth Amendment, and that prisoner release was necessary to remedy the situation ("Schwarzeneggar v. Plata," 2010). Subsequently, under Governor Jerry Brown's California Public Safety Realignment program, the state has sought to better align the incarceration rate with the rate of violent crime, giving nonviolent criminals alternative sentences such as mental health treatment, drug rehabilitation programs, community service, or house arrest with GPS tracking ("The Challenges of 'Realignment,'" 2012). As a result, the prison population decreased to 134,211 in 2012, a drop of nearly 10 percent from the preceding year. Nonetheless, prison crowding continued, and the Brown administration looked to prisons run by private corporations GEO Group and Corrections Corporation of America to further alleviate the problem without releasing additional prisoners (St. John, 2013). In many ways, California's history of high incarceration rates and attempts to rectify its problems exemplify the state of the prison system in the United States, as we will see below.

The end result of our change to a punitive approach to crime—and particularly our severe laws on nonviolent crimes such as drug sales or use—is that the U.S. far outstrips every other country in the world in per capita incarcerations. The U.S. incarcerates a much higher proportion of its population than Russia or even China, a country that Smith and Hattery (2007) note has incarceration practices that are "frequently the target of investigations and reports by human rights watch groups such as Amnesty International" (p. 275).

In addition, Frederickson (2008) observes that "the costs of the American penal system are astonishing." Klein and Soltas (2013) note that the average inmate in a federal prison cost twenty-one thousand dollars per year in 2013, and that by 2010, the federal prison system is projected to account for 30 percent of the Justice Department's budget. Thus, we can expect much more tax money to go into the burgeoning U.S. prison system.

Incarceration & Crime Rates

Since our prison population has been rapidly increasing since the early 1990s, it seems logical that the cause would be an increase in the number of violent crimes, but there has not been an increase in violent crimes. In fact, there has been a significant *decrease.* The rate of violent crime dropped steadily from a high of 757.7 per 100,000 inhabitants in 1992 to a low of 429.4 per 100,000 inhabitants in 2009 (Federal Bureau of Investigation, 2010). Clear gives us yet more specific information about the tenuous relationship between incarceration figures and crime rates:

> ...a 500 percent generation-long growth in imprisonment has had little impact on crime. Broadly speaking, crime rates are about what they were in 1973, though they have fluctuated dramatically over the 33-year time span since then. Beginning in 1973, crime rates went up into the early 1980s, went down for a few years at the end of that decade, went back up again, and then experienced a lengthy downward trend starting in the late 1990s. Prison populations, on the other hand, have risen every year since 1990 (Clear, 2007, p. 613).

As noted above, one of the biggest reasons for the increase is our harsh approach to nonviolent crimes—especially our punitive laws on drug distribution, sales, and use. The Pew analysts have determined that the phenomenal growth "is being fueled by mandatory minimum sentences that have stretched prison terms for many criminals, declines in inmates granted parole and other policies that states have passed in recent years to crack down on crime" (Johnson, 2007, para. 2). The Pew report specifically cites harsher drug laws as one of the main factors in increasing the nation's prison population (Johnson, 2007, para. 14).

The Prison Population

The Bureau of Justice Statistics estimates that 1.57 million Americans were serving prison sentences in local, state, and federal prisons in 2012 (Carson & Golinelli, 2013). According to the nonprofit organization the Sentencing Project (2013a), African Americans constituted 38 percent of all prisoners in 2011, and only roughly 7 percent (91,590 of the estimated 1,341,804 sentenced prisoners) that year were female (Carson & Golinelli, 2013). If we examine the statistics by gender, then African American men represent the majority of the male prison population. Yet African Americans comprised only 13 percent of the total U.S. population in 2012, according to the US Census Bureau (2012). This seems a clear indication that something about American culture—a combination of its socioeconomic, legislative, and judicial systems—is causing a significant disproportion in our prison population.

Spear (2006) observes that the United States incarcerates a disproportionately large number of poor and uneducated Americans; thus, nearly all of the prisoners are from poor and uneducated backgrounds, and many of them are African Americans. The Sentencing Project (2013b) also reports that African American men have a one in three chance of being incarcerated during their lifetimes, as compared to a one in six chance for Latino men and a one in seventeen chance for Caucasian men. Spear observes that the "mentally disturbed, lacking support in the community, gravitate toward the prison system, where they will find little help" (2006, p. 22). Clear (2007) observes that people who go to prison "come disproportionately from a handful of neighborhoods, impoverished places where schools are bad, the labor market weak, and housing inadequate" (p. 615). He then concludes that the "social effects of incarceration are hyperconcentrated among young, poor, black men and urban black communities" (Clear, 2007).

Smith and Hattery offer another interesting statistic and comparison. They point out that, in 2006, 450,000 of the more than 2 million inmates were serving sentences in state and federal prisons for nonviolent drug offenses. They also point out that this number (,000) represents more prisoners than the European Union had in prison for *all* crimes combined—and the EU had a larger population than the U.S., by 100 million people (Smith & Hattery, 2007, p. 6). Smith and Hattery note that African American males represented only 9% of the prison population in the 1970s, but after harsher drug law sentencing came into effect, the population climbed to 62% representation by the mid-2000s (Smith & Hattery, 2007, p. 22).

The U.S. jail and prison population has continued to rise sharply. Spear and other researchers concur that a "get-tough" legal approach to the distribution and use of illicit drugs is the primary cause for the increase. Spear notes that many of the prisoners who are there for drug offenses actually have no record of violent offenses; that there are other expanding groups in the prison population. The rise of "tough-on-crime" laws has allowed far more juveniles to be tried in an adult court at much younger ages than previously, and according to the Sentencing Project, these adult sentences that are imposed on minors are "unduly severe." As discussed below, the conditions in juvenile prisons are also unduly severe. Spear notes that the female prison population has also increased significantly and comments that this situation usually leaves their children with a family member or the children end up as wards of the state. This of course weakens or perhaps destroys the family structure of the imprisoned (Spear, 2006, p. 23). To summarize, the prison population is mostly poor and uneducated, predominantly African American, and increasingly consisting of women, children, and the mentally disturbed; and the biggest cause of this increase is the changes in drug laws.

FURTHER INSIGHTS

The Prison Industrial Complex

The private business sector benefits in various ways from increased incarcerations, and this should be examined more closely. Smith and Hattery note that many Fortune 500 companies have taken advantage of the cheap labor resources available through prison populations. The use of prison labor allows corporations to save significantly on labor costs and thereby increase their profits "much like plantations, ship builders, and other industries did during the 200 plus years of slavery in the United States" (Smith & Hattery, 2007, p. 11). Smith and Hattery aptly refer to the prison system as the "prison industrial complex (PIC)," and they argue that the capitalist economy and the prison system that characterizes the PIC create a symbiotic system. Prisons only make money when the prison beds are occupied, and "the more prisons provide labor for corporations, the more prisons will be built." Their conclusion is alarming. They propose that "the PIC and its attendant industries contribute to the increased rates of incarceration in the US and the continued exploitation of labor, primarily African American labor" (Smith & Hattery, 2007, p. 11). It makes basic economic sense that, when there are empty prison cells, the prison loses money, and "prisons beds"—as industry insiders refer to their economic units—need full capacity for optimal profit. The authors argue that the PIC is a self-perpetuating system:

> We must impose harsher and longer sentences and we must continue to funnel inmates into prisons... and this funnel is not being filled with white collar offenders such as Bernie Ebbs (WorldCom), Ken Lay (Enron), or Martha Stewart, but rather by vulnerable, unempowered populations, primarily young, poor, African American men (Smith & Hattery, 2007, p. 13).

A change in inmate labor regulations has created a system wherein inmate labor is increasingly subcontracted for a variety of business sectors. Subcontracting companies act as middlemen for many of the largest companies in the United States. The middlemen subcontracting companies that are hired by America's largest companies use prison labor for telemarketing, call service, manufacturing, packaging, and distributing their products, though in some cases there is no middleman and the companies directly outsource to prison labor. Smith and Hattery note that, although Americans are unaware of it, every day they are the beneficiaries of the work done by ten to fifteen prison laborers, and Americans use about thirty products daily that were produced, packaged, or sold out of a prison (Smith & Hattery, 2007, p. 17). The authors also make an astute observation on the ultimate reach of this economic system by observing "prison industries have truly infiltrated the global market" (Smith & Hattery, 2007, p. 283).

Corporations pay prisoners a subminimum wage (between 23 cents and 1.15 dollars per hour in 2001) and make enormous profits on prison labor (Smith & Hattery, 2007, p. 13; Fox, 2012). Additional advantages to the use of prison labor, besides the obvious advantage of paying very low wages, are that companies who use prison labor do not have to provide health insurance or vacation benefits, and they need not be concerned about severance pay or layoffs (Smith & Hattery, 2007, p. 14; Fox, 2012). They can conveniently increase the number of prison workers during peak sales periods and send them back to their cells whenever sales decline (Smith & Hattery, 2007, p. 19).

Although big companies pay prison workers much less than they pay for workers on the outside, they are not actually reducing the markup to the consumer; of course, they retain the increased profits (Smith & Hattery, 2007, p. 19). The system thus benefits the wealthier citizens who might own stock in these companies, but it does not help the average American worker or consumer. In fact, evidence suggests that, if anything, the system creates negative effects for the average American worker (Fox, 2012). Smith and Hattery note that the exploitation of inmate labor can cause higher unemployment and lower wages in local communities (Smith & Hattery, 2007, p. 17).

Corporations & Prisons

Another benefit to the private sector is the outsourcing of both the construction of prisons and the operation and management of those prisons. For example, the publicly-traded Corrections Corporation of America (CCA), which builds and staffs prisons, managed an estimated ninety thousand beds across sixty-plus facilities in nineteen states and the District of Columbia in 2011 and employed approximately 17,000 personnel in 2013 ("Corrections Corporation of America," 2013).Private corporations such as CCA not only make high profits on building and operating prisons, they also profit on many outsourcing services, such as food service or other services, and they profit on "leasing" prisoner labor to the multinational corporations in the above-described scenario (Smith & Hattery, 2007, p. 21). In short, the PIC is booming in spite of the decrease in violent crime between the late 1980s and early 2000s.

After the loosening of the laws that prohibited the direct competition between prisons and free enterprise, some prisons have also begun directly producing their own goods for the mainstream market. For example, an Oregon prison that started out making denim uniforms for all the inmates in the entire Oregon State Prison system has successfully marketed its own denim clothing line. The Prison Blues Garment Factory operates behind barbed wire, and Americans are ordering the prison factory's "Prison Blues"® clothing online (Smith & Hattery, 2007, p. 16). Supporters of the PIC argue that "this is a positive movement in the evolution of prisons because it provides work, it teaches job skills that are transportable, and it allows inmates to earn some money while they are on the inside" (p. 18). Although these arguments are founded in a rehabilitative mentality, we should ask whether the system is actually based on a rehabilitative philosophy or whether it is entirely based on convenient exploitation of prisoners to maximize corporate profits (Smith & Hattery, 2007).

Exploitation & Corruption

Corporate exploitation of prisoners can also occur from the customer end. For example, for years, prisoners paid much higher fees for making collect calls [CCL2]to speak with their families. According to the *New York Times*, prisons all over the country "goug[ed] inmates and their families when telephone companies started paying legalized kickbacks—called 'commissions'—to the state prison systems for monopoly on the service" ("A Good Call in New York," 2007, Abstract). The state of New York set a national precedent by forcing its corrections department to change its policy of charging prison inmates and their families "more than six times the going rate for collect calls made from prison." As the article observes, "these schemes place a huge financial burden on inmate families, who tend to be among the poorest in the nation, and who must often choose between paying phone bills and putting food on the table" ("A Good Call in New York," 2007, Abstract). In August 2013, the Federal Communications Commission capped rates at 25 cents per minute for interstate collect calls; prior to the ruling, inmates and their families could be charged as much as seventeen dollars for a fifteen-minute call (Gamboa, 2013).

There are also many cases of corruption and scandal from corporations operating prisons. For example, the GEO Group, a publicly traded company that runs private prison facilities across the country, has faced repeated accusations of human rights abuses against inmates in its facilities (Dahl, 2008, para. 1). In 2000, the same company was known as Wackenhut Corrections Corporation, and they were sued for "excessive abuse and neglect" of inmates at the Jena Juvenile Justice Center in Jena, Louisiana (Dahl, 2008, para. 5). A scandal involving the same company also occurred in Texas, where a dozen juvenile girls successfully sued the Wackenhut prison, and two Wackenhut employees pled guilty to criminal charges of sexual assault. Unfortunately, the girl who initiated the lawsuit committed suicide on the day of the legal settlement ("Locked Inside a Nightmare," 2000, para. 10). Apparently, the company used the strategy of changing its name to escape the bad press and then faced new accusations in Oregon in 2008. Despite that and an $6.5-million-dollar wrongful death suit in Oklahoma, the company continued to operate sixty-five facilities and made $1.6 billion dollars in 2011 (Lee, 2012).

Politics & the Prison System

Simon (2007) notes that our program of Mass incarceration threatens to recreate the worst features of post-slavery America while escaping most of the protections provided by the Reconstruction constitutional amendments and the civil rights legacy they produced ... young men, and increasingly women, are being shunted into a system whose not so unintended effect is to cast them into a permanently diminished citizenship (p. 499).

Additionally, our prison system strips the social capital from minority communities by the removal and degradation of their human capital. Simon writes, "It is not difficult to reach the bleak conclusion that the prison has become an engine of social war against some of America's most vulnerable communities" (2007, p. 499).

In other words, the War On Drugs is in reality a politically-based "War on the Poor and Uneducated." Smith and Hattery (2007) note that harsh sentencing guidelines have filled America's prisons with a surprisingly large number of young African American and Latino men who are guilty of little more than untreated drug addictions (p. 21). It should be added that socioeconomic status highly influences whether harsh sentencing guidelines are applied to a person's drug addiction. This becomes quite clear if we consider that, with money and connections, an affluent cocaine user will end up in an expensive private rehab center rather than in the prison system. For example, in 2002, Jeb Bush, former governor of Florida, entered his daughter Noelle Bush into a drug treatment program after she was arrested trying to use a counterfeit drug prescription at a pharmacy. While in the treatment center, she was caught in possession of "a small white rock substance" (crack cocaine), that the police lab-tested as positive for cocaine ("Police Investigate Jeb Bush's Daughter," 2002, para. 2–3), but she served only three days in jail that July and an additional ten in October that year ("Jeb Bush's Daughter out of Rehab," 2009, para. 6). In Florida, there are much harsher laws for possession of crack cocaine than powder cocaine. The poor and uneducated do not receive the same patient and compassionate rehabilitative system when they are caught in possession; rather, they face a quick and very punitive legal and judicial system.

VIEWPOINTS

The Politicization of Crime

A good question to ask is "to what extent has crime been politicized?" Blumstein (2007) writes that, concurrent to the growth period of the prison system, "being 'tough on crime' and especially being able to label one's opponent as 'soft on crime' provided great political advantage in a nation that was becoming increasingly concerned about the crime problem" (p. 4). The author then reminds us of a classic political TV advertisement, which was "a 30-second 'sound bite' showing the candidate vigorously slamming shut a cell door and then proclaiming his toughness on crime." Blumstein observes that this particular form of advertising became so popular that it bordered on cliché, but he reasons that this kind of political ad campaign was effective since it was simple enough to fit the typical thirty-second TV advertising format. The author argues that politicians saw great political advantage in demonstrating their toughness on crime, and because of this, the U.S. experienced a wide variety of legislative changes that directly contributed to increasing our prison population (Blumstein, 2007, p. 5). The author also makes an important distinction between the growth of crime and the growth of punitiveness, which essentially explains how violent crimes could go down even while the number of incarcerated doubled. It is not that violent crimes have increased, but that laws have become much more punitive for nonviolent crimes—and these harsh laws were probably enacted for essentially political reasons.

Jones (2006) brings up another angle to the politicization of crime, and that is the role of lobbying from the prison industrial complex. For example, the "correctional officers union in California has become one of the state's top political contributors, and that their lobbying efforts push for tougher laws and longer sentences" (para. 6), presumably to ensure steady if not increased employment of corrections officers. Jones also notes that "private firms quickly get addicted to the government cash. They, too, have poor rehabilitation rates and spend their time lobbying state legislatures for tougher laws and longer sentences" (para. 8).

Once the tougher laws get pushed through, state governors further benefit the private sector from tax dollars by increasing the prison system budget. Frederickson (2008) notes that growth in spending for the prison system has pushed aside other priorities. For example, between the late 1980s and late 2000s, state spending on higher education increased by 21 percent, but the spending for the prison system increased 127 percent (Frederickson, 2008, p. 11). Politics has changed government into a system of governing through politicized crime in society, and Frederickson (2008) asks what the end result of governing through crime has done to government:

Whether one values American democracy for its liberty or its equality-enhancing features, governing through crime has been bad. First, the vast reorienting of fiscal and administrative resources toward the criminal justice system at both the federal and state levels has resulted in a shift aptly described as transformation from the 'welfare state' to the 'penal state.' The result has not been less government, but a more authoritarian executive, a more passive legislature, and a more defensive judiciary than even the welfare state itself was accused of producing (p. 11).

Blumstein (2007) writes that because the politicization of crime has been occurring for some time and is likely to accelerate, it is all the more urgent to intercept it (p. 14). Jones points out the biggest problem with the PIC by asking a central question and providing the answer: "Where are the financial incentives for prisons to properly perform their rehabilitative function? If anything, the captains of the incarceration industry have a perverse incentive to rehabilitate as few people as possible and keep business booming" (2006, para. 4). Gonnerman and Brown point out that the punitive philosophy reigning within the PIC makes the odds of rehabilitation far less. America's prisons are filled with illiterate men and women who never graduated from high school—68 percent of state inmates in 2003–2004 were dropouts, according to Bureau of Justice Statistics (cited in Tyler & Lofstrom, 2009, p. 88), and they have a very difficult time finding employment after release (Gonnerman & Brown, 2008). The punitive measures continue once a prisoner is released from the prison system: "Once freed, they become second-class citizens. Depending on the state, they may be denied public housing, student loans, a driver's license, welfare benefits, and a wide range of jobs." The authors point out that this may be the reason that, within three years of being released, nearly half of the ex-convicts will be convicted of a new crime (Gonnerman & Brown, 2008, para.7). Between 2004 and 2007, the three-year recidivism rate (including rearrests, reconviction, or returns to custody) was 43.3 percent across thirty-three states (Pew Center on the States, 2011).

Solution to Prison Growth

The most fundamental solution to the unnecessary growth of U.S. prisons lies within Gonnerman and Brown's final analysis: "We've become a two-tier society in which millions of ostensibly free people are prohibited from enjoying the rights and privileges accorded to everyone else—and we continue to be defined by our desire for punishment and revenge, rather than by our belief in the power of redemption" (2008, para. 8).

The most basic change that needs to occur is a change in our belief as to what function prisons should serve for our society and also in our perception of what constitutes crime worthy of lengthy incarceration. Spear suggests that a good starting place for reform is to change the mandatory-minimum drug laws that keep low-level drug offenders incarcerated for decades. He also believes citizens should urge lawmakers to change drug law sentencing to treatment rather than to prison. Spear and other researchers of the prison system believe that "the goal of criminal justice should not be simply to punish, but to prepare prisoners for re-entry into the communities to which they will eventually return" (Spear, 2006, p. 23), meaning rehabilitation.

Education

From a rehabilitative perspective, education in prisons is of primary importance. According to Bracey, research on "the impact of education on recidivism finds positive effects, whether the program provides basic secondary education, vocational education, or college education." The author cites research into the efficacy of education in reducing recidivism and writes that "participation in prison education programs reduced recidivism by about 29% overall" (Bracey, 2006, p. 253). However, education in prisons has significantly diminished since America has taken its punitive approach. From 1972 until the early 1990s, prisoners who were not on death row or sentenced to life without parole could qualify for federal Pell grants and other government funding for postsecondary educational programs, but since their eligibility was eliminated in 1994, the number of programs has dropped from 350 to a dozen in 2005(Gonnerman & Brown, 2008, para. 6; Skorton & Altschuler, 2013). Thus, the most powerful tool to prevent recidivism has been significantly reduced.

Accountability

Jones suggests we begin holding the prison system accountable for reducing recidivism and that we look at any other creative alternatives, such as community-based programs, that seem to hold promise. "If a community-based program can do a better job at keeping people out of prison with dimes than incarcerators have been doing with dollars, let's reallocate those funds," suggests Jones, and he gives the example that YouthBuild USA helps unemployed 16- to 24-year-olds prepare for a high school diploma while they learn job skills. Jones suggests we increase funding into such programs (2006, para. 13). The policy of "zero tolerance" does not work and has fed a perverse prison market system that is counterproductive to American society in many ways. The change will not be easy since the philosophy and sentencing policies are deeply rooted. As Simon observes, "the carceral state is not likely to disappear any time soon. Behind the surface of political rhetoric about crime is a vast and interwoven circuitry of knowledge and power, one that links politicians and media celebrities to security experts and law enforcement, to parents and employers" (2007, p. 503). The first step, however, is to recognize the damage and social injustice that the system has propagated.

TERMS & CONCEPTS

Corrections Corporation of America (CCA): One of the largest private prison providers in the U. S., with sixty-six facilities in nineteen states and the District of Columbia in 2011. CCA runs both prisons and immigrant detention centers.

Fortune 500 Companies: *Fortune Magazine* ranks the top 500 American public corporations as measured by their gross revenue.

Pell Grant Program: A type of postsecondary, educational federal grant program sponsored by the U.S. Department of Education. Named after U.S. senator Claiborne Pell, it was originally known as the Basic Educational Opportunity Grant program. Grants are awarded based on a financial need formula.

Pew Charitable Trusts: Independent nonprofit and nongovernmental organization that serves the public interest by improving public policy, informing the public, and stimulating civic life. One of its many missions is working on issues related to state correction policies.

Prison Industrial Complex (PIC): Refers to the complex of organizations that have financial interest in the operation of the prison facilities, including prison guard unions, construction companies, subcontracting companies, surveillance technology vendors, etc.

Three Strikes You're Out: Also called "three strikes laws" or habitual offender laws. Statutes enacted by state governments requiring the state courts to impose a mandatory and extended period of imprisonment to anyone who has been convicted of a serious criminal offense on three or more separate occasions.

Wackenhut Corrections Corporation: A United States-based private security and investigation firm. Wackenhut was founded in 1954 by former FBI agents. In the 1960s, Wackenhut began providing food services for prisons and in 1984 started a subsidiary to design and manage jails and detention centers for the growing private prison market. Critics claim that the company's guards have abused inmates in many states. Wackenhut has been renamed GEO Group and continues to operate.

War on Drugs: A term first used by President Richard Nixon in 1971, it refers to a prohibition campaign undertaken by the U. S. government to "curb supply and diminish demand" for certain psychoactive substances deemed "harmful or undesirable" by the government. This includes a set of laws that are intended to discourage the production, distribution, and consumption of targeted substances.

Bibliography

"A good call in New York." (2007, Jan. 10). *New York Times* [Abstract].

Albanese, E. (2007). "Texas: Prison bed debate." *Bond Buyer, 359*(32557), 9.

Blumstein, A. (2007). "The roots of punitiveness in a democracy." *Journal of Scandinavian Studies in Criminology & Crime Prevention, 8,* 2–16.

Bracey, G. (2006). "Locked up, locked out." *Phi Delta Kappan, 88,* 253–254.

Carson, E. A., & Golinell, D. (2013, July). *Prisoners in 2012—Advance counts* (NCJ 242467). Washington, DC: U.S. Department of Justice, Bureau of Justice Statistics. http://www.bjs.gov/content/pub/pdf/p12ac.pdf

"The challenges of 'realignment.'" (2012, May 19). *Economist.* http://www.economist.com/node/21555611

Chamberlain, A. (2012). "Offender rehabilitation: Examining changes in inmate treatment characteristics, program participation, and institutional behavior." *JQ: Justice Quarterly, 29,* 183–228.

Clear, T. (2007). "The impacts of incarceration on public safety." *Social Research, 74,* 613–630.

"Corrections Corporation of America." (2013, April). In the Public Interest website: http://www.inthepublicinterest.org/organization/corrections-corporation-america

Dahl, J. (2008, Aug. 5). "Private prison co. again accused of human rights abuses." *The Blotter from Brian Ross.* ABCNews.com: http://abcnews.go.com/Blotter

Federal Bureau of Investigation, U.S. Department of Justice. (2010, September). "Crime in the United States: Table 1." http://www2.fbi.gov/ucr/cius2009/data/table%5F01.html

Fox, E. J. (2012, August 14). "Factory owners: Federal prisoners stealing our business." *CNN Money.* http://money.cnn.com/2012/08/14/smallbusiness/federal-prison-business/

Frederickson, H. G. (2008). "Politics and administration in the penal state." *PA Times, 31,* 11.

Gamboa, S. (2013, August 9). "Feds to slash cost of phone calls made from prison." Associated Press. http://bigstory.ap.org/article/fcc-address-high-phone-charges

Gonnerman, J., & Brown, E. (2008). "Slammed." *Mother Jones, 33,* 44–46.

"Jeb Bush's daughter out of rehab." (2009, Feb. 11). Associated Press. http://www.cbsnews.com/2100-201%5F162-326007.html

Johnson, K. (2007). "Study predicts rise in inmate populations." *USA Today.*

Jones, V. (2006). Con game. *Forbes, 177,* 34.

Klein, E., & Soltas, E. (2013, August 13)."Wonkbook: 11 facts about America's prison population" [Web log]. Washington Post website: http://www.washingtonpost.com/blogs/wonkblog/wp/2013/08/13/wonkbook-11-facts-about-americas-prison-population/

Lee, S. (2012, June 20). "By the numbers: The U.S.'s growing for-profit detention industry." ProPublica: http://www.propublica.org/article/by-the-numbers-the-u.s.s-growing-for-profit-detention-industry

"Locked inside a nightmare" [Electronic version]. (2000, May). *60 Minutes II* . http://www.cbsnews.com/stories/2000/05/09/60II/main193636.shtml

Massoglia, M., & Warner, C. (2011). "The consequences of incarceration." *Criminology & Public Policy, 10,* 851–863.

NAACP. (2013). "Criminal justice fact sheet." http://www.naacp.org/pages/criminal-justice-fact-sheet

Page, J. (2011). "Prison officer unions and the perpetuation of the penal status quo." *Criminology & Public Policy, 10,* 735–770.

Pew Center on the States. (2011, April).*State of recidivism: The revolving door of America's prisons.* Washington, DC: Author. http://www.pewtrusts.org/uploadedFiles/wwwpewtrustsorg/Reports/

"Police investigate Jeb Bush's daughter." (2002, Sept. 10). CNN.com: http://edition.cnn.com/2002/US/09/10/noelle.bush/

St. John, P. (2013, August 8). "California seeks private prison deals." *Los Angeles Times.* http://www.latimes.com/local/political/la-me-pc-ff-brown-private-prison-deal

Saskal, R. (2006). "Calif. Gov. unveils plan for prisons." *Bond Buyer, 358*(32535), 1–40.

Savitsky, D. (2012). "Is plea bargaining a rational choice? Plea bargaining as an engine of racial stratification and overcrowding in the United States prison system." *Rationality & Society, 24,* 131–167.

Schwarzeneggar v. Plata. (2010). Legal Information Institute, Cornell University Law School website: http://www.law.cornell.edu/supct/cert/09-1233#%5FIssues

Sentencing Project. (2013a). *Facts about prisons and prisoners.* http://www.sentencingproject.org/doc/publications/publications/

Sentencing Project. (2013b). *Report of the Sentencing Project to the United Nations Human Rights Committee: Regarding racial disparities in the United States criminal justice system.* http://sentencingproject.org/doc/publications/

Simon, J. (2007). "Rise of the carceral state." *Social Research, 74,* 471–508.

Skorton, D., & Altschuler, G. (2013, March 25). "College behind bars: How educating prisoners pays off." *Forbes.* http://www.forbes.com/sites/collegeprose/2013/03/25/college-behind-bars-how-educating-prisoners-pays-off/

Smith, E., & Hattery, A. (2007). "f we build it they will come: Human rights violations and the prison industrial complex." *Societies without Borders, 2,* 273–288.

Smith, E., & Hattery, A. (2007). "The prison industrial complex." *Sociation Today, 4,* 1–28.

Spear, L. (2006). "Reforming the system." *America, 195*, 22–23.

Steinbuch, A. T. (2014). "The movement away from solitary confinement in the United States." *New England Journal on Criminal & Civil Confinement, 40,* 499–533.

Tyler, J. H., & Lofstrom, M. (2009). "Finishing high school: Alternative pathways and dropout recovery." *America's High Schools, 19* www.princeton.edu/futureofchildren/publications/

United States Census Bureau. State & county quickfacts. http://quickfacts.census.gov/qfd/states/00000.html

SUGGESTED READING

"Forecasting Prison Populations." (2007). *State Legislatures, 33,* 7.

Hartnett, S. J. (2011). *Challenging the prison-industrial complex: Activism, arts, and educational alternatives.* Urbana, IL: University of Illinois Press.

Jacklet, B. (2008). "Prison town myth." *Oregon Business Magazine, 31,* 30–35.

Johnson, K. (2006). "Inmate suicides linked to solitary." *USA Today.*

Loury, G. (2007). "The new untouchables." *UN Chronicle, 44,* 53–55.

McFarlane, D. A. (2012). "The impact of the global economic recession on the American criminal justice system." *International Journal of Criminal Justice Sciences, 7,* 524–549.

Meyer, E. (2008). "Get tough on crime, not on kids." *Corrections Today, 70,* 19.

Taylor, A. (2011). *The prison system and its effects: Wherefrom, whereto, and why?* Hauppauge, NY: Nova Science Publishers.

"Trouble in Tallahassee." (2006). *Economist, 380* (8485), 29.

Sinclair Nicholas, M.A.

RACE, ETHNICITY, AND LAW ENFORCEMENT

ABSTRACT

Race and ethnicity in American society are organized into an indisputable socially constructed power hierarchy. While scholars debate the exact structure of this hierarchy, it is generally agreed upon that the traditional structure is those of European descent are at the top of this hierarchy and that those of African descent are near to the bottom. It is true that other racial groups also occupy the hierarchy, but the primary relationship is that of the white oppressor and the black oppressed. There are many arenas in which this relationship is made clear, but that of criminality and law enforcement is the most clear and surrounded with the most controversy. This article explores the relationship between race, criminality, and law enforcement and highlights some of the issues surrounding the intersection of race and criminal behavior.

OVERVIEW

Background: Race in America

Due to complex histories of contested interactions, issues of race and ethnicity often prove difficult to study. This is especially true in regard to the way criminality is studied in the context of race and ethnicity, but, despite complexity, the relationship between crime and racial or ethnic identity is quite useful for understanding American inequalities.

The concept of race is generally associated with the physical characteristics an individual possesses that set the individual apart from other racial groups: skin pigmentation, eye color, and facial features. Ethnicity, on the other hand, is culturally based and generally associated with regional ancestry: food, dress, or religious practices. Another concept often closely associated with racial and ethnic groups is that of a minority. While the concept of "minority" may seem without need of explanation, the sociological definition of a minority group entails any group of people that is held subservient to a dominant group of people. Thus, the sociological concept of minority is not a matter of numbers; it is a matter of power. For example, while blacks outnumbered whites in the South during the era of segregation, they remained a minority in sociological terms due to their level of relative powerlessness in comparison to whites.

The context in which the racial dynamic developed in America is complicated and has evolved over several centuries. The racial hierarchy in which whites are favored and blacks are oppressed has its basis in the efforts of slaveholders in the American southeast. Unlike other immigrant groups, Africans were transported to North America by force. Once they arrived, they were placed into subservient positions from which they could not escape, and they were forced to perform tasks that were seen as "unfit" for whites (Zinn, 2003). Slaveholders actively subverted African culture among their slaves by preventing them from speaking their own language, learning to read or write English, or from practicing their or any religion in independent ways (Zinn, 2003). After the direct and overt oppression of slavery was ended from a legal standpoint, slightly more subtle forms of domination continued with laws dictating the segregation of blacks from whites in public places. In the workplace, blacks were often pitted against each other by employers who sought to break up labor unions and keep worker wages as low as possible.

During the 1960s when the civil rights movement was most active, civil rights leaders made great strides in achieving equal rights for people of all racial groups. While this goal may have been legislatively achieved, racial privilege remains a significant societal issue: Communities grapple with more subtle forms of racism that are built into the social structure and of which most community members are not aware. These subtle forms of racism are the residual effect of generations of discrimination against blacks perpetrated by whites (Wilson, 1978). The result is class subordination of blacks under whites (Wilson, 1978).

Class Subordination

The class subordination identified by Wilson (1978) is subtle, and not as simple a form of discrimination to recognize as a "Whites Only" sign. In fact, one must carefully catalog demographic data before a clear picture of this subtle discrimination develops. Historically, whites have tended to live in more upscale neighborhoods, with less crime and better educational systems. They have had higher levels of education and higher rates of college attendance and graduation. There is greater access to the cultural capital of the dominant culture, which then fosters increased accrued knowledge through experience with a cultural group.

In distinct opposition to their white counterparts, life circumstances have been primarily harder with fewer opportunities available for African Americans who have historically lived in poor, urban areas with crumbling infrastructures, poor local economies, and lower levels of public services. People living in these areas often have poorer quality education (due to a lack of funding for schools) and higher dropout rates among high school students. There is reduced access to and interest in the cultural aspects of the community or city, which can translate into difficulty in finding meaningful, well-paying employment (Bourgois, 2003). In turn, an inability to get a good job may cause people to turn to crime in order to survive. In this way, sociologists are able to account for higher levels of crime in poor, black, inner-city areas.

Other Race Relations

For many, the term "race relations" as it pertains to the United States often brings white–black relations to mind due to the centuries-old history the two groups share. There are many other racial and cultural groups to consider, however, due in part to the nation's ideological stance on immigration, which has ensured the near constant flux of the racial dynamic of the United States.

In the latter half of the nineteenth century, for example, Irish and Italian immigrants came to the east coast of the United States and were discriminated against and experienced prejudice. Also during this time period, large numbers of Asians immigrated to the West Coast of the United States. This group suffered even greater persecution over many decades from whites who had been in the country for several generations prior. This increased persecution was exacerbated by the tendency of Asian communities to isolate themselves in immigrant enclaves within urban areas. Within these enclaves, immigrants would maintain their own cultures, speak the language of their country of origin, and send money to family back in their country of origin. These enclaves allowed immigrant populations to resist assimilation with the greater Anglo-American culture. While such resistance allowed for a degree of comfort for the immigrants, it caused resident whites to fear the "otherness" of these people. This fear then fed the persecutory tendencies already in place and greatly hindered the acceptance of Asians by the majority of whites for several generations.

In twenty-first-century America, the majority of immigrants hail primarily from Latin America. Much controversy surrounds this group, primarily around the issues of language and illegal immigration. Many feel that this group of immigrants is unable to properly integrate with American society. The fear that newly immigrated Latin Americans may be taking American jobs is not new. Indeed, nearly every previous wave of immigration was accompanied by these same discriminatory apprehensions.

In the background of the American racial turmoil continues to be the plight of the American Indian who have suffered greatly at the hands of the US government and have been pushed from their ancestral lands and onto reservations that are plagued with poverty, alcoholism, and high teen suicide rates (Schaefer, 2006). While efforts in recent decades have been made to preserve and revive American Indian culture, they remain a group pushed to American society's periphery. However, in an effort to spotlight the Native American culture and its importance to the United States as a whole, US president Barack Obama in November 2012 proclaimed that month to be National Native American Heritage Month whereby he called on all US citizens to commemorate Native Americans with programs and activities that highlighted the culture's heritage and celebrated its people.

Race as a Social Construction

The construction of racial group identity by both the group and the dominant culture goes a long way to illustrate the social construction of race. From the sociological viewpoint, race, like other social categories, is socially constructed and heavily dependent on the time period and social setting in which such constructions occur. It is true that a significant component of what we call racial characteristics is based on physical appearance such as skin tone and facial features. However, these characteristics are not as concrete across a racial category as many may think. In the instance of skin tone, individuals who are categorized as black, both in the United States and across Africa, have a wide scope of pigmentation shades. This variance of skin tone of the "black" category is due in large part to the social construction of this category in the United States (Schaefer, 2006). Much debate among scholars of race has centered around various racial categories becoming more or less "white." The argument generally centers around how possible it is for a racial category to shift from the white to the black category or vice versa (Schaefer, 2006). Arab Americans, on the other hand, have been argued to have been forced out of association with the sociologically dominant or "white" category and closer to the sociological minority or "black" category due to racist suspicions surrounding fearful responses to Islamic-fundamentalist terrorism.

APPLICATIONS

The Police

Much controversy has surrounded US law enforcement on issues of race and ethnicity. Much of what police officers do focuses on the detection of lies. Unfortunately, the police often have very little to work with in solving a case other than suspicions and hunches (Rubinstein, 1973). This work can be made more complicated by hostile attitudes from civilian populations. Since the compliance of the population is critical to law enforcement, a hostile neighborhood can make an officer's job quite difficult. Therefore, a hostile neighborhood makes law enforcement difficult and in turn often makes police hostile toward the neighborhood (Rubinstein, 1973). If an officer harbors racist assumptions, even if the assumptions are subconscious and the officer is unaware of them, hunches that a case may be based on then have the potential to be racially motivated (Rubinstein, 1973). These racist assumptions are further complicated by the fact that individual police officers have a great deal of discretion when deciding to arrest the individuals they encounter (Rubinstein, 1973). It stands to reason, then, that a white police officer, for example, who is subconsciously racist may be more likely to arrest a black suspect than a white suspect because a hunch may or may not be based in the reality of the situation. The officer feels validated by society because the law allows the arrest to be made and validated by their profession, which often relies on hunches when following a case.

In certain jurisdictions, race relations between police and civilians are not limited to hunches and extend to a practice known as "racial profiling." Racial profiling is the process through which individuals of a particular race or ethnic group are targeted and singled out by law enforcement as part of routine patrols, checkpoints, and arrests. This practice has in the past been subtly sanctioned by the police department (Rubinstein, 1973). Examples of racial profiling could include police pulling over a car of young black males or searching people of Middle Eastern descent in an airport for no reason other than the fact that they are members of a particular race or ethnic group.

The US government requires by law that individuals over the age of fourteen who are not legal residents of the United States must register with the US government if they are in the country more than thirty days. Additionally, these individuals must have in their possession at all times registration documents. In April of 2010, the state of Arizona enacted SB 1070, which made it a misdemeanor crime for a nonresident of the United States to be in Arizona without carrying the required documents. The act also allowed officers to determine an individual's immigration status during a lawful stop or arrest (Archibold, 2010). The act, which was written primarily to address Arizona's influx of illegal immigrants, was the strictest and most controversial anti-illegal immigration legislation at the time and prompted debate worldwide regarding the potential for racial profiling. The Supreme Court upheld the requirement in 2012, and five other states (Alabama, Georgia, Indiana, Utah, and South Carolina) adopted similar legislation (Billeaud & Berry, 2012). In 2015, a US district court dismissed the seventh of seven challenges to SB 1070.

An act to deter racial profiling was passed in 2012 in the state of Connecticut. SB 364, "An Act Concerning Traffic Stop Information," forces local and state law enforcement to enact policies that disallow the search, detention, or stopping of any person based solely on their race, ethnicity, age, gender, or sexual orientation. Additionally, police are required to note in a report the racial makeup of every individual stopped or detained. The legislation was passed after an incident in East Haven, Connecticut, where police were accused of beating, harassing, and falsely arresting Latinos who threatened to report police misconduct.

Racial Profiling

In order to better understand the relationship between crime and race, Kowalski and Lundman

(2007) conducted a study that monitored vehicle stop search data and recorded citizen observational reporting of police traffic stops. The goal was to understand the phenomenon commonly known as "driving while black," which refers to the belief that African Americans are targeted and pulled over simply because of their race. Initial research seemed to indicate that African Americans were being pulled over in a disproportionate number of cases when compared to whites. Kowalski and Lundman then observed reports of police pulling cars over at night under the premise that race could not be as easily determined in darkness. The findings for this phase of the study showed that blacks continued to be pulled over with greater frequency when compared to whites. The evidence would point to some that blacks do indeed drive faster than whites, but upon reviewing the citations given to the accused, however, Kowalski and Lundman found an important trend in understanding this phenomenon: When comparing similar offenses across racial groups, such as comparing a white male individual driving 80 miles per hour to a black male going the same speed, the black individual tended to be given a harsher sanction than his white counterpart. Kowalski and Lundman theorized in their study that after the pullover had occurred, police tended to sanction African Americans with harsher penalties than they did other racial groups due to subconscious racism and a tendency to issue stronger sanctions (in this case, traffic tickets) to black individuals than to people of other racial groups. Kowalski and Lundman explained this phenomenon by theorizing that young black males are more likely to break traffic laws because of their discontent for a legal system that they feel to be unjust.

VIEWPOINTS

Controversies of Law Enforcement & Race

After discussing issues of race and crime in a sociological way, we are left with a number of troubling moral questions about our society. First, is our society fundamentally racist? There are governmental policies that clearly favor whites over blacks and other racial groups. While the objectives of these policies may not be intentionally racist, they are inadvertently so because they were created by whites without consulting other racial groups. If we live in a racist society, how valid is racial profiling? In such a society, racial profiling would merely serve as a mechanism through which the dominant group furthers the oppression of the subservient group. Furthermore, a disproportionate number of African Americans are in the prison system when compared to the greater society, and this disproportion becomes even greater when examining death row inmates (Schaeffer, 2006). According to the NAACP, as of 2016, almost six times more African Americans are imprisoned that whites. This suggests that society more severely punishes black men. If this is the case, it is not only a scathing indictment on capital punishment; it calls into question many elements of the criminal justice system.

TERMS & CONCEPTS

Anglo-American Culture: The dominant culture of the United States; a culture that stresses the attitudes and behaviors typical of those of European descent.

Cultural Capital: knowledge an individual possesses by virtue of being exposed to life experiences.

Ethnicity: The cultural characteristics that set a group of people apart from others.

Eurocentrism: The attitude that the peoples and cultures of European descent are superior to those people of other parts of the world.

Immigrant Enclaves: Small communities in which immigrants may isolate themselves so that they may maintain the cultures of their home country and speak their own language.

Minority: Any group of people that is treated differently because of characteristics that the individuals have little or no control over.

Race: A group of people defined by similar physical characteristics.

Racial Profiling: A practice through law enforcement treats members of a particular racial or ethnic groups with greater suspicion.

Social Construction of Race: The process through which racial categories are created by society.

Bibliography

Archibold, Randal C. (2010, April 23). "Arizona enacts stringent law on immigration." *New York Times.* http://www.nytimes.com/2010/04/24/us/politics/24immig.html

Armaline, W. T., Vera Sanchez, C. G., & Correia, M. (2014). "'The biggest gang in Oakland': Rethinking police legitimacy." *Contemporary Justice Review, 17,* 375–399.

Billeaud, J., & Berry, W. (2012, September 5). "Judge OKs Arizona's show-me-your-papers law." *NBC News.* http://www.nbcnews.com/id/48920114/#.UoPUvHCsiSo

Bourgois, P. (2003). *In search of respect: Selling crack in El Barrio.* New York, NY: Cambridge University Press.

Brooms, D. R., & Perry, A. R. (2016). "It's Simply Because We're Black Men." *Journal of Men's Studies, 24*(2), 166-184.

Chan, J. (2011). "Racial profiling and police subculture." *Canadian Journal of Criminology & Criminal Justice, 53,* 75–78.

Chaney, C., & Robertson, R. V. (2014). "'Can we all get along?' Blacks' historical and contemporary (in) justice with law enforcement. ' *Western Journal of Black Studies, 38,* 108–122.

Franklin, T. W. (2015). "Race and ethnicity effects in federal sentencing: A propensity score analysis." *JQ: Justice Quarterly, 32*(4), 653–679.

Hackney, A. A., & Glaser, J. (2013). "Reverse deterrence in racial profiling: Increased transgressions by nonprofiled whites." *Law & Human Behavior (American Psychological Association), 37,* 348–353.

Higgins, G. E., & Gabbidon, S. L. (2012). "Exploring untested measures on public opinion on the use of racial profiling during traffic stops to identify criminals." *Journal of Ethnicity in Criminal Justice, 10,* 71–85.

Jordan, K. L., & Freiburger, T. L. (2015). "The effect of race/ethnicity on sentencing: Examining sentence type, jail length, and prison length." *Journal of Ethnicity in Criminal Justice, 13*(3), 179–196.

Kowalski, B. & Lundman, R. (2007). "Vehicle stops by police for driving while black: Common problems and some tentative solutions." *Journal of Criminal Justice, 35,* 165–181.

Lundman, R. J. (2004). "Driver race, ethnicity, and gender and citizen reports of vehicle searches by police and vehicle search hits: Toward a triangulated scholarly understanding." *The Journal of Criminal Law and Criminology, 94,* 309–350.

MacDonald, M. (2000). *All souls: A family story from southie.* New York: Ballantine Books.

Rubinstein, J. (1973). *City police.* New York: The Noonday Press.

Schaefer, R. (2006). *Racial and ethnic groups.* 10th ed. Upper Saddle River, NJ: Prentice Hall.

Wilson, W. J. (1978). *The declining significance of race: Blacks and changing American Institutions.* 2nd ed. Chicago: University of Chicago Press.

Zinn, H. (2003). *A people's history of the United States: 1492 to present.* New York: Harpercollins.

Suggested Reading

Barkan, S. E. (2001). *Criminology: A sociological understanding.* 2nd ed. New Jersey: Prentice Hall.

Crank, J. P. (2011). "Scholarly debate on racial profiling: To what end?" *Canadian Journal of Criminology & Criminal Justice, 53,* 79–85.

Gabbidon, S. L., & Higgins, G. E. (2011). "Public opinion on the use of consumer racial profiling to identify shoplifters: An exploratory study." *Criminal Justice Review (Sage Publications), 36,* 201–212.

Hanser, R. D., & Gomila, M. (2015). *Multiculturalism and the criminal justice system.* Boston: Pearson.

Ibe, P., Ochie, C., & Obiyan, E. (2012). "Racial misuse of 'criminal profiling' by law enforcement: Intentions and Implications." *African Journal of Criminology & Justice Studies, 6* (1/2), 177–196.

Purpura, P. (2001). *Police and community.* Boston: Allyn and Bacon.

Rothenberg, P. (2002). *White privilege: Essential readings on the other side of racism.* New York: Worth Publishers.

Smith, B. W., & Holmes, M. D. (2014). "Police use of excessive force in minority communities: A test of the minority threat, place, and community accountability hypotheses." *Social Problems, 61,* 83–104.

Whitehead, S. N. (2015). "The specter of racism: exploring White racial anxieties in the context of policing." *Contemporary Justice Review, 18*(2), 121-138.

Jeremy Baker, M.A.

Rational Choice Theory

ABSTRACT

Rational choice theory is an economic model of human decision making which assumes that people are motivated by their own self-interests and, through a process of weighing costs and benefits, work to maximize their gain. While economists would view this gain in monetary and market exchange terms, rational choice theorists might include less tangible outcomes like enhanced reputation, time saved, peer approval, and other possible desirable outcomes. In criminology, rational choice theory is used to understand when crime is profitable and how to decrease criminal action by making its risks too high. Theoretically speaking, if the difficulty in achieving a criminal objective is increased along with the risk of being caught and punished, the criminal will seek out some other means of obtaining money or reward—maybe even a legal one.

OVERVIEW

Rational-Choice Theory in Economics

Rational-choice theory developed in the discipline of economics, where it remains the foundational premise for understanding individual human decision making. In the late 1700s, Jeremy Bentham, an English economist, argued that human beings are highly individualistic and surprisingly lazy when it comes to meeting their everyday needs. Given this desire not to work too hard, human beings are usually intent upon maximizing their utility, that is, producing the greatest amount of happiness with the least amount of suffering. According to this theory, two mechanisms govern human behavior: the desire for pleasure and the fear of pain. In order to make optimal utilization decisions, then, the individual must be a reasoning actor who weighs the costs and benefits of particular actions before acting in a manner that achieves the best possible outcome with the least likelihood of pain or failure. Since individuals cannot achieve all of the things they desire, they must choose to pursue specific goals and determine the best way to reach those goals. On the surface, the process by which an individual makes a decision and acts on it may seem like a rational process subject to scientific measurement and analysis. For economists and social scientists eager to have a model to understand human decision-making processes, this basic principle has served a profound purpose. However, in practice, individuals can act with misinformation, disregard obvious failings and flaws in their plans, or act with emotion and haste.

Rational-Choice Theory in Sociology

The application of rational choice in sociology is more formal and tries to statistically quantify human behavior. It argues that people's preferences can be evaluated and prioritized in relation to other options and that individuals seek to maximize the utility of these preferences, though they are subject to various constraints. Each choice is given a numerical value as a possible outcome. In order to maximize utility, for example, a robber will wish to rob the most lucrative business on Main Street. Preference A is the bank that is known to have the most cash on hand. Preference B is the less desirable liquor store. Preference C is the least desirable local coin laundry. Mathematically speaking, because the compelling goal of human behavior is to maximize utility, there is no rational reason for the robber to choose preference C over preference A. Because this is so, the rational-choice model has explanatory and predictive value in understanding the human decision-making processes. If preference C is chosen over preferences A and B, the model takes this into account by arguing that specific constraints affected the actor, such as time, money, access to special equipment, the need for co-conspirators, or the likelihood of getting caught. When these circumstances are taken into consideration, it is possible for preference C to become the rational choice for a robbery.

This idea of special circumstances affecting the outcome of an actor's decision is important, since the economist Adam Smith, Bentham's Scottish contemporary, argued that value is intrinsic or innate to a given object; gold, for example, would always be more valuable than water, he claimed. Bentham and others disagreed, arguing that the value of an object could vary according to circumstances. To a man dying of thirst, for example, a drink of water would have greater value than gold. Rational-choice theorists, then, try to given statistical values to an individual's preferences for predictive purposes. Not surprisingly, since it is premised on the idea that people are motivated by making money and maximizing their financial gain in a deliberative manner, economists can use this model to optimize their own market-driven goals and objectives. By determining the factors that cause a consumer to purchase one car over another, car manufacturers and marketing executives can retool their products or merely modify their advertising to move their car higher up in consumers' preferential priorities. The value of any theoretical framework that could discern human thought processes in decision making, delineate them in detail, predict outcomes, and account for special circumstances that might make this rational process seem irrational is, and has been, incalculable. In essence, rational-choice theory denies the existence of any action that is not rational, deliberate, calculated, and motivated by the pleasure of gain or the fear of pain. Altruism, morality, trust, social connections, social identity, past history, and human goodness have no place in the model unless they enter the equation in a practical, measurable manner.

Methodological Individualism

Since rational-choice theory is based on the decision-making processes of the individual, it stems from the theory of methodological individualism, which believes that "the elementary unit of social life is the individual human action. To explain social institutions and social change is to show how they arise as the result of the action and interaction of individuals" (Elster, 1989, p. 13). One flaw in this logic is the attribution of social phenomena to discrete, individual actions committed by individuals who supposedly have no social identity. Similarly, many would argue that the theory is flawed in its assumption that individual behavioral studies can predict aggregate social phenomena. Complicated theories of "social structures, collective decisions, collective behavior, and systems of cultural ideas" are thus made dependent on self-interested individuals (Turner, 2006, p. 497). Through the lens of rational-choice theory, war, peace, environmentalism, and all other social phenomena become solely utilitarian. Additionally, others have noted that once the social system emerges, it redistributes resources and places restraints on individuals' seemingly rational choices and actions. The relationship between the individual and the collective whole described by rational-choice theory is completely disrupted. Nevertheless, rational-choice theory has played a significant role in the social sciences since the late 1960s. As noted below, rational-choice theory has provided criminologists with several mechanisms for predicting crime and devising methods of crime prevention. The model is extremely useful and powerful, and its predictions are frequently accurate.

APPLICATIONS

Control Theory

Rational-choice theory has a foundational presence in classical criminological control theory, which assumes that people will always act in their own self-interest. According to Rock's (2002) explanation of control theory's underpinnings, "people ... seek to commit crime because it is profitable, useful, or enjoyable for them to do so, and ... they will almost certainly break the law if they can" (Rock, p. 56). One major problem with rational-choice theory is its central assumption that self-interest or egoism is the driving force of human behavior. No understanding of the role of altruism is possible within this framework. However, rather than discussing theory, control theorists are much more interested in creating practical policy interventions by analyzing the specific factors that deter people from committing crimes. Travis Hirschi (1969), for example, reframed the debate of criminal conduct by shifting the focus away from why people commit crimes to why they do not. Thus, deterrence and deterrence theory also are aspects of rational-choice theory.

Ron Clarke & Crime Reduction

Some of the most practical considerations of fluctuating crime rates have come out of Ron Clarke's (1992) work. As a situational control theorist, Clarke focused on the circumstantial dynamics of a given setting in order to predict criminal activity. He argued that three main factors affect criminal outcomes. The first is the effort needed to commit a given crime. Making a crime more difficult to commit and forcing a criminal to put forth more effort to commit it, Clarke thought, would dissuade the criminal actor. Several techniques could be used to increase the difficulty of committing a crime:

- Target hardening, which involves making sure that the object or person being targeted is better protected. For example, encasing a toy in a large, hard plastic package that is difficult to open would make it more difficult for a thief smuggle the toy out of the store.

- Access control, which entails impeding a criminal's access to a target through fencing, concrete barricades, or other physical objects of deterrence.
- Deflecting offenders, which involves providing other outlets for an undesirable behavior. A building that generally prohibits smoking, for instance, could allow smoking in designated areas.
- Controlling factors, which includes methods of prohibiting or limiting access to undesirable items. Gun control regulations, for example, could be used to prevent violent gun crimes, and a prohibition on minors purchasing spray paint could be used to deter graffiti.

Clarke's second tactic for crime reduction involves increasing the risk of being caught. Mechanisms in this category include screening individuals at national borders, using metal detectors at school entrances, and implementing various forms of surveillance: formal surveillance by police and guards, informal surveillance by employees trained to be alert to crime, and "natural surveillance," such as cutting hedges, installing closed-circuit cameras, and enhancing lighting around the target.

Clarke's third tactic for crime reduction is to make crime less profitable for criminals. Techniques for achieving this include:

- Target removal, which makes the target less accessible to the criminal. Rather than keeping all its cash on hand, for example, a liquor store might, throughout the day, place large sums of cash in a safe that cannot be unlocked by an attendant.
- Property identification, which is the process of making a stolen object identifiable so that it can be returned to its owner, such as by etching serial numbers on it.
- Removing inducements, which involves eliminating factors that might attract crime. Quickly removing graffiti, for instance, can frustrate the satisfaction of the perpetrator and cause future vandals to look elsewhere. Similarly, quickly repairing broken windows can also deter vandals.
- Rule setting, which entails articulating expected behaviors and the consequences of illegal action. Income tax returns and custom declarations, for example, outline the laws governing these forms as well as how violations of these laws are punished.

Routine-Activities Theory

Another offshoot of rational-choice theory is routine-activities theory. This, too, is an environmental criminal theory, rather than one that focuses on the nature of the individual. Routine-activities theory holds that in order for a crime to occur, three elements must be present:

- A suitable target (person, place, or thing).
- A lack of suitable guardians, such as owners, law enforcement personnel, neighbors, or security cameras. Some of these guardians are intentional, like law enforcement; others, such as neighbors, are more informal.
- A motivated offender.

As Rock (2002) described the theory, "crime was taken to be embedded in the very architecture of everyday life" (p. 61). Out of this theoretical framework came the crime triangle, also called the problem analysis triangle (PAT). The crime itself is the center of the triangle; the three sides are labeled "offender," "target/ victim," and "place." Superimposed over this is another triangle that names interventions.

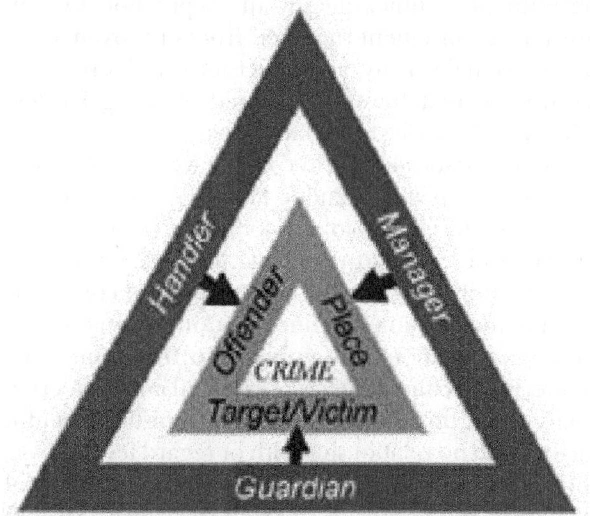

(taken from Center for Problem-Oriented Policing, 2008)

Figure 1: The Problem Analysis Triangle

"Manager" is over "place," "guardian" is over "target/victim," and "handler" is over "offender." This framework is used to describe both the elements necessary to create criminal situations and those necessary to prevent and respond to criminal situations.

While routine-activity theory is useful in crime prevention and deterrence analysis, many criminologists and sociologists fault it for failing to look at the social causes of crime.

VIEWPOINTS

In the past, rational-choice theory has been criticized for its lack of measurable, empirical analysis to prove its efficacy. Through game theory and experimental economics, however, extensive documentation now demonstrates its usefulness as a tool to analyze and predict human behavior. It continues to receive criticism within the social sciences, however, because of the difficulty of mathematically quantifying and analyzing human behavior in real-life settings.

Not all social-control theorists explain criminal conduct in situational terms. Hirschi (1969), for example, argued that "delinquent acts result when the individual's bond to society is weak or broken" (p. 16). Four aspects of social relationships caused the individual to obey the law, according to Hirschi. "Attachment reflected a person's sensitivity to the opinions of others; commitment flowed from an investment of time, energy, and reputation in conformity; involvement stemmed from engrossment in conventional activity; and belief mirrored a person's conviction that he or she should obey legal rules" (Rock, p. 57). Given that all four of these factors involve strong social links, in contrast to rational-choice theory, it is possible under Hirschi's theory for an individual to choose to not commit a crime, even if it would be easy and rewarding. Later in his career, Hirschi (1990) looked to lack of impulse control as a basis for criminal conduct. Lacking the ability to delay gratification and attracted to the immediate, powerful, exciting realities of criminal conduct, criminals under this analysis were opportunistic, deceitful actors with no relationship with or regard for their victims. By focusing on forms of control over individual behavior as they relate to criminal activity, Hirschi and similar theorists ignored numerous traditional criminological questions relating to class, ethnicity, gender, environment, personality, and social systems.

Deterrence Theory

Given that rational-choice theorists believe pleasure and pain govern individual behavior, it is not surprising that their perspectives on crime control include these two dimensions in what is known as deterrence theory. This theoretical perspective argues that the threat of punishment or the promise of a reward should motivate individuals to modify their behavior just as much as actual punishments or rewards. In order for these threats to be effective, however, there has to be a strong likelihood of being caught, along with severe and swift punishment. Otherwise, the deterrent would be too weak to modify action. In the public-policy realm, deterrence theory has led to "use a gun, go to jail" laws and other mandatory sentencing requirements. It has also led to the public posting of criminal consequences, such as signs in stores stating that shoplifters will be prosecuted and radio announcements informing the public that drunk-driving crackdowns will occur during certain holidays. The assumption of deterrence theory in these instances is that, because of the threat of being caught, for every person arrested and swiftly prosecuted, dozens of others will have been deterred from committing the crime in the first place.

Under deterrence theory, it follows that jurisdictions that have enacted the death penalty should see lower homicide rates than those that have not, since the threat of punishment by death should be the ultimate deterrent. However, Tittle (1995) found that this is not the case. A study reported on by Bonner and Fessenden (2000) showed that when US states enact the death penalty, their homicides rates increase. Many researchers have concluded that the death penalty has a brutalization effect on individuals, causing them to devalue human life (King, 1978). Additionally, those who commit murder may go on to eliminate witnesses in an effort to avoid capital punishment. Bonner and Fessenden (2000) also mention the disproportionate representation of African American men on death row and its implications of racism.

If aspects of deterrence theory sound like B. F. Skinner's work on animal behavior from the 1940s, the similarity is intentional. Skinner's theories on conditioning behavior—reinforcing certain behaviors through rewards and punishments—mirrored Bentham's economic beliefs from the 1700s. In one of his experiments, Skinner used a system of rewards to train pigeons to play a version of ping-pong. Homans (1961) and other proponents of rational-choice theory believed that conditioning mechanisms could be applied to humans as well as pigeons, even if the natures of the rewards were more diverse for people. Respect, freedom, money, approval, and material objects might all be used to motivate humans, but the process of motivation itself was the same as it was with the pigeons. The strength of the reinforcement is not as easy to quantify, but its utility, or value to the individual, remains central to the analysis. Homans also argued that if individuals are not engaging in a profitable exchange, they might withdraw from an interaction or refuse to engage in subsequent interactions. This observation brought in the concept of mutual profitability, which states that a social interaction can only be sustained if all participants find it profitable. Thus, in addition to competition and exploitation, the concept of cooperation is prevalent in rational-choice theory.

Social-Exchange Theory & Game Theory

Thus far, we have focused on the individual in this discussion of rational-choice theory. Exchange theory is similar to rational-choice theory, but instead of focusing purely on the individual, it also considers the individual or entities with which the individual interacts. It is economic exchange when goods or services are being negotiated. It is social exchange when other intangible, yet valued, behaviors are negotiated, such as respect, antipathy, tolerance, love, or approval. In both instances, the reward or desired outcome can have both monetary and non-monetary value. Negotiating for peace, for example, can reduce monetary expenditures on war and also provide a more stable and safe living environment for citizens. Self-interest governed by pain and pleasure remains the motivating force, but now concepts of cooperation, competition, and exploitation enter the discussion. The players act with strategic intent to achieve their goals under uncertain conditions by exerting their perceived optimal choices. These same principles apply in game theory, which is another dimension of rational-choice theory. The cast of characters in game theory can include two individuals, two corporations, two countries, or any other number of players.

It is important to remember that social-exchange theory and game theory can make some rather unrealistic assumptions. The first assumption is that actors have all of the information necessary to make a rational choice regarding their self-interests. Second, the theories assume that every actor has the mental and psychological ability to effectively weigh each choice against the others. Third, the actor is assumed to be aware of every possible choice that pertains to the exchange or interaction and how it relates to the actor's self-interest. Certainly, theorists do not actually assume all of the above, but they rely on these assumptions as if they were true in every analysis as a means of predicting behavior. Of course, one consistent outcome has been that people and entities act in ways that deviate from their best self-interests, but that, too, is accounted for in the various models. When it was found that the death penalty does not serve as the ultimate deterrent of crime, theorists looked for reasons to explain this apparently nonrational outcome.

Free Riders

One issue constantly present in the development of rational-choice theory is the concept of the free rider. Free riders are individuals who exert little or no energy to realize their self-interests, relying instead on society for support. Later in his own life's work, Bentham worried that social welfare programs that provided handouts and assistance to the poor would appeal to the innate laziness of the human actor and deter the poor from seeking gainful employment. The reliance on public assistance as a rational choice for subsistence remains an ongoing debate in society centuries later.

CONCLUSION

Rational-choice theory is the dominant theoretical framework for the analysis of individual human behavior in the field of economics, and it has a strong following in the social sciences as well. It offers a simple, quantifiable evaluation of human behavior and, more importantly, offers significant predictive value. By understanding how people select their morning cereal, for example, manufacturers and marketing experts can modify their product or their advertising to augment sales. Criminologists can predict high-crime situations and deter such action through specific interventions or severe, effective punishments. On a larger, societal level, though, rational-choice theory arguably has severe limitations. Why people might join together to act collectively is difficult to explain within this theoretical structure, as are altruism, social norms, trust, and other related but intangible forces that have some place in individual motivation. How and why individuals might subvert their own self-interests for the collective good are enduring challenges to the rational-choice theoretical framework.

TERMS & CONCEPTS

Access Control: Intentionally making it difficult for a criminal to gain entry to or to approach places that are desirable for criminal purposes.

Deflecting Offenders: Forcing potential offenders to redirect their undesirable attention and actions into an alternative outlet.

Exploitation: The practice of taking selfish or unfair advantage of a person or situation, usually for personal gain.

Impulse Control: The ability to exert authority over one's sudden desires, urges, or inclinations.

Methodological Individualism: The belief that the elementary unit of social life is the individual human action, and criminological and sociological research should seek to explain social institutions and social change in relation to the individual human action.

Target Hardening: Providing better protection for a person or an object in order to deter crime.

Target Removal: Eliminating the object of criminal desire in order to reduce criminal behavior.

Bibliography

Bonner, R., & Fessenden, F. (2000, September 22). "Absence of executions: A special report: States with no death penalty share lower homicide rates." *New York Times.* http://www.nytimes.com/2000/09/22/us/absence-executions-special-report-states-with-no-death-penalty-share-lower.html

Clarke, R. (1992). *Situational crime prevention.* New York: Harrow & Heston.

Elster, J. (1989). *Nuts and bolts for the social sciences.* Cambridge: Cambridge University Press.

Gottfredson, M. & Hirschi, T. (1990). *A general* theory *of crime.* Stanford, CA: Stanford University Press.

Hirschi, T. (1969). *Causes of delinquency.* Berkeley, CA: University of California Press.

Homans, B. (1961). *Social behavior: Its elementary forms.* London: Routledge.

King, D. R. (1978). The brutalization effect: Execution publicity and the incidence of homicide in South Carolina. Social Forces, 57(2), 683-687. Retrieved November 7, 2013, from EBSCO Online Database SocINDEX with Full Text. http://search.ebscohost.com

Maimon, D., Antonaccio, O., & French, M. T. (2012). "Severe sanctions, easy choice? Investigating the role of school sanctions in preventing adolescent violent offending." *Criminology,* 50(2), 495-524.

Manzo, G. (2013). "Is rational choice theory still a rational choice of theory?" *A response to Opp. Social Science Information,* 52(3), 361-382.

Nagin, D. (1990). "Prisons and alternatives to incarceration" In D. Ebley, (Ed.). *Leading Pennsylvania into the 21st century.* PA: Commonwealth Foundation.

Rock, P., (2002). "Sociological theories of crime." In M. Maguire, M. Morgan, & R. Reiner (Eds.), *Oxford handbook of* criminology. (3rd ed., pp. 51-82). Oxford: Oxford University Press.

Scott, J. (2000). "Rational choice theory." In G. Browning, A. Halcli, & F. Webster (Eds.), *Understanding contemporary society:* Theories *of the present.* Thousand Oaks, CA: Sage.

Snook, B., Dhami, M., & Kavanagh, J. (2011). "Simply criminal: Predicting burglars' occupancy decisions with a simple heuristic." *Law & Human Behavior,* 35(4), 316-326.

Sutherland, E. (1947). *Principles of* criminology (4th ed.). Philadelphia, PA: Lippincott.

Tittle, C. (1995). *Control balance: Toward a general* theory *of deviance.* Boulder, CO: Westview Press.

Turner, J. (2006). "Rational choice theory." In B. Turner (Ed.), *The Cambridge dictionary of sociology.* London: Cambridge University Press.

Warren, M., & Hindelang, M. (1979). "Current explanations of offender behavior." In H. Toch (Ed.), *Psychology of crime and criminal justice.* (pp. 166-182). Prospect Heights, IL: Waveland Press.

Wilson, J. (1975). *Thinking about crime.* New York, NY: Basic.

Suggested Reading

Allingham, M. (2002). *Choice theory*: A very short introduction. Oxford: Oxford University Press.

Archer, M., & Tritter, J. (Eds.), (2001). *Rational choice theory*: Resisting colonization. London: Routledge.

Clarke, R., & Felson, M. (Eds.), (2004). *Routine activity and* rational choice*: Advances in criminological* theory—Volume 5. New Brunswick, NJ: Transaction Books.

Green, D., & Shapiro, I. (1996). *Pathologies of* rational choice theory*: A critique of applications in political science.* New Haven, CT: Yale University Press.

Hastie, R., Dawes, R. (2001). *Rational choice* in an uncertain world: The psychology of judgment and decision-making. Thousand Oaks, CA: Sage.

Lilly, J., Cullen, F., & Ball, R. (2007). *Criminology Theory*: Context and Consequences. (4th ed.). Thousand Oaks, CA: Sage.

Ritzer, G. (Ed.), (2007). *Classical sociological* theory. (5th ed.). New York, NY: McGraw-Hill.

Ritzer, G., & Goodman, D. (2007). *Sociological* theory. (6th ed.). New York, NY: McGraw-Hill.

Sato, Y. (2006). *Intentional social change: A* rational choice theory. Victoria, Australia: Trans Pacific.

Stinchcombe, A. (1987). *Constructing social* theories. Chicago, IL: University of Chicago Press.

Van Gelder, J. (2013). "Beyond rational choice: The hot/cool perspective of criminal decision making." *Psychology, Crime & Law,* 19(9), 745-763.

Karen Harbeck, Ph.D., J.D.

Rational Control Theory

ABSTRACT

Early studies on deviance largely ignored the intersections of deviance and gender in society. However, recent researchers have been able to better understand and define deviance by examining the points where deviance and gender converge. Although theories regarding social deviance have been generated for decades, it is only recently that theorists have begun to explore the intersections between deviance, crime and gender. This article describes the tenets of Control Balance Theory, Self Control Theory, Differential Association Theory (as described in Social Learning Theory), and Strain Theory and examines these theories using a gender specific lens.

OVERVIEW

By definition, deviance is any action or activity that differs from accepted social standards or what society deems to be normal (Webster's New World College Dictionary, 2001). Early studies on deviance largely ignored the intersections of deviance and gender in society. However, recent researchers have been able to better understand and define deviance by examining the points where deviance and gender converge.

Upon hearing the phrase "deviant behavior," most people immediately think of criminals. And when speaking of criminals, most people will envision males as the criminals. In fact, males are more often found to be involved in criminal behavior than females. For research purposes, criminality is often divided into various categories, such as violent crimes, substance-abuse crimes, and property crimes, all of which tend to be dominated by males (Baron, 2003). Yet a lot of non-criminal behaviors are also, by definition, deviant, while others were considered deviant in the past and are now considered to be acceptable behavior. Defiant behavior, rebellious behavior, causing harm to oneself, and acting outside of roles assigned by society are all considered to be deviant behavior. Due to its location in social attitudes and practices, the definition of deviance changes as society evolves. For example, women who chose to exert themselves in an effort to preserve their constitutional rights were considered to be social deviants from the inception of the United States until the early twentieth century (Kerber, 2000). As society changed and accepted women's claims to personal rights and freedoms, the definition of deviance slowly began to exclude these women.

Today what is considered to be deviant behavior continues to evolve. Consider how views of homosexuality have changed over the past decades. Once considered deviant behavior by the majority of people and the American Psychological Association (APA), it is now viewed as an innate trait and accepted by many people in society, and the APA has dropped it from its diagnostic manual (Cummings, 2006). The evolving nature of what is considered to be deviant makes deviance a bit difficult to understand from a sociological perspective. However, understanding deviance and its impacts on people within a society helps to inform how people deal with the roles imposed on them by society and how society works to maintain these social roles. Hence, many theories of deviance have been developed, and many researchers have examined the differences in perceived deviance in males and females. Some of the more prevalent theories here discussed are control balance theory, self-control theory, differential association theory, and strain theory,

APPLICATIONS

Control Balance Theory

This theory, devised by Charles Tittle (1995), claims that the types of deviance in which one engages are based on a control ratio (i.e., the amount of control that one is under versus the amount of control one commands). Control is placed along a gradient line, with too little control (i.e., a control deficit) to the left of center and too much control (i.e., a control surplus) to the right. It is only when achieving a balance in the center of this gradient that a person will be motivated to conform to social conventions. Tittle hypothesized that when deviance is examined along lines of gender, most females will be subjected to constraints in their ability to exercise control and will most likely violate social conventions via predation or defiance. Conversely, males will more often experience an excess of control and will most likely violate social conventions via predation or exploitation (Tittle, 1995; Hickman & Piquero, 2001). In other words, because women are relegated to social positions in which they are forced into a role of submission relative to males, they are more likely to violate social conventions by defying the structures that control them or by manipulating the structures to get what they want. Men, who are located in social positions that largely afford them control or dominance, are more likely to manipulate the social structure or engage in the outright exploitation of others to get what they want. Figure 1, below, illustrates this hypothesis.

Control balance theorists believe deviance will occur when all three of the following factors are present:

- The person is motivated toward deviance by virtue of temperament or situational circumstances,
- Constraint (i.e., the risk of being caught or punished) is perceived as low, and
- Opportunity is present.

If one of these factors is absent, the deviance is less likely to occur. This theory clearly reveals the convergence of deviance and gender by taking into account the differences in how females and males are socialized in society. Females are generally socialized to care for others, consider the needs of the group as opposed to the individual, and provide support and maintenance for the social group. Males are generally socialized to occupy a position of dominance and privilege in which competition and acquisition of material goods are valued. Though this position provides greater motivation for males to conform, thus maintaining the status quo, it also moves them to commit acts of deviance that are more often categorized as criminal activity within the society (Beutel & Marini, 1995).

Self-Control Theory

This theory purports to have identified one of the major causes of deviant behavior. Gottfredson and Hirschi (1990) hypothesize that the amount of self-control one has is predictive of how likely one will engage in socially deviant behavior (Gottfredson & Hirschi, 1990). They suggest that people who are "insensitive, physical (as opposed to mental), risk-taking, shortsighted, and nonverbal" (Gottfredson & Hirschi, 1990, p. 90) will have less self-control than other people in the general population. Intuitively, this makes sense. A person with low self-control would seem more likely to break a law or engage in behavior that is exciting or gratifying without a thought of future consequences.

Self-control theorists suggest that propensity for self-control is established during childhood, is correlated to the quality of child rearing practiced by parents, and is unlikely to change much during one's lifetime. They also claim that parents must exert strong influence over a child's level of self-control by setting and adhering to strict behavioral expectations until the child is eight years old (Unnever, Cullen, & Pratt, 2003). An adult with low levels of self-control will have difficulty refraining from temptations that arise when working to create long-term personal or working relationships within a societal structure. People with low self-control will not have the fortitude to pass up opportunities to cheat on spouses, lie for personal gain, steal from work, or execute other breaches of the social contract.

This theory has been challenged and tested several times in the past decades and remains a valid predictor of social deviance (Pratt & Cullen, 2000; Grasmick, Tittle, Bursik, & Arneklev, 1993; Hay, 2001). A few studies have indicated gender to be a significant, indirect factor correlated with criminal and delinquent behavior (Unnever, Cullen, & Pratt, 2003; Tittle, Ward, & Grasmick, 2003). It is suggested that parents are more attentive and controlling of their daughters' behaviors due to their more vulnerable position in society, supporting the finding that females are involved in fewer criminal offenses while manifesting similar levels of self-control as boys (Tittle, Ward, & Grasmick, 2003; Gibbs, Giever, & Martin, 1998; LaGrange & Silverman, 1999). Notably, these studies focused more on criminal behaviors than other types of socially deviant behaviors (e.g., smoking, eating disorders, alternative lifestyles, etc.). It has been noted in the literature that people reporting low self-control tend to form friendship groups with similar people, with whom they tend to engage in deviant behaviors as a group (Gottfredson & Hirschi, 1990). This observation led to the development of the differential association theory, which argues that deviance is a product of socialization (i.e., social learning) and group association.

Differential Association Theory

Older people always have a saying that helps describe what they have learned from life experience, such as "Birds of a feather flock together," meaning people who are similar will hang out with each other. That is the gist of the differential association theory, except in reverse: according to the theory, people tend to adopt the behaviors of the group, rather than deviant people seeking out groups who are deviant. This is more a case of peer influence than one of peer pressure. People who hang out with each other will come to adopt the attitudes and behaviors of those with whom they associate; social deviance is learned from direct and indirect association with one's friends (Akers & Lee, 1996; Sutherland, 1940). In other words, one will adopt the deviant attitudes and behaviors displayed by the majority of one's friends, and this adoption will usually begin with forms of mild experimentation that are rewarded and encouraged by the peer group. Once mild forms of deviance have been noticed by other groups, those groups will come to exclude the person exhibiting the deviance from further membership, leaving that person largely associating with the original group.

Unfortunately, the "learning" referred to in social learning theories, of which differential association is one, often means that the person is being excluded from groups who find the deviant behavior unacceptable. Instead of learning more socially accepted behaviors, the deviant person will be forced to seek out peers who manifest similar behaviors (Akers & Lee, 1996). People will seek out friendship groups whose members generally agree on what is deemed to be fun, acceptable behavior. Good students will join clubs that honor and value good students, while religious students seek out groups that study and value religion. Adventure seekers will locate themselves in a group of friends who skateboard, snowboard, and surf, while emo kids will hang out and listen to their own brand of alternative music while discussing who is into cutting.

Once a person has found a group based on certain interests and proclivities, the group will help socialize that person to the attitudes, beliefs, and behaviors its members believe to be normal or comfortable while providing opportunities to experiment with and refine their participation in those behaviors. It is in this way that a person with tendencies toward deviant behaviors will become involved in a group with similar interests and attributes and will come to adopt the attitude of the group majority. A deviant peer group is likely to encourage similar deviant and criminal behaviors within the group while seeking opportunities to exhibit those behaviors (Evans, Cullen, Burton, Dunaway, & Benson, 1997).

Males tend to gravitate toward the development of large groups that are governed by physical and competitive interactions. Females tend to interact in smaller groups that are organized around cooperation and relationship maintenance. This difference in associative preference tends to provide more opportunity and support for deviant and criminal behavior in males (Broidy & Agnew, 1997). Additionally, females are more likely to adopt the deviant behaviors of their love interests than are males. Some critics of this theory disagree that people with similar attributes and interests will find each other and form a self-supporting social group. They suggest that the groups are actually imposed on people via the social barriers in place within the society. These opponents call this competing theory the strain theory.

Strain Theory: Classic & General
Based on Emile Durkheim's "anomie" and developed by Robert Merton, classic strain theory predicts that people who have high long-term aspirations coupled with low long-term economic expectations will be most likely to engage in criminal and deviant behavior as they attempt to beat the odds society has imposed on them (Merton, 1938). These theorists believe that much of crime and social deviance is directly or indirectly related to social class, more specifically the strain of being a member of a lower social class. However, this theory was not easily validated because many of the people included in strain studies were not manifesting deviant or criminal behaviors and women were dismissively regarded as being insulated against the effects of strain due to their positioning in the social structure (Broidy & Agnew, 1997).

Subsequent theorists realized that strain cannot be simply measured by absolute deprivation (i.e., level of poverty) but must also be examined from the perspective of the person's perception of the gap between expectations and reality and his or her reactions to strain. Studies began to suggest that strain did indeed contribute to criminal and deviant behavior (Pratt & Cullen, 2000). Agnew (2001) revised classic strain theory to create general strain theory, extending the theory to allow researchers to further explore the factors that influence how a person reacts to strain. These new factors add the loss of positive stimuli (jobs, friends, romantic partners, etc.) and the acquisition of negative stimuli (excessive demands, stress, all types of abuse, etc.) to the original strain of failing to achieve aspirations and goals (Broidy & Agnew, 1997).

Once the theory was extended, researchers were better able to identify and measure strain unique to females, such as abortion, sexual abuse, unjust treatment based on gender, burdens associated with private-realm responsibilities, et cetera, and to examine both objective and subjective levels of strain. Evidence suggests that females are subjected to as much or more strain than males, negating the assertion that the level of strain correlates positively with commission of crimes. Related research suggests that the differences between how males and females experience the world will predict whether strain will correlate with deviant/criminal behaviors. Men are more focused on fairness in outcomes, while females are more focused on fairness in the process that results in the outcome (Broidy & Agnew, 1997). Recent research in general strain theory suggests that it is one's emotional response to strain that is the true predictor of criminal behavior.

Anger is the driving emotion that leads to crime; anger lowers inhibitions, moves a person toward action, and increases individual energy (Broidy & Agnew, 1997; Sharp, Brewster, & Love, 2005). Anger is acknowledged to be both situational and trait-based. While situational anger is a robust predictor of shoplifting and assault, trait-based anger only predicts assault. Researchers assert that all people experience similar levels of anger. However, differences between how females and males are socialized account for their different responses to anger (Sharp, Brewster, & Love, 2005). Given this assumption, it follows that criminal acts are more prevalent in males due to their learned responses to strain: they have been taught that it is okay to be angry. Females are taught that their anger is less appropriate, and less effective, than men's. They tend to turn their anger inward, resulting in depression or guilt, thus reducing non-criminal activities but resulting in more covert types of deviant behavior, such as eating disorders, drug abuse, and ignoring or reframing problems (Sharp, Brewster, & Love, 2005; Broidy & Agnew, 1997).

VIEWPOINTS

In 1969, a well-respected psychologist, Lawrence Kohlberg, was deeply involved in research that described moral development. His research suggested that personal morality involves a complex mix of how stringently a person is willing to follow societal conventions and how willing that person is to defy those conventions when faced with a situation in which one must choose between upholding conventions or upholding a personal respect for human life and welfare.

Kohlberg's research outcomes suggested that adult females remained morally immature throughout their lives; based on his operationalized definition of morality, only men tended to reach the pinnacle of morality. His lab assistant, Carol Gilligan, criticized his work heavily, noting that based on their place of relative oppression within American society, women were not morally deficit. Indeed, these women developed a morality that was firmly grounded in care for the ongoing needs of society (i.e., sacrificing the good of the individual in favor of society), which differed from Kohlberg's biased analysis. Kohlberg believed the pinnacle of moral behavior was reached when a person was able to value the needs of the individual over the general benefit of society (Gilligan, 1982).

In this debate lies the seed of how females and males may be socialized in ways that differ, creating differing levels of potential deviance. It is also an important example of how personal perspective can introduce bias into research and theories. Studies on deviance and crime often have biases based on gender, race, socioeconomic status, and class. Crime, for instance, is usually regarded as acts for which one is prosecuted and sent to jail. This definition precludes the examination of what is typically referred to as white-collar crime. In reality, crimes are committed by many people in the upper class, but these crimes are prosecuted in civil courts or are handled by administrative boards or commissions (Sutherland, 1940). However, these activities are still crimes and should be carefully considered as such when one is determining whether a theory can be generalized to all types of deviant behavior.

TERMS & CONCEPTS

Control Ratio: The amount of power one has to limit other people's realization of their goals or to escape external limitations of one's own goals versus the extent to which one is subject to real and potential goal limitations by others (Hickman & Piquero, 2001).

Defiance: Deviant acts that reject societal norms in an effort to avoid the infliction of serious harms (e.g., political protest, vandalism, etc.) without providing apparent benefits to the actor (Hickman & Piquero, 2001).

Deviance: Any action or activity that differs from accepted social standards or what society deems to be normal (Webster's New World College Dictionary, 2001).

Exploitation: The act of using other people or organizations to coerce, manipulate, or extract property from others, creating personal benefit while disregarding the desires or well-being of the exploited (Hickman & Piquero, 2001).

Operationalize: To define abstract concepts in concrete ways so that they can be more easily measured.

Oppression: The empowering or privileging of one group at the expense of another.

Predation: Deviant acts that include direct physical violence, manipulation, or acquisition of property to provide apparent benefits to the actor. Predation includes harm against both self and others (Hickman & Piquero, 2001).

Social Convention: Behaviors and customs generally accepted by a society or conforming to a larger set of rules, whether written or unwritten.

Bibliography

Agnew, R. (1992). "Foundation for a general strain theory of crime and delinquency." *Criminology*, 30, 47-87.

Akers, R. L., & Lee, G. (1996). "A longitudinal test of social learning theory: Adolescent smoking." *Journal of Drug Issues,* 26(2).

Augustyn, M., & McGloin, J. (2013). "The risk of informal socializing with peers: Considering gender differences across predatory delinquency and substance use." *JQ: Justice Quarterly,* 30(1), 117-143.

Baron, S. W. (2003). "Self-control, social consequences, and criminal behavior: Street youth and the general theory of crime." *Journal of Research in Crime and Delinquency,* 40 (4), 403-425.

Beutel, A. M., & Marini, M. M. (1995). "Gender and values." *American Sociological Review,* 60 (3), 436-448.

Broidy, L., & Agnew, R. (1997). "Gender and crime: A general strain theory perspective." *Journal of Research in Crime and Delinquency,* 34(3), 275-306.

Carstens, L. (2011). "Unbecoming women: Sex reversal in the scientific discourse on female deviance in Britain, 1880-1920." *Journal of The History Of Sexuality,* 20(1), 62-94.

Cummings, N. A. (2006). *The APA and Psychology Need Reform.* APA Convention. New Orleans.

Evans, T. D., Cullen, F. T., Burton, V. S., Dunaway, G., & Benson, M. L. (1997). "The social consequences of self-control: Testing the general theory of crime." *Criminology,* 35 (3), 475-501.

Gibbs, J. J., Giever, D., & Martin, J. S. (1998). "Parental management and self-control: An empirical test of

Gottfredson and Hirschi's General Theory." *Journal of Research in Crime and Delinquency*, 35 (1), 40-70.

Gilligan, C. (1982). *In a different voice.* Cambridge, MA: Harvard University Press.

Gottfredson, M., & Hirschi, T. (1990). *A general theory of crime.* Stanford, CA: Stanford University Press.

Grasmick, H. C., Tittle, C. R., Bursik, R. J., & Arneklev, B. J. (1993). "Testing the core empirical implications of Gottfredson and Hirschi's general theory of crime." *Journal of Research in Crime and Delinquency,* 30 (1), 5-29.

Hay, C. (2001). "Parenting, self-control, and delinquency: a test of self control theory." *Criminology,* 39 (3), 707-736.

Hickman, M., & Piquero, A. (2001). "Exploring the relationships between gender, control balance, and deviance." *Deviant Behavior: An Interdisciplinary Journal,* 22 (4), 323-351.

Kerber, L. K. (2000). *No Constitutional right to be ladies* (2nd Edition ed.). New York, NY: Hill and Wang.

LaGrange, T. C., & Silverman, R. A. (1999). "Low self-control and opportunity: Testing the general theory of crime as an explanation for gender differences in delinquency." *Criminology,* 37 (1), 41-72.

Merton, R. (1938). "Social structure and anomie." *American Sociological Review,* 3 (5), 672-682.

Posick, C., Farrell, A., & Swatt, M. L. (2013). "Do boys fight and girls cut? A general strain theory approach to gender and deviance." *Deviant Behavior,* 34(9), 685-705.

Pratt, T. C., & Cullen, F. T. (2000). "The empirical status of Gottfredson and Hirschi's general theory of crime: A meta-analysis." *Criminology,* 38 (3), 931-964.

Sharp, S. F., Brewster, D., & Love, S. R. (2005). "Disentangling strain, personal attributes, affective response and deviance: A gendered analysis." *Deviant Behavior,* 26 (2), 133-157.

Sutherland, E. H. (1940). "White-collar criminality." *American Sociological Review,* 5 (1), 1-12.

Tittle, C. R. (1995). *Control balance: Toward a general theory of deviance.* Boulder, CO: Westview.

Tittle, C. R., Ward, D. A., & Grasmick, H. G. (2003). "Gender, age, and crime/deviance: A challenge to self-control theory." *Journal of Research in Crime and Delinquency,* 40 (4), 426-453.

Unnever, J. D., Cullen, F. T., & Pratt, T. C. (2003). "Parental management, ADHD, and delinquent involvement: Reassuring Gottfredson and Hirshci's General Theory." *Justice Quarterly,* 20 (3), 471-500.

Webster's New World College Dictionary (4th Edition ed.). (2001).

SUGGESTED READING

Alarid, L. F., Burton, V. S., & Cullen, F. T. (2000). "Gender and crime among felony offenders: Assessing the generality of social control and differential association theories." *Journal of Research in Crime and Delinquency,* 37 (2), 171-199.

Hagan, J. & Foster, H. (2003). "S/he's a rebel: Toward a sequential stress theory of delinquency and gendered pathways to disadvantage in emerging adulthood." *Social Forces,* 82(1), 53-86.

Young, R. L., & Thompson, C. Y. (2011). "Gender, attributions of responsibility, and negotiation of deviant labels in small groups." *Deviant Behavior,* 32(7), 626-652.

Sherry Thompson, Ph.D.

RE-ENTERING SOCIETY FROM PRISON

ABSTRACT

The United States has the highest rate of incarceration in the world, and the majority of incarcerated offenders will eventually be released back into society. While much attention has been paid to the dramatic increase in the incarceration rate since the mid-1970s, comparatively little attention has been paid to the corresponding increase in ex-prisoners who are rejoining society. The terms of a prisoner's release—whether release comes from exoneration, serving an entire sentence, or early conditional release through a parole board—have an impact on how an ex-prisoner reintegrates into society. Generally ex-prisoners face many problems, from disenfranchisement to difficulties finding employment and housing, to high recidivism rates and health problems.

OVERVIEW

The United States has one of the largest prison populations in the world (Reiman, 2004). From 1970 to 2008, the number of prisoners went from around 300,000 to around 2.5 million, which means that the United States has the highest imprisonment rate in the world. According to data from the International Centre for Prison Studies, approximately 716 per 100,000 people were incarcerated in the United States in 2012. Although these numbers had been decreasing slightly up to that point, the Bureau of Justice Statistics announced in 2013 that the total number of prisoners had climbed to 1,574,700, an increase of about 4,300 inmates (Carson, 2014); the official number declined somewhat to 1,561,500 at the end of 2014. A 2016 report from the Prison Policy Initiative noted that counting all forms of imprisonment—from local jails and juvenile correction centers to military prisons—the United States held over 2.3 million people incarcerated. There are many explanations for this high rate: the excessive rate of violent crime in the United States; the association of crime with stigmatized groups; increasingly harsh penalties for nonviolent crimes, especially drug crimes; and a focus on punishment rather than rehabilitation (Mauer and Coyle, 2004).

Still others have pointed to what activist Angela Davis dubbed the prison-industrial complex, the powerful political lobbying groups that promote the interests of the businesses involved in operating and supplying government prison agencies, by advocating for strict sentencing laws and other policies designed to increase the prison population and thereby prison revenues. Despite the attention paid to the increased number of prisoners, little public discussion exists about the inevitable result of this increase: there has also been an enormous increase in the number of former inmates who have re-entered society. Most prisoners will eventually re-enter society, a process that has changed substantially in the last few decades. The increase in the incarceration rate, decreases in funding for many social programs, a harsher societal attitude toward crime, and stricter legal penalties for reoffending have all made the experience of re-entry different and more difficult than in the past (Seiter & Kadela, 2003).

Felons are people who have been convicted of a felony, a crime that has been characterized by the state as serious in nature and warrants a prison term over one year. Classification of crimes as misdemeanors or felonies differs from state to state. Minorities are charged with felonies at a higher rate than whites (Walker, Spohn and DeLone, 2004). Minorities are more likely to be arrested, more likely to be convicted, and more likely to receive stiffer sentences for the same crimes as their white counterparts. This results from both racial profiling and also from legislation that is written in such a way as to disproportionately affect minority groups (Mauer, 2007). Social attitudes toward race create yet another obstacle to reintegration into society after prison. In addition to barriers based on pre-existing racial and ethnic divisions, there are also barriers to obtaining adequate housing and well-paying jobs created by one's felony status (Liker, 1982; Copenhaver, Edwards-Willey, & Byers, 2007).

Many felons are released back into the communities in which they previously lived. Some ex-offenders are monitored by the Board of Parole, or by halfway houses that offer social services and provide some education, job training, and reintegration programs to help ex-felons learn the social and work skills necessary to stay out of prison. In some cases, halfway houses function as a step toward addiction management, and in other cases they provide low-cost living for those who have no other options. Unfortunately, many ex-felons are returned to a life of poverty, which increases the risk of re-offending (Berk, Lenihan, & Rossi, 1980).

Exoneration

According to the Innocence Project, more than three hundred people have had their convictions overturned through the use of DNA testing since 1989. Evidence gathered by the *New York Times* on ex-prisoners who were exonerated by DNA evidence, while not generalizable, suggests that exonerees face a unique set of problems upon release. There are not generally organized transition or support programs for those who have been declared innocent. Additionally, many exonerees convicted by states are not awarded compensation by the state for their time wrongly served, although there is now federal legislation that guarantees compensation for anyone exonerated of a federal conviction (Roberts & Stanton, 2007).

Transitional Programs

Programs that aid re-entry to society can begin in prisons themselves and carry over into the outside community, or they can focus only on the post-release transition. Most prisons have some sort of release curriculum, although these can range from brief interviews or orientations to more tailored programs dealing with employment, drug use, health issues, and life skills. Vocational training programs, work release, halfway houses, and drug treatment programs reduce recidivism. Educational programs and programs aimed at ex-offenders have more mixed results (Seiter & Kadela, 2003).

Recidivism

The Bureau of Justice Statistics has operationalized recidivism as "rearrest, reconviction, resentence to prison, and return to prison with or without a new sentence" (Langan & Levin, 2002, p. 1). As Maltz (2001) argues, the definition and measurement of recidivism has serious implications. Older measures captured rearrest rates within a year of a prisoner's release, which overestimated the effectiveness of the corrections system's goals of protection and rehabilitation.

In a study of prisoners released in 1994, Langan and Levin (2002) found that within three years, 67.5 percent had been rearrested, and slightly more than half were back in prison for either a new crime or a parole or probation violation. Those who had been in prison for homicide, rape, and driving under the influence had the lowest recidivism rates. Women (compared to men), Hispanics (compared to non-Hispanics), whites (compared to blacks), and younger prisoners also had lower rates of recidivism. The highest rearrest rates were for prisoners convicted of robbery, burglary, and similar property crimes.

These high rates indicate that the traditional system fails in terms of rehabilitation. Maltz (2001) points out that recidivism data has contributed to a sense that "nothing works" by not paying enough attention to the type of crime most likely to be repeated and the demographics of offenders likely to reoffend.

In 2014, the Bureau of Justice Statistics released a report containing data on the recidivism rates of prisoners released in 2005. Within three years, 67.8 percent of these individuals were locked up once more; within five years, 76.6 percent had returned to prison (Dickson, 2014).

Parole

The parole process—the conditional release of a prisoner before his or term is finished, under court supervision, with rigid behavioral requirements for continued freedom—varies from state to state. Generally, decisions to grant parole are made by a parole board set up by the state. Parole became more popular through the first half of the twentieth century, as corrections philosophy focused more on rehabilitation. When the parole rate hit its highest point in 1977, 72 percent of prisoners were granted parole. Seiter and Kadela (2003) argue that parole had many positive functions. Parole was part of a larger corrections structure aimed at reintegrating ex-prisoners back into society; as such, it worked as a "gatekeeper" to keep more dangerous prisoners behind bars while allowing others out only under supervision. Parole boards made sure that released prisoners had a residence lined up before release and connected parolees to social services and treatment options. In the late twentieth and early twenty-first centuries most states moved away from the parole system and back to a system of set sentences, which means that many former inmates are released without any post-prison supervision or state-sponsored transition.

Parole is not always granted fairly. For example, Huebner and Bynum (2008) found that parole boards are more likely to grant earlier parole dates to white offenders than to black offenders, and Maltz (2001) pointed out that parole rates increased when prisons became overcrowded, suggesting that it is more tied to the needs of the prison system than to individual prisoners' readiness for release.

FURTHER INSIGHTS

Labeling

Once an individual is convicted of a felony his or her life changes in many ways. Time away from society can affect ones' social skills, work-related abilities, and connections to the community. In some cases, being labeled an ex-felon increases the likelihood of recidivism, and in other cases there are consequences for voting rights and job opportunities. Regardless, the label of "ex-felon" negatively affects ones' life chances (Chiricos, Barrick, & Bales, 2007).

Labeling theory suggests that people often react to labels placed on them by others by adopting the labels as their self-identities. Thus, the label of felon might result in an ex-offender identifying as such and committing acts of deviance that conform to this self-image.

Being labeled a felon transforms a subject on both the micro- and macro- level. On the micro-social level, the label can cause the subject to self-identify as a criminal and embrace the concept of what it means to be and act like a felon. This can cause offenders to engage in more risky behaviors and commit more crimes since they have adopted the lifestyle they perceive to be consistent with the label of felon. Second, the label of felon will have a structural impact on an offender's life: bringing about changes ranging from increased surveillance to a loss of citizenship rights such as voting, serving on a jury, or owning a gun (Chiricos, Barrick, & Bales, 2007).

Being labeled as a felon increases the likelihood of recidivism. In a study comparing adults who were convicted of a felony with those who were found guilty yet had adjudication of guilt withheld, Chiricos, Barrick, and Bales (2007) found that being officially labeled a felon led to significantly higher rates of recidivism, especially among whites and women.

Felon Disenfranchisement

Along with the rapid growth in the prison population has also been an increase in the number of felons who have lost their right to vote. In many states, election laws bar anyone convicted of a felony (whether currently serving time or released from prison) from voting. It is estimated by the Sentencing Project that nearly six million Americans are unable to vote because of their felony convictions as of 2014.

Scholars who investigate the impact of felon disenfranchisement on electoral outcomes (Havey, 1994; Manza & Uggen, 2004; Manza, Brooks, & Uggen 2004; Manza & Uggen, 2007) have found empirical evidence that suggests the electoral decisions in many gubernatorial and presidential contests would have been different had there not been the systematic disenfranchisement of ex-felons throughout the United States.

Central to these concerns is the issue of race and felon disenfranchisement in terms of voting rights. Because minorities are far more likely to be charged with and convicted of a felony, disenfranchisement of felons has a disproportionate impact on minority groups. These findings are troublesome when we consider that a felony conviction can remove one from civic participation and potentially lead to the total exclusion of certain racial and ethnic groups from participating in the democratic process of electing local, state, and national representatives.

Given the close presidential elections of 2000, 2004, 2012, and 2016, this imbalance is of growing concern to many who value the notion of an open democracy (Manza & Uggen, 2004). Manza and Uggen (2002; 2004; 2007) have demonstrated that the disenfranchisement of black (and some Latino) ex-felons in southern states has resulted in electoral outcomes that favor Republican candidates over Democratic and Independent candidates. Their data show that the disenfranchisement of minority voters has had a significant impact in both senate elections as well as the 2000 presidential election. The 2016 US presidential election was yet another example of a close contest that many observers felt was impacted by minority voter disenfranchisement.

Health Risks

Rosen and Wohl (2008) found that the mortality rate for men released from state prisons was higher than the mortality rate for other men residing in the state, although black ex-prisoners had lower-than- expected rates of lung cancer, heart and respiratory diseases, and diabetes.

Discrimination in the Work Place

Employers who conduct background checks for criminal history are much less likely to hire ex-offenders, especially if the employer is legally required to conduct such a check (Stoll & Bushway, 2008). The effect of a criminal record on employment is further compounded by race. Pager (2007) has demonstrated several noteworthy trends in employment opportunity by race and having a criminal label. First, she looks at how accessing jobs differs for black and white applicants with and without a criminal conviction. The data suggest that even when the experience and skills for each job candidate are exactly the same, a white man with a criminal record is more likely to be called in for an interview than a black man without any previous convictions. This demonstrates widespread discrimination against black applicants by many employers, and especially for black job applicants who have a criminal conviction.

Scholarship in the area of penology has demonstrated that one way to reduce crime and recidivism is to help ex-felons reintegrate into society through meaningful work and suitable housing. Pager's work may account for some of the disparity in recidivism rates between black and white ex-felons. Liker (1982) found that ex-felons re-entering society suffered less emotional distress if they were employed. Employment reduced their sense of stigma and helped reintegrate them into society, while also providing the security of income.

Discrimination in Housing

Pager (2007) studied whether black and white men with criminal convictions are treated differently with respect to obtaining credit and access to housing by sending black and white actors to apply for credit and rental housing. She randomly assigned some of them fictitious criminal records. The actors were wearing nearly identical clothing and had exactly the same credit scores and work experience to try and obtain lines of credit and/or rental housing. When black applicants showed up, they were told that there were no apartments available or that the advertisement was incorrect. This was exacerbated when black applicants reported having a criminal conviction on their rental applications. White applicants had no such experience when they attempted to get credit lines or enter a contract for rental housing. Even with a criminal conviction, white applicants were met with less hostility and suspicion than their black counterparts.

Previous scholarship has demonstrated that stable housing helps to minimize criminal involvement. When people feel connected to their communities or at the very least feel as though engaging in crime can adversely affect their lives, they are less likely to engage in criminal activity.

Access to Higher Education

Copenhaver, Edwards-Willey, and Byers (2007) found that there is a stigma associated with being labeled a felon which negatively affects individuals' experiences in the classroom. Access to financial aid is restricted for those who have been convicted of drug-related crimes (FAFSA 2009). Though intended to prevent the wrongful use of aid money, limiting access to financial aid puts forth yet another barrier for those felons who are trying to turn their lives around by learning new trades or skills in order to enter the workforce. Given what is known about access to meaningful employment and the links between higher education and job opportunities, these types of policies negatively affect the opportunities for ex-felons and disproportionately affect the opportunities for poor minorities who are trying to work their way out of impoverished, crime-ridden neighborhoods.

Additionally, the accessibility and number of correctional education programs have decreased since the elimination of the Pell Grants in the early 1990s. As studies have shown that a large number of people imprisoned are undereducated (oftentimes because of the young age at which they are incarcerated) and, in some cases, illiterate, the reduction of these programs has also negatively affected prisoners' abilities to achieve higher levels of functionality and employment upon release (Pryor & Thompkins, 2013).

VIEWPOINTS

Social & Political Consequences of Labeling Felons

By labeling and stigmatizing those who are convicted of a felony as felons, society is limiting individual access to employment opportunities, basic citizenship rights, and education. Policies that support limiting access to these basic services exacerbate the likelihood of recidivism and continue to perpetuate the cycle of violence and the revolving door that has come to typify the US criminal justice system. If real change is to be done to help offenders reintegrate into society and leave a life of crime behind, the United States needs to put in place policies and resources that help ex-felons obtain meaningful work, adequate housing, job training, and social development. Through these types of policies one can be assured of developing community ties and reducing crime at the same time.

The United States has the largest prison population in the world. The majority of offenders, violent and nonviolent, will be released back into society; most never received any rehabilitative services while in prison. With the increasing number of ex-felons being released back into society the question remains what do to help reintegrate those who are leaving prison? The issues of discrimination in employment and housing and voter disenfranchisement play into the revolving door that has become stereotypical of the country's criminal justice system. Until greater attention is given to the loss of citizenship rights and access to opportunities, crime and recidivism will continue to be a problem facing the United States. Much has yet to be learned as to how society can intervene and increase the odds of ex-felons making it rather than returning to a life of crime.

TERMS & CONCEPTS

Disenfranchisement: The removal of one's citizenship rights, especially the right to vote.

Felony: In the United States, a crime serious enough in nature to warrant more than one year in prison.

Labeling theory: Labeling theory states that people perceive the labels that others place on them and these labels become part of their identities, influencing their future actions.

Parole: Conditional release before the completion of a prison sentence, under the supervision of the court system, with stringent behavioral conditions.

Probation: The suspension of all or part of a jail sentence, whereby the offender will remain under the supervision of the court for a specific period of time.

Recidivism: Generally described as the act of reoffending once released from jail or prison, it can include rearrest, reconviction, resentencing, and any return to prison.

Social Control: The formal or informal processes that regulate individual and group behavior

Stigmatization: Severe social disapproval of personal characteristics that violate cultural norms and shared values.

Bibliography

Berk, R., Lenihan, K., & Rossi, P. (1980). "Crime and poverty: Some experimental evidence from ex-offenders." *American Sociological Review, 45,* 766–786.

Carson, A. (2013, September). *Prisoners in 2013.* Washington, DC: US Department of Justice. http://www.bjs.gov/content/pub/pdf/p13.pdf

Chiricos, T., Barrick, K. & Bales, W. (2007). "The labeling of convicted felons and its consequences for recidivism." *Criminology, 45,* 547–581.

Copenhaver, A., Edwards-Willey, T., & Byers, T. (2007). "Journeys in social stigma: the lives of formerly incarcerated felons in higher education." *The Journal of Correctional Education, 58,* 268–283.

Dickson, C. (2014, April 22). "America's recidivism nightmare." *Daily Beast.* http://www.thedailybeast.com/articles/2014/04/22/america-s-recidivism-nightmare.html

Duwe, G., & Clark, V. (2013). "The effects of private prison confinement on offender recidivism: evidence from Minnesota." *Criminal Justice Review, 38,* 375–394.

FAFSA—"Free application for federal student aid: FAQs: eligibility" (2009). http://www.fafsa.ed.gov

Hallett, M. (2012). "Reentry to what? Theorizing prisoner reentry in the jobless future." *Critical Criminology, 20,* 213–228.

Harvey, A. (1994). "Ex-felon disenfranchisement and its influence on the black vote: The need for a second look." *University of Pennsylvania Law Review, 142,* 1145–1189.

Huebner, B., & Bynum, T. (2008). "The role of race and ethnicity in parole decisions." *Criminology, 46,* 907–938.

Koschmann, M. A., & Peterson, B. L. (2013). "Rethinking recidivism: a communication approach to prisoner reentry." *Journal of Applied Social Sciences, 7,* 188–207.

Kroner, D. G., & Yessine, A. K. (2013). "Changing risk factors that impact recidivism: in search of mechanisms of change." *Law and Human Behavior, 37*, 321–336.

Langan, P. A. & Levin, D.J. (2002). "Recidivism of prisoners released in 1994." *Bureau of Justice Statistics.* http://www.ojp.usdoj.gov/bjs/pub/pdf/rpr94.pdf

Liker, J. (1982). "Wage and status effects of employment on affective well-being among ex-felons." *American Sociological Review, 47*, 264–283.

Maltz, M.D. (2001). *Recidivism.* Originally published by Academic Press, Inc., Orlando, Florida. Internet edition available http://www.uic.edu/depts/lib/forr/pdf/crimjust/recidivism.pdf

Manza, J. & Uggen, C. (2004). "Punishment and democracy: Disenfranchisement of non-incarcerated felons in the United States." *Perspectives on Politics, 2*, 491–505.

Manza, J., Brooks, C. & Uggen, C. (2004). "Public attitudes toward felon disenfranchisement in the United States." *Public Opinion Quarterly 68*, 275–86.

Manza, J. & Uggen, C. (2007). *Felon disenfranchisement and American democracy.* Boston, MA: Oxford University Press.

Mauer, M. (2007). "Racial impact statements as a means of reducing unwarranted sentencing disparities." *Ohio State Journal of Criminal Law, 5*, 19–46.

Mauer, M., & Coyle, M. (2004). "The social cost of America's race to incarcerate." *Journal of Religion & Spirituality in Social Work, 23*(1/2), 7–25.

Pager, D. (2007). *Marked: Race, crime, and finding work in an era of mass incarceration.* Chicago, IL: University of Chicago Press.

Plante, J. (2015). "Problems prisoners face in the reentry industry." *Perspectives (University Of New Hampshire)*, 52–59.

Pryor, M., & Thompkins, D. (2013). "The disconnect between education and social opportunity for the formerly incarcerated." *American Journal of Criminal Justice, 38*, 457–479.

Reiman, J. (2004). *The rich get richer and the poor get prison: Ideology, class, and criminal justice.* 7th (Ed.). Boston, MA: Allyn and Bacon.

Roberts, J. & Stanton, E. (2007, November 25). "A long road back after exoneration, and justice is slow to make amends." *New York Times*, http://www.nytimes.com/2007/11/25/us/25dna.html?%5fr=1.

Rosen, D., Schoenbach, V., & Wohl, D. (2008). "All-cause and cause-specific mortality among men released from state prison, 1980-2005." *American Journal of Public Health, 98*, 2278–2284.

Seiter, R. P., & Kadela, K. R. (2003). "Prisoner reentry: What works, what does not, and what is promising." *Crime & Delinquency, 49*, 360–388.

Stoll, M., & Bushway, S. (2008). "The effect of criminal background checks on hiring ex-offenders." *Criminology & Public Policy, 7*, 371–404.

Uggen, C. & Manza, J. (2002). "Democratic contraction? Political consequences of felon disenfranchisement in the United States." American *Sociological Review, 67*, 777–803.

Uggen, C. (2008). "Editorial introduction: The effect of criminal background checks on hiring ex-offenders." *Criminology & Public Policy, 7*, 367–370.

Walker, S., Spohn, C. & DeLone, M. (2004). *The color of justice: Race, ethnicity, and crime in America.* Belmont, CA: Thompson and Wadsworth.

Wyse, J. B., Harding, D. J., & Morenoff, J. D. (2014). "Romantic relationships and criminal desistance: Pathways and processes." *Sociological Forum, 29*(2), 365–385.

Suggested Reading

Liem, M., & Sampson, R. J. (2016). *After life imprisonment: Reentry in the era of mass incarceration.* New York, NY: New York University Press.

Martin, L. (2013). "Reentry within the carceral: Foucault, race and prisoner reentry." *Critical Criminology, 21*, 493–508.

McCleary, R. (1992). *Dangerous men: The sociology of parole.* New York, NY: Harrow and Henson.

Price, J. M. (2015). *Prison and social death.* New Brunswick, NJ: Rutgers University Press.

Schutt, R. K., Deng, X., & Stoehr, T. (2013). "Using bibliotherapy to enhance probation and reduce recidivism." *Journal of Offender Rehabilitation, 52*, 181–197.

Simon, J. (1993). *Poor discipline: Parole and the social control of the underclass, 1890–1990.* Chicago, IL: University of Chicago Press.

Vanstone, M. (2008). "The international origins and initial development of probation: An early example of policy transfer." *British Journal of Criminology, 48*, 735–755.

Westervelt, S., & Cook, K. (2008). "Coping with innocence after death row." *Contexts: Understanding People in Their Social Worlds, 7*, 32–37.

Jennifer Christian, M.A., and
Katherine Walker, Ph.D.

Sex Differences in Crime

ABSTRACT

The study of sex differences in crime involves multiple levels of inquiry, both qualitative and quantitative, into the rates at which the two genders are victimized by crime and the rates at which each gender perpetrates crime. In addition, researchers study differences in how each gender experiences crime as perpetrator and victim. Research into the intersection of gender and crime is to some extent descriptive, as it seeks to provide an accurate picture of the current state of affairs, but it can also be prescriptive, providing implications about the reasons for crime among each gender and by proposing methods for reducing crime's effects.

OVERVIEW

The study of the relationship between gender and crime has a complex history, intertwined as it is with evolving social views regarding the sexes and the roles available to them. For most of human history, women have been forced to occupy a position subordinate to that of men in patriarchal societies. Some attribute this to biological factors such as different levels of body mass and hormones related to aggressive behavior, while others see it more as a consequence of socialization, with women placed in the role of nurturer and caregiver and men tasked with hunting and fighting. Both sides of this debate generally agree that while in past eras there may have been some logic to the gender hierarchy (from an evolutionary, if not ethical, perspective), in the modern world there is no longer any reason to maintain it, apart from blind adherence to tradition (LeClerc & Wortley, 2014). Nevertheless, the consequences of gender inequality persist, as is evidenced by the study of sex differences in crime.

One aspect of the field focuses on defining and determining the reasons for differences in risk factors for criminal behavior between men and women. Throughout history, the conventional wisdom has been that women are much less likely to exhibit criminal behavior than men. In part this can be attributed to the system of patriarchy which has prevailed almost everywhere in the world. One of the central features of patriarchy is that men have been the ones considered to set the standard for human behavior and "normality." This has left women to be treated as embodying either deviations from normal (male) behavior or as a kind of sub-species which can only be defined by comparing it unfavorably to men. Thus, women are often described as more emotional than men, less physically aggressive, less rational, and–to return to the present context–less inclined to criminal behavior. This conceptual frame of reference is deeply problematic in many ways (Renzetti, Miller & Gover, 2013). It tends to ignore the fact that women's lower reported rates of criminal behavior are likely to be an effect of their narrower confinement within social boundaries. That is, women have historically been excluded from many activities, both personal and professional, as a consequence of patriarchy. It is at least possible that if women and men had enjoyed access to the same range of activities, then their crime rates would have been less disparate.

It is also important when analyzing sex differences in the commission of crimes to remain aware that rates change significantly depending on the type of crime involved. Many of the crimes for which perpetration rates are higher among women, such as prostitution, are related to women's sexuality. This is explained by the fact that throughout history, society in general and the criminal justice system in particular have spent more energy regulating female sexuality than on controlling men's sexual behavior. One way of exercising such control has been through criminalizing behavior that does not conform to the expectations of the patriarchal system. A famous example of this phenomenon can be seen in Italy, which for many years made it a crime for a woman to commit adultery but not for a man to do so (Walklate, 2012). Obviously, this caused women to have a much higher rate of criminality than men within this category (Cusack, 2015). Such a pattern has been repeated in other types of crime.

At the same time, men tend to have much higher rates of committing crimes of violence, such as murder, assault, and so forth. This is often attributed to their greater physical stature, which makes it easier for them to engage in physical conflict with a reasonable chance of success, and to their greater freedom in society, which provides them with more opportunities to engage in activities that culminate in violence (Hayes, Luther & Caringella, 2015).

The other side of the coin, sex differences in rates of victimization by crime, is in many ways a mirror image of crime commission rates. Men are more likely to commit violent crimes, which are by their very nature more detectable, more likely to have witnesses, and in general more visible to society. There is also a tendency for law enforcement officials, and to some extent judges and the court system, to treat criminal defendants in a way that is based on traditional stereotypes of men and women (Walklate, 2012). This means that men often receive harsher sentences or are less likely to be shown leniency than are women. Over time, this behavior tends to solidify itself in place, because the effects it produces appear to provide justification for its continuance: More males are convicted of crimes, based partly on widespread assumptions about gender-based behavior, and the fact that more men are incarcerated then reinforces the belief that men are more prone to certain types of crime (Russell, 2013). Overall, what can be said with confidence is that while men do commit crimes at higher rates than women in almost every category except prostitution, many of these crimes are ones which have male victims, so it is important to distinguish crime commission statistics from crime victimization statistics.

VIEWPOINTS

For many years there has been concern in the fields of gender studies and criminology that traditional notions about women's participation in crime may be skewed by the fact that almost all of the research done in the past was conducted on men, and the results were later either simply assumed to apply to women also, or were somewhat haphazardly extrapolated to include women. Part of the reason for this was the effect of patriarchy discussed above: Male researchers tended to assume that men are the "standard" human and that it was not necessary to study women as well as men (LeClerc & Wortley, 2014). Critics have also suggested that there may have been some reluctance in the scholarly community toward studying women and criminality, caused by fear that the findings of such research would differ so markedly from the assumptions based on a male-only population that they would not be taken seriously. It was much easier to concentrate scholarly attention on male populations, for to do otherwise would be seen as at best impolite and at worst deviant.

The view of sex differences in relation to crime that has predominated in recent years is sometimes referred to as the gender equality hypothesis. By looking at historical crime rates, researchers have noted that, as already stated, men commit most crimes at a higher rate than women do (Andersen & Hill, 2013). Taking the analysis a step further, it has also been shown that when the crime rates for a particular category of offense go up for men, they tend to go up for women by roughly the same amount. So, if an average of twenty men and two women commit murder each year, and the figure for men suddenly increases to forty per year, the number for women that year would likely double also. This realization has had profound implications for those who argued that the basis for the difference in crime rates between the two sexes is based purely on biology rather than on circumstances in society (Russell, 2013). If biology were indeed the sole explanation for differences in crime rates between genders, then one would expect that in a year when men's crime rates increased, women's would stay the same. However, the fact that male and female rates tend to remain in proportion to each other suggests that both men and women are being influenced by the same social factors (unemployment rates, inflation, availability of illicit drugs, etc.). This awareness laid the foundation for the gender equity hypothesis, which proposes that male and female crime rates are different because of society's unequal treatment of women, and that as women move closer to parity with men, female crime rates can be expected to rise until they are on a par with those of males (Cusack, 2015).

Proponents of the marginality theory see the situation for female perpetrators from the opposite direction. While gender equality theory states that greater equality for women will provide more women with more opportunities to commit crimes, marginality theory states that many of the crimes women commit are desperate acts rather than the result of rational deliberation (Pasko & Chesney-Lind, 2012). Poverty, substance abuse, and physical and sexual abuse drive many women to commit crimes in order to survive or escape their circumstances. According to marginality theory, as the overall condition of women improves through the creation of new opportunities and the removal of gender-based barriers to success, fewer women out of the population will find themselves in circumstances dire enough to motivate them to commit crimes. More recently, researchers have begun calling for a "gendered" theory of crime–one that takes into account the context of crime, prevailing norms of gender in the context being studied, antecedents of crime particular to women, and biological influences (Steffenmeier & Allan, 1996). The goal of those pursuing a gendered theory is not to determine the underlying reason for the difference in crime rates between men and women but to study the phenomena of male crime and female crime in depth and in their own contexts.

There is also an expanding body of research into the different effects each gender experiences as a consequence of being victimized by crime. Studies conducted in recent years show that women are almost twice as likely as men to suffer from post-traumatic stress disorder (PTSD) in the aftermath of victimization. This is particularly surprising because men are the ones at greater risk of exposure to trauma-inducing events, yet women appear to be more vulnerable to trauma itself. PTSD research has shown that whether or not an individual develops PTSD after a traumatic experience is closely related to the way the individual mentally processes the trauma (Andersen & Hill, 2013). Studies are ongoing into the ways men and women cognitively process events, in the hopes of determining the nature of the difference in their cognition, as it is presumed that this may reveal why women appear more susceptible to PTSD. It appears that women have a greater tendency to view the traumatic event as having a negative impact on their lives, thus making it more difficult for them to process emotionally what happened (Russell, 2013). Men, in contrast, tend to have a greater chance of being able to bring to mind positive consequences that emerged from a negative event.

Another difference that has emerged in some studies is in men and women's attitudes about the likelihood of being victimized by crime. For men, it appears more common to think about crime as something that is so widespread that there is a significant possibility that it will affect everyone at some point or other (Gartner, 2014). This appears to make it easier to deal with the aftermath of crime, because there is less of a tendency to question oneself and one's fate, and to wonder "Why did this have to happen to me?" Women, on the other hand, frequently report that they were always aware of the potential for being a victim of crime but on an abstract level, so that they did not truly think it would happen to them. This suggests the possibility that when these women were victimized by crime, the shock was all the more intense and thus more difficult to recover from.

Sex differences in crime is an active area of research, and developments are expected on a number of fronts in the years to come. A great deal of psychological research now underway uses recent discoveries in neuroscience and brain imaging to gather heretofore unavailable information about the inner workings of the brains of crime victims and perpetrators. These studies seek to delve further into physiological differences in brain function that may exist between men and women, and between those who commit crimes and those who do not. At the same time, other developments in the realm of sociology and civil rights suggest that there is no cause for concern that criminality can or should be defined as nothing more than the result of a few misplaced neurons. There is growing awareness in the United States and elsewhere of the sociological, economic, and educational factors that together act upon young people, shape their identities, and help to incline them either toward or away from criminal behavior. In particular, the concept of the "school to prison pipeline" has captured the attention of large numbers of teachers, who are working to find ways to help children develop into mature and productive adults even as they lack many of the social support systems that were available to previous generations. There is no doubt that the debate will continue over the causes of crime–nature or nurture–and the reasons for sex differences in crime–biology or socialization. It is to be hoped that before too much more time passes, some concrete conclusions can be drawn from the research that is ongoing and from the debate, to reduce the incidence of criminality and victimization for both genders while continuing to maintain the societal trend toward greater equality for women.

TERMS & CONCEPTS

Gender equality hypothesis: This hypothesis suggests that as women's status in society comes closer to equaling that of men, rates of female criminal behavior will also rise to comparable levels.

Gender neutral theory of crime: A theory of crime is gender neutral if it places its emphasis on the factors that motivate a person to commit a crime without regard to the person's gender. Most gender neutral theories of crime were developed by studying populations composed almost exclusively of men.

Gender specific theory of crime: A theory of crime is gender specific if it attempts to account for the reasons a particular gender group commits crimes, often in an effort to understand which aspects of gender identity either encourage or inhibit criminal behavior by persons of that gender. Gender specific theories of crime often focus on female subjects in an effort to understand the forces that cause them to engage in criminal behavior.

Marginality theory: This theory suggests that rates of crimes committed by women fall as women's socioeconomic status increases to equal that enjoyed by men. This is because a majority of crimes by women are committed among those at the margins of society due to poverty, discrimination, or abuse. As women's status rises on average, the theory goes, there will be fewer women driven to crime through desperation.

Patriarchy: A social or political system of organization in which power is vested in males to the detriment of females.

Post-traumatic stress disorder (PTSD): Often referred to by its acronym, PTSD, this disorder afflicts millions of people each year. PTSD is triggered by a traumatic event such as a car crash, a violent attack, or the prolonged conflict of war. Those suffering from PTSD experience a variety of symptoms, which can include difficulty sleeping, anxiety, depression, and flashbacks to the traumatic event.

Bibliography

Andersen, M. L., & Hill, C. P. (2013). *Race, class, and gender: An anthology.* Belmont, CA: Wadsworth Cengage Learning.

Cusack, C. M. (2015). *Criminal justice handbook on masculinity, male aggression, and sexuality.* Springfield , IL: Charles C. Thomas.

Gartner, R. (2014). *The Oxford handbook of gender, sex, and crime.* Oxford, UK: Oxford University Press.

Hayes, R. M., Luther, K., & Caringella, S. (2015). *Teaching criminology at the intersection: A how-to guide for teaching about gender, race, class and sexuality.* New York, NY: Routledge.

LeClerc, B., & Wortley, R. (2014). *Cognition and crime: Offender decision-making and script analyses.* New York, NY: Routledge.

Pasko, L., & Chesney-Lind, M. (2012). *The female offender: Girls, women, and crime.* Thousand Oaks, CA: Sage.

Renzetti, C. M., Miller, S. L., & Gover, A. R. (2013). *Routledge international handbook of crime and gender studies.* London, UK: Routledge.

Russell, B. L. (2013). *Perceptions of female offenders: How stereotypes and social norms affect criminal justice responses.* New York, UK: Springer.

Steffenmeier, D. & Allan, E. (1996). "Gender and crime: Toward a gendered theory of female offending." *Annual Review of Sociology* 22: 459-87.

Walklate, S. (2012). *Gender and crime.* London, UK: Routledge.

Suggested Reading

Bisi, S. (2002). "Female criminality and gender difference." *International Review of Sociology* 12: 23-43.

Boisvert, D., Vaske, J., Wright, J. P., & Knopik, V. (2012). "Sex differences in criminal behavior: A genetic analysis." *Journal of Contemporary Criminal Justice,* 28, 293-313.

Frisell, T., Pawitan, Y., Långström, N., & Lichtenstein, P. (2012). "Heritability, assortative mating and gender differences in violent crime: Results from a total population sample using twin, adoption, and sibling models." *Behavior Genetics,* 42, 3-18.

Jacobsen, S. K. (2012). "The differential representation of women and men in crime, victimization, and the criminal justice system." *Sex Roles,* 66, 293-295.

Rebellon, C. J., Wiesen-Martin, D., Piquero, N. L., Piquero, A. R., & Tibbetts, S. G. (2015). "Gender differences in criminal intent: Examining the mediating influence of anticipated shaming." *Deviant Behavior,* 36, 17-41.

Scott Zimmer, MLS, M.S., J.D.

Social Disorganization Theory

ABSTRACT

Unlike most theories of crime that focus on the individual, social disorganization theory focuses on place and tries to explain why some communities experience high levels of crime while others do not. The theory attends to the ecologies or environments of communities in which social institutions succeed or fail in maintaining order in public places. Arguably, the success of a given neighborhood or community is based upon the effective collective use of skills, resources, focus, and energy to solve problems and enhance the quality of life in order to deter criminal activity. Social disorganization theory argues that because of failures in the skills and networking abilities of community organizations, whether they be educational, business, law enforcement, social services, health care, or religious organizations, a specific neighborhood or community can experience high crime rates through a breakdown in social order and a lack of compliance with social rules.

OVERVIEW

Adolphe Quetelet

According to Michael Gottfredson and Travis Hirschi (1990), the basis of social disorganization theory emanates from the statistical work of Belgian sociologist Adolphe Quetelet in the early nineteenth century. Quetelet studied various urban geographical areas and determined that the crime rates in each area were stable over long periods of time regardless of the race, nationality, or national origin of an area's residents at a given point in time. Quetelet concluded from this data that there were features unique to each area or to the groups adapting to reside in an area that were responsible for the area's crime rate.

The Chicago School

Theorists in economics, geography, sociology, and criminology built upon Quetelet's work and used maps of geographical areas to show the spatial distribution of crime in a given area. This approach was known as the "Cartographic School," and it was popular with scholars at the University of Chicago during the first half of the twentieth century. William Isaac Thomas and Florian Znaniecki added to the theoretical framework around 1919 by arguing that people's beliefs and attitudes were shaped by their interactions with their "situation," or the environment, as well as their behavior. This acculturation process, they said, takes place on both an individual level and within a group as a whole.

Building on their colleagues' work, in 1925 Robert Ezra Park and Ernest W. Burgess adapted Darwinian evolutionary concepts to this Chicago School Sociology, as it had by then become known. They argued that urban environments mirrored natural ecosystems and that careful analysis would reveal distinctive ecological niches or zones throughout a city. "Ecology" is defined by the Encarta English Dictionary "as the study of the relationships between living organisms and their interactions with their natural or developed environment" (Soukhanov, 2004). Ecological studies of crime view "the physical structure of communities as shaping the routine activities of inhabitants in ways that affect the likelihood of crime" (Gottfredson, 1990, p. 82). Through the interplay of humans with their environment and its resources, the theory holds, the zones evolve into diverse, unique areas with the residents sharing similar social characteristics. This process can be said to mirror the evolutionary changes experienced by plants and animals as they adapt to varied ecological niches in a diverse landscape.

Park and Burgess used their cartographic research on the City of Chicago to argue that urban areas have five distinct zones of natural competition:

- The central business district;
- The transitional zone;
- The working-class zone (single family tenements);
- The residential zone (single family homes with yards and garages); and
- The commuter zone (suburbs).

Their theory, which they called "the concentric zone theory," held that as a city evolves through outward expansion, the more desirable and successful zones are those that avoid the intense concentration and competition for land and resources within the inner city. Zone Two, the transitional zone, is therefore arguably the most disadvantaged and thus evidences the highest rates of crime and delinquency. Park and Burgess described the transitional zone as being driven by industrial expansion; it serves as a residential entry point for immigrants and has a wide variety of cultural groups, high unemployment and welfare rates, low educational and occupational attainment levels, low real estate rental values, and social institutions with poor community organization abilities. Despite high rates of movement in and out of the zones, Park and Burgess argued that each zone retained its characteristics. Subsequent efforts to duplicate their findings in different countries have successfully linked high delinquency rates with areas of economic decline. Park's and Burgess's analysis of concentric zones, however, has proven to be flawed in cities where "the wealthy are often near the center of the city, while the poorer zones of the city are found near its fringes" (Wong, 2007, p. 3).

Shaw & McKay

In 1942, Clifford R. Shaw and Henry D. McKay became the most famous members of the Chicago School by trying to explain the spatial distributions of crime and delinquency set forth by their predecessors. In seeking a social causation of crime, Shaw and McKay focused on social institutions—educational, law enforcement, business, social services, healthcare, and religious entities—rather than on individual perpetrators and their social characteristics. Shaw and McKay argued that social institutions in Zone Two–type locales are too disadvantaged and disorganized to perform their major social function of training or socializing individuals to be law-abiding members of the community. Secondarily, they also fail to monitor the behavior of individuals in order to ensure lawful behavior. One major assumption of social disorganization theory, then, is that crime is caused by social factors or bad places rather than bad people. Another term for this perspective is "environmental determinism."

Within this context, social disorganization is defined as "the inability of local communities to realize common values of their residents or solve commonly experienced problems" (Shaw & McKay, 1942, qtd in O'Connor, 2006, ¶ 13). In an attempt to explain why these communities faced social disorganization to such a level that criminal traditions became embedded, three reasons were set forth:

- residential instability/mobility;
- racial/ethnic heterogeneity; and
- poverty.

Residential instability/mobility was defined as individuals having no commitment to their locale since they moved frequently and intended to leave the area as soon as possible. The mid-twentieth century "white flight," the migration of working- and middle-class Caucasian residents out of areas with growing numbers of African American residents, left the poorest members of these communities behind in an even more depressed environment. Racial, cultural, and language barriers were erected as a result of racial/ethnic heterogeneity to such an extent that residents isolated themselves from dissimilar community members in small pockets of minority areas. In consequence, they forfeited the meaningful interactions that might have led to solutions to overarching community problems such as crime. Finally, because of poverty due to a low tax base and restricted local resources, community members did not have the resources to solve their social problems, and residents continued to seek housing in less disorganized residential zones. Poverty itself does not cause crime, according to Shaw and McKay, but it does facilitate it due to a lack of the resources necessary to eradicate criminal behavior. Subsequent researchers have added family disruption and urbanization as additional factors to the theory.

One major feature of a socially disorganized zone was that it offered an explanation for how high crime and delinquency rates can cause further disruptions in a community due to the high levels of incarceration of its residents. Obviously, according to social disorganization theorists, a pattern of frequent, repeated incarceration adds to the residential instability factors in a given community and only worsens a community's social ills. Thus, a major policy implication of social disorganization theory is to find alternatives to incarceration and crime control. Expanded remedial educational programs, youth athletic leagues, community youth services and clubs, summer camps, youth employment services, recreation programs, and other types of social service and educational interventions are championed by social disorganization theorists to create the positive socialization opportunities for youth that the community is unable offer on its own.

VIEWPOINTS

Strain Theory

Social disorganization theory concerns itself with the abilities of a community's social institutions to inculcate common values of lawfulness and to monitor compliance with those values. One major criticism of the theory focuses on its foundational premise "that people will commit criminal acts when the surrounding 'society' is unable to prevent them from doing so" (Gottfredson, 1990, p. 82). No empirical basis has been offered for this assumption, and several subsequent theorists have argued that the absence of social organization does not adequately account for crime and delinquency. Instead of social disorganization as impetus for crime, Robert Merton and other strain theorists argued that societal pressures and frustration drive crime and delinquency. Strain theory (also referred to as anomie theory) asserts that there is "a universal aspiration to accumulate material wealth," but because our society is stratified into various classes, those in the lower economic levels to not have an equal opportunity to realize the American dream (Gottfredson, 1990, p. 78). Under pressure to reach these culturally inculcated goals, some individuals adapt by turning to crime as a means of material gain. Merton argued further that since middle-class values conflict with engaging in criminal activities generally, individuals will experience higher levels of strain should they consider engaging in criminal conduct. Arguably, crime is higher in Zone Two–type areas because their residents do not have the same socialization or, in fact, because their cultural processes hold a different view of crime altogether and, as a result, they feel less strain against the "dominant" cultural value of behaving in a law-abiding manner. With subcultural values different from or even in opposition to the dominant norm of behaving in a law-abiding manner, Zone Two–type communities may even give law-breakers a high status within the community due to their material success. Interestingly, strain theory argues that individuals residing in socially disorganized zones are aware of the dominant culture's values toward material wealth but are frustrated in achieving the same ends. Social disorganization theorists, on the other hand, would say that the dominant culture's values have not been instilled and, therefore, are not an aspiration.

Cultural Transmission Theory

Elements of these arguments also can be found in cultural transmission theory, which has dominated discussions in criminal causation to this day. According to O'Connor (2006), this theory states that "traditions of delinquency are transmitted through successive generations of the same zone in the same way language, roles, and attitudes are transmitted" (Shaw & McKay, 1942 qtd. in O'Connor, 2006, ¶ 13). One can see from these arguments, and from the assertions of the social disorganization theorists, why there has been controversy and criticism over issues of class and criminality since the 1950s. Given their application to Zone Two–type areas with high immigrant populations experiencing high unemployment levels, charges of racial and ethnic bias were made as well. In fairness, Shaw and McKay argued that a high crime rate was not related to any given racial or ethnic population's presence in the community. Their original theory held that the crime rates of Zone Two–type areas were high regardless of the races or ethnicities of the areas' residents at a given time. Nevertheless, social disorganization theory became unpopular by the 1960s because of its subjective evaluations, negative terminology, and race/class bias.

Although social disorganization theory was meant to be a scientific explanation of crime and delinquency, in the public policy arena it has deteriorated into accusations that individuals residing in high crime areas are immoral. Evidence of this perspective is clear in recent debates over juvenile crime. In a 1995 article in the *Conservative Weekly*, public policy analyst John DiIulio coined the word "super-predator" to describe what he believed to be a new breed of juvenile criminal. Described as having no conscience and capable of killing at the slightest whim or provocation, super-predators, according to DuIlio, were the result of children being raised in "abject moral poverty... surrounded by deviant, delinquent, criminal adults in abusive, violence-ridden, fatherless, Godless, and jobless settings" (Satterthwaite, 1997, p. 20-21). While this rhetoric has gone a long way in heightening the public's fear of juvenile criminals, it has done little to address the social causes of crime or alleviate the hardship conditions in high crime areas.

Methodological Flaws

Another failing of social disorganization theory is that the methodology employed to establish the theory was based upon circular reasoning. Using crime and juvenile delinquency as an index of social disorganization, Shaw and McKay then argued that social disorganization caused crime and delinquency. Compounding this difficulty was an inability to measure social organization and disorganization within a given community. This challenge remains, and recent efforts focus on "levels of involvement across age-levels in activities coordinated by representatives of the communal institutions (e. g. family heads, pastors, school organizations, and local officials" (Jensen, 2003, p. 1). A community is deemed to be especially organized when it offers high levels of these types of activities. Another difficulty with the theory, however, is that even in communities with high rates of crime, social organization exists: it may simply be structured or operate in a way that does not fit into the methodological framework of social disorganization theorists.

Measuring Social Organization

One outgrowth of social disorganization theory has been the effort to find less pejorative terminology for describing community structure in criminality studies. By the late 1980s, these efforts made social disorganization theory again tremendously popular as a contextual explanation of crime and delinquency. Sampson (1997), for example, coined the words "collective efficacy" to assess a community's ability to control crime in public places. Within Sampson's analysis, in order for a community to be efficacious, "social capital" is needed within the community, meaning that there is significant interdependence, extensive informal networks, and strong social ties that allow community members to work together to achieve common goals of law enforcement. Robert D. Crutchfield, Michael R. Geerken, and Walter R. Gove (1982), among others, focused on "social integration" levels within communities, hypothesizing that high population turnover negatively affects a community's ability to be integrated enough to fight crime. Related theorists, including Rodney Stark and colleagues (1983) and Marvin D. Krohn (1986), suggested a focus on "social networks" and "network density." Their methodology of studying direct relationships between individuals within a community provided another tangible means of determining social organization levels. The scientific means to show the direct relationship between social ties and community control, however, are still undergoing development. The intent of all of these efforts is to go beyond the negative connotations of "social disorganization" and place the theoretical framework within more scientific and measurable contexts. Each of these contributions, however, can be traced back to social disorganization theory.

With the resurgence of interest in social disorganization theory, numerous studies have been undertaken that support the empirical framework. In 1980, James Q. Wilson undertook a study of delinquency in Birmingham, England, and concluded that when parents exercised "chaperonage" they significantly lowered the risk of their child becoming delinquent. Chaperonage was defined as parents keeping a close watch on their children and sheltering them from the negative aspects of neighborhood life. This was accomplished by escorting children to and from school and forbidding them to play with troublemakers. Similarly, a 1982 British Crime Survey by Robert Sampson and W. Byron Groves (1989) "became a criminological classic," according to Christopher T. Lowenkamp and his colleagues (2003, ¶ 1), who set out to replicate the study. Their 1994 analysis offered even greater support for social disorganization theory as a means of understanding criminal causation on a contextual basis. Given advances in statistical studies, economics, and urban policy analysis, Charles E. Kubrin and Ronald Witzer (2003) predicted that groundbreaking work can be expected on the relevance of social disorganization theory, including its application to non-urban areas. Kubrin's article should be required reading for anyone interested in testing this theoretical framework.

Social Control Theory

Because social disorganization theory emphasized the obligation of the community to train or socialize individuals and to then monitor individual behavior to ensure lawful action, it gained significant interest within "social control" theory circles. Social control theorists hypothesize that an individual can turn to crime when his or her connection to or identification with the dominant culture is ineffective. In fact, like their social disorganization counterparts, they believe that people find crime useful, profitable, and enjoyable unless they are influenced by larger societal values to forego these urges. Their ideal is to preserve values about lawful personal conduct.

To do this, control theorists argue for interventions that control deviance and reorganize communities in order to advance and enhance traditional cultural values. Identification with these traditional values instills mechanisms of internal, individual control through a social bond that helps group well-being. In addition to policing mechanisms, external social control is exerted through enhanced involvement in community activities and by creating role models and peer pressure so that the individual will not want to disappoint the other members of the group. Many contemporary control theorists, like Gottfredson and Hirschi (1990), also focus on the individual's lack of self-control over impulsive urges as a cause of crime and delinquency, but these perspectives move even further from the social disorganization theory's attention on community-level analysis.

Social Disorganization Theory & Immigrant Populations

Family breakdown was considered an important aspect of social disorganization until the 1930s, but interest in this variable waned until the 1980s, according to Wilson (1974). He argues that family dysfunction always was a compelling variable to explain criminal conduct, but that public policy advocates were convinced that other social institutions, like schools, religious organizations, and recreational groups, were the keys to solving social ills. Although the social disorganization theorists tried to be neutral toward the various immigrant populations within their zones of study, reliance on social institutions to develop American values in youth has had a long and hostile anti-immigrant history in social and educational policies since the early 1800s. Standardized educational settings with health education, showers, the Pledge of Allegiance, and numerous other socialization tasks were institutionalized in schools to inculcate American values and behaviors in immigrant youth. The American family may have lost its exclusive influence over child development, but an even greater concern has been that the foreign values and behaviors of immigrant families might alter our dominant culture's identity to an even greater degree. New insights into the motivations and beliefs of the social disorganization theorists might be gained by comparing their writings with those of educational theorists intent upon Americanizing immigrant youth since the early 1800s. At the very least, it would be interesting to know if the social disorganization theorists were aware of the strong anti-immigrant themes in American educational policies and how they contextualized those Americanization goals within their supposedly bias-free socialization processes that looked to schools as one mechanism of social cohesion for survival.

CONCLUSION

By weaving cartographic data on juvenile delinquency and crime with theoretical analysis, members of the Chicago School Sociology laid a framework that has dominated criminology discussions throughout the twentieth century. Beginning in the 1930s, these theories were put into practice by Shaw, McKay, and their colleagues with the advent of the Chicago Area Project (CAP). Project workers were recruited from the local community to help organize against crime and to provide advocates and role models who would assert larger social interests. Through increased recreational facilities and equipment, community cleanup endeavors, and juvenile justice advocacy linked with social service assistance, CAP efforts established models for community improvement that are still practiced today. O'Connor (2006) has argued that contemporary "public housing tenant councils; citizen task forces; citizen patrols; and neighborhood watch groups" come the closest to mirroring the CAP perspectives and activities (¶ 22). This interest in the role of community action remains a salient feature of criminology theory to date. A prominent example in the tradition of social disorganization theory is Wilson and Kelling's (1982) broken window theory. They argued that "abandoned buildings and automobiles, the accumulation of trash and litter, broken windows and lights, and graffiti or profanity (signs of crime or incivilities) all invite criminal behavior" (O'Connor, 2006, ¶ 23). Unfortunately, since such programs do not generate direct economic gain and they are not naturally self-sustaining, their failure rate is high unless they receive sustained financial support and augmented structural assistance.

Even with a brief introduction to social disorganization theory, it is easy to see the influence the theoretical framework has on our everyday lives in terms of using community organizations to steer youth into law-abiding behaviors. A bumper-sticker on a YMCA van, for example, states "Keep boys and girls in sports and out of courts." Like so many other aspects of our culture, we know the values and beliefs but not the underlying theoretical frameworks that both analyze our society and influence it.

TERMS & CONCEPTS

Acculturation: A change in the cultural behavior and thinking of a person or group of people through contact with another culture.

Collective Efficacy: The group's ability to accomplish a goal; more specifically, the ability of a community to maintain order in public places.

Delinquency: Antisocial or illegal acts caused by youth under the age of eighteen years.

Ecology: The study of the interactions between living organisms and their environments.

Environmental Determinism: The idea that all behavior, including human action, is caused by the surroundings of the acting subject.

Social Capital: The many informal, interdependent networks that help a community or individual function effectively and achieve its goals.

Subculture: An identifiably separate group within a larger culture, especially one regarded as existing outside of mainstream society.

BIBLIOGRAPHY

Crutchfield, R., Geerken, M., & Gove, W. (1982). "Crime rates and social integration." *Criminology, 20,* 3-4.

Fox, K. A., Rufino, K. A., & Kercher, G. A. (2012). "Crime victimization among gang and non-gang prison inmates: examining perceptions of social disorganization." *Victims and Offenders, 7,* 208–225.

Gibbons, D., & Krohn, M. (1986). *Delinquent behavior.* (4th ed.). Englewood Cliffs, NJ: Prentice-Hall.

Gottfredson, M. & Hirschi, T. (1990). *A general theory of crime.* Stanford, CA: Stanford UP.

Jensen, G. (2003). "Social disorganization theories." In R. Wright (Ed.), *Encyclopedia of criminology.* Boca Raton, FL: Fitzroy Dearborn.

Krohn, M. (2001). "The web of conformity: A network approach to the explanation of delinquent behavior." *Social Problems, 33,* 81-93.

Kubrin, C. (2003). "New directions in social disorganization theory." *Journal of Crime and Delinquency, 40*(4), 374-402.

Lowenkamp, C., Cullen, F., & Pratt, T. (2003). "Replicating Sampson and Grove's test of social disorganization theory: Revisiting a criminological classic." *Journal of Research in Crime and Delinquency, 40,* 351-373.

O'Connor, T. (2006). "Social disorganization theories of crime." *MegaLinks in Criminal Justice.* http://www.apsu.edu/oconnort/crim/crimtheory10.htm

Rock, P., (2002). "Sociological theories of crime." In M. Maguire, M. Morgan, & R. Reiner (Eds.), *Oxford handbook of criminology.* (3rd ed., pp. 51 - 82). Oxford: Oxford University Press.

Regoeczi, W. C., & Jarvis, J. P. (2013). "Beyond the social production of homicide rates: extending social disorganization theory to explain homicide case outcomes." *Justice Quarterly, 30,* 983–1014.

Satterthwaite, M. (1997). *Juvenile crime.* Philadelphia, PA: Chelsea House.

Sampson, R., & Gove, W. (1989). "Community structure and crime: Testing social disorganization theory." *American Journal of Sociology, 94* , 774-802.

Sampson, R., Raudenbusch, S., & Earls, F. (1997). "Neighborhoods and violent crime: A multilevel study of collective efficacy." *Science, 227,* 918-924.

Soukhanov, A. (Ed.). (2004). "Ecology." *Encarta Webster's dictionary of the English language* . (2nd ed.). New York: Bloomsbury.

Stark, R., Bridges, W., Crutchfield, D., Doyle, D., & Finke, R. (1983). "Crime and delinquency in the roaring twenties." *Journal of Research in Crime and Delinquency, 20,* 4-23.

Sutherland, E. (1947). *Principles of criminology* (4th ed.). Philadelphia, PA: Lippincott.

Teasdale, B., Clark, L., & Hinkle, J. (2012). "Subprime lending foreclosures, crime, and neighborhood disorganization: beyond internal dynamics." *American Journal of Criminal Justice, 37,* 163–178.

Warner, B. D., Beck, E., & Ohmer, M. L. (2010). "Linking informal social control and restorative justice: moving social disorganization theory beyond community policing." *Contemporary Justice Review, 13,* 355–369.

Warren, M., & Hindelang, M. (1979). "Current explanations of offender behavior." In H. Toch (Ed.), *Psychology of crime and criminal justice* (pp. 166 - 182). Prospect Heights, IL: Waveland Press.

Wilson, J. (1975). *Thinking about crime.* New York, NY: Basic.

Wong, C. (2007). "Clifford R. Shaw and Henry D. McKay: The social disorganization theory." http://www.csiss.org/classics/content/66.

Suggested Reading

Benko, G., & Strohmayer, U. (Eds.), (1997). *Space and social theory: Interpreting modernity and postmodernity.* Oxford, UK: Blackwell.

Calhoun, C. (Ed.), (1994). *Social theory and the politics of identity.* Cambridge, MA: Blackwell.

Coleman, J. (1990). *Foundations of social theory.* Cambridge, MA: Belknap Press.

Edberg, M. (2007). *Essentials of health behavior: Social and behavioral theory in public health.* Sudbury, MA: Jones & Bartlett.

Farganis, J., (2004). *Readings from social theory: The classic tradition to post-modernism.* (4th ed.). New York, NY: McGraw-Hill.

Kaylen, M. T., & Pridemore, W. A. (2013). "The association between social disorganization and rural violence is sensitive to the measurement of the dependent variable." *Criminal Justice Review, 38,* 169–189.

Kivisto, P. (Ed.), (2007). *Social theory: Roots and branches: Readings.* (3rd ed.). New York, NY: Oxford UP.

Lilly, J., Cullen, F., & Ball, R. (2007). *Criminology theory: Context and consequences.* (4th ed.). Thousand Oaks, CA: Sage.

Ritzer, G. (Ed.), (2007). *Classical sociological theory.* (5th ed.). New York, NY: McGraw-Hill.

Ritzer, G., & Goodman, D. (2007). *Sociological theory.* (6th ed.). New York, NY: McGraw-Hill.

Stinchombe, A. (1987). *Constructing social theories.* Chicago, IL: U. of Chicago Press.

Karen M. Harbeck, Ph.D., J.D.

Sociology of Addiction

ABSTRACT

According to the World Health Organization (WHO), addiction is a worldwide problem. Indeed, over seventy-six million people suffer from alcohol abuse, and more than fifteen million people confront drug abuse issues internationally (World Health Organization, 2008). A British Social Trends report (2002) notes that drinking, smoking and drug addictions are rising in the UK, especially among young people, with more than 50% of teenage boys consuming these substances regularly by the age of 15. In the U.S., the incidence of addiction is so high that there are insufficient trained professionals to assist those affected by drug abuse (Brandeis University Institute for Health Policy, 1993), precipitating a crisis in treatment. "Fewer than one-fourth of the persons in need of alcohol and drug abuse services in the United States actually receive treatment" (p. 60, as cited in American Psychiatric Association, 2008). Yet, according to WHO, such rehabilitation is cost effective, saving seven dollars in "health and social costs" for every one dollar invested in drug treatment programs (WHO, 2008). The establishment and endorsement of addiction prevention and treatment programs are somewhat compromised by debates and controversies over cause.

OVERVIEW

According to the World Health Organization (WHO), addiction is a worldwide problem. Indeed, more than 15.3 million people confront drug abuse issues internationally, and the abuse of alcohol results in 2.5 million deaths every years (World Health Organization, 2012). A British Social Trends report (2002) notes that drinking, smoking, and drug addictions are rising in the United Kingdom, especially among young people, with more than 50 percent of teenage boys consuming these substances regularly by the age of fifteen. In the United States, the incidence of addiction is so high that there are insufficient trained professionals to assist those affected by drug abuse (Brandeis University Institute for Health Policy, 1993), precipitating a crisis in treatment. "Fewer than one-fourth of the persons in need of alcohol and drug abuse services in the United States actually receive treatment" (p. 60, as cited in American Psychiatric Association, 2008). Yet, according to WHO, such rehabilitation is cost-effective, saving seven dollars in "health and social costs" for every one dollar invested in drug treatment programs (WHO, 2008). The establishment and endorsement of addiction prevention and treatment programs are somewhat compromised by debates and controversies over cause.

Defining Addiction

Addiction is "a chronic relapsing illness with onset typically occurring in the early teenage years, followed by cycles of drug use and abstinence" (Elkashef, Biswas, Acri and Vocci, 2007). The source of addiction is complex and entails interactions between biological factors (specifically genes) and environmental factors. Some research suggests that some people are born with a higher tendency to become addicted (NIDA, 2008). According to this argument, addiction is a biological disease, much like diabetes or hypertension, and acquiring the tendency (or predisposition) to addiction is as much out of a person's control as the predisposition to some other diseases.

Alternately, the environment in which people develop (including how they are parented, their socioeconomic status of origin, peer group influences, traumatic or stressful experiences and their levels of education) produces protective or risk-enhancement effects (Elkashef, Biswas, Acri and Vocci, 2007). While many laypeople may view addictive behavior as a choice, there is a growing consensus that both biology and environment are factors in addiction.

Nonetheless, even with explanations about brain chemistry and genetic predisposition, certain images of addiction prevail: the beggar on skid row or the drunk driver. Those images are powerful, and scientific jargon does not erase them from the cover of newspapers or the lead story on the six o'clock news. Concomitantly, Alan I. Leshner (1997) notes the difficulty in addressing such stereotypes:

> One major barrier [to treatment] is the tremendous stigma attached to being a drug user or, worse, an addict. The most beneficent public view of drug addicts is as victims of their societal situation. However, the more common view is that drug addicts are weak or bad people, unwilling to lead moral lives and to control their behavior and gratifications ... We need to face the fact that even if the condition initially comes about because of a voluntary behavior (drug use), an addict's brain is different from a nonaddict's brain ... Recall that as recently as the beginning of this century we were still putting individuals with schizophrenia in prison like asylums, whereas now we know they require medical treatments (par. 4).

Amphetamine-type stimulants are the second most widely abused drugs worldwide, after cannabis (United Nations Office on Drugs and Crime, 2011). According to the WHO Report on the Global Tobacco Epidemic (2013), 19 percent of Americans smoked nicotine in 2012 and tobacco kill nearly six million people each year, up to half of all tobacco users. In many instances, people who become addicted first use substances voluntarily. As Linda S. Cook (2001) noted, most teenagers have used some substance by the time they turn eighteen. One recent study (Sweeting & West, 2008) on the lifetime prevalence of drug use among a cohort of people in the United Kingdom (which tracked use over twenty years), found that drug use, in general, rose from 9 percent at the age of fifteen to 58 percent by age twenty-three.

Many addicts go through a cycle of abuse and recovery that is difficult to explain. As Leshner (2008) observes:

> Many people equate addiction with simply using drugs and therefore expect that addiction should be cured quickly, and if it is not, treatment is a failure. In reality, because addiction is a chronic disorder, the ultimate goal of long-term abstinence often requires sustained and repeated treatment episodes (p. 10).

This cycle of repeated treatment and relapse is difficult for individuals with addiction, their families, and the general public to understand and can also be viewed as an excuse for an addict's behavior. Davies (1997) notes that the biological source of addiction may be accepted for the wrong reasons, as a means to absolve people who behave badly because the disease is out of their control.

FURTHER INSIGHTS

Neurobiology

The biological explanation for addiction is based on research linking addiction to significant changes to brain chemistry caused by repeated substance use. Different kinds of drugs produce particular responses in precise areas of the brain, although the mechanisms underpinning these responses vary, as do the outcomes (Elkashef, Biswas, Acri & Vocci, 2007). For instance, Leshner (1997) notes:

> Virtually all drugs of abuse have common effects, either directly or indirectly, on a single pathway deep within the brain ... Activation of this system appears to be a common element in what keeps drug users taking drugs. Not only does acute drug use modify brain function in critical ways, but prolonged drug use causes pervasive changes in brain function that persist long after the individual stops taking the drug ... The addicted brain is distinctly different from the nonaddicted brain, as manifested by changes in brain metabolic activity, receptor availability, gene expression, and responsiveness to environmental cues ... That addiction is tied to changes in brain structure and function is what makes it, fundamentally, a brain disease (p. 45).

According to Nora Volkow (2008), director of the National Institute on Drug Abuse (NIDA), the recognition of addiction as a biological disease has not only changed the way of thinking about addiction for the scientific community but also the options for treatment.

> When science began to study addictive behavior in the 1930s, people addicted to drugs were thought to be morally flawed and lacking in willpower. Those views shaped society's responses to drug abuse, treating it as a moral failing rather than a health problem, which led to an emphasis on punitive rather than preventative and therapeutic actions ... addiction is a disease that affects both brain and behavior. We have identified many of the biological and environmental factors and are beginning to search for the genetic variations that contribute to the development and progression of the disease (Volkow, 2008, n.p.).

Genetics

In addition to biochemical factors and the cycle of addiction outlined above, according to D. Ball, M. Pembrey, and D. Stephens (2005), genetics is also a causal factor linked to addiction. For instance, they note:

> Twin and adoption studies show that genetics contributes (along with environment) to our vulnerability to different types of addiction, probably via genes that regulate the metabolism of psychoactive drugs and the brain neurotransmitter systems on which they act (as cited in Hall, 2006, p. 1530).

To clarify any confusion about genetics, though, Hall (2006) makes the distinction that,

> ...it is not the case that if you have 'the gene' you will become addicted and if you do not then you will not. Instead, addiction is most likely to be a polygenic disorder that results from interactions between the environment and the effects of a large number of genes ... that affect a variety of personal characteristics such as: drug metabolism, levels of brain neurotransmitters and transporters, preparedness to use drugs, school performance, susceptibility to peer influence, and so on (2006, p. 1530).

Biology & Environment

Focusing on the combination of biology and environment, J. Shedler And J. Block (1990) conducted a longitudinal study to look at drug use in relation to psychological characteristics. Specifically, they assessed both ego and cognitive development during seven different interviews with each of the 101 participants at ages three, four, five, seven, eleven, fourteen, and eighteen years (p. 195). Shedler and Block note that at the age eighteen interview:

> Of the 101 subjects for whom information about drug use was available, 68 percent had

> tried marijuana ... 39 percent ... reported using marijuana once a month or more, and 21 percent reported using it weekly or more than weekly (p. 196).

Based on this data, the researchers created the following three categories of participants—frequent users, abstainers, and experimenters (p. 197) and they were able to make comparisons based on information they collected over the fifteen-year period of the study.

Throughout most of the study, frequent users displayed characteristics that were unique when compared to subjects in the other two categories. For instance, frequent users were identified as:

- Not dependable or responsible
- Not productive
- Deceitful
- Opportunistic
- Unpredictable
- Unable to delay gratification
- Rebellious and nonconforming
- Feeling cheated and victimized by life
- Having fluctuating moods (Shedler & Block, 1990, p. 197).

When compared with subjects who had experimented with marijuana, the subjects in the frequent user group were identified as having adverse characteristics at the age eighteen interviews. Furthermore, "the frequent users appear to be relatively maladjusted as children. As early as age 7, the picture that emerges is of a child unable to form good relationships, who is insecure, and who shows numerous signs of distress" (p. 200). As children, these subjects exhibited similar characteristics as when they were eighteen.

In addition to assessing the child participants in the study, Shedler and Block also assessed the participants' mothers and observed that "compared with the mothers of experimenters, both the mothers of frequent users and the mothers of abstainers were perceived to be cold, critical, pressuring, and unresponsive to their children's' needs" (p. 205). Such research suggests that how a person is treated by his or her primary caregiver when he or she is a child will most likely affect the way he or she behaves in later life, although it is not certain how that behavior will manifest. What is clear from this research, however, is that "the relative social and psychological maladjustment of the frequent users predates adolescence, and predates initiation of drug use" (p. 200). It is probable that the drug use leading to addiction is most likely the symptom of a greater issue.

VIEWPOINTS

Blame & Biology

One of the problems with addiction is that many people do not understand it and place blame on those who are addicted. Attribution theory explains the rules that people use to infer the causes of behavior. While people tend to attribute their own behaviors to their social circumstances (or environment) they attribute other people's behaviors (especially socially problematic behaviors) to personality or biology (Davies, 1997).

John Monterosso, Edward B. Royzman, and Barry Schwartz (2005) tested attribution theory in a study to determine if people would be more willing to accept negative behavior if it was the result of physiology (biological make-up) rather than experience (environmental factors) (p. 139). Almost two hundred subjects participated with an almost even split between university undergraduates (n=96) and middle-class white adults in a suburban area (n=100) (p. 142). The participants were presented with several written scenarios that depicted characters intentionally behaving in negative ways. Each scenario randomly offered one of two explanations for the character's behavior, and participants were asked to determine whether they thought the behavior was voluntary. For instance, in one scenario, a man killed a store clerk in an argument. The explanation given for this behavior was that either he had an exceptionally high quantity of a particular neurotransmitter or had a history of being severely abused as a child (Monterosso, Royzman & Schwartz, 2005, p. 143). The researchers were not surprised by their findings:

> Observers judged actors as less responsible for misdeeds explained physiologically than for those explained experientially ... Physiological explanations resulted in ... less judged volition, greater sympathy, greater blame mitigation, more positive treatment, and a greater expressed likelihood by the participants that they would also behave in

> the undesirable way if the antecedent were true of them (Monterosso, Royzman & Schwartz, 2005, p. 150).

Specifically, one of the participants explained, "I don't think it can be willpower or character if it is a brain thing" (Monterosso, Royzman & Schwartz, 2005, p. 153). In other words, the characters in the scenarios were considered less responsible for their actions—even when they murdered someone—when a physiological basis rather than an environmental basis was cited as the reason for their actions. In addition, subjects in the study felt sympathy for the characters based on the circumstance of biology.

Treating Addiction

There are three main approaches to treating addiction: behavioral (cognitive behavioral therapy or motivational enhancement), pharmacologic, and immunologic therapies, such as vaccines, especially for stimulant use disorders and nicotine addiction (Elkashef, Biswas, Acri & Vocci, 2007).

Research in the field of genetics suggests that there are biological underpinnings to drug abuse disorders, and, concomitantly, biological markers that can be identified (for instance, through brain imaging techniques) and used to plan more precise treatment regimes (Schumann, 2007). However, the routine use of genomic medicine is limited until future research further develops a proper methodology. In the meantime, there is no magic treatment for substance addiction, and while many people find success with twelve-step programs, in-patient programs, outpatient programs, or a combination of any of these, no program offers individuals suffering from addiction or their families a guarantee of sobriety.

Indeed, treatment for addiction is as complex as the causes of addiction and typically includes a mix of pharmacologic (e.g. non-addictive stimulant substitution, such as nicotine replacement products) and behavioral/psychological therapy, such as motivational enhancement and cognitive behavior therapy, which focuses on "patterns of thinking that are maladaptive and the beliefs that underlie such thinking" (NAMI, n.d.).

However, according to Wayne Hall, Lucy Carter, and Katherine Morley (2003), neuroscience research offers hope that a cure and possibly even a vaccine for addiction may eventually be developed (p. 867). Such research:

> ... may lead to more effective ways of helping drug dependent people to withdraw from their drug of dependence and it may increase their chances of remaining abstinent (Koob, 2000). We may also have immunological prostheses for relapse prevention—'drug vaccines'—that help former addicts remain abstinent by preventing their drug of choice from acting on receptors in their brains during the period when they are most vulnerable to relapse (Fox, 1997; Hall, 2002) (Hall, Carter & Morley, 2003, p. 867).

Preventing Addiction

Addiction has a very good chance of ruining a young person's life (Cook, 2001). In a study looking at criminal behavior and adolescents, F. A. Esbensen, D. Huizinga, and S. Menard (1999) identified that "chemical dependence played a greater role in the number and types of crimes committed than criminal behavior did in the development of addiction" (as cited in Cook, 2001, p. 151). What is even more alarming is that substance use among this population is pervasive. Cook (2001) notes statistics gathered by the National Household Survey on Drug Abuse from 1995 to show how prevalent substance abuse is within this population.

By the age of fourteen, over one-third of the student population has tried an illegal drug. The numbers rise to 46 percent by the age of sixteen and 52 percent by the age of eighteen. The figures for alcohol use are higher: 55 percent of fourteen-year-olds, 71 percent of sixteen-year-olds, and 81 percent of eighteen-yearolds. For those children who do become dependent upon drugs or alcohol, however, the consequences are devastating. All aspects of the child's life are affected. Academic performance typically drops as absenteeism increases. Hawkins, Catalano, and Miller (1992) allude to an increased school dropout rate among adolescent drug users. The cessation of education places limits on the child's future employment and earning potential, making it more difficult to support oneself and making poverty more likely (Cook, 2001, p. 152).

The link between substance abuse and criminal behavior should make it clear that a population so impressionable needs intervention before abuse or dependence is an issue as recognized by campaigns such as the National Youth Anti-Drug Media Campaign. Researchers know that just because children inherit a predisposition to addiction does not mean that they will become addicted. Nor can anyone be sure that being neglected as a child leads to life-avoidance patterns such as substance abuse. However, what is known is that links have been made between biological and environmental factors. With that knowledge, society as a whole—doctors, psychologists, educators, neighbors—can focus resources on those youth who are predisposed to dependency before the disease takes over their lives.

TERMS & CONCEPTS

Abstinence: Restraint from a behavior or activity.

Abuse: Using something in a harmful (often habitual) way.

Addiction: Being physiologically or psychologically dependent on a drug or habitual behavior.

Chronic: An illness or condition (often medical) that lasts over a long period of time and which can cause changes in the body.

Compulsion: The inability to resist a desire to do something.

Disease: A disorder that is pathological in nature.

Predisposition: Susceptibility to an illness or disease based on genetic factors.

Relapse: A return to undesirable behavior that was once stopped.

Volition: The ability to make choices, whether positive or negative.

Bibliography

Adan, A. (2013). "A chronobiological approach to addiction." *Journal of Substance Use, 18*(3). 171–183.

American Psychiatric Association. (2008). "Training needs in addiction psychiatry." Position Statement: 199512. APA website: http://www.psych.org/ Departments/ EDU/Library/APAOfficialDocumentsand Related/ PositionStatements/199512.aspx

Appel, J., Backes, G. & Robbins, J. (2004). "California's Proposition 36: a success ripe for refinement and replication." *Criminology and Public Policy,* 3(4): 585-592.

Cook, L. (2001). "Adolescent addiction and delinquency in the family system." *Issues in Mental Health Nursing,* 22(2), 151-157.

Davies, J. (1997). *The myth of addiction.* 2nd edition. New York: Harwood Academic Publishers.

Elkashef, A., Biswas, J., Acri, J.B. & Vocci, F. (2007). "Biotechnology and the treatment of addictive disorders." *Biodrugs,* 21(4):259-267.

Hall, W. (2006). "Avoiding potential misuses of addiction brain science." *Addiction,* 101(11) 1529-1532.

Hall, W., Carter, L., & Morley, K. (2003). "Addiction, neuroscience and ethics." *Addiction,* 98(7), 867-870.

Kovac, V. B. (2013). "The more the merrier: a multi-sourced model of addiction." *Addiction Research and Theory, 21*(1), 19–32.

Leshner, A. I. (2008). "Principles of drug addiction treatment: A research based guide." National Institute on Drug Abuse. website: http:// www.nida.nih.gov/PDF/PODAT/PODAT.pdf

Leshner, A. (1997). "Addiction is a brain disease, and it matters." *Science,* 278(5335), 45.

Monterosso, J., Royzman, E. B. & Schwartz, B. (2005). "Explaining away responsibility: Effects of scientific explanation on perceived culpability." *Ethics & Behavior,* 15(2), 139-158.

National Alliance on Mental Illness. (2003). "Cognitive Behavior Therapy." http://www.nami.org

National Institute on Drug Abuse. (2008). "Addiction: Drugs, brains, and behavior: The Science of addiction." NIDA website: http://www.nida. nih.gov/scienceofaddiction/

Office for National Statistics. (2002). *Social trends.* London: The Stationary Office.

Reinarman, C. (2005). "Addiction as accomplishment: The discursive construction of disease." *Addiction Research & Theory,* 13(4), 307-320.

Richter, L., Foster, S. E. (2013). "The exclusion of nicotine: closing the gap in addiction policy and practice." *American Journal of Public Health, 103*(8), E14–E16.

Shedler, J. & Block, J. (1990). "Adolescent drug use and psychological health: A longitudinal inquiry." In, Duntley, J. & Shaffer, L., eds. (1995). *Human Development Across the Life Span* (3rd ed.). [194-211]. Acton, Massachusetts: Copley Custom.

Schumann, G. (2007). "Okey Lecture 2006: identifying the neurobiological mechanisms of addictive behavior." *Addiction*, 102, 1689-95.

United Nations Office on Drugs and Crime (2003). "Global illicit drug trends." New York: United Nations Publication. http://www.unodc.org

United Nations Office on Drugs and Crime (2011). "ATS: second most commonly abuse drug type worldwide." UNODC website: http://www.unodc.org/unodc/en/frontpage/2011/ September/ats-second-most-used-drug-type-in-the-world. html

Volkow, N. D. (2008). "Preface: Addiction: Drugs, brains, and behavior—The Science of addiction." National Institute on Drug Abuse. NIDA website: http://www.nida.nih.gov/scienceofaddiction/

World Health Organization (2008). "Facts and figures. Management of substance abuse." WHO website: http://www.who.int/ substance%5fabuse/facts/en/

World Health Organization (2012). "Facts and figures. Management of substance abuse." WHO website: http://www.who.int/

Suggested Reading

Allamani, A. (2007). "Addiction, risk, and resources." *Substance Use & Misuse*, 42(2/3), 421-439.

Astramovich, R. L., & Hoskins, W. J. (2013). "Evaluating addictions counseling programs: promoting best practices, accountability, and advocacy." *Journal of Addictions and Offender Counseling, 34*(2), 114–124.

Ball D., Pembrey, M. & Stephens, D. (2005). *Foresight state of the art science review: Genomics.* London: Department of Trade and Industry.

Brandeis University Institute for Health Policy. (1993). *Substance abuse: The nation's number one health problem.* Princeton, N.J.: Robert Wood Johnson Foundation.

Hawkins, J. D., Catalano, R. F., & Miller, J. Y. (1992). "Risk and protective factors for alcohol and other drug problems in adolescence and early adulthood: Implications for substance abuse prevention." *Psychological Bulletin*, 112(1), 64-105.

Johnson, B. D., Wish, E. D., Schmeidler, J., & Huizinga, D. (1991). "Concentration of delinquent offending: Serious drug involvement and high delinquency rates." *Journal of Drug Issues*, 21(2), 205-229.

Keire, M. (1998). "Dope fiends and degenerates: The gendering of addiction in the early twentieth century." *Journal of Social History*, 31(4), 809.

Read, D., & Roelofsma, P. (1999). "Hard choices and weak wills: the theory of intrapersonal dilemmas." *Philosophical Psychology*, 12(3), 341.

Stephenson, A. L., Henry, C. S. & Robinson, L. C. (1996). "Family characteristics and adolescent substance use." *Adolescence*, 31(121), 59-77.

Sabini, J., & Silver, M. (1982). *Moralities of everyday life.* New York: Oxford University Press.

Shultz, T., Schleifer, M., & Altman, I. (1981). "Judgments of causation, responsibility and punishment in cases of harm-doing." *Canadian Journal of Behavioural Sciences*, 13, 238-253.

Strawson, P. (1962). "Freedom and resentment." In G. Watson (Ed.), *Free will* (pp. 59-80). New York: Oxford University Press.

Tweed, S. H. (1998). "Intervening in adolescent substance abuse." *Nursing Clinics of North America*, 33(1), 29-45.

Weiner, B. (1995). *Judgments of responsibility: A foundation for a theory of social conduct.* New York: Guilford Press.

World Health Organization. (2002). "Policy Recommendatoins for Smoking Cessation and Treatment of Tobacco Dependence." Geneva: WHO.

Maureen McMahon, M.S., and Alexandra Howson

Subcultural Theories of Deviance

ABSTRACT

Subcultural theories of deviance emerged in the 1950s and were popular for only 20 years before they were charged with ethnocentrism. Instead of adopting the traditional perspective within criminology that individuals turn to crime because their access to legitimate opportunity structures is limited or nonexistent, subcultural theorists argued that lower-class individuals form completely different, collective views on the nature of criminal behavior, making the class a unique subculture within American society. Access to legitimate opportunity structures is blocked for this group, but since the entire group feels the same frustrations, it forms its own values and norms that make delinquent behavior and membership in gangs acceptable and rewarding. By 1964, critics were arguing that subcultural theories of deviance were the work of middle class intellectual elites who were trying to impose their norms and values upon lower-class groups. Similarly, it was argued that the values attributed to these subcultural groups are not universal or constant either within the group or within any given individual's life experience. Thus critics argued that membership in gangs is transitory, and that the excitement of crime is classless.

OVERVIEW

Culture is a complex term with many different meanings, but sociologists studying culture tend to focus on the norms, beliefs, customs, and values shared by a group of likeminded individuals. Culture is transmitted socially between members of a given group as well as to subsequent generations. It is a "majority rule" framework in which dominant values and beliefs are deemed normal and acceptable, and alternative perspectives are viewed on a continuum ranging from mere eccentricism to outright immorality. A *subculture,* then, is a subgroup within the larger cultural population. It shares some of the norms and beliefs of the dominant group, but it also holds values that are distinctly different from the majority.

Subcultural theories of *deviance* focused on minority populations that sociologists and criminologists labeled as holding views of crime and *delinquency*different from those held by the white, Anglo-Saxon, Protestant (WASP) majority in American and English society. An articulation of these dominant WASP values drives these societies' criminal laws, along with their social mores about proper behavior. Labeling the dominant cultural values as WASP is intentional, since most of the subcultural theories of deviance focused on lower-class individuals, youth, and minority populations. These subgroups, it was argued, develop their own cultural values, particularly in regard to deviance and crime. Miller (1958), for example, argued that the working-class youth in his study had a different "focal concern" that was pervasive in their subculture around concepts of trouble, toughness, excitement, smartness, fatalism, and autonomy. Because of these different norms or values, high crime rates could be explained as consistent with their subcultural values. Critics of Miller's arguments said that not all working-class youth resort to lives of immediate need-fulfillment and crime, especially women, leading them to conclude that high crime rates cannot be explained by pervasive subcultural values. Subcultural theorists also were criticized for being insensitive to issues of race, class, gender, and ethnicity, since many of the studies regarded inner-city crime as having a place of value uniformly within a given population.

HISTORY

The Anomie Theory

Subcultural theories of deviance grew out of the work of French sociologist Émile Durkheim (1858–1917), who laid the foundation for what is called the *structural-functionalist* perspective on crime. According to Durkheim, since a society in part consists of shared values, the sources of crime and deviance also can be found within that social structure. Durkheim argued that crime is a normal and universal part of all cultures and that it even has some positive functions in a society. Political protests about racial inequality, for example, might move a society to be more racially inclusive and just. In pre-industrial societies, though, the general uniformity of roles and values promoted conformity;

although crime existed within the culture, its role was limited. But Durkheim and other sociologists were concerned with industrial times and what they believed was a weaker collective conscience around values, norms, and rules. Specifically, Durkheim argued that *normlessness,* or *anomie,* permits crime to flourish because "the disciplines and authority of society are so flawed that they offer few restraints or moral direction" (Rock, 2002, p. 52.). This became known as anomie theory in sociology and criminology.

Strain Theory

Robert Merton (1910–2003) built upon Durkheim's anomie theory to create what is known as *strain theory.* Merton asserted that there is "a universal aspiration to accumulate material wealth," but because our society is stratified into various classes, those in the lower economic levels do not have an equal opportunity to realize their desires for wealth (Gottfredson, p. 78). Under strain to reach these culturally induced goals, some individuals adapt by turning to crime as a means of material gain. Merton argued further that middle-class values generally conflict with engaging in criminal activities, causing members of the middles class to experience especially high levels of strain should they consider engaging in criminal conduct. In the inner-city where crime is highest, the theory holds that because lower-class individuals do not have the same socialization—or in fact, because their cultural processes hold a different view of crime altogether—they feel less strain when not adhering to *dominant* cultural values, such as behaving in a law-abiding manner. With subcultural values different from or even in opposition to the dominant norms, these lower-class communities might give law breakers high status because of their material success.

Social Disorganization Theory

Strain theory argues that individuals in the lower classes are aware of how the dominant culture values material wealth, but are frustrated in realizing this value by acquiring wealth for themselves. Another group of theorists who focus on social disorganization would say that the dominant culture's values have not been instilled in these groups and, therefore, are not an aspiration. *Social disorganization*theories came out of the Chicago Sociology School that dominated criminology for much of the twentieth century. Working from data on juvenile crime, this school mapped crime rate areas throughout the city of Chicago and discovered that certain zones or areas of the city experience high rates of crime regardless of their communities' racial or ethnic makeup at any period of time. This methodology, when combined with ecological theories, views "the physical structure of communities as shaping the routine activities of inhabitants in ways that affect the likelihood of crime" (Gottfredson, p. 82). Through the interplay of people and the environment and its resources, the various zones of the city would evolve into diverse, unique areas with the residents sharing similar social characteristics. This process could be said to mirror the evolutionary changes plants and animals undergo as they adapt to the varied ecological niches in a diverse landscape.

Social Control Theory

Because social disorganization theory emphasizes the obligation of the community to train or socialize individuals and then monitor their behavior to ensure lawful actions, it received significant attention from *social control* theory circles. Social control theorists hypothesize that an individual can turn to crime when his or her connection or identification with the dominant culture is ineffective. In fact, like their social disorganization counterparts, they believe that people find crime useful, profitable, and enjoyable unless they are influenced by larger societal values to forego these returns. Their ideal is to preserve what many would call "WASP" values about lawful personal conduct. To do this, control theorists argue for interventions that control deviance and reorganize communities so that traditional cultural values are encouraged and enhanced. Identification with traditional values instills mechanisms of internal, individual control through a social bond that helps group wellbeing. In addition to policing mechanisms, external social control is exerted through involving people in community activities, displaying role models, and using peer pressure. These mechanisms create social bonds that can dissuade the individual from engaging in activities that would disappoint the other members of the group.

Gang Theory

The last theoretical element needed for the development of subcultural theoriesof deviance is *gang theory,* which was first articulated by Frederick Thrasher in 1927. Thrasher was a member of the Chicago Sociology School and an adherent to social disorganization theory. He undertook a systematic study of gangs and concluded that they originate spontaneously from adolescent play groups that get into mischief. As these groups' activities increasingly focus on illegal and delinquent behavior, opposition to their existence increases, which in turn augments and cements their group identities. *Cultural transmission theory,* which has dominated discussions in criminal causation into the twenty-first century, was offered as the mechanism by which each subsequent generation learns gang values and behavior. According to O'Connor (2006), this theory states that "traditions of delinquency are transmitted through successive generations of the same zone in the same way language, roles, and attitudes are transmitted" (p. 4). This *acculturation* process builds communities of individuals who view criminal acts in ways that significantly differ from the dominant norm. A successful drug dealer within a given community, for example, might be respected for his wealth and business abilities rather than be reviled as a thug and a criminal. Since these gangs were prevalent in inner-city areas experiencing high population turnover, poverty, and racial/ethnic heterogeneity, Thrasher argued that these groups provide members with a sense of identity and belonging.

VIEWPOINTS

Albert Cohen

Drawing on various aspects of the theoretical frameworks discussed above, Albert Cohen set forth the foundational work on subcultural theories of deviance in 1955. Studying gangs of delinquent boys from working class sums, Cohen set forth the argument that these gangs form a distinctive subculture within American society. Cohen believed that crime is a structural element of society, and, like Merton, he believed that the youth in these gangs suffer from cultural strain because of their unequal access to opportunity in American society. Cohen's views differed from Merton and others, though, because he argued that the delinquency he witnessed was not just an individual response to cultural strain. Rather, he believed, it is a collective response. By weaving in the Freudian idea of *reaction formation,* Cohen argued that these young men, facing the prospect of profoundly failing to achieve the dominant culture's monetary aspirations, undergo a psychological transformation that makes them reject the dominant culture's values and create their own centered around crime and personal advancement. According to Rock (2002), "the practical and utilitarian in middle-class life was transformed into non-utilitarian delinquency; respectability became malicious negativism; and the deferment of gratification became short-run hedonism" (p. 54).

Cohen's theoretical framework falls within the *reactive subculture* structural argument about subgroup formation. As noted above, Cohen believed that the new subculture is formed "as both a response to and opposition against the prevailing norms and values that exist in a wider (predominantly middle-class or 'conventional') culture" (Livesey, n.d., p. 2). This perspective fits within Merton's strain theory framework as an explanation of how a group can create values that are in opposition to the dominant culture. An alternative to reactive subculture is the notion of *independent subculture,* wherein "the members of the group are held to adopt a set of norms and values which are effectively 'self-contained' and specific to the group" (Livesey, p. 8). Miller's work on gangs provides an example of this form of subcultural grouping, since he argued that their subcultural norms are merely a solution to problems faced by group members in their everyday lives. Gangs, he believed, are an independent cultural phenomena based upon lower-class beliefs and experiences.

In addition to advancing the theory that a collective solution to status frustration creates subcultures within the larger society, Cohen also argued that it is possible for crime to have no utilitarian or monetary function. Rather, it could be used to consolidate group loyalty and to foster bonding between individuals within the gang. Graffiti and other forms of vandalism, for example, are seen as expressions of malice and defiance toward the dominant cultural as well as mechanisms to express group identity. Because they cannot have the American dream as it is expressed through the dominant culture's values and norms, Cohen argued, youth gangs reject the majority beliefs and pursue values that are in direct opposition to them. Thus, because of the groups' subcultural norms, instant gratification, malice, disruptive and destructive behavior, and intent to injure are all rewarded with prestige, recognition, and greater authority within the group.

Richard Cloward & Lloyd Ohlin

In 1960, Richard Cloward and Lloyd Ohlin also argued that delinquent working class youth gangs are a subculture. They, too, agreed with Merton that the development of subcultures is related to the limited opportunities members of the lower classes have to legitimate means for success in the dominant society. While Merton had focused on the *legitimate opportunity structure* of the dominant culture, Cloward and Ohlin argued that there are three parallel *illegitimate opportunity structures* within the lower class subcultures that steer working-class youth into crime. In other words, instead of one grand subculture, Cloward and Ohlin argued that there are three, each with a different mechanism and structure to attract youthful members. The first illegitimate structure is *criminal* and refers to the existence of well-organized, adult, utilitarian criminal networks intent upon crime as a means of material gain. Within this subculture, youth learn the "tricks of the trade" and become socialized in the subculture's values and beliefs. The second subculture is *conflict* focused and involves gangs of youth destructively acting out their frustration at their inability to access both legitimate and illegitimate opportunity structures. The third subculture involves *retreat.* Illegal drug use and prostitution are the fate of these individuals who are "double failures" since they cannot access legitimate or illegitimate opportunity structures.

Walter Miller

The third major contributor to subcultural theories of deviance was Walter Miller, whose work is mentioned above. Miller agreed that delinquency is a subculture for working class youth, but he argued that the subculture is an outgrowth of lower-class values and norms passed on to young males, not a reaction to the dominant middle-class culture. Since unskilled labor is boring and unrewarding, Miller argued that little satisfaction could come from adhering to the middle-class work ethic. Instead, Miller believed, young males are taught to focus on other concerns like street smarts, recognition, making trouble, and prestige within the gang. The gang becomes the unit of identification; more than the family, work, school, or the community, it allows the members to feel like they belong to something and provides a means for status enhancement within its ranks. The subculture, in Miller's opinion, is the lower-class collective that sees gang affiliations as a normal response to a lack of opportunities for economic advancement. Miller went on to argue that it is unfortunate that the dominant society labels the actions of the delinquents as criminal, since within the subculture the label is not relevant or accurate.

As noted above, Miller introduced the concept of *focal concerns* to the discussion of lower-class culture. Six characteristics make up this analysis. The first is *trouble,*which assumes that lower-class males have a tendency to become involved in acts of violence, so they quickly learn how to handle it. *Toughness* is the second subgroup focal concern, since the boy has to be able to handle trouble with masculine abilities relating to strength and endurance. *Smartness* is related to being "street smart" and able to cope with trouble. It also means the ability to look good and impress others, especially women. *Excitement* involves the constant search for thrills and having fun. According to Miller, this is an expressive outlet for the lack of meaningful self-expression through education or an occupation. *Fate* is the fifth focal point and involves an assumption that life is out of the individual's control so nothing can be done to create change or assert control. Livesey argued that this lack of control produces a focus on hedonistic leisure activities that seem to occur as a result of chance or fate. The sixth focal concern, according to Miller, is *autonomy.* Since group members are fatalistic about the life circumstances, they resent authority figures and rules. Instead, they seek ways of exercising freedom and independence in situations where they do have some control or influence. Usually these situations involve delinquency and crime. Obviously, one major area of criticism of Miller's work involves his complete acceptance of heightened definitions of masculinity, while at the same time ignoring the lower-class female experience within the study populations. Collinson (1990) and others argued that Miller's findings have nothing to do with a different subculture, but rather are a reflection of heightened masculine values that are the underpinnings of deviant behavior.

Critical Views

In 1964, David Matza provided the first major criticism of subcultural theories of deviance, a trend that led to a rapid retreat from their acceptability. Matza argued that young people in gangs are not adherents to unique or different subculturalvalues. Rather, they drift in and out of conventional and unconventional behavior based upon their life circumstances. This is called an *interactionalist* perspective on criminal behavior. Even though the dominant culture's values and expectations are clear, Matza argued that individuals have ways of ignoring those demands in order to avoid feeling guilty about not adhering to them. This process of ignoring the dominant culture, however, falls far short of the formation of unique subgroups with alternative values and expectations that could be considered subculture entities. Matza also argued that delinquent behavior is fun and exciting, and any interest in this thrill has little to do with class considerations. Arguably, anyone could make a rational choice to commit vandalism, for example, knowing that structural restraints are in place to prohibit vandalism and that he or she might be arrested and punished.

Subsequent studies of working-class adolescents by Downes (1966) found little support for Cohen's arguments that working class gang members are frustrated with their status in life or "resentful of their lack of legitimate employment prospects" as argued by Cloward and Ohlin (Livesey, p. 11). Downes did find unplanned, petty acts of crime that seemed to add excitement to otherwise boring life circumstances, but none of these actions was a predictor of a life of crime.

As noted above, the influence of subcultural theories of deviance lasted from 1950 through the late 1960s. Closer scrutiny of lower-class youth gangs revealed little evidence to prove that distinct and oppositional subcultures form around differing attitudes toward criminal behavior. Not only were defined, shared values lacking within these gangs, but membership in the gangs also proved to be transitory. The theoretical framework also was challenged by anthropologists, who argued that the subcultural theorists' analysis of culture and subcultures was shallow and failed to adhere to more rigorous disciplinary considerations. The most significant criticism of subcultural theories of deviance, however, had to do with the theories' *ethnocentric* adherence to the values of middle class individuals over those of the lower class. By suggesting that lower-class individuals adhere to differing views of criminal action, subcultural theorists downplayed the hardships and tragedies wrought on communities facing high levels of crime and delinquency. By building their theories solely on young, male gang members, the subculturaltheorists also failed to look at the larger issues of criminal conduct in a society, violence within families and towards women and children, and white collar and middle-class crime.

TERMS & CONCEPTS

Adherents: A supporter of a cause or a leader.

Acculturation: A change in the cultural behavior and thinking of a person or group of people through contact with another culture.

Delinquency: Antisocial or illegal acts performed by youth under the age of 18.

Deviance: Activities that do not conform to the norms of a particular community or society.

Ecology: The study of interactions between living organisms and their environment.

Ethnocentric: A belief in or assumption of the superiority of one's social or cultural group over others.

Reactive Subculture: A new subculture that is formed "as both a response to and opposition against the prevailing norms and values that exist in a wider (predominantly middle-class or 'conventional') culture" (Livesey, n.d., p. 2).

Subculture: An identifiably separate group within a larger culture, especially one regarded as existing outside of mainstream society.

Bibliography

Cloward, R., & Ohlin, L. (1960). *Delinquency and opportunity*. New York: Free Press.

Cohen, A. (1955). *Delinquent boys: The culture of the gang*. Glencoe, IL: Free Press.

Collinson, D., Knight, D., & Collinson, M. (1990). *Managing to discriminate.* London: Routledge.

Downes, D. (1966). *The delinquent solution.* London: Routledge and Kegan Paul.

Gottfredson, M. & Hirschi, T. (1990). *A general theory of crime.* Stanford, CA: Stanford University Press.

Livesey, C. (n.d.). "Deviance and social control: Subcultural theories." http://www.sociology.org.uk/devteco.pdf

Matza, D. (1964). *Delinquency and drift.* New York: Transaction Press.

Miller, W. (1958). "Lower-class culture as a generating milieu of gang delinquency." *Journal of Social Issues, 14* (3), 5–20.

O'Connor, T. (2006). "Social disorganization theories of crime." http://www.apsu.edu/oconnort/crim/crimtheory10.htm.

Petre, R. (2013). "Criminalization of youth in Romania: The creation and amplification of youth deviance." *Social Work Review / Revista De Asistenta Sociala,* (1), 153–162.

Piquero, A., Intravia, J., Stewart, E., Piquero, N., Gertz, M., & Bratton, J. (2012). "Investigating the determinants of the street code and its relation to offending among adults." *American Journal of Criminal Justice, 37* (1), 19–32.

Rock, P. (2002). "Sociological theories of crime." In M. Maguire, M. Morgan, & R. Reiner (Eds.), *Oxford handbook of criminology.* (3rd ed., pp. 51–82). Oxford: Oxford University Press.

Spencer, D. (2011). "Cultural criminology: An invitation... to what?" *Critical Criminology, 19* (3), 197–212.

Suggested Reading

Banks, C. (2013). *Youth, crime, and justice.* New York, NY: Routledge.

Deflem, M. (2006). "Sociological theory and criminological research: Views from Europe and the United States: Vol. 7." *Sociology of crime, laws and deviance.* Oxford: Elsevier.

Downes, D., & Rock, P. (2007). *Understanding deviance.* (5th ed.). Oxford: Oxford University Press.

Downes, D., & Rock, P. (2011). *Understanding deviance: A guide to the sociology of crime and rule-breaking.* (6th ed.) Oxford, UK: Oxford University Press.

Farganis, J. (2004). *Readings in Social Theory: The classic tradition to post-modernism.* (4th ed.). New York, NY: McGraw-Hill.

Frelich, M., Raybeck, D., & Savishinsky, J. (Eds.). (1991). *Deviance: Anthropological perspectives.* New York: Greenwood.

Hendershott, A. (2004). *The politics of deviance.* San Francisco, CA: Encounter Books.

Kaplan, H., & Johnson, R. (2001). *Social deviance: Testing a general theory.* New York: Kluver Academic.

Kivisto, P. (Ed.). (2007). *Social theory: Roots and branches: Readings.* (3rd ed.). New York, NY: Oxford University Press.

Lilly, J., Cullen, F., & Ball, R. (2007). *Criminology theory: Context and consequences.* (4th ed.). Thousand Oaks, CA: Sage.

Ritzer, G. (Ed.). (2007). *Classical sociological theory.* (5th ed.). New York, NY: McGraw-Hill.

Ritzer, G., & Goodman, D. (2007). *Sociological theory.* (6th ed.). New York, NY: McGraw-Hill.

Stinchombe, A. (1987). *Constructing social theories.* Chicago, IL: University Of Chicago Press.

Karen M. Harbeck, Ph.D., J.D.

VICTIM BLAMING

ABSTRACT

The term "victim blaming" refers to the act of attributing blame or responsibility to victims for their victimization. Many reasons exist for victim blaming, such as avoiding feelings of guilt, fear of vulnerability or misfortune, the desire to exculpate aggressors, and the need to believe that the world is a just and fair place in which people get what they deserve. Sometimes victim blaming also serves to maintain or restore social status.

OVERVIEW

People react to victims in various ways, such as empathizing with the victim, supporting the victim and providing assistance. On the other hand, people may react by holding the victim fully or partially responsible for the event in which he or she has been victimized. In short, the victim is attributed responsibility for his or her condition. This reaction is known as victim blaming (Vynckier, 2012). The situations for which victims are blamed are many: poverty, crime, illness, violence, harassment, stalking, economic exploitation, and many others.

Marginalization

Victim blaming has existed for a very long time and has always been a mechanism of emotional distancing and moral disinterest. Historians point out that slaveholding societies dehumanize enslaved people, creating a sometimes vast machinery of discourse, theories, and ideology to attribute enslaved people some degree of responsibility for their condition. In such situations, the victims are positioned as less than human and even happy with their condition. This allows people who benefit from slavery to live comfortably without having to question their own self-image and brutal acts of oppression (Romito, 2008).

Victim blaming is similarly used to legitimate poverty and marginalization. As with slavery and racial oppression, myriad scientific and social theories have been created to justify the condition of poor people, such as the "culture of poverty" theory, which attributes the condition of poor people to factors such as the prevalence of a single-parent family structure and behavioral issues such as lack of control. These instances of victim blaming often hide the very material effects of institutionalized racism, discrimination, economic exploitation, and overall oppression (Romito, 2008).

Sexual and Domestic Violence

Victimized children also suffer instances of victim blaming, for example, when they are made responsible for acts of physical or sexual abuse against them. There are whole discourses of blame to legitimize domestic violence against women and children, for example, in which they are often blamed for violence aimed at them for having provoked it with their behavior, or else accused of secretly enjoying it. After more than a decade of recurrent scandals regarding the sexual abuse of children within the Catholic Church by clergy, prominent church leaders gave statements adducing that the children might also have born at least partial responsibility for the abuse, by inviting or provoking it (Blaming the Victim, 2008). In some cases, despite the vulnerability of the victim, he or she is blamed for "allowing it to happen," a scenario common in bullying cases. Instances of victim blaming are often compounded by prejudiced attitudes, such as racism, sexism, and homophobia, so that individuals from discriminated against groups bear the brunt of the worst instances of victim blaming.

Women victims of domestic violence are often blamed for staying with their victimizer, and her mental health and intelligence are called into question. It was commonplace, up to the late twentieth century, for many to quote psychological theories positing that pathological dysfunctions led some women to cleave to an abusive relationship. Despite contemporary evidence to the contrary, this myth remains commonplace. In fact, studies consistently show that most people surveyed believe women to be responsible for the violence they suffer in relationships as well as in cases of sexual violence.

Institutionalized Indifference

These stereotypes influence public health and legal institutions, and are part of the legal system in some countries. For example, some psychological theories support the argument that when women say no, they really mean yes; also pertinent are rape corroboration laws (Romito, 2008). Corroboration laws requires additional corroboration of essential facts that have been initially evidenced in court. Rape victim advocates charge that such laws are used to dismiss the testimonial validity of a victim's statement by requiring further evidence. Although corroboration laws in may localities have been eliminated or reformed, in many places they are still effective in blocking rape prosecutions (Falk, 2014).

Institutionalized instances of victim blaming often discourage victims from appealing to legal redress. Even in advanced countries with enlightened justice systems, victims of violence are often denigrated and alienated through the legal process. In the case of minors who are victims of sexual abuse, they are often removed from their home and placed in foster care or an institution. In less developed societies, abused women and children often become outcasts. Their shame may extend to their families, compounding the marginalization, while aggressors remain unaccountable for their victimizing acts.

Therefore, psychological and legal theories dovetail coherently with social attitudes; in other words, victim blaming may be a prevalent ideology. As such, it has very real social and material impacts. An ideology is a set of concepts and beliefs mostly used to support or defend the status quo, that is, the interests of a dominant group. Its ulterior aim, in the case of victim blaming, is to exculpate the aggressor. International cooperation organizations find these attitudes extend across countries and regions. A report published by the Human Rights Interamerican Commission, for example, shows police authorities, court officials, and other government representatives often blame victims of violence and abuse for their situation, adducing reasons such as their lifestyle, attire, and behavior. In other words, victim blaming becomes an ideology that contaminates the mindsets of authorities and legal institutions.

This has deleterious results for victims and perpetuates injustice. For example, a body of research shows that in cases of rape, jurors regularly use evidence of the victim's voluntary intoxication to attribute responsibility, even when such attributions contradict the intent of the law. In other words, jurors hold a victim partially responsible for her sexual assault if she was voluntarily intoxicated, even when the law states that an intoxicated victim cannot be held responsible for her victimization (Carlson, 2014). After all, individuals do not relinquish the right to bodily integrity and protection against sexual assault or bodily harm when they consume intoxicants.

FURTHER INSIGHTS

Experts have argued that too often, the treatment or remedies granted to victims seem to be a sort of punishment. Moreover, the commiseration of others for the victim's plight is tinged with the belief that the suffering is due to the victim's bad choices or personal faults, rather than to contextual and structural issues that lead to abuse. These beliefs are compounded by the systemic shortcomings of legal and state institutions, which deflect culpability away from aggressors and the state (Sered, 2014).

Shame is an important element in victim blaming. For example, when women are victims of rape, they are often accused of having been intoxicated or provocatively dressed, or somehow placed themselves in a state of vulnerability to rape. All of these serve to suggest she invited the aggression. The actions of the aggressors are often depicted as the "unavoidable" result of having been unduly provoked by the victim. Moreover, victims are often ostracized and shamed. These attitudes deter victims from coming forward to file charges against their victimizers.

Shame is a common feeling for victims. Victims may blame themselves, and often internalize the victim blaming attitudes of others. In other words, they end up believing that they are in fact fully or partially responsible for the event. Feelings of blame may be triggered or worsened by the attitudes of others. Feelings of blame may also ensue from believing themselves–rightly or wrongly–to have been participants in their own victimization. Victims also experience trauma upon realizing the world is not the safe and just place they may have believed it to be, and that misfortune is often random. Often, in order to accommodate belief in a just world, victims grow to believe they somehow deserved the event.

The coalition of victim blaming and shame has particularly horrifying consequences in some traditional societies. Honor killings are not uncommon in some countries, in which women victims of sexual assault are killed. Their killing is viewed as necessary in order to cleanse the family's sense of shame. Although honor killings are not sanctioned in the legal code of any country, the practice is traditional and persistent in many cultures. According to experts, the murder of women to repair a family's honor stems from social pressure and expectations felt by the killers. The aim of an honor killing is that the family may regain its lost social status. In order to eliminate honor killings, some countries, such as Jordan, have successfully moved to harsher prison sentencing for honor killings and human rights awareness campaigns.

VIEWPOINTS

Even victims of non-violent crimes are frequently held responsible for their part in becoming a victim. For example, upon reporting the event, victims of theft are often asked by authorities if they had taken appropriate preventive measures to avoid the crime. Experts find that these inquiries serve to measure the extent to which victims should have foreseen the crime and failed to prevent it (Vynckier 2012).

Much research has been done to understand victim blaming. Results show that there are many different reasons for the phenomenon. Some experts point to the desire to believe in personal invulnerability and also, a just world. That is, the idea that random misfortune does not happen to good people (Vynckier, 2012).

Fundamental Attribution Error

Other types of victim blaming ascribe the harm done to something other than the event, such as the oversensitivity of the victim or other personal flaw. Social scientists call this phenomenon fundamental attribution error (Vynckier, 2012). For example, victims are believed to have worsened the event by their actions or motivations. Ulterior motivations may be ascribed to the victim, such as desire for notoriety or revenge against a possibly innocent defendant. In the latter instance, a woman victimized by abuse may be accused of being a spurned woman out for revenge, or somebody victimized by workplace harassment may be accused of being a disgruntled employee.

Fundamental attribution error applies when victim blaming ascribes inherent fault to victims, such as perceived or real intelligence deficits, genetic flaws, and so on. No reputable contemporary scientist relies on such deterministic factors to explain human behavior, the same way few scholars ascribe poverty to the inherent characteristics of poor people. Nevertheless, as many studies demonstrate, these perceptions still survive in different societies in the form of stereotypes. In a 1990s study, close to half of the American college students surveyed agreed that the main cause of poverty is that some individuals are simply not apt or intelligent enough to make it in modern society. Others ascribe poverty and other inequalities to bad habits and lacking appropriate values. On the other hand, most people, upon becoming victims, tend to blame the incident contextually, that is, on external factors. In other words, when it occurs to others it tends to be viewed as if the victim is somehow or to some extent, to blame. However, when it occurs to oneself, the blame tends to rest entirely on others or on the situation (Wright & Rogers, 2015).

Other Theories

Other theoretical explanations for victim blaming exist, such as defensive attribution theory and the above-mentioned just world theory. Defensive attribution theory assigns responsibility to the victim based on a perceived similarity and likelihood of victimization. For example, an individual may assume that the sexual assault on a person whom they perceive as similar to themselves would not have occurred were it not for the victim's intoxication; hence, the victim's intoxication is partially to blame. A person's belief in just world theory may be threatened by the proposition that misfortune is random. Most people have a basic need to believe that the world is fundamentally a just place. That is, people get what they deserve (Carlson, 2014).

Marxist theory explains victim blaming as the effect of economic, cultural, and social processes. For example, poverty is caused by complex social factors, especially an economic and ideological structure that is set to benefit some groups at the expense of others. Nevertheless, people are led to believe that for poverty to end, it is poor people who need to change, rather than the social structure. Blaming the victim serves to explain complex social conditions easily, support the status quo, and decrease feelings of personal guilt.

Internalizing Blame

In time, many people living in poverty grow to subscribe to this set of beliefs about their own condition.

Internalizing victim blaming erodes the victim's self-esteem and motivation. Poverty is usually the result of many economic and social factors that curtail educational and employment opportunities for people, including the disappearance of manufacturing jobs in urban centers and their relocation to other countries, the move of the middle class to the suburbs, the decline of public education, and other factors. In other words, poverty exists as a consequence of social structures, rather than because of lack of incentive and values among the poor. Despite evidence to the contrary, however, many people continue to blame victims for their situation (Wright, 1993).

TERMS & CONCEPTS

Attribution: To assign causation, credit or blame to an individual, object, or incident.

Blame: Assigning responsibility for a wrong, infraction, or fault. Blame may be used to make somebody accountable for a wrong. However, blaming others may also be used to hide a person's own faults or misbehavior, or to sustain a set of assumptions or beliefs. Blaming others is known to reduce empathy.

Defensive Attribution: A psychological mechanism or set of beliefs that helps the individual forestall the anxiety associated with believing he or she may be at risk of causing or being victimized by something negative.

Fundamental Attribution Error: Also known as attribution effect. A psychological mechanism that leads people to place undue emphasis on a person's character to explain some incident or behavior, rather than considering the situation or context.

Honor Killings: In some traditional cultures, the murder of a relative, usually a woman, who is accused of bringing shame and dishonor to the family. It is perceived that her death will cleanse the possibility of blame and restore status to the family.

Ideology: A set of concepts and beliefs, based in part on a minuscule element of reality and the rest based on myth and unsupported arguments. They often function unconsciously.

Just World Theory: Also known as Just World Hypothesis. People have a strong need to believe the world an orderly, just place, so that bad things do not occur to good people. In other words, people get what they deserve, be it good or bad. This psychological mechanism often serves to explain away gross injustices as deserved by the victims.

Shame: Feelings of chagrin, mortification, humiliation, and stress with the belief of having done something wrong. As a verb, to make others feel ashamed.

Stereotypes: Fixed, simplistic, and over-extended concepts of or images of certain groups of people. They tend to be negative and harmful and are used to explain away imposed disadvantages as character traits.

Bibliography

Barak, G., Leighton, P., Cotton, A. (2014). *Class, race, gender and crime: The social realities of justice in America.* Lanham, MD: Rowman and Littlefield.

"Blaming the Victim–Again." (2008). *New Oxford Review,* 75(6), 22-25.

Carlson, C. (2014). "'This bitch got drunk and did this to herself:' Proposed evidentiary reforms to limit 'victim blaming' and 'perpetrator pardoning' in rape by intoxication trials in California." *Wisconsin Journal of Law,* Gender and Society, 29(2), 286-315.

Davis, R., Lurigio, A. J., Herman, S. (Eds.). (2012). *Victims of crime.* Sage Publications.

Doermer, W. G., & Lab, S. P. (2014). *Victimology,* 7th ed. London, UK: Routledge.

Falk, P. J. (2014). "'Because ladies lie': Eliminating vestiges of the corroboration and resistance requirements from Ohio's sexual offenses." *Cleveland State Law Review,* 62(2), 343-371.

Lupo-Ocando, J. (2014). *Blaming the victim: How global journalism fails those in poverty.* London, UK: Pluto Press.

Pennington, L. (Ed). (2015). *Everyday victim blaming: Challenging media portrayals of domestic sexual violence and abuse.* Glenside, PA: EVB Publishing.

Romito, P. (2008). *A deafening silence: Hidden violence against women and children.* Cambridge, UK: Polity Press.

Sered, S. (2014). "Suffering in an age of personal responsibility." Contexts: *Understanding People in Their Social Worlds,* 13(2), 38-43.

Vynckier, G. (2012). "Victim blaming revisited: Beyond the explanation of self-protection." *International Perspectives in Victimology*, 7(1), 38-46.

Wallace, H., & Robertson, C. (2014). *Victimology: Legal, Psychological, and Social Perspectives*, 4th ed. Upper Saddle River, NJ: Prentice Hall.

Wright, S. E. (1993). "Presidential Address, Blaming the victim, blaming society or blaming the discipline: Fixing responsibility for poverty and homelessness." *Sociological Quarterly*, 34(1), 1-16.

Wright, E. O., & Rogers, J. (2015). *American society: How it really works*. 2nd ed.. New York, NY: W. W. Norton & Company.

Suggested Reading

Hayes, R. M., Lorenz, K., & Bell, K. A. (2013). "Victim-blaming others: Rape myth acceptance and the just world belief." *Feminist Criminology*, 8(3), 202-220.

Jackson, A., Lucas, S. L., & Blackburn, A. G. (2009). "Externalization and victim-blaming among a sample of incarcerated females." *Journal of Offender Rehabilitation*, 48, 228-248.

Johnson, L. M., Mullick, R., & Mulford, C. L. (2002). "General versus specific victim blaming." *The Journal of Social Psychology*, 142(2), 249-263.

Kushmider, K. D., Beebe, J. E., & Black, L. L. (2015). "Rape myth acceptance: implications for counselor education programs." *Journal of Counselor Preparation & Supervision*, 7(3), 7-30.

Trudy Mercadal, Ph.D.

Victimless Crime

ABSTRACT

How does society determine what is harmful enough to be illegal and what is not? Defining what is and is not a criminal offense is often subject to interpretation, cultural norms, and values, as well as the historical context in which the actions occur. Many behaviors we consider commonplace today were once criminalized, while others were not. Understanding the process by which some actions are declared criminal and others are not provides the foundation for investigating the controversies surrounding "victimless" crimes. This article reviews the social construction of crime and sociological research on victimless crime. It also touches on the broader study of crime and deviance and theories regarding the social construction of crime and criminology.

Keywords Consensual Behavior; Criminalization Theories; Decriminalization; Drug Addiction; Drug Use; Gambling; Prostitution; Social Construction; Status Offense; Vice; Victimless Crime

OVERVIEW

In the United States, what actions are criminalized? Should only actions that are truly harmful be illegal? What about drugs? Should some drugs be legal because they are relatively harmless? How about polygamy? Gambling? Pornography? If nobody gets hurt, why should these activities be criminal? Moreover, what is the process of criminalization? How does society determine what is harmful enough to be illegal and what is not? Are laws created to protect people or control people? Is determining what is and is not a crime a political act?

You may have thought about these very issues, or even just simply wondered why the driving age is set at sixteen in some states and fifteen in others, or why the drinking age is twenty-one and not eighteen, or why tobacco is legal and marijuana is not. Questions like these fit into the broader study of crime and deviance and theories regarding the social construction of crime and criminology (Vago, 2000).

The concept that binds these questions together and relates to the study and analysis of victimless crime is the notion that crime is a social construct. That is to say, no one behavior is inherently criminal or illegal; rather, through a process in which members of society come to agree that certain actions are worthy of regulation, laws are passed that make certain behaviors criminal.

Many scholars who study the social construction of crime and deviance use questions like these as a starting point for investigating the politics and controversies surrounding the criminalization or decriminalization of victimless crimes. Wertheimer (1977)

describes how advocates of decriminalizing victimless crime, once thought of as a controversial issue, advanced their position on the grounds of what has been described as the philosophy of law and function of the criminal justice system. These scholars contend that the purpose of criminal law should be limited to pursuing those who victimize others and that the criminal justice system should not be involved in matters where there is no victim or no harm is done.

On the other side of the debate are those who argue that it is the government's responsibility to ensure an orderly community and supervise moral conduct through legislation. Such proponents argue that nearly every crime causes some harm, either directly to an individual or to society at large.

There is still much debate in sociology, criminology, law, and criminal justice about what should and should not be criminal and how victimless crimes are to be handled, if at all, by the criminal justice system.

FURTHER INSIGHTS

Victimless Crime: A Definitional Issue

Understanding what constitutes a victimless crime is a complex issue. Many sociologists who study crime and victimization suggest that it is imperative to have a clear and concise definition of the criminal event from the perspectives of both law enforcement and the victim (Mosher, Miethe, & Phillips, 2002). However, many also recognize that what is criminal is not universally understood and agreed upon. For example, some people who are thought to be victimized do not think of themselves as victims. This is often the case with drug use, surrogacy, and prostitution. In such examples, while a crime may have occurred, it is difficult to distinguish who is the criminal and who is the victim.

One of the most widely accepted definitions of a victimless crime was first proposed by Edwin M. Schur in 1965. He maintained that a victimless crime is any illegal action that is largely consensual between two parties and lacks a complaining participant (Schur, 1965). While we may be able to think of dozens of behaviors that fit into this category, the most commonly studied are prostitution, gambling, drug use, and pornography (Veneziano & Veneziano, 1993).

While this definition provides scholarly guidance, it is still ambiguous in practice. For example, law enforcement officials and the judiciary are faced with the difficult decision of what to do with individuals who engage in victimless crimes as the pressure from society regarding these types of offenses changes over time and across communities. In some cases, such as drug addiction and gambling, those who engage in behaviors that lead to problems with the law are thought to need special attention and help. Some communities even offer treatment and counseling. In other cases, such as prostitution, individuals are chastised for engaging in behaviors that are far from what is considered normal by members of a society. People who engage in such behaviors are often thought to deserve punishment, or at least to be taken off the streets.

Victimless Crime and Changing Times

The notion of what constitutes a victimless crime is ever changing (Conklin, 1982), as it varies in the eyes of the public, political officials, and the police. Practically speaking, when law enforcement officials are investigating victimless crimes, these crimes tend to be drug use, prostitution, illegal gambling activities, public drunkenness, and/or vagrancy (Hagan, 2008).

However, these activities have not always been criminalized. In fact, many drugs that are currently illegal have previously been prescribed or recommended by doctors for legitimate medical issues (Inciardi, 1992). For example, cocaine and amphetamines were routinely prescribed for allergies and sinus-related ailments. Drugs such as cocaine were given to soldiers to fight fatigue and improve concentration during World War II. It was only when society became concerned with the social and political ramifications of drug use and abuse that such drugs became outlawed.

In addition to the definition of victimless crime changing over time, it also varies based on geography. In many countries, having more than one wife is considered legal and even encouraged by religious and government officials. Prostitution is not illegal in certain countries; in these places, it is highly regulated, taxed, and viewed as a legitimate occupation. In the twenty-first century, surrogacy has come under fire and been made illegal in several countries in an effort to protect women who had previously turned to surrogacy as a way to earn income. Gambling, public intoxication, and vagrancy are viewed by many as symptoms of social problems and not themselves criminal offenses in certain locales. Consequently, rehabilitation and treatment are often prescribed to help individuals in dire situations, rather than sending them off to prison or jail.

Issues like these, buttressed against the absence of an identifiable victim, beg the question of why such behaviors and activities are criminal. Should the government decriminalize victimless crime? The answer is inherently political (Dombrink, 1993).

As a society, it is arguably important to have a shared set of values and beliefs to help regulate undesirable behavior, whether through formal pressures such as laws and city ordinances or by informal mechanisms such as social pressure. The pressure to conform is rooted in institutional ideologies about appropriate behavior and grounded in political theories about social control and domination. Some scholars have argued that the process of criminalizing behavior and victimless crime is a political move to control some segments of the population at the expense of others. Karl Marx, for example, while never explicitly theorizing about crime, has been widely cited for his belief that the government has a vested interest in maintaining a working class and uses its power to force people into the labor pool through the use of laws and moral codes.

The following section will provide concrete examples of how scholars from both sides of the debate on victimless crime describe the construction of crime as a social problem and how they suggest society should respond though policies, procedures, and legislative change.

VIEWPOINTS

The Debate over Victimless Crime

There are two major factions in the debate over victimless crime and the need to regulate it. There are those who advocate for the decriminalization of crimes in which no formal complaint is leveled and harm is unlikely to have occurred. These scholars and activists point to the role of the government and the capacity of the criminal justice system, which, they argue, is critically understaffed and frequently inconvenienced by focusing on victimless crimes when there are more serious offenses and offenders to be pursuing.

In contrast, there are those who reject the notion that the government should not attempt to protect the people even in the absence of a complaint. These scholars and activists argue that allegedly victimless crimes do in fact have victims and that ignoring such offenses does cause harm. Central to these arguments is the notion that it is the state's responsibility to legislate morality.

Decriminalization and Victimless Crime

Two victimless crimes that have received the most attention from advocates, scholars, and the media are gambling and the use of marijuana. Central to the arguments for decriminalizing each offense is the notion that prosecuting these activities is draining resources that could otherwise be put to better use in controlling violent crime. Proponents for the decriminalization of marijuana and gambling also point to changing values and norms regarding these behaviors. Much has been made of marijuana's medicinal value. As for gambling, it offers the opportunity for states suffering from deficits to increase their tax base. These issues came to the forefront of political debate in the wake of Proposition 215, which in 1996 decriminalized marijuana in the state of California for medicinal purposes, and in the aftermath of Hurricane Katrina, when Mississippi legislation allowing damaged offshore casinos to rebuild on land played a fundamental role in bringing money to the state, provided jobs to local residents, and assisted in rebuilding efforts.

Marijuana

Grassroots organizer Dennis Peron advocated extensively for the decriminalization of marijuana. His efforts, which ultimately led to the passage of California's Proposition 215 in 1996, originated in San Francisco, where Peron campaigned to permit the use of marijuana by terminally ill AIDS patients. The law decriminalized using, growing, and distributing marijuana for those who had a doctor's prescription for its use. Opponents of Proposition 215 included many members of law enforcement, drug prevention groups, and elected officials, who thought that the decriminalization of marijuana would ultimately lead to other, more dangerous drugs being decriminalized and an overall breakdown in the obligation of the government and law enforcement to protect the community.

After much debate, the electorate of California passed Proposition 215. The final legislation provided legal protection for patients, caregivers, and physicians who possess or grow marijuana for medical purposes. This shift in legislation illustrates how a behavior that was once criminalized and fit the definition of victimless crime has been decriminalized in a carefully crafted way based on changes in values and norms among the majority of Californians, as expressed in their support for legislative change. As opinions on marijuana began to shift, legislation also changed elsewhere in the country: over the following two decades, twenty-three states and the territory of Guam legalized marijuana for medical use, and Washington, Colorado, Oregon, Alaska, and the District of Columbia legalized recreational use. In 2015, the Pew Research Center reported that 53 percent of Americans supported legalization.

Gambling

The notion that gambling is a victimless crime has been around for a long time. However, most scholars would argue that gambling has also long been tied to organized crime and corruption. Once the action of gambling is isolated from the organization of gaming, it is easer to see how some advocates have come to view it as a victimless crime. Gambling, broadly defined, involves an individual making a bet or wager based on the probability that a game or a sporting event could result in a payoff or prize. Proponents of decriminalizing gambling argue that individuals are capable of making their own decisions about potential risks and benefits and that it is not the government's responsibility to legislate such decisions (Hagan, 2008).

The issue of gambling gained more attention in the media and among political officials after the devastation to the Gulf Coast due to Hurricane Katrina. Gambling had long been a contentious issue in Mississippi; supporters of legalized gambling wanted their historically poor state to gain access to jobs and tax revenue that casinos provide, while many conservative religious leaders believed that gambling is a sin, harmful to the individual, the family, and the community. Others argue that casino gambling inherently favors the house, allowing the casino operators and state to benefit financially primarily off of individuals with gambling addictions, and that gambling's social and economic costs do not outweigh the economic gain in the form of additional tax revenue. In order to compromise, the state of Mississippi decided to allow some highly regulated gaming facilities to open, but only on barges located offshore. This provided an enormous amount of tax revenue while at the same time preserving the state's anti-gaming image. Over time, the locals shifted their attitudes toward the facilities, and new laws were proposed to expand the gaming facilities. Much of this legislation stagnated in the state legislature until Hurricane Katrina destroyed or heavily damaged all of the gaming barges. In an attempt to help bring money and jobs back to the state, Senator Trent Lott facilitated a legislative change that allowed casinos to build on land with the assistance of federal funds. This change is yet another example of the process of decriminalizing victimless crimes in the wake of political necessity and changing attitudes (Veneziano & Veneziano, 1993).

All Crimes Have Victims

While the previous section illustrates how some crimes have been decriminalized in some US states, the following section will highlight areas around the United States where the same activities have met with far more resistance. Opponents of decriminalization in these states argue that all crimes have victims, regardless of whether or not they voice a complaint. In order to see the real harm that drug use and gambling cause, they argue, we need to look beyond the individual and consider the harm such actions cause the family and community. Moreover, scholars who look at these issues have also noted that when asked if victimless crimes are harmful, most people say yes, which is proof that Americans support the notion that the government should regulate such behavior.

Drugs and Addiction

Many people who advocate for the strict enforcement of drug laws point to the multitude of victims affected by drugs. They contend that drug use leads to social isolation and a removal of oneself as an active participant in society. Moreover, many advocates of enforcement suggest that drug use can lead to criminal activity such as theft and robbery, or even child neglect and marital problems that cause harm to both children and families and eventually lead to the deterioration of morals and commitment to the community. Accordingly, those who oppose the notion of victimless crimes, particularly with respect to drug use, assert that such behaviors do not fit the definition of a victimless crime, as there clearly is harm—if not specifically to the individual drug user, then certainly to family members and the community. There is a place for a complaint to be leveled on behalf of children and those who are directly and indirectly affected by the drug user's behavior.

Compulsive Gambling

In response to those who advocate for the decriminalization of gambling, proponents of banning it often see the actions of gamblers and the organizations that facilitate gaming as part of a larger social problem that undermines gamblers' work ethic, destroys local businesses, perpetuates addiction, invites fraud, and propagates social decay. Similar to the example of drug use, those who oppose the decriminalization of gambling believe that both harm and victims can be identified, and therefore this activity does not meet the criteria of a victimless crime.

Victims in the case of gambling are often the gamblers themselves, who are often viewed has having an addiction or compulsion that interferes with their ability to appropriately assess the risks of participating and the likelihood of winning (Bloch, 1951). The harm that scholars often point to when discussing gambling can be limited to the individual, or it can be applied more globally. For the individual, gambling can result in the loss of a substantial amount of money and, in extreme cases, the need for public assistance or charity to provide the basics of survival. On a global level, gambling affects society insofar as it arguably attracts a deeper criminal element, in the form of loan sharks and corruption. Additionally, opponents to the legalization of gambling also contend that the presence of casinos impedes the formation of social bonds in a community and prohibits individuals from establishing a sense of community with their neighbors.

CONCLUSION

Understanding the scholarly arguments about victimless crime requires one to first understand that crime is a social construct, subject to change over time, between individuals, and across communities. Theories on the social construction of crime suggest that social norms and values play a central part in determining what actions are criminalized and what are not. There is much debate over how to define victimless crime and what role the criminal justice system should have in regulating behavior and legislating morality. Future research in this area will continue to look at the factors that contribute to individual perceptions of what should and should not be criminalized and how these views affect social policy.

TERMS AND CONCEPTS

Consensual Behavior: Behavior that is agreed upon by two or more willing, capable, and reasonable adults.

Criminalization Theories: Theories that pertain to the process of understanding why some actions are determined to be criminal and others are not.

Decriminalization: The process of abolishing criminal penalties for an action that was at one time illegal.

Social Construction: The Durkheimian notion that any phenomenon that is agreed upon by participants in a particular culture or society exists and therefore becomes embedded into the institutional fabric and structure of society, subject to the rules and regulation thereof.

Status Offense: A crime that can only be committed by people occupying a particular status.

Vice: A practice, behavior, or habit that is considered immoral by society.

Victimless Crime: An infraction of criminal law that occurs without causing damage or harm to any identifiable individual (victim).

Bibliography

Bloch, H. (1951). The sociology of gambling. *The American Journal of Sociology, 57* 215–221.

Conklin, J. (1992). *Criminology (4th ed).* New York, NY: MacMillan.

Dombrink, J. (1993). "Victimless crimes and the 'culture wars' of the 1990s." *Journal of Contemporary Criminal Justice, 9,* 31–40.

Dysart, T. L. (2014). "Child, victim, or prostitute? Justice through immunity for prostituted children." *Duke Journal of Gender Law & Policy, 21,* 255–288.

Hagan, F. (2008) *Introduction to criminology: Theories, methods, and criminal behavior* (6th ed.). Thousand Oaks, CA: Sage.

Hughes, B. T. (2015). "Strictly taboo: Cultural anthropology's insights into mass incarceration and victimless crime." *New England Journal on Criminal and Civil Confinement, 41*(1), 49–84.

Huisman, W., & Nelen, H. (2014). "The lost art of regulated tolerance? Fifteen years of regulating vices in Amsterdam." *Journal of Law & Society, 41,* 604–626.

Inciardi, J. (2000). *The war on drugs II: The continuing epic of heroin, cocaine, crank, crime, AIDS, and public policy.* Woodland Hills, CA: Mayfield.

Lowman, J., & Louie, C. (2012). "Public opinion on prostitution law reform in Canada." *Canadian Journal of Criminology & Criminal Justice, 54,* 245–260.

Luna, E. (2012). "Prosecutorial decriminalization." *Journal of Criminal Law & Criminology, 102,* 785–819.

Mosher, C., Miethe, T. & Phillips, D. (2002). *The mismeasure of crime.* Thousand Oaks, CA: Sage.

Mostyn, B., Gibbon, H., & Cowdery, N. (2012). "The criminalization of drugs and the search for alternative approaches." *Current Issues in Criminal Justice, 24,* 261–272.

Pöysti, V. (2014). "Comparing the attitudes of recreational gamblers from Finland and France toward national gambling policies: A qualitative analysis." *Journal of Gambling Issues, 29,* 1–24.

Schur, E. (1956). *Crimes without victims: Deviant behavior and public policy.* Upper Saddle River, NJ: Prentice Hall.

Schur, E. & Bedau, H. (1974). *Victimless crimes, two sides of a controversy.* Upper Saddle River, NJ: Prentice Hall.

Vago, S. (2000). *Law and society (6th ed.).* Upper Saddle River, NJ: Prentice Hall.

Veneziano, L & Veneziano C. (1993). "Are victimless crimes actually harmful?" *Journal of Contemporary Criminal Justice, 9,* 1–14.

Wertheimer, A. (1977). "Victimless crimes." *Ethics, 87,* 302–318.

Suggested Reading

Braasch, P. (2012). "Margin of appreciation or a victimless crime? The European Court of Human Rights on consensual incest of adult siblings." *German Yearbook of International Law, 55,* 613–623.

Miethe, T. (1982). "Public consensus on crime seriousness." *Criminology, 20*(3/4), 515–526.

Orrick, E., & Vieraitis, L. (2015). "The cost of incarceration in Texas: Estimating the benefits of reducing the prison population." *American Journal of Criminal Justice, 40*(2), 399–415.

Schur, E. & Bedau, H. (1974). *Victimless crimes two sides of a controversy.* Upper Saddle River, NJ: Prentice Hall.

Weitzer, R. (2003). *Current controversies in criminology.* Upper Saddle River, NJ: Prentice Hall. [RT1]1.15

Jennifer Christian, M.A.

Vigilantism

ABSTRACT

There is no concrete definition for vigilantism, although it tends to identify a series of actions that serve to impose order and control on society, and punish transgressors and criminals. Vigilante behavior may occur at the group or at individual levels, illicitly and secretly or as sanctioned by the state. Vigilantism may also be accompanied by instances of public lynching, shaming, and moral policing. Vigilantism may become part of a culture and surface in popular culture products, in which it may be legitimized, criticized, and/or perpetuated.

OVERVIEW

The term "vigilante" is a Spanish word from the verb "vigilar," which means to watch or maintain surveillance over. A vigilante, then, is somebody who guards, watches over, or controls. In its current conception as a social practice, it was attributed to William Lynch in the nineteenth century. The term was first used to refer to controlling and penalizing the socially proscribed actions of out-groups such as African Americans and abolitionists. It is also closely linked with practices such as "lynching" (Lynch law) and moral policing. These practices are rooted in the idea of groups abrogating their own law independently of the established legal authority.

Vigilantism, then, is the philosophy or standpoint that led to the practice of surveillance and punishment of others by individuals who have taken it upon themselves to execute their own brand of authority or justice. The traditional definition refers to the use or threat of violent extralegal action by private citizens independent of state authority or even in the absence of the state; moreover, one of the conditions for vigilantism, according to scholars, is the absence of state authority or the presence of a weak state. Therefore, vigilantes serve several purposes that under normal circumstances would be the jurisdiction of the state, such as policing, protection, maintenance or community order and values, and others. Vigilantism may be exerted by a group of people as well as by individuals. Notwithstanding that vigilantism implies proactive surveillance and violence, however, the idea remains that vigilantism and lynching are forms of self-defense by a community against illicit actions by others that are allowed to occur unchecked by the state (Arrigo, 2014).

Scholars explain that vigilantism is typically a temporary or short-lived phenomenon and tends to occur in borderline or frontier areas, where the state is corrupt or weak. Experts also find that vigilantism transcends a behavior by private individuals in the absence of state crime control. For example, vigilantism may include mercenary action, that is, groups that offer legal or extralegal protection beyond that of the state. Their services may be hired by private or government organizations. Other scholars view vigilantism as forms of community self-defense or self-help. Whichever the case, vigilantes seldom operate openly, and often use illicit force against those they deem as offenders or violators of laws or social norms. Because they operate in obscurity, in some cultures, vigilantes have been romanticized and become part of popular lore, offering characters such as the Lone Ranger in the United States.

According to some scholars, vigilantism is not merely the result of a lack of state intervention. While the idealization of vigilante figures is a result of community need for security, it also reflects an overall approval of the ideals of self-help and the ability to take care of oneself. Moreover, it vigilantism reflects a subversion of the social order and the authority of the state. In some cases, the state is actually so strong as to be excessively authoritarian or autocratic. In such cases, people who result to vigilantism may feel victimized by the state or find the government and legal authorities untrustworthy. People are more inclined to cooperate with the state and authorities when they trust that justice will be administered fairly. On the other hand, when people do not trust the police, for example, they are less likely to cooperate and comply, and tend to view extrajudicial actions with approval and arrogate police authority for themselves (Tankebe, 2009).

The average level of education attained in a community may also be crucial to the development of vigilantism. Data support that populations with average higher levels of educational attainment and literacy also show higher support for government and are less inclined to favor vigilante behavior. Education helps people gain better awareness and critical thinking skills, understanding of democracy and due process practices (the principles of which may seem abstract, especially regarding short-term or personal interests), and better informed principles of democratic governance (Tankebe, 2009).

Vigilantism is a worldwide problem. In Latin America, vigilantes often appeared as state-sponsored death squads in charge of preventing citizen uprisings against dictatorial right-wing states. They also continue to appear in the form of lynch mobs among communities that take the law into their hands, having lost trust in corrupt governments and police. The rise of illicit drug trade in Mexico and Central America is related to a rise in vigilantism in the region, which enjoys a groundswell of popular support. Vigilantism, then, is both cause and effect of violence and repression, especially in countries in which corrupt and weak government, police repression, and profound poverty and inequality stoke the cycles of violence (Grayson, 2014).

FURTHER INSIGHTS

Vigilantism, under other names, has existed as long as documented history. In the United States, it rose during the nineteenth century in the expansion of the developing Western frontier. With little government representation in the form of police, courts, and schools, small mining camps grew into towns populated by settlers from many ethnic and national backgrounds. This included an influx of individuals who would take advantage of the ineffectual policing to make their fortunes illegally; nominally illegal but common activities included thievery, prostitution, gambling, counterfeiting, and drug trafficking. In order to control the expansion of criminal activity, citizens began to organize themselves in vigilante groups and exert different forms of street law, such as flogging, expulsion, beatings, and lynching. Although in appearance based on a groundswell mob action, vigilantism was often supported by the local commercial and professional elites, who were invested in the development of an orderly society (Scully and Moorman, 2014).

In the late 1800s, vigilantism, lynching, and other forms of open violence became a way to control and repress African Americans. In fact, lynching became public spectacles that served to instill fear in non-white populations. Although lynching was not limited exclusively to African Americans, the latter were the majority victims of the practice. Vigilante violence was often accompanied by a discourse that posited it as necessary to protect the virtue of white womanhood from the potential depredations of over-sexualized others. As anti-lynching crusader Ida B. Wells posited after her in-depth examination of lynching dynamics, however, lynching tended to surge when African American males began to prosper economically in a community, often independently and autonomously from whites. In other words, it served not only as a warning to allay white fears of African American competition for the attentions of white women, but also as a deterrent threat to African Americans not to become too independent in a white-dominated society.

By the inception of the twentieth century, vigilante violence in America was often equated with patriotism and loyalty, especially when directed against groups considered politically radical. This sentiment created fertile terrain for the creation of organizations such as the American Protective League (APL), which rose during the World War I period fueled by the martial spirit of the era. Organized with the sponsorship of the U.S. government, the APL was a vigilante paramilitary group that, at a given point, reached a reported 250,000 members. Any U.S. citizen could join. The government considered them "agents" and had them work with other state agencies, such as local police forces. Among the purposes of the APL was to organize and participate in raids against political suspects such as socialists and anarchists, anti-war activists, and union organizers, among others (Cohen 2007).

The state-sanctioned attacks against political and labor activists in particular, then, brought vigilantism to a new level, transcending localized community-based activity. It turned into a project of organized violence as a way to create national cohesiveness by unifying citizens in opposition to a "common enemy." Not only were groups such as the APL created, but also marginal and illicit groups such as the Ku Klux Klan gained new prominence and legitimacy (Cohen, 2007).

In time, the "Old West" and a culture of individualism gained a strong foothold in the American value system, further entrenching vigilantism in popular culture. Vigilante characters have long held sway in popular culture in such figures as the Lone

Ranger, Batman, Green Arrow, and many others, the popularity of which expanded worldwide. This is also reflected in representations of rogue cops in film, such as in Rogue Cop, Lethal Weapon, and Robocop, and iconic stars of vigilante themed films like Charles Bronson and Clint Eastwood.

In 1979, as a response to a surge in street crime in New York City, a group of citizens led by Curtis Sliwa organized an unauthorized vigilante crime patrol called the Guardian Angels. The group patrolled the subways and famously rejected the use of arms in their activities. Acts of violence by real-life vigilantes were often met with widespread approval, as in the case of Bernhard Goetz, who in 1984 shot four African American adolescents in a subway station whom he perceived as trying to rob him. The incident caused widespread debate; however, it was notable for the overwhelming public support that Goetz received (Sculley & Moorman, 2014).

Vigilantism exists around the world and unceasingly adapts to contemporary dynamics. For example, in societies governed by authoritarian regimes, such as China, technology is regulated and Internet access suffers censorship to different extents. On the other hand, citizens also use the Internet to engage in vigilantism against government abuses, and identify and expose corrupt government officials as well as private citizens caught in acts of transgression. In such cases, vigilantism tends to be organized through networks of people who share common concerns and act upon them mainly by inflicting public shame or calling for action.

Besides lynching, vigilantism also fuels acts of shaming. With technological expansion and ever-faster Internet access comes a vast proliferation of social networks. Online networks are often used for public exposure and shaming of those who violate laws and social norms. The latter may include violence against animals, adultery, unsafe driving, and others. The purpose of these vigilantes, then, is social control, by way of enforcing conformism and compliance with laws and with community values. In fact, the practice has become so popular that there are online sites completely dedicated to shaming for specific violations. Some experts analyze these dynamics as communal acts of self-regulation and peer-surveillance. However, others warn that their effect may be limited: Shaming usually works only on those who already adhere strongly to societal norms and values.

VIEWPOINTS

Many scholars have sought to study and explain vigilante behavior and the different ways in which it is expressed in societies around the globe. One of the ways in which experts examine vigilantism is through its expression in popular culture. In 1980s United States, for example, vigilantism became very popular by way of comic book superheroes, especially in New York City, which at the time was suffering high rates of street crime. Fear in New York City increased, stoked by crime and the media. Moreover, real acts of vigilantism took place, both individual and organized, and were heavily publicized. Coincidentally, New York City was the center of comics' publication; not surprisingly, their authors created superheroes that reflected the fears and fantasies prevalent among the public (Scully & Moorman, 2014).

Mainstream comic book heroes such as Vigilante, Punisher and Green Arrow served to illustrate the new vision of vigilantism in America. The character named Vigilante, for example, was driven by idealism and rejected the use of lethal force in the beginning, but constantly ran afoul of police authorities. In the end, he inevitably ends acting in lethally violent ways and horrified by his actions, commits suicide. Other characters, such as Punisher and Green Arrow, also pursue vigilante justice and end up engaging in acts of extreme violence (Scully & Moorman, 2014).

Various scholars have examined film and fantasy heroes in order to understand the ways in which vigilantism affects popular culture. In many of the stories, for example, police forces request vigilante intervention, as can often be seen in comics and films in which characters such as Batman are at play. In fact, the superhero often intervenes when police forces are already at work, but acting slowly and fecklessly. Sometimes, official forces are portrayed as corrupt and inept, so that the vigilante must break the law in order to get justice accomplished. It is unsurprising, then, that the representation of vigilantism in motion pictures and popular culture has often served to both reflect and perpetuate an idealized version of vigilantism in American society.

Some scholars ascribe this to an instrumental view of the role of government in a democracy such as the United States. In this view, the role of the government is to exercise control over society through laws and policing. Given the failure of such, citizens ought to take control into their own hands. In other words, in a society in which control and order appear to be arbitrary, people may believe they must take control themselves. A theory of the instrumental role of government responds to a teleocratic view of politics and society, one in which grand narratives or great myths prevail, with the final goal of achieving national unity. Teleocratic views, according to scholars, become very persuasive in times of social conflict, when people may become concerned with survival. Following the rule of law may appear ineffectual and even an impediment to prompt justice (Beard, 2015). Therefore, in times of fear and crisis, it may become legitimate to break the law in order to achieve justice and order (Mendenhall, 2013). In a world in which grand narratives are attractive, fantasies in which vigilante behavior turns perpetrators into superheroes may easily proliferate despite their sociopathic and unlawful implications.

Other scholars have sought to understand the role of the oppressed in vigilante behavior, such as the role of women in vigilantism in patriarchal societies. Even though under certain circumstances vigilante behavior may meet with popular approval, it has strong connotations of violence and unlawfulness; as such, they run against conventional images of women as maternal, peace-oriented, and in need of masculine protection. Despite these images, however, vigilante behavior by women has been on the rise in traditional societies such as in India and Mexico. India has seen the rise of groups of women vigilantes such as the Gulabi Gang–also known as the Pink Gang–founded by Data Sadbodh Sain in Uttar Pradesh. The Gulabi Gang's mission is to fight against violence against women. In Mexico, a vigilante woman murdered two bus drivers in Juarez, Mexico, allegedly on a mission of justice. The vigilante's crimes were met with sympathy by many Mexican women bus passengers, making it more difficult to dismiss them as just random acts of violence (Baldritch, 2014). These cases are doubly interesting, since they have taken place in societies in which vigilante behavior tends to occur among men, such as fathers, brothers and other male figures who "police" women's behavior.

These cases have raised a lively debate about issues of justice, oppression, and violence against women. In fact, some scholars have posited that when the oppressed engage in acts of vigilantism in the face of inaction by authorities, it may be framed as an issue of Just War. That is, it raises questions such as, are these actions necessary? Are they proportional to the crime they pretend to redress?

Finally, vigilante behavior is also examined under the aegis of "global vigilantism." Some experts argue that vigilante behavior has extended to the global sphere, by way of the expansion of private policing forces at the international level, accompanied by the erosion of social investment and widespread deregulation, and growing inequality worldwide.

TERMS & CONCEPTS

Arbitrary: Random, capricious, or unpredictable. Based on a whim, rather than on standardized and impartial procedures.

Instrumental Value: The value of an object, action, or system as a means of gaining something else.

Just War Theory: A doctrine and philosophical field that deals with examining the instances in which wars are justified.

Lynching: An illicit mob action that involves beating and often putting to death an individual. The purpose is usually to punish or and instill fear in others to deter them from engaging in conduct the group finds threatening or unruly.

Moral Police: Vigilante groups that aim to enforce their own religious or moral codes. These may be informal or state-sanctioned groups.

Policing: Controlling, supervising and/or ordering the law, morals, and safety for the common good of a society.

Bibliography

Abrahams, R. (1998). *Vigilant citizens: Vigilantism and the state.* Cambridge, UK: Polity.

Arrigo, B. (2014). *The encyclopedia of criminal justice ethics.* Thousand Oaks, CA: Sage.

Baldritch, R. (2014). "Taking the law into our own hands. Female vigilantism in India and Mexico." (Masters thesis). http://www.sciencespo.fr/psia/sites/sciencespo.fr.psia/files/

Beard, M. (2015). "The Arrow and Philosophy, part one: The morality of vigilantism." *The Conversation.* http://theconversation.com/the-arrow-and-philosophy-part-one-the-morality-of-vigilantism-43355

Cohen, M. (2007). "'The Ku Klux Klan government': Vigilantism, lynching, and the repression of the IWW." *Journal for the Study of Radicalism,* 1(1). 31-56.

Grayson, G. W. (2014). *Threat posed by mounting vigilantism in Mexico.* Washington, DC: U.S. Department of Defense.

Mendenhall, A. (2013, December 30). "Nomocracy and Oliver Wendell Holmes, Jr. Nomocracy in Politics." http://nomocracyinpolitics.com/2013/09/30/nomocracy-and-oliver-wendell-holmes-jr/

Scully, T.A., & Moorman, K. (2014). "The rise of vigilantism in 1980s comics: Reasons and outcomes." *Journal of Popular Culture* 47(3), 634-652.

Tankebe, J. (2009). "Self-help, policing, and procedural justice; Ghanaian vigilantism and the rule of law." *Law and Society Review* 43(2), 245-270.

SUGGESTED READING

Gazit, N. (2015). "State-sponsored vigilantism: Jewish settlers' violence in the occupied Palestinian territories." *Sociology,* 49(3), 438-454.

Hass, N. E., de Keijser, J. W., & Bruinsma, G. J. (2014). "Public support for vigilantism, confidence and police, and police responsiveness." *Policing & Society,* 24(2), 224-241.

Marazi, K. (2015). "Superhero or vigilante? A matter of perspective and brand management." *European Journal of American Culture,* 34(1), 67-82.

Sridharan, E., & Cerulli, A. (2014). "Editors' introduction to the roundtable on intellectual freedom, vigilantism, and censorship in India." *India Review,* 13(3), 274-276.

Trudy Mercadal, Ph.D.

VIOLENT CRIME IN THE U.S.

ABSTRACT

According to the United States Justice Department, violent crime includes murder, rape and sexual assault, robbery, and assault. Detailed crime data concerning all types of violent offenses is provided. Research data and theoretical analysis about murder is considered along with a brief review of the relationship of organized crime and gang violence to the overall rate of violent crime in the United States.

OVERVIEW

What is Violent Crime?

Violent crime is defined in the FBI's Uniform Crime Reporting (UCR) Program as offenses involving "force or the threat of force," categorized into: murder and non-negligent manslaughter, rape, robbery, and aggravated assault (United States Department of Justice, 2016). The classification of all of the Justice Department crime data is based upon the decisions of police investigators rather than upon any final determination by a coroner, court, or other judicial body. State by state data is available from the Department of Justice, as well as the Kaiser Family Foundation (See figure 1).

According to the Merriam-Webster Dictionary, murder is defined as "the crime of unlawfully killing a person especially with malice aforethought" (2018). Manslaughter is distinct from murder in that manslaughter is the unlawful killing of one person by another without intention or advance planning. Negligence entails failing to use a proper level of care, so accidents that result in death do not come under the governmental definitions of violent crime. In summary, then, governmental data on murder does not include deaths caused by negligence, suicide, accidents, justifiable homicide (such as a police officer killing a felon in the line of duty), or attempts to commit murder (United States Department of Justice, 2007d). Rape is defined as non-consensual sexual intercourse, and robbery is the illegal taking of money or property belonging to another. Keep in mind that in both of these offenses violence or the threat of violence is a necessary component of the

Violent Victimization by Type of Crime, 2016

Type of crime	Number	Rate per 1000[a]
Violent crime[b]	5,749,330	21.1
Rape or sexual assault[c]	323,450†	1.2†
Robbery	500,680†	1.8†
Assault	4,925,200	18.1
Aggravated assault	1,084,340†	4.0†
Simple assault*	3,840,860	14.1
Domestic violence[d]	1,109,610	4.1
Intimate partner violence[e]	597,740	2.2
Stranger violence	2,232,260	8.2
Violent crime involving injury	1,366,250	5.0

Note: Violent crime classifications include rape or sexual assault, robbery, aggravated assault, and simple assault. Other violent crime categories in this table, including domestic violence and violent crime involving injury, are not mutually exclusive from these classifications. Detail may not sum to total due to rounding. Total population age 12 or older was 272,174,080 in 2016. Total number of households was 133,271,310 in 2016.

*Comparison group for violent crime. Simple assault is compared to rape or sexual assault, robbery, and aggravated assault.

†Significant difference from comparison group at 95% confidence level.

[a]For violent and serious violent crime, rate is per 1,000 persons age 12 or older. For property crime, rate is per 1,000 households.

[b]Excludes homicide because the NCVS is based on interviews with victims and cannot measure murder.

[c]See Methodology for details on the measurement of rape or sexual assault in the NCVS.

[d]Includes victimization committed by intimate partners and family members.

[e]Includes victimization committed by current or former spouses, boyfriends or girlfriends.

Figure 1: Comparison of violent crimes.

 Source: Bureau of Justice Statistics, National Crime Victimization Survey (NCVS), 2016.

crime. Similarly, while simple assault involves a physical attack or threat of attack, it does not involve a dangerous weapon or serious injury; aggravated assault involves a higher level of violence, one that could cause death or serious bodily harm, making it a violent crime.

The United States Department of Justice estimated that in 2016, 1,248,185 violent crimes occurred in the United States, or 386.3 violent crimes per 100,000 inhabitants. 6The national violent crime rate in 2016 was more than 12 percent lower than ten years earlier, in 2007, but 2.6 percent higher than five years earlier, in 2012 (United States Department of Justice, 2016).

Prevalence

According to the 2016 government data, aggravated assault accounted for 64.3 percent of violent crime in the United States, or 248.5 offenses per 100,000 individuals. The rate of aggravated assaults decreased 13.5 percent from 2007 to 2016.

Robbery accounted for 26.6 percent of all violent crimes in 2016, or 102.8 offenses per 100,000 individuals. The most common locations for acts of robbery were streets and highways (108,957 offenses, 38.9 percent of the total), while 4,982 offenses occurred in a bank (1.8 percent of the total). On average, the stolen property value per crime was $1,400 dollars, while bank robberies averaged $3,531 per offense. Total loss estimates for the year 2016 were $465 million.

Rape accounted for 7.7 percent of all violent crime, or 41.2 offenses per 100,000 individuals. Included in these figures are each reported victim of a rape, attempted rape, or assault with intent to rape. Statutory rape, defined as sex with a minor, is not included in the data unless force was used in the commission of the crime; nor is incest. The historical definition used by the Department of Justice concerning rape used the words "female" and "forcible" until the 2013 revision, at which time the definition was amended to "penetration, no matter how slight, of the vagina or anus with any body part or object, or oral penetration by a sex organ of another person, without the consent of the victim" (United States Department of Justice, 2016).

Although a detailed analysis of the causes of sexual offending is beyond the scope of this article, criminologists Tony Ward and Anthony Beech provide a useful integrated theory that includes genetic predisposition; adverse developmental experiences (such as child abuse and rejection); psychological dispositions/trait factors (interpersonal problems, mental disorders); social and cultural structures and process (sexism, masculinity, and other learned behaviors); and contextual factors (such as stress or intoxication) (2008). While their theoretical framework is related to sexual offending exclusively, it is useful in considering the development of theories of violent crime in general.

Finally, an estimated 17,250 people were murdered in the United States in 2016. Murder was the least common violent crime, making up only 1.4 percent of the overall violent crime, or 5.3 murders per 100,000 inhabitants. Of murder offenders, 10,310 were male, 1,295 were female, and in 5,359 cases the offender's sex was not known. Most of the offenders were individuals eighteen years of age or older. Around half of all murder victims were African American, and slightly less than half were white (United States Department of Justice, 2016).

VIEWPOINTS

How Does Violent Crime Occur?

In this book on homicide in Australia, *When Men Kill,* Kenneth Polk (1994) offers an excellent summary of crime statistics from the United States, along with contemporary theoretical analysis. In his summary of studies by Wolfgang (1958), Wallace (1986), and Daly and Wilson (1988), for example, a picture of emerges of a male offender, over the age of twenty-five, who is from a poor economic background and who has a 54 percent chance of being unemployed.

Sexual Intimacy

Violence often arises out of sexual intimacy, and in Polk's study about 23 percent of the murders committed in Victoria, Australia between 1985 and 1989 involved "sexual ownership" and control issues. The first type of sexual ownership and control was violence triggered by jealousy or the threat of separation from a sexual partner. Four percent of these murders were of perceived rivals, while the majority involved the murder of a current or former sexual partner. In both of these instances, numerous acts of physical assault and threats usually preceded the actual murder, and the use of temporary restraining orders and police interventions was ineffective (Polk, 1994). The second type of sexual partner murders involved suicidal thinking and depression on the part of the offender, whose issues of ownership of and control over his or her sexual partner led to the assumption that the partner would be better off dead too. Often, these murderers were older and in failing health, but younger killers facing medical and/or economic problems resorted to this murder/suicide pattern as well. Most of the killings related to sexual partner control involved premeditated planning on the part of the murderer, even those that seemed to be based on violent, immediate expressions of anger.

Confrontations

The vast majority of homicides are "confrontational" in nature, involving strangers, acquaintances, family members, or friends (Polk, 1994). Often these interpersonal disputes are spontaneous arguments sparked by some perceived threat to the "honor" of one or both of the participants. Alcohol or drug impairment plays a significant role is these dynamics. Many murders occur outside of bars and clubs, and often youth gang violence is a factor. In analyzing these confrontation murders, Luckenbill set forth a multistep transactional analysis of the actions of both the offender and the victim that lead to the death (1977).

- The first step involves an opening move by the victim that is perceived by the offender to be some act of dishonor. Intentional and unintentional acts, gestures, facial expressions, or comments by the victim can set off the offender regardless of how trivial or meaningless.
- In the second step, the offender takes the victim's behavior as meaning offense.
- The offender making some retaliatory move against the victim rather than ignoring the situation is step three.
- In step four, though the victim may have numerous options, he or she chooses to stand up to the offender's challenge, leading to the killing of the victim. Usually, these murders are resolved in three ways: the killer flees, remains to face the police, or is held by observers until the police arrive (Polk, 1994).

Sociologist Randall Collins also argues that traditional views of crime are not helpful in understanding violent situations (2008). Rather than focusing on the pathology of the individuals involved, he also engages in a transactional analysis of the violent situations. Violence, according to Collins's analysis, "is a set of pathways around confrontational tension and fear" (2008, p. 8). In contrast to traditional criminological theory, however, Collins argues that violence is not easy even if the motivation exists because so many conditions are required for violence, and there are numerous turning points that could diffuse the event. Social control and routine activities theorists, for example, say that "the formula for crime is a coincidence in time and space of a motivated offender, an accessible victim, and the absence of social control agents who deter crime" (Collins, 2008, p. 21).

Others might argue that violence stems from poverty and low status in a capitalist economy. Social learning theorists argue that the techniques of violence are learned and acquired through "deliberate tutelage, training, and socialization of offenders" (Akers & Silverman, 2004, p. 19). Collins, however, argues that "most violence is bluster and standoff, with little actually happening, or incompetent performance with mostly ancillary and unintended damage" (2008, p. 32). Like David F. Luckenbill, Collins takes a micro-sociological view of violence by analyzing each step each an actor might take that either diffuses violence or causes it to escalate. Unlike Luckenbill, though, Collins believes that each comment or action by the parties is important in the analysis, not just the process that steps up the violence. The significance of acts such as griping, whining, arguing, and quarreling all receive extensive regard under Collins's theoretical framework.

Unplanned Violence

The third category of homicides involves what Polk refers to as "exceptional rush" killings that occur during some other high-risk criminal activity, such as an armed robbery. In these situations, the victim is most likely a stranger to the murderer. Smaller categories of homicides include victims killing their attackers, professionals killing for hire, prison murders, serial killings, mass murders, and law enforcement officers killed in the line of duty.

Family Violence

In most situations in which children are the victims of a murder, they fall into a category labeled "family killings" (Polk, 2004, p. 141). In these instances, female perpetrators are as frequent as male killers. According to Polk, there are four sub-themes in parental murders of their children.

- The first type involves parents who batter or beat their children; the murder occurs as an outgrowth of this conduct.
- The second type mirrors the murder of a sexual partner as noted above; the murderer is suicidal and believes that the children need to die along with him or her.
- The third subcategory of parental murder involves neonaticide, or the killing of an infant during the first twenty-four hours of its life. Mothers are the most typical killers in these instances.
- The final subcategory involves neglect of a child leading to his or her death (Polk, 2004).

Organized Crime

Thus far, the discussion of violent crime in the United States has focused on individual perpetrators. Violent crime also occurs in the course of organized crime, including gang violence. *The Blackwell Dictionary of Sociology* defines organized crime as having several essential elements. First, some formal organizational structure has to exist, including a hierarchical governance process and a division of duties or labor. The organization also has to have management systems in place, including rules of conduct and record keeping (Blackwell, 2000, p. 216). It would seem that an additional element necessary would be a purpose or focus for the organization. These characteristics fit both traditional organized crime, such as the Mafia and youth gangs.

The Organized Crime Control Act of 1970 defines organized crime as "The unlawful activities of ... a highly organized and disciplined association" (U.S., 1970). It can and does exist in any setting, local, state, national, or international. It also can flourish within prisons. In order to thrive, however, organized crime has to have strong ties with legitimate business entities so that money can be moved throughout the economy. Cooperation from respected members of the business community is sometimes gained through bribery, extortion, and blackmail. Criminal endeavors are additionally protected by bribing judicial and law enforcement officials. In order to achieve its goals and to protect its interests, organized crime may resort to violence.

In an effort to combat organized crime, in 1970 the federal government passed the Racketeer Influenced and Corrupt Organization (RICO) Act (18 U. S. C. A., § 1961 et seq.) In addition to crimes deemed to be white collar in nature, RICO addresses gambling, extortion, prostitution, narcotics trafficking, loan sharking, and murder. Punishment under RICO can be extremely harsh and include fines and up to twenty years in prison. Additionally, the defendant must forfeit any claims to the money or property obtained from the criminal enterprise or obtained from any criminal enterprise barred under RICO (White-Collar Crime, 2008).

Gang Violence

Although any in-depth discussion of gang violence falls outside the scope of this article, some degree of violence in the United States is caused by gangs.

In 2011 the National Gang Intelligence Center estimated that there were nearly 1.4 million active gang members in cities, prisons, and outdoor motorcycle clubs—making up over 33,000 gangs. Street gangs are often made up of youth and urban criminal organizations. Prison gangs operate within the penal system and prison institutions. Outlaw motorcycle gangs (OMG) are made up of individuals who conduct activities using motorcycle clubs. These varieties of gangs are responsible for a percentage of violent crime that ranges from 48 to 90 percent, depending on the region. Some of the violent crime perpetrated by gangs includes murder, home invasions, armed robbery, aggravated assault, carjackings, and drive-by shootings.

In his studies of youth gangs in Chicago, Illinois, John Hagedon, argued that instead of relying on traditional sociological theories of crime, scholars should be engaged in cultural studies of the gang populations (2008). Hagedon believes that "if gangs are indeed made up of alienated youth who are angry with an unresponsive government, undying racism, and a blank future," then focusing on geographic zones of social disorganization or attributing rational choice analysis to these situations not only fails to provide a meaningful explanation of gang violence, it also affects the interventions posed to help alleviate crime in the United States (2008, p. 135).

While some gang violence is related to drug trafficking, the "vast majority of violent incidences involving gang members continue to result from fights over turf, status, and revenge" (Gang Violence, 2002, ¶1). Successful methods of intervention are necessary. The State of California's SafeState: Preventing Crime in California task force, for example, calls gang violence "one of the greatest threats to the safety and security of all Americans" (SafeState, 2008, ¶2). Although gang violence is a law enforcement problem, it also is a community problem that requires the involvement of educators, health care professionals, business leaders, politicians, and other community-based organizations.

TERMS & CONCEPTS

Aggravated assault: An attack on an individual that usually involves a weapon and is likely to produce death or serious bodily harm.

Bribery: Offering someone money to act in an illegal manner.

Carjacking: The crime of taking control of someone's car while the owner is present, either to steal the automobile, rob the owner, or force the driver to go someplace against his or her will.

Disposition: An inclination or tendency to act in a certain manner.

Negligence: Causing harm or the failure of an actor to use reasonable care when a duty is owed to another.

Neonaticide: The killing of an infant within the first twenty-four hours of his or her life.

Rationalizations: Explanations provided for behavior that is illegal or inappropriate.

Turf: A geographical area claimed by a gang as under their ownership and control.

BIBLIOGRAPHY

Akers, R., & Silverman, A. (2004). "Toward a social learning model of violence and terrorism." In M. Zahn, H. Brownstein, & S. Jackson (Eds.), *Violence: From theory to research.* Cincinnati, OH: Anderson.

Briggs, S., & Opsal, T. (2012). "The influence of victim ethnicity on arrest in violent crimes." *Criminal Justice Studies, 25,* 177–189.

Collins, R. (2008). *Violence: A micro-sociological theory.* Princeton, NJ: Princeton University Press.

Daly, M., & Wilson, M. (1988). *Homicide.* New York, NY: Aldine de Gruyter.

Gilliard-Matthews, S., Nolan, J. J., Haas, S. M. (2013). "Assessing the risk of nonsexual and sexual victimization using incident-based police reports." *Victims and Offenders, 8,* 23–41.

Gottfredson, G., & Gottfredson, D. (2002). *Gang problems and gang programs in a national sample of schools: 2001 summary.* Ellicot City, MD: Gottfredson.

Gottfredson, M., & Hirschi, T. (1990). *A general theory of crime.* Stanford, CA: Stanford University Press.

Johnson, A. (Ed.). (2000). Organized crime. *The Blackwell dictionary of sociology.* Malden, MA: Blackwell.

Kaiser Family Foundation. (2007). *Violent crime offenses.* http://www.statehealthfacts.org/

Klein, M., & Maxson, C. (2006). *Street gangs patterns and policies.* Oxford, England: Oxford UP.

Luckenbill, D. (1977). "Criminal homicide as a situated transaction." *Social Problems, 25,* 176-186.

Polk, K. (1994). *When men kill: Scenarios of masculine violence.* Cambridge, England: Cambridge University Press.

Pyrooz, D. C., Moule, R. K., & Decker, S. H. (2014). "The contribution of gang membership to the victim–offender overlap." *Journal of Research in Crime & Delinquency, 51,* 315–348.

United States Department of Justice, Federal Bureau of Investigation. (2016). "Violent crime." *Crime in the United States, 2016.* https://ucr.fbi.gov/crime-in-the-u.s/2016/crime-in-the-u.s.-2016/topic-pages/violent-crime.

Violence Prevention Coalition of Greater Los Angeles. (2002). *Gang violence: Report on the Status of Los Angeles Street Gangs.* Los Angeles County Interagency Task Force, 1999-2000. http://www.vpcla.org/factGang.htm.

"Violent crime reports up 1.2 percent in US last year, FBI finds." (2013). *Corrections Forum, 22,* 8–10.

Wallace, A. (1986). *Homicide: The social reality.* Sydney, Australia: New South Wales Bureau of Crime Statistics and Research.

Ward, T., & Beech, A. (2008). "An integrated theory of sexual offending." In D. Laws, & W. O'Donohue (Eds.), *Sexual deviance: Theory, assessment and treatment* (2nd ed.), pp. 21–36. New York, NY: Guilford.

"White-collar crime." (2008). In *West's encyclopedia of American Law* (2nd ed.). The Gale Group. http://legal-dictionary.thefreedictionary.com/White-collar+crime.

Wolfgang, M. (1958). *Patterns of criminal homicide.* Philadelphia, PA: University of Pennsylvania Press.

Zimring, F. E. (2013). "American youth violence: A cautionary tale." *Crime and Justice, 41,* 265–298.

Suggested Reading

Brownstein, H. (1999). *The social reality of violence and violent crime.* Boston, MA: Allyn & Bacon.

Burke, J. (2007). *Rape: Sex, violence, history.* Washington, DC: Shoemaker & Hoard.

DeLisi, M., & Conis, P. (2007). *Violent offenders: Theory, research, policy, and practice.* Sudbury, MA: Jones & Bartlett.

Eller, J. (2005). *Violence and culture: A cross-cultural and interdisciplinary approach.* Florence, KY: Wadsworth.

Hamm, M. (2007). *Terrorism as crime: From Oklahoma City to Al-Queda and beyond.* New York: New York University Press.

Hunter, R., & Dantzker, M. (2005). *Crime and criminality: Causes and consequences.* Monsey, NY: Criminal Justice Press.

Jones, S. (2001). *Understanding violent crime.* Philadelphia, PA: Open University Press.

Laver, T. (2002). *The truth about rape.* Gold River, CA: Raperecovery.com.

Laws, D., & O'Donohue, W. (Eds.). (2008). *Sexual deviance: Theory, assessment and treatment.* (2nd ed.). New York, NY: Guilford.

Miller, M. (1996). *Drugs and violent crime.* New York, NY: Rosen.

Moore, M. D., & Bergner, C. M. (2016). "The relationship between firearm ownership and violent crime." *Justice Policy Journal, 13*(1), 1-20.

Palermo, G., & Kocsis, R. (2005). *Offender profiling: An introduction to the sociopsychological analysis of violent crime.* Springfield, IL: Charles C. Thompson.

Reidel, M., & Welsh, W. (Eds.). (2007). *Criminal violence: Patterns, causes, and prevention.* (2nd ed.). Oxford, England: Oxford University Press.

Singer, S. (1996). *Recriminalizing delinquency: Violent juvenile crime and juvenile justice.* Cambridge, England: Cambridge University Press.

Tilly, C. (2003). *The politics of collective violence.* New York, NY: Cambridge University Press.

Van Kesteren, J. N. (2014). "Revisiting the gun ownership and violence link." *British Journal of Criminology, 54,* 53–72.

"Violent crime, mobility decisions, and neighborhood racial/ethnic transition." (2013). *Social Problems, 58,* 410–432.

Weiner, M., & Wolfgang, M. (1989). *Violent crime, violent criminals.* Thousand Oaks, CA: Sage.

Karen M. Harbeck, Ph.D., J.D.

WHITE COLLAR CRIME

ABSTRACT

Although white collar crime costs an estimated $300 billion annually in the United States alone, few perpetrators are caught and even fewer of receive any sort of punishment. Analysis of white collar crime focuses on two types: the individual perpetrator having special knowledge or occupational expertise or access that permits him or her to gain illegal financial advantage over others and corporate or organizational perpetrators, including organized and governmental crime. Since white collar crime is intermingled with legitimate business activities and often involves complex and sophisticated technical actions and internal networks, detection is difficult. Estimates are that less than 10 percent of perpetrators are caught. Analysis of federal sentences of corporations convicted of crimes during the late 1980s showed that 80 percent of the offending entities received fines of $25,000 or less, regardless of the severity or impact of their crimes. While the public has demanded greater accountability and more severe punishment, the reality is that white collar crime occurs with little likelihood of punishment compared to street crime. With the passage of the Sarbanes-Oxley Act in 2002, the US Congress instituted severe penalties for some types of corporate fraud and financial report falsification. Following the global financial crisis that began in late 2007, many people were angered over the fact that few financial institutions or executives were brought to trial over the systemic mismanagement of high-risk investments and widespread securities and mortgage fraud.

OVERVIEW

According to the Federal Bureau of Investigation (FBI) data, white collar crime costs the United States more than $300 billion dollars annually. While this total greatly exceeds the annual costs of crimes in the streets, estimated by the FBI to be $3.8 billion a year, most people are not as concerned about "crime in the suites." Despite the cost to society, white collar crime often goes undetected. If discovered, white collar criminals frequently are dealt with within the civil law framework rather than the criminal law system. Under civil law, regulations deal with economic losses between private parties, so repayment becomes the focus rather than punishment.

Although criminologists continue to debate which specific crimes qualify as white collar crime, in general white collar crime encompasses a variety of nonviolent crimes usually committed in commercial situations for financial gain. Types of white-collar crime include:

- Financial fraud
- Mail fraud
- Computer and Internet fraud
- Counterfeiting
- Public corruption
- Money laundering
- Price fixing
- Tax evasion
- Kickbacks
- Securities fraud
- Insider trading
- Bribery
- Embezzlement
- Trade secret theft
- Back-dating stock options
- Phone and telemarketing fraud
- Consumer fraud
- Credit card fraud
- Bankruptcy fraud
- Health care fraud
- Environmental law schemes
- Insurance fraud
- Government fraud
- Blackmail
- Investment schemes
- Extortion
- Racketeering
- Welfare fraud
- Weights and measures fraud

The tools of the trade are fast-talking, internal networks, accounting systems, and computers. Usually, criminal complaints are brought against individuals, but sometimes corporations are held accountable as well, especially in terms of restitution and fines. Technically speaking, however, offenses committed by a corporation are called corporate crime or organizational crime. Both are considered one type of white collar crime. This division of white collar crime categories into two types—occupational and corporate—was advanced by criminologists Marshall B. Clinard and Richard Quinney in the 1960s, and it remains influential to this day.

Although most individuals conceptualize white collar crime as being nonviolent, in reality this definition is faulty. Corporations that knowingly engage in the production of substandard food, drugs, or building materials or who intentionally expose their employees to dangerous working conditions can be held liable for crimes that fall into the white collar framework of analysis. According to data from the US Bureau of Labor Statistics, nearly three million nonfatal workplace injuries and illness were reported by private employers in 2014, with more than 4,600 fatal work injuries. Despite this staggering loss of life, however, few corporations or their leaders are held criminally liable for their misconduct. There are numerous reasons explaining why little is done about white collar crime in general, and these deaths in particular, and they will be discussed later in this article.

Given the current condition of federal and state data collection methods, it is difficult to perform statistical analyses of white collar crime. There are no socioeconomic or occupational data about offenders in the Uniform Crime Reporting (UCR) data, for example, and no information other than the arrest records of corporate criminal actors. Similarly, FBI crime statistics collect information on only three categories of what is considered to be white collar crime: fraud, counterfeiting and forgery, and embezzlement. All other related crimes are encompassed in the category of "other." The FBI's estimate of $300 billion in losses a year, therefore, is probably low. The collapse of the savings and loan industry, for example, cost the American public between $300 and $500 billion dollars, while some estimates place health care fraud alone at between $100 billion and $400 billion per year (Mokhiber, 2007). The cost of the 2008 global financial crisis, which was spurred by widespread insurance, mortgage, and securities fraud and mismanagement by financial institutions, has been estimated to be in excess of $30 trillion.

FURTHER INSIGHTS

Edwin H. Sutherland

The term "white collar crime" was used first in 1939 by sociologist Edwin H. Sutherland, who defined it as "a crime committed by a person of respectability and high social status in the course of his occupation." Since colored dress shirt fabrics did not come into use until the 1960s, executives and office workers across the nation wore white shirts to work every day, resulting in the label "white collar crime."

Because the term "white collar crime" has gained such acceptance with the public and scholars, it is hard to appreciate the revolutionary nature of Sutherland's arguments. Previously, crime analysis had focused on street crime and violence, rather than on the illegal actions of the rich and powerful. Sutherland sought to expose these crimes and bring justice to individuals harmed by those with powerful social, political, and economic connections. Edward Ross had articulated these same concerns in an article published in the *Atlantic Monthly* in 1907, but Sutherland's presidential address to the American Sociological Association's national convention in 1939 made front page news nationwide (Wong, 2005). Albert Morris had also examined upper-class criminals in his 1935 book on crime, but Sutherland's public platform, catchy terminology, and theoretical research framework launched the sub-discipline. Suddenly, the theoretical analyses of crime based upon poverty and poor socioeconomic conditions were shown to be inadequate as general explanations of criminal conduct (Wong, 2005).

Sutherland's Critics

Although the term "white collar crime" has gained public acceptance over the decades, sociologists and criminologists have engaged in an extensive debate over how to define the concept. Sutherland's argument that white collar criminals were of high status and respectability was challenged with research of the wide variety of individuals who engaged in white collar crime. Sutherland's argument that murder, robbery, and burglary were "blue-collar crimes" also was challenged. Similarly, scholars argued that the terms "respectability" and "high social status" were too vague and subjective for scholarly study. Thus, Sutherland's efforts to make a class-based definition of crime that focused on the perpetrator failed to withstand scrutiny. In part, this failure can be attributed to each individual's right to equal protection under the law.

Sutherland's assertion that white collar crime was related to occupation has been accepted in both sociological literature and in criminal practice. In 1981, for example, the United States Department of Justice's definition of white collar crime was dependent upon the professional status and/or special knowledge of the offender. It stated that white collar crime was:

Nonviolent crime for financial gain committed by means of deception by persons whose occupational status is entrepreneurial, professional or semiprofessional and utilizing their special occupational skills and opportunities; also, nonviolent crime for financial gain utilizing deception and committed by anyone having special technical and professional knowledge of business and government, irrespective of the person's occupation. (Bureau of Justice Statistics, 1981, p. 215)

Under this definition, then, white collar crime includes someone who provides fraudulent goods or services to the public. It also includes someone who works for a business or corporation and commits a crime against that entity, such as an employee who embezzles money from his or her employer.

VIEWPOINTS

While the dual definition of white collar crime as either occupational or corporate enjoys wide acceptance, since the 1970s there has been a move to further refine the definition to focus on the actual act committed, rather than on the occupation or corporate role of the actor. In 1989, for example, the FBI changed its definition of white collar crime to:

Those illegal acts which are characterized by deceit, concealment, or violations of trust and which are not dependent upon the application or threat of physical force or violence. Individuals and organizations commit these acts to obtain money, property, or services; to avoid the payment or loss of money or services; or to secure personal or business advantage. (p. 3)

Corporate Crime

Thus, in addition to nonviolent actions, the abuse of trust has surfaced as a major element in the definition of white collar crime (Spalek, 2000). Another important development has been a focus on white collar crime as "power crimes," whether they are committed by individuals, corporations, or gangsters (Ruggiero, 2007). Criminologists Gary Slapper and Steve Tombs (1999) have added to the debate by analyzing criminal and non-criminalized wrongdoings. Much of the harmful conduct committed by corporations, such as polluting the environment, often violates American regulatory policies rather than actual criminal statutes. Because the intent of these regulations is to prohibit conduct rather than to punish it, the fines often are remarkably low. Some argue that by making these harmful actions criminal, too great a strain is placed upon law enforcement agencies, which can lack sufficient resources to deal with these problems. Slapper and Tombs, however, argue that the threat of criminal prosecution and adverse publicity would put pressure on corporations to police themselves. Though the likelihood of being caught and prosecuted would be statistically low, the corporations would still assume the costs of regulating themselves rather than the public. Celia Wells (2001) argues further for the criminalization of regulatory violations since, by sending a message about what kinds of conduct society deems to be worthy of sanctions and condemnation, it might serve as some additional deterrence.

Intent

While it may seem logical to hold organizations and corporations to the same standards individuals are held to, how this is done is not clearly defined within the theories of criminal law. Often, for example, in order to be convicted of a particular crime, it must be shown that the perpetrator had a guilty mind or "mens rea" to commit the crime. To be convicted of first-degree murder, for example, the accused must have had the intent to murder or to cause serious bodily injury resulting in death. If the intent is lacking, the perpetrator can only be charged with a lesser offense, such as manslaughter. But all too often in corporate crimes the leadership lacks the specific intent to harm its victims. Instead, corporate executives weigh the risks involved in their actions, both the risks of harming others and of getting caught. Doctrines that hold corporations liable are less well developed than those pertaining to individuals in part because some would argue that there is no intent possible in a nonhuman legal entity. Eli Lederman (2001) offered an extensive discussion on developing legal theories to hold corporate entities criminally liable for their actions. One argument, for example, is that a corporation's intent or culpability can be gleaned from the leadership's directives to employees, whether verbal, written, or through everyday behaviors. It is important to realize that this entire legal development is relatively new. The first conviction in the United Kingdom for the offense of corporate manslaughter, for example, occurred in 1994 following an industrial death (Tombs, 1995). This development occurred as a response to a wave of business enterprise deaths at sea and on the nation's rail network. Often a corporate crime is portrayed as a unique accident rather than as the outcome of systemic wrongdoing and intentional neglect. Media images of street violence are intense, immediate, and personalized so that the public feels the threat of danger and becomes outraged; in contrast, corporate-related deaths are portrayed as rare, specific to a unique set of circumstances, and without culpability.

Individual Crime

Like their corporate counterparts, individual white collar offenders face remarkably few consequences for their illegal behavior. Most individual white collar offenders are people who "got into financial difficulty and who saw their way out of it through illegal and fraudulent means" (Keel, 2008, p. 2). These relatively small operators are more likely to get caught, while major criminals have the connections and resources to escape detection and prosecution. In fact, estimates are that less than 10 percent of the perpetrators are ever caught and convicted. Of these, an even smaller percent go to jail. According to the American Bar Association, for example, 91 percent of convicted bank robbers go to jail, while only 17 percent of those convicted of embezzling bank funds do. And individual white collar criminals are still more likely to be convicted and, once convicted, to serve long jail sentences than corporate offenders, who often get off with a shorter sentence or simply a fine (Gottschalk & Rundmo, 2014). Even when building contractors knowingly use substandard materials that result in injury and death, they face fines rather than jail time (Long, 2007). Penalties have increased over the past few years, but severe punishment still remains unlikely.

There are several reasons why white collar criminals are not as severely punished as their street crime counterparts. Sometimes the status and wealth of a perpetrator does afford him or her special protections. Cronyism, or favors from politically elite friends, may influence whether a prosecutor decides to bring criminal charges against an individual or whether local law enforcement resources are allocated to pursue certain types of crime. Access to excellent, expensive, and well-connected lawyers also plays an important role in protecting these criminals from severe punishment. Since white collar individuals write the laws concerning white collar crime, vague terms and light sentences are established. And because these crimes are usually nonviolent and do not fit society's image of purposefully evil, illegal conduct, the public perception of white collar crime is different and the demand for severe punishment less vocal.

Detecting and Prosecuting White Collar Crime

White collar crime often is difficult to discover. Special experts are required to trace bank fraud, securities fraud, and other complex and technical illegal transactions. Usually the offenses are hidden within normal business practices and easily kept secret through occupational controls. Additionally, white collar criminals often commit illegal acts that are regulated by government agencies, such as the US Treasury and the Environmental Protection Agency. Understaffed and lacking resources, these agencies often fail to detect white collar crime. However, following the global financial crisis, the US government has increased funding and resources for the US Department of Justice to investigate and prosecute cases of white collar crime more thoroughly.

When corporations are the perpetrators, it can also be difficult to assign blame to specific individuals within the organization. More often than not, corporations make arrangements to pay some relatively small fine as their only punishment. In these cases, it is believed that the removal of corporate officers guilty of the criminal conduct might disrupt the function of the entity, harming employees and shareholders who played no role in the crimes. Similarly, requiring the corporation to pay a huge fine also might affect its stability and the livelihoods of hundreds or thousands of employees. The Federal US Sentencing Commission, for example, found that between the years 1984 through 1987, nearly half of convicted corporations paid fines of $5,000 or less, while 80 percent were fined $25,000 or less (Keel, 2008).

Because white collar crime is so difficult to detect and investigate, numerous federal and state agencies work together to control it. In fact, the National White Collar Crime Center (NW3C) exists to:

Provide a nationwide support system for agencies involved in the prevention, investigation, and prosecution of economic and high-tech crimes and to support and partner with other appropriate entities in addressing homeland security initiatives, as they relate to economic and high-tech crimes (2008, ¶8).

Organizational Deviance

Although Sutherland and his colleagues were concerned about crime perpetrated by business entities, all too often their theoretical or legal analysis of corporate crime focused on the criminal actions of individuals within an organization rather than the criminal actions of corporate entities. In 1976, however, president-elect of the American Sociological Association, Stanton Wheeler, used his public platform to promote the study of organizational crime (Wong, 2005). Then, in 1981, Ermann and Lundman introduced the concept of organizational deviance (Wong, 2005, p. 15). Under their analysis, an organization is deviant if

- It commits an act that is in violation of external norms and the organization's stated goals, but "supported by internal operating norms"
- It socializes new members to consent to the organizations "rationalizations and justifications" for the deviant act
- It gives peer support to the individuals who committed the act, and
- Its dominant leadership supports deviant acts (Wong, 2005, p. 15–16).

Later theorists distinguished between organizations with deviant goals and those "that approved illegitimate means in the achievement of organizational goals" (Wong, 2005, p. 16). Organized crime syndicates fit into the category of organizations with deviant goals, although not all of the offenses committed by organized crime syndicates fall into the category of white collar crime.

Organized Crime

The Organized Crime Control Act (U.S., 1970) defines organized crime as "the unlawful activities of... a highly organized and disciplined association." It can and does exist in any setting, whether it be local, state, national, or international. In order to thrive and move money throughout the economy, however, organized crime has to have strong ties to legitimate business entities. Often, cooperation from respected members of the business community is gained through bribery, extortion, and blackmail. Added protection for the criminal endeavors is achieved by bribing judicial and law enforcement officials.

In an effort to combat organized crime, in 1970 the federal government passed the Racketeer Influenced and Corrupt Organization (RICO) Act (18 U. S. C. A. § 1961 et seq.) In addition to crimes deemed to be white collar in nature, RICO encompasses gambling, extortion, prostitution, narcotics trafficking, loan sharking, and murder. Punishment under RICO can be harsh, including fines and up to twenty years in prison. Additionally, the defendant must forfeit any claims to the money or property obtained from the criminal enterprise, or obtained from any criminal enterprise barred under RICO (White-collar, 2008).

Political Crime

Another aspect of white collar crime that can be either individual in nature or organized is governmental or political crime. Lawmakers are frequently in a position to trade their influence and legislative votes for money and gifts. Again, the risks of being caught are low, and given politicians' elite political connections within a governmental entity, even the loss of one's political career is not a given. Similarly, entire governments, or groups within a government, can commit acts that fall into the broad category of white collar crime. The Watergate break-in during the Nixon administration and the Iran-Contra scandal during the Reagan administration are both examples of illegal action performed by an organized group of individuals within our government.

Despite decades of corporate criminal offenses, it was not until 2002 that Congress enacted legislation that seriously penalized corporate wrongdoing. The Public Company Accounting Reform and Investor Protection Act, also known as the Sarbanes-Oxley Act (Pub.L. 107-204, 116 Stat. 745) increased penalties for mail and wire fraud to twenty years in prison. Acts of securities fraud could be punished by up to twenty-five years in prison. Additionally, the act criminalized the falsification of corporate financial reports, making it punishable with fines of up to five million dollars and ten years in prison (White-collar, 2008). Also contained within the act was the directive that the Federal US Sentencing Commission increased the penalties for other white collar crimes. The huge financial losses from the Enron and WorldCom scandals, combined with the evidence of extensive financial report falsification by the accounting firm of Arthur Andersen, finally moved the government to take white collar crime seriously, in large part to shore up public confidence in the stock market and in corporate America. These new regulations changed the landscape of both public and law enforcement attitudes towards white collar crime. However, there was widespread disappointment following the 2008 global financial crisis that few financial executives or institutions were brought to trial for systemic mortgage and securities fraud, reinforcing the idea that white collar crime is extremely difficult to prosecute.

TERMS AND CONCEPTS

Bribery: The act of attempting to induce someone to do something, especially something illegal, by offering money or some other enticement.

Cronyism: Preferential treatment given to one's friends or colleagues regardless of their abilities or qualifications.

Embezzle: To take for personal use and without permission the money or property belonging to others with which one has been entrusted.

Extortion: The use of threats, force, or other illegal methods to gain money or information from someone.

Mens Rea: Also known as criminal intent. The requirement that, to be found guilty of a criminal offense, the accused must have intended to commit the offense and known that it was a crime. Literally, a "guilty mind."

Bibliography

Bureau of Justice Statistics, United States Department of Justice. (1981). *Dictionary of criminal justice data terminology.* (2nd ed.). Washington, DC: Government Printing Office.

Bureau of Labor Statistics. (2012). "Workplace injuries and illnesses—2011." Washington, DC: Government Printing Office.

Charon, J. (1986). *Sociology: A conceptual approach.* Boston, MA: Allyn and Bacon.

Faichney, D. (2014). "Autocorrect? A proposal to encourage voluntary restitution through the white-collar sentencing calculus." *Journal of Criminal Law & Criminology, 104,* 389–430.

Federal Bureau of Investigation. (1989). *White collar crime: A report to the public.* Washington, DC: Government Printing Office.

Gottfredson, M. & Hirschi, T. (1990). *A general theory of crime.* Stanford, CA: Stanford University Press.

Gottschalk, P. (2012). "White-collar crime and police crime: Rotten apples or rotten barrels?" *Critical Criminology, 20,* 169–182.

Gottschalk, P., & Rundmo, T. (2014). "Crime: The amount and disparity of sentencing—A comparison of corporate and occupational white collar criminals." *International Journal of Law, Crime & Justice, 42,* 175–187.

Keel, R. (2008). "White collar crime." http://www.umsl.edu/~keelr/200/wcolcrim.html.

Kostelnik, J. (2012). "Sentencing white-collar criminals: when is shaming viable?" *Global Crime, 13,* 141–159.

Lederman, E. (2001). "Models for imposing corporate criminal liability: From adaptation and imitation toward aggregation and the search for self-identity." *Buffalo Criminal Law Review, 4,* 641-708.

Long, R. (2007). "Introductory sociology: White-collar crime." http://www.delmar.edu/socsci/rlong/intro/wc-crime.htm.

Michel, C., Heide, K., & Cochran, J. (2015). "Socidemographic correlates of knowledge about elite deviance." *American Journal of Criminal Justice, 40*(3), 639–660.

Mokhiber, R. (2007). "Twenty things you should know about corporate crime." www.alternet.org/story/54093.

Perri, F. (2011). "White-collar criminals: the 'kinder, gentler' offender?" *Journal of Investigative Psychology & Offender Profiling, 8,* 217–241.

Rock, P. (2002). 'Sociological theories of crime.' In M. Maguire, M. Morgan, & R. Reiner (Eds.), *Oxford handbook of criminology.* (3rd ed., pp. 51 - 82). Oxford: Oxford University Press.

Slapper, G., & Tombs, S. (1999). *Corporate crime.* London: Pearson Education Ltd.

Spalek, B. (2001, October). "White-collar crime victims and the issue of trust." *British criminology conference: Selected proceeding, 4,* 1-15.

Strader, J. (2002). *Understanding white collar crime.* Newark, NJ: Matthew Bender & Company.

Sutherland, E. (1947). *Principles of criminology* (4th ed.). Philadelphia, PA: Lippincott.

Wells, C. (2001). *Corporations and criminal responsibility* (2nd ed.),. Oxford: Oxford University Press.

"White-collar crime." (2008). *West's encyclopedia of American law* (2nd Ed.). The Gale Group. http://legal-dictionary.thefreedictionary.com/White-collar+crime.

Wong, K. (2005). "From white-collar crime to organizational crime: An intellectual history." *Murdoch University Electronic Journal of Law, 12* (1/2).

SUGGESTED READING

Benson, M. & French, J. L. (2008). *White collar crimes (Criminal investigations).* Philadelphia, PA: Chelsea House.

Coleman, J. (2005). *The criminal elite: Understanding white-collar crime.* New York, NY: St. Martin's.

Davis, J., & Holland-Davis, L. (2015). "Beyond neighborhoods and crime: Expanding the scope of social disorganization to explain occupational deviance." *Sociological Inquiry, 85*(2), 262–284.

DeAngelis, G., & Sarat, A. (1999). *White-collar crime (Crime justice and punishment).* Philadelphia, PA: Chelsea House.

Geis, G., Meier, R., & Salinger, L. (1995). *The white-collar crime: Offenses in business, politics, and the professions* (3rd ed.). New York, NY: Free Press.

Gibbs, C. (2010). "Transnational white-collar crime and risk." *Criminology & Public Policy, 9,* 543–560.

Hunter, R., & Dantzker, M. (2005). *Crime and criminality: Causes and consequences.* Monsey, NY: Criminal Justice Press.

Leap, T. (2007). *Dishonest dollars: The dynamics of white-collar crime.* Ithaca, NY: Cornell University Press.

Pontell, H., & Geis, G. (Eds.). (2006). *International handbook of white-collar and corporate crime.* New York, NY: Springer.

Sachner, M. (2009). *The FBI and white-collar crime.* Broomall, PA: Mason Crest.

Salinger, L. (Ed.), (2004). *Encyclopedia of white-collar and corporate crime.* Thousand Oaks, CA: Sage.

Simon, D., & Hagan, F. (1999). *White-collar deviance.* Boston, MA: Allyn & Bacon.

Steffensmeier, D. J., Schwartz, J., & Roche, M. (2013). "Gender and twenty-first-century corporate crime: Female involvement and the gender gap in Enron-era corporate frauds." *American Sociological Review, 78,* 448–476.

Young, M. (2008). *White-collar crime.* San Diego, CA: Greenhaven.

Karen M. Harbeck, Ph.D., J.D.

Race & Ethnicity

Introduction

The conversation about race and ethnicity has long been a heated one. Like with other highly debated topics, emotional viewpoints and uncomfortable feelings cause people to lash out, often denying the history, impact, and continued experience of racial struggles. This section explores how race and ethnicity has impacted minorities throughout history, specifically in America.

Often debated during this conversation is the lack of scientific evidence that race and ethnicity actually exist. Some believe that race and ethnicity are both socially constructed elements, and the term "race" was developed as a tool to categorize people based on common physical characteristics. Others, struggle with this idea, finding comfort in the differences between them and minorities.

Although slavery existed worldwide for all of history, modern (English) slavery brought forth "an extreme denial of recognition that slaves were human beings; they were seen as property and the laws treated them as such." This is an example of *ethnocentrism*—the tendency to see your own group as superior to others. Although slavery was officially abolished by the Emancipation Proclamation in 1865, the next hundred years of *segregation* demonstrated a battle for equality and rights. Although laws change from one day to the next, societal acceptance takes longer.

This section also discusses the impact of slavery, including *cultural prejudice, racism,* and *discrimination* in modern day society. These are all reactions to the dehumanization of black slaves, and other minority groups. The term *white privilege* means that certain privileges and benefits are given to a person simply because of their skin color. A white male teenager going into a bank wearing a hoodie and baggy jeans will probably be greeted by the guard with a smile and helped by the teller without question. If a black male teenager went into the same bank wearing the same outfit, he may be followed by the guard, questioned about his purpose, and asked for additional identification to withdraw funds. White privilege makes it easier to move throughout American society.

Other topics covered in this section include how racism continues to be present in society, often covertly. *Scapegoating* is when minorities are unfairly targeted or blamed. If there are five news stories of women being attacked, and four of the attackers were white, the media may choose to report only the incident of the black attacker. Highlighting minority crimes and downplaying crimes by a person of privilege is common. When a Muslim person is caught committing a crime, his ethnicity and religion are focused on; when a white male commits a mass murder his race is downplayed in favor of his mental health. This is an example of *minority group threat,* s stressing the negativity of minority groups in a disproportionate manner. *Institutional racism* looks at racism on a large scale such as in organizations or politics. *Racial profiling* is when a police officer pulls over a black man for no other reason than the color of his skin.

These articles also discuss research theories that attempt to explain the psychology and relational reasoning behind hierarchy and oppression. *Realistic Conflict Theory* looks at the competition between resources as a reason for ethnocentrism and negativity towards others. For example, if you are waiting to be interviewed, sitting in a room with other people who are interviewing for the same job you might think that someone looks less attractive, less smart, or less nice, creating a reason to dislike them because you are in competition for the job.

Our society has a long way to go to reach race equality. Social justice is based on education, understanding of similarities and differences between races, and acceptance. For a minority population to gain higher social status, the majority population has to accept their role in oppression and use their voices to challenge discrimination.

Kimberly Ortiz-Hartman, Psy.D., LMFT

Adorno's Authoritarian Personality

ABSTRACT

A group of authors published a study on the Authoritarian Personality in 1950. Theodor W. Adorno was one of them. They combined Freud's idea that suppression of instincts during childhood can have adverse effects in later life with an explanation for the rise of fascism and anti-Semitism. The AuthoritarianPersonality is the relationship of the Authoritarian structure of families at the core of Authoritarian states that could turn prejudice into fascist action, such as what happened in Germany. The study employed the so-called F-scale or (pre)fascism scale, which structured the Authoritarian personalities into several traits. Adorno's contribution is deeply rooted in his intellectual biography.

OVERVIEW

The Frankfurt School

Theodor W. Adorno (1903–1969) was a leading member of the so-called Frankfurt School who proposed critical theory. Adorno, Max Horkheimer and Friedrich Pollock comprised the inner circle of that group. Horkheimer and Adorno were born into fairly wealthy bourgeoisie families and formed the intellectual core, while Pollock, son of a factory worker, stayed mostly busy with the finances and certain administrative tasks on which he and Horkheimer worked. After the Second World War, Horkheimer was left with little time for writing and the bulk of intellectual production was left to Adorno and offshoots of critical theory; the second and third generation of the Frankfurt School.

Both Horkheimer and Adorno had studied in the 1920s in Frankfurt under the Neo-Kantian scholar Hans Cornelius. Horkheimer, slightly older, became Cornelius's assistant and much of Adorno's work ever since that time was worked out in direct answer to problems introduced to Adorno by Horkheimer. The intellectual background of Adorno's writings as well as of the majority of the members of the Frankfurt School is clearly rooted in Hegel-Marxism. Given that most members of the Frankfurt School and Marxist circles at the time were descendants of rather wealthy families, it is often ironically remarked upon that social criticism was something that one must be able to afford.

Adorno's Background

Adorno wrote his dissertation in 1924, trying to prove that Husserl's Phenomenology is part of the positivist movement due to its roots in Greek philosophy. To become a full professor, German PhDs had to undergo (and still do) a second process after their dissertation which is called habilitation. Adorno had to enter two habilitation scripts since his first one was rejected by Cornelius.

Adorno biographers differ on the importance of this fact for his life's work. The most dominant interpretation sees Adorno's second habilitation on Kierkegaard in light of his last and unfinished book on aesthetic theory. It is widely considered that Adorno saw art as the one field that still allowed for escape and free thought, which could break the cage of total ideology that mass society and its culture-industry had lured the entirety of society into (Mueller-Doohm, 2003).

Another interpretation suggests that his rejected first habilitation on the concept of the unconscious in Kant and Freud foreshadowed the fundamental issues to which Adorno would later dedicate most of his work. Alexander Stingl goes so far as to suggest that Adorno's entire publishing career can be perceived as a continuous defense of his first habilitation, and thereby as a continuous defense against the authority of the hierarchy of the university (Stingl, 2009).

A central aspect of that first habilitation is Adorno's warning about the use of psychotherapy by the "wrong groups." The celebration of psychoanalysis and psychotherapy by a large group of people glossed over the danger that these techniques and the insight they offered into the human mind could also be used to manipulate society. The veiling or blinding that these techniques produced, for example, applied by the entertainment or advertisement industry, were addressed in his own writings, as well as in his famous 1944 co-production with Horkheimer, *The Dialectic of Enlightenment.* The culture industry, under the guise of helping individualism, pre-structures the world into decisions which are therefore no longer free and autonomous. The perfidy of the culture-industry and its manipulation is that the effect of the blinding is so total (totaler Verblendungszusammenhang) or can be called a total ideology, that people do not even realize this effect but instead celebrate the culture industry and its products as an agent of freedom and individual choice. This illusion has become so total that there is no escaping. The sole route of escape that Adorno and Horkheimer allowed for was either in some works of art and music—although Adorno was himself very selective in what he would allow to count as art; for example, he absolutely hated jazz. An intellectual route of escape was critical theory or its method of immanent criticism, which Adorno and Horkheimer would consider their "message in a bottle," which they would not live to see arrive. However, later generations would decipher and break the circle.

Adorno's cynicism is of course explained in his bearing witness to the horror of the Third Reich and his own fate as a refugee.

FURTHER INSIGHTS

In 1950, a group of scholars from the University of California, Berkeley published *The Authoritarian Personality*, a study that Adorno helped create. The work is of course deeply influenced by Adorno's personal experiences, but also by his readings of Freud and his colleague and former member of the Frankfurt School, Erich Fromm.

During the Second World War, anti-Semitism was a subject of concern for the Jewish community in the United States, not only in regard to what was happening in the concentration camps in Nazi-Germany, but world-wide. Before 1933, German anti-Semitism was not the worst in Europe. Actually, German anti-Semitism was a relatively late development in Europe and many European Jews considered moving to Germany as a relatively safe territory. Additionally, anti-Semitism was felt to be on the rise in the United States, which had just experienced one of its worst financial crises and many angry people were looking for scapegoats.

Roosevelt's New Deal was not initially as popular as common history now paints it. Its critics went as far as calling it the Jew Deal, hoping to play on latent anti-Semitism (Feingold, 1995). A series of "Studies in Prejudice" sponsored by Horkheimer's committee was intended to uncover the roots of prejudices such as anti-Semitism, as well as its roots in the United States, while exposing how and why people move from internal sentiments of prejudice to outwardly acting on it. This project was lucrative and Horkheimer wrestled to get his friends involved. Adorno was actually a late addition; he was known for his lack of skill in empirical research and his distrust of the "American empirical orientation" in sociology, which came from his brief work on Paul Laszarsfeld's radio project; one of the first jobs Horkheimer could land for Adorno in the United States after he fled Germany via Britain.

The Authoritarian Personality

The subject matter of the *Authoritarian Personality* by Adorno, Else Frenkel-Brunswik, Daniel Levinson, and R. Nevitt Sanford was the relationship of the Authoritarian structure of families as the core of Authoritarian states that could turn prejudice into fascist action, such as what happened in Germany. The study employed the so called F-scale or (pre)fascism scale, which structured the Authoritarian personalities into several traits.

The F-scale was a psychometric Personality test designed to give a quantitative (measured in numbers) representation of tendencies that could be qualified as Authoritarian. Among the variables measured were:

- Authoritarian aggression;
- Sex;
- Superstition;
- Conventionalism;
- Cynical attitude;
- Leaning to stereotypes; and
- Destructive attitude.

The approach followed the work of Sigmund Freud, Wilhelm Reich, and Erich Fromm in several ways. The Freudian model predicts that a high severity of punishment in the family will result in a child's increased susceptibility to authority in later life, because children will then identify strongly with Authoritarian figures. Reich transformed this mode into an explanation for the rise of Fascism. The most developed model can actually be found in Erich Fromm's study, *Escape from Freedom*. Fromm not only provided the most thorough analysis, but his idea confirms a certain aspect argued in the long-standing tradition of enlightenment philosophy; that people shun the responsibility that goes along with freedom and making choices and rather, transfer this responsibility to somebody they assume to have authority. This is not that far from Kant's postulation that the enemy of enlightenment and reason is comfort or convenience.

Neither Fromm nor Reich was adequately mentioned by the authors of the Authoritarian Personality. In the case of Reich, this may pertain to the fact that he was considered somewhat of a maverick in academic circles. In the case of Fromm, this was largely due to his split with the core group of the Frankfurt school over a grave dispute with Horkheimer on the correct interpretation of Freud. The famous psychologist Karen Horney, whose work was close to Fromm's, became occasionally a target for Adorno's attacks on positions on Freud he disagreed with. This line of attack was actually a weapon of choice for Adorno. He and Horkheimer rarely addressed the person or his work they were criticizing directly, but looked for somebody applying a similar or related theoretical construct to criticize.

Influence from Psychoanalysis

The divergence between Adorno and Fromm means that there was a common source in Freudian psychology which Fromm developed first. Adorno and his group took the lead from Fromm and developed the Authoritarian Personality in another direction.

In the work of psychoanalysis, the family structure was the primary agent of suppressing aggression and instinct and to develop a tendency in the child to follow Authoritarian characters and release aggression onto minorities and weaker opponents. In the sociological view, society and the state promote this tendency by enforcing hierarchical structure throughout society. The group around Adorno seemed to believe that the family was to blame and that these aspects were almost impossible to revert in later life. Their research and the F-scale largely confirmed their postulates and could show that prejudice and the potential for Authoritarianism existed.

VIEWPOINTS

The Authoritarian Personality was a study that received a lot of attention in the United States after its publication. In many regards this attention is well deserved. The awareness that Authoritarian tendencies and prejudice are a common phenomenon (and not just in Nazi Germany) is certainly an important contribution. Secondly, the interdisciplinary nature of the study, as well as several novel approaches and applications deserved praise.

Criticism

But on the other side, there was also a lot to criticize in that study. One of the major criticisms was that the Freudian premise was overstretched into an all-out explanation. The work of important predecessors such as Fromm was unduly ignored, it seemed, for there was no respective mention made in the publication. In regard to the statistical methods applied, several scholars have questioned the representation and reliability of the results.

One particular criticism was made in regard to the political ideology of the authors. It was argued that they were themselves leftist scholars and respectively had been searching for a connection between right wing extremism and the Authoritarian Personality, while neglecting that leftist extremism, too, could lean towards Authoritarianism.

It must also be said that the F-scale was an untested instrument and has been subject to disputes ever since. Several important aspects are not taken into proper account by the F-scale, such as education, socioeconomic status, etc. A large number of individual variations can be much better explained by these other factors.

Adorno abandoned empirical research after the publication of the report and even began to preach against this kind of research. The often harsh critique in American sociological journals turned him against American science, and after his return to Germany, he would never set foot on American soil again. The reason for this can be identified in an essay by Edward Shils, which was a clear-cut and brutally honest analysis of *The Authoritarian Personality* (Wiggershaus, 2003).

True to form, instead of answering to this critique or taking up a discussion with Shils, Adorno picked another target. In 1951, Shils was one of the coauthors of the seminal structural-functionalist work, *Toward a General Theory of Action*, an effort to create a common frame of reference for social and behavioral sciences put together by a Harvard discussion group financed by the Carnegie Foundation and spearheaded by sociologist Talcott Parsons and anthropologist Clyde

Kluckhohn. Instead of attacking Shils or his psychological premises directly, Adorno wrote a critical review of an essay Parsons wrote in 1955 on the relation between sociology and psychology, which addressed the same points as did Shils. Not once does Adorno make mention of the influential *Toward a General Theory*, while at the same time the review defends in many aspects the central ideas of Adorno's failed first habilitation.

In sum, *The Authoritarian Personality* was an insightful project that can still serve as a template for similar studies. But the weaknesses of the methodology and application of psychology as an explanation are obvious. Adorno's reaction to criticism is unfortunate, for had he perceived this study as a work in progress, he would have had the unique chance of working on a lasting influence on empirical research and not only in philosophy and abstract sociological theory. However, in this regard, we also see the difference between German and American scholarship. American scholarship is generally more open to criticism and improvement and accepts that methods are in stages of transition, while German scholarship is itself very Authoritarian and hierarchical, and the critical theorists from Frankfurt were no exceptions.

TERMS & CONCEPTS

Authority: Concepts of authority, domination, hierarchy and ruling classes have long been subjects of social ethical and sociological thought. The classic work on authority in sociology is Max Weber's distinction of ideal-types of political leadership and authority:

- The charismatic type;
- The traditional type; and
- The legal-bureaucratic type.

These ideal-types do not occur in their pure form, but are heuristic devices for analysis. Horkheimer and Adorno used Weber's ideas implicitly. For critical theorists and their Hegel-Marxist or Freudo-Marxist background, authority and leadership always leads back to theoretical abstractions of the idea of oppression.

Critical Theory: In 1937, Max Horkheimer defined the difference between traditional and critical theory. Traditional theory, according to Horkheimer stops at explaining the social facts, while critical theory hopes to change society through critical analysis. Horkheimer hoped to counter the climate of positivist science of his era and that critical theory could unmask the historic specificity of society and its dominating ideology as a total entity.

Frankfurt School: The original critical theorists began studying and working in Frankfurt am Main, Germany. In 1930, Max Horkheimer became the director of the Frankfurt Institute of Social Research, which he and his colleagues used to promote the study of society from Marxist theoretical positions. Many original members such as Herbert Marcuse, Erich Fromm, Otto Kirchheimer and Franz Neumann developed their own version of critical theory over time, splitting with Adorno and Horkheimer who remained the intellectual core of the Frankfurt School.

Immanent Criticism: Immanent criticism denotes a method of critical theory. This method means that criticism must come from within the system or within the frame of reference. Measuring and evaluating a system in its own categories and values, exposing its ambiguities is the process of immanent criticism, which will lead to change, according to critical theory.

Personality: The history of the concept of Personality in the social sciences lies deep in the history of biology and philosophy in the nineteenth century and the German scholar Rudolf Hermann Lotze (1817 –1881), who thought that while resting in the soul, Personality is shaped by civilization and society. The most important transformations occur in the works of William James (Principles of Psychology) and Pierre Janet (Les névroses), before modern psychology emerges from the work of Freud as a discipline, and the concept of Personality is taken for granted.

Phenomenology: Created by Edmund Husserl (1859–1938), the philosophical discipline of phenomenology seeks to show that in "bracketing" away the assumptions we hold about the external world when viewing a phenomenon, we can actually reach the essence of this phenomenon. The consciousness as an act and the direction to the objects are two different things; there is no thought that is not directed at something or does not have intentionality. Therefore, our directedness to the object in intentionality also constitutes it. This speculation lead Husserl to another question, namely what happens when several people refer to an object in communication, what is it that they are referring to, if each subjective mind has its own intentionality and constitutes the object for each person in a unique way.

Structural Functionalism: Structural functionalism argues that various elements in a social system evolved to perform certain tasks within the society by resolving a problem or the other. The economy as a subsystem of society for example emerged to resolve the problem of efficient allocation of resources. Systems can be analyzed in accordance to a presupposed from of order and the elements of the system are in state of mutual interdependence. Systems tend toward establishing or re-instating equilibrium.

Totalitarianism: A state in which all aspects of life are governed by the state and no private life exists anymore we speak of totalitarian states, such was the case in the Communist Soviet Union or Nazi Germany.

Bibliography

Adorno, T. W. (2003/1973). *Gesammelte Schriften I: Philosophische Frühschriften.* Frankfurt aM: Suhrkamp.

Adorno, T. W. (2003/1962). *Gesammelte Schriften II: Kierkegaard Konstruktion des Ästhetischen.* Frankfurt aM: Suhrkamp.

Adorno, T. W. (2003/1951). *Gesammelte Schriften IV: Minima Moralia Reflexionen aus dem beschädigten Leben.* Frankfurt aM: Suhrkamp.

Adorno, T. W. (2003/1970). *Gesammelte Schriften VII: ästhetische Theorie.* Frankfurt aM: Suhrkamp.

Adorno, T. W. (2003 /1972*). Gesammelte Schriften VIII: Soziologische Schriften 1.* Frankfurt aM: Suhrkamp.

Adorno, T. W. (1997/1975). *Gesammelte Schriften IX.1 u. IX.2: Soziologische Schriften II* (2 Vols.). Frankfurt aM: Suhrkamp.

Benhabib, S. (1986). *Critique, Norm and Utopia. A study of the foundations of Critical Theory.* New York: Columbia University Press.

Feingold, H. L. (1995). *Bearing Witness: How America and its Jews responded to the Holocaust.* Syracuse, NY: Syracuse University Press.

Foucault, M. (2003). *In Defense of Society.* London: Palgrave MacMillan.

Fromm, E. (1941). *Escape from freedom.* New York: Holt, Rinehart & Winston.

Fromm, E. (1976). *To Have or to Be?* New York: Harper & Row.

Horkheimer, M. (1947). Eclipse of Reason. Oxford: Oxford University Press.

Horkheimer, M., & Adorno, T. W. (2000/1944). Dialektik der Aufklärung Philosophische Fragmente. Frankfurt aM: Fischer.

Jay, M. (1996/1973). The dialectical imagination: A history of the Frankfurt School and the Institute of Social Research 1923 - 1950. Berkeley: University of California Press.

Jay, M. (2003). Refractions of violence. New York: Routledge.

Ludeke, S. G., & Krueger, R. F. (2013). "Authoritarianism as a Personality trait: Evidence from a longitudinal behavior genetic study." *Personality & Individual Differences, 55*(5), 480-484.

McCarthy, T. (1978). *The Critical Theory of Jürgen Habermas.* Cambridge, MA: MIT Press.

McCarthy, T. (1991). *Ideals and Illusions. On Reconstruction and Deconstruction in contemporary Critical Theory.* Cambridge, MA: MIT Press.

Müller-Doohm, S. (2003). *Adorno.* Frankfurt aM: Suhrkamp.

Stingl, A. (2009). "The Enlightenment in Adorno, Horkheimer and Focault: Immanent Critics versus Interpretative Analytics." Online Publication (in German) at pompeii-project.eu.

Stoner, A., & Lybeck, E. (2011). "Bringing Authoritarianism back in: Reification, latent prejudice, and economic threat." *Conference Papers—American Sociological Association,* 247.

Wiggershaus, R. (2001). *Die Frankfurter Schule.* Munich: dtv.

Ziege, E. (2012). "Patterns within prejudice: Antisemitism in the United States in the 1940s." *Patterns Of Prejudice, 46*(2), 93-127.

Suggested Reading

Adorno, T. W. (2003). *Vorlesung über negative Dialektik.* Frankfurt aM: Suhrkamp.

Adorno, T. W. (1975/1966). *Negative Dialektik.* Frankfurt aM: Suhrkamp.

Demirovic, A. (1999). *Der nonkonformistische Intellektuelle Von der Frankfurter Schule zur kritischen Theorie.* Frankfurt aM: Suhrkamp.

Marcuse, H. (1998 /1956)). *Eros and civilization: A philosophical inquiry into Freud.* London: Routledge.

Martinussen, M., & Kroger, J. (2013). "Meta-Analytic Studies of Identity Status and Personality: Introduction and Overview." *Identity,* 13(3), 189-200.

Richey, S. (2012). "Campaign advertising and the stimulation and activation of the Authoritarian Personality." *Political Communication, 29*(1), 24-43.

Wolin, R. (1992). *The Terms of Cultural Criticism: The Frankfurt School, Existentialism, Poststructuralism.* New York: Columbia University Press.

Alexander Stingl, Ph.D.

Assimilation

ABSTRACT

Assimilation is the process by which immigrants become part of the mainstream culture of their new country, lessening the differences between immigrants and native born Americans. Research often distinguishes between cultural Assimilation, in which ethnic and cultural norms from the previous country become less prevalent, and other factors such as socioeconomic success and educational equity, referred to under the umbrella of structural Assimilation. Assimilation, especially cultural Assimilation, has been a controversial debate in American policy making, affecting education, health policy, and other areas. Previously, many believed that total Assimilation was necessary for the healthy functioning of American society. Today, many embrace multicultural or segmented Assimilation theories, which view multiculturalism and distinct ethnic identity as a strength rather than a weakness.

OVERVIEW

Assimilation is the process by which immigrants to the United States become part of mainstream American culture, lessening the distinctions between the various ethnic and racial groups. There are several characteristics by which Assimilation of an individual or group is measured, including language proficiency, the decision to become a citizen, and the concentration of ethnic groups in any one geographic region or area. Immigrants are classified as those who have relocated from their country of birth to live and work in another country. The immigration rate in the United States is measured by the percentage of those who were born outside of the country who are currently residing in the United States, either legally or illegally (Wadsworth & Kubrin, 2007).

Immigration has been a significant issue throughout United States history. Historically, the United States has been a country of immigrants, with groups of people coming to live in and work in the country from all over the world. Many countries' citizens have also been barred from entering the United States by various laws throughout the course of history. Immigrant groups have faced and continue to battle racism and negative treatment subsequent to entering the United States.

Today, immigration to the United States has changed drastically from the first half of the twentieth century. Since a low point in the 1940s, the immigration rate has risen dramatically. The population of immigrants in the United States has quadrupled since 1970 and doubled in number since 1990. Furthermore, today's immigrants differ in ethnicity, skills, and education. Most immigrants in the early 1900s emigrated from Europe, and were largely Caucasian. In 2011, most immigrants entered the United States from Latin America and all over Asia (Vigdor, 2008; Office of Immigration Statistics [OIS], 2012). Immigration continues to be a salient policy issue because there continues to be no consensus on whether immigrants have a positive or negative impact on United States society.

The idea of Assimilation has been connected to the metaphor of a "melting pot," or a blurring of differences between different ethnic and racial groups, creating a society where one group cannot necessarily be differentiated from another. Conversely, the idea of pluralism encourages retaining ethnic differences, embracing various aspects of one's original ethnicity and culture, and celebrating the diversity as a unique attribute to the United States. A poll taken in 1994 found that the country evenly supported Assimilation, pluralism, and a blend of the two (Spain, 1999). A Gallup poll conducted in 2012 found that 66 percent of American respondents thought that immigration was a positive thing for the United States (Jones, 2012).

Research regarding immigration and its impact on society has laid the foundations of American sociology. Generally, sociologists recognize three distinct groups of immigrants who entered the United States. The first group, mostly northern and western Europeans, immigrated up to the nineteenth century to set up the American colonies, states, and to move westward. These groups often made their living as farmers. Subsequently, from the end of the nineteenth century to the beginning of the twentieth, the United States experienced massive industrialization. Immigrants to the United States during this period were largely from southern and eastern Europe, settling in urban areas of the country. Finally, in the post-1965 era of immigration, following the 1965 Immigration Act, immigrants entered the United States largely from Latin America and Asia, and new immigrants were largely focused on service professions. Sociologists also recognize and study the south to north migration of black Americans during the beginning of the twentieth century (Pedraza, 2005).

Those who study Assimilation often distinguish between socioeconomic, cultural, and structural Assimilation, in addition to other categories, and there are several Assimilation theories that have been developed. Until recently, complete Assimilation has been seen as imperative to the success of our economy and society (Portes & Zhou, 1993).

FURTHER INSIGHTS

Socioeconomic Assimilation

Socioeconomic status refers to the "measure of an individual or family's relative economic and social ranking" (NCES, 2008). The three major measures of socioeconomic status in the United States include education level, occupation, and income level. When discussing the economic success of immigrants, Assimilationexperts refer to these measures. In a society in which all immigrants were completely socioeconomically assimilated, there would appear to be little or no differences in socioeconomic status between immigrants and native born individuals and families (Spain, 1999).

Vigdor (2008) presents a report measuring the socioeconomic similarities and differences between native-born and foreign-born adults in the United States. Utilizing census data since 1900, many differences have emerged in socioeconomic measures of Assimilation rates since the turn of the twentieth century. The study analyzes data regarding education, home ownership, English-speaking ability, naturalization rates, and marriage patterns. The study also found that immigrants who have arrived in more recent years are more likely to arrive less assimilated; however, non-native born individuals assimilate at a quicker rate than in the past, especially culturally.

Further research shows that immigrants in the United States are slightly more likely than non-immigrants to hold an advanced degree; however, native-born individuals are much more likely to have a high school diploma. Additionally, low-skilled immigrants who enter the country are much less likely than native-born individuals to be unemployed (Orrenius, 2004).

Studies have also found that immigrants become economically assimilated after living in the United States for approximately sixteen to twenty years, reaching the socioeconomic levels of those who are native born. Research has also suggested that non-Hispanic groups make the largest gains in education, but Hispanic groups made the most overall economic gains from generation to generation (Orrenius, 2004).

Cultural & Structural Assimilation

Cultural Assimilation refers to the Assimilation of cultural patterns, including language and value systems. Structural Assimilation refers to the Assimilation of non-native-born individuals and their families into the structural customs of American society, including intermarriage. In the past, cultural and structural Assimilation has been seen as necessary to the economic and social health of the country, but also as a process by which non-native-born individuals and families merge themselves into American mainstream society (Pedraza, 2003).

Transnationalism & Diasporic Citizenship

Today, many sociologists have refocused from classical theories of Assimilation towards "transnationalism" and "diasporic citizenship." Transnationalism and diasporic citizenship refer to the "process by which immigrants forge and sustain multi stranded social relations that link together their societies of origin and settlement" (Basch, Schiller, & Szanton, 1993) and the "set of practices that a person is engaged in and a set of rights acquired or appropriated that cross nation-state boundaries and that indicate membership in at least two nation states" (Laguerre, 1998), respectively.

Previously, classical theories of Assimilation held that immigrants became more assimilated into mainstream American culture the longer they resided in the United States. However, newer theories of Assimilation differ. For example, transnationalism and diasporic citizenship purport that during the Assimilation process, the immigrant not only adopts customs and practices of the society into which they are integrating, but they also change and enrich the society in which they live by introducing different customs and points of view. Furthermore, these theories contend that many immigrants do not completely assimilate culturally or structurally, choosing to retain parts of their identity prior to arrival in the United States and create hybrid identities that meld aspects of both cultures into one, and also help transform embedded cultures and structures. Many researchers argue that these practices have actually been common for many years, but until recently have rarely been formally studied.

Sociologists also now study varying paths of Assimilation, and argue that individuals and different segments of the population assimilate at varying rates depending on a variety of factors. Thus, understanding the Assimilation process has become much more complex and not only involves whether an immigrant group has become assimilated but also which groups are assimilating and the degree to which they are assimilating.

THEORIES OF ASSIMILATION

Classical Theory

The classical theory of Assimilation, attributed largely to Gordon (1964), viewed Assimilation into mainstream culture as imperative to success of the immigrant and for the rest of the country. The primary step towards success was cultural Assimilation, which was purported to lead to other types of Assimilation, though this did not always occur. Gordon (1964) also acknowledged that complete Assimilation was dependent on reception from and recognition by the principal population, or white Americans.

Classical Assimilation theory viewed being able to distinguish ethnic differences and traits of immigrants as detrimental to the individual and the larger society. However, beginning in the 1960s, classical Assimilation was challenged due to the many anomalies that were observed in immigrant populations. First, classical Assimilation theorists argued that the longer one stayed in a country, the more assimilated one became; that this trend would follow across generations; and that children of immigrants would see more economic success than their parents. However, recent studies found opposite patterns as well. Additionally, educational success declined in certain cases, especially children from less fortunate immigrant families in comparison to those in the middle class. Certain immigrant groups and families were consistently found to have lower educational success. Even those who were successful were sometimes seen to exhibit high risk behaviors such as involvement in gang activity (Zhou, 1993).

As a result of these anomalies, critics of classical Assimilation argue that complete Assimilation of an individual into mainstream culture may actually be harmful and have a negative impact on the individual and society. This view has spawned another theory of Assimilation, the segmented theory of Assimilation, which argues that there are three paths that an individual can follow when they immigrate:

- Acculturation and integration into the middle class,
- Assimilation into the lower class resulting in permanent poverty, or
- Economic advancement while consciously holding onto aspects of their previous culture (Zhou, 1997).

Many experts, often called multiculturalists, believe distinct cultural attributes are not and should not be seen as inferior and harmful to the individual or society.

Zhou (1997) also points out that while immigrant groups to the United States have changed, so have the opportunities available to them. Immigrants today come to a vastly different country than those who arrived in the late 1800s and early 1900s. In the last half century, we have seen a widening gap between the rich and poor, a severe distinction and concentration of poverty in inner cities, lower class mobility, and availability of educational and economic resources are closely tied to current socioeconomic status and race and ethnicity.

Multiculturalism

The topic of Assimilation, especially cultural Assimilation, has had a great impact on various policy issues, including immigration, education, health care, and government aid programs. In the past, there was much support for classical Assimilation theory—that immigrants would leave their customs and culture behind, and become "Americans." In recent years however, there has been a movement towards multiculturalism and acceptance of new cultures and practices into American culture. Those who support multiculturalism focus on the cultural aspects of immigrant patterns, recognizing that they often become a permanent part of American society, reinvented from the original culture to meld into a new society (Zhou, 1997).

Education & Assimilation

Research has also focused on the effects of different levels and types of Assimilation on a variety of factors. Previously, educators and policymakers held the belief that retaining one's customs and traditions and not assimilating completely into American culture would hinder one's academic performance. There was an assumption that it was impossible to successfully manage being a part of both cultures at once, and that those who clung to their previous traditions would not become familiar let alone embrace aspects of American culture. However, studies have actually shown the opposite to be true—students who retain aspects of their culture and background previous to arriving in the United States actually perform at a higher educational level. Immigrant students can become skilled at utilizing resources in aspects of each culture and community, successfully navigating both to assist in their educational aspirations. Additionally, bilingualism has also been shown to boost a child's ability to think and learn complex subjects, and contribute to the success of their education (Akiba, 2007).

Schools have played the largest role for assimilating immigrant children into the culture of the United States. In the early twentieth century, America was known as a melting pot—a country where many people arrived, and blended with a new culture to form a new identity. The binding of this melting pot was the language, English, and schools were the primary purveyors of the language as well as transmitting the knowledge and values of American culture to immigrants. However, many argue today that Assimilation into the mainstream culture is in the best interest of the country.

Educationally, there has been an increased movement towards accepting a variety of cultures and backgrounds. Globalization of the economy and the subsequent increased exposure to different cultures in the latter half of the twentieth century has contributed to the trend towards the incorporation of multiculturalism in educational practices. This is a departure from the early portion of the twentieth century, when immigrant families felt the pressure to completely leave their culture behind, to become as Americanized as possible, including disposing of language and customs (Akiba, 2007). Souto-Manning (2007) also cites research that shows that speaking multiple languages is an academic resource and not a detriment.

Other studies have researched different types of Assimilation, and how they impact non-native individuals and families. Vigdor (2008) reports on economic and civic Assimilation versus cultural Assimilation of immigrants, finding that the former can often occur successfully without the latter. In other words, studies have found that immigrants can attain socioeconomic levels similar to that of native-born individuals and families, while participating and engaging in their new communities, while holding onto their previous culture and customs. However, studies have also found that post-1995 immigrants to the United States are assimilating faster, culturally, than those who came before them.

ISSUES

Growing Hispanic Immigration

As the Latino and Hispanic populations in the United States have vastly increased in numbers over the years due to increased immigration, the concerns of policymakers and researchers have also grown regarding the Assimilation process for Latino and Hispanic groups. Souto-Manning (2007) cites research that found children of Mexican immigrants had a high failure rate in American schools. Rather than actually having academic deficiencies, researchers also suggest that these groups are seen by their teachers and schools as missing certain skills and having a lack of knowledge. Vigdor (2008) also found that Mexican immigrants assimilate more slowly than other immigrant groups, and that while rates for of cultural Assimilation for this group is normal, economic and civic Assimilation are much lower than other immigrant groups. There is much research to be accomplished in this area, as immigrant demographics are shifting rapidly in the United States, and educating immigrant populations will continue to be a serious educational policy issue in the years to come.

Suicide

The discussion of immigration additionally impacts policies on health and health care. For example, researchers have argued that immigrants are at an increased risk for suicide compared to native-born individuals due to the emotional and economic stress of living and working in another country, leaving behind customs and family when immigrating to the United States. Countering those arguments are those who believe that immigrants would have lower suicide rates due to their resiliency and increased ability to overcome obstacles. Wadsworth & Kubrin (2007) report that suicide rates in the Hispanic community may be related to cultural Assimilation—the higher the rates of cultural Assimilation, the higher the suicide rate. However, economic Assimilation, for Hispanics and all other groups, decreases the rate of suicide. Additional research into the protective factors offered by retaining certain parts of one's cultural and ethnic identity, while also increasing one's economic stability and civic engagement, is a necessary step to discover more about these health policy concerns.

Generational Factors

Matters of generational differences also come to light when discussing Assimilation. Zhou (1997) focuses on a middle ground between the classical Assimilationist theory that concentrates on immigrants assimilating totally into mainstream culture, and multiculturalists who support immigrants reshaping and reinventing their cultures, and permanently integrating them to be a part of American society. This theory, called segmented Assimilation theory, centers on a variety of individual factors that influence how immigrants assimilate, including educational level, language, the age of the individual when they immigrate, length of residency, and other factors such as socioeconomic status, location in the United States, and racial/ethnic background.

Zhou (1997) recognizes that immigrants and their willingness and ability to assimilate culturally may depend heavily upon the aforementioned factors. For example, younger immigrants may assimilate at a faster rate than their elders. However, this may also lead to generational dissonance, increasing conflict within families. Increased Assimilation by immigrant youth may also divest them of the resources within their family and within immigrant group communities which potentially act as protective factors for various negative behaviors, including drug abuse, suicide, and gang involvement. However, in other ways, belonging to an ethnic community may hinder other important Assimilation processes, such as socioeconomic Assimilation.

Segmented Assimilation

Segmented Assimilation theory can be seen as a middle ground between classical Assimilation and multiculturalism—immigrants and how they assimilate into mainstream culture is certainly a complex issue that encompasses social, economic, and cultural factors. It also appears that all types of Assimilation are not always beneficial to an immigrant. The benefits are heavily dependent on a host of other important factors, both constant and shifting.

Immigration and Assimilation are increasingly complex issues in an era of shifting demographics and immigrant patterns, as the world becomes more familiar and accommodating of various groups and identities. The Assimilation debate is multifaceted and encompasses policies in education, health, and civic engagement. Questions linked to Assimilation include how students should be taught in schools, how much money and resources schools and government agencies should spend on communicating with those who speak other languages besides English, and what message should be sent about assimilating culturally versus economically versus structurally once arriving in the United States. These questions, and others like them, will continue to have a strong impact on how immigrants are treated in the United

States, not only when they first enter the country, but as they continue to live, work, and raise families. The policies created in answer to these questions will affect one's ability to receive an education, work, and rewarding personal lives. While Assimilation has been studied for many years, there continues to be questions left to answer, and research will continue to shed light on the debate.

TERMS & CONCEPTS

Assimilation: The process by which immigrants become part of the culture of their new country.

Cultural Assimilation: Cultural Assimilation refers to relinquishing one's own cultural norms and embracing the new cultural norms of the country one immigrates to.

Immigrant: An immigrant is an individual who currently resides in a country other than the individual's country of birth.

Melting Pot: The *melting pot* is a term referring to the widely accepted notion that America's culture was built on the premise that those who immigrated would give up their customs to become part of American culture.

Multiculturalism: Multiculturalism supports retaining certain aspects of one's culture after immigration.

Segmented Assimilation: Segmented Assimilation argues that not all immigrants can assimilate at the same rate, nor is it beneficial for all immigrants to assimilate culturally.

Socioeconomic Status: Socioeconomic status refers the economic/social ranking of a family, individual, or group.

Structural Assimilation: Structural Assimilation factors include structural customs including marriage patterns and place of residency.

Bibliography

Akiba, D. (2007). "Ethnic retention as a predictor of academic success: Lessons from the children of immigrant families and black children." *Clearing house: A journal of educational strategies, issues and ideas*, 80(5), 223-225.

Basch, L., Schiller, N. & Szanton Blanc, C. (1993). *Nations unbound: Transnational projects, postcolonial predicaments, and deterritorialized nation states.* New York: Routledge.

Gordon, M. (1964). *Assimilation in American life: The role of race, religion, and national origins.* New York: Oxford University Press.

Jones, Jeffrey M (2012). "Americans more positive about immigration." http://www.gallup.com/poll/155210/Americans-Positive-Immigration.aspx

Laguerre, M. S. (1998). *Diasporic citizenship: Haitian Americans in transnational America.* New York: Palgrave Macmillan.

National Center for Education Statistics. (2008). "Glossary." National Center of Education Statistics Web Site: http://nces.ed.gov/programs/coe/glossary/s.asp.

Office of Immigration Statistics (2012). *2011 yearbook of immigration statistics.* http://www.dhs.gov/sites/default/files/publications/immigration-statistics/yearbook/2011/ois%5Fyb%5F2011.pdf

Orrenius, P. M. (2003). "U.S. Immigration and economic growth: Putting policy on hold." *Southwest Economy*, 6, 1-5.

Pedraza, S. (2005). "Assimilation or transnationalism? Conceptual models of the immigrant experience in America." The University of Texas website: http://lanic.utexas.edu/project/asce/pdfs/volume15/pdfs/pedraza.pdf.

Portes, A. & Zhou, M. (1993). "The new second generation: Segmented Assimilation and its variants among post-1965 immigrant youth." *Annals of the American Academy of Political and Social Science*, 530, 74-98.

Restifo, S. J., Roscigno, V. J., & Qian, Z. (2013). "Segmented Assimilation, split labor markets, and racial/ethnic inequality: The case of early-twentieth-century New York." *American Sociological Review, 78*(5), 897-924.

Souto-Manning, M. (2007). "Immigrant families and children (re)develop identities in a new context." *Early Childhood Education Journal*, 34(6), 399-405.

Wadsworth, T. & Kubrin, C.E. (2007). "Hispanic suicide in U.S. metropolitan areas: Examining the effects of immigration, Assimilation, affluence, and disadvantage." *American Journal of Sociology*, 112(6),1848-1885.

Vigdor, J.L. (2008, May). "Executive Summary. Measuring immigrant Assimilation in the United States." *Civic Report* 53. Manhattan Institute for Policy Research Web Site: http://www.manhattan-institute.org/html/cr%5f53.htm.

Zhou, M. (1997). "Segmented Assimilation: Issues, controversies and recent research on the new second generation." *International Migration Review*, 31(4), 975-1008.

SUGGESTED READING

Archdeacon, T.J. (1983). *Becoming American: An ethnic history.* New York: The Free Press.

Berrol, S. C. (1995). *Growing up American: Immigrant children in America, then and now.* New York: Twayne Publishers.

Booth, A., Crouter, A. C., & Landale, N. (ed.). (1997). *Immigration and the family: Research and policy on US. immigrants.* New Jersey: Lawrence Erlbaum Associates, Publishers.

Hatton, T. J. (1997). "The immigrant Assimilation puzzle in late nineteenth-century America." *Journal of Economic History*, 57, 34-62.

Kwok-bun, C., & Plüss, C. (2013). "Modeling migrant adaptation: Coping with social strain, Assimilation, and non-integration." *International Sociology*, *28*(1), 48-65.

Ogbu, J. U. (1991). *Minority status and schooling: A comparative study of immigrant and involuntary minorities.* New York: Garland Publishing.

Perlmann, J. & Waldinger, R. (1996). "Second generation decline? Children of immigrants, past and present—a reconsideration." *International Migration Review*, 31(4), 893-922.

Xi, J. (2013). "English fluency of the US immigrants: Assimilation effects, cohort variations, and periodical changes." *Social Science Research*, *42*(4), 1109-1121.

Rana Suh, M.Ed.

CULTURAL PREJUDICE & DISCRIMINATION

ABSTRACT

Cultural prejudice and discrimination continue to present complex challenges in American society. One of the great barriers to tackling issues of racial discrimination in the United States is the legacy of the Trans-Atlantic Slavery Trade. The effects of slavery were not resolved with emancipation or with the Civil Rights Act of 1964. Prejudice and discrimination against people of color persists in America today. Along with problems experienced by African-Americans, people of other Cultural backgrounds such as Jewish people, Hispanic-Americans, people with disabilities, and many others have experienced widespread discrimination. America's immigration policy introduced millions of people into the country, but also resulted in increased prejudice and discrimination among disparate cultures.

OVERVIEW

Prejudice is the belief or perception that people of different cultures are inferior or have negative characteristics because of their skin color, religious belifs, or Cultural background. Discrimination is the act of denying someone their rights on the basis of prejudice.

The Impact of Slavery

In the United States, the legacy of slavery has resulted in tremendous suffering. The social and political upheaval caused by slavery led to the Civil War, one of the bloodiest chapters in American history. When emancipation came, 350 years of abuse and enslavement could not be easily forgotten. On January 1, 1863, President Abraham Lincoln abolished slavery, but African-Americans continued to suffer from discrimination well into the 20th century and after the passage of the Civil Rights Act of 1964.

Continued Segregation

From 1863 until 1964, America was a segregated society. African-Americans were forced to sit at the back of buses, were prevented from attending white schools, had to drink at separate water fountains, eat in racially-designated restaurants Moreover, African-Americans were prevented from attending certain universities, colleges and from hold various forms of employment.

Landmark legislative efforts have helped to reverse the legacy of prejudice and discrimination suffered by African-Americans. Affirmative action initiatives have worked to redress the inequality African-Americans have faced in education, housing and employment.

Native Americans & Prejudice

When British settlers first landed in North America, they appropriated land from Native Americans. Untold numbers of Native Americans were slaughtered or forced to relocate as a result of British and American colonization. Some Native American stereotypes remain prevalent. Many television programs and movies continue to portray Native Americans in a negative or stereotypical light, perpetuating false and romanticized images.

History textbooks that discuss the European discovery of the Americas often reveal a Eurocentric bias that disregards the histories of the Indigenous nations of North America. Books and videos that exploit Native American Cultural and spiritual traditions for profit. Some 'New Age' spiritual guides commit this error, which many Native Americans find offensive (Almeida, 1996, p. 4).

Anti-Semitism

Although Jewish people are well integrated into American life they still face prejudice and discrimination. Cohen (2008) states, "Anti-Semitism is a form of race or national prejudice that crystallized in the nineteenth century." (Cohen, 2008, pp. 48-49).

Historical stereotypes of Jews are deeply ingrained in Western culture. Research suggests that one of the reasons for prejudice against Jewish people is that some Christians have developed and promulgated the misconception that Judaism challenges the values of Christianity.

FURTHER INSIGHTS

Although Friedman (2007) does not necessarily disagree with this theory, he states that prejudice and discrimination are an innate part of the human condition. It is his belief that they have always been a part of human society.

Scapegoating

Friedman (2007) theorizes that scapegoats and prejudicial stereotyping is psychologically based. He cites the fact that societies usually develop scapegoats and strong prejudicial beliefs about certain minority groups during difficult social and economic times. He goes on to state that even the most rational person can develop prejudicial attitudes under stress. Times of great stress and economic uncertainty can lead people to become less logical, even paranoid, and at risk for developing prejudicial attitudes. Discriminatory acts can and often do follow.

Media Stereotyping: Islamaphobia & September 11th

The terrorist attacks of September 11, 2001 caused a nationwide increase in discrimination against Arab-Americans. In response to the fact that the attacks were undertaken by Islamic fundamentalists, political organizations and individuals throughout America chose to take out their anger on the larger American Islamic community. Many Muslim Americans were forced into the position of defending their faith and themselves. Verma (2005), a teacher of South Asian background comments on the ways in which Arab-Americans and Arabic people in general have been the victims of prejudice since 9/11: "I have observed trends in television, radio, and print media that saturate popular culture with images of terror and war and encourage racial stereotyping" (Verma, 2005, p. 12).

One of the more damaging and unfortunate results of 9/11 has been the stereotyping of people of Arabic background; assumptions made about their culture based on the actions of a few people. As Verma states, segments of American media culture engaged in a dramatic spectacle and a disinformation campaign that dehumanizes and victimizes Arabs and portrays stereotypical images of the "civilized West" and "barbaric Arabs." Rallying and mobilizing fear of this fabricated vision of evil, these representations contribute to a discourse of violence against Arabs and others who resemble them (Verma, 2005, p. 12).

Other individuals, people of color who may look Arabic are also being discriminated against. This is the insidious way in which stereotyping works. A negative perception is developed, it becomes embedded in popular culture through the media (and especially today with the widespread and immediate power of the Internet) and the stereotype becomes real to far too many people. Verma (2005) points out that one of the more dangerous symptoms of stereotyping and prejudiceis hate crimes.

Salaita (2005) suggests that the passage of the Patriot Act contributed to making Arab-Americans feel discriminated against and unwanted in America. Suddenly, the spotlight was on them to defend themselves even if they had not done anything. He also suggests that many feel their patriotism towards America is being questioned and they are often discriminated against with the use of racial profiling. People of Arabic background have become a target for those who fear terrorist violence.

VIEWPOINTS

Eliminating Cultural Prejudice & Discrimination

The primary question that emanates from this research is; 'how can we effectively cope with and eliminate prejudice and discrimination'? While the first is certainly possible, the latter may not be probable. America's history is rife with racial prejudice and discrimination. It seems that our differences divide us rather than give us strength and the desire to learn about one another. There are practical steps that can be taken. The recurring theme in this essay is a lack of understanding about different Cultural groups. Almeida (1996) and Fleming (2006) point out that the average American knows little to nothing about Native Americans and their cultures. The research of Gross (2008) highlights the need to understand prejudice and discrimination in a racial context and the importance of slavery to history. Verma (2005) writes about the implications of 9/11 and the stereotypes, prejudice and discrimination against Arab-Americans that has followed.

Research by Zebrowitz (2008) on exposure to people of other races suggests that when people have greater exposure to persons of various races, they have a reduced tendency to develop ideas of racial prejudice. Thus, it is perhaps, at least to some degree, the fact that many people do not have direct connections with persons of other racial and ethnic backgrounds that increases tendencies towards prejudice and discrimination. Utsey, Ponterotto and Porter (2008) state that there is a need for social scientists to conduct in-depth research into the connections between racism, prejudice and discrimination in order to develop a better understanding of how they work and possible social remedies.

All of these researchers suggest a similar theme; a need for more education and understanding of other cultures, their ways of life, their belief systems and the historical context for their lives today. This increased education coupled with greater exposure may be a path toward eliminating prejudice and discrimination among cultures.

CONCLUSION

Barriers to Eliminating Cultural Prejudice

One of the major barriers to eliminating prejudice and discrimination against the Native Americans is a lack of knowledge about their cultures. White people often make the mistake of generalizing about Native Americans as if there is one big 'culture' that embraces all Native American tribes. This is something that sociologists and social anthropologists have been trying to change through their direct studies with Native American cultures. The second major barrier is the distinct lack of Native Americans in positions of authority and power in American society. There are very few Native Americans in congress, the senate or serving as governors. In addition, there are few Native American teachers and university professors so that their Cultural knowledge is not being introduced to mainstream American educational institutions. This means that we are still hearing about Native American issues from White voices; rarely do we hear about them from Native American voices.

The Debate on Reparations

One of the primary issues today is that of reparations. According to Gross (2008),

An emphasis on the continuing legacies of slavery animates all arguments in favor of reparations for slavery, but these have taken three forms with regard to legal claim: debt (contract), unjust enrichment (restitution), or corrective justice (tort). All three of these legal and moral approaches rely on a version of history in which slavery is the direct cause of continuing harm (Gross, 2008, p. 305).

There are opinions on both sides of the debate on reparations. One side argues that this would provide a sense of redress—that is, correcting the injustice of slavery. The other side of the argument claims that reparations for slavery do a disservice to African-Americans and suggest that injustice towards African-Americans was only in the past, a fact that is blatantly untrue (Gross, 2008). Yet, there is no denying that slavery continues to affect the lives of African-Americans today. The lives of so many families were disrupted and there is no doubt that the stereotypes of centuries ago have not yet been fully destroyed. As Gross (2008) states:

> Slavery is still the touchstone for all of our discussions about race in America-as it should be, because race was born out of slavery. It is our nation's original sin. Through the telling and re-telling of the history of slavery, we judge our own responsibility for the continuing injustices of racial inequality (p. 321).

TERMS & CONCEPTS

Affirmative Action: Not one law or one piece of legislation, but rather a series of initiatives and policies which have attempted to redress the social, political and economic disadvantages that people such as African-Americans have endured.

Anti-Semitism: Prejudicial attitudes, stereotyping and discrimination towards people of the Jewish faith and culture.

Civil Rights Act of 1964: This was the piece of legislation that finally made segregation illegal in America. Schools, public places and places of employment were now expected to fully integrate African-Americans and it became illegal not to.

Emancipation Proclamation: The declaration made by President Abraham Lincoln on January 1, 1863 which effectively abolished slavery in America.

Discrimination: To treat a person or group of people with prejudice.

Hate Crimes: Crimes committed by someone against another person because of their inclusion in a specific group or culture. Hate crimes have been and continue to be perpetrated on people of color, people who are gay, lesbian, bisexual or transgendered, Arab-Americans, Jewish people and others.

Islamaphobia: The prejudice and discrimination leveled at people who practice the faith of Islam or those people known as Muslims.

Patriot Act: Enacted by President George W. Bush on October 26, 2001 as a response to the events of 9/11. It has been a controversial piece of legislation that has given the country's law enforcement agencies enormous power to try to deal and weed out any potential acts of terrorism at home or abroad.

Prejudice: When we make a judgment about someone or something without having the facts. Racial prejudice is to make assumptions or hold specific beliefs about a person or group based on a lack of information. Today we often think of it as outright hostility or hatred for a person or group based on race.

Racial Profiling: To use racial characteristics when considering whether or not someone is likely to commit a certain type of crime.

Racism: The belief that a person's race is the source of their attributes or characteristics. It also promotes the notion that certain races are superior while others are inferior and that race is a determinant of this superiority or inferiority.

Scapegoating: Used to describe the blaming of a culture or other group of people for the dominant culture or country's social ills. It is a means to deflect from the real and root causes of the problem.

Stereotype: A notion, conception, idea or image that someone has of another person, group or culture based on assumptions and misconceptions. They are usually overly simplified ideas and generalizations about a group of people which have no basis in reality.

Zionism: Refers to the international political movement to create a homeland for Jewish people. It gained international support after World War II.

BIBLIOGRAPHY

Ahmed, S., Kia-Keating, M., & Tsai, K. (2011). "A Structural Model of Racial Discrimination, Acculturative Stress, and Cultural Resources Among

Arab American Adolescents." *American Journal Of Community Psychology*, 48(3/4), 181-192

Almeida, D.A. (1996). *Countering prejudice against American Indians and Alaska.*

Bardoel, E., Drago, R., Cooper, B., & Colbeck, C. (2011). "Bias Avoidance: Cross-Cultural Differences in the US and Australian Academies." *Gender, Work & Organization*, 18e157-e179.

Caughy, M., Nettles, S., & Lima, J. (2011). "Profiles of Racial Socialization Among African American Parents: Correlates, Context, and Outcome." *Journal Of Child & Family Studies*, 20(4), 491-502.

Cohen, M. (2008). "Anti-Semitism and the left that doesn't learn." *Dissent, 55* (1), 47-51.

Deng, S., Kim, S., Vaughan, P., & Li, J. (2010). "Cultural Orientation as a Moderator of the Relationship Between Chinese American Adolescents' Discrimination Experiences and Delinquent Behaviors." *Journal Of Youth & Adolescence*, 39(9), 1027-1040.

Fleming, W. C. (2006). "Myths and stereotypes about Native Americans." *Phi Delta Kappan, 88* (3). 213-217.

Friedman, C. (2007). "An object relations approach to studying prejudice with specific reference to anti-Semitism: The long-term use of a lethal apocalyptic projection." *International Journal of Applied Psychoanalytic Studies, 4* (1), 31-40.

Gross, A. (2008). "When is the time of slavery? The history of slavery in contemporary legal and political argument." *California Law Review, 96* (1), 283-321.

Lai, L., Cummins, R., & Lau, A. (2013). "Cross-Cultural Difference in Subjective Wellbeing: Cultural Response Bias as an Explanation." *Social Indicators Research*, 114(2), 607-619.

Lewis, R. (2006). "The emancipation proclamation: Communicate to motivate." *Black History Bulletin, 69* (2), 15-20.

Pargament, K.I., Trevino, K., Mahoney, A., & Silberman, I. (2007). "They killed our Lord: The perception of Jews as desecrators of Christianity as a predictor of anti-Semitism." *Journal for the Scientific Study of Religion, 46* (2), p143-158.

Salaita, S. (2005). "Ethnic identity and imperative patriotism: Arab Americans before and after 9/11." *College Literature, 32* (2), 146-168.

Shore, L. (2005). "The enduring power of racism: A reconsideration of Winthrop Jordan's white over black." *History and Theory, 44,* 195-226.

Sindik, J. (2012). "Data Analysis Strategies for Reducing the Influence of the Bias in Cross-Cultural Research." *Collegium Antropologicum*, 36(1), 31-37.

Utsey, S.O., Ponterotto, J.G., & Porter, J.S. (2008). "Prejudice and racism, year 2008- still going strong: Research on reducing prejudice with recommended methodological advances." *Journal of Counseling & Development, 86* (3), 339-347.

Verma, R. (2005). "Dialogues about 9/11, the media and race: Lessons from a secondary classroom." *Radical Teacher, 74.* 12-16.

Zebrowitz, L.A., White, B., & Wieneke, K. (2008). "Mere exposure and racial prejudice: Exposure to other-race faces increases liking for strangers of that race." *Social Cognition, 26* (3), 259-275.

SUGGESTED READING

Borgida, E. & Fiske, S. (Eds.). *Beyond common sense.* Boston, Massachusetts: Blackwell Publishing.

Chin, J. L. (2004). *The psychology of prejudice and discrimination.* Westport, Connecticut: Praeger Publishers.

Payne, J. (2007). "The function of public policy." *International Journal of Diversity in Organizations, Communities & Nations, 6* (6), 23-29.

Reicher, S. (2007). "Rethinking the paradigm of prejudice." *South African Journal of Psychology, 37* (4), 820-834.

Simpson, G. E., & Yinger, J. M. (1965). *Racial and Cultural minorities: An analysis of prejudice and discrimination,* Third Edition. New York, N.Y.: Harper & Row.

Waller, J. & Brinkley, D. (2000). *Prejudice across America.* Jackson, Mississippi: University Press of Mississippi.

Ilanna Mandel, M.A.

Ending Racism & Discrimination in the United States

OVERVIEW

This article addresses the prospect of ending racism and discrimination in the United States. It begins by defining racism and discrimination and differentiating individual prejudice from institutional racism. It then reviews the extent of social change that has lead to a decline in racism and discrimination since the middle of the twentieth century, as well as the continuing significance of racism and discrimination in the lives of people of color. People have proposed various ways of reducing or ending racism and discrimination. This article reviews three such proposals: increased multicultural education, reforms to the legal system, and radical social change. It also considers the argument that eradicating racism and discrimination in the United States is impossible as well as the argument that eradicating racism and discrimination is unnecessary.

When most people think about the term racism, they think of the various attitudes and beliefs individuals may hold about different racial groups, particularly negative stereotypes about one or more racial groups as well as the opinion that one's own racial group is superior. To sociologists, this common understanding of racism is more accurately termed "prejudice." It is hard to get a good sense of what percentage of Americans continue to hold prejudiced views about other racial groups. When asked survey questions about their opinions of other races, few Americans give answers that suggest that they hold prejudiced views, and these figures have declined substantially over the since the mid-to-late twentieth century. However, there is evidence that surveys designed to elicit individuals' racist views suffer from something called interviewer effect. What this means is that when surveyors ask certain questions, survey respondents will give what they believe are the socially desirable responses rather than their actual beliefs or opinions.

Despite both our uncertainty about how many Americans continue to hold racist views and the fact that the percentage of Americans holding such views has declined over time, racism continues to have significance in American life. In addition to individual racism, institutional racism occurs within organizations like the government, corporations, and schools. While individual prejudice may result in a person experiencing a racial slur or a hate crime, institutional racism is responsible for many of the inequalities between racial groups, such as poverty and segregation. Institutional racism can continue even when there is no individual racist person within an institution. Instead, institutional racism is manifested in the policies and practices built into an institution that lead to racist outcomes. For example, if a mortgage company redlined a neighborhood forty years ago based on the fact that the neighborhood was heavily black, and if, as a consequence, African Americans living in that neighborhood could not get mortgages and could not sell their homes, that neighborhood today will likely continue to be run down and have low property values–even if the people working for the mortgage company today are committed to racial equality.

Both individual prejudice and institutional racism can lead to discrimination. Discrimination is what the group experiencing the prejudice or institutional racism encounters. For instance, if an individual who is prejudiced against African Americans refuses to hire a black employee, that individual has discriminated. For the most part, racial discrimination is illegal in the contemporary United States. Individuals are permitted to think racist thoughts and write racist texts, but they are not permitted to make hiring decisions, sell real estate, or engage in other sorts of differentiation on the basis of race. This legal prohibition does not, however, mean that discrimination has ended. In order to penalize an individual or a company for discrimination, the person who has been discriminated against must prove not only that discrimination occurred, but also that the individual or company accused of discrimination intended to discriminate (Crenshaw, 1995). This makes it very difficult for individuals to win racial discrimination law suits.

Thus racial discrimination continues in many aspects of life in the contemporary United States. For instance, in fiscal year 2007 alone, the US Equal Employment Opportunity Commission (EEOC) received over 30,000 charges of racial discrimination in employment; in FY2012, this figure increased to over 33,000, while in FY2017 the figure decreased to 28,528. Other areas of life in which racial discrimination continues to play a particularly significant role include housing, the criminal justice system, and healthcare. Yet despite the continuing significance of racial discrimination, discrimination has declined considerably since the middle of the twentieth century.

In 1950, it was still completely legal for school districts and schools to segregate education from kindergarten through graduate school–if graduate schools were even available for nonwhite students. It was legal for real estate agents to refuse to show homes or apartments to members of certain races, and individuals could even write language into the deed of their home prohibiting its sale to nonwhite buyers. Classified ads for employment could say "whites only," and several states still prohibited interracial marriage. Things have come a long way.

These changes did not come easily. They required concerted efforts by social movements, lobbyists, religious leaders, educators, and others. The civil rights movement of the 1950s and 1960s played a key part in effecting the social changes that led to the end of legal discrimination. For instance, the leaders of the movement coordinated sit-ins and other acts of civil disobedience that led to the desegregation of lunch counters and public transportation throughout the South. They also led voter registration drives that helped elect black candidates to public office. These black politicians then became instrumental in passing laws that reduced discrimination. Among the crucial legal gains of the civil rights movement were:

- The Civil Rights Act of 1964, which prohibited discrimination based on race,
- The Voting Rights Act of 1965, which made it easier for southern African Americans to vote,
- Executive Order 11246, which established affirmative action for government contractors,
- The Civil Rights Act of 1968, which specifically prohibited housing discrimination.

Inspired by the civil rights movement, social movements representing American Indians, Asian Americans, and Latinos emerged during the 1960s and 1970s, and these movements also pushed for an end to discrimination. Among other things, these groups pushed immigration reform, changes in college and university admissions policies, the honoring of treaties with American Indian tribes, and the establishment of ethnic studies departments that would expand knowledge and teaching about people of color. Many–though far from all–of these goals were attained. For example, the US Supreme Court has ruled in favor of affirmative action policies in higher education in three cases: Regents of the University of California v. Bakke(1978), Gratz v. Bollinger et al. (2003), and Grutter v. Bollinger (2003) (Pitt & Packard, 2012). It is important to not understate the gains these movements made in reducing racism and discrimination in the United States, but the problem has not disappeared. In fact, the Supreme Court invalidated part of the Voting Rights Act (1965) when they voted in June 2013 to allow nine states to change their election laws without getting federal approval in advance (Liptak, 2013). In 2013, the American Civil Liberties Union (ACLU) was challenging changes in voting laws in North Carolina, Kansas, Pennsylvania, and Wisconsin, that the ACLU says threaten the rights of voters including minority voters (ACLU, 2013). In 2018, the ACLU identified ballot access, voter suppression, voter restoration, the Voting Rights Act, and gerrymandering as issues affecting equal voting rights in the United States.

APPLICATIONS

How to End Racism & Discrimination

If racism and discrimination continue to make a significant impact on the lives of people of color in the contemporary United States, what can be done about it? Scholars and activists have made several proposals. Some focus on the importance of education and diversity or multiculturalism for changing the culture of racism. Others point to legal reforms as a way to make it easier to challenge acts of discrimination or institutional racism. A third group argues for more substantial social change aimed at repairing the effects of past discrimination. Finally, some people believe that racism has become such an integral part of the fabric of American society that it cannot be removed.

For the first group, racism and discrimination can be eliminated through education. In particular, advocates of this perspective include educators who are committed to multiculturalism and diversity in their classrooms. Such educators believe that the American society will eventually accept people of color as it did white immigrant groups, and all that is needed is to educate about difference and celebrating the diverse cultural backgrounds that make up the United States. Advocates of this perspective believe that multicultural education will change American culture to make it more inclusive. Affirmative action is one of the specific policy proposals that multiculturalists propose. They believe that affirmative action will lead to schools and workplaces that value diversity and individuals in such diverse environments will be able to overcome any prejudiced views they may hold. In fact, there is evidence that exposure to diverse educational circumstances may change the views of white students (Bowen & Bok, 1998)and have a positive impact on all students (Pitt & Packard, 2012). For the multiculturalists, education and exposure alone will create the changes necessary to rid American society of racism and discrimination. This view, then, is focused on the role of individual prejudice. Many scholars and activists note that focusing only on individual prejudice ignores the continuing presence of institutional racism. As a result, their proposals aim to change the institutional structures that enable discrimination to continue.

Some believe that these changes can occur within our legal system. As noted above, discrimination law currently requires that allegations of discrimination prove discriminatory intent in order to prevail in a court of law. In addition, allegations of discrimination must prove that the discrimination occurred due to race itself, rather than some other factor related to race (such as economic status or linguistic style). One scholar, Kenji Yoshino, proposed a different standard in his 2006 book Covering. He argued that discrimination law should focus on discriminatory outcomes rather than discriminatory intent. More importantly, he argued that discrimination law should be focused on providing equality to all people, not just those who act, talk, or look like majority groups.

Other scholars take this logic a step further. For them, changing the legal system would be insufficient for eradicating racism and discrimination. Instead, they advocate more substantial social and political changes. The particular policy proposals such scholars advance vary. For instance, in Whitewashing Race (2003) Michael Brown and his coauthors advocated remedying the legacy of past discrimination and establishing new government agencies to respond to racism and discrimination. Eduardo Bonilla-Silva advocated for the creation of a new civil rights movement that would militantly challenge racism both "from within" whiteness and from outside of it (2004). Discussions of reparations and the role that they could play in reducing racial disparities also fall into this category (Darity & Meyers, 1998). Many social movement activists fit into this category as well, since they advocate substantial social change to respond to continuing racism and discrimination.

Despite the often-radical proposals for social change that this diverse group of scholars and activists has made, some people believe that there is nothing we can do to fully eradicate racism and discrimination from US society, politics, and culture. For instance, Howard Winant has argued that the United States was formed as a racist country on the backs of enslaved African Americans (2002). While he affirmed that antiracist mobilization can and has continued to have an effect, he also argued that pervasive racial inequality and the racial consciousness behind individual prejudice and discriminatory acts will not disappear. While this position may appear to be fatalistic, most scholars who believe in the persistence of racism do still advocate for social movements and progressive social change aimed at eradicating racism and discrimination.

VIEWPOINTS

Ignoring Racism & Discrimination

Not everyone agrees that racism and discrimination are a continuing problem that requires a societal response. There are three main groups of people who do not believe any response to racism is necessary. First, there are the ideological racists. Second, there are libertarians. And finally, there are those who believe we have already resolved the problems of racism and discrimination and who thus attribute continuing racial disparities to other causes.

Both ideological racists and libertarians agree that racism and discrimination are continuing realities in the lives of people of color in the United States. Ideological racists, however, openly defend racism and discriminatory practices. They believe that racial groups are inherently unequal and that people should be allowed to discriminate against groups they believe are inferior. Libertarians, in contrast, are more likely to say that they ethically or morally disapprove of racism and discrimination. However, libertarians also have an ideological commitment to small government and a lack of government interference.

Therefore, they argue that even if racism and discrimination are reprehensible, it is not a governmental responsibility to eradicate them.

The third group who believe that racism and discrimination do not require a social or political response are those who believe that the problems of racism and discrimination have already been resolved. These people point to the gains of the civil rights movement, the growing numbers of black professionals and members of the black middle class, the declining numbers of white people who are willing to publicly state racist views or opinions, and such notable events as Barack Obama's presidential election as proof that racism has been overcome. Most people who believe that racism is a thing of the past do admit that sometimes discrimination occurs. However, they attribute such discrimination to individuals from older generations or who have been improperly educated by parents who never gave up their own racial beliefs. Give it another generation or two, their argument goes, and discrimination will be a relic of the past as well.

Some individuals who fall into this category may be unaware of the continuing inequality between racial groups in the United States. For instance, Abigail and Stephan Thernstrom (1997) have argued that reports of racial inequality are exaggerated by black activists to increase public sympathy, and that, in reality, disparities are small and primarily due to the actions of illogical, prejudiced individuals. Many others, however, are aware that African Americans, Latinos, and American Indians earn less money, have less accumulated wealth, receive less education, have worse health care, are more likely to be involved with the criminal justice system, and face many other aspects of inequality. Instead of attributing these disparities to the workings of institutional racism, though, this group attributes them to a variety of other factors, such as genetics or culture. For instance, when the Thernstroms do admit that racial disparities exist, they argue that culture is responsible for their continuation. They believe that African Americans, particularly poor African Americans, have unique cultural values focused on dependency and instant gratification that prevent them from resolving their own economic problems. There is little evidence to support such claims, but a few scholars and many conservative pundits and politicians have continued to make them. There is one more defining factor relevant to this argument. Those who argue that racism and discrimination are no longer problems in contemporary American society also tend to argue that it is public discussions of race and racism that lead to what little persistent racism there is. Thus, they say that we should avoid collecting data on race, measuring racism, or talking about these issues, and instead focus our attention on issues such as economic inequality and educational problems.

Brown and his coauthors (2003) call such individuals "color-blind racists." Color-blind racists are individuals who believe that racism is no longer a problem in society and believe that they themselves do not see or act on race. Yet they continue to live in a society that is racially stratified and to benefit from this stratification. At a time when few people will openly admit to racist opinions or beliefs, color-blind racists argue that we should avoid talking further about race in order to effect its complete disappearance. The evidence suggests, however, that racism and discrimination are unlikely to disappear without considerable effort on the part of antiracist activists–if it is possible for them to disappear at all.

TERMS & CONCEPTS

Civil Rights Movement: The civil rights movement was a social movement with the goal of gaining legal, social, and political equality for African Americans in the United States. The civil rights movement lasted roughly from 1955 to 1968. Many marches, demonstrations, and acts of civil disobedience were part of this push towards desegregation and political rights.

Color-Blind Racism: According to Bonilla-Silva, a form of racism more subtle than the overt racism of the past that allows whites to maintain white racial privilege by denying the continuing significance of race and racism in the lives of people of color. Color-blind racism relies on the notions that racial problems have been solved, that racial disparities are due to culture or are inevitable, and that talking about race is responsible for creating racial problems.

Civil Disobedience: Deliberate, public, nonviolent acts that violate a law, such as sit-ins, usually undertaken because of a belief that the law in question is unjust.

Discrimination: Differentiating between individuals or groups on the basis of prejudicial attitudes and beliefs rather than on the basis of individual merit. Discrimination generally carries the connotation that one group is disadvantaged by such treatment in comparison to another.

The Equal Employment Opportunity Commission (EEOC): The EEOC is a federal regulatory agency which was created by Title VII of the Civil Rights Act of 1964 to monitor and investigate claims of employment discrimination. The EEOC is concerned with other types of discrimination besides race, including gender and religion.

Ethnic Studies: Ethnic studies refers to a group of academic disciplines that are concerned with the experiences and history of particular racial and ethnic groups. They include black or African American studies, Asian American studies, Latino/Chicano studies, and American Indian studies. Ethnic studies disciplines have developed their own methodologies and literatures that foreground the groups they study, and they have often retained ties to communities and activists of color.

Institutional Racism: Structural factors like policies and procedures that are built into organizations and institutions and lead to racially disparate outcomes. Institutional racism can continue even in the absence of any individuals holding racist views or opinions.

Interviewer Effect: This term refers to any time when the results of a survey, interview, or other social research instrument are altered due to the presence of the researcher. Such situations can include interviewer bias or improper actions of the interviewer. They can also include social desirability effects, when research participants choose to answer questions in a way they believe the interviewer will approve of rather than sharing their true feelings or opinions.

Prejudice: Technically, prejudice refers to any instance in which an individual makes a decision before they know all of the facts and details relevant to that decision. However, the term is most frequently used in reference to people having preconceived ideas, generally negative and unrelated to fact, about a particular social group.

Privilege: Privilege refers to any special advantage or benefit that some, but not all, people get. In the context of race, white privilege refers to advantages or benefits that white people get in society by virtue of their skin color and that are not available to people of color. These benefits can range from the mundane (such as the ability to buy skin-toned bandages that are similar to one's actual skin tone) to the highly significant (such as avoiding being followed by shopkeepers while in a store).

Race: A system of stratification based on real or imagined physical differences between groups that are believed to be essential and permanent.

Racism: Racism refers to discrimination and other beliefs and practices that assume differences between racial groups and/or which lead to racially disparate outcomes for different racial groups. Racism includes both individual racial prejudice and institutional racism.

Redlining: An institutional policy and practice of not making mortgages or other loans in specific neighborhoods because these neighborhoods are seen as poor investments. While on the surface the decision to redline an area may appear to be based on the economic qualities or the property value of the area, it has often been the case that redlined neighborhoods are predominantly black or multiracial or have growing African American populations. The term "redlining" comes from the practice of outlining such neighborhoods on a map in red to alert lenders to the locations in which they should avoid making loans.

Reparations: Reparations generally refers to any payment of money in compensation for a past wrong. In the context of race in the United States, discussions of reparations are generally focused on whether or not African Americans should be paid a sum of money to compensate them for the harms their ancestors suffered under slavery.

Segregation: The arrangement of groups into separate geographical areas, schools, or other facilities based on race or some other characteristic not related to individuals' own choices and skills. Segregation can be maintained by law and policy or it can exist informally through the institutionalized actions of social groups.

Social Movement: An organized effort to create changes in social, cultural, or political life by a group who is excluded from the power structure of society.

Stereotype: An exaggerated belief about a group of people which holds that all members of a group share the same characteristic. While stereotypes do sometimes have a grain of truth to them, they are more often based on assumptions or prejudices. Stereotypes can be both positive and negative, but are more often negative.

Bibliography

American Civil Liberties Union (2007). "Race & ethnicity in America: Turning a blind eye to justice." http://www.aclu.org/files/pdfs/humanrights/cerd%5Fexecutive%5Fsummary.pdf

American Civil Liberties Union (2013). "Voting rights: Your vote, your voice." https:// www.aclu.org/voting-rights

American Civil Liberties Union (2018). "Voting rights." https://www.aclu.org/issues/voting-rights#current.

Bonilla-Silva, E. et. al. (2004). *"I Did Not Get that Job Because of a Black Man…": The Story Lines and Testimonies of Color-Blind* Racism.

Bowen, W. G. & Bok, D. (1998) *The shape of the river: Long-term consequences of considering race in college and university admissions.* Princeton, NJ.: Princeton University Press.

Brown, M. K. et al. (2003). *Whitewashing race: The myth of a color-blind society.* : Berkeley: University of California Press.

Burke, M. A. (2017). "Racing left and right: color-blind racism's dominance across the U.S. political spectrum." *Sociological Quarterly,* 58(2), 277-294.

Crenshaw, K. (1995). *Critical race theory: The key writings that formed the movement.* New York: New Press.

Darity, W. A., Jr. & Meyers, S. L., Jr. (1998). *Persistent disparity: race and economic inequality in the United States.* Cheltenham, UK: Edward Elger.

Leonardo, Z., & Harris, A. P. (2013). "Living with racism in education and society: Derrick Bell's ethical idealism and political pragmatism." *Race, Ethnicity & Education,* 16, 470-488.

Liptak, A. (2013). "Supreme Court invalidates key parts of Voting Rights Act." *New York Times.* http://www.nytimes.com/2013/06/26/us/supreme-court-ruling.html?%5Fr=0

Pitt, R. N., & Packard, J. (2012). "Activating diversity: The impact of student race on contributions to course discussions." *Sociological Quarterly,* 53, 295-320.

Thernstrom, S. & Thernstrom, A. M. (1997). *America in black and white: One nation, indivisible.* New York: Simon & Schuster.

US Equal Employment Opportunity Commission (n.d.). "Race-based charges (charges filed with EEOC) FY1997-FY2017." https://www.eeoc.gov/eeoc/statistics/enforcement/race.cfm.

Williams, D. R., & Mohammed, S. A. (2013). "Racism and health I: pathways and scientific evidence." *American Behavioral Scientist,* 57, 1152-1173.

Winant, H. (2002). *The world is a ghetto.* New York: Basic Books.

Yoshino, K. (2006). *Covering: The hidden assault on our civil rights.* New York: Random House.

Suggested Reading

Back, L. & Solomos, J. (2000). *Theories of race and* racism*: A reader.* New York: Routledge.

Blank, R. M., Dabady, M., & Citro, C. F. (2004). *Measuring racial* discrimination. Washington, DC: National Academies Press.

Jones, E. (2018). "Racism, fines and fees and the US carceral state." *Race & Class,* 59(3), 38-50.

O'Brien, E., & Korgen, K. (2007, August). "It's the message, not the messenger: The declining significance of Black-White contact in a 'colorblind' society." *Sociological Inquiry,* 77, 356-382.

Lipsitz, G. (2006). *The possessive investment in Whiteness.* Philadelphia: Temple University Press.

McIntosh, P. (1988) "White privilege and male privilege: A personal account of coming to see correspondences through work in women's studies." *Wellesley Centers for Women.* Working Paper Number 189.

Ponds, K. T. (2013). "The trauma of racism: America's original sin." *Reclaiming Children & Youth,* 22, 22-24.

Rainey-Brown, S. A., Johnson, G. S., Latrice Richardson, N. N., Stinson, T. G., & Ellis, N. P. (2012). "New American racism: A microcosm study of a small town (Clarksville, Tennessee)." *Race, Gender & Class,* 19(3/4), 266-291.

Mikaila Mariel Lemonik Arthur, Ph.D.

Ethnocentrism & Racism

ABSTRACT

Ethnocentrism describes an individual or group's tendency to see their own group or culture as superior in culture and practices. Racism is a belief that human beings can be divided into various races, and that certain races are inferior to others. Racism has been blamed for various discriminatory policies throughout American history, including eugenics, slavery, segregation, and immigration. Today, Ethnocentrism and Racism continue to be important in discussions pertaining to issues such as education and social justice.

OVERVIEW

The term Ethnocentrism was first coined by American sociologist William Graham Sumner in 1906. Sumner described Ethnocentrism as an individual's tendency to see his own group or culture as central or most important, relating all other groups to his own. Today, the definition of Ethnocentrism also includes a belief that one's own culture or group is superior to others. Most social scientists believe that some degree of Ethnocentrism is unavoidable in humans; it is inherent in how people see and organize their concept of the world (Kam & Kinder, 2007). One of the challenges of social science research is the impartiality imparted by ethnocentric tendencies. Scientists' goal is to see the world from an unbiased, objective point of view; however, impartiality may be impossible due to previous experiences. While a certain degree of Ethnocentrism is natural and unavoidable, extreme Ethnocentrism can be very dangerous and have ill effects on individuals and societies, leading to discrimination or persecution, or in extreme cases, war or genocide.

Human Nature

Ethnocentrism is related to ethnicity. Ethnicity refers to one's nationality, where one is born or raised, and the culture that an individual identifies with. The United States is one of the most ethnically diverse countries in the world. Cindy D. Kam and Donald R. Kinder (2006) believe that viewing outside groups as dissimilar and inferior to one's own is part of human nature. Survey studies have proven that when humans refer to and discuss groups outside their own, they often do so in negative terms. Ethnocentrism is measured by how an individual feels toward groups in general rather than a specific group and what stereotypes or beliefs that individuals hold about these outside groups.

Racism is a belief that humans can be divided into various groups by race, and that the members of certain races are inferior to those of others, whether by intelligence, morals, culture, or physical abilities. Racism, unlike Ethnocentrism, is directed at a certain group or groups, or at individuals. The term was first used in the 1930s, primarily as a response to the treatment of Jews by the German Nazis. However, Racism as it is defined today can be identified much earlier in human history (Rattansi, 2007). Modern-day Racism is largely seen as a product of the development of race categories and how people came to view those of different races. Racism has been a driving force behind many conflicts around the world, including colonialism by Great Britain, the Holocaust in Europe, and slavery and segregation in the United States.

As one of the most ethnically and racially diverse countries in the world, the United States has struggled with issues driven by Racism and Ethnocentrism throughout its history into the present day. Today, the terms are often used interchangeably. In order to understand these issues further, it is important to discuss the development of racial categories and their historical significance, as well as the part that these concepts have played in various events and continue to play today.

HISTORY

The Development of Race

An individual's race is imperative to their social identity, as well as their interaction with others, whether they recognize it or not. Most scientists today do not see race as a useful biological concept. However, it is an important cultural construct, invented and further developed by humans (Smedley, 1999).

Racial categories and the act of dividing people into races became prevalent during the fifteenth century when travel and colonization of other continents were on the rise, especially by European nations. Exploration, imperialism, and colonialism led to a curiosity about others who looked different from oneself. Audrey and Brian Smedley (1999) trace Ethnocentrism in North America, the development of racial categories, England's treatment of the Irish, and English explorers' interactions with groups met through travel, trade, and colonization. For example, the English exhibited extreme Ethnocentrism toward the Irish and treated them as second-class people. When explorers met the American Indians during the beginning of the colonization of the Americas in the sixteenth century, this Ethnocentrism continued, coupled with Racism—Indians were often generalized as savage, corrupt, or inferior.

The North American slave trade had some of the greatest impacts on the development of racial categories and Racism. Slavery had existed long before the colonization of North America. However, slavery in this new context had a much larger impact on the construction of race and Racism. From the beginning of the American colonies, there was a system of indentured servitude through which poor Europeans exchanged several years of labor for passage, room, and board. When indentured servants fulfilled the terms of their contract, their servitude ended and servants were granted freedom dues, which usually included plots of land and supplies as payment for their service. The first black Africans arrived in Virginia in 1619. At this time, there were no slave laws in place in the American colonies, and black Africans and poor white colonists were both treated as indentured servants. Many wealthy landowners began to feel threatened by the growing economic power of former indentured servants and sought to limit freedoms and opportunities for the poorest colonists. The earliest slave laws were passed several decades after the first black indentured servants arrived in colonial America, first in Massachusetts in 1641 and then in Virginia in 1661. In the early years of American slavery, English colonists typically enslaved only non-Christians, not black Africans in particular. At this time, slaves could typically earn their freedom by converting to Christianity. As a way to limit the freedoms and mobility of indentured servants and slaves, racial slavery created a permanently dependent labor force of black slaves who were clearly set apart from their poor white counterparts. Under the slave system, while poor Europeans who came to the colonies as servants could eventually gain freedom, black slaves had no opportunities to earn their freedom and remained permanently enslaved. As slavery became more ingrained, slaves were stripped of more and more rights and increasingly seen as less than human. Some historians have argued that racial slavery served an important role in preventing cooperation and solidarity between poor black and poor white colonists, thereby solidifying the economic power of the wealthy, landowning elite. For these critics, racial categories in the early American colonies served as a way of obscuring class distinctions, so that poor white indentured servants felt they had more in common with the white landowning elite than the black slaves whom they worked alongside.

While slavery had existed around the world long before the English colonies in America, English slavery was very different—there was an extreme denial of recognition that slaves were human beings; they were seen as property and the laws treated them as such (Smedley, 1999).

English colonists began viewing people hierarchically and exhibited Ethnocentrism toward other countries. This mindset is often connected with how slavery developed in the United States. Slavery placed black individuals in a different category from white individuals and attributed all sorts of differences in characteristics and abilities between the two. By the eighteenth century, reputable European scientists, who had little exposure to individuals of different backgrounds and few facts based in sound scientific practices, had begun to classify human beings into racial categories and connected cultural, physical, and behavioral attributes to each race, creating a hierarchy of races. Through this hierarchy, white individuals received paternalistic justification for treating black slaves as sub-human. Slavery was a precursor to how the ideology of race pervaded North America; it compounded the differences between white and black individuals, and established the English at the top of any hierarchy of human beings (Smedley, 1999).

Government & Race

In 1790, the Naturalization Act was passed in the United States, restricting citizenship to only free white people. This law was not fully eliminated until 1952 with the passage of the Immigration and Nationality Act, which prohibits racial discrimination in immigration and naturalization processes, over which time many people tried to prove themselves as white in order to gain the benefits afforded to citizens. Other laws were set into motion to prevent black Americans and other minority groups from gaining the same privileges as white Americans. These laws addressed such basic freedoms such as marriage and education (Smedley, 1999).

The end of slavery brought other issues of race and ethnicity to the United States. After slavery was outlawed, many states instituted Jim Crow laws to segregate black Americans and restrict their freedom. Even though the Fourteenth Amendment ensured that all individuals born in the United States were US citizens and granted them equal protection under the law, many injustices continued to prevail. In other parts of the country, black Americans continued to face discrimination and limits on their freedoms. However, they were not the only ones who faced the negative impact from Ethnocentrism and racist attitudes. In the late nineteenth century through the early twentieth century, twenty-three million immigrants from central and eastern Europe arrived in the United States. These groups, though they were white, faced backlash from white Americans and were consequently labeled as inferior intellectually and different from those groups who were already in the United States. However, people from this migration, one of the largest in history, eventually identified as white and were able to attain higher social positions than African Americans or American Indians (Smedley, 1999).

By the end of the nineteenth century, the idea of intelligence testing became popular, and scientists began to measure the intelligence of various groups in an attempt to further separate races and establish hierarchy. Scientists began testing all immigrants, and testing to enter into the US Army also became common. Many advocated eugenics, or the idea that all things were inherited, including intelligence, criminality, reason, and there were advocates for the forced sterilization of those people who exhibited negative behaviors or traits (Smedley, 1999). All of these developments fueled the concept of Racism towards non-white groups.

Between World War I and World War II, the Ku Klux Klan used intimidation tactics to scare and control black Americans. Furthermore, demographic changes were occurring, as more middle- class whites moved to the suburbs, away from cities, fueling racial tensions even further. However, as the twentieth century progressed, changes began to occur. First, the ideas behind the science of race—the notion that different races were biologically different and thus were born into a naturally hierarchical order—began to meet more opposition and fall apart under scientific scrutiny. Scientists and others began to think of race as a socially constructed phenomenon and challenged previous ideas regarding the hierarchy of races. Furthermore, people in the United States were exposed to new cultures and different people all over the world as the country became more diverse and people traveled more widely and came into contact with other cultures. Finally, the atrocities committed by Nazi Germany against Jews and other minority groups created a wave of antiracist activism among Americans that made it clear that individuals and communities were reassessing values and ideas that they had once accepted as fact (Smedley, 1999).

In the latter half of the twentieth century, the civil rights movement gained momentum, and various groups demanded the repealing of certain laws that continued to create racial hierarchies and corralled all people of color as second-class citizens. Many laws were passed during this time, granting rights that had been denied to groups of Americans for many years. While people in the United States have made many inroads on dealing with Racism and Ethnocentrism, there are still prominent issues that arise and are intertwined with race and ethnicity.

Types of Racism

There are several different types of Racism that are discussed throughout the literature. The three major types include:

- Individual Racism;
- Institutional Racism; and
- Cultural Racism.

Individual Racism refers to the prejudices toward other groups that an individual displays or believes in (Franklin, Boyd-Franklin, & Kelly, 2006). These actions or behaviors are fueled by beliefs that there are hierarchical differences between races. Institutional Racism encompasses policies or procedures of a certain institution such as a company, a community, or a governing body that restrict or discriminate against certain groups (Franklin, Boyd-Franklin, & Kelly, 2006). Cultural Racism is a third type of Racism that is a result of one group's advantageous position in society over another. This type of Racism refers to one group's ability to determine how certain values or practices become legitimate parts of a culture. Slavery in the United States and apartheid in South Africa are examples of cultural Racism (Franklin, Boyd-Franklin, & Kelly, 2006).

Prejudice & Discrimination

Prejudice and discrimination are words often used in association with Racism and Ethnocentrism. Prejudice is defined as an attitude toward or judgment about a person based on a belief one has about the group that the person identifies with. Discrimination is behaving a certain way toward a person or a group because of the values or ideas that you associate with that group. Both are fundamentally linked to the concepts of Ethnocentrism and Racism. While Ethnocentrism and Racism are similar, Ethnocentrism is broader. Racism is targeted at specific groups, while Ethnocentrism is a more general outlook rejecting groups outside one's own. Ethnocentrism has often been closely connected to nationalism, or the idea that one's own nation has practices or norms that make it superior to others (Kam & Kinder, 2006).

VIEWPOINTS

While the United States has made large strides in combating both Racism and Ethnocentrism, and attitudes toward other groups outside one's own have certainly changed, Racism and Ethnocentrism continue to be important and present concepts. The United States is one of the most diverse countries in the world, racially and ethnically, with a long history of clashes between racial and ethnic groups.

The racial and ethnic demographics of the United States are changing rapidly. In 2012, the US Census Bureau reported that just over 63 percent of Americans identified as white alone. By 2050, that number is projected to be closer to 50 percent, meaning that white Americans will no longer make up the majority of the United States population. This diversity presents unique challenges in areas such as education, health care, and public policy.

Furthermore, in today's global economy, there are benefits as well as threats. While the United States has largely enjoyed success in the world market, this status does not preclude the United States from tensions. On September 11, 2001, terrorists attacked the United States, and fears from these attacks have affected how Americans feel about non-Americans around the world and US policy-making strategy in wake of these threats.

Racism in the United States has mostly been directed at minority groups by the white majority in various areas such as educational, housing, and employment opportunities. These groups include American Indians, African Americans, Asian Americans, and Hispanic and Latino Americans. All of these groups have struggled against Racism and exclusion from the American story.

Color-Blindness

Today, one of the major arguments pertaining to Racism is the idea of "color-blindness." Color-blindness is a term that has become associated with law-making bodies, arguing that race should not matter in making decisions in public matters, even if the goal is to improve inequalities or amend previous inequities. Many people believe that Racism and race are no longer important issues in US society, or that discussing race actually holds back progress, that Racism is a thing of the past, and involving race in decision-making procedures is actually racist itself and counterproductive (Doane, 2006). As a result of these ideas, many laws and practices such as affirmative action or using quotas at colleges and universities have been challenged in courts.

Others believe that color-blindness is simply a cover up or a denial that Racism still exists and race continues to matter in US society, and allows claims of Racism to be blamed on hypersensitive minorities. Critics of color-blindness also contend that denying that race matters or that Racism continues to exist allows existing racist policies to stay in place, limiting the progress toward a more egalitarian society (Doane, 2006).

Issues

Further relevant issues regarding the question of Racism in the United States revolve around the idea that anyone can be a racist, even those who belong to minority groups. While it is true that all human beings can harbor beliefs and ideas about certain racial groups, critics of this rationalization contend that while anyone can certainly be racist, using this explanation as a reasoning for not continuing to address Racism in the United States removes the burden of past racist policies and actions that were largely focused on mistreatment of non-white groups (Doane, 2006). McIntosh (1988) argues that white Americans, unlike other minority groups, are systemically conferred certain everyday privileges because they are white, while these privileges are denied to other racial groups simply because of the color of their skin. These privileges alone prove that there continues to be a problem of Racism in the United States and that race continues to matter. McIntosh (1988) labels this privilege as "white privilege," a social power held by whites that is unearned but given at birth and is ingrained into US culture and society.

Research on Racism and its effects on the victims of Racism have also shown that those who are affected by racist beliefs can suffer from invisibility syndrome and can also internalize racist attitudes. Invisibility syndrome occurs when individuals feel they cannot express their own identity because of existing stereotypes about their group. Victims may also begin to internalize certain viewpoints about their group and accept certain stereotypes as true, which can have harmful effects such as stunting achievement (Franklin, Boyd-Franklin, & Kelly, 2006). While there has been much research regarding Racism and its impact, in light of many arguments surrounding Racism today, more research will need to focus on pertinent issues such as the impact of color-blindness or the withdrawal of specific policies such as affirmative action.

Ethnocentrism differs from Racism but also continues to be a salient discussion in the United States today. The tragic terrorist attacks of September 11, 2001, were not only shocking, but the event and reactions to it redirected US policy. First, President George W. Bush and the United States government declared a war on terrorism. One of the first outcomes of that war was the passage of the Patriot Act by a huge majority in both houses of Congress. The Patriot Act allowed the government new powers to gather intelligence, including some that certain groups declare unjust. The countries of Afghanistan and Iraq were targeted as strongholds for terrorism, and both countries were attacked (Kam & Kinder, 2007).

The September 11th terrorist attacks drastically changed the foreign policy of the United States and, for some, heightened ethnocentric and racist beliefs against Arabs and Muslims. Kam and Kinder (2007) conducted research that addresses how Ethnocentrism relates to an individual's support of the new foreign policy. In the past, studies relating Ethnocentrism to public opinion have been few and far between, especially in the United States. In conducting this analysis, Kam and Kinder (2007) studied survey data from the 2000–2002 National Election Study, which contains information on how the American public's political leanings. Ethnocentrism was tested for in this survey data, and the timing proves useful as the surveys were taken before and after September 11, 2001, so changes in attitudes can be compared and contracted.

Ethnocentrism is measured through the prevalence of stereotypes, or the negative beliefs about another group, that one holds. These beliefs can include factors such as trustworthiness, intellectual acumen, or physical talents. Kam and Kinder (2007) found that Americans who support the war on terror do so for various reasons, and Ethnocentrism had a significant impact on this support. What is interesting about this study however, is that the research focused on how Americans rate other Americans who are part of different groups than they are. The individuals were most likely to rate Americans who were outside their own groups negatively were more likely to support the new foreign policy. This research presents that Ethnocentrism continues to have significant effects on what people believe, and this affects how people translate their political opinions. However, more research on ethnocentric attitudes in the United States may be necessary to understand further consequences.

TERMS & CONCEPTS

Color Blindness: Color blindness means to ignore race in creating policies and laws.

Discrimination: Discrimination is behaving a certain way toward a person or a group because of the values or ideas that you associate with that group.

Ethnicity: Ethnicity is defined by one's nationality and the culture that an individual identifies with.

Ethnocentrism: Ethnocentrism is the belief that one's own group is most important and that all other groups are inferior to one's own group.

Eugenics: Eugenics is a belief that all traits are inheritable and that the human race can be improved through selective breeding.

Racism: Racism is a belief that humans can be divided into various groups by race and that the members of certain races are inferior to those of other races.

Segregation: Segregation is the separation of people, in this context, by race or ethnicity.

White Privilege: White privilege is the concept that white people in certain societies are born with unearned privileges because they are white.

BIBLIOGRAPHY

Araújo, M., & Maeso, S. R. (2012). "History textbooks, Racism and the critique of Eurocentrism: beyond rectification or compensation." *Ethnic & Racial Studies, 35*(7), 1266–1286.

Doane, A. (2006). "What is Racism? Racial discourse and racial politics." *Critical Sociology, 32* (2-3), 255-274.

Franklin, A., Boyd-Franklin, N., & Kelly, S. (2006). "Racism and invisibility: Race-Related stress, emotional abuse and psychological trauma for people of color." *Journal of Emotional Abuse, 6* (2/3), 9-30.

Greitemeyer, T. (2012). "Boosting one's social identity: effects of social exclusion on Ethnocentrism." *Basic and Applied Social Psychology, 34*(5), 410–416.

Habtegiorgis, A. E., Paradies, Y. C., & Dunn, K. M. (2014). "Are racist attitudes related to experiences of racial discrimination? Within sample testing utilising nationally representative survey data." *Social Science Research, 47,* 178–191.

Kam, C., & Kinder, D. (2007). "Terror and Ethnocentrism: Foundations of American support for the war on terrorism." *Journal of Politics, 69* (2), 320-338.

McIntosh, P. (1990). "White privilege: Unpacking the invisible knapsack." *Independent School, 49* (2), 31.

Nelson, J. K. (2013). "Denial of Racism and its implications for local action." *Discourse and Society, 24*(1), 89–109.

Rattansi, A. (2007). *Racism: A very short introduction.* New York, NY: Oxford University Press, Inc.

Rodenborg, N. A., & Boisen, L. A. (2013). "Aversive Racism and intergroup contact theories: cultural competence in a segregated world." *Journal of Social Work Education, 49*(4), 564–579.

Smedley, A.(1999). *Race in North America: Origin and evolution of a worldview* (2nd Ed.). Boulder, CO: Westview Press.

U.S. Census Bureau. (2004), *U.S. Interim Projections by Age, Sex, Race, and Hispanic Origin.* U.S. Census Bureau Web site: http://www.census.gov/ipc/www/usinterimproj/

SUGGESTED READING

Blauner, R. (2001). *Still the big news: Racial oppression in America.* Philadelphia, PA: Temple University Press.

Campbell, D. T., & LeVine, R.A. (1961). "A Proposal for Cooperative Cross-Cultural Research on Ethnocentrism." *Journal of Conflict Resolution* (5), 82-108.

Hirschfeld, Lawrence A. 1996. *Race in the making.* Cambridge: MIT Press.

Omi, M. & Winant, H. (1994). *Racial formation in the United States from the 1960s to the 1990s.* New York, NY: Routledge & Kegan Paul.

Stewart, T. L., et al. (2012). "White privilege awareness and efficacy to reduce racial inequality and improve white Americans' attitudes toward African Americans." *Journal of Social Issues, 68* (1), 11–27.

Taras, R. (2013). "'Islamophobia never stands still': race, religion, and culture." *Ethnic & Racial Studies, 36*(3), 417–433.

Rana Suh, M.Ed.

Genocide

ABSTRACT

This article is an overview of the history and the concept of genocide. It reviews several episodes of genocide in modern world history, including the Holocaust as well as genocides in Bosnia, Rwanda, Armenia, and Darfur. The article then considers several controversies in Holocaust and Genocide studies. First, it discusses what factors cause genocides to occur, including national character, the development of modernity, and individual compliance. Second, it considers various responses to genocide, including trials, reparations, and truth and reconciliation commissions. Finally, it considers the relationship between the Holocaust and other genocides.

OVERVIEW

In general terms, the word "genocide" is used to refer to instances in which one group or nation sets about systematically exterminating a specific ethnic, racial, national, or religious population. It is undoubtedly true that such killings have happened all throughout history, but genocide as a term did not come into existence until near the end of World War II. The horrors of the Holocaust, the Nazi German campaign of extermination of Jews, Roma, individuals with disabilities, and a wide variety of others, led scholars and commentators to seek a new language to describe what had occurred. Raphael Lemkin, a lawyer of Polish-Jewish descent, coined the term "genocide" to describe the Nazi atrocities. Genocide combines the prefix geno-, from the Greek term for race or tribe, with the suffix -cide, from the Latin term for killing.

In the years following World War II, genocide was used as a descriptive term by scholars, commentators, and prosecutors. In particular, the prosecutors at the International Military Tribunal at Nuremberg (an international trial in which Nazi officials were tried for their participation in atrocities) used the term genocide to describe the acts encompassed by the charge "crimes against humanity." In 1948, genocide as a concept took on a more permanent life when the United Nations (UN) established the Convention on the Prevention and Punishment of the Crime of Genocide. This international treaty document defined genocide as an international crime that nations can attempt to prevent and punish.

Article 2 of the Convention defines genocide as follows:

In the present Convention, genocide means any of the following acts committed with intent to destroy, in whole or in part, a national, ethnical, racial or religious group, as such:

(a) Killing members of the group;
(b) Causing serious bodily or mental harm to members of the group;
(c) Deliberately inflicting on the group conditions of life calculated to bring about its physical destruction in whole or in part;
(d) Imposing measures intended to prevent births within the group;
(e) Forcibly transferring children of the group to another group (Office of the High Commissioner for Human Rights, 1948, ¶ 3).

While the Convention has made it possible for the International Criminal Court to prosecute individuals who participate in the commission of genocide, not much success has been had in terms of preventing genocide. In part, this is because it remains hard to predict when genocide will occur. Perhaps more important, however, is the fact that genocides frequently occur within an individual nation's borders, and the international community is often reluctant to interfere in what it sees as an internal matter.

APPLICATIONS

Episodes of Genocide

Genocide is not as rare as some people think. In fact, over the past century quite a number of episodes of genocide have occurred.

Since the Holocaust is the episode of genocide that sparked the invention of the term itself, it has had a central place in the study of genocide. The Holocaust, sometimes called the Shoah, refers to the period between 1933 and 1945 in Europe, during which the Nazis consolidated their political power in Germany; invaded and subjugated other European nations; and systematically exterminated Jews, Roma, homosexuals, those with mental and physical disabilities, and various political prisoners such as Catholic priests, resistance fighters, Communists, and dissident intellectuals. It is estimated that the Nazis killed six million Jews as well as several million others. Some died due to forced overcrowding in ghettos, where they succumbed to disease and starvation. Others were executed by roving death squads or were imprisoned in concentration camps where they died from starvation, disease, or overwork. A key element of the Nazi extermination campaigns was the development of gas chambers in which large numbers of prisoners could be killed at once through the application of Zyklon-B, a pesticide.

There have probably been over a dozen instances of genocide in the years since the Holocaust ended, occurring in nations all across the globe. Two of the most recent episodes occurred in the former Yugoslavia and in Rwanda. In the early 1990s, a conflict developed between Serbs and Croats, two ethnic groups living in Bosnia-Herzegovina, a small Eastern European nation making up one portion of the former Yugoslavia. In part due to their connections with the neighboring nation of Serbia, the Serbs were able to develop a military force that attacked the Croats. Thousands were displaced and many women and girls were raped. Despite the intervention of peacekeeping troops, the death toll numbered in the thousands, though the exact number is still uncertain.

The Rwandan genocide also has its roots in the political boundaries of the nation. During the years when Rwanda was a British colony, the colonial government differentiated between two ethnic groups, the Hutus and the Tutsis. These differentiations led to resentment and civil war. A ceasefire that was supposed to end the violent conflict was reached in 1993. However, in 1994 the Rwandan president's plane was shot down, and this event triggered genocidal action. Hutus, including civilians, were encouraged to kill their Tutsi neighbors. Up to one million people were killed, despite the presence of a UN force that had little ability to intervene.

While most commentators agree that the Holocaust and the events in Bosnia and Rwanda qualify as genocide, there is more controversy over other episodes. The existence of a clear definition of genocide as laid out by the UN Convention has not made people any more likely to agree. For instance, some activists and scholars have argued that the deaths that occurred among indigenous populations during periods of colonization as well as those that occurred during the Middle Passage, the period during which Africans were transported to the Americans as slaves, represent episodes of genocide. These controversies are often shaped by the maxim that "the victors write the history." In other words, these activists and scholars argue that we see the Holocaust as an episode of genocide because Nazi Germany lost the war and the victorious Allies wrote the history. In contrast, Great Britain, the United States, and other nations that have been accused of genocides during the colonial era have little motivation to assume responsibility for their role in these deaths because, as dominant powers, they have framed discussion about them.

An example that might make this problem of identifying genocide clearer is the actions of the Turkish government in Armenia, a small country wedged in between Turkey and Asia, during and just after World War I. After protracted conflicts between Turkey and Russia over their respective national borders, which lay in territory occupied by Armenians, a new Turkish government arose in 1908. Seven years later, in the midst of World War I, this new government began a campaign of systematically expelling Armenians. Many were killed outright; others were forced to march until they died. By 1923, Western Armenia was emptied of Armenians. Some fled to seek refuge in other nations, but over a million were killed. However, to this day, the Turkish government claims that no genocide occurred. Due to their reluctance to anger Turkey, which is seen as a valuable ally, few other nations have recognized this episode as genocide either. In total, just over twenty nations—including Argentina, Belgium, Canada, France, Italy, Russia, and Uruguay—and forty-three US states recognize the events as genocide as of 2011.

One of the most recent controversial episode has been the events in Darfur, a region in the western part of Sudan, a nation that borders Egypt in northern Africa. A group called the Janjaweed, a militia comprising nomadic Arabic tribes from northern Sudan, has set about systematically killing and expelling non-Arab populations from Darfur. While the Sudanese government claims that it is not supporting the Janjaweed, there is evidence suggesting that the government provides financial and military resources to the militia. This instance of genocidewas precipitated by decades of civil war as well as severe drought that intensified land conflicts between ethnic groups. Between the beginning of the conflict in 2003 and 2013, it is estimated that between 200,000 and 400,000 people have been killed; as many as 2.5 million people have been displaced. Many of the displaced are living in refugee camps in neighboring nations. While many advocacy groups have been active in drawing attention to Darfur, international governments are still undecided about whether to treat this episode as a genocide or as a civil war ("Q&A: Sudan's Darfur Conflict," 2008).

VIEWPOINTS

What Makes Genocide Possible?

Sociologists and other scholars who study genocide are particularly interested in understanding what makes genocide possible. If a model could be developed to predict when and where genocide would happen, it would make it much easier for the international community to take advanced action to prevent genocide from occurring. Such a model does not yet exist. However, scholars have proposed a variety of explanations that help to explain what might make genocide possible.

Some scholars have argued that genocide occurs because of unique flaws within the particular nation or population committing genocide. For instance, in his book *The Germans*, German sociologist Norbert Elias argued that the Holocaust occurred because of cultural attributes unique to Germany (1996). Elias argued that the culture of violence and dueling in Germany, the code of honor governing social life, and the rigid and authoritarian personality of German individuals led to the development of the Nazi party and, ultimately, the Holocaust. This sort of argument tends to be reassuring, as it assumes that there is something unique about groups that will engage in genocide. As a society, most people do not like to think that they could be likely to participate in genocide. However, the historical record shows that many episodes of genocide have occurred over the past century. If it were true that genocide occurs because the unique attributes of a nation, it is unlikely that so many could have occurred within such a short period of time.

Other scholars argue that the development of modernity made genocide possible. While it is true that some episodes of genocide—or something like it—did occur prior to the modern era, they say that it was much harder for one population to systematically exterminate another. In fact, the dynamics of these mass killings were quite different from those of today. In the pre-modern era, a nation that wished to oppress another nation might choose to kill the population, but it also might choose another form of oppression, such as slavery or forced conversion and assimilation. In part, this distinction arises from the difference between the xenophobia, or fear of foreigners, which was a key element of ethic relations in the pre-modern world, and the modern development of racial ideologies. Racial ideologies allow nations to distinguish between different groups of foreigners and declare some fit for continued existence and others for extermination. Furthermore, they encourage nations to see foreigners as essentially or biologically different and thus unfit for assimilation.

Another aspect of modernity is the development of advanced technologies for extermination. Committing genocide effectively requires the availability of surveillance technologies like censuses and personal identification cards so that those singled out for extermination can be located. It also requires the availability of effective and efficient technologies with which individuals can be killed. The Nazis developed many of these technologies, including racial censuses, personal identification cards, and gas chambers, as the Holocaust progressed. In contrast, in pre-modern societies without surveillance, it was easier for individuals to escape detection and thus survive an attempted genocide. Before the development of bombs, accurate guns, and gas chambers, killing was much more individualized and slower—the Nazi death toll would have undoubtedly been lower in the absence of modern technology.

Still, all of the modern technology and racial ideology in the world cannot create genocide without a population that is willing or compliant enough to carry it out. Social scientists and historians since the Holocaust have been exploring what it takes to get people to participate in an atrocity. A variety of different investigations have all found that about one third of people would enthusiastically participate in an atrocity, slightly less than one third would refuse to go along, and the remaining third would participate but not enthusiastically. Some of the earliest of these studies were conducted by experimental psychologists Stanley Milgram, who found that 65% of his test subjects were willing to administer what they believed to be seriously harmful shocks to a confederate, and Phillip G. Zimbardo, who, by creating a simulated prison in the basement of the psychology building at Stanford University, found that the personalities of psychologically "normal" college students were drastically altered as they carried out their assigned roles as guards and prisoners in the course of the experiment (1974, 1972). Similar results were found by Christopher Browning, who studied the actions of a particular killing squad that operated in Poland during the Holocaust (1992).

Responding to Genocide

Despite the fact that it occurs more often than we like to think, genocide remains an extreme event in human experience. Historians, artists, poets, novelists, and designers of memorials have all sought ways to memorialize and comprehend episodes of genocide. In addition, the victims of genocide along with the international community have sought ways to legally respond. These responses have varied, but there are three general forms that have been tried: perpetrator trials, reparations, and truth and reconciliation commissions.

Perpetrator Trials

The Nuremberg trials after the Holocaust were the first perpetrator trials. At these trials, the international community came together to try those accused of perpetrating genocide during the Holocaust. More recently, the International Criminal Court was established in the Hague in the Netherlands to serve as a permanent facility for trying those accused of perpetrating genocide as well as crimes against humanity and war crimes. While not all nations, including the United States, have ratified the treaty bringing the International Criminal Court into existence, it is engaged in several investigations and prosecutions. However, the lack of participation by some nations, coupled with the difficulties of international debates about issues like the death penalty—a penalty not assessed by the International Criminal Court—makes its work more difficult. In addition, as Lawrence Douglas has argued, some survivors of genocide find that the trial process and its commitment to legal procedure do not properly represent survivors' experiences and their suffering (2001).

Reparations

Others believe that survivors deserve compensation for their suffering and advocate for reparations as another legal method of response to genocide. Reparations refer to the idea that individual survivors and their descendants should receive payments to compensate for their losses. Reparations have been most notable in the case of the Holocaust, but have been used in other situations as well. Not all situations involving reparations have been genocides. For instance, the United States paid reparations to Japanese Americans who were placed in internment camps during World War II, and activists have argued that the United States should also pay reparations to the descendants of those brought here as slaves. Despite the fact that reparations do offer tangible benefits to survivors and their descendants, they have remained controversial. Among the many objections to reparations that Christian Pross outlined in his book Paying for the Past are the ideas that suffering cannot be so easily quantified, that reparations allow the offenders to assuage their own guilt, and that reparations create a situation in which survivors are re-victimized and made dependent upon the country that tried to kill them (1998).

Truth & Reconciliation Commission

A final and more modern method of responding to genocide is the truth and reconciliation commission. South Africa developed the first truth and reconciliation commission in the aftermath of the severe segregation that was legally enforced in the country between 1948 and 1990 and known as apartheid. Truth and reconciliation commissions function as hearings in which perpetrators of genocide admit openly to their crimes in return for a guarantee that they will not face criminal prosecution. Though some argue that this approach allows perpetrators to avoid being punished for their crimes, truth and reconciliation commissions do allow for the possibility of communal healing and they do allow survivors to have their voices heard. Rwanda is one nation that has used this approach in response to genocide.

Scholarly Understandings of Genocide & the Holocaust

Scholars of genocide often struggle with how to understand comparisons between the Holocaust and other instances of genocide. As noted above, the Holocaust was the episode that lead to the development of the concept of genocide; it probably also had the highest death toll of any modern genocide. These distinctions have led some scholars to argue that the Holocaust is different from other genocides and that it should be considered apart from them. However, others argue that the Holocaust was like other genocides, and that seeing it as different trivializes other genocides that have had equally devastating effects. Partially for this reason, the academic discipline that studies genocide is often called "Holocaust and Genocide Studies" so as to avoid taking a side in this dispute. Perhaps the most noteworthy statement on the subject comes from Tzvetan Todorov, who has argued that "Jews should emphasize the ordinariness of the Holocaust, Germans its uniqueness" (1996; p. 117). Why? Because, as Todorov has said, the only moral position one can have with respect to the Holocaust is to refuse to seek advantage from it.

TERMS & CONCEPTS

Ethnic Group: Ethnic groups are groups of people who see themselves as sharing some sort of common ancestry, identity, and/or culture.

Holocaust: The word "Holocaust" derives from the Greek terms meaning "completely burnt." It generally refers to the period between 1933 and 1945 when Nazi Germany exterminated six million Jews and several million others. Some scholars have expanded the term to include the extermination of other, non-Jewish people, like Roma, communists, and people with disabilities, whom the Nazi party also deemed "undesirable."

International Criminal Court: An international tribunal established in 2002 in The Hague, Netherlands to prosecute individuals accused of genocide, crimes against humanity, and war crimes.

Modernity: Modernity refers to the period of human history ranging roughly from the end of the Middle Ages until the mid to late twentieth century. Modernity is marked by four primary characteristics: rapid and extensive social change, a new set of social institutions, the de-localization of social relations, and the development of new technologies that allow for increasing standardization and surveillance.

Nazis: The German National Socialist German Workers' Party. It came to power in Germany under Adolf Hitler and perpetrated the Holocaust.

Nuremberg Trials: A series of trials in which Nazi officials were prosecuted for their involvement in crimes against humanity, including genocide, and war crimes. The trials were held in Nuremberg, Germany between 1945 and 1949 and were presided over by officials from the United States, France, Russia, and Great Britain.

Roma: An ethnic group with origins in South Asia, often referred to as Gypsies.

Shoah: A Hebrew word meaning "calamity" that is the preferred term for the Holocaust in Israel and among some scholars.

United Nations Convention on the Prevention & Punishment of Genocide: An international treaty that established the concept of genocide in international law and authorized member nations of the United Nations to seek to prevent and punish it.

Xenophobia: Literally, "fear of foreigners." Figuratively, it used to refer to situations in which members of an ethnic group or a nation are prejudiced against or feel superior to other ethnic groups or nations.

Bibliography

Bauman, Z. (2000). *Modernity and the Holocaust.* Ithaca: Cornell University Press.

Browning, C. (1998). *Ordinary men: Reserve police battalion 101 and the Final Solution in Poland.* New York: Harper Collins.

Clark, J. (2012). "The 'crime of crimes': Genocide, criminal trials and reconciliation." *Journal Of Genocide Research, 14*(1), 55–77.

Douglas, L. (2001). *The memory of judgment: Making law and history in the trials of the Holocaust.* New Haven: Yale University Press.

Elias, N. (1996). *The Germans: Power struggles and the development of habitus in the nineteenth and twentieth centuries.* New York: Columbia University Press.

Haney, C., Banks, C. & Zimbardo, P.G. (1973). "Interpersonal dynamics in a simulated prison." *International Journal of Criminology and Penology,* 1, 69-97.

Milgram, S. 1(983). *Obedience to authority: An experimental view.* New York: HarperCollins.

Office of the High Commissioner for Human Rights. (1948). "Convention on the prevention and punishment of the crime of genocide." United Nations. http://www.unhchr.ch/html/menu3/b/p%5fgenoci.htm

Pross, C., & Cooper, B. (1998). *Paying for the past: The struggle over reparations for surviving victims of the Nazi terror.* Baltimore: Johns Hopkins University Press.

"Q&A: Armenian genocide dispute." (2008). *BBC.* http://news.bbc.co.uk/2/hi/europe/6045182.stm

"Q&A: Sudan's Darfur conflict." (2008). *BBC.* http://news.bbc.co.uk/2/hi/africa/3496731.stm

Schneiderhan, E. (2013). "Genocide reconsidered: A pragmatist approach." *Journal For The Theory Of Social Behaviour, 43*(3), 280–300.

Shaw, M. (2012). "From comparative to international genocide studies: The international production of genocide in 20th-century Europe." *European Journal Of International Relations, 18*(4), 645–668.

Todorov, T. (1996). *Facing the extreme: Moral life in the concentration camps.* New York: Henry Holt.

Zimbardo, P. G. (1972). "Pathology of imprisonment." *Society,* 9(6), 4-8.

Suggested Reading

Gerson, J. M. & Wolf, D. L. (Eds.). (2007). *Sociology confronts the Holocaust: Memories and identities in Jewish Diasporas.* Durham, NC: Duke University Press.

Gourevitch, P. (1999). *We wish to inform you that tomorrow we will be killed with our families: Stories from Rwanda.* New York: Macmillan.

Hagan, J. & Rymond-Richmond, W. (2008). *Darfur and the crime of genocide.* Cambridge, UK: Cambridge University Press.

Hovannisian, R. G. (Ed.). (2003). *Looking backward, moving forward: Confronting the Armenian Genocide.* New Brunswick, NJ: Transaction Publishers.

Nielsen, C. (2013). "Surmounting the myopic focus on genocide: The case of the war in Bosnia and Herzegovina." *Journal Of Genocide Research, 15*(1), 21–39.

"Remembering Feinstein." (2007). *Center for Holocaust and genocide studies.* http://www.chgs.umn.edu/

Vollhardt, J., & Bilewicz, M. (2013). "After the genocide: Psychological perspectives on victim, bystander, and perpetrator groups." *Journal Of Social Issues, 69*(1), 1–15.

Mikaila Mariel Lemonik Arthur, Ph.D.

INSTITUTIONAL PREJUDICE

ABSTRACT

This article defines race and ethnicity and discusses instances in which these factors have played a role in situations of prejudice and institutional prejudice. Both race and ethnicity are defined as socially constructed categories, with race focusing on biological and societal characteristics and ethnicity focusing on those who share the same religion, language or dialect, or customs, norms, practices, and history. Institutional prejudice involves preconceived thoughts and emotions about an outgroup regarding social policies like hiring and firing, police and legal policies, and housing. These occurrences are discussed.

OVERVIEW

The Social Construction of Race

Race is best described as a socially constructed category. Groups that are treated as distinct within society based on various characteristics, including biological characteristics, are considered races. Assumed culturally or biologically inferior characteristics, as noted by powerful social groups, generally cause races to be singled out as being different. This thinking brings on great distress to the individual members of a race due to being treated differently and unfairly. Consequently, the manner in which groups have been treated both historically and socially defines the racial groups rather than individual biological characteristics (Andersen & Taylor, 2006).

Racial categories like 'Black' and 'White' are assigned to people by society, rather than by science, fact, or even logic. These decisions are generally based on opinion and social experience and explain what is meant by race being a "socially constructed" term. Though perceived biological differences like skin color, lip form, and hair texture typically define the meaning of race between groups, the social categories used to divide racial groups are not exactly fixed and vary from society to society. Laws defining who is African American, for example, have varied historically based on the laws of the state in which one resides. This suggests that racial differences are not merely biological (Andersen & Taylor, 2006; Washington, 2004).

For example, for years Tennessee and North Carolina law defined people as Black if they had at least one great-grandparent who was Black. Having any Black ancestors (even one great-great-great-grandparent) satisfied the conditions for other Southern states, which were based on the so-called "one drop" rule (Taylor, 2006; Malcomson, 2000). More complexity comes into play when the meaning of race is considered in other countries, as race is defined more so by one's social class. For example, a dark brown-skinned Black person in Brazil could be considered White, particularly if he or she has a high economic status. Brazilians are considered Black only if they are descendants of Africans and have no apparent White ancestry. Under the Brazilian rule, the majority of African Americans would not be considered Black in Brazil (Surratt & Inciardi, 1998; Omi & Winant, 1994; Sowell, 1983; Blalock, 1982). To add, the social constructionist view argues that a classification system based only on skin color, body shape, hair style, and the like does not fully justify meaningful and biological evidence, but has been used to justify the unequal treatment of diverse groups (Machery & Faucher, 2005).

Ethnicity

Like race, ethnicity is considered a social category of people who share various characteristics. For example, an ethnic group may share a common religion, a common language or dialect, or common customs, norms, practices, and history. Examples of ethnic groups that reside in the United States include Mexican Americans, Japanese Americans, Italian Americans, Arab Americans, Polish Americans, Greek Americans, and Irish Americans. However, ethnic groups are found in other societies as well. The Shiites and Sunnis in Iraq, whose ethnic classifications are based on their religious differences, serve as one example (Andersen & Taylor, 2006).

Unique historical and social experiences cause the development of ethnic groups, and these experiences make up the group's ethnic identity. An example of ethnic identity is the way Italian immigrants came to identify themselves as a group. Before immigration, Italian immigrants did not consider themselves an ethnic group with similar experiences and interests, as they came from different villages and cities.

Instead, their family backgrounds and communities of origin were the identifiers of the groups they belonged to. The immigration process, however, and the experiences Italians underwent in the United States, influenced the creation of a new identity for Italians as they now shared similar experiences in a foreign land (Waters, 1990; Alba, 1990).

The intensity level of ethnic development and identification can vary. If ethnic groups face prejudice or some type of hostility from other groups, they tend to unite around common interests politically and economically. In addition, voluntary or involuntary development of ethnic unity may occur as a result of ethnic group exclusion by ingroups with more power in various residential areas, social clubs, or occupations. These instances typically cause ethnic identity to strengthen (Andersen & Taylor, 2006).

Prejudice

Before we can discuss institutional prejudice, we must first define prejudice. It is, however, important to differentiate prejudice from other related terms. Terms like discrimination and stereotypes are similar to prejudice, but they each have different meanings. For example, discrimination is a matter of action, whereas prejudice is about one's attitude. Stereotypes, on the other hand, are sets of beliefs about social group members that have been overly simplified. They are normally intended to describe a typical member in the group, but they typically provide inaccurate descriptions (Andersen & Taylor, 2006).

Steele, Choi, and Ambady (2004) define prejudice as a preconceived negative attitude or feeling toward an outgroup (group from a different racial, ethnic, religious, or socioeconomic group from one's own). Prejudice is driven by emotion (Johnson, Musial, Hall, Gollnick, & Dupuis, 2004), and it is further described as an evaluation of a social group based on misjudgments that are believed, even if facts have proven the believer wrong (Allport, 1954; Pettigrew, 1971; Jones, 1997). For example, having negative thoughts about people solely because they belong to a certain group is considered prejudice. Though negative predispositions usually define prejudices, prejudices can sometimes be positive. For example, a negative feeling about someone in a different group from one's own is often associated with a positive disposition for someone who is in one's own group (Andersen & Taylor, 2006).

Though most people fail to own up to racial and ethnic prejudices, the majority of citizens hold some form of prejudice against other groups different from them. Whether it is on the basis of race, ethnicity, gender, age, class, or sexual orientation, almost everyone holds a prejudice against another in some way (Andersen & Taylor, 2006).

Prejudice based on race or ethnicity, in particular, is referred to as racial-ethnic prejudice. An example that would constitute prejudice in this case is if a Latino person dislikes an Anglo person, only because he or she is White. The Latino person would be considered a member of the ingroup and the White person would be part of the outgroup. Statements from the Latino like, "all Whites behave badly," indicate that the Latino is using a stereotype to justify his or her prejudice. It is a negative prejudgment based solely on race and ethnicity (Andersen & Taylor, 2006).

Some forms of prejudice can lead to intergroup hostility and violence, the dehumanization of others different from oneself, and can even lead to mass murders and group destruction. The Holocaust, the genocide of the Tutsis by the Hutus in Rwanda, the conflict that continues between the Israelis and Palestinians, and the terrorist attacks of September 11, 2001, are all examples of what intergroup hatred can cause (Steele, Choi, & Ambady, 2004).

In the United States, the most physically violent forms of prejudices that continue to persist tend to involve African Americans, Hispanics, and homosexuals. Each of these groups has suffered instances of beating or even murder as a result of their group membership. The fatal beating of Matthew Shepard, a gay student at the University of Wyoming, is an example of the prejudices the homosexual community has experienced. Shepard was brutally beaten and left in freezing temperatures to die, just because of his sexual orientation. The incident that happened to Rodney King, an African American, is another example of how prejudicial attitudes have caused harm to an outgroup member. In this case, several White Los Angeles police officers beat King severely in an act that seemed to be driven by racial motives. Based on incidents such as these, researchers have asked questions about where these attitudes originate, form, and develop over the years (Steele, Choi, & Ambady, 2004).

Research findings suggest that the very first signs of prejudice have been seen in children at very early stages in their lives (Aboud, 1988). Around age five, a child's prejudice level is high and begins to decrease or become more flexible as the child matures. Some research indicates that by the time a child becomes a teenager and older, the prejudices they held at an early age return. This is particularly true if the prejudice is around their social environment. For instance, if a child's mother shows some form of ethnic prejudice, more than likely the child with display the same prejudice. In addition, children of highly authoritative parents with great rigidity and intolerance for difference typically are more prejudiced than other children who don't have that type of family structure (Steele, Choi, & Ambady, 2004).

APPLICATIONS

Institutional Prejudice

When one considers prejudicial attitudes held in and among institutions, the term institutional prejudice appears. Institutional prejudice involves preconceived thoughts and emotions about an outgroup regarding social policies like hiring and firing, police and legal policies, housing, and the like. It occurs in public bodies like corporations, universities, and state and government agencies, or simply among various ingroups (Johnson, Musial, Hall, Gollnick, & Dupuis, 2004; Andersen & Taylor, 2006).

Minority Group Threat

Institutional prejudice on the basis of race and ethnicity has taken many forms. When race has been at the forefront of the prejudice, the topic of minority threat and perceived police force size needed is one example that sheds light on this problem and highlights the minority group threat theory. Minority group threat explains the types of social controls that affect racial minorities disproportionately, such as felon disenfranchisement laws (Behrens et al., 2003), incarceration rates (Greenberg & West, 2001), or arrest rates of minorities (Eitle et al., 2002).

Mainstream thinking suggests that the larger the number of minority (often African American) members in an area, the more majority members should feel threatened. This form of institutional prejudice in turn increases the perceived level of crime control needed in that area, and eventually increases the size of the police force. This causes larger criminal justice costs, more arrests, and increased imprisonment rates of minorities (Stults & Baumer, 2007).

Examples

There are many examples of institutional prejudice on the basis of ethnicity and negative bias that have surfaced as a result of immigration to the United States. Between 1890 and 1924, for example, Japanese people were able to immigrate to the United States. Many first-generation immigrants employed in agriculture came from farming families and wanted to purchase their own land. The 1913 Alien Land Law of California, however, held that Japanese aliens could only lease land for three years, and even those who already owned or were leasing land could not leave the land to their heirs. So even though the second generation of Japanese Americans became more educated than their parents, spoke in American English, and essentially assimilated to American culture, they still faced prejudice, specifically in areas with the largest populations of Japanese Americans, on the West Coast from Washington to southern California (Glenn, 1986).

The most significant examples of institutional prejudice among Japanese Americans occurred following the Japanese attack on Pearl Harbor in 1941. After the attack, the loyalty of Japanese Americans was questioned. Their assets were frozen, and in many cases, their real estate was confiscated, and they were labeled by the media as "traitors" and "enemy aliens" (Glenn, 1986). Numerous Japanese Americans were forced to leave their homes and were taken to relocation camps. These relocation efforts destroyed many Japanese families and ruined their finances (Glenn, 1986; Kitano, 1976; Takaki, 1989).

In the late 1960s, more Koreans came to the United States following amendments made to the immigration laws. These amendments allowed increased immigration from Asia. At least half of the adults that immigrated to the U.S. came with a college education and had been successful professionals prior to arriving. Institutionalprejudice surfaced, however, when Koreans sought employment. Despite their level of education, many immigrants had no choice but to take unskilled jobs. Similarly, in the 1970s, numerous Vietnamese refugees immigrated to the United States. Like other Asian immigrants before them, they were routinely faced with institutional prejudice because of the way many Americans perceived them. Americans perceived Vietnamese as competitors for their jobs, which were scarce at the time. Therefore, Vietnamese immigrants often faced various prejudices and hostility based on the motives Americans thought the Vietnamese had (Kim, 1993; Winnick, 1990). In each case, there was a negative bias against the other group.

VIEWPOINTS

Allport's Contact Hypothesis of Intergroup Interactions

Allport's Intergroup Contact Theory (Allport, 1954) lends some explanation for how institutional prejudice occurs. It explains the process by which diverse groups (ingroups and outgroups) interact with one another. The theory posits that a specific type of setting must be created to encourage groups to develop positive interactive relations. The setting should consist of four conditions: cooperation between groups, equal status, common goals, and support from authority figures in the program or institution in which the interaction takes place. Less bias and a greater possibility for cross-group interactions have resulted when these conditions have been met, including a reduction in prejudices (Allport, 1954; Pettigrew & Troop, 2000). Allport (1954) suggests that ingroups are "psychologically primary," meaning that familiarity, preference, and attachment for one's ingroups is established before the development of attitudes toward specific outgroups.

Advice to Individuals Working Toward Eliminating Prejudice

One line of thought in reducing prejudice suggests simply making a determined effort not to be prejudiced. Though this is typically a very difficult task for many, suppressing negative thoughts and removing them from one's mind is recommended as a key effort to eliminating prejudice in oneself. One must be cognizant, however, that in some cases, this strategy leads to one having somewhat of a rebound effect. Now, the area of prejudice is focused on more rather than ignored, because the individual is purposely trying not to think about the issue (Macrae, Bodenhausen, Milne, & Jetten, 1994).

TERMS & CONCEPTS

Allport's Intergroup Contact Theory: Allport's Intergroup contact theory posits that a specific type of setting must be created to encourage diverse groups to develop positive interactive relations. This setting should consist of four conditions: cooperation between groups, equal status, common goals, and support from authority figures in the program or institution in which the interaction takes place.

Discrimination: Discrimination is a matter of action and consists of overt negative and unequal treatment of members of members of the outgroup.

Ethnic Identity: Ethnic identity refers to the way in which a group sees themselves sharing common cultural bonds with one another.

Ethnicity: Ethnicity is considered a social category of people who share various characteristics, such as a common religion or language.

Ingroups: A sociological term used to describe a group that people identify with and feel some form of attachment to. In many instances, the attachment is based on opposition toward outgroups.

Institutional Prejudice: Institutional prejudice involves preconceived thoughts and emotions about an outgroup regarding social policies like hiring and firing, police and legal policies, housing, and the like. It occurs in public bodies like corporations, universities, and state and government agencies, or simply among various ingroups.

Intergroup: Intergroup refers to the state of being or occurring between two or more social groups.

Minority Group Threat: Minority group threat explains the types of social controls that affect racial minorities disproportionately, such as felon disenfranchisement laws, incarceration rates, or arrest rates of minorities.

Outgroups: A group of individuals toward which members of an ingroup harbor a sense of opposition, resistance, and even hatred. Outgroups are required for ingroups to exist.

Prejudice: Prejudice is a preconceived negative attitude or feeling toward an outgroup (group from a different racial, ethnic, religious, or socioeconomic category than one's own), and is driven by emotion. Prejudice is further described as an evaluation of a social group based on misjudgments that are believed, even if facts have proven the believer wrong.

Race: Race is best described as a socially constructed category. Groups that are treated as distinct within society based on various characteristics, including biological characteristics, are considered races.

Racial-ethnic Prejudice: Racial-ethnic prejudice is prejudice based on race or ethnicity only.

Socially Constructed: Socially constructed refers to decisions that are generally made based on opinion and social experience. It is a social process used to define racial groups.

Stereotype: A stereotype is a belief about members of a social group or division that is often oversimplified.

BIBLIOGRAPHY

Aboud, F. (1988). *Children and prejudice.* Oxford, UK: Basil Blackwell.

Alba, R. (1990). *Ethnic identity: The transformation of ethnicity in the lives of Americans of European ancestry.* New Haven: Yale University Press.

Allport, G. W. (1954). *The nature of prejudice.* Reading: Addison-Wesley.

Andersen, M. L. & Taylor, H. F. (2006). *Sociology: Understanding a diverse society,* 4th ed. New York: Wadsworth.

Behrens, A., Uggen, C. & Manza, J. (2003). "Ballot manipulation and the 'Menace of Negro Domination': Racial threat and felon disenfranchisement in the United States, 1850–2002. *American Journal of Sociology,* 109(3), 559–605.

Chen E. Y. F. (1991). "Conflict between Korean greengrocers and Black Americans." Unpublished thesis. Princeton University, Princeton, NJ.

Duriez, B., Vansteenkiste, M., Soenens, B., & De Witte, H. (2007). "The social costs of extrinsic relative to intrinsic goal pursuits: Their relation with social dominance and racial and ethnic prejudice." *Journal of Personality,* 75(4), 757–782.

Eckert, R., & Rowley, A. (2013). "Audism: A theory and practice of audiocentric privilege." *Humanity & Society, 37*(2), 101–130.

Eitle, D., D'Alesso, S. & Stolzenberg, L. (2002) "Racial threat and social control: A test of the political, economic, and threat of Black crime hypotheses." *Social Forces,* 81(2), 557–76.

"Future directions in research on institutional and interpersonal discrimination and children's health." (2013). *American Journal of Public Health, 103*(10), 1754–1763.

Glenn, E. N. (1986). *Issei, Nisei, War Bride: Three generations of Japanese American women in domestic service.* Philadelphia: Temple University Press.

Greenberg, D. & West, V. (2001) "State prison populations and their growth, 1971–1991." *Criminology* 39(3), 615–53.

Harrison, F. (1995). "The persistent power of race in the cultural and political economy of racism." *Annual Review of Anthropology,* 24(1), 47–74.

Johnson, J. A., Musial, D., Hall, G. E., Gollnick, D. M., & Dupuis, V. L. (2004). *Introduction to the foundations of American education.* Boston: Allyn & Bacon, Inc.

Jones, J. (1997). *Prejudice and racism,* (2nd Ed.). New York: McGraw-Hill.

Kim, E. H. (1993). "Home is where the Han is: A Korean American perspective on the Los Angeles upheavals." In Robert Gooding-Williams (Ed.), *Reading Rodney King/reading urban uprising,* (pp. 214–235). New York: Routledge.

Kitano, H. (1976). *Japanese Americans: The evolution of a subculture.* (2nd Ed.). New York: Prentice Hall.

Machery, E., & Faucher, L. (2005). "Social Construction and the Concept of Race." *Philosophy of Science,* 72(5), 1208–1219.

Macrae, C. N., Bodenhausen, G. V., Milne, A. B., & Jetten, J. (1994). "Out of mind but back in sight: Stereotypes on the rebound." *Journal of Personality and Social Psychology,* 67(5), 808–817.

Pettigrew, T. F. (1971). *Racially separate or together?* New York: McGraw-Hill.

Pettigrew, T. & Troop, L. (2000). "Does intergroup contact reduce prejudice? Recent meta-analytic findings." In S. Oskamp (Ed.), *Reducing prejudice and discrimination* (pp. 93–114). Mahwah, NJ: Erlbaum.

Shavers, V. L., Fagan, P., Jones, D., Klein, W. P., Boyington, J., Moten, C., & Rorie, E. (2012). "The state of research on racial/ethnic discrimination in the receipt of health care." *American Journal of Public Health, 102*(5), 953–966.

Steele, J., Choi, S. J. & Ambady, N. (2004). "Stereotyping, prejudice, and discrimination: The effect of group based expectations on moral functioning. In T.A. Thorkildsen, J. Manning, & H.J. Walberg (Eds.), *Children and Youth Series: Nurturing Morality*, New York: Kluwer Academic.

Stults, B., & Baumer, E. (2007, September). "Racial Context and Police Force Size: Evaluating the Empirical Validity of the Minority Threat Perspective." *American Journal of Sociology*, 113(2), 507–546.

Takaki R. (1989). *Strangers form a different shore: A history of Asian Americans*. New York: Penguin.

Taylor, H. F. (2006). "Defining race." In E. Higginbotham and M. L. Andersen (Eds.). *Race and ethnicity in U. S. Society*. Belmont: Wadsworth.

Utsey, S., Ponterotto, J., & Porter, J. (2008). "Prejudice and racism, year 2008—still going strong: Research on reducing prejudice with recommended methodological advances." *Journal of Counseling & Development*, 86(3), 339–347.

Washington, S. (2004). "Racial taxonomy." Unpublished manuscript. Department of Sociology, Princeton University, Princeton, NJ.

Waters, M. C. (1990). *Ethnic options: Choosing identities in America*. Berkeley: University of California Press.

Winnick, L. (1990). "America's model minority." *Commentary*, 90, 222-229.

SUGGESTED READING

Blodorn, A., O'Brien, L. T., & Kordys, J. (2012). "Responding to sex-based discrimination: Gender differences in perceived discrimination and implications for legal decision making." *Group Processes & Intergroup Relations, 15*(4), 409–424.

Brewer, M. (1999). "The psychology of prejudice: Ingroup love or outgroup hate?" *Journal of Social Issues*, 55(3), 429.

Brown, R. & Hewstone, M. (2005). "An integrative theory of intergroup contact." In M. P. Zanna (Ed.), *Advances in experimental social psychology* (255–343). San Diego: Elsevier Academic Press.

Duckitt, J., Wagner, C., du Plessis, I., & Birum, I. (2002). "The psychological bases of ideology and prejudice: Testing a dual process model." *Journal of Personality and Social Psychology*, 83, 75–93.

Hirschman, C., & Alba, R. (2000). "The meaning and measurement of race in the U. S. census: Glimpses into the future." *Demography*, 37(3), 381–393.

Pilkington, A. (2013). "The interacting dynamics of institutional racism in higher education." *Race, Ethnicity & Education, 16*(2), 225–245.

Roberts, D. (2007). "Constructing a criminal justice system free of racial bias: An abolitionist framework." *Columbia Human Rights Law Review*, 39(1), 261–685.

Scheepers, D., Spears, R. Doosje, B. & Manstead, A. S. R. (2006). "The social functions of ingroup bias: Creating, confirming, or changing social reality." *European Review of Social Psychology*, 17, 359–396.

Turner, J. C., Brown, R. J., & Tajfel, H. (1979). "Social comparison and group interest in ingroup favoritism." *European Journal of Social Psychology*, 9, 187–204.

Belinda Bennett McFeeters, Ph.D.

Interminority Racism

ABSTRACT

A brief description of the global city and the increasing diversity represented in these cities is followed by an example of interminority conflict. This is then followed by a discussion and definition of the concept of race and racism in the United States and how it has historically been studied. Theories of interminority racism are then discussed. The ways in which interminority conflict has been addressed and is understood are dealt with. This discussion includes how rapid demographic shifts have led to contests for political representation and how they have often led to violent conflict between minority groups. The idea of the model minority and resentment among different minority groups and how it has led to conflicts is discussed. Finally, this article deals with differing views of interminority conflict including the ideas of multiculturalism, hierarchy, and positionality.

OVERVIEW

As the world has become increasingly globalized through increased trade and migration, people from varied backgrounds are interacting with one another more and more. This is especially true in the emerging global cities where many immigrants from all around the world settle. In these cities many different racial and ethnic groups as well as native and foreign-born residents live alongside each other (Orum & Chen, 2003). As many scholars have noted, this has meant that competition for scarce resources within these cities is becoming more diversified. In the United States especially, this has meant that historically marginalized racial and ethnic groups who occupy the urban landscape are competing amongst themselves, rather than against the historically dominant white majority, for those scarce resources (Davis, 2006; McClain, 2006, Natapoff, 1995).

This competition has manifested itself in various forms. For example, there have been nationwide and localized boycotts of Korean American–owned businesses by the African American community; these boycotts were particularly prevalent in the 1990s. Further, there was an increase in violence between African Americans and Latinos in the first decade of the twenty-first century, particularly in the Los Angeles area. While violence between the two communities has been less prevalent since then, it still exists. The increased instances of conflict between these historically socially subordinate groups has led, in turn, to an increase of investigation into what is variously known as *interminority racism* or *interminority conflict*. Because of this, scholars have begun to pay more attention to this phenomenon.

Race & Racism in the United States

Although in the past many scientists attempted to define *race* as a biological category, it is now understood that race is socially constructed. Macionis (2001) explains: "a race is a socially constructed category composed of people who share biologically transmitted traits that members of a society consider important" (p. 354). So although we may consider a person to be of a particular race because they have certain physical traits, these traits are not inherently a part of some biological schema of race. Instead, racial traits are dependent upon the society in which a person lives. For example, in the United States, for a long time a person was defined as black if they had "one drop" of African ancestry. This is what is known as the "one drop rule." Some states also defined black as having one-eighth African ancestry. Today, in the United States, it is generally accepted that a person's race is defined by the racial community he or she identifies with. This means that racial constructions are fluid and are differently understood by different societies.

In the United States, racial and ethnic conflict has generally been viewed in terms of white racism toward African Americans and other people of color. This is because historically white Anglo society has dominated and marginalized other non-white groups, especially African Americans. *Racism* is best understood as a relationship between races, and refers to the ways in which one racial group gains social, economic, and/or political advantage in society. Racism can be overt violence against one racial group by another or it can be more subtle, as in the way that job promotions are awarded because a person shares the same race as the boss and is therefore viewed more positively. The term *minority* refers to social groups "who have unequal access to positions of power, prestige, and wealth in a society" (Knox, Mooney & Schacht, 2002, p. 156). The term does not specifically have to refer to a numerical minority, but instead only to a group that lacks equal access to social resources. *Ethnicity,* unlike race, is not characterized by phonotypical traits but rather is defined by a group's shared sense of culture and history. For example, white Americans in the United States are considered to be a race, but within that race there are many different and distinct ethnicities. Someone may consider themselves to be racially white, but ethnically Irish American, for example.

FURTHER INSIGHTS

Interminority Conflict Theory

Theories regarding interminority conflict generally view this conflict as a competition for resources. These include theories about *in-group/ out-group* conflict. This theory claims that groups, in this case racial/ethnic groups, see themselves as competing for scarce resources against other groups. Racial conflict is also seen as a result of proximity. Here, the theory is that groups who perceive themselves as in competition with one another for resources are more likely to perceive the other groups negatively and conflict may occur between them (Morris, 2000, pp. 80–81). Conflict, then, is a result of either real or perceived threats to a group's sense of security. In the case of interminority conflict this can be a result of contests for political power through *demographic shifts* or perceived *power differentials* in economic and social status. These conflicts will be more likely to occur, according to this theory, if groups are in closer proximity to one another.

Changing Demographics

The passage of the 1965 immigration bill, which led to a sharp increase of immigrants from Latin America and Asia, has been seen as one of the reasons for rising tensions in US cities between minority groups (Davis 2007; Kim, 2004). Kim (2004) states "the post 1965 demographic revolution generates increasingly complex racial antagonisms among historically subordinated groups..." (p. 997). Davis (2007) likewise, points out that "in 1965 the Voting Rights Act and the Immigration and Nationality Act were passed, creating at the same time a sharp increase in Black voter registration and the largest Korean community in the United States" (p. 219). These conditions of increasing African American political power and rapid demographic shifts, both through increased immigration and *white flight* from US cities, have created situations in which minority groups have increasingly come into conflict with one another. Indeed, it has been noted that many US cities are either majority-minority or will be soon if trends continue.

These changing demographics have led to changing political and economic power in cities, which at times has also led to violence. Many historically African American neighborhoods have seen dramatic changes because of this. For example, Davis (2007) points out that in the Los Angeles Unified School District (LAUSD) from 1992 to 2006 the percentage of African American students dropped from 14.6% to 11.7%, while at the same time the Latino population increased from 65% to 73.3% (p. 222). Davis quotes a *Los Angeles Times* article that highlights the increasing conflict between Los Angeles' minority populations:

> The acrimonious relationship between Latinos and African Americans in Los Angeles is growing hard to ignore...just last August, federal prosecutors convicted Latino gang members of engaging in a six-year conspiracy to assault and murder African Americans in Highland Park. During the trial, prosecutors demonstrated that African American residents (with no gang ties at all) were being terrorized in an effort to force them out of a neighborhood now perceived as Latino (Maddox, 2007 as cited in Davis, 2007, p. 223).

Political Factors

Beyond the violence that is associated with these shifts there are political factors as well. The political importance of these demographic shifts is discussed by Natapoff (1995). In her discussion of how the Supreme Court has dealt with racial politics she highlights several cases that dealt with racial politics.

Historically fights over racial politics and political districts have been very contentious. In many cases political districts were either drawn or redrawn to limit minority groups' political power. This was done by carving up minority neighborhoods into many different districts so that a minority group could never gain a majority in a district and subsequently elect someone to represent their interests. This practice is known as *gerrymandering.* In the cases Natapoff discusses she points out that the court has not dealt well with race and ethnicity as constructs. She states that the court has either dealt with race as a black and white issue or has dealt with it in a *multiculturalist* and *pluralist* way in which white people are treated as just another racial/ethnic group competing equally among others. This, she argues, leads to decisions that lack a consideration of the dynamics of race in the United States. These decisions fail to acknowledge that in the US, white Americans have historically been the dominant group, which should be considered, but also that different minority groups have their own unique and distinct interests. In one redistricting case, she explains that the court failed to recognize that the scheme for redistricting did not deal well with interminority conflict because it lumped the Puerto Rican community into a district with the African American community of New York. She argues that in this case, the court failed to see that each community has its own interests that while distinct from white interests, are also distinct from one another's. Thus, because of the way politics functions in the US, minority interests are closely related to demographics. As these demographic shifts continue, scholars argue there is likely to be more interminority conflict (Davis, 2007; Mclain, 2006; Natapoff, 1995).

Economic & Social Power Shifts: The African American & Korean American Communities

It has also been noted that beyond the sheer numbers of demographics there have also been differentials in economic and social power that have created conflicts. Instances in which this has become most acute include fights over Korean American–owned businesses in African American neighborhoods (Davis, 2007; Joyce, 2003; Kim, 2004; McClain, 2006; Morris, 2002).

In the 1980s and 1990s there were a series of boycotts of Korean American–owned businesses led by the African American community. The boycotts were precipitated themselves by various events but often became linked to African American unity and nationalism (Joyce, 2003). Davis (2007) describes one situation in Los Angeles in which a young African American girl was shot by a Korean American shop owner over an argument in which the shop owner accused the girl of trying to steal something from the store. She also points out that beyond this incident, many in the African American community in Los Angeles thought that they were treated unfairly in Korean American–owned businesses. She explains that most of the Korean American shopkeepers who did business in African American neighborhoods did not live in those neighborhoods (p. 221). These facts led to a feeling among African American community leaders and activists that this was robbing the African American community of their own economic livelihood and well-being. Joyce (2003) describes it this way:

> ... a common thread ran through nearly all the boycotts: protesters made demands that went beyond initial provocations, explicitly linking their actions to the impact of stores on the surrounding community. Boycott leaders almost always claimed that they were defending the economic self-sufficiency of black neighborhoods or the dignity of black residents, twin themes in ideologies of black nationalism (p. 221).

The African American community, then, came to view all of these boycotts together and framed the existence of so many Korean American–owned businesses in African American neighborhoods as an affront to the entire community. In 1992 simmering tensions between the African American and Korean American communities exploded during the Los Angeles riots. During these riots, which were sparked by the acquittal of four Los Angeles Police Department officers who were videotaped beating an African American man, African American and Latino residents burned and looted many Korean-owned businesses. Many commentators saw this as an inevitable outcome of the interminority tension that had been building (Davis, 2007; Joyce, 2003).

Further fueling the fire of conflict between the African American and Korean American communities is the idea of the *model minority* myth. Model minority refers to the idea that some minorities are more successful or more deserving than others because they posses characteristics that have enabled them to succeed financially or socially and integrate into mainstream society. In the United States Asian Americans are often held up as model minorities because they have gained more financial and educational success on average than other minority groups. Rim (2007) quotes a 1966 *US News and World Report* article that highlights the idea of the model minority well. It states: "At a time when it is being proposed that hundreds of billions be spent to uplift Negroes and other minorities, the Nation's 300,000 Chinese Americans are moving ahead on their own, with no help from anyone" (as cited in Rim, 2007, p. 40). Although she points out that the model minority is a myth, it is often used to divide minorities into competing camps. It also serves to create resentments between different minority groups because it implies that other minorities just are not working hard enough to get ahead or are even deficient in some way.

A further illustration of interminority animosity can be seen in the way in which different minority groups have gained political access and power. For example, following the civil rights movement African Americans were very organized politically and have been perceived by other minority groups as having gained more access to formal political channels than others. Kim (2004) explains that although African Americans may see themselves at the bottom of a perceived *racial hierarchy*, other minorities do not necessarily see it the same way. The author states, "There is a sense among some Asian Americans and Latinos that all minorities are comparably oppressed and/or that blacks not only dominate civil rights circles and electoral politics but also act (inappropriately) as gatekeepers in these arenas" (p. 999). Within different minority groups, then, there are differing opinions about levels of oppression and about which group is more or less deserving of social and/or political benefits.

Viewpoints & Discussion

Although there has seemingly been much evidence of interminority conflict, from riots and protests to interethnic killings and beatings, such conflict is not necessarily inevitable. Many scholars have argued that although it does seem like there has been ever-increasing conflict among growing minority populations, there are some studies that conclude that this conflict has not been occurring to the degree that it may seem. Others claim that evidence of it is not that strong. Some argue that the conflict that has been occurring may not be inherently bad. For example, conflict theorists see conflict as an inherent part of any unjust society. Joyce (2003) sees conflict as normal and instead examines the political structures and opportunities that have allowed for certain types of conflict to emerge in some cities while being discouraged in others. In New York, for example, old-style machine politics allowed for nonviolent African American mobilization whereas in Los Angeles, the reform-style government led to more violent outbursts such as the 1992 riot.

Morris (2000) examines interminority conflict as it played out in voting patterns regarding California's Proposition 187, to bar undocumented workers from receiving state services except in cases of emergencies. The rhetoric surrounding the proposition was highly racialized and Morris saw it as an opportunity to examine how different ethnic groups voted on the proposition and, in turn, interminority conflict. The author found no evidence within this context that African Americans, and especially poor African Americans, would be more likely to vote for the proposition. Thus, he argues that theories of interminority conflict are not necessarily accurate in every situation.

Dissecting the Term

Another critique of interminority racism is that the term itself is misleading because it masks power in society. Because racism is usually understood to be a term that refers to the domination of one race over another, it may not be accurate to describe interminority discrimination or prejudice as racism. This is because it is not clear which group would be the group in power in interminority racism. Not only does it hide power relations, but it also tends to *reify* social difference. The theories of competing group interests do not take into account to a great degree that these differences are constructed and can be reconstructed accordingly. Kim (2004) addresses the idea of interminority conflict and its relation to official multiculturalist discourse. The author argues that instead of dealing with the diverse experiences of minorities in the US and striving to solve social conflict that arises from these vast experiences, official multiculturalist discourse (that is, the discourse of multiculturalism that emanates from the government and other powerful institutions) creates a triumphalist narrative. In this narrative the power differences between racial and ethnic groups are flattened, claiming instead that the United States is a uniquely multiculturalist and pluralist society where diversity creates a stronger nation. Kim argues that instead of this flat multiculturalist discourse, which hides power relations, a counter-narrative of racial *positionality* should be created. This positionality discourse would position racial and ethnic groups in context to one another. Instead of viewing racial difference as without power differences or in a simple hierarchy, it would position them in relation to their differing experiences. Kim argues that racial positionality:

...will be a less politically divisive concept than that of racial hierarchy. Rather than arguing about which group occupies which rung of a rigid vertical ladder, communities of colour can proclaim the specificity of their respective experiences, acknowledge complex relationality, and focus on how they would all benefit from dismantling the structure of racial difference (2004, p. 1000).

So, rather than minority groups seeing themselves as in competition with one another, instead they would see their mutual benefit from creating new structures entirely.

CONCLUSION

As scholars have noted and as many have probably noticed, the world in which we live is becoming increasingly interconnected. This interconnectivity has lead to rapid changes in the way people live and where they live. Increasingly our cities are becoming microcosms of the world, where people from many different nationalities, ethnicities, and races live side by side. In many cases these groups have entirely different views, not only about race, but also about politics and conflict. As our cities become more diverse it will be increasingly important to understand, not only historic relations between white Americans and African Americans, but also just as importantly, the multiplicity of different experiences of many different races and ethnicities. A whole new set of racial understandings is necessary to understand racial conflict. Rather than viewing racial conflict as a dichotomous relationship between black and white, interminority conflict can be understood as a part of an emerging diversity. Some scholars have argued that interminority conflict is caused by minority groups that have traditionally lacked equal access to resources competing for scarce resources. Others have argued that racial constructs themselves create these strains. Whatever the case, it is clear that at times the tension that exists between different racial and ethnic groups explodes to the surface in often violent ways. Only by understanding these conflicts can we hope to avoid the violence that often results.

TERMS & CONCEPTS

Ethnicity: A group's shared sense of history and culture.

Gerrymandering: Refers to the odd-shaped political districts that were drawn so that minority groups' political power was diminished by spreading their numbers into several white-dominated districts.

Minority: Refers to a group that lacks full access to social, political, and economic resources of any given society. This does not mean that a group must be a numerical minority.

Model Minority: Label given especially to Asian Americans in the United States. This label implies that they are more hardworking and fit in better to mainstream society than other minorities.

Multiculturalism: A view of society as made up of many different races, ethnicities, and cultures, which all participate peacefully and equally in society.

Race: A social construction based on phonotypical traits that society has deemed important.

Racism: The practice or belief in elevating one race over others either socially, economically, or politically.

Redistricting: When politicians or courts redraw political boundaries for election purposes.

White Flight: Refers to the rapid migration of white Americans out of the inner cities and into the suburbs.

Bibliography

Alexander, B. K. (2012). T*he performative sustainability of race: Reflections on black culture and the politics of identity*. New York: Peter Lang.

Davis, D. M. (2007). The Los Angeles riots revisited: The changing face of the Los Angeles Unified

School District and the challenge for educators. *Educational Studies. 42* (3), 213–22.

Jones, J. A. (2012). Blacks may be second class, but they can't make them leave: Mexican racial formation and immigrant status in Winston-Salem. *Latino Studies, 10* (1-2), 60–80.

Joyce, P. D. (2003). *No fire next time: Black-Korean conflicts and the future of America's cities.* Ithaca: Cornell University Press.

Kim, C. J. (2004). Imagining race and nation in multiculturalist America. *Ethnic & Racial Studies, 27* (6), 987–1005.

Knox, D., Mooney & L. A. & Schacht, C. (2002). *Understanding social problems* (8th ed). Stamford, CT: Wadsworth.

Macionis, J. J. (2001). *Sociology* (8th ed). Upper Saddle River, New Jersey: Prentice Hall.

Markert, J. (2010). "The changing face of racial discrimination: Hispanics as the dominant minority in the USA – a new application of power-threat theory." *Critical Sociology, 36* (2), 307–327.

McClain, P. D. (2006). Presidential Address. Racial intergroup relations in a set of cities: A twenty-year perspective. *Journal of Politics, 68* (4), 757–770.

Morris, I. L. (2000). "African American voting on Proposition 187: Rethinking the prevalence of interminority conflict." *Political Research Quarterly, 53* (1), 77–98.

Natapoff, A. (1995). "Trouble in paradise: Equal protection and the dilemma of interminority group conflict." *Stanford Law Review, 47* (5), 1059–1096.

Orum, A. M. & Chen, X. (2003). *The world of cities: Places in comparative and historical perspective.* Malden, Massachusetts: Blackwell Publishing.

Rim, K. H. (2007). "Model, victim, or problem minority? Examining the socially constructed identities of Asian-origin ethnic groups in California's media." *Asian American Policy Review, 16,* p37–60.

Thornton, M. (2011). "Meaningful dialogue? The *Los Angeles Sentinel*'s depiction of black and Asian American relations, 1993–2000." *Journal of Black Studies,* 42 (8), 1275–1298.

SUGGESTED READING

Brueggemann, J. (2012). *Inequality in the United States.* Boston, MA: Allyn & Bacon.

Chew, C. M. (2008). "Deconstructing the politics of race." *Diverse: Issues in Higher Education, 25* (5), 9.

Kim, D. H., Lee, E. S., Mendieta, E., Perina, M., & Sheth, F. A. (2012). "An unruly theory of race." *Hypatia, 27* (4), 898–921.

McClain P. D. & Stewart Jr, J. (1999). *Can we all get along? Racial and ethnic minorities in American politics.* Boulder, CO: Westview Press.

Omi, M. & Winant, H. (1994). *Racial formation in the United States form the 1960s to the 1990s.* New York: Routledge.

Sheth, F. A. (2009). *Toward a political philosophy of race.* Albany, NY: SUNY Press.

Wells, A. S. & Frankenberg, E. (2008). "The public schools and the challenge of the Supreme Court's integration decision." *Education Digest, 73* (8), 4–13.

Jonathan Christiansen, M.A.

Intersectionality

ABSTRACT

Intersectionality, one of the foundational concepts within the social sciences, complicates traditional approaches toward the study of race, gender, class, and sexuality by treating these factors as interconnected variables that shape an individual's overall life experiences, rather than as isolated variables. Power, privilege, and oppression are often much more complex than has been traditionally thought, as an individual may be relatively privileged in one or more aspects of their life, while simultaneously experiencing prejudice, discrimination, or oppression stemming from other aspects of their social background or identity. Intersectionality seeks to explain how these different variables come together to shape experience, identity, and society.

OVERVIEW

Intersectionality is one of the most important concepts in sociology, cultural anthropology, psychology, and other social sciences pertaining to the study of social inequalities and the nature of life experiences among members of a particular society. Race, ethnicity, social class, and religion have been central topics of study within sociology and anthropology since the late nineteenth and early twentieth centuries, and gender and sexual orientation have become a major focus of social science research since the late 1960s. Historically, however, these various markers of identity were treated by researchers and social theorists as isolated variables, without consideration as to how these different factors interact (or intersect) with one another in shaping an individual's overall life experiences and circumstances. Prior to the mid-to-late 1970s, much scholarship within the social sciences spoke of various social groups (for example, African Americans, women, the working class, or LGBT people) as undifferentiated, monolithic entities. In other words, up until the 1970s, most social scientists categorized and identified individuals according to what they believed was their master status—that is, the marker of identity that was assumed to be the most important or fundamental in a person's life. This simplistic categorization then served as the basis for conducting research and speaking about various groups within American society.

Sociologists, anthropologists, and other scholars, however, have recognized the inherent flaws in such an approach; principally, the focus on assumed master statuses leads researchers to ignore important markers of variation within a racial, religious, gender, or sexual orientation group, thus providing a very limited understanding of the complexities and intricacies of social life within the United States or elsewhere. For example, consider the hypothetical example of three African American individuals. In the early years of the social sciences, the common approach would be to think of these three individuals as sharing a common identity, a common culture (stemming from their common racial and ethnic heritage, which would be assumed to be their common master status), and a common set of social experiences. Yet such a limited view obscures other possible important variables of difference. Suppose that these three individuals each was of a different religious heritage-such as a Roman Catholic, a Baptist, and a Muslim. These religious distinctions would consequently result in different social identities and distinct cultural experiences for these three individuals, despite their common ethnic background. These social differences would be further complicated if we also took the individuals' gender, social class, age, and other factors into consideration.

FURTHER INSIGHTS

Although intersectionality has become a central principle in contemporary social science disciplines, it is oftentimes still overlooked or ignored in public conversations and media discourses about particular groups of people. The media still commonly speaks of individuals and groups in terms of master statuses, choosing to emphasize certain markers of identity while ignoring others. A prominent example of this occurred during the 2008 presidential campaign, which featured Arizona senator John McCain (a white male), Illinois senator Barack Obama (a biracial male of white and black parentage, but simply considered "black" under the "one-drop rule" of racial classification in the United States), New York senator Hillary Rodham Clinton (a white female), and Alaska governor Sarah Palin (also a white female). As sociologists Patricia Hill Collins and Margaret

Andersen have pointed out, media coverage of these candidates identified and spoke of each candidate in terms of their master status. The media referred to Obama as the black or African American candidate, while Clinton and Palin were identified as the female candidates. The implication of such discourses was that Obama's race was visible, but not his gender, while the reverse was true for Clinton and Palin-their gender was visible, but not their race. On the other hand, the media did not highlight McCain's race or gender; if any attention was paid to McCain's identity, it was focused on his age (71 years old throughout most of the campaign).

Intersectionality is an important concept within the social sciences precisely because it challenges traditional, often takenfor- granted assumptions about privilege and oppression in American society. While it is true that, in the aggregate, African Americans and Latinos experience more societal discrimination and inequalities than white Americans, such a generalized statement overlooks the wide range of lived experience and social realities that structure the daily lives of millions of individuals within these broadly defined racial and ethnic categories. Working class, lower income, and impoverished whites have a vastly different set of social experiences in the United States than do middle- and upper-class whites, and economically disadvantaged whites do not experience the same degree of "white privilege" as more affluent whites, though this marker is often portrayed, uncritically, by the media as the experience shared by whites as a whole in American society. An upwardly mobile African American female who has earned a Master's Degree or a PhD and works as tenured college administrator or professor is obviously more socially privileged than a homeless white male, despite the fact that the former will likely encounter racism and/or sexism throughout her life. By the same token, middle-class African Americans who were born and raised in a suburban environment have a vastly different social reality and set of life experiences than do African Americans who were born and raised within a lower income, inner-city neighborhood.

Aside from experiences of privilege and oppression, intersectionality also highlights cultural variation within socially defined groups. Since the publication of Edward Burnett Tylor's *Anthropology* (1881), culture has been defined as "the complex whole, which includes knowledge, beliefs, arts, laws, morals, customs, habits, and any other capabilities that an individual acquires as a member of his or her society." Culture is thus a worldview, a way in which an individual comes to understand the world, as well as their place within it; culture therefore enables individuals to make sense of their social realities. Historically, anthropologists, psychologists, and sociologists perceived culture as a monolithic entity that unified an entire nation or ethnic group and was shared equally and uniformly by the members of that group. This notion grew out of British structural-functionalist theorists, who emphasized social cohesion and unity within societies, and American "culture and personality" theorists, who sought to identify and describe the basic personality type among citizens of particular nations, from the 1920s through the 1940s. This logic, now understood to be excessively rigid and overly deterministic, was popularized by high-profile American anthropologists Ruth Benedict and Margaret Mead and was based on the simple, linear notion that an individual's national heritage or ethnic background determined their culture, which in turn shaped their personality type.

Psychological research has indicated that personality types differ among members of individual families, let alone entire ethnic groups or nations. Since the 1970s, social scientists, particularly cultural anthropologists, have shifted away from viewing "culture" as a static, timeless, and homogeneous feature of a racial, ethnic, or national group in favor of a much more modified and nuanced view of culture. This new understanding of culture recognizes that culture is highly fluid and dynamic (in other words, something that is subject to change over time). This new understanding of culture also recognizes that people are producers of culture through agency (that is, the actions that people take- both as individuals and as collective members of groups-to influence and change their lives and the society around them); this contrasts sharply with the older notion of culture that ignored agency altogether and viewed individuals as simply the products of culture. The basic view in cultural anthropology and other social sciences today is that socialization (the process by which a person acquires his or her cultural background) is an ongoing, lifelong process-not simply a phenomenon that occurs in childhood and then abruptly stops-and that people use agency to actively produce cultural change. Culture is contested and negotiated, rather than static, because different individuals and groups are positioned differently within society and therefore have different views as to what is considered most desirable for their society.

Another hallmark of contemporary understandings of human culture is that a tremendous amount of cultural variation also exists within socially defined groups, as opposed to traditional notions of culture that only understood cultural differences as existing between groups. For example, a Latino senior citizen and a Latino teenager will, in some important respects, have more commonalities with white and African American senior citizens and teenagers, respectively, than they will with one another, given their age/generational differences. Latinos are also highly culturally diverse among themselves in many other respects, in terms of specific ethnic-national heritage (Mexican, Puerto Rican, Cuban, etc.), citizenship or immigration status (U.S.-born citizen or immigrant), linguistic orientation (monolingual English speaker, monolingual Spanish speaker, or bilingual), social class, sexual orientation, region or geographic locale, religion, and other important variables. These variables shape an individual's overall culture, and these variables exist within all racial and ethnic groups.

Intersectionality thus has lead social scientists to understand oppression and culture in very different manners than was common in the early years of many academic disciplines. As such scholars no longer treat race, ethnicity, gender, social class, and sexual orientation as separate and isolated variables, but rather as an interconnected web that shapes cultural background and experiences with social privilege and/or oppression.

Discourse

Although intersectionality is a relatively new term within the social sciences, the concept that different factors or variables interact in shaping one's life experiences dates back much earlier. The German sociologist Max Weber, one of the pioneering figures of modern sociology in the early twentieth century, noted that social class was a much more complicated phenomenon than had traditionally been thought. According to Weber, social class consisted of three distinct, but interrelated elements-wealth prestige, and power. Whereas wealth refers to the amount of financial assets one possesses, prestige refers to the degree of social respect and admiration that one accrues from their society on the basis of their social standing. Power refers to one's ability to have their social, political, or financial interests promoted and defended within their society. While these three elements are interrelated in shaping one's social class background, they do not necessarily go hand in hand. For example, an experienced long-haul truck driver working for a unionized company may, in fact, earn higher wages than a college professor. However, the latter career has traditionally carried more social prestige than the former-particularly since professors have often come from middle- and upper-middle class family backgrounds (especially in past generations), while truck drivers often come from working class backgrounds.

Black legal theorist Kimberlé Williams Crenshaw, who would go on to become a professor of law at the University of California, Los Angeles, coined the term "intersectionality" in a famous 1989 essay titled "Demarginalizing the Intersection of Race and Sex: A Black Feminist Critique of Antidiscrimination Doctrine, Feminist Theory and Antiracist Politics." Focusing on the experiences of black women in American society, Crenshaw pointed out that the unique lived experiences of this group had largely been marginalized and overlooked by scholars, since studies of feminism had tended to center on white women, while studies of racism centered largely on the experiences of black men. While being both female and black, the experiences of black women differ in important respects from others who share their sex or race.

Crenshaw argues that the prejudice and discrimination that black women experience in American society is not always easily and clearly identifiable as strictly an act of racism or sexism but, instead, could be a complex combination of both. Although Crenshaw was the first to use the term "intersectionality," criticisms of the mainstream feminist movement as reflecting the ideals, interests, and agenda of middle-class, heterosexual, white women were first raised as early as the 1970s by black, Chicana, and lesbian feminists who felt excluded from the women's movement in the United States. Women from such historically marginalized backgrounds raised objections that feminist activism essentialized (assuming homogeneity within a group) males and females while ignoring important social differences among males and among females-such as race, social class, religion, age, and so on. Growing attention to these matters led to the rise of Third Wave feminism in the 1980s and 1990s, which asserted the viewpoints that neither women nor men were homogeneous groups, and that experiences of femininity and masculinity co-exist alongside one another within society (based on the intersection of gender with other variables of identity, such as race and class). This produces a range of gendered experiences, just as there are a wide range of African American experiences, white experiences, and gay and lesbian experiences.

Sociologists Maxine Baca Zinn, Pierrette Hondagneau-Sotelo, and Michael Messner term this novel approach towards understanding the complexities of gender, race, class, and sexuality as the "prism of difference." Zinn, Hondagnaeu-Sotelo, and Messner contend, "Gender is no longer viewed simply as a matter of two opposing categories of people, male and female, but as a range of social relations among differently situated people." Different forms of masculinity and femininity are interconnected with other variables, such as race, ethnicity, class, sexuality, nationality, age, etc. This reality accounts for "multiple masculinities" and "multiple femininities." A middleage, middle-class, white, heterosexual female living as a single mother in suburban Long Island has a very different set of life experiences than a twenty-five year-old working-class lesbian Mexican immigrant female living in an inner-city Los Angeles neighborhood. By the same token, President Barack Obama and former Secretary of State Colin Powell articulate different versions of black masculinity than hip hop producer Sean "Puffy" Combs or rapper 50 Cent, despite all four men being black males in the United States.

These arguments notwithstanding, several cultural anthropologists have criticized multicultural programming and cultural diversity training, which have become quite common in schools and on college campuses, as well as part of employee orientations at many companies nationwide, for often neglecting intersectionality and instead presenting simplistic, essentialized depictions of various racial and ethnic groups. Judith Goode, a former professor of anthropology at Temple University, has been an outspoken critic of multiculturalism and cultural diversity programs for reinforcing the public's notion that each racial or ethnic group can be characterized by a singular, distinct culture and personality type. According to Goode, this approach inadvertently ends up promoting stereotypes of racial and ethnic groups. A much more accurate approach, according to anthropologists, would be to educate the public that a considerable degree of cultural variation also exists within groups-rather than simply focusing on cultural differences assumed to exist between groups.

TERMS & CONCEPTS

Culture: Broadly defined, the total accumulation of knowledge, beliefs, values, and information that an individual acquires as part of their life experiences

Discourse: The nature of a conversation about a particular subject; the way in which people commonly talk about, define, or label a particular social topic such as race, gender, sexuality orientation, or social class.

Essentialism: The simplistic assumption of homogeneity within a specific group of people

Ethnicity: A social identity based on a sense of common, shared ancestry with others-usually (but not always) connecting to an ancestral country of origin or common cultural characteristics (such as a linguistic or religious heritage)

Gender: The socially constructed differences between males and females within a society, consisting of the culturally defined roles and identities associated with each sex

Intersectionality: The complex ways in which social variables, such as race, ethnicity, gender, sexual orientation, social class, and other factors combine to shape a person's overall life experiences-particularly with respect to the prejudice and discrimination that one may face within society

Master status: The marker of identity that is usually assumed (perhaps incorrectly) by society to be the most important variable in a person's life; the variable that is assumed to be the core of one's identity

Race: A socially constructed category of classifying members of a society on the basis of a few arbitrarily selected physical or biological traits, such as skin color or eye shape

Sex: The biological distinction between male and female, based on chromosomal differences (XY for males; XY for males)

Social class: A segment of society characterized as having a relatively common economic and educational background, which is seen as a basis for similar social outlook and experiences that distinguish it from other classes. In the United States, social classes have traditionally been defined as upper class, middle class, working class, and impoverished.

Third Wave feminism: An approach toward feminist theory that emerged in the 1980s and 1990s that argued that neither males nor females were homogeneous and promoted taking intersectionality into account in studies of gender

Bibliography

Andersen, M. L., & Hill Collins, P. (2013). *Race, class, & gender: An anthology,* 8th edition. Belmont, CA: Wadsworth.

Corus, C., et al. (2016). "Transforming poverty-related policy with intersectionality." *Journal of Public Policy and Marketing, 35*(2), 211–222.

Garcia, J. D. (2013). "'You don't look Mexican!': My life in ethnic ambiguity and what is says about the construction of race in America." *In Multicultural Perspectives, 15,* 2013: 234–238.

Goode, J. (2001). "Teaching against culturalist essentialism." In *Cultural diversity in the United States.* Ida Susser and Thomas C. Patterson (Eds.). Maiden, MA: Blackwell Publishers, pp. 434–456.

Hancock, A.-M. (2013). *Solidarity politics for millenials: A guide to ending the oppression Olympics.* New York, NY: Palgrave Macmillan.

Mitchell, D. (2014). *Intersectionality & higher education: Theory, research, & praxis.* New York, NY: Peter Lang.

Smith, S. (2012). "Black feminism and intersectionality." *International Socialist Review,* 91.

Williams, P. (2014). "Life is complicated, and other observations." In *Intersectionality: A foundations and frontiers reader.* Patrick R. Grzanka (Ed.). Boulder, CO: Westview Press.

Zinn, M. B., Hondagneau-Sotelo, P., & Messner, M. (2010). *Gender through the prism of difference,* 4th ed. New York, NY: Oxford University Press.

Suggested Reading

Delgado, R., & Stefancic, J. (2012). *Critical race theory: An introduction,* 2nd ed. New York, NY: New York University Press.

Garcia, L. (2012). *Respect yourself, protect yourself: Latina girls and sexual identity.* New York, NY: New York University Press.

Garcia, L. (2016). Intersectionality. *Kalfou, 3*(1), 102–106.

Kimmel, M. S., & Ferber, A. (2013). *Privilege: A reader,* 3rd ed. Boulder, CO: Westview Press.

Lykke, N. (2012). *Feminist studies: A guide to intersectional theory, methodology, and writing.* New York, NY: Routledge.

Ore, T. E. (2013). *The social construction of difference and inequality: Race, class, gender, and sexuality,* 6th ed. New York, NY: McGraw-Hill.

Samuels, D. (2014). *The culturally inclusive educator: Preparing for a multicultural world.* New York, NY: Teachers College Press.

Justin D. García, Ph.D.

Prejudice Theory: Bogardus & the Social Distance Scale

ABSTRACT

The following article provides a summary of the work of sociologist Emory Bogardus, focusing on his contributions to the study of race relations and racial prejudice. Although Bogardus made many contributions to the field in general—he began an academic journal and a student honor society, for example—he is best known for the development of the social distance scale. The social and historical origins of the scale, its technical development, and its application to the study of early twentieth-century race relations are discussed. Recent research using the scale is also introduced, as are some of the philosophical and methodological critiques.

OVERVIEW

Emory Bogardus's contribution to sociology was immense. In 1911, after graduating with his doctorate from the University of Chicago, Bogardus accepted a teaching position at the University of Southern California. Just four years later, he was asked to found and chair the department of sociology. He continued to lead the department for over thirty years and served as a full-time faculty member for forty-two years. But Bogardus was a leader outside USC as well; in 1916, he created and became editor of the second sociological journal, Sociological Monographs, which today is known as the Journal of Applied Sociology. He founded Alpha Kappa Delta, a sociological honor society whose aim was to identify undergraduate and graduate students who demonstrated promise in the social sciences (Bogardus, 1956). None of these achievements, however, brought him as much notoriety as his contribution to the study of race relations. It was his interest in the relationship between social groups, particularly social groups of different ethnic and language origins, and his accompanying development of the social distance scale for which he became well-known.

Bogardus first developed the social distance scale in 1925 as part of a larger cooperative study of race relations, led by colleague Robert Park. The impact of the scale was due in part to the fact that Bogardus continued to use it beyond its original intent. With the help of over 25 professors at various universities across the country, Bogardus administered the scale every ten years, from 1926 to 1966, making it one of the first longitudinal studies of "America's experience with diversity and difference" (Wark & Galliher, 2007). In addition, Bogardus's social distance scale was one of the first scales developed to measure attitudes. Campbell (1952) writes, "Only the Harper test of liberalism-conservatism is older among attitude tests that have been used beyond the research in which they were originally presented" (as cited in Wark & Galliher, 2007, p. 391). Bogardus (1947) described competing measurements this way: "Many so-called attitude tests are not much more than personal opinion tests. But [social distance] measures something more deep-seated than a person's opinions—if not his attitudes then something very similar to attitudes" (p. 309). The social distance scale continues to be used today in a variety of academic disciplines, including education, psychology, political science, and sociology, and with a variety of different social groups, such as individuals with disabilities, occupational groups, religious sects, and ethnic groups. As Wark and Galliher (2007) conclude, "the Social Distance Scale has...had a profound influence on the landscape of American sociology" (p. 393).

Development of the Social Distance Scale

Before taking a closer look at the scale itself, it might be worthwhile to pause and investigate the contexts—both Bogardus's personal experiences as well as the broader academic and cultural landscape—in which the scale was developed. Wark and Galliher (2007) attempt to show, for example, that "the invention of the Bogardus Social Distance Scale was the result of a unique convergence of biographical and historical circumstances" (p. 393). First and foremost, around the same time Bogardus was being educated and starting to teach, America was beginning to pay more attention to race relations. African Americans were migrating north in larger numbers, and while they did not face the same legal barriers there as in the South, they were not treated on equal terms with whites either. In addition, a second wave of immigrants flooded the country, and unlike their predecessors, they were largely non-Protestant and/or Asian. In 1913, for example, just after Bogardus joined USC, California passed a law prohibiting Chinese and Japanese people from land ownership. In his own words, Bogardus (1931) explains, "There was not much cooperative research in the social-science fields on the Pacific Coast before 1923. In that year, however, culture conflicts between Orientals and Americans reached a climax of intensity up and down the Coast. It was this conflict that gave the setting for an extensive piece of [cooperative race-relations research]" (p. 563).

America's increasing interest in race was also shared by academics. Prior to this time, scholars paid the subject little attention; if race was studied, it was typically in an attempt to validate the different mental abilities of people of varying ethnic backgrounds. Indeed, "at the beginning of the 20th century the flagship journal of the profession was the American Journal of Sociology. It published only one article per year on [race] issues. For this generation of sociologists, racial conflict was considered inevitable" (Wark & Galliher, 2007, p. 386). At the University of Chicago, where Bogardus earned his doctorate, scholars began questioning the idea that mental abilities varied by race and started studying attitudes and prejudicestoward racial and ethnic groups instead. Written evidence of Bogardus's personal interest in race relations can be found in his 1922 publication A History of SocialThought, predating the development of the scale. He identified race relations as one of the major social problems confronting Americans (Wark & Galliher, 2007). Bogardus's interest in race, however, was not purely academic. He was motivated to use his knowledge to improve social conditions for all Americans.

Bogardus's interest in social reform fit well with the prevailing mindset of early 20th-century sociologists. The discipline's interest in reform, however, came at the expense of its academic reputation. Specifically, sociology was viewed as unscientific and subjective (Wark & Galliher, 2007). As Bogardus entered the profession, it was making a concerted effort to reshape itself into a social science, with a focus on objectivity and research. As Bannister (1987) writes, Bogardus'ssocial distance scale was one manifestation of the "1920s craze for measurement" (as cited in Wark & Galliher, 2007, p. 388).

The Social Distance Scale

Specifically, the early twentieth-century relations between the immigrant Japanese and West Coast Caucasian Americans set the stage for the development of the social distance scale. Bogardus (1931) explains, "While a number of Americans were openly expressing prejudice against the Orientals, there were other Americans who felt that the Japanese were being unjustifiably insulted. [The latter] urged that an investigation of the problem be made, feeling that a scientific inquiry would undermine much of the unfair tactics of those opposed to the Japanese" (p. 563). The Institute of Social and Religious Research in New York City hired Dr. Robert Park of the University of Chicago to head the study; he in turn hired Bogardus for the specific purpose of developing a quantitative measure of racial attitudes. Bogardus explained that they used the generic title "race relations survey," with specific inclusion of the term "survey," for conventional reasons and to present a face of objectivity and scientific methodology. More surreptitiously, he had "undertaken the tabooed procedure of penetrating hidden subjective fields of experience and their resultant attitudes...and attempted to make those attitudes ... measurable" (p. 567).

Thus, it was important to Bogardus to make a distinction between "thinking" and "feeling" and to keep the goal of "attitude measurement" in the forefront of his mind as he developed the social distance scale (Bogardus, 1947). Social distance, he argued, focuses on the feeling reactions of people toward another individual or group of people. Feelings, he explained, are "spontaneous expressions of the autonomic nervous system to whatever is happening in the organism. They are expressions in part of the urge for security" (p. 306). Importantly, Bogardus (1947) believed that feelings were indicative of attitudes and that they might shed more light on attitudes than anything except actual behavior, hence their predictive power. The challenge in the implementation of the scale was to capture the respondent's "first feeling reaction." In other words, Bogardus asked respondents to complete the scale "without thinking." "Feeling reactions," he wrote, "indicate how a person would express himself toward his fellows if he acted 'without thinking,' 'just the way he feels,' and without regard to politeness, social amenities, or his own status" (Bogardus, 1947, p. 307).

Before jumping into the nuances of how the scale was administered, however, its development should be discussed first. Bogardus asked 100 people—faculty members and graduate and undergraduate students—to rate 60 statements according to the social distance each statement described. The types of relationships described by the statements—"all of which were heard in ordinary conversations where a person was expressing himself about other persons," Bogardus explained—included contacts with family members, political groups, occupational groups, and recreational groups (Bogardus, 1933, p. 265). Some sample statements were:

- Would have as chums;
- Would have as my pastor, or religious guide;
- Would invite to my home;
- Would take as guests on automobile trips;
- Would dance with in public regularly.

Each person was asked to place each statement into one of seven social distance categories, with 1 representing the least amount of social distance and 7 representing the greatest amount of social distance. Bogardus computed means for each statement; those having means nearest the whole numbers from 1 to 7 were selected to represent the seven nearly equidistant social distance situations. The final seven social distance categories were:

1. Would marry.
2. Would have as regular friends.
3. Would work beside in an office.
4. Would have several families in my neighborhood.
5. Would have merely as speaking acquaintances.
6. Would have live outside my neighborhood.
7. Would have live outside my country.

In his first administration of the scale, Bogardus (1933) asked 110 businessmen and public school teachers to rate 40 different ethnic groups, 30 occupations, and 30 religious groups using the social distance scale. Both businessmen and public school teachers gave Canadians the lowest social distance score, indicating the highest level of social contact, and persons of Turkish descent the highest socialdistance score, indicating the lowest level of social contact. African Americans received the second-highest social distance score. In a follow-up study, Bogardus(1925) attempted to determine "just how and why these grades of understanding and intimacy vary" (p. 216). He asked each student to "describe in detail the circumstances as nearly as he could recall them under which this dislike [for a particular group] originated and developed" (Bogardus, 1925, p. 219). Even though students were explicitly asked to describe experiences, as opposed to secondhand evidence or hearsay, the vast majority were unable to do so. Bogardus (1925) concluded that "it is clear after reading the data that hearsay evidence coming from both one's personal friends and from relative strangers in one's own 'universe of discourse' who possess prestige in one's own eyes are widely influential in creating social distance" (p. 219).

Bogardus spent as much time brainstorming solutions for reducing racial prejudice and tension as he did studying it. He made particular effort, without much success, to discredit the notion of race altogether. Specifically, Bogardus(1954) argued that "the term race . . . is a misnomer" because "there are no pure races" (p. 317). In response, Sellew (1950) wrote, "Bogardus appears to complicate the problem unnecessarily. What is important is the reaction to these evident traits, not an attempt to prove that a racial nature does not exist" (p. 272). Whether race exists or not, Bogardus believed prejudices could be eliminated through increased social contact between groups. Importantly, however, he believed such contact had to occur in the absence of competition for resources. "When the competition is removed," he wrote, "then race prejudice will be alleviated" (Bogardus, 1954, p. 329). In an article titled "Reducing Racial Tension," Bogardus outlines nine processes that might help alleviate "antagonism between racial groups" (Sellew, 1950, p. 271). These include commonsense suggestions such as legislation, elimination of stereotypes, and full participation in the democratic process across racial groups.

APPLICATIONS

As previously mentioned, the social distance scale continues to be used in research today. Even as its application has expanded to other disciplines and types of social groups, it remains a popular tool for the study of race relations. The following section will serve as a brief introduction to recent research on racial prejudice using Bogardus's scale.

In a study titled "As the World Turns: Ethnoracial Distances after 70 Years," Kleg and Yamamoto (1998) attempted to replicate Bogardus's original study. Like Bogardus, Kleg and Yamamoto sampled public school teachers and asked them to complete a nearly identical social distance scale using 24 of the original 40 ethnic groups. Their results suggest that "the majority of Americans today may not only (a) hold attitudes that are more socially accepting (the mean distances being 3.82 in 1925 and 1.43 in 1993, t = 8.05, d.f. = 46, p <.001), but also (b) express them more uniformly (the standard deviations being, respectively, 1.43 and.28)" (Kleg & Yamamoto, 1998, p. 185). Although such results were encouraging and suggest less social distance between various ethnic groups today than in the past, the authors provided one caveat. The sequential ordering of social distance from the 24 ethnic groups mirrored the ordering of the 1925 results. Thus, "those who had earlier enjoyed a higher level of permissible intimacy stayed the more preferred. In the same vein, those who had been more distanced in the 1920s"—such as "Arabs, Turks, Orientals, Mexicans, and African-Americans"—"were still the less preferred in the 1990s," (Kleg & Yamamoto, 1998, p. 185). On the basis of these mixed results, they concluded that they could not respond to the question of whether ethnoracial attitudes in the United States had improved over the past seventy years "in an unequivocally affirmative manner" (p. 185).

In another example, Morgan (1996) used a modified version of the social distance scale to investigate friendship preferences among black and white students in Georgia public schools. He was particularly interested in understanding how different public policies and school practices might influence the degree of socialcontact among racial groups. He found that white students generally reported greater social distance than black students and that "social distance was least in the lowest grades and progressed as children progressed through the grades" (Morgan, 1996). Citing Gary Orfield, director of Harvard University's Project on School Desegregation, Morgan (1996) explained these findings as partial outcome of the fact that "1995 marked the first time in 40 years that black children and white children in the south became less likely to go to school together than their older brothers and sisters had been" (p. 4). Furthermore, Morgan argues that desegregation—attending the same school—is qualitatively different from integration. Integration, which suggests interaction among social groups, is more likely to lead to improved attitudes. Practices such as tracking, however, keep ethnic groups largely separate, even in desegregated schools. Thus, "the longer children in this study remained in desegregated [as opposed to integrated] school environments, the less likely they were to value interracial friendships" (Morgan, 1996, p. 5).

Cover (1995) tested the relationship between social contact and social distance more directly. Using a small sample of college students in an introductory sociology course, Cover (1995) asked respondents to complete the social distance scale with respect to 11 different groups and also asked them to indicate whether they had had any interactions with any members of the 11 groups. In support of his hypothesis, results demonstrated that "noncontact groups reported having higher average social distance than contact groups." He also found social distance ratings to be similar across all 11 groups for those who indicated higher levels of contact. Like Bogardus, however, Cover (1995) qualified these findings by arguing that social contact in and of itself is not enough to lower social distance. Rather, lack of competition is necessary as well. "If social distance is to be lessened by contact, the groups involved should not be competitors, and their status must be relatively equal" (Cover, 1995, p. 404).

Randall and Delbridge (2005) investigated the relationship between social contact and social distance using members of a fast-growing and increasingly diverse southern community as their sample. Their research provides an important contribution to the literature in this area; whereas past studies looked at socialdistance largely from the perspective of white Americans, Randall and Delbridge (2005) studied social distance from the perspective of Latinos and African Americans as well. More specifically, they were interested in knowing whether groups with greater interaction and greater knowledge of one another culturally were likely to report greater social intimacy, and therefore less social distance. They found that African Americans and whites report less social distance from each other than from any other racial or ethnic group. They also found that African Americans express greater social distance from Mexicans than whites. Delbridge and Randall (2005) provided a two-fold explanation of these results: Mexicans were a new subpopulation within the community and therefore had had less social-contact with other groups, and Mexicans and African Americans were competing at the time for economic resources.

VIEWPOINTS

Despite the popularity of the social distance scale and its continued use across a variety of academic disciplines, there are scholars who take issue with it on both methodological and philosophical grounds. Lee, Sapp, and Ray (1996), for example, argue that social distance between two groups should be measured from the perspective of the minority group, rather than the perspective of the majority group, as Bogardus's original scale does. They write, "The social distance between a minority group and the majority group...has been postulated by the present authors to be based on the minority group's reaction to its perceived rejection or acceptance by the majority group, rather than on the majority group's reaction to the minority group" (Lee, Sapp & Ray, 1996, p. 17). Lee et. al (1996) modified the questions from the original scale—changing "Would have as a neighbor" to "Do they mind you living in their neighborhood," for example—and administered the scale to African Americans, Hispanics, and students identified as "other." African American students perceived a greater distance between themselves and Caucasian Americans than either of the other two groups. Findings such as these, Lee et. al. (1996) argue, provide a more complete picture of the relationship between social groups. The Randall and Delbridge (2005) study described above is another example of how the use of the scale has been extended in this manner.

Weinfurt and Moghaddam (2001) also take issue with the social distance scale, but for methodological reasons rather than philosophical ones. Specifically, they argue that the meaningfulness of the scale depends on the assumption that respondents view the social distance between categories—neighbor and friend, for example—in the same way as those who developed the scale. Weinfurt and Moghaddam (2001) write, "A number of cross-cultural researchers have asserted, often explicitly, that research methods and instruments are themselves cultural products. An implication is that the methods and instruments developed by researchers who share a particular culture may involve assumptions that are not valid in other cultures" (p. 102). People from non-Western societies in which collectivism is typically emphasized over individualism, for example, may interact with very few people outside their immediate and extended families, while people from Western societies interact with strangers frequently and have less contact with extended families. All of this may impact how particular people view social categories such as "friend," "neighbor," and "family member." Indeed, Weinfurt and Moghaddam (2001) found that Indian, Algerian, and Greek participants exhibited response patterns least consistent with the assumptions of the instrument designers; compared to other ethnic groups included in their study, their respective cultures were most dissimilar from the Western culture Bogardus's inhabited.

Despite these criticisms, the impact of the social distance scale is undeniable. Bahr, Johnson, and Seitz (1971), in a publication titled "Influential Scholars and Works in the Sociology of Race and Minority Relations," identified Bogardus as one of the heavyweights in the field between 1944 and 1968. Of twenty-eight authors whose work was most frequently cited, Bogardus was listed in the top five. Perhaps more significantly, the scale continues to be used by scholars today, even though it was first conceived in 1925.

TERMS & CONCEPTS

Attitudes: In developing the social distance scale, Bogardus was making an attempt to measure attitudes. He encouraged respondents to complete the scale "without thinking," relying instead on their first feeling reaction. This feeling reaction, which he described as involuntary and automatic, was more representative of underlying attitudes than a "thinking response," which he believed would be a more socially desirable, less accurate one.

Prejudice: As Bogardus entered the field of sociology, prejudice was currently being defined as the "more or less instinctive and spontaneous disposition to maintain social distances from other groups" (Wark & Galliher, 2007, p. 390). Bogardus believed that every person possessed racial prejudices but that they could be eradicated if competition for resources was also removed.

Race: According to Bogardus, the concept of "race" was a misnomer. Because there are no pure racial types and people have multiple racial/ethnic origins, he argued, individuals should not categorize each other into distinct groups. He recognized the existence of racial prejudice, however, and believed that increased social contact and the absence of competition would help eradicate it.

Racial Distance: Bogardus's social distance scale measures perceived distance/intimacy between members of two groups. Because it can be applied to any type of social group, including ethnic groups, occupational groups, and religious groups, the scale was given the generic title "social distance." However, it was originally developed to measure distance between racial groups and thus is sometimes referred to as a racial distance scale.

Social Distance: Bogardus borrowed his definition of social distance from colleague Robert Park, who defined it as "the grades and degrees of understanding and intimacy which characterize pre-social and social relations generally" (Bogardus, 1925, p. 216). For Bogardus more specifically, social distance is indicative of underlying attitudes and prejudices.

Bibliography

Ani, C., Ola, B. A., & Coker, R. (2011). "School children's stigmatizing attitude towards peers with epilepsy in Nigeria." *Vulnerable Children & Youth Studies*, 6(4), 330–338.

Bahr, H.M., Johnson, T.J., & Seitz, M.R. (1971). "Influential scholars and works in the sociology of race and minority relations, 1944-1968." *The American Sociologist, 6* (4), 296-298.

Bogardus, E.S. (1925). "Measuring social distance." *Journal of Applied Sociology, 9,* 299-308.

Bogardus, E.S. (1925). "Social distance and its origin." *Journal of Applied Sociology, 9,* 216-226.

Bogardus, E.S. (1929). "Public opinion as a social force: Race reactions." *Social Forces, 8,* 102-105.

Bogardus, E.S. (1931). "Cooperative research on the Pacific Coast." *Journal of Educational Sociology, 4* (9), 563-568.

Bogardus, E.S. (1933). "A social distance scale." *Sociology and Social Research, 17,* 265-271.

Bogardus, E. S. (1947). "Measurement of personal-group relations." *Sociometry, 10,*306-310.

Bogardus, E. S. (1954). *Sociology.* New York, NY: The MacMillan Company.

Bogardus, E.S. (1956). "The aim of Alpha Kappa Delta." *Alpha Kappa Deltan, 27,*18-19.

Cover, J.D. (1995). "The effects of social contact on prejudice." *The Journal of Social Psychology, 135,* 403-405.

Kleg, M., & Yamamoto, K. (1998). "As the world turns: Ethno-racial distances after 70 years." *Social Science Journal, 35,* 183-190.

Lee, M. Y., Sapp, S. G., & Ray, M.C. (1996). "The reverse social distance scale." *The Journal of Social Psychology, 136,* 17-24.

Morgan, H. (1996, April). "Social distance and race in public schools: Grades five through twelve." Paper presented at the Annual Meeting of the American Education Research Association, New York, NY. Education Resources Information Center: http://www.eric.ed.gov/ERICDocs/data/ericdocs2sql/content_storage_01/0000019b/80/16/d0/d0.pdf

Parrillo, V. N., & Donoghue, C. (2013). "The national social distance study: Ten years later." *Sociological Forum,* 28(3), 597–614.

Potdar, R., & Elliott, D. (2011). "Online education and the promotion of diversity: Using the Bogardus scale to measure student attitudes." Conference Papers—*American Sociological Association,* 1435.

Randall, N.H., & Delbridge, S. (2005). "Perceptions of social distance in an ethnically fluid community." *Sociological Spectrum, 25,* 103-122.

Sellew, G. (1950). "Reducing racial tension." *American Catholic Sociological Review, 11,* 271-273.

Wark, C., & Galliher, J.F. (2007). "Emory Bogardus and the origins of the social distance scale." *American Sociologist, 38,* 383-395.

Weinfurt, K. P., & Moghaddam, F. M. (2001). "Culture and social distance: A case study of methodological cautions." *The Journal of Social Psychology, 14,* 101-110.

Suggested Reading

Bogardus, E. S. (1923). *Essentials of social psychology.* Los Angeles, CA: The press of Jesse Ray Miller.

Bogardus, E.S. (1926). *The new social research.* Los Angeles, CA: The press of Jesse Ray Miller.

Bogardus, E.S. (1928). "Teaching and social distance." *Journal of Educational Sociology, 1,* 595-598.

Bogardus, E.S. (1930). "Social-distance changes in educational procedure." *Journal of Educational Sociology, 3,* 497-502.

Bogardus, E. S. (1931). *Contemporary sociology: A companion volume to history of social thought.* Los Angeles, CA: University of Southern California Press.

Bogardus, E. S. (1960). *The development of social thought.* New York, NY: Longmans, Green, and Company.

Fee, H. R., & Nusbaumer, M. R. (2012). "Social distance and the formerly obese: Does the stigma of obesity linger?" *Sociological Inquiry,* 82(3), 356–377.

Iyengar, S., Sood, G., & Lelkes, Y. (2012). "Affect, not ideology." *Public Opinion Quarterly,* 76(3), 405–431.

Neumeyer, M.H. (1974). "A tribute to Dr. Emory S. Bogardus." *Sociological Inquiry, 44,* 3-5.

Jennifer Kretchmar, Ph.D.

Prejudice Theory: Realistic Conflict Theory

ABSTRACT

Psychological, social, and cultural theories of the development of prejudice emerged in the early twentieth century with a focus on individual psychopathology. Arguing that only a few, disturbed individuals could be guilty of war crimes, social scientists were reluctant to consider the wider significance of prejudice. By the mid-1950s, scholars recognized the pervasiveness of prejudice and began to look at intergroup dynamics in terms of attitude formation and discrimination. Realistic conflict theory focused on competition between groups over actual or perceived scarce resources, but more contemporary theorists believe that prejudice is more systemic and does not require actual competition.

OVERVIEW

Conflict between groups has been studied for centuries, especially in terms of war, economics, and governmental clashes. However, there was very little sociological or psychological analysis concerning prejudice and conflict between different racial and ethnic groups until the horrors of World War II affected the world. In light of the atrocities committed during the Holocaust, social scholars began to try and understand what would make one group devalue the humanity of another group of individuals and commit such heinous acts of torture and murder. These horrible acts prompted a new subdiscipline in sociology that focuses on theories of prejudice, discrimination, and stigma as they relate to intergroup conflict.

Prejudice is defined by Weinberg as the "systematic and durable assessments of groups, or members of those groups, in unfavorable terms" (2006, p. 470). In fact, prejudice, or prejudgments, can be positive or negative, but because unfavorable stereotypes can lead to hostility and discrimination against another group, they tend to hold the greatest interest for scholars. Prejudices are attitudes and beliefs, either conscious or unconscious, and interventions focus on attitudinal change as the key to mitigating hostility between groups and their members. Interwoven with the concept of prejudice are those of discrimination and stigma. Discrimination is "prejudicial or injurious behavior" that occurs because of hostile attitudes towards others (Weinberg, 2006, p. 470). Stigma, on the other hand, entails the "experiences and behaviors of those who are victimized" by prejudice and discrimination (Weinberg, 2006, p. 470). Scholars focusing on discrimination look at the institutional and structural aspects of society which reinforce its prejudicial attitudes, while those who study stigma look at the individual's experience of prejudice and discrimination. One can see that the focal point of inquiry provides differing perspectives on the characteristics and causes of prejudice and discrimination, so this article will focus on theories of prejudice.

One early look at the role of prejudice in intergroup dynamics was set forth by Durkheim in his

1895 study of crime entitled *The Rules of Sociological Method.* Durkheim argued that there was a "certain social functionality in explicitly designating and discriminating against groups other than one's own" (Weinberg, 2006, p. 470). Durkheim then went on to consider group solidarity as it related to crime, but ultimately he was more interested in group social cohesion than he was in inter-group conflict. It was not until 1939, and John Dollard's book *Frustration and Aggression* that serious analysis commenced on prejudice theory. Weinberg and others have argued that the impetus for the development of prejudice theories was the Nazi German atrocities of the Holocaust. But since World War II did not commence until 1939, it may be the case that it was the Armenian genocide prior to World War II that served as Dollard's focus. Subsequent scholars, of course, were influenced by the death of over 17 million individuals in the Holocaust.

Dollard observed the harsh treatment of Germany and Eastern European countries by the Allies after World War I, and argued that "an agent frustrated at the hands of a more powerful actor will sublimate the sentiments of aggression created by the frustration by focusing them on less powerful scapegoats" (Weinberg, 2006, p. 470). All of the theories which suggest that frustration leads to prejudice can be categorized as scapegoat theories of prejudice. Scapegoating is an important tool of propaganda. Essentially, one group blames the other for any and all calamities or injustices that have occurred and seeks retribution for those harms, even if the targeted group is not actually at fault.

While sociologists were examining group dynamics, Freudian psychoanalytic theories were also being set forth which focused on the childhood development of personality traits. Theodor Wiesengrund Adorno, for example, argued that an "authoritarian personality" was the cause of the development of prejudicial feelings. In early childhood, a "highly regimented, strictly disciplined household" caused children to learn propensities toward "rigid, inflexible, and prejudicial attitudes towards certain minority groups and their members" (Weinberg, 2006, p. 470). This, in turn, created a person who was "highly submissive to the dictates of established authority figures and intolerant of people(s) who do not conform to those dictates" (Weinberg, 2006, p 471). Through this analysis, Adorno explained both how a person can act upon inhumane orders from authority figures and this process can reinforce intolerance towards specific minority individuals and groups through the development of a personality trait. Simply stated, "extreme prejudice is a personality trait linked to personas who conform rigidly to cultural norms and values" (Macionis, 2007, p. 359). According to Weinberg, most of the theoretical analysis of prejudice up to this point focused on the psychopathology of a few deviant individuals who were able to influence others to commit terrible acts of genocide (2006). Thus, feelings of prejudice were presented as rare and extreme until Allport argued it was more commonplace and universal in 1954.

In *The Nature of Prejudice,* Gordon Allport argued that a "routine and pervasive learning process" was the cause of prejudicial feelings (1954; Wienberg, 2006, p. 471). Allport believed that "categorical thinking," or stereotypical thinking as it is now called, was a mechanism by which the mind processed complex sensory and cognitive materials in a simple and systematized manner. Prejudice was based upon "faulty and inflexible generalizations," according to Allport, but it was the mind's way of organizing information efficiently (Weinberg, 2006, p. 471). Allport believed that individual prejudices were learned from cultural, social, economic, and psychodynamic influences, but that correcting the harm done by prejudice and discrimination should focus on restructuring the individual's learning process. Little attention was paid to the overall failings of a given social structure.

A similar phenomenon occurred in other cultural theories of prejudice set forth in the first half of the twentieth century. Simmel, Park, and Bogardus, for example, all believed that prejudice was learned from one's culture, but to assess this view, they looked at individual experiences in relation to racial attitudes. Simmel introduced the concept of "social distance" to understand both the geometric relationships between people of different races and their metaphorical distances. Focusing on community and the processes of conflict, reciprocity, and interaction, Simmel tried to understand the actual interactive processes between individuals of differing racial backgrounds. Following Simmel's framework, Bogardus developed the Borgardus Social Distance Scale, which remains the most widely used measure of interpersonal psychological interactions in sociology today (Ethington, 1997). In addition to actual interpersonal distance, the Bogardus Scale looks at psychological distance as seen from the actor's point of view and the subjective distances as evidenced by the actor's motivations and temperament. In his essay "Understanding Conflict," Rummell elucidated four types of distances (material, psychological, social, and cultural) and eleven subtypes, although he acknowledges significant overlap for each conceptually (2008). Throughout these methods of analysis, however, the focus remains on the individual actor's experience and attitudes. It was not until Sherif introduced Realistic conflict theory that a group-level or macrostructural view of group prejudice began to emerge.

VIEWPOINTS

Realistic conflict theory is a social psychological analysis of prejudice, discrimination, and stereotyping. It is based upon the premise that conflict over materials goods and resources leads to ethnocentrism and hostility towards other groups competing for those same resources. In 1954, Muzafer Sherif and Carolyn Sherif created an experiment to test Realistic conflict theory. Known as the "Robbers Cave Experiment," Sherif posed as a camp janitor and had two busloads of eleven-year-old boys brought to different remote campsites; each group was unaware of the other. Within about three days, both groups had developed a hierarchical internal group structure, and individuals showed a strong loyalty to their specific ingroups. During the "Friction Phase" of the experiment, Sherif introduced the two groups to each other and engaged them in competition, especially athletic events. In many ways, the experiment worked too well, as the groups became so hostile to each other that Sherif concluded that the experiment needed to end for the safety of his subjects. Rather than leave the boys with hostile feelings, however, the Sherifs engaged them in joint tasks and created "false" emergencies that required the two groups to work together in order for them to succeed. One such task, for example, was to tell the youth that the camp truck had broken down on the road and needed to be towed back to camp, requiring the labor of all camp participants. By giving the twenty-two boys a superordinate task to accomplish jointly, Sherif's experiment also became famous for providing one mechanism to reduce intergroup conflict through joint efforts and shared goals.

Sherif concluded from the study that newly constituted groups will adopt a hierarchical internal structure and that members will show heightened loyalty to their ingroups. When competition is introduced, those groups will show heightened hostility to the each other, develop stereotypes about the other group, and overvalue the performance of the ingroup relative to the outgroup. For Sherif, the key to eliciting these feelings and behavior in each group was competition over actual or perceived scarce resources.

In his group position model, Blumer argued that prejudice is based upon perceptions and its development does not require the impetus of competition for tangible scarce resources. Blumer believed that four elements were needed for one group to become prejudiced against another:

(1) a feeling of superiority;
(2) a belief that the outgroup is intrinsically different and alien;
(3) a sense of proprietary claim to certain privileges and resources; and
(4) a sense of threat from members of the subordinate group upon the dominant group's prerogatives (Weinberg, 2006, p. 471).

Since all individuals have a sense of the "color line," as Blumer called it, or a sense of their position relative to other racial groups, Blumer believed that it would be very difficult for the civil rights movement to succeed. Not only would there have to be profound efforts to change the public layers of the color line, but until that was accomplished, it would be hard to change the private feelings of exclusivity and entitlement. Blumer's work launched discussions about both the emotional qualities of prejudice and their instrumental functions in intergroup conflicts.

Also, in contrast to Realistic conflict theory, Henri Tajfel argued in his social identity theory that competition is not necessary for prejudice to occur. Tajfel believed that individuals desire a "psychological distinctiveness" in which our identity is differentiated from and positively compared to other groups. According to him, the psychological manner in which one's social identity is formed has four elements and occurs in the following manner:

- First, the individual puts himself or herself and everyone else he or she encounters into categories and labels those categories.
- Second, the individual identifies and associates with certain groups in order to bolster self-esteem.
- Third, the individual engages in comparisons between groups with a favorable bias towards their own group.
- Fourth, the "psychological distinctiveness" emerges, making the ingroup the most desirable for membership at the expense of the outgroup.

Tajfel also believed that individuals gain emotional satisfaction and tangible benefits from self-identifying with their ingroup at the expense of an outgroup. In fact, in his studies, Tajfel demonstrated that individuals would work hard to outdo the outgroup even if there was no benefit to them personally for their own group to succeed. He argued, then, that our self-esteem is generated from the group with which we identify, and that we overvalue our group in order to enhance our group's status and, thereby, our own status. Rather than being motivated by a real or potential threat from the outgroup, individuals are compelled by a "sense of entitlement felt by in-group members to dominance" (Weinberg, 2006, p. 472). This model is also the "social dominance model" of prejudice.

Goffman, in his major work, *Stigma*, also focused on the process by which an individual is "disqualified from full social acceptance" (1963, p. i). According to Goffman, as socialized individuals we constantly categorize people in terms of attributes we expect them to exhibit. This "social identity" allows us to anticipate human interactions without excessive conscious thought and nervous confusion, since we expect and demand very specific behaviors in terms of an individual's social identity. An internal conflict arises, however, when the outgroup individual expresses incongruous attributes from those that we anticipate and thus frustrates our expectations and demands. Quite often, our response to these unanticipated attributes is to further categorize the individual as less desirable than those individuals who conform to our social identity stereotype. The individual "is thus reduced in our minds from a whole and usual person to a tainted, discounted one" (Goffman, 1963, p. 2-3).

Goffman grouped these negative characteristics into three types:

- The various physical abnormalities.
- The character disorders such as dishonesty, weakness, or evilness, which are perceived to be expressed through behavior such as prostitution, homosexuality, drug addiction, alcoholism, unemployment, welfare dependency, and political radicalism.
- The group stigmas based upon race, color, religion, ethnicity, and gender, which are usually transmitted through familial lineages and affect all members of the family group.

Because of these perceived negative characteristics, we "tend to impute a wide range of imperfections on the basis of the original one" (Goffman, 1963, p. 4-5). If an ethnic or racial group does not speak English in the same way as the ingroup, for example, intellectual inferiority, laziness, carelessness, and divisiveness can be attributed to the group and compound the ingroup's impression of them. Our beliefs about the original characteristic, plus the imputed additional negative images, allows us to self-righteously exclude and discriminate against stigmatized people, thus further reducing their chances of full participation in normative social dynamics. Having been pushed to the negative fringes, individuals suffer from the lack of access to more traditionally available resources, and they may adopt the negative societal context into which they are thrust. A young, African American male from the inner city, for example, may engage in crime because it is expected of him and he has few other alternatives. Racial profiling by the police would enforce this disesteemed situation. Thus, the cultural stereotype takes on a larger power that reinforces the discriminatory process.

Modern theorists interested in personality theories of prejudice, like Stephen and Rosenfield, believe that experiences of interracial or interethnic contact are more likely to influence feelings of prejudice than early childhood psychodynamics related to parenting processes (1978). The more positive the interactions between racial and ethnic groups the less likely the individual is to exhibit negative prejudicial attitudes and discriminatory behaviors.

Two other similar models of prejudice theory deserve mention: the paternalism model and the ideological control model. Both of these models build on the sense of intergroup superiority noted above, but they also focus on the process by which the ingroup devalues the abilities and nature of the outgroup, much like the discussion concerning Goffman's theory. These models explain racism and classism by arguing that the ingroup sees outgroup members as less intelligent, less capable, and less compelled to work for a living, and that it is the ingroup's obligation to "look after" the outgroup members. These models do not focus on conflict, and they add the emotional dimensions of caretaking and warmth to the paternalistic mix concerning prejudicial affect.

Some scholars like to focus on the cognitive or information processing details of prejudice formation. In terms of the development of stereotypes, the "illusory correlations" factor is often cited. In illusory correlations, as Hamilton and Gifford have argued, make individuals prone reading the correlations that they expect into sets of data, even when the actual correlation is much smaller than the expected one or nonexistent (1979). This is because individuals tend to remember unusual events and people much more readily than they do everyday events and people, leading them to develop of generalizations and stereotypes that are based on rare rather than common events. Individuals in a suburb, for example, having seen stories about African American criminals in the news, may see an African American male on the street and assume that he is pursuing some criminal purpose. With our culture's intense mass media, people's stereotypes are influenced by nondirect experiences more than ever before.

Two other cognitive processes maintain the existence of stereotypes: encoding bias and recall bias. In encoding bias, the individual takes in objective sensory data, like sights and sounds from an outgroup member. The ingroup member then begins the complex mental process of converting that objective data into a subjectively meaningful experience. Because of prior experiences and developed stereotypes, though, the ingroup member fails to take in this new, unique experience and thus maintains his or her prejudices. The same phenomena occurs in recall bias, or reporting bias, which is most often related to survey studies. In this case, the individual maintains a systemic bias to such an extent that, when asked a question, they are not only influenced by the possible correct answer but also by their memory and stereotypical thinking. Thus, regardless of the "truth" of a given situation, the answer is colored by previous, deeply believed experiences, feelings, and beliefs. Obviously, given the profound influence of these affective and experiential opinions, it is difficult to change people's minds merely by pointing out the flaws in their thinking.

The very process of socialization instills in each of us a desire to be normal, to belong. This power to define normalcy is the basis of the success of stigmatization, since all persons go through the cultural process. In his contact hypothesis, Stephen argued that sustained, repeated, frequent, and non-stereotypical interactions between members of the ingroup and outgroup will reduce prejudiceand discrimination (1978). As more and more members of the ingroup encounter the nonstereotypical members of the outgroup, the whole normative belief system about the entire class of people is challenged.

In all of this discussion of norms and power, however, it must be remembered that the contest is not merely an intellectual conflict over ideology. Social control and the power to define normalcy have as their extension the power to control personal actions, determine access to employment and financial security, regulate the rights to have intimate relationships legitimized and supported by the government, and the power to intrude into a person's very sense of self-worth and self-respect.

TERMS & CONCEPTS

Cognitive: Of or related to the processes through which individuals perceive experience, reason through it, and learn from and about it.

Ethnicity: A shared cultural heritage.

Genocide: The systematic killing of a racial, ethnic, religious, or national group of people by another.

Institutional Discrimination: The bias inherent to any society's institutions, such as its legal, educational, medical, or political systems.

Race: A category comprising people who share biologically transmitted traits that members of a society deem socially significant.

Racism: The belief that one racial category is innately superior or inferior to another.

Scapegoating: The act of holding a person, group of people, or thing responsible for a multitude of problems.

Stereotypes: Prejudicial views or descriptions of some category of people, often based upon strong emotions and misinformation.

Bibliography

Allport, G. (1954). *The nature of prejudice.* Cambridge: Addison-Wesley.

Blumer, H. (1946). "Collective behavior." In A. Lee (Ed.), *New outline of principles of sociology.* New York: Barnes and Noble.

Blumer, H. (1955). "Social Movements." In A. Lee (Ed.). *Principles of sociology.* New York: Barnes and Noble.

Conger, A. J., Dygdon, J. A., & Rollock, D. (2012). "Conditioned emotional responses in racial prejudice." *Ethnic & Racial Studies, 35*(2), 298-319.

Ethington, P. (1997). "The intellectual construction of 'social distance': Toward a recovery of George Simmel's social geometry." *Cybergeo,* 30. Retrieved October 8, 2008 from: http://www.cybergeo.eu/index227.html

Gaunt, R. (2011). "Effects of intergroup conflict and social contact on prejudice: The mediating role of stereotypes and evaluations." *Journal Of Applied Social Psychology, 41*(6), 1340-1355.

Goffman, E. (1963). *Stigma: Notes on the management of a spoiled identity.* Englewood Cliffs, NJ: Prentice-Hall.

Hurst, C. (1992). *Social inequality: Forms, causes and consequences.* Boston, MA: Allyn & Bacon.

Macionis, J. (2007). *Sociology.* (11th ed.). Saddle River, NJ: Pearson Prentice-Hall.

Martiny, S. E., Kessler, T., & Vignoles, V. L. (2012). "Shall I leave or shall we fight? Effects of threatened group-based self-esteem on identity management strategies." *Group Processes & Intergroup Relations, 15*(1), 39-55.

Rummel, R. *Understanding conflict and war: Vol. 2: The Conflict Helix.* Retrieved October 8, 2008 from: http://hawaii.edu/powerkills/THC.CHAP16.htm.

Sherif, M., & Sherif, C. (1969). *Social psychology.* New York: Harper & Row.

Stephan, W., & Rosenfield, D. (1978). "Effects of desegregation on racial attitudes." *Journal of Personality and Social Psychology,* 36, 795-804.

Tajfel, H., & Turner, J. (1979). "An integrated theory of intergroup conflict." In W. Austin, & S. Worchel (Eds.), *The social psychology of intergroup relations.* Monterey, CA: Brooks-Cole.

Weinberg, D. (2006). "Prejudice." In B. Turner (Ed.), *The Cambridge dictionary of sociology.* Cambridge, UK: Cambridge University Press.

Suggested Reading

Binning, K. R., & Sherman, D. K. (2011). "Categorization and communication in the face of prejudice: When describing perceptions changes what is perceived." *Journal Of Personality & Social Psychology, 101*(2), 321-336.

Brown, R. (2001). *Group processes: Dynamics within and between groups.* (2nd ed.). Malden, MA: Wiley-Blackwell.

Heatherton, T., Kleck, R., Hebl, M., & Hull, J. (Eds.). (2003). *The social psychology of stigma.* New York: Guilford.

Korstelina, K. (2007). *Social identity and conflict: Structures, dynamics, and implications.* Hampshire, UK: Palgrave Macmillan.

Moghaddam, F.; Harre, R.; & Lee, N. (Eds.). (2007). *Global conflict resolution through positioning analysis.* New York: Springer.

Pruit, D., Rubin, J., & Kim, S. (2003). *Social conflict: Escalation, stalemate, and settlement.* Columbus, OH: McGraw-Hill.

Ritzer, G. (Ed.). (2007). *Classical sociological theory* (5th ed.). New York, NY: McGraw-Hill.

Ritzer, G., & Goodman, D. (2007). *Sociological theory* (6th ed.). New York, NY: McGraw-Hill.

Rodenborg, N. A., & Boisen, L. A. (2013). "Aversive racism and intergroup contact theories: Cultural competence in a segregated world." *Journal Of Social Work Education, 49*(4), 564-579.

Sidanius, J., & Pratto, F. (2001). *Social dominance: An intergroup theory of social hierarchy and oppression.* New York: Cambridge University Press.

Stinchombe, A. (1987). *Constructing social theories.* Chicago, IL: University of Chicago Press.

Karen M. Harbeck, Ph.D., J.D.

PREJUDICE THEORY: SCAPEGOAT THEORY

ABSTRACT

Scapegoating is the process through which frustration and aggression are directed at a group that is not the causal agent of the frustration. Scapegoat theory emerged during the 1940s as a way for social psychologists to explain why prejudice and racism occur. Though many scholars today choose to study racism from a social cognitive or institutional perspective, some continue to use Scapegoat theory to study responses to affirmative action and immigration policies.

OVERVIEW

For over a century, social psychology has concerned itself with the intersection of the individual with society. One of the field's preeminent theorists, Gordon Allport, explained in 1954 that "social psychologists regard their discipline as an attempt to understand and explain how the thought, feeling and behavior of individuals are influenced by the actual, imagined or implied presence of other human beings" (quoted in Lubek, 2000, p. 320). Racism and its social effects have been significant areas of study for social psychologists. Scholars in the field have put forth a number of theories about racism, but this article will concentrate on Scapegoat theory.

According to Echebarria (1997), Scapegoat theory emerged during the 1940s as social psychologists began their first attempts to conceptualize racial prejudice. During this time, prejudice was largely seen as being rooted in psychology, not society; it was "the result of defense mechanisms through which internal conflicts were resolved" (Echebarria, 1997, p. 1). The Scapegoat theory was introduced during this time as a means of explaining why frustration and aggression are deflected toward other, less powerful groups in the form of prejudice, even if those groups are not the source of the frustration. For example, an economic downturn may cause a group to become aggressive towards immigrants, whom it blames for taking its jobs, since it is unable to express its anger toward the cause of its frustration. Thus, anger, and even violence, is deflected away from the true source of the frustration—which Echebarria defined as the "interruption or impossibility to obtain certain desired goals" (p. 2)—because it is either impossible or too difficult to address the source of this frustration (Echebarria, 1997, McMannus, 2008).Thus, Scapegoat theory introduced societal aspects into the period's purely psychological approach to prejudice.

Allport

Gordon Allport further advanced the theory during the 1950s with his work on ingroups and outgroups in *The Nature of Prejudice* (1954). He drew on William Graham Sumner's work in *Folkways* (1906) to outline a theory of prejudice that is based upon ingroup and outgroup conflict. According to Allport, the need for defined ingroups and outgroups grew out of our evolutionary development as an obligatorily interdependent species. Because humans rely on one another for the information and resources they need to survive, we must be willing to trust and cooperate with one another. But indiscriminate trust isn't a good survival strategy, since it is necessary to have some degree of certainty that the obligation is mutual. Therefore, ingroups are formed in which members are obligated to reciprocate any aid given to them in a system of "contingent altruism" (Brewer, 1999, p. 433). At the most basic level, members expect the ingroup to treat them with kindness and fairness so long as they cooperate with other group members. As groups become larger, signs and symbols are created to differentiate ingroup members from outgroup members so that outgroup members will not accidentally receive the benefits given to ingroup members. At the same time, the group's institutions and rules gain a degree of moral authority within the group. And as that authority becomes more absolute, the ingroup members' tolerance for the institutions and rules of the outgroup declines, leading to disapproval of or outright hostility toward the outgroup (Brewer, 1999).

Scapegoating can occur when an ingroup perceives itself to be interdependent with an outgroup. When the two groups are forced to work together to achieve a common goal or face a common threat, the lack of mutual trust between the groups becomes particularly noticeable. Since neither group can trust the other to not exploit the relationship, the relationship becomes one of distrust. This distrust can lead to Scapegoating as one group blames the other for the difficulties or failures it encounters while working to achieve the groups' mutual goal or ward off a mutual threat (Brewer, 1999).

One of Allport's unique insights was that aggression directed against an outgroup does not serve a cathartic function. Instead, he believed that aggression feeds on itself, resulting in ever worse relationships between the two groups (Pettigrew, 1999).

Girard

The French anthropologist and philosopher, Rene Girard, revived Scapegoat theory during the 1980s (Wagner, 1986). Drawing on sources ranging from Greek mythology to the Biblical Passion, he claimed that:

> ....human communities maintain their order—language, status, possession and so forth—through a system of differences. These differences are threatened by violence within the group. Sacrifice is a momentary reversion to the chaos of violence in order to maintain the system of differences (Williams, 1989, p. 452) and The Scapegoat allows the social group to achieve unanimity by imputing its sin (=violence) to the sacrificial victim. Violence is thus both checked and maintained through a ritual act that itself is a form of violence (Williams, 1989, p. 451).

Girard used his most controversial writings—*Violence and the Sacred* (1977), *The Scapegoat* (1986), and *Things Hidden Since the Foundation of the World* (1987)—to show how sacrificial Scapegoats function in areas as wide ranging as law, literature, politics, and religion. He focused on sacrificial foundational myths, embedding them with critical importance:

> These myths operate [by turning] certain targeted 'others' into 'aliens'. Holding these aliens responsible for the ills and divisions of society, the Scapegoaters proceed to isolate or eliminate them. This sacrificial strategy furnishes many communities with their sense of collective identity—that is, with the basic sense of who is included (us) and who is excluded (aliens). But the price to be paid is often the demonising of an innocent outsider: the immolation of the 'other' on the altar of the 'alien' (Kearney, 1999, p. 251-252).

Thus Scapegoats unite divided groups against a perceived "other," and the violence directed at the "other" allows the community to forget its internal divisions. And while examples of the "immolation of the 'other'" are abundant in Greek or Roman mythology, Girard also argued that the same dynamic is in play today, too, albeit in less obvious ways. Indeed, Girard argued that all modern societies take part in Scapegoating at some level. Whether the Scapegoating is carried out via a witch hunt or in the name of national security, the tendency to persecute the "...fantasy of the evil adversary" (Kearney, 1999) is a part of an ancient tradition.

APPLICATIONS

Affirmative Action

Just as scholars were beginning to formally study prejudice and racism, America was entering into the civil rights era. In 1955, *Brown v. The Board of Education,* 349 U.S. 294 ended de jure segregation in schools, and nine years later the Civil Rights Act of 1964 banned segregation in public places, the government, and workplaces.

In the years after the civil rights era, some activists and legal scholars sought to realize further changes by expanding the scope of affirmative action, often through legal means. These programs are designed to increase the representation of groups who have historically been excluded from participation in certain employment sectors, companies, or educational institutions. Affirmative action programs can take many forms, ranging from programs that encourage employers and admissions committees to report on the racial and gender breakdown of those who apply and those who are accepted to strict quota programs requiring that a specific number or percentage of those accepted come from underrepresented backgrounds.

While many affirmative action programs remain legal, strict quota programs were ruled unconstitutional in the landmark affirmative action case was *Regents of Univ. of Cal. v. Bakke,* 438 U.S. 912 (1978). Allan Bakke, a white man, had applied to the University of California, Davis Medical School in 1973 and 1974 through its general admissions program and was rejected both times. He sued, claiming that the university's special admissions program, which each year admitted sixteen applicants with lower test scores and grade point averages than applicants to the general program, operated as a racial and ethnic quota system and had discriminated against him because of his race. While the Court found that it is a positive good for colleges and graduate schools to work to achieve diversity in the student body, it ruled that colleges and universities cannot have rigid "quota" systems, unless "the facts established there was a specific constitutional reason to do so" (Jones, 2002, p. 15).

Legal scholar and critical race theorist Derrick Bell has suggested that the Supreme Court's largely formalist approach toward affirmative action is a modern version of Scapegoating.

> ...when conservative white elite privilege is protected, it deflects anger onto unprivileged people of color and prevents white class warfare....Because white racial privilege promises poorer whites the possibility of upward mobility, they gain a stake in the system. For that reason, they are fooled into seeing people of color as the enemy. In cases like *Bakke* blacks are Scapegoated, becoming the enemy, shifting the focus away from the children of elites who benefit far more from a legacy admission policy (Jones, 2002).

According to critical race theorist scholars, the formalist's preference for completely race neutral policies understands affirmative action as nothing more than a "...system of spoils for people of color to gain unfair advantages over others" (Jones, 2002, p. 12).

However, Associate Justice of the Supreme Court Clarence Thomas has defended the court's formalist rulings, saying that the constitution is "color blind" and should not be used "simply as an efficiently functioning instrument that parcels out goods to different competing interest groups," (quoted in Jones, 2002, p. 19). Instead, he argued, "justice and conformity to the Constitution, not 'sensitivity,' should be the object in race relations" (quoted in Jones, 2002, p. 19-20).

Still, critical race theorists like Bell have countered that it is impossible for the law to be race neutral. Because racial discrimination has been a part of society for so long, they say, its effects are still with us today, even after the civil rights movement. Jurisprudence that does not take into account racism and its effects, then, is in fact no more than covert discrimination (Jones, 2002). They see the current state of civil rights laws as "a vast array of race-neutral rules intended to advantage whites while excluding or greatly limiting access to blacks" (Bell, 1998, quoted in Jones, 2002, p. 17).

Echebarria (1997) has suggested that racism and Scapegoating serve a social purpose, that they are used to justify and maintain dominant groups' position of power and privilege. Bell seconded this notion, writing that:

> even when non-racist practices might bring a benefit, whites may rely on discrimination against blacks as a unifying factor and a safety valve for frustration during economic hard times.....Whites, rather than acknowledge the similarity of their disadvantage, particularly when compared with that of better-off whites, are easily detoured into protecting their sense of entitlement vis-á-vis blacks for all things of value (Bell, 1998, quoted in Jones, 2002, p. 53).

Immigration

In the late twentieth century and early twenty-first century, immigration has become as controversial subject as affirmative action within the United States. While critics like Samuel P. Huntington (2004) charge illegal aliens with being a drain on the nation's economy and public services and failing to assimilate to US culture, others say that illegal aliens are being made into Scapegoats for societal ills on which they have little bearing. Mexican American journalist Ruben Navarrette (2005) has been a supporter of strong borders, but he sees racism at the root of much of the debate over illegal immigration. Illegal immigrants, he has said, "are being unfairly attacked and blamed for everything from traffic jams, to overcrowded schools, to the spread of infectious diseases" (2005, p. 80).

Judis (2006) has observed that immigrants' failure or refusal to assimilate into US culture may be at the root of critics' concerns. Speaking of immigration in Arizona, journalist Dave Wagner commented:

> Mexicans and Mexican-Americans have their own culture and stores. It is possible if you are Spanish-speaking to disappear into that culture. That scares the hell out of some people...Arizona has changed dramatically in the last 20 years, and a lot of people are uncomfortable with that. (Judis, 2006, p. 18)

Pyong Gap Min (1996) has also studied prejudice among what he calls "middleman minorities," or minorities that occupy an intermediate position in racially stratified societies and offer goods and services made by dominant groups to low status groups. His work on Korean business owners in black neighborhoods as shown that racial conflict and Scapegoating can occur not just within dominant groups, but also among minority groups.

VIEWPOINTS

As Brewer (199) has pointed out, Allport's work on ingroups and outgroups differs from Sumner's in one very important aspect: whereas Sumner had argued that the love of one's own group necessitated the hatred of others, Allport posited that identification with one's own group doesn't necessitate hostility toward members of other groups. In contrast to Sumner, who believed that one must be hostile towards an outgroup in order to identify with an ingroup, Allport claimed that while one's attachment to one's ingroup is "primary," it is not predicated upon negative beliefs about or attitudes toward outgroups. He believed while an ingroup must identify an outgroup in order to define itself, it does not have to hate or fear this outgroup. While Allport is considered one of the early and most important thinkers within Scapegoat theory, this insight demonstrates that, unlike Girard, he did not see Scapegoating as innate to the human condition (Brewer, 1999).

Certainly, not all theorists agree with Gerard that every myth and every modern society is founded upon a Scapegoating relationship. Kearney (1999) has asked if there might be some myths that try to "express a genuinely creative impulse to imagine other possibilities of existence" rather than just a desire to dominate the world as it is (p. 253). Similarly, not all social psychologist accept Scapegoat theory as a comprehensive theory for understanding interracial relationships. Zawadzki (1948) asked four questions that challenge the foundations of the theory:

- Why is one minority chosen as a Scapegoat when there are many to choose from?
- Why is there sometimes a significant difference in the level of animosity directed at minorities?
- Why are some minorities respected or liked while others are found objectionable or even despised?
- Why do minorities have prejudices against majorities?

Zawadzki (1948) claimed that Scapegoat theory is an incomplete theory, for it is entirely focused on the drives which cause a person to become prejudiced, ignoring the characteristics unique to the group against which he or she becomes prejudiced. He argued that any theory of prejudice which does not account for both the factors peculiar to the prejudiced individual and those peculiar to the minority against which he or she is prejudiced is too narrowly focused and cannot fully explain violence or aggression.

Today, Scapegoat theory is no longer a predominant theory among social psychologists; rather, since the 1980s, most scholars have subscribed to social cognition theories. They believe that racism is a natural and normal part of human thought processes, and seek to overcome it by disproving stereotypes through psychosocial interventions like intergroup contact (Echebarria, 1997). In addition, racism and prejudice have become a topic of interests to a broader range of sociologists who have studied it from a more institutional perspective. Racism, in other words, is no longer seen only in terms of the prejudice that may develop inside individuals' minds, but also as a product of social and institutional relationships that advantage some groups and disadvantage others.

TERMS & CONCEPTS

Affirmative Action: Policies designed to improve access to education and employment opportunities among groups that have historically been targets of discrimination, such as women and racial minorities. These policies can take a variety of forms from targeted recruiting to explicit preferential treatment.

Critical Race Theory: A legal theory that focuses on racial discrimination within the legal system. Among other tenets, it holds that "race neutral" legal decision making in fact provides a way for the legal system to maintain White privilege.

De Jure Segregation: Racial segregation that is enforced by the law.

De Facto Segregation: Racial segregation that is not enforced by the law, but that occurs anyway through social custom, business practices, or economic conditions.

Formalism: A legal theory which holds that judges should limit themselves to interpreting what the law says about a particular case rather than seek to determine what the law should say about a particular case. Formalists argue that this limitation serves to uphold the separation between the judiciary and legislative branches of government; they do not consider the social or political history behind a law when making judgments.

Ingroup: A group in which an individual has membership and toward which the individual feels loyalty and respect. Strong ingroup feelings generally lead to a bias towards the ingroup. Ingroups are often formed on the basis of social relationships such as family, religion, or ethnic and racial identities. However, social psychologists have found that ingroup bias can develop even on the basis of traits we normally do not consider to have social meaning, such as eye color. Ingroup loyalty can thus explain behavior such as that of sports fans or people who follow certain fashion trends.

Outgroup: A social group in which one does not have membership and does not seek to have membership. Outgroups are the opposite of ingroups, and ingroup members tend to feel contempt, opposition, and other negative emotions towards outgroup members.

Prejudice: An opinion or attitude about a particular group or object that is founded upon incorrect stereotypes, incomplete knowledge, or irrational emotions.

Racism: The term *racism* can be used in two different contexts. In individual terms, racism refers to the notion that people of different races necessarily possess certain qualities or abilities which make them superior or inferior to other races. Institutional or structural racism, on the other hand, refers to racial inequality that is built into social institutions and which continues to produce racially disparate effects even in the absence of any racist feelings or actions on the part of individuals.

Scapegoating: A term describing the process through which frustration and aggression are directed at a group that is not the causal agent of the frustration.

Stereotype: A set of oversimplified beliefs about a group or person.

Bibliography

Allport, G. (1954). *The nature of prejudice.* New York: Basic Books.

Bell, D. (1998). "The Burger Court's place on the bell curve of racial jurisprudence." In B. Schwartz (Ed.), *The Burger court: Counter-revolution or confirmation?* (pp. 57-65) Oxford: Oxford University Press.

Brewer, M. (1999, Fall). "The psychology of prejudice: Ingroup love or outgroup hate?" *Journal of Social Issues,* 55(3), 429-429.

Caple James, E. (2012). "Witchcraft, bureaucraft, and the social life of (US)AID in Haiti." *Cultural Anthropology, 27*(1), 50-75.

Echebarria, A. E. (1997) "Socio-psychological approaches to racism: A critical review." *Papers on Social Representations,* 6. http://www.psr.jku.at/

Huntington, S. P. (2004, March/April). "The Hispanic challenge." *Foreign Policy.* http://www.foreignpolicy.com

Jones, A., & Ewing, D. (2005). "The ghost of Wards Cove: The Supreme Court, the Bush administration, and the ideology undermining title VII." *Harvard Black Letter Law Journal,* 21, 163-184.

Jones, B. D. (2002). "Critical Race Theory: New Strategies for Civil Rights in the New Millennium?" *Harvard Black Letter Law Journal,*18, 1-90. www.law.harvard.edu/students/orgs/blj/vol18/jones.pdf

Judis, J. (2006, January 16). "Border war." *New Republic,* 234(1), 15-19.

Kearney, R. (1999). "Aliens and others: Between Girard and Derrida." *Cultural Values,* 3(3), 251-262.

Lubek, I. (2008). "Understanding and using the history of social psychology." *Journal of the Behavioral Sciences,* 36(4), 319–328.

Min, P. G. (1996). *Caught in the middle: Korean communities in New York and Los Angeles.* Berkley: University of California Press.

Murakawa, N. (2012). "Phantom racism and the myth of crime and punishment." *Studies In Law, Politics & Society, 59,* 99-122.

Navarrette Jr., R. (2005, October). "A healthy division." *Hispanic,* 18(10), 80-80.

Pettigrew, T. (1999). "Gordon Willard Allport: A tribute." *Journal of Social Issues,* 55(3), 415-415.

Rothschild, Z. K., Landau, M. J., Sullivan, D., & Keefer, L. A. (2012). "A dual-motive model of Scapegoating: Displacing blame to reduce guilt or increase control." *Journal Of Personality & Social Psychology, 102*(6), 1148-1163.

Wagner, M., & Fletcher, J. (1986, November 1). "Review of the book The Scapegoat." *Library Journal,* 111(18), 102.

Williams, J. (1989). "The Scapegoat." *SA: Sociological Analysis,* 49(4), 451-453.

Zawadzki, B. (1948). "Limitations of the Scapegoat theory of prejudice." *Journal of Abnormal and Social Psychology,* 43, 127-41.

Suggested Reading

Cameron, Jessica & Trope, Yaacov. (2004) "Stereotype-biased search and processing of information about group members." *Social Cognition,* 22(6), 650-672. http://www.psych.nyu.edu/

Deo, M. (2006). "Ebbs & flows: The courts in racial context." Conference Papers—*American Sociological Association;* 2006 Annual Meeting, Montreal.

Delgado, R., & Stefancic, J. (2007). "Critical race theory and criminal justice." *Humanity & Society,* 31(2/3), 133-145.

Didech, K. (2004). "The extension of disparate impact theory to White men: What the Civil Rights Act of 1991 plainly does not mean." *Texas Journal on Civil Liberties & Civil Rights,* 10(1), 55-81.

"Illegal immigrants add to states' economies." (2008, April 4). *USA Today.*

Janowitz, N. (2011). "Inventing the Scapegoat: Theories of sacrifice and ritual." *Journal Of Ritual Studies, 25*(1), 15-24.

Kanat, K. (2012). "'War on Terror' as a diversionary strategy: Personifying minorities as terrorists in the People's Republic of China." *Journal of Muslim Minority Affairs, 32*(4), 507-527.

Kosterlitz, J., & Caruso, L. (2008, March 29). "We love you, now leave." *National Journal,* 40(13), 19-19.

McManus, J. (2008, March 4). "The battle against illegal immigration." *New American,* 24(5), 10-13.

Renfro, C., Duran, A., Stephan, W., & Clason, D. (2006). "The role of threat in attitudes toward affirmative action and its beneficiaries." *Journal of Applied Social Psychology,* 36(1), 41-74.

Ruggiero, K. (1999). "The personal/group discrimination discrepancy: Extending Allport's analysis of targets." *Journal of Social Issues,* 55(3), 519-519.

Cheryl Bourassa, M.A., and
Mikaila Mariel Lemonik Arthur, Ph.D.

Race, Ethnicity & Income Inequality

ABSTRACT

It is a fact of American life that income is not distributed evenly. Along with sex, race, and ethnicity are key determinates in income distribution. Myriad reasons are presented to explain this phenomenon. Many sociologists look to historic patterns of discrimination that are responsible for lower levels of wealth accumulation, leading to stunted cultural, human and social capital. Also considered are group threat theory and failures of great society-based welfare programs. While there isn't agreement on cause, there is widespread agreement that lower income levels set up a cyclical pattern, making it equally difficult for the next generation to escape from poverty.

OVERVIEW

It has been said, "Logic dictates that if opportunities and resources were available equally and freely to all US residents, the proportional distribution of representatives of various ethnic cultures would be spread across economic levels, throughout occupations, across educational levels" (Cuyjet, 2006, cited in Strayhorn, 2008, p. 52). Fifty years after the passage of the Civil Rights Act of 1964, which was designed to end discrimination in employment, black unemployment rates are almost twice as high as they are for whites. In 2012, white families earned approximately 58 percent more than black families (US Census Bureau, 2012a). There is widespread agreement that income inequality between races exists; there is less agreement about the causes.

A net result of income inequality is that far more black than white families live in poverty. Increasingly, there are calls for more federal spending to combat the effects of poverty. The term *poverty* is often used in a broad sense to describe deprivation, but the federal government has a specific definition: in 2012, an individual under sixty-five years of age with an annual income of less than $11,945 was considered poor. Officially, 15 percent of Americans were poor by this definition in 2012 (US Census Bureau, 2012b).

Glazer argues that American opposition to the welfare state and support for patterns of small government go back many generations and can be traced back to the end of the nineteenth century. This could be the result of the structure of the US economy, its political system, or other behavioral characteristics, which include uniquely American belief systems. One might be the idea that it is possible to achieve upward mobility. While there is some evidence that this mobility is more easily achieved in Europe than in the United States, "71 percent of Americans, but only 40 percent of Europeans, believe that the poor have a chance to escape from poverty" (Glazer, 2005, p. 9). One aspect that seems to separate Americans from Europeans is 'racial fractionalization.' Comparing welfare benefits across states, there is a direct correlation between the percentage of the black population and the size of the welfare benefit: "Race seems decisive in explaining indifference to inequality" (Glazer, 2005, p. 9).

Alesina, et al., puts it bluntly:

> Americans redistribute less than Europeans for three reasons: because the majority of Americans believe that redistribution favours racial minorities, because Americans believe that they live in an open and fair society, and that if someone is poor it is his or her own fault, and because the political system is geared toward preventing redistribution (cited in Glazer, 2005, p. 10).

HISTORY

Since the late 1970s, sociologists have employed various measures to determine whether class or race has the greater impact on life chances. Even a suggestion that class is the more salient factor is controversial (Wilson, 1980). What is clear though, is that blacks still lag on many critical scales. In 2010, for instance, high school graduation rates showed that 83 percent of whites graduated from high school while 66 percent of blacks graduated. That same year, 62 percent of whites were enrolled in accredited post-secondary institutions while only 15 percent of blacks were enrolled (National Center for Education Statistics, 2013). Blacks face unemployment rates have been almost double those of their white counterparts since the US government began keeping track of such data in 1972 (Fletcher). In 2012, 33 percent of blacks held professional or managerial positions compared with 39 percent of whites Bureau of Labor and Statistics, 2013). Median family income for blacks was 66 percent that of white median family income (US Census Bureau, 2012a). Conley (2001) argues that one significant reason for the glacial pace of change concerns differing rates of accumulated family wealth.

Accumulated Wealth

Accumulated wealth is one of the most salient factors that determine socioeconomic status. Its impact ranges from family stability to educational options and all areas of employment as well as welfare dependency. The twentieth century witnessed a modest dispersal of wealth, but the Great Recession in the first few years of the twenty-first century widened the gap considerably. According to the US Census Bureau, the median household net worth for black families was $4,995, while the median white family held a household net worth of $110,729 (Luhby, 2012).

Because accumulated wealth multiplies in a way that wages do not, the gap has continued to grow, even after the victories of the civil rights era (Conley, 2001). As a result, even blacks with similar incomes to whites are far less likely to own their home; a critical step for amassing wealth.

Conley looks to a history that deprived blacks of all ownership, even of their own bodies and labor. The stated goal of Reconstruction was to help blacks toward "economic self-sufficiency." Since plantations were never divided, this did not happen. Eventually, share-cropping forced many former slaves and their descendants into a vicious cycle of debt and dependency on white landholders. When Social Security was created in 1935, agricultural and domestic workers were excluded, thus ensuring that 42 percent of black workers would be excluded from the system of old age pensions, compared to 22 percent for whites (Conley, 2001). Reflecting Glazer's argument, Contez (1992) contended that Franklin Roosevelt knew that the only way he could get the insurance plan past conservative southern Democrats was if a substantial portion of blacks were excluded. Without Social Security, blacks had to spend what little they might accumulate supporting themselves in old age rather than passing on an inheritance. Even more frequently, elder and destitute blacks were a financial drain on the next generation.

One of the landmark achievements of the civil rights movement was passage of the Civil Rights Act of 1964. The two most important segments of the law outlawed discrimination in public accommodations (Title II) and in employment (Title VII). In the two decades following its passage, the Supreme Court interpreted Title VII quite broadly, finding that along with intentional discrimination, practices that have a "racially disparate impact" were also banned (Hall, 2005, p. 172). This had the effect of invalidating many employment tests and requirements that kept minorities out of the workforce. The Equal Employment Opportunity Commission was created and charged with investigating possible cases of discrimination. As the composition of the Court changed during the Reagan Administration, increasingly, decisions in discrimination cases favored employers; none more so than *Ward's Cove Packing Co. v. Atonio* 490 U.S. 642 (1989). As a result, Congress passed the Civil Rights Act of 1991. The goal of this legislation was to clarify Congress's support for consideration of disparate impact. Both laws helped to open up the employment playing field; yet neither has succeeded in creating a completely level field (Conley, 2001; King & Wheelock, 2007; Strayhorn, 2008).

FURTHER INSIGHTS

Residential Segregation

Residential segregation between blacks and whites is a persistent problem that can be seen in many areas of the United States. Substantial research documents show that predominately black communities provide very different social environments than their white counterparts, with higher levels of unemployment, unwed motherhood, dilapidated housing, and crime common features of African American neighborhoods. In addition, these neighborhoods are marred by higher taxes and substandard schools (Peterson & Krivo, 1993).

Sociologists Blau, Blau, Logan and Messner (1987) describe how residential segregation limits opportunities:

> Racial segregation imposes a significant barrier to black upward mobility and quality of life. Places of residence locates people not only in geographical space but also in networks of social opportunities—it influences prospects for employment, for public

> services, for educational advancement, ... Residential segregation by race accordingly implies that opportunities for achievement are limited for certain groups, and it conflicts with basic American value commitments which encourage members of all groups to strive for socioeconomic success. Such a 'disjuncture' between structural arrangement and fundamental cultural values.... tends to undermine the legitimacy of social norms and thereby promotes deviant behavior (cited in Peterson & Krivo, 1993, p. 1004).

Education Opportunities

One of the most immediate consequences of segregated housing patterns is schools that are further separated by race and poverty. Orfield (2012) reports that in the first decade of the twenty-first century, 43 percent of Latino and 38 percent of black students attended schools that contained 0 to 10 percent white students. Additionally, blacks typically attended schools that were over 60 percent low income, whereas white or Asian students were found to attend schools that were on average just above 35 percent low income. Consistently, high poverty schools are connected with the problems of high turnover rates, less qualified teachers, and removal from mainstream society (Orfield & Eaton, 2003).

Employment Patterns

The implications of segregated housing patterns leading to diminished educational opportunities plays a role in income inequality at virtually all levels of employment. Since many black and Latino families find themselves in the inner city, they have been particularly hard hit as industrial jobs, once the mainstay of the cities, have disappeared. This has had a devastating impact on the employment options for many non-white men, indirectly contributing to an equally dramatic decline in the norm of a two parent household (Woldoff & Cina, 2007). Children born to single parents have a significantly higher chance of living in poverty than do children born into two-parent households.

Occupational Segregation

Occupational segregation for black and white men began moving in opposite directions in the 1980s. On one hand, more than ever before, black men were entering elite professions that had long been dominated by whites; on the other, the wage gap was growing when measured for all men. A widely held belief has been that as more blacks enter higher paid professions, the wage gap would decrease, but the trend seems to be moving in the opposite direction. Kaufman used the 1970 census to show that "black men face the greatest disadvantage in labor market at the high end of the earnings hierarchy" (cited in Grodsky & Pager, 2001, p. 543). Thus, as black men move into higher paying professions, the wage gap stands to intensify rather than shrink. Grodsky and Pager found largely the same process at work with newer data, contradicting the long standing principle that occupational selection is key to determining economic well being.

Grodsky and Pager also draw on the work of Tomaskovic-Devey who argues that as an occupation is selected either by more women or more minorities, the composition of the workforce itself "becomes a fundamental aspect of the job, influencing the work done as well as the organizational evaluation of the worth of the work" (Grodsky & Pager, 2001, p. 544). As the percentage of women or minorities shift upward, the prestige, and thus the pay, shifts downward. Wilson (1980) takes a notably different approach; he sees that as blacks enter the professions, new opportunities for blacks to gain the sorts of human capital necessary for intergenerational success accrue to them. While he acknowledges that high income blacks still have a more difficult time finding housing than do their white counterparts, they do, nonetheless, have a way to escape the inner city, and the limited educational opportunities found there.

Minority Women

As the research on black men shows, there remains a significant gap between employment rates based on race; this gap is not nearly as obvious for women. Historically, race has had minimal impact on employment levels for women. This however has been evolving over the last several decades. In 1969, white and black women with low levels of work experience were employed at the same rate; by 1991, these two groups faced divergent employment opportunities, with white women far outpacing black women. Ferrell and Glynn (2013) reported that African American women earned close to 40 percent less than white men, and Latinas earned 45 percent less. This is a particularly disturbing trend, given increasing numbers of minority women who have sole financial responsibility for their families (Reid & Padavic, 2005).

Hispanics

Hispanics are another group that has long faced difficult odds in the labor market. First and second generation Mexican immigrants have traditionally clustered in border cities along the Rio Grande and in the barrios of the Southwest border cities. As they have slowly moved from these traditional locations to newer venues in the Midwest, they still find that low educational levels leave them stranded in low-wage jobs, often depressing already inadequate wages. With restrictions aimed at noncitizens in the 1996 Welfare Reform Act, options became ever more limited (Crowley, Lichter & Qian, 2006). As Tomaskovic-Devey points out, cities with large concentrations of Hispanics, such as Los Angeles, California, have become more segregated with time, creating what has come to be called "browncollar jobs" (2006, p. 568). Beginning in the early 1990s, as low-wage jobs reached a saturation point at the same time that antiimmigrant sentiment was peaking in California, with Proposition 187, new opportunities were opening up in meat packing plants in regions once outside the traditional destinations.

As demand for processed meat has increased, meat packers have looked to reduce cost by eliminating skilled jobs, replacing them with mechanized, low skill operations, outside of cities that had high concentrations of unionized workers. Native white workers have shown limited interest in these dangerous and generally unpleasant jobs. Year round work with benefits appealed to Mexican workers, even if the wages were low, and allowed them to gain a standard of life that had not been easy to achieve elsewhere. Crowley, et al. (2006) note that meat packers actively pursued this labor source, seeing in Mexicans a willingness to "work hard, put in long hours, and endure unpleasant working conditions for low wages" (p. 347).

VIEWPOINTS

Group Threat Theory

There are myriad possibilities to consider when attempting to discern why income inequality continues to exist. One explanation involves a theory called group threat. King and Wheelock explored the role this can play in shaping income inequality between races. The theory, first put forth by Blumer in 1958, holds that "prejudice and inter-group hostility are largely reactions to perceived threats by subordinate groups" (in King & Wheelock, 2007, p. 1256). For example, whites, historically the dominant group in the United States, may try to maintain their social advantages when they sense competition (such as for jobs) from a minority population. The perception of threat increases in areas where the minority population is relatively high. One way that the dominant group can preserve its control is through punitive measures, such as harshly punishing criminal behavior. High rates of incarceration have a significant impact on all other aspects of life, most notably in the areas of family stability, civil participation, and employment. States with larger black populations tend to have higher rates of incarceration; this holds true when other variables such as crime and unemployment rates are held constant. Incarceration rates tend to increase as unemployment levels rise, especially in regions prone to income inequality (King & Wheelock, 2007).

Social Capital

Connected to the theory of group threat is Putnam's theory of social capital. He defines social capital as "connections among individuals—social networks and the norms of reciprocity and trustworthiness that arise from them," creating "civic engagement and levels of mutual trust among community members" (Weaver & Rivello, 2006, p. 21). In areas of the country with higher concentrations of blacks or Latinos, for example, there tends to be less social capital, since groups of people who differ tend not to come together often across ethnic or racial lines. To change this, a history of racism would have to be acknowledged to build trust across groups. As group threat theory implies, building trust can be quite difficult. Weaver and Rivello argue that areas with low social capital tend to have high levels of income inequality. Importantly, this is also an impediment to effecting democratic action (Weaver & Rivello, 2007).

The Digital Divide

A divergent approach involves understanding how access to information technology is divided by race. Access to computers and to the knowledge required to adequately make use of them is yet another way to determine one's chances of economic success. Servon and Nelson explain: "access to information technology and the ability to use it [have] increasingly become part of the toolkit necessary to participate and prosper in an information-based society" (cited in Chakraborty & Bosman, 2005, p. 395). In 2008, the US Bureau of Labor Statistics estimated that almost half of all jobs will be in industries that produce or depend upon intensive use of information technology. Yet, the United States faces a troubling digital divide between those who have access to these new technologies and those who do not. (Chakraborty & Bosman, 2005).

Larry Irving, Assistant Secretary of Commerce for Communications and Information during the Clinton administration in the 1990s, believes that the 'digital divide' between black and white Americans is "one of America's leading economic and civil rights issues and we have to take steps to redress the gap between the information haves and have-nots" (cited in Chakraborty & Bosman, 2005, p. 396). It is not simply a matter of all citizens gaining access as the price of the technology falls; there is also the issue of the price of network access, and equally critical, access to the skills necessary to make the technology a worthy investment. New technologies only intensify the divide, and the pace of new technology is always accelerating. It is important to note that this has implications that expand beyond incomeinequality, while at the same time reinforcing that inequality. One of the critically important uses of information technology is in the field of democratic action. Without adequate access, low income Americans have a reduced opportunity to participate in this ever more important venue for political dialogue and action. Thus, they miss out on the option of organizing for political change that could affect their economic wellbeing (Chakraborty & Bosman, 2005).

Welfare & the Non-Working Poor

Finally, it is important to recognize that some scholars believe there is not a tie between race and income inequality. Mead (2007) argues that we only have a tenuous understanding of the roots of poverty and income inequality; thus while there seems to be almost obligatory rhetoric about addressing the problems that stem from poverty, there are few fresh ideas, and less confidence that a solution can be found. He suggests that the 'solutions' of the War on Poverty were not really solutions at all; rather a robust economy made work pay, at least for those who choose to work. His focus is on those who opted against working. He explains:

> In 1959, 68 percent of the heads of poor families worked, 31 percent of them full-time and year-'round. By 1975 those figures had fallen to 50 and16 percent respectively, and they have changed little since then. For the nonworking poor, a hot economy was no solution (Mead, 2007, p. 46).

He blames welfare for this increase in the number of the non-working poor, since the rolls exploded just as the economy boomed in the 1960s.

Mead outright rejects the notion that poverty and relatively higher unemployment rates for racial and ethnic minority groups are a result of racial bias in hiring. He acknowledges that a quarter of all poor are black, and another quarter are Hispanic, far beyond their representation in the population. He contends that the most destructive forms of poverty—that marked by lower work levels and higher levels of crime and substance abuse—are a hallmark of the post-civil rights era. Although Daniel Patrick Moynihan's explanation for black poverty, one that put the blame on the family, especially on women who took leadership roles within the family is no longer widely accepted (Contz, 1992), Mead agrees with him that it is the "dissolution" of the black family that is the root cause of their poverty. In 1965, when Moynihan issued his report, 25 percent of black children were born into single parent households; in 2007, 68 percent of black children were born into fatherless families. Even during the 1990s, as the labor market boomed, young black men were less apt than ever to join the workforce. Instead, a third of black men have criminal records, and half are not parenting their children (Mead, 2007).

Although civil rights era legislation has helped to narrow the gap between white workers and those of other races, most notably blacks and Hispanics, there remains a significant difference in the wages that each group earns. When one generation accrues less wealth than would be possible under more ideal circumstances, there is an intergenerational impact, since the family of origin's wealth plays a substantial role in determining its children's economic chances, as they pass on the human, social and cultural capital necessary for success. Reasons for the gap abound, ranging from segregated neighborhoods and schools, to computer ownership and group threat theory.

TERMS & CONCEPTS

Civil Rights Act of 1964: Landmark legislation of the civil rights era, designed to end discrimination in public accommodations and in employment.

Cultural Capital: The beliefs, tastes, and preferences that come from one's family, helping to define class status (Strayhorn, 2008).

Equal Employment Opportunity Commission (EEOC): Collects yearly data on the sex by race/ethnic composition of private sector employment as part of federal efforts to monitor compliance with the Civil Rights Act and similar legislation (Tomaskovic-Devey, 2006).

Fragile Family: A family that is formed when the parents are not married, and their economic situation is precarious.

Group Threat Theory: "Prejudice and inter-group hostility are largely reactions to perceived threats by subordinate groups. Dominant groups seek to preserve their advantaged social position and view encroachments on their prerogatives by minority groups as disrupting to the existing social order" (King & Wheelock, 2007, p. 1256).

Poverty: The federal government uses a formula that considers the cost of basic housing, food and other essentials. It is this measure that determines eligibility for a host of social services.

Segregation: A policy in which residential areas, places of employment and schools that are separated by race. Segregation can be achieved through legal strategies (de jure) or through customs and norms (de facto).

Social Capital: "Connections among individuals—social networks and the norms of reciprocity and trustworthiness that arise from them," creating "civic engagement and levels of mutual trust among community members" (Weaver & Rivello, 2006, p. 21).

Undocumented Workers: These are workers who entered the United States without proper immigration documentation. They cannot legally work, and they are subject to deportation.

War on Poverty: During the Johnson Administration there was a concerted effort made to combat the effects of long term, intergenerational poverty. Included were Aid to Families with Dependent Children (AFDC), Medicare and Medicaid. Eventually commitment to the Great Society programs of the War on Poverty gave way to funding for the Vietnam War.

Bibliography

Bureau of Labor Statistics. (2013, February 3). "Labor force statistics from the current population survey." http://www.bls.gov/cps/cpsaat10.htm

Chakraborty, J., & Bosman, M. (2005). "Measuring the digital divide in the United States: Race, income, and personal computer ownership." *Professional Geographer*, 57(3), 395–410.

Conley, D. (2001). "Decomposing the black-white wealth gap: The role of parental resources, inheritance, and investment dynamics." *Sociological Inquiry*, 71(1), 39–66.

Contz, S. (1992). *The way we never were: American families and the nostalgia trap.* New York: Basic Books.

Crowley, M., Lichter, D., & Qian, Z. (2006). "Beyond gateway cities: Economic restructuring and poverty among Mexican immigrant families and children." *Family Relations*, 55(3), 345–360.

Farrell, Jane, & Glynn, S. J. (2013, June 7). "The gender pay gap by race and ethnicity." *Center for American Progress.* http://www.americanprogress.org/issues/ext/2013/06/07/65727/the-gender-pay-gap-by-race-and-ethnicity/

Fletcher, Michael A. (2012, December 14). "Black jobless rate is twice that of whites." *Washington Post.* http://articles.washingtonpost.com/2012-12-14/business

Glazer, N. (2005). "Why Americans don't care about income inequality." *Irish Journal of Sociology*, 14(1), 5–12.

Grodsky, E., & Pager, D. (2001). "The structure of disadvantage: Individual and occupational determinants of the black-white wage gap." *American Sociological Review*, 66(4), 542–567.

Hall, K. (2005). *The Oxford companion to the Supreme Court of the United States*. New York: Oxford University Press.

Killewald, A. (2013). "Return to being black, living in the red: A race gap in wealth that goes beyond social origins." *Demography, 50*(4), 1177–1195.

Kim, C., & Tamborini, C. R. (2012). "Do survey data estimate earnings inequality correctly? Measurement errors among black and white male workers." *Social Forces, 90*(4), 1157–1181.

King, R., & Wheelock, D. (2007). "Group Threat and social control: Race, perceptions of minorities and the desire to punish." *Social Forces*, 85(3), 1255–1280.

Luhby, Tami. (2012, June 21). "Worsening wealth inequality by race." *CNNMoney*. http://money.cnn.com/2012/06/21/news/economy/wealth-gap-race/

Luttig, M. (2013). "The structure of inequality and Americans' attitudes toward redistribution." *Public Opinion Quarterly*, 77(3), 811–821.

Mead, L. (2007). "Crying poverty." *Commentary*, 124(2), 45–49.

National Center for Education Statistics. (2013). "The condition of education." http://nces.ed.gov/programs/coe/

Orfield, G., & Eaton, S. (2003). "Back to segregation." *The Nation*, 276(8), 5–7.

Orfield, G., et al. (2012, September 19). "E pluribus . . . separation: Deepening double segregation for more students." *The Civil Rights Project*. http://civilrightsproject.ucla.edu/research/k-12-education/integration-and-diversity/mlk-national/e-pluribus...separation-deepening-double-segregation-for-more-students/

Peterson, R., & Krivo, L. (1993). "Racial segregation and Black urban homicide." *Social Forces*, 71(4), 1001–1026.

Pop, I., Ingen, E., & Oorschot, W. (2013). "Inequality, wealth and health: Is decreasing income inequality the key to create healthier societies?" *Social Indicators Research, 113*(3), 1025–1043.

Reid, L., & Padavic, I. (2005, Dec.). "Employment exits and the race gap in young women's employment." *Social Science Quarterly*, 86, 1242–1260.

Strayhorn, T. (2008). "Influences on labor market outcomes of African American college graduates: A national study." *Journal of Higher Education*, 79(1), 28–57.

Tomaskovic-Devey, D., Zimmer, C., Stainback, K., Robinson, C., Taylor, T., & McTague, T. (2006). "Documenting desegregation: Segregation in American workplaces by race, ethnicity, and sex, 1966-2003." *American Sociological Review*, 71(4), 565–588.

US Census Bureau. (2012a). "Income, poverty, and health insurance in the United States: 2012–detailed tables." http://www.census.gov/hhes/www/income/data/incpovhlth/2012/dtables.html

US Census Bureau. (2012b). "Poverty." http://www.census.gov/hhes/www/poverty/about/overview/

US Department of Education, National Center for Edudcation Statistics. (2009–2010). "State dropout and completion data file, table 125." http://nces.ed.gov/programs/coe/indicator%5Fcoi.asp

Wallace, M., & Figueroa, R. (2012). "Determinants of perceived immigrant job threat in the American states." *Sociological Perspectives, 55*(4), 583–612.

Weaver, R., & Rivello, R. (2006). "The distribution of mortality in the United States: The effects of income (inequality), social capital, and race." *Omega: Journal of Death & Dying*, 54(1), 19-39.

Woldoff, R., & Cina, M. (2007). "Regular work, underground jobs, and hustling: An examination of paternal work and father involvement." *Fathering: A Journal of Theory, Research, & Practice about Men as Fathers*, 5(3), 153–173.

Suggested Reading

Kim, C., & Tamborini, C. (2006). "The continuing significance of race in the occupational attainment of whites and blacks: A segmented labor market analysis." *Sociological Inquiry*, 76(1), 23–51.

Langdon, D., & Klomegah, R. (2013). "Gender Wage Gap And Its Associated Factors: An Examination Of Traditional Gender Ideology, Education, And Occupation." *International Review of Modern Sociology, 39*(2), 173–203.

McVeigh, R. (2004). "Structured ignorance and organized racism in the United States." *Social Forces*, 82(3), 895–936.

Rohde, N., & Guest, R. (2013). "Multidimensional racial inequality in the United States." *Social Indicators Research, 114*(2), 591–605.

Rosenfeld, J., & Kleykamp, M. (2012). "Organized labor and racial wage inequality in the United States." *American Journal of Sociology,* 117 (5), 1460–1502.

"Trading action for access: The myth of meritocracy and the failure to remedy structural discrimination." (2008). *Harvard Law Review,* 121(8), 2156–2177.

Cheryl Bourassa, M.A.

RACIAL PROFILING

ABSTRACT

Racial profiling is a contentious issue in US law enforcement policy. The practice of using race as a part of a profile when attempting to identify or curb criminal activity has been used in various ways, including pulling individuals over on highways and questioning airline passengers and individuals at border crossings. Racial profiling has been used to justify finding drug smugglers, terrorists, and undocumented immigrants. Many contend that Racial profiling severely hampers civil rights, while others believe it is necessary police practice.

Racial profiling has become a contentious issue in law enforcement practices over the last twenty years. An increasing number of reported instances in which law enforcement personnel have been accused of targeting certain minority groups has cast a spotlight on Racial profiling, as well as increased tensions and debate over the legitimacy of the practice for various reasons (Institute on Race and Justice, 2008).

OVERVIEW

Defining Racial Profiling

There is no single agreed upon definition of racial profiling. The definition across the literature ranges from including race, ethnicity, or nationality as a consideration when deciding to apply law enforcement procedures, to using race, ethnicity, or nationality as the only consideration when deciding to apply law enforcement procedures. A similar term is Racially-biased policing, and the line between what communities find acceptable and unacceptable is influenced by a wide range of factors (Anderson & Callahan, 2001). The public perception of the acceptability of racial profiling varies under circumstances. For example, a poll conducted in 1999 said 81 percent of individuals reported that they disapproved of racial profiling when law enforcement officials pulled over motorists solely based on their race and ethnicity. On the other hand, another poll conducted after the September 11 terrorist attacks showed that the majority of those polled supported increasing security and investigation of individuals from Arab backgrounds on planes (Pampel, 2004).

The practice of racial profiling by law enforcement agencies was begun during the late 1970s, as police officers worked to capture drug traffickers. A profile is a collection of gathered facts that help law enforcement officers target individuals who are likely committing criminal acts. Law enforcement officers have long used profiling to help them gain understanding about the likely characteristics of the perpetrator of a crime, including but not limited to age, sex, race, and observed behaviors (Institute on Race and Justice, 2008). Police have used profiling to target the characteristics of certain individuals as more likely to commit certain types of crimes, often observed by police officers. For example, a poor individual who spends a large amount of time in affluent enclaves may be targeted as someone likely to commit a crime. While this type of profiling has often been seen as unfair and biased, law enforcement agencies consider it a necessary practice to intercept possible criminal activity before it occurs (Pampel, 2004).

Racial profiling was first termed during the war on drugs in the 1970s and 1980s, when police officers were accused of pulling over motorists based on race and then searching their vehicles for illegal substances. However, there are incidents of racial profiling in other situations and instances throughout American history. For example, during World War II, hundreds of thousands of Japanese immigrants and Japanese-Americans were interned in camps throughout the United States even though many were American citizens and had never had any negative interactions with law enforcement officers in the past (Anderson & Callahan, 2001). Even more currently, after the September 11 attacks in 2001, the War on Terrorism was announced and individuals across the country were arrested, questioned, or detained by federal law enforcers. Many advocacy groups have derided the government for what they believe is questioning or harassment based solely on an individual's race, ethnicity, or national origin (Anderson & Callahan, 2001).

Other instances of racial profiling include pulling over Hispanics near the Mexico border in an attempt to capture illegal immigrants en route to the United States or questioning or searching minorities in high-crime urban areas (Pampel, 2004). In April 2010, Arizona enacted SB 1070, which made it a misdemeanor crime for a a nonresident of the United States to be in Arizona without carrying required documents. The act also allowed officers to determine an individual's immigration status during a lawful stop or arrest (Archibold, 2010). The act, which was written primarily to address Arizona's influx of illegal immigrants, was the strictest and most controversial anti-illegal immigration legislation at the time and prompted debate worldwide regarding the potential for racial profiling. The Supreme Court upheld the requirement in 2012, and five other states (Alabama, Georgia, Indiana, Utah, and South Carolina) adopted similar legislation (Billeaud & Berry, 2012).

The arguments that surround the issue of racial profiling are connected to the inherent racism found in our communities and the tensions between law enforcement officials and various communities of color. Statistics have shown that African-American individuals are much more likely to be arrested and imprisoned than white Americans. As of 2012, 60 percent of all imprisoned men were African American, and 1 in every 15 African American men was in prison versus 1 in every 106 white men. Additionally, 1 in every 3 black men can expect to go to prison as some point in their lives, and convicted blacks receive sentences that are 10 percent longer than their white counterparts. Blacks were also three times more likely than whites to be searched during traffic stops (Kerby, 2012). Other ethnic groups in the United States have also experienced negative effects from racial profiling.

Background

While the term racial profiling has only recently come into use, law enforcement agencies have long used race, ethnicity, and national origin as grounds for police action in the United States. During the years of slavery, blacks were not allowed to leave their plantations without passes, and they could be questioned or detained by any white individual without any reason for suspicion. After slavery was outlawed, many states continued to control African Americans through curfews and the use of Jim Crow laws throughout the South (Pampel, 2004).

Throughout history, conflicts and tensions between police officers and communities of color have endured. Hispanics and Latinos have faced intense scrutiny from law enforcement officials under suspicion that they are illegal residents; Asian-Americans were discriminated against by police officers in the communities in which they lived when they began immigrating to the United States in large numbers in the 1800s. Those of Middle Eastern descent face profiling in the wake of the September 11 terrorist attacks.

APPLICATIONS

The Police Public Contact Survey

A report released by the United States Department of Justice's Bureau of Justice Statistics (BJS) provided results from a 2002 survey in which contacts between police officers and close to 17 million drivers were analyzed. The results were significant for several reasons. First, although white drivers were more likely than both black and Hispanic drivers to be stopped by police for speeding, both blacks and Hispanics were more likely to receive a ticket. Among the young, males drivers to be stopped, blacks and Hispanics were more likely to be searched. These statistics are in spite of the fact that in 2002 a higher percentage of white drivers were licensed in the United States (76.2 percent) than black drivers (10.5 percent) and Hispanics (9.7 percent).

Many people equate the war on drugs as beginning the controversy regarding racial profiling. The war on drugs gained intensity in the 1980s, with the introduction of crack cocaine into mainstream America (Pampel, 2004). In 1985, as the war against drugs continued, the Drug Enforcement Agency (DEA) began training police officers across the country in recognizing a profile of a drug courier, based on intelligence gathered in how drugs were transported and introduced to various drug markets. The intelligence garnered by the DEA gave birth to

Operation Pipeline, the knowledge of the relationship between drug networks and drug markets, and how drugs were transported between each. Local and state police were trained to target individuals and vehicles that met certain characteristics, including but not limited to age and race characteristics of possible transporters. When the profiling lesson was distorted, officers began targeting black and Hispanic drivers, pulling over male drivers with these racial characteristics under the guise of traffic violations in order to search their cars for drugs (Institute on Race and Justice, 2008).

Government officials also began an effort to halt the smuggling of drugs through airports. Customs agents were provided profiles that drug couriers were often black women with certain physical characteristics. However, due to intense scrutiny from the public, this profile was eventually changed to focus on behavior rather than race and ethnicity of the individual (Pampel, 2004).

Many critics of the drug wars believe that law enforcement officials relied too heavily on Racial stereotypes in searching for those trafficking and using drugs. Others also contend that the problem in minority communities was blown out of proportion, while drug use in white suburbs was largely ignored as a problem (Pampel, 2004).

Community Policing

While law enforcement agencies answer calls of distress or solve crimes, they also engage in another area of community life imperative to preventing crime before it happens, often called community policing or quality of life policing. Community policing involves officers directly in the community they police, improving the neighborhood, reducing factors that fuel the fear of crime, and bettering the neighborhood to discourage crimes from taking place (Pampel, 2004). Community policing has sometimes focused around the "broken windows" theory–that if one window is broken and left broken, all of the other windows will soon be broken because it shows that there is no penalty for disorderly conduct. This theory was first introduced by criminologists James Wilson and George Kelling and purports that when there appears to be no consequences for crime, crime will rise. Thus, police officers take harsh measures against those who commit even the slightest crimes to prevent further criminal activity (Wilson & Kelling, 1992).

This theory was put into place in New York City in the mid-1990s, with a great amount of success. However, critics often suggested that police were using stereotypes and racial discrimination to choose who they suspected and questioned about crimes. While city officials deny using racial profiling, many believe that race was a component in many police actions (Pampel, 2004).

Immigration & Terrorism

According to a US Census Report, there were over 40 million legal and illegal immigrants in the United States in 2010, which is a 28 percent increase from 2000. The United study completed by the Pew Research Center indicates that there were over 11 million undocumented residents in the United States (Passell & Cohn, 2011). The high numbers of undocumented immigrants from Mexico and Central and South America have led to some controversy on racial profiling when identifying undocumented immigrants. Using the criteria of race or ethnicity in checking for legality has contentious arguments on both sides. While the Supreme Court in previous years has refrained from making a decision on whether race and ethnicity could be a criteria in attempts to identify undocumented immigrants, starting in the mid-1970s the Court upheld that race and ethnicity could not be sole factors in consideration. Even more recently, courts have upheld that it is unconstitutional to use Hispanic appearance as a factor in determining whether or not an individual is legally in the country. While the US Border Patrol denies use of racial profiling, there are groups who contest this claim, including civil rights groups and many members of the Hispanic and Latino community (Pampel, 2004).

More recently, the aftermath of the September 11 terrorist attacks has many groups arguing that current policies encourages law enforcement officials to unfairly profile individuals of Middle Eastern descent, using race and ethnicity as the largest factor in questioning individuals (Harris, 2002).

Case Probability & Class Probability

Racial profiling inherently relies on the use of stereotypes: casting often innocent people as suspects because of how they look. Anderson & Callahan (2001) describe the difference between case probability and class probability when discussing racial profiling.

Case probability relies on variables that are relevant or applicable to a certain event or to making a guess based on some of the evidence at hand. Class probability relies on statistics used to make inferences about a certain event, but does not take into account evidence of the particular event. For example, if the police are investigating a crime in which bystanders saw a young Asian woman fleeing the scene, they will employ case probability in searching for a young Asian woman. In this scenario, the police have hard facts and suspicions on which to build an investigation. On the other hand, pulling over minorities on the highway and hoping to increase the chances of decreasing crime falls under the umbrella of class probability. This shift represents a loss in civil protection for a certain class of people, in this case, based on race.

VIEWPOINTS

There are vehement arguments both for and against racial profiling. On one hand, supporters believe that the gains of using race or ethnicity in profiling outweigh the consequences. Others believe that racial profiling is ineffective and destroys civil rights for certain groups of people.

For example, there are statistical factors that show that while whites have higher total numbers of arrests than blacks, the percentages of arrests are higher for blacks for various types of infractions including drug abuse, weapons violations, driving while intoxicated, and vehicular fatalities. Proponents of Racial profiling address these statistics as proof that minorities often commit more crimes than whites; others argue that there is inherent bias in the police activity towards minorities and that these statistics cannot be taken at face value. There is well documented evidence that minorities are arrested more often, and receive harsher sentences for similar crimes committed by Whites (Pampel, 2004).

Costs & Benefits

Another factor in support of racial profiling addresses the costs and benefits of the practice. Many argue that the gains outweigh the losses. For example, it may indeed be too unfair to subject those of certain Racial or ethnic backgrounds to searches or questioning, but if it prevents a large scale crime from occurring, it may be worth burdening other individuals (Anderson & Callahan, 2001). The major areas of law enforcement where Racial profiling has been used, such as in the drug wars and in anti-terrorism activity, have both had severely negative impacts in communities such as a high number of lives lost (Pampel, 2004).

The arguments against racial profiling are also numerous, and those who oppose the practice come from diverse backgrounds. Critics of using race, ethnicity, or nationality as a precursor for random checks and questioning contend that the practice is inherently unfair, has a negative impact on communities, and is also an ineffective investigation practice (Pampel, 2004).

An act to deter racial profiling was passed in 2012 in the state of Connecticut. SB 364, An Act Concerning Traffic Stop Information, forces local and state law enforcement to enact policies that disallow the search, detention, or stopping of any person based solely on their race, ethnicity, age, gender, or sexual orientation. Additionally, police are required to note in a report the racial makeup of every individual stopped or detained. The legislation was passed after an incident in East Haven, Connecticut, where police were accused of beating, harassing, and falsely arresting Latinos who threatened to report police misconduct.

Statistical analysis also provides doubt that racial profiling is effective. For example, Harris (2002) reports on "hit rates" for drug searches for different minority groups, or the percentage of searches by law enforcement officials that resulted in finding drugs. In two studies, the hit rates for drug searches on the highway turned out nearly identical numbers between whites and blacks. Similarly, in customs searches for drugs found a hit rate of 6.7 percent for whites, compared to 6.2 percent and 2.8 percent for blacks and Hispanics, respectively.

Consequences in the Community

Racial profiling can also have psychological effects and negative effects on the community. Minorities who are innocent victims may feel intimidated, with little control over their lives. Some psychologists have likened the effects to post-traumatic stress disorder, in which individuals who have experienced a traumatic event will experience a host of stressful reactions to the memory of the event including but not limited to negative thoughts, dreams, avoidance of social situations, or change in their daily activities to avoid re-experience of the situation. While many people may view Racial profiling as a minor inconvenience, for others it may have more serious consequences (Pampel, 2004).

The community and the effectiveness of law enforcement officials can additionally be adversely affected. In the most basic sense, all individuals in the United States have the right to certain civil liberties; profiling separates people into groups based on injustices that Americans have been attempting to fight for hundreds of years. Many argue that when law enforcement officials use Racial profiling, they risk antagonizing the very communities they serve and work with, staunching the flow of information from those who are skeptical that police officers are working to help them (Pampel, 2004).

Curbing Racial Profiling

Those who oppose racial profiling most often believe that it is practiced often within the law enforcement community. While federal and state governments have not necessarily addressed the issue, there are others who are working to stop the practice. Racial profiling is being combated through a variety of practices, including data collection, trainings, and litigation.

Law enforcement agencies who hope to decrease racial profiling have taken measures such as conducting trainings for officers regarding diversity and cultural norms, limiting when officers can search vehicles, and increasing recruitment and hiring of diverse individuals from an array of backgrounds. Some of these measures, especially limiting officers' abilities to search vehicles or question random individuals are seen as controversial; proponents say that allowing these actions actually promotes racial profiling while those who believe police officers need these powers contend that limiting this power limits the ability to do the work effectively (Pampel, 2004).

Litigation

A number of lawsuits have been brought concerning the practice of racial profiling. These include cases in which individuals believe they were wrongly pulled over on the highway or searched or detained during flying. Opponents of these practices claim that they are unfair, demeaning, and ineffective at finding actual criminal activity. Various lawsuits across the country have thrust the practice of using racial profiling into the spotlight. Many groups who work on behalf of victims of racial profiling hope that if the practice does not actually become illegal, it will become too expensive to continue (Pampel, 2004).

The debate over racial profiling has a long history and will continue to have an impact on how law enforcement agencies in the United States work to keep citizens safe. While there are many who are working to stop Racial profiling, calling it an unfair, irresponsible, and ineffective practice, public opinion in the wake of events such as the September 11 attacks and political issues such as those surrounding undocumented immigration will continue to affect how the public feels about the practice of using race, ethnicity, or national origin as a reason to take police action against certain individuals.

TERMS & CONCEPTS

Broken windows theory: The broken windows theory was developed by criminologists and purports that when it is apparent that there are no consequences for crimes, crime will escalate.

Case probability: Case Probability refers to the reliance on variables that are relevant or applicable to a certain event, or using evidence to help make an assumption.

Class probability: Class probability uses statistical evidence to make inferences, but does not take into account evidence of the particular event.

Community policing: Community policing refers to the work of law enforcement officials to improve community relations, decrease opportunities for crime, and address crime before it happens in a certain community.

Post-traumatic stress disorder: Post-traumatic stress disorder occurs to individuals after a traumatic event, and is characterized by symptoms including negative thoughts, reliving the event, social withdrawal, and panic.

Profiling: Profiling is used by law enforcement officers to gather facts that will help them determine the type of person who is likely to commit a certain crime.

Terrorism: Terrorism refers to the use of terror tactics and violence as a means to achieve a political goal.

Undocumented immigrants: Undocumented immigrants, also called illegal immigrants, are those who are have entered the country without the proper identification.

War on Drugs: The war on drugs refers to the drive by law enforcement officials in the 1970s and 80s to apprehend those involved in the drug trade. Many believe that officials used Racial profiling to pull over and search vehicles during this time.

BIBLIOGRAPHY

Anderson, W., & Callahan, G. (2001). "The roots of racial profiling: Why are police targeting minorities for traffic stops?" Reason Online Web Site: http://www.reason.com/news/printer/28138.html.

Archibold, R. C. (2010, April 23). "Arizona enacts stringent law on immigration." *New York Times.* http://www.nytimes.com/2010/04/24/us/politics/24immig.html

Billeaud, J., & Berry, W. (2012, September 5). "Judge oks Arizona's show-me-your-papers law." *NBC News.* http://www.nbcnews.com/id/48920114/#.UoPUvHCsiSo

Camarota, S. A. (2007). "Immigrants in the United States, 2007: A profile of America's foreign-born population." Center for Immigration Studies Web Site: http://www.cis.org/immigrants%5Fprofile%5F2007

Chan, J. (2011). "*Racial profiling* and police subculture." *Canadian Journal of Criminology & Criminal Justice*, 53, 75-78.

Hackney, A. A., & Glaser, J. (2013). "Reverse deterrence in racial profiling: Increased transgressions by non-profiled whites. Law & Human Behavior." (American Psychological Association), 37, 348-353.

Harris, D. A. (2002). *Profiles in injustice.* New York: The New Press.

Higgins, G. E., & Gabbidon, S. L. (2012). "Exploring untested measures on public opinion on the use of Racial profiling during traffic stops to identify criminals." *Journal of Ethnicity in Criminal Justice*, 10, 71-85.

Higgins, G. E., Vito, G. F., Grossi, E. L., & Vito, A. G. (2012). "Searches and traffic stops: Racial profiling and capriciousness." *Journal of Ethnicity In Criminal Justice*, 10, 163-179.

Institute on Race and Justice. (2008). "Background and current data collection efforts: History of Racial profiling analysis." RacialProfiling Data Collection Resource Center Web Site: http://www.Racialprofilinganalysis.neu.edu/background/

Kerby, S. (2012, March 13). "The top 10 most startling facts about people of color and criminal justice in the United States." *Center for American Progress.* http://www.americanprogress.org/issues/race/news/2012/03/13/11351/the-top-10-most-startling-facts-about-people-of-color-and-criminal-justice-in-the-united-states/

Pampel, F. C. (2004). *Racial profiling.* New York: Facts on File, Inc.

Passel, J. S., & Cohn, D. (2011, February 1). "Unauthorized immigrant population: National and state trends, 2010." *Pew Research Hispanic Trends Project.* http://www.pewhispanic.org/2011/02/01/unauthorized-immigrant-population-brnational-and-state-trends-2010/

Rojek, J., Rosenfeld, R., & Decker, S. (2012). "Policing race: The Racial stratification of searches in police traffic stops." *Criminology*, 50, 993-1024.

Thomas, S. A., Burgason, K. A., Brown, T., & Berthelot, E. (2017). "Is it all about race? Intergroup threat and perceptions of Racial profiling." *Criminal Justice Studies*, 30(4), 401-420.

Source Ultimate. http://search.ebscohost.com

Wilson, J. Q., & Kelling, G. L. (1992). "Broken windows." *Atlantic Monthly*, 249, 29-38.

SUGGESTED READING

Asim, J. (ed). (2001). *Not guilty: Twelve black men speak out on law, justice, and life.* New York: Harper Collins.

Cole, D. (1999). *No equal justice: Race and class in the American criminal justice system.* New York: The New Press.

Crank, J. P. (2011). "Scholarly debate on Racial profiling: To what end?" *Canadian Journal of Criminology & Criminal Justice*, 53, 79-85.

Engel, R. S., Calnon, J. M., & Bernard, T. J. (2002). "Theory and racial profiling: Shortcomings and future directions in research." *Justice Quarterly* 19, 249-273.

Gabbidon, S. L., & Higgins, G. E. (2011). "Public opinion on the use of consumer racial profiling to identify shoplifters: An exploratory study." *Criminal Justice Review* (Sage Publications), 36, 201-212.

Ibe, P., Ochie, C., & Obiyan, E. (2012). "Racial misuse of 'criminal profiling' by law enforcement: Intentions and implications." *African Journal of Criminology & Justice Studies*, 6(1/2), 177-196.

MacDonald, H. (2003). *Are cops racist?* Chicago: Ivan R. Dee.

Nier, J. A., Gaertner, S. L., Nier, C. L., & Dovidio, J. F. (2012). "Can racial profiling be avoided under Arizona immigration law? Lessons learned from subtle bias research and anti-discrimination law." *Analyses of Social Issues & Public Policy*, 12, 5-20.

Seigel, M. (2017). "The dilemma of 'racial profiling': an abolitionist police history." *Contemporary Justice Review*, 20(4), 474-490.

Willbanks, W. (1987). *The myth of a racist criminal justice system*. Monterey, CA: Brooks/Cole Publishing.

Rana Suh, M.Ed.

Segregation

ABSTRACT

For a century after the Civil War, white and black Americans worked to sort out the nature of the relationships they would create to govern their interactions. It is overly simplistic to see the creation of de jure segregation that came to rule those relationships in the South as an inevitable by-product of the demise of slavery; instead, both the formal and informal rules of Jim Crow evolved slowly through the remainder of the 19th century. One result was the impoverishment of the region, for both whites and blacks. As blacks fled from the racial violence that became a hallmark of Jim Crow, they found themselves locked in a new pattern of discrimination in the North and Midwest: de facto segregation also limited the options opened to black citizens. The Civil Rights movement challenged both types of segregation, resulting in substantial changes in the social and economic realities for both races, but lingering vestiges of discrimination remain.

OVERVIEW

The decades before the Civil War found the vast majority of African Americans in a state of slavery in the Southern and mid Atlantic states. An inevitable by-product of slavery was a high degree of physical and social proximity between whites and blacks. Slave owners and slaves lived on the same property, sharing work space; owners had their most intimate needs tended to by their slaves. When the Thirteenth Amendment abolished slavery, a new system of relationships between whites and blacks had to be established. By the beginning of the 20th century, de jure segregation created a protocol, much of it formalized in law, which regulated almost every aspect of those relationships.

When blacks started migrating North, no such formal system was in place. What emerged instead was a system of de facto segregation, one which could be every bit as restricting as the more legally binding system found in the South. The social and economic consequences of both systems of segregation were significant and affected both races. By mid-20th century, the Civil Rights Movement arose to challenge both systems of segregation. While the changes have been immense, vestiges of segregation can still significantly impact the lives of black Americans today.

HISTORY

19th Century America

In his seminal work, *The Promise of the New South: Life After Reconstruction,* Edward Ayers argued that race relations after Reconstruction were far more complex and fluid than they appear at first glance. Still, the rituals of race relations colored every aspect of personal interactions. For instance, when a young boy referred to a respected black man as "Mr. Jones," his aunt told him: "No, son, Robert Jones is a nigger. You don't say 'mister' when you speak of a nigger.... [You] say 'nigger Jones'" (Ayers, 1992, p. 132). Even certain days of the week were segregated. By custom, blacks were expected to come into town to shop only on Saturday afternoons; white shoppers knew to stay away. Nonetheless, civil relationships were possible, even in the face of general and mutual dislike, and periodic, outright violence. Elderly and "worthy" blacks were treated with kindness; doing so was seen as a sign of good character on the part of whites (Ayer, 1992). The question remains: how did race relations change to such a degree as to give rise to the Civil Rights Movement?

Consider one of the more famous images from the Civil Rights movement: African Americans were peacefully protesting in Birmingham, Alabama, when Bull Connor, the city sheriff who became synonymous with racial antipathy, used dogs and water cannon to break up the demonstration. With that image it is possible, even easy, to see a single straight narrative from slavery to viciously enforced segregation. Jane Dailey (2002), writing of interracialism in 19th century Virginia, disagreed with this view. "It [has become] easy to see white supremacy as irresistible," she wrote, arguing that this view is too limiting (quoted in Kelly, 2004, p. 4). By focusing on the inevitableness of white supremacy, she believed, one misses the moments of possibility, sensed by both races, for greater equality during the decades between emancipation and Jim Crow.

Brian Kelly (2004) suggested that it is ironic that Birmingham has become a symbol of white supremacy; the city was founded after the Civil War as a modern beacon of industrialism. The elite of the city were repeatedly shaken by interracial strikes in which blacks and whites came together against enormous obstacles to challenge the racial and class hierarchies of the city. In 1908 and 1920, the state declared martial law to break up labor protests. Kelly saw the use of troops as a means of legitimizing vigilante justice. Thus, he suggested, the "visceral racism" that was so visible by 1963, was not a "natural, inevitable feature of Southern society," but rather a "historic consequence" of the aftermath of the strikes (Kelly, 2004, p. 5).

Southern industrial elites understood that their ability to compete with the more technologically advanced mills of the North was dependant on a continual exploitation of both white and black labor that maintained a "racial hierarchy." Jacquelyn Hall suggested that Jim Crow should be understood as racial capitalism, "a system that combined de jure segregation with hyper exploitation of black and white labor" (quoted in Kelly, 2004, p. 7).

In the 1870's, vast reserves of coal and iron ore were discovered in Birmingham, making feasible the dream of a Southern city to rival Pittsburgh. To make that dream a reality, though, the new industrialists needed one more factor: an endless supply of cheap labor.

"Nowhere in the world is the industrial situation so favorable to the employer as it is now at the south," a typical editorial in the *Manufacturers' Record* boasted. The black worker, in particular, represented to industrial élites the "most important working factor in the great and varied resources of the [region]," whose labour would "yet aid his white friends ... to take the lead in the cheapest production on this continent." (Kelly, 2004, p. 8)

In short, according to industrial historian David W. Lewis (1984), Birmingham became "an iron plantation in an urban setting" (quoted in Kelly, 2004, p. 8).

As the industrial class solidified its political control through the 1880s, it was faced with a new threat: agrarian discontent that drove poor white farmers and sharecroppers from the Democratic Party. As the new Populist Party tried to build a base of support to challenge the Democrats, it also sought votes from African Americans, drawing them away from the Republican Party. In northern Alabama, the Greenback-Labor party, many of whose members were later absorbed into the Populist Party, became "the strongest advocates of the rights of blacks in the Deep South" (Kelly, 2004, p. 9).

Willis Johnson Thomas, a prominent black leader of the Greenback Party, often spoke at interracial meetings. The economic elites who knew that their power was sustained by racial antipathy were horrified. As Kelly (2004) recounted:

"Three years ago," one dejected Democrat complained after a brush with Thomas in 1878, "if a negro dared to say anything about politics, or public speaking, or sitting on a jury ... he would be driven out of the county, or shot, or hung in the woods. ... Now white people are backing them in doing such things" (p. 9).

The elite response to this and every subsequent interracial lower class uprising was the same: white Populists were race baited and intimidated with vigilante justice of the sort used by the Ku Klux Klan. Appeals were made to their pride in their Anglo Saxon heritage. Black populists were bribed or physically intimidated into abandoning the struggle (Ayers, 1992).

The defeat of the Populists in 1896 began the period of the worst interracial relations in the new South. As the 1890's began, segregation was still largely a matter of custom. Few laws formally circumscribed relationships. Ayers (1992) suggested that the word "segregation" cannot truly be applied to the South until the beginning of the twentieth century. Although the races lived largely separate lives, few whites saw it as desirable to complicate their lives by enshrining separation into law; they also foresaw that legal separation would antagonize friendly and co-operative blacks. Prior to 1896, only Mississippi formally disenfranchised black voters; after the Populists were defeated all Southern states moved to do so (Ayers, 1992). The de facto segregation in place since Emancipation, only loosely observed, became tightly woven into law.

The new de jure segregation laws separated the races in all public accommodations. For instance, blacks were frequently excluded from white owned hotels. However, blacks could still turn to a black owned hotels, and generally preferred to do so. Where railroads were concerned, though, there were no alternatives. As railroads began spreading rapidly after the Civil War, local customs had to give way to state laws. Between 1887 and 1891, nine states enacted segregation laws that applied to the rails—the first concrete, state-wide efforts to legislate separation. Blacks were confined to third class cars that were filled with tobacco smoke and spit and often filthy with soot from the train's engine. There was no access to drinking water or comfortable seats (Ayers, 1992). Ultimately, train travel lead to the Supreme Court decision, *Plessy v Ferguson* 163 U.S. 537 (1896), that enshrined the legal doctrine of "separate but equal." In its decision, the Court upheld the legality of an 1890 Louisiana law that required railroads to provide "equal but separate accommodations for the white and colored races" (Hall, 2005, p. 739). Justice Brown wrote that laws requiring separation did not imply inferiority, just difference. According to legal historian Kermit Hall (2005), the law upheld "long established customs of society" (p. 739).

Racial violence increased at the turn of the century to levels not seen since the early days after the Civil War. White supremacy continued unchallenged, as well as the economic order which benefited only the most elite (Kelly, 2004). The frameworks created by Jim Crow contributed to a much lower standard of living among Southern industrial workers of both races in comparison to their Northern counterparts:

> The South remained the most impoverished region of the United States, with per capita wages for industrial workers at about one third the national average as late as 1935. And, while white workers generally received higher wages than blacks, by any measure (mortality, literacy levels, exposure to disease, access to health care), they endured worse conditions than their counterparts anywhere else in the country. (Kelly, 2004 , p. 11)

Early 20th Century America

Between 1914 and 1918, as the United States geared up to supply armaments to the Allied forces during the First World War, almost a half million blacks moved from the South to the industrial cities of the Midwest and the North. This was the beginning of the "Great Migration." Draw by the lure of good jobs during wartime labor shortages, as well as by the hope of political and social freedom, millions of black fled the South (Brinkley, 1997). Wages were higher in the North, but with periods of unemployment and risk of injury or death, black lives were still marked by peril. To help counter these risks, they settled together in the same buildings and neighborhoods. Yet as their numbers swelled, they met with increasing hostility from urban and educational administrators. Municipal laws and restrictive covenants limited their options for housing and education. As Fassil Demissie (1995) describes it, the resulting shift toward segregated, African American neighborhoods was:

> Not the result of impersonal market forces ... or ... the desires of African Americans themselves ....On the contrary, the black ghetto was constructed through a series of well-defined institutional practices, private behaviours, and public policies by which whites sought to contain growing urban black populations. (¶ 22)

By 1919, as the war time jobs were drying up, violence was on the rise: lynching increased in the South, while racial animosity continued to intensify in the factory cites as whites came to believe that blacks had "stolen" their jobs. Chicago was the scene of some of the worst violence of that summer, with the city in a state of virtual warfare for over a week (Brinkley, 1997).

After World War II, federal programs lead to a significant movement of the white population from urban centers to the suburbs, leaving an ever greater concentration of poor people, especial racial minorities, in the cities. Massey and Denton (1993) write:

What is striking about these transformations is how effectively the colour line was maintained despite the massive population shifts. The white strategy of ghetto containment and tactical retreat before an advancing colour line, institutionalized in the 1920s, was continued after 1945: the only change was the rate at which the leading edge of the ghetto advanced (quoted in Demissie, 1995, ¶ 23).

An assortment of mechanisms existed for 'ghetto containment': racially restrictive covenants, red-lining, as well as discriminatory real estate and banking policies.

Ending De Jure Segregation

It wasn't until 1954 that the Supreme Court decisively reversed itself on *Plessey v. Ferguson,* beginning the end of de jure segregation. Prior to the Court's decision in *Brown v. the Board of Education* (1954), the federal government financially supported a segregated America through payments to separate schools, segregated public housing, and separate farm support programs. President Truman understood that the "racial caste system" was detrimental to the fabric of our society, and to our image abroad. Although a lame duck, he took courageous steps to dismantle the system, strengthening federal equal employment opportunity laws, desegregating the military, and using the Justice Department to intercede with the courts in cases that ranged from restrictive racial covenants, segregated railroad dining cars, and segregated public graduate schools. Critically, he filed an amicus brief in *Brown v Board of Education* (1954) in 1952. His Justice Department argued that racial discrimination "inevitably tends to undermine the foundations of society dedicated to freedom, justice, and equality" (quoted in Landsberg, 1995, p. 628). Legal scholar Brian K. Landsberg has argued that Truman's concern was less centered on the individual, and that rather "President Truman's actions reflected the understanding that the racial caste system was shredding the fabric of national life" (Landsberg, 1995, p. 628).

Eisenhower's Justice Department concurred with the amicus brief already on file. In a subsequent ruling, *Brown v. Board of Education II,* his administration urged the Court to secure constitutional rights as quickly as feasible, arguing the "right of children not to be segregated because of race or color...is a fundamental human right, supported by considerations of morality as well as law," and that "racial segregation affects the hearts and minds of those who segregate as well as those who are segregated, and it is also detrimental to the community and the nation" (quoted in Landsberg, 1995, p. 629).

During the 1950s, Kenneth Bancroft Clark, an African American psychologist, developed a unique testing method to determine the impact of segregation on personality development. By presenting black children with white and black dolls, Clark found that the majority of the children demonstrated a preference for the white dolls, and shame toward the black dolls. He argued that the children's reactions were the result of a social system in which, in general, whiteness has positive connotations and blackness is linked to inferiority. He was convinced that white children internalized this social system as well, claiming that they developed negative beliefs about blacks as a result of segregation, learning that whiteness was not just different but better. As sociologist Henry Allen Bullock wrote:

Social isolation, occupational immobility, and the rigid enforcement of interracial etiquette-generated within Negroes the personality inclinations that now form the basis for the various negative stereotypes, so often used against them. Negroes and whites became different because they were kept apart. White Southerners insisted that they be kept apart because they were different. Segregation begat segregation. (quoted in Meyers & Nidiry, 2004, p. 268 - 269)

Clark's testimony in *Brown v. Board of Education* (1954) later gained fame as "Footnote #11," which supported the Court's ruling that "Separate educational facilities are inherently unequal" (Meyers & Nidiry, 2004, p. 266).

The federal government used several tools to hasten desegregation: it filed amicus briefs in every case before the Supreme Court; developed a statewide litigation process as a means for rapidly obtaining decrees for a large number of school districts; and offered a financial incentive for desegregation by paying for its related costs like the teacher training and curriculum development (Landsberg, 1995). Perhaps the most substantial example of that support was found in the Justice Department's amicus brief in *Green v County School Board* (391 U.S. 430, 1968). Kent County, Virginia had created a "freedom of choice" plan that kept almost completely segregated schools in place. The Justice Department argued:

Against the background of educational segregation long maintained by law, the duty of school authorities is to accomplish "the conversion of a de jure segregated dual system to a unitary, nonracial (nondiscriminatory) system–lock, stock, and barrel....the Fourteenth Amendment bars State action which unnecessarily creates opportunities for the play of private prejudice" (quoted in Landsberg, 1995, p. 630).

Ending De Facto Segregation

Resistance to integration in Northern school systems could be just as intense as that found in the legally separated systems of the South. Plans to end de facto segregation and more fully integrate schools and school districts through busing were hotly debated. In 1974, the Supreme Court had a chance to weigh in when it considered *Milliken v Bradley* (1974). The case centered on the Detroit school system's plans to merge its metropolitan center with two largely white suburban districts. In a very divisive ruling, the Court in effect limited integration at a district's boundary. As a result, the predominantly white suburban districts were exempted from integrating with the predominately black inner-city school districts. The ruling also reinforced "white flight" as white families living in the city moved to the suburbs to avoid integration (Hall, 2005).

In 1964 Congress passed its landmark Civil Rights Act, forthrightly declaring an end to discrimination in public accommodations and employment. Repeatedly, the Supreme Court has taken a broad view of Title II, eventually defining a public accommodation as any facility open to the public.

FURTHER INSIGHTS

Slowly, federal support for school desegregation has slackened. In the 1980s, the Justice Department lost funding for its programs overseeing desegregation efforts. The same has been true of the Department of Education: its programs were dismantled and their funding was moved into general grants that did not specifically support desegregation efforts (Landsberg, 1995).

Brown's impact has always been more judicial; it has not reshaped the way that education is delivered. Some scholars see its very premise as an acceptance of white cultural norms that leaves little room for honoring African American culture or integrating it into formerly all white school systems. Whether or not Brown has succeeded depends upon one's outlook. According to Landsberg (1995):

"If equal opportunity means the end of racial isolation and the achievement of equal funding or outputs, the Court long ago gave a negative answer...If equal opportunity means freedom from present intentional racial discrimination in the public schools, its future is secure. If it also means freedom from the lingering effects of past discrimination, its future hangs in the balance." (p. 631)

Of course, education is not the only topic considered under desegregation efforts. One of the lingering effects of segregation and racism is deeply entrenched poverty. Douglas Massey and Nancy Denton's *Apartheid: Segregation and the Making of the Underclass* focuses on the underlying mechanisms that have created an underclass. They forcefully argue that if residential segregation is permitted to continue, urban poverty cannot be eliminated, nor can the problems that result from the tolerated existence of the underclass (Demissie, 1995). During the 1960's, the United States made great progress eliminating legally sanctioned segregation, yet poverty and racism go on unabated. Beginning in the 1970s, the income gap between whites and blacks began to increase once again. During the 1980s and early 1990s, residential segregation increased in Chicago, St. Louis, Los Angeles, Philadelphia, and New York (Demissie, 1995). Massey and Denton use census records to show that varying degrees of segregation affect all racial minorities in the United States; however segregation by and large only affects African Americans (Demissie, 1995).

Though the Fair Housing Act was passed in 1968, residential segregation remains high. Massey and Denton found that even suburbs became segregated once a visible presence of African Americans appeared. As time went on, more blacks than whites move to these newly segregate enclaves within the suburbs. As support for social programs dwindled through the 1980s, the poor slipped further from mainstream America. As Massey and Denton (1993) observed, "Segregation and rising poverty interact to deliver an exogenous shock to black neighbourhoods that push them beyond the point where physical decay and disinvestment became self-perpetuating" (as quoted in Demissie, 1995, ¶ 27). The authors went on to argue that many different groups in America benefit from these patterns of segregation; thus they tolerate them, or even support the continuation of segregation in American cities.

In the 1980s, a number of conservative scholars attempted to tackle the problem of urban poverty. Most concurred to some degree with Charles Murray (1984), a fellow of the American Institutes for Research, that poverty is a pathological problem, made worse by social programs designed to lessen the burdens of poverty. For these scholars, the "welfare state" did nothing but allow the number of poor to proliferate by fostering a culture that supports illegitimate births, female headed households, and dependence on welfare (Demissie, 1995). Massey and Denton suggested this explanation is based on a flawed understanding of urban poverty. They instead proposed considering the structural changes in the inner cities: the loss of high wage industrial jobs; job migration to the suburbs; and the rise of the low wage service economy have all combined to shred the economic vitality of inner city neighborhoods. Even more important, the persistence of poverty can't be explained without a consideration of residential segregation. This, they posited, must be at the center of any understanding of urban poverty: "residential segregation [plays]...a special role in enabling all other forms of racial oppression...[to organize themselves] into a coherent and uniquely effective system of racial domination" (quoted in Demissie, 1995, ¶ 17).

CONCLUSION

The impact of racial segregation, both in terms of social and economic welfare, has been enormously significant in American history. Prior to the Civil Rights Movement, segregation was tolerated as legal policy, custom, and as a byproduct of policies that subtly resulted in the separation of the races. Even after the legal doctrine of "separate but equal" was deemed unconstitutional, the legacy of segregation remains part of the fabric of American life, seen in education, residential patterns, and poverty levels.

TERMS & CONCEPTS

***Brown v Board of Education* (1954):** A landmark United States Supreme Court decision that overturned the legal concept of separate but equal. The case challenged six legally segregated school districts. Writing for a unanimous Court, Chief Justice Earl Warren declared that segregation was harmful to the social development of black students and cannot be permitted under the Fourteenth Amendment.

Civil Rights Act of 1964: Still regarded as the bedrock of civil rights law, this law outlawed discrimination based on race, ethnicity, national origin, religion and sex in public accommodations and in employment.

De Facto Segregation: Literally, segregation that occurs "by fact" rather than by law. Outside of the South, very few states had systems of formal, legal discrimination. Instead, school segregation emerged informally as a result of residential patterns that grew out of discrimination.

De Jure Segregation: Literally, segregation that occurs "by law." It emerged slowly in the post-Civil War South and was legitimated in 1896 with the *Plessy* decision. Eventually it came to govern many aspects of daily life for Southerners of both races as it grew to encompass public accommodations, transportation, education and employment.

Federal Fair Housing Act: Passed in 1968, the goal of this law was to ensure that discrimination in lending and renting would no longer be permitted. It prohibits landlords from refusing to rent to a tenant based on race, ethnicity, religion, or national origin unless the building is owner occupied and has four or fewer units.

Fourteenth Amendment: It grants citizenship to all persons born or naturalized in the United States, including former slaves, and it offers equal protection under the law. Southern states provided the three quarters majority needed to ratify the amendment in 1868 as a condition for readmission to the Union,. The amendment should have overruled Jim Crow legislation, but as earlier as the 1880s the Supreme

Court began to back away from the equal protection clause, not enforcing it until the *Brown* decision in 1954 (Hall, 2005).

Jim Crow: A system of both legally mandated and informal practices that separated black and white citizens. It gained and lost strength through the decades after Reconstruction, but by the beginning of the 20th century was completely entrenched in all of the Southern states.

***Milliken v Bradley* (1974):** A 1974 United States Supreme Court decision that limited the extent of Court authorized desegregation plans. In a five to four ruling, the Court declined to support efforts to end de facto segregated schools in the North by busing students between school districts. The case grew out of Detroit's efforts to combine its largely black city school districts with the predominately white districts in the surrounding suburbs.

***Plessy v Ferguson* (1896):** A 1896 United States Supreme Court decision regarding a Louisiana law requiring blacks to ride in third class train compartments with no restroom facilities, dining options, or sleeper compartments. The Supreme Court ruled that segregation was permitted in "separate but equal" facilities. Even though these facilities were far from equal, the law was allowed to stand. The ruling became the basis for all future Jim Crow legislation.

Reconstruction: Lasting from the end of the Civil War in 1865 until the Compromise of 1877, the period during which the Federal government maintained control of the states that had constituted the Confederacy. One essential component of Reconstruction was the integration of former slaves into the social, economic, and political landscape of the new South. The period ended in 1877 as federal troops were withdrawn, leaving the states with fairly extensive power to regulate the lives of black citizens. Around the same time, the Republican Party shifted its priorities to focus on encouraging industrial development and moved away from protecting civil rights.

Redlining: This practice was used to deny blacks access to mortgages in certain parts of cities, effectively resulting in de facto segregation. Although now illegal, a substantial body of research shows that it still exists as an informal practice (Peterson & Krivo, 1993).

Bibliography

Ayers, Edward. *The Promise of the New South: Life After Reconstruction.* New York: Oxford University Press. 1992

Brinkley, Alan. *The Unfinished Nation: A Concise history of the American People.*2cd Edition. New York: McGraw Hill Companies, Inc. 1997

Demissie, F. (1995, August). Book reviews. *Social Identities, 1* (2), 407.

Hall, Kermit, *The Oxford Companion to the Supreme Court of the United States.*New York: Oxford University Press, 2005.

Harrison, J., & Lloyd, S.E. (2013). "New jobs, new workers, and new inequalities: Explaining employers' roles in occupational segregation by nativity and race." *Social Problems, 60*(3), 281–301.

Kelly, B. (2004, June). "The Isaac and Tamara Deutscher Memorial Prize Lecture: Materialism and the Persistence of Race in the Jim Crow South." *Historical Materialism, 12* (2), 3-19.

Landsberg, B. (1995, Summer95). "The federal government and the promise of Brown." *Teachers College Record, 96* (4), 627-636.

Massey, D.S. (2012). "Reflections on the dimensions of segregation." *Social Forces, 91*(1), 39–43.

Meyers, M., & Nidiry, J. (2004, Spring2004)." Kenneth Bancroft Clark: The Uppity Negro

Integrationist." *Antioch Review, 62* (2), 265-274.

Peterson, R., & Krivo, L. (1993, June). "Racial Segregation and Black Urban Homicide." *Social Forces, 71* (4), 1001-1026.

Quillian, L. (2012). "Segregation and poverty concentration: The role of three segregations." *American Sociological Review, 77*(3), 354–379.

St. John, C. (1995, March). "Interclass Segregation, Poverty, and Poverty Concentration: Comment on Massey and Eggers." *American Journal of Sociology,* pp. 1325,1333.

Wilson, T.M., & Rodkin, P.C. (2013). "Children's cross-ethnic relationships in elementary schools: Concurrent and prospective associations between ethnic segregation and social status." *Child Development, 84*(3), 1081–1097.

SUGGESTED READING

Bell, J. (2013). *Hate thy neighbor: Move-in violence and the persistence of racial segregation in American housing.* New York: New York University Press.

Higginbotham, F.M. (2013). *Ghosts of jim crow: Ending racism in post-racial America.* New York: New York University Press.

Jones, J. (2006, December). "From Racial Inequality to Social Justice: The Legacy of Brown v. Board and Lessons from South Africa." *Journal of Social Issues, 62* (4), 885-909.

McConnell, M. (1996, Winter96). "Segregation and the original understanding: A reply to Professor Maltz." *Constitutional Commentary, 13* (3), 233.

Orfield, G., & Eaton, S. (2003, March 3). "Back to Segregation." *Nation,* pp. 5, 7.

Cheryl Bourassa, M.A.

Society & Technology

Introduction

This section explores the impact of modern technology on society. Researchers and scholars have long predicted significant advancement in technology. French scholar Jacques Ellul wrote in the 1950s about this technological advancement, exploring how this may change humanity and what the future of human beings may bring. His work has long been known as a cornerstone of ideas of science, technology and the "technical phenomenon."

The technological revolution has transformed all aspects of our functioning and truly changed the course of globalization and how the world operates. Days or weeks to send a message changed to seconds—a positive change. American jobs being affected by products being manufactured overseas and quickly transported back to the U.S.—a negative change.

In the 1990s the World Wide Web was born and today, impacts nearly, every single aspect of the human experience, affecting communication, connectivity, and daily operation. One minute we talk, face to face with someone halfway across the world and the next minute we talk to our family across town. You can "travel" across the world in a moment, do business anywhere and anytime, and make connections it previously would have been impossible or taken a lifetime to make. The internet has also forced the *digital divide*—evidenced by countries or individuals who have the means to technologically advance far more quickly and easily than those who can not afford these advancements. An American child with access to the internet has much more continued opportunity than a child born in poverty in a small rural town in Africa without no access to modern technology.

Digital sociology looks specifically at the impact of the internet and social media on relationships with others. Social media is a new-found medium of internet-based interactions with others. Facebook, Instagram, dating apps etc., have completely transformed how people meet and interact, develop relationships, and maintain connection. Although the internet is responsible for opening up a world of new opportunities, it has also opened up new paths for oppression, self-worth struggles and cyber-crime. Teenagers, for example, now have a new path to be bullies. Bullying is not a new activity, however before modern technology, bullying usually ended after kids left school; today, bullying continues 24/7, via social media.

Modern technology is not only responsible for transforming relationships. It has changed surveillance, the judicial system, the media, education, and news reporting. Access to real-time video and information replaced next day newspaper and radio reports.

The changes caused by modern technology has created a multitude of new behavior to study and explore. Advancements will continue to cause changes in the human experience. The magnitude of these technological changes will provide a greater difference in this current generation than possibly any other age-gap in history.

Kimberly Ortiz-Hartman, Psy.D., LMFT

THE DIGITAL DIVIDE

ABSTRACT

Information and communication technology (ICT) has pervaded almost every aspect of society, from dating and the labor market to governance and shopping. However, not every member of society has been successfully integrated into the information society. The increasing isolation of those suffering from this digital inequality continues to deepen the divide. While information technology persists in conquering ever more aspects of social life, the new form of inequality is affecting the social and economic prospects of those left without ICT knowledge or access. Without access to digital information or resources, these people face a digital divide that sociologists are working to overcome.

OVERVIEW

The term digital divide rose to fame in the mid-nineties, predominantly due to its use by Vice President Al Gore in a 1996 speech. Originally, it referred to the distribution of personal computers in American households. With the turn of the century, however, the question of Internet access became a crucial aspect of the debate in the United States and around the world.

In its simplest explanation, one could say that the digital divide represents the division between people with and without access to and practical knowledge about modern technology, specifically the Internet and technology categorized as information technology (IT). But further elaboration is, of course, necessary. There exists, for example, a digital divide between developed and underdeveloped countries, for example the difference in available digital resources between the U.S. and Ethiopia. Pick and Azari have analyzed the effects of IT usage in 71 developing and developed countries to specifically identify steps that can be taken to help developing countries in their progress (2008). They have also managed to elaborate on the effects that investment and information technology has on a country's progress.

IT Access

In a global perspective, the difference between developed and developing nations in regard to IT access is immense. While in developed countries it is perfectly normal for more than half of households to own computers, in many developing nations it may be nearly impossible to find more than two people out of a hundred who own a computer. This disparity became the topic of two World Summit on the Information Society conferences hosted by the United Nations in Geneva and Tunis (2003, 2005) as well as a series of further related events. The continuing aim of these conferences, whose reports can be found online, is to find workable solutions for bridging the international digital divide. In the same spirit, a group of faculty members of the Massachusetts Institute of Technology (MIT) began an initiative called One Laptop per Child, which builds inexpensive, rugged, energy-efficient laptop computers and distributes them to children in countries such as Uruguay, Rwanda, and Mongolia. These computers enable teachers worldwide to better educate children about technology and their world.

But the term "digital divide" does not just describe a global disparity. Within developed nations, too, access to information technology can be unequal, and this inequality's effects are becoming increasingly grave. Within the United States itself, attempts have been made to bridge the gap in Internet access, including trying to regulate the companies supplying this access. In 2011, one of the nation's largest Internet providers, Comcast, released a product called Internet Essentials as part of a Federal Communications Commission mandate issued upon the company's acquisition of NBC Universal. Internet Essentials, priced at ten dollars per month, was designed to allow low-income families the ability to purchase an affordable subscription (Anderson, 2014). While many argued that the company did not make a genuine effort to reach out and market this product and initially included too many restrictions, leading to a minimum impact, Comcast did loosen one of the eligibility requirements and ran a special back-to-school promotion for the program in 2014 (Fung, 2014). As information technology continues to pervade everyday life and the job market, those without access are left further and further behind.

Causes of the Digital Divide

The causes behind the national digital divide are manifold. Poverty and social class are issues that come into play even within the most developed nations. These issues can be described in terms of access to cultural capital or symbolic capital, a theoretical conception originally formulated by French sociologist Pierre Bourdieu (1986). According to Bordieu's model, members of a lower social class have little or no opportunity to acquire the traits, habits, or information necessary to accomplish a rise in status, income, class, or livelihood. In the worst cases, a lack of information, which is increasingly available only online, would bar these classes from informed participation in civic life and democracy.

In the case of the digital divide, a lack of cultural capital would make it much harder for children born into low socioeconomic classes to gain the knowledge necessary to command information technology. Possessing this command, according to the Bourdieu theory, is a necessary form of capital if one is to be a part of modern society, which increasingly relies on the use of technology such as email and Internet videophones. From arranging a date to securing job information to handling client agendas, the demands of everyday private and professional life require not only the capability to use information technology but also the ability to do so with ease.

From the point of view of those already fluent in the use of this technology, it may seem very simple to be able to handle technology. But even something as simple as reading a website and finding its significant content requires a thorough initiation.

Media-Multitasking

The requirements have reached a level designated as media-multitasking. Successfully performing a variety of simultaneous tasks, such as coordinating activities on a cell phone while simultaneously surfing the Internet, requires a great deal of prior learning. Further, the learning process for such habitual routines is fairly time-consuming and gets harder with the increased age of the learner.

Therefore, we have to think of other factors besides mere class status when considering the digital divide, such as those of age and generation. Elderly people often have difficulty adjusting to swift changes in technology. The two major problems they are facing, even when they are presented with access, are a) their own fear or resentment, and b) a form of technological illiteracy. As Foehr and Roberts have argued, reading web content requires a multitude of learned skills (2008). For those who weren't educated into this cultural technique at an early age, the learning process can be long and difficult.

Symbolic-Capital Theory

The symbolic-capital theory applies in these cases, too. Consider the following analogy: buying into a fledgling market requires only a small amount of start-up capital, but once a market has gained momentum, it becomes much more difficult and requires an ever higher margin of investment to buy into it. It is the same with IT. If a person has not grown up within the development of the technology, then more effort and more symbolic capital will be required of them in order to obtain even a moderate amount of technological knowledge.

In other words, those on the losing side of digital inequality will face a widening gap between themselves and the technologically literate as well as an increasingly steep learning curve as they try to catch up.

This effect is visible in the impact that Internet use has on U.S. workers, as Paul DiMaggio and Bart Bonikowski (2008) have shown. Just demonstrating the ability to use Internet technology, whether at work or at home, has a significant positive impact on workers' earnings and chances on the job market. The ability to use the Internet, symbolized, for example, by possessing one's own e-mail address, can not only serve as an indicator to employers that a worker is computer literate and therefore more employable but also enable workers to find better job opportunities.

In sum, it is necessary to shrink the digital divide, for knowledge of ICT must now be considered a condition of participation not only in the labor market, but also within the political and social spheres in the forms of access to certain markets as well as government services. However, ICT must not be seen as only a mechanism of exclusion. ICT can also be a means to empower those who have been excluded. Many citizens, previously barred from certain forms of political and social participation, or, because of age or disability, dependent on others when it comes to fulfilling certain administrative requirements, now have a chance at participation and independence through technology in the form of e-government. Even if this goal is not equally realized across all U.S. states, as Rubaii-Barret and Wise have shown, efforts are being made all over the U.S. to ensure that more people have easy access to government information and services (2008).

APPLICATIONS

Consumer Empowerment

Because spreading information about consumer products becomes more difficult in a globalizing market, consumer empowerment has become increasingly important. Take the example of health care: a number of cheap generic medical products, for example, are only available through Internet sources. Studies, like one undertaken by Rains, have shown that Internet access and use can be positively correlated with personal health care (2008). Specifically, access to broadband Internet in correlation with age and area of residence (whether rural or urban) are factors that contribute to personal health. In this regard, the promotion of personal health is negatively affected by digital inequality. On the other hand, though, access and use can be linked to better health as well as increased opportunities for social and economic participation. Enabling access to e-health is therefore a crucial factor to reduce the effects of digital inequality.

According to Matusitz and Breen, e-health now covers a wide range of fields. As an ever greater number of aspects of healthcare are relocated to the Internet (which increases digital inequality), the amount of actual discourse between patients and doctors is decreasing, making e-health an often problematic social transformation (2007). Notwithstanding, those on the down-side of digital inequality, who have less access to Internet technology or no accurate knowledge of how to use the Internet, are unable to access new developments in treatments or the comparative resources and support offered by patient groups.

E-Health

This question of e-health touches upon the basic question of citizens as consumers, not only of healthcare products, but of products in general. Social participation has transformed in large part into consumption. Therefore, it can be said that in a global, political economy that is increasingly dominated by so-called multinational corporations, the remaining counter-power, as Ulrich Beck suggests, lies not so much in the hands of national governments, but in those of the consumers themselves, who ultimately decide which products they will buy (2008). The currency they use to exercise this power is information. The role of national governments, therefore, lies in ensuring that consumers can obtain and distribute information about products and services. Nation-states must then create IT access for everyone, or bridge the digital divide, if they wish to restore the democratic power of the people.

One group of actors in particular is struggling with the new digital age and represents a special dimension of the digital divide: the print media. Newspapers, magazines, and journals have in the past been perceived as the agents that upheld a system of critical control over political and commercial developments. But, faced with the free-floating information of the Web, print media have a hard time adapting. With every major paper now maintaining its own website, readers are beginning to question whether buying a paper at the newsstand is truly an efficient way of accessing up-to-date information. Further, with dwindling sales and subscribers, the number of advertisers willing to financially support quality publishing is also decreasing.

The effect on journalism has been fairly grave, most importantly in the dimension of the quality. The quality of information (including contextualization, critical perspectives, reliability, validity, and thoroughness of research) is one of the least explicitly discussed, yet most important, factors in the functioning of modern economies and political systems. To some commentators, iconic publications such as the *New York Times* and the *New Republic* have represented the shift from organized, in-depth editorial content to providing more space for images in conjunction with coverage of popular trends and seemingly "innocuous trivia" (Hollander, 2014). The quality of information itself also contributes to the digital divide, since those who have access to or can afford high quality information can more easily increase their activities and gains.

VIEWPOINTS

Bridging the Digital Divide

On the global scale, bridging the digital divide will be an effort that is wrought with conflict. One must factor in questions of gender, ethnicity, race, and religion, all of which are addressed differently from one nation to another. In some countries, Internet access is regulated by the state, and content considered harmful, whether for political or ideological reasons, is banned. Governments often fear the Internet's potential for aiding democratic and revolutionary movements in spreading their ideas and creating a coherent power base. This fear was proven to be warranted when dissenters used the Internet to organize and report on massive protests during the Arab Spring uprisings that began in late 2010 and early 2011.

But at the same time, the progress of information technology itself makes it much harder to bridge this divide. More and more intricate Internet content demands not only better hardware, but also ever faster broadband connections. Delivering these to every region in the world is an enormous challenge.

The circuits of modern societies are in a state of transformation in regard to time, space, and meaning. The shipping and transportation of material goods is of less importance than the access and distribution of information. These circuits constitute the economies of social relations in regard to questions of ethnicity, gender, social justice, etc. In the transformation of the circuits, the social relations are also being transformed, as Lash and Urry predicted in their analysis of the "economies of signs and space" in 1994.

In summary, we are witnessing a profound change in the way our societies and democracies are functioning. In 1962, the German sociologist and philosopher Juergen Habermas published his groundbreaking study The Structural Transformation of the Public Sphere. Habermas described the transformation of the bourgeois public sphere, which emerged in the eighteenth century, came to full bloom in the nineteenth century, and then fell into decline. Within this process of the rise and fall of a culture or form of public discourse, Habermas argued, were the two major social and political transformations that shaped modern western societies: the shift from a feudalistic society to a liberal public sphere on the one hand, and, on the other, yet another shift from the liberal bourgeois public discourse to the democratic social welfare state.

Following Habermas's account, it can be argued that we are witnessing another structural transformation of the public sphere. The looming question for this transformation, which is of course reflected in the emergence of the public sphere of the digital age or information society, is the problem of mechanisms of inclusion and exclusion in participation. Inclusion means herein the acquisition of cultural capital or the means to gain access to knowledge of the use of information technology. Exclusion describes either a lack of access, either through indigence or through intentional separation. Non-democratic regimes may find incentives for providing access only to a privileged few who are assumed to be loyal to the regime. Neo-Marxist critics, however, hold that even in democratic societies, forces exist that supposedly keep mechanisms of exclusion in place.

Several economic theorists subscribing to rather simple accounts of the digital divide often hold to theories of access, claiming that merely providing everyone with technology such as personal computers and broadband connections will eventually solve the problem of exclusion. But studies like Habermas's and Bourdieu's have shown that just providing technological access is not enough to guarantee inclusion. Even in the nineteenth century, simply being literate was not sufficient for active civic, social, or political participation. In the same regard, owning a computer with Internet access is unlikely to solve the problems of poverty either globally or nationally. Additionally, the problems caused by the digital divide on the one hand, and by information technology itself on the other—for example, information overload, invalid information distribution, identity theft, etc.—lead to a transformation of the political structure of modern societies themselves.

TERMS & CONCEPTS

Cultural Capital: The concept of cultural capital as a form of symbolic capital was made popular by French sociologist Pierre Bourdieu. In his work, Bourdieu showed that besides money, other forms of capital regulate access to social classes. Cultural capital comprises knowledge, network connections, and experiences.

Digital Divide: The difference in access to and practical knowledge of information technology, especially the Internet. The divide exists between different kinds of groups. Internationally, it describes the differences between developing and developed nations. Within nations, it exists between rural and urban areas or between densely and sparsely populated areas that are of different economic interest to Internet service providers. Finally, it also exists between social classes.

Digital Inequality: A new form of inequality springing from the digital divide in which those denied access to or practical knowledge of information technology suffer from political, social, or economical disadvantages as a consequence of that exclusion.

Digital Society: A form of society in which electronically stored and processed information is a main constituent for the functions of society, replacing material constituents (e.g. products of craftsmanship) in most sectors. Is contrasted with the analogue society, a form of society in which material objects constitute the main functions of society. The distinction stems from the distinction between analogue and digital components in information theory

E-Government: E-Government, also known as e-gov, digital government, or online government, refers to the government use of information and digitaltechnologies to promote the free exchange of political information, communication between citizens and government agencies, and the use of government services. Different branches of government have also used information technology internally in order to increase efficiency. Private citizens have also found e-government more convenient for using government services or participating in political activities. In particular, people whose mobility is impaired by age, illness, or disability have been enabled to participate in the democratic process as well as independently work with government agencies.

E-Health: Healthcare that is supported by information technology. This can take a variety of forms, from electronic medical records to health related websites for patients to surgeons using robot arms to operate from remote locations.

E-Learning: A form of education in which learning takes place through the use of computer technology. Among other things, it encompasses the integration of computer technology into the traditional classroom, online courses and online colleges, free online education resources, and online corporate learning tools.

The concept of making knowledge freely available to everyone is a central tenet of the humanist ideal. E-learning, some say, can realize that promise by allowing everyone able to access the Internet to make use of e-learning resources. However, not all e-learning services are free. Online courses can come with high fees, and the quality of education available online, whether from commercial or nonprofit sources, is quite variable. Still, the goal of providing everyone with the opportunity for higher education, regardless of factors like social status or work schedules, may be realizable with Internet technology.

Generic Medical Products: Generic medical products are drugs that are produced without patent protection; their active agents are proven to be bioequally effective in comparison to their brand name counterparts.

Information & Communication Technology (ICT): Summary names for technologies such as the Internet, mobile phones, personal digital assistants (PDAs), and personal computers that allow users to manipulate and communicate information.

Information Society: A form of society in which the production, distribution, use, and conservation of knowledge and information is a main factor in all social aspects from the political and economic sectors to the cultural sector.

BIBLIOGRAPHY

Anderson, J. (2014). "Fighting to bridge the digital divide." *Social Policy, 44*(1), 56–57.

Baudrillard, J. (1983). *Simulations.* Los Angeles, CA: Semiotext(e).

Beck, U. (2006). *Power in the global age: A new global political economy.* Cambridge: Polity Press.

Bourdieu, P. (1986). "The forms of capital." In J. C. Richardson (Ed.), *Handbook of theory and research in the sociology of education* (pp. 241–58). New York: Greenwood.

Castells, M. (2001). *The Internet galaxy: Reflections on the Internet, business and society.* New York: Oxford University Press.

Chen, W. (2013). "The implications of social capital for the digital divides in America." *Information Society, 29*(1), 13–25.

Crossley, N. & Roberts, J. (2004). *After Habermas: New perspectives on the public sphere.* Oxford: Blackwell Publishing.

Crouch, C. (2004). *Post-Democracy.* Oxford: Polity Press.

Epstein, D., Nisbet, E. C., & Gillespie, T. (2011). "Who's responsible for the digital divide? Public perceptions and policy implications." *Information Society, 27*(2), 92–104.

Fung, B. "Comcast is expanding its $10-a-month internet program for the poor." (2014, August 4). *Washington Post.* http://www.washingtonpost.com/blogs/the-switch/wp/2014/08/04/comcast-is-expanding-its-10-a-month-internet-program-for-the-poor/

Habermas, J. (1991). *The structural transformation of the public sphere.* Cambridge, MA: The MIT Press.

Hadley, G. & Mars, M. (2008). "Postgraduate medical education in paediatric surgery: Videoconferencing—A possible solution for Africa?" *Pediatric Surgery International,* 24(2), 223–226.

Hollander, P. (2014). "Popular culture, the *New York Times* and the *New Republic*". *Society,* 51(3), 288–296.

Horrigan, J. (2008). "Home broadband adoption 2008." Pew Internet & American Life Project. http://www.pewinternet.org/PPF/r/257/report%5fdisplay.asp

Kong, S. C. (2008). "A curriculum framework for implementing information technology in school education to foster information literacy." *Computers & Education,* 51(1), 129–141.

Lash, S. & Urry, J. (1994). *Economies of signs and space.* London: Sage

Logue, D., & Edwards, M. (2013). "Across the digital divide." *Stanford Social Innovation Review, 11*(4), 66–71.

Masic, I. & Suljevic, E. (2007). "An overview of e-health implementation in countries, members of the European Union." *Acta Informatica Medica,* 15(4), 242–245.

Matusitz, J. & Breen, G. M. (2007). "E-health: A new kind of telemedicine." *Social Work in Public Health,* 23(1), 95–113.

McLuhan, M. (1962). *The Gutenberg galaxy: The making of typographic man.* Toronto: University of Toronto Press.

Pick, J. B. & Azari, R. (2008). "Global digital divide: Influence of socioeconomic, governmental, and accessibility factors on information technology." *Information Technology for Development,* 14(2), 91–115.

Rains, S. A. (2008). "Health at high speed: Broadband Internet access, health communication, and the digital divide." *Communication Research,* 35(3), 283–297.

Rubaii-Barrett, N. & Wise, L. R. (2008). "Disability access and e-government: An empirical analysis of state practices." *Journal of Disability Policy Studies,* 19(1), 52–64.

Wei, L., & Hindman, D. (2011). "Does the digital divide matter more? Comparing the effects of new media and old media use on the education-based knowledge gap." *Mass Communication & Society, 14*(2), 216–235.

World Summit on the Information Society. (2005). "Report on the WSIS stocktaking." Geneva, Switzerland: Authors. http://www.itu.int/wsis/docs2/tunis/off/5.pdf

SUGGESTED READING

Acemoglu, D. (2002). "Technical change, inequality, and the labor market." *Journal of Economic Literature,* 40(7), 40:7–72.

Aghion, P. & Howitt, P. (2002). "Wage inequality and the new economy." *Oxford Review of Economic Policy* 18, 306–23.

Agnew, I., & Ripper, L. (2011). "Using embedded outreach to bridge the digital divide." *Working With Older People: Community Care Policy & Practice, 15*(3), 127–134.

Autor, D.H. (2001). "Wiring the labor market." *Journal of Economic Perspectives* 15, 25–40.

Autor, D.H., Katz, L.F. & Krueger, A.B. (1998). "Computing inequality: Have computers changed the labor market?" *Quarterly Journal of Economics,* 113, 1169–83.

Bresnahan, T.F., Brynjolfsson, E. & Hitt, L.M. (2002). "Information, technology, workplace organization and the demand for skilled labor: firm-level evidence." *Quarterly Journal of Economics* 117, 339–76.

Brown, J.S. & Thomas, D. (2006, April). "You play world of warcraft? You're hired! Why multiplayer games may be the best kind of job training." *Wired,* 14 (4). http://www.wired.com/wired/archive/14.04/learn.html

Dickerson, A. & Green, F. (2004). *The growth and valuation of computing and other generic skills.* Oxford Economic Papers 56, 371–406.

DiMaggio, P. & Bonikowski, B. (2008). "Make money surfing the web? The impact of internet use on the earnings of U.S. workers." *American Sociological Review,* 73 (2), 227–250.

DiMaggio, P. (2004). "Cultural capital." In, *Encyclopedia of social theory,* edited by G. Ritzer. 167–70. Thousand Oaks, CA: Sage Publications.

Downs, D. (2006, March). "Dragnet, reinvented." *Wired,* 110–16.

Eastin, M.S. & LaRose, R. (2000). "Internet self-efficacy and the psychology of the digital divide." *Journal of Computer-Mediated Communications.* http://jcmc.indiana.edu/vol6/issue1/eastin.html

Fairlie, R.W. (2004). "Race and the Digital Divide." Contributions to *Economic Analysis & Policy.* Article 15. http://www.bepress.com

Fountain, C. (2005). "Finding a job in the internet age." *Social Forces,* 83(3), 1235–62.

Fountain, J. (2001). "Paradoxes of public sector customer service." *Governance,* 14(1), 55-73.

Goss, E.P. & Phillips, J.M. (2002). "How information technology affects wages: Evidence using internet usage as a proxy for IT skills." *Journal of Labor Research,* 23, 463–74.

Hoffman, D.L. & Novak, T.P. (1998). "Bridging the digital divide: The impact of race on computer access and internet use." *Science,* 280:390–91.

James, J. (2011). "Are changes in the digital divide consistent with global equality or inequality?" *Information Society, 27*(2), 121–128.

Jung, J-Y, Linchuan Qiu, J., & Kim, Y-C. (2001). "Internet Connectedness and Inequality." *Communication Research,* 28, 507–35.

Kapitzke, C. (2000). "Information technology as cultural capital: Shifting the boundaries of power." *Education and Information Technologies* 5, 49–62.

Krueger, A.B. (1993). "How computers have changed the wage structure: Evidence from microdata, 1984–1989." *The Quarterly Journal of Economics,* 108, 33–60.

Kuhn, P. & Skuterud, M. (2004). "Internet job search and unemployment durations." *American Economic Review,* 94, 218–32.

Lenhart, A., Horrigan, J, Rainie, L., Allen, K., Boyce, A., Madden, M., & O'Grady, E.. (2003). "The ever-shifting internet population: A new look at internet access and the digital divide." Washington, DC: Pew Internet and American Life Project. http://www.pewinternet.org/

Levy, F. & Murnane, R. (2004). *The new division of labor: How computers are creating the next job market.* Princeton, NJ: Princeton University Press and Russell Sage Foundation.

Lin, N. (2001). *Social capital: A theory of social structure and action.* New York: Cambridge University Press.

McDonald, S. & Crew, R.E. Jr. (2006). "Welfare to web to work: internet job search among former welfare clients." *Journal of Sociology and Social Welfare,* 33(1), 239–53.

Niles, S. & Hanson, S. (2003). "The geographies of online job search: Preliminary findings from Worcester, MA." *Environment and Planning* 35, 1223–43.

Ono, H. & Zavodny, M. (2003). "Gender and the internet." *Social Science Quarterly,* 84 (1), 111–21.

Rifkin, J. (2000). *The age of access.* New York, NY: Tarcher.

Sanz, E., & Turlea, G. (2012). "Downloading inclusion: A statistical analysis of young people's digital communication inequalities." *Innovation: The European Journal of Social Sciences, 25*(3), 337–353.

Turner, F. (2006). *From counterculture to cyberculture: Stewart Brand, the whole earth network, and the rise of digital utopianism.* Chicago, IL: University of Chicago Press.

Van Dijk, J.A. G. M. (2005). *The deepening divide: Inequality in the information society.* Thousand Oaks, CA: Sage.

Warschauer, M. (2003). *Technology and social inclusion: Rethinking the Digital Divide.* Cambridge, MA: MIT Press.

Alexander Stingl, Ph.D.

Digital Sociology

ABSTRACT

Digital sociology refers to the branch of sociology that examines the impact of the Internet and, more particularly, social media outlets in the perception and even formation of the relationships that have long been studied within the field: friendship, love, family, marriage, community, and also the perception and definition of the self. Given the immense impact of social media on virtually every aspect of social relations, digital sociology acknowledges that the constructs of intimacy, relationships, sexuality, community, self, and gender have been affected by the massive influence of the Internet.

OVERVIEW

Sociology has long been interested in the relationship between the self and the social construct that the self inhabits. How does an individual's perception of self—a well as that of marriage, family, sexuality, professional success, even death—respond to and involve a broader social network? If a person is born in, say, Philadelphia, would that individual be the same had he or she been born in, say, Papua, New Guinea? Sociology was a discipline grounded in real time, real space. Although other academic curricula were quick to acknowledge and embrace the opportunities offered by the Internet and the impact of digital media to heighten long-established protocols and to radically alter methodologies and the presentation of their academic materials, sociologists sought to scrutinize that impact.

Can the Internet create a community or society? Perhaps because sociology had long been concerned with defining the dynamics of social constructs, viable in a certain time and at a certain place, and the influence such constructs had on the integrity and viability of the self, sociologists perceived in the created spaces of the Internet an eccentric exception: Is the reach of the Internet to be considered a valid kind of community? Are exaggerated re-creations of the self through the agencies of Facebook a valid measure of the real self? What does a stream of Twitter messages from an individual reveal about that individual? Is an individual tweeting to a non-specific broad audience alone or connected? Because sociologists had for more than two centuries explored the dimensions and impact of social constructs on the individual, the Internet posed a significant, even systemic dilemma. Is the space defined virtually commiserating to real-time geographic and temporal space? Can the Internet create a culture?

Accepting the Internet as a professional resource posed additional dilemmas to traditional old-school sociologists. After all, the Internet had become by the early twenty-first century a virtually unlimited resource bank of data that might help define, redefine, and re-characterize the elements of any given social construct. The emerging concept of big data—that is, the unimaginably large data sets generated virtually daily by Internet activity, there to be analyzed for patterns, for trends, for some sustaining and defining logic about human behavior and human interaction—posed a most tempting challenge for sociologists (see Duggan et al., 2014). For the first time in human history, the accumulation of data about humans within their social organizational patterns exceeded the ability of processing it. Beginning in the middle 1990s, at the threshold of what would become the digital age, the data measured and filed by an ever increasing global platform of information doubled every two years. That was an unprecedented volume of data. What might sociologists do with such reservoirs of information? Are they valid materials akin to the decades long painstaking gathering of data performed under the scrutiny of professionals in the field? Can such an apparently careless grab-bag of unexamined responses be considered as viable data for sociological inquiry? Traditional, conventional sociologists had long prided themselves on developing specific protocols to ensure that whatever data might be gathered had significant and probative value. What now to do with this tsunami of unfocused, unfiltered, and unsponsored data? Bluntly, "the relations between social life and its analysis are changing in the context of digitization and digital sociology offers a way of engaging with this" (Marres, 2013).

Embrace it, according to the argument of a new wave of sociologists, the digital sociologists. These pioneers argued passionately that the Internet had significantly redefined traditional notions of the self, the community, gender, even space itself. And that, as sociology had done with other major social upheavals triggered by the introduction of new technology (such as the printing press, locomotives, the telephone, the airplane, and television), the time had come for the discipline to recognize a field devoted to studying the patterns and habits of human behavior within specific technological and social constructs. The principal difference between the digital environments and those of other technological innovations was speed: Compared to the pace of other major cultural and sociological ages, such as the Renaissance or the Industrial Revolution, the computer age developed with remarkable rapidity, barely thirty years, new technologies redefining the reach of the digital world exponentially. Obsolescence of computer software and applications, as well as the gadgets that sustain and maintain them, could now be measured in a span of months. As social media, the Internet, and the global links of instantaneous communication accelerated their influence on everyday lives, a new generation of sociologists posited the dramatic notion that their field needed to redefine some of its foundations to accommodate the new era of information, networking, and access (Davies, 2014).

APPLICATIONS

With the embrace of digital technologies in the field of sociology came concerns that resisting the obvious influence of such technologies on everyday life would lead to a revisiting of a striking and apparently irresolvable dichotomy within the academic community between the humanities and the sciences, a binary approach to education that was sustained with some acrimony a generation before. In the advent of the digital era, the hard sciences appeared once again to split off from the humanities. Could machines with their elaborate algorithms define human communities? Could a community be sustained among people who never actually met, never actually bonded in real time and within real space? Sociology, although obviously reliant on hard data, was centrally a humanities discipline, investigating as it did real peoples involved in real communities and acting and reacting with one another in ways that defined real patterns. With the introduction of cyber-communities, the disciplines were poised again inevitability to collapse into an all new civil war.

Beginning at the turn of the twenty-first century, digital sociology offered a strategy to negotiate such inevitability. The term itself was not used within academic discourse until 2009—sociologists raised entirely within the argument of digital realities were far more attuned to the implications of the digital environment. By 2009, the larger public had gone a long way toward embracing social media as a way to engage others and to forge a community that was at once real and not real. By 2009, the message pipelines provided by and facilitated by the Internet—Twitter, blogging, emails, iPhones, LinkedIn, tablets, personal and professional websites, Facebook, Pinterest, as well as the constant stream of information via Internet sources, to name only a handful of the available social media platforms operating by 2009—had become standard communication vehicles for people with Internet access, a rapidly increasing demographic.

At the beginning of a new century, the industrialized world was converting into a mediated environment; that is, a global, culturally diverse community linked by digital communication technologies, rather than the traditional face-to-face sharing, into community that had long defined societies in real time and in real place. For the new age sociologists, who had termed their emerging field digital sociology, the key was far from ignoring the impress of social media and the data reservoir of the Internet rather to embrace such resources and such realities. Space, community, identity, family, gender, intimacy, relationships—all had undergone radical redefinition. The vocabulary of traditional sociology needed to be reconfigured. Indeed, observers know that digital natives use the resources and the reach of the Internet to pursue not narrow and individual initiatives (such as Facebook or blogs or Instagram) but perceive that the Internet can be used to forge an international community of the likeminded to direct and even encourage activism, promote social agendas and political causes, to use the Internet and social media to actually create a community.

No academic has so engaged the challenge and possibilities of digital sociology as Deborah Lupton, of Australia's University of Queensland. In her pioneering work which has gone a long way in codifying the new discipline, she wrote in 2012, "Digital sociology can offer a means by which the impact, development and use of these [digital] technologies and their impact upon and incorporation into social worlds and concepts of selfhood may be investigated, analyzed and understood." ("What Is Digital Sociology?").

These were potentially template-changing issues for the science of sociology, in a field where the digital capabilities were redefining themselves with unprecedented rapidity. New software applications, new gadgets, new access portals appeared with such frequency that any stable approach would undergo complete reinvigoration. Using websites and professional conferences, sociologists began to investigate how to use social media within their discipline. Quickly, proponents cited four areas in which traditional sociology and the digital era might overlap. First, sociologists needed to study how users of social media define and in some cases entirely create their sense of self (dubbed cyber-self) and their sense of identity as part of a larger, albeit digital, community. Second, professional observers needed to define precisely the import and reliability of the massive amounts of data retrievable from Internet resources. Third, sociologists as professionals needed to exploit the pipeline of the Internet to create an international body of like-minded researchers with shared areas of inquiry, a network of cooperative sociologists taking advantage of the communication opportunities of the Internet. And fourth, sociologists, whatever their personal predisposition or biases toward the emerging technology, needed to recognize that an entirely new era of their science had opened and that, as a collective, sociologists needed to codify precisely how to approach the impact of social media on traditional notions of community and self, not only to gather the data but to respond critically to the instruments of social media. Within a scant decade, social media had entirely recreated the traditional conceptions of relationships, although that revolution certainly had not included everyone. If the traditional assumption behind sociology was that participation in communities as the shaping influence on a range of constructs from self to family, the new age of digital technologies posed a particularly stubborn barrier. Some people had the technology; some did not. If formerly sociologists could assume wide inclusive participation in a social construct given space and time (if a person lived in, say, Melbourne, Australia, in the early twentieth century, then participation in that social construct could be assumed), digital sociologists could not. Having computers and digital technology did not presume computer literacy. Among the earliest terms introduced into the field of digital sociology was the concept of the digital divide.

The digital divide is a concept that describes the unequal access to technology that exists as a result of the stratification of society into different economic classes. Many people are unable to afford their own computers, tablets, smartphones, and similar gadgetry, and even when some of these devices are available (most libraries have computers for public use, for example), not everyone has the time or the educational background to be able to make use of them. This means that a large segment of society is without the equipment, skills, and confidence to access the variety of digital media. Furthermore, according to Jan A. G. M. van Dijk, an early advocate of the field of digital sociology, access to digital resources is not the same as connectivity, and connectivity is not the same as competence, and competence is not the same as skill. A line divides users from non-users. That line, as it turned out, cut across a number of traditional sociological barriers—those without digital access included the economically disadvantaged who could not afford the gadgets crucial to full Internet access; those who lacked the education, the training, and the competency to fully realize the opportunities of the Internet; Luddites who simply refused to embrace the implications and opportunities of the Internet; and most broadly those not digital natives, those born before 1980s, those who came at technology with a deeply ingrained bias and/or anxiety. Sociologists needed to create new dynamics to measure both those within and without the digital environments.

Professionally, sociologists needed to confront the vast reservoirs of information cataloged daily, even hourly, by the Internet. If sociologists had long prided themselves on the meticulous and careful gathering of data from which to extrapolate guiding theories about behavior, this new resource posed considerable challenges. How much of the data were even reliable? Do people within the comfortable anonymity of social media deal with accurate information, honest responses, and reliable observations? How much of a person's Internet identity is a construct? Rather than dismissing the sum total of Internet data as unreliable as they were gathered without professional supervision, digital sociologists determined that the field was at the threshold of a new discipline protocol that would deal with rather than ignore these questions.

VIEWPOINTS

Of course, a big part of the challenge to those in the field of digital sociology is the field's newness. For advocates, introducing social media and digital cultures into sociology represents a way to "enliven" standard sociological research (Daniels, 2014). It is at the stage—as exhilarating as it is frustrating—in which its advocates can formulate critical and intriguing questions but must wait for the hard data to be gathered to make the necessary conclusions. As Jonathan R. Wynn, professor of Digital Sociology at Smith College, has outlined (2009), the challenges in the field are continually expanding with the growth of digital communications itself. Inevitably, digital sociology will evolve as an interdisciplinary field, drawing together fields as far ranging as computer software engineering and communication. The field is as ambitious as it is complex, and digital sociologists have only begun to contend with the tonnage of data available from social media sources, have only begun to formulate a code of ethics regarding the use of social media data and the sticky issue of privacy, have only begun to pattern out the contradictions and complexities of behavior that first responds to the opportunity of social media and then without deliberate plan or supervision come together to form an entirely new social construct, a digital nation, one that crosses not only geographical boundaries but political, social, religious, cultural, and economic boundaries as well.

TERMS & CONCEPTS

Big data: A very large, complex set of contradictory data points gathered by a variety of digital platforms and available for analysis as a way to reveal patterns or to suggest trends.

Cybercommunity: A quasi-nation culture that defies traditional national, political, military, or geographical boundaries, a culture shaped and sustained entirely by the links available through the Internet.

Cyberself: The reconstruction, even recreation of the self and the repurposing of identity through the use of social media outlets.

Digital divide: A concept that describes the unequal access to technology that exists as a result of the stratification of society into different economic classes. Many people are unable to afford their own computers, tablets, smartphones, and similar gadgetry, and even when some of these devices are available (most libraries have computers for public use, for example), not everyone has the time or the educational background to be able to make use of them.

Mediated environment: The reconstruction of cultures and societies through the infiltration of visual media, digital technologies, and the Internet.

Bibliography

Davies, H. C. (2014, February 25). "Introducing digital sociology." http://thesocietypages.org/sociologylens/2014/02/25/introducing-digital-sociology/

Duggan, M., et al. (2015, January 9). "Social media update." http://www.pewinternet.org/2015/01/09/social-mediaupdate-2014/

Knoblach, H. (2014, November 20). "Pioneering digital sociology: Contexts." http://contexts.org/articles/pioneering-digitalsociology/

Lupton, D. (2012, July 8). "What is digital sociology?" https://simplysociology.wordpress.com/2012/07/08/digitalsociology-part-1-what-is-it/

Marres, N. (2013, January 21). "What is digital sociology?" http://www.csisponline.net/2013/01/21/what-is-digitalsociology/

Marres, N., & Gerlitz, C. (2016). "Interface methods: renegotiating relations between digital social research, STS and sociology." *Sociological Review, 64*(1), 21–46.

Wynn, J. (2009). "Digital sociology: Emergent technologies in the field and the classroom." *Sociological Forum, 24*(9), 448–456.

Van Dijk, J. A. G. M. (2013). "Inequalities in the network society." In K. Orton-Johnson & N. Prior (Eds.). *Digital sociology: Critical perspectives*: 105–124. Basingstoke, UK: Palgrave Macmillan.

Suggested Reading

Fuchs, C. (2013). *Social media: A critical introduction.* Thousand Oaks, CA: Sage.

Kirkpatrick, G. (2008). *Technology and social power.* Basingstoke, UK: Palgrave-Macmillan.

Lupton, D. (2015). *Digital sociology.* New York, NY: Routledge.

Orton-Johnson, K, & Prior, N. (Eds.). (2013). *Digital sociology: Critical perspectives.* Basingstoke, UK: Palgrave-Macmillan.

Parmeggiani, P. (2009). "Going digital: Using new technologies in visual sociology." *Visual Studies, 24*(1), 71–81.

"Pioneering digital sociology." (2014). *Contexts: Understanding People in Their Social Worlds, 13*(4), 6–8.

Sanjek, R., & Tratner, S. W. (2016). *eFieldnotes: The makings of anthropology in the digital world.* Philadelphia, PA: University of Pennsylvania Press.

van Heur, B. (2010). "From analogue to digital and back again: Institutional dynamics of heritage innovation." *International Journal of Heritage Studies, 16*(6), 405–416.

Joseph Dewey

The Internet & Society

OVERVIEW

Nothing has changed the social world since the 1990s as profoundly as has the global spread of Internet technology. The Internet has begun to reshape the social structure of modern society. It has proliferated the process of globalization and pervaded everyday life with the miniaturization of technology. It has created new forms of social interaction, expression of the self and political organization. At the same time, this new technological advancement is responsible for a new form of social inequality, which has become known as the digital divide.

Internet technology has changed the world profoundly. Distances of time and space have shrunk dramatically. Information has become readily available at any time and nearly every location. At the same time, one can–via email, chat, or video-phone–communicate with a person at any time and nearly every geographic location. The idea of distance is slowly dissolving. News travels in split seconds into every household at the very moment it is made, enabling a feeling of synchronicity.

Estimates have it that in 2012, 2.4 billion people (of an estimated global population of 7 billion) had access to the Internet (Miniwatts Marketing Group, 2013). According to the Pew Research Center in 2015, 84 percent of adults used the Internet while 96 percent of young adults reported using the Internet (Perrin & Duggan, 2015). At the same time, this technological advancement is responsible for a newer form of social inequality, which has become known as the digital divide. For example, in the United States 81 out of every 100 people have access to the Internet; Iceland has the highest rate, with 95 of every one hundred having access. Developed countries generally have high rates of usership; however developing countries–especially those in Africa–often have very low percentages of Internet users; Eritrea has the lowest ratio: less than one of every one hundred persons has access to the Internet (World Bank, 2013). For example, theories of access, like Jeremy Rifkin's, and theories of cultural capital, such as Pierre Bourdieu's, have guided economists and sociologists alike in accounting the reasons for and effects of the digital inequality (2000, 1986). At the same time, political as well as civic efforts are underway to enable every person to have access to information and communication technology (ICT).

However, studies such as that by Roberts and Foehr show that in households with children, Internet access rose from 22 percent to 63 percent between just 1997 and 2003 and up to 86 percent by 2010 (Economics and Statistics Administration, 2011). There remains the question, though, of whether the people in these households are merely exposed to the Internet or able to actually use it. Roberts and Foehr were able to show that when it came to the question of the ability to use media, aspects of socioeconomic status, race, and ethnicity all play important roles independent of the question of mere exposure. Hsieh, Rai and Keil also suggested that there are certain caveats to the idea that merely providing access to Internet technology will enable participation and thereby reduce digital inequality (2008). They specifically criticize initiatives that Mandviwalla and others have described as municipal broadband wireless networks (MWNs) (2008). MWNs are wireless Internet access networks that are funded and maintained by local governments or by civic activists in order to enable constituencies that have been neglected by profit-oriented providers to participate in the digital age. Mandviwalla and others have argued that MWNs are necessary because "private sector Internet service providers tend to focus their services toward more financially attractive markets and consumers, and thus tend to neglect certain constituencies" (p. 72-73). However, Hsieh, Rai, and Keil have argued that merely providing access is not enough to bridge the divide; rather, users must also accept the technology and be able to use it.

But the digital divide has been only one outgrowth of the Internet. The Internet is also dramatically changing the worlds of both business and labor as well as private life. Modern financial markets have become globally intertwined due to web technology and have subsequently become more important to the global economy, as the recent economic crises have shown. Internet technology affects the lives and livelihoods of most participants in the labor market, too. The ability to use web-based technology is being demanded in nearly every occupation today, as even dentist appointments are being canceled and confirmed via email. Just having an email account increases a job-seeker's chances of finding a job and finding a well-paid job, as DiMaggio and Bonikowski have illustrated (2006).

The transformation of personal lives since the beginning of the 1990s has been equally fast-paced. Of course, reports of children becoming lost in the virtual world of online gaming or being harassed by classmates via Facebook unbeknownst to their parents come to mind, but in sociology one should think first of more basic changes. For instance, traveling or moving to a new town no longer means that one has to leave behind friends. Today, relationships can be maintained over long distances with the assistance of instantaneous communication from nearly everywhere. The concept of distance, temporal as well as spatial, is being dissolved. Life in the global village is experienced in a mode of synchronicity.

One should also not forget the topic of the entertainment industry. Music, television, and other entertainment platforms are now available through the Internet, a fact that has significantly changed our viewing and listening habits. This capability in turn affects the conditions of production and sale of entertainment products and, as a result, the structure of the entertainment industry. The current generation of children and teenagers is being raised in a world in which music and movies can be downloaded for free from some source on the Internet. This will likely change how future generations will think about intellectual property and copyrights claims.

The Internet certainly has created new means of social interaction, greatly impacting the political field. With chat-rooms and interactive forums that allow for new forms of debate, politics have become more strongly grounded in grassroots movements. No politician in a democratic country can ignore the Internet; each must establish a web presence. Social media gives many voters a chance to ask questions of candidates directly. This novel development has set a standard for future elections. It also has created a feeling of participation that voters have previously not been able to enjoy. However, it also opens the new forums for political extremists. In the long run, however, the public sphere itself will be transformed and open up to a variety of constructive debates and dialogues.

The Internet has also enabled new forms of self-expression. Through avatars in online-games and chat rooms, people cannot only freely express their opinions, but also assume different personalities and express themselves as they never would dare to in real life. This may not in every case be a positive development, as some people may deliberately cloak their true identities in order to commit criminal activities. But the positive effects certainly lie in the ability to express and find one's identity beyond questions of ethnicity, gender, race, or social status. Conflicts in identities can be discussed with like-minded people openly and anonymously.

In sum, the world is shrinking, while new opportunities arise. This is in itself not an entirely new thought. In 1962, before the Internet was even conceived, Marshall McLuhan–famous for his phrase, "the medium is the message"–described the Gutenberg-Galaxy, a concept which describes a state in which the world is shrunk down to a global village as people's minds are transformed by the invention of the printing press. In 2001, sociologist Manuel Castells spoke of the Internet Galaxy, which describes a similar state in which the Internet has taken the transformations initiated by the printing press even further. Castells is the leading sociological analyst of the network society and the information age, terms which describe societies or time periods in which information is the key to all social action, and social action is enabled and structured by network connections. Castells analyzed society along three variables:

production, power, and experience in regard to collective action.

Jean Baudrillard, however, offered a contrary position. According to Baudrillard, postmodern societies create levels of the hyperreal through so-called "simulacra" (1983). A simulacrum is not just a copy or a simulation of some reality, but it becomes a truth in itself, because it is treated as truth by social actors. In other words, the copy replaces the original.

Critics therefore ask whether the world we are creating, a simulacrum (a world without substance), must not ultimately fail.

APPLICATIONS

Permanence/Durability

One of the major and paradoxical issues about web-content is the question of durability of permanence. This has become an issue for young people who, upon entering the job market, worry that outdated, occasionally embarrassing information about them is available on the Internet for everyone to access. This information, which may have been initially posted by themselves or others, may range from fairly harmless but negative comments about a concert they attended years ago to literally career-destroying pictures taken at a student party.

On the other hand, some critics wonder if it is wise to have so many aspects of our culture, as well as important data, stored only electronically. Electronic media, it has been argued, are easily destroyed and often have a very short half-life. If these contents are lost, they are gone forever.

Medical Aspects of Internet Use

In the medical field, Internet technology has brought several innovations. Of the many positive effects is the possibility that patients will be able to consult with experts worldwide at any moment. Surgery could be supported through robotic technology, or even performed by a surgeon on a different side of the planet than the patient (Hadley & Mars, 2008).

It is also possible for medical practitioners to access the latest medical information from the moment it is available through the vast resources of the Internet. However, this information is available not only to experts but also to private citizens, an aspect that has both positive and negative sides. Of course, patients can be enabled with a better understanding of and control over their treatment. Yet at the same time, they can also be misled by false or yet unproven information. In some cases, they are intentionally misled by profiteers who advertise costly, but ineffective treatments. The most positive effect for patients seems to be that the Internet allows them to contact other people who are suffering from the same ailments in order to exchange information and experiences. For instance, parents of children suffering from attention deficit hyperactivity disorder, which is an increasing phenomenon in the United States, are becoming a focus of interest to medical sociology in this regard. Exchanging information and experiences often proves crucial when it comes to the psychological aspect of treatment.

In short, the "telemedicine" and "e-health" businesses are booming (Matusitz & Breen, 2007). The one thing that the sector of e-health often seems to lack, in Matusitz and Breen's opinion, is actual patient-doctor interaction, which can more often than not lead to misunderstandings, incorrect self-diagnoses, and miscalculations of risks. However, increasingly, patients are able to interact with doctors, nurses, and other medical personnel via health information exchange networks.

Scientific Use of Wikipedia

Public Internet databases and encyclopedias such as Wikipedia have made knowledge accessible for everybody and seem thus to fulfill a humanistic ideal. But these databases also suffer criticism from academics since the articles are written through a community effort in which everyone can participate whether or not they have actual competence or expertise in a subject. Academics and teachers have repeatedly pointed out that, because of their authorship, sources like Wikipedia are highly unreliable because they do not adhere to established procedures, such as peer-review. At the same time, it has been noted that students rely increasingly on such sources, up to the point of copying and pasting portions of online articles into the papers they write for school.

VIEWPOINTS

Statistical Data of Internet Access & Use

How many people use the Internet is in itself a matter of debate, for it cannot be clearly determined who has access where and when. The number of people who are computer-literate within a household may vary enormously, while there are many public access points that do not record who uses them. The number of Internet users is also growing at such a fast rate that reliable sources that rely on census data are quickly outdated. Internet consultancy companies usually operate with the most current estimates, which are usually published on the Internet for client use. But these estimates are only valid to some degree, and, again, because of the fast-paced growth of the Internet, the data available is as short-lived as it is uncertain.

This is not to say that certain trends cannot be found in the comparison of different data sets over time. For example, South Korea has overtaken the United States. in persons per one hundred who have access to the Internet, and Asia has two times as many Internet users as Europe and nearly four times as many as North America (World Bank, 2013; Miniwatts Marketing Group, 2013). Meanwhile, the African continent is left behind dramatically in all forms of ICT.

Identity Theft

The term "identity theft" is a neologism and actually somewhat inaccurate, for it is not one's identity that is being stolen. Rather, it is one's crucial personal data, such as social security or credit card numbers, which are accessed by people who then use them for the purpose of fraud.

Identity Theft is commonly differentiated into four categories:

- Financial identity theft, or using another person's data, such as a credit card number, to purchase goods or services
- Criminal identity theft, or using another person's data to pose as him or her when arrested for a crime
- Identity cloning, or using another person's data to pose as him or her in daily life
- Business/commercial identity theft, or using the data of another business to obtain credit in that business's name.

The actual annual damage in the United States cannot be exactly measured, but the Bureau of Justice Statistics reported that 17.6 million Americans were victims of identity theft in 2014 alone (Bureau of Justice Statistics, 2015).

Social Network Providers & Private Information

Both neo-Marxist critics and citizenship rights activists have emphasized that Internet users are educated into a culture of sharing private information freely with both companies and governmental agencies. Web providers offering personal web space or acting as social network providers often require their clients to hand them information that is otherwise considered highly sensitive. Participants openly reveal their private addresses and phone numbers, personal tastes, sexual and political orientations, and so forth. They have often no control over how this information is used or by whom it is accessed. In the gravest of cases, the providers of such services have opened their client data to commercial enterprises. This information is also often available to actual or future employers, who are otherwise banned from obtaining it directly.

Terrorist Websites & Communication

One of the gravest political concerns since the September 11, 2001, terrorist attacks has been the fact that terrorist organizations, as well as other radical and ideological organizations, use the Internet to distribute their propaganda material to their followers. They apply web technology as a means of communication as well as use the web to recruit new members. Organizations like al-Qaeda have used the Internet to distribute images of acts of terrorism.

TERMS & CONCEPTS

Cultural Capital: The concept of cultural capital as a form of symbolic capital was made popular by French sociologist Pierre Bourdieu. In his work, Bourdieu showed that, besides monetary capital, other forms of capital–those comprising knowledge, network connections, and experience–can regulate access to social classes.

Digital Divide: The differences in access to and practical knowledge about the use of information technology, especially the Internet. The divide may exist between different kinds of demographic groups (e.g. age groups), between social classes, nationally, between rural and urban areas, or between areas of greater or lesser economic interest to Internet service providers, or internationally, between developing and developed nations.

Digital Inequality: An effect of the digital divide in which those denied access to the use of or knowledge about Internet technology suffer political, social, or economic disadvantages as a result of that denial.

E-Government: E-Government, also known as e-gov, digital government, or online government, refers to the government use of information and digital technologies to promote the free exchange of political information, communication between citizens and government agencies, and the use of government services. Different branches of government have also used information technology internally in order to increase efficiency. Private citizens have also found e-government more convenient for using government services or participating in political activities. In particular, people whose mobility is impaired by age, illness, or disability have been enabled to participate in the democratic process as well as independently work with government agencies.

E-Learning: A form of education in which learning takes place through the use of computer technology. Among other things, it encompasses the integration of computer technology into the traditional classroom, online courses and online colleges, free online education resources, and online corporate learning tools.

Gutenberg-Galaxy: Media theorist Marshall McLuhan coined this term in 1962 along with the concept of the global village. In his description, the invention of the printing press had a lasting and transformative effect on human consciousness, for through this invention, concepts like nationalism, dualism, and rationalism could actually become widespread ideas that would transform entire cultures and societies. Later, the Gutenberg-Galaxy expanded into the Internet-Galaxy, according to Manuel Castells.

Information & Communication Technology (ICT): Summary names for technologies such as the Internet, mobile phones, personal digital assistants (PDAs), personal computers, and tablets that allow users to manipulate and communicate information.

Municipal Broadband Wireless Network (MWN): A wireless Internet access network that is funded and maintained by a local government or by civic activists in order to enable constituencies that have been neglected by profit-oriented providers to participate in the digital age.

Bibliography

Baudrillard, J. (1983). *Simulations.* Los Angeles, CA: Semiotext(e).

Beck, U. (2006). *Power in the global age: A new global political economy.* Cambridge, England: Polity Press.

Bureau of Justice Statistics. (2015). "Victims of identity theft, 2014." https://www.bjs.gov/content/pub/pdf/vit14%5Fsum.pdf

Castells, M. (2001). *The* Internet *galaxy: Reflections on the* Internet, *business and* society. New York, NY: Oxford University Press.

Crossley, N., & Roberts, J. (2004). *After Habermas: New perspectives on the public sphere.* Oxford, England Blackwell Publishing.

DiMaggio, P., & Bonikowski, B. (2006). "Does Internet use affect earnings?" Paper presented at the meeting of the American Sociological Association Montreal, CA.

Economics and Statistics Administration & National Telecommunications and Information Administration. (2011, Nov). "Exploring the digital nation: Computer and Internet use at home." Washington, DC: U.S. Department of Commerce. http://www.esa.doc.gov/sites/default/files/reports/documents/exploringthedigitalnation-computerand-Internetuseathome.pdf

Hadley, G., & Mars, M. (2008). "Postgraduate medical education in pediatric surgery: Videoconferencing–A possible solution for Africa?" *Pediatric Surgery International,* 24, 223-226.

Hsieh, J. J., Rai A., & Keil, M. (2008). "Understanding digital inequality: Comparing continued use behavioral models of the socio-economically advantaged and disadvantaged." *MIS Quarterly,* 32, 97-126.

Kong, S. C. (2008). "A curriculum framework for implementing information technology in school education to foster information literacy." *Computers & Education,* 51, 129-141.

Kruikemeier, S., van Noort, G., Vliegenthart, R., & de Vreese, C. H. (2014). "Unraveling the effects of active and passive forms of political Internet use: Does it affect citizens' political involvement?" *New Media &* Society, 16, 903-920.

Lash, S., & Urry, J. (1994). *Economies of signs and space.* London: Sage.

Mandviwalla, M., Jain, A., Fesenmaier, J., Smith, J., Weinberg, P., & Meyers, G. (2008). "Municipal broadband wireless networks: Realizing the vision of anytime, anywhere connectivity." *Communications of the ACM,* 51, 72-80.

Masic, I., & Suljevic, E. (2007). "An overview of e-health implementation in countries, members of the European Union." *Acta Informatica Medica,* 15, 242-245.

Matusitz, J., & Breen, G. M. (2007). "E-Health: A new kind of telemedicine." *Social Work in Public Health,* 23, 95-113.

McLuhan, M. (1962). *The Gutenberg galaxy: The making of typographic man.* Toronto, Ont.: University of Toronto Press.

Millham, M. H., & Atkin, D. (2018). "Managing the virtual boundaries: Online social networks, disclosure, and privacy behaviors." *New Media &* Society, 20(1), 50-67.

Miniwatts Marketing Group. (2013). "Internet World Stats: Usage and Population Statistics." http://www.Internetworldstats.com/stats.htm

Perrin, A., & Duggan, M. (2015, June 26). "Americans' Internet access: 2000-2015." Pew Research Center. http://www.pewInternet.org/2015/06/26/americans-Internet-access-2000-2015/

Pick, J. B., & Azari, R. (2008). "Global digital divide: Influence of socioeconomic, governmental, and accessibility factors on information technology." *Information Technology for Development,* 14, 91-115.

Rains, S. A. (2008). "Health at high speed: Broadband Internet access, health communication, and the digital divide." *Communication Research,* 35, 283-297.

Roberts, D. F., & Foehr, U. G. (2008). "Trends in media use." *Future of Children,* 18, 11-37.

Robinson, L. (2014). "Freeways, detours, and dead ends: Search journeys among disadvantaged youth." *New Media &* Society, 16, 234-251.

Rubaii-Barrett, N., & Wise, L. R. (2008). "Disability access and e-government: An empirical analysis of state practices." *Journal of Disability Policy Studies,* 19, 52-64.

World Bank. (2013). "Internet users (per 100 people)." Washington, DC: World Bank. http://data.worldbank.org/

Suggested Reading

Abedini, S. (2011). "Sociological approach to Internet usage: The case of university students, Khalkhal." *OIDA International Journal of Sustainable Development,* 3, 23-29.

Acemoglu, D. (2002). "Technical change, inequality, and the labor market." *Journal of Economic Literature,* 40, 7-72.

Aghion, P., & Howitt, P. (2002). "Wage inequality and the new economy." *Oxford Review of Economic Policy,* 18, 306-23.

Autor, D. H. (2001). "Wiring the labor market." *Journal of Economic Perspectives,* 15, 25-40.

Autor, D. H., Katz, L. F., & Krueger, A. B. (1998, Nov). "Computing inequality: Have computers changed the labor market?" *Quarterly Journal of Economics,* 113, 1169-83.

Bresnahan, T. F., Brynjolfsson, E., & Hitt, L. M. (2002, Feb). "Information, technology, workplace organization and the demand for skilled labor: Firm-level evidence." *Quarterly Journal of Economics,* 117, 339-76.

Brown, J. S., & Thomas, D. (2006). "You play world of Warcraft? You're hired! Why multiplayer games may be the best kind of job training." *Wired,* 14. http://www.wired.com/wired/archive/14.04/learn.html

Davidson, J., & Martellozzo, E. (2013). "Exploring young people's use of social networking sites and digital media in the Internet safety context." *Information, Communication &* Society, 16, 1456-1476.

Dickerson, A., & Green, F. (2004). "The growth and valuation of computing and other generic skills." *Oxford Economic Papers,* 56, 371-406.

DiMaggio, P., Bonikowski, B. (2008). "Make money surfing the web? The impact of Internet use on the earnings of U.S. workers." *American Sociological Review,* 73, 227-250.

DiMaggio, P. (2004). "Cultural capital." In G. Ritzer (Ed.), *Encyclopedia of Social Theory* (pp. 167-70). Thousand Oaks, CA: Sage.

Downs, D. (2006). "Dragnet, reinvented." *Wired,* 14, 110-16. http://www.wired.com/wired/archive/14.03/lapd.html

Eastin, M. S., & LaRose, R. (2000). "Internet self-efficacy and the psychology of the digital divide." *Journal of Computer-Mediated Communications,* 6. http://jcmc.indiana.edu/vol6/issue1/eastin.html

Fairlie, R. W. (2004). "Race and the digital divide." *Contributions to Economic Analysis & Policy,* 3, Article 15. http://www.bepress.com/bejeap/contributions/vol3/iss1/art15

Fountain, C. (2005). "Finding a job in the Internet age." *Social Forces*, 83, 1235-62.

Fountain, J. (2001). "Paradoxes of public sector customer service." *Governance*, 14, 55-73.

Goss, E. P., & Phillips, J. M. (2002, Summer). "How information technology affects wages: Evidence using Internet usage as a proxy for IT skills." *Journal of Labor Research*, 23, 463-74.

Graham, M., Schroeder, R., & Taylor, G. (2013). Re: *Search. New Media &* Society, 15, 1366-1373.

Hoffman, D. L., & Novak, T. P. (1998, April 17). "Bridging the digital divide: The impact of race on computer access and Internet use." *Science*, 280, 390-91.

Holmgren, H. G., & Coyne, S. M. (2017). "Can't stop scrolling!: Pathological use of social networking sites in emerging adulthood." *Addiction Research & Theory*, 25(5), 375-382.

Jung, J.-Y., & Qiu, J. L., & Kim, Y.-C. (2001, Aug). "Internet connectedness and inequality." *Communication Research*, 28, 507-535.

Kapitzke, C. (2000). "Information technology as cultural capital: Shifting the boundaries of power." *Education and Information Technologies*, 5, 49-62.

Krueger, A. B. (1993). "How computers have changed the wage structure: Evidence from microdata, 1984-1989." *Quarterly Journal of Economics*, 108, 33-60.

Kuhn, P., & Skuterud, M. (2004). "Internet job search and unemployment durations." *American Economic Review*, 94, 218-32.

Lenhart, A., Horrigan, J., Rainie, L, Allen, K., Boyce, A., Madden, M., & O'Grady, E. (2003). "The ever-shifting Internet population: A new look at Internet access and the digital divide." Pew Internet and American Life Project, Washington, DC. http://www.pewInternet.org/

Levy, F., & Murnane, R. (2004). *The new division of labor: How computers are creating the next job market.* Princeton, NJ: Princeton University Press and Russell Sage Foundation.

Lin, N. (2001). *Social capital: A theory of social structure and action.* New York, NY: Cambridge University Press.

McDonald, S., & Crew, R. E., Jr. (2006). "Welfare to web to work: Internet job searching among former welfare clients." *Journal of Sociology and Social Welfare*, 33, 239-53.

Niles, S., & Hanson, S. (2003). "The geographies of online job search: Preliminary findings from Worcester, MA." *Environment and Planning*, 35, 1223-43.

Ono, H., & Zavodny, M. (2003). "Gender and the Internet." *Social Science Quarterly*, 84, 111-21.

Rifkin, J. (2000). *The age of access.* New York, NY: Tarcher.

Turner, F. (2006). *From counterculture to cyberculture: Stewart brand, the whole earth network, and the rise of digital utopianism.* Chicago, IL: University of Chicago Press.

Van Dijk, J. A. G. M. (2005). *The deepening divide: Inequality in the information* society. Thousand Oaks, CA: Sage.

Warschauer, M. (2003). *Technology and social inclusion: Rethinking the digital divide.* Cambridge, MA: MIT Press.

Alexander Stingl, Ph.D.

Jacques Ellul's *The Technological Society*

ABSTRACT

Jacques Ellul (1912–1994) was an illustrious French scholar who wrote about social philosophy and theology. In his highly acclaimed book *The Technological Society* (1954/1964), he addressed the question of what it means to live within a society that is run by an ever larger number of technicians. He tried to elucidate what this may mean to present and future human beings. According to Ellul, technique must be understood as the set or regime of means (or techniques) that are employed to execute a rationale toward a predetermined end. Risk and uncertainty are increasingly excluded from the world of the Technical Man. At the same time, ends themselves are turned into means, while means become ends. The criterion that determines these processes is the idea of efficiency. Economics and governance become subject to this doctrine, which places performance above achievement. With the acceleration of standardization, technique pervades an ever larger segment of social life until it becomes a global phenomenon. Along this course, Ellul introduced the controversial thesis that both American and Soviet society are increasingly ruled by the idea of efficiency and by technique, therefore both becoming illiberal societies in which technology becomes a new god, replacing the god of Christianity. In his own words, in the end "technique is nothing more than means and the ensemble of means."

OVERVIEW

It is nearly impossible to separate *The Technological Society* from its author and his illustrious biography. On occasion, the book has been criticized for its subjective attitude and tone. Ellul himself openly admitted that he made strong statements, yet maintained that he had never done so without elaborate reasoning. The book managed to transcend the genre of pure sociological analysis and became a milestone of critical thought on modernity and technology.

Jacques Ellul was both a social philosopher and a theologian. He was active in the Ecumenical Movement and a follower of Karl Barth (1886–1968). During the Second World War he was one of the intellectual leaders of the French Resistance. Because of his critical attitude towards technology and his literate references to Karl Marx, he was often described as being a socialist or Marxist. However, his work, particularly *The Technological Society,* shows that he was very cautious and critical in his reception of Marx and highly adverse to the totalitarian impetus of practiced socialism.

Aside from his technological critique, Ellul became famous for his statement that anarchy and Christianity had the same goal. He believed that science, and more importantly what he calls technique, have "desacralized" not only the scriptures but also humanity itself. In their stead, he argued, the object of worship has become the phenomenon of *technique.* Ellul promoted this conviction, most explicitly expressed in *The Technological Society,* throughout out his career.

The Technological Society was published in French in 1954, and translated into English ten years later thanks to the efforts of influential American scholars like Robert M. Hutchins, Scott Buchanan, and Robert K. Merton, who wrote the foreword. In it, Ellul outlined his view of technique, which he described as "the totality of methods rationally arrived at and having absolute efficiency (for a given stage of development) in every field of human activity" (1964, p. xxv). Thus, even if it originated with machines, technique means more than just "machines" or some technological procedures or devices that have been crafted to achieve some goal. Rather, technique increasingly interpenetrates with every aspect of social life. Though the machine stood as the ideal-type of the nineteenth century, in the twentieth century technique has taken over people and the entirety of their activities. Thus, in Ellul's view, capitalism is not to blame for the developments that followed it, for capitalism itself has become governed by technique. It is technique that integrates capitalism into the fabric of society, just as it integrates the machine into society, for it "clarifies, arranges, rationalizes" (Ellul, 1964, p. 5).

In this regard, Ellul viewed reason and science as the combined forces behind the development of technique. Traditionally, claimed Ellul, technique is perceived as the application of science: it is the medium between material reality and scientific formula. However, Ellul stands this relation on its head.

He argued that technique preceded science, thus reducing the gains of nineteenth century physical science to just a tiny period in the history of technique. In truth, Ellul said, technique had to wait for science to develop in human civilization, for technique rendered explicit problems of human progress that only science could solve. According to Ellul's account, if technique had not preceded science, science would only be hypothesis and speculation.

Essential for technique is its relation to organization, which is a central feature of modern society. The two processes that organization enables and that take hold of society's progress are standardization and rationalization. Society's progress itself is intertwined with the progress of technique. The technological societydiffers from prior forms of society in that it is characterized by technique, which rests not on tradition but rather on prior technical procedures. Therein, technique has reached its own form of autonomy.

According to Ellul, every technical operation, every actual application of technique in the real world, produces a "technical phenomenon." This phenomenon is rendered explicit in the two processes that lie within each actor: consciousness and judgment (i.e., reason). Consciousness creates the awareness of the advantages and accomplishments of the application of technique, while reason enables the progress towards new methods as well as the efficient use of existing means. The concrete phenomenon that emerges from the relation between reason and consciousness is found in the "one best means" to accomplish a task.

Aside from the application of technique as "mechanical technique" (machines) and "intellectual technique" (the storage of knowledge, e.g. in libraries, data-bases, and the like), Ellul discusses three interdependent divisions, he calls economic technique, technique of organization (or of the state), and human techniques.

Economic Technique

Ellul was an attentive reader of Marx, yet he was also a critical one. In Ellul's iconoclastic interpretation of Marx, it is not the economy or capitalism that produces technique. Quite the contrary, only through technique can the economy develop. Economics must therefore be seen from two angles: as the dynamic force behind technical innovation, and as innovation's static counterpart, the organization of economy.

Marx and his followers believed that a society's economic base determined its superstructure, or its socio-political institutions. Ellul called this belief a "self-deception." Ellul viewed Marx's analysis as correct only in regard to the nineteenth century and not relevant for other periods. Instead, he held that technique is the actual base, in that it guides not only production, but also distribution.

Thus, economics is subsumed to technique and, as it intervenes in the sphere of the state through political economy, efficiency becomes the criterion for political agendas. Just as technique pushes economists to establish "exact procedures," so policy-making becomes characterized by "exact procedures" meant to make policy-making more efficient.

In following the ideals of physics, economists hope to establish "exact procedures." Thereby, in political economy, this ideal is adapted to be the maximum of efficiency in policy-making. But at the same time, economics fails to accomplish this goal, as is illustrated in the repeated occurrence of economic crises. What remains is the public's trust in the force (i.e. technique) behind both the science of physics and economics, even while it loses faith in economics. The basic instruments that policy-makers and economists in the "technical state of mind" therefore rely upon are the means of statistics, accounting and the likes—all methods that can be broken down to technical performances.

In this regard, Ellul argued, both planning and liberty are in a conflict, wherein both socialist and democratic societies increasingly drift toward planning and away from liberty, for the two techniques of intervention into macro-relations—norm and plan—have proven their ability to increase efficiency.

Planning suggests itself in all forms of modern society, for it is not the best economic but rather "the best technical solution" (Ellul, 1964, p. 184). The two remaining types of economy, corporate economy and planned economy, display equal characteristics that relate back to the prerequisites of technique. However, both types of economy are not found in the real world in their extremes. Instead they are ideal-types, or heuristic devices. For even in a planned society, not "every detail is integrated into the plan."

In actuality, there will be a highly unstable equilibrium between technique and freedom, state and private enterprise. This tendency, however, seemed for Ellul to be a pendulum swing toward technique. In this pendulum swing, the conflict between politics (or better: the polity) and economics is forced into a mulled synthesis where "politics disappears and economics is forced into submission" (1964, p. 197). Subsequently, both the market and the state are organized and structured by technique. That the Soviet Union of Ellul's era was in his view very close to the fulfillment of that state, he supplemented by the controversial statement that the United Sates was also "oriented in this direction very rapidly" (Ellul, 1964, p. 197).

The realization of technique would therefore be the end of liberal economy, which aims at profit, since the goal of technique is found in a combination of rationality and efficiency.

Additionally, technique is anti-democratic. The engineers, statisticians, accountants, judges and other technicians who are responsible for the proliferation of technical progress are not elected, but merely join their creed through another increasingly technical process of education.

According to Ellul, production, consumption and education alike are increasingly subject to the same technical process: standardization. While the "price" for a consumer good or to attain an education is reduced, the number of possible choices (diversity) is at the same time reduced. The effect is felt both in market circumstances and education issues. It is finalized in the creation of the same technical state of mind.

And, finally, since civilization is becoming a mass civilization with the progress of technique, the problems of economy must be posed, suggests Ellul (in 1954, long before modern theories of globalization), "in global terms, in terms of global income, global employment, global demand, and so." (1964, p. 205)

Technique & the State

In the historic evolution of the state, its own forms of technique emerged: financial, administrative, and judicial technique. Each emerged to fulfill a specific function. Yet during the nineteenth century and early twentieth century, they were conflated in administrative law, with the political function providing the general direction that combined the other functions toward a global perspective.

The state, in the course of history, began to wedge into areas it had previously ignored and had so far left to the interest and care of individuals, including education, faith, and so on. With the "massification" of the individuals into society, large areas of the "private sphere" merged with the public sphere. The state in turn became a technical organism. The techniques need and make the state, and the state needs and makes the techniques. The technical organism is similar to a biological organism in which the organs and the body as a whole are mutually dependent: the organs are defined by the function they perform for the whole body, while the whole body is dependent upon the organs.

The motive force behind the state, and therefore behind technique, is the human being. But people-in-mass are eliminated from the actual processes of the state. The politician's capacities are reduced from decision making to the mere application of technique. Each politician is left with a choice: uphold democracy, which will eventually lose importance and diminish the role of the politician; or become a political technician and transform statesmanship into a synthesis of technique and politics.

But "the state machine," as Ellul called his era's state, "is not yet well adjusted." He saw the transformed state as being in its infancy. However, he also believed that the transformation is a steadily growing process that is changing the state into a synthesis of technical organizations at the expense of the autonomy of decision-making. The latter is a capacity that will decrease, while an ever increasing number of processes and goals are predetermined by the available technical processes.

This transformation will eventually affect the progress of justice and law, until the guiding rationale becomes: "Better injustice than disorder" (Ellul, 1964, p. 295). The criterion for laws and law-making will thus become the establishment of order, which is nothing else but, once again, the criterion of efficiency. Law would thus transform the institutions that regulate the organization of individual life and social relations at an ever higher rate. This is the result, on the one hand, of the general belief in the power of "facts" in the realm of public opinion on the one hand, and, on the other, of the subsequent general belief that only technical problems are to be taken seriously, and that, therefore, every problem or conflict has a technical solution.

Human Techniques

Ellul emphasized the demand that the increasing amount of technique makes on the human mind and life: never before have so many mechanisms demanded to be integrated into the process of everyday labor. According to him, technique pervades and structures even the basic components of life: time, space, and motion. And at the same time, in accordance with the processes of massification and standardization, the effects of technique have become inescapable. It is increasingly impossible to evade participation in the rhythms and attitudes of a society that is regulated by technique. To even try would result in either neurosis and/or total exclusion.

The actual goal of participation in society is set towards the elimination of the "nightmare of industrial labour": the fatigue factor. Therefore, the application of *technique* runs from state to individual, contrary to the romantic idea of humanism and democracy that rested on the idea of bottom-up decision making and thought that social resolution can be found in art. Action has subsequently three criteria:

- **Generality:** The elimination of the importance of individuals
- **Objectivity:** Independence from subjective motives
- **Permanence:** Each person must be immersed in the technical complex all his life

This is exemplified in the changing educational technique. The actual goal of technical education, which replaces the liberal arts, is for the child to adapt to technological society: "it is not the child in and for himself who is being educated, but the child in and for society. And the society, moreover, is not an ideal one, with full justice and truth, but society as it is." (Ellul, 1964, p. 348). Therefore, society becomes totalitarian. Society creates an increasing number of problems that further the process of adaptation and require conformism.

This process is promoted by propaganda. While this technique had previously been studied as a tool of the totalitarian states of Nazi-Germany or Soviet Communism, Ellul claimed that every form of government employs some means of propaganda. The effects of propaganda are difficult to discern, and only a few corollaries seem obvious:

- That the creation of "collective passions" undermines the development of the capability of critical thought in individuals.
- Additionally, a collective conscience appears. People who have adapted their personality to technique will share a universal idea of what is collectively good and just.
- Finally, a new "sphere of the sacred and sphere of taboo" is created.

What follows is that technique will not only structure the psyches of people, but it will increasingly rule the body and the biological functions. Technique will establish a biocracy. It will make the person into a machine. This will result in a loss, though. Creativity and spontaneity—and with them, real innovation—will disappear. This must lead to "disequilibration." Feeling unfulfilled, humanity will end in psychological crisis. The modern society seeks to counter this effect in the concept of "leisure." People supposedly are enabled to realize creative power in their spare time. But leisure itself becomes part of technique: rationalized, efficient, and predetermined.

Ellul's book was a controversial, but certainly also to a large degree, a prognostic effort. In 1954, he saw clearly how the processes of standardization and globalization would progress in the future while his contemporaries lacked the same foresight. Even over fifty years after its initial publication, Ellul's book offers insightful elaborations of the development of modern society in regard to the progress of social techniques that are still worth reflecting upon when thinking about our own future.

FURTHER INSIGHTS

While being highly pessimistic, Ellul's book was also very much ahead of its time. The proliferation of technique can be certainly be diagnosed today. Even still, one must not necessarily share Ellul's perspective that this will lead—or has led—to the total elimination of liberty. But in a few instances, the effects of Ellul's technique should give rise to critical reflection.

Starting with science itself, it is necessary to look at the question of how scientific progress is guided today. It is not much of a secret that the demands of efficiency and utility have gained strength in the choices that researchers make. Additionally, there is a tendency to eliminate risk and uncertainty in advance. Institutions that finance science require more and more detailed research proposals that feature ever more bureaucratic standards of science along with exhaustive research proposals that feature results and possible applications, all before the actual research has even been executed. This process affects not only the natural sciences, but has also become common within the social sciences and humanities alike.

Since one of the largest organizations enabling science is the state, we can see clearly that technique is becoming a universal aspect of policy-making. Current political debates are less and less about what goal is to be accomplished, but rather whether a suggested policy makes sense in regard to budgeterian constraints, or whether an existing system is efficient.

The question of health care, for example, currently centers not on what it means to be a healthy human being, but rather whether the existing system efficiently includes all of those who actively participate in society as self-sustaining laborers and, if it does not do so, whether a financially sound transformation can be effected to reach this predetermined goal. The question of the quality of life, whether physical or psychological, is not so much the issue. It is still left to the decreasing amount of leisure time.

But even within leisure time, the effects of standardization can be felt. The technical demands of modern life require schedules to be synchronized and standardized. Temporal slots for meeting with friends must be negotiated according to sports clubs' opening hours, the availability of daycare for one's children or pets, or the time it takes to download a movie off of the Internet. Cell phones render people available at all times, but this can only seem to increase leisure. In reality, each person is rendered available to be called to work at any moment. Cell phones can be turned into instruments for tracking the movements of one's own children. Similarly, integrated GPS can tell a driver the most efficient route to his or her destination, though it is not necessarily the most picturesque one. GPS can lead shoppers directly to the shops they are looking for, disabling the possibility for a surprise discovery on the way. But standardization has reached into the stores as well, limiting shoppers' choice of warehouses, supermarkets, and so forth. Within stores, too, choice is limited. In comparison to the actual number of products on the market, shelf-space is restricted. Rationalization and standardization in the shelves follows complicated technical processes. For instance, a chain of grocery stores may collect information about shoppers' zip codes and document their purchases with privileged customer-cards that offer discounts.

The effects of technique pervade everyday life, still and increasingly. But technique itself is neutral. Even Ellul made this point. Therefore, the issue at hand is not so much the pessimism of Ellul. Rather, it is the critical attitude in making explicit the effects of technique and showing where they lead to a reduction of freedom.

CONCLUSION

Certainly, most of Ellul's criticisms and concepts are, in themselves, not original, yet he still managed to apply them in a unique and provocative way.

Many of Ellul's "leitmotifs" were present in the prior literature. Titchener's psychological writings (1918, 1972) feature similar depictions of the roles of, on the one hand, the scientist and the politician, and, on the other, the ordinary person, with the new breed of the technological person having an intermediate role between the two. Also foreshadowing Ellul's work is G. Stanley Hall's *Fall of Atlantis* (1920), which told the tale of the negative effects that came from the turn from independent research to a research guided only by "practical goals." Additionally, the idea of total integration is very close to the concept of total ideology criticized by Ellul's contemporaries, especially the members of the Frankfurt School.

But certain corollaries of Ellul are unique and prognostic. Two decades after Ellul, Michel Foucault was (and his successors are still) discussing the concept of biopolitics. Ellul's concept of biocracy is more than an accidental resemblance. At the same time, modern theories of globalization that are now taken for granted in social and political science, as well as in public discourse, were not conceived of when Ellul inferred that technique would eventually require its effects to attain a global reach. Finally, Ellul definitely must be counted as a forerunner of the current debate on "post-democracy" (Crouch, 2004). The disillusionment with democracy that many people in Western countries presently experience has created anti-democratic sentiments, which yet seek to receive proper explication in new concepts of government.

What emerges in these discussions as "solutions" often resembles the diagnosis of Ellul.

Ellul certainly was not a prophet, but he was a keen observer and analyst, whose insights still have validity. His work's influence in current debates can still be felt.

TERMS & CONCEPTS

Biocracy: Technique that has shaped political economy as the technique of policy-making and administration as well as propaganda as the technique of the adaptation of the psychological makeup of its members. But this does not satisfy the totalitarian impetus of technique. It seeks to regulate the organism of societyand of the people that make society, so that a person is turned into a man-machine. The political invasion of the organism occurs in the form of biocracy, a forerunner of the biopolitics, identified by Michel Foucault.

Equilibrium: The concept of equilibrium is introduced by Ellul without further specification and without any evaluation. Although in sociology the concept has a long history, it became controversial in the 1960s. Leftist critics of that time interpreted the idea of equilibrium as a static and conformist state of society. The concept, which was introduced into social and economic thought in the nineteenth century with Cournot's adaptation of Lagrange's mechanics, and was made popular first by Vilfredo Pareto and then by Talcott Parsons. For these scholars, it was a dynamic concept that allowed for social conflict and change, while for later critics the idea of equilibrium displayed the inability of sociological theory to account for progress, conflict, and social change.

Economic Man: With the differentiation of anthropology and economics in the nineteenth century, the concept of the economic man became the leitmotif of liberalism. Every person, being a homo economicus, would seek to increase his or her own (monetary) profit. The new economic man, which Ellul saw emerge, does not follow this goal. Since, in Ellul's view, economics had changed from the profit-motive to efficiency, the new economic man no longer seeks profit maximization, but rather increased efficiency. He or she lives in an artificial paradise where he or she has become human capital

Fact: According to Ellul, the raw material that constitute the justifications of the technological society. These facts are the uninterpreted data from instruments like statistical analyses or public opinion polls.

Mass vs. Community: In the traditional account, social cohesion is constituted within and via communities. When communities start engaging another on a social level (e.g. in trade), potentials of freedom are enabled within these communities. Mass is the opposite of community. Sociologically, mass means not simply a great number of people. It means that these people are not organized in separate communities, but rather are following a common rationale. Ellul claimed that the process of massification has standardized individual goals to the point where a single person no longer follows an individually unique and private goal, but rather a goal that is the same as that of each anonymous next person, even if the illusion of individuality is upheld through the means of propaganda.

Propaganda: In 1954, research into mass communication was still young. This kind of research had its first climax with the analysis of the rise of fascism. The first studies on the effects of propaganda, however, can be found in Gustav Le Bon's *The Crowd* (1895) and Walter Lippman's *Public Opinion* (1922). For Ellul, propaganda is a human technique. But in spite of the fact that propaganda studies usually focus on the Third Reich or communism, Ellul claimed that every form of government employs propaganda techniques to achieve adaptation of all of a society**'s** members.

Technique: Ellul's conception of technique describes an ensemble or a regime of means that constitute a rationale towards the realization of predetermined goals.

Zweckwissenschaft : Originally applied by the Nazis, the concept means "practical or purposive science." However, according to Ellul, this was a premature application. Only now, with the eradication of the possibility of "independent research," has the concept reached its realization. The opportunities to find a public forum for one's research decrease and are increasingly regulated by technical procedures (peer-review, standardized research proposals etc.).

Research involves ever higher costs that preclude private researchers from entering into new projects. Research must now be previously marketed to "potential financiers," who in turn seek to derive applicable results from the research.

Bibliography

Crouch, C. (2004). *Post-democracy.* Oxford: Polity.

Ellul, J. (1964). *The technological society.* (J. Wilkinson, Trans.). New York: Knopf. (Original work published 1954).

Hall, S. G. (1920). "The fall of Atlantis." In *Recreations of a psychologist* (pp. 1-127). New York: Appleton.

Melman, S. (1975). "The impact of economics on technology." *Journal of Economic Issues, 9*(1), 59–72.

Rustum, R. (2005). "Scientism and technology as religions." *Zygon, 40*(4), 835–844.

Titchener, E. B. (1972). *Systematic pychology.* Ithaca, NY: Cornell Univerisity Press. (Original work published 1929).

Titchener, E. B. (2005). *A beginner's psychology.* Boston: Adamant Media Corporation. (Original work published 1915).

van der Laan, J. M. (2012). "Language and being human in technology." *Bulletin of Science, Technology & Society, 32*(3), 241–252.

Vanderburg, W. H. (2012a). "The desymbolization of human life in contemporary mass societies." *Bulletin of Science, Technology & Society, 32*(3), 213–221.

Vanderburg, W. H. (2012b). "The life and work of Jacques Ellul." *Bulletin of Science, Technology & Society, 32*(3), 183–186.

Suggested Reading

Ellul, J. (1955–56). *Histoire des institutions* (Vols. 1–5). Paris: Presses Universitaires de France.

Ellul, J. (1967). *Political illusion.* (K. Kellen, Trans.). New York: Knopf. (Original work published 1965).

Ellul, J. (1972). *The politics of God, the politics of man.* (G. W. Bromiley, Trans.). Grand Rapids, MI: Eerdmans. (Original work published 1966).

Ellul, J. (1973). *Propaganda: The formation of men's attitudes.* (J. Lerner, Trans.). New York: Vintage. (Original work published 1962).

Ellul, J. (1984). *Money & power.* (L. Neff, Trans.). Downers Grove, IL: Inter-Varsity Press. (Original work published 1954).

Ellul, J. (1991). *Anarchy and Christianiy.* (G. W. Bromiley, Trans.). Grand Rapids, MI: Eerdmans. (Original work published 1988).

Ellul, J. (2010). *On freedom, love, and power.* W. H. Vanderburg (Ed.). Toronto: University of Toronto Press.

Foucault, M. (2008). *The birth of biopolitics.* (G. Burchell, Trans.). New York: Palgrave Macmillan. (Original work published 1978).

Rose, N. (2008). *The politics of life itself: Biomedicine, power, and subjectivity in the twenty-first century.* Princeton: Princeton University Press.

Alexander Stingl, Ph.D.

Knowledge-Based Economy

ABSTRACT

Modern society has become a network society that runs on the basis of knowledge and information. It stands to reason that the underlying economy is intertwined with this transformation. Two aspects must be distinguished: the aspect of knowledge economy, in which knowledge is the product of economic action, and that of knowledge-based economy, in which knowledge is the means of production. Not only economies and societies but also human personalities are changing, as people are becoming knowledge entrepreneurs.

OVERVIEW

The historians of economic processes have made note of a relatively recent change: the switch from a physical-labor-based economy to a knowledge-based economy. This has of course not been the first such transformation to occur, and maybe it is not even the most significant in human history. Nonetheless, its importance in regard to human affairs cannot be underestimated.

The very first transformation that was a significant step toward creating the prerequisites for modern society was the decline of feudalism, which existed in Europe between the fourteenth and seventeenth centuries. As Maurice Dobbs argued in his classic *Studies in the Development of Capitalism* (1963), the landowning nobles in England were struggling to reconstitute their privileges and prerogatives at the time, as well as their income, so to speak. They transferred direct control of agricultural production to rent-paying commoners, who at first were thought of as being nothing but peasants, quickly turned into yeomen and freeholders, and eventually became what is known as gentry. As a result, the landed nobility declined, and the modern market economy **based** on capitalism was able to emerge in the process.

Growth of the Market Economy

The nineteenth century saw this once-potential consequence become a reality that shaped social structures all over Europe and America in the "Great Transformation," as Karl Polanyi (1944) called it. Polanyi suggested that the emergence of the market society and the modern nation-state are not to be seen as separate occurrences. On the contrary, both were deeply intertwined in the single and coherent process of the creation of market society. With the creation of modern statehood and its subsequent transformation of social structures and institutions, competitive markets could be stabilized in the "civilizing process," as it has been called by Norbert Elias (2000).

However, the classic idea of capitalism itself declined between 1880 and 1930, as Livingston (1997) has argued, for capitalists tried to reconstitute their prerogatives and income in light of the social transformations occurring around them during that time. In that transformation, they reconstructed production and distribution under the guiding metaphor of the corporation and created an age of surplus. The post-capitalist society after World War II and its discontents became a much-discussed topic, beginning in the 1960s when the differences in the modes of production became endemic and physical labor began to decline, at least in the Western world. This seems to be even more the case now with the process known as globalization, or the "Flattening of the World" (Thomas L. Friedman). This new modern age, or "Fourth Epoch" (C. Wright Mills), began with a shift in the way the production of knowledge became fused with governance on the one hand and industrial and military production on the other.

In the context of the American effort and involvement in World War II and the following Cold War between the Western nations and the Communist Soviet Union, theories of communication and information spilled from cryptography and cybernetics into the physical and biological sciences. Decoding the "book of life" became a promising future project, funded by CalTech, the Rockefeller Foundation, and other similar organizations as well as the government, which had great hopes that the new information technology would give America a cutting edge in the Cold War. The rise of computer technology that resulted from the very same development gave the transformation of economy its determining nudge. An ever-larger part of industrial production became subject to automation. In the end, the revolution occurred not only within the language of science itself but also in the way our economies and modes of production actually function.

Midcentury sociological shop talk from Raymond Aron to Amitai Etzioni, Daniel Bell, or Ralf Dahrendorf, coined the now-popular terms "post-industrial society" and "post-capitalist society." Peter Drucker, in his seminal book *The Age of Discontinuity* (1969), popularized the concepts of the knowledge economy and the knowledge-based economy, as well as their inherent distinction: whether knowledge is viewed as a product or as a tool.

FURTHER INSIGHTS

Knowledge Economy vs. Knowledge-based Economy

Mid-20th-century knowledge itself became a problem of social science. Its use and production, the role it played in government and economy, and how it was mutually affected by those fields suddenly emerged as explicit fields of study. The distinction between economy of knowledge and knowledge-based economy is crucial, yet their interrelation must also be recognized:

- Economy of knowledge treats knowledge as a product and asks for the conditions of its construction and transformation.
- Knowledge-based economy sees knowledge as an applicable device, tool, or technique that can be used to benefit economic production and market exchange.

Modern information society is the product of the interrelation of both economies. The expansion of these economies, geographically and in ever more sectors of society, has become subsumed under the heading of globalization. The determining factors of a global economy are no longer the traditional factors (land, natural resources, and physical labor); instead, they are expertise, intellectual property (rights), and technique.

Education as a Resource

Education has turned into the most fundamental resource a nation can offer to its citizens. Contrary to the earlier belief that globalization would abolish the need for container concepts such as nation-states, the early twentieth century—in the wake of 9/11, the pending threat of a global recession, and the looming oil crisis—has seen a reinvigoration of the concept of the national, and the economies in question are actually national knowledge-based economies that interact on a global market, despite the existence of a variety of so-called multinational corporations.

These developments have left their imprint on educational institutions. In many European countries, such as Germany, the hope lies in an increase in student numbers and a shortening of the time spent at a university by increasing each student's courses per semester. Ultimately, this trend moves away from a broad, future-oriented education and toward focused training for specific jobs in existing markets—in other words, from the creation of new knowledge to the application of existing knowledge. This describes a trend toward a reduced definition of innovation, which no longer entails invention and merely rests on the expansion of existing technology. Intellectuals and scholars are being reduced to experts and technicians.

The New Economy

The social sciences have to adapt to these developments, taking into account the fact that the economic system is moving from a material economy to a symbolic economy. The prerequisites and rules that accounted for the production, distribution, and consumption of material resources and products are of course entirely different from those governing the dynamics of knowledge production, access, and consumption. This does not mean that the material factors and material economy will disappear. But certainly their importance is continually diminishing and has, at least in Western countries, reached a point where their economic importance is overshadowed by the dynamics of the symbolic economy. This can be verified by the history of the recent economic crises, from the bursting of the 1990s "new economy" bubble to the 2007–8 crisis in the US housing market.

However, Nico Stehr (2002) has argued that between this economic reality and the public and political discourses there exists what can be called a cultural lag. Public discourse and political decision making often rest on outdated theories and data, because the translation of the actual development into theory and data sets is a time-consuming process that is subject to politicking from different parties and interest groups, each with its own agenda. Knowledge of these agendas and groups subsequently factors into the dynamics of the modern economy itself.

The "new economic sociology" that is often associated with Mark Granovetter (1973; 1985) has therefore taken note that not only do modern economies function by laws of supply and demand, of wants and needs, but a most decisive factor lies in the existing social networks within which markets and economies are embedded. The navigation of these markets requires knowledge about them in the same way that knowledge about the application of a technological device is required for its proper use. Such knowledge, described as "soft skills," can be acquired as a form of human or cultural capital, a concept introduced by Pierre Bourdieu.

The Network Society

The importance of such networks, which serve as channels and mechanisms of exclusion and inclusion, became an explicit topic for sociology in 1991, when Dutch social scientist Jan van Dijk coined the term "network society," which was then picked up by Manuel Castells in his renowned trilogy on the information age.

In many respects, the prerequisites of the knowledge-based economy and those of the network society are very similar, beginning with the changes in the concepts of property, the importance of nonmonetary forms of capital, and the rise of the digital age through the increasing importance of information and communications technology (ICT). The latter development, however, brought with it its own form of inequality. Prior epochs have seen inequalities in land ownership, access to the physical resources of production, and social class. Similarly, the digital divide circumscribes some people's access to means of using or knowledge about ICT. Those people excluded from the knowledge of how to use this technology, or deprived of access to the technology itself, are denied participation in the knowledge-based economy and therefore barred from modern labor markets. This phenomenon is a global one.

The Commercial-Industrial-Academic Complex

It is a cliché to say that "knowledge is power," yet there is evidently some truth to it. Knowledge and information are turned into the currency that our societies and economies increasingly thrive upon. But it is critical to understand that in an economy and society, whoever controls access to and distribution of knowledge wields a substantial power. It seems therefore imperative to ascertain the autonomy of educational and research institutions. But as we can see in regard to the biological sciences and the advances made in pharmacology, genetics, and so on, a commercial-industrial-academic complex is already in existence.

For example, the irony is noted that research into alternative forms of energy production at private universities is funded by oil companies, the very entities who seem to have the least financial interest in this kind of research. This demonstrates that the emergence and proliferation of a knowledge-based economy entails a dimension of moral and ethical questions that are not easily answered or free of biases. Companies that invest in certain kinds of research that seem to contradict their current financial goals may have other motivations. It may be seen as manipulation of data or clever marketing, but it could also be seen as genuine concern for ethical and environmental issues, or a clever investment in future technology to ensure the company's long-term survival.

The larger problem seems to be whether or not a society with a knowledge-based economy allows for a truly open public discourse of these moral issues. Nico Stehr (2002; 2005) argues that while knowledge is being increasingly transformed into the basis of economic production, the resulting products, services, and technologies embody social norms and values. In other words, they are moral objects as well as ethical subjects.

Language & Economy

It should be mentioned that economy has never been independent from knowledge, and vice versa. Economic action is dependent on the use of language, and language itself is shaped in economic ways and by economic metaphors. This shows an interrelation that suggests a co-evolution of economy and knowledge throughout human history. An exemplary discussion of this concept is found in the work of linguist Florian Coulmas (1993).

In his seminal work *The Logic of Writing and the Organization of Society* (1986), Jack Goody argued that the emergence of written language was tied to the emergence of organized markets, and subsequently both have made possible the emergence of larger organized societies. From this perspective, the current shift toward a knowledge-based economy would have to be viewed not as a novelty but merely as a move toward new forms of knowledge and information distribution, coupled with new ways of controlling the channels and any access to them. Goody suggests that this control was formerly in the hands of states and is now in the hands of the market. The critical moral issue, then, is whether or not the market can guarantee autonomous knowledge production and free and fair access to knowledge.

Aside from critical theory and neo-Marxism, it is the field of sociology of knowledge that is most concerned with this question. The social production and application of knowledge and the relevant conditions and prerequisites are the field's primary concerns. This field of sociology was developed in the 1920s by Max Scheler and Karl Mannheim, two German sociologists and philosophers, and carried into American sociology by Germans fleeing the Nazi regime as a result of the influence of sociologists such as Robert K. Merton and Talcott Parsons, who had studied with Mannheim in Heidelberg. With Peter Berger and Thomas Luckmann's *The Social Construction of Reality* (1966), the whole field was revised. Modern conceptions in sociology of knowledge, such as research into the knowledge-based economy, may be regarded as the outcome of the Berger and Luckmann contribution on the one hand and Daniel Bell, Ralf Dahrendorf, and Peter Drucker on the other.

VIEWPOINTS

A critical question is whether these developments are necessarily for good or for ill. While it is true that participation in modern economy and society can be strictly regulated by those who control access to information and education, at the same time, the increasing availability of knowledge opportunities gives people the freedom to make their own choices, whether about their life course or in individual acts of consumption. The Internet has opened up the possibility of comparing prices and qualities of a vast amount of goods and services. It has created entirely new fields of services that in turn enable people to act economically on a global scale in ways that could not previously have been conceived of. In other words, the transformation is not in itself good or bad. What is of utmost importance is that the institutions that control access to channels of information and education remain autonomous, while inequalities in the knowledge markets must be addressed by reasonable governance.

The outcome of all these developments is another form of subjectivation, with personalities adapting through the process of socialization (the learning and integration of social norms) to the interpenetrating demands of information and network societies and a knowledge-based economy. The concept of self that is taking shape is a concept of a knowledge entrepreneur. Every person, every acting subject, understands him- or herself to be in all social matters using and producing knowledge in an economic or market-related fashion. Claims are not made, argued, and reasoned until consensus is found. Instead, ideas are increasingly marketed, budgeted, and **based** on prior ideas that were the outcome of the same knowledge-market economy that has pervaded all social reality.

But aside from these theoretical matters, it should be taken into consideration that physical labor and material products and factors did not disappear. A critical approach would suggest that the specifically Western knowledge-based economy rests on the outsourcing of material economy to poorer countries that run on low wage structures. From a critical point of view, this could be seen as a new form of colonization. However, even such a critical perspective would have to allow that bringing jobs to these countries could serve as a stabilizing force and create demand for more service- or knowledge-oriented markets in these countries as well. This, therefore, functions as a factor for development. This is a question that will not be entirely answered in the decades to come and certainly provides for ongoing research opportunities.

TERMS & CONCEPTS

Civilizing Process: Norbert Elias wrote *The Civilizing Process* in the late 1930s. The book became a sociological bestseller in 1976 upon the release of a new edition. This meticulous study of Western civilization describes the interdependent processes of state formation and psychological development over time, from the Middle Ages to modern civilization. In other words, the transformation of social structures and personality structures are mutually dependent and deeply intertwined.

Cultural Capital: The concept of cultural capital as a form of symbolic capital was made popular by French sociologist Pierre Bourdieu, who showed that in addition to money, other forms of capital exist that regulate access to social classes, such as knowledge, network connections, and experiences.

Digital Divide: This term describes the disparity in access to and practical knowledge about the use of information technology, specifically the Internet. The divide exists between different kinds of groups. Internationally, it exists between developing and developed nations. On the community level, it exists between rural and urban areas, or populated areas that are of more or less economic interest for Internet service providers. Finally, it exists between social classes.

Economy of Knowledge: Economy of knowledge treats knowledge as a product and asks for the conditions of its construction and transformation.

Embeddedness: Markets are, according to Mark Granovetter, not closed-off entities. Instead, their functioning depends on the context and conventions of the social networks in which they are embedded.

Great Transformation: Karl Polanyi's theory of the great transformation argues that the historical development of the modern nation-state is interlinked with the development of market economy. They are but two aspects of the same development in human society: the emergence of market society.

Information Technology (IT)/ Information and Communications Technology (ICT): These terms are summary names for technologies such as the Internet, mobile phones, PDAs, and personal computers, as well as the ability to command standard programs such as e-mail and office or data management.

Information Society: This concept describes a form of society in which production, distribution, use, and conservation of knowledge and information is the main factor in all social aspects, from the political to the economical and cultural sectors.

Knowledge-based Economy: This form of economy sees knowledge as an applicable device, tool, or technique that can be used to benefit economic production and market exchange.

The Social Construction of Reality: In 1966, Berger and Luckmann published their landmark study The Social Construction of Reality. In their view, the reality that exists for members of a society is based on phenomena they construct by their social actions, by behaving as if they are following conventional rules and the phenomenon does exist. The most famous example is perhaps the assumption of the existence of social status.

Bibliography

Berger, P., & Luckmann, T. (1966). *The Social Construction of Reality.* Garden City, NY: Anchor Books.

Coriat, B., & Weinstein, O. (2012). "Patent regimes, firms and the commodification of knowledge." *Socio-Economic Review,* 10(2), 267–292. Coulmas, F. (1993). Language and Economy. Oxford: Blackwell Publishing.

Dobbs, M. (1963). *Studies in the Development of Capitalism.* New York, NY: International Publishers.

Drucker, P. (1969). *The Age of Discontinuity: Guidelines to our Changing Society.* New York: Harper and Row.

Goody, J. (1986). *The Logic of Writing and the Organization of Society.* Cambridge: Cambridge University Press.

Granovetter, M. (1973). "The strength of weak ties." *American Journal of Sociology,* 78(6), 1360-1380.

Granovetter, M. (1985). "Economic action and social structure: The problem of embeddedness." *American Journal of Sociology,* 91(3), 481-510.

Graz, J., & Hartmann, E. (2012). "Transnational authority in the knowledge-based economy: Who sets the standards of ICT training and certification?" *International Political Sociology,* 6(3), 294–314.

Polanyi, K. (1944). *The Great Transformation: The Political and Economic Origins of Our Time.* Boston: Beacon Press.

Stehr, N. (2002). *Knowledge & Economic Conduct.* Toronto: University of Toronto Press.

Stehr, N. (2005). *Knowledge Politics: Governing the Consequences of Science and Technology.* Boulder, CO: Paradigm Publishers.

Tocan, M. C. (2012). "Knowledge based economy assessment." *Journal of Knowledge Management,* Economics & Information Technology, 2(5), 188–201.

Suggested Reading

Autor, D. H. (2001). "Wiring the labor market." *Journal of Economic Perspectives,* 15. 25-40.

Autor, D. H., Katz, L.F. & Krueger, A.B. (1998). "Computing inequality: Have computers changed the labor market?" *Quarterly Journal of Economics,* 113(4), 1169-83.

Bashehab, O., & Buddhapriya, S. (2013). "Status of knowledge based economy in the kingdom of Saudi Arabia: An analysis." *Journal of Social & Development Sciences,* 4(6), 268–277.

Beck, U. (2006). *Power in the Global Age: A New Global Political Economy.* Cambridge: Polity Press.

Bourdieu, P. (1986). "The forms of capital." In, *Handbook of Theory and Research in the Sociology of Education,* J. C. Richardson, ed. 241-58. New York: Greenwood.

Bresnahan, T. F., Brynjolfsson, E. & Hitt, L.M. (2002). "Information, technology, workplace organization and the demand for skilled labor: Firm-level evidence." *Quarterly Journal of Economics,* 117(1), 339-76.

Castells, M. (2001). *The Internet Galaxy:Reflections on the Internet, Business and Society.* New York: Oxford University Press.

De Muro, P., Monni S., & Tridico, P. (2011). "Knowledge-based economy and social exclusion: Shadow and light in the Roman socio-economic model." *International Journal of Urban & Regional Research,* 35(6), 1212–1238.

Elias, N. (2000). *The Civilizing Process.* Oxford: Backwell.

Pick, J. B., & Azari, R. (2008). "Global digital divide: Influence of socioeconomic, governmental, and accessibility factors on information technology." *Information Technology for Development,* 14 (2), 91-115.

Van Dijk, J. A. G. M. (2005). *The Deepening Divide: Inequality in the Information Society.* Thousand Oaks, CA: Sage.

Warschauer, M. (2003). *Technology and Social Inclusion: Rethinking the Digital Divide.* Cambridge, MA: MIT Press.

Alexander Stingl, Ph.D.

Posthumanism

ABSTRACT

Posthumanism is an ethically ambiguous concept that refers to social movements and ideas about transcending the concept of what it means to be human by technological manipulation or augmentation. While skeptics fear new forms of oppression, enthusiasts not only promote the possibilities, but also claim that with a pending environmental collapse, transforming ourselves beyond humanity may be the only option of securing our species' survival.

OVERVIEW

Explicit caution is needed to speak scientifically about a concept such as posthumanism. The concept immediately calls up in one's mind images from the science fiction movies and novels that have pervaded modern culture. While sometimes these images have offered apt warnings of dangers that scientific progress can entail, more often than not they are fictionally projected dangers or innovative myths and legends rather than true to actual scientific or social fact. This warning must precede any scientific contribution on the matter, for it is also a fact that very often academic authors, specifically sociologists and philosophers, have made either over-cautious or overzealous arguments on the subject that are based on very little actual understanding of the scientific facts.

The term *posthumanism* refers to conceptions of what it means to be human that transcend traditional concepts of the human or come close to abolishing them. As is the case with most laden concepts that have such theoretical magnitude, posthumanism comprises several complementary aspects.

Conceptions of posthumanism entail social aspects that can be traced back to Thomas More's *Utopia* (1516) and Immanuel Kant's *Anthropology from a Pragmatic Point of View* (1798), which both lead to the often misunderstood philosophical idea of Nietzsche's *Übermensch,* or *Overman.* Newer versions of this concept discuss the need for technological augmentation of the human body, resulting in the idea of a man-machine organism known as the *cyborg.* In other versions, the debate circumscribes the question of the intervention into the biological processes through the manipulation of the brain or the body with hormones and drugs, or even meddling with the genetic makeup. All these different areas can be viewed as deeply intertwined as well as discretely isolated, and they are in any event the subject of both grave fear and skepticism on the one hand and great optimism and hope on the other. *Transhumanists* like Nick Bostrom tend to hail the possibilities, while skeptics like Jürgen Habermas warn against the manipulation of "prepersonal life" on instrumentalist intentions.

The idea of improving ourselves as a species, of improving our bodies and mental capabilities, is certainly not in itself a new concept. The quest for immortality is the stuff of legend and is found in ancient sacred and fictional texts, such as the Sumerian *Epic of Gilgamesh.* In the Western world, the alchemists of the Middle Ages sought potions and elixirs that could extend life or improve the human organism beyond its natural capabilities. Francis Bacon, in his *Novum Organon*(1620), instituted the scientific method as the way to gain control over all the things of nature in order to improve human livelihoods. The subject was given a new turn when, in 1923, the biochemist Haldane published an essay that projected that in the future science would not only take control of nature as the environment for humans, but also that it would make human nature itself an object of manipulation through genetics. He predicted that humans would grow in artificial wombs, where they would be manipulated to be stronger and healthier.

About ten years later, such fantasies were reined in by novelists like Aldous Huxley, whose *Brave New World* depicted the future of such manipulation as leading to a less desirable form of society. The combination of emerging biotechnological capabilities on the one hand and, on the other, the hygiene movement—which sought to counter the much feared concept of degeneration that the Vitalist movement had set up as a counterforce in light of conservation of life-energy—led to the eugenics programs and finally to the purification scheme of the Third Reich that is known today as the Holocaust.

After the end of World War II, the discovery of DNA and its subsequent applications to the Human Genome Project, prenatal diagnosis, reproductive medicine, cybernetics, and the new research methods in neurology have renewed questions that the eugenics movement raised and that are now "coming through the back door." But this development is in itself not necessarily bad or good, for, as Nikolas Rose has argued, it harbors just as many pitfalls and dangers as it does possibilities for freeing individuals to make better life choices (2007).

APPLICATIONS

In his seminal *The Order of Things,* Michel Foucault gave an account of how and when the sciences began to problematize what it means to be human and what it means to be a subject (1966). His study showed that all human eras contained certain conditions that regulated what was understood to be the truth. These implicit regimes of truth conditions were called *epistémes* by Foucault. Accordingly, what we have come to know as scientific discourse is in itself only a specific kind of regime of truth production. It is this discourse, however, that had made explicit the question of "what it means to be human": in closing the book, Foucault hints at the possibility that this way of thinking about ourselves as human subjects may "be erased like a face drawn in sand at the edge of the sea."

Foucault can be read here as making a prophetic statement about an upcoming age of posthumanism, an age in which the category of the human subject is no longer the primary category of social or scientific action. Whether the human category will indeed completely dissolve is a question about which Foucault's later works have been a little less clear. Yet today we live in the face of the possibilities of manipulating our genetic makeup before birth or changing memories with drugs, as has been done to treat posttraumatic stress disorder (PSD) in soldiers who served in Iraq and Afghanistan. Meanwhile it has been debated whether such drugs should be made available to victims of rape, molestation, or horrible accidents (Glannon, 2006). These treatments could be called dramatic interventions into identity and personality. It may indeed be argued that with our subjective identity being rendered fluid and plastic in such a way, the concept of identity itself—which can be considered a prerequisite of the concept of the human subject—is dissolved. Nick Bostrom has introduced similar conjectures that look beyond technological developments to draw on both works of fiction and speculative science (2005).

Discussing the Prospects of Nanotechnology & Uploading

Nanotech is already being applied to small-scale products, such as new fabrics and certain computer components, but we are still far away from realizing the possibilities of nanobots performing delicate brain surgery, or of directly rewiring the mind. Even greater complexity lies in the question of *uploading*. Since the "mind" is often conceived to be constituted by neural activity, which is largely a form of electricity, some bold scientists have postulated that the mind can be uploaded into a computer, if only that computer holds a large enough storage space and offers enough processing capacity. Transhumanist philosophers like Bostrom have engaged in discussions over whether or not such a "virtual copy" of the mind would, on the one hand, be conscious and, on the other, if that conscious mind would have a personality identical to the original. However, it must be said that without a human body and with new possibilities of meddling with the datastream, a Foucauldian perspective would suggest that the concept of "identity" or "the human subject" would no longer apply to such an entity.

Another way in which scholars have envisioned the effacement of the human subject was introduced by Richard Dawkins through his book *The Selfish Gene*(1976) in the concept of the *meme*. The term is often misunderstood as being a mere neologism for cultural trait. However, having illustrated how genes propagate themselves over other genes in the "struggle for survival," Dawkins introduces the concept of the meme by postulating that society and culture are constituted by certain units or elements that struggle with each other for survival and domination in ways that much resemble Darwinian variation, competition, and natural selection. However, these memes do not have a concrete substrate. In other words, one cannot just put a finger on what they are. The melody of a famous motif from Bach can be written down in various ways—e.g., for a complex symphony orchestra or for a single flute—demonstrating that there is something transcending these variations that allows the melody to be recognizable whether played by an orchestra or simply whistled. So, too, the meme is recognizable across its variations and is perhaps much closer to the idea of *gestalt* than those of chromosomes or DNA.

Concept of the Meme

The concept of the meme was originally used in a similar fashion in 1904 by a German zoologist, Richard Semon, who was certainly familiar with the era-specific discussions between *Gestaltpsychologie* and *Voelkerpsychologie,* which had tried to tackle similar questions. It has many variations and siblings within the history of science in the nineteenth and twentieth centuries, from French philosopher Gabriel de Tarde to economist John Maynard Keynes. Picking up on Dawkins' work, in 2000 Susan Blackmore published her seminal *The Meme Machine,* proliferating in particular the idea that memes can group together and function in unison toward their group survival under the term *memeplex*.

Since neuroscience has made popular the idea that consciousness itself may be a mere illusion or simulation, the existence of culture would similarly be reduced to memes. It is argued that these reductions are by far the simplest explanation for the existence of human culture. Consequently, if human culture and consciousness can be reduced to such a naturalist version, and therefore eliminated, the category of "human" dissolves in the process.

VIEWPOINTS

Extropy

In 1988, Max More and Tom Morrow created a public forum for scholars engaged in the debate about futurist concepts and ideas about humanity and technology. This journal was called *Extropy*. In their work, they sought to promote transhumanism in the light of libertarian ideas, which they dubbed*extropianism*. By promoting the rights and possibilities for self-transformation and questioning legal and biological boundaries set before human expansion, they hoped to create "spontaneous order." Because of growing concerns that any concept of order would be too authoritarian, More latched onto the concept of the *open society,* a term originally coined by Karl Popper.

Dissatisfaction with movements such as *Extropy* led to Nick Bostrom's and David Pearce's founding of the transhumanist movement in 1998. Their issues with their predecessors rested in particular on the fact that they had tended to create cults rather than academic debate. With the Transhumanist World Association, Bostrom and Pearce hoped to create a forum that would allow for political and scientific discussion under academic guidelines. Bostrom and his colleagues have continually stressed that, aside from cultural conservatism, they can associate and converse with most existing social philosophies as long as the proliferation of developing human evolution in the form of a "transformative agenda" remains central. It could be argued, though, that transhumanism is but another version of pragmatism.

In the voice of Donna Haraway, the feminist perspective has become prominent in the debates surrounding posthumanism. The feminist critique has challenged the traditional ascription of technology and culture to men and nature to women. Haraway thus famously stated that she would "rather be a cyborg than a goddess" (1991). Feminists have subsequently taken stances on both sides. Some claim the liberation potential of transhumanism plays in favor of the feminist agenda, while others perceive the movement as driven by masculine ideas and values.

Oppression & Violence

A more classic humanist perspective, represented by Habermas (2003) or Francis Fukuyama (2002) also urges caution. Their fear is that eliminating the binding factor that makes us equal in our humanity will ultimately lead to new forms of oppression and violence. Specifically, they believe that biotechnological intervention into our genetic or neurological makeup will destroy the human factor. Scholars like Nikolas Rose, on the other hand, argue that such interventions have taken place for centuries, that humans have always sought ways to improve their physical conditions. The new biotechnologies merely add to the toolbox, thereby enriching the choices individual people can make in their lives.

One crucial aspect, however, lies in the issues raised by the elimination of consciousness and the reduction of culture to memeplexes. Neuroscience respectively presents a challenge to the justice system, for, without consciousness and free will, how can there be legal accountability? If the defendant in a murder case can claim that it was not him or her, but a neurologically deficient brain that made the kill happen and that he or she is therefore not responsible, what would prevent other criminals from making use of this same defense? And, indeed, it is easy to find the odd historian who would claim that even the Holocaust must be viewed as a neurological event.

Within sociology, Bruno Latour's contributions have made a strong impression. Latour, originally a science historian whose work focused on the construction of objects in science, has become associated with the concept of *actor-network-theory (ANT).* He has suggested dropping "society" as the explanatory device of sociology and instead reconstructing the options for action in regard to the network ties that the object itself offers and enables. In other words, nonhuman entities are attributed with agency, which other sociologists have perceived as controversial. In this regard, Bruno Latour has suggested the creation of a new sociology, not as a sociology for humans, but as a sociology for earthlings.

Therapeutic Effects

In all of the various perspectives on posthumanism, Sherry Turkle has probably offered one of the most modest approaches to certain aspects of the debate. In her view, the use of technology, in particular computers and the Internet, can have therapeutic effects. However, one must be alert not to fall victim to addiction or crime. At the same time, she warns against what she calls *sociable robots,* and the subsequent dangers of an encroaching devaluation of social relationships, which could lead to an eventual destabilization of society.

TERMS & CONCEPTS

Biopower: The term *biopower* was introduced by Michel Foucault to describe a technology of power that states apply to govern a population by subjugating the body itself through a form of discipline and a regulative regime of biopolitics.

Cyborg: Cyborg is the abbreviation for *cybernetic organism,* a concept that derived from the 1950s discourse on cybernetics, the study and theory of complex, self-regulating systems. Commonly, the term cyborg is used to describe the technological augmentation of human bodies.

Gestaltpsychologie & Völkerpsychologie: The so-called *gestaltpsychologie* of the Berlin School was inspired by Johann Wolfgang von Goethe and Ernst Mach and founded by Christian von Ehrenfels and Max Wertheimer in the late nineteenth century. A gestalt is a "whole form," which cognitively comprises the mind, that is governed by laws of perception that form a global process as well as by a principle of totality and the idea that conscious experience has a correlate in cerebral activity.

The *Völkerpschologie* was founded by Wilhelm Wundt and promoted by Moritz Lazarus and Heymann Steindahl. It was concerned with the investigation of cultural traits as expressions of a people's spirit. It and *Gestaltpsychologie* were engaged in the struggles for intellectual domination among German academia during the late nineteenth century. *Völkerpsychologie* eventually diminished when the fledgling field of sociology began addressing questions of culture.

Governmentality: The French term *gouvernementalité* was introduced by Michel Foucault in his later years. It became well known long after his death, along with the concept of biopower, when it was declared that the turn of the twenty-first century would be marked by advances in biotechnology. According to most Foucault interpretations, *governmentality* refers either to the modes of production that governments install to bring forth citizens that fit into the governments' policies, or to the discursive practices (disciplines) that govern subjects. What is often neglected in the literature is the subject's active part in creating an attitude or mentality to actively and creatively govern himself or herself within the discipline by choosing from among the possibilities that the governing framework offers.

Human Genome Project (HGP): The HGP was an international project, begun in 1990, to determine the structure of human DNA and its supposed 25,000 genes in their functional and physical aspects. Headed by James Watson and financed by the National Institute for Health (NIH), the project was finished in 2003. However conclusive the results of this "cartography," though, there is a lot of work left because having a genome map is only the start. Much research remains to be done on the interrelational effects of genes, epigenetics, and the study of the proteom (the sum of proteins and enzymes that are the products of gene expression and that regulate the organism)

Nanotechnology: Technology at the nano level involves the application of science to the manipulation of matter on the scale of molecules and atoms (smaller than 100 nanometers). This technology has been applied to materials and fabrics. It is hoped that at some point nano-machines can be built for mainstream commercial, medical, and industrial use.

Transhumanism: The transhumanism movement promotes the idea of human enhancement through science and technology. Its goal is to overcome the physical and mental limitations of the human organism and transform humans into beings with enhanced capabilities, a goal that transhumanists see as the overall goal for humanity. Some argue that, in the face of an impending extinction through either natural disasters or the damage humans have caused to the environment, technological augmentation is the sole solution to save humanity. Critics have argued that transhumanism will dissolve the "common factor" people share and lead to new forms of oppression.

Übermensch (Super-human, Overman): In modern philosophy, this concept was coined by Friedrich Nietzsche. It is often misunderstood as being a direct influence on the racist concepts that governed Nazi ideology. However, this view gravely misinterprets Nietzsche, whose intention was to describe an idealized version of human existence, where the need for believing in another-worldly existence, as promised by religion, is transcended. The *Übermensch,* described in *Thus Spoke Zarathustra* (1883), manages to create new values in order to overcome the death of God and the subsequent danger of falling into nihilism.

Uploading: Uploading is more fiction than science. In theory, it is assumed that a human mind can be uploaded to a computer because cerebral activity is nearly identical with electrical activity and can thus be represented in algorithms and binary structures that a computer can translate.

BIBLIOGRAPHY

Blackmore, S. (2000). *The meme machine.* Oxford: Oxford University Press.

Bostrom, N. (2005). "A history of transhumanist thought." *Journal of Evolution and Technology, 14*(1). http://www.nickbostrom.com/papers/history.pdf

Crary, A. (2012). "What is posthumanism?" *Hypatia, 27*(3), 678–685.

Dawkins, R. (1976). *The selfish gene.* Oxford: Oxford University Press.

Deckha, M. (2012). "Toward a postcolonial, posthumanist feminist theory: Centralizing race and culture in feminist work on nonhuman animals." *Hypatia, 27*(3), 527–545.

Foucault, M. (1970). *The order of things.* New York: Pantheon Books.

Fukuyama, F. (2002). *Our posthuman future.* New York, NY: Farrar, Strauss and Giroux.

Habermas, J. (2003). *The future of human nature.* Cambridge: Polity.

Haraway, D. (1991). *Cyborgs, simians, and women: The reinvention of nature.* New York, NY: Routledge.

Glannon, W. (2006). "Psychopharmacology and memory." *Journal of Medical Ethics, 32,* 74–78.

Latour, B. (2006). *Reassembling the social.* Oxford: Oxford University Press.

Rose, N. (2007). *The politics of life itself.* Princeton, NJ: Princeton University Press.

Shu-mei, S. (2012). "Is the post-in postsocialism the post-in posthumanism?" *Social Text, 30*(1), 27–50.

SUGGESTED READING

Beilharz, K. (2011). "Tele-touch embodied controllers: Posthuman gestural interaction in music performance." *Social Semiotics, 21*(4), 547–568.

Coyle, F. (2006). "Posthuman geographies? Biotechnology, nature, and the demise of the autonomous human subject." *Social & Cultural Geography, 7*(4), 505–523.

Foucault, M. (2008). *Security, territory, population.* Basingstoke: Palgrave MacMillan.

Fukuyama, F. (1999). *The great disruption.* New York: Free Press.

Kay, L. (2000). *Who wrote the book of life?* San Francisco, CA: Stanford University Press.

Shaviro, S. (2007). "The souls of cyberfolk: Posthumansim as vernacular theory." *Modern Language Quarterly, 68*(3), 457–460.

Wolfe, C. (2010). *What is posthumanism?* Minneapolis, MN: University of Minnesota Press.

Alexander Stingl, Ph.D.

SOCIAL ASPECTS OF TECHNOLOGY IN EDUCATION

OVERVIEW

Technology in education is more than an advantage. While the No Child Left Behind Act of 2001 (replaced by the Every Student Succeeds Act in 2015) required US schools to graduate students with technology experience at an eighth grade level, specific education organizations have said that level is not enough. To be prepared for–and competitive in–a global workforce, students need to demonstrate technology skills that show advanced levels. Furthermore, access to technology education is not universal; as such, not all students will achieve even the minimum requirement. This is especially true for the students who do not have computers at home. In addition, teachers and librarians need administrative support in order to pursue professional development opportunities that lead to teaching advanced computer skills.

Innovations like Baby Einstein®, Leap Frog®, Microsoft Power Point®, and SMARTboards®, were created to further the education of people from infancy to adulthood. Those who cannot adequately utilize the innovations may have a crumbled foundation on which to contend with their peers. Almost every subject from preschool to college can utilize technology as an instrument of instruction, development, or function. And those who lack the skills to teach or implement the resources are left out of a continuous conversation that will become more extensive in the future. The most important topic of that conversation should be whether or not high school graduates are proficient enough in technology applications to earn jobs once they leave high school.

While many people view technology proficiency as being able to research journal articles, create spectacular looking presentations, or utilize databases, A Nation at Risk (1983)–a report created by the National Commission on Excellence in Education (NCEE)–notes that many occupations require proficiency of a level beyond what is common to high school activity. Even in 1983, fields like "health care, medical science, energy production, food processing, construction, and the building, repair, and maintenance of sophisticated scientific, educational, military, and industrial equipment" were identified as those requiring levels of technology higher than what most high school graduates achieved (NCEE, as cited in Allen, p. 26).

Allen (2008) notes that since the A Nation at Risk report was published, the "student-to-computer ratio has certainly improved, from about 60-to-1 in 1983 to about 4-to-1 nationwide in 2007" (Office of technology Assessment, 1988 (1983 data), Nagel, 2007 (2007 data), as cited in Allen, p. 611). The ratio improved again in 2008 with three students for every one desktop or laptop computer. As of 2018, several schools in the United States and across the world were implementing and experimenting with a one-to-one laptop program, with Maine being one of the first states to do so in 2002; experts were still assessing the level of success of these programs (Doran & Herald, 2016). While this is a positive trend that shows a change toward allowing academic institutions the ability to develop and maintain technology curricula, it also promotes the disparity between haves and have-nots once students leave school, as many do not have computers at home.

In 2005, for example, only 11.4 percent of households with an income of $29,900 or lower had high-speed Internet access, while 62 percent of those with incomes of $100,000 or more had high-speed access (United States Government Accountability Office). As long as this informational playing field is not level, the inequity of access to educational resources will remain (Allen, 2008, p. 611). According to the Pew Research Center, in November 2016, 53 percent of adults making less than $30,000 used broadband internet at home while 93 percent of those making at least $75,000 used broadband internet at home (Pew Research Center, 2018).

The Partnership for Twenty-First Century Skills is an organization of public and private groups established in 2002 to create a standard for successful learning. The Partnership recommends that each state focus closely on the students who do not have access to technology, insisting that meeting the (technology) needs of such students requires a matter of policy (p. 20). Further, as research notes that students are more motivated in the classroom when the Internet and other technologies are utilized (Leu, 2002, as cited in Partnership for 21st Century Skills, 2008, p. 4), teachers also require support for improving their skills.

Many teachers still lack ongoing professional development support needed to fully integrate existing technology into instructional practice. States should support these professionals with sustained, strategic professional development that enables them to incorporate twenty-first century skills into their standards, curricula, and assessments (Partnership for 21st Century Skills, 2008, p. 20).

More students than ever before can use computers at school; however, working at home is limited to those in specific income levels. Furthermore, depending on the budget of the school district, limitations with technology may not be exclusive to household incomes. The Partnership for 21st Century Skills and the National Education Association address this issue:

> While most states and school districts have made remarkable progress in installing computers in schools, many still do not have ready access to the Internet or adequate technical support to make access reliable all day, every day. Today, desktop computers in classrooms represent the bare minimum in terms of technology equipment that schools need. Classroom telephones, laptops, wireless technology, scientific devices, and video conferencing centers for distance learning are just a few of the tools that can improve and expedite learning (Partnership for 21st Century Skills, 2008, p. 20).

With regard to the No Child Left Behind Act of 2001, which legislated that students achieve technological literacy by the eighth grade, the Partnership argued that "states need to think much bigger and go much further to prepare young people adequately for the future. Eighth-grade technology literacy is just a starting point" (Partnership for 21st Century Skills, 2008, p. 10). The organization insists that,

> [s]tandards must encompass more than technology proficiency, which is too narrow a skill for the world today. Instead, students must be competent in ICT [information and communication technology] literacy-using 21st century tools and learning skills (information and communication skills, thinking and problem solving skills, and interpersonal and self-directional skills) that will enable them to learn how to learn in school and throughout their lives (p. 10).

It is not clear within the 21st Century Skills document how the Partnership defines literacy with regard to information and communication technologies (ICT). As such, other terms that are defined may show how different levels of proficiency are considered when working with technology is concerned. Computer literacy is the most basic form of computer proficiency. Someone who is computer literate can understand rudimentary applications, like Power Point® and Microsoft Word®. A slightly more advanced person would have information literacy in order to determine which information resources are needed in various contexts. This is a necessary skill since technology is a constantly changing field. Finally, someone with information technology literacy (ITL) is effective at utilizing various technologies. Someone at this advanced level can write HTML code or can find a lost file within data storage components.

As far as the National Education Association (NEA) is concerned, students "need to know how to learn new skills as quickly as technology creates new challenges" (2008). While such skills do not require the acquisition of information technology literacy (ITL), it is essential that all students acquire the skills necessary to utilize different technologies according to the context of the tasks they are completing. Indeed, the information-literate student will be successful with many applications and with various technologies. To create an information-literate student body (and, ultimately, workforce) the NEA (2008) takes the following stance concerning technology and education in the United States.

- More funding is needed at all levels to better integrate technology into schools and classrooms.
- The technology available to educators and students should be compatible with, and at least on the same level as, technology in general use outside of schools.
- Education technology budgets should reflect the importance of professional development. At least a third of all tech budgets should be reserved for school staff to become proficient in using and integrating technology into their classrooms.
- Educators themselves should be involved in decisions on planning, purchasing, and deploying education technology.
- Teacher education programs need to embrace educational technology and help prospective teachers use it effectively in the classroom.
- Technology should be deployed and applied equitably among all students and educators, regardless of geography or demographics.
- Students should also be taught the appropriate and safe use of technology. (National Education Association, 2008).

FURTHER INSIGHTS

Required technology

The Individuals with Disabilities Education Act (IDEA), established in 1990, requires that all schools provide equal access to education for all students with documented learning or physical disabilities. Students with learning or physical disabilities are allowed what is known as accommodations–devices or services that level the playing field between the disability and the lack thereof for other students. For example, a student with attention deficit disorder (ADD) may require extra time for tests or a private testing room; someone with dyslexia or a visual impairment might need assistive technology to perform similarly to their peers. Computerized learning systems can scan texts, essays, and notes and present the information to students in the form of a digital voice. Students can take notes manually or within the system while the text or notes are being read. In addition, once the digital software becomes accustomed to students voice (pitch, speaking speed), the system actually types in large print and/or in various colors when necessary according to what the student has said.

Moreover, with specific programs, [s]tudents can highlight key points and bookmark areas they feel are important; further, notes and highlights are easily copied and pasted to text files for later review. Either instructors or students may create audio CDs to facilitate listening to books "on the go." The program may also be used by students for writing assignments. For example, students can type their ideas into the program, use the spell-check function, and have the program read back the text so that they can self-edit their work... Spell-checking is available in multiple languages (Ludlow & Foshay, 2006, p. 79).

While students who do not know English as a first language are not granted "official" accommodations by schools, they can purchase the software for home use and practice language learning whenever they want. Many such programs provide dictionary and thesaurus utilization as well. What needs to be clear is that for students with disabilities, schools can provide access to these programs, usually within an academic service office. However, students with disabilities, as well as those learning English as a second language, have to purchase the software themselves. The accommodation is that their work with the assistive technology is accepted for a grade. Many of these software packages are costly and unaffordable for many, and while schools that purchase the technology can avert the cost of the programs through grants or waivers, individuals cannot.

Integrated Learning Systems (ILS)

Integrated technology systems also assist with learning capabilities without the requirement of a documented disability: if a school purchases the software, teachers can work ILS lessons into already established or new classroom programming. What is beneficial about the programs is that in most cases, they offer a supplemental resource for student learning on an individualized basis. For example, if a fourth grader is reading at a sixth grade level but performs at grade level in other subjects, a learning system can provide the student with sixth grade reading assignments that test, review, and introduce more challenging material at an advanced level. Thus, the student is not bored by the classroom instruction (leveled at fourth graders) and is challenged by the material. The software has the capability to assess a student's work, and if the reading level does not increase, for example, the software will only provide reading activities within the level the student is currently attaining.

In addition, teachers input data for each student based on the student's ability in certain subjects. Because programs are available in numerous subjects, students can work independently and at their level, which also allows for students to increase performance in weak subject areas as a way to catch up. Furthermore, each student's work is saved in each subject and within various lessons to facilitate beginning where the student left off. As the student logs back into the lesson, a review is offered and new information presented. Additionally, ILS software stores individualized scores within a database for the instructor's use. Thus, if there is a concept that several students do not understand, the teacher can provide instruction on that specific topic. Using ILS systems increases the technological ability of both instructors and students and keep class lessons on schedule while challenging stronger students and assisting weaker students. This is especially helpful in large classes.

VIEWPOINTS

Keeping Current

According to Kenney (2008), the people expected to know the most about technology are librarians, sometimes referred to as media specialists. With technological advances occurring almost daily in education and research settings, it is nearly impossible to keep up with each change. Yet, someone has to in order for those resources to make the difference for which they were intended. Utilizing a school's database to access an online journal can be tricky to the new searcher. When intimidation sets in, discouraged students often ask for the assistance of the people behind the desk, the specialists.

Kenney (2008) suggests that experts in the field of library science keep current in two ways: The first is to review the latest research; the second involves developing proficiency with new programs and with new features of old programs as soon as changes or additions are made. Indeed, it is important to be able to maneuver through sites, document changes, and teach others to do the same. This involves the hands-on capabilities of someone who has worked with the technology advances that are changing constantly. In order for a library to be successful, then, librarians need to be supported by school administration and encouraged to access professional development opportunities.

Cyber Cheating

If online learning becomes even more prominent in high school courses, young teenagers will be facing the organization issues that come with not seeing a teacher for scheduled classes, time management, and procrastination to name two. In addition, teachers (and schools in general) will be balancing the concepts of student privacy and academic honesty. Several colleges require proof that the students enrolled in online courses are the same students submitting work for those courses. How is that kind of proof acquired? With technology.

Securexam Remote Proctor is a monitoring device utilized by many colleges and universities in their online courses. The device gathers a 360-degree image around the person taking the test and has the ability to scan fingerprints. If the student's fingerprint does not match the student's print on file at the college, the student cannot continue with the test. The student is also prevented from visiting Internet sites while the test is in session.

Another monitoring device used by colleges and universities in their online courses is Proctor101, developed by Kryterion Incorporated. This system utilizes webcams that are linked to live proctors who monitor the test taker. Webcams must show the test taker's face, computer screen, keyboard, mouse, and any allowed materials for the test. In addition, the system includes software that can recognize a student's typing ability, like whether or not he pauses between certain letters and how quickly he types. When a student's typing ability conflicts with the one he or she demonstrated at registration or his or her image does not match his or her enrollment photograph, he or she will be unable to take the exam. If, by chance, the student acts "suspiciously," the proctor can inhibit him or her from finishing the test and reports the activity to the course's instructor.

Other systems that have been developed to confirm a test taker's identity collect information from various databases–including property records and criminal histories–in order to test a student's knowledge of information specific to him or her, such as what street he or she lived on when he or she was five years old and what his or her first job was. Correct responses yield progression to the exam. This system does not use a camera.

While nobody wants students to cheat, there are several concerns regarding these systems. First, the cost or application requirements will limit accessibility. Second, Lori McNabb, assistant director of student and faculty services at the online division of the University of Texas, notes that "there's no evidence that cheating or fraud happens more often with... [online] students than with students in face-to-face classes" (Foster, 2008). Most course management systems store a bank of test questions that randomly generate distinctive exams for each student. In addition, teachers who require writing will agree that a student's writing style is almost as predictive as a fingerprint, making cheating identifiable without the use of a webcam. A final concern lies within legislation: If Congress requires monitoring of online testing, it could also require a specific type of system, forcing colleges and universities to purchase and maintain technology they may not want or want to budget for.

The Future

It is difficult to predict whether or not devices will be required to monitor younger students when they are testing at home. What is not difficult to determine is that technology is going to improve, and students, teachers, and employers will benefit. For those who are currently out of the technology loop, trying to get inside is going to become more difficult as each innovation does more, does it faster, and does it with less physical material than was previously thought possible. It seems that there will always be something new to learn when it comes to technology. While learning, people become ready for the rigors of higher education, steady employment, or advances in their careers, and more technology-literate people are produced. There is no standard for who should experience such learning, but there is the expectation that those who need to learn it will meet a standard of competence. In turn, there should also be the expectation that access to meet that standard is supplied as a universal policy.

Teachers and students need access to laptops and handheld devices, digital cameras and microscopes, Web-based video equipment, graphing calculators, and even weather-tracking devices. They need to become responsible and savvy users and purveyors of information. They need to know how to collaborate successfully across miles and cultures. The technology environment of today's public schools should match the tools and approaches of the work and civic life that students will encounter after graduation.

This will ensure that schools stay relevant to today's students, as well as equip them for success in life after school ("Technology in Education," 2008).

Andrea Foster (2006) from the Chronicle of Higher Education notes that "students preparing to enter college are sorely lacking in the skills needed to retrieve, analyze, and communicate information that is available online." Without more than the minimum technological experience, some students will not be accepted into the colleges of their choice and will not be hired for positions in which they would be otherwise qualified. That is not the answer the US federal government or school administrators are willing to accept. However, without the financial backing of education institutions, teachers will not learn the technology they need to teach their students for increased proficiency.

TERMS & CONCEPTS

A Nation at Risk (1983): A report created by the National Commission on Excellence in Education focusing on education in the United States.

Computer Assisted Instruction (CAI): Teaching that incorporates the use of a computer (specific application, the Internet, course management systems) into a curriculum.

Computer Literacy: Understanding the basic processes of computers and technology and being able to use those processes.

Individuals with Disabilities Education Act (IDEA): Legislation established in 1990 that requires equal access to education for any student with learning or physical disabilities.

Information and Communications technology (ICT): A field of education that requires students to learn skills (and comprehend) in various sectors.

Information Literacy: The ability to determine what information is needed for what purpose—as different contexts require different objectives—and having the ability to use that information appropriately.

Information Technology Literacy (ITL): The advanced capability of manipulating technology for various purposes (writing HTML, taking apart a hard drive, communicating, managing information).

Integrated Learning Systems (ILS): Software or hardware packages containing different content, such as reading, mathematics, or social studies. Assessment tools measure and monitor the delivery of the content.

No Child Left Behind Act of 2001 (NCLB): Federal legislation created to ensure that all students (regardless of ethnicity, socioeconomic status, or disability) have access to instructional approaches that have been proven to be successful; it was replaced in 2015 by the Every Student Succeeds Act.

Partnership for 21st Century Skills: The primary national education/business affiliation promoting the need for twenty-first century skills in American education.

Technology Education: The study of technology (understanding its uses, developing skills for proficiency).

US Department of Education: Federal organization created to promote achievement in US education as a competitive global resource; ensures equal access to education.

Bibliography

Allen, L. (2008). "The technology implications of a nation at risk." *Phi Delta Kappan*, 89, 608-610.

Doran, L., & Herald, B. (2016, May 18). "1-to-1 laptop initiatives boost student scores, study finds." *Education Week*, 11.

Foster, A. (2006, Oct). "Students fall short on 'Information Literacy,' Educational Testing Services finds." *The Chronicle of Higher Education.*

Kenney, B. (2008). "Leaping into technology." *School Library Journal*, 54, 11.

Kumar, M. (2012). "The new landscape for the innovative transformation of education." *Social Research*, 79, 619-630.

Ludlow, B. & Foshay, J. (2006). "Kurzweil 3000." *Journal of Special Education Technology*, 21 79-81.

McNeil, P. W. (1998). "Implementation of the Adult Education and Family Literacy Act and the Perkins Act of 1998." Memo to State Directors of Adult Education and State Directors of Vocational Education, U. S. Department of Education. U. S. Department of Education website: http://www.ed.gov/policy/sectech/guid/cte/implemen.html

Nickolai, D. H., Hoffman, S. G., & Trautner, M. (2012). "Teaching & learning guide for 'can a knowledge sanctuary also be an economic engine? The marketing of higher education as institutional boundary work'." *Sociology Compass*, 6, 596-600.

Partnership for 21st Century Skills. (2008). "The road to twenty-first century learning: Policymakers' guide to twenty-first century skills. NEA and the twenty-first Century." NEA website: http://www.21stcenturyskills.org

Pew Research Center. (2018, February 5). "Internet/broadband fact sheet." Pew Research Center. Retrieved from http://www.pewinternet.org/fact-sheet/internet-broadband/

Rivera, C. J., Hudson, M. E., Weiss, S. L., & Zambone, A. (2017). "Using a multi-component multimedia shared story intervention with an iPad to teach content picture vocabulary to students with developmental disabilities." *Education & Treatment of Children*, 40(3), 327-352.

Still, K., & Gordon, J. P. (2012). "Focusing on teacher perspectives through dialogue about the meaningful integration of literacy & technology." *National Social Science Journal*, 38, 80-97.

"Technology in Education." (2008). National Education Association (NEA). NEA website: http://www.nea.org/technology/index.html

Trotter, A. (2008). "Online education cast as 'Disruptive Innovation'." *Education Week*, 27, 1-13.

SUGGESTED READING

Berrett, J. (2008). "Are we there yet?" *Technology* & Children, 12, 3.

Childress, V. & Rhodes, C. (2008). "Engineering student outcomes for grades 9 - 12." *Technology Teacher*, 67, 5-12.

Christensen, Horn & Johnson (2008). *Disrupting class: How disruptive innovation will change the way the world learns.* McGraw-Hill Education: Europe.

Cuban, L. (2001). *Oversold and underused: Computers in the classroom.* Cambridge, Mass.: Harvard University Press.

Dowd, H., & Green, P. (2016). *Classroom management in the digital age: Effective practices for technology-rich learning spaces.* Irvine, CA: EDTechTeam Press.

Ferreira, G. M. d. S. (2008). "Crossing borders: Issues in music technology education." *Journal of Music, Technology & Education*, 1, 23-35.

Fox, N. J. (2011). "Boundary objects, social meanings and the success of new technologies." *Sociology*, 45, 70-85.

Jones, K. (2008). "Ideas for integrating technology education into everyday learning." *Technology & Children*, 12, 20-21.

Jacobsen, M., Clifford, P. & Friesen, S. (2002). "Preparing teachers for technology integration: creating a culture of inquiry in the context of use." *Contemporary Issues in Technology and Teacher Education*, 2, 363-88.

Leu, D. J., Jr. (2002). "The new literacies: Research on reading instruction with the Internet and other digital technologies." In J. Samuels & A. E. Farstrup (Eds.). *What research has to say about reading instruction.* Newark, DE: International Reading Association.

Litowitz, L. S. & Warner, S. A. (2008). technology education: A contemporary perspective. Phi Delta Kappan, 89, 519-521.

Nagel, D. (2007). "Groups respond to proposed EETT cuts." *T.H.E. Journal.* website: http://thejournal.com/articles/20166

National Commission on Educational Excellence. (1983). "A nation at risk: The imperative for educational reform." Washington D.C.: U.S. Department of Education, 10.

Office of technology Assessment. (1988). "Power On! New Tools for Teaching and Learning." Washington D.C.: U.S. Government Printing Office, OTA-SET-379, 7.

Slade, S., & Prinsloo, P. (2013). "Learning analytics: Ethical issues and dilemmas." *American Behavioral Scientist*, 57, 1510-1529.

Slade, S., & Prinsloo, P. (2013). "Learning analytics: Ethical issues and dilemmas." *American Behavioral Scientist*, 57, 1510-1529.

United States Government Accountability Office. (2006). "Broadband deployment is extensive throughout the United States, but it is difficult to assess the extent of deployment gaps in rural areas." Report to Congressional Committees, Telecommunications. GAO website: www.gao.gov/cgi-bin/getrpt?GAO-06-426.

Wynn, G. (2008). "Avenues to success–Developing a thriving technology education program." *Technology Teacher*, 67, 29-33.

Maureen McMahon, M.S.

Social Impacts of Cyber Crime

ABSTRACT

Cyber criminals take full advantage of the anonymity, secrecy, and interconnectedness provided by the Internet, therefore attacking the very foundations of the modern information society. Cyber crime can involve botnets, computer viruses, cyber bullying, cyberstalking, cyberterrorism, cyberpornography, Denial of Service attacks, hacktivism, identity theft, malware, and spam. Law enforcement officials have struggled to keep pace with cyber criminals, who cost the global economy billions annually. Police are attempting to use the same tools cyber criminals use to perpetrate crimes in an effort to prevent those crimes and bring the guilty parties to justice. This essay begins by defining cyber crime and then moves to a discussion of its economic and social impacts. It continues with detailed excursions into cyberbullying and cyberpornography, two especially representative examples of cyber crime, and concludes with a discussion of ways to curtail the spread of cyber crime.

OVERVIEW

Computer-related crime dates to the origins of computing, though the greater connectivity between computers through the Internet has brought the concept of cyber crime into the public consciousness of the information society.

In 1995, when the World Wide Web was in its early stages of development, futurist Dr. Gene Stephens wrote about the present and future reality of cyber crime and made several predictions: "Billions of dollars in losses have already been discovered. Billions more have gone undetected. Trillions will be stolen, most without detection, by the emerging master criminal of the twenty-first century–the cyberspace offender" (Stephens, 1995, p. 24).

Reflecting on his predictions in a 2008 article, Stephens noted that he and others foresaw much of the cyber crime to come:

> I correctly forecast an explosion of cellular phone time theft and phone fraud; increased cyberattacks and fraud against government and business; massive credit card theft and fraud; internal theft of clients' identities by financially struggling and/or greedy financial service employees; more cyberporn, cyberstalking, cyberharassment, and cybervengeance; and the use of biometrics and encryption as methods of protecting data in cyberspace (Stephens, 2008, p. 33).

Defining Cyber Crime

Cyber crime, as distinguished from computer crime, is an umbrella term for the various crimes committed using the World Wide Web, such as:

- The theft of one's personal identity (identity theft) or financial resources;
- The spread of malicious software code such as computer viruses;
- The use of others' computers to send spam email messages (botnets);
- Denial of Service (DoS) attacks on computer networks or websites by the hacker;
- Hacktivism, or attacking the computer servers of those organizations felt by the hacker to be unsavory or ethically dubious;
- Cyberstalking, by which sexual predators use Internet chat rooms, social networking sites, and other online venues to find and harass their victims;
- Cyberbullying, where individuals are harassed by others, causing severe mental anguish;
- Cyberpornography, the use of the Internet to spread child and adult pornography;
- Internet gambling and software piracy; and
- Cyberterrorism, the use of the Internet to stage intentional, wide-spread attacks that disrupt computer networks; using the Internet to spread violent messages, recruit terrorists, and plan attacks.

Cyber crime can be divided into four sub-categories:

- Cyber-trespass (hacktivism, viruses, Denial of Service attacks)
- Cyber-deceptions (identity theft, fraud, piracy)
- Cyber-pornography
- Cyber-violence (cyberbullying, cyberstalking) (based on Wall, 2001, p. 3-7, cited in Yar, 2006, p. 10).

Several of these activities have a long history that predates the Internet, and they also have technological antecedents. "Some of the nineteenth-century wire frauds perpetrated by tapping into the early electric telegraph systems, for example, bear an uncanny resemblance to modern day hacks" (Wall, 2007, p. 2).

Media reports since the 1990s have documented the many methods by which criminals have used the Internet to commit crimes. Cyberthieves have become skilled at using the anonymity and secrecy of the Internet to defraud their victims of their money, their peace of mind, and indeed even their lives. When victims let their guard down by muting a healthy skepticism and caution, cyber crime takes place. As one FBI spokeswoman noted, "The scammer tries to prey on victims who are kind of in tune with what's going on in the world. The scam changes, but ultimately they're preying on the good will of people" (quoted in Simmons, 2008).

The Scope of Cyber Crime

Law enforcement officials have struggled to identify, arrest, and prosecute these tech-savvy offenders, even as sociologists have sought to get to the root of cyber crime. The Federal Bureau of Investigation (FBI) created a special cyber division in 2002 to "address cyber crime in a coordinated and cohesive manner (Federal Bureau of Investigation, 2013) with cyber squads in each of its fifty-six field offices, "cyber action teams" that travel worldwide to address cyber attacks, and nationwide computer task forces. The field of cybercrime has spawned the field of cyber criminology, defined as "the study of causation of crimes that occur in the cyberspace and its impact in the physical space" (Jaishankar, 2007, p. 1).

The scope of cyber crime remains staggering, and it continues to grow. In 2012, for instance, the US economy lost $525.5 million to cyber crime (Federal Bureau of Investigation, 2013), up over 40 million from 2011 with the most common complaints in 2012 being impersonation email scams, intimidation crimes, and scams that attempted to extort money from computer users. In 2012, cyber crime cost British businesses €21 billion (Morris, 2012), and over one million computer users in the European Union were affected every day by cyber crime (EruActive, 2012). According to the Federal Bureau of Investigation's Internet Crime Complaint Center's 2016 report, victims of cybercrime lost a total of $1.33 billion that year; by that point, the organization was receiving an average of 280,000 complaints of cybercrime victimization per year (Internet Crime Complaint Center, 2017).

As more and more people have used the Internet to do their shopping, communicating, banking, and bill paying, they have become targets for cybercriminals. There are common-sense steps that can prevent or reduce having one's financial information stolen online, as well as to avoid other scams and threats, but cyber crime in these areas persists largely due to a lack of consumer education.

Some varieties of cyber crime, such as hacktivism, are ostensibly motivated by noble intentions, such as protest against perceived abuses by governments and corporations. Often these attacks involve posting comments on official government websites and are not motivated by a desire for monetary gain. However, other forms of cyber crime have a much more violent intent. These include cyberstalking, cyberbullying, and cyberterrorism.

Cyber Crime & Society

While the economic impact of cyber crime is beyond dispute, rather less attention has been given to the social implications of cybercrime. Psychologists and psychiatrists can help victims cope with the fallout from identity theft, sexual abuse, or financial ruin, whereas sociologists are well-positioned to look at the broader social impacts and explanations of cyber crime.

Cyber crime attacks the very foundations of modern, technological societies, bound up as they are with the rapid flow of computer data facilitated by the Internet. At the most basic level, cyber criminals often take advantage of technologically unsophisticated individuals who nonetheless find themselves in a world where the Internet plays an increasingly central role in both community and private life. Cybercrime depends, at this level, on the ability of those who are more technologically sophisticated to use that knowledge to trick others into surrendering vital information, such as their bank account information or Social Security number. While it is possible in some situations for the victim of cyber crime to restore stolen money or even their personal online identity, the event often leaves the victim traumatized and deeply suspicious of the Internet and other trappings of modern life. In this way the cyber criminal deprives his or her victim of many of the conveniences of today's information economy.

Experts in cyber crime have noted that its impact occurs on multiple levels. First, on a purely economic level, cyber crime involves the theft of millions, and in some instances billions, of dollars every year. In addition, cyber crime requires individuals and institutions to take on the added cost of security software and other means by which to frustrate the cyber criminals.

Second, on a broader cultural level, cyber crime helps to sour general perceptions about the Internet in particular and new technology in general. Paradoxically, it can also make those who have been victims of one type of cyber crime more vulnerable to other types of cyber crime because of their lack of awareness of new and evolving cyber crime methods.

Third, and perhaps most alarming of all, cyber crime creates traumatized individuals who are less able to cope with the demands of life. Whether one is the victim of identity theft, a credit card scam, or cyberbullying, and regardless of whether restitution is made, the effects of cyber crime can impact the psyche as much as any crime.

APPLICATIONS

Cyberbullying

Cyberbullying can best be described as the extension of physical bullying in cyberspace. However, the individual often is not physically assaulted but rather psychologically harassed. Perhaps not surprisingly, cyberbullying most often occurs between teenagers and other young adults. According to a 2011 Pew Research study, 88 percent of teenagers surveyed reported witnessing cruelty from one individual to another on a social networking site. The bullying was through online posts, text messages, email messages, or instant messages (Liebowitz, 2011). In 2017, the Pew Research Center reported that by that point, 41 percent of American adults had been directly subjected to online harassment while 66 percent had witnessed harassment of others online (Duggan, 2017).

Cyberbullying is defined as the activity by which an individual or group of individuals is targeted for insulting, offensive, or threatening messages sent through Internet-enabled equipment such as computers or hand-held devices like mobile phones or tablets. According to cyberspace expert Parry Aftab, "Cyber-bullying is when one child or teen targets another for embarrassment, humiliation, fear, blackmail. Something designed to hurt the other using an interactive technology. That's made a big difference because kids have learned that they can use the internet as a weapon" (quoted in "Battling the online bullies," 2008). Sometimes cyberbullying continues and extends a fight or disagreement that takes place at school, at a party, or in some other social situation.

In the opinion of many victims and experts, cyber bullying is worse than in-person bullying because the perpetrators can hide behind a cloak of anonymity provided by the Internet. Two victims of cyber bullying conveyed the harshness of the tactic:

> "It's more harsh over the Internet because they don't have to see your reaction when they say those mean words to your face. So over the Internet you're more likely to say the meanest possible things you can say, and then you don't even regret it," said cyber-bully victim Abby.
>
> "I would get messages on IM [Instant Messenger] and they would be 'you're really mean' or 'you're ugly', until I just couldn't take it anymore," says Ralph who was also a victim of cyber-bullying (quoted in "Battling the online bullies," 2008).

A disturbing extension of cyberbullying occurs when physical assaults, such as rapes or beatings, are posted online. The goal is to show the power and control of the perpetrators over the victim or victims, as well as to shame and humiliate them. A related practice is publishing photos, phone numbers, and other personal information about the cyberbullying victim on certain websites.

The trauma felt by victims of cyberbullying is very real, and it often exacerbates preexisting insecurities felt by young people going through adolescence. There have been several reported incidents of a cyberbullying victim committing suicide after suffering unrelenting attacks (Pokin, 2007), including Lakeland, Florida, teen Rebecca Sedwick, who committed suicide in September 2013 after being harassed for months through online message boards and texts (Stanglin & Welch, 2013).

Given the proliferation of Web-enabled devices, parents, child advocates, politicians, and law enforcement officials are uncertain about how to reduce instances of cyberbullying. Some proposed solutions include more parental involvement in their child's online activities, such as texting and instant messaging, while others suggest that positive peer pressure is the best long-term method for reducing cyberbullying.

Cyberpornography

Although there are no universal laws regulating pornography on the Internet, individual nations have laws regulating the possession and distribution of pornographic materials. Most countries have laws regarding child pornography, and groups such as Interpol and the US Department of Justice often coordinate to apprehend and prosecute Internet child pornographers. Child pornography on the Internet generally refers to images and videos of individuals under the age of eighteen. While courts in the United States and Europe have found adult pornography on the Internet to fall within legal boundaries, there is a virtually unanimous legal, moral, psychological, and social consensus that children are not to be involved in the global sex industry.

Just as the rise of the Internet facilitated a new and expansive type of bullying, so too has it led to a proliferation of child pornography. Various websites have become repositories of sexually explicit pictures of children, where the images are bought and sold (Simons, 1998).

There is evidence that the rise of cyberpornography has led to increased instances of child abuse in the world ("Internet porn," 2004). Countries like Great Britain have been particularly impacted:

Children's charity NCH–formerly National Children's Homes–said there was evidence that the 1,500 percent rise in child pornography cases since 1988 would be reflected in more children being abused to produce the pictures.

"The scale of the problem has changed beyond recognition in just over a decade," said NCH's Internet consultant John Carr. The increased demand has made child pornography into big business and the consequences for children in all parts of the world are horrifying" ("Internet porn," 2004, par. 1-3).

A newer form of cyberpornography on the Internet involves online communities such as Second Life, where avatars, or three-dimensional representations of computer users, interact with one another in realistic online environments. Prosecutors have brought charges against individuals in Second Life who bought virtual sex with other Second Life users represented as children. In some countries, such as Germany, virtual child pornography is illegal, while the law is much less clear elsewhere (Johnston, 2007).

VIEWPOINTS

Stopping Cyber Crime

In his 1995 essay, Gene Stephens offered what one might call a traditionally libertarian way to combat cyber crime that fits well with the open ethos of cyberspace: "the only real help is... conscience and personal values, the belief that theft, deception, and invasion of privacy are simply unacceptable" (quoted in Stephens, 2008, p. 2).

Given the massive proliferation of cyber crime since 1995, Stephens began in 2008 to see things differently and argued that stopping cyber crime will depend largely on two factors: a more secure Internet infrastructure, redesigned with security foremost in mind; and coordinated, global policing of cyberspace to back up other security methods such as biometrics.

One prediction Stephens made is for a more secure, second generation Internet:

Stephens also argued that fighting cyber crime involves tackling a larger and more fundamental issue: How can one police an area, such as cyberspace, that very obviously no one person owns and has jurisdiction over? The answer, he argues, is voluntary, multinational policing, with the price of failure being too great to ignore:

> The exponentially improving capabilities of emerging Web technologies spotlights the long-ignored issues of who owns the World Wide Web, who manages it, and who has jurisdiction over it. The answer now is: Nobody! Can the world's most powerful socio-politico-economic network continue to operate almost at random, open to all, and thus be excessively vulnerable to cybercriminals and terrorists alike? Yet any attempt to restrict or police the Web can be expected to be met by extreme resistance from a plethora of users for a variety of reasons, many contradictory., ... Biometrics and more-advanced systems of ID will need to be perfected to protect users and the network. In addition, multinational

> cybercrime units will be required to catch those preying on users worldwide, as Web surfers in Arlington, Virginia, and Victoria, British Columbia, may be victims of cyber-scams perpetrated in Cairo or Budapest. Coordination and cooperation will be keys to making the Internet a safer place to travel and conduct business (Stephens, 2008, p. 3).

Although the task is daunting, governments worldwide are taking steps. In 2012, the European Union (EU) announced the establishment of a cyber crime centre aimed at stopping identity thieves and other online criminals (EurActiv, 2012). The policy-making arm of the EU, the European Commission, proposed mandatory jail time for online crimes (Morris, 2012), and the cyber crime centre was expected to staff fifty-five personnel with an annual budget of €3.6 billion.

Can one be optimistic about the containment of cyber crime? If history is any judge, the same Internet technology that empowers criminals to evade the law can enable law enforcement to defend the law.

TERMS & CONCEPTS

Botnet: A collection of computers that have been infected with software by computer hackers to force those computers to commit crimes, such as sending out computer viruses or unsolicited email (spam).

Computer Virus: A piece of rogue computer code that, when allowed to operate on a computer, causes the computer to malfunction, often leading to the loss or compromising of sensitive electronic data such as banking information or SocialSecurity numbers.

Cyber Crime: An umbrella term for the various crimes committed using the World Wide Web.

Cyberbullying: The use of the Internet and other Web-enabled mobile technologies to harass and insult others, sometimes leading to or resulting from in-person confrontations.

Cyberstalking: The use of the Internet and other Web-enabled mobile technologies to track the movements of another individual, often with the intent of doing that person harm.

Cyberterrorism: The use of the Internet and other Web-enabled mobile technologies to plan terrorist activities.

Cyberpornography: The use of the Internet to distribute and solicit sexually explicit images and videos. The laws of one's country dictate the legality of possessing or distributing pornography.

Denial of Service Attack: A method by which computer hackers send a swarm of data to a certain website to overwhelm its servers and prevent the company for transacting normal business online.

Hacktivism: A term used to describe electronic attacks by computer attackers on certain business or electronic websites, with the aim of spreading their message about the organization through online graffiti.

Identity Theft: The theft of an individual's personally identifying information, such as their Social Security number, through electronic means, including email.

Information Society: A term used to describe the economies in the United States and elsewhere in the developed world, based as they are on the flow of information via the Internet.

Internet: The global electronic communications infrastructure that facilitates the rapid flow of data between computers and other Web-enabled devices around the world.

Malware: A term used to describe computer software created for nefarious purposes, such as turning computers into botnets or causing them to crash.

Spam: A term used to describe unsolicited email.

Bibliography

"2007 Internet Crime Report." The National White Collar Crime Center. Bureau of Justice Assiatnce. Federal Bureau of Investigation. http://www.ic3.gov/media/annualreports.aspx.

"Battling the online bullies." (2008, June 27). *BBC-News.* http://news.bbc.co.uk

Duggan, M. (2017, July 11). "Online harassment 2017." Pew Research Center. http://www.pewinternet.org/2017/07/11/online-harassment-2017/

Dupont, B. (2017). "Bots, cops, and corporations: On the limits of enforcement and the promise of polycentric regulation as a way to control large-scale cybercrime." *Crime,* Law & *Social* Change, 67(1), 97-116.

EurActive. (2012, March 29). "EU prepares to launch first cybercrime centre." http://www.euractiv.com/infosociety/eu-prepares-launch-cybercrime-ce-news-511823

Federal Bureau of Investigation. (2012). "Cyber crime: Computer intrusions." http://www.fbi.gov/about-us/investigate/cyber/computer-intrusions

Federal Bureau of Investigation. (2013, May 14). "2012 internet crime report released: More than 280,000 complaints of online criminal activity reported in 2012." http://www.fbi.gov/sand-iego/press-releases/2013/2012-internet-crime-report-released

Heath, N. (2008, April 16). "FBI cyber crime chief on botnets, web terror and the social network threat." Management.silicon.com. Computer Crime Research Center: http://www.crime-research.org/news/16.04.2008/3312/.

Internet Crime Complaint Center. (2017). "2016 Internet Crime Report." https://pdf.ic3.gov/2016%5FIC3Report.pdf

"Internet porn 'increasing child abuse.'" (2004, January 12). *Guardian.* http://www.guardian.co.uk/technology/2004/jan/12/childprotection.childrensservices

Jaishankar, K. (2007). "Cyber criminology: Evolving a novel discipline with a new journal [Editorial]." *International Journal of* Cyber *Criminology,* 1. www.geocities.com/cybercrimejournal/editorialijcc.pdf

Johnston, C. (2007, May 10). "Brave new world or virtual pedophile paradise? Second Life falls foul of law." *The Age.* http://www.theage.com.au/news/technology/can-an-avatar-commitacrime/2007/05/09/1178390390098.html.

Lenhart, A. (2007, June 27). "Cyberbullying and online teens [Data Memo]." Pew Internet & American Life Project. CyberLaw website: http://www.cyberlaw.pro/docs/pewcyberbullying.pdf.

Liebowitz, M. (2011, November 9). "Online bullying rampant among teens, survey finds." *Security News Daily.* http://www.technewsdaily.com/3396-online-bullying-teens-facebook.html

Marcum, C., Higgins, G., Freiburger, T., & Ricketts, M. (2014). "Exploration of the cyberbullying victim/offender overlap by sex." *American Journal of Criminal Justice,* 39, 538-548.

Morris, H. (2012, March 12). "Europe cracks down on cybercrime." *International New York Times.* http://rendezvous.blogs.nytimes.com/2012/03/29/europe-cracks-down-on-cybercrime/

"National economies threatened by cybercrime, According to EU Information Security Agency." (2008, June 9). *AVG Anti-Virus and Internet Security* website. http://www.grisoft.com

Pokin, S. (2007, November 11). "'My Space' hoax ends with suicide of Dardenne Prairie teen." *Suburban Journals.* http://suburbanjournals.stltoday.com/articles/2007/11/13/news/

Simmons, C. (2008, April 7). "Losses rise in internet-related scams." *CIO Today.* http://www.newsfactor.com

Simons, M. (1998, July 19). "Dutch say a sex ring used infants on internet." *The New York Times.* http://query.nytimes.com/

Stanglin, D., & Welch, W. M. (2013, October 16). "Sheriff says he made arrests after one suspect posted on Facebook that she didn't care the victim had died." *USA Today.* http://www.usatoday.com/story/news/nation/2013/10/15/florida-bullying-arrest-lakeland-suicide/2986079/

Stephens, G. (1995). "Crime in cyberspace." *Futurist,* 29, 24-31.

Stephens, G. (2008). "Cybercrime in the year 2025." *Futurist,* 42 32-36.

Swartz, J. (2008, April 11). "Online crime's impact spreads." *USA Today.*

Wall, D. (2007). Cybercrime: The transformation of crime in the information age. Cambridge, UK: Polity.

Wall, D. S., & Williams, M. L. (2013). "Policing cybercrime: networked and social media technologies and the challenges for policing." *Policing & Society,* 23, 409-412.

Wayne L., A., & Johnson, L. A. (2011). "Current United States presidential views on cyber security and computer crime with corresponding Department of Justice enforcement guidelines." *Journal of International Diversity*, 116-119.

Yar, M. (2006). *Cybercrime and society*. Thousand Oaks, CA: SAGE.

Suggested Reading

Gray, D., Citron, D. K., & Rinehart, L. C. (2013). "Fighting cybercrime after United States v. Jones." *Journal of Criminal Law & Criminology*, 103, 745-801.

Levi, M. (2017). "Assessing the trends, scale and nature of economic cybercrimes: Overview and issues." *Crime*, Law & *Social* Change, 67(1), 3-20.

Litwiller, B., & Brausch, A. (2013)." Cyber bullying and physical bullying in adolescent suicide: The role of violent behavior and substance use." *Journal of Youth & Adolescence*, 42, 675-684.

McQuade, S. (ed.). (2008). *Encyclopedia of cybercrime*. Westport, CT: Greenwood.

McQuade, S. (2006). *Understanding and managing cybercrime*. Boston: Allyn & Bacon.

Pattavina, A. (ed.). (2005). *Information technology and the criminal justice system*. Thousand Oaks, CA: SAGE.

Van Wilsem, J. (2011). "Worlds tied together? Online and non-domestic routine activities and their impact on digital and traditional threat victimization." *European Journal of Criminology*, 8, 115-127.

Weimann, G. (2011). "Cyber-fatwas and terrorism." *Studies in Conflict & Terrorism*, 34, 765-781.

Williams, M. (2006). *Virtually criminal*: Crime, *deviance and regulation online*. London, UK: Routledge.

Matt Donnelly, M.Th.

Social Impacts of Wireless Communication

ABSTRACT

Wireless technologies use electromagnetic waves to send information. Ever since the development of radio, new wireless technologies have changed every aspect of human life from communication, family life, and social interaction to military strategies, medical treatments, and policing. Critics allege that wireless technologies have destroyed the sense of community and turned modern citizens into passive consumers of the culture industry, and that computer-mediated communication has created a digital divide between technology's haves and have-nots. Technophiles believe that wireless technologies have connected the world's citizens while improving their standards of living and increasing their social capital and access to information. Without a doubt, wireless technologies have changed the nature of social interaction.

OVERVIEW

Wireless technologies such as broadband Internet, cell phones, television, and radio have reshaped all aspects of society since radio was first introduced at the end of the nineteenth century. As new technologies have been introduced, people have created new uses for them, which in turn cause new forms of social interaction to evolve. Wireless technology is currently reshaping the fields of medicine, law enforcement, sports, and education, among others, while reconfiguring interpersonal communication and changing the norms of public behavior. Technology provides the social context for interaction.

What Is Wireless Technology?

Wireless technology is any technology that transmits information using electromagnetic waves (which can include radio, infrared, laser, acoustic, or light waves) instead of using wire-based technology. This includes such diverse technologies as AM and FM radios, video conferencing, satellite television, cell phones, GPS systems, and text messaging.

Summarizing the impact of wireless technology can be difficult because the category "wireless" is merely one of many ways to categorize new technology. Some media forms use both wireless and wired technologies. This means that analytically it is useful to look at the social impact of one particular medium, for example, the Internet (which can be delivered through cable, phone lines, or wireless technology) or television (delivered through satellite, cable, traditional broadcast), in addition to examining the wired/wireless distinction. At other times, the wireless/wired distinction is salient; at the minimum it usually creates a difference in the cost, access, regulation, bandwidth, capacity, portability, speed, and convenience.

When studying the impact of wireless technology, it is also important to pay attention to the multiple forms of communication it enables, which can vary by size of audience, synchronicity, and direction of transmission (one-way versus two-way). A cell phone, for example, enables two-way communication between two or more individuals, while a television can only receive (not send) a signal, which is potentially sent out to millions of televisions. The direction of a particular technology can change; for example, recommendation lists on newspaper website have turned a formerly one-way form of communication into a two-way form (Thorson, 2008). Synchronous communication means that the people communicating are participating at the same time; asynchronous communication means that messages are sent back and forth with temporal gaps between sending and reception. Video conferencing is an example of synchronous communication while email is an example of asynchronous communication.

It can be easier to understand the impact that wireless technology has had on the world by looking at the roots of wireless communication. Radio and television both began as wireless media (although wired versions of television evolved later), so a close look at their development will illuminate the many ways in which these advances changed society.

The Development and Dissemination of Radio and Television

The history of modern wireless technology begins in 1899, when Guglielmo Marconi debuted his "wireless telegraph," which eventually came to be known as radio. The potential uses of this technology caught the public imagination; scores of other inventors scrambled to improve wireless technology. Radio did not come into its own for two decades after its creation, although in the first years of the twentieth century the industrialized world realized that wireless technology could create major social change and most countries struggled to anticipate and prepare for these changes.

From the beginning, the military applications of radio technology were seen as immense; the US Navy asked Marconi for demonstration of his devices a few months after he introduced it to the public. The military's concern was prescient; wireless technology was used in the Boer War (1899–1902) and the Russo-Japanese War (1904). wireless technology was seen as so important to international relations that Germany hosted International wireless Conferences in 1903 and 1906 and the Institute of International Law in Belgium crafted guidelines to control wartime wireless use. In the United States, as the Army, Navy, journalists, the Weather Bureau, and other agencies began to compete for control of the airwaves, President Theodore Roosevelt formed an Interdepartmental Board of wireless Telegraphy to handle problems arising from competition for the new technology. No regulations were actually created in the United States until a collision between two ocean liners in 1909 resulted in the wireless Ship Act of 1910. This required that larger ships carry wireless equipment. It became evident that problems remained with the implementation of radio technology after sinking of the *Titanic* 1912; while the ships that arrived to rescue surviving passengers heard the *Titanic*'s distress call over the wireless, demonstrating its usefulness, closer ships either lacked equipment to receive the signals or lacked twenty-four-hour monitoring of the equipment they possessed. The tragedy led to a public outcry for more regulation of radio, which resulted in the Radio Act of 1912, requiring for the first time that radio operators obtain licenses to broadcast over the airwaves (Douglas, 1987).

Inventors also applied themselves to less practical uses for radio. One of the first entrepreneurs to push the idea that radio could be used as a means of transmitting entertainment was Lee De Forest. His ideas were ahead of available technology, as his attempts to broadcast music from 1907 on were often panned by journalists of the day. Commercial radio broadcasting took off in 1922; the years 1922 through 1925 were the boom years of early radio. In 1921, one in five hundred households owned a radio; in 1926 that increased to one in six. Stations came and went. Early fare on radio stations consisted mainly of music, variety shows, vaudeville routines, drama, and some news and political programming. Commercial broadcasting stole audience share from other entertainment industries, such as phonograph sales and live entertainment. Radio advertising also became widespread during the economic strains of the Great Depression (Douglas, 1987; Sterling and Kittross, 1990).

Television was pioneered and first publicly demonstrated in 1926, although the technology remained experimental for years. Commercial television broadcasting began in 1941, but almost immediately the government instituted a wartime freeze on expansion of stations and the production of television sets. The freeze was lifted in 1945, and television's boom began in 1947, slowed temporarily by another freeze, this time to control the number of new stations from 1948 until 1952. Because consumers were already adept at radio use, television use required little further socialization. Advertisements in magazines hyped TV sets as the center of family life before most consumers owned one, making suggestions about where to locate TV sets and advising that television would help to bring the family together (Spigel, 1990).

ADOPTION OF WIRELESS TECHNOLOGY

Generally, when a new technology is introduced, people first interpret its usefulness in terms of older technologies. Gradually, as people develop new uses for new technologies, their behavior changes and the new technologies feel indispensable to them. The new uses then bring about changes in social norms. For example, the telephone was first used in the same way as the telegraph; the idea of a central exchange linking households was slow to develop. Of course, once house-to-house communication was established, telephones became seen as necessary (Aronson, 1977). Likewise, the wireless nature of cellular telephones was first used in much the same way as land lines; it took a few years for people to develop uses for the cell phone that could not be replicated on a land line.

As cell phones have become widespread, they have changed social behaviors. For example, studies show that the convenience and accessibility of cell phone communication leads people to spend less time planning their schedules; their use of time becomes more spontaneous. This lack of planning in turn creates a need to continue using the cell phones; people feel dependent on them. Some people report a need to engage in "digital fidgeting" by constantly checking messages (Croal, 2008; Thulin & Vilhelmson, 2007).

As cell phones first became popular, a debate emerged about changing norms concerning appropriate behavior in public. The major point of dispute revolves around the politeness of answering the phone when in public: is it rude to do so when out with friends or on a date? When is it permissible to screen calls? Is it rude to talk on a phone while waiting in line, eating in a restaurant, riding public transportation, or using public restrooms? Such questions are still being negotiated, as the perception of cell phones shifts from the exotic to the humdrum (Humphreys, 2005). For younger users of technology, availability and accessibility are markers of higher social status (Quan-Haase & Collins, 2008). For older users, they are often a public annoyance, although they have become seen as necessary.

Social Interaction

Radio created a mass public. While newspapers and books also created mass audiences, radio was unique since it created an audience that participated in broadcast events simultaneously yet without sharing physical space. This effect has led to some of the major social impacts of all subsequent wireless technologies: humans can create bonds with each other without the need for "physical co-presence" (Cerulo, 1997, p. 49). From the beginning, then, wireless technology changed the concept of interaction.

Joshua Meyrowitz points out that the creation of new forms of communication change the pattern and character of social interaction (1997). Television and radio changed the nature of socialization, shifted the public sense of shared experiences and group identity, eliminated distinctions between public behavior and private behaviors, and changed in-group and out-group boundaries. Radio and television created shared experiences between groups that had been separated by print media. Whereas there had been men's magazines and women's magazines, and children's books and adult books, the programming of electronic media was initially aimed at a general audience. This has changed since the invention of cable television and subsequent technologies have re-splintered the audience.

The Family

Television was initially welcomed as an aid to family togetherness. The American family changed rapidly after the Second World War. Suburbanization isolated people from their extended family networks, married women entered the workforce in larger numbers even while gender roles underwent retrenchment, men dealt with the after-effects of combat, and the family was increasingly socialized to become a unit of consumption to jumpstart the postwar economy. Studies at the time showed a strong belief that television viewing drew families together, helping them resist the centripetal forces of modern life. At the same time, many people expressed the same ambivalence toward the television that they expressed toward other forms of technology. There were concerns that television would create passivity, increase violence, and weaken the influence of parents. This ambivalence was not misplaced; television united families and also divided them (Spigel, 1990).

The Internet has further shifted family dynamics. Meyrowitz argues that the boundaries of family life have become blurred by electronic media:

> We and computer networks. We "travel" through, or "inhabit," electronic landscapes or setting that are no longer defined fully by walls of a house, neighborhood blocks, or other physical boundaries, barriers, and passageways (1997, p. 65-6).

Social Ties

These changes serve to unite people around the globe, in a surface sense, while eroding local homogeneity. On the other hand, while people's exposure to these different experiences has increased the heterogeneity of families, it also can keep families more connected. Many households use wireless technology to keep in touch and manage their schedules. While this means they are in frequent contact, it also means that households now function more as networks of individuals rather than as unified groups (Kennedy & Wellman 2007).

Of course, being connected electronically is not the same as sharing a social connection. Because wireless technologies make it possible for people to access each other, advances in communications technologies are often greeted with the belief that they will bring people together. While the phone and the Internet have created new ways of maintaining social relationships and enable new types of relationships, the extent to which people take advantage of the ability to connect with others was overestimated in early hype over these technologies. Just because people are available to each other online or over the phone does not mean that they will become socially close to each other. In this sense, wireless communication is much like face-to-face communication; physical propinquity does not guarantee social closeness (Zhao & Elesh, 2008).

Research that tries to understand the connection between Internet use and offline social ties has been contradictory. Sociologist Shanyang Zhao suggests that this is because the concept of Internet use is overly broad (2006). There are heavy users and light users, people who use the Internet for solitary purposes and people who use it to connect with others through email, chat, and discussion forums. When controlling for usage patterns, Zhao found that people who spend more time online engaged in nonsocial purposes had fewer social ties than those who used the Internet more lightly, or who used it for primarily social reasons. Overall, findings seem to suggest that use of the Internet enhances or exaggerates pre-existing preferences for isolation or interaction (Dimaggio et al., 2001).

APPLICATIONS

According to CTIA–the wireless Association, the use of wireless devices is growing in US households; as of December 2012, there were 326.4 million active wireless devices, including smartphones, tablets, and Wifi hotspots; with a total population of 316 million Americans, the United States has a wireless penetration rate of 102.2 percent (CTIA, 2012). Furthermore, CTIA indicated that more than one-third of American households (35.8 percent) were wireless-only, meaning they no longer had a landline phone (CTIA, 2012). As wireless technology is used for an ever-increasing number of new devices, it permeates more and more areas of daily life. Examples of recent innovations include these areas:

- Olympics: Cyclists training for the 2008 Beijing Olympics used wireless technology: power meters integrated with their bicycles captured data on the force they exerted on different parts of their course (Murray, 2008).
- Education: The San Francisco Department of Public Health partnered with Internet Sexuality Information Services, Inc., to create a text-messaging system to provide educational information about sexual health after noticing that sexual

transmitted infections were on the rise in the same demographics that reported increasing use of cell phones (Levine et al., 2008).

- Medicine: Hospitals report using "a single network infrastructure that supports data, voice, video, cellular, fire- and life-safety systems, telemetry, and real-time location systems for patients, staff and equipment . . . an ambulatory electronic health record with e-prescribing capabilities . . . automation in the supply chain combined with computerized provider order entry . . . IT-powered payer transactions and revenue-cycle activities . . . [automation of] the supply chain, the revenue cycle and public health surveillance . . . a picture archiving and communication system . . . medication safety . . . [and] direct feeds from biomedical equipment" (Coye, 2008; "Wow," 2008). Transmitters can download data from implanted heart devices and send it automatically into patients' hospital records, effectively replacing the need for frequent in-person checkups (Pedersen 2008).
- Crime & Policing: wireless technologies have been used by police teams during crises such as hostage negotiations, allowing teams more mobility and faster information processing. Police cars are increasingly replacing or augmenting their radio systems with Mobile Data Terminals so that officers can download data directly instead of having to relay information through a dispatcher (Shinder, 2005).

VIEWPOINTS

Just as it is hard to separate the social impact of wireless from the impact of each technological form, it is hard to separate criticisms of each. Separate criticisms have been made of each new media form carried through wireless technologies: radio, television, the Internet, and cell phones specifically, and wirelesstechnologies in general have been condemned.

The Culture Industry

At times, criticisms of the social impacts of new technologies are actually criticisms of the mass production of culture. For example, Theodor Adorno and Max Horkheimer, writing during World War II, criticized the culture industry, believing that the mass production of cultural products stifled individualism and led to a conformity that supported fascism (1993). While their critique was aimed at all forms of mass culture (of which wireless technology was a small part) they disliked the one-way communication and passivity of the audience exemplified by radio.

Critiques of Television

Television has probably come in for more censure than other technologies. At various times, people have claimed that television dumbs down the public, increases violence, distorts reality, encourages conformity, isolates viewers, and induces political apathy (Berger, 2007). Studies looking for overt media effects suggest that heavy watchers of television do have a distorted view of reality, insofar as they believe that the high level of violence on television reflects reality and are likely to see society as more violent than it actually is (Ryan & Wentworth, 1999).

Neil Postman believes that television has had a negative influence on US society (1985). He believes that the form of media shapes its content; that is, the same sorts of ideas cannot be expressed by each form media takes. The printed word can express complex, logical thoughts; smoke signals can only communicate the briefest messages. Television is good at entertaining, perhaps too well, because it has led viewers to expect everything to be entertaining, including religion, education, and politics. As a result, people vote based on image and appearances, religion has lost its sacred quality, and education has become more like television: an institution that avoids complexity, critical thinking, and exposition. Postman believes that the age of television has reduced public discourse to nonsense and that the lack of an informed public able to think critically will eventually threaten democracy.

OTHER CURRENT WIRELESS DEBATES

Security

Wireless networks are more vulnerable to security breaches than wired networks. This risk is exacerbated by the tendency of many people to use mobile devices in public without considering issues of privacy and security (Urbas & Krone, 2006).

The Digital Divide

As the Internet first became popular and the advantages conferred by Internet access became apparent, researchers became concerned about the potential exacerbation of inequality caused by unequal access to the Internet. This concern faded as availability of Internet has become more widespread through public wireless access such as Internet in schools and libraries. A different digital divide has appeared, one concerning how effectively people can use the Internet. This divide is correlated with the amount of education a person has, and has implications for ability to effectively retrieve and use information found online (Robinson, Dimaggio, & Hargittai, 2003).

Wireless technology has been embraced by schools and universities trying to prepare students for the workforce, and is especially useful in supporting the move toward problem-based learning. However, technology improves at such a fast pace that it can be hard for school systems to keep up with the changes (Blackbourn et al., 2008).

Wireless technology is seen by some as an invaluable aid in the spread of human rights round the globe (Lane, 2008). Former Federal Communications Commission chair Kevin Martin thinks that wireless communication has become so important that he wants to mandate that at least 25 percent of the wireless airwave spectrum coming up for auction to be set aside for free broadband, thus addressing the needs of lower-income households and rural areas that are currently underserved by the broadband industry (Cauley, 2008).

Ownership, Access, and Globalization

In the United States, the public owns the airwaves (although many citizens are unaware of this fact) and the Federal Communications Commission regulates the use of the airwaves for communication in the United States. Many of this agency's decisions have ignited political controversy. For example, the Fairness Doctrine, which mandated equal time for issues of community importance, was eliminated in 1987, and caps on the number of radio stations that one corporate entity could own nationwide have also been eliminated. While supporters of these actions claim that the multiple media outlets of the present day make issues of ownership and access less pressing, opponents claim that concentrated media ownership and lack of attention to equal time have weakened citizens' ability to gain the knowledge needed to anticipate in a healthy democracy (McChesney, 2004).

CONCLUSIONS

Two things are certain: wireless technologies have changed the face of the United States and the world, and the rate of change is speeding up all the time. wireless technologies have connected the world and made the old idea of globalism real. At the same time, they encourage cultural imperialism and reify older forms of inequality. Social interaction has shifted, as cell phones mean that everyone can be accessible at all times. The Internet has increased access of information to the point that information overload has become a problem. Identities and group boundaries have been rearranged by wireless technologies. Critics believe that these seismic shifts have weakened Americans' ability to think critically; others claim that the information and connection provided by these advances have made the world smaller and a much more hospitable place for humans.

TERMS & CONCEPTS

Computer-Mediated Communication (CMC): Any communication carried out over the Internet, for example email, social media, instant messaging, and web conferencing.

Cultural Imperialism: Domination or obliteration of one culture by another culture's products.

Culture Industry: The entirety of industries involved in the production and distribution of articles of mass culture. The term generally carries negative connotations.

Digital Divide: Originally describing a gap in Internet access, this now also refers to a gap in information literacy.

Information & Communication Technologies (ICT): Popular catchall term for both wireless and wired new media technologies.

Social Capital: The extent to which a person belongs to and participates in community networks.

Synchronous Communication: Communication in which participants take part simultaneously.

Wireless Technology: Any technology that transmits information using electromagnetic waves such as radio, infrared, laser, acoustic or light waves, instead of using wire-based technology.

Bibliography

Adorno, T., & Horkheimer, M. (1993). "The culture industry: enlightenment as mass deception." In S. During (Ed.), *The cultural studies reader* (pp. 29–43). New York, NY: Routledge.

Aronson, S. H. (1977). "Bell's electric toy: What's the use? The sociology of early telephone usage." In I. Pool (Ed.), *The social impact of the telephone* (pp. 15–39). Cambridge, MA: MIT Press.

Bacigalupe, G., Camara, M., & Buffardi, L. E. (2014). "Technology in families and the clinical encounter: Results of a cross-national survey." *Journal of Family Therapy, 36*(4), 339–358.

Bergdall, A. R., et al. (2012). "Love and hooking up in the new millennium: communication technology and relationships among urban African American and Puerto Rican young adults." *Journal of Sex Research, 49*(6), 570–582.

Berger, A. A. (2007). *Media and society: A critical perspective* (2nd ed.). New York, NY: Rowman and Littlefield.

Blackbourn, J., Fillingim, J., McCelland, S., Elrod, G., Medley, M., Kritsonis, M., et al. (2008, June). "The use of wireless technology to augment problem-based learning in special education preservice teacher training." *Journal of Instructional Psychology, 35* (2), 169–176.

Cauley, L. (2008, August 20). "Martin wants broadband across USA." *USA Today.*

Cerulo, K. A. (1997). "Reframing sociological concepts for a brave new (virtual?) world." *Sociological Inquiry, 67,* 48–58

Coye, M. (2008). "Getting IT Right." *H&HN: Hospitals & Health Networks, 82*(7), 26.

Croal, N. (2008, July 21). "The peril of digital fidgeting." *Newsweek, 64.*

CTIA—The wireless Association. (2012, December). "Early release of estimates from the National Health Interview Survey, January–June 2012." *National Center for Health Statistics.* http://www.ctia.org/

Dilaver, O. (2014). "Making sense of innovations: A comparison of personal computers and mobile phones." *New Media & Society, 16*(8), 1214–1232.

DiMaggio, P., Hargittai, E., Neuman, W. R., & Robinson, J. P. (2001). "Social implications of the internet." *Annual Review of Sociology, 27* (1), 307–336.

Douglas, S. J. (1987). *Inventing American Broadcasting 1899-1922.* Baltimore, MD: Johns Hopkins University Press.

Dulin, P. L., et al. (2013). "Development of a smartphone-based, self-administered intervention system for alcohol use disorders." *Alcoholism Treatment Quarterly, 31*(3), 321–336.

Humphreys, L. (2005). "Cellphones in public: Social interactions in a wireless era." *New Media & Society, 7,* 810–833.

Islam, Y. M., & Doyle, K. (2008). "Distance education via SMS technology in rural Bangladesh." *American Behavioral Scientist, 52,* 87–96.

Kennedy, T. L. M & Wellman, B. (2007). "The networked household." *Information, Communication and Society,* 10, 645–670.

Lane, E. (2008). "Summit promotes wireless technology as human rights tool." *Science, 320* (5884), 1732.

Laposky, J. (2008, July 21). "CEA tracks accessories growth." *TWICE: This Week in Consumer Electronics, 23* (15), 60.

Levine, D., McCright, J., Dobkin, L., Woodruff, A., & Klausner, J. (2008, March). "SEXINFO: A sexual health text messaging service for San Francisco youth." *American Journal of Public Health, 98,* 393–395.

McChesney, R. (2004). *The problem of the media: US communication politics in the 21st century.* New York, NY: Monthly Review Books.

Meyrowitz, J. (1997). "Shifting worlds of strangers: Medium theory and changes in 'them' versus 'us'." *Sociological Inquiry, 67* (1), 59–71.

Murray, C.J. (2008). "Olympic cyclists go wireless." *Design News, 63* (10), 52–54.

Pedersen, A. (2008). "Merlin@home gets FDA approval for remote monitoring of ICDs." *Medical Device Daily, 12* (136), 1–6.

Postman, N. (1985). *Amusing ourselves to death.* New York: Penguin Books.

Przybylski, A. K., & Weinstein, N. (2013). "Can you connect with me now? How the presence of mobile communication technology influences face-to-face conversation quality." *Journal of Social and Personal Relationships, 30*(3), 237–246.

Quan-Haase, A., & Collins, J. (2008), "I'm there, but I might not want to talk to you." *Information, Communication & Society, 11,* 526–543.

Robinson, J. P., Dimaggio, P., & Hargittai, E. (2003). "New social survey perspectives on the digital divide." *IT& Society, 1,* 1–22.

Ryan, J., & Wentworth, W. M. (1999). *Media and society: the production of culture in the mass media.* Boston: Allyn and Bacon.

Shinder, D. L. (2005). "Using new wireless technologies to aid in negotiation tasks." *Journal of Police Crisis Negotiations, 5,* 23–33.

Spigel, L. (1990). "Television in the family circle." In P. Mellencamp, (Ed.), *Logics of television: Essays in cultural criticism* (pp. 73–97). Bloomington, IN: Indiana University Press.

Sterling, C. H., & Kittross, J. M. (1990). *Stay tuned: A concise history of American broadcasting* (2nd ed.). Belmont, CA: Wadsworth.

Thorson, E. (2008). "Changing patterns of news consumption and participation." *Information, Communication and Society, 11,* 473–489.

Thulin, E., & Vilhelmson, B. (2007, August). "Mobiles everywhere." *Young, 15* (3), 235–253.

Urbas, G., & Krone, T. (2006). Mobile and wireless technologies: Security and risk factors. *Trends & Issues in Crime & Criminal Justice,* 329, 1–6.

Wahl, A. (2008). "Why-max?" *Canadian Business, 81* (12/13), 19–20.

"Wow! Ten years on the most wired list (2008)." *H&HN: Hospitals & Health Networks, 82* (7), 35.

Zhao, S. (2006). "Do Internet users have more social ties? Call for differentiated analyses of Internet use." *Journal of Computer Mediated Communication 11,* 844–862.

Zhao, S. & Elesh, D. (2008). "Copresence as 'being with'." *Information, Communication & Society, 11,* 565–583.

SUGGESTED READING

Davis, L., Shapiro, J. J., & Steier, F. (2012). "Shaping boundaries within the flow: Workspaces, environments, identities." *Spaces & Flows: An International Journal of Urban & Extra Urban Studies, 2*(3), 71–83.

Croteau, D., & Hoynes, W. (2003). *Media and society* (3rd ed.). Thousand Oaks, CA: Pine Forge Press.

Martinez-Pecino, R., Lera, M. J., & Martinez-Pecino, M. (2012). "Active seniors and mobile phone interaction." *Social Behavior and Personality: An International Journal, 40*(5), 875–880.

Merton, R.K.; Lowenthal, M. F., & Curtis, A. (1946). *Mass persuasion: The social psychology of a war bond drive.* New York, NY: Harper.

Meyrowitz, J. (1985). *No sense of place: The impact of electronic media on social behavior.* New York, NY: Oxford University Press.

Rheingold, H. (2003). *Smart mobs.* New York, NY: Perseus.

Katherine Walker, Ph.D.

Social Media and News Reporting

ABSTRACT

Social media has changed how people find out about the news, how they access the news, and how the news is made. News gathering and news reporting has undergone a process of radical democratization, but critics assert that the quality of news reporting has been sacrificed along the way (Streitmatter, 2012). Many who have been in the business of journalism for their entire lives have lamented the fact that, "Now that just anyone can report the news, they are having just anyone report the news."

OVERVIEW

In little more than a decade, social media sites such as Twitter and Facebook revolutionized the way society stays current with world events. Prior to the advent of social media, most people relied on newspapers, radio, and television news programs to find out what was going on in their communities or around the world. Now, people frequently find out about major events on social media before they hear about them on television, and certainly before they read about them in the newspaper. The speed with which news can travel via the Internet explains why so many more people now get their news, or at least learn of it initially, via social media (Zion & Craig, 2015). Large newspapers used to have an evening edition in addition to the morning paper, but this has now become rare, and most papers that continue to operate are printed only once a day. For many people, hearing about an event or witnessing once often had less of an impact than reading about it in the news–winning a track meet might make a high school athlete feel good, but getting her picture in the paper with the other winners was truly something special (Briggs, 2013). A social media post, however, has the charm of instant gratification, offering a kind of immediacy and response that is simply not available from a print newspaper and which can be broadcast by a participant or eyewitness.

Accessing the news has also undergone radical changes due to the influence of social media. A social media user can, for example, use a key term tagged with a hashtag (#) to find posts on Twitter about a news item. The most popular news items are said to be "trending." Social media platforms, such as Facebook, also provide a marketplace to draw potential news customers in (Bullard, 2015). One of the most effective marketing gimmicks is the "listicle"—that is, a short, quirky list of informational items intended to arrest and capture the interest of a Social media user and drawn him or her to a commercial site.

Social media makes it possible for users to follow specific news sources that use a perspective that they find agreeable. Sociologists are finding that social media users get much of their political news through sites such as Facebook (Bode, 2016). Further, instead of having to buy a newspaper that tries to cover all of the topics that people are likely to be interested in, with sections devoted to sports, business, local news, national news, world news, and so on, social media users can choose to follow only those social media news sites that fit within their areas of interest. A person who only cares about sports news can follow dozens of sports news outlets using Twitter, Facebook, and similar sites, while a person interested in science and technology news can find numerous sites that serve up all the latest discoveries. Only a few decades ago, futurists foresaw a time when people would be able to have personalized newspapers, full of stories about the topics they most cared about, delivered to them each day. For the most part, social media news reporting has made this prediction a reality, even though there is an argument to be made that reading only news about narrow topical areas does not make for a well-informed citizenry (Hayes, Battles & Hilton-Morrow, 2013).

FURTHER INSIGHTS

News reporting before the days of social media was a specialized field requiring many different skills. Reporters had to be skilled researchers and writers to be able to look into the background of their subjects and discover relevant information and then write about it in ways that make dry or confusing material interesting and accessible to the public. Journalists also had to have a talent for talking to people from all walks of life and, perhaps more important, getting those people to talk to them. Finally, the profession required quick wits and an ability to react to changing circumstances, making intuitive leaps about the real significance of seemingly innocuous facts.

The modern state of news reporting is far, far different. The widespread availability of cheap, small cameras capable of recording high quality photos, audio, and videos have put into the hands of almost everyone tools that were once accessible only to small numbers of people and only usable with considerable preparation (Shaw, 2012). This disruptive innovation has led to the rise of the amateur reporter, often a person who just happens to be in the right place at the right time, with a fully charged cell phone battery and a clear view of events. Eyewitness accounts and visuals of major events, such as riots, uprisings, and natural disasters, are frequently crowdsourced in real time or shortly after from people on the ground rather than gathered by a reporter who arrives later.

To understand the magnitude of the change that has occurred, one need only recall the assassination of President John F. Kennedy in Dallas, Texas, in 1963. That tragic event was captured on a handheld movie camera by Abraham Zapruder, and Zapruder's footage has been endlessly replayed and dissected ever since. When tragedy strikes in the modern world, however, those looking for information about the events can rest assured that they were most likely recorded on not one or two cameras that happened to be nearby, but dozens. Having access to more information about current events in the form of pictures and videos taken by those nearby, however, very rarely provides the public with any kind of heightened understanding of those events. It is quite literally a case of greater access to information resulting in less comprehension (Wenger & Potter, 2012; Browne, Stack & Ziyadah, 2015).

VIEWPOINTS

Though some argue that the availability of the Internet and social media have made news reporting much less important an activity than it used to be, the opposite may be true. That is, the fact that society is now awash in information of every sort from events all over the world, practically within seconds of their occurring, means that there is a greater need for talented journalists to sort through this sea of information and filter out the redundancies and irrelevancies in order to present the public with a coherent picture of events. Journalism schools seem to be well aware of the new realities. After several years in which journalism cast a gimlet eye upon social media, viewing it as unreliable at best and an inane distraction at worst, journalism faculty are now beginning to incorporate the use of Social media into their curriculum.

These classes do not focus on specific technologies such as Twitter, since the particulars of technology change rather frequently and are often not directly relevant to the study or practice of journalism. Instead, the focus is on the principles of journalism and how they can be applied to new methodologies of newsgathering made possible by increased access to information (Reimold, 2013).

A significant area of focus has become the importance of exercising ethics when making use of social media to gather news and report it. Social media works because people are anxious to interact with one another and to share information about themselves, but it frequently happens that people only want to share certain information with certain people. In many cases, reporters can easily use social media to gain access to information that could be very damaging to any number of people. Some reporters take the approach that if people put information about themselves online–even if they don't fully understand what it means to do so, or how many people will be able to access it–then they have assumed the risk of making that information public, and deserve whatever repercussions occur.

Other journalists, perhaps more familiar with the frailty of human nature and less interested in making headlines at any cost, understand the importance of considering the circumstances before using information as part of their story. Journalism students are being confronted with such dilemmas with increasing frequency, thanks to social media. Part of the reason for this has been attributed to the relative informality that reigns in social media communications (Streitmatter, 2015).

Social media posts and messages, not unlike email, tend to use a style and tone that is more conversational, even chatty, than the typical newspaper article or television news script. Younger reporters, accustomed to communicating with peers using social media, sometimes find it difficult to maintain a professional bearing when using social media for work related communications. Social media also offers unique opportunities for information gathering, and these open whole new ethical dilemmas for journalists to consider (Anderson, 2013). For example, it is common knowledge that when dealing with Internet communications, all is not necessarily as it seems. It is fairly easy for one person to impersonate someone else, for example, especially when the communication is happening between user accounts belonging to people who have never met face to face. This means that for a reporter investigating a person suspected of wrongdoing, it would be all too easy to create a fictitious social media account posing as another person entirely, and use this account to approach the subject of the investigation, in the hope of enticing the person to reveal information that the subject would almost certainly never reveal to one who was known as a journalist.

Like many of the thorniest ethical dilemmas, this scenario is one which could be perpetrated and never discovered, making it all the more important for journalists to consider well in advance, so they can decide for themselves, after careful reflection, what kind of journalists they want to be. It is almost certain that the technology and the profession of news reporting will continue to evolve in ways as drastic as have been seen during the rise of social media, and it is just as certain that journalists will continue to face new dilemmas they will need to carefully weigh (Shepard, 2013).

TERMS & CONCEPTS

Crowdsourcing: Crowdsourcing is a model of financing or project development that draws on contributions of some resource (e.g., money or information) from large numbers of people. News reporting has begun to take advantage of crowdsourcing as well, with footage and photographs for many stories being contributed by amateurs armed with cell phone cameras.

Disruptive Innovation: Disruptive innovation is a phenomenon discussed in the fields of business and the social sciences. It refers to a new technology that arrives on the scene and provides new methods of performing tasks. While the technology is usually helpful and therefore a welcome change, it also disrupts established ways of doing things, traditional hierarchies within organizations, and can even change the way people relate to one another.

Hashtag: A hashtag is the symbol #. It is used on the social networking site Twitter to mark a keyword that many people are tweeting about, so that other users can search for the hashtag and quickly find all the tweets that mention it. For example, if a member of Britain's royal family were getting married, news reporters tweeting from the ceremony might use the hashtag, #RoyalWedding. That way, any Twitter user could search for that hashtag and find all the tweets that use it.

Listicle: This term is meant to be a contraction of the words "list" and "article," and it describes the many Internet news postings that are little more than lists of bullet points. These listicles have titles such as "Five Things You Need to Know About Planting a Garden," or "The Twelve Best Restaurants in Alaska." In a style indicative of much Internet news reporting, a small amount of effort is expended to create the article, in the hope that Internet users will glance at it and then share it with their friends online. Some have pointed to the growing prevalence of listicles as signs of the declining quality of journalism.

Platform Specialization: Platform specialization refers to the way that users of social media tend to use different social networking communities for different purposes when it comes to finding and evaluating news. Twitter is the service of choice for people who think of themselves as extremely interested in the news, and it is the site most often mentioned when people are asked how they found out about a particular news topic, such as a political scandal or a natural disaster. Facebook, on the other hand, is the social network that most people say they use to share news stories with their friends. In most cases, platform specialization is a property that emerges without having been intentionally designed; people use the social networking tool that happens to work best for their needs, not the one that has been most painstakingly designed for a particular purpose.

Social Networking: Social networking refers to the use of various technology platforms on the Internet to create and use online communities of friends and shared interests. After the Internet boom of the late

1990s and early 2000s, social networking sites quickly sprang up to offer users the means to easily interact with each other, without having to know arcane commands to connect. Social networks now account for a large amount of all Internet traffic, and for many people they are the primary means used to find out about news and events in their home towns and all around the world.

BIBLIOGRAPHY

Anderson, C. W. (2013). *Rebuilding the news: Metropolitan journalism in the digital age.* Philadelphia, PA: Temple University Press.

Bode, L. (2016). "Political news in the news feed: Learning politics from Social Media." *Mass Communication & Society,* 19(1), 24-48.

Briggs, M. (2013). *Journalism next: A practical guide to digital reporting and publishing.* Los Angeles, CA: Sage/CQ Press.

Browne, M., Stack, L., & Ziyadah, M. (2015). "Streets to screens: Conflict, Social media and the news." *Information, Communication & Society,* 18(11), 1339-1347.

Bullard, S. B. (2015). "Editors use social media mostly to post story links." *Newspaper Research Journal,* 36(2), 170-183.

Hayes, J. E., Battles, K., & Hilton-Morrow, W. (2013). *War of the worlds to Social Media: Mediated communication in times of crisis.* New York, NY: Peter Lang.

Reimold, D. (2013). *Journalism of ideas: Brainstorming, developing, and selling stories in the digital age.* New York, NY: Routledge.

Shaw, I. S. (2012). *Human rights journalism: Advances in reporting distant humanitarian interventions.* Houndmills, UK: Palgrave Macmillan.

Shepard, S. B. (2013). *Deadlines and disruption: My turbulent path from print to digital.* New York, NY: McGraw-Hill.

Streitmatter, R. (2015). *A force for good: How the American news media have propelled positive change.* London, UK: Rowman & Littlefield.

Streitmatter, R. (2012). *Mightier than the sword: How the news media have shaped American history.* Boulder, CO: Westview Press.

Wenger, D. H., & Potter, D. (2012). *Advancing the story: Broadcast journalism in a multimedia world.* Washington, DC: CQ Press/Sage.

Zion, L., & Craig, D. (2015). *Ethics for digital journalists: Emerging best practices.* London, UK: Routledge.

SUGGESTED READING

Campbell, R., Martin, C. R., & Fabos, B. (2014). *Media & culture: Mass communication in a digital age.* Boston, MA: Bedford/St. Martin's.

Mosca, L., & Quaranta, M. (2016). "News diets, Social media use and non-institutional participation in three communication ecologies: Comparing Germany, Italy and the UK." *Information, Communication & Society,* 19(3), 325-345.

Reich, Z. (2013). "The impact of technology on news reporting: A longitudinal perspective." *Journalism & Mass Communication Quarterly,* 90(3), 417-434.

Van Leuven, S., Heinrich, A., & Deprez, A. (2015). "Foreign reporting and sourcing practices in the network sphere: A quantitative content analysis of the Arab Spring in Belgian news media." *New Media & Society,* 17(4), 573-591.

Zhuang, Z. (2014). "The importance of citizen journalists in new media when reporting on catastrophes." *Global Studies Journal,* 7(3), 21-39.

Scott Zimmer, MLS, M.S., J.D.

Social Media and Self-Worth

ABSTRACT

The excessive use of social media can have negative impacts on the self-esteem of adolescents. Specifically, experts point to the phenomenon of psychological addiction to social media, the proliferation of and preoccupation with selfies, the effects of cyberbullying, and the role of social media sites in allowing individuals to construct false and fantasy images of themselves to be presented to others, and the proliferation of sexist, racist, and homophobic messages and content circulated on social media as particular points of concern.

OVERVIEW

There is no question that social media is now a central feature in the lives of many people around the world. Facebook remains, by far, the largest and most popular social media site, but many other social media exist, including Twitter, Tumblr, Instagram, Pinterest, MySpace, and LinkedIn, among others. Additionally, the popular site YouTube allows the public to upload videos of themselves and others for the entire world to view. Statistics compiled by Jennifer Beese of SproutSocial.com claim that more than 1.4 billion people worldwide log in to Facebook at least once a month (a total greater than the entire population of China and almost representing one-fifth of the world's total population). Beese also estimates that approximately 936 million people log in to Facebook on a daily basis, and the average Facebook user spends 40 minutes per day on the site (Beese, 2015). These staggering numbers have been bolstered by the growing number of people with smartphones; Beese estimates that out of the total number of daily Facebook users, 85 percent (798 million people) log in to the site on mobile phones.

These global statistics are impressive, but use of social media in the United States is even more apparent. The Pew Research Center notes that 65 percent of all American adults over the age of 18 used social media in 2015, compared with only 7 percent in 2005 (Perrin, 2015). Breaking these numbers down by age bracket, 89 percent of Americans between the ages of 18 and 29 and 82 percent of Americans aged 30 to 49 use social media (Pew Research Center, 2015). Furthermore, Americans of all racial and ethnic backgrounds use social media in relatively equal numbers: 65 percent of whites, 56 percent of blacks, and 65 percent of Latinos report using social media (Perrin, 2015).

Although each social media site has its own unique idiosyncratic features, a common feature is that they allow users to post photographs, status updates, and personal thoughts and reflections that capture an individual's mood and actions at a particular moment in time. Posts, in effect, serve as online "snapshots" of a person that capture and preserve their respective emotions and activities at a specific moment in their lives. Another common feature of these sites is that they allow users to establish a close network of colleagues who are given the ability to access the content a user has posted. Facebook refers to these colleagues as "friends," while Twitter uses the term "followers."

People are more mobile than ever before and often must relocate for work, school, or other purposes. Among the many positive aspects of social media is that it allows people to reestablish or remain in frequent contact with old friends and colleagues despite being separated by distance. Social media also makes it relatively easy for users and organizations to organize events and to share news stories, announcements, and other important information to a wide network of individuals.

However, major criticisms of social media have emerged in recent years, particularly with regards to the harmful impacts that excessive use of social media can have on its users, especially teenagers and young adults. Some critics contend that a major problem with social media is that it allows users to construct a false image of their lives in an effort to impress others, hide one's own unhappiness or depression, or to boost one's self-esteem. These concerns seem to be even more common among middle school and high school students, whose daily lives unfold at a very impressionable time of identity development and the seeking of social inclusion.

Many users of Facebook, Instagram, and Twitter often post pictures they have taken of themselves, popularly known as selfies, to their sites; selfies can be used innocently to capture one's visit to a popular tourist destination or attendance at a music concert, for example, but some critics allege that excessive taking of selfies can affect one's self-esteem in seemingly contradictory ways. On one hand, individuals who take and post dozens of selfies to their social media accounts may start to develop inflated egos by beginning to think of themselves as a constant and ongoing center of attention. Celebrities such as singers Justin Beiber and Rihanna, but perhaps most famously the reality TV star Kim Kardashian, have drawn large amounts of attention to themselves through their regular posting of selfies online. The general public has followed suit, as 79 percent of teenagers posted selfies online in 2006; by 2013 that figure had increased to 91 percent according to the Pew Research Center (BBC, 2013). Various types of selfies are common, including one snapped from a high angle that show one's arm extended overhead, a head shot that resembles a mirror image, and more lighthearted selfies where individuals make faces, gesture with their hands, or pout their lips.

Social media sites typically allow users to indicate that they approve, find impressive, or support messages, pictures, and content posted by their colleagues. For example, Facebook users can "like" a "friend's" posts, while other sites allow users to click on a star. Posting a picture that generates many "likes" from one's network of colleagues can boost one's self-esteem, but conversely, uploading a picture of oneself that generates few or no "likes" can decrease self-esteem or make an individual feel depressed or angry, particularly if they spent a considerable amount of time preparing for the "perfect shot." Additionally, the use of selfies for purposes of sexting has become a major concern among parents and counselors. Sexting, a portmanteau of "sex" and "texting," is sending sexually themed text messages or provocative nude or semi-nude selfies of one's full body or genitals to others. This practice is not limited to teenagers, but much of the concern over sexting focuses on the dangers—emotional as well as potentially physical—that sending naked selfies to romantic interests or partners can ultimately lead to. Snaking occurs when an individual privately sends a nude or sexually provocative selfie to someone, who in turn shares this image with their wider network of friends or posts the picture online for a wide audience to view (Weale, 2015). This can deeply embarrass the person depicted in the photo, generate negative rumors about their character, or make them a laughingstock among their peers, becoming a source of profound psychological stress.

VIEWPOINTS

Since its development, social media has generated debate and controversy over its affects on children and adolescents. Initially, the site MySpace sparked concerns over minors revealing sensitive personal information to complete strangers who might seek to take advantage of them. However, these fears had largely subsided by 2010. In a May 2010 column in the *Los Angeles Times*, Melissa Healy argued that social media sites provided teenagers with an important and positive way of developing friendships and social bonds with others, as well as contributing positively to a teenager's development of self-identity, that far outweighed the risks of strangers using social media to prey on teenagers. Without referencing or citing specific studies, Healy claimed that a growing body of empirical research indicated that teenagers who spent "lots of time" on social media sites were more psychologically well-adjusted and exhibited better mental health than teenagers who do not regularly use social media. Healy also claimed that most social media users, including minors, connected only with people they knew in real life on social media sites (Healy, 2010).

However, the majority of experts have never shared Healy's unbridled optimism and enthusiasm regarding the extensive use of social media in the lives of adolescents. Many disagree with the idea that excessive amounts of time spent on social media enhances one's self-esteem; in fact, most analysts argue the exact opposite. A common theme among these critics is that individuals, particularly teenagers and young adults, often do not reveal their "true selves" on social media, but instead often seek to craft an idealistic, censored, overly positive image of their lives that either is intended to, or has the effect of, giving off the impression that their lives are more exciting and glamorous than they really are. One aspect of this consists of altering, editing, or airbrushing selfies to conceal blemishes and other physical traits considered undesirable or ugly.

Teenagers and young adults, particularly females who often face greater social pressure to conform to powerful culturally-defined standards of beauty, may compare the quality of their selfies with those of their peers, and experience a loss of self-esteem if they consider their pictures less attractive or appealing than self-images posted by others. Another source of frustration and angst for social media users is the discouragement one experiences from posting pictures or messages on social media that fail to gain a desired number of "likes" from their friends. This can reinforce perceptions that one is unattractive to others or is not as popular or liked as wished. Kathy Young, a journalist with Britain's Telegraph periodical, points out that approximately 50 percent of 18-23 year olds admit that social media makes them feel more negative about their physical appearance. Young also reports that adolescent females spend an average of 12 minutes to prepare and edit a single selfie, and that one million adolescent females in the United Kingdom experience low self-esteem (Young, 2015).

Katy Waldman of Slate.com contends that social media has now largely replaced glamour beauty magazines, such as Cosmopolitan, Elle, Allure, and Vogue, as the major culprit contributing to poor self-esteem regarding physical appearance and body image among teenage females and young women. Waldman cites a study conducted by the American Academy of Facial Plastic and Reconstructive Surgery that revealed that 13 percent of plastic surgeons in the United States treated patients in 2013 who wanted plastic surgery procedures because they were unsatisfied with the way their pictures looked on social media. Additionally, 58 percent of plastic surgeons claimed to have seen an increase in patients under the age of 30 (Waldman, 2014). Against this backdrop, the skin care product manufacturer Dove announced in the fall of 2015 that it was launching a public relations campaign titled "#NoLikesNeeded" in an effort to bolster the self-esteem of young women by encouraging them not to measure themselves or their sense of self-worth by the number of "likes" their profile pictures generate on Facebook and other sites.

Others claim that social media contributes to low self-esteem and psychological issues in other ways. Kelsey Sunstrum argues that the tremendous effort expended by teenagers and young adults in crafting an idealized image of their lives on social media causes them to lose sight of their "real" self; she uses the term smiling depression to refer to individuals who present public profiles of themselves as happy and upbeat, but who experience depression in their true lives. Socialmedia, in many ways, serves as a means for individuals to gain the attention of others, and when one fails to attract this attention, the psychological response can be mildly to moderately traumatizing for some. Two-thirds of social media users admit having trouble falling asleep or relaxing shortly after spending time on sites, and half of social media users in the United States claim that the time spent on these sites negatively impacted their self-esteem (Gummow, 2014).

Interestingly, research indicates that having a larger number of friends on Facebook may lead to greater stress and, ultimately, a higher risk for depression. A study of 12-17 year olds revealed that persons with three hundred or more friends on Facebook had higher levels of the stress-causing hormone cortisol in their bloodstream than those with fewer Facebook friends; the study also found that anxiety was higher among persons with more than three hundred Facebook friends and that excessive amounts of time spent on Facebook also correlated with higher levels of cortisol (Kowalski, 2015). Furthermore, new warnings from doctors cite the taking of group selfies as a major source of lice transmission among teenagers in the United States. Since lice cannot jump, the close huddling that occurs when people attempt to fit into the photo frame for a selfie, which results in the hair of different people to come into contact, allows lice to spread to others.

Cyberbullying, the harassing or issuing of threats or efforts to destroy another person's reputation through the Internet, has also become a concern. Almost a quarter of American teenagers indicate that they are, or have been, the victim of cyberbullying, while 15 percent of teenagers admit that they have engaged in cyberbullying at some point (Ring, 2015). Many social media sites, including Facebook, have terms of agreement that prohibited the use of their sites for purposes of bullying and harassment of others, but the sheer number of users makes it virtually impossible to effectively monitor how individuals use their accounts.

Social media has additionally been criticized for serving as a digital cauldron of online bigotry, reflected in the posting of messages and content with explicit racist, sexist, misogynistic, and homophobic slurs and rhetoric. Yik Yak, a college-based social media site that allows users to post anonymous messages after downloading its app to one's mobile phone, has been more sharply criticized for enabling abusive and hateful comments to be posted with relative impunity. This drew nationwide attention in October 2015 when students at American University in Washington, D.C. launched campus-wide protests in opposition to the regular volume of racist and homophobic slurs and hate speech posted on its Yik Yak site. Similar incidents have occurred at several other colleges and universities.

TERMS & CONCEPTS

App: Downloadable software applications that allow users to install various programs or features on their smartphones or computers.

Cyberbullying: The use of social media sites to harass, insult, threaten, or negatively affect the reputation of another person.

Likes: A Facebook feature that signifies a user's approval or positive impression of pictures, messages, or other content posted by other users; other social media sites have similar features.

Selfie: A picture taken of oneself via the forward-facing camera feature now found on cell phones and iPads; selfies are often uploaded to one's social media accounts to be shared with others.

Sexting: The sending of sexually provocative or nude pictures of oneself to others via text messages.

Smartphone: A cell phone equipped with Internet capabilities that allow the phone to operate, in effect, as a mini computer.

Smiling Depression: A false public image that results when a person projects a sense of happiness to others around them, but in reality is secretly and internally depressed.

Snaking: The sharing of nude pictures that an individual receives through "sexting" with others for whom the image was not originally intended.

Tweets: Messages posted on an individual's Twitter account; these messages are limited to 140 characters.

Yik Yak: A social media site founded by Brooks Buffington and Tyler Droll in 2013 that allows users to post anonymous messages.

Bibliography

Baruth, K. (2014). "Psychological aspects of social media and mental well-being." *Journal of Human Services*, 34(1), 84-88.

Beese, J. (2015, June 20). "17 powerful Facebook stats for marketers and advertisers." SproutSocial.com. http://sproutsocial.com/insights/facebook-stats-for-marketers/

Gummow, J. (2014, March 7). "7 telltale signs social media is killing your self-esteem." Alternet.org. http://www.alternet.org/personal-health/7-telltale-signs-social-media-killing-your-self-esteem

Healy, M. (2010, Mau 18). "Teenage social media butterflies may not be such a bad idea." *Los Angeles Times*. Retrieved December 21, 2015 from http://articles.latimes.com/2010/may/18/science/la-sci-socially-connected-kids-20100518

Kowalski, K. (2015, December 9). "Too many Facebook friends?" *Science News for Students*. https://student.societyforscience.org/article/too-many-facebook-friends

Manago, A., Ward, L., Lemm, K., Reed, L., & Seabrook, R. (2015). "Facebook involvement, objectified body consciousness, body shame, and sexual assertiveness in college women and men." *Sex Roles*, 72(1/2), 1-14.

Perrin, A. (2015, October 8). "Social media usage: 2005-2015." PewInternet.org. http://www.pewinternet.org/2015/10/08/social-networking-usage-2005-2015/

Pew Research Center (2015). "Social networking fact sheet." PewInternet.org. http://www.pewinternet.org/fact-sheets/social-networking-fact-sheet/

Ring, M. (2015, August 6). "Teen depression and how social media can help or hurt." CNN.com. http://www.cnn.com/2015/08/05/health/teen-depression-social-media/

Ross, J. (2015, November 12). "Yik Yak might not encourage racism and threats. But it certainly enables them." *The Washington Post*. https://www.washingtonpost.com/news/the-fix/wp/2015/11/12/yik-yak-might-not-encourage-racism-and-threats-but-it-certainly-enables-them/

Salinger, T. (2015, August 25). "Selfies lead to 'social media lice' spreading head lice infestations among teens: Experts." *New York Daily News.* http://www.nydailynews.com/life-style/health/selfies-lead-social-media-lice-experts-article-1.2337345

"Self-portraits and social media: The rise of the 'selfie'." (2013, June 7). *BBC News.* http://www.bbc.com/news/magazine-22511650

Sunstrum, K. (2014, March 14). "How social media affects our self-perception." PsychCentral.com. http://psychcentral.com/blog/archives/2014/03/14/how-social-media-affects-our-self-perception/

Svrluga, S. (2015, October 22). "After racist comments online, American University criticizes popular social media site Yik Yak." *The Washington Post.* https://www.washingtonpost.com/news/grade-point/wp/2015/10/22/after-racist-comments-online-american-university-criticizes-popular-social-media-site-yik-yak/

Tobin, S. J., Vanman, E. J., Verreynne, M., & Saeri, A. K. (2015). "Threats to belonging on Facebook: Lurking and ostracism." *Social* Influence, 10(1), 31-42.

Waldman, K. (2014, March 14). "Move over glossy magazines. Now social media makes young girls hate themselves." Slate.com. http://www.slate.com/

Weale, S. (2015, November 10). "Sexting becoming 'the norm' for teens, warn child protection experts." *The Guardian.* http://www.theguardian.com/society/2015/nov/10/sexting-becoming-the-norm-for-teens-warn-child-protection-experts

Young, K. (2015, October 7). "#NoLikesNeeded: Dove's self-esteem project to protect our selfies." *The Telegraph.* http://www.telegraph.co.uk/beauty/body/Dove-No-Likes-Needed-campaign/

Suggested Reading

Bine, A. (2013, October 28). "Social media is redefining 'depression'." *The Atlantic.* http://www.theatlantic.com/health/archive/2013/10/social-media-is-redefining-depression/280818/

Boyd, D. (2015). *It's complicated: The* social *lives of networked teens.* New Haven, CT: Yale University Press.

Perez, J. (2015, March 17). "To like, or not to like: How social media affects self-esteem." *The Daily Sundial.* http://sundial.csun.edu/2015/03/to-like-or-not-to-like-how-social-media-effects-self-esteem/

Tiidenberg, K., & Gómez Cruz, E. (2015). "Selfies, image and the re-making of the body." *Body & Society,* 21(4), 77-102.

Tolly, K. (2014, October 21). "Does social media affect students' self-esteem?" *USA Today.* http://college.usatoday.com/2014/10/21/does-social-media-affect-students-self-esteem/

Justin D. García, Ph.D.

The Technological Revolution

ABSTRACT

This paper takes a look at the effects of modern technological developments on the evolution of the global economy. As a result, the reader gleans a better understanding of the links between human sociopolitical and economic development and the introduction of relevant technologies.

OVERVIEW

In 1985, US president Ronald Reagan stood before a group of Nobel Prize–winning scientists who had gathered at the White House. "You, on the cutting edge of technology," he said, "have already made yesterday's impossibilities the commonplace realities of today" (Simpson, 1988).

Those who had gathered on the White House lawn that day were among the most exceptional minds on the planet, presenting ideas that would change the course of history. Indeed, the scientific and technological breakthroughs humanity have marked extraordinary steps forward in its evolution. The steam engine ushered in a new era in transportation. The telephone linked together people who lived great distances from one another. More recently, the Internet and satellite technologies have created extensive networks throughout the globe. Humanity and technology seem to evolve together.

In the last two decades, modern technological advancements have done more than just benefit business, economic development, and public health. It has helped forge together the countless economies and political systems into one, global network. The process of "globalization" has created one broad-reaching economic institution, operating beyond the limitations of the modern nation-state.

This paper investigates the effects of modern technological developments on the evolution of the global economy. As a result, the reader gleans a better understanding of the links between human sociopolitical and economic development and the introduction of relevant technologies.

The Internet

History

In 1962, it was assumed that communications networks via telephonic technologies were about as far as science would go. At the World's Fair in 1964, a "Picturephone" was displayed proudly by communications giant AT&T, a mere update of a picture phone that was introduced at another World's Fair thirty years earlier.

Meanwhile, however, researchers were working behind closed doors to find a way to not only speak with colleagues over great distances, but to exchange data and information as well. The Advanced Research Projects Agency (ARPA) was established for this purpose as a means to create links between US military interests looking to defend against attacks by the Soviet Union. Gradually, ARPANET (the ARPA network) began to take on a less militaristic application, as only a few thousand computer terminals increased exponentially in volume. People were using the earliest forms of the Internet for data transfer, commerce, and other applications. As more and more people acquired computers, the Internet continued to grow exponentially. By the last decade of the twentieth century, the number of Internet host centers grew from four in the 1960s to 300,000 spanning the globe (Computer History Museum, 2006). Today, with the overwhelming number of personal and portable computers, tablets, and integrated cellular phone devices, there are few nations on earth in which one cannot find one or more avenues of access to the Internet.

E-Commerce

The Internet has done more than simply enhance communications capabilities for the post-industrial world. In truth, it has created entirely new markets and industries around the globe. By 2003, Internet "e-commerce" generated nearly US$7 billion in revenues, almost 10 percent of all sales. E-commerce has become the dominant form of business-to-business transactions, due in no small part to the fact that businesses can connect from all over the world without onerous interstate regulations and national interference. The relative simplicity, efficiency, and speed by which transactions take place over the Internet, therefore, have created a sort of "peer pressure" for those political institutions that do not embrace e-commerce in its current form are considered to be less of a value to potential business partners (Mann, 2001).

Hope for the Impoverished

In sub-Saharan Africa great potentials are seen to exist with the introduction of Internet access. In a region that has a poverty rate of 45 to 50 percent, countless individuals lack access to educational resources, social services, and business connections. They lack an ability to tap into key regional and international markets as well as training programs that can help them participate in the development of their own regional and national economies (The World Bank Group, 1996).

It is widely held, therefore, that facilitating access to the Internet can help reverse this trend (Juma & Moyer, 2008). In fact, many nations are investing in the development of information science technology to increase Internet activity. In South Africa, for example, a Soweto project was recently implemented to ensure that all 1.5 million students of that school district have access to the Internet. President Thabo Mbecki has made bridging the gap between those who have such access and those who do not (known as the "digital divide") a top priority, saying that technological literacy is key to the country's participation in the global economy (Itano, 2001).

What is it that the Internet does to alleviate poverty in the developing world and ensure continued prosperity in the industrialized world? The vast networks created by the Internet deliver information of vital import to virtually every industry. From increasing the speed by which payments are being made to monitoring outbreaks of disease, the Internet has critical applications for the agricultural sector. Education, the media, and manufacturing are among the myriad of industries that benefit on many levels from the possibilities offered by the "information superhighway" (Thomas, 2007). While the United States continues to lead the world in terms of Internet users and hosts, many more nations are becoming strong players in the new marketplaces created by this technological juggernaut. Brazil and China, for example, have long been considered on the cusp of economic power in the high technology industries but, thanks to their increased investment in this continuously evolving market, are now shifting the market profile away from a singularly dominated institution (Inarritu, et al., 2007).

Indeed, the Internet has become arguably the crown jewel in the global economy. Then again, as this paper has suggested, there are many nations that have less of a stake in the Internet market. For them, there are still other aspects of this post-industrial "technological **revolution**" that have relevance for the global economy.

Telecommunications

A decade after the American Civil War came to an end, Alexander Graham Bell, a speech expert, contacted a senior official at the Smithsonian Institution to seek his advice about a concept upon which he had stumbled. By passing an electrical current through a copper wire, Bell explained, a noise could be heard at the other end. When he brought his device to the Smithsonian, the secretary of the institution listened and indeed heard the transmission of a voice through Bell's technology. Bell, who was not an engineer or even all too familiar with electricity, asked the official, Joseph Henry, for his advice about how to develop the technology. Henry's response of Bell's "telephone" was one of the greater understatements in human history: "You have the germ of a great invention," he said. "Work at it" (MacKenzie, 2003).

Less than half a century after Bell's telephone was developed, there were fifteen million of the devices around the globe.

By the mid-twentieth century, however, land lines were not the only form of telephony. The development of "cellular" technology (which is based on the division of service areas into "cells") has been slow, to be sure. It was first introduced in 1947 but not widely researched as a private mode of communication until the late 1970s. Once it had been developed accordingly, however, demand far outstretched the supply of cellular technology within a decade (Bellis, 2008).

As of 2012, the number of cellular phones exceeded six billion around the globe (by contrast, in 1991, that figure reached sixteen million, according to the International Telecommunication Union). Forecasts have projected that the total number of cell phones worldwide will surpass the global population by 2014. In 2013, out of the world's estimated seven billion people, more than six billion had access to cellular phones.

As landline telephones linked people around the world beginning in the nineteenth century, cellular communications technology has successfully created linkages between people across the globe, even in the most remote locations, in the twenty-first century. While landline telephones have facilitated many forms of commerce, wireless technology takes communication to the next level, enabling business to be conducted in virtually any location and at any time. It has created a new degree of convenience for customers and entrepreneurs alike, facilitated corporate operations, improved competitiveness, and even helped enhance marketing abilities (Keng, Nah & Hong, 2006). Cellular technology, which today integrates telecommunications, Internet access, and other computing abilities, in essence creates small, mobile offices and, as a result, radically transforms the way business is conducted in the global economy.

While cellular technology first flourished in industrialized nations in North America, Europe, Australia, and East Asia, it is no longer localized to the wealthier countries of the world. Indeed, the developing world is increasingly becoming proficient with this technology, and it has helped their populations in a similar vein. Indeed, the introduction of cellular telephony has had a positive effect on the lives of those who live at or below the poverty level. Telephone poles used for landline phone networks, which are less extensive and far less reliable in rural areas, are being replaced with cell towers and consistent service. Trade networks have been increasingly forged and employment searches significantly aided. Even the cost of using a telephone is reduced with the myriad subscriber resources.

It is no surprise, therefore, that less developed countries (LDCs) are increasingly adopting cellular technologies in their pursuit of participation in the global economy. In four years, for example, the number of Nigerians with cell phones jumped exponentially from 370,000 in 2001 to 16.8 million in 2005. The Philippines has seen a similar explosion in cellular use, from about seven million subscribers in 2000 to forty million in 2006, making cellular technologies the preferred form of communication in that country (World Bank, 2006).

The contributions of cell phones and other modern forms of telecommunications technologies to the global economy are not limited to the confines of the business environment, either. Commerce can only successfully take place in a stable, conducive economic environment. Few regions can sustain indefinitely both global commerce and sociopolitical stability. It is in this arena that improved telecommunications also plays a beneficial role. Conflict prevention, mitigation, and resolution all require communication, and the extensive networks offered by cellular and other modern telecommunications systems mean parties will be able to connect and address divisive issues before they can cost a society a stake in the global economy (Wehrenfennig, 2007). From local crisis hotlines to international networks, modern telecommunications capabilities help maintain stability in an ever-developing international marketplace.

The world has come a great distance since the mid-nineteenth century when Alexander Graham Bell introduced his prototype telephone to the world. Since then, the international community has used it to connect to one another, both for personal contact and for business development. Modern applications of telecommunications technologies have taken this evolution even farther, enabling people in every corner of the world to connect to the global economy.

Indeed, modern technology has been a central figure in the development and maintenance of the global economy. Still, commercial connectivity is but one part of the international business system. There is still an issue regarding how best to transfer goods and services to international contacts.

Transportation

Technical innovations such as the Internet and cellular communications have made globalization much easier in a number of critical arenas. Arguably, one of the most important of these areas is that of cost: email is much less expensive than regular postal services and cellular subscriptions are less expensive than long-distance calling plans. As the global economy still requires methods for transferring goods and services between participating international parties, transportation must also be modernized to mitigate costs.

While the world may have changed significantly over the past two millennia, the need to transport people and goods has not. Humanity has long needed to find ways to traverse long distances, whether by land, sea ,or air. In the new global economy of the twenty-first century, the need for transportation is moot; the real issue is how to transport in a way that is both quick and inexpensive.

Shipping

In 2006, a controversy over foreign-owned shipping terminals in the United States cast a light on the evolution of transportation in the post-industrial era. In addition to the obvious implications of a foreign company operating a major port in another country as evidence of the burgeoning globalization of shipping, the attempt by a Dubai-based company to operate a port in the coastal United States also presents an interesting illustration of the increasing ease by which shipments are offloaded and transported.

Previously, shipping consisted of multiple legs—for example, a shipment of goods was delivered to a distribution port, where it was broken up and held in storage facilities awaiting placement onto trucks or trains (or both). The process was considered onerous, expensive, and time-consuming, not to mention localized to only a few ports that had the capacity to offload large bulk orders. The subsequent modification of shipping systems is reflective of the need to simplify the process, improve technologies, and increase the number of available ports.

As the computer became the primary conduit by which information is transferred, the shipping container (a lightweight casing that contains trailer-sized shipments) became the preferred method by which goods are distributed. One scholar noted that the simplification of shipping and transportation of goods with such containers has made an important impact on the global economy by making the process easier, less expensive, and far more adaptable to ports around the globe:

> You can call one of the big international ship lines, tell them to pick up your container in Bangkok, which is not a port, and tell them to deliver it in Dallas, which is not a port, and they will make the arrangements to get it ...where it needs to be (Levinson, cited in Postrel, 2006, par. 8).

Land Transport

Despite the obvious benefits of the global economy on commerce, and the great examples of new technologies that contribute to globalization, transportation technologies have remained more modest and, at times, outdated. The cause is something that is intrinsic to a "global" economy—geography. Goods and products must often travel great distances from port to port and they must still be transported over land to the customer. There are but two avenues for this transportation, trucks and train, and both are expensive. Trucks are the preferred land transportation, reaching virtually any location, whereas trains run along a set of transcontinental rail lines.

As suggested earlier, both of these modes of transport are indeed expensive. Rail transportation, for example, is faced with a difficult challenge by the volume of containers that can be carried on each car. As demand in the global economy continues to rise, more and more shipments must be carried on the rails. As a response, railroad cars with double the cargo capacity are being built and introduced, and more efficient train engines are being developed (Everett, 2008). In the preferred transportation field (trucking), increased volume also calls for more trucks on the roads, which requires the use of more fuel. Here too, engineers and policymakers are seeking more efficient engines as well as trucks that run on alternative fuel sources (Tucker, 2008). Then again, such technological developments are experiencing some hesitation from the industry, as some changes are being met with skepticism about the impact on business ("Surviving and thriving," 2008).

In an ever-developing global economy, it only follows that technology has evolved alongside it. In the case of shipping transportation, however, it appears that overwhelming demand for goods and products that come from this new world order has not yet fostered significant change. There have been some technological improvements, to be sure, but the world of transportation is still slowly adjusting to the changes in global commerce.

CONCLUSION

The British scientist William Kelvin was known as an expert in a variety of disciplines, including engineering and physics. However, his view of the future was somewhat uninformed and, in hindsight, ironically comedic. At the beginning of the twentieth century, he declared, "radio has no future"; "heavier-than-air flying machines are impossible"; and "x-rays will prove to be a hoax" ("Lord Kelvin's bad predictions," 2008).

Indeed, Lord Kelvin's prognostications proved far from the truth—technology has evolved far beyond the expectations of those who lived only a century ago. These advancements have coincided with the further evolution of international commerce. With the development of the global economy over the last few decades, the link between technology and the international economic system has been further strengthened, particularly as new innovations have been central to building on that new international regime.

This paper has taken a look at three areas of pivotal importance to the global economy. The Internet, for example, has provided strong links between business partners and individuals alike from every corner of the world. Cellular technology has also largely answered the limitations of the wire-based telecommunications world as well as facilitated mobility. Even transportation has seen upgrades that are vital to delivery of shipments to customers in even the most remote of locations.

As the global economy continues to take shape based on technological innovations, the question that remains for international participants is one of access. Fortunately, the prevalence of such technology has made such access more affordable for most socioeconomic strata. There remains considerable development to be done, particularly regarding delivery and increased access to such technology. Still, with the constant introduction of new systems, networks, and devices, the number of participants entering into and prospering as a result of their involvement will likely continue to grow.

TERMS & CONCEPTS

Cellular Technology: Telephony that relies on regional centers rather than land-based telephone networks.

Digital Divide: Differential between those who have Internet and other high technologies and those who do not.

E-Commerce: "Electronic commerce," a form of business transaction that takes place via the Internet.

Globalization: Economic trend by which national markets are increasingly being centralized on a global scale.

LDCs: Less developed countries.

Bibliography

Bellis, M. (2008). "Selling the cell phone." About.com: Inventors. http://inventors.about.com/library/weekly/aa070899.htm

Computer History Museum. (2006). "Internet history." http://www.computerhistory.org/internet%5fhistory/index.shtml

Ducruet, C., & Notteboom, T. (2012). "The worldwide maritime network of container shipping: spatial structure and regional dynamics." *Global Networks, 12*(3), 395–423.

Everett, B. (2008). "Talk of transport challenges is not all good." *Supply and Demand Chain Executive,* 9(4), 10.

Goodman, D.N. (2006). "Used phones drive third world wireless boom." *MSNBC.* http://www.msnbc.msn.com/id/ 15434609/

Inarritu, A.G., et al. (2007). "America no longer owns globalization." *New Perspectives Quarterly,* 25(1), 78-81.

Itano, N. (2001, August 15). "Fighting poverty online in South Africa." *Christian Science Monitor.* http://www.csmonitor.com/2001/0815/p6s3-woaf.html

Jin, B., & Park, N. (2013). "Mobile voice communication and loneliness: cell phone use and the social skills deficit hypothesis." *New Media and Society, 15*(7), 1094–1111.

Juma, C. & Moyer, E. (2008). "Broadband internet for Africa." *Science,* 320(5881), 1261.

Keng, S., Nah, F. & Hong, S. (2006). "Implications of wireless technology for mobile and ubiquitous commerce." *Journal of Database Management,* 17(4).

"Lord Kelvin's bad predictions." (2008). In Fripp (ed.) *Speaking of science.* Retrieved August 26, 2008, from Anecdotage.com. http://anecdotage.com/index.php?aid=14035

MacKenzie, C. (2003). Alexander Graham Bell. Kessinger Publishing. Google Books. http://books.google.com/

Mann, C.L. (2001, April). "The Internet and the global economy." International Symposium on

Network Economy and Economic Governance. http://unpan1.un.org/intradoc/groups/public/documents/UN/UNPAN000696.pdf

Postrel, V. (2006, March 23). "The container that changed the world." *New York Times* Online Edition. http://www.nytimes.com/2006/03/23/business/

Sharar, J. (2012). "Let them have their cell phone (and let them read to it too): technology, writing instruction and textual obsolescence." *Changing English: Studies in Culture and Education, 19*(4), 415–422.

Simpson, J.B. (1988). "Ronald Reagan." In J.B. Simpson (ed). *Simpson's Contemporary Quotations.* Bartleby.com. http://www.bartleby.com/63/17/3217.html

"Surviving and thriving." (2008). *Trailer/Body Builders,* 49(6), 28-34.

Thomas, D. (2007). "Teaching technology in low socioeconomic areas." *Technology Teacher,* 67(3), 4-8.

Tucker, R. (2008). "GAO cites transit shortfalls." *Women's Wear Daily,* 195(52), 10.

Wehrenfennig, D. (2007). "Do you hear me now?" Conference Papers -International Studies Association, 1.

World Bank. (2006). "2006 information and communications for development." World Bank Publications. Retrieved August 25, 2008, from Google Books. http://books.google.com/

The World Bank Group. (1996, May). "Poverty in sub-Saharan Africa." http://www.worldbank.org/afr/findings/english/find73.htm

Suggested Reading

Burnson, P. (2002). "Hong Kong seizes on the technology tool." *World Trade,* 15(12).

Campbell, H. A. (2013). "Religion and the Internet: a microcosm for studying Internet trends and implications." *New Media and Society, 15*(5), 680–694.

"E-commerce yet to improve developing world." (2002). *World Trade,* 15(4), 14.

"Going digital." (1998). *Fortune,* 137(1), 19-24.

Hoske, M.T. (2000). "Technology enables economic success, responsibilities: Economist." *Control Engineering,* 47(7).

Michael P. Auerbach, M.A.

Technology & Medicine

Overview

The development of technology, medicine, and social structures has been intertwined since the creation of the research university in the eighteenth century. One of the most significant changes has been the transformation of the clinical perspective to the molecular perspective. The challenge lies, therefore, in the ethical implications of the development of biotechnologies that can change the human organism on a genetic and molecular level.

It is not easy to decide where to begin a history of science, especially when speaking about the relations between medicine, society, and technology. One could begin with the first classical physicians, Hippocrates (ca. 460 BC- 379 BC) and Galen (ca. 129 AD-216 AD). Indeed, into the mid-eighteenth century, the pendulum of medical wisdom swung between these two names, since knowledge until that time had to be proven by reference to a classical text.

In the history of medicine, Galen is known not only as the first practitioner with a vast anatomical knowledge but also for performing difficult operations that required the use of sophisticated instruments. He is even reputed to have undertaken the first brain surgeries (Toledo-Pereyra, 1973). For centuries, his and Hippocrates's ideas were most often referred to as the defining criteria of all medical knowledge. Up to the mid-eighteenth century, much progress was made in the application of instruments, devices, and drugs that would, in many ways, have been readily available for scholars in line with Galen or Hippocrates.

However, another beginning could be made in the nineteenth century, when modern science was combined with industrialization and technology came to the forefront with the emergence of electricity. Other accounts could focus on the discovery of penicillin or make the case that with the discovery of DNA, a new age dawned in which life could increasingly be directly manipulated, thus pinpointing the decisive moment in medical development to the twentieth century.

However, the incident that may have been most crucial for the development of medicine, and subsequently the use of technology in medicine, came in 1737, when the newly founded University of Goettingen persuaded the famous anatomist Albrecht von Haller to become one of the key figures of its faculty. While at the university, von Haller pioneered an important innovation in the education system by combining both research and education within his professorship (Lenoir, 1981a; Cunningham, 2002, 2003).

From that time forward, in ways they never had before, students lived and worked in close proximity to the creation of knowledge and the innovative application of instruments. For two elemental fields of medical knowledge–anatomy and physiology–this resulted in a spurt in knowledge creation, and by the end of the century, knowledge about physiology had exploded at such a rate that the scientific vocabulary could not keep up. Toward the end of the century, physiologists and anatomists–on the verge of creating the ultimate life science, biology–resorted to the language of the new critical philosophy of Immanuel Kant to find ways of expressing their findings (Lenoir, 1981; Stingl, 2008). It was this course that prepared the way for the breakthrough development of medicine.

Birth of the Clinic

After the emergence of anatomy and physiology, the next important step certainly was the "birth of the clinic" and the emergence of the clinical gaze, as it was called by Michel Foucault (1963). Following the French revolution, two developments set in: the myth of a nationally organized medical profession and the myth that in an untroubled and therefore healthy society, disease would disappear. The effort to realize these two myths, Foucault claimed, rendered the medical doctor a politician. The doctor's gaze became a force; the doctor, considered as all-wise, could see through the veil that covered the eyes of normal men and see the underlying reality. The effectual change from ancient to modern times thus lay not in a transformation of this idea of the doctor as wise but in the theory behind it.

As scientific research increased during this period, knowledge was increasingly perceived as fragile and dynamic. With the installation of the clinic, however, an abode was created for the accumulation of knowledge and its changes. The clinic was also storage for the technological devices employed in modernity. When the clinic was then turned into a facility for research and education as well, it became the prime force behind medical innovation.

Genetics & Biotechnology

This turn was amplified by the emergence of genetics and biotechnology, where the anonymous laboratory became a second stage for the creation of what can be called biopolitics, a political system in which populations' bodies are subject to government control.

Nikolas Rose has argued that as of the early twenty-first century, doctors, clinicians, and researchers have essentially changed their gaze (2007). While most people are still tied to the molar or somatic level, clinicians and experimenters view the human organism as a DNA-based bio-chemical system that needs to be optimized. They have, according to Rose, a molecular gaze, rather than a clinical gaze (2007).

APPLICATIONS

The Clinic versus the Laboratory

Whether the clinic or the laboratory is the main stage for the development of medical research and technology–and whether the two should be integrated into one site–has been disputed. In the history of physiology, anatomy, neurology, medicine, and psychology, the distinction between the practices of the clinic and the laboratory continued throughout the nineteenth century. Clinicians would not trust "artificial" lab results, while experimenters shunned the individualized experiences and ideas of clinical practitioners as lacking validity and universality. Pitted against each other by their own versions of objectivity and naturalism, clinicians and experimenters divided and reunited time and again.

This theme was repeated in the narrative structure of medical discourse and the technological development of medicine. In the early decades of the twentieth century, the discourse involved renowned scholars from related fields like Lawrence Henderson and Walter Cannon, whose experimental works in physiology became seminal. Henderson, an "occasional sociologist," is also credited with, at least in part, having introduced the idea that the patient-doctor relationship must be described in terms of "an equilibrating social system" (to apply the terminology of Vilfredo Pareto) in which the doctor helps the patient return to normal functioning within society. Whether Henderson or his younger Harvard colleague Talcott Parsons (who worked on the idea around the same time and had approached Henderson for advice on his project) was the actual author of this idea is not entirely clear, but both men used it in their lectures (Stingl, 2008). Parsons introduced the idea that a patient must be seen as occupying a social role, the sick role. Changes in technology, therefore, can be described in regard to the changes in the sick role as part of the social system in which it is embedded. This took a new turn in the 1960s in American medicine, when critical scholars began arguing that progress in medical technology does not necessarily translate into better health care for everyone. Quite the contrary, it can lead to a widening of the gap between social classes with only the wealthy able to afford expensive new treatments and the poor unable to receive other, less expensive treatments because medical progress has made them obsolete.

Certainly, surgical medical technology has already progressed to a stage that not long ago was considered science fiction. The classic idea of the surgeon's job being equitable to that of a "butcher with precision" has become outmoded due to the evolution of less invasive surgical instruments. Contemporary surgeons may employ micro-surgery and robots, as well as telemedicine, a technique in which the surgeon is not even in direct contact with the patient but controls a robot from some other location. These developments require more than just a steady hand and knowledge of human anatomy; they also necessitate that surgeons keep up with the fast paced changes of computers and software tools. The latest developments in medical technology seem to realize the dream of nano-surgery, which allows the direct manipulation of single tissue cells or neurons. To keep pace with all of these developments, surgeons' education and training has had to change.

Medication & Drugs

One of the most major changes in the late twentieth and early twenty-first centuries is the industry around, and the application of, medication and drugs. The traditional model of campus-based academic research is long past. While governments still finance much research taking place at universities and state-run laboratory facilities, the bulk of research is done either at pharmaceutical companies or, at the very least, largely financed by these companies, even if the research does occur on college or university campuses. A major difference in this regard between Europe and the United States must be taken into account, since in many European countries higher education is state sponsored, while in the US, many facilities of higher education are private entities with their own economic interests at heart. This also means that researchers in European countries, such as Germany, cannot benefit in the same way from the profits garnered by their innovations.

The use of drugs and medication has also been subject to change. Pharmaceuticals are now often used not to cure or treat an illness but to improve conditions of life and livelihood. Whether used for enhancement (e.g. sexual or sports performance) or to overcome a cognitive disability, new drugs have enabled individuals to intentionally intervene into their own neuro-chemical processes, thus re-creating personhood in the image of neuro-chemical selves, as Nikolas Rose (2007) has argued.

Biopolitics

This recreation of the self is being increasingly addressed within the field of biopolitics, which, according to Michel Foucault, describes the technologies of power or style of government that regulate a population by disciplining its biological aspects. Beginning in the eighteenth century, these technologies began emerging in the form of dispositives of power/knowledge that account for the possibility of modifying and controlling the processes of life or the living being. In light of biopolitics and in the wake of Foucault, Girogio Agamben has argued that one must therefore distinguish between bios (a the biological/organic life) and zoe (which is life itself, purposeful and, to some degree, can be called the "spiritual life").

Recent developments in technology have also opened access to the "inner self" in another way, namely through devices such as Computed Axial Tomography (CAT), Postitron Emission Tomography (PET), and (functional) Magnetic Resonance Imaging (fMRI). Having come a long way from the classic X-Ray, these technologies enable a wealth of insight into the body, even into the processes of the human brain. While some enthusiasts hope that it will one day be possible to even read minds by use of these technologies, interpreting the images these technologies deliver is often as complicated as interpreting a literary classic, as Joseph Dumit has illustrated with PET scans (2004).

VIEWPOINTS

Developments in medical technology spur dreams in other directions also. Members of the post-humanist or trans-humanist movement believe that the salvation of human race lies in the technological augmentation of the human body, whether it is through memory chips that transfer human consciousness into computers or through the creation of cybernetic organisms (cyborg). Technological developments in recent years, at the very least, point to innovations that will replace lost limbs or equip blind people with nearly perfect artificial eyes.

At the same time, access to the genetic make-up of human beings has created a situation where certain physical or mental impairments can be discovered before birth through prenatal diagnosis and treated at a very early stage. In other cases, parents can choose not to have a child because of the likelihood of it having an impairment. These developments have incited heated debates in the field of bioethics in the past decades, as Fox and Swazey (2008) have recounted.

Social Effects of Medical Technology

The development of less- or non-invasive surgeries has had several social effects. First of all, it requires different kinds of training for doctors. Beyond medical training, an ever higher rate of "computer literacy" has to be considered a prerequisite for medical practice. This puts an older generation of surgeons at a disadvantage as well as prospective doctors and students from developing countries or of lower social classes.

But this question, which certainly falls into the realm of social justice, not only affects those who may be excluded from medical education but also, at an even larger degree, affects patients' access to medical care, including their choice of doctor. For example, the Internet has made it also possible for patients to consult with experts worldwide, and even surgery can be undertaken remotely from any location in the world by application of robot-arms, but these technologies are also available only to those who have the information and resources to access them.

Another important player in medical development is the advance of pharmaceutical companies. A multi-billion dollar business, the pharmaceuticals market is one of the most profitable in the world. These corporations are the most important source of financing for medical research and have faced criticism for their influence on scientific studies on the effectiveness and side effects of medications and their political lobbying efforts. Critical voices such as David Healy have made a case against the new "medical oikumene" of researchers, government, and the pharmaceutical industry, with pharmaceutical companies often commissioning ghostwriters to write articles published under the names of renowned researchers (2004).

Increasingly, patients are turning toward alternative medicine. Though Asian healing traditions are often either overestimated or discounted, thorough scientific investigation reveals that they can have genuine benefits. Body disciplines such as yoga or Qi-gong can help attune the senses to the body, helping individuals locate pain or sub-optimal functioning long before damage becomes permanent or life-threatening, thereby also making these practices cost-effective. In cases of children with ADHD or autism spectrum disorders (see Levenson), practicing Aikido has proven to be an effective technique for improving motor and social skills.

An important issue in medical ethics is the question of human test subjects. Since pharmaceuticals are a competitive business and, at the same time, safety regulations demand ever higher numbers of participants to increase reliability and validity, testing new drugs on human subjects has become more precarious for pharmaceutical companies. Many turn to developing countries, where they can find large numbers of willing subjects who will accept small financial compensations. These subjects are also "medication naïve," meaning that they have not previously been exposed to similar medication and are therefore better test subjects. Of course, this outsourcing of human testing is not without ethical concerns. Critics of pharmaceutical companies have questioned whether test subjects are apprised of what they are actually agreeing to participate in and whether experimental treatments undertaken in developing countries are unnecessarily dangerous to test subjects.

TERMS & CONCEPTS

Bioethics: Ethical concerns regarding human subjects.

Biopower: A term introduced by Michel Foucault to describe a technology of power that states apply in order to govern a population by subjugating the body itself to the discipline and regulative regime of biopolitics.

Functional Magnetic Resonance Imaging (fMRI): Technology that measures brain activity by recording changes in blood oxygenation and blood flow within the brain in response to certain stimuli. The images produced by fMRIs are subject to interpretation, however, and the technology is somewhat imperfect as there can be a temporal gap of up to a second between a stimulus and the observed reaction in the blood flow.

MRI: Magnetic Resonance Imaging (MRI) makes use of the magnetic specificity of elements in the human body to create images of the internal structures and functions of the body, offering imaging technique similar to, but more clear than, Computer Tomography.

Neuroethics: The ethical questions raised by modern neurology and its capacities to not only provide an insight into the processes of thought, putting into question the idea of autonomy, but also of manipulating mind and memory through enhancement drugs.

Positron Emission Tomography (PET): Like MRI and fMRI, PET is an imaging technique that makes visible certain processes occurring within the body. For this purpose, a slightly radioactive substance is introduced into the body to travel through the bloodstream. Given a certain stimulus, the bloodstream can then be mapped, producing an image of the region of activity.

Sick Role: In his 1940 lectures on medical sociology, Harvard sociologist Talcott Parsons (1902-79) introduced the concept of the sick role, which he later wrote about in The Social System (1951). Being sick, from this perspective, is for the patient not simply a matter of fact, but rather comes with a set of social expectations which constitute an actual role in society. In this role, the sick person is exempted from other roles in society (e.g. his or her role at work or in the family) and considered to not be responsible for his or her condition. On the other hand, a sick person is expected to actively pursue treatment and seek out expert help.

Bibliography

Agamben, G. (1998). *Homo sacer.* Stanford, CA: Stanford University Press.

Blackman, T. (2013). "Care robots for the supermarket shelf: A product gap in assistive technologies." *Ageing & Society,* 33, 763-781.

Blume, S. S. (2013). "Medical innovations: Their diffusion, adoption, and critical interrogation." *Sociology Compass,* 7, 726-737.

Cross, S. J., & Albury, W. R. (1987). *Walter B. Cannon, L. J. Henderson, and the organic analogy.* Osiris, 3, 162-192.

DeGrandpre, R. (2006). *The cult of pharmacology.* Durham, NC: Duke University Press.

Dumit, J. (2004). *Picturing personhood.* Cambridge, MA: MIT Press.

Foucault, M. (1963). *Naissance de la clinique* [*The birth of the clinic*]. Paris, France: Presses Universitaires de France.

Fox, R., & Swazey, J. P. (2008). *Observing bioethics.* Oxford, UK: Oxford University Press.

Healy, D. (2004). *Let them eat Prozac.* New York, NY: New York University Press.

Kay, L. (2000). *Who wrote the book of life?* Stanford, CA: Stanford University Press.

Lenoir, T. (1980). "Kant, Blumenbach, and vital materialism in German Biology." *Isis,* 71, 77-108.

Lenoir, T. (1981a). "The Göttingen School and the development of transcendental naturphilosophie in the romantic era." *Studies in the History of Biology,* 5, 111-205.

Lenoir, T. (1981b). *The strategy of life.* Chicago, IL: Chicago University Press.

Lupton, D. (2014). "The commodification of patient opinion: the digital patient experience economy in the age of big data." *Sociology of Health & Illness,* 36, 856-869.

Nielsen, C., Funch, T., & Kristensen, F. (2011). "Health technology assessment: Research trends and future priorities in Europe." *Journal of Health Services Research & Policy,* 16(s2), 6-15.

Noury, M., & López, J. (2017). "Nanomedicine and personalised medicine: Understanding the personalisation of health care in the molecular era." *Sociology of Health & Illness,* 39(4), 547-565.

Phillips, C. (2012). "The constitutive nature of vital signs: An examination of the sociality of technology in medicine." *Qualitative Inquiry,* 18, 868-875.

Rose, N. (2007). *The politics of life itself.* Princeton, NJ: Princeton University Press.

Safire, W. (2002). "Visions for a new field of neuroethics." In S. J. Marcus (Ed.), *Neuroethics: Mapping the field* (pp. 3-9). Washington, DC: Dana Press.

Starr, P. (1982). *The social transformation of American* medicine. New York, NY: Basic Books.

Stingl, A. (2008). *The house of Parsons: The biological vernacular from Kant to James, Weber and Parsons.* Lampeter, UK: Edward Mellen Press.

Toledo-Pereyra, L. H. (1973). "Galen's contribution to surgery." *Journal of the History of* Medicine *and Allied Sciences,* 28, 357-375.

Warner, J. H. (1991). "Ideals of science and their discontents in late nineteenth-century America." *Isis,* 82, 454-478.

Suggested Reading

Ashcroft, R. E. (2003). "Kant, Mill, Durkheim? Trust and autonomy in bioethics and politics." *Studies in the History and Philosophy of Biological and Biomedical Sciences,* 34, 359-366.

Beaulieu, A. (2002). "Images are not the (only) truth: Brain mapping, visual knowledge, and iconoclasm." *Science,* Technology *and Human Values,* 27, 53-87.

Blakemore, C. (2002). "From the 'public understanding of science' to the scientist's understanding of the public." In S. J. Marcus (Ed.), *Neuroethics: Mapping the field* (pp. 212-221). Washington, DC: Dana Press.

Broman, T. (1989). "University reform in medical thought at the end of the eighteenth century." *Osiris,* 5, 36-53.

Craver, C. F. (2005). "Beyond reduction mechanisms, multi-field integration and the unity of neuroscience." *Studies in the History and Philosophy of Biological and Biomedical Sciences,* 36, 373-395.

Cross, S. J., & Albury, W. (1987). "Walter B. Cannon, L. J. Henderson and the organic analogy." *Osiris,* 3, 165-192.

Cunningham, A., & Williams P. (1993). "De-centring the 'big picture': The origin of modern science and the modern origins of science." *British Journal for History of Science,* 26, 407-432.

Cunningham, A. (1988). "Getting the game right: some plain words on the identity and invention of science." *Studies in the History and Philosophy of Science,* 19, 365-389.

Cunningham, A. (2002). "The pen and the sword: Recovering the disciplinary identity of physiology and anatomy before 1800 I: Old physiology - the pen." *Studies in History and Philosophy of Biological and Biomedical Science,* 33, 631-665

Cunningham, A. (2003). "The pen and the sword: Recovering the disciplinary identity of physiology and anatomy before 1800 II: Old anatomy - the sword." *Studies in History and Philosophy of Biological and Biomedical Science,* 34, 51-76

Elia, J., Ambrosini, P., & Berettini, W. (2008). "ADHD characteristics I: Concurrent comorbidity patterns in children and adolescents." *Child and Adolescent Psychiatry and Mental Health,* 2, 1-9.

Frazzetto, G.,Keenan, S., & Singh, I. (2007). "'Il bamini e le droghe': The right to ritalin vs. the right to childhood in Italy." *Biosocieties,* 2, 393-413.

Gross, M. (2014). "Communitarian bioethics: Three case studies." *Society,* 51, 354-361.

Harrington, A. (1987). *Medicine,* mind and the double brain. Princeton, NJ: Princeton University Press.

Hunt, R. D. (2006a). "The neurobiology of ADHD." *Medscape Psychiatry and Mental Health,* 11.

Hunt, Robert D. (2006b). "Functional roles of norepinephrine and dopamine in ADHD." *Medscape Psychiatry and Mental Health,* 11.

Illes, J., & Racine, E. (2005). "Imaging or imagining? A neuroethics challenge informed by genetics." *American Journal of Bioethics,* 5, 5-18.

Ioannidis, J. P. A. (2008). "Effectiveness of antidepressants: A myth constructed from a thousand randomized trials?" *Philosophy, Ethics, and Humanities in* Medicine, 3.

Kristoffersson, A., Coradeschi, S., Loutfi, A., & Severinson-Eklundh, K. (2011). "An exploratory study of health professionals' attitudes about robotic telepresence technology. "*Journal of* Technology *in Human Services,* 29, 263-283.

Levenson, M. (2003). "Choosing Aikido: An opportunity for children with Asperger's syndrome." www.aiki-extensions.org

Michael, M., & Rosengarten, M. (2012). "Medicine: Experimentation, politics, emergent bodies." *Body & Society,* 18(3/4), 1-17.

Rabinbach, A. (1990). *The human motor: Energy, fatigue and the modernity.* Berkeley, CA: University of California Press.

Rabinow, P. (1989). *French modern: Norms and forms of the social environment.* Cambridge, MA: MIT Press

Rabinow, P. (1996). *Making PCR: A story of biotechnology.* Chicago, IL: University of Chicago Press.

Yock, P. G., et al. (2015). *Biodesign: The process of innovating medical* technologies. Cambridge, UK: Cambridge UP.

Alexander Stingl, Ph.D.

Technology & Societal Development

OVERVIEW

It has been convincingly argued that the development of societies rests at least in part on the developments of their technologies. For example, preindustrial societies developed from nomadic familial units to more extended villages and towns as they were enabled by technology to advance from hunting and gathering societies to horticultural and eventually to agrarian societies. With the advent of the Industrial Revolution, society experienced a more marked and less gradual change as jobs and populations became more centered around the artifacts of technology. As a result, a shift occurred from extended to nuclear families and the concomitant development of societal institutions to take the place of the extended family in many instances. Society continues to change and development as postindustrial technology requires society to rethink such basic concepts as gender roles. Sociologists today must take a multidisciplinary approach in order to better study and understand the processes and effects of the influence of postindustrial technology on globalization, and the way that society must develop and change in order to meet the needs of its members in the postindustrial age.

> I remember as recently as the 1980s giving a speech at a convention regarding the use of technology and how it had changed our lives. As an example, I referred to a once-popular science-fiction franchise in which the crew of a spaceship boldly walked up to doors that automatically opened and put magical three-inch square plastic disks into their computer workstations to call up data from stored memory. Although these things had been science-fiction wonders in the 1960s when they were first introduced, I reminded my audience that although we might not be sailing through space, the doors to the convention center had automatically opened for us that morning, and we all put three-inch disks into our own computer workstations every day. Several decades later, we can add other common uses of technology to the list: computers that take dictation and even talk back to us, wireless communication devices, and electronic pads that can display books automatically downloaded from afar or take notes as we work in the field. These tools are more than toys, however.

In many ways, they have changed the way that we do business and live our lives. Because of technological advances, our society has moved from one that is primarily industrial to one that is primarily postindustrial in nature. Jobs today increasingly require one to be able to use newer technologies, and growing numbers of jobs require one to be able to develop new technology. As technology advances, society changes and grows in response, adapting to and incorporating it.

It would be difficult to argue that technology does not shape the development of society. At its most basic, technology is the application of scientific methods and knowledge to the attainment of industrial or commercial objectives. Technology includes products, processes, and knowledge.

According to Gehard Lenski, societal development occurs along a continuum of sociocultural evolution, the process by which a society develops through the growth of its stores of cultural information. One of the catalysts for societal growth, in this theory, is the society's level of technology, a specially defined term referring to information about the ways in which material resources of the environment can be used to satisfy the needs and desires of human beings.

Stages of Sociocultural Evolution

Preindustrial

In Lenski's theory, there are several stages of sociocultural evolution. The first stage, preindustrial, comprises several levels, starting with the hunting-and-gathering society. These societies have minimal technology (e.g., spears, gathering baskets), and their members rely on whatever food and fiber they can easily acquire. Hunting-and-gathering societies are typically organized into nomadic groups, often composed primarily of extended family members, to better help them sustain themselves without actually cultivating the land. To further aid in the endeavors of hunting and gathering, these groups are typically geographically widely dispersed so that each group can have the best possible range of environmental resources to sustain its members. Because hunting-and-gathering societies tend to be organized around blood ties, family is particularly important, issues of authority and influence revolve around kinship, and social differentiation is usually based on such variables as gender, age, and family background.

The next preindustrial stage of society is the horticultural society. These societies subsist not only on readily available foods, as in hunting-and-gathering societies, but also on plant seeds and crops. The advent of a horticultural society is enabled by the development of the appropriate technologies, including basic digging and cultivation tools, irrigation systems, and fertilization techniques. Horticultural societies are typically much less nomadic than hunting-and-gathering societies because of their need to cultivate the land, at least through one growing season. They place greater emphasis on producing technology in the shape of tools and household objects than do hunting—and-gathering societies.

As the tools of the horticultural societies advance beyond the basics necessary to cultivate the land, they move into the final preindustrial stage of society: the agrarian society. Although agrarian societies are also engaged in the production of food from crops, technological innovations such as plows and irrigation allow them to do so much more efficiently. In addition, because of improvements in technology, agrarian societies tend to be larger than either hunting-and-gathering or horticultural societies. Technology also encourages the members of agrarian societies to become more specialized than in other types of preindustrial societies, as the wider use of technology combined with these societies' relative stability allows their members to focus on specialized tasks. This leads to higher degrees of specialization and even greater stability. Agrarian societies are marked by a greater permanence than hunting-and-gathering or horticultural societies, which allows them to store greater surpluses and create artifacts (e.g., statues, monuments) that can be passed from one generation to another.

Industrial Revolution

Societies remained in one of the three preindustrial modes until the Industrial Revolution in the late 18th and early 19th centuries. Industrialization brought with it new sources of power to perform tasks, a dependence on mechanization to produce goods and services, and new inventions to facilitate agricultural and industrial production. Because the technology associated with industrialization tended to be centralized, the populations of these societies became more centralized as well. This led to increasing urbanization and the creation of more and larger cities. For many societies, the concentration of technology and the jobs that it produced within urban centers resulted in an irrevocable transition from an agrarian economy to an industrial one. Due to the advances in technology and the resulting industrialization, it was no longer necessary for a single individual or even a single family to focus on producing a single product or service. This enabled factory production, division of labor, and the concentration of industries and populations within certain geographical areas. Society became less dependent on the family as many workers left home to work in the new industrial centers, and the family lost its unique position as a source of power and authority within society. Industrialization meant that villages and other small communities became increasingly less independent, relying on each other for the exchange of goods and services. Industrialization also necessitated the creation of a more formalized education system in order to teach its members to use and advance its technology. A summary of Lenski's theory of technology's effects on societal development is shown in Table 1.

Postindustrial Society

Perhaps the best illustrations of the effects of technology on societal development are those that we have seen in our own lifetimes. Although Lenski's theory ends with the industrialization of society, most observers now think that we have entered a new era of technology and concomitant sociocultural development. Today's postindustrial societies have an economy that is primarily based on the processing and control of information and the provision of services rather than the production of goods or other tangible products.

The development of digital computer technology and its evolution into the powerful computers, tablets, and smartphones of today have in many ways revolutionized the way that we live our lives. In the 1980s and 1990s, it was considered a luxury for a teenager to have a phone in her or his own bedroom, and to have one's own phone number at that age was remarkable. A mere ten or twenty years later, it seemed that virtually all teenagers (and many children much younger) had their own phones that they carried with them everywhere. The teenager of the twentieth century was often restricted to using the phone for a set period of time each day. In the twenty-first century, not only do many teenagers not have such restrictions, they seemingly try to constantly keep in touch with others via calling, text messaging, e-mailing, and social networks.

In many ways, these are minor changes. However, when one thinks about, the culture of modern youth increasingly demands not only constant contact but a greater monetary investment in equipment than ever before. Societal norms are gradually changing to expect these things, while the person who prefers to remain at home and read a book becomes someone who does not fit in with the rest of society.

Similarly, the use of computers and other technological innovations in the workplace has changed not only the way that we do business but also some basic

Table 1: Lenski's Analysis of Technology, Division of Labor, & Stratification of Society

Type of Society	Level of Technology	Division of Labor	Amount of Economic Surplus	Political Domination by a Few over the Masses	Extent of Stratification
Hunting and gathering	Simple tools lor gathering food and hurtling animals	Minimal, except for that based on age and sex	Minimal	Raic	Minimal
Horticultural	More advanced than hunting and gather ing (includes digging tools. Iiocs, some irrigation and fertilization of crops)	Greater than in hunting and gathering societies	Greater than in hunting and gathering societies	Greater than in hunting and gathering societies	Greater than in hunting and gathering societies
Agrarian	More advanced than horticultural societies (includes metallurgy pious, arid harnessing of animals)	Greater tlun in horticultural societies	Greater than in horticultural societies	Extensive	Much greater than in other types of societies
Industrialized	Highly advanced	Extensive	Extensive	Less than in agninan societies	Less than in agninan societies

(from Stockand, p. 166)

tenets of more traditional societies. For example, although the historical norms regarding the division of labor between the sexes are similar across cultures, to a great extent these norms are changing in postindustrial societies. Many of the jobs in industrial and postindustrial societies no longer require the physical strength necessary in hunting- and-gathering societies for one to support one's family. Success frequently depends on mental rather than physical skill, an area in which neither gender has an innate advantage.

Further, as women earn more gender equality in the workplace, they expect (and need) more gender equality in the home as well. Although some couples continue to work best within the traditional paradigm of a wife and mother who stays home and tends to the children and household while the husband and father goes out and works for a living, relatively new educational opportunities for women and the changing nature of many jobs mean that more and more women are also working outside the home. Some families handle this situation by having the woman not only work at a full-time job but also try to fulfill the domestic responsibilities at the same pre-career level. Other families attempt to compromise by having the woman only work part time outside the home, lowering their standards at home, or hiring someone to do the domestic tasks for them, such as a housecleaner, a personal chef, or a nanny. Still other families attempt to work out a more equitable division of domestic responsibilities between wife and husband. Because of postindustrial reliance on high technology, telecommuting is another option that can help couples balance these responsibilities. Modern society can adapt in order to accommodate all these approaches. Because of technology, society's expectations for gender roles are changing, becoming much less rigidly defined than they have traditionally been in the past.

Today's technological advances have implications not only for economically developed postindustrial societies but for societies that are still developing economically as well. Modernization theory posits that less developed countries will eventually industrialize in the manner of more developed countries and that the process of modernization will gradually improve the quality of life for their citizens due to political and economic forces. Modernization is thought to affect virtually all countries that have been affected by technological change. Thompson examines this phenomenon in terms of technology and societal development (1974). He contends that large social groupings of human beings have been growing larger throughout history. At first, families bonded together to form small communities so that they could hunt better and have a higher probability of success. As societies progress from horticultural to agricultural, these groups tend to get larger as specialization takes place, with some families continuing to farm, others making and selling products, and so forth; this eventually leads to the rise of villages and larger communities, all of which require societal development to progress. Although these changes may be evolutionary, the advent of industrialization in a society often has revolutionary effects on society. For example, the opportunity to find better jobs in industry than in agriculture leads many individuals leave the farm and head to the city. This creates urban centers that require different approaches to living together. The extended family is replaced by the nuclear family, and young couples move out of their parents' homes to start their own families. In some ways, this also contributes to the number of people living in poverty, as young women in particular choose to raise families on their own rather than return to their families of origin. Urbanization also lends itself to greater migration and social mobility, which in turn results in greater social distance, again requiring society to adapt and change in response to the new requirements of its members as based on their responses to technology.

APPLICATIONS

The globalization enabled by modern advanced technology is another such revolution. Technological innovations mean that in many cases, individuals no longer need to be collocated in order to work together, resulting in social isolation in some ways and the creation of a larger, global society in others as communications around the world occur almost instantaneously. The advances in technology also may mean that to get ahead, more education is required, not only to use technology but to develop it as well. This may result in an inversion of status between adult children and their parents, leading to a cult of youth and the need to develop social institutions to take care of the elderly, as their geographically and socially mobile offspring are no longer able to take care of them personally.

In addition, the globalization enabled by advances in modern technology can affect less developed societies as well. In many ways, once-separate societies are becoming closer despite their geographical separation. With business practices such as outsourcing and offshoring and technologies that make inexpensive and instantaneous communication a reality, a business in India or the Philippines, for example, can provide customer service for a corporation located in the United States. For this to be successful, however, the societies will have to become more similar so that they can more easily work together.

CONCLUSION

Throughout recorded history and even prehistory, technology has affected the development of societies. Far from being only a fact of historical interest, however, this phenomenon is still occurring today. However, to truly be able to understand and respond to the rapid changes in society that result from rapid advances in technology, sociologists need to become more multidisciplinary. As pointed out by Hansen (2004), early pioneers of sociology such as Marx, Durkheim, and Weber all drew on various academic fields to conduct systematic studies of the development processes of industrialized society. Similarly, modern sociologists must take a multidisciplinary approach in order to study and understand the processes and effects of the shift from industrial to postindustrial societies, the influence of technology on globalization, and the ways that society must develop and change in order to meet the needs of its members in the postindustrial age.

TERMS & CONCEPTS

Economic Development: The sustainable increase in living standards for a nation, region, or society. More than mere economic growth, economic development is sustainable and positively impacts the well-being of all members of the group through such things as increased health, education, environmental protection, and per capita income,. Economic development is progressive in nature and positively impacts the socioeconomic structure of a society.

Gender Roles: Separate patterns of personality traits, mannerisms, interests, attitudes, and behaviors that are regarded as "male" and "female" by one's culture. Gender roles are largely products of the way in which one was socialized and may not be in conformance with one's gender identity.

Globalization: The process by which businesses or technologies spread across the world. This creates an interconnected global marketplace operating outside constraints of time zone or national boundary. Although globalization means an expanded marketplace, products are typically adapted to fit the specific needs of each locality or culture to which they are marketed.

Industrialization: The use of mechanization to produce economic goods and services within a society. Historically, industrialization is a society's transition between farm production and manufacturing production. Industrialization is associated with factory production, division of labor, and the concentration of industries and populations within certain geographical areas and concomitant urbanization.

Modernization Theory: A sociological perspective of globalization that posits that less developed countries will eventually industrialize in the manner of more developed countries and that the process of modernization will gradually improve the quality of life in these countries due to political and economic forces.

Norms: Standards or patterns of behavior that are accepted as normal within the culture.

Postindustrial: The nature of a society whose economy is no longer dependent on the manufacture of goods and is instead primarily based on the processing and control of information and the provision of services.

Preindustrial: The nature of a society that has not yet been industrialized. Preindustrial societies tend to be small and family oriented. There are three types of preindustrial societies: hunting- and-gathering societies, horticultural societies, and agrarian societies.

Society: A distinct group of people who live within the same territory, share a common culture and way of life, and are relatively independent from people outside the group. Society includes systems of social interactions that govern both culture and social organization.

Sociocultural Evolution: The process by which a society develops through the growth of its stores of cultural information.

Social Stratification: A relatively fixed hierarchical organization of a society in which entire subgroups are ranked according to social class. These divisions are marked by differences in economic rewards and power within the society and different access to resources, power, and perceived social worth. Social stratification is a system of structured social inequality.

Technology: The application of scientific methods and knowledge to the attainment of industrial or commercial objectives. Technology includes products, processes, and knowledge.

Bibliography

Hansen, X. (2004). "Back to the future: The origins and return of sociology as the scientific study of societal development." Conference Papers—*American Sociological Association* 2004 Annual Meeting, San Francisco, 1-22.

Jing, S. (2012). "Study on the interaction of enterprise technological innovation and regional economic development in China." *Studies in Sociology of Science,* 3(2), 39-43.

Madueke, C., Ezenezi, R. E., & Ehiobuche, C. (2011). "Information technology and the societal development in Africa: A review of literature." *Journal of International Diversity,* 4, 77-104.

Milligan, C., Roberts, C., & Mort, M. (2011). "Telecare and older people: Who cares where?" *Social Science & Medicine,* 72(3), 347-354.

Schaefer, R. T. (2002). *Sociology: A brief introduction* (4th ed.). Boston: McGraw-Hill.

Stockard, J. (2000). *Sociology: Discovering society* (2nd ed). Belmont, CA: Wadsworth/Thomson Learning.

Thompson, J. D. (1974). "Technology, polity, and societal development." *Administrative Science Quarterly,* 19 (1), 6-21.

Suggested Reading

Bubou, G. (2011). "Platform technologies and socio-economic development: The case of information and communications technologies (ICTs) in Nigeria." *International Journal of Emerging* Technologies *& Society,* 9(1), 35-49.

Corea, S. (2007). "Promoting development through information technologyinnovation: The IT artifact, artfulness, and articulation." *Information* Technology *for* Development, 13 (1), 49-69.

Laszlo, A. (2003). "The evolutionary challenge for technology." *World Futures,* 59 (8), 639-645.

Mont, O. & Bleischwitz, R. (2007, Jan). "Sustainable consumption and resource management in the light of life cycle thinking." *European Environment,* 17, 59-76.

Nooteboom, B. (1988). "The facts about small business and the real values of its 'life world': A social philosophical interpretation of this sector of the modern economy." *American Journal of Economics and Sociology,* 47 (3), 299-314.

Stehr, N. (1991). "The power of scientific knowledge—and its limits." *Canadian Review of Sociology and Anthropology,* 28 (4), 460-482.

Ruth A. Wienclaw, Ph.D.

TECHNOLOGY & SURVEILLANCE

ABSTRACT

The co-evolution of technologies of power and technologies of surveillance has generated various forms of criticism. In some ways, society has come to accept elements of the infamous surveillance state described by novelist George Orwell in his seminal work *Nineteen Eighty-Four.* Many argue that society in the age of information has already a surveillance society.

OVERVIEW

There have always been critical voices in the social sciences that have viewed technological developments with skepticism and warned of their potential negative influence on the private sphere. The debate over how advancements in technology influence liberty, democracy, and autonomy has occurred for decades. Michel Foucault, in his investigations into the technologies of power, in his lectures at the Collège de France, and in his famous book *Surveillenir et punir* has described the invasion these technologies make, beginning from the somatic punishment of the Inquisition via Bentham's Panopticon towards the biopower and disciplining of our physical bodies, which we could nowadays supplement with the surveillance and discipline of our "neuro-chemical selves."

Social movements in the late 1960s were concerned with the influence and power wielded by governments and the political-industrial-military complex. If governments were equipped with the right devices to monitor their citizens every move, they could wield tremendous influence over citizens' lives. In the years following the terrorist attacks of September 11, 2001, the terrorist bombings of Madrid (2004) and London (2005), and the inception of the American Patriot Act, it has been argued that citizens are beginning to welcome restrictions on their freedom and autonomy that, they believe, will ensure their security. This, coupled with the research commercial companies undertake on the private lives and behavior of customers, has made more amendable to transparency of information.

Further, it is not just governments and companies that are using surveillance technologies: an increasing number of people are using surveillance technologies within their homes to monitor the activities of their children and spouses. In a time and age in which the polity, the economy, and the zone of infringement between the private and the public sphere are all constituted by capillaries of information made transparent by the progressive digitalization of all facts of life, modern society has come to embody a surveillance society.

APPLICATIONS

Public vs. Private Sphere

The distinction of a public and a private sphere is crucial to understand surveillance as a sociological issue as well as an ethical one. Also, it must be understood that the conception of privacy, as we take it for granted today, is a modern concept. As Jürgen Habermas has shown in his *Structural Transformation of the Public Sphere* (1962), the 18th and 19th centuries were a crucial historic time during which cultural transformations shaped the distinctions between public and private that we recognize today.

In *The Civilizing Process* (1939/1994), Norbert Elias cited many examples of behavior typical of prior centuries that would nowadays be considered intrusions into privacy, such as servants being present during a king's or queen's wedding night. With the emergence of privacy, however, there came the potential of using this privacy to gain and maintain control over groups of people. Of course, these groups would largely comprise people considered harmful to society: deviants, outcasts, criminals.

Panopticon

In this regard, the idea of a total control of the incarcerated was epitomized in the Panopticon, the prison Jeremy Bentham designed in 1785. The cells in such a prison are arranged in a circle around a central watchtower from which the prisoners can be observed at all times. Prisoners are unable to know, though, when they were being watched and when they are not. Because of this uncertainty, a sense of omniscience pervades the prison: since the prisoners cannot know when they are being watched, they tend to act under the assumption that they are being watched all the time.

Michel Foucault used the Benthamite Panopticon as an example for the emergence of the modern "disciplinary" society. In a disciplinary society, norms are "inscribed into the body," rather than merely taught. The discipline constructs the body. In a critical interpretation, the body is thus formed to adhere to the functions of an industrial community and of labor based capitalism.

In a historical perspective, we should be mindful of the methods that were applied by organizations such as the Gestapo, the Stasi, and the KGB to spy on their own countries' citizens in order to establish total control. Extreme historical cases of surveillance being used as a tool for oppression can be found in the Nazi's Gestapo and communist East Germany's Stasi. Both groups relied heavily on the citizens' surveillance of each other. Out of fear (or sometimes opportunism), people spied on their neighbors and friends and reported suspicious activity, which then led to the incarceration or murder of the spied upon. The Stasi meticulously documented the lives of the citizens of the German Democratic Republic through taped conversations, interrogation protocols, and other means. They developed many techniques of surveillance, a number of which were documented in the motion picture *The Lives of Others* (Das Leben der Anderen).

Microchips

In recent years, critical thinkers and skeptics have become highly critical of a potential surveillance method: the use of micro-chips to track citizens' movement. While many commercial products are already equipped with micro-chips to prevent theft, these chips can potentially be used for other purposes, too. By now it has become a matter of fact that new American passports are issued with an RFID chip that contains personal information. These chips can be identified within a radius of ten meters. However, similar chips have already been implanted in humans also. A few clubs and discotheques have spearheaded this use by injecting micro-chips into the arms of regular customers in order to provide them with easier access and an electronic tab that does away with the need to carry money or credit cards. Ironically, it follows that surveillance can be used not only as an implicit and secret form of control, but has been accepted in business circles as a way to provide explicit 360° feedback. This type of feedback involves the evaluation of managerial performance through auditing the entire organizational context. However, this process can give rise to micro-politics within an organization and invite denunciations and blackmail.

It has been argued that this is the perfect form of discipline in that it makes the subject of disciplinary power feel welcome and invite discipline openly. Similarly, skeptics fear that we are willingly creating the transparent human or the "Man of Glass" by laying bare every personal detail and making these details subject to control by outside forces.

VIEWPOINTS

Foucault

Foucault's *Discipline and Punish* was originally published in 1975. It begins with an account of a torturous execution in the 18th century, which is then contrasted with a 19th century prisoner's schedule, a highly regulated daily routine. Taken together, the two accounts illustrate the changes that had occurred in the penal system over the course of the intervening century.

The transformation from punishment to discipline, Foucault argued, was a change from one technology of power to the other. However, Foucault's concept of power has often been gravely misunderstood. In Foucault's account, power is not a means of domination, but rather a productive force. In themselves, the bodies and practices that disciplinary power produces are not to be viewed as good or bad effects of power. Foucault is an ardent student of Nietzsche in this regard. As such, if one seeks to follow a Foucauldian analysis, one should first study the changes in surveillance techniques today, rather than study them from the point of view of domination. This, however, must not be the only perspective.

Mills

Leftist and Marxist oriented critical thinkers have held—and increasingly hold—deep reservations about the invasion of the private sphere by either the government or multinational companies. In 1956, the American sociologist C. Wright Mills warned of a conflation of the political, military and economic elites in his book *The Power Elite*. Delineating the emergence of a shared world view among these elites, he foresaw a military metaphysic that would guide all three institutions in a "community of interests" in a permanent "war economy."

C. Wright Mills' work on political sociology and Alvin Gouldner's on the history of social theory together drove a major shift within sociology during the 1960s and early 1970s. The classical theories of Max Weber, Emile Durkheim, and Talcott Parsons, the last of which had dominated sociology from the mid-1940s into the 1960s, were denounced as being authoritarian and conservative, oriented toward the establishment, and set on upholding social order and rigid social control by providing "grand theories" that offered the empty promise of an explanation for every social fact. Such views were grave misconceptions of Parsons, but they prevailed nonetheless (Stingl, 2008).

Anti-Psychiatry

A very similar development, the Anti-Psychiatry movement, was a sort of 1960s corollary rebellion against established theory in the humanities and social sciences. This movement mimicked the early Adorno's skepticism about the misuse of psychoanalysis and psychotherapy towards the domination and control of people through capitalism. Leftists Anti-Psychiatrists viewed psychiatry as a method of surveillance, while the "moderate main-stream," in the wake of Thomas Szazs and R.D. Laing (Foucault is often erroneously named in this context as well), has argued that the application of certain medical conceptions and tools in psychiatry is to a large degree too broad to be called "scientific."

The concept of the misuse of psychiatry as a tool for social control is echoed in the term "the therapeutic state," which was coined by Szazs in 1963 to refer to a state system in which unwanted emotions and thoughts among citizens are "cured" by the means of psychotherapy as a metaphor for "pseudo-medical interventions." However, Szazs himself came under scrutiny when he was found to be associated with an organization that had close ties to Scientology, a religious organization often criticized for the control and surveillance it exerts over its members.

Some critics today would claim that the political actions (e.g. the Patriot Act) after the attacks of September 11, 2001 have led to a regime in which the war economy has realized a new potential as it has come to be applied within the U.S. itself. Under Title II of the Patriot Act, options of surveillance were widely opened up to government agencies. For example, the investigation of private computer data became available through a legal redefinition of the term "protected computer" which allows law enforcement agents to access information through Internet Service Providers.

Satellite Images

One should also certainly cite the controversy over the use of satellite images by companies like Google. It has been pointed out by some critics that the detailed imagery available of Google Maps (e.g. individual homes) seem to be a clear invasion into the private sphere.

A recent development in surveillance is found in the commercial use of global positioning systems (GPS) and tracking devices, especially when children are tagged with these devices. Child locator systems use the same technology as cell phones to track the movement of people. These systems are now readily available and can be installed in a child's knapsack or clothing, though they are usually worn as wristband. But the application of this technology comes with a price, and it can be taken too far. Parents surely have legitimate concern in preventing their child from wandering off and making sure that he or she is safe on the way home from school, but at what age does a child or adolescent gain the right to a private sphere? If parents track the movement of their teenage child with a hidden chip in his or her knapsack or through a mobile phone, at some stage this technologymay raise doubts about the family's ability to trust one another. Further, it can be argued that trust is the major integration factor of a family—maybe even within an entire society.

Other Surveillance

But surveillance is also an issue of commercial interests, and it is interesting to note how willing people in Western countries share personal data. One should remember that in Germany in 1987, a nation-wide census (originally planned for 1981) was the cause of a major social protest as critics thought the census would prove an invasion of privacy. Yet the questions that comprised the questionnaire were rather docile in comparison to the questions people nowadays readily answer to register with websites like

Facebook and YouTube. Supermarket bonus cards are yet another way that companies gather personal information.

Early in the 20th century, novelists had begun to warn about the totalitarian potential of super-surveillance societies. George Orwell's *Nineteen Eighty-Four* is perhaps the most famous of these, depicting a world in which all life and knowledge itself was under the surveillance and control of the thought police and a ministry of truth. With individuals in politics or the economy controlling the capillaries of information, truth, and knowledge construction and distribution, the realization of a new from of totalitarianism may not be too far.

In the digital age, the information trails we leave everywhere are not only subject to constant surveillance, but also, through this surveillance, to a new form of discrimination, as David Lyon, author of *The Surveillance Society* (2001), has shown. The odd consequence of surveillance is that it demarcates a new and unique form of inclusion/exclusion in society. According to Lyon, only those who have (and want) access to modern information technology, such as the Internet and cell phones, and thereby only those who actively invite the kind of surveillance these technologies impose, can fully participate in modern society. Those who have no access to this kind of technology fall on the losing side of what is called the digital divide.

Following the case that Lyons argues, it can be said that we have entered an age of post-privacy. This means that we have entered an age in which we use markers of identification to such a degree, and that—unbeknownst to us—the data collected about us has reached such a significant mass, that the concept of privacy can no longer be upheld. Consumerism itself is a driving force behind these developments. A surveillance society thus thrives on the willing participation of its members, at the very least in so far as they turn a blind eye to the consequences of the distribution of their information and the question of who controls the channels through which their information runs.

United States National Security Agency

In 2013, former U.S. National Security Agency (NSA) contractor Edward Snowden began providing the international media with details about the agency's mass surveillance of American citizens and foreign countries. In order to avoid an effort by law enforcement to arrest him, Snowden flew to Russia, where he was granted official permission to reside. Snowden was formally charged with espionage and theft of government property in June 2013. Among the information leaked by Snowden to the media was evidence that the NSA collected internet activity information and phone call data from billions of people in countries all over the world. In addition to collecting data on both American and foreign citizens, the NSA has collected information on foreign leaders and their colleagues. Based on the information provided by Snowden, it became clear that employees within the NSA and government officials endorsed the surveillance efforts with the understanding that it would aid in the goal of preventing terrorist attacks and help ensure global economic security. Nevertheless, critics of the NSA programs maintain that the United States government has used the issue of terrorism as a pretext to invade the personal lives of millions of people and put them under surveillance without their knowledge.

While U.S. President Barack Obama reacted to the NSA controversy with assurances that the government does not exceed legal boundaries of privacy in its surveillance practices, the issue of government spying is likely to inform the debate about security and privacy well into the future.

TERMS & CONCEPTS

360° Feedback: 360° feedback or "multi-rater feedback"/"multi-source assessment" is a Human Resource (HR) tool that utilizes reports from a variety of sources, including supervisors, co-workers, and supervisees, to evaluate an employee's job performance. This method has been criticized as an unreliable tool because it can give rise to intensive politicking, denunciations, and peer pressure, all of which are counter-productive to a working environment. Additionally, the method has been criticized as a form of illegitimate surveillance and social control. The method, it is claimed, mirrors the strategies of the Gestapo or the Stasi, even if it is supposedly only used to "enhance" work performance in corporate contexts.

Biopower: Introduced by Michel Foucault to describe a technology of power that states apply to govern a population by subjugating the body itself to forms of discipline and a regulative regime of biopolitics.

Consumerism: Consumerism is a postmodern description of a form of society in which self-realization and happiness are identified with the ability to purchase material goods and consume services. The constitutive factor is comprised by the opportunities for consumption.

Digital Divide: The difference in access to and practical knowledge of information technology, especially the Internet. The divide exists between different kinds of groups. Internationally, it describes the differences between developing and developed nations. Within nations, it exists between rural and urban areas or between densely and sparsely populated areas that are of different economic interest to Internet service providers. Finally, it also exists between social classes.

Discipline: The term, as used by Michel Foucault, has a slightly different meaning than it does in common usage. According to Foucault, disciplinary power is the process that enables the subjectification of the individual by constructing his or her body and his or her somatic identity through a regime of practices. Disciplinary power as such, therefore, is not visible.

Forms of Power: (Marxists, Weber, Parsons, Foucault, Mann) The concept of power itself is disputed within the social and political sciences. In the common-sense understanding, it is usually synonymous with terms such as domination and influence. This usage is actually very close to the Marxist and Neomarxist definition, which equates power with domination and material ownership.

Max Weber defined power as the ability to influence or control the behavior of others. A main means of doing so lay in the ability to coerce behavior through force, whether this force is realized or merely potential. Power rests on different types of authority: charismatic (people obey on grounds of the qualities of a leader), traditional (people obey to continue a pattern or uphold a value) and rational-legal (people obey on the grounds that authority giving the order holds an institutionalized office which fulfills a function in society).

Talcott Parsons conceived of power as a social medium among three others, each, according to his AGIL-scheme (Adaption, Goal-Attainment, Integration, Latency/Pattern-Maintenance), fulfilling a specific function in society.

Power as a medium fulfills the function of Goal-Attainment in the social subsystem of the polity. Money is the medium of the economy (A), the societal community (I) works on influence, while the fiduciary system (L) applies the medium of value commitments. In a tentative description, power in Parsons' frame of reference is about the ability to set goals, while influence is all about the promotion of the goal.

Foucault's concept of power is based on the relations between power, truth, and knowledge. For Foucault, power is a force that cannot simply be equated with the intentions of people, but is rather a current in the interchanges of knowledge and a formative and productive force that even enables its own counter-forces.

For Michael Mann, power comes in four subforms of resources for power: military, political, economical, and ideological. He integrates these in an analysis of the logistics of distribution in networks to explain the rise of political regimes, such as the fascist regimes of the early 20th century and the phenomenon of ethnic cleansing.

Micro Chip Tagging: The application of microchips with Radio Frequency Identification (RFID) and global positioning system (GPS) technology is becoming increasingly common.

The use of RFID in passports and consumer products is now very common. And while proponents of the technology claim that the operational radius of the devices is very limited, tests have shown that this radius can be easily expanded.

Panopticon: The Panopticon is a prison building designed by Jeremy Bentham. Architecture can play a central role as a technology of surveillance, and Bentham's Panopticon creates a space in which a feeling of invisible omniscience is achieved. With such a dominance over its subjects established, the prison does not simply incarcerate the body, but, as Bentham himself claimed, also exerts power over the mind. Michel Foucault used the Panopticon to illustrate the shift to disciplinary power between the 18th and 19th centuries.

Patriot Act: The U.S. Patriot Act was signed into law on October 26th 2001 in response to the terrorist attacks of September 11, 2001. The name is an acronym for "Uniting and Strengthening America by Providing Appropriate Tools Required to Intercept and Obstruct Terrorism Act of 2001." The act increases the rights of law enforcement agencies to act within the U.S. and abroad, specifically with regard to aspects of surveillance. It also affects the Secretary of the Treasury's rights of the regulation of financial assets, including those of foreign entities. The Patriot Act is still controversial, since its critics assert that it destroys the very liberties and rights it was enacted to protect.

Political-Industrial-Military Complex: According to Sociologist C. Wright Mills (1916—1962), the political, military, and economic elites share an ideology that defines them as a superior sector of society that supposedly knows best and is guided by a military outlook on foreign relations and social reality. To promote the interests of their "better community," as Mills states in The Power Elite (1956), this complex works to change the structure of the general economy into a "state of war economy."

Bibliography

Ball, K. S., & Wood, D. (2013). "Political economies of surveillance." *Surveillance & Society, 11*(1/2), 1–3.

Bright, J. (2011). "Building biometrics: Knowledge construction in the democratic control of surveillance technology." *Surveillance & Society, 9*(1/2), 233–247.

Cannon, M., & Witherspoon, R. (2005). "Actionable feedback: Unlocking the power of learning and performance improvement." *Academy of Management Executive, 19*(2), 120–134.

Eichinger, R. (2004). "Patterns of rater accuracy in 360-degree feedback." *Perspectives, 27*(4), 23–25.

Elias, N. (1994). *The civilizing process.* (Edmund Jephcott, Trans.). Oxford, UK: Blackwell. (Original work published 1939).

Farman, J. (2014). "Creative misuse as resistance: Surveillance, mobile technologies, and locative games." *Surveillance & Society, 12*(3), 377–388.

Fuchs, C. (2013). "Societal and ideological impacts of deep packet inspection internet surveillance." *Information, Communication & Society, 16*(8), 1328–1359.

Foucault, M. (1995). *Discipline and punish: The birth of the prison.* New York, NY: Vintage.

Foucault, M. (2006). *Psychiatric power.* New York, NY: Picador.

Furnham, A. (1998, April). "Congruence in job-performance ratings: A study of 360 degree feedback examining self, manager, peers, and consultant ratings." *Human Relations, 51*(4), 517–530.

Guru, S. (2012). "Under siege: Families of counterterrorism." *British Journal of Social Work, 42*(6), 1151–1173.

Habermas, J. (1962). *The structural transformation of the public sphere.* Cambridge, UK: Polity Press.

Hallinan, D., Friedewald, M., Schütz, P., & de Hert, P. (2014). "Neurodata and neuroprivacy: Data protection outdated?" *Surveillance & Society, 12*(1), 55–72.

Lyon, D. (2001). *The surveillance society.* Philadelphia, PA: Open University Press.

Mills, C. W. (1956). *The power elite.* Oxford, UK: Oxford University Press.

Stingl, A. (2008). *The house of Parsons: The biological vernacular from Kant to James, Weber and Parsons.* Lampeter, UK: Edward Mellen Press.

Suggested Reading

Elias, N. (1994). *The civilizing process.* (Edmund Jephcott, Trans.). Oxford, UK: Blackwell. (Original work published 1939).

Lyon, D. (2003). *Surveillance as social sorting: Privacy, risk and digital discrimination.* New York, NY: Routledge.

Luther, C., & Radovic, I. (2012). "Perspectives on privacy, information technology and company/governmental surveillance in Japan." *Surveillance & Society, 10*(3/4), 263–275.

Mann, M. (2004). *Fascists.* Cambridge, UK: Cambridge University Press.

Pallitto, R. M. (2013). "Bargaining with the machine: A framework for describing encounters with surveillance technologies." *Surveillance & Society, 11*(1/2), 4–17.

Parsons, T. (2007). *American society.* Boulder, CO: Paradigm.

Rose, N. (2007). *The politics of life itself.* Princeton, NJ: Princeton University Press.

Surveillance studies: An overview. (2007). Cambridge, UK: Polity Press.

The dark side of democracy: Explaining ethnic cleansing. (2005). Cambridge, UK: Cambridge University Press.

Weber, M. (1978). *Economy and society.* Berkeley, CA: California University Press.

Alexander Stingl, Ph.D.

Technology & the Judicial System

ABSTRACT

While technology has long been used to uncover evidence germane to the commission of crimes and the adjudication of the accused at trial, the past several decades have resulted in an exponential increase in the technical sophistication of exploratory and explanatory methods in criminology and their use in the American judicial system. These methods include DNA testing and forensics in general, as well as the use of cell phone records and GPS tracking. As for judicial management, assistive technologies and tele-justice have brought a new level of accessibility to, and participation in, the US judicial system. Finally, from a strategic perspective, computer information systems and the Semantic Web hold the potential to provide richer data sets about those accused of crimes.

OVERVIEW

Like most other aspects of modern life, the American judicial system has been touched by technology. Indeed, the field of criminology in general has benefited from the rapid pace of technological advances made since the twentieth century.

Technology has been broadly used to provide legal evidence for centuries, and not only in the West. For example, it has been known for centuries that fingerprints are unique identifiers. Since at least the 7th century in China (Laufer, 2000), fingerprints were placed on credit slips by debtors so the latter could not evade repayment. In 13th- and 14th-century Persia, it was customary to put fingerprints on all legal contracts ("Laying on of hands," 1919). Forensic science in general dates back at least to the time of Archimedes (c. 287 BCE-212 BCE), at least in a crude form, when the great philosopher proved a king's crown was not made entirely of gold by measuring the amount of water it displaced (Vitruvius).

The same technology that has benefited countless people both at home and at work has been employed by law enforcement and the judicial system in the investigation and prosecution of crimes in the United States. This technical evidence includes well-known examples such as DNA testing, video and audio recordings, cell phone records, and GPS tracking, but there are also other, perhaps less glamorous, uses of technology in the judicial system. These include centralized record-keeping systems for courts, improved access to the legal system for those with disabilities, and the use of videoconferencing systems.

DNA Testing

DNA testing is perhaps the most well-known use of technology in the judicial system. It relies on the fact that while most of the base pairs of DNA shared by humans are identical, there are segments of DNA in humans that are quite variable. These segments, known as variable number tandem repeats (VNTR), are unlikely to be the same in any two individuals, and thus they have become highly reliable evidence in criminal proceedings. Working from a sample of material such as skin, blood, or semen, forensic scientists are able to determine with a high degree of confidence whether or not the sample came from a particular individual.

DNA testing was invented by Dr. Alec Jeffreys at the University of Leicester in 1984 and was introduced into criminal proceedings later that decade. Between 1989 and 2013, it was used to overturn 311 wrongful convictions in the United States, 244 of them in 2000 or later. Furthermore, in nearly half of those cases, the same process that acquitted the wrongly accused led law enforcement to identify the truly guilty ("DNA exonerations nationwide," 2013). According to the Innocence Project, there have been tens of thousands of other cases in which the cloud of suspicion was lifted from a prime suspect through DNA testing ("DNA exonerations nationwide," 2013). As of 2017, the Innocence Project reported that 354 people had been exonerated through DNA testing ("DNA exonerations in the United States," 2017). It is still important to note, however, that more often than not, DNA testing actually confirms the guilt of those who have been suspected or convicted of a crime (Jacobi & Carroll, 2007, p. 2).

DNA analysis has come to be widely regarded as the most trustworthy type of evidence, indeed much superior to eyewitness testimony. Nearly 80 percent of the persons vindicated by DNA evidence in the United States prior to 2008 were put in prison due to faulty eyewitness testimony (Pribek, 2008). No one is certain of the total number of wrongful convictions due to faulty eyewitness testimony, but the percentage may be as high a 6 percent (Pribek, 2008).

Traditionally there have been two main types of DNA testing: restriction fragment length polymorphism (RFLP) analysis and polymerase chain reaction (PCR) analysis. "PCR is less direct and somewhat more prone to error than RFLP. However, PCR has tended to replace RFLP in forensic testing primarily because PCR based tests are faster and more sensitive" (Riley, 2005). Another method is short tandem repeat (STR) analysis, which compares DNA sequences called microsatellites. DNA testing is especially useful when there are no other types of forensic evidence available, such as fingerprints, which are also unique to individuals and have been used to secure convictions of the guilty and exonerate the innocent in the United States since 1911 ("Laying on of hands," 1919).

Audio & Video Evidence

Audio and video evidence has become another tool frequently used in court. Prosecutors use it to place the accused at the scene of a crime, while defense attorneys may use it to cast doubt on the prosecution's reconstruction of events. Audio evidence can be obtained from any number of devices, such as nearby microphones, digital or cassette recorders, or even the audio from a digital camera. Video evidence typically comes from video cameras, closed-circuit television cameras, and mobile phone cameras.

Video evidence, while compelling, suffers from two potential drawbacks: quality and integrity. First, depending on the environmental conditions, such as the level of light or the quality of the camera, video evidence can be grainy, blurry, or otherwise unclear, making the identification of individuals and activities on the video difficult or even impossible. Second, modern video-editing technology makes it easier than ever to doctor video evidence. For video evidence to be legally admissible in the United States, it must be clear and compelling and retain its original integrity.

The quality of video evidence can be improved to some extent using computer software. One popular way to demonstrate the integrity of video is the use of digital signatures, wherein the video is electronically marked while being recorded in such a way that evidence of tampering becomes readily apparent (Beser, Duerr, & Staisiunas, 2003).

Regarding audio evidence, some of the same rules apply: Was the tape altered? Is it possible to identify those speaking on the tape? Does the recorded conversation implicate the defendant or defendants in any criminal activity? Since the 1958 Supreme Court ruling in United States v. McKeever, US courts have applied the following seven-pronged standard to ensure that an audio tape is authentic:

1. Recording device was capable
2. Operator was competent to operate the device
3. The recording is authentic and correct
4. Changes, additions or deletions have not been made in the recording
5. The recording has been preserved in a manner shown to the court
6. The speakers are identified
7. The conversation elicited was made voluntarily and in good faith without any kind of inducement (Owen et al., 2005, p. 4)

Of course it is not always an easy task to answer such questions of audio and video authenticity. In this case, as in other instances where technology plays a role in jurisprudence, the role of the expert witness has become vital. Owen et al. explain:

Usually a prosecutor or a defense lawyer will contact an expert and ask for assistance in determining whether an audio or video recording has been edited, whether the voice on the tape is that of his/her client, or whether it is possible to tell if that is really the defense attorney's client in the video robbing the 7-11 store. He or she will send a tape that has been provided by the government, or by the opposing attorney or agency. The attorney will expect the expert to conduct an examination and present conclusions and opinions. (Owen et al., 2005, p. 1)

The US Supreme Court has ruled that trial judges are the gatekeepers, or arbiters, of the scientific soundness of expert witnesses. As such, judges can either allow or disallow expert witnesses from appearing and testifying at trial. As Owen et al. point out, "most judges rely on the expert to provide the information they need to assess the science and technology" (2005, p. 4).

Cell Phone Records

The use of cell phone records has become another important tool in judicial proceedings. In the United States, each cell phone is connected to the carrier's system through cell phone towers located throughout the country. Because each cell phone signal is sent from the closest available cell tower when a call is made, law enforcement can identify the general area the caller was in at the time of the call. According to Tisch (2005), "In urban areas crowded with cell towers, the records can pinpoint someone's location within a few blocks" (par. 3).

Cell phone records, in conjunction with DNA and eyewitness testimony, have been used successfully to acquit individuals of criminal activity in US courts (Brick, 2007). They have also been used to establish that the accused was in fact in the area when the crime was committed (Tisch, 2005), though other types of evidence were required to prove that this was more than merely coincidental. A subpoena is required to compel cell phone carriers to release an individual subscriber's cell phone records, though this process can be circumvented in kidnappings and other extreme cases where time is of the essence.

Beyond cell phone towers, the Global Positioning Satellite (GPS) systems that are built into many cell phones allow cell phone carriers and law enforcement to pinpoint the exact location of a cell phone on a grid. Cell phones such as these use the same satellite-powered GPS technology used by mapping services. In addition, starting in September 2012, US cell phone carriers were required to be able to provide a specific caller's latitude and longitude within three hundred meters upon request, which raised the issue of potential invasion of privacy:

> The FCC's Wireless 911 rules require that all US cell phones be equipped with a global positioning system (GPS) or other technology so that emergency personnel can locate people who call 911 from their mobile phone. When the system is fully implemented, 911 operators will know your longitude and latitude, which is a good thing if one needs help and cannot report an exact location. But there's nothing in the rules that say that the technology can only be used for emergency services. In fact, there are numerous commercial services that are already piggybacking on this E911 location technology. And it is not just cell phones that can track one's location. Laptop PCs, PDAs, Internet phones and other WiFi (wireless networking)-enabled devices can also be used to locate someone, thanks to a company that has mapped out the location of millions of wireless Internet adapters around the US. (Magid, 2007, par. 3-4)

Civil libertarians have noted that such methods contain within them the potential for abuse, although law enforcement officials and politicians maintain that the benefits of geo-tracking for consumers outweigh any potential dangers from unjust violations of privacy.

Assistive Technology

Attempts are underway to make the US judicial system more accessible to the country's aging population, as well as to Americans with disabilities. In 2007, the Center for Legal and Court Technology (CLCT) and the American Foundation for the Blind (AFB) Consulting Group partnered together to launch the Accessible Courts Initiative, which was:

> ... a partnership aimed at getting government agencies, law firms, law schools, judges, lawyers, and other members of the legal professions to make use of appropriate access technology in the courts in addition to making their web sites and other services accessible to people with disabilities. ("New program," 2007, par. 2)

Their aim was to take the spirit of the federal Americans with Disabilities Act (ADA), which requires physical access to courts for all, and extend it to the realm of technology. Under the Accessible Courts Initiative, the CLCT and AFB Consulting Group provided consultation, training, and support services to courts, law firms, and others to ensure compliance with the legal requirements of the ADA and other mandates.

FURTHER INSIGHTS

Gathering Data on the Accused: Integrated Data Technology is an essential part of judicial management. One of the most important, albeit less recognized, uses of technology in the judicial system is the use of integrated electronic data sets related to the accused. This technology has the potential to make all the computerized records relevant to the accused--child-support data, arrests in other states, drunk-driving records, and so on–available when his or her case is tried.

As of the early twenty-first century, such a goal remained more a dream than a reality, though stated support for it remained strong. Historically, the various parts of the criminal justice system have purchased and deployed computerized systems that were unable to communicate with other systems in other jurisdictions or departments. Since then, many of these computerized systems have become antiquated and inefficient, with no upgrades or replacements planned because of political, budgetary, or other concerns.

Computerized records did not replace paper records in a seamless manner. Some areas continue to retain both paper and electronic records, with perhaps predictable results. In Maryland, as of July 2008, it remained the case that "prisoner-release and detention instructions [were]... managed with handwritten notes," a method that has resulted in several convicted criminals being improperly released due to paperwork errors (Harris, 2008, par. 1).

Lack of Coordinated Data

Due to these various technological, economic, and political realities, it has been commonplace for some or all of the data relevant to a defendant's trial to be unavailable due to the presence of data silos. While the exact number is impossible to calculate, there is little doubt that a lack of integrated data on the accused has led to justice not being served in more than a few cases.

In an attempt to address the problem of siloed data, some states have adopted measures to centralize their records. Several federal government departments have pursued such measures as well, especially in the wake of the September 11, 2001, terrorist attacks, when the lack of coordination between various federal agencies became apparent. These efforts have met with varying degrees of success.

The Semantic Web

A newer frontier in data collection involves the concept of the Semantic Web, which Tim Berners-Lee, the inventor of the World Wide Web, first described in 1999 (Berners-Lee & Fishetti, 1999) and has more recently restated:

> The Semantic Web looks at integrating data across the Web... The Web can reach its full potential only if it becomes a place where data can be shared and processed by automated tools as well as by people. For the Web to scale, tomorrow's programs must be able to share and process data even when these programs have been designed totally independently. The Semantic Web is a vision: the idea of having data on the web defined and linked in a way that it can be used by machines not just for display purposes, but for automation, integration and reuse of data across various applications. (Berners-Lee, as cited in Carvin, 2005, par. 6)

That is, machines will help share the burden of collecting, integrating, and contextualizing information relevant to the judicial system. If history is any indication, the private sector will continue to do the pioneering work on the Semantic Web, with the public sector following suit some time later.

Telejustice

A related and emerging field of technology as applied to the judicial system is what some have called telejustice (Tinnin, 2005). Telejustice takes advantage of modern, Web-based videoconferencing technologies to allow attorneys to perform such tasks as taking depositions over the Internet. This method reduces travel costs and decreases the time it takes to get depositions from key individuals in a case. It also allows defendants to enter a plea from a secure location, while perhaps also making it less dangerous for witnesses to testify and be cross-examined.

Mathias and Twedt (1997) provide a helpful list of other uses of telejustice:

- Probable cause/bond hearings/appointment of indigent counsel/setting of arraignment date (misdemeanors and felonies)
- Misdemeanor arraignments/guilty pleas/sentencing

- Felony arraignments
- Parole interviews, parole revocation, victim input, and other post-conviction hearings
- Juvenile detention hearings (delinquent, child in need of assistance)
- Mental health hearings (emergency detention, review)
- Pretrial conferences and motion hearings with out-of-town attorney(s)
- Taking trial testimony of witnesses at other locations
- Depositions of out-of-town witnesses
- Law enforcement officer swearing under oath to facts alleged in affidavit or complaint
- Law enforcement officer testimony before grand jury
- Prosecutor interview of law enforcement officer regarding facts in police report
- Federal social security disability hearings
- Federal veterans benefits hearings
- Signing or language interpretation
- Training of detained juveniles, court staff, law enforcement officers & staff, or other staff (Mathias & Twedt, 1997, Table 1)

No advocate of telejustice sees it as a complete replacement for in-person judicial proceedings. Regarding its use in depositions, one attorney noted that the technology can be useful in certain situations where depositions need to be monitored. However, it was felt that there is still no real substitute for the physical presence of the attorney. The technology can then be applied so that others can view it, thus simplifying the scheduling and logistics and saving on travel expenses (Tinnen, 2005).

TERMS & CONCEPTS

Assistive Technology: An umbrella term used to describe technology and other measures that make institutions of society more accessible to the elderly and people with disabilities.

Cell Phone Records: Records of the times, dates, recipients, and general locations of calls made on a cellular phone. Such records are often used in court to establish the general whereabouts of a suspect at the time a crime was allegedly committed.

Criminology: The science of criminal investigation, encompassing the crime itself as well as the social causes and ramifications of the crime.

DNA Testing: A scientific method that can be used to try to match DNA material from a crime scene to one or more individuals accused of a crime.

Forensics: A shorthand way of referring to forensic science, a collection of scientific methods used to investigate questions relevant to the judicial system. One such method is DNA testing.

GPS Tracking: A feature of some cell phones, in-car navigational systems, and other high-tech devices in which an individual's location is mapped and tracked by satellite. GPS tracking is more accurate than cell phone records for establishing a geographical location, though both methods have their place.

Judicial Management: A term used to describe the practice of maintaining a well-run judicial system. Many of these practices involve the use of computers and other high-tech devices to streamline the administration of justice.

Semantic Web: A term used to describe the extension of the World Wide Web in which machines would reach across the Internet to gather data related to a particular need or question.

Telejustice: The use of videoconferencing in court proceedings. Some uses of telejustice include felony arraignments, parole interviews, and depositions.

Videoconferencing: A technique by which two or more individuals in different physical locations can communicate, through audio and video, with one another.

BIBLIOGRAPHY

Berners-Lee, T., & Fischetti, M. (1999). *Weaving the web.* San Francisco: HarperSanFrancisco.

Beser, N. D., Duerr, T. E., & Staisiunas, G. P. (2004). "Authentication of digital video evidence." *Forensic Science Communications,* 6. http://www.fbi.gov/

Brick, M. (2007, August 24). "Cellphone records help to clear a murder suspect." *New York Times.* http://www.nytimes.com/2007/08/24/nyregion/24phone.html

Carvin, A. (2005, February 1). "Tim Berners-Lee: Weaving a Semantic Web." The Digital Divide Network. http://www.digitaldivide.net/articles/view.php?ArticleID=20.

"DNA exonerations nationwide." (2013). The Innocence Project. http://www.innocenceproject.org/Content/DNA

DNA exonerations in the United States. (2017). Innocence Project. Retrieved from https://www.innocenceproject.org/dna-exonerations-in-the-united-states/

Harris, M. (2008, July 10). "Jail computer upgrades urged." *Baltimore Sun.* http://articles.baltimoresun.com/2008-07-10/news/

Jacobi, T., & Carroll, G. (2007). "Acknowledging guilt: Forcing self-identification in post-conviction DNA testing." *American Law & Economics Association Papers,* 40, 1-35.

Laufer, B. (2000). "History of the finger-print system." [1912 Reprint]. *The Print,* 16, 1-13. Southern California Association of Fingerprint Officers. http://www.scafo.org/

"The laying on of hands for fingerprints; woman expert thinks system will not be confined to criminals, but will become universal–Chinese used it for identification sixteen centuries ago." (1919, June 29). *New York Times Magazine,* p. 80. http://query.nytimes.com/

Magid, L. (2007, May 1). "Is your cell phone exposing where you are?" *CBS News.* http://www.cbsnews.com/stories/2007/05/01/scitech/pcanswer/main2746509.shtml

Mathias, J. T., & Twedt, J. C. (1997, September). "TeleJustice: Videoconferencing for the 21st Century." Paper presented at the Fifth National Court TechnologyConference (CTC5), National Center for State Courts. http://ncsc.contentdm.oclc.org/cdm/ref/collection/tech/id/674

"New program seeks to make courts and the legal system more accessible to people with disabilities." (2007, October 2). The Center for Legal and Court Technology (CLCT) and the American Foundation for the Blind (AFB) Consulting Group. American Foundation for the Blind. http://www.afb.org/Section.asp?DocumentID=3638

Owen, T., Owen, J., Lindsay, J., & McDermott, M. (2005). "Law and the expert witness: The admissibility of recorded evidence." Paper delivered at the AES 26th International Conference, Denver, CO. 2005 July 7-9. http://tapeexpert.com/pdf/owendenver2005.pdf

Pribek, J. (2008, June 2). "Error may be in the eye of the beholder." *Wisconsin Law Journal* (Milwaukee, WI).

Riley, D. E. (2005, April 6). "DNA testing: An introduction for non-scientists." *Scientific Testimony: An Online Journal.* http://www.scientific.org/tutorials/articles/riley/riley.html

Robertson, C. (2012). "The Facebook disruption: How social media may transform civil litigation and facilitate access to justice." *Arkansas Law Review,* 65, 75-97.

Shelby, R. M. (2016). "Whose rape kit? Technological innovation, materialization, and barriers to social justice." Conference Papers–*American Sociological Association,* 1-22.

Short, G. (2011). "A judicial use of technology." *American City & County Exclusive Insight.*

Tinnin, A. (2005, October 12). "Video conferencing gains ground in legal community." *The Daily Record* (Kansas City, MO).

Tisch, C. (2005, September 17). "Cell phone trails snare criminals, call or no." [Electronic version]. *St. Petersburg Times.* http://www.sptimes.com/2005/09/17/

Vitruvius (c. 100 B.C.). *The ten books on architecture.* M. H. Morgan, trans. (1914). Cambridge, MA: Harvard University Press. New York University: http://www.math.nyu.edu/~crorres/Archimedes/Crown/Vitruvius.html

SUGGESTED READING

Cohn, M., & Dow, D. (1998). *Cameras in the courtroom: Television and the pursuit of justice.* Jefferson, N.C.: McFarland & Company.

Mohr, R., & Contini, F. (2011). "Reassembling the legal: 'The wonders of modern science' in court-related proceedings." *Griffith Law Review,* 20, 994-1019.

Ressl-Moyer, T. (2016). "The intersection of forensic science and technology with criminal justice in

Massachusetts: Interview with David Siegel." *New England Journal on Criminal & Civil Confinement*, 42(1), 51-64.

Sammons, J. (2012). *The basics of digital forensics: The primer for getting started in digital forensics.* Waltham, MA: Syngress.

Smith, F. C., & Bace, R. G. (2002). *A guide to forensic testimony: The art and practice of presenting testimony as an expert technical witness.* Boston: Addison Wesley Professional.

Stepniak, D. (2008). *Audio-visual coverage of courts: A comparative analysis.* Cambridge: Cambridge University Press.

Matt Donnelly, M.Th.

TECHNOLOGY & THE MASS MEDIA

ABSTRACT

The evolution of technology, mass media, and society is deeply intertwined. Technological advances flourished with the invention of the printing press, a process of social transformation that enabled scientific and political revolutions by promoting the ideas of the nation-state and democracy. Radio and television have enabled the propaganda of authoritarian leaders on the one hand, and the world of advertising and consumerism in modern capitalism on the other. Society is in the information age, with generations of digital natives coming of age.

OVERVIEW

Recent decades have seen a drastic change in the technological distribution of information, a change that has had a lasting effect on our social structures and cultural memory. A similar change occurred nearly 600 years ago with the advent of the printing press, though less rapidly. With Johann Gutenberg's printing press, which was modeled on Chinese presses and popularized through clever marketing, the technology became a tool for mass-production.

However, it took the better part of another century for the technology to become a "mass medium," meaning that the majority of people accepted the content it produced as possessing a certain truth value. In other words, a long process of validation had to occur before it became socially accepted to reference printed content as a source of knowledge. Only at the conclusion of this process could the printing press itself become a motor of social transformation.

Prior to this acceptance of the printed word, writing itself had little value in comparison to the spoken word. Even Plato, in the voice of Socrates, had initially voiced skepticism about the written word, arguing that it would cause the mind and memory to deteriorate. However, when writing itself was accepted into societies, it changed the social structure insofar that it enlarged the social relations both spatially and temporally. Spatially, insofar as it became possible to transport lengthy and complicated messages over longer distances, thereby, for example, increasing the territory over which a monarch could effectively rule. Temporally, insofar as it became possible for a writer to transcend the present moment by leaving a message for a future reader, as well as making the message accessible to an unintended reader.

But up until the times when the printed word became widely accessible and socially acceptable, reading and writing were highly specialized practices that many cultures and societies permitted only their ruling elites and clergy to engage in. With the ready availability of written material through the printing press, though, the pressure to attain literacy grew among a wider audience while the output of information gradually increased.

From Scripture to Printing

In her seminal, *The Printing Press as an Agent of Change,* Elisabeth Eisenstein described in meticulous detail the effects of the shift from scripture to printing, including the influence this technology had on the rise of the major movements that shaped early modernity (1980). Actually, only with the printing press and the mass production of literature did concepts like the author and authorship, the authenticity of writing, and the reader, readership, and audience–concepts that are taken for granted–arise. These concepts did not really exist in the world before the printing press. With its invention, though, the processes of standardization began to restructure the intellectual world. In a way, before the printing press, there existed several "Aristotles" or "Platos," and several Holy Scriptures. Depending on where one resided in the world, the scriptures could have significant variations, and the Aristotle one encountered in Paris was not the same Aristotle encountered in Rome. With the advent of the printing press, however, a technology arose that could create the one, canonical "Holy Bible" or "Aristotle" that is known today.

With these developments concerning authorship and audience, the idea of the "public" emerged, which was a necessary condition for the development and proliferation of the ideas of a "nation" and a "modern democracy." The structural transformation of the public sphere, as Juergen Habermas would come to call it, began during this time and progressed throughout the eighteenth and nineteenth centuries within the culture of the tea-circle and the salon. The bourgeois, or burgher class, during this period had ample leisure time to discuss the formation of the "nation" and the ideas of "republic" and "democracy." Alongside the formation of "public sphere" was the emergence of a new conception of "privacy": when "private citizens" came together and "reason" became the tool of science and the control of state power, it was thought that both the church's and the monarchy's power would be demystified.

With the twentieth century, however, this public sphere was gradually eliminated by capitalist consumerism as corporations began to take control of the old and the new mass media like radio, movies, and television. According to Habermas, the critical public, recruited from active citizens, was transformed by capitalist consumerism into a passive consumerist mass public. Thereby, people turned inward in pursuit of self-interest and instrumentalist reason, discarding a consensus-based communicative reason, which, according to Habermas, could further the democratic welfare of society and its citizens. Today, in light of the effects other media have had on society, the nature of the Internet is still hotly disputed, with some critics seeing it as a beacon of hope for direct democracy and others as a symbol of increasing consumerism.

FURTHER INSIGHTS

Mass Media

The mass media has played and continues to play an important role in the formation and proliferation of democratic and liberal ideas. Next to the legislative, executive, and judicative branches of government, the media have been named the fourth power. As such, modern democracy cannot remain unaffected by the technological changes that have transformed media.

Many social theorists have stated their high hopes that the new information and communication technologies (IT/ICT) will offer new forms of democracy. E-government and e-learning, they claim, will not only greatly improve government efficiency, but also enable entirely new and improved forms of democratic participation. At the same time, though, critics such as Jean Baudrillard have voiced concern about the effects that digital technology will have on our perception of reality, arguing that it will turn reality itself into a mere simulation. Most perversely, Baudrillard has argued that it could even transform reality into the simulation of a simulation. His position is typified in his statement that the First Gulf War of 1990 was an event that actually "did not take place," for the media presented recycled images of the war in real time, thereby creating the notion of two enemies fighting, while in reality very little was happening on the ground. The media thus created the simulation of the war, as the war existed only in the real time transmissions of the mass media.

Positions such as Baudrillard's are often decried as being merely a deeply philosophical, speculative account. On a different and more sociological note, others have argued that the development of mass media has affected the metaphors and symbols that structure the narratives of biographies and identities (Stingl, 2007).

Effects of Mass Media on Identity

These effects of the mass media on identity can also be seen in the work of Palfrey and Grasser, which has argued that a new generation of digital natives came of age in the early 2000s. The generation was born into a world in which digital technology was already so widespread that its use became part of their initial socialization and is thus second nature to them. This socialization has affected how they perceive and interact with social, cultural and economic structures in the most profound ways, especially with regard to the exchange and the use of information. To the older generation, called digital immigrants, this new generation can appear as a strange paradox, for its members simultaneously appear very apt and sophisticated, yet also narrow in scope and shallow in understanding. In many ways, the technological evolution of the mass media over the past several decades has created a digital generation gap.

This shift has also created new forms of collective memory and new temporal structures in our culture. In many ways, as Elena Esposito has shown in her works, these changes have affected how people perceive and react to contingencies (2003). Esposito has repeatedly explored the shift from the "static past and uncertain/dynamic future" structure to a new one in which the use of technology requires intense planning and organization to the point that all future contingency has to reduced (2003). In contrast, this same shift has made the past fluid and constantly reinterpretable, as is exemplified in Esposito's explication of how Internet search engines repeatedly create new catalogues of past events in constellations that had never before been thought of. Through planning and technology, the future has become static and the past fluid, and, therefore, cultural memory has found a new form.

VIEWPOINTS

In a consumerist culture, positive identification is tied within material possessions and the acquisition of services. It is arguable that the increasing speed of mass media development has been the engine behind the development of consumerism. First of all, the mass media is in itself–either through hardware components (e.g. desktop computers, cell-phones, DVD players, and satellite dishes) or through related services (e.g. weather forecast, and music downloads)–made up of consumable items. Second, the mass media comprises the channels of advertisement. As a result, progressing technology has led to an increase in the volume and frequency of exposure to advertising.

Inequality

Of course, as society enters the digital age and becomes more dependent on information, new forms of inequality are arising, too. Just as the transformation of medieval society into the Gutenberg Galaxy necessitated that people learn to read, those who would not or could not acquire those skills sooner or later became a social underclass. This will also happen with those who do not learn to effectively use mass media technologies like the Internet. As a result, they will likely end up on the losing side of the so-called digital "divide."

Similarly, the digitalization of information and the progress of technology in mass media have caused older forms of the mass media to enter an age of decline. The traditional newspaper is losing its audience as ever more readers get their news online. For new outlets, this development has caused them to lose profits on the one hand and to develop an Internet presence on the other.

With the latest technological innovations, it has become possible for people in nearly any location to record images and sound and even write comments. Information, even news information, can be created by anyone with access to the right tools and send into the global data stream where, again, anyone with the right tools can access it. In effect, everyone has the potential to become an i-reporter, able to create content distributed through mass-media channels.

This would seem to be a realization of Andy Warhol's famous quip that, "In the future everyone will be famous for fifteen minutes." At the same time, though, as the mass of content produced and distributed inflates, the number of actual receivers of each contribution deflates, raising the question of where the mass is in these media.

Rise of Celebrities

Yet, with the expansion of mass media, the number of celebrities has risen. Today, celebrities are ranked on A, B, and C lists, and while i-reporters often help "make" these celebrities in the first place, they also often disregard the most basic rights of privacy. The classic paparazzo is increasingly being replaced by an army of amateur i-reporters who, instead of selling their pictures and footage to news organizations, post them directly on the web. The contents of these photos and videos very often jeopardize the security of personal information, and, overall, the effect has been the advent of a post-privacy society. In another ethically fraught issue, these same developments in mass media technology can be used for surveillance purposes.

CONCLUSION

The socio-critical aspect of these developments lies in the question of who controls the technology and the channels of information. In an economy that increasingly rests on the flow of information, access to mass media technology and control over the distribution of content through media channels have become crucial foci of power. If the powers of access and regulation rest in the hands of the same entities that produce media technology or content (such as the owners of major news corporations), then the mass media may prove to be counterproductive to freedom and democracy. Indeed, political scientist Colin Crouch has proclaimed that the information age has created a society in a state of post-democracy (2004).

TERMS & CONCEPTS

Cultural Capital: The concept of cultural capital as a form of symbolic capital was made popular by French sociologist Pierre Bourdieu. In his work, Bourdieu showed that, besides monetary capital, other forms of capital–those comprising knowledge, network connections, and experience–can regulate access to social classes.

Digital Divide: The differences in access to and practical knowledge about the use of information technology, especially the Internet. The divide may exist between different kinds of demographic groups (e.g. age groups); between social classes; nationally, between rural and urban areas or between areas of greater or lesser economic interest to Internet service providers; or internationally, between developing and developed nations.

Digital Inequality: An effect of the digital divide in which those denied access to the use of or knowledge about Internet technology suffer political, social, or economic disadvantages as a result of that denial.

Digital Native: A term for people who are born into societies in which information technology permeates all aspects of everyday life, thus influencing socialization patterns. The reception and application of digital information is often second nature to digital natives.

Digital Society: A form of society in which electronically processed and stored information is a main constituent for the functions of society. Often discussed in contrast to the analogue society, of which material products (i.e. the products of craftsmanship) are main constituents. The distinction stems from that between analogue and digital in information theory.

E-Government: E-Government, also known as e-gov, digital government, or online government, refers to the government use of information and digital technologies to promote the free exchange of political information, communication between citizens and government agencies, and the use of government services. Different branches of government have also used information technology internally in order to increase efficiency. Private citizens have also found e-government more convenient for using government services or participating in political activities. In particular, people whose mobility is impaired by age, illness, or disability have been enabled to participate in the democratic process as well as independently work with government agencies.

E-Learning: A form of education in which learning takes place through the use of computer technology. Among other things, it encompasses the integration of computer technology into the traditional classroom, online courses and online colleges, free online education resources, and online corporate learning tools.

The concept of making knowledge freely available to everyone is a central tenant of the humanist ideal. E-learning, some say, can realize that promise by allowing everyone able to access the Internet to make use of e-learning resources. However, not all e-learning services are free. Online courses can come with high fees, and the quality of education available online, whether from commercial or nonprofit sources, is quite variable. Still, the goal of providing everyone with the opportunity for higher education, regardless of factors like social status or work schedules, may be realizable with Internet technology.

I-Reporter: A citizen journalist, or a person who, without professional journalism training or employment, researches and publishes news. As a movement, the practice is known as citizen journalism. In an information society, given the right technology, anyone can be an i-reporter. However, some critics call into question the quality of the products of citizen journalism, claiming that they are more sensational than actually newsworthy. Some i-reporters have even gotten themselves into dangerous situations trying to get sensational footage or photos. Critics also worry that i-reporters can infringe on privacy rights, (e.g. in the case of celebrity news stories).

Information & Communication Technology (ICT): Summary names for technologies such as the Internet, mobile phones, personal digital assistants (PDAs), and personal computers that allow users to manipulate and communicate information.

Information Society: A form of society in which the production, distribution, use, and conservation of knowledge and information pervade all aspects of society from the political to the economic and cultural sectors. The main source of power in this society is the control of the capillaries of access and transmission of information.

Media: In sociology, one can distinguish three different types of media: media of transmission, mass media, and symbolically generalized media. This distinction relates back to the works of Talcott Parsons and Niklas Luhmann among others. In a very simple depiction of the distinction, one can say that media of transmission are the form in which information is stored and related from one sender to one receiver (oral speech, written word, or print or digital media). Mass media are technologies and social institutions that relate information from a sender to a mass of people (such as radio, newspapers, or the Internet). Symbolically generalized media are media that increase the likelihood of the acceptance of a communication, such as money, power, or influence.

Bibliography

Baudrillard, J. (1983). *Simulations.* Los Angeles, CA: Semiotext(e).

Beck, U. (2006). *Power in the global age: A new global political economy.* Cambridge: Polity Press.

Beck, U., Giddens, A., & Lash, S. (1994). *Reflexive modernity.* Cambridge: Polity Press.

Bolin, G. (2012). "The labour of media use." *Information, Communication & Society,* 15, 796-814.

Bourdieu, P. (1986). "The forms of capital." In J. C. Richardson (Ed.), *Handbook of theory and research in the sociology of education* (pp. 241-58). New York: Greenwood.

Crouch, C. (2004). *Post-democracy.* Oxford: Polity Press.

Eiseinstein, E. (1980). *The printing press as an agent of change.* Cambridge: Cambridge University Press.

Esposito, E. (2003). "The arts of contingency." *Critical Inquiry,* 32, 7-25.: http://criticalinquiry.uchicago.edu/features/artsstatements/arts.esposit to.htm

Habermas, J. (1991). *The structural transformation of the public sphere.* Cambridge, MA: The MIT Press.

McLuhan, M. (1962). *The Gutenberg Galaxy: The making of typographic man.* Toronto: University of Toronto Press.

Nguyen, A. (2012). "The digital divide versus the 'digital delay': Implications from a forecasting model of online news adoption and use." *International Journal Of* Media*& Cultural Politics,* 8(2/3), 251-268.

Palfrey, J., & Grasser, U. (2008). *Born digital: Understanding the first generation of digital natives.* New York: Basic Books

Pick, J. B. & Azari, R. (2008). "Global digital divide: Influence of socioeconomic, governmental, and accessibility factors on information technology." *Information* Technology *for Development,* 14, 91-115.

Prokopović, A. M. (2017). "Media and technology: Digital optimists and digital pessimists." *Facta Universitatis: Series Philosophy, Sociology, Psychology & History,* 16(2), 117-127.

Sommer, D. (2013). "Media effects, interpersonal communication and beyond: An experimental approach to study conversations about the media and their role in news reception." *Essachess,* 6, 269-293.

Stingl, A. (2007). "Procedural memory in reflexive modernities: The transformation of the 'opfer'-semantic and the genesis of the 'opfer'-/survivor-narrative in the current German discourse." Paper presented at the 8th Interdisciplinary, International Graduate Conference, Nuremburg, Germany. www.gradnet.de/events/webcontributions/stingl.pdf

Sznaider, N. & Levy, D. (2005). *Holocaust and memory in the global age.* Philadelphia, PA: Temple University Press.

SUGGESTED READING

Bittman, M., Rutherford, L., Brown, J., & Unsworth, L. (2012). "Digital natives? New and old media and children's language acquisition." Family Matters, 18-26.

Brienza, C., & Revers, M. (2016). "The field of American media sociology: Origins, resurrection, and consolidation." *Sociology Compass,* 10(7), 539-552.

Castells, M. (2001). *The Internet galaxy: Reflections on the Internet, business and society.* New York: Oxford University Press.

Crossley, N. & Roberts, J. (2004). *After Habermas: New perspectives on the public sphere.* Oxford: Blackwell Publishing.

Lash, S. & Urry, J. (1994). *Economies of signs and space.* London: Sage

Sanz, E., & Turlea, G. (2012). "Downloading inclusion: A statistical analysis of young people's digital communication inequalities." *Innovation: The European Journal Of Social Sciences,* 25, 337-353.

Van Dijk, J. A. G. M. (2005). *The deepening divide: Inequality in the information society.* Thousand Oaks, CA: Sage.

Warschauer, M. (2003). *Technology* and social inclusion: Rethinking the digital divide. Cambridge, MA: MIT Press.

Alexander Stingl, Ph.D.

WEAPONS OF MASS DESTRUCTION

ABSTRACT

The specter of nuclear weapons and similar weapons of mass destruction (WMD) looms like a dark shadow for people around the world, even for those who have never even seen the images of Hiroshima and Nagasaki. Stockpiles remain, while some countries are only beginning to build caches of their own. Even more concerning is that terrorist networks are known to be developing the capacity for building and using nuclear weapons. This paper will take an in-depth look at weapons of mass destruction in the twenty-first century. The reader will glean a better understanding of the types of such weaponry, as well as a stronger appreciation of the forces that push leaders to either dismantle or build their WMD arsenals.

OVERVIEW

Tomiko Morimoto remembers the day as if it was yesterday. The sky was clear, and despite the fact that the familiar drone of an American B-29 bomber hummed from the sky, she had little fear. After all, Hiroshima had not yet been bombed during the war but countless reconnaissance airplanes had flown over her city. What happened next, however, forever scarred her. She saw a flash as bright as the sun followed by a loud explosion. "Everything started falling down," she recalls. "All the buildings started flying around all over the place." As she escaped the growing fire, she watched helplessly as her city burned. The next day, she and the other children were released from their exile to find their way home. She crossed a railroad bridge, and saw what was once a river had become "a sea of dead people." She lives now in a quiet town in upstate New York, grateful for her life but fearful of the fact that nuclear weapons still exist. "I'm always afraid as more countries have the atomic bomb. I fear the end of the world" (Phillips, 2005).

The horrific scenes of Hiroshima and later Nagasaki were indeed traumatic to those who viewed their images as well as those who witnessed them firsthand. Even those who had dropped the bomb had no idea of the devastation the atom bomb would cause when detonated over the enemy. Then again, the two bombs used in Japan during World War II were far less powerful than the ones that would be built after the war. The United States and its allies built up an enormous stockpile of these nuclear weapons (as well as the cutting-edge technologies used to deliver them), and their primary competitor in the Cold War, the USSR and its Warsaw Pact allies, did the same.

In the post-World War II world, the term, "weapons of mass destruction" refers to a weapon capable of inflicting massive destruction to property and/or the human population. Long after the Cold War came to a close and after many of these arsenals were dismantled, the specter of nuclear weapons and similar weapons of mass destruction (WMD) looms for people around the world, even for those who have never seen the images of Hiroshima and Nagasaki. Stockpiles remain, while some countries are only beginning to build caches of their own. Even more frightening is that terrorist networks are known to be developing the capacity for building and using nuclear weapons.

This paper will take an in-depth look at weapons of mass destruction in the twenty-first century. The reader will glean a better understanding of the types of such weaponry, as well as a stronger appreciation of the forces that push leaders to either dismantle or build their WMD arsenals.

Chemical & Biological Weapons Use

In 1937, German bombers, at the behest of the Spanish government, laid siege to the ancient Basque city of Guernica, dropping thousands of pounds of explosives on the Spanish town, including thousands of two-pound incendiary projectiles. In their pursuit of crushing insurgents, the Germans literally razed the city in an attack that lasted for three hours. People attempting to escape were either gunned down at the city limits or pushed back into the city to be buried under fiery rubble. George Steer of the *London Times* commented on the devastation, coining a term that would become a household phrase for generations to come: "Who can think without horror of what another widespread war would mean, waged as it would be with all the new weapons of mass destruction?" (Macfarlane, 2005, p. 2).

Of course, Steer's use of the term was in reference to the devastation of Guernica. The Germans used conventional weapons of the era, such as grenades and artillery that were non-nuclear, non-biological, and non-chemical. The destruction was total, to be sure, but it was not of an unconventional nature. In the post-World War II world, however, "weapons of mass destruction" refers to a weapon that is capable of inflicting massive destruction to property and humans. Although Steer referred to conventional weaponry, the phrase has long since been equated with nuclear, chemical, or biological arms.

Interestingly, one of the manifestations of WMDs pre-dated the conventional weapons use at Guernica. Early in the First World War, the French fired tear gas canisters at their German enemies, and the Germans used similar tear gas weaponry in much larger quantities shortly thereafter. One year into the war, however, the Germans built upon their use of chemical weapons, launching chlorine gas attacks on the Western Front and either killing or severely wounding large numbers of Allied troops. The attacks were quickly condemned, but the British retaliated with their own chlorine weaponry. As the war escalated, so too did the use of chemical weapons. Chlorine was mixed with phosgene, and mustard gas soon followed. Had the war not come to an end when it did, historians believe, some 30-50 percent of all manufactured artillery shells would have contained poison gases (Duffy, 2007).

The Armistice of 1918 and the Geneva Conventions banned such weaponry. However, not all segments of humankind put their faith in such older treaties during the course of their own wars. In fact, they were used almost immediately in the Pacific War of the 1930s, when the Japanese are alleged to have used them on the Chinese. The United States had employed a policy of no-first-use for chemical weapons, threatening to use them only if they were used against US forces. However, a German bombing run on an American ship in Italy destroyed thousands of 100-pound mustard bombs.

During the Vietnam War, the United States used defoliants and riot-control chemical weapons, but it also ratified the Geneva Protocols pertaining to such weapons in 1975. The Protocols also gave the United States the right retaliate using such chemical WMDs if they were used against the United States.

In 1993, the United States signed the United Nations Chemical Weapons Convention, agreeing to completely dismantle its chemical stockpiles (Federation of American Scientists, 2000). A great many other nations also ratified the treaty, but many others did not. In fact, the broad-scale ratification of international treaties designed to halt production and dismantle existing stockpiles of chemical and biological weapons are in a way making the environment more complicated. Some believe that the many states that have not ratified the treaties may in fact be continuing their chemical and biological weaponry development programs.

Chemical and biological weapons remain some of the more elusive forms of WMDs, due in part to their constant evolution and to the technological limitations in tracking their production and transport. As so-called rogue nations (those that are perceived to have sponsored various forms of international terrorism or act outside of other international laws) become increasingly isolated, their propensity to provide such weaponry to non-state or extra-national armed groups or use them on an open battlefield becomes less of an option to them (Slesnick, 2007). Nevertheless, their continued presence among those who refuse to comply with international bans signifies that they remain a threat to global security.

Nuclear Weapons

When Robert Oppenheimer first saw the destructive power his atom bomb demonstrated at Alamogordo, New Mexico, in 1945, he famously invoked the words of the Hindu epic Bhagavad Gita: "If the radiance of a thousand suns were to burst forth at once in the sky, that would be like the splendor of the Mighty One," he said, adding, "I am become Death, the shatterer of worlds" (Center for Defense Information, 2008).

The bomb that was detonated over Hiroshima yielded about 12 kilotons of explosive power on that city, the equivalent of about 4.8 million sticks of dynamite (Allison, 2005). Today, there are thousands of nuclear weapons tipped with warheads that are hundreds of times more powerful than that bomb (Roth, 2006).

Mutually Assured Destruction

Traditionally, the world's nuclear powers have remained hesitant to deploy nuclear weapons during a war. Cold War adversaries, for example, understood that any war they fought with nuclear weapons would be won at too great a cost. With this fact in mind, a long-standing policy between the US-led West and the Soviet Union-led East kept the two countries from engaging in open warfare with one another. This policy, known as Mutually Assured Destruction, was by and large successful in this regard—neither side wanted to risk launching its nuclear arsenal at the other, so neither side would allow a direct confrontation to occur (Downing, 2008). This approach would be the dominant mode of thought for much of the Cold War years.

With the exceptions of the Cuban Missile Crisis and President Reagan's resurgent rebuilding of the American nuclear arsenal, US and Soviet nuclear stockpiles began shrinking with the introduction of several UN-sponsored non-proliferation and disarmament treaties. When the Cold War came to an end, the greatest nuclear powers in the world saw no need to continue building their stockpiles, and the world began to feel as if the specter of nuclear war was fading.

The United States and the Soviet Union were not, however, the sole nuclear powers in the world. China tested its first nuclear bomb. India, Israel, and Pakistan would not be far behind. Interestingly, India, Israel, and Pakistan would not sign the landmark nuclear Non-Proliferation Treaty (NPT), but many more would (although they would disarm not long after declaring their nuclear capabilities), such as the former Soviet states, South Africa, and Iraq. Three states, however, have captured international attention as so-called "states of immediate proliferation concern," which means that they are alleged to continue to develop their nuclear programs in defiance of the demands of the international community: Syria, Iran and North Korea (Arms Control Association, 2007).

With the continued development of nuclear weapons by sovereign nation-states, concerns remain not only about the warheads being constructed but about the methods by which such weapons might be delivered. Two decades after President Reagan fought for a space-based missile defense system, President George W. Bush fought for missile interceptor installations in Europe. In fact, the issue of weapons delivery remains just as paramount in terms of interstate relations as does the nature of the weapons themselves. One missile defense advocate maintains that the best policy in this regard is not diplomacy, mutually assured deterrence, or even a measured response. Rather, he argues, the best response is to use modern technology to its fullest to create an impenetrable missile shield to protect American interests (Ellison, 2008).

The end of the Cold War also created a nuclear security situation. With the breakup of the Soviet Union, the stockpiles of many of that former collective's members were left in questionable states of security. Such risks create opportunities for subnational groups, such as terrorist organizations, to obtain weapons of mass destruction for their own purposes.

FURTHER INSIGHTS

WMDs & Terrorism

The horrific results of the use of chemical, biological, and nuclear weapons would seem to fit perfectly into the plans of sub-national armed organizations and networks seeking to instill fear into their targets. For a long time, however, these groups eschewed the use of such WMDs for two major reasons: The technologies used to create WMDs were not easily obtained since state security organizations held them under tight guard. Also, targeting of innocent individuals is believed to have deterred sub-nationals from using WMDs, especially in an era in which such images would be quickly viewed around the world, which could then create a backlash among would-be sympathizers and supporters (Cronin, 2003).

This latter concern among terrorist groups was cast aside by the Japanese group Aum Shinrikyo, whose leader sought to destroy Japan in order that he would reemerge as its new leader. In 1994 and 1995, the group launched a series of chemical and biological weapons attacks on their perceived enemies as well as innocent targets in a residential neighborhood and, most infamously, on a crowded subway in Tokyo. The two attacks killed nearly twenty people and injured thousands. Had the group not made a series of logistical mistakes, the death toll would almost certainly have been much higher. Police cracking down on the group after the subway attack discovered that Aum Shinrikyo was attempting to create powerful biological agents and already had enough sarin gas to kill more than four million people (Choy, 2002). In a world in which such groups had previously proven unable to use WMDs in their activities, the Japanese terrorist group became the first to use them almost exclusively.

Indeed, several spectacular terrorist attacks in the latter twentieth and early twenty-first centuries suggest that their fear of losing support among likely constituents was subsiding. With the willingness to use WMDs increasing among some terrorist groups, all that was lacking was access to either the technology to build WMDs or the weapons themselves.

For example, the fall of the Soviet Union and the subsequent instability among its former satellite states exacerbated fears that a terrorist group might obtain nuclear technology or materials through black market networks and create a crude but more easily assembled weapon.

Dirty Bombs

Dirty bombs use radioactive material in a conventional explosive. When the bomb detonates, it does not yield the destructive power of a nuclear bomb—rather, it simply disperses radioactivity upon detonation. Such a device is easily constructed within and/or transported across borders into a target zone. Larger amounts of casualties and injuries would occur if a dirty bomb was set off in a crowded area, and if the attack was large enough, entire city blocks would need to be razed, decontaminated, and buried (Acton, Rogers & Zimmerman, 2007).

Certainly, the fear of such WMD attacks is both quantifiable and justifiable. Since the terrorist attacks of September 11, 2001, municipalities have weaved into their emergency preparedness plans contingency plans for radiological dispersal device (RDD) weapons attacks.

International security investigators continue to identify facilities in former Soviet states in which materials are at risk of theft. Some several hundred material-producing generators, most in former Soviet states, are at risk of terrorist infiltration (Myers, 2007). Most stated targets remain on guard for such devices, as well as other WMDs, as rogue nations and terrorist organizations continue to press forward with nuclear development and use.

CONCLUSIONS

"Weapons are like money; no one knows the meaning of enough" ~ Martin Amis

Indeed, the history of humankind has coincided with an evolution of sorts, creating bigger and more powerful weapons seemingly with every generation. Chemical, biological, and nuclear weapons have long been a part of the weapons caches of many major industrialized nations. With only a few exceptions in the twentieth and twenty-first centuries, however, WMDs have, not been deployed in state military operations since the Geneva Accords. Still, as long as the weapons (and the money, materials, and schematics used to help people and nations build their own) remain in the open and on the marketplace, few nations with WMDs will unilaterally dismantle their own programs until their competitors do.

With this inter-state equilibrium concerning the use of WMDs, attention naturally turns to those who do not follow internationally-accepted rules. Subnational armed organizations may not have had the wherewithal to conduct an operation that involves WMDs until Aum Shinrikyo's attacks, but terrorist networks worldwide have expressed an interest in obtaining such technologies and using them against their perceived enemies.

In addition to watchdog-style investigation and inspections, an increasingly globalized international community is well-advised to work collectively against WMD development and proliferation (Bernstein, 2008) and to enhance security around existing stockpiles.

TERMS & CONCEPTS

Aum Shinrikyo: Japanese terrorist group responsible for a series of 1990s chemical and biological weapons attacks on civilian targets.

Mutually Assured Destruction: Cold War deterrent doctrine that signified that any confrontation between NATO and Warsaw Pact forces would result in the mutual annihilation.

Nuclear Non-Proliferation Treaty (NPT): Originally signed in 1968.

Radiological Dispersion Devices (RDD): Also known as dirty bombs—conventional explosives mixed i with radioactive materials to spread radiation rapidly upon detonation.

Rogue Nation: A state that poses a risk to international security due to destabilizing activities such as supporting terrorism and authoritarianism.

Weapon of Mass Destruction (WMD): A device designed to cause large-scale damage and casualties upon deployment.

Bibliography

Acton, J. M., Rogers, M. B. & Zimmerman, P. D. (2007). "Beyond the dirty bomb." *Survival*, 49(3), 151-168.

Allison, G. (2005). *Nuclear Terrorism: The Ultimate Preventable Catastrophe.* New York: MacMillan Press.

Arms Control Association. (2007, Oct.). "Nuclear weapons: Who has what at a glance." *Strategic Arms Control and Policy Fact Sheet.* http://www.armscontrol.org/factsheets/Nuclearweaponswhohaswhat.

Bernstein, P. I. (2008). "Combating WMD collaboratively." *JFQ—Joint Force Quarterly*, 51, 37-45. http://search.ebscohost.com/

Byman, D. (2008). "Iran, terrorism, and weapons of mass destruction." *Studies in Conflict & Terrorism, 31*(3), 169-181.

Center for Defense Information. (2008). "Selected nuclear quotations." http://www.cdi.org/nuclear/nukequo.html.

Choy, S. (2002, July 23). "In the spotlight: Aum Shinrikyo." Center for Defense Information. http://www.cdi.org/terrorism/aumshinrikyo.cfm.

Cronin, Audrey Kurth. (2003, March 28). "Terrorist motivations for chemical and biological use." Congressional Research Service. http://www.fas.org/irp/crs/RL31831.pdf.

Downing, T. (2008). "Under the mushroom cloud." *History Today*, 58(8), 22-23.

Duffy, M. (2007). "Weapons of war: poison gas." Firstworldwar.com. http://www.firstworldwar.com/weaponry/gas.htm.

Ellison, R. (2008, July/August). "The best defense. [Letter to the Editor]." *Foreign Policy*, (167), 12-15.

Federation of American Scientists. (2000, June 15). "Chemical weapons." http://www.fas.org/nuke/guide/usa/cbw/cw.htm.

Fick, N. (2008, March 16). "Worries over being 'slimed'." *New York Times.*

Glazov, J. (2008, August 26). "Iran and the dirty bomb." *Front page Magazine.* Frontpagemagazine.com. http://www.frontpagemag.com/

Macfarlane, A. (2005, July). "All weapons of mass destruction are not equal." *Audit of the Conventional Wisdom.* MIT Center for International Studies, http://web.mit.edu/

Myers, L. (2007, March 12). "Report: Dirty bomb materials still available." *MSNBC*.com. http://www.msnbc.msn.com/id/17583305/.

Phillips, A. (2005, August 5). "Hiroshima survivor recalls day atomic bomb was dropped." Voice of America. http://www.voanews.com/english/archive/2005-08/2005-08-05-voa38.cfm.

Roth, N. (2006, August 9). "The modern nuclear threat." *Nuclear Age Peace Foundation.* http://

www.wagingpeace.org/articles/2006/08/09%-5froth%5fmodern-threat.htm

Slesnick, I. (2007)." Chemical and biological weapons of mass destruction." *NSTA Reports*! 19(4).

Stone, J. (2009). ":Al Qaeda, deterrence, and weapons of mass destruction." *Studies in Conflict & Terrorism, 32*(9), 763-775.

Van der Heide, L. (2013). "Cherry-picked intelligence. The weapons of mass destruction dispositive as a legitimation for national security in the post 9/11 age." *Historical Social Research, 38*(1), 286-307.

Suggested Reading

Asal, V. H., Ackerman, G. A., & Rethemeyer, R. (2012). "Connections can be toxic: Terrorist organizational factors and the pursuit of CBRN weapons." *Studies in Conflict & Terrorism, 35*(3), 229-254.

Cressey, D. (2008). "Chemical weapons agency shifts focus." *Nature*, 452(7188), 671.

Gorman, S. & Crawford, D. (2008). "WMD panel urges focus on biological threats." *Wall Street Journal—Eastern Edition*, 252(59), A4.

Johnson, K. (2008). "WMD/hazardous materials evidence awareness." *Fire Engineering*, 161(9), 28-30.

Magnarella, P. J. (2008). "Attempts to reduce and eliminate nuclear weapons through the nuclear Non-Proliferation Treaty and the creation of nuclear weapon-free zones." *Peace and Change*, 33(4), 507-521.

"Military is called unprepared for attack." (2008, February 1). *New York Times.*

Mousavian, S. (2013). "Globalizing Iran's fatwa against nuclear weapons." *Survival (00396338), 55*(2), 147-162.

Michael P. Auerbach, M.A. and
Jonathan Christiansen, M.A.

Sociology of Health & Medicine

Introduction

These articles explore how society is impacted by a variety of public health issues, which are defined as struggles impacting society on a large scale. For example, one of the biggest public health issues impacting Americans today is obesity, in both adults and children. Obesity is determined when a person's body mass index (BMI) is 20% higher it should be. The continuous rise in obesity is mostly due to the consumption of unhealthy/fatty foods and a sedentary lifestyle. There is a disproportionate number of minorities who are obese, possibly due to the inaccessibility of healthy, affordable food and limited opportunity for physical activity. A Mexican boy living in a low-income area whose family works long hours, might eat fast food for dinner and spend free time playing video games, possibly due to the cost of participating in school sports. Not only is it unhealthy to be overweight, but it causes a lifetime of increased medial issues, costs huge amounts in health care and creates other dynamic issues.

Other public health issues include poor drinking water, climate change, and bioterrorism. Another topic discussed is *medicalization*—medicine being an institution of social control, due to the power it has over the physical, emotional, and social norms of a society. Many theories look at the power of modern medicine to shape society, as well as the *social construction* of medical ideas, interpretations and practices. The *anti-vaccination movement* challenges the need, benefit and long-term effects of vaccinations for children. Vaccinations have become increasingly controversial as medical findings are challenged and doctor's advice is not followed. Should individual desires be sacrificed for the good of society, as laws require children to be vaccinated before attending school? Increased distrust of the medical perspective has led to more *holistic medicine*, which has long been the popular route in Eastern cultures. Holistic medicine treats the "whole person" from a "mind-body-spirit" perspective, for example, using herbs or essential oils for pain rather than turning to pharmaceutical medicines.

Other highly emotional topics also covered in this section are substance abuse and suicide. Substance abuse is an especially complicated social issue, due to the wide acceptance and even encouragement of using certain substances, such as alcohol, a widely used and promoted substance in most social and professional settings. If a woman is struggling to control her alcohol consumption and invited to a professional meeting where everyone is drinking, it may be unacceptable and affect her job if she does not have a drink. Suicide, especially among young people, is a national health tragedy. The decision to take your own life generally comes from an unbearable amount of emotional pain and distress. This becomes a social issue when we see patterns of this decision, exploring how societal impacts may be causing this pain. A homosexual teenager who is being cyber-bullied via social media is a situation that should lead to a discussion of what can be done to regulate this on a larger scale.

It is important to explore these public health issues and work together to increase understanding and acceptance, and decrease negative impact. Understanding gives professionals the tools they need to make a difference. With increased accessibility of mental health, now available through teletherapy (phone) or E-therapy (online), we should encourage all people we know struggling with issues to seek out support.

Kimberly Ortiz-Hartman, Psy.D., LMFT

ANTI-VACCINATION MOVEMENT

ABSTRACT

The development of vaccines has long been considered to be one of the most significant advances in modern medicine. However, the anti-vaccine movement has challenged the prevalent assumption that vaccines are a panacea or universal remedy. In fact, concerned anti-vaccination supporters argue that vaccinations are overused and may be harmful in excess or even in any dosage; many believe conspiracies exist between the pharmaceutical industry, doctors, and governments in order to hoodwink the public. Landmark court cases from 2008 to 2010 have further nuanced the debate.

OVERVIEW

The inception of modern vaccines dates to the late 1700s, with the development of anti-smallpox vaccination by Edward Jenner. Since then, there have been those who opposed vaccination, chiefly out of concern that they might cause ills worse than those they purported to cure. Most vaccination opponents in the twenty-first century are parents concerned for their children. They run the gamut from people who want to delay or space out vaccination to those who reject only some types of inoculation to those who refuse any type of vaccination (Blume, 2006). A rise in the numbers of people who refuse to vaccinate their children worldwide has caused grave concern in the medical and public health fields. Experts point to the popular spread of anti-vaccination conspiracy theories as one of the main causes for declines in immunization rates in some societies.

In 1998, *The Lancet,* a respected medical journal, published an article authored by Andrew Wakefield raising the possibility of a link between the Measles, Mumps and Rubella (MMR) vaccination to autism. Even though the article was eventually retracted and the research behind it discredited, many claim the article was one of the main causes of a decline in vaccinations worldwide. As a consequence, according to experts, diseases such as measles, which had been halted in most regions, have become endemic in some areas again. For example, the United Kingdom declared in 2008 that measles had reappeared in its population.

Conspiracy theories—elaborate plots based on unfounded suspicions that nevertheless find common cause with adherents who find them compelling and believable—tend to be based on a fear and mistrust of governments, corporations, and other special interests, such as the scientific and medical communities (Mar-hánková, 2014; Camargo, 2015). Anti-vaccination movement detractors argue that proponents base their concerns on conspiracy theories, in particular, that pharmaceutical corporations cover up detrimental information about vaccines or exaggerate their benefits in order to protect and increase their profits. Proponents, in fact, are able to present real historical examples to bolster their position that cover ups are nothing novel. In the 1940s, the U.S. government was involved in experimenting with inoculating unsuspecting people in Guatemala with venereal diseases in order to run a clinical trial. The Tuskegee Syphilis study ran from 1932 to the early 1970s, following the progress of syphilis in hundreds of African Americans, from whom treatment was deliberately withheld even after it became available so that the study might continue. Incontrovertible scientific evidence, however, exists that vaccines are reasonably safe and effective. Vaccines are also necessary for long-term maintenance of public health.

Faced with a heavy schedule of routine vaccinations for their young children, parents are often more likely to seek information about vaccines on the Internet and other media outlets than from medical personnel. Internet sites that disseminate anti-vaccine theories have been especially influential in dissuading parents from protecting their children from serious childhood diseases with vaccinations (Jolley & Douglas, 2014).

Pediatrics researchers, on the other hand, urge parents who refuse vaccination for their children to reconsider. In a 2010 pediatrics study showing that unvaccinated children played a role in the spread of a whooping cough epidemic, the researchers argued that vaccination is one of the greatest public health achievements in medical history, playing an indispensable role in eradicating smallpox and controlling polio, measles, rubella, and other infectious diseases (Hellman, 2014).

FURTHER INSIGHTS

Vaccines protect inoculated people from various infectious diseases caused by bacteria and viruses. Widespread vaccination led to the eradication of smallpox, one of the deadliest diseases in the world, and has led to significant decreases in rates of many other diseases that were once common. The more people who are vaccinated in a community, the smaller the risk of infection for the whole community. Community immunity relies on safety in numbers, provided the numbers of vaccinated people are high enough. There are always some unvaccinated individuals in a community for several reasons. For example, vaccination may be potentially dangerous to certain individuals because of personal health issues, and infants may be too young to vaccinate. If the numbers of unvaccinated individuals in a community are low enough, the unvaccinated may in a sense "ride free" on the backs of the vaccinated. That is, because most of the people in a community are vaccinated, the spread of disease is halted or controlled, and the small number of unvaccinated individuals are unlikely to encounter the disease or spread it to others if they do contract it. When vaccination rates decline from the ideal rate, the safety in numbers effect weakens. In consequence, diseases spread (Understanding Community Immunity, 2015).

Not all communities are able to reach an ideal immunization rate. Lack of access to immunization is one of the main reasons for mortality in children younger than five in developing countries. In fact, close to 100 percent of these deaths occur in low-income countries, and about 70 percent are caused by diseases that are preventable by vaccines widely available in other countries. Moreover, with widespread international travel, new and old diseases can be contracted in one location and spread around the world by travelers, making immunization and vaccination critical in preventing the reestablishment of formerly common serious illnesses.

Many experts argue that anti-vaccine movements take place almost exclusively in advanced countries, among parents who probably have never seen a child harmed or killed by preventable diseases such as polio, measles, or meningitis. Many of these diseases have become rare in advanced countries, and the chances of encountering them in a largely vaccinated country may seem to be very small. A misconception also persists that because many of these diseases were once common, they were also fairly harmless.

Until the late twentieth century, measles was a common childhood disease. It can lead to grave complications such as brain swelling, seizures, pneumonia, and hearing loss in close to 30 percent of cases. Measles is highly contagious, but it was overwhelmingly reduced after a vaccine was developed in the 1960s. The MMR vaccine was developed in the early 1970s, leading to a significant decline in mumps, measles, and rubella worldwide. In fact, according to the U.S. Centers for Disease Control, vaccination of children with MMR vaccine led to a 75 percent decrease in measles around the world at the inception of the twenty-first century and was eliminated in the United States at that time.

Because the MMR vaccine is not widespread in some countries, measles continues to cause close to 150,000 annual deaths. Despite the decline and disappearance of measles in many advanced nations, several of these suffered outbreaks of measles in the second decade of the twenty-first century. The United States, for example, suffered a new measles outbreak in seventeen states, with nearly 180 cases. These cases were linked to the decline in vaccination rates. Measles is so contagious that in order to maintain community immunity it is necessary to maintain a 95 percent immunization rate. Nevertheless, measles immunization rates in the United States are steadily declining, and experts explain that in some communities, they are no longer high enough to protect vulnerable members of the population (Understanding Community Immunity, 2015).

Parents who have chosen not to vaccinate their children tend to live in clusters. This is reflected in a mapping of infectious disease outbreaks, several of which occurred in California, one of the states in which the anti-vaccination movement is most prevalent. In fact, some of the schools in California have a vaccination rate of less than 50%. In 2010 California had the highest epidemic of whooping cough since the 1940s, and scientists found that unvaccinated children were linked to the spread. Outbreaks have also occurred in New York and other states (Hellman 2014; Tighter Laws, 2015).

In the United States, all states require parents or guardians to comply with vaccine regulations as established by the American Academy of Pediatrics prior to their children attending public schools. Most states require the same for daycare centers. However, many states provide legal opt-out options, which run the gamut from children who cannot be immunized for health reasons—for example, their immune system is compromised—to waivers for religious or even philosophical reasons (Hellman, 2014).

The tide may be turning for the anti-vaccination movement. In 2015, California legislators signed a mandate for all children enrolling in daycare or school to be vaccinated, including those who have philosophical or religious objections. Other states, such as Vermont, allowed some religious opt-outs based along strictly established parameters, while opt-outs for philosophical or personal reasons continued to be allowed in eighteen states.

Parents who refuse to vaccinate their children argue that they are protecting their children from health risks they believe are posed by vaccination. Supporters of the anti-vaccination movement are mostly well-educated and affluent people who have engaged in research (Kluger, 2014). These parents are supported by some physicians. For example, many parents and some doctors argue that it might be better to acquire immunization the natural way, by experiencing and coming through the disease by way of contagion.

On the other hand, most doctors and other experts argue that insufficient evidence exists for these claims and that parents are placing their children at risk for diseases spread not only by their peers but also by travelers from abroad. They also argue that anti-vaccination activists are influenced by unsound theories and do not fully comprehend the risks of terrible infectious diseases (Tighter Laws, 2015).

VIEWPOINTS

In 1957, there were close to 60,000 cases of polio in the United States. By 1961, six years after the polio vaccine became widespread, it was reduced by 98 percent. There were fewer than 200 cases reported in the United States in the last two decades of the twentieth century and none since 1999. Similarly in the 1950s, up to 4 million were infected with measles every year, with close to 50,000 requiring hospitalization. By 2012, 55 cases were reported. Nevertheless, outbreaks of nearly-eradicated infectious diseases in the United States have occasionally been reported, such as measles and whooping cough in California, mumps in Ohio, and measles in New York (Kluger, 2014).

Even vaccination advocates acknowledge that some of the concerns of anti-vaccine activists are legitimate. For example, some vaccines do pose risks for some people, and the live polio vaccine has a small risk of inadvertently causing the disease. Vaccinations against polio and rotavirus, however, were made safer and other vaccinations have been proven to be reasonably safe. Nevertheless, many parents are more scared of the potential or perceived risks posed by vaccines than by the more certain risks posed by the diseases the vaccines are meant to prevent.

Vaccines, throughout their history, have raised fears and suspicions by skeptics who view vaccinations as, at best, overused and, at worst, toxic. Anti-vaccination adherents claim that vaccines cause a wide range of health problems, including autism, bipolar disorder, and attention deficit disorders. Some doctors support the anti-vaccine movement and state that vaccination should be elective. Others argue that for a healthy child, childhood disease that used to be commonplace should not be a serious risk and would naturally immunize the child. The latter position has been adamantly refuted by the Centers for Disease Control.

Associated assertions commonly made by anti-vaccination advocates include that pharmaceutical corporations are aware of the serious risks posed by vaccines and are covering them up. Moreover, some argue that the medical field and the government aid and abet the pharmaceutical industry out of greed, expediency, and other ulterior interests (Kluger, 2014).

Scientists argue that the anti-vaccination movement relies on unfounded arguments. They mention, for example, a prevalent rumor that 97 percent of people who have suffered mumps were vaccinated for it; hence, it was pointless to get vaccinated against the disease. The CDC counters that, while some people will contract mumps even after vaccination, those who received two doses of the MMR vaccine are nine times less likely to get mumps if exposed and that those who do get sick suffer milder symptoms. In response to the assertion that vaccines cause autism, it is argued that the disorder usually appears about the time that children start their vaccinations and the apparent correlation is a matter of timing rather than cause and effect.

Interestingly, most anti-vaccination supporters are better educated and more affluent than the average person. It has been suggested that people with higher education levels believe that risk may be eliminated if all variables are under control. In other words, rather than believing in the randomness of adversity, they trust nothing bad will happen to them, and if it does, they will have the resources to handle it. Nevertheless, it is important to note that anti-vaccination supporters are a diverse group that spans a wide social, cultural, and ideological spectrum.

The link-to-autism controversy had widespread effects. In 2001, over 5,000 families filed a claim arguing that MMR vaccines triggered autism in their children, specifically due to the thimerosal ingredients in some of the vaccines, possibly in addition to other factors. Evidentiary hearings were conducted in 2007. Thousands of pages of evidence were analyzed and the testimony of dozens of experts was heard. In 2009, the courts ruled that the MMR vaccine, whether alone or in combination with other vaccines, was not a cause in the development of autism or any of the autism spectrum disorders (ASD). A second set of rulings was issued in 2010, finding that thimerosal in vaccines was not a causal factor in the development of autism or ASD.

The ruling was also critical of doctors who, in the opinion of the judges, peddled hope to parents rather than sound opinions based on science. Public health officials also expressed hope that the rulings would reassure parents that vaccination was safe and put to rest the rumors linking vaccinations to autism and related disorders (Barrett, 2010).

Moreover, a scientific study published in the journal Pediatrics analyzed 20,000 scientific reports published between the years 2010 to 2013. It determined that vaccinations do not trigger autism and that they present very low risk factors. The study found no link between immunization and allergies or leukemia. Nevertheless, an analysis by the RAND Corporation acknowledges that some rare side effects may occur, including fever or seizures. The MMR vaccine is not associated with autism (Hell-man, 2014).

In 2008, however, the U.S. federal government settled a case in federal vaccine court before it went to trial. The government agreed that vaccines aggravated an underlying mitochondrial disorder suffered by the claimant, Hannah Poling. In the statement, the government claims that in aggravating her then-undiagnosed condition, it resulted in autism even though it did not cause it. It is not known how many children may have similar undiagnosed conditions.

Scientists and policymakers continue to work to eliminate the rare risks related to vaccinations and to reassure the public of the efficiency, need, and safety of vaccination. They claim some inroads have been made, in particular by being explicit about the specific consequences of contagion with infectious diseases. For example, mumps can cause hearing loss and infertility, measles and meningitis can have serious lifelong consequences, and most of the diseases at issue pose a risk of death.

By 2015, the movement seemed to be slowly losing traction. Parents who refused to vaccinate complained of becoming outcasts in their communities, feared by other parents who saw their unvaccinated children as risks to their own. Doctors and public health officials hope that availability to up-to-date sound scientific information will slowly turn vaccine opponents around.

TERMS & CONCEPTS

Autism: A neuro-developmental disorder, the onset of which starts in early childhood. Symptoms include difficulty interacting with others in normative ways.

Conspiracy Theories: Trvine to explain social—often random—events as the secret acts of powerful, evil forces. They tend to include mistrust of government or corporate entities.

Immunization: A process by which an individual is made resistant to an infectious disease, such as by vaccination. Individuals may also become immune to a disease after suffering contagion.

Opt-outs: Express instructions provided in order to refuse to participate in a service, program, process, or contract.

Thimerosal: Also known as thiomersal or merthiolate. An antiseptic and antifungal agent used in vaccines that was erroneously implicated as a possible cause of autism in vaccinated children. Childhood vaccines have not contained thimerosal since 2001.

Vaccine: Vaccines are made from the same organisms that cause a disease. They help a person develop immunity to the disease by causing the immune system to respond to a dead or weakened form of a virus without producing full-blown symptoms.

BIBLIOGRAPHY

Barrett, S. (2010). "Omnibus court rules against autism-vaccine link." *Autism Watch.* http://www.autism-watch.org/omnibus/overview.shtml

Blume, S. (2006). "Anti-vaccination movements and their interpretations." *Social Science & Medicine,* 62(3), 628-642.

Camargo Jr., K., & Grant, R. (2015). "Public health, science, and policy debate: Being right is not enough." *American Journal of Public Health, 105(2),* 232-235.

Hellman, M. (2014). "Study: Measles, mumps and rubella not associated with autism." *Time.*com, 1.

Jolley, D., & Douglas, K. M. (2014). "The effects of anti-vaccine conspiracy theories on vaccination intentions." *PloS ONE,* 9(2). 1-9.

Kluger, J. (2014). "Who's afraid of a little vaccine?" *Time, 184(13),* 40-43.

Marhánková, J. H. (2014). "Postoje rodičů odmítajících povinná ockování svych dětí: případová Studie krize důvěry v biomedicínské vědění." *Czech Sociological Review, 50(2),* 163-187.

Offit, P. (2012). Deadly choices: *How the anti-vaccine movement threatens us all.*New York, NY: Basic Books.

Poland, G., Jacobson, R. M., & Ovsyannikova, I. G. (2009). "Trends affecting the future of vaccine development and delivery: The role of demographics, regulatory science, the anti-vaccine movement, and vaccinomics." *Vaccine, 27(25/26).* 3240-3244.

Sears, R.W. (2011). *The vaccine book: Making the right decision for your child.*New York, NY: Little, Brown and Company.

"Tighter laws on vaccines are just what the doctor ordered." (2015). *USA Today.*

"Understanding community immunity." (2015). *VAX, 13 (2).* 4.

Youngdahl, K., Hammond, B., Sipics, M., Hicks, R., & Cicchini, D. (2013). *The history of vaccines.* Philadelphia, PA: College of Physicians of Philadelphia.

SUGGESTED READING

Baker, A. (2013). "Pakistani polio hits Syria, proving no country is safe until all are." *Time.*com, 1.

Grant, A. (2010). "Vaccine phobia becomes a public-health threat." *Discover, 31(1),* 18-19.

Rieder, M. J., & Robinson, J. L. (2015). "'Nosodes' are no substitute for vaccines." *Paediatrics & Child Health*(1205-7088), 20(4), 1-2.

Ward, J. K., Peretti-Watel, P., Larson, H. J., Raude, J., & Verger, P. (2015). "Vaccine-criticism on the Internet: New insights based on French-speaking websites." *Vaccine, 33(8),* 1063-1070.

Trudy Mercadal, Ph.D.

Body Image and the Media

ABSTRACT

Body image refers to people's judgments about their own bodies. It is formed as people compare themselves to others. Because people are exposed to countless media images, media images become the basis for some of these comparisons. When people's comparisons tell them that their bodies are substandard, they can become depressed, suffer from low self-esteem, or develop eating disorders. The influence of media on body image is ironic, given that as people in the United States and other countries have become heavier and more out of shape, female models have become thinner and male models have become more muscled. Sociologists and psychologists have developed several theories describing how the media influences body image, including social comparison theory, self-schema theory, thirdperson effects and self-discrepancy theory. They also have developed interventions to offset the negative impact of unreal media images. Sociologists theorize that the media have an investment in promoting body dissatisfaction because it supports a billion-dollar diet and self-improvement industry.

OVERVIEW

The study of body image—how people perceive their bodies and how these opinions develop—was pioneered by Paul Schilder in the 1920s. His working definition of body image was "the picture of our own body which we form in our mind, that is to say, the way in which the body appears to ourselves" (as quoted in Grogan 2008, p. 3). Many contemporary researchers feel that this definition downplays the complexity of the field, since body image can refer to a variety of concepts from judgments about weight, size, appearance and normality, to satisfaction with these areas. The term "body image" includes both how people perceive their bodies cognitively and also how they feel about their bodies. Studies of body image show that it influences many other aspects of life. People live their lives in bodies, and understanding how they experience embodiment is crucial to understanding their quality of life (Pruzinsky & Cash, 2002). Dissatisfaction with one's body image can lead to many problems, ranging from depression to low self-esteem and eating disorders.

People feel increasingly pressured by the media about their bodies. The average person is exposed to thousands of beauty images weekly, and these images reflect an unreal body image that becomes more and more removed from the reality of contemporary people, who on average weigh more and exercise less than people did decades ago. At the same time, bodies depicted by the media have become thinner and fitter. Pressure about body image is not new, and even in the days before the electronic mass media expanded to its current size and speed, messages about body image were carried in magazines, books, newspapers, and—looking back even further—in paintings and drawings. Modern-day media do have a financial investment in promoting body dissatisfaction. Advertising revenues from the body industry contribute a great deal to media profits. This connection means that the link between media and body image is a health issue but also raises questions about the end results of consumer culture.

Changing Body Norms in the Media

The ideal body presented by the media has become thinner since the 1960s, particularly for women. At the same time, Americans have become much heavier. Since the 1980s, the percentage of overweight and obese children has doubled and that of overweight and obese teenagers has tripled. Adults show similar trends; according to the Centers for Disease Control and Prevention, as of 2016 more than 36 percent of adults were obese (Centers for Disease Control and Prevention, 2016). The trend toward thinner and thinner models has developed slowly since the early 1900s. In the 1920s through magazines and in the new medium of film, a thinner, almost androgynous female form was promoted, epitomized in the flat-chested flapper. The ideal female form became curvier during the hard times of the Great Depression in the 1930s, although it remained relatively slender through World War II. The postwar revival of domesticity led to the media hyping heavier, ultra-feminine images such as Marilyn Monroe, with larger breasts and hips but small waists. This was only a temporary interruption of the century's trend toward increasingly thin bodies as the ideal. Models shrank more throughout the 1980s and 1990s. In these latter decades, models also became fitter, adding muscles and tone to the preferred image. Images of men have followed the same pattern since the 1980s with male models displaying slightly less fat, much more muscled bodies. A study comparing the changing body-mass index of Miss America contestants, *Playboy* and *Playgirl* centerfolds, and average Americans and Canadians since the 1960s found that especially during the 1980s and 1990s, the female centerfolds became dangerously thin, while male models increased in size, and average people gained weight (Spitzer & Henderson, 1999). Through changing norms of beauty images, women are told to be thin; men are told to have little body fat and sculpted muscles (Grogan, 2008; Hesse-Biber, 2007; Soulliere & Blair, 2006).

Modern people live media-saturated lives. Studies suggest that a large percentage of women and girls read fashion magazines, most people watch several hours of television a day, and people are exposed to countless images while walking down the street, glancing through the newspaper, and browsing online. This constant exposure affects viewers. Studies suggest that the effect is felt in several areas. People compare themselves to images, internalize these idealized images as the norm, and absorb the message that they should judge themselves based on their appearance. This process of comparison, internalization, and acceptance leads to other effects: distortion of accurate body perception (for example, girls who are normal weight may think they are overweight), negative emotional effects, a tendency to overemphasize messages about appearance, and changes in eating and exercise habits (Tiggemann, 2002).

FURTHER INSIGHTS

Psychological Theories on How Media Affects Body Image

The effect of media on body image is complex; it is not simply the equation that exposure makes people feel worse about their own bodies. For one thing, people are not affected equally by exposure to media images. Some react quickly and strongly to beauty images and others are resistant. Some of the difference in reactions to media images has to do with people's individual traits. People who are more self-conscious, who place more importance on appearance, who are heavier, and who have symptoms of eating disorders are more swayed by these images (Tiggemann, 2002).

Three psychological theories are particularly useful in understanding how media images affect people differently:

- Social comparison theory was developed by Leon Festinger in the 1950s. Festinger theorized that to evaluate themselves, people compare themselves to others. Psychologists have expanded this theory and suggested that people compare themselves not only to others in face-to-face interactions, but also to media images.
- Self-schema theory says that people develop a sense of self by considering what makes them unique and valuable and arranging these into schemas, which are used to process social encounters. Some people prioritize appearance in their self-schemas; these people are more likely to place more importance on media images and messages about body image.
- Self-discrepancy theory says that people carry an idealized image of the person they want to be; discrepancies between this ideal and their perceptions of themselves can cause them unhappiness and stress. Media images can contribute to the formation of the idealized image (Grogan, 2008).

Studies have shown that women identify the media as the major source of the perceived social pressure to maintain a thin body image. Thin models are a major source of this pressure; in one study women who viewed images of heavier models were less likely to judge their own bodies negatively (Posavac, Posavac & Weigel, 2001).

Cusumano and Thompson (2001) developed the Multidimensional Media Influence Scale (MMIS) to measure media effects on body image in children. Their research indicated that media effects occur in three distinct areas: awareness, internalization, and pressure. These areas capture the extent to which children are aware that the media promote thinness as an ideal, the extent to which they internalize this ideal as applying to themselves, and the extent to which they feel pressured by the media to conform to the idealized image. Interestingly enough, Cusumano and Thompson found that these three items vary independently; that is, it is possible to be aware of media images without internalizing them. Children who internalized media images were most likely to feel dissatisfied with their own bodies.

Sociological Theories on How Media Affects Body Image

There are many explanations for why some people feel more pressure from media beauty images. Many of these have to do with social dynamics rather than individual traits. Media products' messages are not fixed; different social groups will take varying messages from the same media products. Interpretation of media images is partially dependent on a person's interpretive community (Milkie, 1999).

Milkie points out that many studies of media effect on body image examine the content of media images and assume that negative content automatically will have a negative impact on viewers, without actually measuring and explaining how this takes place. On the other hand, other studies examine whether people are aware of the unreality and negative or unrealistic images shown by the media, and assume that awareness of potential harm somehow prevents viewers from negative effects. As with the content analyses, these studies do not specify how being media savvy protects the audience.

Reflected Appraisals & Third-Person Effect

Milkie theorized that people are influenced by media content through reflected appraisals. Reflected appraisals are how people think they are viewed by others. These appraisals can have an influence on the self-image and action of individuals, if they are seen as relevant, and if they come from individuals or groups that are valued. People generally think that they are less influenced by media images than others. This is called the third-person effect. Media images can thus have an impact on people through the third person effect and reflected appraisals. This means that people might understand that media images are unrealistic and negative, yet still be influenced by these images because they believe that others will use these images to judge them.

Studies of teenage girls show that white girls tend to be more influenced by beauty images in the media than African American girls, largely due to the absence of black girls in the media. Without such images, black girls feel that the beauty images are not aimed at them, and also feel that others will not judge them against such images. White girls—even those who acknowledge the unreality of such images—still aspire to look like the images and believe that others will judge them based on this media ideal (Milkie, 1999).

Objectified Body Consciousness

Studies have shown that women and girls tend to be more affected by media images than men and boys. One explanation for this is that females have higher levels of *objectified body consciousness*—that is, women are trained to view their bodies from the point of view of outsiders, practice self-surveillance, and feel shame about their bodies for not matching the ideal (Knauss, Paxton & Alsaker, 2008). But research shows that males are also negatively affected when exposed to idealized body images in the media and also become depressed and dissatisfied with their own bodies when exposed to idealized images (Agliata & Tantleff-Dunn, 2004). Men are exposed to idealized images of other men at a higher and higher rate all the time. According to Soulliere and Blair (2006), one source of this increase is popularity of televised professional wrestling. Wrestling puts highly muscled and partially clad male bodies on display for a mostly male audience. Not only are heavily muscled, large, and strong bodies put on display, but play-by-play commentary emphasizes that these physical qualities are important for men to be considered "real men" (Soulliere & Blair, 2006). Both men and women are exposed to unrealistic images that often are outside the range of normal human variation.

Schudson (1989) found that cultural messages are most effective when they are easy to retrieve, memorable, resonant (that is, somehow familiar, or compatible with other aspects of the viewers' lives), institutionalized, and tied to some suggestions for action. Media messages about body image meet all these criteria. Effective and ubiquitous, media beauty images have a powerful impact. They generally:

- Combine eye-catching photography with memorable slogans,
- Complement messages about health and fitness received from schools, doctors and family,
- Are echoed in most areas of leisure,

- Tied to major institutions from public education to the health care industry, and
- Come with specific suggestions about how to change behavior—eat less, follow a specific diet, and workout more.

Body Image & the History of Consumer Culture

The growth of the modern mass media is inseparable from the growth of modern advertising and consumer culture, especially in the twentieth century. As the United States further industrialized in the late nineteenth and early twentieth centuries, the rate of industrial production eliminated the old problem of scarcity of goods and created a new problem of overproduction. The higher wages and shorter hours of "Fordism" gave modern industrial workers the time and money to acquire goods. Advertising was created to teach them to desire the products that were rolling off the assembly lines. In its infancy, advertising merely told people what products did; as it matured, it began to tell people about themselves. That is, advertisers learned that the most efficient way to sell products was to make people feel that there were serious lacks in their lives that could be satisfied through purchasing a product. Because advertising needed to create more and more new needs, everything about people was fair game: homes, clothes, food, and bodies. Early ads created a concern with body odor, misplaced hair, bad breath, wrinkles and other social "tragedies" of this ilk. Both men and women were targeted in ads that suggested that poor hygiene would ruin them in the business and social worlds (Ewen, 1976).

These ads were part of what Lears (1983) calls a "therapeutic ethos" that emerged from the social dislocations caused by mass urbanization and industrialization. The ethos rested on three assumptions:

1. Farmers, children, and others who were "close to nature" enjoyed an enviable state of health and vitality compared to modern urban dwellers;
2. People could return to this state of vigorous health by following the advice of modern experts; and
3. A person's primary goal in life should be the quest for self-fulfillment (p. 11).

People felt that modern urban life was somehow "unreal."

Advertisers used this concern with health and this willingness to spend more time searching for secular self-fulfillment to promote a new obsession with the body and its imperfections.

Social Media's Affect on Body Image

Social media platforms—be it Facebook, Twitter, or Instagram—have come to dominate the ways in which members of younger generations interact with one another. These are essentially visual platforms and ones that induce a higher level of self-observation than other forms of media. College-age individuals who use sites such as Facebook seem not only to have a heightened awareness of their physical images but also, as a result, experience a degree of "body shame and decreased sexual assertiveness" than those who do not spend as much time on social media (Manago, Ward, & Lemm, 2015). Thus, social media has the potential to make people more aware of their body image than even television advertisements, for example.

Discussion: Avoiding the Negative Effects

Interventions can decrease the impact of media images on self-perception. A study grounded in social comparison theory tested interventions designed to stave off the negative effects of unreal body images by disrupting the process of comparison. Since people are unlikely to compare themselves to others who they believe are not similar, the researchers created an experimental intervention that would suggest dissimilarity between the experimental subjects and the media images. Using subjects who already displayed body dissatisfaction (the group that has been shown to be the most influenced by beauty images in the media), the researchers found that exposing the subjects to information on the artificiality of media images and the genetic realities of weight control before exposing them to media beauty images reduced the likelihood that the subjects would make negative statements about their own weight or appearance (Posavac, Posavac & Weigel, 2001).

CONCLUSION

Consumer culture is the engine that sustains the modern economy. Advertising, carried in mass media's numerous outlets, stimulates consumer demand by creating new needs. The beauty industry and the related therapeutic industry (exercise, cosmetics, health and fitness, diet, relaxation and leisure) promote images of the idealized figure. These are generally aimed at women, who have historically been judged more by how they look than what they can do. Women's strides in the workplace have not changed this old equation.

Pressure to maintain an idealized body image supports a major industry in the United States. The number of diet books in print has exploded, with many becoming run-away best sellers, selling millions of copies and earning millions of dollars for their authors and publishers.

In the late-capitalist economies, the media function primarily to sell space to advertisers. When choices are presented to readers and viewers, they are usually choices between different products. The option of not participating in consumer culture is rarely offered. Having the perfect body is linked to buying things, and corporations are constantly finding new areas of the human body to improve. (For example, consumers have been bombarded with messages that their teeth are disgusting unless they are bleached to a whiteness rarely if ever found in unprocessed teeth.) Theorists who study the relationship between body image and consumer culture question whether lasting interventions are even possible when consumers are confronted by an industry that makes billions of dollars a year by making them dissatisfied with their bodies.

TERMS & CONCEPTS

Body Dissatisfaction: Unhappiness with one's own body shape, size, weight, or attractiveness.

Body Image: How a person visualizes his or her own body. This can have emotional and cognitive aspects and may be related to appraisal of height, weight, size, attractiveness, and other aspects related to appearance and function.

Body Image Disturbance: Distortion in the cognitive or emotional appraisals of the body.

Objectified Body Consciousness Viewing one's body from the perspective of others.

Reflected Appraisals: What people believe others think about them.

Self-discrepancy Theory: The idea that people carry an idealized image of the person they want to be; discrepancies between this ideal and actual perception of themselves can cause unhappiness and stress. Media images can contribute to the formation of the idealized images.

Self-schema Theory: The idea that people develop a sense of self by considering what makes them unique and valuable and arranging these into schemas, which are used to process social encounters.

Social Comparison Theory: Leon Festinger theorized that people evaluate themselves by comparing themselves to others. Recent theorists believe that people also evaluate themselves by comparing themselves with media images.

Therapeutic Ethos: Cultural trend of the early twentieth century concerned with health, vigor, professional expertise and self-realization.

Third Person Effect: People believe others are more influenced by the media than they are themselves.

Bibliography

Agliata, D. & Tantleff-Dunn, S. (2004). "The impact of media exposure on males' body image." *Journal of Social and Clinical Psychology 23*, 7–22.

Bazzini, D., Pepper, A., Swofford, R., & Cochran, K. (2015). "How healthy are health magazines? A comparative content analysis of cover captions and images of women' s and men's health magazines." *Sex Roles, 72*(5/6).

Bell, B., & Dittmar, H. (2011). "Does media type matter? The role of identification in adolescent girls' media consumption and the impact of different thin-ideal media on body image." *Sex Roles, 65*(7/8), 478–490.

Capodilupo, C. M. (2015). "One size does not fit all: Using variables other than the thin ideal to understand black women's body image." *Cultural Diversity & Ethnic Minority Psychology, 21*(2), 268–278.

Centers for Disease Control and Prevention. (2016, September 1). "Adult obesity facts." *CDC.* https://www.cdc.gov/obesity/ data/adult.html

Conlin, L., & Bissell, K. (2014). "Beauty ideals in the checkout aisle: health-related messages in women's fashion and fitness magazines." *Jour. of Magazine & New Media Research, 15,* 1- 19.

Cusumano, D.L. & Thompson, J.K. (2001). "Media influence and body image in 8–11-year-old boys and girls: A preliminary report on the multidimensional media influence scale. *International Journal of Eating Disorders 29,* 37–44.

Ewen, S. (1976). *Captains of consciousness: Advertising and the social roots of consumer culture.* New York: McGraw-Hill Book Company.

Farley, S. (2011). "Mass media and socio-cultural pressures on body image and eating disorders among adolescent women." *Perspectives,* 100–107.

Grogan, S. (2008). *Body Image: Understanding body dissatisfaction in men, women, and children.* 2nd edition. New York: Routledge.

Hesse-Biber, S.N. (2007). *The cult of thinness.* 2nd edition. New York: Oxford University Press.

Knauss, C., Paxton, S., & Alsaker, F. (2008). "Body dissatisfaction in adolescent boys and girls: Objectified body consciousness, internalization of the media body ideal and perceived pressure from media." *Sex Roles, 59*(9/10), 633-643.

Lears, T.J.J. (1983). "From salvation to self-realization: Advertising and the therapeutic roots of the consumer culture, 1880–1930." In W. Fox and T.J.J. Lears, (Eds.), *The culture of consumption: Critical essays in American history 1880-1980* (pp. 1–38). New York: Pantheon Books.

Manago, A., Ward, L., Lemm, K., Reed, L., & Seabrook, R. (2015). "Facebook involvement, objectified body consciousness, body shame, and sexual assertiveness in college women and men." *Sex Roles, 72*(1/2), 1–14.

Milkie, M. A. (1999). "Social comparisons, reflected appraisals, and mass media: The impact of pervasive beauty images on black and white girls' self-concepts." *Social Psychology Quarterly 62,* 190–210.

Ogden, C.L., Carroll, M.D., Kit, B.K., & Flegal, K.M. (2012). "Prevalence of obesity and trends in body mass index among US children and adolescents, 1999-2010." *Journal of the American Medical Association 307,* 483–490. Centers for Disease Control and Prevention. http://www.cdc.gov/ nchs/data/databriefs/db82.pdf

Posavac, H.D., Posavac, S.S. & Weigel, R.G. (2001). "Reducing the impact of media images on women at risk for body image disturbance: Three targeted interventions." *Journal of Social and Clinical Psychology 20,* 324–340.

Prichard, I., & Tiggemann, M. (2012). "The effect of simultaneous exercise and exposure to thin-ideal music videos on women's state self-objectification, mood and body satisfaction." *Sex Roles, 67*(3/4), 201–210.

Pritchard, M., & Cramblitt, B. (2014). "Media influence on drive for thinness and drive for muscularity." *Sex Roles, 71*(5/8), 208–218.

Pruzinsky T. & Cash T. F. (2002). "Understanding body images: Contemporary and historical perspectives." In T. F. Cash & T. Pruzinsky (Eds.) *Body image: A handbook of theory research and clinical practice* (pp. 3–12). New York: Guilford Publications, Inc.

Schudson, M. (1989). "How culture works." *Theory and Society 18,* 153–180.

Snapp, S., Hensley-Choate, L., & Ryu, E. (2012). "A body image resilience model for first-year college women." *Sex Roles, 67*(3/4), 211–221.

Soulliere, D., & Blair, J. (2006). "Muscle-mania: The male body ideal in professional wrestling." *International Journal of Men's Health, 5,* 268–286.

Spitzer, B., & Henderson, K. (1999). "Gender differences in population versus media body sizes: A comparison over four decades." *Sex Roles, 40*(7/8), 545–565.

Tiggemann, M. (2002). "Media influence on body image development." In T. F. Cash & T. Pruzinsky (Eds.), *Body image: A handbook of theory, research, and clinical practice* (pp. 91–98). New York: Guilford Publications, Inc.

Wright, J., Halse, C., & Levy, G. (2016). "Preteen Boys, body image, and eating disorders." *Men & Masculinities, 19*(1), 3–21.

Wykes, M., & Gunter, B. (2005). *The media and body image: If looks could kill.*. Thousand Oaks, CA: SAGE.

Suggested Reading

Barlett, C., & Harris, R. (2008). "The impact of body emphasizing video games on body image concerns in men and women." *Sex Roles, 59*(7/8), 586–601.

Bell, B., & Dittmar, H. (2011). "Does media type matter? The role of identification in adolescent girls' media consumption and the impact of different thin-ideal media on body image." *Sex Roles, 65*(7/8), 478–490.

Dworkin, S.L. & Wachs, F.L. (2009). *Body panic: Gender, health, and the selling of fitness.* New York: New York University Press.

Farley, S. (2011). "Mass media and socio-cultural pressures on body image and eating disorders among adolescent women." *Perspectives,* 100–107.

Grogan, S. (2017). *Body Image: Understanding body dissatisfaction in men, women and children* (3rd ed.). New York, NY: Routledge.

Harris-Moore, D. (2014). *Media and the rhetoric of body perfection: Cosmetic surgery, weight loss and beauty in popular culture.* Farnham, Surrey: Ashgate.

Lears, J. (1994). *Fables of abundance: A cultural history of advertising in America.* New York: Basic Books.

Perloff, R. (2014). "Social media effects on young women's body image concerns: theoretical perspectives and an agenda for research." *Sex Roles, 71*(11/12), 363–377.

Katherine Walker, Ph.D.

BODY WORK IN CONTEMPORARY SOCIETY

ABSTRACT

The appearance and functioning of the human body is central to the establishment and maintenance of social life. In order to present ourselves as competent social actors, people engage in body work—activities and practices associated with grooming and hygiene, as well as exercise and dietary management (Giddens, 1991). These activities help to maintain our bodies according to prevailing scientific standards of nutrition, growth, development and hygiene, and because of their aesthetic component, help us to present ourselves to others as particular kinds of people. Therefore, our participation in certain kinds of bodywork helps us to create social identities for ourselves. Labor markets favor particular kinds of bodies, which are, in turn, surveyed and managed in the workplace in order to ensure that organizational values are on display to the customer. In the workplace, bodily performance is also typically gendered. Therefore, the embodied capabilities of workers are harnessed by contemporary work practices, especially in the service industry, in ways that researchers call "aesthetic labor" (Warhurst et al., 2000) because of the emphasis within these work practices on bodily performance and presentation (Witz, et al., 2003).

OVERVIEW

The appearance and functioning of the human body is central to the establishment and maintenance of social life. In order to present ourselves as competent social actors, people engage in body work—activities and practices associated with grooming and hygiene, as well as exercise and dietary management (Giddens, 1991). These activities help to maintain our bodies according to prevailing scientific standards of nutrition, growth, development and hygiene, and because of their aesthetic component, help us to present ourselves to others as particular kinds of people. Therefore, our participation in certain kinds of body work helps us to create social identities for ourselves. Schilling (1993) describes body work as activities and practices associated with grooming and hygiene, as well as exercise and dietary management which include a range of practices such as dietary control and exercise that enable people to work on the body as a vehicle of self-expression and encourage the view that the body is an unfinished product.

However, body work is also what sociologists call morally charged. For instance, research demonstrates that physical appearance, body shape, and size influence the likelihood of people entering particular occupations or being promoted (Nickson et al., 2005). Or, put another way, labor markets favor particular kinds of bodies, which are in turn surveyed and managed in the workplace in order to ensure that organizational values are on display to the customer. Moreover, in the workplace, bodily performance is typically gendered, in that there are expectations about employees' appearance and conduct in ways that conform to idealized notions of masculinity and femininity (Tyler & Abbot, 1998). Therefore, the embodied capabilities of workers are harnessed by contemporary work practices, especially in the service industry, in ways that researchers call "aesthetic labor" (Warhurst et al., 2000) because of the emphasis within these work practices on bodily performance and presentation (Witz et al., 2003).

Social Aspects of the Human Body

Although the social sciences in general, and sociology in particular, are generally interested in ration actors (Weber), collective conscience (Durkheim), and social structure (Marx), since the 1980s, sociologists have become much more interested in the role the human body plays in contemporary (modern, Western) social life. This interest has, in particular (though not exclusively) drawn from interpretive traditions and focused on the cultural meanings bestowed on the body, how the body is 'lived' or experienced in everyday life (or, as phenomenologists such as Marcel Merleau-Ponty put it, how people experience "being-in-the-world"), and how the body is used to represent meaning and identity.

Historically and cross-culturally the human body has been and is, used symbolically. For instance, drawing on Durkheim's work on religious ceremony, anthropologist Mary Douglas (1970) observed that because the human body is common to all human beings, it is used as a natural symbol to classify and express ideas about the social order. In particular, the kinds of beliefs that societies hold about the body reveal something about what is deemed important for that society, or that it classifies as sacred or profane. For instance, we attribute social and cultural meaning to bodily states and products (tears can be interpreted as signs of sadness or joy) and the body can be used as a physical symbol of social values. As Warner (2000) observes, the Statue of Liberty, gifted to the people of the United States by the people of France in 1886, *embodies* social values of freedom and liberty.

Many cultures make marks on or modify the body in ways that signify meaning, such as changes in social status or social identity. In contemporary society, which some researchers have argued is characterized by anxiety and self-consciousness (e.g. Beck, 1992; Giddens, 1991), there is a tendency for people to become ever more concerned with bodily appearance and to view the body as a vehicle of self-expression (Lasch, 1979). This self-expression is nurtured through consumption activities associated with the cultivation of the body as an outward manifestation of self-identity (Shilling, 1993). This shift toward the body as a vehicle of self-expression has been tied to the birth of cinema, photography, and women's cosmetics (Wolf, 1990) that emphasize the importance of looking and being looked at (Featherstone, 1991). These technologies contribute to idealized images of the human body (often in ways that emphasize current notions of what it means to be fit and healthy) that create points of comparison for people between who they are and who they might become, and in so doing, stimulates the importance of bodywork or maintenance, through which the human body can be transformed.

Body maintenance includes a range of practices such as dietary control and exercise, pursuing healthy regimes in response to health messages about risky behaviors (such as stopping smoking, eating a "heart-healthy" diet, and engaging in "safer sex"). These strategies enable people to work on the body as a vehicle of self-expression and encourage the view that the body is an unfinished product (Shilling, 1993) that can be endlessly modified through the application of technologies (ranging from exercise to cosmetic surgery).

The Social Significance of the Body

The BodyScholarly interest in the human body has emerged in part as a consequence of social changes that force us to think about it (Howson, 2004). First, demographic changes, such as an aging population and increased life expectancy, mean that a greater proportion of the population is living longer, albeit with expectations of poorer health and perhaps disability. Researchers have argued that this shift toward an older population forces society to acknowledge and care for the aging body in new ways that maintain productivity and aesthetic appeal.

Second, contemporary society is characterized by its emphasis on physical and outward appearance about which people are consumed with anxiety (what to wear, what not to wear, am I too fat, too thin, too tall, too hairy?). Indeed, the human body is one of the key resources that people use to classify and categorize each other and therefore people spend a great deal of time and effort—and money—on maintaining their bodies. Moreover, in a world characterized by chaos and flux (i.e., unanticipated economic recession, natural disasters, 9/11), for many people, their own body is one area of life over which they may feel they have some control, especially in terms of food consumption. As Shilling (1993) puts it, we may not be able to influence global politics but we can show our significant others how disciplined we are by restricting our calorie and food intake. Similarly, we can influence or even manipulate others' responses to us by 'working' on our bodies—through diet, exercise and even surgical modification—often in ways that conform to idealized notions of beauty or work against them.

Finally, social scientists have become increasingly interested in the significance of the human body in social life because of the emergence of new technologies that stretch the limits of what the body is capable and of what the body can become. Genes can be manipulated, body parts replaced with parts from other humans or even animals (xenotransplantation), our faces reshaped, skin tightened, and limbs built. These developments influence the meanings that people attach to their own bodies and the bodies of others. If I have plastic surgery am I pandering to the beauty myth (Wolf, 1990) or taking control of my own life? While these technologies offer the potential to transform and redefine the physical body, they also raise questions about the boundary between nature and culture (Haraway, 1991).

FURTHER INSIGHTS

The Self & Body Work

Within a social interactionist tradition, self and society are constituted or constructed through the practical work that that people do in interaction with others and with their physical environments. This interaction involves body work at many levels and includes the visual information we make available to others and how they interpret it. In Erving Goffman's (1971) dramaturgical model, the body is a central resource to how people manage the information they provide to others through facial cues or expressions, physical gestures and mannerisms. For Goffman, the setting in which focused interaction takes place is deemed a front region. In such a setting (a classroom, a party) people use the body's potential for expressiveness, such as appearance, dress, and demeanor in ways that help define the situation as being of a particular sort.

People manage this micro-level body work through a shared inventory or vocabulary of gestures and expressions to which a common set of meanings is attributed. This common understanding helps people make sense of everyday interactions and classify the visual information that is being presented to them, in ways that allow people to modify their own presentations in social encounters. While Goffman refers to these bodily gestures and expressions as body idiom, anthropologists refer to body idiom as techniques of the body (Mauss, 1973) and emphasize that there is distinct cross-cultural variation in the meanings that people attribute to bodily gestures and expressions. For instance, while eye contact is especially important for white, English-speaking Westerners, for some other ethnic groups eye contact is interpreted as aggressive or hostile. Therefore, while people are able to engage in body work in ways that shape social encounters because, largely, they share common understandings of what bodily gestures mean, they may also find themselves in contexts where their bodies work against the flow of smooth interaction. This tension is apparent in studies of the importance of bodywork in the context of employment.

Body Work & Emotional Labor

The concept of aesthetic labor has been developed from Arlie Hochschild's work on emotional labor, which she defined as "the management of feeling to create a publicly observable facial and bodily display" (1983, p. 7). Through a study of flight attendants and their work, Hochschild argued that in Western culture people in certain occupations become alienated from their emotions through the commercialization of labor because they are expected and perhaps even required to manage and control their emotions. The naturalistic or orgamismic model of emotions emphasizes emotions as feelings that are experienced universally, and which express a range of physiological and biochemical responses to certain kinds of stimuli. In contrast, Hochscild argued that while sensations occur within the body, they have to be acknowledged and interpreted in order to have *meaning* as feelings. She notes that people may be aware of certain responses or sensations, like the heart beating faster or having a sense of tightness in our stomachs (what some might describe as a "knot"), but argues that these sensations derive their meaning from the social context in which they are experienced. And, as with bodyidiom, people are able to interpret these sensations through a shared cultural vocabulary of emotion; or as Harré (1991) puts it, through a shared repertoire of emotional language that guides us toward and prompts us to label a feeling in a particular way.

An Example: Flight Attendants

Hochschild uses this model of emotions to explore the work of people in service occupations (such as airline attendants) and in particular, drawing on a Marxist perspective, how modern market relations shape human feelings and incorporate them into the service of capitalism. The occupational restructuring and the expansion of the service sector that began to emerge in North America and Europe in the period after the Second World War has increased market demand for personal and relational skills (Adkins, 1995), particularly those oriented toward the physical and emotional comfort of customers. This phenomenon is what led Hochschild to the example of flight attendants who, twenty years ago, seemed to epitomize this kind of body work and emotional labor. She was especially interested in the relation between emotional labor and femininity, and how flight attendants were trained to deploy what are (still) regarded as feminine traits (that is, expressing sympathy, responding to the feelings of others and taking care of the feelings of others).

Central to the emotional labor of flight attendants is the emphasis on helping others relax. The techniques flight attendants were trained to use largely required attention to facial expressions and bodily gestures that would "look friendly" to customers and put people at their ease. Hochschild found that company documentation spelled out techniques to support the display of friendliness, and that flight attendants were constantly having to monitor their internal feelings and adjust their facial expressions to make sure they were in line with company policy on how to look friendly (a later study by Tyler and Abbott, 1998, had similar findings). This monitoring consisted of at least three key elements.

First, the techniques provided to flight attendants for managing emotional expression reflected norms about what people *should* feel in a given situation, or as Hochschild puts it, 'feeling rules.' Second, the techniques emphasized particular ways of expressing feelings that Hochschild calls "techniques of interpersonal exchange," such as smiles, tears and physical touch. Crucially, these techniques involve two forms of acting. Surface acting involves modifying one's external appearance, often by adopting a strategy of pretence to give an impression of a particular feeling. For instance, in service occupations, in situations where customers are giving employees a hard time, employees are required to manage what they feel (such as irritation or anger) and instead, work on their faces and bodies to display neutrality, civility, or whatever the organizational code insists on. Deep acting involves working on the way one feels to transform from one feeling into another (for instance, anger into compassion).

The cost of engaging in these forms of body and emotional work include feelings of insincerity and ultimately, for some, burn-out from the constant necessity to create an outward appearance of friendliness while internally dealing with negative feelings. Moreover, such body work and emotional labor can contribute to poor health, such as sleep deprivation and eating disorders (Freund, 1998). More recently, Tyler and Abbott (1998) described the on-going effort and time needed to maintain the female airline attendant's body; specifically the labor of dieting to maintain the company's ideal body weight.

Finally, people who are expected to do emotional labor and the body work that accompanies it may experience stress. The commercialization of feeling associated with service occupations and the ways this work is bought and sold in the marketplace is inherently stressful. Since Hochschild published her seminal workon emotional labor, other scholars have taken up her observations about the role of the body in certain kinds of occupations and developed the concept of aesthetic labor.

Aesthetic Labor

Aesthetic labor refers to the phenomenon that employees are collectively encouraged to embody the desired aesthetic of an organization (or are "made up" to do so) and in so doing, to commercially benefit the organization (Warhurst, et al., 2000). Witz (2003) defines aesthetic labor as "the mobilization, development and commodification of embodied 'dispositions'" (p. 37) and entails the face-to-face interactions between employees and customers in which the service provider is "packaged" for the customer (Warhurst & Nickson, 2007, p. 112). As such, aesthetic labor is inherently embodied, first because it requires the characteristics associated with different kinds of bodies (that display certain racial, gendered and class-associated demeanors and attitudes) and second because bodily conduct is central to the practice of aesthetic labor. That is, employers look for racial, gender and class "markers" in prospective employees that signal to customers, or service recipients, the nature of the service they are consuming (MacDonald & Merrill, 2009, p. 122).

Aesthetic labor occurs when an organization hires people for their particular physical or bodily characteristics and then requires those employees to further develop those characteristics in ways that bring value to the company through specific training in dress or style, body language, or personal grooming (Nickson et al., 2005). Such a process is most notable in industrial sectors such as retail and hospitality, which explicitly recruit "customer-facing employees with the right attitude and good appearance, both of which employers perceive as skills to be employed and then deployed at work" (Warhurst, no date, n.p). For instance, one study interviewed employees working in the hospitality industry to explore whether organizations hired staff on the grounds of their attractiveness and if so, how these organizations exploited employee attractiveness (Quinn, 2008). The study found that employers did hire on the basis of attractiveness and that they used this attractiveness (as well as overall staff appearance, customer empathy, and the physical environment) to build subliminal messages that encourage customers to feel "special" and therefore more likely to use the company's services.

Clearly, in the context of aesthetic labor, the body work that employees are being asked to perform entails transforming themselves in ways that serve organizational interests; there is an ongoing tendency within capitalism to extract value from bodies (Harvey, 1998). Thus, in the context of service industries, employers are not just interested in 'good looking' employees but also employees with the 'right look', or stereotypes (Oaff, 2007).

VIEWPOINTS

The Body as Commodity

However, such body work has implications of and may even contribute to workplace discrimination on grounds of appearance (Oaff, 2007). For instance, there are many studies that show how certain kinds of young women (deemed "attractive" according to idealized notions of femininity) are given preferential treatment in certain categories of face-to-face service work (Entwistle & Wissinger, 2006). This is most discernible, not surprisingly, in the fashion industry, where models literally "sell" their bodies as work.

One study (Entwistle & Wissinger, 2006) details the narrow parameters by which models are hired in the fashion industry (e.g. predominantly young, white European men and women) and the very specific physical requirements that prospective models must meet (for women, a thin, pre-pubescent figure). In order to meet these requirements, prospective models engage in body work or, "commodify themselves" precisely because what they are selling to employers is how their bodies look. Moreover, models must do so in ways that meet the fluctuating demands of the fashion industry and the shifts in the kind of image that is selling at a particular point in time. However, the authors of this study point out that while it is tempting to see the kind of work that models do as surface body work (for instance, dressing in a particular way, cultivating a certain image through make-up, hair and demeanor, diet, exercise and perhaps even using cosmetic surgery), in fact, such body work is indivisible from work on the self. The body, they note (drawing on Merleau-Ponty, 1981), is the vehicle for "being-in-the-world" (p. 82) and "the visible form of our intentions" (Entwistle & Wissinger, 2006, p. 784). What they mean by this is that the body is not an *expression* of self, or an outward manifestation of an internal state of being, but that body and self are intertwined and that the body's appearance and conduct is who we are.

Research suggests that body work is an inescapable aspect of contemporary life. Managing appearance and working on one's body is key to establishing self and social identity and to presenting ourselves to others as particular kinds of people. However, it also seems inescapable that, at least from materialist or Marxist perspectives, contemporary capitalism requires people to manage and work on their bodies, because so much of what capitalism sells is embodied. The service sector epitomizes embodied labor and, as many researchers observe, extracts exchange value from people's bodies. That is, employees are hired because their appearance, demeanor and emotional expressiveness helps organizations build and sell a particular brand or idealized experience. This argument is especially evident in the fashion and airline industries, where employees are on display and have to actively manage their emotional and bodily expressions and gestures in the service of their employers. Body work entails both a physical component (diet, exercise, surgery, managing facial expressions and bodily gestures) and an emotional component that can be tiresome and even damaging to people. After all, from a phenomenological perspective on the social world, the body is indivisible from self, and indeed, our bodies *are* ourselves.

TERMS & CONCEPTS

Aesthetic Labor: The phenomenon in which employees are collectively encouraged to embody the desired aesthetic of an organization for the commercial benefit of the organization.

Body Work: Activities and practices associated with grooming and hygiene, as well as exercise and dietary management. Includes a range of practices such as dietary control and exercise that enable people to work on the body as a vehicle of self-expression and encourage the view that the body is an unfinished product (Shilling, 1993).

Dramaturgical Model: Erving Goffman's model of how people manage information through performances in order to present particular impressions to those with whom they interact.

Emotional Labor: "The management of feeling to create a publicly observable facial and bodily display" (Hochschild, 1983, p. 7).

Feeling Rules: Social and cultural rules that govern the sorts of emotions people are expected to display and how they are expected to display them.

Profane: Categorically distinct from the sacred by religious ceremonies in traditional societies and by pollution beliefs and taboos in secular societies.

Sacred: Ideas, events, objects or persons that are considered special and beyond the ordinary. Things that are considered sacred are typically treated differently and kept physically apart from the profane.

Techniques of Interpersonal Exchange: Forms of performance through which feelings are expressed (e.g. smiles, tears).

Bibliography

Adkins, L. (1995). *Gendered work: Sexuality, family and the labour market.* Buckingham: University Open Press.

Beck, U., (1994). *Reflexive modernization: Politics, tradition and aesthetics in the modern social order.* Polity Press: Cambridge.

Chrisler, J. C. (2011). "Feminist psychology and the "body problem": Sexuality, physical appearance, and women's physical and mental health." *Psychology of Women Quarterly, 35*(4), 648–654.

Coffey, J. (2013). "Bodies, body work and gender: Exploring a Deleuzian approach." *Journal Of Gender Studies, 22*(1), 3–16.

Douglas, M. (1970). *Natural symbols: Explorations in cosmology.* New York: Pantheon.

Entwistle, J. & Wissinger, E. (2006). "Keeping up appearances: Aesthetic labour in the fashion modeling industries of London and New York." *Sociological Review. 54*(4), 774-794.

Entwistle, J., & Mears, A. (2013). "Gender on display: Peformativity in fashion modeling." *Cultural Sociology, 7*(3), 320-335.

Featherstone, M. (1991). "The body in consumer culture." In Featherstone, M., Hepworth, M. and Turner, B. (eds). *The Body: Social Process and Cultural Theory.* London: Sage.

Freund, P. A. (1998). "Social performances and their discontents: Reflections on the biosocial psychology or role playing." In G. Bendelow and S. Williams (eds). *Emotions in social life: Critical themes and contemporary issues.* London: Routledge.

Giddens, A. (1991). *Modernity and self-identity: Self and society in the late modern age.* Cambridge: Polity Press.

Goffman, E. (1971 [1959]). *The presentation of self in everyday life.* Harmondsworth: Penguin.

Harré, R. (1991). *Physical being: A theory for a corporeal psychology.* Oxford: Blackwell.

Haraway, D. (1991). *Simians, cyborgs and women.* London: Free Association Press.

Harvey, D. (1998). "The body as accumulation strategy." *Environment and Planning D: Society & Space, 6* (4): 401-421.

Hochschild, A.R. (1983). *The managed heart: Commercialization of human feeling.* Berkeley: University of California Press.

Howson, A. (2004). *The body in society: An introduction.* Cambridge: Polity Press.

Lasch, C. (1980). *The culture of narcissism: American life in an age of diminishing expectations.* London: Abacus Press.

Mauss, M. (1973). "Techniques of the body." *Economy and Society.* 2: 70-88.

MacDonald, C.L. & Merrill, D. (2009). "Intersectionality." In C. L. MacDonald and M. Korczynski (eds). *Service work: Critical perspectives.* 113-133. New York: Routledge.

Merleau-Ponty, M. (1981). *The phenomenology of perception.* London: Routledge and Kegan Paul.

Nickson, D., Warhurst, C. & Dutton, E. (2005). "The importance of attitude and appearance in the service encounter in retail and hospitality." *Managing Service Quality, 15*(2):195-208.

Nickson, D., Warhurst, C., Witz, A. & Cullen, A. M. (2001). "The importance of being aesthetic: Work, employment and service organization." In A. Sturdy, I. Grugulis, and H. Willmott (eds). *Customer Service.* Basingstoke: Palgrave.

Oaff, B. (2003, 25 January). "Opening the locked doors." *Guardian: Jobs & Money.* 7.

Quinn, B. (2008). "Aesthetic labor, rocky horrors, and the 007 Dynamic." *International Journal of Culture, Tourism and Hospitality Research, 2*(1): 77 - 85.

Shilling, C. (1993). *The body and social theory.* London: Sage.

Tyler, M. & Abbott, P. (1998). "Chocs away: Weight watching in the contemporary airline industry." *Sociology. 32*(3): 441-469.

Warhurst, C. (n. d.). "Aesthetic Labour." *Work and SocietyResearch Network.* University of Strathclyde http://www.workandsociety.com/downloads/bodywork/aeslab.pdf.

Warhurst, C. & Nickson, D. (2007). "A new labour aristocracy? Aesthetic labour and routine interactive service." *Work, Employment and Society. 21*(4): 785-798.

Warhurst, C., Nickson, D., Witz, A. & Cullen, A.M., (2000). "Aesthetic labour in interactive service work: Some case study evidence from the 'New' Glasgow." *Service Industries Journal, 20* (3): 1-18.

Warner, M. (2000). The slipped chiton. In L. Schiebinger (ed). *Feminism and the Body.* Oxford: Oxford University Press.

Witz, A., Warhurst, C. & Nickson, D. (2003). "The labour of aesthetics and the aesthetics of organization." *Organisation. 10*(1).

Wolf, N. (1990). *The beauty myth.* London: Vintage.

Suggested Reading

Entwistle, J. (2002). "The aesthetic economy: The production of value in the field of fashion modeling." *Journal of Consumer Culture, 2*(3): 317-339.

Freeman, C. (2000). *High tech and high heels in the global economy: Women, work and pink-collar identities in the Caribbean.* Durham, NC: Duke University Press.

Hancock, P. & Tyler, M. (2000). "Working bodies." In P. Hancock, B. Hughes, E. Jagger, K. Patterson, R. Russell, E. Tulle-Winton and M. Tyler (eds). *The Body, Culture and Society.* Buckingham: Open University Press.

Maidman, S. (2012). "Governing the female body: Gender, health, and net-works of power." *Foucault Studies,* (13), 193–195.

Nixon, D. (2009). "'I can't put a smiley face on': Working class masculinity, emotional labour and service work in the 'new economy'." *Gender, Work & Organization, 16*(3): 300-322.

Shilling, C. (2011). "Afterword: Body work and the sociological tradition." *Sociology of Health & Illness, 33*(2), 336–340.

Thomas, H. (2003). *The body, dance and cultural theory.* London: Palgrave Macmillan.

Alexandra Howson

CHILD OBESITY

ABSTRACT

Obesity has become a contentious topic in contemporary Western societies. While it is viewed as a medical and public health concern, it is also accompanied by social connotations and moral judgments. To be obese is to be fat, overweight, plump, large, or big: these are all words that vary in meaning across time and place, as suggested by debates about how to accurately measure and differentiate overweight and obesity. Moreover, while obesity has been associated with wealth and affluence at different historical periods, in contemporary Western society it is symbolically linked with poverty and laziness, while leanness tends to be equated with discipline and moral virtue (Turner, 1984). People who are obese experience discrimination–for instance, in relation to employment hiring and even pay–while popular culture parodies, ridicules, and vilifies overweight individuals on television and in film. Moreover, treatments for weight loss (programs, pills, surgery) play on people's anxieties about obesity and send a message about its undesirability (Sanstad, 2006).

OVERVIEW

Obesity has become a contentious topic in contemporary Western societies. While it is viewed as a medical and public health concern, it is also accompanied by social connotations and moral judgments. To be obese is to be fat, overweight, plump, large or big: these are all words that vary in meaning across time and place, as suggested by debates about how to accurately measure and differentiate overweight and obesity. Moreover, while obesity has been associated with wealth and affluence at different historical periods, in contemporary Western society it is symbolically linked with poverty and laziness, while leanness tends to be equated with discipline and moral virtue (Turner, 1984). People who are obese experience discrimination–for instance, in relation to employment hiring and even pay–while popular culture parodies, ridicules, and vilifies overweight individuals on television and in film. Moreover, treatments for weight loss (programs, pills, surgery) play on people's anxieties about obesity and send a message about its undesirability (Sanstad, 2006).

However, amid the contention about the cultural meanings attributed to obesity, there is public and professional concern about obesity in the United States and throughout the world.

The Centers for Disease Control and Prevention (CDC) reports that from the early 1980s through 2011, obesity in children more than doubled and more than tripled in adolescents. Indeed, some public health professionals and government agencies argue that this rise in child obesity has reached epidemic proportions with about 17 percent of US children and adolescents obese in 2011 to 2012. obesity is problematic because it is correlated with hypertension, diabetes, heart disease, osteoarthritis, and other conditions that are costly in both dollars and in quality of life. Consequently, social, political, and economic responses to obesity have emerged that are, according to the Institute for the Future, transforming consumption, business and health practices (Sanstad, 2006).

Measuring obesity

According to the CDC, overweight and obesity refer to weight ranges that are greater than what is generally considered healthy for a given height. Overweight and obesity are gauged in terms of elevated Body Mass Index (BMI), which in adults is determined by first squaring one's height in meters then dividing one's weight in kilograms by the squared height. There are online calculators as well as conversion charts to simplify the procedure. For children and teens, height and weight are plotted against a gender-specific growth chart, which indicates the relative position of the child's BMI number among children of the same sex and age. Overweight for children is defined as having a BMI in the 85th to 95th percentile, while obesity for children is defined as having a BMI in the 95th percentile.

Some researchers (e.g. Ebbeling & Ludwig, 2008) have questioned the usefulness and accuracy of BMI in predicting obesity-related illness, since it does not provide key data such as body composition and fat distribution, nor do its interpreters routinely take confounding variables, such as racial and ethnic considerations, into account. Nonetheless, BMI has become the gold standard for measuring overweight and obesity. Using BMI, the US government has been tracking child height and weight since the 1970s as part of the National Health and Nutrition Examination Survey (NHANES). NHANES uses an in-person interview conducted in the home and in a private mobile examination center, where trained interviewers conduct a physical examination (including weight and height measures) and medical tests.

Rising Obesity Rates and a Leveling Off

According to data collected from a 2008 National Center for Health Statistics (NCHS) survey, the CDC reported a trend in increased obesity in the United States between 1980 and 2008, where the percentage of obese two- through five-year-olds more than doubled from 5 percent in 1980 to 10.4 percent in 2008. The percent of obese six- to eleven-year-olds more than tripled during those years from 6.5 percent in 1980 to 19.6 percent in 2008, as did the twelve- through nineteen-year-olds with 5 percent in 1980 and 18.1 percent in 2008. Data from a 2014 NCHS survey shows that the prevalence of obese two- through five-year-olds and six- through eleven-year-olds decreased to 8.4 percent and 17.7 percent, respectively, while the prevalence of obese twelve- to nineteen-year-olds increased to 20.5 percent.

This rise in obesity among children has been one of the fastest emerging public health issues of the last few years in the United States and is presented as "a relentless upward slope that threatens to undo progress on heart disease and exacerbate other killer illnesses influenced by weight, including diabetes, high blood pressure and some types of cancer" (Zarembo, 2008).

Racial disparities are sharp. According to the 2008 NCHS survey, among girls aged twelve to nineteen, 29.2 percent of African Americans and 17.4 percent of Mexican Americans were obese, compared with 14.5 percent of whites. Among boys in the same age group, 19.8 percent of African Americans and 26.8 percent of Mexican Americans were obese, compared with 16.7 percent of whites (Ogden & Carroll, 2010). According to the 2014 NCHS survey, among girls aged two to nineteen, 20.5 percent of non-Hispanic African Americans and 21.1 percent of Mexican Americans were obese, compared to 15.6 percent of non-Hispanic white Americans in 2011 to 2012.

Evidence from the CDC suggests, however, that obesity rates among children in the United States are leveling off as there was not a significant rise in obesity levels between 2008 and 2012 (Ogden, Carroll, Kit, & Flegal, 2012; CDC 2014). Although this is taken as a positive sign by many, the goal to reduce childhood obesity rates is still unmet.

Obesity as a Global Issue

Childhood overweight and obesity are also problems seen on a global scale. For instance, childhood obesity levels in boys and girls between eleven and fifteen almost doubled in Britain between 1995, when 13.9 percent of boys and 15.5 percent of girls were obese, and 2004, when 24.3 percent of boys and 26.7 percent of girls were obese. From 2004 to 2011, however, those rates fell slightly in boys to 23.8 percent and more dramatically among girls to 16.5 percent (Eastwood, 2013).

A January 2013 study from the Australian Bureau of Statistics reported that between 2011 and 2012, 24 percent of Australian boys and 27 percent of Australian girls aged five to seventeen were overweight. The World Health Organization (WHO) has also identified obesity as an epidemic, even in developing countries–where in 2011 it was estimated that over 30 million children were overweight as opposed to 10 million overweight children in developed countries (World Health Organization, 2013). In 2014 WHO reported that, worldwide, 42 million children under five years of age were overweight or obese in 2013 and that childhood obesity in emerging economies has been increasing at a rate 30 percent higher than that of developed countries (World Health Organization, 2014). Obesity is especially a problem for children because their eating and physical activity habits become entrenched in ways that can contribute to life-long health problems.

FURTHER INSIGHTS

Implications of Overweight & Obesity

Overweight and obesity contribute to a raft of health, social, and economic problems that are costly and sometimes debilitating (Sanstad, 2006). Elevated BMI is correlated with hypertension, diabetes, heart disease, osteoarthritis, and other conditions that are costly in both dollars and quality of life. According to the Surgeon General, "risk factors for heart disease, such as high cholesterol and high blood pressure, occur with increased frequency in overweight children and adolescents compared to children with a healthy weight," and overweight adolescents have a 70 percent chance of becoming overweight or obese adults. This increases to 80 percent if one or more parent is overweight or obese (Office of the Surgeon General, 2007).

One study found overweight was associated with the early appearance of cardiovascular disease risk factors among children between the ages of five and ten and also with an increasing incidence of type 2 diabetes (Kaplan, Liverman & Kraak, 2005). Type 2 diabetes, previously considered an adult disease, has increased dramatically among children and adolescents. Diabetes is the seventh reported cause of death in the United States according to the CDC in 2015, and increases the risk of heart disease and stroke, contributes to hypertension and nervous system diseases, and can cause blindness, kidney disease, peripheral vascular disease (potentially leading to amputation), and dental complications (Sanstad, 2006). One implication of the link between obesity and the early appearance of risk factors for these conditions is that children will live with the burden of disease for considerably longer periods of time than adults who develop these conditions. Researchers have shown that managing diabetes as a sixteen-year-old is quite distinct from managing it as an older person and has implications for self-identity and social status (e.g. Greene, McKiernan and Greene, 2008). Also, heart disease and other conditions take a physical toll that may contribute to comorbidity (Lobstein, 2008) and even reduced life expectancy.

However, children view social discrimination as the most immediate consequence of overweight and obesity, which in turn is associated with poor self-esteem and even depression. For instance, studies from Yale University and Monash University in Australia have reported that obese people experience a "culture of blame" in which they feel overwhelmed and disheartened by media portrayals of obesity(Doheny, 2008) and that women are more likely to feel prejudice if they are obese (Puhl & Andreyava, 2008).

obesity also creates "significant economic burdens . . . [on] total health care costs in the United States" (Oliver & Lee, 2005, p. 924). It is estimated that hospital costs of treating children for obesity-associated conditions rose from $35 million in 1979 to $127 million in 1999 (Wang & Dietz, 2002) and rose again to $237.6 million in 2005 (Trasande & Liu, 2009). Overall, the economic costs of dealing with obesityrelated conditions are high, since this expenditure is funded mainly through Medicare and Medicaid (Sanstad, 2006).

The Causes of Obesity

There is considerable debate about the causes of obesity and overweight. On the one hand, obesity is viewed as a consequence of individual actions, such as poor nutritional choices and limited physical activity. On the other, there is some consensus that obese children especially are innocent victims of changes in their environment–in the food market, in schools and in child care settings, and in the role of parents–that ill serve them (Anderson & Butcher, 2006). Overweight and obesity in children and adolescents is generally caused by a combination of the lack of physical activity and unhealthy eating patterns with genetics and lifestyle playing important roles in determining weight. Children who eat more "empty calories" and expend fewer calories through physical activity are more likely to be obese than other children (Anderson & Butcher, 2006). Moreover, contemporary Western societies have become very sedentary. For instance, children's leisure time typically involves access to television, computer and video games, which, some suggest, have produced a generation of "couch potatoes."

Crouch, O'Dea, and Battisti identify the prevalence of an "obesogenic" environment, whereby modern lifestyles tend to foster an imbalance between energy intake and energy expenditure, resulting in excessive fat deposition (2006). The engendering of this environment is complex, but is, according to Paxson, Donahue, Orleans, and Grisso, attributable to a powerful cocktail that includes the proliferation of fast-food restaurants, many of which market their products to children through media campaigns organized around tie-ins to children's movies and TV shows (2006). In addition, there has been an increase in sugary and fat-laden foods displayed at children's eye level in supermarkets and advertised on television. Similarly, in some schools there is an increasing availability of energy-dense, high-calorie foods and drinks, while at the same time, physical education classes and recess opportunities have been reduced.

Additionally, changes in the family–particularly an increase in dual-career or single-parent working families–may have increased demand for food away from home or for pre-packaged foods (Anderson & Butcher, 2006). Indeed, market demands on working parents have made it difficult for many to find the time or energy to cook nutritious meals or supervise outdoor play. Grocery stores have shifted their locations from urban centers, reducing access to affordable fresh fruits and vegetables, especially for low-income households; and suburban sprawl and urban crime have limited the extent to which children engage in outdoor, physical activities, even such as walking to school (Paxson, Donahue, Orleans & Grisso, 2006). These problems engender an even greater obesity burden for ethnic minority and low-income groups (Kumanyika & Grier, 2006).

VIEWPOINTS

Measures & Policies to Tackle Obesity

There is often the misperception that obesity is a moral failure. Hence, overweight and obese people are generally stigmatized for transgressing prevailing social ideals of appropriate body weight. Consequently, both public and professional opinion seem divided on whether overweight and obesity are individual and personal issues or whether government interventions should be instituted–such as regulating advertising aimed at children or monitoring public school lunches–in order to reduce the problems associated with childhood obesity and overweight. One 2005 study of public opinion found that Americans were generally less concerned by obesity as a public health problem than other issues such as cancer and heart disease, and although participants reported being aware of their own health (for instance, they exercised and paid attention to nutritional information), they were relatively unconcerned about obesity as a national health issue. Additionally, government intervention into the problems of obesity and overweight at both the national and state levels was limited at that time and was a low priority for most law makers (Oliver & Lee, 2005). By 2012, however, Americans considered obesity second to cancer as the nation's most serious health issue, and obesity-related health concerns (such as diabetes and heart disease) were listed as third. And while the individuals surveyed did not support being taxed on "unhealthy" food nor did they support restrictions on consumer choices, they did support government intervention in the public schools (requiring, for example, more physical activity during the school day) and policies such as providing incentives to the food industry to create healthier choices (Associated Press-NORC, 2013).

In the United States, an expert committee comprised of representatives from fifteen professional organizations appointed experienced scientists and clinicians to recommend evidence-based approaches to the prevention, assessment, and treatment of childhood obesity and overweight (Washington, 2008). These recommendations emphasized obesity prevention messages, behavioral measures to promote healthy weight maintenance (accompanied by annual BMI monitoring), and weight-control interventions for those with excess weight. These measures focused on tracking individual children and offering messages and measures to prevent increases in or to maintain current weight. However, other interventions, which are supported by health, consumer, and public interest groups, focus on the cultural and physical environment and emphasize the role of regulatory constraints on what can be said–and how–about food.

In 2003, the US Food and Drug Administration (FDA) required that all trans fats be listed on the food labels of products, but only if there was more than one half a gram of trans fats per serving. Ten years later, in November of 2013, the FDA announced that it would be instituting a timetable for the food industry to begin to completely remove all trans fats from their products. In June 2015, the FDA deemed partially hydrogenated oils, the main source of trans fat, no longer safe for use in food and ruled that companies would have until 2018 to remove them from all food products.

In the United States, some schools have eliminated soda machines, media coverage of obesity has proliferated, and even fast-food restaurants have introduced low-fat meals. For instance, "the Child Nutrition and WIC (Women, Infants, and Children) Reauthorization Act of 2004, required school districts that participate in the National School Lunch Program or School Breakfast Program to develop a local wellness policy by the beginning of the 2006-2007 school year" (Paxson, Donahue, Orleans & Grisso, 2006, p. 4).

Other proposals also include taxing sodas and snack foods, setting health mandates for school lunches, instituting standards for physical fitness education within schools, extending health and disability protections for the morbidly obese, requiring food labeling in restaurants, limiting food advertisements, and promoting greater levels of physical activity among adults through the creation of bike paths, sidewalks, or other programs (Oliver & Lee, 2005).

In 2010, President Barack Obama signed the Healthy, Hunger-Free Kids Act into law and First Lady Michelle Obama instituted the "Let's Move!" campaign with the goal of eradicating child obesity. Mandates of the act that were put into effect in the 2012-13 school year included a requirement that children receive at least a half serving of fruits and vegetables with every meal served at school and that schools only serve fat-free or low-fat milk, whole grains, and reduced portions of meat. However, these adjustments have also faced increased lunch prices and reductions in the number of children purchasing lunch at school. Additionally, part of the "Let's Move!" campaign has aimed at offering more resources for nutritional education available to child care providers; these trainings focus on daily physical activity, less screen time, and the encouragement of breastfeeding (Bobrovnyk, 2014).

Concern over childhood obesity has also prompted leaders outside of the United States to implement a number of initiatives. In England in 2005, for instance, the Department of Health (DH) announced a plan called the National ChildMeasurement Programme that would monitor and observe children's weight and record a child's weight and height upon entry into the school system and again in the final year of elementary school. In 2009, England implemented its first national marketing campaign, Change4Life, with the sole purpose of addressing the causes of obesity and promoting healthy behaviors in children and adults in order to prevent obesity and reduce obesity rates in that country.

In 2012, the World Health Organization (WHO) presented approaches to prevent childhood obesity (World Health Organization, 2012). WHO member countries were urged to analyze and take their respective cultures and political and economic climates in to consideration when determining which approaches to implement. WHO suggested that in order to prevent obesity and overweight in children, governments should make population-wide policies such as requiring nutrition labeling on foods or restrict marketing unhealthy foods and beverages to children.

Overall, these measures point to a shift towards public regulation of private practices that have a bearing on individual health and that manage the public burden for disease (Sanstad, 2006). Government intervention in food markets and restaurant chains seems especially controversial. However, some researchers argue (e.g. Cawley, 2006) that markets and restaurants need to be persuaded to increase the information they provide to consumers in order to enable them to make more informed choices about the food they eat. Since children are not what Cawley calls "rational consumers" who can evaluate information and weigh the long-term costs, the government has a role to play in directing choices. Moreover, since society bears the economic costs of obesity, the government may have a role to play in lowering the cost to taxpayers.

TERMS & CONCEPTS

Body Mass Index: Calculated from measurements of height and weight, usually taken by health professionals—weight in kilograms divided by height in meters squared.

Comorbidity: The extent to which two conditions or diseases occur together in a given population.

Epidemic: When a condition or disease occurs in a population in numbers that exceed normal expectations.

Incidence: The number of new cases of a condition appearing in a population during a particular period.

Obesity: Range of weight that is greater than what is generally considered healthy for a given height. An adult with a BMI between twenty five and twenty-nine is considered overweight.

Overweight: A range of weight that is greater than what is generally considered healthy for a given height. An adult with a BMI of over thirty is considered obese.

Prevalence: The number of cases of a condition that are present in a given population at a particular point in time.

Prevention: Averting the occurrence of health problems and diseases.

Bibliography

Anderson, P. M. & Butcher, K. (2006). "Childhood obesity: Trends and potential causes." *Childhood* Obesity, 16, 19-45. Future of Children http://www.futureofchildren.org/

Associated Press-NORC Center for Public Affairs Research. (2013). "Obesity in the United States; Public perception of causes, solutions, and consequences." *Associated Press.* http://www.apnorc.org/about-the-center/Pages/default.aspx

Australian Bureau of Statistics. (2013). "Health risk factors: Overweight and Obesity." *Gender Indicators.* http://www.abs.gov.au/ausstats/abs@.nsf/Lookup/4125.0main+features3330Jan%202013

Bobrovnyk, M. (2014). "Confronting childhood obesity." *Policy & Practice,* 72(5), 28-30.

Cawley, J. (2006). "Markets and childhood obesity policy." *Childhood* Obesity, 16, 69-88. Future of Childrenhttp://www.futureofchildren.org/

Cooper, S. (2008, June 11). "Healthy towns can cut child obesity." *Children* & Young People Now, p 2.

Doheny, K. (2008). "Stigma of obesity not easy to shed." WebMD. http://www.webmd.com/balance/news/20080619/stigma-of-obesity-not-easy-to o-shed

Eastwood, P. (2013). "Obesity among children." *Statistics on* Obesity, *Physical Activity and Diet: England, 2013,* 1, 22-27. http://www.bhfactive.org.uk/userfiles/Documents/obes-phys-acti-diet-eng-2013-rep.pdf

Ebbeling, C. B. & Ludwig, D. S. (2008). "Tracking pediatric obesity." *Journal of the American Medical Association.* 299:2442-2443.

Eyler, A. A., Nguyen, L., Jooyoung, K., Yan, Y., & Brownson, R. (2012). "Patterns and predictors of enactment of state childhood obesity legislation in the United States: 2006-2009." *American Journal of Public Health,* 102, 2294-2302.

Fryar, C. D., Carroll, M. D. & Ogden, C. L. (2014). "Prevalence of overweight and obesity among children and adolescents: United States, 1963-1965 through 2011-2012." http://www.cdc.gov/nchs/

Greene, A., McKiernan, P. & Greene, S. (2008). "The nature of reciprocity and the spirit of the gift: Balancing trust and governance in long-term illness." In J. Brownlie, A. Greene and A. Howson (eds). *Researching Trust and Health.* New York: Routledge.

Gollust, S. E., Niederdeppe, J., & Barry, C. L. (2013). "Framing the consequences of childhood obesity to increase public support for obesity prevention policy." *American Journal of Public Health,* 103, e96-e102.

Haden, R. (2006). "Pandora's lunchbox." *Food, Culture & Society,* 9, 265-274.

Koplan, J.P., Liverman, C.T. & Kraak, V.A. eds. (2005). Preventing childhood obesity: Health in the balance. Washington: National Academies Press.

Kumanyika, S. & Grier, S. (2006). "Targeting interventions for ethnic minority and low-income populations." *Childhood* Obesity 16, 187-208. Future of Children http://www.futureofchildren.org/

Lobstein, T. (2008). "Obesity in children." *British Medical Journal,* 337(7668): 472-473.

"Local targets to stop child obesity." (2008, February 27). *Children* & Young People Now, p11.

Luck, A. (2006, June 30). "Stigma of topping the fat league." *Times Educational Supplement,* 4692, 2.

Matthews, A. E. (2008). "Children and obesity: A pan-European project examining the role of food marketing." *European Journal of Public Health,* 18, 7-11.

MITGANG, M. (2011). "Childhood obesity and state intervention: An examination of the health risks of pediatric obesity and when they justify state involvement." *Columbia Journal of Law & Social Problems,* 44, 553-587.

National Center for Health Statistics. (2004). National Health and Nutrition Examination Hyattsville, Maryland: National Center for Health Statistics.

Ogden, C. L., Carroll, M. D. & Flegal, K. M. (2008). "High body mass index for age among us children and adolescents, 2003-2006." *Journal of the American Medical Association,* 299, 2401-2405.

Ogden, Cynthia, & Caroll, Margaret. (2010). "Prevalence of obesity among children and adolescents: United States, trends 1963-1965 through 2007-2008." Centers for Disease Control and Prevention http://www.cdc.gov/

Ogden, Cynthia L., Carroll, Margaret D., Kit, Brian K., & Flegal, Katherine M. (2012). "Prevalence of obesity in the United States, 2009-2010." NCHS Data Brief, 82. Centers for Disease Control and Prevention http://www.cdc.gov/

Oliver, J. & Lee, T. (2005). "Public opinion and the politics of obesity in America." *Journal of Health Politics, Policy & Law,* 30, 923-954.

Paxson, C., Donahue, E., Orleans, T., Grisso, J. (2006). "Introducing the issue." *Childhood* Obesity,16, 3-17. Future of Children http://www.futureofchildren.org/

Puhl, R.M., Andreyeva, T. & Brownell, K. D. (2008). "Perceptions of weight discrimination: prevalence and comparison to race and gender discrimination in America." *International Journal of* Obesity, 32, 992-1000.

Sanstad, K. (2006). *Obesity*: Mapping the life-cycle of response. Palo Alto: Institute for the Future.

Stewart, K., Gill, P., Treasure, E. & Chadwick, B. (2008). "Understandings about food among 6-11 year olds in

South Wales." *Food, Culture and Society,* 9, 265-274.

Trasande, L., Liu, Y., Fryer, G., & Weitzman, M. (2009). "Effects of childhood obesity on hospital care and costs, 1999-2005." *Health Affairs* 28, 751-760. http://www.nccor.org

Turner, B.S. (1984). *The body and society.* Oxford: Blackwell.

U.S. Department of Health and Human Services. Office of the Surgeon General. (2007). "Overweight in children and adolescents." http://www.surgeongeneral.gov/topics/obesity/calltoaction/fact%5Fadolescents.htm

Wang, G. & Dietz, W.H. (2002). "Economic burden of obesity in youths aged 7 to 17 years: 1979-1999." *Pediatrics,* 109, E81.

Washington, R. (2008, September). "Overview of the expert committee's recommendations for prevention, diagnosis, and treatment of child and adolescent obesity." *Progress in Pediatric Cardiology,* 25, 125-128.

World Health Organization. (2012). "Population-based approaches to childhood obesity prevention." Geneva: WHO Document Production Services. http://apps.who.int/iris/bitstream/

World Health Organization. (2013, March). "Obesity and overweight." *Media Centre,* N.311. http://www.worksheetworks.com/miscellanea/calendars/hour.html

World Health Organization. (2014, August). Obesity and overweight. *Media Center,* N. 311. http://www.who.int/mediacentre/factsheets/fs311/en/

Zarembo, A. (2008, May 28). "Child obesity rate in U.S. hits plateau, researchers say." *Los Angeles Times.* http://articles.latimes.com/2008/may/28/science/sci-obesity28

Suggested Reading

Brownell, K.D., Puhl R., Schwartz, M.B. & Rudd, L. eds. (2005). *Weight bias: Nature, consequences, and remedies.* New York: Guilford Publications.

Finkelstein, E.A.,. Fiebelkorn, I.C. & Wang, G. (2003). "National medical spending attributable to overweight and obesity: How much, and who's paying?" [Electronic version]. *Health Affairs.* http://content.healthaffairs.org/cgi/content/full/hlthaff.w3.219v1/DC1

Jackson, S. L., & Cunningham, S. A. (2015). "Social competence and obesity in elementary school." *American Journal of Public Health,* 105(1), 153-158.

Mori, N., Armada, F., & Willcox, D. (2012). "Walking to school in Japan and childhood obesity prevention: New lessons from an old policy." *American Journal of Public Health,* 102, 2068-2073.

Novotny, R., Fialkowski, M. K., Fenfang, L., Paulino, Y., Vargo, D., Jim, R., & ... Wilkens, L. R. (2015). "Systematic review of prevalence of young child overweight and obesity in the United States-affiliated Pacific region compared with the 48 contiguous states: the Children's Healthy Living Program." *American Journal of Public Health,* 105, e22-e35.

Parizkova, J. and Hills, A. (2000). *Childhood* obesity: *Prevention and treatment.* Boca Raton: CRC Press.

Spruijt-Metz, D. (2011). "Etiology, treatment, and prevention of obesity in childhood and adolescence: A decade in review." *Journal of Research on Adolescence* (Wiley-Blackwell), 21, 129-152.

Staniford, L., Breckon, J., & Copeland, R. (2012). "Treatment of childhood obesity: A systematic review." *Journal of*Child *& Family Studies*, 21, 545-564.

Alexandra Howson

Doctor-patient Communication

ABSTRACT

Doctor-patient (or client-professional, practitioner-patient, lay-professional) communication has been the focus of scholarly study and public concern for several decades. Within medicine, communication is increasingly seen as a critical skill set in the delivery of care. The Doctor-patient relationship is a special kind of relationship; while patients may not know their doctors in a personal sense (and often, vice versa) they are nonetheless asked to disclose intimate details of their personal lives and reveal their bodies for examination. This vulnerability is not reciprocated from doctors to patients. There is, therefore, a degree of social imbalance in this relationship (albeit one that is socially sanctioned), which may have a bearing on communication. Barriers to effective communication between doctors and their patients, including such factors as class, gender, race, and health literacy, are discussed.

OVERVIEW

Doctor-patient (or client-professional, practitioner-patient, lay-professional) communication has been the focus of scholarly study and public concern for several decades. Within the medical field, communication is increasingly seen as a critical skill set in the delivery of care. The Doctor-patient relationship is a special kind of relationship; while patients may not know their doctors in a personal sense (and often, vice versa) they are nonetheless asked to disclose often intimate details of their personal lives and reveal parts of their bodies for examination. This vulnerability is not reciprocated from doctors to patients. There is, therefore, a degree of social imbalance in this relationship (albeit one that is socially sanctioned). This may have a bearing on communication; that is, the full range of spoken, facial, bodily, and symbolic expressions that people use when they interact and exchange information with each other.

Classic studies in sociology have highlighted the potential for conflict in Doctor-patient communication and identified how assumptions about patients based on class, gender, age and race influence the content and tone of communication. Moreover, research has shown that patients who understand their doctors are more likely to acknowledge their health problems, understand their treatment options, modify their health-related behaviors at their doctor's recommendation, and adhere to treatment recommendations. Given this compelling evidence, two-thirds of medical schools now provide their students with instruction on how to communicate with patients and how to develop interpersonal skills to support effective communication (Travaline et al., 2005). Such skills, which include listening, explaining, questioning, counseling and motivating patients, are becoming core competencies for medical practice, and in the United States, demonstration of such skills is required for licensure and board certification. Nonetheless, there continue to be many barriers to effective communication between doctors and their patients, including such factors as gender, race, and health literacy.

Communication & the 'Ceremonial Order of the Clinic'

Physician-patient communication has been central to scholarly research for at least fifty years and the ideal medical encounter (for which effective communication is critical) is increasingly viewed as one that is patient-centered (Mead & Bower, 2000) from obtaining the patient's medical history to conveying a treatment plan. The medical or clinical encounter entails much information sharing about symptoms, diagnosis, and treatment options in what has been historically and is increasingly recognized as a therapeutic relationship that provides the first step toward healing (Travaline, Ruchinskas & D'Alonzo, 2005). However, studies of patient-doctor communication demonstrate that communication is rarely patient-centered and is in fact influenced by many characteristics and ideas.

There is a surprising degree of regularity and ritual associated with communication between doctors and patients, or, more correctly, with the medical encounter. In a classic study of outpatient clinic visits in Scotland, Phil Strong (1979) found that there is an unspoken set of rules and rituals that guide the medical encounter or consultation. These rituals, encoded as role formats (or as sociologist Erving Goffman might put it, social scripts), provide tacit resources that both patients and doctors call upon, depending on their assessment of the encounter (that is, what kind of consultation they consider it to be). Strong identifies four such formats:

- Bureaucratic (doctor and patient are both polite and avoid conflict, though doctors assume patients to be less than competent);
- Charity (doctors draw attention to patients' incompetence);
- Clinical (in which the doctor and patient tacitly agree on the doctor's expertise and authority); and
- Private (in which the doctor focuses on "selling" his competence).

Core to these formats is the way the doctor typically asserts control over the communication process and directs the conversation by the following tactics: interrupting patients or breaking off conversation; excluding the patient by writing while they tell their story; and eliciting information from patients but not explaining why such information was required. Strong (1979) notes that such tactics cement the asymmetry between doctor and patient, and subsequent studies in social psychology have confirmed their use.

Conflict & Power

Indeed, studies of Doctor-patient communication often begin with the observation that the relationship between doctors and their patients is unequal in terms of power, status, and knowledge. For instance, in Talcott Parsons's (1951) discussion of the sick role (a socially deviant state) the patient is entitled to be sick, provided she or he assumes certain obligations, such as making an effort to get well. Accordingly, doctors are obliged to help patients get well. How they interact and communicate with each other is central to how the sick role is negotiated, since doctors occupy a position of authority in relation to the patient (Nettleton, 1992). While such asymmetry is unproblematic in a functionalist view of the social world, it ignores the potential for conflict between doctor and patient, or of the potential for value judgments to influence the process of making clinical decisions.

For instance, doctors may discount information that patients provide and be dismissive toward them. In studies of how patients use emergency rooms, researchers have found that doctors are often dismissive of patients because in their view, based on the symptoms that patients describe, some patients should not be in the emergency room in the first place. That is, patients are judged as being overanxious (especially mothers of young children, see Roberts, 1992) or, in certain situations (such as patients who are injured but who have also been drinking alcohol) may be judged for behaving in ways that are seen as irresponsible. In such cases, patients may be judged as "normal rubbish" (Jeffery, 1979); that is, they are seen as presenting with symptoms that are considered inappropriate or trivial. While doctors usually do not explicitly inform patients of what they are thinking or what their value judgments are, they may communicate disapproval nonverbally by not listening to patients or not demonstrating empathy. More recent research confirms that in situations characterized by prejudice and fear, such as in the case of consultations about HIV risk, doctors may handle communication ineffectively in ways that make patients feel uncomfortable or even stigmatized (Epstein et al., 1998).

Barriers to Doctor-patient Communication

Social characteristics such as gender and race influence the content and tone of Doctor-patient communication, and many studies have demonstrated how the social backgrounds of both patients and doctors create barriers to effective communication. Many studies have found social class, gender, and racial differences in physician communication style, that is, how physicians talk with patients and communicate nonverbally.

Social Class

First, social class differences are significant in determining how doctors communicate with their patients. Although there have been some changes in medical school recruitment, medicine is largely practiced by members of the middle, upper-middle, or upper class and as such, reflects values associated economic independence and autonomy (Mechanic, 1974). These values influence communication style, especially in terms of the language and the forms of expression used by doctors. For instance, members of the middle class tend to be more verbally explicit, while working class members tend to rely more on nonverbal communication. This means, in Doctor-patient encounters between middle-class physicians and working-class patients, physicians may be more likely to talk than their patients (Cooper & Roter, 2003). In addition, patients whose health literacy levels are low (that is, they have difficulties reading and understanding written medical information), which is often associated with social class, are more likely to report poor communication with doctors in face-to-face encounters (Schillinger et al., 2004).

Gender

Second, there are differences between male and female physicians in the way they interact with their patients in general (Brody & Hall, 2000). Male physicians have been found to engage less in nonverbal gestures that communicate warmth and empathy, such as smiling, eye contact, nodding, hand gesturing, direct body orientation (facing the patient), and "back-channel responses" (such as saying "mm-hmm" to acknowledge what the patient is saying) (Cooper & Roter, 2003). Similarly, observation studies have found that male physicians talk more than female physicians and when they do so, they are more likely to provide the patient with biomedical information than to engage in psychosocial conversation that explicitly invites comment from patients about their expectations, feelings, and life circumstances (Krupat et al., 2000). On the other hand, female patients are more likely to ask questions than male patients, which may explain why they are given more information than male patients (Waitzkin, 1985) or given information rather than emotional support. These differences in communication style may translate into differences in how physicians treat their female patients, which researchers have historically explained in terms of patriarchal or sexist ideologies (Nettleton, 1992).

Time Factors

Third, doctors may lack the time and skills to communicate effectively with patients. Patient consultations are generally short and doctors learn to describe and understand disease and illness in a specialized language, which patients may view as "jargon." Such jargon gets in the way of establishing common ground between doctors and patients (Stacey, 1988) and may contribute to patient dissatisfaction (Williams, Weinman & Dale, 1998).

Race

Finally, there are differences in race and ethnicity. For instance, doctors and patients are more likely to communicate effectively with each other if they share a similar racial or ethnic background, or are "race concordant" (Cooper-Patrick et al., 2000). In particular, African American patients experience less participatory visits with their doctors (that is, they are less likely to be included in making decisions about their care) than are other racial or ethnic groups. Indeed, one study found that when African American and Hispanic patients are able to choose their physician, they are more likely to choose a physician who is racially concordant (Saha et al., 1999), because they feel such physicians are more likely to be culturally sensitive to their needs and more likely to share their values, beliefs, and experiences. When patients and physicians do not share a similar racial and ethnic background, visits are likely to be shorter, patients are less likely to participate in decisions about their care, and tend to be less satisfied with their physician (Cooper-Patrick et al., 2000).

However, racial concordance between doctor and patient does not necessarily, on its own, contribute to quality of communication between doctor and patient (Misra-Hebert, 2003) and it is not necessarily the case that if the patient and physician are of the same race, there are no barriers to communication. In part, racial or ethnic similarity is a marker for cultural similarity, whereby members of a group share beliefs, values, mannerisms, and behaviors that are learned and shared by the members of a group (Misra-Hebert, 2003) and extends beyond racial, ethnic, or gender boundaries. Accordingly, cultural competence has become increasingly important in Doctor-patient communication.

FURTHER INSIGHTS

Patient-Centered Care

Communication matters because it has consequences for patient health and health outcomes. Broadly, studies have found that when communication is effective (i.e., when patients are able to ask questions, doctors talk less than patients and provide socio-emotional support along with providing biomedical information), care is more patient-centered. When care is patient-centered, there is some evidence that patient outcomes are better, such as pain control, blood pressure, health status (Stewart, 1995), and patient satisfaction (Kaplan et al., 1995). Concomitantly, communication lies at the heart of patient-centered care. Patient-centered care emerged in the late twentieth century as an approach to medicine that is sensitive to patients' cultural and personal preferences and values, family relationships, and lifestyles (Institute of Medicine, 2001). Patient-centered care includes the patient and his or her family as part of the health care team and emphasizes participation and collaboration, and encourages patients to take responsibility for being involved in decisions about their care. Consequently, communication skills are increasingly taught as a set of technical skills, not only in medical schools but also as part of continuing medical education. Behaviors that are thought to be associated with effective communication include:

- Gathering data from the patient, for instance through open-ended questions;
- Building rapport with patients, by using empathy, reassuring patients and responding when patients express emotions;
- Building partnerships with patients by asking for their input and opinion and inviting patients to solve problems jointly; and
- Counseling (Roter, 2000).

Teaching Communication Skills

While many medical schools teach communication skills to their students, there is considerable debate over which skills to teach and how to teach them. For instance, some training tools focus on improving communication in the context of poor health literacy and emphasize using plain, nonmedical language, slowing down speech, limiting information and offering it in different formats, such as images as well as text (Weiss, 2009). Other tools emphasize how racial and ethnic issues affect communication and focus on cultural competency and the need to understand, respect, and empathize with the patient's perspective, or focus more generically on patient-centeredness and the need to incorporate the patient as a key player in the health care team.

Overall, there is a growing body of behavioral research to support training approaches and content, and at least some agreement on core skills, such as listening, using open-ended questions to elicit patient information, providing and explaining information, counseling and educating patients, and taking patient preferences into account. Moreover, teaching these skills has become more of a priority in relation to health care disparities. The Institute of Medicine ("Unequal Treatment," 2002) published a report that identified Doctor-patient communication as a possible source of disparities for minority patients. A consequence of this report, and the research that supports it, is that in addition to teaching communication skills to medical students and practitioners, skills in cultural competence are also required.

Communication & Cultural Competence

Cultural competence emerged in medicine as a way to bridge "cultural distance" between physicians and patients in the interest of reducing racial disparities in health care. Racial disparities are "racial or ethnic differences in the quality of healthcare that are not due to access-related factors or clinical needs, preference, and appropriateness of intervention" ("Unequal Treatment," 2002). Cultural competence includes ways of addressing interpersonal and institutional sources of racial disparities in health care (Saha et al., 2008) and is becoming especially pertinent as the proportion of ethnic minorities in the United States continues to increase and is viewed as a national priority in health care. Cultural bias has been identified as a potential source of disparities or at least a barrier to communication between patients and physicians and cultural competence may be a way to overcome this barrier.

Cultural competence has many definitions, but generally refers to the ability of physicians to provide patient-centered care by "adjusting their attitudes and behaviors to the needs and desires of different patients and account for the impact of emotional, cultural, social, and psychological issues on the main biomedical ailment" (Misra-Hebert, 2003, p. 293). In practice, cultural competence means different things, but includes, first, language sensitivity—for instance, using interpreters when language barriers exist—and learning about how different cultures treat nonverbal communication (Misra-Hebert, 2003). For instance, bodily and social gestures differ across cultural groups, as do concepts about appropriate personal space. While personal space for many Anglo-Saxon Americans is generally considered to be about eighteen inches, personal space in many cultures is often considered to be much closer.

Second, cultural competence in communication includes finding out more about the patient experience of disease. In a classic study, medical anthropologist Arthur Kleinman and colleagues (1978) argued for a distinction between disease (a biological concept) and illness (an experiential state), in which the latter is influenced by cultural norms (whether, for instance, it is acceptable to express pain in front of other people) and personal health belief systems. This argument is increasingly taken seriously by medical educators who suggest that in culturally competent care, doctors need to be able to understand the patient experience and their own interpretation of what ails them (what Kleinman et al., refer to as the "cultural construction of clinical reality").

Finally, culturally competent communication is designed to help doctors negotiate with patients in terms they understand and to which they subscribe. In practice, this means respecting patient preferences (for instance, for complementary or alternative therapies such as herbal remedies, or for including family members in decision-making).

VIEWPOINTS

Improving Patient Communication

While teaching communication skills to doctors is an important corrective to the power imbalance that may be an inherent part of the Doctor-patient relationship, some researchers argue that patients also need to be taught communication skills, especially among populations for whom health literacy levels are low. In part, this drive to communication may be because poor communication between doctors and patients can lead to malpractice suits, where communication errors include inadequate understandings of diagnosis or treatment or where patients feel their concerns have been ignored (Weiss, 2009). Consequently, some studies have used waiting-rooms as places to talk to and coach patients about communication and in particular, which questions to ask and how to ask them during the clinical consultation (e.g. Cegala et al., 2000). One study found that following such an intervention, patients' overall perceptions of their health improved and their blood sugar decreased (Greenfield et al., 1988), which suggests that empowering patients to participate in their care can lead to better communication and perhaps even better health outcomes.

CONCLUSION

Doctor-patient communication has long been of concern for medical practitioners, educators, and researchers. Ineffective communication has been found to affect patient experience and outcomes and is associated with social factors such as gender, class, and race. These differences have been explained in different ways. Scholars in the political economy of health have argued that poor communication is a result of the social distance between middle-class doctors and working-class patients. The recognition that race and ethnicity also affects communication has brought new urgency to the debate because of evidence that links ineffective communication to racial disparities in health care. Consequently, there is a shift toward training doctors in both cultural competency and patient-centeredness, which have both been found to improve communication in ways that might reduce disparities. However, communication is a two-way street, and some patient groups advocate that patients too, need to be coached in how to best communicate with their doctors, so that they feel comfortable asking questions and participating in decisions about their treatment options and care.

TERMS & CONCEPTS

Communication: The full range of verbal, facial, bodily and symbolic expressions that people use when they interact and exchange information with each other.

Concordance: Shared identity between patient and physician based on demographic attributes such as age, gender, or race.

Cultural Competence: The ability of physicians to provide patient-centered care by taking the needs and desires of different patients into account as well as how emotional, cultural, social, and psychological issues affect the main biomedical ailment.

Functionalism: A sociological perspective based on application of scientific method to the social world that sees the world as a social system with needs that need to be met in order to maintain order and stability.

Health Care Disparities: Racial or ethnic differences in the quality of health care not due to access-related factors or clinical needs, preference, and appropriateness of intervention.

Patient-centered Care: An approach to medicine that is sensitive to patients' cultural and personal preferences and values, family relationships, and lifestyles.

Role Format: Rituals that guide Doctor-patient communication and that both patients and doctors call upon, depending on their assessment of the encounter.

Sick Role: A special role that sanctions the absence of people from production until they are considered (by physicians) well enough to return.

Bibliography

Bergen, C., & Stivers, T. (2013). "Patient disclosure of medical misdeeds." *Journal of Health and Social Behavior, 54*(2), 220–239.

Brody, L.R. & Hall, J.A. (2000). "Gender, emotion, and expression." In, M. Lewis & J. Haviland-Jones (Eds.), *Handbook of emotions*, 2nd ed. (pp. 338–349). New York: Guilford.

Cegala, D.J., McClure L., Marinelli, T.M., & Post, D.M. (2000). "The effects of communication skills training on patients' participation during medical interviews." *Patient Education and Counseling*, (41), 209–222.

Cooper, L. & Roter, D. (2003). "Patient-provider communication: The effect of race and ethnicity on process and outcomes of healthcare." In Smedley, B.D., Smith, A.Y. and Nelson, A.R. (eds). *Unequal Treatment: Confronting racial and ethnic disparities in health care.* Washington, D.C.: The National Academies Press.

Cooper, L. A., Roter, D. L., Carson, K. A., Catherine Beach, M., Sabin, J. A., Greenwald, A. G., & Inui, T. S. (2012). "The associations of clinicians' implicit attitudes about race with medical visit communication and patient ratings of interpersonal care." *American Journal of Public Health, 102*(5), 979–987.

Cooper-Patrick, L., Ford, D.E., Vu, H.T., Powe, N.R. Steinwachs, D.M. & Roter, D.L. (2000). "Patient-physician race concordance and communication in primary care." *Journal of General Internal Medicine.* (15), 106.

Epstein, R.M., Morse, D.S., Frankel, R.M., Frarey, L., Anderson, K., Beckman, H.B., (1998). "Awkward moments in patient-physician communication about HIV risk." *Annals of Internal Medicine, 128*(6), 435–42.

Greenfield, S., Kaplan, S.H., Ware, J.E., Jr., Yano, E.M., Frank, H.J.L. (1988). "Patients' participation in medical care: Effects on blood sugar control and quality of life in diabetes." *Journal of General Internal Medicine.* (3), 448–457.

Gregory, R., Peters, E., & Slovic, P. (2011). "Making decisions about prescription drugs: a study of Doctor-patient communication." *Health, Risk and Society, 13*(4), 347–371.

Institute of Medicine. (2001). *Crossing the chasm: A new health system for the 21st century.*

Institute of Medicine. (2002). *Unequal treatment: Confronting racial and ethnic disparities in healthcare.*

Jefferson, L., Bloor, K., Birks, Y., Hewitt, C., & Bland, M. (2013). "Effect of physicians' gender on communication and consultation length: a systematic review and meta-analysis." *Journal of Health Services Research & Policy, 18*(4), 242–248.

Jeffery, R. (1979). "Normal rubbish: Deviant patients in casualty departments." *Sociology of Health and Illness, 1* (1), 90-107.

Kaplan, S.H., Gandek, B., Greenfield, S., Rogers, W., Ware, J.E. (1995). "Patient and visit characteristics related to physicians' participatory decision-making style: Results from the Medical Outcomes Study." *Medical Care,* (33), 1176–1183.

Kleinman, A., Eisenberg, L., Good, B. (1978). "Culture, illness, and care: Clinical lessons from anthropologic and cross-cultural research." *Annals of Internal Medicine. 88* (2), 251–258.

Krupat, E., Rosenkranz, S.L., Yeager, C.M., Barnard, K., Putnam, S.M., Inui, T.S. (2000). "The practice orientations of physicians and patients: The effect of Doctor-patient congruence on satisfaction." *Patient Education and Counseling. 39* (1), 49–59.

Mead, N. & Bower, P. (2000). "Measuring patient-centredness: A comparison of three observation-based instruments." *Patient Education and Counseling. 39*(1):71–80.

Mechanic D. (1974). *Politics, medicine, and social science.* New York: John Wiley & Sons.

Misra-Hebert, A. (2003). "Physician cultural competence: Cross-cultural communication improves care." *Cleveland Clinic Journal of Medicine. 70*(4): 289–303. http://www.dhss.mo.gov/SpecialNeedsToolkit/PublicHealth_Health_Hospitals/Misra-Hebert403.pdf.

Nettleton, S. (1992). *The sociology of health and illness.* London: Routledge.

Parsons, T. ([1951] 1991). *The social system.* London: Routledge.

Roberts, H. (1992). "Professionals' and parents' perceptions of A&E use in a children's hospital." *Sociological Review. 40*(1): 109–131.

Roter, D.L. (2000). "The enduring and evolving nature of the patient-physician relationship." *Patient Education and Counseling, 39*(1), 5–15.

Saha, S., Beach, M. C. & Cooper, L. A. (2008). "Patient centeredness, cultural competence, and healthcare quality." *Journal of the National Medical Association. 100*(11),1275–85.

Schillinger, D., Bindman, A., Wang, F., Stewart, A., & Piette, J. (2004). "Functional health literacy and the quality of physician-patient communication among diabetes patients." *Patient Education and Counselling. 52*(3), 315–23.

Strong, P. (1979). *The ceremonial order of the clinic.* London: Routledge and Kegan Paul.

Stewart, M.A. (1995). "Effective physician-patient communication and health outcomes: A review." *Canadian Medical Association Journal.* (152), 1423–1433.

Stacey, M (1988) *The sociology of health & healing: A textbook.* London: Unwin Hyman.

Travaline, J.M., Ruchinskas, R., D'Alonzo, G.E (2005). "Patient-Physician communication: Why and how." *Journal of the American Osteopathic Association.* 1105(1):13–18. http://www.jaoa.org/cgi/content/full/105/1/13.

US Census Bureau. (2000). http://www.census.gov/main/www/cen2000.html.

Waitzkin, H. (1985). "Information giving in medical care." *Journal of Health and Social Behavior,* 26 (2), 81–101.

Weiss, B.D. (2007). *Health literacy and patient safety: Help patients understand.* AMA Foundation.

Wilkerson, J. M., Rybicki, S., Barber, C. A., & Smolenksi, D. J. (2011). "Creating a culturally competent clinical environment for LGBT patients." *Journal of Gay and Lesbian Social Services, 23*(3), 376–394.

Williams, S., Weinman, J., Dale, J. (1998). "Doctor-patient communication and patient satisfaction: A review." *Family Practice. 15*(5), 480-92. http://fampra.oxfordjournals.org/cgi/reprint/15/5/480.

SUGGESTED READING

Arora, N. K. (2003). "Interacting with cancer patients: The significance of physicians' communication behavior." *Social Science and Medicine.* 57, 791-806.

Fisher, S. (1993). "Doctor talk/patient talk: How treatment decisions are negotiated in Doctor-patient communication." In, *The Social Organization of Doctor-patientCommunication.* 2nd Edition. Norwood, New Jersey: Ablex Publishing Corporation.

Lee, R. G. & Garvin, T. (2003). "Moving from information *Transfer* to information *Exchange* in health and health care." *Social Science and Medicine.* 56: 449–464.

Mick, P., Foley, D. M., & Lin, F. R. (2014). "Hearing loss is associated with poorer ratings of patient-physician communication and healthcare quality." *Journal of the American Geriatrics Society, 62*(11), 2207–2209.

Naidoo, J. & Wills, J. (Eds). (2001). *Health studies: An introduction.* Basingstoke: Palgrave.

Noel, L. T., & Whaley, A. L. (2012). "Ethnic/racial differences in depression among US primary care patients: cultural considerations in screening and detection." *Journal of Ethnic and Cultural Diversity in Social Work, 21*(4), 314–330.

Shoou-Yih D. L., Arozullah, A.M. & Young, I. C. (2004). "Health literacy, social support and health: A research agenda." *Social Science and Medicine.* 58: 1309–1321.

Alexandra Howson

HOLISTIC MEDICINE

ABSTRACT

There is perhaps no experience so human as that of dealing with illness and/or injury. Our very existence is predicated on being able to function so that we can do all that is expected of us on a daily basis. When we have to cope with a serious injury or illness, there are many choices to be made. Many people are increasingly moving toward the use of treatments and medicine that are covered under the broad term of "holistic medicine." This is a philosophy that believes in treating the whole person and not just an injured body part or an illness. The notion of the integrated mind-body-spirit is integral to holistic medicine. An important distinction to make is that of the difference between alternative medicine and complementary medicine. The first is used in place of traditional Western medicine, whereas the latter is given in conjunction with traditional medicine and not in place of it.

OVERVIEW

Holistic medicine has become far more popular in Western countries than it ever has before. There may be many reasons why people are choosing to investigate alternative and complementary medicine. One of these may be a sense of dissatisfaction with what modern or conventional medicine can and cannot do. Many people feel that a traditional Western doctor (usually known as an allopath) is limited by the very focused, scientific training he or she receives. While there is respect for the technological innovations and surgical techniques, many feel that Western biomedical science is limited when it comes to a wide range of issues. These often include conditions that are difficult to treat and/or resistant to modern pharmacological medicines such as fibromyalgia, Lyme disease, chronic fatigue syndrome (sometimes called Epstein-Barr Syndrome), chronic pain, cancer, recurring muscular pains and injuries, among others.

There have been some misunderstandings about what holistic medicine is. Some misinterpret it as a group of treatments that are basically "natural remedies" with no science behind them whatsoever. However, homeopathy, herbalism, Chinese medicine, massage therapy, and other treatments are very much rooted in science, albeit in different scientific beliefs than those that serve as the foundation for Western or conventional medicine.

The Philosophy of Holistic Medicine

The terms *holistic medicine, alternative medicine,* and *complementary medicine* have often been used interchangeably. In fact, *alternative medicine* and *complementary medicine* are different (as explained below), and holistic medicine is a term that tends to embrace the larger definition of a system of treatment and practitioners who do not work within the system of conventional medicine.

A more precise definition of the term is that holism is a philosophy that believes in treating the whole person and in the integration of mind, body, and spirit. Holism promotes the belief that these three elements of a human being must be treated together in order to achieve any notion of "healing," rather than simply treating a person for a specific illness or injury.

In the holistic belief system, illness and injury are often the result of disharmony in the mind-body-spirit relationship. The disharmony can often come about from a dysfunction in any one of these areas. Holistic medicine believes that a dysfunction in one area affects the whole person and not just that one area of the body.

Research in Australia demonstrated that one of the reasons so many Australians seek out alternative and complementary medicine is because of the holistic philosophy that guides their work. It is also the reason why many Australians are becoming less enthusiastic about Western or conventional medicine, which is seen as non-holistic in nature (Hassed, 2004).

One of the terms that is increasingly popular in Western culture is "wellness." It is not only a term we see in popular magazines advertising day spas and on the shelves of health food stores, wellness is also becoming a philosophy that is permeating Western society. Universities, colleges, and even corporations are beginning to offer wellness programs for their staff. The notion of "holistic" is the foundation for this growing movement of wellness. Many people have become tired of waiting long hours in an emergency room only to be treated by a tired doctor. They want to take their well-being into their own hands, and they feel empowered when they do.

Holistic medicine is as much about a way of life as it is about medical treatment. The holistic philosophy embraces an approach that promotes overall body wellness.

Alternative medicine

This term refers to alternative medical systems other than allopathic or traditional (conventional) Western medicine. These include traditional Chinese medicine, homeopathy, and herbalism. These all require certification, and the practitioner is referred to as a doctor. He or she might carry the title of naturopathic physician or doctor of chiropractic. Alternative medicine is used in place of traditional or conventional medicine, although some people use them together.

Homeopathy

The growing popularity of alternative medicine is due in large part to the growth of homeopathy. This science was developed in the late eighteenth century by the German doctor and biologist Dr. Samuel Hahnemann. One of the primary principles in homeopathy is the *law of similars*. The premise states that "like cures like." In other words, "a substance produces symptoms of illness in a well person when administered in large doses. If we administer the same substance in minute quantities, it will cure the disease in a sick person" (Novella et al., 2008, p. 9). Hahnemann had very different ideas about the body from his colleagues who practiced conventional medicine. He believed in the concept of the "constitution," the notion that the body must be treated as a whole and that the right remedy would literally "kick start" the system into healing itself at the most basic level. In this way, homeopathy would not treat disease; it would heal the body. The second principle is the *law of infinitesimals*, which states that "substances become more potent when diluted" (Novella et al., 2008, p. 9).

Of course, Hahnemann did not have the technological advantage that modern doctors and scientists enjoy. Over the years since its inception, homeopathy has always been somewhat controversial. Some scientists have suggested that the remedies are so highly diluted that there is actually nothing of the original substance left. There are doctors who have criticized homeopathy and suggested that people get well only because they have convinced themselves they are better (the placebo effect). An interesting roundtable discussion of scientists took place at Penn University in 2008. After much initial skepticism, their conclusion was that homeopathy is indeed a valuable form of medical science. Novella (2008) states:

> ... homeopathy is very plausible and there is both ample clinical and epidemiological evidence that it works. Homeopathy *will* become an integral part of medicine despite the paradoxical nature of its remedies and all other prejudices against it, *simply* because homeopathy is safe, efficacious, and cost effective (p.13).

The concept of the constitution is an important one in homeopathy. In many ways, this is the vital life force that Hahnemann believed exists in all of us. As a result of this belief, the classical homeopath engages in a highly detailed discussion with every patient especially during the initial visit. The homeopath is concerned with everything, not just the physical symptoms occurring at the time. They want to know about the person's emotions, their personal interactions, work life, stressors, dreams, and anything else of importance in the person's life. They also take into account the person's appearance, demeanor, and body language. "Homeopaths use the vital force assessment to guide dose (potency) selection and treatment pace and to judge the likely clinical course and prognosis" (Bell et al., 2004, p. 124).

This notion of a vital force or constitution indicates that Hahnemann may have already known or understood (at least to a degree) what happens to the body on the atomic or molecular level. This is something that not even our present-day scientists can measure. The inability to measure this notion of the "life force" or "constitution" has been one of the criticisms leveled at homeopathy. The other has been its use of substances that are toxic in their natural state, such as arsenic, but are medicinal and safe in their diluted form, such as *Arsenicum Albun,* a well-known homeopathic remedy.

Jobst (2005) states her conclusions thusly:

> In the meantime, if patients are recovering through the use of nontoxic homeopathic medicines and using the homeopathic method, let us, as physicians, get on and heal in the truest sense of that word, while as scientists we search to understand the mechanisms by which our activities might be working, and let us strive to always remain open (p. 274).

Traditional Chinese medicine

Traditional Chinese medicine (TCM) may be one of the world's oldest medical systems. It was developed over 2,000 years ago and has only become popular in Western cultures in the late twentieth and early twenty-first century. One of the key concepts in TCM is the notion of the *qi,* or life-force. In some ways, this notion of a life-force is somewhat similar to the notion of the vital force in homeopathy, but they are understood and treated differently. There is no doubt that TCM is fundamentally different from Western medicine in many essential ways. Even with a small similarity to homeopathy, it is also distinctly different from any other form of medical treatment. It is important to take into account that TCM is a reflection of a specific culture, like Ayurvedic medicine developed in India. Some of the components that are essential to TCM include:

- Personal observations of the physician,
- A subjective basis for diagnosis,
- Healing as a way to balance the body's processes,
- Measuring the outcomes of treatment qualitatively (versus quantitatively), and
- Gearing the treatment to the individual and not the condition (Shea, 2006).

One of the criticisms of TCM is that it is based on a physician's subjective observations rather than an in-depth examination of the person (Shea, 2006). This observation has even been made in China, where many are beginning to question its efficacy. A second criticism has been regarding the herbs used to treat. A typical Chinese pharmacy has thousands of remedies made from a wide array of herbs, animal parts, and other pharmacopeias.

Herbalism

Herbal medicine may have been humanity's first attempt at a synthesis of conditions and corresponding treatments. The very first treatments may have been the herbs and flowers that people found in their immediate surroundings. However, herbal medicine has come a long way since those early days of human civilization. In fact, the words "herbal" and "natural" seem to be everywhere. People in Western countries are flocking to the stores to buy lotions with lavender, tea with chamomile, and even cleaning products are being infused with natural and herbal elements. Modern-day herbalists engage in training, and they must be certified to practice. Although many advancements have been made in our understanding of what herbs can do and our preparations of herbal remedies, there are still concerns about the safety of these remedies.

Ernst (2004) explains, "Safety issues related to herbal medicine are complex: possible toxicity of herbal constituents, presence of contaminants or adulterants, and potential interactions between herbs and prescription drugs" (p. 985). Given these concerns, why is it that herbal remedies have become so popular, and what is it that people and practitioners can do to ensure the remedies are safe and appropriate? One of the reasons for the increasing popularity of herbal remedies is the same reason for the boom in homeopathy and TCM. People are looking for natural answers to their problems. In fact, there is a larger irony here. On the conventional side of medicine, there are concerns over the safety of herbs and other alternative remedies. Yet, many people carry the same concern regarding pharmaceutical medicines and conventional treatments. People worry about radiation from CT scans and MRIs. They wonder whether the medicines they are taking will cause serious side effects, as has been the case with many medicines that have had to be taken off the shelf permanently.

Ginkgo biloba, echinacea, garlic, ginseng, and saw palmetto were among the most commonly used herbal or dietary supplements in 2007 (Nahin, Barnes, Stussman & Bloom, 2009), and the herbs most researched on the National Center for Complementary and Alternative medicine (NCCAM) website in 2012 were evening primrose oil, St. John's wort, fenugreek, echinacea, and aloe vera. One important concern is that unlike homeopathic remedies, herbs have the potential to interact with pharmaceutical drugs.

Complementary medicine

These are treatments that are given in conjunction with and not in place of allopathic treatment.

Complementary medicine prides itself on being noninvasive and non-pharmaceutical. It should be noted that some (but not all) practitioners in this field of medicine are also highly regulated, undergo rigorous training, and must be certified in order to practice.

Chiropractic

While many people might think of chiropractic care as a relatively recent treatment, it was actually developed back in the late nineteenth century (Cooper & McKee, 2003). For decades, chiropractors fought to be accepted as a legitimate form of medical treatment by mainstream conventional medicine. In the twenty-first century, conventional medicine is becoming more supportive of chiropractors, and many doctors and some surgeons refer their patients to chiropractors before considering more invasive procedures such as surgery. Still, there are medical practitioners and patients who are skeptical (and some even fearful) of chiropractic manipulations. The technique used is called spinal manipulative therapy (SMT).

The primary reason people go to chiropractors is for musculoskeletal pain. Most often, this is back or neck pain. They rely on the chiropractor's use of SMT to alleviate their pain and hopefully avoid more invasive treatments. SMT is based on the principle that the spine experiences "subluxations" of the joints. This literally means that joints go out of place and must be manipulated back into place. When they are out of alignment, these joints can cause muscular, joint, and nerve pain (Cooper & McKee, 2003). Unfortunately, some studies have suggested that SMT is not always reliable and has sometimes demonstrated adverse side effects, and there is a problem with consistency of treatments among chiropractors, which makes the treatments questionable (Cooper & McKee, 2003). Many insurance companies in the U.S. will not pay for chiropractic treatment, and there are still concerns among conventional doctors about the efficacy of chiropractic care.

Massage Therapy

The growing popularity of massage therapy is not surprising. To lie on a firm, supportive table, while soft music plays and someone kneads out the knots in your body has a soothing ring to it. The question is whether or not massage therapy has any medical purpose. There are many different forms of massage, including deep tissue, Swedish, and shiatsu. Some doctors and researchers suggest that while having a massage is a nice experience and provides short-term pain relief, it does not have any long-term medical advantage. Others would disagree. Massage therapy is neither new nor unusual in Western culture. Unlike other complementary and alternative forms of medicine that have only emerged relatively recently, massage therapy seems to be an almost universal form of treatment. According to Kaye et al. (2006), "Massage therapy, especially deep tissue massage (DTM), has been used for centuries to relieve myofascial syndromes including muscle spasm, muscle strain, and pain associated with numerous neuromuscular pathological processes" (p. 128).

Doctors are becoming less skeptical about the long term benefits of massage therapy. People are being referred to massage therapists for a wide range of physical and psychological conditions. There have been clinical studies to suggest that massage therapy has both physical and emotional benefits. The use of massage therapy has broadened from being a luxury for an occasional ache or pain to being used for people with multiple sclerosis, cancer, HIV/AIDS, neurological trauma, sciatica, depression, anxiety disorders, and many others. While some people do experience bruising, soreness, fatigue, and increased discomfort (Cambron, Dexheimer, Coe, & Swenson, 2007), most people feel better after massage therapy.

Acupuncture

The most famous treatment in traditional Chinese medicine is probably acupuncture. This treatment has gained increasing popularity in Western countries. Acupuncture is thought to be primarily helpful for aches and pains or to alleviate the problems from an injury; however, it has a much broader medical application. Acupuncture has been used in clinical trials for a wide range of moderate ailments to life-threatening conditions. These include arthritis, chronic back pain, sciatica, HIV/AIDS, and many others. The technique involves using various sized needles that the acupuncturist inserts into points along meridians in the body. These meridians are energy points and designed to stimulate the *qi*, or the person's life-force, and the healing process. The "needling" can be done dry or using electricity. "Acupuncture has established a reputation among the public for being a safe and effective treatment for a range of conditions. It relies greatly on its reputation for its widespread acceptance and growth as a valuable treatment technique" (White, 2007, p. 9).

Additional treatments in complementary and alternative medicine include aromatherapy, ear candling, energy healing, crystal healing, reflexology, lymph drainage, and cranial sacral therapy.

FURTHER INSIGHTS

Integrating holistic medicine into Conventional Medical Training

One of the most promising applications is that of integrating these alternative and complementary medical treatments and philosophies into conventional medical training. By 2004, a majority of allopathic and some osteopathic medical schools provided some kind of complementary and alternative medicine curriculum to their students (Saxon, Tunnicliff, Brokaw, & Raess, 2004). Although this represents an intriguing and perhaps promising concept, skepticism remains strong among students and practitioners of conventional medicine concerning alternative forms of medicine such as herbalism and TCM. Critics question the efficacy and reliability of complementary and alternative medicine practices, and researchers at NCCAM and other organizations seek to legitimize them by subjecting them to the scientific scrutiny and proof of efficacy required of conventional Western techniques.

Despite this ongoing skepticism, given the increasing popularity of alternative medicine, and the fact that many people are turning to alternative practitioners, it is to the advantage of conventional doctors that they have at least some level of knowledge regarding these medical systems. At the very least, they are enabled to communicate with their patients in an informed and understanding way and assist them as they pursue a more holistic approach to their health care.

CONCLUSION

Holistic medicine is a growing field all over the world. Many people are turning to holistic medicine out of frustration with some of the failures of conventional medicine. Some people feel that conventional medicine is impersonal, while holistic medicine is personal and more attentive. The reasons for turning to holistic medicine may be due, in part, to the fact that some people are becoming skeptical of pharmaceuticals and do not like taking pharmaceutical medications. The growth of the "natural" industry is very much a part of the holistic approach that many people find comforting. While there are still conventional practitioners who maintain a skeptical attitude toward natural products that they feel are insufficiently tested or regulated, many are beginning to accept the benefits of the holistic approach. The notion of attending to the mind-body-spirit is one that gives people a sense that the practitioner cares.

TERMS & CONCEPTS

Acupuncture: A practice in traditional Chinese medicine that uses needles of various sizes to stimulate points along the body's energy streams, called meridians.

Allopath: Refers to a doctor of medicine who practices conventional or traditional Western medicine.

Alternative medicine: A branch of medicine that embraces a wide range of various medical systems from different cultures that are not based in biomedicine. Some of these include Chinese medicine, homeopathy, and herbalism.

Aromatherapy: A treatment that uses essential oils to help restore balance to body, mind, and spirit. Essential oils come from plants, and the premise is that they stimulate the sense of smell, which can impact how we feel.

Chinese medicine: Also referred to as traditional Chinese medicine, this is a system of medical treatment developed over 2,000 years ago in China and embraces the use of Chinese herbs, acupuncture, and a unique system of diagnosis. Over the centuries, there have been several forms of Chinese medicine, and the unified system known as TCM only emerged in modern times.

Chiropractic Care: A non-pharmaceutical, hands-on approach that uses spinal manipulations as the core of its treatments. The chiropractor trains for the same number of years as a medical doctor and is accorded the title doctor of chiropractic medicine.

Complementary medicine: Various health care techniques and strategies such as physical therapy, massage therapy, and many others that are used as a complement to either traditional or alternative medicine.

Energy Healing: Is based on the belief that the practitioner uses his or her intuition and intent to create a flow of energy through his or her hands and to the client. The premise is to stimulate energy flow and a sense of well-being.

Herbalism: A system of treatment that uses herbs in specific formulations to produce natural medicines. The practitioner of this form is generally known as an herbalist or certified herbalist.

Holism-holistic: The term that refers to the philosophy underlying all complementary and alternative medicines. In the holistic belief system, illness and injury are often the result of disharmony in the mind-body-spirit, which practitioners see as one.

Homeopathy: A form of alternative medicine that uses minute dosages of substances that produce the symptoms of the illness. They are given to the person in the belief that doing so will stimulate the body's own healing power. The primary purpose of homeopathy is to stimulate the body's own healing responses or the "constitution."

BIBLIOGRAPHY

Bhargava, V., Hong, G., & Montalto, C. P. (2012). "Use of practitioner-based and self-care complementary and alternative medicine in the United States: A demand for health perspective." *Family & Consumer Sciences Research Journal, 41*(1), 18–35.

Bell, I. R., et al. (2004). "Strength of vital force in classical homeopathy: Bio-psycho-social-spiritual correlates within a complex systems context." *Journal of Alternative & Complementary medicine, 10* (1), 123–131.

Cambron, J. A., Dexheimer, J., Coe, P., & Swenson, R. (2007). "Side-effects of massage therapy: A cross-sectional study of 100 clients." *Journal of Alternative & Complementary medicine, 13* (8), 93–796.

Cooper, R. A., & McKee, H. J. (2003). "Chiropractic in the United States: Trends and issues." *Milbank Quarterly, 81* (1), 107–138.

Ernst, E. (2004). "Prescribing herbal medications appropriately." *Journal of Family Practice, 53* (12), 985–988.

Fries, C. (2013). "Self-care and complementary and alternative medicine as care for the self: An embodied basis for distinction." *Health Sociology Review, 22*(11), 37–51.

Hassed, C. S. (2004). "Bringing holism into mainstream biomedical education." *Journal of Alternative & Complementary medicine, 10* (2), 405–407.

Jobst, K. A. (2005). "Homeopathy, Hahnemann, and the Lancet 250 years on: A case of the emperor's new clothes?" *Journal of Alternative & Complementary medicine, 11* (5), 751–754.

Kaye, A. D., et al. (2008). "The effect of deep-tissue massage therapy on blood pressure and heart rate." *Journal of Alternative & Complementary medicine, 14* (2), 125–128.

Nahin, R. L., Barnes, P. M., Stussman, B. J., & Bloom, B. (2009). "Costs of complementary and alternative medicine (CAM) and frequency of visits to CAM practitioners: United States, 2007." *National Health Statistics,* 18, 1–6. http://www.cdc.gov/NCHS/data/nhsr/nhsr018.pdf

National Center for Complementary and Alternative medicine. (2013, January). "NCCAM's 5 most searched-for herbs of 2012: What the science says." *NCCAM Clinical Digest.* http://nccam.nih.gov/health/providers/digest/topsupplements-science

Novella, S., et al. (2008). "A debate: homeopathy—Quackery or a key to the future of medicine?" *Journal of Alternative & Complementary medicine, 141* (1), 9–15.

Possamai-Inesedy, A., & Cochrane, S. (2013). "The consequences of integrating complementary and alternative medicine: An analysis of impacts on practice." *Health Sociology Review, 22*(11), 65–74.

Saxon, D. W., Tunnicliff, G., Brokaw, J. J., & Raess, B. U. (2004). "Status of complementary and alternative medicine in the osteopathic medical school curriculum." *Journal of the American Osteopathic Association, 104*(3), 121–126 http://www.jaoa.org/

Shea, J. (2006). "Applying evidence-based medicine to traditional Chinese medicine: Debate and strategy." *Journal of Alternative & Complementary medicine, 12* (3), 255–263.

White, A. (2007). "The safety of acupuncture techniques." *Journal of Alternative & Complementary medicine, 13* (1), 9–10.

Wu, E. S. (2013). *Traditional Chinese medicine in the United States: In search of spiritual meaning and ultimate health.* Lanham, MD: Lexington Books.

SUGGESTED READING

Cloninger, R. C. (2004). *Feeling good: The science of well-being.* New York, NY: Oxford University Press.

Coulter, I. D. (1999). *Chiropractic: A philosophy for alternative health care.* Oxford, England: Butterworth-Heinemann.

Cummings, S., & Ullman, D. (1984). *Everybody's guide to homeopathic medicines.* Los Angeles, CA: Jeremy T. Archer.

Heller, T., et al. (Eds.). (2005). *Perspectives on complementary and alternative medicine: A reader.* London, England: Routledge.

Juvva, S., & Newhill, C. E. (2011). "Rehabilitation contexts: A holistic approach." *Journal of Human Behavior in the Social Environment, 21*(2), 179–195.

Kendall, D. E. (2002). *Dao of Chinese medicine: Understanding an ancient healing art.* New York, NY: Oxford University Press.

Merrick, J. (2013). *Textbook on evidence-based holistic mind-body medicine: holistic practice of traditional Hippocratic medicine. New York, NY: Nova Science Publishers, Inc.*

Ziment, I., & Rotblatt, M. (2002). *Evidence-based herbal medicine.* Philadelphia, PA: Elsevier Health Sciences.

Ilanna Mandel, M.A.

LEGAL & ETHICAL ISSUES OF LIFE & DEATH

ABSTRACT

As advances in medicine expand the possibilities of life, postpone death, and expand the knowledge of the genetic and molecular makeup of human beings, new issues emerge in the legal and ethical issues of life and death. The United States Supreme Court has legalized the right of every individual to prepare health care directives concerning the nature and extent of end-of-life treatment and care. Less accepted is the concept of physician-assisted suicide, in which the health care provider assists the individual in selecting the time and manner of his or her death. These issues are complicated further when the patient is poor or mentally or physically challenged. Additionally, there may be limits on financial and medical resources, further requiring individuals and their families to make hard decisions about life and death. This article will explore some of the contemporary legal and ethical issues of life and death in the United States.

OVERVIEW

A large metropolitan hospital receives a call that an infant in critical condition is arriving for care. All of their extracorporeal membrane oxygenation (ECMO) machines, which give blood oxygen outside the body when a ventilator is not sufficient, are in use. What is the ethical thing to do? Place the new patient on an ECMO machine because they are critical? First come, first served? Or should the doctor consider which children have the better prognosis and treat them first?

Famed New York Yankees slugger Mickey Mantle was inducted into the Baseball Hall of Fame in his first year of eligibility in 1974. Mantle suffered from alcoholism, cirrhosis of the liver, and hepatitis C, and seems to have been inducted into the liver transplant program at Baylor University Medical Center in Dallas, Texas, with equal ease in 1995. Despite a terrible prognosis and a long line of patients also waiting for a liver transplant, Mantle received the transplant and lived only another two months. Public outcry over the power of celebrity and how transplant organs are allocated raged for months.

The legal and ethical considerations of life and death are numerous and without absolute answers. They can be complicated further if the patient is elderly, mentally or physically challenged, poor, and/or without sufficient health insurance. In an ideal world, none of these conditions would be the basis for making life and death decisions. But as society makes unimaginable medical advances, the price tag for these life-saving treatments continues to soar. Individuals, and state and federal governments, are staggering under the huge bill for health care insurance and treatment.

Sociologists, legal theorists, politicians, and the public are interested in these matters as evidence of social change and the tensions between personal freedom and public constraints upon those freedoms. Although the Declaration of Independence mentions "life, liberty, and the pursuit of happiness," for example, there is no mention of privacy rights or individual freedoms pertaining to biological and/or medical issues. Given our country's Puritan/Protestant religious background, rule by the majority has dominated many of these ethical and legal matters for centuries. Over the last forty years, however, emergent medical advances and beliefs in privacy and personal decision-making have changed the landscape of debate. All across the nation, scholars see evidence of the struggles between traditional values and emergent personal freedoms on local, state, and national levels. On the other hand, some of these issues, such as the allocation of transplant organs or setting limits on medical interventions, are caused by relatively recent medical breakthroughs that have no precedent in modern society. In some ways, it is difficult for society to debate these issues since the two means of resolution have been the courts and legislative action. How different groups conceptualize each of these issues, and how the larger society engages in the debate and temporary resolution of these matters is of major interest to sociologists interested in social change and ideological/social conflicts.

FURTHER INSIGHTS

Advance Care Directives

In terms of end-of-life care, normative statements from the American Medical Association state that "the primary consideration should be what is best for the individual patient" (American Medical Association, 2007b). Physicians are not required to provide care that has no "reasonable chance of benefiting the patient" (American Medical Association, 2007c). If the medical interventions are viewed as futile, then the process changes into one of making the patient comfortable and pain free, both mentally and physically.

Advance care directives are formal, written, and signed documents that provide legal and medical instructions concerning an individual's wishes for their medical treatment, even when they are no longer able to actively participate in those decisions. Often called a "living will," "health care proxy," or "medical power of attorney," these types of documents empower a surrogate decision-maker or caregiver and delineate the treatments desired or refused during illness or at the end of life. Often included in these documents are "do not resuscitate (DNR)" instructions in the event that a patient suffers cardiac or respiratory arrest and their medical condition does not warrant cardiopulmonary resuscitation. Individuals with inoperable, terminal medical conditions or those facing a long-term coma with no hope of recovery are most likely candidates for DNR orders.

State and federal laws encourage these types of patient decision-making in order to avoid court-ordered determinations of the patient's wishes. In 1991, the US Congress passed the Patient Self-Determination Act (PSDA), which mandates that any health care institution receiving Medicaid or Medicare funds must inform patients of their right to self-determine their end-of-life care. Despite this law, and the ugly legal battles played out in media and political circles, estimates are that fewer than 29 percent of adult Americans have advance directives. The failure to make these important medical and legal decisions can place the patient, the family, and medical care providers in an expensive and complex legal battle over what should be done on the patient's behalf.

That was the situation in the famous Terri Schiavo case, in which both the state of Florida and the then-conservative United States Congress intervened to try and stop the removal of feeding tubes for Schiavo, who had been in a persistent vegetative state for fifteen years. In 1990, Schiavo suffered irreversible brain damage after experiencing both respiratory and cardiac arrest. In 1998, Schiavo's husband petitioned the court to remove the feeding tubes, arguing that Schiavo would not have wished to continue to be kept alive in such a condition. Schiavo's parents disagreed, and the ensuing legal battle took seven years and involved both the Florida and the United States Supreme Courts. Although both federal and state congresses attempted to pass laws prohibiting the removal of the feeding tubes (and some ardent Congress members sought to have Schiavo qualified for the federal witness protection program), ultimately the courts permitted the feeding tubes to be withdrawn. Two weeks later, Terri Schiavo died at the age of forty-one. Pro-life advocates called the court's decision "judicial murder," while disability advocates were on both sides of the debate.

ISSUES

Physician-Assisted Suicide (PAS)

Physician-assisted suicide (PAS) is "when a physician facilitates a patient's death by providing the necessary means and/or information that enable the patient to perform the life-ending act" (American Medical Association, 2007). Arguments in favor of PAS are that individual autonomy should be respected, as well as individual liberties, and that it is simple justice since the individual already has the right to refuse treatment. Why should they not have the right to choose when they die? Some consider PAS to be a compassionate solution to terrible pain and suffering. Finally, others argue that PAS already is occurring, particularly in the use of morphine drips that lessen pain but also negatively impact the respiratory processes. To make PAS legal would be to bring the discussion of end-of-life options out into the open for both the patient and the physician ("Physician Assisted," n.d.).

Opponents of PAS argue for the sanctity of life and make the distinction between letting someone refuse further medical treatments and actively taking an action that will end his or her life. They also argue that it is necessary to preserve the integrity of the medical profession as healers, and, in fact, the American Medical Association disagrees with PAS for this reason. Anti-PAS advocates argue that mistakes might be made through an erroneous diagnosis or colored by a patient's deep depression and that with the proper treatment, the patient might live a full life. And finally, they argue that abuses might occur so that poor or elderly patients might be offered PAS as a means of avoiding more expensive medical treatments and palliative care ("Physician Assisted," n.d.).

Oregon, Washington, and Vermont are the only states that permit a physician to aid in a suicide, while suicide attempts and suicide are not criminal acts in any state. In *Dying v. State of Washington*, a federal appeals court ruled that individuals do have the right to choose how and when they die. Similarly, another federal appeals court found that a New York law barring PAS violated the Fourteenth Amendment, which states that no state can "deny to any person within its jurisdiction the equal protection of the laws." The United Stated Supreme Court, however, ruled that there is no constitutional entitlement to physician-assisted suicide, although patients do have the right to refuse medical treatment. The Supreme Court made it clear that the decisions about physician-assisted suicide should be left to each state under the state's rights doctrine ("Physician Assisted," n.d.).

Organ Transplants

Organ donors can be living or deceased. The major organs and tissues transplanted are the heart, kidneys, liver, lungs, pancreas, and intestines. Also transplanted are blood, bone marrow, bone, tendons, corneas, heart valves, veins, and skin (US Department of Health and Human Services, n.d.). Transplant rejection of the new organ or tissue historically has been a significant bar to long-term, successful transplants, until the development of the drug cyclosporine. Today, 90 percent of patients survive for a year after the transplant, and 72 percent survive for five years ("Heart Transplant," 2008). Many patients live for more than a decade following an organ transplant. In 2006 2,192 patients received heart transplants; the following year 2,210 patients received transplants ("Heart Transplants: Statistics," 2009). Now that organ transplants have become routine and drug protocols have been developed that reduce the likelihood of transplant rejection, a lack of organs and tissues for transplant has become a critical problem. The legal and ethic considerations now are who should receive priority donee status and which living individuals should be allowed to be donors.

There are several processes by which human organs and tissue are obtained legally. One of the most successful is a donation made by a living relative of the recipient. Because of similar genetics and strong emotional ties and the possibility of saving the life of a loved-one, these exchanges are not only biologically favorably, but emotionally as well. Because the tissue has the highest possibility of being genetically similar, the odds of tissue rejection can be diminished considerably. Unfortunately, not all living relatives are a match, just as marital partners are not a match usually. In these situation, one favored procedure is called a "paired-exchange." The donee's spouse or other willing donor is matched with another individual in the larger transplant community who needs the same organ, and their donor is matched with the original donee. Harvesting of the two donated organs and their subsequent transplantation are all timed simultaneously to diminish the possibility that one of the organ donors will back out of the deal once their loved one has received a transplant. Because of the national organ transplant registry and a plethora of additional websites, individuals can be "good Samaritans" and voluntarily provide organs or tissue to someone unknown or less known to them ("Kidney Transplant-Paired Exchange," 2009).

In some countries, the buying and selling of transplant organs is legal, although in developing countries the donor is often paid very little for their organ because they may not fully understand the consequences of their actions since they are desperate financially. In the United States, the National Organ Transplant Act of 1984 made the sale of organs illegal in this country. It also formed the Organ Procurement and Transplantation Network (OPTN), that determines who should receive the next available organ ("Legislation and Legislative History," n.d.). Potential kidney recipients are holistically evaluated by a number of factors like blood type, age, geography, and how long they have been on the waiting list; potential liver donation recipients are evaluated by an empirical disease score to determine necessity ("Matching Process-The Waiting List," n.d.).

One final form of organ acquisition is forced donorship. Up until a few years ago, most Chinese organ donations came from executed prisoners. In October 2007, under pressure from the World Health Organization and other advocates, the Chinese Medical Association agreed to a moratorium on the forced harvesting of organs from prisoners, and it is unknown if this process continues (Shimazono, 2007).

In order to bypass altogether the need for organ donorship from humans, scientists are working on xenotransplantion, the transplanting of tissue from the body of another species into the human who needs the new organ. To date, the transplant of a baboon heart into a human body has failed, as have other variations on this effort. Not surprisingly, this process is very difficult and it will be years before it is established as a viable option.

Medical Use of Marijuana

Over the past decade, the debate over the medical benefits of marijuana (cannabis), and cannabinoids (substances that are chemically similar to and that mimic the effects of marijuana) has increased. Although a majority of Americans are familiar with smoking marijuana, health professionals agree that the act of smoking causes respiratory damage. Thus, significant research is being undertaken to develop synthetic drugs from the cannabis plant or to use its herbal properties for tinctures and other ingestible medications. Recent studies have shown that marijuana may be useful in the treatment of nausea caused by chemotherapy, glaucoma, cachexia, chronic pain, epilepsy, and multiple sclerosis. (American Medical Association, 2001; National Institute of Health, 1997; National Institute of Health, 2007).

In the United States, marijuana possession, use, or distribution is illegal on the federal level due to the Controlled Substance Act. Exercising their constitutional state's rights, however, the following twenty states have adopted medical use marijuana laws, along with the District of Columbia: Alaska, Arizona, California, Colorado, Connecticut, DC, Delaware, Hawaii, Illinois, Maine, Massachusetts, Michigan, Montana, Nevada, New Hampshire, New Mexico, Oregon, Rhode Island, Vermont, and Washington. California was the first state to adopt such laws in 1996. Several states also have adopted laws that reduce the penalties for marijuana possession for individuals with proven medical necessities. Most of these states limit the quantity that any individual may possess for medical purposes to less than one or two ounces and a dozen homegrown plants. Support of medical marijuana is growing nationwide, in both medical and political circles, and one can expect an increase in the legalization and use of this medical treatment in the future (National Organization for the Reform of Marijuana Laws, 2008).

Antitrust Laws

Antitrust laws are intended to protect the public from unfair business practices and lack of competition in the marketplace. The health care industry is becoming more vertically integrated, meaning that there are monetary relationships between the individuals and entities at the commencement of care, related to those in the management and insurance, and related to hospitals, clinics, and laboratories. Doctors, for example, may own the laboratories to which they send their patients, and therefore, order expensive tests to be conducted. Conversely, the insurers or health care institutions may penalize the doctor for ordering too many or too expensive tests, and thus restrict the care needed for the public. Heightened federal or state regulation scrutiny may occur if the entity has:

- Significant market share;
- Joint action with other actors;
- Denial or limitation of professional privileges of other practitioners; and,
- Involvement in a merger, acquisition, joint venture, provider Network, or other integrated delivery system (American Medical Association, n.d.).

Obviously, sociologists interested in the medical delivery system would find these issues of interest, as should those who are concerned with unequal medical care based upon age, race, class, gender, or disability.

Patients with Disabilities

Special circumstances arise when the patient has mental or physical challenges that complicate his or her medical situation. In 1990, the Americans with Disabilities Act (ADA) was passed by Congress and is the first civil rights protections for people with disabilities. The ADA prohibits discrimination in employment and services based upon one's disability status. In terms of legal and ethical considerations of life and death, it means that a physician must make a reasonable effort to accommodate a patient with disabilities. As part of a requirement to provide "auxiliary aids and services," physicians must make an effort to communicate to the patient with disabilities through an appropriate means. In terms of a patient with hearing difficulties, for example, this means that the physician must assess whether written communication, telecommunication devices, or an sign-language interpreter would provide the necessary assistance, and then provide that resource for the patient. If this obligation places an undue burden upon the physician, such as significant expenses or difficulty, or it fundamentally alters the nature of the services normally offered, then alternatives are possible so long as the communication is effective. Obviously, the choices of the patient should bear serious consideration and the physician cannot pass the expense of the accommodation on to the patient.

TERMS & CONCEPTS

Autonomy: Independence or freedom.

Extracorporeal: Occurring or situated outside the body.

Palliative Care: End-of-life care provided to relieve or lessen pain or symptoms without curing them.

Protocols: The plan for a course of medical treatment or for a scientific experiment.

Resuscitate: To revive from apparent death or unconsciousness.

BIBLIOGRAPHY

American Medical Association. (2001). "Report 6 of the council on scientific affairs (a-02) medical marijuana." http://www.ama-assn.org/ama/no-index/about-ama/13625.shtml

American Medical Association. (n.d.). "Americans with Disabilities Act and hearing interpreters. Regulatory Compliance Topics." http://www.ama-assn.org/ama/pub/physician-resources/legal-topics/regulat tory-compliance-topics/the-americans-disabilities-act-hearing-interprete ers.shtml

American Medical Association. (n.d.). "Antitrust. Business Management Topics." http://www.ama-assn.org/ama/pub/physician-resources/legal-topics/busines ss-management-topics/anti-trust.shtml

American Medical Association. (2007a). "Physician-assisted suicide. Code of Medical Ethics: Opinions on Social Policy Issues." http://www.ama-assn.org/

American Medical Association. (2007b). "Quality of life. Code of Medical Ethics: Opinions on Social Policy Issues." http://www.ama-assn.org/

American Medical Association. (2007c). "Futile care. Code of Medical Ethics: Opinions on Social Policy Issues." from http://www.amaassn.org/

Garwood, P. (2007). "Dilemma over live-donor transplantation." *Bulletin of the World Health Organization,* 85(1).

"Heart transplant." (2008). Mayo Clinic. http://www.mayoclinic.com/health/heart-transplant/

"Heart transplants: Statistics." (2009). American Heart Association. http://www.americanheart.org/

Himchak, M. V. (2011). "A social justice value approach regarding physician-assisted suicide and euthanasia among the elderly." *Journal of Social Work Value and Ethics, 8*(1), 57–70.

"Kidney Transplant-Paired Exchange." (2009). University of California, San Francisco Medical Center. http://www.ucsfhealth.org/adult/special/k/113180.html

National Institutesof Health. (2006). "Marijuana." http://teens.drugabuse.gov/

National Institutes of Health. (1997). "Workshop on the medical utility of marijuana." http://www.nih.gov/news/medmarijuana/MedicalMarijuana.htm

National Organization for the Reform of Marijuana Laws. (2008). http://norml.org/

"Physician Assisted Suicide." (n.d.). *Ethics in Medicine,* University of Washington School of Medicine. http://depts.washington.edu/bioethx.pas.html

Pozar, G. (2005). *Legal and ethical issues for health professionals.* Sudbury, MA: Jones & Bartlett.

Scherer, Y., Jezewski, M., Graves, B., Wu, Y., & Bu, X. (2006). "Advance directives and end-of-life decision making." *Critical Care Nurse,* 26(4), 30-40.

Shimazono, Y. (2007). "The state of the international organ trade: A provisional picture based on integration of available information." *Bulletin of the World Health Organization,* 85(12).

Supiano, K. P. (2013). "Weaving interdisciplinary and discipline-specific content into palliative care education: one successful model for teaching end-of-life care." *Omega: Journal of Death and Dying, 67*(1/2), 201–206.

U.S. Department of Health and Human Services. (n.d.). "What can be donated." OrganDonor.gov. http://www.organdonor.gov/donation/what%5f-donate.htm

U.S. Department of Health and Human Services. (n.d.). "Legislation and legislative history." OrganDonor.gov http://www.organdonor.gov/research/legislation.htm

U.S. Department of Health and Human Services. (n.d.). "The Matching Process-The Waiting List." OrganDonor.gov http://www.organdonor.gov/

Westerfeld, J. S., et al. (2013). "Physician-assisted death and its relationship to the human services professions." *Journal of Loss and Trauma, 18*(6), 539–555.

Suggested Reading

Baird, R., & Rosenhaum, S. (2001). *The ethics of abortion: Pro-life vs. Pro-Choice.* (3rd ed.). Amherst, NY: Prometheus.

Braun, K., Pietsch, J., & Blanchette, P. (Eds.), (1999). *Cultural issues in end-of-life decision making.* Thousand Oaks: CA: Sage.

Cherry, M. (2005). *Kidneys for sale by owner.* Georgetown, Washington, D.C.: Georgetown UP.

Csikai, E., & Chaitin, E. (2005). *Ethics in end-of-life decisions in social work practice.* Chicago, IL: Lyceum.

de Boer, M. E., et al. (2011). "Advance directives for euthanasia in dementia: How do they affect resident care in Dutch nursing homes? Experience of physicians and relatives." *Journal of the American Geriatrics Society, 59*(6), 989–996.

Holtkamp, S. (2001). *Wrapped in mourning: The gift of life and donor family trauma.* New York: Routledge.

Kleespies, P. (2003). *Life and death decisions: Psychological and ethical considerations in end-of-life care.* Washington, D.C.: American Psychological Association.

Kuebler, K., Heidrich, D., & Esper, P. (2006). *Palliative and end-of-life care: Clincial guidelines.* (2nd ed.). Philadelphia, PA: Mosby.

Muth, A. (1999). *Death and dying sourcebook: Basic consumer health information about end-of-life care and related ethical and legal issues.* Detroit, MI: Omnigraphics.

Taylor, J. (2005). *Stakes and kidneys: Why markets in human body parts are morally imperative.* Burlington, VT: Ashgate.

Karen M. Harbeck, Ph.D., J.D.

Long-term & Institutional Care

OVERVIEW

Long-term and institutional care in the United States is provided to people with chronic health issues, terminal illnesses, and serious mental health conditions such as schizophrenia or dementia. Institutions can vary greatly, and they include nursing homes, hospices, and other institutional environments. Institutions may be run by the private sector, the government, or faith-based services. The primary difference between long-term and institutional care is that long-term care is often a community-based model whereas institutions are typically closed environments.

For some, the mention of institutional care options, such as hospice or palliative care, creates worrisome images. However, these services exist to provide important care functions in our communities. Yet not all people who require care want to go into a nursing home, and many feel they can be taken care of more effectively in their own home. While home care is definitely a viable and important option, one has to take into account the level of care required and how best to provide it. This requires an assessment of the community care services available so that family members do not burn out trying to support their loved ones who require round-the-clock care.

The various options for long-term care require a strict and constant review. It is absolutely vital that the nation's most vulnerable individuals receive professionally appropriate care. However, there have been concerns in the past and in the present as to whether the highest professional standards are being met by care providers.

Understanding Long-term & Institutional Care

A wide range of people benefit from care services, from children and young adults who require home care services due to a chronic condition or disability to people who are elderly and require at least some level of care that may be too complicated to provide at home. Many people who need long-term care rely on a combination of family support and formal long-term care, including home care, adult day care, assisted living, and nursing home care.

Individuals require long-term care for many reasons, but it is a misconception to think that only persons who are elderly require these services. Children who are born with disabilities, people with severe mental health issues, young adults who acquire a disabling condition such as multiple sclerosis, and seniors all can require some form of long-term care.

The broad range of assistance that constitutes long-term care results in confusion and disagreement about what long-term care is and how it is distinct from medical care. Other examples of long-term care can range from skilled nursing facility care provided after hospitalization to housing arrangements for healthy seniors and special transportation services (Tumlinson et al., 2007, p. 1).

There is no doubt that most people would rather be in their own environment, but unfortunately it is not always possible. According to a report by the National Commission for Quality Long-term Care, "many older people with disabilities simply do not have the financial resources to obtain the services they need, either in the community or in long-term care facilities. In some cases, their care options are limited, if available at all" (2007, p. 13).

The choice to provide long-term care at home can be a difficult one. It is often driven by a combination of emotional, financial, and practical considerations. Many families cannot bear to place a loved one into a nursing home or other care facility. In addition, the quality services are very expensive and many families simply do not have the money. Yet, trying to provide the care at home can often be just as costly.

ADL Assessment

The level of care required is driven by an assessment of activities of daily living (ADL). The assessment must be provided by a home-care professional. The assessment identifies the medical, psychological, functional, and social needs of the client (Phillips, Smith, & Cournoyer, 2004, p. 42).

Home care is not always possible even if a family member prefers to stay in his or her own environment. It is the ADL assessment that determines whether a person can be cared for in the home, who will provide that care, the parameters of care, and the standards that must be adhered to. Although home care sounds like a simpler option (and less expensive), the reality is that home care is often financially and emotionally difficult on family members. An individual may lose income depending on the amount of time they need to be home to care for a relative (or to hire a home care provider) and the emotional toll can sometimes be extremely taxing on a family.

LTC Professionals

The long-term care workforce includes physicians, nursing home and assisted living coordinators and administrators, registered nurses, licensed practical and vocational nurses, physical therapists, home health aides, and social workers, with nurses providing the majority of professional long-term care. The professionals who work in long-term care facilities are also under a great deal of pressure especially as the US health care system comes under increasing scrutiny. The training required to work in long-term care is highly specialized. In addition, the providers of these services must develop an infrastructure that supports quality-level care. Presently, there is a dire shortage of professionals capable of working in long-term care facilities. The state of many long-term care facilities is thus a cause for concern.

Many providers maintain that inadequate funding makes it difficult for them to upgrade their infrastructures and their care practices. In particular, providers say that they lack the necessary resources to recruit, train and retain quality staff, especially those direct care workers who provide day-to-day care to long-term care consumers. These workers are in short supply, in large part because their demanding jobs don't offer adequate salaries, benefits, training or opportunities for advancement (National Commission

Report, 2007, p. 13). According to a 2013 congressional report prepared by the Commission on long-term Care, the professional workforce trained to provide long-term care will quickly become inadequate as the population of the United States ages: "There were only 7,356 board-certified geriatricians in the United States in 2012, and there is only 1 geriatric psychiatrist for every 11,000 older adults. If these rates continue, there will only be 1 for every 20,000 older persons by 2030" (Commission on Long-term Care, 2013, p. 18).

FURTHER INSIGHTS

Types of Long Term Care Assisted Living

One option open to persons with the financial means is assisted-living facilities. These are private residences in which an individual who does not need twenty-four-hour or intensive care but may need a small level of assistance or supervision. The consumers who live in assisted-living residences such as these range from young adults with some form of disability who are otherwise independent to older adults (with or without disabilities) who also need some form of assistance with their daily tasks such as cleaning, grocery shopping, transportation, medication management, and other activities of daily living. However, these residences are expensive. The average cost for a private one-bedroom apartment in an assisted-living residence is $3,022 per month, according to the 2009 Overview of Assisted Living (American Association of Homes and Services for the Aging, 2009).

Another option is continuing-care retirement communities. In these residences there are nurses on staff and assisted living is available. Most residents are independent and live in their own apartments within a supportive community.

Unfortunately, the bottom line in long-term care comes back to finances. Someone must pay the bills, and that is usually the state and federal governments. There are, of course, private facilities owned and managed by companies and corporations, but the federal government pays a large portion of long-term care in the United States. The federal and state governments pay for approximately 62 percent of paid long-term services and supports, amounting to more than $130 billion a year (Commission on Long-term Care, 2013, p. 3). That may sound like a staggering amount, but considering the population of the United States that is quickly aging, that number is likely to increase substantially.

Nursing Homes

Nursing homes have evolved since the 1950s when standards for care were enforced by the Hill-Burton Act of 1946. The act was a necessity, since nursing homes actually had their beginnings in the old poorhouses of the nineteenth century. The poorhouses were the beginnings of institutionalized care and a place to send people who literally had nowhere else to go (White, 2005). While nursing homes have steadily improved over the last fifty years, it is clear that the term "nursing home" continues to suffer from the social stigma of being a rather gloomy and negative environment despite increased regulations and improved standards of care.

An ongoing problem for nursing homes (as it is for health care in general) is the acute shortage of qualified nurses (Stoil, 2007). Nursing homes are always in competition with home health care services, hospices, hospitals, and one another for qualified personnel.

A common misconception is that nursing homes are places for the elderly or other individuals who have become ill as a result of a stroke or other serious condition, and therefore cannot take care of themselves on an independent basis. Nursing homes provide treatment for people on a temporary basis as well. One of their functions is to provide a place for recovery after serious injuries or surgeries. This is known as subacute care, and nursing homes are increasingly serving in this capacity, which "is supported by the fact that the number of nursing homes with specialized sub-acute units for residents requiring short-term recovery after serious trauma or accident has been increasing in the last 15 years" (Bernstein, et al., 2003, p. 55).

The majority of the services provided by nursing homes are for people who have extremely high-level personal needs. Some of the conditions that can lead people to require long-term care in a nursing home include multiple sclerosis, amyotrophic lateral sclerosis, dementia, and Alzheimer's disease. People with debilitating conditions often have a high level of complex needs ranging from assistance with daily tasks to regular physical therapy and constant supervision to ensure they do not endanger themselves.

One of the more recent advances in nursing care is in the way it has become a form of cooperative care with home care services. Since most people would prefer to remain at home as long as they can, home care services are often required. Unfortunately, home health care services and nursing homes became bitter adversaries during the 1980s when home health care professionals lobbied to convince legislators that Medicare costs would go down if more home health care services were utilized. Unfortunately, their case lost some credibility when certain scandals became public. "A few high-profile cases were used to illustrate that home healthcare agencies could, and did, bill for services not actually delivered or for poor-quality, neglectful care" (Stoil, 2007, p. 12).

Hospices

Hospices offer quality end-of-life care. Some hospices are private institutions that provide palliative (end-of- life) care, and there is also hospice care available within certain nursing homes. Nursing homes also function as a referral service for persons who require hospice/palliative care. These are extremely difficult services to provide and professionals who work in hospices require extensive training to work on the highly sensitive issues related to end of life. Some of the issues include medication use, pain management, end-of-life counseling, bereavement counseling (for families and partners), and coping with dying patients.

The primary distinction between nursing home care and palliative care offered by hospices is that the latter focuses on providing quality care as a person's end of life approaches, while the former focuses on life-prolonging techniques and technologies. Thus, when a person enters into a hospice or palliative care, they do so with the firm recognition that they are in the final stages of life and they do not wish to prolong it further. Some would suggest it is a more natural approach, but others would state it is merely a different approach (Keay & Schonwetter, 1998, p. 491).

Although hospice care has been recognized for some time as a positive and appropriate environment for persons facing end of life, the fact is that the majority of Americans who die in an institution do so in a nursing home.

The rapid growth in the number of hospice patients served and the acceptance of hospice as a legitimate health-care provider for patients near the end of life is evident. It was estimated that 44 percent of Medicare beneficiaries who died in 2010 were under hospice care at the time of death, up from 23 percent in 2000 (Report to the Congress: Medicare Payment Policy, 2012).

The reality of institutional care is that some nursing homes (as noted above) may not be fully equipped or have a staff that is sufficiently trained to provide quality end-of-life care. However, research into hospice care and the reasons why more people decide to enter or stay in a nursing home are still unclear. The National Hospice Organization has published guidelines to help determine who is an appropriate candidate for hospice care and the parameters of that care. One of the most important criteria is that the individual has been determined to have less than six months to live (Keay & Schonwetter, 1998).

To aid individuals who are dying, there is the Medicaid Hospice Benefit. While it is limited, it provides financial support. For example, persons in a nursing home can receive visits by hospice personnel (provided that the nursing home has a contract with the hospice) and receive the medication and technical equipment necessary to make end of life comfortable for them. Unfortunately, not all nursing homes have a relationship with a hospice and therefore they cannot provide palliative care with the same skill. "When a nursing home resident is identified as having a limited life expectancy, it is appropriate to plan for end-of-life care...Specially trained hospice professionals and volunteers can provide many services that are beyond those usually offered in nursing homes" (Keay & Schonwetter, 1998, p. 492).

Standards of Care

In addition to the constant shortage of nurses and other qualified personnel, long-term care services must deal with a high level of scrutiny on their standards of care. There is an ongoing concern over the lack of quality in some nursing homes. Research has demonstrated that quality is not uniform across states. While consumers certainly benefit from information on quality and improvements in nursing homes across the nation, the question is whether, in the end, consumers even have a choice as to where they go. "The number of nursing home beds is tightly controlled in most states in an effort to minimize Medicaid expenditures. Desirable nursing homes have long waiting lists. Most nursing home patients are admitted from hospitals" (White, 2005, p. 28).

VIEWPOINTS

Recommendations

In order to improve and maintain high quality of care in nursing homes and other institutional settings, there is a definite need to address a wide range of issues. A 2007 report on this subject by the Institute for the Future of Aging Services (2007) made a broad range of recommendations. These included:

- Reducing the stereotypical images people have of long-term care,
- Modernizing the system of long-term care,
- Attracting and hiring qualified personnel,
- Improving working conditions,
- Promoting career mobility for long-term care workers,
- Introducing technology that can save time and empower consumers to be more independent, and
- Providing financial incentives for further training and education

It is absolutely imperative that the highest standards of care be adhered to in long-term care services and institutions. Many people in nursing homes and other services (and even many at home) are vulnerable to the point where they might not even be aware of who they are or of their surroundings. Professionals must have the training necessary not only to provide quality care but compassionate care. They must be able to deal with the patients and their families, friends and partners. It is often the case that the family is going through a difficult time and the long-term or end-of-life care being provided is a crucial time in their lives as well.

In terms of specific educational standards there are major recommendations that emanated from the above-mentioned report. Some of these include:

- Improving the performance of doctors who serve as medical directors in long-term care services,
- Developing model standards for nursing home administrators,
- Strengthening long-term care nurse competencies in geriatrics, administration, management and supervision, and
- Reassessing scopes of practice of registered nurses and licensed practical nurses working in long-term care settings (Institute for the Future of Aging Services, 2007, p. 17).

Another means to continue the enforcement of high standards and quality of care is consumer involvement. Consumers have a strong, collective voice and the ability to affect legislation. When consumers band together they provide a strong incentive for their elected representatives to listen. This is especially true in an election year. Families, partners, and friends of consumers who use these services are the most important voices of all. Their experiences with the system are absolutely vital to understanding the ways in which the system does or does not work and what can be done to improve the situation.

CONCLUSION

To enter into long-term care is a significant and life-altering decision. It implies that there are important activities of daily living that can no longer be performed independently. Some individuals have required long-term care since childhood. In either situation, the standard of care is absolutely critical. The nation's most vulnerable people–people with disabilities, the elderly, and people with terminal illnesses are in need of long-term care. Whether these services are provided in the home, a nursing home, a hospice, or other long-term facility, the persons using these services are extremely vulnerable. It is essential that the country continues to press for the highest standards in quality of care and the credentials of the professionals providing this care. Long-term care has evolved a great deal over the past century and especially over the last half century. This evolution has been for the better but the system is still in need of improvement.

TERMS & CONCEPTS

Activities of daily living: The most basic tasks of everyday life and include bathing, eating, dressing, using the toilet, and transferring from one place to another inside the house. ADLs include meal preparation, managing money, managing medications, using the telephone, doing light housework, and shopping for groceries.

Assisted living: The residences that emerged since the independent living movement for persons with disabilities began to have an effect in the 1970s. Assistive living refers to residences where persons live independently but utilize personal caregivers with some of their activities of daily living such as shopping and cleaning. People who live in AL residences do not need twenty-four hour care and do not need the services of a nurse or doctor in their daily lives.

Continuing care retirement communities: A community in which residents live together in a complex of units such as apartments, cottages, or other residences. There are both independent and group living arrangements and community care(medical or assistive care) is centralized in a building within the complex. There may be shops, dining rooms, or other amenities as well.

Faith-based services: Services that are based on a particular religious or spiritual belief and the people within those communities donate to and arrange for the upkeep of the home or institution.

Hospices: Either private institutions or part of a larger institution established to provide quality end-of-life (palliative) care.

Licensed practical nurse (LPN): A nurse who does not undergo the same level of rigorous training as a registered nurse (RN). LPNs must work under the supervision of an RN or a licensed physician. Although they are lower than RNs, they have more responsibilities than certified nursing assistants. They also work in a wide range of health care settings including hospitals and nursing homes.

Nursing homes: A generic name for a broad range of Long-term care services, although they sometimes provide subacute or short-term rehabilitation services. This is usually a place for individuals who require constant care especially with respect to a significant portion of their activities of daily living.

Palliative care: The term for end-of-life care, usually provided by a hospice organization.

Registered nurse (RN): An individual who has completed a specific level of training to earn the designation of 'registered nurse'. They work in a wide range of health care settings including hospitals, nursing homes and hospices. RNs can also be highly specialized such as emergency nursing, pediatric nursing, palliative nursing, psychiatric nursing, and many other specializations. They are highly valued in the health care system.

Retirement living communities: A broad term for a wide range of communities for persons in retirement. Retirement communities are for persons of a certain age and a certain level of physical functioning. They often have an extensive list of amenities such as pools, clubhouses, and on-site medical facilities. The residents live in their own independent apartments.

Subacute care: Generally considered to be short-term care and/or rehabilitation.

Bibliography

American Association of Homes and Services for the Aging. (2009). "2009 overview of assisted living." Washington, DC: American Association of Homes and Services for the Aging.

Atkins, G. L., Tumlinson, A., & Dawson, W. (2016). "Financing for Long-term services and supports." *Generations*, 40(4), 38-44.

Bernstein A. B., Hing, E., Moss A. J., Allen, K. F., Siller, A. B., & Tiggle R. B. (2003). "Health care in America: Trends in utilization." Hyattsville, Maryland: National Center for Health Statistics. http://www.cdc.gov/nchs/data/misc/healthcare.pdf

Chen, H., Haley, W. E., Robinson, B. E., &. Schonwetter, R. S. (2003). "Decisions for hospice care in patients with advanced cancer." *Journal of the American Geriatrics Society*, 51, 789-797.

Commission on Long-term Care. (2013, September 30). "Report to the Congress." http://ltccommission.org/ltccommission/wp-content/uploads/2013/12/Commission-on-Long-term-Care-Final-Report-9-26-13.pdf

Gibbs, L. M., & Mosqueda, L. (2004). "Confronting elder mistreatment in Long-term care." *Annals of* Long-term Care, 12, 26-33. http://www.annalsoflongtermcare.com/

Hanson, L. C., Sengupta, S., & Slubicki, M. (2005). "Access to nursing home hospice: Perspectives of nursing home and hospice administrators." *Journal of Palliative Medicine*, 8, 1207-1213.

Institute for the Future of Aging Services. (2007). "The Long-term care workforce: Can the crisis be fixed?" *A Report for the National Commission for Quality* Long-term Care. http://www.qualitylongtermcarecommission.org/

Kane, R. L., Lum, T. Y., Kane, R. A., Homyak, P., Parashuram, S., & Wysocki, A. (2013). "Does home- and community-based care affect nursing home use?" *Journal of Aging and Social Policy*, 25, 146-160.

Keay, T. J., & Schonwetter, R.S. (1998). "Hospice care in the nursing home." *American Family Physician*, 57, 491-496.

Livne, R. (2014). "Economies of dying: The moralization of economic scarcity in U.S. hospice care." *American Sociological Review*, 79, 888-911.

Luo, H., Lin, M., & Castle, N. G. (2013). "The correlates of nursing staff turnover in home and hospice agencies: 2007 National Home and Hospice Care Survey." *Research on Aging*, 35, 375-392.

National Commission for Quality Long-term Care. (2007). "From isolation to integration: Recommendations to improve quality in Long-term care." Commission website: http://www.qualitylongtermcarecommission.org/

Pesis-Katz, I, Phelps C. E., Temkin-Greener, H., Sepctor, W. D., Veazie, P. & Mukamel, D. B. (2013). "Making difficult decision: the role of quality of care in choosing a nursing home." *American Journal of Public Health*, 103, E31-E37.

Phillips, S. L., Smith, D., Cournoyer, B., & Hillegass, B. E. (2004). "Chronic home care: A health plans experience." *Annals of* Long-term Care, 12, 41-45. http://www.annalsoflongtermcare.com

Report to the Congress: Medicare Payment Policy. (2012). "Chapter 11: Hospice services." *MedPac*. http://www.medpac.gov/docs/default-source/reports/march-2012-report-to-the-congress-medicare-payment-policy.pdf

Stoil, M. (2007). "Nursing homes and home care: A shotgun marriage." *Nursing Homes:* Long Term Care *Management*, 56, 12-14.

Tumlinson, A., Woods, S., & Avalere Health LLC. (2007). *Long-term care in America: An introduction.* http://www.qualitylongtermcarecommission.org/

Washington, K. T., Wittenberg-Lyles, E., Parker Oliver, D., Baldwin, P. K., Tappana, J., Wright, J. H., & Demiris, G. (2014). "Rethinking Family Caregiving: Tailoring Cognitive–Behavioral Therapies to the Hospice Experience." *Health & Social Work*, 39, 244-50.

White, H. (2008). "Promoting quality care in the nursing home." *Annals of Long-term Care*, 13, 26-33. http://www.annalsoflongtermcare.com/altc/attachments/3999.pdf

Suggested Reading

Dennis, M. K., Washington, K. T., & Koenig, T. L. (2014). "Ethical dilemmas faced by hospice social workers." *Social Work in Health* Care, 53, 950-968.

Garre-Olmo, J., et al. (2012). "Environmental determinants of quality of life in nursing home residents with severe dementia." *Journal of the American Geriatrics Society*, 60, 1230-1236.

Gaugler, J. E. (2005). *Promoting family involvement in* Long-term care *settings a guide to programs that work.* Baltimore, Maryland: Health Professionals Press.

Kunkel, A., & Wellin, V. (Eds.). (2006). *Consumer voice and choice in* Long-term care. New York, N.Y.: Springer Publishing Co.

Lattanzi-Licht, M., Mahoney, J. J., & Miller, G. W. (1998). *The hospice choice: In pursuit of a peaceful death.* New York, N.Y.: The National Hospice Association.

Lepore, M., Knowles, M., Porter, K. A., O'Keeffe, J., & Wiener, J. (2017). "Medicaid beneficiaries' access to residential care settings." *Journal of Housing for the Elderly*, 31(4), 351-366.

Salamon, M. J., & Rosenthal, G. (2003). *Home or nursing home making the right choices.* New York, N.Y.: Springer Publishing Co.

Wunderlich, G. S., &. Kohler, P. O. (Eds.). (2001). *Improving the quality of* Long-term care. Washington, D.C.: The National Academies Press.

Ilanna Mandel, M.A.

MEDICALIZATION

ABSTRACT

Medicalization is central to the idea that medicine is an institution of social control, implying that all knowledge, including scientific and medical knowledge, is a social product, developed through processes of interpretation and negotiation that play a critical role in evaluating and legitimizing deviance. In this social constructionist perspective, illness and disease are forms of social deviance that need to be controlled or regulated through specially sanctioned agencies such as medicine. Medicalization is a concept that captures the processes through which medicine and medical culture categorize physical, emotional and social phenomena as normal or not-normal, and thus encroach on various aspects of social life. Political economists have argued that medicalization occurs primarily in capitalist societies that are characterized by processes of specialization and differentiation through which medicine expands its boundaries and colonizes new areas of the body and mind. Similarly, medicalization has proved a valuable analytic tool for feminists interested in exploring and explaining the relationship between medicine and the female body. Finally, while medicalization processes are not without conflict, medicalization is increasingly driven forward by the pharmaceutical industry.

OVERVIEW

Medicalization is central to the idea that medicine is an institution of social control. Irving Zola (1972), whose work explores medical authority and power in capitalist societies, originally developed the concept. In Zola's framework, illness and disease are viewed as forms of social deviance that need to be controlled or regulated through specially sanctioned agencies such as medicine. Medicalizationis a concept that captures the processes through which medicine and medical culture categorize physical, emotional, and social phenomena as normal or not-normal. In doing so, medicine encroaches on various aspects of social life and, to a degree, wins social consent from members of society for doing so (de Swaan, 1990). Diagnosis is important in the process of medicalization because it is through diagnosis that claims are made about what is considered normal and what is not.

Political economists have argued that medicalization occurs primarily in capitalist societies that are characterized by processes of specialization and differentiation, through which medicine expands its boundaries and colonizes new areas of the body and mind (Illich, 1976). Similarly, medicalization has proved an invaluable analytic tool for feminists interested in exploring and explaining the relationship between medicine and the female body. Central to the concept of medicalization is the idea that all knowledge, including scientific and medical knowledge, is a social product, developed through processes of interpretation and negotiation that play a critical role in evaluating and legitimizing deviance.

The Medicalization Thesis

The medicalization thesis emerged primarily in the 1970s as a way of explaining the expansion of modern medicine and its apparent ever-increasing reach into corners of social life. The concept of medicalization is derived from two main approaches to the study of health, illness and disease. First, medicalization is related to the political economy of health, in which good health (in capitalist societies) is viewed as a resource, as well as a state of being. As such, struggles between different social groups ensue over access to and control over whatever is required to produce and maintain good health (such as housing, food, medical care). Those who experience poor health, disabilities and/or advanced age, have less capacity to engage in this struggle for health (or to contribute to the production of commodities) and therefore come to be marginalized by society, or are viewed as deviant.

Political Economy

In the political economy perspective, certain social groups (e.g. minorities, women, people with disabilities, low income groups) have less access to resources that support good health and consequently experience poorer health. In this view medicine contributes to and reproduces social inequalities because its primary focus is on returning those who are sick (deviant) to the labor force, rather than addressing the conditions that create disease in the first place. Thus, medicalization plays a key role in labeling already marginalized social groups as socially deviant, and in securing social power, authority and status for doctors as members of a prestigious profession. Indeed, as more resources are devoted to disease and illness (deviance), medicine's status and power as a profession has grown, such that members of society tend to view medicine as a panacea for life's problems, rather than turning their attention to what is making them sick in the first place; that is, in the political economy perspective, social inequalities. While the political economy perspective was predominant in the 1970s, social constructionist perspectives largely displaced it in the 1980s and 1990s.

Social Constructionism

Social constructionism underpins the second element of the medicalization thesis. This perspective assumes that definitions of illness are the products of social processes and interactions between social groups. These interactions are characterized by inequality, in the sense that not all social groups have equal access to the capacity to produce knowledge or define what counts as knowledge about the human body and its vicissitudes (Nettleton, 1992). Medical practitioners have the power to define what counts as disease and illness as a consequence of negotiations with the state, which have resulted in their designation as professional groups, or experts (Witz, 1992). Such expertise can be considered a social resource, since all societies have social groups that are viewed as experts in relation to illness and disease (with the expertise to heal), from shamans to surgeons. However, the expertise that is conferred on medical practitioners by society also enables them to pass considerable judgment on which phenomena (be they behaviors or symptoms) come to be categorized as disease or illness, and how phenomena that are defined as medical should be handled. This power can have detrimental consequences, as we see especially in the case of childbirth.

APPLICATIONS

The Example of Childbirth

Many researchers, especially those from feminist perspectives, have argued that childbirth and pregnancy have been socially constructed as a medical problem. In pre-modern societies it is generally noted that pregnancy was not viewed as a separate or special kind of experience. Researchers have argued that women expected pregnancy and childbirth to be accompanied by pain and discomfort (Donnisson, 1977) and there was very little formal advice given to women before or during pregnancy and childbirth. Instead, women tended to rely on each other for support through pregnancy and childbirth and they learned informally about what to expect through oral sharing of information.

Historically, childbirth attendance was mainly the preserve of women known as midwives who specialized in assisting friends and kin in giving birth. However, medical men who also practiced birthing wished to formalize the knowledge and practices of midwives as a way of developing a specialized, professional group (Witz, 1992). This process of formalization challenged the primacy of midwives in the early eighteenth century and subsequently, in the nineteenth century, as medicine became increasingly scientific, pregnancy and childbirth came to be seen as a pathological-and therefore clinical-event, in part because the men who attended births were largely associated with hospitals and hospital based medicine (Turner, 1987).

This specialized location enabled them to create a systematic knowledge base that supported the view that pregnancy needed to be managed via medical interventions and not allowed to simply happen as a natural event. The development of forceps (Wajcman, 1991) was critical in this process as it allowed doctors to deliver babies that would not otherwise have survived. However, it also allowed doctors to discredit midwives and marginalize them from the process of pregnancy and childbirth and in doing so, redefine pregnancy and childbirth from a natural event to a pathological event requiring medical surveillance and management. As Oakley (1980) argued in her classic study of the history of childbirth, the development of birthing technologies, from forceps to Cesarean sections, provided a way of restricting the informal practice of midwifery and cementing technical intervention as the hallmark of modern obstetrics.

In the twenty first century, pregnancy and childbirth continues to epitomize the significance of medicalization, as new technologies ensure that the pregnant woman and the baby she carries is supervised and monitored from early in conception through to delivery and even beyond (Apple, 1995). Nonetheless, there has been backlash against the medicalization of pregnancy and childbirth and growth in midwife deliveries as an alternative to medical supervision. For instance, in New Zealand, a majority of women register with a midwife rather than an obstetrician to manage their pregnancy (Jutel, 2006). Such a change allows the medicalization process as one of negotiation rather than as undisputed dominance and social control.

FURTHER INSIGHTS

Medicalization, Deviance & Social Control

Central to the concept of medicalization is the idea that medicine is an institution of social control whose primary function is to deal with illness as a form of social deviance. This claim is based on the observation that areas of life that might be defined as natural or social have increasingly come under the scrutiny of medical culture and practice. For instance, natural human processes such as childbirth, aging and menstruation have all been defined as medical problems that require medical solutions. Zola (1972) argued that medicine has been central to handling social deviance in contemporary capitalist societies as the social power of religious institutions has diminished. In doing so, medicine develops experts upon whom people come increasingly to depend, in ways that diminish their own capacities to make judgments and deal with problems (Illich, 1976).

In medieval and pre-modern Europe and early America, religious institutions were generally charged with identifying and defining behaviors as deviant and dealing with them through punishment and/or marginalization. For instance, in Puritan New England, witches were viewed as deviant, or, in fact, as sick (Gevitz, 2000). In seventeenth century Salem, Massachusetts, they were viewed as dangerous and therefore deviant by religious governors. Consequently, these women and girls were treated in ways that punished them and warned other members of society that such differences would not be tolerated. In modern Western societies, medicine has taken over the role of "processing" deviance, by identifying and labeling certain behaviors as socially inappropriate and/or dangerous (such as homosexuality). In this understanding of deviance, people who are different in ways that society cannot accommodate are not categorized as "evil," as they may have been viewed in the past, but instead they are categorized as "sick."

The Sick Role

Talcott Parsons (1951), the functionalist sociologist, developed a theory for explaining how medicine handles sickness as deviance, and how people participate in the process of managing deviance. In the functionalist perspective, illness is considered deviance and the patient-physician relationship is a primary mechanism of social control that functions to restore social stability. In his view, illness is considered deviant behavior because when people are ill, they threaten the stability of the social order, as they are (often, though not always), unable to perform their usual social roles. Illness, as understood in the functionalist perspective, violates social norms and is potentially disruptive. Therefore, it requires a social response. Medicine provides a social response that treats people who are ill, or sick, with the aim of restoring them to health, or to social functioning. Part of this social response requires people who are sick to take on a special role that permits their absence from production until they are considered well enough to return (by physicians). Therefore, the sick role exists to pull the sick person into a relationship with a physician, who helps to heal the sick person and integrate them back into their normal social roles (e.g. parent, wife, worker).

When people adopt the sick role, they are not viewed as responsible for being sick (that is, their deviance) and therefore, they are not necessarily stigmatized for being sick (or deviant-although there are exceptions in diseases that are viewed as the consequence of social behaviors that are perceived to be deviant, such as sexually transmitted diseases). Consequently, as long as members of society inhabit the sick role appropriately and fulfill the obligations that come with it, including submitting to medical care and intervention, they are not, in Parsons' view, categorized as deviant (just sick). Central to the process of categorizing people as sick or not sick, is the related process of diagnosis.

Medicalization & Diagnosis

Interpretative perspectives on medicine, disease and deviance claim that diagnosis is not a value neutral process. Indeed, diagnostic categories are often imbued with assumptions about social categories such as race, gender and age. Because these assumptions change over time and place, so do the diagnostic categories. For instance, in the nineteenth century, the phenomenon of runaway slaves was understood as a disease-drapetomania-and in the twentieth century, there is a shifting smorgasbord of physical, emotional and social phenomena that are increasingly viewed as medical disorders, such as female sexual dysfunction (Tiefer, 2006) and compulsive shopping (Lee & Mysyk, 2004).

Diagnosis is central to the process of medicalization because it is an interpretative and social process that is built on and helps to build a formal system of classification or nomenclature that serves to legitimate medicine as a profession of authority (Jutel, 2009). This process involves describing a phenomenon in medical terms, which then is incorporated as a disease concept which relies on an understanding of disease categories as socially constructed (Hacking, 2001). It is this process of categorization that lies at the heart of medical authority, because of its role in legitimizing sickness (de Swaan, 1990), and in establishing and modifying the boundaries of what is considered normal or abnormal. Indeed, scholars have argued that social assumptions influence how and which symptom clusters come to be identified as diseases (Aronowitz, 2001).

The case of homosexuality is a classic example of how behaviors that are considered socially deviant have been categorized as disease, and therefore become subject to medical surveillance. The Diagnostic and Statistical Manual of Mental Disorders (DSM) is the key classificatory text of modern psychiatry and until 1973, homosexuality was listed as a psychiatric condition. However, during the preparation of the DSM-III, gay activists protested at American Psychiatric Association conventions against the categorization of homosexuality as mental illness. Ultimately, homosexuality was removed from the DSM-III as a diagnostic category (Kirk & Kutchins, 1992). Diagnosis, then, can be understood as a process that involves fixing diagnostic labels to socially deviant behaviors.

This understanding of diagnosis and its role in medicalization processes is also seen in the case of obesity in the US. Obesity has shifted from being seen primarily as a sign of weakness or moral lassitude arising from gluttony and sexual excess that primarily targeted women in the early twentieth century (Stearns, 1999) to a disease that requires medical treatment at both the level of the individual and public policy (Boero, 2007). Boero argues that the "obesity" label was initially used to designate undesirable or stigmatizable "differences" that could be treated through interventions such as drugs, jaw wiring, or bariatric surgery. However, while obesity was initially treated as a problem for individuals, and interventions designed accordingly, obesity is now seen as a wider social problem-or epidemic-that has the consequence of extending "medical jurisdiction over health itself in addition to illness, disease, and injury" (Clarke et al., 2003, p. 162). In contrast, there are patients and advocacy groups who refute that obesity is a disease and suggest instead that obesity has been medicalized because society discriminates against size (Jutel, 2006).

Medicalization & Pharmaceuticals

In the twentieth century, research on medicalization has turned to the prevalence of pharmaceuticals as panaceas for the ailments and aches of everyday life as well as the controversies and conflicts that accompany their use. In the 1970s, pharmaceuticals were viewed as key objects in the process of medicalization. Ivan Illich (1976) noted, for instance, that if contemporary American society was dependent on medicine and medical experts in general, then the consumption of drugs in particular fuelled that dependence. Yet, as Williams et al. (2008) note, while pharmaceuticals were viewed as part of the problem of the engine of medicalization, they were not viewed as its driver. Increasingly, researchers argue that the pharmaceutical industry plays a key role in medicalization. Consequently there are a number of case studies that follow the development of not only drugs to treat particular diseases but also the creation of new disease categories (such as ADHA, erectile dysfunction and bipolar disorder) to which they can market their products.

While doctors were seen as the drivers of medicalization in the twentieth century, the pharmaceutical industry is seen in the twenty-first century as a key driver because of the direct relationship that "big pharma" has with health consumers as well as with doctors and health care practitioners through direct-to-consumer advertising (DTCA) and Internet purchase via e-pharmacies (Fox et al., 2005). This process of medicalization via pharmaceuticals occurs in two main ways. First, drug consumption in the domestic context has increased, especially drugs that enhance or suppress dietary and increase sexual appetites. Second, consumers increasingly see drugs as a normal-and normalized-means of dealing with everyday life (Fox et al., 2007). Thus, the extension of pharmaceuticals into domestic, everyday life contributes greatly to contemporary medicalization.

ISSUE

The Medicalization of PMS

While medicalization is generally viewed critically as a source of power and undisputed authority, it is also marked by negotiation and conflict. For instance, pre-menstrual syndrome (PMS) emerged as a broad term to encompass a variety of female experiences that have subsequently come under the purview of gynecology (Rodin, 1992). PMS is a diagnostic category that focuses on hormonal imbalance but it reflects ideas about femininity and the female body and about a woman's place in society in terms of career. Rodin argues that just as hysteria was defined in the nineteenth century in terms of its unpredictability (and marriage was offered as a solution), the category of PMS in the twentieth century was sometimes used to legitimate claims that women ought not to be given positions of responsibility in the workplace or in public life. Yet, PMS has also been used to support the legal category of 'diminished responsibility' in the United Kingdom as a defense for women charged with crimes of violence (usually against domestic partners).

Anthropologists have suggested that the cluster of symptoms that women experience that are categorized as PMS may be culturally specific. Johnson (1987) suggested that PMS is a kind of cultural safety valve through which women give expression to the social contradictions of living in capitalist societies which expect citizens to engage in productivity, and also be reproductive. Emily Martin, in her book, Woman in the Body, takes this observation further to argue that in Western capitalist societies the bodily and material disruptions women experience are not readily accommodated. It is difficult for them to carry the burdens of both production and reproduction. Hence, PMS provides women a measure of reprieve. This analysis suggests that women themselves have contributed to the social construction of medical categories (or medicalization) as a way to find solutions to their embodied experiences, especially those that disrupt their lives. The medicalization of symptoms associated with PMS invites further investigation, but it also provides a mechanism through which women have been able to find legitimization and authoritative support for symptoms associated with pain and discomfort. In such circumstances women are not necessarily the victims of medicalization but participants in the construction of discourses that define female embodiment.

CONCLUSION

Although medicalization is central to the idea that medicine is an institution of social control, its power may be modified by social protest (as in the case of homosexuality and the DSM). Further, when people who have symptoms and discomfort do not have the benefit of diagnostic category, this can cause distress and make it difficult for them to claim benefits and legitimacy for their illness (Nettleton, 2006). Thus, medicalization, through the process of diagnosis, may have social benefits. Nonetheless, it seems clear that medicalization continues as a process that defines and categorizes areas of life that have not hitherto been understood in terms of disease. Pharmaceutical companies may play a critical role in this process, as they support the categorization of certain symptoms as disease, in order to promote their products. While professional expansion and the pursuit of prestige may explain medicalization processes in the twentieth century, this "disease-mongering" (Williams et al., 2008) may be the new engine of medicalization.

TERMS & CONCEPTS

Deviance: Differences in behavior from what is generally considered the social norm.

Diagnosis: An interpretative and social process that is built on and helps to build a formal system of classification or nomenclature that serves to legitimate medicine as a profession of authority.

Functionalism: A sociological perspective based on application of scientific method to the social world, that sees the social world as a social system with needs that need to be met in order to maintain order and stability.

Medicalization: The processes through which medicine categorizes physical, emotional and social phenomena as normal or not-normal.

Political Economy of Health: An analytic approach in which health is viewed as a resource, as well as a state of being. As such, struggles between different social groups ensue over access to and control over whatever is required to produce and maintain good health (such as housing, food, medical care).

Sick Role: A special role that sanctions the absence of people from production until they are considered well enough to return (by physicians).

Social Constructionism: A philosophical perspective that views social phenomena as created through social action and interaction.

Social Control: The formal or informal mechanisms that regulate individual and group behavior.

BIBLIOGRAPHY

Apple, R.D. (1995). "Constructing mothers: Scientific motherhood in the nineteenth and twentieth centuries." *Social History of Medicine.* 8: 161-78.

Aronowitz, R. (2001). "When do symptoms become a disease?" *Annals of Internal Medicine.* 134(9), part 2:803-8.

Boero, N. (2007). "All the news that's fat to print: The American 'Obesity Epidemic' and the media." *Qualitative Sociology,* 30(1), 41-60.

Cacchioni, T., & Tiefer, L. (2012). "Why medicalization? Introduction to the Special Issue on the medicalization of Sex." *Journal Of Sex Research,* 49(4), 307-310.

Cartwright, S. (1981 [1851]). "Report of the diseases and physical peculiarities of the negro race." In Caplan, A., Englehardt, H.T. and McCartney, J. (eds). *Concepts of health and disease.* Reading, MA: Addison-Wesley Publishing Company.

Clarke, A., Shim, J., Mamo, L., Fosket, J., & Fishman, J. (2003). "Biomedicalization: Technoscientific transformations of health, illness, and U.S. biomedicine." *American Sociological Review,* 68 (2), 161-194.

Conrad, P. & Schneider, J.W. (1992). *Deviance and medicalization: From badness to sickness.* Philadelphia: Temple University Press.

De Swaan, A. (1990). *The management of normality.* London: Routledge.

Donnisson, J. (1977). *Midwives and medical men: A history of inter-professional rivalries and women's rights.* London: Heinemann.

Farrell, J., & Cacchioni, T. (2012). "The medicalization of Women's Sexual Pain." *Journal Of Sex Research,* 49(4), 328-336.

Fox, N. J. & Ward, K. J. (2008). "Pharma in the bedroom...and the kitchen... The pharmaceuticalisation of everyday life". *Sociology of Health & Illness.* 30(6):856-868.

Fox, N.J., Ward, K.J. & O'Rourke, A.J. (2007). "A sociology of technology governance for the information age: The case of pharmaceuticals, consumer advertising and the Internet." *Sociology.* 40, 315-34.

Gevitz, N. (2000). "'The Devil hath laughed at the physicians': Witchcraft and medical practice in seventeenth-century New England." *Journal of the History of Medicine.* 55(1):5-36.

Hacking, I. (2002). "Inaugural lecture: Chair of Philosophy and History of Scientific Concepts at the Collège de France." *Economy and Society,* 31(1), 1-14.

Jutel, A. (2009). "Sociology of diagnosis: A preliminary review." *Sociology of Health and Illness.* 31(2), 278-299. Available at: http://www3.interscience.wiley.com

Johnson, T. (1987). "Pre-menstrual syndrome as a Western culture-specific disorder." *Culture, Medicine and Society.* 11:337-356.

Kirk, S.A. & Kutchins, H. (1992). *The selling of DSM: The rhetoric of science in psychiatry.* New York: Aldine de Gruyter.

Lee, S. & Mysyk, A. (2004). "The medicalization of compulsive buying." *Social Science and Medicine,* 58(9), 1709-18.

Marshall, B. L. (2012). "Medicalization and the Refashioning of Age-Related Limits on Sexuality." *Journal Of Sex Research,* 49(4), 337-343.

Martin, E. (1989). *The woman in the body.* Buckinham: Open University Press.

Nettleton, S. (2006). "'I just want permission to be ill': Towards a sociology of medically unexplained symptoms." *Social Science and Medicine.* 62, 1167-78.

Oakley, A. (1980). *Woman confined: Towards a sociology of childbirth.* Oxford: Martin Robertson.
Parsons, T. ([1951] 1991). *The social system.* London: Routledge.
Polzer, J. C., & Knabe, S. M. (2012). "From Desire to Disease: Human Papillomavirus (HPV) and the medicalization of Nascent Female Sexuality." *Journal Of Sex Research,* 49(4), 344-352.
Rodin, M. (1992). "The social construction of premenstrual syndrome." *Social Science and Medicine.* 35, 49-56.
Scott, S. (2006). "The medicalization of shyness: From social misfits to social fitness." *Sociology of Health and Illness,* 28(2), 133-53.
Tiefer, L. (2006). "Female sexual dysfunction: A case study of disease mongering and activist resistance." *PLoS Medicine.* 3(4): e178.
Tiefer, L. (2012). "Medicalizations and Demedicalizations of Sexuality Therapies." *Journal Of Sex Research,* 49(4), 311-318.
Turner, B.S. (1987). *Medical power and social knowledge.* London: Sage.
Williams, S., Gabe, J. & Davis, P. (2008). "The sociology of pharmaceuticals: Progress and prospects." *Sociology of Health and Illness,* 30 (6), 813-824.
Wajcman, J. (1991). *Feminism confronts technology.* Cambridge: Polity.
Witz, A. (1992). *Professions and patriarchy.* London: Routledge.
Zola, I.K. (1972) "Medicine as an institution of social control." *Sociological Review,* 20 (4), 487-504.

Suggested Reading

Brown, P. (2008). "Naming and framing: The social construction of diagnosis and illness." In Brown, P. (ed.) *Perspectives in Medical Sociology.* Long Grove, Ill: Waveland Press.
Busfield, J. (2006). "Pills, power, people: Sociological understandings of the pharmaceutical industry." *Sociology,* 40(2):297-314.
Campos, P., Saguy, A., Ernsberger, P., Oliver, E. & Gaesser, G. (2006a). "The epidemiology of overweight and obesity: Public health crisis or moral panic?" *International Journal of Epidemiology.* 35(1):55-60.
Engelhardt, H.T. (1992). "The body as a field of meaning: Implications for the ethics of diagnosis." In Peset, J.L. and Gracia, D. (eds). *The Ethics of Diagnosis.*Netherlands: Springer.
Healy, D. (2006). "The latest mania: Selling Bipolar Disorder." *PLoS Medicine,* 3(4), e185.
Moynihan, R. & Cassels, A. (2005). *Selling sickness: How drug companies are turning us all into patients.* Sydney: Allen and Unwin.

Alexandra Howson

Mental Health & E-Therapy

OVERVIEW

Good mental health is the condition comprising emotional well-being, good behavioral adjustment, relative freedom from anxiety and disabling symptoms, and a capacity to establish constructive relationships and cope with the ordinary demands and stresses of life. When experiencing undue stress or other problems with their mental health, many individuals turn to psychotherapy for help. Although psychotherapy has traditionally been conducted in a clinical setting, today's information technology allows therapists to use the Internet in e-therapy, psychotherapy that is conducted over the Internet rather than in face-to-face sessions. E-therapy may be conducted using real-time messaging, chat rooms, or e-mail messages. Given the fact that many people find information and communicate through the Internet, e-therapy has become increasingly popular. However, much more research is needed to determine the efficacy of this type of therapy, the situations under which it works best, and the types of clients for whom it is best suited.

When meeting a stranger at a party, I rarely reveal the fact that I am a psychologist. Too many times the conversation has quickly turned from the purely social to an attempt at a free diagnosis of self, friends, or family. I suppose this is just one of the hazards of the profession, as is the tendency to psychoanalyze things that do not require psychoanalysis. For example, last evening I was watching my favorite television show, which features a misanthrope well known for his curmudgeonly behavior with others. On more than one occasion I have been drawn into conversations with friends trying to sort out the character's problems as the writers bit by bit give the viewers more insight into his psyche. In the end, of course, I need to step back and remember that he is, after all, just a character on a television show. The writers either got the psychology right or they did not. However, diagnosing a character on a television show does no one any good. This, however, does not keep the other characters on the show from attempting to do so. In the latest episode, the character was listening intently to the current woes of his best friend. Trying to encourage the other man, the character remarked "interesting" at one point in the conversation. The friend took offense. "Why do you say interesting?" he asked. "Because I am interested," the character replied. "But you should have said 'good for you' or something else instead," replied his friend. Frankly, "interesting" was a perfectly reasonable response. However, the character's friend was looking for something else, and took the lack of what he deemed to be an appropriate response to be another example of the character's need for in-depth psychotherapy.

Although on one level, this story is merely about a fictional conversation between two fictional characters, on another level it is a good example of how the expectations of other people determine in part whether or not one is considered "normal" and whether one is considered to be mentally healthy or mentally ill. In another context or with other people, the comment that something was interesting might go unremarked. However, the expectation of the friend was that the character would say something inappropriate. Therefore, he interpreted the character's response as being inappropriate and further evidence of his lack of mental health. In fact, in many ways, mental health and mental illness are little more than social constructs. Through the process of socialization, one is taught to act in a way that is deemed to be acceptable and to act in a manner that is appropriate for the needs of the society.

Psychotherapy

Whether or not mental health and mental illness are social constructs or objective states, we treat them as if they were the latter–that is, with the attitude that the person with mental health issues needs to be treated so that he or she better conforms to the norms and expectations of society in the future. This is often done through psychotherapy, a generic term used to refer to any psychological service provided by a trained professional. Psychotherapy primarily uses communication and interaction to assess, diagnose, and treat the dysfunctional emotional reactions, ways of thinking, and patterns of behavior of an individual, family, or group. From a sociological perspective, this can be viewed as a method of socialization aimed at preserving the stability of society. There are a number of methods of psychotherapy, including the general categories of cognitive behavioral, humanistic, integrative, or psychodynamic. Typically, psychotherapy takes place in the office of a licensed psychotherapist. However, with the increasing advances in information technology today, new approaches are being tried.

Information Technology

In many ways, information technology has transformed our lives over the past few decades. As societies transition from being industrial (using mechanization to produce the economic goods and services within a society) to being postindustrial (primarily based upon the processing and control of information and the provision of services), we frequently find ourselves turning more and more to electronic communications media in general and the Internet in particular to communicate with others. In the workplace, this means a heavy reliance on such things as e-mail and teleconferencing rather than the more traditional written correspondence, faxes, or business travel and meetings. At home, this means such conveniences as the ordering of goods and paying of bills online. However, it is not only correspondence that is carried on over the Internet. One can easily use the knowledge base of a manufacturer to determine how to troubleshoot software or repair an appliance. Even medical sites are available so that one can learn about the possible diagnoses for one's symptoms or research alternative treatments. It is also possible on some sites to chat online with a physician or nurse practitioner by e-mail rather than going into the office. These two features of postindustrial society–greater reliance on non-face-to-face methods of communication and the ability to solve one's problem online rather than in person–have combined in the mental health professions to create a demand for psychological services over the Internet. This approach to psychotherapy has a certain logic to it. People are used to communicating electronically and to receiving their information over the Internet. By extension, chatting with one's therapist online is just the application of these principles in the arena of mental health.

E-Therapy

This distance approach to psychotherapy using the Internet is known as e-therapy or online therapy. This is a form of psychotherapy that is conducted over the Internet rather than in face-to-face sessions. E-therapy may be conducted using real-time messaging, chat rooms, or e-mail messages.

E-therapy has a number of potential advantages including being more convenient than going to a therapist's office as well as being more private than going to an office and waiting in a public waiting room. It is theorized that more people needing psychological help might be willing to receive it over the Internet since they do not have to go into a therapist's office with the risk of being seen by others, fear of embarrassment, or unwillingness or inability to get to the office. The Internet allows the therapy client relative anonymity and, perhaps, engenders a concomitant greater willingness to open up to the therapist for the very reason that he or she does not have to see the therapist's reaction.

E-therapy can also provide a more convenient alternative for getting the help needed to those in rural areas where access to a therapist is exceedingly difficult. In addition, e-therapy tends to be less expensive than in-office therapy, another factor that might increase the likelihood that it will be used by those who need it.

As attractive as e-therapy may sound to overly busy professionals in today's society, it is also not without its drawbacks as well. Despite the fact that many of us in the twenty-first century are used to communicating through e-mail, online chat, or instant messaging, these communication methods have the drawback of not allowing the two parties in communication to receive important cues about what the other person is trying to communicate such as tone of voice, facial expression, and body language. In general, this can lead to potential miscommunication. This risk may be acceptable most of the time for normal communications. However, nonverbal cues are often essential to the task of the psychotherapist and not having these cues can potentially lead to an incorrect diagnosis. In addition, psychotherapists frequently use proprietary clinical assessment instruments to help them diagnose a client. However, many of the tests and instruments used in diagnosis tend to be not only ethically but legally required to be given by a credentialed professional in a controlled situation. This cannot be done over the Internet because there is no control over who will see the test, how long the client takes to answer the questions, or even whether it was the client or someone else who took the test.

APPLICATIONS

Treating Mental Disorders

The literature shows evidence that e-therapy can be successfully used to treat a number of mental disorders including panic disorder, social phobia, child adjustment after traumatic brain injury, and complicated grief. However, a great deal more research is needed in order to answer questions such as what types of disorders as best suited to the e-therapy approach, what type of clients are most likely to benefit from e-therapy, what methods can be used to successfully overcome the disadvantages to diagnostic and therapeutic progress that result from the inability of the client and therapist being able to see each other. In addition, e-therapy is currently performed using a variety of electronic media. Research is needed to determine the relative efficacy of each approach in various circumstances.

This research has begun. Pier, Austin, Klein, Mitchell, Schattner, Ciechomski, et al. (2008), for example, performed a controlled trial of Internet-based cognitive behavioral therapy (an approach to psychotherapy that emphasizes the correction of distorted thinking patterns and changing one's behaviors accordingly) for panic disorder with both face to face support from a general practitioner and e-mail support from a psychologist. Panic disorder is an anxiety disorder in which an individual experiences sudden, debilitating attacks of intense fear. This is one of the most common anxiety disorders that are seen by general practitioners today. Previous research has indicated that cognitive behavioral therapy is the most effective approach to treating this disorder. However, most general practitioners are not trained in this method. In addition, in the area in which the research was conducted, access to a psychotherapist trained in cognitive behavioral therapy is not always available and often prohibitively expensive. Such a situation is a good example where e-therapy–if effective–could do great good.

Panic Online Research Study

Subjects in the study were 65 individuals with panic disorder who participated in the Panic Online research study. The program included six modules: an introductory module, four learning modules, and a relapse prevention module. The material covered in the program included techniques typically covered in cognitive behavioral therapy (e.g., control breathing, progressive muscle relaxation, cognitive restructuring, and situational exposure). Audio material for the muscle relaxation techniques with downloadable off the Internet and gradual exposure exercises were also available. Thirty-one of the subjects are placed in the Panic Online with psychological assistance group. Each subject in this group was assigned to a treating psychologist who communicated with the subject using e-mail. This e-mail support was intended to allow the therapist to provide support and feedback to the subject as well as to guide the subject through the program based on the individual's needs. Although the psychologists initiated contact with each subject at least weekly, the subjects were allowed to e-mail their therapists as frequently as they desired. The therapists responded to all e-mail from the subjects within a 24-hour period. The remaining 34 participants were put in the Panic Online general practitioner group. Interaction with the general practitioners occurred face-to-face. The general practitioners provided support and feedback to each participant as well as guided him or her through the program according to each individual's needs a request. Subjects and the general practitioners were encouraged to consult each other on a regular basis for the duration of the 12 weeks of the study.

The study showed similar results for those subjects who worked with the online materials with the support of their general practitioner as did those who worked with the online materials with the support of an online psychologist. The researchers interpreted these results to mean that the online tools were a useful adjunct to the support given by general practitioners to clients with panic disorder, making e-therapy a helpful tool for situations in which there is little or no face-to-face access to trained psychotherapists. Both groups of subjects experienced significant improvements in their experience of symptoms include depression, anxiety, stress, and frequency of panic attacks. In addition, both groups experienced significantly increased quality of life. However, although the results of the study are encouraging, they are limited by several methodological considerations. One of the most important of these is the fact that the study included no control group to compare the efficacy of the use of a therapist in an online setting with use of a therapist in a traditional face-to-face setting using the same tools.

Whether or not e-therapy is effective is a moot point, however, if those who need therapy do not trust it enough to participate. Skinner and Latchford performed a study to compare the attitudes to e-therapy of those clients currently using e-therapy, individuals who participate in support groups on the Internet and who are familiar with talking about mental health issues online and individuals who were used to face-to-face psychotherapy but not e-therapy (2006). The factors included in the study were:

- The use of computers to facilitate therapy,
- The ability to meet for therapy at a convenient time,
- The advantage of therapy being conducted anonymously,
- The advantage of being invisible during therapy, and
- A greater ability to concentrate on the therapy.

Subjects included 39 individuals who were face-to-face therapy clients and 130 individuals who participated in Internet support groups. Although the study was originally designed to include a third group comprising e-therapy clients, only three individuals meeting this criterion agreed to participate, so the group was dropped from the study. Results of the study indicated that although clients of face-to-face therapy tended to be more likely to disclose personal information, both groups had similar self-disclosure styles. Members of Internet support groups tended to be more positive about e-therapy than were the subjects who were only used to face-to-face therapy. The study further found that attitudes toward e-therapy were more positive if the individual had experience both with online support groups and with face-to-face therapy.

CONCLUSION

Although mental health and psychotherapy in many ways is the domain of psychologists, sociologists have an interest in this area as well, particularly from the point of view that the concept of mental health is a social construct and that society socializes its members to behave within acceptable norms and parameters. Further, the concept of e-therapy is of particular interest to sociologists as an artifact of post-industrialization. Given the fact that many of us today live our lives in great part based on the availability of information on the Internet and by communicating through the Internet, e-therapy certainly makes sense. E-therapy is becoming increasingly popular. However, much more research is needed to determine the efficacy of this type of therapy, the situations under which it works best, and the types of clients for whom it is best suited.

TERMS & CONCEPTS

Chat Room: A space on a web site or network server that allows multiple people to communicate by entering text messages at their individual computers. The messages are viewable by all in the virtual "room," and messages appear almost instantaneously once they are sent.

Electronic Therapy (E-Therapy): A form of psychotherapy that is conducted over the Internet rather than in face-to-face sessions. E-therapy may be conducted using real-time messaging, chat rooms, or e-mail messages. Internet-based therapy is also called online therapy or Internet-based therapy.

Electronic Mail (E-Mail): A system for sending and receiving messages electronically through personal computers or other computer network. Usually, it takes only a few seconds or minutes for e-mail to be sent from one computer and received at another.

Information Technology: The use of computers, communications networks, and knowledge in the creation, storage, and dispersal of data and information. Information technology comprises a wide range of items and abilities for use in the creation, storage, and distribution of information.

Instant Messaging: A method of electronic communication that allows two or more people to communicate nearly instantaneously without using a chat room. Instant messaging is much like a telephone conversation with text messages conducted using a computer rather than a phone. The sender types a message at his or her computer, which is then sent to and received at the other person's computer. Instant messaging can be used in much the same way as a private chat room.

Mental Disorder: A psychological illness that is characterized by any one or more of the following: abnormal behavior, impaired functioning, or psychological symptoms.

Mental Health: The condition comprising emotional well-being, good behavioral adjustment, relative freedom from anxiety and disabling symptoms, and a capacity to establish constructive relationships and cope with the ordinary demands and stresses of life.

Norms: Standards or patterns of behavior that are accepted as normal within the culture.

Postindustrial: The nature of a society whose economy is no longer dependent on the manufacture of goods (i.e., industrial), but is primarily based upon the processing and control of information and the provision of services.

Psychotherapy: A generic term used to refer to any psychological service provided by a trained professional. Psychotherapy primarily uses communication and interaction to assess, diagnose, and treat the dysfunctional emotional reactions, ways of thinking, and patterns of behavior of an individual, family, or group. Within this broad categorization there a number different types of specific approaches to psychotherapy, most of which fall into one of four general subgroups: cognitive behavioral, humanistic, integrative, or psychodynamic.

Socialization: The process by which individuals learn to differentiate between what the society regards as acceptable versus unacceptable behavior and act in a manner that is appropriate for the needs of the society.

Social Construct: Any phenomenon that is invented (i.e., constructed) by a culture or society. Social constructs exist because the members of a society behave as if it exists rather than because of the availability of criteria that are necessarily obvious to an objective outside observer. Race and ethnicity are both examples of social constructs. (Also referred to as a social construction.)

Society: A distinct group of people who live within the same territory, share a common culture and way of life, and are relatively independent from people outside the group. Society includes systems of social interactions that govern both culture and social organization.

Subject: A participant in a research study or experiment whose responses are observed, recorded, and analyzed.

Bibliography

Morrison, A. (2017). "Online therapy: friend or foe for social work?" *New Social Worker,* 24(2), 18-19.

Pier, C., Austin, D. W., Klein, B., Mitchell, J., Schattner, P., Chiechomski, L., et al. (2008). "A controlled trial of Internet-based cognitive-behavioral therapy for panic disorder with face-to-face support from a general practitioner or email support from a psychologist." *Mental Health* in family Medicine, 5, 29-39.

Skinner, A. E. G. & Latchford, G. (2006). "Attitudes to counseling via the Internet: A comparison between in-person counseling clients and Internet support group users." *Counseling and Psychotherapy Research,* 6, 92-97.

Wienclaw, R. A. (2007). "Internet-based therapy." In L. J. Fundukian & J. Wilson (Eds), The Gale *Encyclopedia of* Mental Health (2nd ed.). Detroit: Thomson/Gale.

Suggested Reading

Aneshensel, C. S. & Phelan, J. C. (1999). "The sociology of mental health: Surveying the field." In C. S. Aneshensel & J. C. Phelan (Eds). *Handbook of the Sociology of* Mental Health. New York: Kluwer Academic/Plenum Publishers, 3-17.

Bell, V. (2007). "Online information, extreme communities and Internet therapy: Is the Internet good for our mental health?" *Journal of* Mental Health, 16, 445-457.

Borcsa, M., & Pomini, V. (2017, December). "Virtual relationships and systemic practices in the digital era." *Contemporary Family* Therapy*: An International Journal.* pp. 239-248.

Brown, T. N., Sellers, S. L., Brown, K. T., & Jackson, J. S. (1999). "Race, ethnicity, and culture in the sociology of mental health." In C. S. Aneshensel & J. C. Phelan (Eds). *Handbook of the Sociology of* Mental Health. New York: Kluwer Academic/Plenum Publishers, 167-182.

Faja, S. & Likcani, A. (2006). "E-health: An exploratory study of trust building elements in behavioral health web sites." *Journal of Information Science and Technology,* 3, 9-21.

Horwitz, A. V. (1999). "The sociological study of mental illness: A critique and synthesis of four perspectives. The sociology of mental health: Surveying the field." In C. S. Aneshensel & J. C. Phelan (Eds). *Handbook of the Sociology of* MentalHealth. New York: Kluwer Academic/Plenum Publishers, 57-78.

Manhal-Baugus, M. (2001). "E-therapy: Practical, ethical, and legal issues." *Cyber Psychology and Behavior,* 4, 551-563.

Rogers, A., Lewis, L., & Woodward, L. (2007). "Relocating the sociology of mental health and illness." *Journal of* Mental Health, 16, 287-289.

Welfel, E. R. (2003). "E-therapy: A question of ethics." *Behavioral* Health *Management,* 23, 17-19.

Ruth A. Wienclaw, Ph.D.

Public Health Issues

OVERVIEW

The subject of public health conjures up myriad issues. In this paper, some of the most salient issues are addressed. First, there is a growing crisis in America over the issue of healthy weight. Americans are also increasingly concerned about the problem of environmental change–toxins in air, water, and foods; climate change affecting weather patterns; the threat of secondhand smoke; and buildings that are so toxic, they are called "sick buildings." In addition to these concerns, superbugs and pandemics that can potentially threaten the health of millions have begun to appear. These diseases can also be spread through another contemporary threat–bioterrorism. The concern is how much is known about this threat and what can be done about it. In the end, it may come down to effective health education–educating Americans about what's out there, how to keep healthy, and what to do in the case of health threats.

Public Health Issues

There are numerous issues that could be included in an overview of public health. This paper presents some of the most pressing issues facing the American public. The existence of so many health issues is due to the complexity of the lives we lead and the changes taking place in our environment. The interconnection between environmental changes and human health problems are making it difficult for governments and policy makers to come up with effective solutions. In order to address these issues, the environmental problems must be effectively dealt with, but at the same time, there must be practical and appropriate measures to protect the public's health.

In addition to environmental problems, Americans are facing an enormous problem with the growing threat of obesity. Not only adults but children are gaining weight in record numbers. The use of sugar and fats in a wide range of products means that people ingest far too much of this combination of ingredients.

The final part of the picture is health education and the ways the public can learn to adopt healthy behaviors and healthy lifestyles.

Obesity

There is a growing threat from obesity in America. A startling number of both adults and children are not just overweight but dangerously obese. The lifestyle we lead is increasingly sedentary. Fewer kids walk to school; they are driven by their parents, or they take the bus. At school, they sit all day and eat during lunchtime. When they return home, they sit in front of the television or a computer. For adults, it is very much the same. Many people spend an enormous amount of the day sitting at desks with little opportunity for exercise.

According to Oliver & Lee, health policy experts have recently sounded the warning about the severe health and economic consequences of America's growing rates of obesity. This concern appears to resonate with much of the American public. In 2006, the Pew Research Center found that 8 percent of surveyed American adults were dieting, 40 percent were exercising to lose weight, and 17 percent were attempting to do both. Of those who reported being overweight, 47 percent were then dieting and 53 percent were exercising. Despite this, respondents also indicated ongoing dissatisfaction with their weight and many reported needing to get more physical activity (Pew Research Center, 2006).

The problem, unfortunately, goes far deeper than overeating and too little exercise. It is also a result of the ways foods are manufactured, with far too much sugar and unhealthy fats, and data from a study by Gearhardt, Grilo, DiLeone, Brownell, and Potenza (2011) suggests that certain "hyperpalatable" foods may even have addictive qualities. Obesity is gaining recognition as a serious problem, although it has been building for a long time. Additional factors include lack of public education as to reading and understanding ingredients and labeling of foods and the fact that healthy foods tend to be more expensive and there are populations of people who do not have access to healthy foods (e.g., the urban poor, the homeless).

Perhaps even more disturbing is the growing trend in obesity in kids. With obesity comes a long list of health problems including heart disease, diabetes, musculoskeletal problems, cancer, and the possibility of a decreased life span. According to the US

Centers for Disease Control and Prevention (CDC), 36.5 percent of American adults and 17 percent of children and teens were obese in 2011-2014 (Ogden, Carroll, Fryar & Flegal, 2015). The CDC and state governments have implemented a variety of programs and initiatives to promote fruit and vegetable consumption, physical activity, and breastfeeding, and to discourage the consumption of sugary drinks and high-calorie foods, especially in schools and workplaces (National Center for Chronic Disease Prevention and Health Promotion, 2011). Such efforts may be having a positive impact, as the rate of obesity among low-income preschoolers declined in nineteen states of forty-three surveyed states between 2008 and 2011 (National Center for Chronic Disease Prevention and Health Promotion, 2013). However, much work still needs to be done.

Social Effects

Obesity costs the United States billions of dollars in health care costs. It is connected to myriad health problems, and these problems, in turn, must be dealt with. The question is: what do we do about the problem of obesity in America? The Pew Research Center for the People and the Press (2013) found that a slight majority (54 percent) of surveyed Americans disfavor government intervention in the fight against childhood obesity, although 69 percent agree that obesity is a major health concern and 61 percent believe that government policies can reduce obesity. Americans are supportive of some sanctions and unsupportive of others. The Pew findings show widespread support for requiring restaurant chains to list calorie counts on menus (67 percent) and banning commercials for unhealthy foods during children's television programming (55 percent), but trans fat prohibitions in restaurants met 52 percent opposition; taxing snacks and soft drinks, 64 percent; and limiting soft drink sizes in retail establishments, 31 percent. It is entirely possible that stringent measures and tougher policies are going to have to be instituted in order to help the country combat the epidemic of obesity that threatens its adults and children.

The Environment & Public Health

It might seem obvious that the environment could pose potential health problems to the public. After all, the subject of pollution and the decreasing ozone layer are nothing new. However, the growing specter of climate change must be added to the mix, as well as a relatively new phenomenon–sick building syndrome. Another concern is toxins in our drinking water. That water we take for granted that pours out of our kitchen faucet might be more dangerous to our health than we realize.

Poor Drinking Water

Research has begun to appear about the concern for pharmaceuticals, chemicals from personal care products, pesticides, and hormones, among other chemicals in our drinking water. While steps have been taken for some time to improve the quality of our drinking water, not all municipal water treatment facilities have the capability to removal these contaminants of emerging concern (CECs), as the Environmental Protection Agency (EPA) terms them. The EPA reports that "treated drinking water is disinfected to inactivate and/or remove pathogens. Like municipal wastewater treatment plants, although drinking water treatment plants are not designed to remove CECs; however, removals do occur. The extent of removal varies with the specific CEC and type of drinking water treatment" (2010, p. 2). Marhaba notes that "such compounds ... may accumulate in the environment. Although the concentrations of these compounds in drinking water are low today, their eventual impact on public health should not be ignored" (2008, p. 20).

Public concerns over the safety of drinking water has led to a boom in the business of bottled water. Yet some suggest that even bottled water is not necessarily safe; all bottled water is not equal. Marhaba (2008) warns that bottled water could be even less healthy than tap water: "Be very careful about drinking bottled water. First, purchase only bottled water from deep aquifers not impacted by pharmaceuticals. Not all bottled water comes from deep aquifers, so read the small print carefully" (p. 20).

Climate Changes

A host of environmental problems connected to climate change or global warming will not only affect water but many other aspects of our lives as well. There is generally a scientific consensus that the world's climates are changing. Of course, climate has affected human existence for millennia:

Weather and climate have been known to affect human health since the time of Hippocrates. Heat causes hyperthermia, cold causes hypothermia and droughts cause famine. Injuries, displacement, and death result from floods, hurricanes, tornadoes and forest fires. An entire category of diseases–the tropical diseases–is named for a particular climate; climate and weather affect the distribution and risk of many vector-borne diseases, such as malaria (Frumkin et al., 2008, p. 435).

The international media is reporting life-altering droughts in places such as Australia, where the weather has been predicted to steadily worsen. There have also been reports of the loss of ice in Antarctica, where the ecosystem is undergoing a radical change. As the earth's climate changes, we will have to respond, but in the meantime, there may be consequences to public health that could be next to impossible to cope with. There could be large-scale famines and loss of animal and plant life, not to mention the continued rising cost of food.

The effects of greenhouse gas emissions on the earth's climate have been debated for some time; more recently, the concern over what we can do has set in. As difficult as it is to accept, these climactic changes will spell long-term difficulties for the public's health. Frumkin et al. report that "changes in the patterns of pests, parasites, and pathogens affecting wildlife, livestock, agriculture, forests, and coastal marine organisms can alter ecosystem composition and functions, and changes in these life-support systems carry implications for human health" (Frumkin et al., 2008, p. 435).

These climactic changes create the necessity for public health preparedness. The federal and state governments must develop protocols in order to deal with the ramifications of these massive changes. For example, longer, hotter summers may sound nice to some who live in cold climates. But they can be difficult too. Many people do not cope well with heat, and it also changes the cycles of local flora and fauna. One of the strategies that Frumkin et al. (2008) suggest is a public impact assessment. Governments should study how these long-term weather changes will affect people and the environment. They point out that even one environmental change can have huge results for public health. For example, if we can reduce greenhouse gases, we can improve air quality, thus reducing respiratory disorders.

In 1994, the American Public Health Association developed the 10 Essential Services of Public Health in order to coordinate local, state, and federal responsibilities to cope with serious health care issues (Frumkin et al., 2008). However, one problem with climate change is that it will continue to take place over a long period of time. Even if we are able to respond effectively in the present, it may not be enough to stem all of the changes that may (or may not) take place.

Bioterrorism

While some would suggest that the events of September 11, 2001, aroused our fear and concern around possible acts of terrorism, the fact is the world's population has been living with terrorist acts for a very long time. The difference is in the weaponry available and the reasons for committing acts of terrorism. Historically, terrorism has been used to subdue cultures and enslave people. In the twentieth and twenty-first centuries, it seems to be almost exclusively to incite fear. Certainly, the specter of September 11 hangs over the heads of Americans every day. Yet, while the thought of such a large-scale attack is frightening, an even more damaging attack could take place using biological or chemical weapons. It is not only the weapons that are at issue here, but the seemingly increased preponderance for violence in our world. Some see it as a response to the rising tensions of a world with too many people and too few answers for how to address everyone's problems. In some cultures, a person is defined as a terrorist abroad, but at home he or she is hailed as a hero and a freedom fighter. It can be difficult to gain perspective on this highly complex issue. Nevertheless, the threat of bioterrorism is real, and it could truly be dangerous to public health.

The first issue that relates to public health is preparedness. How prepared are the cities in America for a bioterrorist attack? To be prepared means to have a solid plan in place that will mitigate the ramifications of such an attack. This means that first responders (professionals who work in emergency services) have to be thoroughly trained and have the necessary equipment. It also implies that vaccines and other treatments should be available, and there needs to be way to get them to the people who need them as quickly as possible.

Bioterrorism is still a relatively new concept and as such "our lack of experience with biological attacks leaves considerable room for controversy regarding the magnitude of their threat..." (Epstein, 2008, p. 357). Bioterrorism would not exist if it were not for the continued development of new and exciting technologies meant to benefit humankind. Unfortunately, like nuclear energy, which can also be used in a positive or negative way, such technology has devastating negative applications as well.

Hellmich and Redig (2007) believe that a bioterrorist attack may be inevitable. However, understanding the ways in which terrorist organizations work and the ideology behind their acts may help us to ward off these attacks and to be more prepared in case they do occur. From a public health perspective, bioterrorism is the kind of health threat that would have enormous ramifications. Therefore, we must develop a greater understanding of the ways in which various biological organisms function and how they can possibly be used in such a fashion. There must also be tight controls on the professionals who work with these substances in order to prevent people from selling the scientific data and components that can make such an attack possible.

VIEWPOINTS

Public Health & Education

One of the keys to coping with these critical issues is to provide ongoing, effective public health education. However, the ability to provide that education is an ongoing issue. First, there are financial considerations–updating websites, writing, printing, publishing, and disseminating literature, and providing ongoing education for health care professionals and community services costs a great deal of money. Second, there are continually new public health issues to deal with. Fee and Bu remind us,

Global public health in the beginning of the 21st century has been threatened by SARS, avian influenza, wars and bioterrorism, to name but a few dangers. To deal effectively with new as well as existing public health challenges would seem to require an international army of qualified public health workers, as well as an educated public mobilized to deal with health hazards (2007, p. 977).

Another issue in public health education is the socioeconomic gap between rich and poor. Not everyone is capable of accessing the same array of information on an equitable basis. Public health is not only about responding to crises, but also about promoting health and healthy practices such as proper hygiene, nutrition, and exercise. How prepared are we to provide the public health education necessary to address the complicated issues of contemporary society? "The challenge is to scale up the production of public health professionals with appropriate skills and competencies" (Petrakova & Sadana, 2007, p. 964).

In 1997, the Partners in Information Access for the Public Health Workforce was formed to aid in the training of workers and the necessary dissemination of health information. Some of the key issues they have worked on include responses to HIV/AIDS, children's environmental health, creating 'e-learning' solutions (wired communities), public health outreach projects, and the Healthy People 2010 Initiative (Cahn et al., 2007). As new health concerns arise, as well as to address some long-standing health concerns, there is always a need to update the public. Without this information, people can make incorrect assumptions about what to do with respect to a specific health concern. The public must always have access to credible, up-to-date information in a meaningful and user-friendly way (Cahn et al., 2007).

A key element to keeping the public informed is to continually update the training and skills of the nation's health care professionals. New training modules (and models) as well as publications must be continually developed and disseminated in order to provide them with the training they require. "A secondary goal is to build collaborative relationships among health librarians and health education specialists to improve planning, implementing, and evaluating disease prevention or health promotion programs in their regions" (Cahn et al., 2007, p. 305).

To promote healthy lifestyles, proper nutrition, maintaining a healthy weight, communicate how to deal with a health crisis, and address other key issues, there must be a considerable effort devoted to developing and maintaining the resources that can support people in these endeavors. One goal is to provide the critical information, but this must be balanced with the support services to help make these goals a reality. Public health education requires vision and balance. Both of these will be necessary to keep America healthy and informed through the twenty-first century.

CONCLUSION

There is probably no age in human history that has not witnessed its own worries over public health issues. In the Middle Ages, it was the bubonic plague. Later, diseases such as polio, cancer, multiple sclerosis, and many others have presented. While there is still no cure for many of these conditions, we manage them better and research is progressing. In many ways, humanity has become its own biggest health threat. We have overpopulated the planet, depleted resources, hunted animals to extinction, poisoned our waters with pharmaceuticals and other toxins, and, many believe, created almost irreversible damage through global warming and climate change.

Public health education is not as straightforward or simplistic as it used to be. It is no longer about simply washing one's hands, eating one's basic diet, and getting a good night's sleep. While these three concepts remain important, the complexity of our lives must be matched by public health education that can address these issues on a practical level that people can understand.

TERMS & CONCEPTS

Bioterrorism: The term for terrorism through the use of a biological agent such as bacteria or a virus.

Flora and Fauna: Flora are plants that are all of the same region or period considered part of a group. Fauna are animals of a region or period that are considered part of a group.

Global Climate Change: In its simplest definition, the changes in the earth's climate patterns generally considered to be a result of gradual increasing temperatures of the earth's air and water. The extent to which human activity contributes to global warming and climate change remains the subject of much debate.

Greenhouse Gases: Gases that are in the earth's atmosphere and that prevent the venting of heat into space. They affect global temperature in what is called the greenhouse effect.

Obesity: When a person accumulates excess fat to the point that his or her health may become negatively affected. This is a clinical condition and a public health issue.

Pathogens: An infectious agent; a biological agent that causes disease to its infected host.

Trans Fats: The common name for unsaturated trans fatty acids, which have a trans, or opposing, arrangement of functional groups. They may be monounsaturated or polyunsaturated and generally are created during hydrogenation or partial hydrogenation of vegetable oils. According to the American Heart Association, consumption of trans fats has been associated with higher levels of LDL cholesterol and increased risk of cardiovascular disease, stroke, and diabetes.

Bibliography

Almeida, C. (2011). "Health and foreign policy: The threat from health securitisation." *Australian & New Zealand Journal of Public Health,* 35, 312.

Cahn, M. A., et al. (2007). "The partners in information access for the public health workforce: A collaboration to improve and protect the public's health, 1995-2006." *Journal of the Medical Library Association,* 95, 301-309.

Chatwood, S., Bjerregaard, P., & Young, T. (2012). "Global health–A circumpolar perspective." *American Journal of Public Health,* 102, 1246-1249.

De Senarciens, P. (1984). "Population and security." *International Social Science Journal,* 46, 439.

Ellingson, K., McCormick, K., Sinkowitz-Cochran, R., Woodard, T., Jernigan, J., Srinivasan, A., & Rask, K. (2014). "Enhancement of health department capacity for health care-associated infection prevention through Recovery Act-funded programs." *American Journal of Public Health,* 104, e27-e33.

Environmental Protection Agency. (2010, August). "Treating contaminants of emerging concern: A literature review database." http://water.epa.gov/scitech/swguidance/ppcp/upload/cecliterature.pdf

Epstein, G. L. (2008). "Whither bioscience? Benevolence or bioviolence?" *Bioscience,* 58, 357-359.

Fee, E., & Bu, L. (2007). "Models of public health education: Choices for the future?" *Bulletin of the World Health Organization,* 85, 977-979.

Finkelstein, E. A., & Trogdon, J. E. (2008). "Health interventions for addressing childhood overweight: Analysis of the business case." *American Journal of Public Health,* 98, 411-415.

Frumkin, H., Hess, J., Luber, G., Malilay, J., & McGreehin, M. (2008). "Climate change: The public health response." *American Journal of Public Health,* 98, 435-445.

Gearhardt, A. N., Grilo, C. M., DiLeone, R. J., Brownell, K. D., & Potenza, M. N. (2011). "Can food be addictive? Public health and policy implications." *Addiction,* 106, 1208-1212.

Gerst-Emerson, K., & Jayawardhana, J. (2015). "Research and practice: Loneliness as a public health issue: The impact of loneliness on health care utilization among older adults." *American Journal of Public Health,* 105(5), 1013-1019.

Hellmich, C., & Redig, J. A. (2007). "The question is when: The ideology of Al Qaeda and the reality of bioterrorism." *Studies in Conflict & Terrorism,* 30, 396.

Hruby, A., Manson, J. E., Lu, Q., Malik, V. S., Rimm, E. B., Qi, S., & ... Hu, F. B. (2016). "Determinants and consequences of obesity." *American Journal of Public Health,* 106(9), 1656-1662.

Leider, J. P., Resnick, B., Kass, N., Sellers, K., Young, J., Bernet, P., & Jarris, P. (2014). "Budget- and priority-setting criteria at state health agencies in times of austerity: A mixed-methods study." *American Journal of Public Health,* 104, 1092-1099.

Marhaba, T. H. (2008). "Dangerous pharmaceutical compounds in water cannot be ignored any longer." *NJBIZ,* 21, 20.

National Center for Chronic Disease Prevention and Health Promotion. (2011). "Obesity: Halting the epidemic by making health easier–At a glance 2011." Atlanta, GA: Centers for Disease Control and Prevention. http://www.cdc.gov/

National Center for Chronic Disease Prevention and Health Promotion. (2013, August 6). "Progress on childhood obesity." Centers for Disease Control and Prevention website: http://www.cdc.gov/VitalSigns/ChildhoodObesity

Ogden, C. L., Carroll, M. D., Fryar, C. D., Flegal, K. M. (2015, November). "Prevalence of obesity in the United States, 2011-2014 (NCHS Data Brief no. 219)." https://www.cdc.gov/nchs/data/databriefs/db219.pdf

Oliver, J. E., & Taeku, L. (2005). "Public opinion and the politics of obesity in America." *Journal of Health Politics, Policy & Law,* 30, 923-954.

Petrakova, A., & Sadana, R. (2007). "Problems and progress in public health education." *Bulletin of the World Health Organization,* 85, 963-970.

Pew Research Center. (2006, April 25). "In the battle of the bulge, more soldiers than success." Washington, DC: Author. http://www.pewsocialtrends.org/files/2010/11/Exercise.pdf

Pew Research Center. (2013, November 12). "Public agrees on obesity's impact, not government's role." Washington, DC: Author. http://www.people-press.org/

VanDerslice, J. (2011). "Drinking water infrastructure and environmental disparities: Evidence and methodological considerations." *American Journal of Public Health,* 101(S1), S109-S114.

Suggested Reading

Batra, R., Strecher, V. J., & Keller, P. (2011). *Leveraging consumer psychology for effective health communications: The obesity challenge.* Armonk, NY: M.E. Sharpe.

Camargo, K., Jr., & Grant, R. (2015). "Public health, science, and policy debate: Being right is not enough." *American Journal of Public Health,* 105(2), 232-235.

Figert, A. (2014). "Governing how we care: Contesting community and defining difference in US public health programs." *American Journal of Sociology,* 119, 1780-1781.

Henderson, D. A., O'Toole, T., & Inglesby, T. V. (2002). *Bioterrorism: Guidelines for medical and public health management.* Chicago, IL: American Medical Association.

Kessel, A. (2006). *Air the environment and public health.* New York, NY: Oxford University Press.

Laverack, G. (2015). *A-Z of public health.* New York, NY: Palgrave.

McKee, M., & Sim, F. (2011). *Issues in public health* (2nd ed.). Maidenhead, England: McGraw-Hill/Open University Press.

Oliver, J. E. (2006). *Fat politics: The real story behind America's fat epidemic.* New York, NY: Oxford University Press.

Smith, J. (2005). *Integration of public health with adaptation to climate change: Lessons learned and new directions.* Leiden, Netherlands: Aa Balkema.

Turnock, B.J. (2007). *Public health: What it is and how it works.* Sudbury, MA: Jones and Bartlett Publishers.

Ilanna Mandel, M.A.

RELIGION & HEALTH

ABSTRACT

Although religion and health are historically intertwined, secular society has involved a decrease in the formal influence of religion over everyday lives. At least two of sociology's founding fathers studied the role of religion in social life and predicted that its significance would decline. However, sociological and public interest in the link between religion and health has grown since the 1990s, and research has found that in matters of health, religion largely exerts a positive influence. In general, people who participate in religious activities and events live longer, experience less poor health, and are found to cope better with stress. Although the mechanisms associated with this relationship are unclear, researchers argue that religious beliefs and practices likely protect people from disease and ill health. For instance, membership in certain religious groups encourages moderation in diet and exercise and actively discourages behaviors that are known to be potentially harmful to health, such as excessive alcohol consumption, drug and tobacco use, and premarital sex.

OVERVIEW

Although religion and health are historically intertwined, secular society has involved a decrease in the formal influence of religion over everyday lives. At least two of sociology's founding fathers studied the role of religion in social life and predicted that its significance would decline. However, sociological and public interest in the link between religion and health has grown since the 1990s, and research has found that in matters of health, religion largely exerts a positive influence. In general, people who participate in religious activities and events live longer, experience less poor health and are found to cope better with stress. Although the mechanisms associated with this relationship are unclear, researchers argue that religious beliefs and practices likely protect people from disease and ill health. For instance, membership of certain religious groups encourages moderation in diet and exercise and actively discourages behaviors that are known to be potentially harmful to health, such as excessive alcohol consumption, drug and tobacco use, and premarital sex (e.g., see Musick, Traphagan, Koenig & Larson, 2000). Before exploring this link, however, it is necessary to identify what researchers are referring to when they discuss "religion."

Historical Perspectives on Religion & Health

Historically, religion and health have been closely intertwined, and as the historian Andrew Wear has noted, the words "salvation" and "health" were interchangeable (1985, p. 67). On the one hand, drawing on biblical perspectives, seventeenth-century English writers and artists depicted the human body as a temple to be glorified and cared for through appropriate and careful dietary and physical practices. On the other, medical metaphors were used to describe the sinner as a sick man (Lupton, 1994, p. 57). In the Middle Ages, people with chronic ailments and illness often turned to religious healing systems via pilgrimages and direct contact with the relics of saints (Lupton, 1994). Religion played a crucial role in offering reasons for illness and disease, with explanations ranging from poor health and disease as the result of demonic possession to disease as punishment from God. Indeed, like the Puritans, who saw illness or disease as correctives or punishments from God, many twentieth-century conservative politicians in the USA and the UK viewed the emergence of HIV as evidence of God's wrath on a wicked and sinful world. In 1986, John McKay, at that time Secretary of State for Health in the UK, asserted that AIDS was a "punishment from God" (Howson, 2004, p. 83).

Despite increasing secularization, religion continues to provide a framework for understanding health and disease. Since the 1990s, researchers have become increasingly interested in how adherence to religious beliefs and practices are linked to the experience of health and to health outcomes. This emerging interest in the relationship between religion and health explores both physical and mental health. At least two of sociology's founding fathers, Emile Durkheim and Max Weber, identified religion as a factor contributing to general health and well-being because of its overarching role in influencing how members of a particular society think and act. They viewed religion as a human endeavor that helped people make sense of their lives, by giving them explanations for social life that help them cope or by providing ways of behaving that enable people to express the desire for meaning in everyday life (Bilton et al., 1996). However, their approaches to the significance of religion differ.

Durkheim's Functionalist View of Religion

In the functionalist view, religion is an institutionalized form of thinking and acting that functions to regulate and integrate members of society for the purpose of securing social solidarity and order. Durkheim argued that, first, religion has a *regulative* function that helps to create and sustain social order through rules and regulations that prohibit (proscribe) or permit (prescribe) certain behaviors and practices. These rules typically govern practices and behaviors around sexual intimacy, eating, and drinking. They help integrate people by providing meaningful and tangible connections to others. Moreover, as Ellison and Levin (1998) point out, by internalizing religio-ethical norms, people are likely motivated to conform to rules and regulations and avoid breaking them through fear of embarrassment and social sanctions (such as formal rebukes from their church or informal sanctions such as gossip or ostracism by others in their religious network).

Second, religion has an *integrative* function that binds people to the societies of which they are members. By publicly attending and participating in religious ceremonies, people affirm the beliefs they hold in common with others. This shared value and belief framework may, in turn, create the potential for sharing tangible and intangible resources (housing, food, transport, and clothing on the one hand, and intangibles like intimacy, affection, and touch on the other). Some researchers argue that these regulative and integrative functions may have a direct bearing on people's health and well-being.

Phenomenology

Drawing on the tradition of phenomenology, some sociologists in the 1960s (e.g., Berger, 1967) argued that humanity is characterized by an inherent religiosity that drives people to interpret the world by allocating meaning to events and experiences through symbolic means, such as language and rituals. Religiosity involves the creation of a symbolic world, or a "sacred canopy" under which people live their lives. In the modern, secularized world, people continue to search for meaning, whether through collective membership of formal religious organizations or through looser, more informal practices (e.g., meditation). Within the phenomenological view, religion provides a means of creating individual meaning in a world where people feel dislocated from others; it helps to bring coherence to an otherwise chaotic world, especially in times of stress or sickness; and relieves emotional suffering by providing a worldview (Marsh et al., 1996).

Religion, Religiosity & Spirituality

In modern research on religion and health, the concept of religion (from the Latin root *religi*) can mean different things. Religion is generally considered to include both individual and institutional aspects of the search for the sacred and refers to beliefs, attitudes, and practices that are a part of or constitute membership in an organization or religious institution (Ziegler, 1998).

The concept of religiosity is important in exploring the relationship between religion and health, since researchers use it to capture both attendance at and participation in public ceremonies (such as going to church) and the holding of religious beliefs and values. As Hardy and Carlo (2005) note, there are three types of religiosity:

- Intrinsic;
- Extrinsic; and
- Quest religiosity.

Intrinsic religiosity refers to people who see religion as the answer to life's questions. Extrinsic religiosity refers to people who use religion as a means to an end (e.g., to develop social contacts). Quest religiosity refers to the religious seeker who constantly asks questions and may not believe there are any clear answers. Broadly, the dimensions of religiosity used by researchers include:

- Belief,
- Practice (acts of worship conducted publicly, such as communion, or privately, such as meditation or prayer),
- Experience (a personal of connection and communication with a transcendent or divine being),

- Knowledge (understanding basic teachings of the religion of which one is a member), and
- Consequences (visible indicators of religious membership, such as a particular way of dressing or diet) (Marsh, et al., 1996).

Typically, researchers use the frequency of religious attendance as the main measure of religiosity or religiousness.

Finally, spirituality refers to the individual search for the sacred (Emmons & Paloutzian, 2003) and denotes views and behaviors that express relatedness to something greater than the self (Ziegler, 1998). Therefore, a person can be described as spiritual without participating in formal religious membership. Nonetheless, much of the research that explores the relation between religion and health tends to use the term "religion" or "religiousness" to refer to practices and beliefs associated with formal religious organizations. For instance, researchers view attendance at religious services (and the frequency of attendance) as an indicator of a person's religiousness—that is, the sum of beliefs, practices and attitudes that might be described as religious.

FURTHER INSIGHTS

Mortality

The empirical evidence for the positive impact of religion on physical health is strong, and there are hundreds of studies that show how high levels of religious involvement are associated with better health status across gender, age, ethnicity, and religious affiliation. First, participating in religious activities and holding religious beliefs reduce the likelihood of an early death and reduce mortality rates from hypertension circulatory, digestive and respiratory diseases (Oman, Kurata, Strawbridge & Cohen, 2002), and other various chronic diseases. In addition, researchers have shown that members of specific religious groups (e.g., Zen Buddhist priests, Catholic monks and nuns, and Orthodox Jews) have lower mortality rates than the general population (Fraser & Shavlik, 2001). One key study followed 5,000 respondents over 28 years and examined the association between frequent attendance and mortality (Strawbridge, Cohen, Shema & Kaplan, 1997); frequent attendees had lower mortality rates than did nonattendees. Similarly, a 2008 study using data from the Women's Health Initiative (Schnall et al., 2008) found that women aged 50 and older were 20% less likely to die in any given year if they attended religious services weekly, compared to those that never attend religious services. Infrequent attendees of religious services also appear to have mortality rates similar to infrequent attendees of nonreligious groups (Shor & Roelfs, 2013), suggesting that mortality is more strongly linked to frequent social interaction rather than religiosity.

Such studies raise the question of whether healthier people are more likely to participate in religious activities. In addition, researchers have wrestled with the question of what it is about religion that appears to have this positive impact. For instance, in the Women's Health Initiative study, the lower mortality rates observed among those who participated in religious activities more frequently were explained by differences in personal and social behaviors—those with lower mortality rates and high religious participation rates were also among those more likely to cease smoking, increase exercise, increase social contacts, and remain married. The range of social and personal behaviors associated with religious participation is more evident in research on morbidity.

Morbidity

Religiosity, or religiousness, has also been found to protect people against diseases such as heart disease, hypertension, diabetes, and stroke (Hummer, 1999). Generally, people who hold religious views and practice religion tend to report greater subjective well-being, life satisfaction, and ability to cope with stress, and fewer symptoms of depression (Koenig et al., 2001). Moreover, the more frequent attendance and the greater the level of religiousness, the stronger the benefits appear to be for health. For instance, studies have found that there is a relationship between the frequency of attendance and blood pressure: higher attendance is associated with lower blood pressure (Gillum & Ingram, 2006). For adherents of religions with firm and specific behavior guidelines, such as Seventh-Day Adventists and Mormons, the risk of chronic diseases such as hypertension (Brathwaite, Fraser, Modeste, Broome, & King, 2003) and stroke is lower still.

While many studies on the association between religion and health have focused on elderly or seriously ill patients, more recent research is suggesting that these patterns of association hold for younger people as well, although it is spirituality that is important. For instance, one study published in 2005 examined the roles of spirituality and religiosity on cardiovascular responses during stress and self-reported illness and health in a sample of young women. The study found that while spirituality had a health protective effect for this population, religiosity did not. These findings suggest that spirituality may be more important to younger groups than membership of and participation in formal religious organizations (Edmondson et al., 2005).

Depression

Since the nineteenth century, researchers have also found a positive association between religion and improved mental health regardless of age, gender, ethnicity, class, and geography. In particular, religiousness appears to have a protective effect against depression, and studies report fewer depressive symptoms among the religiously active, especially among the elderly (Koenig et al., 2001).

VIEWPOINTS

Explaining the Impact of Religion on Health

Broadly, there are three mechanisms through which religion appears to affect health:

- The promotion of health behaviors;
- The provision of social support; and
- The provision of coherence (George, Larson, Koenig, & McCullough, 2000).

Research suggests that people who participate in religious activities and practices are also more likely to participate in positive health practices and avoid harmful practices (McCullough & Smith, 2003). Certain religious groups (e.g., Mormons) actively encourage moderation in eating and exercise and discourage potentially harmful behaviors, such as smoking, drug use, excessive alcohol consumption, and premarital sex (Musick, Traphagan, Koenig, & Larson, 2000). Some groups avoid diets that are known to be harmful to health (e.g., Seventh-Day Adventists consume low amounts of red meat). In addition, "simply believing or expecting religious practice to benefit health, or by expecting God to reward expressions of devotion" or obedience with health and well-being—"learned optimism"—"may be enough to account for positive health outcomes among more religiously committed populations" (Ellison & Levin, 1998, p. 708). Therefore, researchers argue that the doctrine and teaching of certain religious groups may regulate lifestyles in ways that have the effect of promoting health.

Several studies have documented the relationship between social support, coping, and religion (McCullough & Smith, 2003). Social support is typically measured objectively (e.g., the size of one's social network, the frequency of interaction with one's network) and subjectively (e.g., satisfaction). People who are frequent attendees of and participants in religious activities are also more likely to be part of larger and denser social networks, which offer the potential for more support through exchanges of goods, services (e.g., transport, meals), and information. Religious groups also provide a source of friendship and kindness through both formal programs and intangible mechanisms such as touch and prayer. Therefore, both objective measures of support and subjective measures, such as how people feel about this support and whether they feel loved, accepted, and cared for, may be important predictors of mental and physical well-being and help explain why religiousness has a positive effect on health. Religious beliefs provide a buffer against distress, especially among those who experience multiple life stressors (such as divorce, death, etc.), symptoms of depression, and also against the sense of hopelessness that accompanies depression (McCullough & Smith, 2003). "Piety indicators" such as frequency of prayer, feelings of closeness to God, and subjective religious identity create a sense of meaning and purpose and provide a source of coping with everyday life, which is linked to well-being (McCullough & Smith, 2003).

Religion may provide "a sense of coherence and meaning so that people understand their role in the universe, the purpose of life, and develop the courage to endure suffering" (George et al., 2000, p. 108). In Durkheim's terms, the shared values and practices that emerge through religious participation contribute to group solidarity by affirming common values and beliefs on a regular basis (e.g., weekly church attendance). They provide a framework that helps people manage and respond to stressful events and conditions. In particular, devotional practices (such as prayer or meditation) may protect against disease and speed illness recovery because they help people establish a sense of control or "reassess the meaning of potentially problematic conditions as opportunities for spiritual growth or learning, or as part of a broader divine plan, rather than as challenges to fundamental aspects of personal identity" (Ellison & Levin, 1998, p. 708). In addition, McCullough and Smith (2003) note that studies have suggested certain religious practices, such as prayer and worship, may induce the experience or expression of certain emotions such as forgiveness, contentment, and love, as well as to release negative emotions such as guilt and fear. There is some evidence that religion, through complex sequences of events, may give rise to positive emotions and release negative emotions.

CONCLUSION

Although the relationship between religion and health is strong, and that relationship appears to mainly have a positive impact on health, it is difficult to isolate specifically what it is about religious participation that affects physical and mental health. The main pathway through which religion appears to affect health is through observable, behavioral aspects of religious involvement, such as frequency of religious attendance. That is, religion affects health largely through the choices that participants make, the social support they receive through religious membership, and the emotional support they receive from people who share a similar worldview. A second pathway suggests that religious participation, especially through devotional practices such as prayer and meditation, may affect biological and physiological mechanisms (e.g., hormone release and stress responses) in ways that are beneficial to health. A third emerging pathway involves examining how religious interventions, such as intercessory prayer—which 89% of praying adults in the United States practice (Schafer, 2013)—affect health outcomes. As one leading researcher in this field has commented, the study of religion and its impact on health is just beginning, since critical questions remain about how and why it works (Aten & Schenk, 2007).

TERMS & CONCEPTS

Integrative Function: Social practices that bind people to the societies of which they are members (e.g., through participating in ceremonies and sharing values and belief systems).

Phenomenology: An approach in sociology that focuses on consciousness and experience from the first-person perspective.

Religion: An institutionalized form of thinking and acting that functions to regulate and integrate members of society for the purpose of securing social solidarity and order.

Religiosity: Involves the creation of a symbolic world that provides people with meaning in the modern world, whether through collective membership of formal religious organizations or through looser, more informal practices (e.g., meditation).

Sacred Canopy: A symbolic world that provides meaning in a context of secularization.

Social Solidarity: The extent to which a society is integrated.

Spirituality: The individual search for the sacred (Emmons & Paloutzian, 2003) and denotes views and behaviors that express relatedness to something greater than the self (Ziegler, 1998).

Bibliography

Aten, J. D., & Schenk, J. E. (2007). "Reflections on religion and health research: An interview with Dr. Harold G. Koenig." *Journal of Religion and Health, 46*(2):183–190.

Bell, R. A., Suerken, C., Quandt, S.A., Grzywacz, J. G., Lang, W., & Arcury, T. A. (2005). "Prayer for health among U.S. adults: The 2002 National Health Interview Survey." *Complementary Health Practice Review, 10*(3):175–188. Sage Journals http://chp.sagepub.com/cgi/reprint/10/3/175

Berger, P. (1967). *The Sociology of Religion.* Harmondsworth: Penguin.

Bilton, T., Bonnett, K., Jones, P., Skinner, D., Stanworth, M., & Webster, A. (1996). *Introductory Sociology.* London: Macmillan.

Brathwaite, N., Fraser, H. S., Modeste ,N., Broome, H., & King, R. (2003). "Obesity, diabetes, hypertension, and vegetarian status among Seventh-Day Adventists in Barbados: Preliminary results." *Ethnicity and Disease, 13*(1), 34–39.

Edmondson, K. A., Lawler, K. A., Jobe, R. L., Younger, J. W., Piferi, R. L., & Jones, W. H. (2005). "Spirituality predicts health and cardiovascular responses to stress in young adult women." *Journal of Religion & Health, 44* (2):161–171.

Ellison, C. G., & Levin, J. S. (1998). "The religion-health connection: Evidence, theory and future directions." *Health, Education and Behavior, 25*(6):700–720. http://www.religionomics.com/

Emmons, R. A., & Paloutzian, R. F. (2003). "The psychology of religion." *Annual Review of Psychology, 54* (1), 377–402.

Fraser, G. E., & Shavlik, D. J. (2001). "Ten years of life: Is it a matter of choice?" *Archives of Internal Medicine 161*(13), 1645–1652. website http://archinte.ama-assn.org/cgi/content/full/161/13/1645

Ganga, N. S., & Kutty, V. (2013). "Influence of religion, religiosity and spirituality on positive mental health of young people." *Mental Health, Religion & Culture, 16*(4), 435–443.

George, L. K., Larson, D. B., Koenig, H. G., & McCullough, M. E. (2000). "Spirituality and health: What we know, what we need to know." *Journal of Social and Clinical Psychology, 19*(1), 102–116.

Gillum, R. F., & Ingram, D. D. (2006). "Frequency of attendance at religious services, hypertension, and blood pressure: The third National Health and Nutrition Examination Survey." *Psychosomatic Medicine. 68,* 382–385. http://www.psychosomaticmedicine.org/

Hardy, S. A., & Carlo, G. (2005). "Religiosity and pro-social behaviors in adolescence: The medicating role of prosocial values." *Journal of Moral Education, 34*(2): 231–249.

Howson, A. (2004). *The Body in Society.* Cambridge: Polity Press.

Hummer, R. A., Ellison, C. G., Rogers, R. G., Moulton, B. E., & Romero, R. R. (2004). "Religious involvement and adult mortality in the United States: Review and perspective." *Southern Medical Journal 97*(12), 1223–1230.

Koenig, H. G., McCullough, M. E., & Larson, D. B. (2001). *Handbook of religion and health.* Oxford: Oxford University Press.

Lupton, D. (1994). *Medicine as Culture: Illness, disease and the body in Western cultures.* London: Sage.

Marsh, I., Keating, M., Eyre, A., Campbell, R., & McKenzie, J. (1996). *Making sense of society: An introduction to sociology.* London: Longman.

McCullough, M. E., & Smith, T. B. (2003). "Depressive symptoms and mortality as case studies." In Dillon, M. (Ed). *Handbook of the sociology of religion.* Cambridge: Cambridge University Press.

Merrill, R. M., & Lyon, J. L. (2005). "Cancer incidence among Mormons and non-Mormons in Utah (United States) 1995–1999." *Preventative Medicine, 40*(5):535–541.

Musick, M. A., Traphagan, J. W., Koenig, H. G., & Larson, D. B. (2000). "Spirituality in physical health and aging." *Journal of Adult Development, 7,* 73–86.

Oman, D., Kurata, J. H., Strawbridge, W. J., & Cohen, R. D. (2002). "Religious attendance and cause of death over 31 years." *International Journal of Psychiatry in Medicine, 32*(1), 69–89.

Schafer, M. H. (2013). "Close ties, intercessory prayer, and optimism among American adults: Locating God in the social support network." *Journal for the Scientific Study of Religion, 52*(1), 35–56.

Schnall, E., Wassertheil-Smoller, S., Swencionis, C., Zemon, V., Tinker, L., . . . & Goodwin, M. (2008). "The relationship between religion and cardiovascular outcomes and all-cause mortality in the women's health initiative observational study." *Psychology and Health, 23* (8), 1001–1006.

Shor, E., & Roelfs, D. J. (2013). "The longevity effects of religious and nonreligious participation: A meta-analysis and meta-regression." *Journal for the Scientific Study of Religion, 52*(1), 120–145.

Strawbridge, W. J., Cohen, R. D., & Kaplan, G. A. (2001). "Religious attendance increases survival by improving and maintaining good health behaviors, mental health, and social relationships." *Annals of Behavior in Medicine, 23*(1):68–74.

Wear, A. (1985). "Puritan perceptions of illness in seventennth century England." In R. Porter (ed). *Patients and Practitioners: Lay perceptions of medicine in pre-industrial society.* (pp. 55–99). Cambridge: Cambridge University Press.

Ziegler, J. (1998). "Spirituality returns to the fold in medical practice." *Journal of the National Cancer Institute.* 90:1255–1257.

Suggested Reading

Blasi, A. (Ed.). (2011). "Toward a sociological theory of religion and health." Leiden, Netherlands: Brill.

Dillon, M., & Wink, P. (2007). *In the course of a lifetime: Tracing religious belief, practice, and change.* Berkeley, CA: University of California Press.

Koenig, H., King, D., & Carson, V. B. (2012). *Handbook of religion and health* (2nd ed.). New York, NY: Oxford University Press.

Krause, N. (2004). "Religious doubt and health: Exploring the potential dark side of religion." *Sociology of Religion, 65* (4), 35–56.

McFarland, M. J. (2009). "Religion and mental health among older adults: do the effects of religious involvement vary by gender?" *The Journals of Gerontology, Series B.* 10:1093.

Schnittiker, J. (2001). "When is faith enough? The effects of religious involvement on depression." *Journal for the Scientific Study of Religion* 40, 393–411.

Wuthnow, R. (1994). *Sharing the journey: Support groups and America's new quest for community.* New York: Free Press.

Yeary, K., Ounpraseuth, S., Moore, P., Bursac, Z., & Greene, P. (2012). "Religion, social capital, and health." *Review of Religious Research, 54*(3), 331–347.

Alexandra Howson

Substance Abuse Prevention & Education

ABSTRACT

In the U.S., substance abuse permeates society with tremendous intensity. This article introduces alcohol as a phenomenon that seeps into common, everyday functions (such as the U.S. workforce) with remarkable acceptance. However, once the invisible line into dependency is crossed and alcohol usage becomes an addiction, insobriety is no longer condoned. Drug use is more concretely refuted due to its illegal status, although there is heated disagreement on whether or not marijuana should be legalized. Drug and alcohol abuse patterns in the U.S. and the U.K. are presented, followed by social implications, such as violence, criminal activity, and incarceration. Based on "risky" behavior that accompanies substance abuse, preventative strategies are discussed, which include intervention through "Boys & Girls Club" involvement, Fetal Alcohol Syndrome prevention, and school-based initiatives that target children of alcoholics. In conclusion, "Amethyst Initiative" is highlighted, a controversial proposal set forth by several university presidents who would like the drinking age to be lowered in order curb binge drinking among college students.

The Nature of Substance Abuse

In the United States, society transmits mixed messages about alcohol that simultaneously reward and admonish alcohol use. Alcohol is a legally sanctioned substance that commonly serves as a social lubricant to ease personal anxieties, promote uninhibited expressions of lighthearted conviviality, or temporarily reduce the edginess of life's painfully harsh realities. Alcohol is a binding force that can unite people in communal celebration. For example, it is not uncommon for many corporate organizations to host regular happy-hour functions, during which employees intermingle with each other in order to instill a relational alliance that might not organically flow within the confines of their departmental workspaces. In the absence of such pre-planned gatherings, staff members might initiate casual outings with their colleagues in order to unwind after a long and stressful day over cocktails and office talk, by rehashing the frustrations and scandals of their work lives. Additionally, annual holiday parties are frequently sponsored by company headquarters, in which good cheer and spirit are channeled through gala events that are elaborately furnished and sufficiently stocked with a variety of intoxicating refreshments.

Despite all of the reinforcing alcohol-related references that correspond with corporate America, an implicit expectation mandates that employees refrain from crossing the obscured line into the realm of dependency. Workers who are deemed "heavy drinkers," or those who drink alcohol with frequent and overzealous fervor, constitute 7.6 percent of the fulltime workforce (Roman & Blum, 2002). When their levels of productivity quantitatively or qualitatively decline, communication with coworkers and clientele becomes strained, or when they are habitually late or absent from work, they might find themselves subjected to onsite alcohol testing or referred to peer and/or employee assistance programs (EAPs) in order to mend faulty drinking patterns (Elliott & Shelley, 2005; Greenwood, DeWeese, & Inscoe, 2005). Likewise, employers might commission punitive consequences such as withholding pay and other job-related privileges, or termination.

On an additional work-related note, there may be some connection between alcoholism and certain occupations, and Smith (2003) suggests that lawyers are more prone to falling in to alcohol's titillating grip. Whereas 10 percent of the general population suffers from alcohol dependency, this rate skyrockets to 15 to 18 percent among attorneys, even up to 26 percent in select regions (e.g., Florida). This is perhaps due to the demanding pressures that correspond with an attorney's characteristics, lifestyle, and work demands, in that the traits that make them successful in their field such as an argumentative deportment, workaholic tendencies, and a heightened ego, simultaneously prevent them from pursuing rehabilitative measures once their drinking patterns escalate to an unmanageable extent.

The ramifications of drug abuse are just as daunting, although the illegal status of narcotics automatically thrusts illicit chemical dependency into a definitively unacceptable standing. Society demonstrates its defamation of drug usage by the harsh penalties that are placed upon offenders (Stephen, 2004), as well as political movements that indicate its reckless and unscrupulous eminence—such as Nancy Reagan's "Just Say No" campaign that saturated the 1980s ("Reagan, GOP," 1995). A possible exception to this statute surrounds marijuana usage, which some people consider benign ("Legalizing Marijuana," 2002) and have initiated campaigns to decriminalize its standing. According to Kirk Muse (2005),

> If marijuana were sold in licensed business establishments where it could be regulated, controlled, and taxed, the bootleg 'grow operations' would disappear in a heartbeat—just as our bathtub gin operations disappeared in a heartbeat when alcohol was re-legalized (p. 8).

The Case of Marijuana

Advocates of this process feel as though court cases targeting marijuana offenders congest the legal system and assert that marijuana usage achieves certain medicinal purposes (McKinley, 2007). Since contingent usage is supported by politicians such as former Washington DC mayor Marion Barry ("Barry endorses," 1997), and US Representatives Barney Frank ("Medical-Marijuana," 2005) and Dennis Kucinich (Hardison, 2004), some feel that our society is one step away from aggregated legalization ("Medical Marijuana," 1994). Critics of marijuana legalization point to health risks that accompany its use, including stressful emotional withdrawal and cognitive impairment such as short-term memory loss and marred physical coordination that may interfere with driving (Joffe & Yancy, 2004). Furthermore, smoking marijuana imparts lung damage akin to long-term tobacco usage. In endorsing the legitimization of marijuana, many people point to the fact that marijuana has less perilous societal consequences than alcohol and is not as physically harmful or addictive as either alcohol or tobacco, rendering its slanderous reputation undeserved. However, Alain Joffe and W. Samuel Yancy point out that legal recognition of marijuana would not eradicate the ill effects of alcohol and tobacco; quite the contrary, it would cause more collective health-related damage. One might examine weaponry as an analogy to illustrate this point: during the course of a physical altercation, guns are more powerful and efficient in imparting damage, therefore rendering them more lethal than an average fistfight. However, the rationale that a weaponless physical assault should be legally sanctioned is dangerous and unconvincing.

In a nationwide poll examining substance abuse patterns among thirty-five-year old Americans, a significant gender configuration emerged, in that men outnumbered women on heavy alcohol consumption (32 percent for men, 13 percent for women) and illicit drug use, including marijuana (13 percent to 7 percent) and cocaine (6 percent to 3 percent). However, women reported a slightly higher dependency (8 percent) toward prescription drugs compared to their male counterparts whose reliance rate was 7 percent (Prevalence of Alcohol, 2004). Substance abuse patterns among adolescents in the

United States have slightly dropped since the 1990s, although a considerable amount of youth are still using drugs and alcohol. According to the 2011 Youth Risk Behavior Survey, 39 percent of high school students reported drinking within the past thirty days, and 40 percent have smoked marijuana at least on one occasion during their lives.

In a study conducted by Alastair Roy, Chris Wibberley, and Jon Lamb (2005) that took place over five years (1997-2001), students between the ages of fifteen and sixteen years old and enrolled in several Manchester schools were examined on both the prevalence of their current substance use, as well as their views surrounding such matters. During this five-year time-frame, there were several notable pattern shifts, particularly regarding an increase in cannabis usage, while alcohol consumption remained consistently high throughout the course of the study. For example, in 1997 the student body was polled and 45.8 percent indicated that they had, at some point in their lives, experimented with cannabis, a figure that rose to 53.5 percent in 2001. During this same span of time almost all students had consumed alcohol at least once, including 97.4 percent in 1997 and 96.5 percent in 2001. Furthermore, there was an increase in ecstasy experimentation (3.2 to 8.3 percent), and a decline in amphetamine usage (23.1 to 8.3 percent). When asked if they agreed with the following statements about a hypothetical friend dabbling with cannabis, results changed significantly throughout the study's five-year duration. Statements included: "It wouldn't bother me, because I don't see anything wrong with it"—with which student agreement increased from 47.7 to 58 percent over the five-year period, and "It wouldn't bother me, it's their choice, nothing to do with me"—which also grew substantially (60.6 to 76.7 percent). At the same time, results to the following statements decreased: "I would be worried and I'd talk to them, to try to stop them using it," (46 to 32.1 percent) and "I would be worried if they brought it into school" (67.6 to 54.8 percent) (Roy, Wibberley & Lamb, 2005, p. 310, Table III).

FURTHER INSIGHTS

Social Implications

Substance abuse and acts of violence correlate together considerably, and in one study researchers examined the relationship between these two phenomena ("Substance Abuse a Significant," 1997). Specifically, in Memphis, Tennessee, investigators examined a variety of demographics surrounding domestic abuse allegations. Upon reporting abuse to officials, both the perpetrators and victims were surveyed on significant information to elucidate the nature of their claims, including the types of substances in their blood systems at the time of the offense. The majority of these cases included a man attacking a woman with whom he was romantically/sexually involved. Two-thirds of the perpetrators had weapons, and 92 percent were under the influence of a mind-altering substance (i.e., alcohol and cocaine), or some combination thereof; 14 percent had used cocaine that day, while 86 percent had consumed alcohol. Conversely, the victims reported alcohol consumption at a 42 percent rate, and cocaine use at a 15 percent rate. Indeed, the Center for Substance Abuse Treatment (CSAT) corroborated the merge between domestic violence and substance abuse (Rose, 1998), indicating that anywhere between 25 to 50 percent of men charged with domestic violence also have a chemical dependency. As such, Rose recommends that mental health professionals should merge the two realms together in terms of prevention and treatment, as opposed to approaching the two domains as though they were distinct entities.

For example, clinicians specializing in domestic violence should be aware of the diagnostic criteria involved in substance abuse, and substance abuse therapists should have a firm understanding of the red flags associated with behavior executed by both abusers and their victims. An essential statistic of which experts should be mindful is that a staggering 30 percent of women hospitalized for severe body trauma not accounted for by traffic accidents are victims of domestic violence. Rose indicates that while substance and domestic abuse are both serious issues, matters that relate to a person's imminent safety are of utmost importance and should be subsequently followed by substance-related inquiries and intervention.

Substance Abuse & Violence

Logically, an increased tendency toward violence predisposes substance abusers to engage in augmented levels of criminal behavior, and various research findings support this premise (Bales, Van Slyke, & Bloomberg, 2006; Copur, Turkcan, & Erdogmus,

2005). For example, an estimated 25 percent of the violent crimes that take place in Sweden are instigated by those with alcohol and drug dependency ("Substance Abuse Linked," 2004). Likewise, 54 percent of Canadian inmates were under the influence at the time of their arrest, 38 percent of them were addicted to alcohol and drugs together, and it is estimated that this chemically dependent population engages in the highest frequency of weekly criminal activity (7.1 violations). The following table offers a more precise interaction between drugs, alcohol, and crime ("Canadian Study," 2002, p. 3):

	Alcohol only	Illicit drugs only	Alcohol and drugs
Assault	39%	9%	24%
Homicide	34%	7%	21%
Attempted Murder	30%	9%	24%

According to Steven Belenko and Jordan Peugh (1998), 47 percent of Americans are under the influence of drugs or alcohol at the time of their arrest, which can be explicated from various angles. Being intoxicated can provide an inborn alibi to their wrongdoings (e.g., "it wasn't me, it was the alcohol"). Moreover, alcohol lowers inhibitions while neurologically altering brain chemicals that heighten aggressive tendencies, and drug and alcohol use blurs social cues that contribute toward misconstruing other people's behavior and motivations. Alcohol tempers frontal lobe functioning, which, under normal circumstances, enables people to adequately interact with unforeseen circumstances. Belenko and Peugh surmise that 80 percent of prisoners have substance abuse problems, while only one in six inmates receive sufficient care during their incarcerated terms, causing escalated recidivism rates. They suggest that it would behoove correctional facilities to invest $6,500 on psychological, educational, treatment-based, and aftercare programs for each inmate; in the long run this would save $68,800 per person that the government would otherwise extend toward ongoing litigious matters. Furthermore, they calculate that if only 10 percent of the prison population successfully enacted this plan, it would prove to be financially prudent. Of particular concern is their approximation of the exponential growth of prison populations. They hypothesize that if incarceration rates continue to incline in accordance with its current pace, 20 percent of Americans that were born in 1997 will be imprisoned at some point in their lives.

Preventative Strategies

Alcohol and drugs allow people who would otherwise be categorized as law-abiding citizens to engage in "risky" behavior, and teenagers seem particularly vulnerable to sacrificing sensible behavior under such circumstances (Rashad & Kaestner, 2004). According to research set forth by Kaiser Permanente, five million young adults engaged in unprotected sex while they were intoxicated ("SubstanceAbuse," 2002). Also, according to research by Laura Kann and her colleagues (2000), 33 percent of teenagers reported that they had been passengers in vehicles driven by an inebriated driver, and 13 percent had gotten behind the wheel themselves after drinking or drugging. As such, many preventative strides have been undertaken by researchers and clinicians to pinpoint demographic characteristics that make certain populations vulnerable to the lure of substanceabuse and to mitigate prospective involvement in the drug and alcohol underground.

Tena L. St. Pierre and colleagues (2001) conducted a substance abuse prevention study in which they targeted second- and third-grade students who came from low-income neighborhoods, since this population typically has higher rates of risk factors that predispose a person toward substance use. The students in the current study were no exception, in that their social-skill set, communication, and decision-making proficiencies were laden with aggressive or disruptive undertones, and both they and their parents lacked involvement in the educational process. Further, parent-child bonds tended to be severed, parenting skills and discipline tactics initiated by parents were less than desirable, and the neighborhoods in which families resided were riddled with drug use and sales.

The SMART Framework

To combat the unpropitious environmental forces with which these students continually contend, they were enlisted to participate in the Boys & Girls Club in order to examine situational factors that might absolve their desolate situations. In order to impart that which was deficient in these children's lives, a trifold SMART framework was used as the primary source of intervention. The three components of the SMART model included a SMART kids faction that focused on pro-social enrichment and supplemental educational services (e.g., tutoring), and SMART teachers who served to monitor student progress and mediate between the school and home. Finally, SMART parents concentrated on establishing a positive sense of kinship toward families who otherwise sat on the outskirts of community affairs, while instilling proactive parenting skills. After two years of such involvement, the program proved to enhance children's ability to distance their involvement in behavioral wrongdoings, refine decision-making skills, improve respectful interactions with authority figures, ameliorate their overall ethical demeanor, and even demonstrate certain academic advancements. These developmental strides were primarily conveyed through both the SMART kids and teachers components, although parental involvement was less consistent based on the busy schedules of both the program coordinators and the parents themselves (St. Pierre, Mark, Kaltreider, & Campbell, 2001).

Fetal Alcohol Syndrome (FAS)

Fetal Alcohol Syndrome (FAS) is a physical condition that develops in utero, during which time the fetus is exposed to harmful alcoholic properties. There are distinct physical characteristics that children who suffer FAS tend to possess, including a smaller physique, cranial abnormalities, and intellectual disabilities, as well as central nervous system damage that manifests through infant irritability, hyperactivity, and seizures. The time at which the mother drinks alcohol depends on the type of FAS symptoms that will abound. For example, the first trimester of a baby's development equates with the formation of the skull, and mothers who drink alcohol during this period increase the risk that their child will have a smaller head and abnormal facial features. Brain development takes place during the second and third trimesters, and women who drink during this timeframe expose their unborn children to potential cognitive deficiencies. Long-term behavioral problems associated with FAS include school-related complications and increased interpersonal difficulties (Elliott, Payne, Morris, et al, 2008; Niccols, 2007; Sigelman & Rider, 2006; Wacha & Obrzut, 2007).

Society shoulders the responsibility of creating programs to enhance the lives of FAS children through various social service initiatives. According to Burgess (1994), schools should apply preventative educational techniques toward children who struggle with FAS. FAS kids who score within the normal range of intellectual functioning still struggle to stay afloat academically, due to the neurological damage that affects their decision-making and judgment skills; the discrepancy between average test scores and low performance generates labels such as "lazy" and "unmotivated." Moreover, FAS children tend not to appropriately correlate causal connections between behavior and punishment and to repeat mistakes and social errors, leading adults to classify them as spitefully errant. Burgess suggests that school officials should recognize this population's specific needs, encourage their progression toward independence, and create programs and curricula to reiterate skills that come naturally to mainstream students, such as cause-and-effect sequences.

Additionally, researchers have studied the preventative attempts to curb or eliminate the occurrence of FAS through a wide range of strategies. Hankin (1994) studied protective mechanisms that inhibit pregnant women from drinking, including the 1989 mandate that the US Surgeon General brandish warning labels on beer, wine, and liquor bottles regarding the harmful health effects that are imparted onto unborn children. Incidentally, these precautionary measures effectively dissuaded "non-risk" drinkers from alcohol consumption; unfortunately, "high-risk" drinkers were not discouraged from ingesting such toxic beverages. Hankin also compiled a list of several successful FAS outreach programs including a training program for helping professionals on the ways they can deter drinking among pregnant women, including non-disparaging counseling techniques that served to enhance women's self-esteem and cognitive-behavioral techniques extended to women who had already given birth to a FAS child in an attempt to restrain them from drinking during future pregnancies.

Educational Approaches

Boulter (2007) organized a FAS prevention research project geared toward seventh- and ninth-grade students that was disseminated by older high school students who were working under a college faculty mentor. Participants underwent an informative presentation highlighting the damage a mother transmits to her unborn fetus when she consumes alcohol. Visual demonstrations included dropping a raw egg, which presenters likened to a developing brain, into a cup of alcohol so that students could witness its dissolution. Students were then tested on their knowledge surrounding FAS facts, provided with life-sized dolls that visually depicted the physical deformities FAS children bear, and engaged in a question-answer forum. Six weeks later, students were given a follow-up post-test that measured their long-term retention on such matters, which revealed significant improvements, particularly among older female students. Results overall were quite favorable, and students summoned the following information from the presentation:

> ... more students knew that no amount of alcohol is safe, more than half of women in the early weeks of pregnancy are consuming alcohol, the debilitating physical, cognitive and behavioral effects of FAS and FAE, the purpose of liquor store warning signs, that the alcohol content in various alcoholic beverages is really the same, and that there is no cure for FAS (Boulter, 2007, p. 16-17).

Geralyn Timler and Lesley Olswang (2001) carried out a qualitative research project whereby they investigated the home and school environments of a young child stricken with FAS in order to understand preemptive educational approaches that would assist his development. The boy, Ian, was eight years of age, had been adopted by a woman named Brenda, and was enrolled in a first-grade special education class at the time that the research was collected. Ian's IQ fell within normal parameters (Verbal: 81, Performance: 90, Full Scale: 83) although his behavior was interspersed with frequent outbursts, a distracted attention span, lack of intrapersonal control, and non-compliant conduct. Brenda explained Ian's behavior through a neurologically defective lens and felt that, through no fault of his own, Ian simply lacked the ability to comprehend certain directives. Moreover, she felt that the positive strides Ian made at school resulted from the vigilant structure that his special education program provided, and she felt as though he would only thrive in subsequent endeavors while under the watchful surveillance of such supervision.

On the other hand, Ian's teacher felt as though Ian had increasingly improved throughout the course of his enrollment in her program, and that this progress would surpass the confines of her class and merge nicely into the future prospects on which he would embark. Despite these divergent views surrounding Ian's ability, the researchers reflected that Ian would excel in an academic setting in which his mother proactively collaborated with teachers through a process called "priming." Priming requires teachers to inform FAS parents ahead of time what the following day's curriculum will entail, and that parents should "prime" their children on such lectures beforehand. For example, if on Tuesday the child is scheduled to learn about "photosynthesis," the child and his parent should review core concepts on Monday night.

In a comprehensive literature review, Kenneth J. Gruber and Melissa Floyd Taylor (2006) noted that 25 percent of American children are raised in families that contain substance abuse, and they delineated various consequences associated with family addiction. Alcoholic parents are often ill-equipped caretakers and more prone toward becoming abusive, which increases the likelihood that their children will eventually suffer from psychological ailments such as depression, anxiety, or low self-esteem. These problems are not exclusive to the home but rather transcend into auxiliary realms of functioning such as school and peer interaction. These effects have a range of outcomes on children, some of whom are more inclined to experiment with substances themselves, others may become "parentified," or assume excessive responsibilities that surpass those that a normal child would undertake. Children are frequently shamed and worried by their parents, who tend to accrue more legal infractions due to their irresponsible lifestyles, which consequently renders these kids helpless, hopeless, or even feeling guilty that they were unable to superimpose more stability into their parents.

VIEWPOINTS

Although research targeting children of alcoholic parents burgeoned during the 1980s and 1990s, relatively few prevention programs were developed. Of those that did exist, Pim Cuijpers (2005) categorizes the objectives that successful programs tend to collectively possess, such as social support, information, skills training, and coping skills elements. Programs reach out to children from various angles, some of which exist through school-based initiatives such as SMAAP, the STAR-project, and 'Images within.' SMAAP, for example, offers children eight film-based lessons during their formative years. According to two distinct program evaluations, the following analyses offer feedback on SMAAP's success rates:

- "Positive effect on: coping, depressive symptomatology, help seeking. No effect on self esteem" (Roosa et al., as cited in Cuijpers, 2005, p. 472)," and
- "Significant effects on knowledge and coping. Stronger effects in high-risk group" (Short et al., as cited in Cuijpers, 2005, p. 472)."

Substance abuse is a complex phenomenon that carries grave consequences, and many experts continually search for preventative strides to diminish its seductive appeal. A controversial measure is currently taking place on several US college campuses in order to combat drinking among college students. While the magnitude of college students partaking in on-campus libation has remained steady, the amount of binge drinking has progressively increased (Age 18, 2008), which yields destructive results including an annual death toll of 1,700 directly pertaining to substance-induced behavior (Levy, 2008).

In response to this dangerous trend, a group of one hundred US university presidents rallied together in attempt to lower the drinking age from twenty-one to eighteen years of age, in a movement titled "Amethyst Initiative" (Waddell, 2008). The theory behind Amethyst Initiative is that underage college students are naturally drawn to the "forbidden fruit," or that which is deemed racy or verboten. Moreover, because these young students are unable to attend alcohol-centered outings at nearby bars and clubs, they relegate themselves to quarantined dorm rooms where they overindulge in drugs and alcohol while "the coast is clear," or outside the bounds of authoritative command. Proponents of the Amethyst Initiative theory point to European countries that generally have younger drinking age restrictions, where parents can model appropriate drinking behavior at home, and that these firsthand demonstrations prevent the emergence of binge-drinking patterns once the living arrangements of young adults become autonomous. This theory is not fool-proof, and some experts fear that granting eighteen-year-old high school students with the ability to access alcohol would encourage younger high school students to follow suit. Moreover, traffic accidents are significantly altered based on the drinking age—in 1984, the drinking restriction was raised from eighteen to twenty-one years and fatal car accidents dropped 16 percent. There is a possibility that if the Amethyst Initiative was enacted, this pattern might reverse itself.

TERMS & CONCEPTS

Amethyst Initiative: A group of one hundred US university presidents who have rallied together to advocate for lowering the drinking age in the United States from twenty-one to eighteen years of age.

Employee Assistance Program (EAP): Programs to help employees grapple with various problems, including substance abuse.

Fetal Alcohol Syndrome (FAS): A physical condition that develops in utero, during which time the fetus is exposed to harmful alcoholic properties.

Priming: An educational method that requires the teacher to inform FAS parents ahead of time what the following day's curriculum will entail so that parents can "prime" their children on such lectures beforehand.

SMART Framework: A tri-fold framework that was used as a primary source of intervention in a study conducted by Tena L. St. Pierre and colleagues (2001) that consisted of kids, teachers, and parents.

SMAAP: A preventative program for children of alcoholics that offers eight film-based lessons.

Bibliography

"Age 18 isn't the answer." (2008, August 27). *USA Today*, 12a.

Bales, W. D., Van Slyke, S., & Bloomberg, T. G. (2006). "Substance abuse treatment in prison and community reentry: Breaking the cycle of drugs, crime, incarceration, and recidivism?" *Georgetown Journal on Poverty Law & Policy,* 13(2), 383-401.

"Barry endorses legalization of medical marijuana." (1997). *Alcohol & Drug* Abuse *Weekly,* 9(45), 8-8.

Belenko, S. & Peugh, J. (1998). "Fighting crime by treating substance abuse." *Issues in Science & Technology,* 15(1), 53-60.

Boulter, L. T. (2007). "The effectiveness of peer-led FAS/FAE prevention presentations in middle and high schools." *Journal of Alcohol & Drug Education,* 51(3), 7-26.

Burgess, D. M. (1994). "Helping prepare children with FAS or FAE for school and beyond." *Alcohol Health & Research World,* 18(1), 73-73.

"Canadian study quantifies link between substance abuse and crime." (2002). *Alcoholism & Drug* Abuse *Weekly,* 14(19), 3-4.

Collins, M. H., Ready, J., Griffin, J. B., Walker, K. G., & Mascaro, N. (2007). "The challenge of transporting family-based interventions for adolescent substance abuse from research to urban community settings." *American Journal of Family Therapy,* 35(5), 429-445.

Copur, M., Turkcan, A., & Erdogmus, M. (2005). "Substance abuse, conduct disorder and crime: Assessment in a juvenile detention house in Istanbul, Turkey." *Psychiatry & Clinical Neurosciences,* 59(2), 151-154.

Cuijpers, P. (2005). "Prevention programmes for children of problem drinkers: A review." *Drugs: Education, Prevention & Policy,* 12(6), 465-475.

Elliott, K. & Shelley, K. (2005). "Impact of employee assistance programs on substance abusers and workplace safety." *Journal of Employment Counseling,* 42(3), 125-132.

Elliott, E. J., Payne, J., Morris, A., Haan, E., & Bower, C. (2008). "Fetal alcohol syndrome: A prospective national surveillance study." *Archives of Disease in Childhood,* 93(9), 732-737.

Greenwood, K. L, DeWeese, P., & Inscoe, P. S. (2005). "Demonstrating the value of EAP services: A focus on clinical outcomes." *Journal of Workplace Behavioral Health,* 21(1), 1-10.

Firesheets, E., Francis, M., Barnum, A., & Rolf, L. (2013) "Community-based prevention support: Using the interactive systems framework to facilitate grassroots evidence-based substance abuse prevention." *American Journal of Community Psychology,* 50(3/4), 347-356.

Gruber, K. J. & Taylor, M. F. (2006). "A family perspective for substance abuse: Implications from the literature." *Journal of Social Work Practice in the Addictions,* 6(1/2), 1-29.

Hankin, J. R. (1994). "FAS prevention strategies." *Alcohol Health & Research World,* 18(1), 62-66.

Hardison, J. (2004, February 5). "Rockers come out for Kucinich." *Rolling Stone,* (941), 14-14.

Joffe, A. & Yancy, W. S. (2004). "Legalization of marijuana: Potential impact on youth." *Pediatrics,* 113(6), 632-638.

Kann, L., Kinchen, S. A., Williams, B. I., Ross, J. G., Lowry, R., Grunbaum, J. A., & Kolbe, L. J. (2000). "Youth risk behavior surveillance—United States, 1999." *MMWR: Morbidity & Mortality Weekly Report,* 49(22), 1-94.

"Legalizing marijuana: Adults can decide for themselves." (2002). [Letters to the Editor]. *USA Today,* 1-1.

Levy, C. (2008, August 29). "College presidents stand up for common sense? I'll drink to that." *Wall Street Journal—Eastern Edition,* 252(51), 9-9.

McKinley, J. (2007, April 3). "The caucus: Constituencies; Marijuana bill attracts a voter." *New York Times,* 16-16.

"Medical marijuana is step toward legalization." (1994). *Human Events,* 50(1), 6-6.

"Medical-marijuana shield bill introduced in house." (2005). *NCADD Washington Report,* 8(7), 1-1.

Merritt, R. J., Jackson, M. S., Bunn, S. M., & Joyner, L. R. (2011). "Substance abuse prevention interventions for pregnant women: a synopsis of a need for collaborative work." *Journal of Human Behavior in the Social Environment,* 21(7), 858-869.

Muse, K. (2005). "Legalization would stem marijuana boom [Letter]." *Christian Science Monitor,* 97(79), 8-8.

Niccols, A. (2007). "Fetal alcohol syndrome and the developing socio-emotional brain." *Brain & Cognition,* 65(1), 135-142.

"Prevalence of alcohol and illicit drug use among 35-year-old U.S. residents, by gender." (2004). *Alcoholism & Drug Abuse Weekly,* 16(27), 7-7.

Rashad, I. & Kaestner, R. (2004). "Teenage sex, drugs and alcohol use: problems identifying the cause of risky behaviors." *Journal of Health Economics,* 23(3), 493-503.

"Reagan, GOP officials politicize war on drugs." (1995). *Alcoholism Report*, 23(4), 2-3.

Roman, P. M. & Blum, T. C. (2002). "The workplace and alcohol problem prevention." *Alcohol Research & Health*, 26(1), 49-57.

Rose, V. L. (1998). "Substance abuse and domestic violence." *American Family Physician*, 57(11), 2887-2888.

Roy, A., Wibberley, C., & Lamb, J. (2005). "The usual suspects: Alcohol, tobacco and other drug use in 15-to 6-year old school pupils—prevalence, feelings and perceived health risks." *Drugs: Education, Prevention & Policy*, 12(4), 305-315.

Schutz, J. A., Pandya, S., Sims, M., & Jones, J. A. (2013). "Participatory monitoring and evaluation within a statewide support system to prevent adolescent substance abuse." *Journal of Prevention and Intervention in the Community*, 41(3), 188-200.

Sigelman, C. K. & Rider, E. A. (2006). *Life-span human development*. USA: Thomson & Wadsworth.

Smith, W. C. (2003). "Pass the bar, flunk rehab." *ABA Journal*, 89(1), 18-19.

St. Pierre, L. L., Mark, M. M., Kaltreider, D. L., & Campbell, B. (2001). "Boys & girls clubs and school collaborations: A longitudinal study of a multi-component substance abuse prevention program for high-risk elementary school children." *Journal of Community Psychology*, 29(2), 87-106.

Stephen, A. (2004). "America." *New Statesman*, 133(4716), 19-20.

"Substance abuse, alcohol linked to unprotected sex." (2002). *Nation's Health*, 32(3), 15-15.

"Substance abuse a significant characteristic in domestic violence assailants." (1997). *DATA: The Brown University Digest of Addiction Theory & Application*, 16(9), 1-3.

"Substance abuse linked to violent crimes." (2004). *Alcoholism & Drug Abuse Weekly*, 16(22), 7- 7.

Timler, G. R. & Olswang, L. B. (2001). "Variable structure/variable performance: Parent and teacher perspectives on a school-age child with FAS." *Journal of Positive Behavior Interventions*, 3(1), 48-56.

Wacha, V. H. & Obrzut, J. E. (2007). "Effects of fetal alcohol syndrome on neuropsychological function." *Journal of Developmental & Physical Disabilities*, 19(3), 217-226.

Waddell, R. (2008). "A legal matter." *Billboard*, 120(36), 20-20.

Suggested Reading

Conyers, B. (2003). *Addict in the family: Stories of loss, hope, and recovery*. USA: Hazelden.

Fisher, G. L. & Harrison, T. C. (2008). *Substance abuse*: Information for school counselors, social workers, therapists, and counselors. USA: Allyn & Bacon.

Jewell, R. (2005). *My way out: One woman's remarkable journey in overcoming her drinking problem and how her innovative program can help you or someone you love*. USA: Capalo Press.

Watson-Thompson, J., Woods, N. K., Schober, D. J., & Schultz, J. A. (2013). "Enhancing the capacity of substance abuse prevention coalitions through training and technical assistance." *Journal of Prevention and Intervention in the Community*, 41(3), 176-187.

Cynthia Vejar, Ph.D.

Youth Suicide

ABSTRACT

This article delves into the tragic subject of youth suicide. Issues related to childhood suicide are introduced, including elements of Jean Piaget's developmental theory, myths surrounding childhood suicide, childhood depression and other preemptive characteristics of suicide, as well as a potential treatment option (play therapy). After segueing into the subject of adolescent suicide, Piaget's theory is once again broached by highlighting a concept known as adolescent egocentrism and its corresponding manifestations (e.g., imaginary audience, the personal fable). Predisposing factors that contribute toward teen suicide and a brief commentary on treatment are included. Finally, gender-related matters are covered, including statistical information and a gender-identity theory, which correlates "event centered" stage of development with suicide.

OVERVIEW

Suicide is the third leading cause of death for people between the ages of fifteen and twenty-four years old, according to the National Institute for Mental Health. Bereaved family members who lose loved ones to suicide are left to scrutinize the emotionally agonizing and mystifying details that contributed toward their child's untimely death. Therefore, research and clinical professionals are often bewildered by child suicide cases. Perhaps one of the reasons why childhood suicide is underestimated relates to the romanticized notion people tend to extend toward childhood itself. Most people view childhood as a carefree, buoyant existence brimming with promise and possibility.

Piaget's Stages of Development

Additionally, many people deem childhood suicide as cognitively unfeasible, given that the brain is still in the process of developing and cannot comprehend concepts that are categorically irrevocable, let alone contrive such destructive schemes. For example, according to renowned child psychologist Jean Piaget, children in the preoperational stage of development (i.e., ages 2-7) are still unable to grasp certain intellectual principles such as reversibility and decentration (Burger, 1991; Gainotti, 1997; Siegler & Ellis, 1996; Sigelman & Rider, 2006; Singer & Revenson, 1996; Favre & Bizzini, 1995), which mentally conceptualizes the multidimensional aspects of problems. By the time children reach the concrete operations stage, which roughly lasts between the ages of 7 and 12, they have made significant strides in their thought processes and can master sequential relationships and classify objects in accordance with their various physical properties (i.e., types of cars; types of dogs) (Mareschal & Shultz, 1999).

However, it is not until children reach adolescence, or the formal operations stage, when they are able to fully enter into the complex realm of abstract thinking. At this age, they can derive conclusions to hypothetical ideas, whereas beforehand they were limited to that which they could tangibly grasp through their five senses. These intellectual augmentations allow the adolescent to "think outside" of the conventional box that had been placed before them throughout their formative years, namely the rules and values that had been imposed upon them by parents, teachers, and society as a whole. It makes "neurological sense," therefore, that the adolescent era is inexorably linked with suicide, since teenagers are more apt to be rebellious and can examine their dilemmas from a variety of angles, thus believing that they had exhausted all options before settling on suicide as a final determination.

Myths of Youth Suicide

According to Greene, there are many myths that accompany childhood suicide, and these myths ultimately serve as barriers toward conquering such a devastating phenomenon (1994). Many people mistakenly presume that children under the age of six do not commit suicide. They also think that children in their latent period of growth (i.e., 6-12 years of age) are not capable of suicide. In reality, Greene eludes to the existence of several documented cases of young children within these age ranges who have committed suicide. Although evidence on this is unclear, Dervic, Friedrich, and Oquendo indicate that children cannot quite grasp the permanence of suicide until age ten (2006). Or, as Fritz indicates, children may be drawn to the prospect of their own mortality, but do not possess the intellectual skill set to interpret and verbalize their destructive motivations (2004). Instead, they habitually choreograph death-defying activities to increase their fatal odds. As Greene points out, when young children make resolute statements such as "I'm going to jump off the house!," they are often perceived as eliciting attention-seeking behavior; but when such misdeeds are actually implemented, they are often regarded as accidental.

Another myth involves the lack of weapons a child has within reach that may facilitate his suicidal pact. To some degree, this assumption has been squashed with the circulation of several media reports regarding the deadly recourse to which many youngsters resort (Children with Guns, 2000). Additionally, children often carry out their deadly, self-imposed intentions through accessible means such as consuming toxic concoctions or bolting into oncoming traffic. Additional myths that circulate around childhood suicide include the belief that children cannot fully understand the finality of death, and that depression, which is a likely antecedent to suicide, does not occur until adolescence (Brådvik, Mattisson, & Bogren, et al, 2008; Herskowitz, 1990). To rebut the first belief while operating in concurrence with Piaget's aforementioned premise, children do, in fact, cultivate an ability to distinguish between that which is reversible and irreversible by age seven. And with regard to depression, it is true that Sigmund Freud elaborated on the roots of adolescent depression, saying that it stemmed from a "diseased superego." Freud also posed that depression was a result of the grievances related to parental attachments that had not been properly resolved (Polmear, 2004). Thus, Freud's inference suggests that the onset of depression coincides with puberty. However, Freud's theories have largely been discredited by modern psychology.

Childhood Depression

A substantial amount of current research proves that childhood depression and correlating suicide rates have significantly increased along with our understanding of the symptomology of depression (Murphy, 2004). For example, because young children tend to discern life's pertinent lessons through the process of play, an absence of such recreational indulgence (i.e., anhedonia) carries tremendous ramifications and is a primary indicator of depression. Indeed, the literature surrounding childhood depression is quite expansive and covers the following categories:

- Utilization of the Berkley Puppet Interview as a diagnostic tool for childhood depression and anxiety (Luby, Belden, & Sullivan, et al, 2007);
- The adverse reactions that some children face when taking psychotropic medication (Bylund & Reed, 2007);
- Family factors that influence childhood depression (Wang & Crane, 2001); and
- The concomitance between childhood depression and other ailments such as cancer (Koocher, O'Malley, Gogan, & Foster, 1980) and ADHD (Redy & Devi, 2007).

In addition to depression, specific motivations surrounding childhood suicidepuzzle experts and the layperson alike. Many decades ago, Gunther reported on possible incentives for childhood suicide by accounts made on behalf of children who had previously plotted suicide (1967; Cytryn & McKnew, 1998; Pelkonen & Marttunen, 2003; Stefanowski-Harding, 1990). A history of prior attempts and sudden personality changes (e.g., shy to talkative; submissive to aggressive) or behavioral changes (in sleep patterns, eating habits, or activity levels) are strong indicators of suicidal ideation, along with feelings of worthlessness, social isolation, hopelessness, and academic failure. These facts tend to couple with a specific trigger, such as the child's perception that he was recipient to undue punishment over a particular event. Family factors that contribute toward suicide consist of parental substance abuse, divorce or separation, physical or sexual abuse, rejection, parental psychopathology (e.g., depression, parental suicide or suicide attempts), as well as good parental intentions that have gone awry, including parents that are either overprotective or those who demand perfection. A child considering suicide may be hypersensitive, depressed, anxious, and angry. Such angst may manifest through health maladies, oppositional behavior, sleep disturbances, or an overriding aversion toward school. Additionally, young children often conjure up enigmatic portrayals to help comprehend the inexplicable nature of death, particularly if they had recently lost a love one. Oftentimes, death is explained to children in ethereal terms such as "Mommy is in heaven now," or "Grandpa is smiling at you from the clouds," and children select suicide as a means to reunite with their loved one.

FURTHER INSIGHTS

Treating the Suicidal Child

Children who have demonstrated some form of suicidal ideation, such as those with a history of previous attempts, would highly benefit from therapy. Since children are ill equipped to both conceptualize and articulate their inner demons, nonverbal therapeutic alternatives such as play therapy (Landreth, 2002; Schaefer & O'Connor, 1983) should be considered. Play therapies have tremendously assisted children who have encountered a variety of psychosocial distress, including survivors of abuse or trauma, those in the throes of grief, and children who are terminally ill. The ways in which therapists elicit pertinent information from children via play therapy includes art (e.g., drawings, clay), as well as puppets, sand and water trays, and through storytelling techniques. The premise behind this therapeutic modality is that although children cannot directly understand or articulate their feelings (e.g., "I'm lonely"), such sentiments will manifest throughout the process of play. For example, the lonely child might portray a solitary puppet who is consistently estranged from the other puppets. The suicidal child might draw graphic depictions of a person getting hit by cars or being held at gunpoint. From that point, the therapist encourages the child and his family to infuse change into the play characters that he has created, which eventually seek to transcend into the child's life. The following passage describes the resolution of a young girl's school phobia through this process:

> Ann and her parents negotiate new solutions via the puppet play. The gorilla agrees to be more patient with the puppy and the cat. When the puppy runs away, the gorilla does not yell at the cat, but they express their worries about the puppy and together go look for the puppy. When they find her, the puppy is excited and hugs the cat and the gorilla. They go home together, the gorilla carrying the puppy on his back. When the therapist processes the play with the family, the dad reports that he used to carry Ann on his back when she was younger and got tired during long walks. The family transfers the "new solution" from the puppet play to their "real" life by changing their morning routine. Dad gets up a little earlier and calmly helps Ann to get ready. Then the family has a brief breakfast together. When it is time to leave, dad pretends to be the "good" gorilla and carries the "puppy" on his shoulder to the front door. There he lets her down, gives Ann a kiss, and sees her off to the school bus (which the parents did not do before, because Ann was a "big" girl). This way Ann feels safer in the transition from home to school and her school fear subsides quickly (Wittenborn, Faber, & Harvey et al, 2006, p. 341).

Adolescent Suicide

Suicide during the adolescent years is much more prevalent and therefore symptoms such as depression are more recognizable. Most people have probably encountered a sullen, disgruntled teenager and attributed such petulance to the influx of hormonal and physical changes that rapidly occur during this time. Furthermore, advancement into Piaget's formal operations developmental stage yields specific characteristics that exacerbate the difficult mood swings and insecurities that teenagers endure. For example, it is common for adolescents to undergo a phenomenon known as adolescent egocentrism, or the inability to operate outside of their internal mechanisms in order to truly align with divergent perspectives (Elkind, 1967).

Adolescent Egocentrism

Two common manifestations that extend from adolescent egocentrism include the imaginary audience and the personal fable (Ryan & Kuczkowski, 1994; Vartanian, 2000). The imaginary audience revolves around the teenager's assumption that the world is preoccupied with his affairs and even garners the same level of attention that he extends toward such matters. To illustrate this premise, let us assume that on the way to school, Brian tripped and ripped the cuff of his pants. Embarrassed, he enters the cafeteria during lunchtime overwrought with fear that his classmates will ridicule his earlier miscalculation, and he modifies his behavior accordingly by quickly exiting the lunchroom. Adolescents who are naturally insecure or feel socially awkward based upon subjective or object criteria feel especially self-conscious during this cumbersome stage, even though in reality their peers are directing the same level of criticism toward themselves.

The personal fable, on the other hand is the adolescent tendency to think that their thoughts, feelings, and experiences are unrivaled. Thus, when they fall in love, they believe it is a love like none that the world has ever seen. Likewise, when they suffer a broken heart, or when they receive the sharp denunciation of peer rejection, they believe that their heightened level of depression is unmatched. Certainly, this reveals insight toward the perplexing nature of adolescent depression and suicide, in that teenagers feel that their social blunders are held under a microscope for the rest of the world to scrutinize. At the same time, they feel that their anguish is unique and that nobody can possibly understand the concentrated level of torment that they encounter.

Predisposing Factors

Bridge, Goldstein, and Brent highlight a variety of predisposing factors that correlate with suicidal behavior (2006). Some of the adolescent family factors mirror those that are prevalent within children and include the following: poor family relations, previous suicide attempts, a family history of suicide, stressful life event or loss, abuse, alcohol and/or drug use, easy access to lethal methods (such as prescription drugs and firearms), and mood disorders. Examples of mood disorders that correlate with suicide are depression and bipolar disorder; other disorders that are risk factors for suicide include substance use disorder, conduct disorder, post-traumatic stress disorder, and eating disorders. Therapeutic treatment plans assist teens who are considering suicide and vary among the various theoretical styles (e.g., psychodynamic, cognitive-behavioral).

Gender also bears tremendous relevance toward the conception and implementation of suicide. The Centers for Disease Control and Prevention (CDC) reported that, for individuals between the ages of ten and twenty-four, almost five times as many boys than girls died from suicide. The gender discrepancy between suicide attempts and actual suicide can be explained through the method of suicide, as boys utilize more lethal means (e.g., guns) in contrast with girls who are more likely to attempt suicide through the over-consumption of pills. Among US students in high school (grades nine through twelve) in 2013, 17 percent reported seriously considering suicide in the previous twelve months, including 22.4 percent of girls and 11.6 percent of boys. In the previous twelve months, 13.6 percent reported having made a plan about how they would attempt suicide, 8 percent reported attempting suicide one ore more times, and 2.7 percent (3.6 percent of girls and 1.8 percent of boys) reported making a suicide attempt that resulted in an injury, poisoning, or overdose that required medical attention, according to the CDC.

In the early 2000s there was a string of high-profile LGBT (lesbian, gay, bisexual, and transgender) teen suicides that were attributed to harassment and bullying, including those of thirteen-year-old Ryan Halligan in 2003, Rutgers student Tyler Clementi in 2010, and fourteen-year-old Jamey Rodemeyer in 2011. In response, projects such as the It Gets Better Project spread messages that the difficult lives of LGBT teens will improve; the project started with video messages from gay adults and some celebrities and includes tens of thousands of videos from a diverse body of contributors. Additionally, policies and programs have been developed in communities and schools to protect LGBT youth from bullying and offer support and resources to prevent this form of youth suicide.

CONCLUSION

Suicide is preventable. The majority of individuals who commit suicide have a mental disorder at the time of their deaths, most commonly depression or bipolar disorder. Any talk of suicide and especially suicide attempts should be taken seriously and treatment should be sought immediately. A combination of therapy and medication is highly effective in reducing the incidence rate of suicide.

TERMS AND CONCEPTS

Adolescent Egocentrism: A teenager's inability to operate outside of his internal mechanisms in order to truly align with divergent perspectives.

Event-centered Stage of Development: The event-centered stage initially surfaces in infancy, but later re-emerges throughout subsequent stages in various forms, and revolves around the belief of omnipotence and creativity.

Imaginary Audience: The teenager's assumption that the world is grossly preoccupied with his affairs.

Personal Fable: The adolescent's tendency to think that his thoughts, feelings, and experiences are unique.

Piaget's Developmental Stages: Piaget's stages that directly pertain to childhood and adolescent suicide include preoperational, concrete operational, and formal operational.

Play Therapy: Although children might not be able to directly understand or articulate their feelings, a therapist can elicit such emotions through the process of play.

BIBLIOGRAPHY

"Alarming rise in youth suicides calls for caring monitors." (2007). *New York Amsterdam News,* 98, 30-31.

Brådvik, L., Mattisson, C., Bogren, M., & Nettelbladt, P. (2008, March). "Long-term suicide risk of depression in the Lundby cohort 1947-1997—severity and gender." *Acta Psychiatrica Scandinavica,* 117, 185-191.

Bridge, J. A., Goldstein, T. R., & Brent, D. A. (2006). "Adolescent suicide and suicidal behavior." *Journal of Child Psychology & Psychiatry,* 47(3/4), 372-394.

Burger, M. L. (1991). "Piaget's developmental theory." *Childhood Education,* 68, 96-97.

Bylund, D. B., & Reed, A. L. (2007, October). "Childhood and adolescent depression: Why do children and adults respond differently to antidepressant drugs?" *Neurochemistry International,* 51, 246-253.

"Children with guns." (2000, March 1). *New York Times,* 22.

Cohen, M. I., Bright, G., Dudenhoeffer, F., Guthrie, A., Hammar, S., Ice, A., Jenkins, R. R., Long, W. A., Shen, J. T., Klein, L., & Felice, M. E. (1980). "Teenage suicide." *Pediatrics,* 66, 144-146.

Cohen, Y. (1991). "Gender identity conflicts in adolescents as motivations for suicide." *Adolescence,* 26, 19-29.

Cytryn, L. & McKnew, D. H. (1998). *Growing up sad: Childhood depression and its treatment.* USA: W. W. Norton & Company.

Dervic, K., Friedrich, E., Oquendo, M. A., Voracek, M., Friedrich, M. H., & Sonneck, G. (2006). "Suicide in Australian children and young adolescents aged 14 and younger." *European Child & Adolescent Psychiatry,* 15, 427-434.

Elkind, D. (1967). "Egocentrism in adolescence." *Child Development,* 38, 1025-1034.

Fast, I. (1984). *Gender identity: A differentiation model.* Hillsdale, NJ: The Analytic Press.

Favre, C. & Bizzini, L. (1995). "Some contributions of Piaget's genetic epistemology and psychology to cognitive therapy. " *Clinical Psychology & Psychotherapy,* 2, 15-23.

Fritz, G. K. (2004). "Suicide in young children." *Brown University Child & Adolescent Behavior Letter,* 20, 8.

Gainotti, M. A. (1997). "Jean Piaget (1896-1980)." *International Sociology,* 12, 373-379.

Girard, C. (1993). "Age, gender, and suicide: A cross-national analysis." *American Sociological Review,* 58, 553-574.

Grzanka, P. R., & Mann, E. S. (2014). "Queer youth suicide and the psychopolitics of 'It Gets Better'." *Sexualities,* 17, 369-393.

Greene, D. B. (1994). "Childhood suicide and myths surrounding it." *Social Work,* 39, 230-232.

Gunther, M. (1967). "Why children commit suicide." *Saturday Evening Post,* 240, 86-89.

Henry, C. S., & Stephenson, A. L. (1993). "Adolescent suicide and families: An ecological approach." *Adolescence,* 28, 291-309.

Herskowitz, J. (1990). "Cries for help." *Learning,* 18, 34-37.

Kiamanesh, P., et al. (2015). "Maladaptive perfectionism: Understanding the psychological vulnerability to suicide in terms of developmental history." *Omega: Journal of Death and Dying,* 71(2), 126-145.

King, R. A. & Apter, A. (1996). "Psychoanalytic perspectives on adolescent suicide." *Psychoanalytic Study of the Child,* 51, 491-512.

Koocher, G. P., O'Malley, J. E., Gogan, J. L., & Foster, D. J. (1980). "Psychological adjustment among pediatric cancer survivors." *Journal of Psychology & Psychiatry & Allied Disciplines,* 21, 163-173.

Landreth, G. L. (2002). *Play therapy: The art of the relationship.* USA: Brunner-Routledge.

Luby, J. L., Belden, A., Sullivan, J., & Spitznagel, E. (2007). "Preschoolers' contribution to their diagnosis of depression and anxiety: Uses and limitations of young child self-report on symptoms." *Child Psychiatry & Human Development,* 38, 321-338.

Mareschal, D. & Shultz, T. R. (1999). "Development of children's seriation: A connectionist approach." *Connection Science,* 11, 149-186.

Miklowitz, D. J., & Taylor, D. O. (2006). "Family-focused treatment of the suicidal bipolar patient." *Bipolar Disorders,* 8, 640-651.

Murphy, K. (2004). "Recognizing depression in children." *Nurse Practitioner,* 29, 18-29.

Pelkonen, M. & Marttunen, M. (2003). "Child and adolescent suicide: Epidemiology, risk factors, and approaches to prevention." *Pediatric Drugs,* 5, 243-265.

Pfeffer, C. R. (2000). "Suicidal behavior in prepubertal children: From the 1980s to the new millennium." In R. W. Maris, S. S. Cannetto, J. L. MvIntosh, & M. M. Silverman (Eds.), *Review of suicidology 2000* (pp. 159-169). New York: Guilford.

Polmear, C. (2004). "Dying to live: Mourning, melancholia and the adolescent process." *Journal of Child Psychotherapy,* 30, 263-274.

Portzky, G., Audenaert, K., & van Heeringen, K. (2005). "Suicide among adolescents." *Social Psychiatry & Psychiatric Epidemiology,* 40, 922-930.

Reddy, P. P., & Devi, S. G. (2007). "Herbal therapy: Children with ADHD (Attention Deficit Hyperactivity Disorder) and depression." *Internet Journal of Alternative Medicine,* 4, 3.

Rhodes, A. E., Boyle, M. H., Bethell, J., Wekerle, C., Goodman, D., Tonmyr, L., & ... Manion, I. (2012). "Child maltreatment and onset of emergency department presentations for suicide-related behaviors." *Child Abuse & Neglect,* 36, 542-551.

Rittner, B. & Smyth, N. J. (1999). "Time-limited cognitive-behavioral group interventions with suicidal adolescents." *Social Work with Groups,* 22(2/3), 55-75.

Ryan, R. M. & Kuczkowski, R. (1994). "The imaginary audience, self-consciousness, and public individuation in adolescence." *Journal of Personality,* 62, 219-238.

Shaffer, D., & Pfeffer, C. R. (2001). "Practice parameters for the assessment and treatment of children and adolescents with suicidal behavior." *Journal of the American Academy of Child and Adolescent Psychiatry,* 40, 24S-51S.

Schaefer, C. E., & O'Connor, K. J. (1983). *Handbook of play therapy.* New York: Wiley.

Schmidt, R. C., Iachini, A. L., George, M., Koller, J., & Weist, M. (2015). "Integrating a suicide prevention program into a school mental health system: A case example from a rural school district." *Children & Schools,* 37, 18-26.

Shaw, C. R. & Schelkun, R. F. (1965). "Suicide behavior in children." *Psychiatry,* 28, 157-168.

Siegler, R. S., & Ellis, S. (1996). "Piaget on childhood." *Psychological Science,* 7, 211-215.

Siegler, C. K., & Ryder, E. A. (2006). *Life span human development.* USA: Thomas and Wadsworth.

Singer, D. G. & Revenson, T. A. (1996). *A Piaget primer: How a child thinks* (Revised edition). USA: Penguin Group.

Singer, J. B., & Slovak, K. (2011). "School social workers' experiences with youth suicidal behavior: An exploratory study." *Children & Schools,* 33, 215-228.

Stefanowski-Harding, S. (1990). Child suicide: "A review of the literature and implications for school counselors." *School Counselor,* 37, 328-340.

Vartanian, L. R. (2000). "Revisiting the imaginary audience and personal fable constructs of adolescent egocentrism: A conceptual review." *Adolescence,* 35, 639-662.

Wang, L., & Crane, D. R. (2001). "The relationship between marital satisfaction, marital stability, nuclear family triangulation, and childhood depression." *American Journal of Family Therapy,* 29, 337-347.

Wherry, J. N., Baldwin, S., Junco, K., & Floyd, B. (2013). "Suicidal thoughts/behaviors in sexually abused children." *Journal of Child Sexual Abuse,* 22, 534-551.

Wittenborn, A. K., Faber, A. J., Harvey, A. M., & Thomas, V. K. (2006). "Emotionally focused family therapy and play therapy techniques." *American Journal of Family Therapy,* 34, 333-342.

Wong, I. C., Besag, F. M., Santosh, P. J., & Murray, M. L. (2004). "Use of selective serotonin reuptake inhibitors in children and adolescents." *Drug Safety,* 27, 991-1000.

"Youth suicides rising, especially among young, teenage girls." (2007). *Nation's Healthy,* 37, 9.

Suggested Reading

Carlson, T. (1995). *The* suicide *of my son: The story of childhood depression.* USA: Benline Press.

Gil, E. (1994). *Play in family therapy.* USA: The Guilford Press.

Moskowitz, A., Stein, J., & Lightfoot, M. (2013). "The mediating roles of stress and maladaptive behaviors on self-harm and suicide attempts among runaway and homeless youth." *Journal Of* Youth *& Adolescence,* 42, 1015-1027.

Pisani, A., Wyman, P., Petrova, M., Schmeelk-Cone, K., Goldston, D., Xia, Y., & Gould, M. (2013). "Emotion regulation difficulties, youth-adult relationships, and suicide attempts among high school students in underserved communities." *Journal of* Youth *& Adolescence,* 42, 807-820.

Scott, M., Underwood, M., & Lamis, D. (2015). "Suicide and related behavior among youth involved in the juvenile justice system." *Child and Adolescent Social Work Journal,* 32(6), 517-527.

Tuggle, A. S. (2006). *Avoiding the path to: Teenage* suicide. USA: Authorhouse.

White, J. (2014). "Expanding and Democratizing the Agenda for Preventing Youth Suicide: Youth Participation, Cultural Responsiveness, and Social Transformation." *Canadian Journal Of Community Mental Health,* 33, 95-107.

Cynthia Vejar, Ph.D.

Sex, Gender & Sexuality

Introduction

Sex is the biological make-up of being male or female, determined by the XX (female) chromosomes or XY (male) chromosomes. Sex determines the ability to reproduce and specific physical traits. Gender, often confused with sex, has no biological basis, rather is the psychological, cultural, and behavioral actions that are socially identified as either male or female. Gender determines how we perform our identity on a spectrum of stereotypically male or female characteristics which are socially constructed, predetermined concepts taught to us throughout our lives. Little girls are often dressed in pink and given dolls to play with, while little boys are often given cars and trucks to play with and told not to cry when they get hurt. These actions teach children how to "do" their assigned gender. When girls and boys engage in behaviors that are more stereotypical of the opposite gender, society often has a hard time accepting this. Parents, teachers and peers might, for example, disapprove of a boy dressing up as a ballerina.

Although gender is a social construct, it is used to identify women and men throughout their lives. Education, treatment in the classroom, sports, domestic responsibility, business relationships, economic expectation, and social characteristics are all affected by gender. Feminist theories support the fact that gender inequality is present in most societies around the world, manifested by women being denied opportunities, making less money than men for the same job, and women being criticized for how they dress, which rarely happens to men.

Sexuality refers to sexual attraction to others, often developing early in childhood. Similar to gender, sexuality can be fluid, in that biological sex and gender do not always predict sexuality. Although we are seeing social movements today that encourage acceptance of different ideas of sexuality and identity, American society remains primarily *heteronormative,* meaning that our systems revolve through a mostly heterosexual understanding of people. Forms ask for names of "mother" and "father" with no option for two mothers or two fathers. *Homophobia* refers to the fear, dislike, and lack of acceptance of people who identify their sexuality differently i.e. lesbian, gay, bisexual, transgender, asexual or queer. Homophobia can take many forms, from internalized feelings and negativity, to hate crimes and violence. Those who identify as non-heterosexual are currently at the forefront of many social justice battles, fighting for equal rights in the workplace, in personal relationships and in the legal arena.

Other topics in this section include attraction and love, prostitution, pornography, contraception, teen pregnancy, sexual harassment, assault and rape. Sociology theories offer insight into these topics, which often include complex psychological issues. Rape, for example, is not a product of someone's sexuality or sexual attraction, but a form of violence that has to do with power and mental health issues.

Kimberly Ortiz-Hartman, Psy.D., LMFT

Attraction & Love

ABSTRACT

We have all felt powerfully attracted to and in 'love' with somebody more than once in our lives. To make sense of the raw emotion experienced during such times, we invariably turn to culturally-mediated constructs—love at first sight, true love, Christian love, etc. Sociologists in turn try to make sense of each amid love and attraction's unique features, and shed light on our underlying motives for and subjective experience of desire. Indeed, at first glance contemporary culture seems head-over heels in love with love. And for good reason, for there are few experiences that match its intensity, that bring us more delight and despair, that confound and conflict us more.

OVERVIEW

Romantic love defies easy explanation. Very few of us, if pressed, could list the exact reasons why we have fallen in love with one person and not another. We just do. But this does not mean we are constantly searching for answers in the great works of literature by Ovid, Dante, Shakespeare, Austen, et al., as well as the pulp-fiction romances, "date" movies, and sentimental music lyrics of pop culture. Indeed, at first glance contemporary culture seems head-over-heels in love with love. And for good reason, for there are few experiences that match its intensity, that bring us more delight and despair, that confound and conflict us more.

Instinct partly accounts for this fixation. Sex ranks alongside aggression and fear as the most basic unconscious urges shaping human behavior. Love, however, is as much an idea as it is an expression of an instinctive drive and therefore a subject of great interest to sociologists as well as psychoanalysts. Each of us filters raw experience through a socially constructed lens and only then assigns it meaning via language, be it verbal, visual, or written.

This premise underlies *symbolic interactionism,* a body of sociology theory that examines how the sociocultural context we refer to in a given situation determines our response, not the situation per se. Quite literarily, reality is largely what other people say it is. Language by its very nature is a collective undertaking, the meaning it conveys culturally arbitrated ("Theories and theorizing," 2003).

And here, one of the most important cognitive representations we as individuals intuit from our milieu is a repertoire of relationship- archetypes. "Falling in love" and marriage are two such models. Extramarital affairs, one-night stands, "friends with benefits" and "living together," though perhaps not as conventional, are nonetheless equally well-defined (Forgas & Dobosz, 1980).

Impression Management

Much like a script an actor works from in creating a character, these models cue us as to how best to win the admiration, acceptance, and love we hunger after. All of us accordingly engage in some form of *impression management:* i.e., project an image of ourselves we think will find the most favor with others, accentuating some traits, downplaying others. The particulars of the character we assume, what's more, change with each person with whom we associate; the powerful underlying motive for adopting these stylized personas never does change ("Socialization, identity, and interaction," 2003).

But what exactly are we looking for most of all in a romantic one-one or *dyadic relationship* that causes us to behave this way? Some researchers believe people look for qualities in a loved one they themselves lack but admire and want. Romantic love in this instance (the theory goes) disguises a more fundamental motive: the attainment of the ego-ideal by proxy. Others posit that people look for mates with needs-patterns that compliment their own (Winch, 1955). Still others have theorized that sharing similar attitudes and beliefs encourages intimacy and that the greater the intimacy the less divisive the remaining differences become (Centers, 1975).

Infatuation

In *infatuation,* alternatively, the normal pattern of disliking people appreciably different from ourselves is temporarily suspended in our haste to idealize the object of our desire. This form of attraction is noted for its suddenness and emotional power but also for its total lack of a concomitant intimacy (McClanahan, Gold, Lenney, Ryckman & Kulberg, 1990). Noticeable differences in specific motives for love have also been observed. The traditionally-minded, in general, find fulfillment in the emotional investment and subsequent dependency of a romantic relationship and the flowing give-and-take of a romantic relationship for fulfillment; more contemporary-types look for intimacy and mutual respect. Women by and large have also been found to be more inclined to a relationship, voice their feelings more, and have greater respect for their partners than men (Critelli, Myers & Loos, 1986).

FURTHER INSIGHTS

The difference between "liking" and "loving" may lie in how long a couple quite literally gazes into each other's eyes. These measurements were taken to confirm the findings of an in-depth attitudinal questionnaire administered to pairs of subjects either dating or "just" friends (Rubin, 1970). Surprisingly, both groups' written responses closely resembled each other; both exhibited affiliative and dependent needs, a predisposition to help, and an orientation toward exclusiveness and absorption.

Romantic & Conjugal Love

The only demonstrated difference was one of degree: dating couples' experiences of each were more intensely felt than their platonic counterparts.' Conceivably, then, an objectively valid "love" scale might be constructed. Results from the controlled experiment supported this hypothesis; as predicted, dating couples' eye-contact did indeed last longer. Romantic love, in effect, may well flow from the same emotional wellspring as *conjugal love.*

By the same token, though, few would dispute that the two also inspire notably dissimilar feeling-states and behavior. Many of us at one time or another have experienced the passion, physical attraction, and idealization of the object of our affections unique to romantic love. Anyone who has ever enjoyed a close friendship, meanwhile, has more than a passing familiarity with the hallmarks of conjugal love: trust, lack of criticalness, mutual appreciation, sharing, loyalty, and genuine knowledge of the other (Driscoll, Davis & Lupetz, 1972).

In either case, we search out the one person who most strongly and fully satisfies our deepest personal needs, chief among which are: sex; affectionate intimacy; the maintenance and enrichment of our sexual identity; acceptance and approval; and validation of our sense of self-worth (Centers, 1975). Such in fact is the strength of these needs that the mere expectation that someone can provide all of this is sufficient enough reason to emotionally engage with him or her. As long as we perceive the resulting relationship does this, for that matter, we continue investing in it even when, objectively speaking, it does not. And therein lies the rub of many a romantic attachment.

Self-esteem

Self-esteem may indeed make someone more or less romantically inclined, along with defensiveness. Less guarded individuals with a strong sense of self-worth arguably are the most likely candidates; naturally defensive ones with low-self esteem the least likely. The former did report greater frequency in some studies but, interestingly, the same degree of satisfaction and fulfillment than the latter. An alternate hypothesis claims that low self-esteem individuals pursue romantic love more fervently for the sense of acceptance and worthiness it bestows.

Much here, though, may depend on the innate defensiveness of the person in question. Intimacy involves self-revelation and possible rejection, a turn of events someone already suffering from low self-esteem would rather avoid. Or it may just be that people with a low opinion of themselves are simply less adept in general at forming relationships. In either case, the end result would be fewer romantic involvements, a conclusion borne out in subsequent studies. Risk has its rewards: respondents on the whole said they were emotionally "genuine," intense experiences. Defensiveness per se though, may actually be the deciding factor, for investigators also found that similarly disposed subjects endowed with high self-esteem reported fewer episodes as well (Dion & Dion, 1975).

The Science of Love

Intense romantic feelings stimulate specific regions of the brain containing high concentrations of dopamine and norepinephrine, the chemical couriers involved in triggering euphoria, craving, addiction, heightened attention, or sleeplessness (Bianchi-Demicheli, Grafton & Ortigue, 2006, p. 92). They have also been linked with dramatic cognitive changes. For, the heights of ecstasy and the depths of despair lovers experience resemble the mood swings of bipolar disorder believed to be linked to sudden upswings in the presence of these two neurotransmitters.

Likewise, our mental preoccupation with the beloved resembles the intrusive thinking characteristic of an obsessive-compulsive disorder marked by an increase in dopamine levels and an accompanying decrease in serotonin. Certainly there is ample reason from the evolutionary perspective for these correspondences. Were it not for a sudden, complete suspension of our natural defensiveness, few of us would emotionally engage much less bond with a complete stranger long enough to procreate and raise a child. But that is exactly what we must do to ensure genetic diversity (Marazziti, 2005, p. 332).

The Archetypes of Love

Because it takes so many different forms, love is perhaps best understood in context. Ever since Max Weber, sociologists have employed *ideal-types* in analyzing real world phenomena, abstracting the predominant characteristics of a thing or event in order to compare and contrast them. Love is no exception. One early attempt at classifying its many varieties—J. A. Lee's six "styles" of love—remains one of the most complete and distinctive. He conceives of each such style not as a constellation of personality traits or characteristic traits but rather as an ideology, a collection of commonly-held beliefs and assumptions underlying existing social institutions (Watts & Stenner, 2005).

The six are:

- Eros;
- Ludus;
- Mania;
- Pragma;
- Agape; and
- Storge.

In *eros,* the lover runs across the flesh-and-blood personification of his or her "ideal" image of physical beauty. The attraction is immediate, powerful, and entirely based on the beloved's looks. Perfection here, the lover reasons, all but ordains the object of his or her ardor will be perfect in every other respect—intellect, temperament, considerateness, etc.—a leap of faith that rarely stands the test of time.

Such immanently practical considerations matter little, however, to someone seeking nothing less than a remedy to our existential loneliness in the physical, emotional, and spiritual union with the "other." This explains the intensity of the longing and the passion felt and why eros disappoints many and drives some to abject despair. But not only is this desired state fleeting at best and unrealistic on the whole, the quest for it also is often self-defeating. For the closer the lover comes to realizing his dream, the more anxious and more precipitous his or her actions may become.

Compared to eros, *ludus* seems an almost cynical pursuit. Its disciples see love as a game, the object of which is enjoyment for enjoyment's sake. One moreover played by a set of rules: avoid involvement and attachment; eschew jealousy expected as a manipulative ploy; always act with taste and good manners; end these casual affairs the minute they are no longer entertaining; and have many lovers. Simply put, pleasure, not fulfillment, is the ultimate prize; ludus therefore is not something people who need to "be in love" should engage in.

Not that those of us who sorely need to be in love are all that inclined to in the first place. For such people seek love in the netherworld of *mania,* in the all-consuming obsession somewhere between eros and ludus. Here he or she "who does not love too much does not love enough" (Lee, 1975, p. 516). Manic love is possessive, dependent love. Countless hours are spent dwelling on a relationship that gives little real satisfaction, punctuated by intervals of intense jealousy and acute anxiety. It can be a particularly unpleasant experience, something perhaps many of us would wish to avoid if we could. The problem, of course, is that the manic lover has no real say in the matter.

Remarkably, though, he or she remains levelheaded and insightful enough to be highly manipulative, wheedling, cajoling, and controlling until his/her fantasies come true. In resorting to such ludic-like tactics the manic lover is at a disadvantage, though, for he or she lacks the accompanying detachment to win this highstakes game yet cannot afford to lose. What then drives him or her to the brink and beyond with such regularity?

Loneliness most certainly enters into it, a lack of self esteem and social status probably as well, and possibly a touch of madness we all experience at one point or another that the manic lover falls afoul of all too regularly.

In eros, ludus, and mania the needs of the self outweigh those of the beloved. Were it not for more other-directed forms of love—storge, pragma, and agape—to counterbalance them the world might be a much sorrier place indeed. *Storge* in classical Greek means filial affection, the love felt by parents for children, brothers for sisters, etc. A wife and husband are friends long before they are lovers, and closeness, commitment and shared values remain more important than physical intimacy.

In *pragma,* considerations of social status, wealth, property, and filial obligation take precedence when selecting a mate. What matters the most here is compatibility and the realization of mutual ambitions. Part storge, part ludus, love only comes after years of living together, and then much more as fondness than passion. It is love rooted in real-world practicality. Romantic love in fact is often an encumbrance, especially in cases of arranged marriages.

Agape, finally, emphasizes the needs of the other to the exclusion of oneself. We have an almost ethical duty to love even the least deserving among us. Combining elements of eros and storge, agapic love extols altruism and self-sacrifice above all else. There is an otherworldliness and moral stridency about it along with a decided prudishness about passion and sex. Both in fact are considered abhorrent to the spiritual nature of agapic love. Physical passion between a husband and wife is considered adultery, sex a strictly procreative act, and pleasure sinful. Dour indeed if taken to extremes, agape embraces divine, not earthly love (Lee, 1975).

In reading these descriptions over you no doubt recollect having felt a version of each or some facsimile at one point or another. You may even recall simultaneously experiencing elements of each in your feelings toward a particular person. Lee (1975) considers mania, pragma, and agape some combination of eros and ludus or storge. You may for that matter be able to discern a change from one style of love to another over time in a given relationship or, perhaps, desire such a change. And, more times than we may care to admit, romantic attraction and love may seem a confusing mix of reality and fantasy, a jumble of conflicting impulses we struggle to control. Nor would Lee be in the least bit troubled by this conclusion, for his six styles are meant as points of reference, much like certain constellations in the night sky were once to seafarers. In the final analysis, there are as many unique experiences of love and therefore as many individual "styles" as there are people in search of it.

VIEWPOINTS

We will always know when and whom we love but probably never fully why or how. And whatever explanations that ultimately emerge will no doubt seem imminently dull compared to the flesh-and-blood experience of "being in love." It is a very powerful feeling that originates deep within the psyche, an expression of our primal urge to procreate. It might just be that to promulgate the species our biochemistry hijacks our conscious selves, exiling us to a temporary state akin to madness we slowly make our way back from. The emotional hardship we endure there may indeed prove our fitness to parent offspring, as evolutionists suggest.

Many of us will, though, nod our heads upon hearing all this and then immediately turn to writers, musicians, and filmmakers for a fuller understanding of what it means to passionately long for and love another. Here we will find explanations that ennoble as much as inform, that give voice to the profound doubt, yearning, ecstasy, and pain we have known firsthand. Love in this sense is a very necessary social construct. The books, movies, and songs remind us of how innately human the experience is.

It in fact can be an unattainable ideal, a manipulative game, a punishing obsession, a marriage of convenience, a celebration of friendship and caring, and a stern religious duty. We may seek love out to bolster our self-esteem, to find our "better half," to validate our values and attitudes, to be sexually gratified, to truly know and be known by someone, to temporarily forget our fundamental existential loneliness, or to simply have someone to talk to who cares. Some will find what they are looking for, others not; their love is requited and unrequited, found and lost. And sociologists will dispassionately document and explain our collective experience of each, enlightening us all the more about the hows and the whys of love.

TERMS & CONCEPTS

Agape: A form of love that emphasizes the spiritual over the physical and the needs of others to the exclusion of one's own.

Conjugal Love: A love relationship in which friendship and sharing matter much more than passion and possessiveness.

Dyadic Relationship: Couples.

Eros: Love inspired by a preconceived ideal of physical beauty.

Ideal-Types: Alike social behaviors grouped together in broad, general categories for the purpose of comparison and contrast.

Ludus: A form of romantic love that extols game-playing in the service of self-gratification.

Mania: Obsessive romantic love characterized by possessiveness, physical longing, and emotional insecurity.

Pragma: Love based on primarily on compatibility and mutual ambition for status, wealth, and social approval where compatibility is the most aspect.

Romantic Love: A concept of love that evolved during the fourteenth century in Europe, characterized by yearning and self-sacrifice for an idealized and often unapproachable other that has since evolved to describe intense sexual and emotional desire for and mental preoccupation with another person real and imagined.

Storge: Friendship-based love.

Symbolic Interactionism: A school of sociological thought that considers meaning to be a culturally-transmitted social construct.

Bibliography

Bianchi-Demicheli, F., Grafton, S., & Ortigue, S. (2006). "The power of love on the human brain." *Social Neuroscience, 1* (2), 90–103.

Centers, R. (1975). "Attitude similarity-dissimilarity as a correlate of heterosexual attraction and love." *Journal of Marriage & Family, 37* (2), 305–312.

Critelli, J., Myers, E., & Loos, V. (1986). "The components of love: Romantic attraction and sex role orientation." *Journal of Personality, 54* (2), 354.

Dion, K., & Dion, K. (1975). "Self-esteem and romantic love." *Journal of Personality, 43* (1), 39–57.

Driscoll, R., Davis, K., & Lipetz, M. (1972). "Parental interference and romantic love: The Romeo and Juliet effect." *Journal of Personality & Social Psychology, 24* (1), 1–10.

Forgas, J., & Dobosz, B. (1980). "Dimensions of romantic involvement: Towards a taxonomy of heterosexual relationships." *Social Psychology Quarterly, 43* (3), 290–300.

Harrison, M. A., & Shortall, J. C. (2011). "Women and men in love: Who really feels it and says it first?" *Journal of Social Psychology, 151* (6), 727–736.

Klesse, C. (2011). "Notions of love in polyamory—elements in a discourse on multiple loving." *Laboratorium: Russian Review of Social Research, 3* (2), 4–25.

Kokab, S., & Asir Ajmal, M. M. (2012). "Perception of love in young adults." *Pakistan Journal of Social & Clinical Psychology, 10* (1), 44–49.

Krain, M. (1977). "Effects of love and liking in premarital dyads." *Sociological Focus, 10* (3), 249–262.

Lee, J. (1975). "The romantic heresy." *Canadian Review of Sociology & Anthropology, 12* (4 Part 2), 514.

Marazziti, D. (2005). "The neurobiology of love." *Current Psychiatry Reviews, 1* (3), 331–335.

McClanahan, K., Gold, J., Lenney, E., Ryckman, R., & Kulberg, G. (1990). "Infatuation and attraction to a dissimilar other: Why is love blind?" *Journal of Social Psychology, 130* (4), 433–445.

Rubin, Z. (1970). "Measurement of romantic love." *Journal of Personality & Social Psychology, 16* (2), 265–273.

"Socialization, identity, and interaction: Understanding socialization, identity, and interaction." (2003). In, *Sociology.* Oxford University Press.

"Theories and theorizing: Academic sociology established." (2003). In, *Sociology.* Oxford University Press.

Watts, S., & Stenner, P. (2005). "The subjective experience of partnership love: A Q Methodological study." *British Journal of Social Psychology, 44* (1), 85–107.

Winch, R. (1955). "The theory of complementary needs in mate-selection: A test of one kind of complementariness." *American Sociological Review, 20* (1), 52–56.

Suggested Reading

Bailey, K., & Nava, G. (1989). "Psychological kinship, love, liking: Preliminary validity data." *Journal of Clinical Psychology, 45* (4), 587–594.

Ben-Ari, A., Lavee, Y., & Gal, Z. (2006). "Midlife perspectives on falling in love: The dialectic of unique experiences." *Journal of Adult Development, 13* (3/4), 118–123.

Buss, D., Shackelford, T., Kirkpatrick, L., & Larsen, R. (2001). "A half century of mate preferences: The cultural evolution of values." *Journal of Marriage & Family, 63* (2), 491.

Duvall, E. (1964, May). "Adolescent Love as a Reflection of Teen-Agers' Search for Identity." *Journal of Marriage & Family, 26* (2), 226–229.

Hassebrauck, M., & Buhl, T. (1996). "Three-dimensional love." *Journal of Social Psychology, 136* (1), 121–122.

Heller, K. (2004). "My choice of a lifetime: finding true love in a sociological imagination." *Human Architecture: Journal of the Sociology of Self-Knowledge, 3* (1/2), 21–31.

Jacobs, J. (1992). "Facilitators of romantic attraction and their relation to love-style." *Social Behavior & Personality: An International Journal, 20* (3), 227–234.

Knobloch, L., Moller, L., & Carpenter, K. (2007). "Using the relational turbulence model to understand negative emotion within courtship." *Personal Relationships, 14* (1), 91–112.

Lacey, R., Reifman, A., Scott, J., Harris, S., & Fitzpatrick, J. (2004). "Sexual-moral attitudes, love styles, and mate selection." *Journal of Sex Research, 41* (2), 121–128.

Lewandowski, G., Jr., J., & Aron, A. (2004). "Distinguishing arousal from novelty and challenge in initial romantic attraction between strangers." *Social Behavior & Personality: An International Journal, 32* (4), 361–372.

Salter, A. (2011). "Virtually yours: Desire and fulfillment in virtual worlds." *Journal of Popular Culture, 44* (5), 1120– 1137.

Solomon, R. (2002). "Reasons for love." *Journal for the Theory of Social Behaviour, 32* (1), 1.

Francis Duffy, MBA

Contemporary Theories of Sexual Orientation

ABSTRACT

Traditional theories on sexual orientation have argued for biological causation and then focused on finding evidence for this perspective in physiological and psychological studies. While some evidence suggests that biology may play some small role in sexual orientation development, theorists recognize the complex interplay between nature and nurture in the formation of both gender orientation and sexual orientation. After a discussion of research on gender orientation, this article presents a multidisciplinary review of the literature on sexual orientation development. As greater professional and public acceptance of homosexuality and bisexuality emerge in our culture, our awareness of the wide diversity of sexual expression is expanding.

OVERVIEW

The nature versus nurture debate is a central theme in any review of contemporary theories of sexual orientation. It centers on the question of whether a person is born heterosexual or homosexual, or if people develop their sexual orientation through childhood interactions with family members and playmates. In part, the answer to this question depends upon how one approaches the issue. Experts in genetics, neurology, and related biological sciences tend to develop perspectives based upon more innate physical qualities that impact human behavior, while social scientists and psychologists tend to focus on human interactions as a basis of social development. Likewise, some individual scholars view one factor as causal in the development of sexual orientation, while others seek a more integrated theoretical analysis that considers several factors.

Thus, although the balance of this article looks at the various factors individually, it is important to consider how complex and interconnected biology and psychology can be. It is also important to consider how most scholars believe that one's sexual orientation is not a fixed or absolute concept. Rather, they believe that one's sexual orientation can differ over time and according to one's life experiences. Many people, for example, have had both homosexual and heterosexual experiences during their lifetime. And though a person may identify himself or herself as homosexual, heterosexual, or bisexual, even this self-definition may differ from that of an outside observer. In thinking about sexual orientation, therefore, it is important to keep one's mind open to the complexities of the human experience.

One important way to deepen our understanding of sexual orientation is to first expand our knowledge of gender orientation. Traditionally, people in Western cultures have believed that there are two genders: male and female. However, Harbeck (2007) and others have argued that "male" and "female" represent two extreme points on a continuum of gender identity. Their work suggests that this continuum can be described in an integrated theory that takes into account a variety of causal factors like:

- Genetic and other biological predispositions;
- Biological and environmental modifications (hormones, surgery, pollution);
- Developmental experiences (family, peers, social institutions);
- Psychological dispositions/trait factors (temperament, identity, lifespan);
- Social and cultural structures and process (masculinity, femininity, gender, and other learned behaviors); and
- Contextual factors (availability, acceptability).

The World Health Organization, for example, indicates that in approximately one out of every 2,000 births in this country, the baby is born visibly intersex. In these cases, a specialist in sex differentiation is to be consulted in order to begin the process of defining the baby's gender. Similar anomalies can be found in internal sex organs, genetic markers, and other neurological and biological materials. Scholars have referred to these conditions as "intersex" or "disorders of sex development," but those eager to abolish the negative connotations of these labels use the phrase "variations of sex development."

While we know that a significant number of individuals have physiological gender variations, little is known about the number of individuals who have psychological gender variations or identify with a gender variation. Additionally, we now know that environmental pollution plays a role in gonad function as well as in the sex development of various species such as green mussels, frogs, sea bass, roaches, rodents, and swallows (Nagarajappa, 2006; Thomas, 1982; Sitzlar, 2008). Thus, some scholars have begun arguing that gender may be more diverse than previously thought, and may even be becoming more diverse.

Thus, bridging the discussion of gender identity and sexual orientation is the topic of intersexuality or transgender identities. Transgender is an umbrella term that encompasses both transvestites and transsexuals. Transvestites are individuals who wear the clothing normally ascribed to the opposite gender in a given society, and adopt the stereotypical mannerisms associated with that gender. For example, a male transvestite might wear a dress, high heeled shoes, and makeup to adopt the persona of a woman. Individuals may engage in this behavior for emotional satisfaction, sexual arousal, or self-identification. Since their pleasure in wearing clothes of the opposite gender is not necessary linked with sexual orientation, transvestites may be heterosexual, homosexual or bisexual.

Transsexuals, or intersexuals, are individuals who identify with a physical sex different from the one with which they were born and raised. These individuals may have aspects of the male/female duality or they may have been assigned the wrong gender at birth. Transsexuals may choose to ignore these feelings, or they may choose to wear the clothing of and pass as the opposite gender. They may or may not choose to undergo gender reassignment through hormone therapy or surgery. Transsexuals and their advocates are somewhat divided over this last point, as some question the need for hormone therapy and surgery to change the gender of an individual, arguing that this process enhances traditional, distorted views of gender in our society rather than supports gender diversity. In terms of their sexual orientation, transgendered individuals who are attracted to women express gynephilia, while individuals attracted to men express androphilia.

FURTHER INSIGHTS

Sexual orientation can be defined in many ways, but the most familiar definitions are also the legal definitions: heterosexuality, homosexuality and bisexuality. Heterosexuality is a sexual attraction to individuals of the opposite gender, while homosexuality is an attraction to individuals of the same gender. Bisexuality is an attraction to both men and women, although some individuals choose to use the words "polysexual" or "pansexual" to avoid bisexuality's implicit assumption that only two genders exist. Asexuality is a lack of sexual interest altogether. In 2013 a Gallup study estimated that the nationwide average of lesbian, gay, bisexual, and transgender individuals in the United States is between 3.5 and 4 percent; estimates in different states range from 1.7 percent (North Dakota) to 10 percent (District of Columbia).

Kauth described sexual orientation as "a biologically based processing bias continuously exploited or challenged by social and cultural conditions," taking into account both sides of the nature versus nurture debate on sexual orientation (2000; LeVay, 2008). Rather than identifying any one factor as a determinant of sexual orientation, such a definition takes in several factors: anatomical brain studies, functional brain studies, genetics/chromosomal, birth order, anatomical, cognitive, developmental, psychoanalytic theories, behaviorism/socialization, sexual experiences, social constructionism, sociocultural, and personal identity.

Anatomical Brain Studies

A number of studies on the anatomical aspects of sexual orientation have focused on the brain. One of the more well-known studies was conducted by LeVay, who argued that the hypothalamus, a part of the underside of the brain which controls hormone production and release, is different in gay and straight men (1991). However LeVay's critics have pointed out that since all of his research was conducted on the brains of individuals who died of AIDS, the results of his study may be invalid. More recently, Savic and Lindstrom suggested that when comparisons are made of left and right brain hemispheres, differences can be seen between heterosexual and homosexual individuals (2008). Similarly, Gorski reported that "the anterior commissure, a bundle of fibers running across the midline of the brain, is larger in women and gay men than heterosexual men" (1978; Odent & Odent, 2006, ¶10).

LeVay has suggested that these differences in brain anatomy may be caused by some prenatal factor (like hormone levels) that affects the fetus' development and, thus, the baby's sexual orientation (2003, 2008). This theory is called the early fixation hypothesis. While studies have failed to find a link between adult's hormone levels and sexual orientation, Dorner and others have argued that prenatal hormone levels may impact the sexual orientation of an individual in later life (1969). Although little empirical evidence is offered, it is the case that certain medical conditions (like congenital adrenal hyperplasia, in which high levels of testosterone-like hormones masculinize external genitalia in female fetuses) and drugs can impact a fetus' physiological gender characteristics. However, so far no research has proven that these conditions or drugs actually increase the person's likelihood of being homosexual (LeVay, 2003, 2008). In fact, research suggests that the majority of women affected by congenital adrenal hyperplasia identity as heterosexual, which would seem to disprove the theory that female fetal exposure to male hormones can cause lesbianism (Peplau, Spaulding, Conley, & Veniegas, 1999).

Functional Brain Studies

Preliminary studies of brain function have found minor differences between heterosexual and homosexual individuals in terms of startle response, sounds produced by the inner ear, sexual arousal and brain activity, neurotransmitter function, and odor response (LeVay, 2003, 2008).

Genetics/Chromosomal

In his studies of male homosexuals in Mormon populations that maintained excellent geologies, Hamer reported that individuals with a certain constellation of genetic material at the Xq28 gene loci on the X chromosome had a 70% likelihood of being gay (1993). If that composition was not present, individuals had a 100% likelihood of not being gay. Note that the gene loci was on the male's X chromosome, meaning that this genetic characteristic is carried in the mother's DNA. However, similar studies conducted on women failed to find any significance, and efforts to replicate Hamer's findings have been inconclusive (Hamer & Copeland, 1994; Hamer & Hu, 1993; LeVay 2008). Another researcher, Mustanski, reported finding evidence of linkage with sexual orientation at markers 8p12, 7q36, and 10q26, with the latter two being affected by equal parts of maternal and paternal genetic influences (LeVay, 2008).

In their review of the literature on genetic studies of twins, Bearman and Bruckner concluded that, while genetics may play a part in sexual orientation, its role is dwarfed by those of other factors, and sexual orientation is more likely socially constructed than biologically determined (2002). Other studies of twins have found that while monozygotic twins are more likely to have the same sexual orientation, this tendency does not prove that sexual orientation is primarily biological (Peplau, et. al., 1999; LeVay, 2008). Studies of siblings have found that lesbians do seem to report a greater number of siblings who also are gay, but, again, this correlation does not prove that genetics is the exclusive cause of homosexuality (Peplau, et. al., 1999).

Birth Order

Focusing on birth order as a causal factor, Blanchard and Klassen reported that gay men are more likely to be among the youngest of their siblings and to have more older brothers than heterosexual men (1997; LeVay, 2008). They argued that because mothers develop male-specific antibodies during each pregnancy with a male child and because the antigens involved in brain masculinization gradually grow weaker with each pregnancy, subsequent male children are more likely homosexually oriented.

Anatomical

Several studies have concluded that lesbian women's index fingers are shorter than their ring finger, whereas most women's ring and index fingers are about the same length (LeVay, 2008). Another study found a difference in fingerprint patterns between straight and gay men, but these findings have not been replicated (LeVay, 2008).

Cognitive

Other researchers have focused on finding differences in how heterosexual and homosexual individuals acquire knowledge through reasoning, intuition and perception. LeVay provided a detailed review of their findings in areas such as:

- Visuospatial tasks (straight men were slightly more able than gay men),
- Object location memory (gay men did better than straight men, and lesbian and straight women were equal),
- Verbal fluency (mixed results, but slight advantage to gay men and lesbians),
- Aggressiveness (gay men were less aggressive than straight men, and lesbian and straight women were equal), and
- Handedness (homosexuals were more likely to be left-handed than their heterosexual counterparts) (LeVay, 2008).

However, these findings are not consistent overall.

Developmental

Daryl Bem, a psychologist from Cornell University, has become known for his argument that children's biologically determined temperaments can cause some to be attracted to activities that are associated with a gender role other than the one that corresponds to their physical sex. Thus, a temperamentally nurturing boy may prefer to play with dolls, or a temperamentally aggressive girl may prefer to play football. Bem argued that because of these temperamental and activity differences, these children will grow up feeling different from their own gender groups and eventually eroticize these differences, leading to same-sex attraction. Bem's theory is based upon numerous studies which suggest that gay males, in particular, report not conforming to gender roles during childhood. However, much of Bem's theoretical framework is based upon an analysis of male behavior, so it may not be applicable to female sexual orientation development (Swidey, 2005).

One interesting related argument put forth by Bem is that sexual orientation need not be based upon gender (Bem, 1996). Attachment theories of sexual orientation development hold that individuals feel sexual arousal toward others and then develop attachment bonds that define their sexual orientation (Zeifman & Hazan, 1997). In other words, a male would feel sexual arousal toward women and then develop attachment bonds that lead to heterosexuality. However, this theory would seem to be contrary to the experience of many lesbian women, who report the opposite experience of forming a strong emotional attachment to another woman that then develops into a sexual relationship (Peplau, et. al., 1999).

Psychoanalytic Theories

Inversion theory is based upon Freudian psychosexual developmental analysis. Under this theory, boys are thought to become homosexual if they have a close relationship with a dominant mother while their father is distant or absent. Girls, on the other hand, become lesbian because they have a strong, unconscious dislike of their mothers or because of penis envy (LeVay, 2008). However, analyst Richard Isay has argued that a same-gender parent's negative behavior toward their pre-gay child may be a response to the child's atypical gender characteristics rather than the cause of them (1996, 1989).

Though not many scholars uphold inversion theory today, it is still important since it has guided biological studies of homosexuality with its assumptions that gay men are physically and emotionally effeminate and lesbians physically and emotionally masculine. Much of the traditional literature on sexual orientation builds upon this premise, seeking affirmation of the view that atypical gender characteristics explain sexual orientation. Over the decades, dozens of studies have compared the masculine and feminine qualities of lesbians and heterosexual women, and a good number have concluded that lesbians score higher on masculine traits such as straightforwardness, sense of honor, direct speech, and voice inflexions (Peplua, 1999). However, others have shown that when study participants are matched upon socioeconomic factors, educational level, and feminist beliefs, the differences between lesbians and heterosexual women are nonexistent.

Behaviorism/Socialization

Behaviorist and socialization theories suggest that gender and sexual orientation are learned behaviors which are consciously and unconsciously inculcated by parents, peers, and society at large. However, critics of these theories argue that while gender identity and roles, sexual orientation, sexual attitudes and beliefs, and sexual knowledge are influenced by cultural attitudes and values, alone they cannot account for homosexuality, since most homosexual individuals are raised by heterosexual role models. Similarly, studies have shown that homosexual parents are no more likely to socialize their child to be homosexual than are heterosexual parents.

Sexual Experiences

Some individuals argue that early sexual experiences can influence one's sexual orientation. A young woman, who has been raped, for example, may be averse to sex with men and become lesbian. Similarly, a young boy who sexually experiments with other boys may come to define himself as homosexual. However, critics charge that this explanation fails to describe most people's sexual experimentation and development. Most scholars believe that this theory is not credible.

Social Constructionism

Others follow Foucault in claiming that gender, gender roles, and sexual orientation are labels, which society imposes upon the individual and which the individual internalizes (1978). As such, sexual orientation labels do not arise from within the individual, but are adopted by him or her (LeVay, 2008).

Sociocultural

In her cross-cultural review of women's sexuality, Blackwood suggested that cultures vary significantly in the extent to which they regulate women's lives, sexuality, and reproduction (1986). For instance, marriage, whether arranged or freely chosen, is often the expected outcome for women in most cultures. Some cultures, however, are accepting of sexual relationships between women who are married to men, as long as they are inconspicuous and informal (Peplua, 1999). Khan, for example, reported that in modern Pakistan, if a woman refuses to marry she is a "pariah," but if she marries and engages in sexual relationships with women, these relationships are overlooked as long as she fulfills her marital and familial obligations (1997).

Personal Identity

Despite whatever role the developmental or physiological processes play in sexual orientation, more and more scholars are emphasizing that it is the individual's self-knowledge, self-acceptance, and identity that ultimately defines his or her sexual orientation. Their research has led them to observe that some individuals may identify with different sexual orientations at various times in their lives, while others may adhere to a heterosexual identity, though they may have had numerous homosexual encounters. For instance, in his study of the "tearoom trade" (sex between men in public restrooms) Humphrey's found that a majority of his study's participants were married and did not define themselves as homosexual (Humphreys, 1970). Some would argue that such men are closeted gay men, but an increasing number of scholars would accept the study participants' heterosexual self-definition by separating personal identity from sexual behavior.

CONCLUSION

Can sexual orientation be changed? Although several "therapeutic" techniques have been applied to alter sexual orientation, there is no evidence that this reparative or conversion therapy works. In fact, the American Psychiatric Association suggests that reparative therapy has numerous risks, including depression, anxiety, and self-destructive behavior. Aversion therapy, for example, may teach one to curb homosexual behaviors, but behavior is only one aspect of an individual's sexual orientation. Those who undergo this sort of therapy may continue to have same-gender feelings of attraction and arousal. These types of therapies generally stem from the belief that homosexuality is a disorder. While this belief remains intact in some socially conservative segments of society, there is a growing professional and public awareness that sexual orientation and gender orientation are multifaceted and complex expressions of human life.

TERMS & CONCEPTS

Androphilia: Having a sexual attraction to males.

Bisexual: Having a sexual attraction to both males and females.

Gonad: An organ that produces reproductive cells, or gametes. In males, these organs are the testes; in females, they are the ovaries.

Gynephilia: Having a sexual attraction to females.

Heterosexual: Having a sexual attraction to members of the opposite sex.

Homosexual: Having a sexual attraction to members of one's own sex.

Monozygotic Twins: Twins who developed from a single egg (also called identical twins).

Neurology: The study of the nervous system.

Polysexual: Having a sexual attraction to both males and females. Some individuals prefer to use this term rather than "bisexual" because they do not believe that there are only two genders.

Bibliography

Bearman, P.S., & Brückner, H. (2002). "Opposite-sex twins and adolescent same-sex attraction." *American Journal of Sociology*, 107, 1179-1205.

Bem, D. (1996). "Exotic becomes erotic: A developmental theory of sexual orientation." *Psychological Review*, 103, 320-335.

Blackless, M., Charuvastra, A., Derryck, A., Fausto-Sterling, A., Lauzanne, K., & Lee, E. (2000). "How sexually dimorphic are we? Review and synthesis." *American Journal of Human Biology*, 12, 151-166.

Collier, K., Bos, H., Merry, M., & Sandfort, T. (2013). "Gender, ethnicity, religiosity, and same-sex sexual attraction and the acceptance of same-sex sexuality and gender non-conformity." *Sex Roles*, 68 (11/12), 724–737.

Dorner, G., & Staudt, J. (1969). "Perinatal structural sex differentiation of the hypothalamus in rats." *Neuroendocrinology*, 4, 278-281.

Frankowski, B., Kaplan, D., Diaz, A., Fisher, M., Klein, J. D., Yancy, W. S., et. al. (2004). "Sexual orientation and adolescents." *Pediatrics*, 113, 1827-1832.

Gorski, R., Gordon, J., Shryne, J., & Santham, A. (1978). "Evidence for a morphological difference within the medial preoptic area of the rat brain." *Brain Research*, 148, 333-346.

Hamer, D., & Copeland, P. (1994). *The science of desire: The search for the gay gene and the biology of behavior.* New York: Simon & Schuster.

Hamer, D., Hu, S., Magnuson, V., & Pattatucci, A. (1993). "A linkage between DNA markers on the X chromosome and male sexual orientation." *Science*, 261 (5119): 321-327.

Harbeck, K. M. (2007). *Gay, lesbian, bisexual, and transgender youth in American schools and colleges.* Malden, MA: Amethyst Press.

Humphreys, L. (1970). *Tearoom trade: Impersonal sex in public places.* Chicago: Aldine-Atherton.

Isay, R. (1989). *Being homosexual: Gay men and their development.* New York: Farrar, Straus and Giroux.

Isay, R. (1996). *Becoming gay: The journey to self-acceptance.* New York: Pantheon.

Kauth, M. (2000). *True nature: A theory of sexual attraction.* The Netherlands: Springer.

Khan, B. (1997). "Not-so-gay life in Pakistan in the 1980s and 1990s." In S. Murray & W. Roscoe (Eds.), *Islamic homosexualities.* New York: New York University Press.

Korchmaros, J. D., Powell, C., & Stevens, S. (2013). "Chasing sexual orientation: A comparison of commonly used single-indicator measures of sexual orientation." *Journal Of Homosexuality,* 60, 596–614.

LeVay, S. (1991). "A difference in hypothalamic structure between heterosexual and homosexual men." *Science,* 253(5023), 1034-1037.

Nagarajappa, Ganguly, A., & Goswami, U. (2006). "DNA damage in male gonads of Green mussel (Perna vividis) upon exposure to tobacco products." *Ecotoxicology,* 15, 365-369.

Odent, M., Odent, P. (2006). "Genesis of sexual orientation." *WombEcology.* http://www.wombecology.com/orientation.html

Peplau, L., Spalding. L., Conley, T., & Veniegas, R. (1999). "The development of sexual orientation in women." *Annual Review of Sex Research,* 10, 70-100.

Reitman, D. (2006). "Sexuality: Sexual orientation." http://emedicine.medscape.com/article/917792-Overview

Savic, I., & Lindström, P. (2008). "PET and MRI show differences in cerebral asymmetry and functional connectivity between homo- and heterosexual subjects." *Proceedings of the National Academy of Sciences,* 105, 9403-9408.

Sitzlar, M., Mora, M., Fleming, J., Bazer, F., Bickham, J., & Matson, C. (2008, August). "Potential effects of environmental contaminants on P450 aromatase activity and DNA damage in swallows from the Rio Grande and Somerville, Texas." *Ecotoxicology.*

Swidey, N. (2005, August 14). "What makes people gay?" *The Boston Globe.* http://www.boston.com/

Thomas, J., Curto, K., & Thomas, M. (1982). "MEHP/DEHP: Gonadal toxicity and effects on rodent accessory sex organs." *Environmental Health Perspectives,* 45, 85 - 88.

Warner, L., & Shields, S. (2013). "The intersections of sexuality, gender, and race: Identity research at the crossroads." *Sex Roles,* 68 (11/12), 803–810.

Zeifman, D., & Hazan, C. (1997). "Attachment: The bond in pair-bonds." In J. A. Simpson & D. T. Kenricks (Eds.), *Evolutionary social psychology.* Hillside, NJ: Erlbaum.

Suggested Reading

Balen, A., Creighton, S., Davies, M., MacDougall, J., & Stanhope, R. (Eds.). (2004). *Paediatric and adolescent gynaecology: A multidisciplinary approach.* Cambridge, UK: Cambridge University Press.

Diamant, L. & McAnulty, R.D. (Eds.). (1995). *The psychology of sexual orientation, behavior, and identity: A handbook.* Westport, CT: Greenwood.

Dreger, A. D. (1998). "Ambiguous sex—or ambivalent medicine? Ethical issues in the treatment of intersexuality." *Hastings Center Report,* 28, 24-35.

Dreger, A. D. (1998). *Hermaphrodites and the medical invention of sex.* Cambridge, MA: Harvard University Press.

Fjelstrom, J. (2013). "Sexual orientation change efforts and the search for authenticity." *Journal of Homosexuality,* 60, 801–827.

Harbeck, K. M. (Ed.). (1991). *Coming out of the classroom closet: Gay and lesbian students, teachers, and curricula.* New York: Haworth.

Harbeck, K. M. (1997). *Gay and lesbian educators: Personal freedoms/Public constraints.* Malden, MA: Amethyst Press.

Intersex Society of North America. (2006). "Clinical guidelines for the management of disorders of sex development in childhood." Rohnert Park, CA: Intersex Society of North America.

LeVay, S. (1993). *The sexual brain.* Cambridge, MA: MIT Press.

LeVay, S. (1996). *Queer science: The use and abuse of research into homosexuality.* Cambridge, MA: MIT Press.

Money, J. (1988). *Gay, straight, and in-between: The sexology of sexual orientation.* New York: Oxford UP.

Priebe, G., & Svedin, C. (2013). "Operationalization of three dimensions of sexual orientation in a national survey of late adolescents." *Journal Of Sex Research,* 50, 727–738.

Karen M. Harbeck, Ph.D., J.D.

Cross-Cultural Perspectives on Gender

ABSTRACT

As economics becomes more globalized, the issue of gender roles remains central to the understanding political and economic evolution. In order to understand cross-cultural differences related to gender, it is important that appropriate research instruments be developed. These research methodologies will support social scientists in the task of better understanding the nature, place, and contribution of gender roles to culture and society.

OVERVIEW

In terms of Western historical tradition, the concept of gender—or the psychological, social, cultural, and behavioral characteristics associated with being female or male—has traditionally been considered unalterably defined by physiology. Males, being the bigger and stronger of the sexes, were taught that they had a biological imperative not only to propagate the species, but to protect it. As a result, boys were taught from an early age to be aggressive, independent, dominant, and achieving. Women, on the other hand, were thought to be limited by their reproductive biology, in particular the constraints placed on them (or believed to be placed on them) by menstruation, pregnancy, childbirth, and lactation. As a result, girls were taught from an early age to be nurturing, sensitive, emotional, and passive. Of course, there have been exceptions to these gender stereotypes throughout history, and many well-known examples of men and women who eschewed accepted gender roles and made their own way in the world. However, such examples were typically looked on as aberrations—exceptions that proved the rule rather than broke it.

Cultural Gender Perspectives

Considerations of gender roles and identity were greatly impacted by the work of Margaret Mead and her research with the native peoples of New Guinea. Her work helped overturn the notion of the biological imperative for gender stereotypes. In the Tchambuli culture of New Guinea, gender roles for women include doing the fishing and manufacturing, as well as controlling the power and economic life of the community. The Tchambuli women also take the lead in initiating sexual relations. On the other hand, Tchambuli men are dependent, flirtatious, and concerned with their appearance, often adorning themselves with flowers and jewelry. In addition, Tchambuli men have a great interest in art, games, and theatrics (Coon, 2001). If gender roles were completely biologically determined, the wide variation between American and Tchambuli gender roles would not be possible, because the physical biology of males is the same in both cultures. In response to the work of Mead and other sociologists, most social scientists reached the conclusion that culture and socialization also play a crucial role in gender role acquisition.

Not all cross-cultural gender role differences are quite as glaring as the comparison between traditional Western culture and the Tchambuli, however. Chuang and Cheng (1994), for example, performed a cross-cultural study to examine differences in gender role attitudes between Chinese and American students. Specifically, the researchers were interested in whether or not these were gender differences in attitudes towards women and gender roles and whether or not they were cultural differences in these attitudes. Subjects in the study came from a predominantly white state university in North Carolina and from the national nniversity in Taiwan. The subjects were given a set of survey instruments (translated into Chinese for the Chinese subjects) that examined attitudes towards women, marital roles, social interaction, male preference (for female subjects only), and expressivity (for male subjects only). Consistent with previous work in this area, the researchers found that all female subjects in both cultures desire to be more equal whereas males desired to continue playing a dominant role in society. The study also found that the Chinese subjects tended to be more conservative than the American subjects and that the Chinese women preferred masculine, dominant males more strongly than did their American counterparts.

Generational & Ethnic Gender Perspectives

International boundaries are not the only parameters that define cultures. Different generations have their own gender cultures as well. To this end, Franco, Sabattini, and Crosby (2004) explore the associations among gender-related ideologies, values, and behaviors and Latino and White families in the United States. Their work examines the correspondence among attitudes, values, and behaviors from two different ethnic groups in order to determine whether or not daughters perceive that their mothers and fathers differ in their gender-based ideology and commitments to gender roles. Subjects were given a survey that asked them to report on their perceptions of their mothers' and fathers' ideologies, values and behaviors. Other standard instruments were used to measure perceived gender role ideology, perceived personal values, perceived commitment to roles, and perceived behaviors of the parents. The results of the study indicated that Latinas were more likely than white respondents to indicate that they believe that their parents had traditional gender roles. Similarly, Latinas also believe that their parents exhibit a more traditional division of household labor. However, Latina participants did not differ significantly from white participants in their perceptions of the amount of time that their mother spent on parenting, although white participants did believe that their father spent more time parenting than did Latino participants.

The Effects of Time on Gender Perspectives

Gender roles also change and evolve within societies. If, as assumed by many theorists, gender role is largely a product of socialization and culture, it would be reasonable to assume that gender roles also will evolve to support these changes. Marini (1990) traces some of the changes between gender roles and the evolution of society from hunter-gatherers to industrialization. Prior to industrialization, the structures of work and family in societies were closely integrated. In such societies, large families were an economic asset because more children meant more workers within the family to plant, cultivate, and harvest. As a result, the reproductive role and productive work of mothers was valued in such societies. However, with the trend toward urbanization, gender roles also shifted. As agricultural productivity improved with greater dependence on tools and animals, women's labor was no longer as necessary for the success of the family farm. As a result, women shifted their focus to other activities, primarily within the home. With the onset of industrialization, institutions outside the family became the centers of productivity and workers left the home for employment. As new labor rights legislation limited the employment of children, they became more dependent on adults as caretakers. Combined with the fact that there was little demand for women's labor outside the home, this led to a greater degree of differentiation of labor within the role, which was absorbed into the gender roles.

APPLICATIONS

Difficulties in Gathering Data

Gathering data in the social sciences can be a challenging task. This is due in part to the fact that although one can in many cases observe and even quantify data regarding an individual's behavior, knowing only what the end behavior is does not explain why the individual behaves that way. For the most part, social scientists are interested in why behavior occurs so that they can better understand the underlying processes that resulted in that behavior and be better able to explain and predict future behavior. For example, suppose that two people are window-shopping on a lazy summer afternoon and the one person turns to the other asks if s/he would be interested in getting an ice cream. The second person politely demurs, and the two continue their leisurely stroll. As social scientists observing this interaction, all we know for certain is that the second person refused to get an ice cream. What we do not know is *why* that person refused. We could, for example, interpret this response to mean that the second person was not hungry at that time. However, a host of alternative explanations are also available. The person might not like ice cream, be lactose intolerant, be on a diet, not have sufficient funds on hand to purchase an ice cream cone at that moment, need to go home soon and not have time to enjoy an ice cream cone, be afraid that the mid-afternoon snack might spoil his/her dinner, or be saving money for another purchase that s/he wants more. The list of possible explanations is endless. Therefore, as social scientists, it would be difficult for us to draw any conclusions or make any generalizations based on this single event. Even if we observed the behavior multiple times in similar situations, we still would not know why the person refused to get an ice cream. Although we might be able to predict that the person would refuse to get an ice cream in a similar situation in the future, we would not know why this was true. Therefore, we would not be able to explain the individual's behavior. However, the goal of social science research is not only to predict behavior, but to explain it as well. For this reason, social scientists develop psychometric instruments that attempt to gather data or make measurements of the attitudes, behaviors, and other intangible mental factors that result in the observed behavior.

Gathering psychometric data about people's attitudes and opinions is a more complex task than gathering behavioral data. It is often difficult for us to articulate our own reasons for doing something, a fact that makes developing questions on a psychometric measurement instrument as difficult. Further, attitudes and opinions can be complex. Going back to the example of the ice cream, we might ask the person who refused whether or not s/he likes ice cream on a scale of 1 to 5. However, that question alone might not tell us whether the person only likes some flavors (which that particular ice cream parlor did not carry). Therefore, we would need to think through what we were really trying to ask, and develop a list of questions that the person could answer regarding the extent to which s/he likes ice cream. Further, different people might have different reasons for the same action. For example, although Person A might only like one flavor of ice cream and Person B might only like another. Person C, however, might all flavors of ice cream but not like the mouth feel of the brand sold at that particular store. To understand the whys of the refusal, therefore, we would have to take such layers of thinking into account. If we were performing our research in a cross-cultural situation, we would experience the further complicating factors such as language and cultural norms and expectations. For example, if we asked a person in Palermo whether or not s/he liked ice cream, we might receive a blank stare because in Italy people are more familiar with gelato, a similar frozen dessert. If we asked a New Guinea tribesperson the same question, s/he might have no idea what a frozen dessert in general was, let alone ice cream in particular.

The Importance of Cross-Cultural Research Tools

Gathering cross-cultural information about ice cream, of course, is much less difficult than gathering cross-cultural information about gender roles and stereotypes. Many researchers have written about the problems attendant on the performance of cross-cultural research regarding gender. There are a number of steps that can be taken in order to help design a psychometric instrument that will be useful in all cultures in which it is used. First, psychometric instruments intended to be used in cross-cultural settings should be designed with this in mind. In addition, such instruments need to be tested for reliability (the degree to which a data collection or assessment instrument consistently measures a characteristic or attribute) and validity (the degree to which a survey or other data collection instrument measures what it purports to measure) within all settings that they will be used. As discussed above, one cannot simply assume that a measurement instrumented designed based on the assumptions of one culture will validly collect data within a different cultural setting. To do this, it is important to have the input of someone who understands the culture (and language, if appropriate) well so that concepts can be expressed in such a way that the data truly measure what the researcher is interested in studying. Further, before an existing instrument that has been developed and validated in a single culture is assumed to be valid in another cultural situation, it must be first validated in that situation.

CONCLUSION

When one has spent one's entire life within a single culture, it is easy to believe that every culture has the same norms and expectations for behavior. This applies not only to the behaviors expected of everyone within a polite society, but also to the gender roles and stereotypes to which the sexes are expected to conform. However, social science research has found that far from being a biological imperative, gender roles and stereotypes are to a great extent a function of socialization and are culturally bound. Further, cross-cultural differences in gender roles are not only defined by international boundaries, but by cultural differences between generations and even ethnicities within a single society. Even within a single culture and generation, social roles can no longer be assumed to be stable: Many researchers have found that gender roles evolve over time, often moving toward more flexibility, adaptability, and androgyny.

Global Gender Knowledge

The cross-cultural aspects of gender roles and stereotypes is much more than an issue for idle contemplation by social scientists, however. There is a practical aspect to this area of study as well. As modern society becomes more and more global in nature and businesses need to learn to survive in cultures around the world, it is important to be able to understand and accommodate the gender role expectations of other societies without losing one's own identity. For example, some Asian countries expect women to be subservient and men to be dominant, and many Muslim counties expect women to wear a *hijab* and be under the protection of a male. In order to be successful in working with people of such cultures, members of Western societies need to understand these cultural assumptions. This does not necessarily mean that the Western individual needs to change to meet the same assumptions, but they must take them into account. Doing so can be a complex and diplomatic process that can only be successful if the gender role assumptions are known and understood.

The fact that there are differences in gender roles and stereotypes between cultures and that these roles and stereotypes may change over time raises a number of interesting issues. First, what is the purpose of gender roles within a culture? To some extent, gender roles must have originally developed in order to support the biological functions of the sexes and to ensure the continuation of the species. However, as societies evolve from being hunter-gatherers to being agrarian, preindustrial, industrial, and postindustrial, is the evolution of gender roles a necessity for the stability of society? Can a society tolerate multiple gender role paradigms (e.g., traditional male/female breakouts versus postmodern androgynous roles), or is it important for society that subcultures (e.g., ethnicities, religions) support the evolution of gender roles as well? At least within American society, there is still much heterogeneity of gender roles. In some quarters, only the traditional gender roles of nurturing, emotional female and aggressive, dominant male will suffice. In other quarters, however, anything goes and the belief is that each individual should be free to express his/her gender in whatever way the individual feels is appropriate. Social scientists are still pondering these and other questions about gender roles. Before they can be answered, however, much more research needs to be done.

TERMS & CONCEPTS

Androgyny: The presence of both feminine and masculine characteristics or traits in one individual.

Cross-Cultural: In the social sciences, cross-cultural refers to any methodological approach or research study that is used to better understand how specific social behaviors are practiced in different cultures.

Culture: A complex system of meaning and behavior that is socially transmitted and that defines a common way of life for a group or society. Culture includes the totality of behavior patterns, arts, beliefs, institutions, and other products of human work and thought of the society or group.

Ethnicity: A social construct used to describe a relatively large group of people that shares a common and distinctive culture such as common history, language, religion, norms, practices, and customs. Although members of an ethnic group may be biologically related, ethnicity is not the same as race.

Gender: Psychological, social, cultural, and behavioral characteristics associated with being female or male. Gender is defined by one's gender identity and learned gender role.

Gender Role: Separate patterns of personality traits, mannerisms, interests, attitudes, and behaviors that are regarded as "male" and "female" by one's culture. Gender role is largely a product of the way in which one was raised and may not be in conformance with one's gender identity.

Gender Stereotype: A culturally defined pattern of expected attitudes and behavior that are considered appropriate for one gender but not the other. Gender stereotypes tend to be simplistic and based not on the characteristics or aptitudes of the individual, but on over generalized perceptions of one gender or the other.

Norms: Standards or patterns of behavior that are accepted as normal within the culture.

Psychometrics: The science and process of mental measurement. The science of psychometrics comprises both the theory of mental measurement as well as the methodology for adequately and accurately capturing and individual's intangible attitude or opinion.

Sex: The biological aspects of being either female or male. Genetically, females are identified by having two X chromosomes and males by having an X and a Y chromosome. In addition, sex can typically be determined from either primary or secondary sexual characteristics. Primary sexual characteristics comprise the female or male reproductive organs (i.e., the vagina, ovaries, and uterus for females and the penis, testes, and scrotum for males). Secondary sexual characteristics comprise the superficial differences between the sexes that occur with puberty (e.g., breast development, hip broadening for women and facial hair and voice deepening for men).

Socialization: The process by which individuals learn to differentiate between what the society regards as acceptable versus unacceptable behavior and act in a manner that is appropriate for the needs of the society.

Society: A distinct group of people who live within the same territory, share a common culture and way of life, and are relatively independent from people outside the group. Society includes systems of social interactions that govern both culture and social organization.

Subject: A participant in a research study or experiment whose responses are observed, recorded, and analyzed.

Survey: (a) A data collection instrument used to acquire information on the opinions, attitudes, or reactions of people; (b) a research study in which members of a selected sample are asked questions concerning their opinions, attitudes, or reactions are gathered using a survey instrument or questionnaire for purposes of scientific analysis; typically the results of this analysis are used to extrapolate the findings from the sample to the underlying population; (c) to conduct a survey on a sample.

Bibliography

Chia, R. C., Moore, J. L., Lam, K. N., Chuang, C. J., & Cheng, B. S. (1994). "Cultural differences in gender role attitudes between Chinese and American students." *Sex Roles,* 31 (1/2), 23-30.

Coon, D. (2001). *Introduction to psychology: Gateways to mind and behavior* (9th ed.). Belmont, CA: Wadsworth/Thomson Learning.

de Lemus, S., Spears, R., Bukowski, M., Moya, M., & Lupiáñez, J. (2013). "Reversing Implicit Gender Stereotype Activation as a Function of Exposure to Traditional Gender Roles." *Social Psychology* (18649335), 44, 109-116.

Franco, J. L., Sabattini, L., & Crosby, F. J. (2004). "Anticipating work and family: Exploring the associations among gender-related ideologies, values, and behaviors and Latino and White families in the United States." *Journal of Social Issues,* 60, 755-766.

Kehn, A., & Ruthig, J. (2013). "Perceptions of Gender Discrimination across Six Decades: The Moderating Roles of Gender and Age." *Sex Roles,* 69(5/6), 289-296.

Marini, M. M. (1990). "Sex and gender: What do we know?" *Sociological Forum,* 5, 95-120.

Szymanowicz, A., & Furnham, A. (2013). "Gender and Gender Role Differences in Self- and Other-Estimates of Multiple Intelligences." *Journal Of Social Psychology,* 153, 399-423.

Suggested Reading

Gibbons, J. L., Hamby, B. A., & Dennis, W. D. (1997). "Researching gender-role ideologies internationally and cross-culturally." *Psychology of Women Quarterly,* 21, 151-170.

Harris, A. C. (1994). "Ethnicity as a determinant of sex role identity: A replication study of item selection for the Bem Sex Role Inventory." *Sex Roles,* 31 (3/4), 241-273.

Klos, L. (2013). "Is Weighing a 'Woman's Thing?' Associations Among Gender, Gender Role Orientation, and Self-Weighing Behavior." *Sex Roles,* 69 (1/2), 16-28.

McHugh, M. C. & Frieze, I. H. (1997). "The measurement of gender-role attitudes: A review and commentary." *Psychology of Women Quarterly,* 21, 1-16.

O'Neil, J. M. (2013). "Gender Role Conflict Research 30 Years Later: An Evidence-Based Diagnostic Schema to Assess Boys and Men in Counseling." *Journal Of Counseling & Development,* 91, 490-498.

Seguino, S. (2007). "Plus ça change? Evidence on global trends in gender norms and stereotypes." *Feminist Economics,* 13, 1-28.

Ruth A. Wienclaw, Ph.D.

Cross-Cultural Perspectives on Sexual Orientation

ABSTRACT

Same-sex relations have existed alongside heterosexual relations throughout history. In Western cultures, it is widely believed that same-sex orientation is an innate, physiological characteristic that cannot be changed. Nevertheless, sexual orientation as a concept is difficult to define. Throughout history, medical science, theologians, legal doctrine and cultural norms have all played a role in influencing how sexual orientation and/or same-sex relations are perceived.

OVERVIEW

Sexual orientation is defined as one's sexual preference for men, women, or both. Although history is replete with literary and religious references to same-sex relations as well as to relations between members of the opposite sex, some societies have not always accepted these different relations, or the sexual orientations of the people who engage in them, as equal (Asia-Europe Foundation, n.d.; Herek, 1997-2008). Indeed, same-sex relations have often been condemned, and those who claim a preference for these relations have been subjected to punishment and discrimination. While attitudes toward homosexuality and bisexuality have become more accepting, the treatment of individuals with sexual orientations toward members of their own sex remains controversial within some cultures.

Defining Sexual Orientations

Defining sexual orientation is not as simple as it seems. While there are common categories used to describe sexual orientation: heterosexual (prefers opposite sex), homosexual (prefers same sex), bisexual (enjoys both), for researchers, it is more difficult to define who fits into each category. This is because an individual's desires and attractions may not always match observable or reported behavior. Take the following cases as examples:

- Interviews have indicated that some men who consider themselves to be heterosexual have had sexual relations with men (Stokes, Miller & Mundhenk, 1998).
- Some men and women who are attracted to members of the same sex marry a member of the opposite sex in order to fulfill cultural expectations or to avoid stigmatization. Sometimes, they have same-sex relations on the side.
- In some cultures, men have reported having same-sex relations in their youth, but as adults, they reject these relations to enter into heterosexual marriages (Cardoso, 2008).

How should individuals in these cases be defined? Should a self-definition as heterosexual be considered accurate when a man says he prefers women but only has sex with men? If one has sex with both men and women, but prefers one over the other, what classification should be given? And what about experimentation in adolescence with members of the same sex? Does sexual orientation change over time? These are some of the complex issues that can arise when defining sexual orientation for the purposes of research and which may cause confusion when individuals are struggling to define their sexual orientation or identity (Stokes, Miller & Mundhenk, 1998).

Choice vs. Innate Quality

The question of whether people have same-sex relations as a result of a biologically determined and innate sexual orientation or as a choice made due to environmental factors which prohibit heterosexual relations or encourage opportunistic behavior is one of the core issues underlying controversies over same-sex relations. Because self-definitions do not always match behavior, and because behavior may be influenced by cultural attitudes toward same-sex relations, answering this question is not easy. Throughout history, theologians, medical professionals, and legal scholars have provided guidance on why people engage in same-sex relations and/or on how cultures should respond to individuals who engage in them. Despite this guidance, and perhaps because of it, today, there is no worldwide consensus on the roots of homosexual and bisexual behavior and even less agreement on how individuals who engage in such behavior should be treated.

APPLICATIONS

Cross-Cultural Research

One reason that many people around the world may view same-sex relations as a product of choice is that in many cultures, same-sex behavior appears to be connected to a lack of gender diversity. In cultures where women are secluded, young men may first experiment with sex through same-sex relations. The reasoning, perhaps, to explain this behavior is that men need to learn about sex in order to function as husbands; once married, this would no longer be necessary and the behavior would be deemed inappropriate. Evidence for this perspective comes from many studies, and was reported in a round-up by Cardoso (2008) that is partially summarized here and which illustrates the many reasons that cultures use to justify same-sex behavior.

- Melanesia—Serves to develop masculinity
- Azande (African people)—Compensates for the lack of women
- Brazil—Increases sexual options for poor fishermen
- India—Allows for the discharge of body tension among truck and taxi drivers
- Morocco—Comprises a stage of sexual development among boys aged 9–17

While the relative unavailability of women seems to account for some instances of same-sex relations among men, throughout all cultures there are women and men who choose homosexual relationships even when heterosexual partners are available. This fact has led cultures around the world to ask what their attitudes should be toward homosexuality in general. Many religions have condemned same-sex relations as being sinful and against the will of God (Asia-Europe Foundation, n.d.; Exodus International, 2005; Myers & Scanzoni, 2005). The natural order of the world, these religions contend, is for men to mate with women.

In some cultures, the violation of traditional gender roles is enough to condemn anyone who considers themselves homosexual to disgrace or punishment. Toro-Alfonso (2007) writes that for Latinos, the "machismo" ideology, which grants males superiority in the culture, is widely accepted. At the same time, the myth is held that gay men want to be women and lesbians want to be men.

In other cultures, a distinction is made between the active and passive actors in same-sex relations, and those who are passive may be considered differently than those who are active (Cardoso, 2008; Stokes, Miller & Mundhenk, 1998). For instance, in some cultures, only the passive actor is considered homosexual. Thus, in Brazil, Turkey, and Thailand, social categories exist for poor, working class boys who have sex with men that do not concur with traditional conceptions of homosexuality. Attitudes toward the passive actor are generally more negative in cultures that make such a distinction. While contemporary Western sociologists have separated sex from gender, with sex being a biologically determined characteristic and gender being socially constructed—meaning that for a man to display "feminine" characteristics is not necessarily unusual—this separation is not always recognized outside of academia or in non-Western cultures (Jandt & Hundley, 2007). Thus, gay men who demonstrate effeminate behaviors may be perceived as passive and as accepting the lower female status. While they may be socially tolerated, they are likely to be viewed more negatively than a masculine gay man who blends into the heterosexual crowd (Cardoso, 2008).

The distinction between active and passive homosexuals is a widespread phenomenon. Other countries which have created a social role for "heterosexual men" who like to have sex with homosexuals include Mexico, the Dominican Republic, Costa Rica, Iran, Argentina, Uruguay, Nicaragua, Syria, and Morocco (Cardoso, 2008).

Religious Perspectives

Perhaps the most influential force in the development of cultural attitudes toward sexual orientation is religion. Religion is the compass by which many people judge whether actions are right or wrong, and many of the world's major religions hold firm positions on whether homosexuality is moral. Indeed, world opinion is sharply divided along religious lines in regard to homosexuality. A 2013 Pew Global Attitudes survey found that large majorities in Africa, Asia, and the Middle East reported the belief that homosexuality should not be accepted by society. In Western Europe, on the other hand, similar majorities said homosexuality should be accepted. In the Americas, individuals indicated mixed views, marked by a significant age gap. Younger respondents were more likely than older respondents to accept homosexuality (Pew Research Center, 2013).

Religious doctrines reflect a diversity of opinion on homosexuality, with divisions occurring among denominations as well as between major religions. The following provides a brief overview of the most pertinent positions of some of the world's religions.

Buddhism

Buddhism does not have a position on homosexuality, but individuals have interpreted texts relating to sexuality and relationships in order to understand how a Buddhist might perceive sexual orientation. The Buddhist precept relating to sexuality is the *panca sila* or moral code. One of the precepts in this code says, "I will take the rule of training not to go the wrong way for sexual pleasure." The code allows the individual to define wrong way. Other Buddhist principles related to relationships indicate that if two adults are consenting, adultery is not involved, and the sexual act is made out of love, respect, loyalty and warmth, then no precepts are broken. While same-sex relationships are not condemned by Buddhism, the Buddha did advise against acts that would be against societal norms or that would raise legal sanctions because of the anxiety and embarrassment that such acts create (Asia-Europe Foundation, n.d.; Gay and Lesbian Counseling Service of New South Wales, n.d.).

Christianity

Multiple positions on homosexuality exist within the various denominations of the Christian faith. Evangelical Christians condemn homosexuality as a sin that goes against the will of God, and many Evangelicals believe that homosexuality can be reversed through reorientation or reparative therapy. Many other mainstream Protestant Christians tend to reject this view, however, believing that homosexuality is an innate, physiological characteristic that cannot be changed (Myers & Scanzoni, 2005). Many Protestants have argued that since God created many sexual orientations, homosexuals should be accepted into the church. Some churches, such as the United Church of Christ and the Episcopal Church, ordain active gays and lesbian members (Gay and Lesbian Counseling Service of New South Wales, n.d.). The Catholic Church formally opposes homosexuality, regarding same-sex attraction as "objectively disordered," according to the church catechism, and asserts that gay people "are called to chastity."

Hinduism

Hinduism does not provide clear guidance on homosexuality. Some interpreters have read the Dharma Shastras, which give three functions of sexuality, as supporting homosexual relations that are based on love. Others have said the text, which says procreation is one function of marriage, indicates that homosexuals should not be allowed to marry. The Manusmriti is a text that does not accept homosexuality, indicating the punishment that might follow from same-sex relations. On the other hand, Vatsyana, a Kama Sutra writer, says that homosexuality is accepted and allowed by the teachings.

Islam

Islam is a religion that condemns homosexuality based on interpretations of the Quran. Islamic law (Shari'ah) provides guidelines for how same-sex behavior is treated. Under this law, four separate legal schools provide slightly different guidelines for punishment, reformation, and standards of proof needed to convict someone of homosexuality. The Hanafite says that no physical punishment is necessary. The Hanbalite requires severe punishment, while the Sha'fi requires a minimum of four adult males as witness before a conviction is possible.

Judaism

Orthodox Jews are strongly against homosexuality, which they believe is forbidden by the Torah.

Conservative, Reconstructionist and Reform Jews have taken more moderate positions, providing support for various gay and lesbian rights.

Taoism

This Chinese religion is based on the beliefs that there is a natural balance in the universe represented by the opposites of yin-yang. Two positions are based on a Taoist viewpoint. One is that a yang-yang (male-male) or yin-yin (female-female) relationship would be out of balance. On the other hand, because all males have some yin and all females some yang, feminine behavior in males or vice versa could be considered a natural phenomenon and thus, homosexuality could be viewed as normal (Asia-Europe Foundation, n.d.; Gay and Lesbian Counseling Service of New South Wales, n.d.)..

Medical Perspectives

In Western cultures, the medical and mental health communities have become strong proponents of the view that sexual orientation is an innate, biological characteristic that cannot be changed. This view is a change from the medical community's earlier position, held from the late 1800s until the 1970s, that homosexuality was a disorder requiring treatment. Following years of research and treatments that failed to change desires or behaviors, the medical community removed homosexuality from its *Diagnostic and Statistical Manual of Mental Disorders* in 1973. Since then, the American Psychological Association, American Academy of Pediatrics, National Association of Social Workers, and the American Psychiatric Association have said that attempting to change one's sexual orientation through therapy can cause harm (Herek, 1997-2008; Myers & Scanzoni, 2005).

ISSUES

Homophobia & Legal Rights

Negative attitudes towards same-sex behavior may manifest themselves as homophobia. Homophobia is, technically, the fear of homosexuality and often leads individuals to reject or socially exclude those who claim gay, lesbian, or bisexual identities (Toro-Alfonso, 2007). Homophobic behaviors and attitudes can result in bullying and discrimination, such as unfair treatment toward homosexuals in the workplace, school, or elsewhere. Homophobia can also result in hate crimes, violent and/or other criminal actions committed against homosexuals. In some countries, widespread homophobic attitudes have been inscribed in the form of laws that make same-sex relations illegal or that deny rights such as marriage or adoption to same-sex couples.

Throughout history, many homosexual and bisexual individuals have hidden their identity in order to avoid negative societal repercussions. Their friends and family members may deny that their loved ones are different, or may accept it as long as it isn't mentioned. The fear of negative reactions to their identity can produce negative mental health effects. It can also make it more difficult for those struggling to understand their sexual orientation to accept a homosexual or bisexual identity (Stokes, Miller & Mundhenk, 1998).

In the past several decades, encouraged by medical views that sexual orientation is innate and normal, and inspired by other minority civil rights movements, gay, lesbian, bisexual, and transgender (LGBT) individuals, have become more politically organized. In the United States, the gay rights movement has been successful in achieving the decriminalization of sodomy and recognition of civil unions and gay marriage on a state-by-state basis since the 1960s, and nationwide based on Supreme Court rulings in 2003 (in the case of sodomy) and 2015 (in the case of gay marriage). Around the world, organizations have formed to advocate for gay rights, including the right to be free from discrimination, the right to civil unions and marriage, and the right to adopt.

These movements have brought sexual orientation into public view and brought about changes in cultural attitudes and behaviors. For instance, in the European Union (EU), wide-ranging anti-discrimination laws have been passed that include sexual orientation as a protected category.

TERMS & CONCEPTS

Bisexual: Describes someone who is sexually attracted to both men and women.

Gay: Synonym for homosexual, or sometimes specifically refers to homosexual men.

Gay rights movement: Umbrella term for the movement for civil rights for lesbian, gay, bisexual, and transgender (LGBT) individuals. This movement has extended around the world where many organizations are making the case for equal treatment for those of nontraditional sexual orientations.

Heterosexual: Describes someone who is sexually attracted to people of the opposite sex.

Homosexual: Describes someone who is sexually attracted to people of the same sex.

Homophobia: The fear of homosexuality.

Lesbian: A homosexual woman.

Reparative therapy: A type of counseling that attempts to change one's homosexual preferences and to replace them with heterosexual desires; sometimes called conversion therapy.

Transgender: Describes someone whose gender identity differs from the one they were assigned at birth; not directly relevant to discussions of sexual orientation.

Bibliography

Asia-Europe Foundation. (n.d.). "Coming out in dialogue: Policies and perceptions of sexual minority groups in Asia and Europe." http://www.civdialogue.asef.org/documents/briefingpaperfinal.pdf

Cardoso, F. (2008). "Some considerations on the limitations confronting the cross-cultural field of sex research." *Sexuality & Culture*, 12, 21-37.

European Commission. (2008). "Discrimination in the European Union: Perceptions, experiences, and attitudes." *Special Eurobarometer 296/wave 69.1- TNS Opinion & Social* . European Commission. http://ec.europa.eu/

Exodus International. (2005). "Policy Statement." http://exodus.to/content/view/34/118/

Gay and Lesbian Counseling Service of New South Wales. (n.d.). "Religions and their attitudes to homosexuality. Information Packet Document #11." http://www.glcsnsw.org.au/documents/Infopack/11_religions.pdf

Halsall, P. (2007). "People with a history: An online guide to lesbian, gay, bisexual, and trans history." http://www.fordham.edu/halsall/pwh/index-eur2.html

Herek, G.M. (1997-2008). "Facts about homosexuality and mental health." http://psychology.ucdavis.edu/rainbow/

Inglehart, R. F., Ponarin, E., & Inglehart, R. C. (2017). "Cultural change, slow and fast: The distinctive trajectory of norms governing gender equality and sexual orientation." *Social Forces*, 95 (4), 1313–1340.

Jandt, F., & Hundley, H. (2007). "Intercultural dimensions of communicating masculinities." *The Journal of Men's Studies*, 15, 216-231.

Korchmaros, J. D., Powell, C., & Stevens, S. (2013). "Chasing sexual orientation: A comparison of commonly used single-indicator measures of sexual orientation." *Journal of Homosexuality*, 60, 596-614.

Murray, R. A., Aberson, C. L., Blankenship, K. L., & Barry Highfield, J. J. (2013). "Beliefs that sexual orientation is a choice and motivation to control prejudice moderates method of disease transmission and sexual orientation effects on reactions to HIV-positive men." *Basic & Applied Social Psychology*, 35, 272-285.

Myers, D. G., & Scanzoni, L. D. (2005). "Changing sexual orientation? A look at the data." *Perspectives, a Journal of Reformed Thought*. http://www.rca.org/

Pew Research Center. (2013, June 4). "The global divide on homosexuality." *Pew Research Center*. http://www.pewglobal.org/2013/06/04/the-global-divide-on-homosexuality/

Platt, L. F., & Lenzen, A. L. (2013). "Sexual orientation microaggressions and the experience of sexual minorities." *Journal of Homosexuality*, 60, 1011-1034.

Priebe, G., & Svedin, C. (2013). "Operationalization of three dimensions of sexual orientation in a national survey of late adolescents." *Journal of Sex Research*, 50, 727-738.

Stokes, J. P., Miller, R. L., & Mundhenk, R. (1998). "Toward an understanding of behaviorally bisexual men: The influence of context and culture." *The Canadian Journal of Human Sexuality*, 7, 101-113.

Toro-Alfonso, J. (2007). "Latino perspectives on sexual orientation: The desire that we do not dare name." *Communiqué Special Section: Psychological Perspectives on Sexual Orientation in Communities of Color*. http://www.apa.org/

Suggested Reading

Badgett, M. V., & Frank, J. (Eds.). *Sexual orientation discrimination: An international perspective.* London; New York: Routledge.

Collier, K. L., van Beusekom, G., Bos, H. W., & Sandfort, T. M. (2013). "Sexual orientation and gender identity/expression related peer victimization in adolescence: A systematic review of associated psychosocial and health outcomes." *Journal of Sex Research,* 50 (3/4), 299-317.

Epstein, R., McKinney, P., Fox, S., & Garcia, C. (2012). "Support for a fluid-continuum model of sexual orientation: A large-scale internet study." *Journal of Homosexuality,* 59, 1356-1381.

Gordon, L. E., & Silva, T. J. (2015). "Inhabiting the sexual landscape: Toward an interpretive theory of the development of sexual orientation and identity." *Journal of Homosexuality,* 62 (4), 495-530.

Halsall, P. (2007). "People with a history: An online guide to lesbian, gay, bisexual, and tran history." *Fordham University:* http://www.fordham.edu/halsall/pwh/index-eur2.html

Omoto, A. M., & Kurtzman, H. S. (Eds.). (2006). *Sexual orientation and mental health: Examining identity and development in lesbian, gay, and bisexual people.* Washington DC: American Psychological Association.

Noelle Vance, M.A.

Feminist Theories of Gender Inequality

OVERVIEW

The term gender inequality refers to the disparities that exist among individuals based solely on their gender rather than objective differences in skills, abilities, or other characteristics. Gender inequalities may be obvious (e.g., not receiving the same pay for the same job) or subtle (e.g., not being given the same subjective opportunities for advancement). Despite the strides taken to eradicate gender inequality over the years, the fact is that it still remains. There are many feminist perspectives of gender inequality, including that of liberal feminism, socialist feminism, radical feminism, and multiracial feminism. Each of these perspectives views the issue from a slightly different angle and offers different insights into the problem in addition to different solutions. However, gender equality is more than a quest for equal pay for equal work. The social roles of females and males are often far from "different but equal." Much more research is needed in order to be able to understand the extent to which gender equality is a good thing for society and how this can best be implemented.

In twenty-first century Western society, it is often difficult to think of women as an oppressed minority group. After all, according to the US Census Bureau current population survey of 2010, females make up 50.8 percent of the total population of the United States: a slim majority, indeed, but a majority nonetheless (Howden & Meyer, 2011). In addition, one can see women in virtually every job and career throughout the levels of social stratification: women are no longer relegated to the positions of wives, mothers, or secretaries, but can and do become doctors, lawyers, and nuclear physicists, as well as truck drivers, welders, and factory workers. Yet despite such advances, women are significantly underrepresented in many segments of twenty-first century society. For example, of the 535 members of the 113th Congress, only 98 of these were women in April 2013 (Center for American Women in Politics, 2013). Although women have achieved positions in other important national leadership roles (e.g., Sandra Day O'Connor, Ruth Bader Ginsburg, Sonia Soto-mayor, and Elena Kagan becoming members of the US Supreme Court; Madeleine Albright, Hillary Clinton, and Condoleezza Rice becoming Secretary of State), they still are significantly underrepresented when compared to their majority status in the population. Sociologically, a minority or a subordinate group is defined by five basic properties:

- Unequal treatment;
- Common physical and cultural characteristics that distinguish them from the dominant group;
- Involuntary membership in the subordinate group;
- Development of a sense of solidarity; and
- Intermarriage within the subgroup.

Women as a general classification fulfill virtually all of these characteristics. Women today still receive unequal treatment when compared to men.

- First, in 2012, the median income for year-round male workers was $50,955 as opposed to $39,977 for female workers (US Census Bureau, 2012).
- Second, women share obvious physical characteristics that distinguished them from men as well as cultural characteristics that also differentiate them from men (e.g., gender roles and stereotypes).
- Third, being a woman is a result of a fact of birth rather than of voluntary membership in a class.
- Fourth, although the fight for women's rights may have been going on since time immemorial, contemporary feminism in many ways has helped women to develop a greater feeling of solidarity.
- Finally, although some women may intermarry within their class, most marriages that take place are heterosexual unions and many women believe that the institution of heterosexual marriage is irrevocably linked with their subordinate position in society.

Gender Inequality

The term gender inequality refers to the disparities between women and men based solely on their gender rather than objective differences in skills, abilities, or other characteristics. These inequalities may be obvious (e.g., not receiving the same pay for the same job) or subtle (e.g., not being given the same subjective opportunities for advancement). There are many answers to the question of why gender inequality exists. For example, the structural functionalist view of gender is that it has a fixed role in society, with men filling instrumental roles and women filling expressive roles. Conflict theorists, on the other hand, view women as being disadvantaged by power inequities that emanate from the social structure. Feminist theorists, however, take exception to both these views of gender inequalities. For example, one of the objections to the functionalist view is that it assumes that such sexist arrangements are functional for society. Feminist theorists differ with conflict theorists because the latter assume that all inequalities stem from the same source.

It would seem that the feminist perspective would have much to say about both gender in general and gender inequality in particular. In general, feminism is an ideology that is opposed to gender stratification and male dominance. Feminist beliefs and concomitant actions are intended to help bring justice, fairness, and equity to all people regardless of gender and aid in the development of a society in which women and men are equal in all areas of life. In general, feminists attempt to understand the nature of women in society in order to bring about social change that will liberate women from being oppressed and bring them parity with men.

Feminist Frameworks

Liberal Feminism

Feminism, however, is far from being a unified perspective, and different feminists view gender inequalities as stemming from different sources depending on their assumptions. Within feminism, there are at least four distinct, major frameworks. Each of these views the issue of gender inequality from a different perspective. Liberal feminists, for example, posit that gender inequality has its origins in historical traditions that have set up barriers to the advancement of women. In addition, liberal feminism emphasizes issues such as individual rights and equal opportunity as a basis for social justice and reform. In addition, this framework assumes that the socialization of women into gender roles contributes to the inequality experienced by women in society. To bring about social change and neutralize gender inequities, feminists advocate removing barriers to the advancement of women within society and developing policies to promote equal rights for women. The liberal feminist framework has been the basis of many legal changes that have been used to bring about greater equality for women within the United States.

Socialist Feminism

A second major feminist perspective is socialist feminism. As with socialist perspectives on other aspects of culture and society, the socialist feminist perspective posits that women's oppression is a result of capitalism. According to this perspective, women are a cheap labor supply that is exploited within the capitalist system. Further, socialist feminists believe that capitalism interacts with the patriarchal system to make women less powerful both within society and as laborers. Socialist feminism is more radical than liberal feminism and critiques the liberal feminist view as being shortsighted because it does not take into account the interaction between capitalism and patriarchal systems. Social feminists believe that gender equality can only be brought about if the economic and political systems on which gender inequality is based are changed.

Radical Feminism

An even more radical view of gender inequality comes from the radical feminists. In this view, patriarchy is seen as the primary cause of the oppression of women. Gender inequality stems, according to the radical feminists, from the fact that men have control over women's bodies. As a result, violence against women (e.g., rape, sexual harassment, physical abuse, sexual abuse) comprises some of the mechanisms by which men assert their power within society. Since the existing social system is dominated by men, radical feminists believe that social change in the form of gender equality cannot be accomplished through the existing social system because it is controlled by men. Although liberal feminists believe that state institutions can be reformed through political action and legislation to bring about gender equality, radical feminists argue that this cannot happen because by its very nature the current state is male.

Multiracial Feminism

The fourth branch of feminism that speaks to gender inequality is multiracial feminism. Although not in and of itself a single theoretical perspective, multiracial feminism has developed new theoretical avenues for studying race, class, and gender. Multiracial feminism grew out of the observation of some theorists that more traditional feminist theories tended to exclude women of color from their analyses, thereby making it difficult if not impossible to truly

Table 1: Four Feminist Views of Gender Inequality

	Liberal Feminism	Socialist Feminism	Radical Feminism	Multiracial Feminism
Are the sexes essentially the same or different?	Essentially the same	Essentially the same	For most, essentially the same	Essentially the same, but not always an issue
Are they equal or hierarchically arranged?	Emphasizes equality as a goal	Emphasizes equality as a goal	Emphasizes equally as a goal	Emphasizes equality as a goal
Sources of differences, similarity and hierarchy	Cultura, social, political, and economic institutions	Patriarchy and capitalism together	Men crealed patriarchy	Patriarchy, capitalism, an racism together
Acceptability of gender differences and inequality	Inequality not acceptable	inequality not acceptable	Patriarchy not acceptable	Inequality not acceptable
Acceptability of Change	Work for equality of all individuals	inequality must be eradicated	Patriarchy must be eradicated	Inequality must be eradicated
Means of Charge	Reform of institutions, education, affirmative action	Remove patriarchy and capitalism together	Technology, legal change individualism	Remove patriarchy, class system, and racism as interlocking systems of domination
What difference does race/ethnicity make for this framework?	Not a major issue	A major issue, but not always the main focus	Not relevant	Often supersedes gender issues
Comments and contributions	Major legislative and institutional changes	Theoretically rich; it implicitly handles women of color ard third world women's issues	Intellectual cutting edge	Closely connected to ethnic activism

(adapted from Jabbra, 2008)

understand and articulate the experience of all women. Multiracial feminism examines the interactive influences of gender, race, and class on various social outcomes and the way that women's and men's experiences differ. Further, multiracial feminism points out the fact that there is no such thing as a common experience for all women. Rather, women's experiences are further complicated by other variables including race and class. The multiracial feminist perspective attempts, for example, to explain why the experience of women of one race differs from the experience of women of another race within the same social class.

APPLICATIONS

Evolving Manifestations of Feminism

As discussed above, feminism is not a unitary concept and there are many feminist perspectives. Jabbra (2008), for example, discusses ten separate feminist perspectives of gender inequality issues. There may be more. In fact, in some ways, although we may group feminist perspectives together under general rubrics such as liberal, socialist, radical, or multiracial, one could almost make an argument that there are as many variants of feminism as there are women pondering the role of women within their culture, society, or world. My grandmother's brand of feminism (although she would be appalled at the appellation), for example, was being allowed to do whatever it took to work alongside her husband and ensure the smooth running of the farm on which their livelihood depended. Although for the most part this meant that she looked after hearth and home and canned the foods that her husband grew; when necessary she stepped out of this expected gender role and donned pants and worked alongside him in the field. Such, in many ways, was the nature of early twentieth century feminism. By the mid-to-late twentieth century, however, many women were involved in a different feminist battle, demanding equal pay for equal work and even attempting to gain the same kind of respect and status that was accorded male colleagues. One of the ways women tried to do this was by "dressing for success," which meant dressing to look like slightly feminized versions of successful males: pinstriped power suits, starched white shirts, and feminine versions of ties. Today's women, of course, are fighting their own feminist battles in their own ways.

Peters (2005) discusses the trends towards gender equality in the latter half of the twentieth century. She observes that gender equality will never occur as long as only one gender strives for such a goal. Women can band together all they want and demand equality, but unless men want it as well—and it is perceived as being advantageous to them—gender equality will not occur. In principle, the twenty-first century society has developed flexible gender roles that can encompass a wide range of variation from stay-at-home moms to stay-at-home dads, from female (or male) secretaries to female (or male) rocket scientists and fighter pilots. In the end, however, this seeming flexibility is gloss, and most individuals see women and men as being bound by their biological distinctions and concomitant behavioral tendencies. Although some fathers prefer to stay home and raise the children, this is still the exception rather than the rule. Further, it is not just the men who cling to traditional gender roles. When given the opportunity to return to work early so that their husbands can stay home and bond with the new baby, most women still prefer to stay home themselves. Further, to the chagrin of their feminist mothers, many young girls today worry not about whether or not they can achieve a position of power, but whether in doing so they will lose the boy.

CONCLUSION

Despite the advances that women have made over the years towards equality with men, the simple fact is that this utopian condition still has not been achieved. Although laws have been enacted to ensure equality in the workplace and the education system continues to attempt to teach everyone that there are no inherent differences between the genders regarding intellectual capacities, most people still view women and men differently and make assumptions about gender roles and abilities based on physiological differences. For this reason, despite their greater numbers, women continue to endure discrimination and gender stratification.

As opposed to some other social theorists who view gender inequality as a good thing that supports and helps maintain society, feminist theorists of all bents view gender inequality as a bad thing and work to eradicate it. However, feminist rhetoric or even legislation is unlikely to be able to do this alone. Gender equality will not become a global reality until both women and men believe that it is true and act accordingly. To do this, more research needs to be done concerning the notion of gender equality not only to empirically demonstrate that there are no important non-physiological differences, but also to understand the psychological and sociological mechanisms whereby obvious differences are inappropriately extrapolated to other areas. Research is also needed to better understand the psychological mechanisms underlying social change. Gender equality by fiat will be a fleeting thing at best unless people believe that the underlying principles are true. In addition, it must be remembered that feminist views of gender inequality—despite the fact that there are many of them—are only one set of ways to look at this issue. Other perspectives yield other views, including the opinion that gender inequality is a good thing and ensures the stability of society. In the end, although the words of the old commercial tell women that "you've come a long way, baby," the truth is that as a society we still have a long way to go before we truly have gender equality.

TERMS & CONCEPTS

Capitalism: An economic system in which the means of production and distribution are privately owned (i.e., not owned by the government or state) either individually or corporately (i.e., by a group of individuals) and operated for profit. In capitalism, investments, distribution, income, production, and pricing are determined by a free market economy.

Class: A group of people or stratum within society that shares a similar level of wealth and income and that have access to the same resources, power, and perceived social worth. Social class is the stratum of the group within the society. (See also: social stratification)

Feminism: An ideology that is opposed to gender stratification and male dominance. Feminist beliefs and concomitant actions are intended to help bring justice, fairness, and equity to all women and aid in the development of a society in which women and men are equal in all areas of life.

Functionalism: A theoretical framework used in sociology that attempts to explain the nature of social order and the relationship between the various parts (structures) in society as well as their contribution to the stability of the society by examining the functionality of each to determine how it contributes to the stability of society as a whole. Also referred to as structural functionalism.

Gender Inequality: Disparities among individuals based solely on their gender rather than objective differences in skills, abilities, or other characteristics. Gender inequalities may be obvious (e.g., not receiving the same pay for the same job) or subtle (e.g., not being given the same subjective opportunities for advancement).

Gender Stratification: The hierarchical organization of a society in such a way that members of one gender have more access to wealth, prestige, and power than do the members of the other gender.

Patriarchy: A social system (e.g., society or group) in which the male is the head of the family, descent is traced through the father's side of the family, and men have power over women.

Physical Abuse: A physical behavior that is violent toward another person (e.g., assault, battery, inappropriate restraint). Sexual Abuse: The violation or exploitation of another person by sexual means. For adults, sexual abuse includes all non-consensual sexual contact. Sexual abuse can arise in relationships of trust (e.g., between a caregiver and the person being cared for).

Social Change: The significant alteration of a society or culture over time. Social change involves social behavior patterns, interactions, institutions, and stratification systems as well as elements of culture including norms and values.

Social Justice: A striving to achieve justice in every aspect of society not merely through the application of the law. Social justice is based on the principle of universal human rights and working to ensure that all individuals receive fair treatment and equally share the benefits of society.

Social Stratification: A relatively fixed hierarchical organization of a society in which entire subgroups are ranked according to social class. These divisions are marked by differences in economic rewards and power within the society and different access to resources, power, and perceived social worth. Social stratification is a system of structured social inequality.

Socialization: The process by which individuals learn to differentiate between what the society regards as acceptable versus unacceptable behavior and act in a manner that is appropriate for the needs of the society.

Society: A distinct group of people who live within the same territory, share a common culture and way of life, and are relatively independent from people outside the group. Society includes systems of social interactions that govern both culture and social organization.

Status: A socially established position within a society or other social structure that carries with it a recognized level of prestige.

Bibliography

Andersen, M. L. & Taylor, H. F. (2002). *Sociology: Understanding a diverse society*. Belmont, CA: Wadsworth/Thomson Learning.

Center for American Women in Politics (2013). "Women in the U.S. Congress 2013." http://www.cawp.rutgers.edu/

Howden, L. & Meyer, J. (2011). "Age and sex composition: 2010 (2010 census briefs)." http://www.census.gov/prod/cen2010/briefs/c2010br-03.pdf

Jabbra, N. W. (2008). "Theories of gender hierarchy for an introductory women's studies class." *Feminist Teacher,* 18(3), 229-233.

Peters, J. K. (2005). "Gender remembered: The ghost of 'unisex' past, present, and future." *Women's Studies,* 34(1), 67-83.

Schaefer, R. T. (2002). *Sociology: A brief introduction* (4th ed.). Boston: McGraw-Hill.

United States Census Bureau. (2001). "Population by region and sex: March 2000." http://www.census.gov/

United States Census Bureau (2012). Table P-24. E"ducation attainment—Full-time, year-round workers 25 years old and over by median earnings and sex: 1991 to 2012." http://www.census.gov/hhes/www/income/data/historical/people/

Suggested Reading

Fox, B. J. (1988). "Conceptualizing 'patriarchy.'" *Canadian Review of Sociology and Anthropology,* 25(2), 163-182.

Hewitt, L. (2005). "Reflections on the role of the scholar-activist in feminist sociology: Dilemmas, frustrations, and visions for the future." *Conference Papers—American Sociological Association Annual Meeting, Philadelphia,* 1-20.

Kainer, J. (1995). "Pay equity strategy and feminist legal theory: Challenging the bounds of liberalism." *Canadian Journal of Women and the Law,* 8(2), 440-469.

Kane, E. W. (1998). "Men's and women's beliefs about gender inequality: Family ties, dependence, and agreement." *Sociological Forum,* 13(4), 611-637.

Lorber, J. (2012). *Gender Inequality: Feminist Theories and Politics.* New York: Oxford University Press.

Tolman, D. (2012). "Female adolescents, sexual empowerment and desire: A missing discourse of gender inequity." *Sex Roles,* 66(11/12), 746-757.

Van der Lippe, T. & Fodor, E. (1998). "Changes in gender inequality in six eastern European countries." *Acta Sociologica,* 41(2), 131-149.

Ruth A. Wienclaw, Ph.D.

Gender and Domestic Responsibilities

ABSTRACT

The gender roles that define what it is to be female or male within a culture have historically placed the responsibility for child care and housework on the woman. This situation originated due to biological considerations such as the need for women to nurse a child and men being physiologically more suited to face the dangers of the outside world. While the reasons for the division of labor as traditionally practiced have changed, mostly due to industrialization, many couples have difficulty with the equal sharing of domestic tasks for a number of reasons, including the close association of gender identity and housework, gatekeeping and managerial responsibility associated with domestic responsibilities, and issues of standards for child care and household chores. Although some couples still use the traditional gender roles to apportion domestic responsibilities, others are trying different divisions of labor, with advancements in modern technology making this easier. As increasing numbers of couples take more egalitarian attitudes toward domestic responsibilities, it is likely that the norms of society will gradually change to make this situation more acceptable.

OVERVIEW

Traditional Division of Labor

Within the home, there has traditionally been a division of labor based on gender. Although in some cultures today this structure is being replaced by a more egalitarian one, traditionally, women and men have each had their own set of responsibilities in the home, typically based on the perceived abilities and demands on each of the sexes. In virtually every culture and society around the planet, women have the primary responsibility for child care. Although alternatives for breast-feeding exist today, historically it has only been the woman who has been able to nurse the child and therefore ensure the survival of the race. Similarly, hunting and waging war are traditional responsibilities for the men of a culture. This division of labor arose due to the physical capacities of women (e.g., their size, shape, and strength), women's psychological and psychological makeup (hypothetically), and women's reproductive biology, all of which made them less suited than men for war and hunting. Conversely, the physical capacities, psychological makeup, and reproductive biology of men made them less suited for home life and more suited for hunting and war. While norms regarding child care tend to be fairly consistent (at least historically) from culture to culture, all the aspects of the division of labor between the sexes are not. For example, in some societies, women care for fowl, small animals, or dairy animals, and in other societies men have these responsibilities. Although the norms for division of labor between the sexes differ from culture to culture, every culture does have norms regarding the division of labor between the sexes.

Sex vs. Gender

To understand the division of domestic labor that occurs between genders in many cultures, one must first understand the differences between sex and gender. Sex is biological in nature and gender is sociocultural in nature. One's sex determines one's biological destiny, such as the ability to bear or sire children. Gender, on the other hand, is the psychological, social, cultural, and behavioral characteristics associated with being female or male; gender is a learned characteristic based on one's gender identity and learned gender role. Gender is a society's interpretation of the cultural meaning of one's sex. In fact, some theories posit that we "do" gender, meaning that gender is a social construct that is interpreted by members of a society through the ongoing social interactions that individuals have with each other. Such constructs can easily give rise to gender stereotypes, or culturally defined patterns of expected attitudes and behavior that are considered appropriate for one gender but not the other. Gender stereotypes tend to be simplistic and over-generalized perceptions of one gender or the other and do not take into account the characteristics or aptitudes of the individual. For example, although the traditional gender stereotype for domestic responsibilities might be that women stay home and clean the house and raise the family while men go out and work, the fact that many women in today's society are successful physicians, scientists, lawyers, business owners, and executives (among other jobs traditionally thought to be "male") while many men share in domestic responsibilities or even stay home with the children demonstrates that it is the abilities and aptitudes of the individual—not the individual's gender or sex—that should prescribe the parameters in which that individual can work.

Despite being social constructs, in some ways, gender roles are biologically based. Physiologically, it is women who must gestate and bear the young of the species. However, it can be argued that biological destiny in many ways ends there, at least when it comes to domestic responsibilities. It is no longer necessary for women to even stay home to nurse an infant. Not only can infants be bottle-fed using formula, women can express breast milk so that the baby continues to get all the immunological benefits of breast feeding without the mother needing to be physically present. Gender does have a biological foundation in the physiological differences between females and males. However, the way that gender is interpreted differs from culture to culture and, in some ways, from individual to individual.

Changing Roles in Developed Societies

Although the historical norms regarding the division of labor between the sexes are similar across cultures, to a great extent these norms are changing in more developed societies. As mentioned above, women are no longer confined by their biology to be physically present with an infant to ensure its survival. Similarly, many of the jobs in industrial and postindustrial societies no longer require the physical strength necessary in hunter-gather societies to go out and literally bring home the bacon. For example, jobs today in information technology require little more physical strength than the ability to sit in front of a computer. In postindustrial societies, success in the job market depends on mental rather than physical skill. Research has repeatedly shown that there is no difference between the sexes in intellectual capacity. As women earn more gender equality in the workplace, they tend to look for more gender equality in the home as well. This attitude affects the division of labor for domestic responsibilities.

APPLICATIONS

Equal Division of Labor in the Home

Although the increasing participation of women in the workplace brings with it a concomitant need in many cases to renegotiate the division of labor within the home, this can be a tricky proposition. Despite the fact that married mothers are increasingly working outside the home, research indicates that wives are still performing many of the domestic responsibilities in the home (Rasmussen, Hawkins, & Schwab, 1996). This phenomenon—sometimes referred to as the "second shift"—can be the source of significant conflict within the home if it is not satisfactorily resolved. Further, research has found that the equal sharing of domestic responsibilities (including both child care and housework) can significantly increase the psychological health of both mothers and fathers.

Difficulties: Male Hang-ups

Coming to the point of equal domestic responsibilities can be a difficult process. First, as discussed above, the traditional division of labor between the sexes has been for men to work outside the home and for women to work inside (including being primarily or totally responsible for both caring for the children and for housework). Since the work of women in the home is typically devalued by many cultures, the adjustment to equally shared domestic tasks is often more difficult for men to make than for women. In many ways, discussions of the division of domestic labor are only the tip of the iceberg and represent deeper attitudes and beliefs held by the wife and husband concerning gender roles and identities in general. For example, although they may be egalitarian in theory, some men find the actual practice of sharing domestic responsibilities to be difficult either to envision or to practice. This typically means that there are deeper issues regarding gender roles and what tasks or activities are or are not masculine.

Difficulties: Female Hang-ups

However, cultural norms and gender roles are deeply ingrained, and it is not necessarily only men who find it difficult to share domestic responsibilities in practice. For example, when their husbands actually take over some of the traditional domestic responsibilities in the family, some women gate-keep, or resist or manage their husband's participation in domestic responsibilities, even if they are working full-time themselves. This situation may arise from the woman's own concepts of traditional gender roles and the reluctance to give them up or from feeling that her gender identity is threatened by her husband's non-traditional participation in the home. It has also been hypothesized that women may gate-keep because the types of jobs that many of them can find outside the home typically do not have as much prestige as those of their husbands. As a result, sharing domestic responsibilities can negatively impact the self-esteem of some women because they see their husband as more competent outside the home and do not want to see him as equally competent inside the home as well. For this reason, gatekeeping can occur even when women work full-time and objectively need help with domestic responsibilities. Similarly, some women attempt to take over managerial responsibility for their husband's domestic tasks. Women may plan the task (such as making appointments with a pediatrician for example) and the man may carry out the task (taking the children to the pediatrician appointment). In fact, research has shown that men are less likely to take managerial responsibility for domestic tasks even when they are the ones carrying out those tasks.

Difficulties: Standards of Domestic Responsibility

Women and men often differ on the standards to which domestic responsibilities need to be performed. For example, one spouse may deep clean every time s/he takes out the vacuum cleaner while the other spouse either performs the task less often (i.e., tolerates more clutter or dirt) or performs it less minutely. This can lead to disagreements over how a task should be done. In many cases, this means that the spouse who has more rigid standards for how the task should be performed either over-manages the task or takes it over her/himself. In such cases, it is often important for the couple to determine the difference between their standards for the performance of a task and set minimum standards. For example, for hygiene reasons, bathroom fixtures need to be routinely cleaned and sanitized. Determining minimum standards for the performance of this task is a more or less objective matter that can be discussed dispassionately. On the other hand, there are other domestic tasks within the bathroom that are more subjective (e.g., streaks on the mirror, placement of objects on the vanity top, or even how one squeezes toothpaste from the tube). Spouses frequently disagree on the standards to which such tasks need to be performed.

Difficulties: Guilt

Women may experience problems with their self-esteem, stress, or guilt when they find that they cannot take on all the domestic responsibilities involved in child care and housework as well as all the duties and activities associated with their careers. The guilt experienced by these women, however, may be more than a personal issue related to gender identity and self-esteem. Some observers have suggested that guilt arising in such situations is actually inherent in society (Guendouzi, 2006). Research in the United Kingdom has found that women often look for employment that will allow them to continue to do their domestic tasks (child care in particular). However, it is unclear whether this trend is due to women choosing to take on a greater portion of the domestic responsibilities in the household or because the pressure of society to do this is difficult to resist. The construct of a "good mother" is prevalent throughout Western society and can be seen in the media and advertising.

The Benefits of Technology

As communication and information technology continue to advance, it is becoming increasingly possible for women to telework from home so that they can continue to play a major role in the lives of their children or do other domestic tasks during the day (e.g., put a load of laundry in the washer while waiting for a fax to come through). In teleworking, an employee works outside the traditional office or workplace—typically at home or while traveling, and the transmission of information and documents occurs via telecommunications or network technology, including the Internet. The teleworker typically has little personal contact with coworkers but communicates with them electronically through email, telephone, teleconferencing, or other communication media. Data, documents, and communication are transmitted via telecommunications or network technology.

CONCLUSION

Although there historically has been little change in the division of labor for domestic responsibilities across cultures, the increasing numbers of women entering the workplace and the changing nature of many jobs in the postindustrial twenty-first century means that this division of labor needs to be rethought in many situations. Some couples continue to work best under the traditional paradigms of a wife/mother who stays at home and tends to the children and household while the husband/father goes out and works for a living. However, increasing levels of education for women and the changing nature of many jobs means that more and more women are also working outside the home. Some women try to handle this situation by working not only at a full-time job but also trying to do all the domestic responsibilities to the same pre-career level. Other women attempt to compromise by not working full-time outside the home, lowering their standards at home, or hiring someone to do the domestic tasks for them (such as a housecleaner, personal chef, or nanny). Still other women attempt to work out a more equitable split of domestic responsibilities with their partner. In today's age of high technology, telework options are also available to help couples balance these responsibilities.

On the one hand, it is important to note that objectively there is no reason to assume that it is the woman's responsibility to make sure that all the domestic responsibilities are completed to a satisfactory standard. Men, too, can participate in doing these tasks. On the other hand, it must also be remembered that the guilt that many women feel when "abdicating" their responsibilities at home so that they can continue in a job or career are socialized and reinforced by the norms of society. However, times are changing as are expectations about the division of labor for domestic responsibilities.

TERMS & CONCEPTS

Culture: A complex system of meaning and behavior that is socially transmitted and that defines a common way of life for a group or society. Culture includes the totality of behavior patterns, arts, beliefs, institutions, and other products of human work and thought of the society or group.

Economic Development: The sustainable increase in living standards for a nation, region, or society. More than mere economic growth (i.e., a rise in output), economic development is sustainable and positively impacts the well-being of all members of the group members through such things as increased per capita income, education, health, and environmental protection. Economic development is progressive in nature and positively impacts the socioeconomic structure of a society.

Gender: Psychological, social, cultural, and behavioral characteristics associated with being female or male. Gender is defined by one's gender identity and learned gender role.

Gender Identity: The recognition that one is either male or female based on both biological and psychosocial considerations, and the internalization of this gender concept into one's self-identity.

Gender Role: Separate patterns of personality traits, mannerisms, interests, attitudes, and behaviors that are regarded as "male" and "female" by one's culture. Gender role is largely a product of the way in which one was socialized and may not be in conformance with one's gender identity.

Gender Stereotype: A culturally defined pattern of expected attitudes and behavior that are considered appropriate for one gender but not the other. Gender stereotypes tend to be simplistic and based not on the characteristics or aptitudes of the individual, but on over generalized perceptions of one gender or the other.

Industrialization: The use of mechanization to produce the economic goods and services within a society. Historically, industrialization is a society's transition between farm production and manufacturing production. Industrialization is associated with factory production, division of labor, and the concentration of industries and populations within certain geographical areas and concomitant urbanization.

Information Technology: The use of computers, communications networks, and knowledge in the creation, storage, and dispersal of data and information. Information technology comprises a wide range of items and abilities for use in the creation, storage, and distribution of information.

Norms: Standards or patterns of behavior that are accepted as normal within the culture.

Postindustrial: The nature of a society whose economy is no longer dependent on the manufacture of goods (i.e., industrial), but is primarily based upon the processing and control of information and the provision of services.

Sex: The biological aspects of being either female or male. Genetically, females are identified by having two X chromosomes and males by having an X and a Y chromosome. In addition, sex can typically be determined from either primary or secondary sexual characteristics. Primary sexual characteristics comprise the female or male reproductive organs (i.e., the vagina, ovaries, and uterus for females and the penis, testes, and scrotum for males). Secondary sexual characteristics comprise the superficial differences between the sexes that occur with puberty (e.g., breast development and hip broadening for women and facial hair and voice deepening for men).

Social Construct: Any phenomenon that is invented (i.e., constructed) by a culture or society. Social constructs exist because the members of a society behave as if it exists rather than because of the availability of criteria that are necessarily obvious to an objective outside observer. Race and ethnicity are both examples of social constructs. (Also referred to as a social construction.)

Socialization: The process by which individuals learn to differentiate between what the society regards as acceptable versus unacceptable behavior and act in a manner that is appropriate for the needs of the society.

Society: A distinct group of people who live within the same territory, share a common culture and way of life, and are relatively independent from people outside the group. Society includes systems of social interactions that govern both culture and social organization.

Telework: A situation in which an employee works outside the traditional office or workplace—typically at home or on travel. Transmission of data, documents, and communication occurs via telecommunications or network technology. Also referred to as telecommuting.

Bibliography

Casinowsky, G. (2013). "Working life on the move, domestic life at standstill? Work-related travel and responsibility for home and family." *Gender, Work & Organization,* 20, 311–326.

Drew, E., & Humbert, A. (2012). "Men have careers, women have babies: Unequal parental care among Irish entrepreneurs." *Community, Work & Family,* 15, 49-67.

Guendouzi, J. (2006). "'The guilt thing': Balancing domestic and profession roles." *Journal of Marriage and Family,* 68, 901-909.

Offer, S., & Schneider, B. (2011). "Revisiting the gender gap in time-use patterns: Multitasking and well-being among mothers and fathers in dual-earner families." *American Sociological Review,* 76, 809–833.

Ranson, G. (2012). "Men, paid employment and family responsibilities: Conceptualizing the 'working father'." *Gender, Work & Organization,* 19, 741–761.

Rasmussen, K. S., Hawkins, A., & Schwab, K. P. (1996). "Increasing husbands' involvement in domestic labor: Issues for therapists." *Contemporary Family Therapy,* 18, 209-223.

Stockard, J. (2000). *Sociology: Discovering society* (2nd ed.). Belmont, CA: Wadsworth/Thomson Learning.

Weisshaar, K. (2014). "Earnings equality and relationship stability for same-sex and heterosexual couples." *Social Forces,* 93, 93–123.

Suggested Reading

Arai, A. B. (2000). "Self-employment as a response to the double day for women and men in Canada." *Canadian Review of Sociology and Anthropology,* 37, 125-142.

Baxter, J. (1997). "Gender equality and participation in housework: A cross-national perspective." *Journal of Comparative Family Studies,* 28, 220-247.

Braun, A., Vincent, C., & Ball, S. J. (2011). "Working-class fathers and childcare: The economic and family contexts of fathering in the UK." *Community, Work & Family,* 14, 19–37.

Dowswell, T., Bradshaw, G., & Hewison, J. (2000). "Child care responsibilities and participation in continuing education and training: Issues relating to motivation, funding and domestic roles." *Journal of Advanced Nursing,* 32, 445-453.

Martens, L. (1995). "Locating gender: Occupational segregation, wages and domestic responsibilities." *The Sociological Review*, 43, 862-863.

Morahan, P. S. (2001). "Career obstacles for women in medicine." *Medical Education*, 35, 97-98.

O'Connor, H. (2011). "Resisters, mimics and coincidentals: Intergenerational influences on childcare values and practices." *Community, Work & Family*, 14, 405–423.

Peterson, R. R. & Gerson, K. (1992). "Determinants of responsibility for child care arrangements among dual-earner couples." *Marriage and Family*, 54, 527-536.

Peterson, R. R. & Gerson, K. (1993). "A social-structural explanation of men's and women's domestic responsibility: A reply to Hawkins and Olsen." *Journal of Marriage and Family*, 55, 508-510.

Schneider, D. (2012). "Gender deviance and household work: The role of occupation." *American Journal of Sociology*, 117, 1029–1072.

Ruth A. Wienclaw, Ph.D.

Gender and Economic Inequality

ABSTRACT

Despite the progress being made to improve the economic equality between the sexes around the world, economic inequality still exists. Although it would be easy to explain this phenomenon in terms of sexual discrimination in the workplace, there are actually a number of potential explanations for this observed inequality including differences in decisions made by the sexes regarding the relative priority of career and family as well as the general preparedness of the genders for being able to compete for better-paying jobs. Some of these factors are likely to change over time as society becomes more accepting of non-traditional gender roles for home and family. Other factors will change as women become better prepared to successfully compete in the job market. More research is needed to better understand the reasons for economic gender inequality so that women and men alike can be better educated about their choices between career and family and can make informed decisions. Such research can also be used to make informed policy decisions to help women become more economically successful and counteract any lingering effects of discrimination in the workplace.

OVERVIEW

Even in the early twenty-first century, women frequently do not receive the same recognition—including salary—for doing the same job a man does. In general, as shown in Table 1, women in the United States earn less income than men do.

The most commonly cited explanations for such statistics are sexual discrimination and glass ceilings, the differential treatment of individuals based on their sex. Although sexual discrimination can occur against either sex, in most cases in contemporary society, it occurs against women. Sexual discrimination can be exhibited in such actions as lower wages being given to one sex for the same work performed by the other sex, discounting of the characteristics or attributes of one sex in comparison with the other, or unfair hiring or promotion policies that are biased against one sex. Although there are undoubtedly cases in which sexual discrimination does account for the differences seen in pay between women and men, it is not the only explanation.

The discrepancy in earnings data is very interesting, particularly given the fact that there are a number of federal laws in place that require employers to not discriminate on the basis of various non-job-related characteristics, such as race, color, religion, sex, or national origin (Title VII), age when one is over 40 (ADEA), or disability (ADA). In addition, the Equal Pay Act of 1963 requires that equal pay be given for equal work regardless of gender. Other laws require

Table 1: Earnings of Full-Time, Year-Round Workers by Selected Gender, 2014 (From US Census Bureau, Current Population Reports, 2015)

Sex	Number	Average earnings ($)
Male	62,455,000	$50,383
Female	46,226,000	$39,621

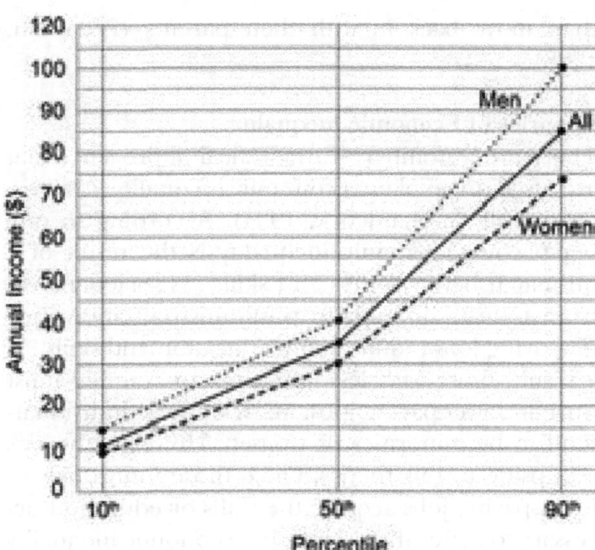

Figure 1: Relative Earnings of Year-Round, Full-Time Workers by Gender: 1999

that various types of businesses take steps for affirmative action to hire various types of people that may be underrepresented in the workplace as well as making sexual harassment in the workplace both illegal and actionable. Despite such legal safeguards that have been created and implemented in order to help ensure gender equality in the workplace and to eliminate sexual discrimination, differences still exist between the average annual income between women and men. As shown in Figure 1, on average, men are paid more money than women in the United States. However, this difference is minimal at the lower end of the scale, but more marked the higher one goes, data that are often interpreted to support the existence of glass ceilings in the United States.

Factors of Inequality: Education & Domestic Responsibility

Although sexual discrimination in the workplace is certainly one explanation for these differences (and it would be difficult in good faith to make the argument that sexual discrimination does not still exist), it is not the only possible explanation nor does it necessarily explain all the data. One explanation for the differences in pay between women and men is that men are more likely than women to attend graduate or professional schools that enable them to obtain high-paying jobs and professional careers. This situation is gradually changing, but men are still more likely to have the received the training or education needed for higher-paying jobs than are women. Yet even those women who do attain higher levels of educational and workplace achievement often continue to earn lower wages relative to men's in the same occupation; for example, US wage data from 2013 indicates female chief executives earned only 80 percent of what their male counterparts took home (Hodgson, 2014). The causes of this phenomenon continue to be the subject of much debate.

One possible explanation is that many women are still forced (or at least feel the need) to choose between career and home. An increasing number of women attempt to work full time in a job or career while still raising a family and tending to the house. Traditionally, there has been a division of labor based on gender (i.e., women have the primary responsibility for child care while men work outside the home). This division of labor supposedly arose due to the fact that the physical capacities of women (e.g., their size, shape, and strength), their psychological and psychological makeup, and their reproductive biology made them less fit for hunting and war than men. When women did begin to work, therefore, it was historically in support roles that did not conflict with the gender roles and stereotypes of the culture: Secretaries, sales clerks, and other jobs that did not offer women the same type of upward mobility as did "male" jobs of business owners, executives, and so forth.

Work Devaluation

Further, the type of work that women typically do is often devalued. The work that women have traditionally done in the home is often seen as support work rather than skilled labor. As a result, "women's work" (e.g., nurse, secretary, flight attendant) is often valued lower than occupations traditionally considered "men's work" (e.g., physician, business executive, airline pilot). Therefore, individuals in these positions are paid less for their work in part because of this devaluation. Further, some women work part time rather than full time so that they can split their attention between career and family. Many women take maternity leave from their job when they are close to term or have just had a baby. Some women also take time off from their careers in order to be at home to raise their children before the children go to school, high school, or college, or reach other benchmark times in their lives. Although these decisions may be good for the woman and her family, they all represent significant time off from the workforce. This means that these women typically do not have the same level of work experience, education, or job skills as their male counterparts (who, for the most part, do not take time off for such activities) and are, therefore, less likely to be promoted or advance as quickly in their career paths as men. Study data appear to bear this out: research found that full-time working mothers in the United States earned 5 percent lower wages per hour per child than did their childless counterparts and working mothers in the United Kingdom earned 11 percent less (Correll, 2013; Darlington, 2012).

Women & Poverty

It is not only in the job market that there is economic inequality between the genders. Women have also shown to be overrepresented among those who live below the poverty line. Although a disproportionate number of the poor has always comprised women and children, the proportion of women and children among those living at or below the poverty line has increased since the mid-twentieth century. For example, in 1960, only 4.42 million heads of family households were women; by 2014, however, this figure had increased to 15.9 million (DeNavas-Walt & Proctor, 2015). This phenomenon of increasing numbers of those living below the poverty line being women and children—referred to as the feminization of poverty—is not only national, but global as well. Within the United States, several factors have led to the feminization of poverty. These include a dramatic growth in families in which a female is the head of the household, a general decline beginning in the 1960s in the proportion of the elderly who are living at or below the poverty level, and continuing gender stratification with concomitant wage inequality between women and men. Of the 9.5 million million households living below the poverty line in 2014, 4.75 million (just over half) were headed by women (DeNavas-Walt & Proctor, 2015). These women tend to be young and without the support of an extended family that was able to help such individuals in the past. Because of the modern tendency to create nuclear rather than extended families, divorced women are more likely to set up their own households rather than move back in with their parents (Pressman, 1988).

Theories of Economic Inequality

There are a number of theoretical approaches that are used to explain economic inequality (Morris, Bernhardt, & Handcock, 1994). According to one perspective, economic inequality is the result of a mismatch between jobs and skills. As society moves from industrialization to postindustrialization, better-paying jobs require more education and skills. As a result, those with less education or training must work in lower-paying jobs. Many of these individuals tend to be minorities or women. However, there is an upside to this theory: Once those individuals in lower-paying jobs acquire the skills or education necessary to better themselves, the economic inequality will decrease. A second popular theory concerning economic inequality is the polarization of skills. According to this theory, the postindustrial shift to a service-based economy will create a two-tiered labor force. In this view, the upper-tier workers (i.e., those with the skills needed for the service industry) not only get the higher-paying jobs, but will also have greater security and opportunities for upward socioeconomic mobility. Those without the skills, on the other hand, will become members of a growing bottom tier of workers who are qualified only for low-skill jobs with concomitantly low pay and little security. Some observers believe that this polarization is caused by the very nature of postindustrial society. As advances in technology continue, these theorists believe that many of the middle-range jobs will disappear because the same tasks will be able to be performed by lower-skilled individuals with the aid of technology. Concomitantly, the demand for highly skilled individuals to design and develop high technology solutions will continue to grow. In this way, the workforce may become polarized into high-level jobs and low-level jobs.

APPLICATIONS

Conducting Income Inequality Studies

Although understanding and reducing economic inequality between the genders is important from the viewpoints of human rights and social justice, much of the information about the causes and nature of this phenomenon is not based on empirical research.

Economic inequality between the genders is not a simple relationship between gender and earnings. Other important determinants of one's economic condition include marital status, number of children, and public income transfers. However, more attention is being given to this important issue. Ozawa and Yoon (2003), for example, investigated gender differences in economic well-being in the United States. The researchers investigated economic inequality using data from the years 1970, 1980, 1990, and 2000 of the Current Population Surveys of the United States Census Bureau. These surveys have been designed to enable investigators to analyze the economic lives of the population in the United States at the level of the household, family, or individual. Ozawa and Yoon's study examined the economic well-being of adults aged 18 to 64.

The Results

The results of the study indicated that not only was there a net difference between the sexes in economic well-being, but that this difference widened during the time period covered by the study (i.e., 3.9 percent difference in 1969 and a 15 percent difference in 1999). This is a particularly interesting finding given the fact that many people believe that economic inequality between the genders is decreasing. This finding existed in every year examined in this investigation. In addition, the findings of the study indicated that the economic well-being of women was affected by two factors: their increasing levels of education and changes in marital status. As could be expected, higher levels of education were positively correlated with a rise in economic status. Further, this correlation was found to be greater for the relationship between these two variables for women than it was for men. Concomitantly, however, single marital status (i.e., divorced or never married) was more negatively correlated with economic well-being for women than for men. Finally, the study found that the economic well-being of women was more adversely affected by children than was that of men.

In addition, economic status depends not only on one's earnings on the job, but on other factors as well, including one's wealth and assets. Deere & Doss (2006) examined the differences in these key variables for the sexes. Wealth and income are typically highly correlated. However, it is important to separate these two variables in order to better understand differences in economic status between the sexes. The distribution of wealth by gender is important because it is an indicator of the prevalence of economic inequality. In addition, wealth is related to both economic and political power. If women are less wealthy, they are by extension less powerful politically and less able to impact policies that will decrease economic inequality between the genders.

CONCLUSION

Economic inequality between the genders remains a fact of life for many people. The problem is so pervasive and so important that Goal 3 of the United Nations Millennium Development Goals is to promote gender equality and empower women. It is easy to stand back and declare that economic gender inequality is a result of sexual discrimination and glass ceilings. However, the phenomenon is more complicated than that. When looking at the economic gender gap, it must be remembered that these statistics are by nature generalized. Just because women are on average less economically well off does not mean that all women are less well off than all men. In addition, many factors can legitimately account for observed differences in the economic well-being of women versus men. Some of these have to do with the decisions that each of the sexes makes regarding career and family. These inequalities may change as gender roles change and domestic responsibilities become more evenly split between the sexes. More research is needed to better understand the reasons for economic gender inequality so that individual men and women and policy makers can make informed decisions to help women become more economically successful and counteract the lingering effects of discrimination in the workplace.

Many activists have argued that companies enforcing pay secrecy rules help to perpetuate the gender wage gap because women cannot determine what they are being paid in comparison to their male coworkers without facing repercussions. These rules, which prohibit workers from sharing information about how much they earn, were either formally or informally enforced at 61 percent of private-sector companies in 2010, according to a survey conducted by the Institute for Women's Policy Research (Kim, 2015). Because of this argument, legislators have attempted to propose laws that would amend the Fair Labor Standards Act (FLSA) to outlaw the policy of pay secrecy. However, as of 2014, these attempts had failed, leading President Barack Obama to issue an Executive Order prohibiting pay secrecy for federal contractors, which activists argued only served a small portion of the working population.

TERMS & CONCEPTS

Correlation: The degree to which two events or variables are consistently related. Correlation may be positive (i.e., as the value of one variable increases the value of the other variable increases), negative (i.e., as the value of one variable increases the value of the other variable decreases), or zero (i.e., the values of the two variables are unrelated). Correlation does not imply causation.

Gender: Psychological, social, cultural, and behavioral characteristics associated with being female or male. Gender is defined by one's gender identity and learned gender role.

Gender Inequality: Disparities among individuals based solely on their gender rather than objective differences in skills, abilities, or other characteristics. Gender inequalities may be obvious (e.g., not receiving the same pay for the same job) or subtle (e.g., not being given the same subjective opportunities for advancement).

Gender Role: Separate patterns of personality traits, mannerisms, interests, attitudes, and behaviors that are regarded as "male" and "female" by one's culture. Gender role is largely a product of the way in which one was socialized and may not be in conformance with one's gender identity.

Gender Stereotype: A culturally defined pattern of expected attitudes and behavior that are considered appropriate for one gender but not the other. Gender stereotypes tend to be simplistic and based not on the characteristics or aptitudes of the individual, but on over generalized perceptions of one gender or the other.

Gender Stratification: The hierarchical organization of a society in such a way that members of one gender have more access to wealth, prestige, and power than do the members of the other gender.

Glass Ceiling: A theoretical societal barrier that prevents able and ambitious individuals from advancing to positions of power and prestige within their job or career path. The glass ceiling can be experienced by individuals because of their race, ethnicity, or gender.

Human Rights Movement: An international movement that promotes the cause of human rights throughout the globe. According to article 1 of the United Nations Universal Declaration of Human Rights: "All human beings are born free and equal in dignity and rights. They are endowed with reason and conscience and should act toward one another in a spirit of brotherhood."

Pay Secrecy: Rules or policies enforced by companies that forbid employees from discussing or sharing information about their salary or wages with others.

Postindustrial: The nature of a society whose economy is no longer dependent on the manufacture of goods (i.e., industrial), but is primarily based upon the processing and control of information and the provision of services.

Poverty Line: Also referred to as the poverty threshold, the minimum annual income necessary for an adequate standard of living. The poverty line is determined by the government and differs from country to country. According to the United States Census Bureau (DeNavas-Walt & Proctor, 2015, p. 43), the poverty line for individuals in the United States in 2014 was $12,071, and for a household of four people, including two children, it was $24,230. This figure in the United Sates is based on income before taxes and does not include capital gains or noncash benefits, such as public housing, Medicaid, or food stamps. If a family's total income is less than the family's threshold, then that family and every individual in it is considered in poverty. Globally, the poverty line is typically considered approximately $1.25 per person per day, according to the World Bank. However, this figure varies depending on the country and its level of economic development.

Sexual Discrimination: The differential treatment of individuals based on their sex. Although sexual discrimination can occur against either sex, in most cases in contemporary society, it occurs against women. Sexual discrimination can be exhibited in such actions as lower wages being given to one sex for the same work being performed by the other sex, discounting of the characteristics or attributes of one sex in comparison with the other, or unfair hiring or promotion policies that are biased against one sex.

Social Justice: A striving to achieve justice in every aspect of society not merely through the application of the law. Social justice is based on the principle of universal human rights and working to ensure that all individuals receive fair treatment and share the benefits of society equally.

Society: A distinct group of people who live within the same territory, share a common culture and way of life, and are relatively independent from people outside the group. Society includes systems of social interactions that govern both culture and social organization.

Socioeconomic Status (SES): The position of an individual or group on the two vectors of social and economic status and their combination. Factors contributing to socioeconomic status include (but are not limited to) income, type and prestige of occupation, place of residence, and educational attainment.

Variable: An object in a research study that can have more than one value. Independent variables are stimuli that are manipulated in order to determine their effect on the dependent variables (response). Extraneous variables are variables that affect the response but that are not related to the question under investigation in the study.

Bibliography

Budig, M. J., Misra, J., & Boeckmann, I. (2016). "Work–family policy trade-offs for mothers? Unpacking the cross-national variation in motherhood earnings penalties." *Work & Occupations,* 43 (2), 119–177.

Correll, S.J. (2013). "Equal pay? Not yet for mothers." *Conference Proceedings—Council on Contemporary Families Equal Pay Symposium,* June 7, 2013. http://www.contemporaryfamilies.org/Economic-Issues/equal-pay-not-yet-for-mothers.html

Darlington, R. (2012, December 23). "Dads earn more while mothers earn less." *Institute for Public Policy* website: http://www.ippr.org/press-releases/111/10113/dads-earn-more-while-mothersearn-less

Deere, C. D., & Doss, C. R. (2006). "The gender asset gap: What do we know and why does it matter?" *Feminist Economics,* 12 (1–2), 1–50.

DeNavas-Walt, C., & Proctor, B. D. (2015). *Income and poverty in the United States: 2014.* https://www.census.gov/content/dam/Census/library/publications/2015/demo/p60-252.pdf

Glynn, S. J., & Wu, N. (2013, Apr. 9). "The gender wage gap differs by occupation." http://www.americanprogress.org/issues/labor/news/2013/04/09/59698/the-gender-wage-gap-differs-by-occupation

Goldberg, G. S. (2010). *Poor women in rich countries: The feminization of poverty over the life course.* Oxford: Oxford University Press.

Hodgson, Paul. "Gender gap in CEO pay is closing." *Fortune.* http://fortune.com/2014/06/03/female-ceo-pay.

Kim, M. (2015). "Pay secrecy and the gender wage gap in the United States." *Industrial Relations,* 54 (4), 648–667.

Lips, H. (2013). "The gender pay gap: Challenging the rationalizations. perceived equity, discrimination, and the limits of human capital models." *Sex Roles,* 68 (3/4), 169–185.

Magnusson, C. (2013). "More women, lower pay? Occupational sex composition, wages and wage growth." *Acta Sociologica,* 56 (3), 227–245.

Mandel, H., & Semyonov, M. (2014). "Gender pay gap and employment sector: Sources of earnings disparities in the United States, 1970–2010." *Demography,* 51 (5), 1597–1618.

Morris, M, Bernhardt, A. D., & Handcock, M. S. (1994). "Economic inequality: New methods for new trends." *American Sociological Review,* 59 (2), 205–219.

Ozawa, M. N., & Yoon, H. (2003). "Gender differences in the economic well-being of nonaged adults in the United States." *Journal of Poverty,* 7 (1/2) 97–122.

Polavieja, J. G. (2012). "Socially embedded investments: Explaining gender differences in job-specific skills." *American Journal of Sociology,* 118 (3), 592–634.

Pressman, S. (1988). "The feminization of poverty: Causes and remedies." *Challenge,* 31 (2), 57–60.

Pressman, S. (2003). "Feminist explanations for the feminization of poverty." *Journal of Economic Issues,* 37 (2), 353–361.

Schaefer, R. T. (2002). *Sociology: A brief introduction* (4th ed.). Boston, MA: McGraw-Hill.

United States Bureau of Labor Statistics, Division of Labor Force Statistics. (2013, February 5). "Household data, annual averages: Median weekly earnings of full-time wage and salary workers by selected characteristics." http://www.bls.gov/cps/cpsaat37.htm

Yang, T., & Aldrich, H. E. (2014). "Who's the boss? Explaining gender inequality in entrepreneurial teams." *American Sociological Review,* 79 (2), 303–327.

Suggested Reading

Bar, M., Kim, S., & Leukhina, O. (2015). "Gender wage gap accounting: The role of selection bias." *Demography,* 52 (5), 1729–1750.

Barkley, A. P., Stock, W. A., & Sylvius, C. K. (1999). "Agricultural graduate earnings: The impacts of college, career, and gender." *American Journal of Agricultural Economics,* 81 (4), 785–800.

Browne, I., & Misra, J. (2003). "The intersection of gender and race in the labor market." *Annual Review of Sociology,* 29 (1), 487–513.

Dorius, S. F., & Firebaugh, G. (2010). "Trends in global gender inequality." *Social Forces,* 88 (5), 1941–1968.

Fadda, S., & Tridico, P. (2016). *Varieties of economic inequality.* Abingdon, UK: Routledge.

Lorber, J. (2011). *Gender inequality: Feminist theories and politics.* Oxford, England: Oxford University Press.

McCall, L. (2001). "Restructuring inequalities: A gender, class, and race perspective." In *Complex inequality: Gender, class and race in the new economy* (pp. 3-26). New York, NY: Routledge.

Nelson, J. A. (1998). "Labour, gender and the economic/social divide." *International Labour Review,* 137 (1), 33–46.

Ruspini, E. (2001). "The study of women's deprivation: How to reveal the gender dimension of poverty." *International Journal of Social Research Methodology,* 4 (2), 101–118.

Tickner, J. A. (2004). "The gendered frontiers of globalization." *Globalizations,* 1 (1), 15–23.

Wharton, A. S. (2011). *The sociology of gender: An introduction to theory and research.* Hoboken, NJ: John Wiley & Sons.

Ruth A. Wienclaw, Ph.D.

Gender and Sexual Orientation in the Workplace

ABSTRACT

An overview of several of the issues generated by gender and sexual orientation challenges in the workplace touching on occupational segregation, the wage gap, glass ceiling, and sexual prejudice all within the context of corporate culture. Both women and those within the LGBTQ community face substantial challenges in the workplace, some stemming from homophobia and heterosexism, others from sexual harassment and the pressures of either adopting the traits of hegemonic masculinity or buckling beneath them. Of course men are not immune to these sociological challenges whether it is sexual harassment as a heterosexual man, or occupying a traditionally female position. The article also touches on the special issues those suffering from Gender Identity Disorder may face as well as the common tactics employers adopt in order to help a transgender individual adapt to the workplace after sex-reassignment surgery. The second part of the paper briefly explores the phenomenon of Pink Corporate Culture and whether it is a viable challenge to the traditional masculine way of business. Ultimately the issues generated by gender and sexual orientation in the workplace reach far beyond the office walls.

OVERVIEW

Gender and sexual orientation in the workplace is an increasingly important topic especially as government policies change and cultural acceptances shift. It is a multidimensional topic that covers early childhood cultural pressures as well as day to day interactions in the office, as the workplace offers a microcosmic snapshot of the cultural atmosphere. Women in particular have long suffered such injustices as wage gaps, sexual harassment, and glass ceilings, while members of the LGBTQ community have only recently been given a voice with which to address the prejudices and disparities experienced within the corporate culture of businesses.

Many sociologists feel that these problems of gender and sexual orientation in the workplace have strong and firmly placed roots in the cultural norms to which we are introduced as children. As adults we bemoan the sexual inequality that we experience every day in the workplace, but we still reinforce and encourage gender traits traditionally exhibited by each sex in our children. Wage gaps and discrimination along with occupational sexism and segregation are still prominent in the workplaces of the 21st century. Women regularly bump their heads on glass ceilings because of a perceived lack of masculine traits that are more suited to management positions, yet parents, society, and educational institutions still encourage traditionally gender-assigned traits to growing boys and girls. Girls are expected to be kind, caring, nurturing and passive while boys are expected to be aggressive, ruthless, ambitious and pragmatic. These traits are then attached to later success or failure as adults in the business world since stereotypically male traits are generally seen as a pathway to success, while stereotypically female traits are seen as necessary for supporting roles in business. Lipsey, et al. (1991) refer to this situation as a "culture trap" since children are nurtured into these socially acceptable roles as children, causing them to adopt certain attitudes and beliefs that may later create professional difficulties.

Interestingly, there have been situations where the concept of hegemonic masculinity has been turned on its head. Corporations who primarily target both women as workers and women as consumers have found tremendous success by favoring feminine traits above masculine ones. Putting family first may seem like a risk in the traditionally masculine world, but these Pink corporations have found that gentle compassion has actually made for a strong inner community as well as well-rounded and enthusiastic workers.

Regardless of the success of Pink corporations, white, heterosexual, cisgender men still appear to have the upper hand in business. Though the tides appear to be turning in favor of those traditionally marginalized populations like women and LGBT people, the business world still has a long way to go before it reaches an atmosphere of true equality.

Women in the Workplace

Though women have been a part of the workforce for well over a century, their presence in the workplace has had many ramifications, and generated many challenges for both men and women in the professional environment. Gender bias has been repeatedly demonstrated through many studies conducted in multiple work environments over the last several decades.

Occupational Sexism

Occupational sexism is essentially any kind of discrimination based on a worker's gender. Most often the term is applied to situations where women are being oppressed by their male co-workers or supervisors, but certain situations allow for men to be discriminated against as well.

One particularly scrutinized issue is that of wage discrimination. Though many had hoped that the days of women earning less money than their male counterparts were long gone, an income disparity still exists. Wage discrimination is still a major issue with women making an average of $0.80 for every dollar earned by white men in the same position in 2016; furthermore, the pay gap increases for women who are Hispanics/Latinas, African Americans, Native Hawaiians/Pacific Islanders, and American Indians/Alaska Natives (AAUW). Wage discrimination is demonstrated in a wide spectrum of occupations.

Though wage discrimination is still a viable concern, research has indicated that the glass ceiling for women workers finally appears to be cracking since there are significantly more women in managerial positions. This increase in the higher positions in the workplace also filters down to benefit the women in non-managerial positions as well. When more women are found in high status positions, the wages of the female employees are effectively raised throughout the managerial hierarchy of a company. However, the absence of females in high-status positions in particular companies or industries leaves the wage gap firmly in place (Cohen & Huffman, 2007).

Sexual Harassment

Sexual harassment has become a highly sensitive area for many corporations because of various lawsuits and protective policies that have developed. In the scope of sociology, sexual harassment becomes an especially charged topic when it takes the rather non-traditional form of women sexually harassing men. Though there has been plenty of documentation to indicate that both dynamics of harassment do occur in the workplace, men are far more likely to be the target of disciplinary action because of the application of sexual stereotypes. Men are less likely to report sexual harassment by a female coworker or boss because of the personal and professional ramifications of their perceived masculinity. The hegemonic male is aggressive and sexually robust, and so any man who reports being sexually harassed by a woman is effectively psychologically castrated by his peers because he is seen as weak and submissive. Some studies have even indicated that the psychological effects of sexual harassment on men are actually more severe than those experienced by women who have been sexually harassed (Street, Gradus, Stafford & Kelly, 2007).

LGBTQ People in the Workplace

Just as women have struggled in the workplace, the LGBTQ community has also met with considerable challenges. The decision to come out to family members and friends is often a troublesome issue for many in the LGBTQ community, but the decision to come out at work may be laced with serious ramifications that affect the individual's day to day life.

Homophobia, Heterosexism & Sexual Prejudice

A large percentage of the gay population has stated that they have experienced harassment and discrimination in the workplace. Gay workers are often denied promotions, pressured to quit, or are held at a lower pay rate that their coworkers. It is also important to point out that this kind of sexual prejudice, or heterosexism, is still a legitimate concern. Even though a federal appeals court ruled in 2017 that the 1964 Civil Rights Act protection against sex discrimination in the workplace extends to protection against discrimination based on sexual orientation, the act does not explicitly prohibit it and the US Supreme Court has not ruled on the issue. As of 2016, thirty states do not explicitly prohibit that form of discrimination. Even those corporations that embrace their gay workers by providing them with domestic partner benefits, support groups, and special training programs are often reluctant to have these workers publicly associated with their company for fear of being considered a gay corporation (Hereck, 2000).

Another interesting phenomenon occurs within the LGBTQ community itself. Many younger LGBTQ workers, who were raised in a culture far more accepting of homosexuality, are more vocal and tend to fight more aggressively to obtain equality in the work place. Those workers who are older and were raised with a cultural stigma of homosexuality are more likely to stay in the closet, or at least be more subtle about their sexual identity. This is true not only among coworkers, but also among customers and business contacts as well (Hereck, 2000).

Gender Identity Disorder in the Workplace

Transgender individuals have an even more complex sociological situation in the workplace since they may have already clearly established themselves as one gender among their coworkers before making the transition. Coworkers and supervisors may actually be witness to the entire sex reassignment process, and as the transition becomes more complete the interoffice relationships that a transgender individual has honed as a member of one sex will inevitably change as they transition to a different sex (Prentiss & McAnulty, 2002).

Many cisgender heterosexuals who have never been exposed to this kind of situation may find it difficult to understand the significant difference between being gay and being transgender. This level of misunderstanding can lead to extreme situations of alienation, harassment, and prejudice. Some transgender employees find it easier to orchestrate a resignation prior to the reassignment process through upper management, and then a rehiring once the sex reassignment is complete (Prentiss & McAnulty, 2002).

Occupational Segregation

Another important dimension of gender and sexual orientation in the work place is gender stereotyping of professional roles, which is referred to as occupational segregation. While some jobs are considered traditionally female (seamstress, waitress, nurse, teacher, secretary, etc.), others are considered traditionally male (doctor, lawyer, pilots, mechanics, architects, etc.). Though there has been significant movement to close the wage gap, there has been little movement towards removing the occupational stereotypes that beget occupational segregation.

Men & Women in Cross-Gender Occupations

Though it has been shown time and time again that women are equally as capable in most occupational roles as men, occupational segregation still persists. For women, obtaining positions that are traditionally male is difficult, and they often find many corporate hurdles that their male counterparts do not experience. In the United States, this is primarily due to the masculine management style that has been socially accepted as equating to success. Kanter (1997) states that women's lack of authoritarian attitudes, lack of aggression, and readiness to accept responsibility are key factors in women being unable to overcome professional hurdles as easily as their male counterparts. All of these factors are polar opposite to the masculine traits considered necessary for success. Lipsey et al (1991) feels that the sex-role socialization discussed earlier is the primary reason women are underrepresented in male-dominated occupations, whereas Gilligan (1982) sees it as a more Freudian problem based in the psychological pressures of women to continue the dependent roles of their mothers while men must make a forceful and clean break from the nurturing to become strong, independent men.

On the other hand, men wishing to find work in traditionally female occupations often experience ridicule and harassment both professionally and personally. Often this harassment and ridicule are attacks on their masculinity, and they are sometimes shamed even within their closest circles of relationships regardless of their dedication and skill in the occupation (Furr, 2002). A typical example of this would be the male nurse. Nursing is a traditionally female occupation, and men who choose to go into this field are looked down upon as if they were not successful enough to become doctors, and thus were forced into "settling" for a position as a nurse. This prejudice is so ingrained in society that it has become part of pop culture as a subplot in the film *Meet the Parents* starring Ben Stiller.

Both men and women are often passed over for promotion when they occupy cross-gender occupational roles because of a perceived issue of abandonment. Women are considered at high-risk for leaving traditionally male positions of extreme responsibility in order to pursue a family, while men are considered at high-risk to leave traditionally female positions to pursue a more fitting position. For example, a male nurse may be passed over for promotion because it may be assumed that they will be pursuing an education to become a doctor, and that the nursing position is simply a stepping stone to bigger and better things (Furr, 2002).

Occupational Segregation as Explanation for Wage Gap

Many theories have been developed as to why the wage gap exists. Erosa, Fuster, and Restuccia (2005) have proposed a strong argument that the wage gap continues to exist because of the perceived value of female workers based on their fertility. In other words, corporations may be less willing to invest in female workers because it is a gamble whether a woman of child-bearing age will continue their work once they have children and if they do continue whether that work will be of the same quality or quantity. In this respect wages are a function of fertility and age. Still others feel that the wage gap is due to educational disparities like men choosing business or other practical classes as minors and electives while women choose liberal or fine art courses that have no perceived practical application (Blau & Kahn, 1997; Wood et al., 1993)

But many feel that occupational segregation may be the culprit. Traditionally female jobs are also some of the lowest paying jobs, so studies that consider income across occupations will not be accounting for the fact that the majority of women in the workforce are simply occupying positions that earn less money than the majority of those that are occupied by men (Cohen & Huffman 2006). While some are relatively satisfied with this explanation, it begs the question of why women have continued to occupy these low-paying positions. One popular explanation to answer this question is that women are often found to exhibit a lower sense of self-confidence when it comes to male-dominated occupations than towards those occupations that are traditionally considered female (Neville & Schlecker, 1988; Stringer & Duncan, 1985; Whiston, 1993)

Gender Conditioning & Reinforcement

Gender traits and what is considered "traditional" are ingrained in our culture and reinforced throughout childhood. In some cases—whether now or in past decades, but not in all families or cultures—girls are encouraged to develop nurturing and household skills by playing with dolls and pretend cookware; little boys, on the other hand, may be encouraged to be assertive and powerful through rough-and-tumble games, or by playing with toys like cars and construction machinery. Children are often asked what they would like to be when they grow up, and girls who want to be plumbers and boys who want to be ballerinas may in some cases be chided or strongly encouraged to reconsider their decisions. Two prominent twentieth century theorists on this aspect of gender socialization are Albert Bandura and Lawrence Kohlberg.

Bandura stressed that the process of gender socialization is achieved through a process called modeling where children imitate the actions of adults and other children around them. Boys often learn masculine behaviors from their fathers and other male role models who exhibit these traits. Girls can learn to be girls by mimicking the feminine behaviors of their mothers and other female role models. Though parents do not necessarily reinforce these gender roles, children tend to learn that behavior exhibiting same-sex traits often reaps rewards, opposite-gender behavior may incur punishment (Bandura, 1977).

Kohlberg, on the other hand, felt that these gender roles developed out of a three-step cognitive process that every child must work through from about the age of two to the age of six. The first step is for the child to recognize their particular gender. At this point they understand that there is a fundamental biological and social difference between a male and a female. Second, a child understands that this gender will not change. If they are female then she is a girl who will eventually grow up to be a woman. Finally, a child understands that no matter which gender traits they choose to exhibit their gender will still remain constant and unchanged (Kohlberg, 1966).

These experiences—whether socially, psychologically, or biologically driven—reinforce what a culture believes to be "normal" for each gender, and since they are carried into adulthood they are often the foundation of our occupational choices. With this in mind, sociologists begin their search for the underlying factors of workplace issues, like wage discrimination, occupational discrimination, glass ceiling effect, and hegemonic masculinity, far before we begin to make any serious career choices. These cultural pressures of gender stereotypes not only shape our career choices, but they also shape our chances of success as well.

APPLICATIONS

Masculine Management Style

Typically, leaders within a corporation are expected to take on the role of the hegemonic male in order to achieve real success. These male traits-like being independent, objective, and competitive-are associated with success to the point that even female managers are expected to either have or learn to assume them. One particularly strong example of a successful, masculine management style can be seen in President Donald J. Trump. The official biography found on his website refers to him as the "archetypal businessman," and reads like a checklist of the most stereotypically male traits ascribed to success in business (Trump, 2008).

Trump had his beginnings working under his father in a small real estate office in Brooklyn, New York, and though his career has been rocky, he has managed to pull his business holdings out of Chapter 11 bankruptcy and into an empire valued at more than $3 billion at the end of 2007 (*Forbes*, 2007). Many, including Trump himself, have declared that the vast majority of this success is a direct result of his aggressive business nature. In fact, in 2006 *BusinessWeek* magazine named Trump as the world's most competitive businessperson.

In his 2007 book, Trump outlines the top ten lessons in success, and not surprisingly, each of these lessons embodies a particularly masculine trait. The first lesson is simply that in order to be successful you must be a workaholic. He insists that an 80-hour work week is the key to reaching business goals, which leaves little time for family. Other hegemonic male attributes that are included in his top ten traits of success are persistence, aggression, and a keen ability to negotiate. He also suggests that any successful business person wishing to marry should only marry someone who understands they will be taking a back seat to business, and who is willing to sign a prenuptial agreement (Trump, 2007).

Competition seems to fuel Trump's aggressive management style. So much so that he created the well-known television show *The Apprentice* , in which he watched young business hopefuls compete for a position in his expanding company. Weakness is not tolerated, and results are rewarded regardless of any morals, principles, or emotional investments that may have been compromised. Though not necessarily well liked and despite several business failures, Trump is considered by many to be an extremely successful businessman. His embodiment of the hegemonic male leaves few to question how he has been able to amass such wealth and celebrity since it is precisely these traits that have been expected from successful men and women in the business world.

Feminine Management Style

The pressures of corporate culture have seen women attempt to adopt the traits of hegemonic masculinity, often at the expense of their perceived status as a woman. While many of these assertive women have achieved quite a bit of success, they are seen as successful in spite of their gender, not because of it. With this in mind, some companies who cater specifically to women as their primary market have begun to rebel against the idea that a successful woman must abandon all her feminine traits. Mary Kay Cosmetics is an excellent example of this movement.

Founded by Mary Kay Ash, the company rose from a one-woman enterprise of less than $200,000 a year to over $2.9 billion in 2011. What is most unique about Ash's company is that she made a conscious drive to elevate the feminine traits generally viewed as weaknesses in the dog-eat-dog world of business into the cornerstones of a successful corporate culture. The Mary Kay motto states that family is more important than business, and that the Golden Rule of treating others as you wish to be treated plays a major role in the decision making process.

Compassion, understanding, caring, and nurturing are all prominent elements of the Mary Kay empire, but the element of recognition is an interesting addition on top of all of these traditionally feminine traits. The women (and few men) who are a part of this pink corporate culture have enjoyed a wide variety of accolades specifically designed to reward the top performers (Mary Kay 2008). Competitiveness is surprisingly not one of the most lucrative traits to possess in this company since cooperation is highly prized and recognized over competition.

What this pink corporate culture demonstrates is that the hegemonic masculinity that we associate with success is not, in fact, a necessity to achieve that success. Though culture may influence women to display traits that many consider to be detrimental in the business world, companies like Mary Kay Cosmetics clearly show that these traits can be just as successful (perhaps even more successful in some cases) as those that embrace traditionally male attitudes.

CONCLUSION

Issues of gender and sexual orientation in the workplace are not simply confined to the office. The challenges and multidimensional experiences that occur within the walls of the work building are rooted in our experiences that occur before we even enter the working world. Regardless of whether the development of gender roles and stereotypes is truly based in biology or traits nurtured in us through our dominant culture, evidence tends to point to the fact that there are strengths and weaknesses in both the hegemonic masculinity and the exaggerated femininity that develop within the corporate culture. Both feminine and masculine traits have had their successes, but it is yet to be seen whether they can exist harmoniously within the same corporate environment, or if they must remain separate and pitted against one another in the world of business.

Though business has seen a dramatic shift over the last few decades to re-incorporate those populations that are traditionally marginalized in corporate cultures, the road to equality is a long one.

Members of the LGBTQ community have a particularly long road ahead of them in respects to seeking out equal treatment, as has been demonstrated by the uphill battle of women in the workplace. Of course these issues will likely never be completely resolved as long as the dominant culture continues to condition children to exhibit traditional gender traits from such early ages. Regardless of the willingness of the population and the growing acceptance of women and LGBTQ people in powerful roles, the shift in gender dynamics in the culture will most certainly not happen overnight. The continued sociological study of the topic of gender and sexual orientation in the workplace will be important in developing corporate techniques and political policies that will help usher in an era of equality that many workers are seeking.

TERMS & CONCEPTS

Corporate Culture: The attitudes, values, and principles that govern the decisions and overall atmosphere of a business or organization.

Gender Identity Disorder: A psychiatric condition where an individual who has been born or assigned one gender, but identifies themselves as being another gender. It is a strong disparity between one's body and one's mind.

Glass Ceiling: Occupational barriers that prevent women who are fully qualified and capable from advancing into another position within a company.

LGBTQ: The common acronym to represent the whole of the lesbian, gay, bisexual, transgender, and queer community.

Hegemonic Masculinity: The respected traits that the dominant American culture defines as masculine. The hegemonic male is assertive, strong, aggressive, a leader, and heterosexual.

Heterosexism: An ideological system that oppresses any behavior, relationship, community, or identity that is considered to be non-heterosexual.

Homophobia: A term falling out of favor, but originally used to describe the heterosexual's discomfort with being near or having any dealings with a gay person. This term may also apply to the homosexual's feelings of self-loathing that are generated by a largely heterosexual culture.

Occupational Segregation: The phenomenon where men and women appear to favor different occupations.

Occupational Sexism: Discrimination in the workplace, which is based solely on an individual's gender.

Sex-Reassignment: An extensive process wherein an individual is given hormones and undergoes surgical procedures so that the physiological expression of their gender matches their gender identity.

Sexual Harassment: Verbal or physical behavior that is of an explicitly sexual nature towards someone who neither invites nor welcomes the behavior from the perpetrator.

Sexual Prejudice: Negative attitudes and assumptions towards an individual or group that is based solely on preconceived notions of their particular gender or sexual orientation.

Transgender: An individual whose gender identity differs from the sex they were assigned at birth

Wage Discrimination: A situation where an individual of one sex is paid more or less than an individual of the opposite sex.

Wage Gap: The difference between the average yearly wages of a man and the average yearly wages of a woman.

BIBLIOGRAPHY

Addison, J. T., Ozturk, O. D., & Wang, S. (2018). "The occupational feminization of wages." *ILR Review, 71*(1), 208–241.

American Association of University Women. (2018). "The simple truth about the gender pay gap." *AAUW.* https://www.aauw.org/research/the-simple-truth-about-the-gender-pay-gap/

Bandura, A. (1977). *Social learning theory.* Englewood Cliffs, NJ: Prentice-Hall.

Blau, F., & Lawrence K. (1997). "Swimming upstream: Trends in the gender wage differential in the 1980s." *Journal of Labor Economics,* 15, 1-42.

Cohen, P. & Huffman, M. L. (2007). "Working for the woman? Female managers and the gender wage gap." *American Sociological Review,* 72, 681-704.

Cohen, P. & Huffman, M. L. (2006). "Working for the man: Management characteristics and the gender wage gap." *Conference Papers—American Sociological Association 2006 Annual Meeting, Montreal,* p 1.

Connell, R.W. (1987). *Gender and power: Society, the person, and sexual politics.* Cambridge: Polity Press.

Endicott, R. C. (2002). "Salary survey." *Advertising Age.* http://adage.com/

Erosa, A., Fuster, L., Restuccia, D. (2005). *A quantitative theory of the gender wage gap.* Federal Reserve Bank, University of Ontario.

Furr, S.R. (2002). "Men and women in cross-gender careers." In Diament, L. & Lee, J.A. (Eds.) *The psychology of sex, gender, and jobs: Issues and solutions.* (pp. 47-68) Westport, CT: Praeger.

Gates, T. G., & Viggiani, P. A. (2014). "Understanding lesbian, gay, and bisexual worker stigmatization: a review of the literature." *International Journal of Sociology & Social Policy,* 359-374.

Gilligan, C. (1982). *In a different voice: Psychological theory and women's development.* Cambridge, MA: Harvard University Press.

Herek, G. M. (2000). "The psychology of sexual prejudice." *Current Directions in Psychological Science,* 9, 19-22.

Hess, K. P. (2013). "Investigation of nonverbal discrimination against women in simulated initial job interviews." *Journal Of Applied Social Psychology,* 43, 544–555. http://www.marykay.com/ (2008). http://www.trump.com/ (2008).

Kanter, R.M. (1997), *On the frontiers of management.* Boston: Harvard Business School Press.

Kmec, J. A., & Skaggs, S. L. (2014). "The 'state' of equal employment opportunity law and managerial gender diversity." *Social Problems,* 61, 530–558.

Kohlberg, L. (1966). "A cognitive-developmental analysis of children's sex role concepts and attitudes." In Eleanor E. Maccoby ed., *The development of sex differences.* Stanford, CA: Stanford University Press.

Lipsey, R.G., Steiner, P.O., Purvis, D.D., Courant, P.N. (1990). *Economics.* New York: Harper & Row.

Lips, H. (2013). "Acknowledging discrimination as a key to the gender pay gap." *Sex Roles,* 68 (3/4), 223–230.

Miller, M. (2007, September 20). *The Forbes 400.*

Nevill, D. & Schlecker, D. (1988). "The relation of self-efficacy and assertiveness to willingness to engage in traditional/nontraditional career activities." *Psychology of Women Quarterly,* 12,(1) 91-98.

Prentiss, C. & McAnulty, R. (2002). "Gender identity disorder in the workplace." In Diament, L. & Lee, J.A. (Eds.) *The Psychology of Sex, Gender, and Jobs: Issues and Solutions* (pp. 171-184). Westport, CT: Praeger.

Somashekhar, S. (April 5, 2017). "In a landmark decision, appeals court finds that federal law bans workplace discrimination against gays." *The Washington Post.* https://www.washingtonpost.com/news/post-nation/wp/2017/04/04/court-discrimination-against-gays-is-prohibited-by-federal-law/

Street, A.E., Gradus, J.L., Stafford, J., & Kelly, K. (2007). "Gender differences in experiences of sexual harassment: Data from a male-dominated environment." *Journal of Consulting & Clinical Psychology,* 75, 464-474.

Stringer, D. & Duncan, E. (1985). "Nontraditional occupations: A study of women who have made the choice." *Vocational Guidance Quarterly,* 35, 241-248.

Tilcsik, A. (2011). "Pride and prejudice: Employment discrimination against openly gay men in the united states." *American Journal of Sociology,* 117, 586–686.

Trump, D.J., & Zanker, B. (2007). *Think big and kick ass in business and in life.* New York: Harper Collins.

Whiston, S. (1993). "Self-efficacy of women in traditional and nontraditional occupations: Differences in working with people and things." *Journal of Career Development,* 19, 175-196.

Wood, R., Corcoran, M., & Courant, P. (1993). "Pay differences among the highly paid: the male-female earnings gap in lawyers' salaries." *Journal of Labor Economics,* 11, 417-441.

Suggested Reading

Bohnet, I. & Greig, F. (2007, April). "Gender matters in workplace decisions." *Negotiations* 4-6.

Buday, S., Stake, J., & Peterson, Z. (2012). "Gender and the choice of a science career: The impact of social support and possible selves." *Sex Roles,* 66 (3/4), 197–209.

Denissen, A. M., & Saguy, A. C. (2014). "Gendered homophobia and the contradictions of workplace discrimination for women in the building trades." *Gender & Society, 28,* 381–403.

Lester, J. (2008). "Performing gender in the workplace." *Community College Review,* 35, 277- 305.

Meyers, J.S.M. (2006). "Diversity and democracy: A model for change in the workplace." *Conference Papers—American Sociological Association,* 2006 Annual Meeting, Montreal, 1, 24p.

Patti, C. (2017). "Hively v. Ivy Tech Community College." *Law & Sexuality: A Review Of Lesbian, Gay, Bisexual & Transgender Legal Issues, 26,* 133–145.

Russo, G., & Hassink, W. (2012). Multiple glass ceilings. *Industrial Relations,* 51, 892–915.

M. Lynette DiPalma

Gender Differences: Biology and Culture

ABSTRACT

As opposed to sex (which comprises only the biological aspects of being either female or male), gender includes the psychological, social, cultural, and behavioral characteristics associated with being female or male. Gender is defined by one's gender identity or the recognition that one is either male or female based on both biological and psychosocial considerations, and the internalization of this gender concept into one's self-identity. Gender role is largely a product of the way in which one was raised and may not be in conformance with one's gender identity. The development of gender differences is a complicated issue including elements of both nature (biology) and nurture (socialization). Far from being straightforward, research is finding that these two factors are interrelated in complex ways. Much more research is needed before the relationship between the two factors and the influence of the relationship on gender is completely understood.

OVERVIEW

"Women are the weaker sex and need to be protected." "Big boys don't cry." "Women and men are different but equal, and each has a unique role within society." These are just a few of the beliefs about gender that can be heard in discussions on the roles of women and men in society. It is difficult to parse out the extent to which any of these beliefs is true, and examples of the entire spectrum of attitudes toward gender can be seen in society: Women who stay at home, keep house, raise the children, and are subservient to their husbands can be seen along with those whose mates stay home with the children while they go out to work. In between is a whole array of other approaches to how individuals and societies "do gender," or interpret what it means to be one gender or another through the ongoing social interactions that individuals have with each other.

Gender vs. Sex

There is a difference between gender and sex. In most cases, it is obvious to the casual observer what the sex of another person is: Biological differences typically make it relatively easy to distinguish adults of one sex from the other. In many cases, it is also relatively easy to tell one gender from another: Women tend to dress and act in one way and men tend to dress and act in another. There are, of course, exceptions to each of these rules of thumb. From a psychosocial point of view, individuals may be androgynous, displaying feminine and masculine characteristics or traits. From a biological point of view, intersex individuals are those born with both female and male sex organs. However, these are exceptions to the rule. Sex is biological in nature and determines one's biological destiny, such as the ability to bear or sire children. Gender, on the other hand, helps define one's role within society. Gender—or the psychological, social, cultural, and behavioral characteristics associated with being female or male—is a learned characteristic based on one's gender identity and learned gender role. Gender can be thought of as a society's interpretation of the cultural meaning of one's sex. In fact, the perspective of "doing gender" posits that gender is a construct that is interpreted by members of a society through the ongoing social interactions that individuals have with each other.

Gender Stereotypes

Such notions can easily give rise to gender stereotypes, or culturally defined patterns of expected attitudes and behavior that are considered appropriate for one gender but not the other. Gender stereotypes tend to be simplistic and based not on the characteristics or aptitudes of the individual, but on over-generalized perceptions of one gender or the other. For example, although the traditional gender stereotype might be that women stay home and clean the house and raise the family while men go out and work, the fact that many women in today's society are successful physicians, scientists, lawyers, business owners, and executives (among other jobs traditionally thought to be "male") demonstrates that it is the abilities and aptitudes of the individual—not her/his gender or sex—that should prescribe the parameters in which s/he can work.

The Basis of Gender

In some ways, gender roles are biologically based. For example, physiologically, it is women who must gestate and bear the young of the species. However, this does not necessarily mean that it is the woman who must take care of the child after it is born, as is demonstrated by stay-at-home fathers who nurture the child while the mother returns to work in a reversal of traditional typical Western gender roles. Although gender has a biological foundation in the physiological differences between females and males, the way that gender is interpreted differs from culture to culture and, in some ways, from individual to individual. For example, although some societies are patriarchal in nature in which the male is the head of the family, descent is traced through the father's side of the family, and men have power over women, others are matriarchal with women holding these roles instead of men.

Nature vs. Nurture

Scientists have long been divided over the relative influences and contributions of nature (i.e., heredity and constitutional factors) and nurture (i.e., sociocultural and environmental factors) in the human development and the degree to which these sets of factors affect his/her eventual personality, abilities, and other characteristics. Part of this issue comprises ongoing questions concerning the extent to which individuals in society ascribe to one gender or another due to biological imperatives such as their sex or to psychosocial factors such as the way that they were raised. One of the assumptions that some people make regarding gender is that because human females in general tend to be not as strong as the male of the species, women are "inferior" in other ways as well. However, scientists have found no gender-based differences in general intelligence between the genders. This does not mean, of course, that every female is as smart as every male or vice versa, but that general intelligence and other mental traits tend to be normally distributed within each group. There is no scientific reason to believe that women and men (as genders) differ from each other on intelligence.

At first glance, it might seem relatively easy to sort out the influences of nature and nurture on the acquisition of gender identity and gender roles. After all, the argument might go, males and females and preprogrammed by the sex organs and hormones to behave in a certain way. Socialization then takes over and determines whether or not these biological predispositions are followed or ignored. However, the interaction between nature and nurture in regard to gender is much more complicated than that. Biosocial theories of gender posit that gender roles are the result of complex interactions between biological and social forces. This interaction helps explain why not every little girl grows up to be a stay-at-home mother or even a mother at all. In one example of a biosocial approach to gender, Udry (2000) hypothesizes that the effect of gender socialization during childhood is constrained by biological processes that produce natural behavior predispositions.

Udry & Biologically Produced Behavior Predispositions

Basing his work on primate research that has been performed with rhesus monkeys, Udry performed a longitudinal study using secondary data and prenatal blood samples that had been collected in the Child Health and Development Study (CHDS) from 1960 through 1969. Udry selected subjects for his study who had mothers with at least two prenatal blood samples in the CHDS study and who had been interviewed themselves at that time. Of 470 daughters who were eligible for participation, 75 percent completed the questionnaire. In addition, subjects completed the Personality Research Form, the Adjective Check List, the Bem Sex Role Inventory, and the Strong Vocational Interest Inventory. Measures of adult gendered behavior included questions in four general factors:

- Importance of home (e.g., ever married to a man, number of live births, importance of career);
- Feminine interests (e.g., feminine appearance factor, likes baby care, score on discriminating factors on Strong);
- Job status (e.g., proportion female in current job and previous job);
- Masculinity-femininity (e.g., feminine and masculine scales on Bem, Adjective Check List, and Personality Research Form).

A 10 ml venous blood sample was also drawn from each subject. Although produced in males in significantly greater amounts, androgens (male hormones that control the development and maintenance of masculine characteristics) are also produced in females by the adrenal glands and ovaries. One of the factors that may affect androgen levels in females is stress. The results of the study showed that mothers' prenatal hormone levels had an effect on the gendered behavior of their adult daughters. In particular, prenatal androgen exposure from the second trimester (but not the other two trimesters) affected gendered behavior, with women who had experienced greater prenatal exposure to androgens exhibiting more typically masculine or androgynous behavior as adults.

APPLICATIONS

One of the venues in which Western society has seen great changes in gender roles over the past century is in the workplace. Traditionally, Western society typically assigned men to the role of breadwinner and head of the family while women were assigned the role of homemaker and mother. When women did work, it was historically in support roles: secretaries, sales clerks, and other jobs that did not offer women the same type of upward mobility as did "male" jobs of business owners, executives, and so forth. This changed to a great extent as a result of the women's liberation movement in the 1960s and 1970s. Women came to believe that they could do anything a man could do, and started going into more technical and professional jobs than ever before. However, although some women today are firefighters, police officers, soldiers, and other professions that were traditionally concerned the domain of men, the fact remains that there is still not equity in many workplaces. Although in some cases this may be due to issues of sexual discrimination, in other cases the argument for the subordinate status of women in the workplace is based on biological factors (Messing, Lippel, Demers, & Mergler, 2000). In general, these arguments revolve around three issues.

- First, it is argued in some situations that the physical capacities of women (e.g., their size, shape, and strength) make them less fit for some jobs that are traditionally performed by men.
- The second argument against gender equity in some workplaces is that many of the occupational illnesses experienced by women on the job may not, indeed, be job-related, but be due to their psychological and psychological makeup.
- The third argument that is often proffered to support seemingly discriminatory practices in the workplace is that women's reproductive biology makes them more likely to be unfit to work than men (Messing, Lippel, Demers, & Mergler, 2000, p. 21).

Physical Strength & Fitness

Objectively, many women are unqualified for jobs that require a great deal of physical strength or a larger than average size body (for a woman). For example, to be a firefighter requires that the individual be able to haul and hold heavy fire hoses, carry people from burning buildings, and perform other tasks that many women cannot perform easily. The muscle mass of most women is less than that of most men, which means that they can lift less weight. That said, it must also be remembered that just because the average woman is not as strong as the average man, it does not mean that no woman has the size and strength necessary to do the job of firefighter or other job requiring these characteristics. Similarly, not every man is physically capable of doing these jobs, either. Further, differences in strength between the sexes vary according the particular muscles and the demands under which they are placed rather than according to a general rule.

The issue of physical characteristics necessary to be a firefighter has gone all the way up to the Supreme Court of Canada. The precedent-setting case concerned a female forest firefighter who had previously been told by her supervisor that her performance was satisfactory for three years. However, when she was required to take a new physical fitness test of strength and aerobic fitness, she was able to meet the strength standards, but failed the 11-minute run to test aerobic fitness by 49 seconds. She was subsequently laid off by the government. She was able to win her appeal based on the argument that the requirement was discriminatory because the aerobic fitness test was not directly related to the job or to the specific tasks of the job. In addition, the test was more likely to exclude women than men.

Employment law can be a complicated thing. Although it might make sense to hire only the "best" person for the job regardless of sex, the reality is that other things need to be taken into account in making this decision. First, many jobs set minimum standards that a person needs to meet in order to be able to adequately do the job. For example, the job of warehouse worker might have a requirement that a person be able to lift 50 pounds to a height of 7 feet. If the warehouse routinely receives 50 pound items that need to be placed on shelves at that height, this might be a bona fide requirement of the job. If, however, the warehouse only receives such items occasionally, this may not be considered a bona fide requirement for the job. In addition, if the worker never needs to be able to lift anything heavier than 50 pounds or higher than 7 feet, it does not matter whether or not someone can lift heavier items to greater heights: Meeting the minimum standard suffices. Further, most employment law requires that an organization make reasonable accommodations for an individual so that s/he can meet the requirements of the job. In the example of the warehouse employee, this might mean that a shorter person could use a step stool in order to be able to reach the higher shelf. In the example of the 2.5 km running test for aerobic fitness discussed above, the test did not meet the requirement of being job related. The 2.5 km distance and concomitant 11 minute limit were randomly determined and not related to such job-requirements as the radius of forest fires or the speed at which they travel. Therefore, the test was determined not to be a bona fide requirement of the job (Supreme Court orders female firefighter rehired, 1999, Sept. 9).

Susceptibility to Occupational Illness

It has been repeatedly observed that although women tend to live longer than men and enjoy similar years of good health, women tend to report more illnesses than do men and take more advantage of health care services (Messing, Lippel, Demers, & Mergler, 2000). Further, although women tend to have significantly fewer accidents on the job than do men, they do tend to have more occupational illnesses such as chemical poisoning, cancer resulting from exposure to toxic substances, and musculoskeletal problems such as carpal tunnel syndrome and back problems. This has been used by some employers to discriminate against women in the workplace based on the assumption that they will be absent more often than male workers.

A number of hypotheses have been posited to explain these differences in occupational illness.

- The first of these is that occupational illnesses are psychologically-based and that women are more likely to report them.
- The second hypothesis is that these are, in fact, real illnesses and that women are more prone to developing them because of their biological make-up (e.g., hormones).
- A third hypothesis also grants that the illnesses are real, but posits that they are related to the work that women do in their homes rather than the work that they do on the job.
- Another hypothesis is that the illnesses are real and related to the working conditions that women encounter on their jobs (Messing, Lippel, Demers, & Mergler, 2000, p. 29).
- A final category of hypotheses posits that the increased occurrence of job-related illness is the result of an interaction between biological specificity and paid or unpaid working conditions.

At this time, research does not point to one of these hypotheses being superior to the other. The difficulty lies in the fact that the working conditions and job requirements vary widely for men and women and it is difficult to sort out their effects.

Fitness & Reproduction

As opposed to arguments that can be made about the differences in size and strength and their relationship with fitness for the job being relative, the differences between the sexes that are due to the nature of their reproductive systems are not. Although some organizations today offer paternity leave in addition to maternity leave, when given the opportunity to return to work early so that their husbands can stay home and bond with the new baby, most women still prefer to stay home themselves (Peters, 2005). Further, although some women may work up until the time that they go into labor, this tends to be the exception rather than the rule.

Although many women are able to continue to work well into their pregnancy, some work environments can negatively impact a fetus, particularly in the early part of the pregnancy when major organs are being established. However, it is not only in the early stages of pregnancy that damage from the external environment can occur: Miscarriage, low birth weight, malformation, or prematurity can be risks from toxic environments throughout a pregnancy. Further, it is not only toxic environments that have been found to have a negative effect on female reproduction. Factors such as extremes in temperature, shift work, heavy work, fast work speed, and irregular schedules can all affect fertility, menstrual regularity or pain, and fetal development.

CONCLUSION

The determination of one's gender is a complicated thing, involving both nature and nurture. Biologically, one's sex organs and concomitant sex hormones determine her/his biological sex. This, in turn, often affects the way that the individual is socialized so that s/he learns to behave in accordance with the gender expectations of society. Gender can be affected in many more ways other than nature or nurture including the environment within the mother's womb to the extent to which one is encouraged to either conform or breakout of gender stereotypes. In addition, the obvious biological differences between females and males have led some people to make assumptions about the capabilities of individuals based on their sex. However, job requirements need to be demonstrably related to the job and developed so not to discriminate between women and men on factors that are not bona fide job requirements.

TERMS & CONCEPTS

Androgyny: The presence of both feminine and masculine characteristics or traits in one individual.

Biosocial Theory: Any theory in the behavioral or social sciences which posits that behavior is the result of a complex interaction between biological and social forces.

Culture: A complex system of meaning and behavior that is socially transmitted and that defines a common way of life for a group or society. Culture includes the totality of behavior patterns, arts, beliefs, institutions, and other products of human work and thought of the society or group.

"Doing Gender": A theoretical perspective on gender which posits that gender is a construct that is interpreted by members of a society through the ongoing social interactions that individuals have with each other.

Gender: Psychological, social, cultural, and behavioral characteristics associated with being female or male. Gender is defined by one's gender identity and learned gender role.

Gender Identity: The recognition that one is either male or female based on both biological and psychosocial considerations, and the internalization of this gender concept into one's self-identity.

Gender Role: Separate patterns of personality traits, mannerisms, interests, attitudes, and behaviors that are regarded as "male" and "female" by one's culture. Gender role is largely a product of the way in which one was socialized and may not be in conformance with one's gender identity.

Gender Stereotype: A culturally defined pattern of expected attitudes and behaviors that are considered appropriate for one gender but not the other. Gender stereotypes tend to be simplistic and based not on the characteristics or aptitudes of the individual, but on over generalized perceptions of one gender or the other.

Intersexuality: A condition of ambiguous sexual identity. Formerly referred to as a hermaphrodite, an intersexual individual possesses both female and male sex organs.

Patriarchy: A social system (e.g., society or group) in which the male is the head of the family, descent is traced through the father's side of the family, and men have power over women.

Sex: The biological aspects of being either female or male. Genetically, females are identified by having two X chromosomes and males by having an X and a Y chromosome. In addition, sex can typically be determined from either primary or secondary sexual characteristics. Primary sexual characteristics comprise the female or male reproductive organs (i.e., the vagina, ovaries, and uterus for females and the penis, testes, and scrotum for males). Secondary sexual characteristics comprise the superficial differences between the sexes that occur with puberty (e.g., breast development and hip broadening for women and facial hair and voice deepening for men).

Sexual Discrimination: The differential treatment of individuals based on their sex. Although sexual discrimination can occur against either sex, in most cases in today's society it occurs against women. Sexual discrimination can be exhibited in such actions as lower wages being given to one sex for the same work when performed by the other sex, discounting of the characteristics or attributes of one sex in comparison with the other, or unfair hiring or promotion policies that are biased against one sex.

Social Role: A set of expectations placed on members of a group of people with a given social position or status within society.

Socialization: The process by which individuals learn to differentiate between what the society regards as acceptable versus unacceptable behavior and act in a manner that is appropriate for the needs of the society.

Society: A distinct group of people who live within the same territory, share a common culture and way of life, and are relatively independent from people outside the group. Society includes systems of social interactions that govern both culture and social organization.

Bibliography

Ayalon, H., & Livneh, I. (2013). "Educational standardization and gender differences in mathematics achievement: A comparative study." *Social Science Research,* 42, 432–445.

Coon, D. (2001). *Introduction to psychology: Gateways to mind and behavior* (9th ed.). Belmont, CA: Wadsworth/Thomson Learning.

Kehn, A., & Ruthig, J. (2013). "Perceptions of gender discrimination across six decades: The moderating roles of gender and age." *Sex Roles,* 69 (5/6), 289–296.

Magee, W. (2013). "Anxiety, demoralization, and the gender difference in job satisfaction." *Sex Roles,* 69 (5/6), 308–322.

Messing, K., Lippel, K., Demers, D., & Mergler, D. (2000). "Equality and difference in the workplace: Physical job demands, occupational illnesses, and sex differences." *NWSA Journal,* 12, 21-49.

Peters, J. K. (2005). "Gender remembered: The ghost of 'unisex' past, present, and future." *Women's Studies,* 34, 67-83.

Schwartz, C. R., & Han, H. (2014). "The reversal of the gender gap in education and trends in marital dissolution." *American Sociological Review,* 79, 605–629.

"Supreme Court orders female firefighter rehired" (1999, Sept. 9). *CBC News.* http://www.cbc.ca/news/canada/supreme-court-orders-female-firefighter-rehired-1.173366

Udry, J. R. (2000). "Biological limits of gender construction." *American Sociological Review,* 65, 443-457.

Yu, W., & Lee, P. (2013). "Decomposing gender beliefs: Cross-national differences in attitudes toward maternal employment and gender equality at home." *Sociological Inquiry,* 83, 591–621.

Suggested Reading

Cole, E. R., Jayaratne, T. E., Cecchi, L. A., Feldbaum, M., & Petty, E. M. (2007). "Viva la difference? Genetic explanations for perceived gender differences in nurturance." *Sex Roles,* 57 (3/4), 211-222.

Miville, M.L. (2013). *Multicultural gender roles: Applications for mental health and education.* Hoboken, N.J.: Wiley.

Nazroo, J. Y, Edwards, A. C., & Brown, G. W. (1998). "Gender differences in the prevalence of depression: Artifact, alternative disorders, biology or roles?" *Sociology of Health and Illness,* 20, 312-330.

Polavieja, J. G. (2012). "Socially embedded investments: explaining gender differences in job-specific skills." *American Journal of Sociology,* 118, 592–634.

Wilcox, W.B., & Kline, K.K. (2013). *Gender and parenthood: Biological and social scientific perspectives.* New York: Columbia University Press.

Wolfe, A. (1994). "The gender question." *New Republic,* 210, 27-34.

Ruth A. Wienclaw, Ph.D.

GENDER IN THE CLASSROOM

ABSTRACT

Despite the fact that research has found no differences in intelligence between males and females, gender differences in the classroom remain. The reasons for this phenomenon are unclear and may be attributable in part both to nature (heredity and constitutional factors) and to nurture (sociocultural and environmental factors). Scientists have proffered at least three potential reasons for the observed differences between genders in the classroom: the hidden curriculum, different expectations for performance and achievement for females and males, and teacher expectancy effect. In truth, more than one factor may be operating at the same time. No matter the underlying causes for gender inequity in the classroom, however, it is important to give both males and females the education that they need, not only as a class but also as individuals within that class, in order to reach their full potential.

OVERVIEW

Not too long ago, little girls were expected to excel in home arts, have high verbal skills, and grow up to be wives and mothers or, if they ventured outside the expectations of their culture, to work in low-level support positions to help their male bosses succeed. Little boys, on the other hand, were told that the world was their oyster and were expected to do well in math and science and go on to become doctors, lawyers, and business leaders. The truth is, of course, that girls can be powerful and assertive, boys can be sensitive and artistic, and nothing is wrong with either of these positions, the old gender stereotypes, or anything in between. In theory, at least, 21st-century society embraces the notion that we should support every child to become the best that he or she can be, based not on cultural expectations but on the interests, aptitudes, and abilities of each child as an individual.

This attitude, however, is often better expressed in theory than in application. For example, as little girls start to do better in mathematics, newspapers write articles about how little boys are falling behind in school achievement, an argument very similar to that advanced by feminists half a century ago regarding little girls. Despite the many advancements in equality and women's rights, practical feminism still has great strides to make in the real world before there is truly equity between men and women, both on the job and in society. Achieving this goal will take action on many levels and in many venues. To be successful, however, it will be necessary to first achieve equity in the classroom. This is not only because the classroom is where both girls and boys learn and acquire skills necessary for later success but also because it is in the classroom that both genders learn to either conform to gender roles and stereotypes or to break free of them and allow others to do the same.

Nature vs. Nurture

Scientists have long been divided over the relative influences of nature (heredity and constitutional factors) and nurture (sociocultural and environmental factors) on the development of an individual and the degree to which these factors affect his or her eventual personality, abilities, and other characteristics. Understanding the basics of this controversy is important to understanding how education may affect how the genders are taught and the expectations that teachers have in the classroom. For example, if the assumption is made that boys are inherently better in math and science than girls—the "nature" side of the argument—it might make sense to emphasize such subjects when teaching boys, set higher expectations for boys in these subjects, and encourage boys to go into careers that require this type of knowledge while doing the opposite for girls. However, if in general girls and boys are equally likely to excel in subjects related to math and science, yet girls are found to do more poorly in these subjects at school, the conclusion might be drawn that there is something within the educational system that is causing the score differential—the "nurture" side of the argument. Therefore, to understand gender differences in the classroom, it is first important to understand to what degree intelligence and other mental capacities are inherently equal—or not—for both genders.

General Intelligence & Gender

In general, scientists have found no gender-based differences in general intelligence. However, just as not every girl is as smart as every other girl and not every boy is as smart as every other boy, all boys and all girls do not start out with the same intellectual capacities. Rather, general intelligence and other mental traits tend to be normally distributed within the group. For example, as a group, girls tend to be better at spelling than boys; by the end of high school, only 30 percent of boys spell better than the average girl. In fact, girls in general tend to be gifted in verbal abilities, whereas boys tend to be overrepresented in the bottom part of the normal distribution for verbal skills. Girls also tend to be more sensitive to touch, taste, and odor than boys, typically learn to talk earlier than boys, and are less likely than boys to stutter. Boys tend to outnumber girls in remedial reading classes by a ratio of three to one and are twice as likely as girls to be underachievers by the time they reach high school. Girls are slightly more likely to graduate high school than are boys, and more women than men graduate from college and receive advanced degrees.

Social Status & Gender

Despite the fact that more women than men complete undergraduate and graduate programs, in the United States, from 2007 to 2011, the median income for women who worked full time ($37,160) was more than $10,000 less than the median income for full-time working men ($47,549) (US Census Bureau, 2011). There are many potential reasons for this phenomenon, including the fact that many women still choose to focus on family over career during their children's formative years. However, many sociologists also interpret this phenomenon as evidence of gender stratification—the hierarchical organization of a society in such a way that members of one gender have more access to wealth, prestige, and power than do the members of the other gender. It is important to note that social stratification by gender is not exactly the same phenomenon as social stratification by race or ethnicity.

This would all be a moot point if education did not play such an important role in one's ability to make one's way in the world. Although there are notable exceptions to the rule, in industrial societies, education is frequently an important predictor of one's eventual socioeconomic status, with individuals who have earned a college degree being more likely to obtain higher-paying jobs than individuals with less education. However, another factor in the pay gap between men and women is what subject they choose to study and, consequently, what field they choose to work in:

> Overall, the most powerful explanation for pay gaps is not so much a failure to pay men and women equally for the same job. Rather, women are more likely to get degrees that lead to positions which are paid less than the positions men are more likely to get following their collegiate specializations. More women end up in education and nursing; more men end up in engineering and computer science. Education and nursing are not as likely to be lucrative as jobs that require engineering and computer science degrees. (Norén, 2012, par. 3)

The question then remains whether women innately prefer fields such as education and nursing over engineering and computer science, or whether women are subtly discouraged from pursing mathematical and scientific fields throughout their educational career. If one gender receives substantially different treatment in school than another gender and this differential treatment results in people of that gender being steered in a direction that makes it difficult for them to obtain higher-status and -income jobs, then the educational system has failed to provide equal opportunities for all.

Gender Differences in the Classroom

Hidden Curriculum

There are at least three potential reasons for the observed differences between genders in the classroom. First, conflict theorists hypothesize that girls and boys are subtly taught from an early age that they are different, not only physically but emotionally and intellectually as well, and that they should expect different things out of life. One of the ways this is done is through what conflict theorists refer to as the "hidden curriculum," which comprises the standards of proper behavior for a society or culture that are taught within the school system. The hidden curriculum subtly reinforces behavior and attitudes that are deemed appropriate by the society or culture, so that girls are reinforced for taking an interest in "feminine" subjects, such as literature and counseling, and boys are reinforced for pursuing more "masculine" subjects, such engineering and science. The hidden curriculum is an example of a nurture theory of individual differences. Whether or not there truly is a hidden curriculum being taught within the school system, many girls emerge from it academically ill prepared to pursue careers in science, mathematics, and technical fields.

Differing Expectations & Teacher Expectancy Effect

Another reason that the different genders may receive different educations within the same classroom is because teachers often have different expectations for performance and achievement for females and males. It has been posited, for example, that based on gender stereotypes, teachers may tend to expect girls to do better in reading and writing and boys to do better in mathematics and science, setting up what is known as the teacher expectancy effect. This is a type of self-fulfilling prophecy in which the student may pick up on subtle (or not so subtle) cues from the teacher about how well he or she should be performing or what areas he or she should be interested in. For example, if a teacher thinks that girls do better in reading and writing than in math and science, the teacher may praise and encourage girls when they do well in courses requiring verbal skills but not when they do well in courses requiring mathematical or scientific skills. Since most children tend to want to please their teachers and receive positive feedback, they tend to work harder in the areas that they know will result in positive reinforcement from the teacher.

APPLICATIONS

Mixed-Gender vs. Single-Gender Educational Settings

Canada and Pringle (1995) performed a study that examined the social construction of gender differences in classroom interactions in the five years immediately following the transition of a former women's college to a mixed-gender institution. Their review of the research literature showed a trend for modern mixed-gender education to place girls and women at a notable disadvantage, while women who attend women-only colleges tend to have greater self-esteem at graduation and less gender-stereotyped career aspirations, are more engaged in college activities, and are more likely to enter certain traditionally male professions, earn higher salaries, and reach high levels of achievement in their careers after college. Research findings also suggest that these advantages may accrue the more time one spends in an all-female institution. However, not only Canada and Pringle but other researchers as well note that much of the research on the success of women's colleges in helping women break away from gender expectations and stereotypes fails to adequately separate the effects of attending an all-women's college from other factors that might also yield these results. Further, it is noted that researchers still do not understand which factors or processes confer these advantages to women.

Canada and Pringle collected data through observation of interactions between students and professors in the classroom. This was done during the middle of the semester; at the beginning of the semester, fewer students would comfortable enough with a subject area and professor to ask questions, while at the end of the semester, there potentially could be a disproportionate amount of interaction between students and professors due to questions about end-of-course requirements. The observers prearranged their visits with the professors and arrived early to each class in order to choose a seat that was peripheral to the main body of seats in the classroom but with a clear view of both the students and the professor. During the first ten minutes of each class, the observer created a diagram of the classroom and marked the positions of the professor and each student as well as the gender of each student. Following this activity, observations were conducted for the next 30 minutes of the scheduled class time.

The researchers found that the behavior of female students, as well as both male and female professors, changes depending on whether or not male students are in the classroom. The behavior of both female and male students in coeducational classes was found to be related to the proportion of male students present, and the gender of the professor was found to be related to classroom dynamics in a complex manner. It appeared that gender was important in coeducational classrooms in ways that it was not in female-only classrooms. The verbal behavior of female students was found to be strongly influenced by the presence of males in the classroom, and gender differences were more obvious in mixed-gender settings.

CONCLUSION

In industrialized societies, education has been shown to be positively linked with various outcomes later in life, including career success, salary level, and socioeconomic status. This linkage is even more likely to hold true in postindustrial societies that are primarily based on the processing and control of information and the provision of services. Further, it is in the classroom that one not only acquires the technical and professional knowledge necessary for success but often also learns the social norms for interactions and gender roles and expectations. This frequently puts women at a disadvantage. On the other hand, when efforts are made to improve the education received by girls and women, male students sometimes suffer as a result. It should be remembered that it is not so much that we as a society need to make sure that women (or men) are given a superior education to make up for past inequities but that any obstacles to educational parity should be removed.

Unfortunately, in many cases, this is easier said than done. Although females may not differ significantly from males in intelligence, in some circumstances it has been found that the genders need to be taught differently in order to understand the same concepts. In addition, research has consistently shown that there are gender-based differences in academic achievement in different subject areas. Much research is still necessary to understand what factors cause these differences and how to create an environment that will foster educational equity between the genders. Whether these observed differences are due to nature or nurture is far from clear.

In addition, it must be remembered that just because men and women do not differ in intelligence does not mean that there are not individual differences both within and between genders. The point is not to make sure that one gender is given a better education than the other; it is to ensure that both genders are offered an education that is free from gender-role expectations and gender stereotyping and helps each person realize his or her potential.

TERMS & CONCEPTS

Conflict Perspective: An approach to analyzing social behavior that explains and understands it in terms of conflict or tension between competing groups.

Culture: A complex, socially transmitted system of meaning and behavior that defines a common way of life for a group or society. Culture includes the totality of behavior patterns, arts, beliefs, institutions, and other products of human work and thought of the society or group.

Feminism: An ideology that is opposed to gender stratification and male dominance. Feminist beliefs and concomitant actions are intended to help bring justice, fairness, and equity to all women and aid in the development of a society in which women and men are equal in all areas of life.

Gender Stereotype: A culturally defined pattern of expected attitudes and behaviors that are considered appropriate for one gender but not the other. Gender stereotypes tend to be simplistic and based not on the characteristics or aptitudes of the individual but on overgeneralized perceptions of one gender or the other.

Gender Stratification: The hierarchical organization of a society in such a way that members of one gender have more access to wealth, prestige, and power than do the members of the other gender.

Hidden Curriculum: The standards of proper behavior for a society or culture that are taught within the school system. The hidden curriculum is not part of the articulated curricula for schools; rather, it is taught subtly through the reinforcement of behaviors and attitudes that are deemed appropriate by the society or culture.

Normal Distribution: A continuous distribution that is symmetrical about its mean and asymptotic to the horizontal axis. The area under the normal distribution is 1.

Reinforcement: An act, process, circumstance, or condition in response to a particular action that increases the probability of a person repeating that action.

Self-Fulfilling Prophecy: A situation in which one's belief or expectation sets up a situation in which the belief or expectation is met. For example, a student who thinks that he or she will not do well on an examination even if he or she studies will not study and, therefore, will not do well on the examination.

Social Stratification: A relatively fixed hierarchical organization of a society in which entire subgroups are ranked according to social class. Divisions are marked by differences in economic rewards, power within the society, and access to resources, power, and perceived social worth. Social stratification is a system of structured social inequality.

Society: A distinct group of people who live within the same territory, share a common culture and way of life, and are relatively independent from people outside the group. Society includes systems of social interactions that govern both cultural and social organization.

Socioeconomic Status (SES): The position of an individual or group on the two vectors of social and economic status and their combination. Factors contributing to socioeconomic status include (but are not limited to) income, type and prestige of occupation, place of residence, and educational attainment.

Stereotype: A set of generalized expectations and beliefs about the qualities, abilities, and other characteristics of people who belong to an identifiable social group or category, such as a certain race, gender, or ethnicity. Although stereotypes can be useful in making simplified and expedited short-term judgments, they tend to be exaggerated and negative, do not take into account individual differences, and are difficult to change. As a result, the application of stereotypes in the long term may be counterproductive. Stereotypes tend to be shared and widely held by the members of a group.

Teacher Expectancy Effect: The impact of a teacher's expectations of a student's performance or achievement on the actual performance or achievement of that student. The teacher expectancy effect is a type of self-fulfilling prophecy.

Bibliography

Canada, K., & Pringle, R. (1995). "The role of gender in college classroom interactions: A social context approach." *Sociology of Education,* 68, 161-186.

Cervoni, C., & Ivinson, G. (2011). "Girls in primary school science classrooms: Theorising beyond dominant discourses of gender." *Gender & Education,* 23, 461–475.

Eliot, L. (2013). "Single-sex education and the brain." *Sex Roles,* 69 (7/8), 363–381.

Kannen, V. (2014). "These are not 'regular places': women and gender studies classrooms as heterotopias." *Gender, Place & Culture: A Journal of Feminist Geography,* 21, 52–67.

Myers, D. G. (2001). *Psychology* (6th ed.). New York: Worth Publishers.

Norén, Laura. (2012, September 4). "Race and gender in higher education: Who gets degrees?" *The Society Pages.* http://thesocietypages.org/graphicsociology/2012/09/04/race-and-gender-in-higher-education/

Stockard, J. (2000). *Sociology: Discovering society* (2nd ed.). Belmont, CA: Wadsworth/Thomson Learning.

Taylor, C. A. (2013). "Objects, bodies and space: gender and embodied practices of mattering in the classroom." *Gender & Education,* 25, 688–703.

Tindall, T. & Hamil, B. (2004). "Gender disparity in science education: The causes, consequences, and solutions." *Education,* 125, 282-295.

United States Census Bureau. (2011). "Selected economic characteristics: 2007–2011 American Community Survey 5-year estimates." http://factfinder2.census.gov/

Suggested Reading

Condravy, J., Skirboll, E., & Taylor, R. (1998). "Faculty perceptions of classroom gender dynamics." *Women and Language,* 21, 18-27.

Drudy, S. & Chatháin, M. Ú. (2002). "Gender effects in classroom interaction: Data collection, self-analysis and reflection." *Evaluation and Research in Education,* 16, 34-50.

Drury, K., Bukowski, W., Velásquez, A., & Stella-Lopez, L. (2013). "Victimization and gender identity in single-sex and mixed-sex schools: examining contextual variations in pressure to conform to gender norms." *Sex Roles,* 69 (7/8), 442–454.

Friend, J. (2007). "Single-gender public education and federal policy." *American Educational History Journal,* 34, 55-67.

Legewie, J., & DiPrete, T. A. (2012). "School context and the gender gap in educational achievement." *American Sociological Review,* 77, 463–485.

Spencer, R., Porche, M. V., & Tolman, D. L. (2003). "We've come a long way—maybe: New challenges for gender equity in education." *Teachers College Record,* 105, 1774-1807.

Whitmore, D. (2005). "Resource and peer impacts on girls' academic achievement: Evidence from a randomized experiment." *American Economic Review,* 95, 199-203.

Younger, M., Warrington, M., & Williams, J. (1999). "The gender gap and classroom interactions: Reality and rhetoric?" *British Journal of Sociology of Education,* 20, 325-341.

Ruth A. Wienclaw, Ph.D.

Gender Issues in Physical Education

OVERVIEW

Low levels of physical activity among young women raises concerns about the negative impact on physical and mental health. The ways in which girls approach physical education classes and physical activity as a whole are related to perceptions of gender differences and teacher attitudes on coeducational PE classes. Alternatives to competitive sports that have helped to raise the interest of girls in both PE classes and in after-school and extracurricular programs.

In 1972, as the women's movement gained force in the United States, Congress passed the Education Amendments. Title IX of those amendments specified that "No person in the United States shall, on the basis of sex, be excluded from participation in, be denied the benefits of, or be subjected to discrimination under any education program or activity receiving Federal financial assistance" (Office for Civil Rights, 2012). From the beginning, Title IX was interpreted to mean that physical education classes should become coeducational. In 2006 as concern mounted over low levels of female participation in PE, the administration of George W. Bush modified that interpretation, giving schools more leeway to establish single-gender classes or single-gender groupings within coeducational classes. Schools are still required to issue biennial reports on the status of gender equality.

Despite significant changes in approaches to female physical activity over the course of history and despite perceptions that barriers to full female participation were removed with the passage of Title IX, physical education classes tend to highlight gender differences, and countries throughout the world are dealing with low levels of physical activity of young females in relation to that of males. As girls age, their level of physical activity continues to decline, and females may take physical education classes only one out of four years in high school. In 1990, the United States National Risk Behavior Survey looked at 11,000 American students to determine how many students were engaging in at least 20 minutes a day of vigorous physical activity at least three days a week, revealing that 31 percent of girls in the 9th grade did so. By the 12th grade, however, the level of physical activity had dropped to 17 percent. Research continues to demonstrate that girls perform better in PE classes when they are given options beyond those of traditional competitive sports.

Even as infants, girls and boys are socialized differently and are encouraged to engage in different forms of play. Those differences may range from the rough-and-tumble play used with male infants to fathers encouraging sons to play football and shoot hoops. At the same time, girls are frequently brought up to value delicacy and are encouraged to engage in more sedentary activities. From a young age, girls are socialized into placing an emphasis on what feminists have identified as the "Barbie doll syndrome," which deals with the need to be thin, pretty, and feminine. From this viewpoint, physical activity may be seen as unfieminine because it is more closely associated with boys than with girls. Schools may exacerbate the problem by creating an environment in which girls are taught to see their bodies as in need of constant improvement (Paechter, 2013). The situation is made even more complicated by the fact that schools sometimes cut programs for male athletes in order to create new programs for females, leading to what has been called reverse discrimination.

Physical education first surfaced as a school subject in Europe in the early nineteenth century. By 1820, some U.S. schools had begun using the European model of physical education to teach gymnastics and hygiene. It was not until after the Civil War that American schools began to introduce physical education classes on a wider scale. Outside the classroom, the Young Men's Christian Association was established by George Williams in London in 1844 as a way to get young men off the street and teach them to respect God, community, and their own bodies. The first YMCA in the United States was established in the historic Old South Church in Boston in 1851, establishing an ongoing pattern for encouraging physical activity among young males.

In 1858, the Ladies Christian Association was established in New York. The familiar YWCA name was not attached to the women's organization until a Boston branch was founded in 1866. Although physical exercise was not generally advocated for females of the period, the YWCA encouraged young women to participate in calisthenics. In Boston, pulleys were installed on the doors of boarding house rooms so that farm girls who were used to physical activity could exercise. During the Great Depression, which began in 1929 and lasted until the outbreak of World War II, many schools were forced to cut out physical education classes in order to remain open.

Even though women finally won the right to vote with passage of the 19th Amendment in 1920, women were still viewed as ill-suited to strenuous physical activity. By World War II (1941-1945), the emphasis in physical education classes was on preparing males for manual labor. The post-war years brought about major changes in education, and new laws such as the Civil Rights Act of 1964, Title IX, and numerous court cases began to mandate sexual equality from a legal perspective. In 1973, tennis player Billie Jean King made history when she defeated Bobby Riggs in a televised match that the media dubbed the "Battle of the Sexes." The following year, King established the Women's Sports Foundation to address gender inequalities in sports.

As female teachers entered the field of physical education, they often faced hostile environments (Verbrugge, 2012) as they sought to encourage girls to engage in more physical activity. Most white teachers left the field when they married (though African American women remained on the job). Historically, the field of women's physical education has been dominated by unmarried females, and this fact has contributed to the homophobia prevalent in the field (Verbrugge, 2012). Because physical education teachers challenged prevailing norms of femininity, they were harshly criticized (Verbrugge, 2012). As late as 2005, menstruation was considered a major drawback for female athletes and perceived of as an obstacle to successful performance in PE classes.

FURTHER INSIGHTS

The Surgeon General of the United States announced in 1996 that levels of physical activity were closely related to overall health, motivating the Centers for Disease Control to create a new unit devoted to promoting physical activity among Americans. Although medical and fitness experts recommend that high school students should do some type of physical activity at least 60 minutes a day on most days, data from various sources suggests that only 27 percent of girls actually do so. Low levels of physical activity among girls have been linked to obesity and teen pregnancy and to heart disease, some cancers, depression, and osteoporosis in adulthood. Only 55.7 percent of girls in the United States regularly attend physical education classes. Illinois is the only state to mandate PE for grades K-12.

The level of physical activity is particularly low for urban and rural females and for minorities and girls from low-income families. By some estimates, Hispanic girls are three times more likely than white girls to be overweight and physically inactive. In 2002, the National Heart, Lung, and Blood Institute Growth and Health Study reported the results of a longitudinal study of 1,166 white girls and 1,213 African American girls. Researchers, who followed girls from the age of nine or ten to the ages of eighteen or nineteen, revealed that the most active girls were those from families with higher levels of education. The least active girls were those who smoked. In 2008, 84 percent of urban girls and 68 percent of rural girls took no PE classes at all (Sabo, 2008). In rural areas, schools may be faced with limited funds for building facilities and purchasing equipment, and the tendency in many areas before the passage of

Title IX was to channel funds to male sports such as football because they were seen as a way to bring attention and glory to rural schools. Even in suburban areas where differences between physical activities of males and females are not as distinct as in urban and rural areas, girls have been found to enter sports at later ages than boys and to drop out of those activities at an earlier age (Sabo, 2008).

In 2004, the Women's Sports Foundation issued a report that focused national attention on the link between levels of physical activity and women's health. That same year, the World Health Organization instituted the Global Strategy on Diet, Physical Activity, and Health. The WSF report was updated in 2009, offering new information documenting continued low levels of female physical activity, particularly among low-income individuals and minorities (Starowsy, DeSouza, and Ducher). That same year, the Barack Obama administration released the first National Physical Activity Plan for the United States.

Researchers have presented overwhelming evidence that physical activity in adolescence is directly related to improved health in adulthood. Those benefits include a 20 percent lower chance of contracting breast cancer and a reduced risk of developing osteoporosis, high blood pressure, diabetes, depression, or anxiety. Among adolescent girls, studies have shown that those involved in athletic activities are also less likely to have unprotected sex with multiple partners, a practice that increases the likelihood of contracting HIV/AIDS or other sexually transmitted diseases. Young athletes also exhibit lower levels of stress and are less likely to attempt suicide.

VIEWPOINTS

Girls who are involved in physical activities outside of physical education classes are more likely than others to express enjoyment of PE. However, girls continue to be less inclined than boys to engage in physical activity because public areas are often taken over by boys (Paechter, 2013) and because community sports teams are still predominantly made up of boys. Despite the passage of Title IX, schools are still more likely to fund sports for boys than for girls since girls express less interest in sports. Even though that interest may be due to limited opportunities to engage in activities other than competitive sports in PE classes, as well as extra-curricular and community-oriented activities, school officials use the low interest level as a rationale for not offering more opportunities for females to engage in physical activities.

Despite the ostensible commitment of governments at all levels to promoting increased physical activity among young females, gender issues have persisted in physical education classes. Some teachers have attempted to level out differences between male and female students in coeducational classes by modifying the scores of female students (Murphy, 2014). For instance, girls may be graded on effort rather than successfully scoring points. Additionally, girls may suffer from the fact that many schools require that grades be based on level of participation. Some teachers divide classes into single-sex groups, particularly in the case of contact sports, to make it possible to match physical skills and ensure the safety of female students.

Girls' attitudes toward physical education are influenced by a number of factors. One of the most important is how friends view the activity. Girls who see physical activity as socially acceptable are more likely to express enjoyment than those whose friends view it as embarrassing (Murphy, 2014). Body image is also a significant influence, and girls who are overweight are particularly reluctant to put themselves on display in front of males. Girls frequently complain that boys make comments about the size of their breasts or call attention to girls' legs or hips. A lack of enjoyment is common among girls who view the military-type exercises preferred by many PE teachers as irrelevant to their bodies and lifestyles (Olafson, 2002).

Competition also becomes a factor in coeducational classes, and girls contend that boys are more competitive than girls. Boys, on the other hand, accuse girls of not being engaged in activities in PE classes. Research reveals that boys gain specific advantages from coeducational classes because they foster confidence, promote group affiliation, and teach helping behaviors (Olafson, 2002). However, boys report that they are more likely to exhibit improved performances and try harder in single-gender classes because of the reduced risk of injuring others (Olafson, 2002). Gender attitudes toward sports may be somewhat skewed by the fact that boys tend to overestimate their interest in sports (Sabo and Veliz, 2008) while girls feel no pressure to engage personally in sports.

Experts on gender differences in physical education recommend involving girls in the design of physical education classes (Murphy, 2014). Research shows that females are more likely to enjoy alternate activities such as dance and drama (Paech-ter, 2013) to the competitive sports preferred by the majority of males. Other options include Pilates, kickboxing, core training (Wilkinson and Bretzing, 2011), gymnastics (Hannon and Ratliffe, 2007), yoga, and spinning. In a study of 83 high school students, Wilkinson and Bretzing (2011) found that almost three out of four girls preferred fitness units to sports units, labeling fitness units helpful, fun, and varied. They also liked the fact that fitness units allowed them to be more physically active, were less demanding than competitive sports, and were easier to ft into busy schedules outside PE classes.

The attitudes of girls toward PE classes and physical activity as a whole are significantly influenced by the presence or absence of positive role models. For girls, common mentors are coaches and PE teachers. For boys, the most important influences are fathers and coaches. Within the context of PE classes, teacher attitudes are considered a major factor in girls' enjoyment. However, PE teachers, particularly male teachers, have often viewed females as problems because they are seen as physically weaker and less skillful than male students. Some researchers insist that the real problem is with curricula rather than female physical abilities (Murphy, 2014).

Girls tend to perform better in PE classes when teachers emphasize effort and participation over skill (Constantinou et al, 2009). Research has shown that teachers interact more often with female students in single-gender classes than in coeducational classes. In coeducational classes, boys may shut girls out of interactive play by not choosing them to be on their teams or refusing to pass them the ball. Contrarily, girls tend to include boys in interactive play because they value their strength.

After-school activities that emphasize physical activity are seen as a way to encourage girls to become more physically active. These programs may include such activities as traditional dance, contemporary dance forms such as hip hop or street dancing, fitness training, or yoga. Participants generally report that they are likely to keep up with such activities outside class, and parents tend to be supportive of such activities.

Non-government organizations (NGOs) are also contributing to the effort to promote greater physical activity among adolescents. For instance, the Women's Sports Foundation partnered with Kaiser Permanente and the Atlanta Women's Foundation to provide $1.5 million to fund a three-year grant project in Atlanta to work with schools, churches, and neighborhood gymnasiums to create programs for 200,000 girls. Atlanta was chosen for the national GoGirlGo project because Georgia ranks 41st out of the 50 states in sports activities for girls, and the state mandates PE only through the fifth grade. In the Atlanta area of DeKalb County, only 25.5 percent of girls attend PE classes at least once a week.

TERMS & CONCEPTS

Barbie Doll Syndrome: Feminist term for the tendency of young girls to attempt to force their bodies into the idealized form of their Barbie dolls.

Civil Rights Act of 1964: Major civil rights bill first suggested by President John Kennedy and steered through Congress by Lyndon Johnson that was designed to end discrimination on basis of race, ethnicity, and national origin. Supporters of women's rights managed to get sex added to the protected classes, and the bill somewhat surprisingly passed with that addition.

Gender socialization: The conscious and unconscious process that begins in infancy of forming gender roles according to attitudes portrayed by social influences such as family, peers, schools, and media.

GoGirlGo: Project created by the Women's Sports Foundation and their partners to work with schools, churches, and communities to develop programs designed to promote physical activity among elementary, middle school, and high school girls as a means of improving health indicators.

Osteoporosis: Medical condition involving thinning of the bones, which results from the reduction of bone mass in response to aging or as a byproduct of taking steroids or steroid drugs.

Title IX: The section of the Education Amendments of 1972 that bans sexual discrimination in any programs receiving federal funds. Title IX led to widespread establishment of coeducational Physical Education classes.

Bibliography

Constantinou, P., Manson, M., & Silverman, S. (2009). "Female students' perceptions about gender-role stereotypes and their influence on attitude toward physical education." *Physical Educator,* v. 66: 85-96.

Hannon, J.C., & Ratliffe, T. (2007). "Opportunities to participate and teacher interactions in coed versus single-gender physical education settings." *Physical Educator,* 64: 11-20.

Murphy, B., Dionigi, R., & Litchfield, C. (2014). "Physical education and female participation: A case study of teachers' perspective and strategies." *Issues in Educational Research,* 24: 241-259.

Office for Civil Rights, United States Department of Education. (2012). "Title IX, Education Amendments of 1972." http://www2.ed.gov/

Olafson, L. (2002). "I hate physical education: Adolescent girls talk about physical education." *The Physical Educator,* 59: 67-74.

Paechter, C. (2013). "Girls and their bodies: Approaching a more emancipatory physical education." *Pedagogy, Culture and Society,* 21: 261-277.

Sabo, D., & Veliz, P. (2008). *Go out and play: Youth sports in America.* East Meadow, NY: Women's Sports Foundation.

Staurowsky, E.J., DeSouza, M.J., & Ducher, G. (2009). *Her life depends on it II: Sport, physical activity, and the health and well-being of American girls and women: Executive Summary.* East Meadow, N Y: Women's Sports Foundation.

Verbrugge, M.H. (2012). *Active bodies: A history of women's physical education in twentieth-century America.* New York, NY: Oxford University Press.

Wilkinson, C., & Bretzing, R. (2011). "High school girls' perceptions of selected fitness activities." *Physical Educator,* v. 68: 58-65.

Suggested Reading

Hardin, M., & Whiteside, E. E. (2009). "The power of 'small stories': Narratives and notions of gender equality in conversations about sport." *Sociology of Sport Journal,* 26: 255-276

Hill, G. M., Harmon, J. C., & Knowles, C. (2012). "Physical education teachers' and university teacher educators' perceptions regarding coeducational vs. single gender physical education." *Physical Educator,* 69: 265-288.

Rich, E., & Evans, J. (2009). "Now I am nobody, see me for what I am: The paradox of performativity." *Gender and Education*, 21: 1-16.

Elizabeth Rholetter Purdy, Ph.D.

HETERONORMATIVITY

ABSTRACT

Social scientists and activists have increasingly challenged heteronormativity bias, including homophobia, heterosexism, and gender stereotyping in American society. Some of the highlights of these struggles have been the repeal of the military's "Don't Ask, Don't Tell" policy and the U.S. Supreme Court's ruling in June 2015 declaring the same-sex couples have a constitutionally protected right to marry. Challenges to heteronormativity also aim to question traditional, simplistic and dichotomized constructs of gender identity by emphasizing that gender is a highly fluid and dynamic social phenomenon.

OVERVIEW

"Heteronormativity" is defined as the hegemonic (socially dominant and prevailing to such an extent that it is generally taken for granted and unquestioned) assumption that individuals are heterosexual – that is, romantically or sexually attracted to members of the opposite sex—without consideration or acknowledgement that other sexual orientations, such as homosexual, bisexual, or asexual orientations, also exist. Sociologists, cultural anthropologists, psychologists, social workers, and other scholars are also increasingly using the term "heteronormativity" to describe, as well as critique, long-standing common perceptions in society that gender identities are clear-cut, rigid, and dichotomous. In short, heteronormative beliefs presume that sexual orientation, biological sex, gender identities, and expressions of these identities are clear-cut and mutually exclusive, and are natural, innate, and biologically discrete.

Social scientists, psychologists, and social activists now openly challenge heterosexism and heteronormative assumptions in light of new genetic information and ethnographic research. However, heteronormative beliefs and ideologies remain powerful and deeply held by certain segments of American society, including, but not limited to, religious fundamentalists, social and political conservatives, and even the mainstream media, who may reinforce heteronormativity in their programming, advertisements, and news coverage. These dynamics fuel contentious and emotionally-charged debates as Americans struggle over the various meanings, understandings, and expressions of gender and sexual identities.

Social scientists, particularly cultural anthropologists, note that popular thinking in Western societies since at least the Middle Ages has often been based on notions of essentialism. Essentialism entails the rigid categorization of the complexities of the social world—such as ethnic identities, cultural customs and backgrounds, gender identities, religious experiences or expressions, and other fluid and dynamic phenomena—into discrete, mutually exclusive labels that are perceived to have innate, fundamental, distinct "essences." Essentialism ignores the range of variation that occurs within socially defined identities and labels (including racial/ethnic, gender, religious, and sexual identities), which ultimately results in a distorted and limited understanding of people's lived experiences and realities.

In terms of gender and sexuality, the prevailing assumption throughout much of Western intellectual and popular thought for many centuries has been that gender is a rigid construct consisting of two mutually opposed categories (male and female) who are naturally sexually attracted to one another. Persons whose lives did not conform to this dichotomization were historically viewed as "deviant," or violating the presumed natural order. Even the American Psychological Association (APA) classified homosexuality as a mental disorder until December 1973, reflecting heterosexist assumptions. The APA now openly condemns prejudice and discrimination on the basis of sexual orientation (Conger, 1975). As such, the APA condemns "conversion therapies" that are sometimes offered by some Christian-based ministers or counselors and some private counseling firms who personally oppose non-heterosexual orientations. Critics of conversion therapy maintain that such practices reinforce heterosexism and heteronormativity, undermine the self-esteem of non-heterosexual individuals, and are ineffective in changing one's sexual orientation (Embry, 2012).

Since the late 1960s, advocates of equality for gays, lesbians, and persons of other sexual expressions and gender identities have aggressively challenged heterosexism and heteronormativity in American society. A flashpoint in the mounting movement for greater social inclusion against heterosexism occurred during the New York City's Stonewall riot in June 1969, in which patrons of a popular bar that catered to gay male customers clashed with officers from the New York Police Department amid a police raid. During the 1980s, the higher rates of HIV and AIDS among gay males relative to heterosexual males and females during the earliest years of the epidemic's discovery led to erroneous assumptions among many Americans that AIDS was exclusively a "gay disease."

Such misperceptions increased homophobia at a time when the religious Right, led by Jerry Falwell and televangelists Pat Robertson, Jimmy Swaggart, and Jim Bakker, had risen to prominence in terms of social and political influence in American society. Falwell and Robertson are among the most outspoken critics of homosexuality in the nation's history; during an episode of Robertson's *700 Club,* both men concurred that gays and lesbians, along with feminists and liberals, bore responsibility for the terrorist attacks of September 11, 2001, by causing God to become angry at the direction of American society (Ambinder, 2001).

In the 1990s, advocates called for the removal of homosexuality as a barrier to military service and grounds for dishonorable discharge. President Bill Clinton implemented a "Don't Ask, Don't Tell" policy in 1993 that allowed gay and lesbian Americans to serve in the military so long as they concealed their sexual orientation; under the policy, soldiers could still be dismissed from duty for openly disclosing their sexual orientation, but superior officers could not question a serviceman or servicewoman. President Barack Obama rescinded "Don't Ask, Don't Tell" in 2011 and allowed persons of any sexual orientation to serve in the U.S. military.

During the 2000s and early 2010s, the topic of same-sex marriage become one of the most divisive political topics in the United States, but on June 26, 2015, the U.S. Supreme Court legalized same-sex marriage in a historic 5-4 decision. The high court's ruling sparked massive public demonstrations of joy and celebration coast to coast, while emboldening opponents of same-sex marriage. By the time of the ruling, according to numerous public opinion polls, the majority of Americans had come to support the right of same-sex couples to marry. Polls conducted by the Pew Research Center in July 2015 indicated that 55 percent of the U.S. population believed that same-sex couples should have the legal right to marry, compared with 39 percent who did not. Support was highest among Americans under the age of 40, persons claiming no religious affiliation, registered Democrats and independent voters, and whites. Approximately 60 percent of Roman Catholics and members of various mainline Protestant denominations support the legal right to same-sex marriage. Support for same-sex marriage is lowest among African Americans (39%), registered Republicans (32%), evangelical Christians (24%), and persons over the age of 70 (39%). This data reveals sharp divides over this topic along generational, ethnic, and religious lines (Pew Research Center, 2015).

However, preoccupation with same-sex relationships or homosexuality can potentially obscure understandings that other sexual orientations exist that are not exclusively heterosexual or homosexual. Cultural anthropologists contend that human sexuality is best understood as a continuum with exclusive homosexuality and exclusive heterosexuality representing the end points of this continuum. According to anthropologists, sexuality is highly fluid. While some individuals may conform to exclusive heterosexual or homosexual orientations, others hold varying degrees of erotic attraction to both males and females. As such, bisexuality does not necessarily require that a person be sexually attracted or romantically involved with males and females equally; rather, bisexuality is fluid and continuous. Furthermore, some individuals identify as asexual or lacking a sense of sexual attraction to either males or females.

Just like sexuality, gender identities and expressions are not clear-cut and self-evident as was once commonly thought in American society. Thus, challenges to heteronormativity increasingly encompasses battles for equality and social inclusion for persons who do not conform to traditional, rigid "cisgender," or biologically conforming, identities. During the summer of 2015, the extensive media spotlight aimed at Caitlyn (formerly Bruce) Jenner, the 1976 Olympic gold medal decathlon champion and reality TV star, raised awareness of the transgender community in the United States and around the world. Transgender identity consists of self-identification with the gender that is opposite of one's biological sex. Although awareness of the transgender community has seen growth as a result of celebrities such as Jenner and Laverne Cox of the popular show

Orange Is the New Black, activists have pointed out that the rate of violence committed against transgender individuals is shockingly high and deserves greater public attention. Approximately 80 percent of transgender individuals are harassed during their high school years; fourteen transgender women were murdered in 2014, while fifteen transgender individuals were murdered during the first eight months of 2015 (Steinmetz, 2015).

It is also important to consider that the biological distinction between male and female is not always easily or precisely discernible in all persons, and the number of intersex individuals is higher than most members of the general public probably realize. The term intersex refers to various biological conditions (either hormonal, genital, and/or chromosomal) that make one's biological sex, to varying degrees, ambiguous and do not allow a person to be identified as exclusively male or female. According to the Intersex Society of North America, approximately 1 out of every 1,666 births is of newborns whose sex chromosomes are not exclusively XX (for female) or XY (for male), and approximately 1 percent of all births result in an individual whose body differs from "standard male or female" (Intersex Society of North America, 2008).

Since the 1990s, the acronym LGBTQ2IA (lesbian/gay/bisexual/transgender/queer/questioning/intersex/ally), or the shorter LGBT, has become more commonly used in reference to the community of people who do not conform to heteronormative identities, heterosexual orientations, or traditional gender identities. Likewise, the term genderqueer has gained increased acceptance as an umbrella term for a range of gender identities that do not conform to the traditional, rigid cisgender identities of "male" and "female." Some genderqueer activists recommend using the gender-neutral pronouns "they" or "zhe" or "hir" in place of "he" and "she" to refer to individuals whose gender identity is either unknown or does not conform to traditional norms of masculinity and femininity.

VIEWPOINTS

More awareness of, and challenges to, heteronormativity now exist in American society than at any previous point in the nation's history. However, despite the Supreme Court's recent legalization of same-sex marriage and the efforts of academics and social activists to fight heteronormativity, heterosexism, and homophobia, bitter opposition remains and the topic remains contentious. Resistance was epitomized by the refusal of Kim Davis, a Kentucky county clerk and a devout evangelical Christian, to issue marriage licenses to same-sex couples in her jurisdiction on the grounds that doing so would violate her religious convictions; she and her supporters asserted that forcing her to issue same-sex marriage licenses would constitute religious discrimination against her. Davis's adamant refusal and subsequent arrest made her a cause célèbre to opponents of same-sex marriage nationwide, even drawing support from Republican presidential candidate and former Arkansas governor Mike Huckabee.

In the run-up and aftermath of the Supreme Court's ruling on same-sex marriage, several states attempted to pass "religious freedom" bills that would allow owners of businesses to deny services to same-sex couples or gay or lesbian individuals, if entrepreneurs felt providing services would violate their religious beliefs. These bills, along with Davis's saga, illustrate that the challenges to heteronormativity will likely continue. As of 2015, twenty states have passed legislation protecting discrimination against individuals on the basis of sexual orientation and gender identities, while three additional states have passed legislation protecting individuals from discrimination on the basis of sexual orientation but not gender identity (American Civil Liberties Union, 2015).

Several scholars and gay rights advocates have asserted that the media and the larger public should refrain from common tendencies toward essentialist thinking about, and perceptions of, the gay and lesbian community and recognize the tremendous variation that exists within the community. Proponents of this view argue that the lives of gay and lesbian individuals are not identical or uniform; rather, gays and lesbians experience a wide range of lived reality, which are shaped by the confluence of multiple variables, such as their racial/ethnic backgrounds, social class, age, religious upbringing, geographic locale, and education level. Recognizing that these variables all play a role in shaping a person's overall lived experiences and sense of identity is known as intersectionality. Chong-suk Han, a professor of sociology and anthropology at Middlebury College, draws attention to this by pointing out the racism he frequently notices demonstrated by gay white men towards gay black men and, conversely, the preference of many gay white men in his community for Asian men. Han also criticizes the higher degrees of homophobia and heterosexism he witnesses among racial and ethnic minorities than among whites (Han, 2013).

Rosaria Bui criticizes the promotion of heteronormativity in the mainstream media by highlighting the ways in which media outlets use language and frame discourses on sexuality and marriage equality issues that reinforce heterosexist and heteronormative assumptions. Three major dimensions of this, according to Bui, include the common phrase "gay marriage" (which she argues reinforces heterosexual marriage as the default norm), expectations that non-heterosexual persons "come out" and publicly disclose their sexual orientations (while no such expectations are placed on heterosexuals to publicly assert their orientation), and references to non-heterosexual orientations as the "gay lifestyle" or "homosexual lifestyle" (as such a framing implies that gays and lesbians are merely "choosing" their orientation; by contrast, heterosexuality is never referred to as a "lifestyle"). Bui contends that to truly become an inclusive society, the media must cease its reinforcement of heteronormativity (Bui, 2015). To Bui's first point, some media pundits have replaced the term "gay marriage" with "marriage equality" or simply "marriage."

On the other hand, Huffington Post columnist and lesbian activist Brooke Sopelsa criticizes what she feels as misguided efforts by the LGBTQ2IA community to chastise heterosexuals for their lack of awareness of the preferred terminology and identity labels favored among members of her community. Sopelsa contends that the LGBTQ2IA community faces greater struggles and battles against discrimination than outrage over group labels. Sopelsa writes, "We are making many of our allies and potential future allies feel as though they have to walk on eggshells because they don't know the latest LGBTQIA lingo (Sopelsa, 2015)." In response, Kelsie Brynn Jones challenged Sopelsa's piece by claiming that no movement for social justice and inclusion in American society has ever achieved success by making its top priority avoiding offending privileged populations or expressing greater concern that privileged groups not feel as if they are walking on eggshells (Jones, 2015).

Educational psychologist Lori Day criticizes heteronormativity from a different angle by challenging the conventional way in which toys are marketed to children. Day challenges the categorization of toys in stores by displaying them in distinct sections labeled for "boys" and "girls" and asserts that such dichotomization compounds the confusion, discomfort, self-esteem, and feelings of belonging for children who do not see themselves as fitting into the traditional gender categories that correspond to biological sex. American toys also routinely reinforce notions of heterosexual identity, encouraging girls to focus on physical attractiveness and beauty in order to attract a male mate and pursue motherhood. Instead, Day advocates that American stores categorize toys by type (e.g., puzzles, building blocks, coloring books) instead of by gender; this practice is already used in a growing number of stores in European countries (Day, 2015).

TERMS & CONCEPTS

Asexuality: The lack of sexual attraction to members of either the same sex or opposite sex.

Bisexuality: Sexual orientation characterized by erotic attraction, to varying degrees, toward both males and females.

Cisgender: A social identity in which one's gender identification and expression conforms with one's biological sex.

Conversion Therapy: Psychiatric and psychological efforts that seek to transform individuals of homosexual or bisexual orientations to a heterosexual orientation; such efforts are now criticized by the American Psychological Association.

Essentialism: The rigid classification of complex social identities and cultural phenomena into discrete, mutually opposing categories and labels, along with the subsequent overlooking of internal differences and variation within these categories/labels.

Gender: The culturally defined norms, behaviors, and expectations that a society associates with ideas of masculinity and femininity.

Genderqueer: A self-referential, catchall term for individuals who do not conform to the traditional, dichotomized identities of exclusively male or female and instead hold a different sense of gender identity, including, but not limited to, identifying as both or neither male/female or shifting between gender identities in different social settings and contexts.

Heterosexual: Romantic and sexual attraction to persons of the opposite sex.

Heterosexism: Prejudice and/or discrimination against non-heterosexual individuals and couples on the basis of their sexuality.

Homophobia: Strong feelings of prejudice and resentment towards gays and lesbians, on the grounds of their sexual orientation.

Intersectionality: The interconnectedness of various factors, including race/ethnicity, gender, social class, sexuality, and age, in shaping one's overall identity and life experiences.

Intersex: Variations in biological features, whether chromosomal, physical, or hormonal, that do not allow a person to be biologically classified as exclusively male or female.

LGBTQ2IA: Acronym commonly used as an all-encompassing term for individuals of non-heteronormative sexual orientations and gender identities.

Sex: The biological distinctions between male and female, based on differences in chromosomes, hormone balances, genitalia, and other physical differences.

Transgender: Self-identification with the gender that is opposite of one's biological sex.

Bibliography

American Civil Liberties Union. "Non-discrimination laws: State by state information – Map." ACLU.org. https://www.aclu.org/map/non-discrimination-laws-state-state-information-map

Ambinder, M. (2001, September 14). "Falwell suggests gays to blame for attacks." *ABC News.* http://abcnews.go.com/

Bui, R. (2015, April 13). "3 ways the news assist heteronormativity." *Media Criticism.* https://blogs.longwood.edu/buirt/2015/04/13/3-times-the-news-assisted-with-hetero-normativity/

Conger, J. J. (1975). "Proceedings of the American Psychological Association, Incorporated, for the year 1974: Minutes of the annual meeting of the Council of Representatives." *American Psychologist,* 30, 620–651.

Day, L. (2015, May 12). "How highly gendered toys present an exclusively heterosexual worldview to children." *Huffington Post.* http://www.huffingtonpost.com/lori-day/how-highly-gendered-toys-_b_7258470.html

Dwyer, A. (2015). "Teaching young queers a lesson: How police teach lessons about non-heteronormativity in public spaces." *Sexuality & Culture,* 19(3), 493–512.

'Embry, L. (2012, August 27). ""Conversion therapy': Therapy that isn't." *Los Angeles Times.* http://articles.latimes.com/2012/aug/27/opinion/la-oe-embry-gay-conversion-20120827

Gender and Education Association. "What is heteronormativity?" *GenderAndEducation.com.* http://www.genderandeducation.com/issues/what-is-heteronormativity/

Han, C. (2013). *Darker shades of queer: Race, class, & gender: An Anthology* (8th ed.), 251–257. Belmont, CA: Wadsworth.

Herz, M., & Johansson, T. (2015). "The normativity of the concept of heteronormativity." *Journal of Homosexuality,* 62(8), 1009–1020.

Intersex Society of North America (2008). "How common is intersex?" *ISNA.org.* http://www.isna.org/faq/frequency

Jones, K. (2015, April 26). "Dear queer people: Stop apologizing to heteronormativity." *Huffington Post.* http://www.huffingtonpost.com/kelsie-brynn-jones/dear-queer-people-stop-ap_b_6744678.html

Liptak, A. (2015, June 26). "Supreme Court ruling makes same-sex marriage a right nationwide." *New York Times.* http://www.nytimes.com/2015/06/27/

Pew Research Center (2015, July 29). "Changing attitudes on gay marriage." PewForum.org. http://www.pewforum.org/2015/07/29/graphics-slideshow-changing-attitudes-on-gay-marriage/

Smith, L. C., & Shin, R. Q. (2015). "Negotiating the intersection of racial oppression and heteronormativity." *Journal of Homosexuality*, 62(11), 1459–1484.

Sopelsa, B. (2015, February 23). "Dear queer people: Let's stop making straight people walk on eggshells." *Huffington Post.* http://www.huffingtonpost.com/brooke-sopelsa/dear-queer-people-lets-st_b_6737294.html

Steinmetz, K. (2015, August 17). "Why transgender people are being murdered at a historic rate." *Time.* http://time.com/3999348/transgender-murders-2015/

SUGGESTED READING

Ferreira, E., & Salvador, R. (2015). "Lesbian collaborative web mapping: Disrupting heteronormativity in Portugal." *Gender, Place & Culture: A Journal of Feminist Geography*, 22(7), 954–970.

Green, E. (2015, June 4). "The real Christian debate on transgender identity." *The Atlantic.* http://www.theatlantic.com/politics/archive/2015/06/the-christian-debate-on-transgender-identity/394796/

Gregory, S. (2015, May 9). "U.S. ranks worst in sports homophobia study." *Time.* http://time.com/3852611/sports-homophobia-study/

Kimmel, M. (2014). *Sexualities: Identities, behavior, and society* (2nd ed.). New York, NY: Oxford University Press.

Teich, N. (2012). *Transgender 101: A simple guide to a complex issue.* New York, NY: Columbia University Press.

Justin D. García, Ph.D.

HOMOPHOBIA

ABSTRACT

This article focuses on homophobia, the fear felt by some heterosexuals toward those with alternative sexual orientation. It provides an overview of sexual orientation including gay, lesbian, bisexual, heterosexual, and transgendered. It also further defines and discusses homophobia and its origins and goes on to discuss various issues surrounding heterosexism or sexual prejudice such as stigmatization, hate crimes, discrimination in the work place, and AIDS stigma.

OVERVIEW

Sexual Orientation

A person's sexual orientation, whether he or she prefers sexual relationships with members of the same sex, or the opposite sex, is considered by some to be determined at birth or learned, and by others as both biological and social. A person can be heterosexual, preferring to have sexual relationships with members of the opposite sex, or homosexual, preferring to have sexual relationships with members of the same sex. Gay people are typically males who prefer to have relationships with other males, while lesbians are women who prefer to have relationships with other women, however some women choose to use the term gay as well. Straight people are referred to as heterosexuals, while bisexuals may have sexual attraction or relationships with both the same and the opposite sex. "Transgender is an umbrella term for persons whose gender identity, gender expression, or behavior does not conform to that typically associated with the sex to which they were assigned at birth" (Pohjanen & Kortelainen, 2016).

However, having a homosexual or bisexual experience does not necessarily mean that a person is homosexual. For some, particularly young people, homosexual or bisexual experiences are experimental and do not continue. For others, however, homosexuality is a way of life. Researchers have found that gay and bisexual men in particular often believed that they were different from other boys from an early age (Savin-Williams, 2004).

What Is Homophobia?

Homophobia, essentially, is the fear of homosexuality. Gays and lesbians experience incidents of homophobia in terms of attacks including verbal assaults, threats, physical and sexual assault, and cyberbullying.

Homophobia includes negative beliefs, attitudes, stereotypes, and behaviors toward gays and lesbians (Espelage, Aragon, Birkett & Koenig, 2008). While homophobia can be defined as heterosexuals' dread of being in close quarters with homosexuals as well as homosexuals' self loathing, homophobia is driven by a rigid gender code (Herek, 2008). Women who break from traditional, culturally defined female roles are often thought of as lesbians, and men who transcend the culturally defined notions of what it means to be male, are punished socially and in the work place (Mottet & Tanis, 2008). Persons of a sexual orientation besides heterosexuality have probably experienced some form of prejudice, or homophobia from heterosexuals. This idea of homophobia may extend past the fear of homosexuality, to include the fear of people who identify as transgender, intersex, asexual or polyamorous.

Gender Roles

While sex is biological, referring to genitalia and to secondary sex characteristics such as breasts, or body hair, gender is a cultural phenomenon. In other words, the notion of male or female is defined by the culture and both sexes are expected to adhere to the rules and norms of society regarding their sex and their gender role—the behavior and attitudes that are considered appropriate for each sex—which are taught from birth through the process of gender socialization.

Being gendered, or identified as being one gender or another can affect a person's life every day from how he or she receives tasks and rewards, the types of education and work available to him or her, and how much wealth and power he or she will receive in the course of a lifetime. The belief systems surrounding gender are embedded within a culture's language and ideas, and are reinforced strongly by religion, science, government and law.

There are popular stereotypes about the genders, such as males being strong, independent and not likely to cry, while women are characterized being weak and emotional. These stereotypes also reinforce the cultural ideas and socialization institutions such as the family, marriage, and religion. For example, as of June 2015 thirty-six states, plus the District of Columbia, recognized same-sex marriage. Prior to 2013, the 1996 Defense of Marriage Act (DOMA) prohibited the federal government from recognizing same-sex marriages, civil unions, and domestic partnerships and allowed states to refuse to recognize them as well, even if the marriages, unions, and partnerships were recognized in other states.

In another example, in 2000, Pope John Paul II criticized gay pride activities in Rome as offensive to Christian values and condemned homosexuality publicly, six years after a closed-door meeting of Christians met to plan attacks on the gay rights movement ("They'll Know," 1994).

Coming Out

Coming out, or claiming publicly to be homosexual, is an intimate detail about a person that can have some positive effects and reduce the stigma related to homosexuality. Social scientists have found that lesbians and gay men who "come out of the closet" to their heterosexual friends and family members help to create these more positive attitudes. People who have a gay friend or relative will think better of homosexuality. But personal contact isn't enough. And one homosexual relative or friend doesn't change much, either. Stereotypes tend to be more easily dispelled among heterosexuals who know, or have contact with more than one gay person and if there is openness about the sexual orientation of the others (Herek, 2008).

Hate Crimes

Coming out also carries danger and risks. Many heterosexual Americans hold strongly negative feelings toward homosexuality, and some commit hate crimes against homosexuals. Hate crimes, or bias crimes, are intended to harm or intimidate people because of their race, ethnicity, sexual orientation, religion, or other minority group status.

FBI statistics show that in 2014—out of a total of 5,462 reported "single-bias" crimes—18.6 percent of hate crimes were based on sexual orientation and 1.8 were based on gender identity. Of all the victims of hate crimes, 36 percent were crimes against property such as robbery, vandalism, theft, or arson. The another 63 percent were victims of crimes against persons, such as assault, rape, and murder. These hate crimes are committed the vast majority of the time by young people who have no criminal record or do not belong to any type of hate group. Their actions are fueled primarily by prejudice and dislike of people who seem different. The offenders tend to believe, too, that their behavior is sanctioned by others, and indeed, with job discrimination on the basis of sexual orientation legal in most U.S. states, that notion could be easily believed (Herek, 2008; American Psychological Association, 2004).

Heterosexism

Heterosexism, or sexual prejudice, is similar to sexism or racism in that it is an ideology that punishes or denies and stigmatizes non-heterosexual behavior or relationships. As long as a person's homosexuality remains hidden, there is no stigma. Once homosexuality is out in the open, gay people are subject to punishment by society.

In the United States, heterosexism and its accompanying discrimination has included:

- The former ban against lesbian and gay military personnel (in December 2013 President Barack Obama enacted the Don't Ask, Don't Tell Repeal Act to end the DADT policy);
- Lack of legal protection in employment, housing, and services; and
- Open hostility to lesbian and gay committed relationships—some US states have had bans on same-sex marriage.

Despite these forms of discrimination, and while many adults in the United States still view homosexual behavior as immoral, the prevailing attitude is changing. In 2015 a Pew Research Center poll also indicated that 57 percent of Americans would back a nationwide law legalizing same-sex marriage—a law many supporters and opponents saw as inevitable.

FURTHER INSIGHTS

Who Is Homophobic?

Those with negative attitudes toward gay people have tended to be more likely to be older, male, less well-educated and living in rural areas or in the Midwestern or Southern U.S. They also attend church frequently and have orthodox beliefs about religion and the literal truth of the Bible (Miller, 2007). Much homophobic behavior is these individuals stems from the fear of implying a pro-homosexual bias. They are also likely to be more politically conservative. Furthermore, those with negative attitudes toward homosexuality tend to display authoritarian personalities, believe in traditional gender roles and divisions of labor, and are less sexually permissive. They often do not believe that homosexuality occurs from birth, and they do not have any close ties to any homosexual people (Herek, 2008).

WHAT MOTIVATES SEXUAL PREJUDICE?

Structural-Functionalist Perspective

The structural-functionalist approach in sociology argues that attitudes about homosexuality serve to help heterosexuals make sense of their interactions with gays and to fit those interactions into a larger world view (Savage & Julien, 1994). Heterosexuals who have not had interactions with homosexuals in a social setting often perceive homosexuality as their opposite, which serves to distance homosexuals as representative of a group to which they do not wish to belong. This gives the heterosexual group a sense of well-being and an identity. In other words, expressing a prejudicial attitude serves as a defense mechanism for heterosexuals who can then separate themselves from any emotional expenditure when homosexuals are discriminated against, or even attacked physically (Herek, 2008).

In the U.S. for example, males may be more likely to reject homosexuality and to align themselves to more socially-acceptable groups that do the same. Research in sports indicates that female team members are more accepting of lesbian teammates than males, and male coaches are able to accept gay team members. While males experience acceptable forms of homoeroticism in the locker room such as slapping one another on the buttocks, or hugging one another, any display of such behavior in another setting could bring accusations of homosexuality and ostracism, or even violence (Demers, 2006).

Conflict Perspective

Conflict theorists argue that sexism allows a system of patriarchy to continue. Strict gender roles reinforce patriarchy, and those who fall outside of the rigid sex roles, such as homosexual, bisexual and transgendered people, are punished by being denied equal rights, or by experiencing prejudice, discrimination and even physical harm. Patriarchy then uses homophobia to oppress people who are perceived as a threat to that system (Schryer & Napier, 1997).

Sodomy Laws

In 1977, a Gallup poll asked about the legality of homosexual relations between consenting adults. Responses were evenly split, with 43% favoring legalization and 43% opposing it.

In the mid-1980s, with the new epidemic of AIDS (Acquired Immunodeficiency Syndrome) affecting

American gay and bisexual males, the trend reversed, with only 32% supporting the legality of homosexual relationships and 57% opposing them, even though the statistics showed that on a global scale, AIDS was more often traced to heterosexuals. In 1986, the Supreme Court of the U.S. upheld the right of states to enact sodomy laws. Sodomy includes sex acts such as anal intercourse or oral sex that are practiced among people including homosexuals. But then the trend began shifting again and in 2003, the Supreme Court overturned the 1986 decision and ruled sodomy laws in Texas to be unconstitutional—it was deemed that due process protects adults' freedom to engage in private, consensual sexual acts, including sodomy. Similarly, public opinion is changing, and by 2015 the majority (over 60 percent) of Americans were accepting of homosexuality in general, with those specifics, of course, varying by gender, age, political affiliation, and religious affiliation, according to the Pew Research Center.

HIV/AIDS

In 2009, more than 45 percent of African American gay and bisexual urban males were infected with HIV. The Centers for Disease Control and Prevention reports that in 2010, the estimated rate of new HIV infections among Black men was 7 times as high as the rate in White men and 3 times as high as that for Black women. That same year 63 percent of the new HIV infections among Americans were attributed to homosexual contact.

Despite the seriousness of the disease in the gay community, particularly among young Blacks, funding for cures and medical attention on the federal level is scarce (Foreman, 2008).

"AIDS-related stigma," or "AIDS stigma," refers to prejudice and discrimination directed at people perceived to have AIDS or HIV. This stigmatization and subsequent discrimination can result in ostracism, violence, and quarantine of persons with HIV. Some would argue that AIDS stigma prevents society from stemming the AIDS epidemic (Herek, 2008).

ISSUES

Gay Marriage

Many have argued that lesbian, gay, bisexual and transgender families deserve the same recognition and legal protection as all other families. In 2003, Massachusetts became the first state in the union to allow same-sex couples to marry. Despite strong opposition, on May 15, 2008, the California Supreme Court made the historic decision to support the freedom of homosexuals to marry (National Center for Lesbian Rights, 2008). In 2015, the US Supreme Court ruled in *Obergefell v. Hodges* that same-sex marriages must be recognized in all fifty states under the Fourteenth Amendment protections of due process and equal protection clauses. As time continues on we are seeing more acceptance and rights for the LGBTQ community.

Sexual Diversity in the Workplace

In many places, homosexual, bisexual, and transgendered people continue to experience discrimination in employment, housing, public accommodation, education, and health care because of a lack of legal protection and a lack of public support for equality in these areas, but the trend is beginning to shift toward more tolerance. As of 2014, eighteen states and the District of Columbia had passed laws banning discrimination on the basis of sexual orientation and gender identity or expression, while another three banned discrimination on the basis of sexual orientation, according to the National LGBTQ Task Force.

One of the most remarkable changes has been in the workplace, where a larger proportion of Americans feel homosexuals should be hired as elementary school teachers; the percentages have increased from 27% in 1977, to 41% in 1992, to 54% in 2005. Other increases in support for employment rights range from 13 percentage points (for clergy) to 34 points (for doctors) (National Gay & Lesbian Taskforce, 2008).

While research indicates that homophobia has decreased over time, there are still segments of society who are homophobic and therefore, many homosexual men and women continue to experience both personal and legal negative effects of being stigmatized because of their sexual orientation.

TERMS & CONCEPTS

Bisexual: People who embrace the notion of being able to love one another irrespective of gender.

Domestic Partner: A person who lives in a domestic relationship with another person of the same or opposite sex without marriage.

Gay: Describes males who prefer sexual relationships with males.

Gender: Culturally defined differences between females and males.

Gender Bias: Prejudice or discrimination against a person based on that person's sex, or gender.

Gender Identity: How a person perceives himself or herself as either male or female

Gender Socialization: The process by which cultural gender roles are taught

Hate Crimes: Criminal actions intended to harm or intimidate people because of their race, ethnicity, sexual orientation, religion, or other minority group status; also referred to as bias crimes.

Heterosexism: Heterosexism began to be used as a term analogous to sexism and racism, describing an ideological system that denies, denigrates, and stigmatizes any non-heterosexual form of behavior, identity, relationship, or community.

Heterosexual: Describes one who has sexual relationships with members of the opposite sex.

Homophobia: Extreme prejudice toward gays, lesbians and bisexuals, anyone perceived as not being heterosexual.

Homosexual: Describes one who has sexual relationships with members of the same sex.

Lesbian: Describes a female who prefers sexual relationships with other females.

Patriarchy: A society where men dominate women.

Sex: The biological differences between males and females.

Sexual Orientation: One's preference for sexual relationships with members of the opposite sex, the same sex, or both.

Sexual Prejudice: Negative attitudes based on sexual orientation, whether the target is homosexual, bisexual, or heterosexual.

Stigma: An attribute that is deeply discrediting.

Straight: Describes a person who is heterosexual.

Transgenderism: Refers to those who do not conform to culturally prescribed norms about what it means to be male or female.

Bibliography

American Psychological Association. (2008). "Position paper on hate crimes, released in 1998." http://www.apa.org/releases/hate.html

Bucher, J. (2014). "'But he can't be gay': The relationship between masculinity and homophobia in father-son relationships." *Journal of Men's Studies,* 22, 222–237.

Costa, A., Bandeira, D., & Nardi, H. (2013). "Systematic review of instruments measuring homophobia and related constructs." *Journal of Applied Social Psychology,* 43, 1324–1332.

Demers, G. (2006). "Homophobia in sport - Fact of life, taboo subject." *Canadian Journal for Women in Coaching Online,* 6.

Espelage, D., Aragon, S., Birkett, M., & Koenig, B. (2008). "Homophobic teasing, psychological outcomes, and sexual orientation among high school students: What influence do parents and schools have?" *School Psychology Review* 37, 202–216.

Foreman, M. (2008). "State of the Movement address by Matt Foreman, Executive Director, National Gay and Lesbian Task Force." Speech given February 8, 2008. http://www.thetaskforce.org/

Herek, G. (2008). "Definitions: Homophobia, heterosexism, & sexual prejudice." http://psychology.ucdavis.edu

MacInnis, C. C., & Hodson, G. (2013). "Is homophobia associated with an implicit same-sex attraction?" *Journal of Sex Research,* 50, 777–785.

McCormack, M., & Anderson, E. (2014). "Homohysteria: Definitions, context and intersectionality." *Sex Roles,* 71 (3/4), 152-158.

McCormack, M., & Anderson, E. (2014). "The influence of declining homophobia on men's gender in the United States: An argument for the study of homohysteria." *Sex Roles,* 71 (3/4), 109–120.

Miller, R. (2007). "Legacy denied: African American gay men, AIDS, and the black church." *Social Work,* 52, 51-61.

Mottet, L., & Tanis, J. (2008). *Opening the door.* Washington, D.C.: National Gay and Lesbian Task Force Policy Institute.

National Gay & Lesbian Taskforce. (n.d.). "The issues: Anti gay industry." http://thetaskforce.org/

National Center for Lesbian Rights. (2008, September 12). "Marriage for same sex couples in California." Nclrights.org: http://www.nclrights.org/

Pohjanen, A., & Kortelainen, T. (2016). Transgender information behaviour. Journal of Documentation: Branford, 72, 172–190. http://dx.doi .org/

Savage, J., & Julien, I. (1994). "Queering the pitch: A conversation." *Critical Quarterly;* 36, 1–11.

Savin-Williams, R. (2004). "Memories of same-sex attractions." In Michael S. Kimmel & Michael A. Messner, (Eds.) *Men's Lives.* Boston: Allyn & Bacon.

Schryer, M., & Napier, O. (1997). "Homophobia: The social basis of male supremacy?" *Unpublished paper, Marshall University Graduate College.* http://www.schryer.com/homophobia/

Tatchell, P. (2000). "Apostles of Unreason settle into their third millennium" [Electronic version]. *Gay and Lesbian Humanist, Autumn.* http://www.pink-triangle.org.uk/glh/201/church.html

"They'll know we are Christians by our sexual orientation" [Editorial]. (1994). *National Catholic Reporter,* 30.

Warriner, K., Nagoshi, C. T., & Nagoshi, J. L. (2013). "Correlates of homophobia, transphobia, and internalized homophobia in gay or lesbian and heterosexual samples." *Journal of Homosexuality,* 60, 1297–1314.

SUGGESTED READING

Fone, B. (2000). *Homophobia: A history.* New York: Picador.

Franklin, K. (2014). "Empathy and reasoning in context: Thinking about antigay bullying." *Law & Sexuality: A Review of Lesbian, Gay, Bisexual & Transgender Legal Issues,* 23, 61–112.

Kantor, M. (1998). *Homophobia: Description, development, and dynamics of gay bashing.* Westport, Conn.: Praeger

Meyer, I. H., Ouellette, S. C., Haile, R., & McFarlane, T. A. (2011). "'We'd be free': Narratives of life without homophobia, racism, or sexism." *Sexuality Research & Social Policy: Journal of NSRC,* 8, 204–214.

Theodore, J. L., Shidlo, A., Zemon, V., Foley, F. W., Dorfman, D., Dahlman, K. L., & Hamid, S. (2013). "Psychometrics of an internalized homophobia instrument for men." *Journal of Homosexuality,* 60, 558–574.

Turner-Frey, W. (2014). "Homophobia is a global issue." *Social Work, 59*(3), 281-282.

Van Dijk, L., & Van Driel, B. (2007). *Challenging homophobia: Teaching about sexual diversity.* London: Trenton Books.

Geraldine Wagner, M.S. and
Kimberly Ortiz-Hartman, Psy.D., LMFT

Kinsey Report

ABSTRACT

In 1948, biologist Alfred C. Kinsey published the groundbreaking research report, "Sexual Behavior in the Human Male", which has served as the impetus for the modern study of human sexuality. Now referred to colloquially as "The Kinsey Report", it remains a controversial and oft-cited body of research. The Kinsey Report challenged many medical and social beliefs about homosexuality and female sexuality, and it contributed heavily to the feminist and gay/lesbian movements of the twentieth century. Kinsey used a taxonomic approach to the classification of human sexual behaviors, which allowed for the first scientific study of what had previously been seen as a moral or medical area of concern.

The Kinsey Report

OVERVIEW

Alfred C. Kinsey (1894–1956) was an American, Harvard-educated biologist and professor of entomology and zoology. In 1947, Kinsey founded the Institute for Research in Sex, Gender, and Reproduction at Indiana University. It was posthumously renamed the Kinsey Institute for Research in Sex, Gender, and Reproduction. Kinsey is best known as the lead researcher and author of the 1948 *Sexual Behavior in the Human Male*, which became an international bestseller and drastically changed the perceptions of human sexuality among both the public and the academic body researching the field. Along with the 1953 volume *Sexual Behavior in the Human Female*, the two reports created a great deal of discussion and controversy and became an enduring part of American culture (Steinberg, 2005; Herzog, 2006).

References to "The Kinsey Report" abound in both the academic literature and in popular culture. In 1964, US poet Ogden Nash titled a piece "The Kinsey Report Didn't Upset Me, Either" in which he wrote, "I won't allow my life to be regulated by reports, whether rosily optimistic or gloomily cadaveric" (Nash, 1964, p.1). In 2004, the critically acclaimed movie *Kinsey*, starring actor Liam Neeson as Alfred Kinsey, portrayed the researcher who revolutionized the study of human sexuality. In addition, there have been academic and trade books published about the studies, their impact on science and culture, and about Kinsey himself.

In the decades following the publication of Kinsey's seminal studies, debates about the methods he used, the conclusions he drew, and about his own sexual practices fueled a controversy that began soon after the reports were first disseminated. Kinsey received a great deal of praise for breaking the silence that had surrounded sexual matters and for making public norms and behaviors that had been considered much more rare and deviant than the research revealed (Herzog, 2006).

Historical Background

The study of human sexuality was considered a moral issue prior to 1890, when the medical community began to address issues of sexual function and sexually transmitted diseases, albeit with a nod to the moral standards of the times. Doctors, with backgrounds in biology, anatomy, and medicine, were seen as the most logical experts in the field (Bullough, 1998). Havelock Ellis and Magnus Hirschfeld were physicians whose research focused on sex through the use of sexual histories, much like Kinsey. The significant difference in their methods, though, is considered to be critical to the divergence in their findings. Ellis compiled histories through correspondence with volunteers, while Hirschfeld relied upon historical data and personal knowledge until late in his career when he began to conduct personal interviews (Bullough, 1998). "Unfortunately, Hirschfeld used only a small portion of his data in his published books, and before he could complete a comprehensive study of sexuality, his files were destroyed by the Nazis" (Bullough, 1994, as cited in Bullough, 1998, p. 127). While some of the data reported in those early studies came from the physicians' own practices and research, it was supplemented by anthropological studies, and much of it was informed by the political and moral standards of the early twentieth century (Bullough, 1998).

Other early research by physicians was published by psychiatrists, especially those trained as psychoanalysts, such as George Henry. These studies lacked validity in that their basic assumptions were flawed (for example, that homosexuals are ill). Furthermore, their questions were designed to determine differences among heterosexuals, but they lacked comparative studies with which to validate them (Henry, 1941, as cited in Bullough, 1998). Despite the difficulties in producing valid research, assumptions about the medical community's authority to explore human sexuality endured. When the Committee for Research in the Problems in Sex (CRPS), a grant-funding organization endowed through the Rockefeller's National Research Council, began awarding funds to researchers to conduct sex surveys, physicians were among the first to receive the monies (Bullough, 1998).

Kinsey was a classically trained scientist who taught courses in general biology, an author who had published several textbooks, and a researcher and world-renowned expert on gall wasps. He began his study of human sexuality in 1938 when he was invited to become a member of an interdisciplinary team delivering a course on marriage and family at Indiana University (Bullough, 1998). In 1941 he received an initial exploratory grant from the CRPS, which was followed by full funding the following year. Kinsey's approach to the study was clinical; he used *taxonomy* to dispassionately classify and describe behaviors and had no moral, ethical, or political agenda to inform his conclusions. The CRPS viewed Kinsey as a favorable candidate for research into human sexuality; he was a bench scientist with impeccable research skills, he was a full professor at a major university, his research into the field had the full support of the university administration, and he was married with adolescent children (Bullough, 1998). According to Bullough (1998), "the CRPS came to be so committed to Kinsey that by the 1946–1947 academic year, he was receiving half of the committee's total budget" (p. 129).

Kinsey's Research Methods

Kinsey's method of data collection involved personal interviews with volunteer subjects. One issue that he faced was in the creation of a representative sample population of American adults. Steinberg (2005) states, "People who agreed to give their sexual histories would necessarily be a self-selected, and therefore skewed, subset of the total population" (p. 19). Kinsey sought to mitigate the problem by using a large number of subjects, hoping that the volume would lessen the bias. This also worked with his methodology as the taxonomic approach required that data from as many subjects as possible be gathered. Although Kinsey had hoped to interview 100, 000 subjects from a variety of distinct cultural subgroups for the report, only 18,000 were completed by the time the Rockefeller Foundation had stopped funding for the research in 1954. Kinsey had personally interviewed 8,000 participants. He believed that self-administered questionnaires encouraged dishonest responses and inaccuracies. He held that participants would only be truthful about their sexual experiences when questioned personally because discrepancies, untruths, and contradictions could be explored by the interviewer (Steinberg, 2005; Bullough, 1998).

Kinsey developed a system of variegated questions and checks to detect lies that respondents might tell, and he believed that his system was effective. Interviewer bias was also a concern, and to mitigate that, he instituted a process through which two interviewers would meet with the same subject independently and at different times and responses would be compared. According to Bullough (1998), there were four interviewers, including Kinsey, and "if there was a bias, it came to be a shared one. The questions, however, were so wide-ranging that this too would limit much of the potential for slanting the data in any one direction" (p. 129).

Kinsey's challenge was to create an interview instrument and environment in which subjects would feel free to discuss a subject on which they had largely remained silent. Kinsey taught his researchers to project a sincere and objective demeanor that would put subjects at ease to disclose their sexual identities. Steinberg (2005) asserts, "his basic method—a contribution to sexual science as profound and longlasting as the data he produced—was to lead people out of their socially enforced silence around sex and into a bubble of free speech where they had permission to speak openly and honestly about sex" (p. 19). In removing the moral overtones from the research, Kinsey removed the taboo that had kept subjects from disclosing their sexual truths; by keeping the research clinical and for scientific use, they were able to elicit more information.

In his reports, Kinsey dismissed sexual practices he deemed outliers, or statistically insignificant. Pregnancy and sexually transmitted diseases were ignored along with sexual behaviors such as swinging, group sex, sadism, masochism, transvestitism, voyeurism, and exhibitionism. Homosexuality, pedophilia, and bestiality, however, were studied in some depth. He treated sex as a part of human behavior, demystifying its discussion and bringing into focus the aspects of sexuality that define individuals by making the study scientific rather than voyeuristic (Bullough, 1998).

FURTHER INSIGHTS

Kinsey's Findings

The Kinsey studies had a profound impact on both American culture and the study of human sexuality. Bethell (2005) states, "Remember the Kinsey sermon: there is no such thing as abnormality, just ceaseless sexual variety" (p. 1), and Steinberg offers, "'Everybody's sin is nobody's sin,' Kinsey proclaimed" (p. 20). The studies brought to light the fact that American sexual activities were radically different from what people believed. "Homosexuality, bisexuality, premarital sex, extramarital sex, oral sex, anal sex, masturbation, sadomasochism, sex with animals, sex with and between pre-adolescent children, sex between older people, sex with prostitutes—all of these were found to be common practices" (Steinberg, 2005, p. 19).

Kinsey's reports challenged many conventional beliefs about human sexual experiences. Romesburg (1998) states, "he also found that nearly 50% of the women had engaged in sex before marriage and more than 25% had experienced extramarital sexual intercourse" (p. 1). In addition, he portrayed extramarital sexual intercourse as a neutral activity rather than as a societal ill. Bullough (1998) suggests, "he questioned the assumption that extramarital intercourse always undermined the stability of marriage... he seemed to feel that the most appropriate extramarital affair, from the standpoint of preserving a marriage, was an alliance in which neither party became overly involved emotionally" (p. 131).

Another convention challenged by Kinsey's research was that of the asexuality (lack of sexual desire) of women. According to Herzog (2006), "American commentators on the female volume were especially distressed by high rates of female marital infidelity and by Kinsey's assertions that female orgasmic response was almost identical to men's" (p. 39). Bullough concurs, stating that among women"40%...had experienced orgasm within the first months of marriage, 67% by the first six months, and 75% by the end of the first year" (p. 131). In addition, "Twenty-five percent had experienced orgasm by the age of 15, more than 50% by the age of 20, and 64% before marriage" (Bullough, 1998, p. 131).

The creation of a taxonomy of human sexual behaviors was one of the many points of controversy when the reports were made public. This scientific approach to the subject allows for the objective classification of all sexual activities in which humans engage and classifies none as abnormal. The classification of human sexuality into a zoological framework fails to incorporate aspects of human psychology and emotion, which impact sexual experiences. Critics argued that defining what is normal for humans in the same manner as what is normal for animals neglects key aspects of human sexuality (Bullough, 1998).

Prevalence of Homosexuality

Kinsey developed a seven-point *bipolar scale*, which was one of the standards means of organizing social science research data at that time. Homosexuality and heterosexuality were seen as points on the seven-point continuum with the only objective indicator being what activity resulted in orgasm. Most people would respond in such a way that they would be in the middle of the scale. Bullough explains, "when one rates heterosexual orgasm as 0 and homosexual orgasm 6, a logical decision in terms of taxonomy, he in effect weights the scale by seeming to imply that exclusive heterosexuality is one extreme and exclusive homosexuality the other" (p. 130). While Kinsey found that most people can be classified exclusively heterosexual, his scale suggests that homosexuality is simply another sexual activity, which was revolutionary at the time. It was his findings that homosexual activity is much more prevalent than it had been believed to be, and his implication that it is within the normal range of behavior, that led to many of the attacks on his research (Bullough, 1998).

According to Romesburg (1998), after Kinsey interviewed nearly 6,000 men, he "concluded that 37% had engaged in at least one homosexual experience to orgasm between the ages of 16 and 55 [but] only 4% of the men were what he called 'exclusively homosexual'" (p. 1). Among women, Kinsey "reported that while 28% of women had "experienced homosexual arousal" by age 45, fewer than 3% could be classified as 'exclusively homosexual'" (Romesburg, 1998, p. 1). The idea that 10% of adult Americans are homosexual arose from these data; the statistic is the average of two numbers, 13% of men and 7% of women who had more homosexual than heterosexual experiences or psychological response for at least three years of adulthood (Romesburg, 1998). The statistics related to the practice of homosexual behavior had a worldwide impact. Herzog (2006) states, "the homophile reception—especially in France and West Germany—was thoroughly enthusiastic...in France, where adult homosexuality was legal but nonetheless subject to social sanction, activists effused about Kinsey's contributions" (p. 42).

Also among the sample population, the research revealed that in rural areas "about 40 to 50% of the males had had at least one sexual encounter with an animal, and 17% had even experienced an orgasm as a result of sexual contact with animals during adolescence" (Beetz, 2005, p. 48). The prevalence among the entire population of American men in the study was closer to 8% (Kinsey, Pomeroy & Martin, 1948, as cited in Beetz, 2005), and the prevalence of sexual contact with animals among women was much lower at 3% (Kinsey et al., 1953, as cited in Beetz, 2005). Given the social stigma of these activities, it is likely that they were underreported to researchers rather than overreported, and many participants indicated that curiosity was their primary motivation rather than sexual attraction (Beetz, 2005).

Numerous challenges to the statistical methods Kinsey employed have been raised in the decades since the first report's publication; however, the report demonstrates that although exact numbers of people engaging in forms of deviant sexual activity may vary, there were significant numbers of Americans engaging in those acts without physical and societal repercussions. "They were not all going crazy, committing suicide, getting pregnant, or dying of grossly disfiguring sexually transmitted diseases, as the popular sex mythology of the day would have predicted" (Steinberg, 2005, p. 20).

VIEWPOINTS

Continuing Criticism

Herzog (2006) states, "American critics variously attacked Kinsey and his associates for methodological insufficiencies (especially in their statistical sampling techniques) or for moral turpitude (for implying that the lived prevalence of non-normative behaviors also suggests that the norms themselves should be adapted)" (p. 40). Indeed, the issue of statistical sampling was a point of contention for the duration of his research. Attempts were made to encourage him to validate his data with a random sample of individuals, but Kinsey refused "on the grounds that not all of those included in the random sample would answer the questions put to them and that, therefore, the random sample would be biased" (Bullough, 1998, p. 132). The sample population on which Kinsey reported is not random, and among the over-represented groups are Caucasians, students, residents of Indiana, and prisoners incarcerated for sexually deviant behavior (Bullough, 1998).

Bethell (2005) challenges Kinsey's statistics, stating that the report maintained "85 percent of American men had sex before marriage, 70 percent had sex with prostitutes, 10 percent were exclusively homosexual. His figures were undermined when it was revealed that he had disproportionately interviewed homosexuals and prisoners (many sex offenders)" Furthermore, when he refused to adopt more valid statistical sampling procedures, the CRPS funding through the Rockefeller foundation was terminated (Bethell, 2005).

A significant incidence of intergenerational sexual behavior (between minor children and adults) was also reported in the study, and this is an area that has remained controversial well after its publication. According to Bullough (1998), "one of his more criticized sections in recent years is the table based on data he gathered from pedophiles. He is accused of not turning these people over to authorities" (p. 131). Further, Kinsey's controversial research demonstrates that many individuals who experienced intergenerational sex as children were not seriously harmed by it (Bullough, 1998). In 1981 questions were raised of how Kinsey and his staff collected data relevant to this area of their study. According to Pool (1996), "Attention was directed to Tables 30–34 of *Sexual Behavior in the Human Male*, which report observations of orgasms in over three-hundred children between the ages of five months and fourteen years" (p. 1). Leadership at the Kinsey Institute confirmed that some of the data were collected from a group of pedophiles whom Kinsey opted not to report to authorities (Pool, 1996).

Kinsey's implication that homosexual behavior was normal and acceptable caused a great deal of debate among homosexual rights activists and those opposed to its decriminalization in both the United States and in Europe. Herzog (2006) explains, "conservative opponents of Kinsey on both sides of the Atlantic were hostile to the notion that the prevalence of a particular sexual practice also implied that it was a morally acceptable practice (in other words, that "what is" was also "what ought to be)" (p. 42). Activists, on the other hand, held that what was natural, normal human sexual behavior should be both legally and socially sanctioned (Herzog, 2006). In the end, Kinsey's report brought to light the high incidence of homosexuality, and helped to spur the movement toward its legal and social acceptance.

Interest in Alfred Kinsey and his research persists into the present day. Biographies, as well as the popular movie, have helped to keep his name and ideas at the forefront of American culture. The impact of the work remains both controversial and profound. In 2005, the conservative publication *Human Events* named the Kinsey Report number 4 on its list of "Top Ten Most Harmful Books of the 19th and 20th Centuries" behind such books as *The Communist Manifesto, Mein Kampf* and *Quotations from Chairman Mao,* and among others like *Das Kapital* and *The Feminine Mystique.* While critics have also called into question the researcher's own sexual proclivities and those of his staff, the fact remains that he removed the taboo from the discussion of sexuality.

Kinsey's reports continue to be cited and his data continues to be used. This includes his bipolar scale, colloquially called the *Kinsey scale.* Numerous scales have been created that describe and measure sexual orientation. Most notable are the Kinsey scale variations created by Michael Storms in 1980 and Fritz Klein in 1987. Storms created a chart with an X and Y axis that includes heteroeroticism and homoeroticism (desire or arousal), as well as asexuality (an asexual is someone who does not experience sexual attraction). Klein developed the Klein Sexual Orientation Grid, which takes into account social and emotional orientation in addition to sexual orientation and acknowledges that one's orientation may change over time.

Among Kinsey's other achievements was the establishment of a library at Indiana University for the collection of sources related to sexuality that is now among the most impressive collections in the world. The Kinsey Institute for Research in Sex, Gender, and Reproduction at Indiana University is among the leaders in research in the field of human sexuality. Bullough (1998) concludes, "Kinsey was the major factor in changing attitudes about sex in the twentieth century. His limitations and his personal foibles are appropriately overshadowed by his courage to go where others had not gone before" (p. 132).

TERMS & CONCEPTS

Bestiality: Bestiality is a term used to describe a sexual act (kissing, petting, intercourse) between a human and an animal.

Bias: A research bias occurs when some members of the overall population are more likely to be included in the research than others. The best way to avoid bias is to use a random sample of the population.

Bipolar Scale: A bipolar rating scale, such as the Kinsey scale, is structured in such a way as to have a transitional midpoint between two extremes. In the case where a preference is indicated, each extreme would indicate a distinct preference, while the midpoint can signify either indifference to both or preference to each. In a bipolar scale, the definition of the midpoint has the potential to impact the meaning of other points as well.

Committee for Research in Problems of Sex (CRPS): The Committee was established in 1922 within the National Research Council's Division of Medical Sciences with the cooperation of the Bureau of Social Hygiene and support from the Rockefeller Foundation. Its central purpose was the investigation of human sexuality in the context of morphology, physiology, and psychology. Due to the support of the committee, a great deal of new data on various aspects of human sexuality was accumulated. The Committee was discharged in 1963.

Homosexual: The term homosexual refers to sexual behavior with or attraction to people of the same sex.

Human Sexuality: Human sexuality refers to the various physical, psychological, intellectual, and emotional ways in which people experience and express themselves as sexual beings, the awareness and expression of themselves as male or female, and the capacity they have for erotic experiences and responses.

Pedophile: The term pedophile refers to a person who either has acted on intense sexual urges toward children, or experiences recurrent sexual urges toward and fantasies about children that cause distress or interpersonal difficulty.

Sample/Sampling: For research purposes, a sample is a subset of the population to be studied. Because overall populations are generally too large to study, a sample of the population is used. A random sample, considered the best way to avoid bias, is one in which any individual member of the total population has the same probability of being selected as any other member of the population.

Taxonomy: Taxonomy is the practice and science of classification. Taxonomies involve the divisions of kinds of things into units, referred to as taxa, which are arranged into a hierarchical structure so that they may be studied.

BIBLIOGRAPHY

Beetz, A. (2005). "Bestiality and zoophilia: Associations with violence and sex offending." *Anthrozoos,* (Special Issue), 46–70.

Bethell, T. (2005). "Kinsey as pervert." *American Spectator,* 38, 42–44.

Bullough, V. (1998). "Alfred Kinsey and the Kinsey Report: Historical overview and lasting contributions." *Journal of Sex Research,* 35, 127–131.

Drucker, D. (2012). "Marking Sexuality from 0–6: The Kinsey Scale in Online Culture." *Sexuality & Culture,* 16, 241–262.

Duberman, M. (1997). "Kinsey's urethra." *Nation,* 265, 40–43.

Foster, T., & D'Emilio J. (2013). *Documenting intimate matters: Primary sources for a history of sexuality in America.* Chicago, IL: University of Chicago Press.

Herzog, D. (2006). "The reception of the Kinsey reports in Europe." *Sexuality and Culture, 10*, 39–48.

Janssen, E., Macapagal, K. R., & Mustanski, B. (2013). "Individual differences in the effects of mood on sexuality: The revised mood and sexuality questionnaire (MSQ-R)." *Journal Of Sex Research,* 50, 676–687.

Nash, O. (1964). "The Kinsey Report didn't upset me, either." *Saturday Evening Post,* 237, 8.

Pool, G. (1996, Sept–Oct). "Sex, science, and Kinsey: a conversation with Dr. John Bancroft - head of the Kinsey Institute for Research in Sex, Gender, and Reproduction." *Humanist.* http://findarticles.com/

Romesburg, D. (1998, June 23). "Kinsey reports sex stats." *Advocate,* 12.

Steinberg, D. (2005). "Origins of the Kinsey Revolution." *Gay & Lesbian Review Worldwide,* 12, 19–21.

"The Ten Most Harmful Books of the 19th and 20th Centuries." (2005, May 30). *Human Events,* 61, 6–7.

SUGGESTED READING

Cloud, J. (2004). "Bondage unbound." *Time,* 163, 104-109.

Crespi, L., & Stanley Jr., E. (1948). "Youth looks at the Kinsey report." *Public Opinion Quarterly,* 12, 687–696.

Del Tredici, P. (2006). "The other Kinsey report." *Natural History,* 115, 22–25.

Jones, J. J. (1997). *Alfred C. Kinsey: A public/private life.* Darby, PA: Diane Publishing Co.

Kinsey, A. C., Pomeroy, W. & Martin, C.E. (1998). *Sexual behavior in the human male.* Bloomington, IN: Indiana University Press.

Kinsey, A. C., et. al. (1998). *Sexual behavior in the human female.* Bloomington, IN: Indiana University Press.

Klein, J. (2004). "Living libido aoca: a Kinsey report." *Chronicle of Higher Education,* 51, B14–B15.

Palmore, E. (1952). "Published reactions to the Kinsey report" (book). *Social Forces,* 31, 165-172.

Pertot, S. (2006). "Sex therapy and the cultural construction of sexuality." *Contemporary Sexuality,* 40, 9–13.

Ramsey, G., & Varley, M. (1951). "Censorship and the Kinsey report." *Journal of Social Psychology,* 33, 279–288.

Yarber, W., Sayad, B., & Strong, B. (2013). *Human sexuality: Diversity in contemporary America.* 8th ed. New York, NY: McGraw-Hill.

Karin Carter-Smith, M.Ed.

POLITICAL INEQUALITY

ABSTRACT

From an egalitarian point of view, the participation of women in the political process—not only as enfranchised citizens but also as candidates and elected officials—is in and of itself an important goal. In addition, from a social justice point of view, the participation of women in the political process is likely to help advance the state of women's issues and gender equality. Theorists posit that the ability of women to be successful in active participation in politics rests upon three types of factors: political, socioeconomic, and cultural. More research is needed to better understand how best to support women in gaining gender equality in this important arena.

OVERVIEW

Looking at things from a gender perspective, it is necessary to note that it was only a couple of generations ago that women in the United States did not even have the right to vote, let alone run for office. Although individual states extended the right to vote to women earlier, women in the United States did not win the national right to vote until 1920 with the ratification of the Nineteenth Amendment to the US Constitution, which states that "the right of citizens of the United States to vote shall not be denied or abridged by the United States or by any State on account of sex. Congress shall have power to enforce this article by appropriate legislation." Since that time, of course, women have made great strides forward in the political arena, not only registering their opinions through their votes, but also by banding together to form political blocs that encourage change or by running for and being elected to political office themselves. Yet, the share of parliamentary seats held by women across the globe remains low. According to data from the International Women's Democracy Center, as of June 2008, Nordic countries had the greatest levels of women legislators in parliament, with an average of 41.4 percent. North and South America had the second highest percentages of female legislators, with an average of 21.8 percent. The Pacific Islands and the Middle East were the regions with the lowest average percentage of female legislators, at 13.4 percent and 9.6 percent, respectively.

According to data compiled by the Inter-Parliamentary Union, as of late 2017, Rwanda had the highest percentage of women in the lower or single house with just over 61 percent, while the United States had just over 19 percent (Inter-Parliamentary Union, 2017).

Making Strides

Although such statistics may appear at first glance to be discouraging, women have actually made significant progress toward political equality over the past few decades. For example, in 2003, women won 48.8 percent of the seats in the lower house of Rwanda's national legislative body (Hughes, 2007-8). As of early 2018, women had also been elected as heads of state in countries such as Finland, Liberia, Chile, Taiwan, Estonia, and Croatia as well as the heads of government in countries including Germany, Jamaica, Poland, Serbia, New Zealand, and South Korea (Gomes, 2007). According to the Pew Research Center, 56 of 146 countries analyzed by the World Economic Forum in 2014 and 2016 had had a woman as the head of state or government for at least one year in the past fifty years (Geiger & Kent, 2017).

FACTORS INFLUENCING FEMALE POLITICAL SUCCESS

Political Factors

The literature posits a number of types of factors that may affect the probability of a woman gaining election to a parliamentary body. The first of these comprises political factors.

- Studies indicate that women are generally more successful in electoral politics in situations where voters choose among party lists and multimember districts rather than in situations in which there are individual candidates and single member districts. In general, political parties are more likely to nominate women candidates (and voters are more likely to vote for them) if women are among other candidates on the party's ticket. It has been found, for example, that many voters vote for a party ticket whether or not some of the individuals on that ticket are women, rather than voting for individual candidates.
- Further, research indicates that the structure of the electoral system is important for the election

of women candidates. For example, there are differences between "the party lists/multimember districts system of balloting and the proportional representation method of seat allocation, whereby each party wins a number of seats in proportion to" its share of the votes cast in the election and the way in which they are perceived by voters (Kenworthy & Malami, 1999, p. 238). As the number of seats in the district becomes smaller, the identity of the individual candidates becomes increasingly important to the voters and, therefore, to the party.

- In addition, the partisan composition of the legislature may also affect the number of women who win seats. More liberal parties typically express greater commitment to reducing gender inequality than do more conservative parties. As a result, liberal parties tend to nominate more women candidates than do conservative parties; therefore, it can be expected that the larger the share of seats held by liberal politicians within the legislature, the greater the proportion of women among those seats.
- Another political factor that can affect the proportion of women elected to the legislature is women's voting rights. Statistics indicate that the longer women have had the right to vote within the country, the greater the percentage of women to vote in the elections.

Socioeconomic Factors. A second set of factors that are important determinants of women's chances of gaining election to the legislature are socioeconomic factors. The progress of women within the political arena is typically correlated with the progress of women in other arenas.

- One important area that appears to be related to women's political progress is their educational progress. Typically, individuals who are able to be successfully elected to the legislature bring with them educational credentials (e.g., law school, business school). Therefore, it has been theorized that in countries where women's educational attainment is high the number of women who are qualified and motivated to run for office, and are, therefore, more likely to win election increases. In addition, voter participation and education tend to be strongly correlated. Therefore, many theorists believe that as women continue to attain higher educational levels, they will concomitantly turn out in greater numbers to vote, which could mean the election of more women to ©ffice.
- Another socioeconomic factor that has been found to be correlated with women's participation as candidates within the electoral process is their activity as part of the labor force. For example, it has been found that women who work outside the home are more likely to be active participants in politics. This can be due to a number of factors. For example, women who are active members of the labor force tend to gain confidence and other skills necessary to be successful in politics. Further, working outside the home could help women obtain funds to help them launch a political campaign. In addition, participating in the labor force affords women the opportunity to network with other individuals who can help them launch and run a successful political campaign. Many theorists believe that as women's participation in the labor force rises, they will turn out in greater numbers to vote and also be more likely to run for office. However, the mere fact of women participating in the labor force is not necessarily sufficient to improve the probability of women running for and winning elected office. For the most part, elected officials typically come from professional fields such as law, education, journalism, and business. Such individuals tend to be better educated, better public speakers, and more knowledgeable of both the law and the political system.
- Another socioeconomic factor that can affect the participation of women in the political process is size and strength of the women's movement within that country. Such organizations not only provide women candidates with a support network to help them win elections, but also can provide women candidates with political and financial resources to help them get elected.
- In addition, another socioeconomic factor that has been suggested to promote gender equality in the political arena is the economic development of the country. It has been suggested that the more wealthy a country is, the less likely it is that its politics will be preoccupied with economic concerns. As a result, both the political parties and the voters may be more likely to consider other factors, such

as gender equality in the election of political officials.

Cultural Factors. In addition to political and socioeconomic factors, the likelihood of success of women in the political arena can also be affected by cultural factors. Simply stated, societies that tend to affirm, promote, or believe in equal political, economic, social, and civil rights for all people tend to be more likely than other societies to promote and foster the active participation of women as candidates and elected officials within the political system. For example, women's willingness to run for political office tends to be higher in European and North American countries than in other areas of the world (Kenworthy & Malami, 1999). The similarities of these cultures and the differences between them and cultures in other areas of the world has been theorized as one of the reasons for the success of women in politics in these regions.

APPLICATIONS

Benefits of Women's Political Participation. Melanie M. Hughes (2008) points out that greater political equality for women is important for several reasons. First, women often focus on the creation and passing of different kinds of legislation than do men. In particular, women are more prone to focus on issues of sexual discrimination and harassment, family leave, reproductive rights, and health care that would otherwise not receive as much attention. The participation of women as candidates in the electoral process has also been hypothesized by some observers to encourage the participation of women in the voting process. For some, voting is considered a matter of human rights and social justice. Unfortunately, women have often been marginalized from political participation.

Increasing Women's Political Participation. In some countries, quota systems have been set up to mandate the proportion of women that are to be elected to legislative office under the assumption that electing women who will pay more attention to women's issues into office will result in greater gender equality. However, Veronica Schild (2000) rightly points out that even when government institutions take steps to reduce discrimination and to open opportunities for women, official strategies do not necessarily translate into true social justice for women on a grassroots level. The political goal of achieving gender equality often becomes a technical task (e.g., creation of laws that prohibit discrimination) rather than one of true social justice for women.

Gender inequality is a situation experienced not only in countries that are still undergoing economic development, but occurs in developed countries as well. Rather than representing real underlying differences in abilities, the inequality of women typically has to do with the gender roles dictated to them by their cultures. Across the globe, women are slowly becoming more able to participate in paid, nonagricultural employment in areas where women have historically had low levels of participation in the labor market. However, in other regions, progress in this area is virtually nonexistent. Despite such advances, however, women tend to be more likely to be unpaid for their labors than men not only within the home but also as unpaid family agricultural workers. Because of this fact, women tend to have less access to social protections, job security, or education. Social observers and theorists believe that these problems can be improved through the election of women to political office (United Nations, 2007).

The 2016 presidential election in the United States was particularly analyzed in terms of gender inequality in politics as Hillary Clinton became the first woman in the developed country's history to be nominated for the role by a major political party. Running as a Democrat, she campaigned against Republican candidate Donald Trump. Gender was a persistent topic of the campaign, as political commentators and the media speculated about the issues championed by each candidate as well as how Americans, particularly, women, might vote in the election. Following the election of Trump in November 2016, debates ensued about why a majority of white women actually voted for Trump rather than Clinton as well as how much Clinton's gender did or did not play a role overall in her defeat. Some argued that the results of the election necessitated a deeper look into the complexity of identity politics, as assumptions based around Clinton's presumed popularity with the female population due to her policies supporting women (paid parental leave, reproductive rights, etc.) and the Republican Party's increased association with policies that do not favor women proved incorrect (McCall & Orloff, 2017).

CONCLUSION

From an egalitarian point of view, the participation of women in the political process—not only as enfranchised citizens but also as candidates and elected officials—is in and of itself an important goal. In addition, from a social justice point of view, the participation of women in the political process is likely to help advance the state of women's issues, children's rights, and gender equality. Although progress is being made in this area, however, there is still a long way to go before women achieve equal rates of political participation as men in many countries. More research is needed to better understand how best to support women in gaining gender equality in this important arena.

TERMS & CONCEPTS

Correlation: The degree to which two events or variables are consistently related. Correlation may be positive (i.e., as the value of one variable increases the value of the other variable increases), negative (i.e., as the value of one variable increases the value of the other variable decreases), or zero (i.e., the values of the two variables are unrelated). Correlation does not imply causation.

Culture: A complex system of meaning and behavior that is socially transmitted and that defines a common way of life for a group or society. Culture includes the totality of behavior patterns, arts, beliefs, institutions, and other products of human work and thought of the society or group.

Economic Development: The sustainable increase in living standards for a nation, region, or society. More than mere economic growth (i.e., a rise in output), economic development is sustainable growth that positively affects the well-being of all members of the group through such things as increased per capita income, education, health, and environmental protection. Economic development is progressive in nature and positively affects the socioeconomic structure of a society.

Gender: Psychological, social, cultural, and behavioral characteristics associated with being female or male. Gender is defined by one's gender identity and learned gender role.

Gender Inequality: Disparities among individuals based solely on their gender rather than objective differences in skills, abilities, or other characteristics. Gender inequalities may be obvious (e.g., not receiving the same pay for the same job) or subtle (e.g., not being given the same subjective opportunities for advancement).

Gender Role: Separate patterns of personality traits, mannerisms, interests, attitudes, and behaviors that are categorized as "male" and "female" by one's culture. Gender role is largely a product of the way in which one was socialized and may not be in conformance with one's gender identity.

Human Rights Movement: An international movement that promotes the cause of human rights throughout the globe. According to Article 1 of the United Nations Universal Declaration of Human Rights: "All human beings are born free and equal in dignity and rights. They are endowed with reason and conscience and should act toward one another in a spirit of brotherhood" (United Nations, 2009).

Marginalization: To relegate a person or subgroup to the outer edge of the group (i.e., margin) by demonstrating through word or action that the person or subgroup is less important and less powerful than the rest of the group.

Sexual Discrimination: The differential treatment of individuals based on their sex. Although sexual discrimination can occur against either sex, in most cases it occurs against women. Sexual discrimination can be exhibited in such actions as lower wages being given to one sex for the same work when performed by the other sex, discounting of the characteristics or attributes of one sex in comparison with the other, or unfair hiring or promotion policies that are biased against one sex.

Social Justice: Efforts to achieve justice in every aspect of society not merely through the application of the law. Social justice is based on the principle of universal human rights and working to ensure that all individuals receive fair treatment and equally share the benefits of society.

Society: A distinct group of people who live within the same territory, share a common culture and way of life, and are relatively independent from people outside the group. Society includes systems of social interactions that govern both culture and social organization.

Socioeconomic Status (SES): The position of an individual or group on the two vectors of social and economic status and their combination. Factors contributing to socioeconomic status include (but are not limited to) income, type and prestige of occupation, place of residence, and educational attainment.

Bibliography

Alexander, A. C., Bolzendahl, C., & Jalalzai, F. (2016). "Defining women's global political empowerment: Theories and evidence." *Sociology Compass,* 10 (6), 432–441.

Fallon, K. M., Swiss, L., & Viterna, J. (2012). "Resolving the democracy paradox: Democratization and women's legislative representation in developing nations, 1975 to 2009." *American Sociological Review,* 77, 380–408.

Geiger, A., & Kent, L. (2017, March 8). "Number of women leaders around the world has grown, but they'restillasmallgroup." *PewResearchCenter.* http://www.pewresearch.org/fact-tank/2017/03/08/women-leaders-around-the-world/

Gomes, A. (2007). "Women in international politics: Glass ceilings." *Social Europe,* 2, 139–141.

Gudhlanga, E. (2013). "Shutting them out: Opportunities and challenges of women's participation in Zimbabwean politics—a historical perspective." *Journal of Third World Studies,* 30, 151–170.

Hughes, M. M. (2007-8). "Windows of political opportunity: Institutional instability and gender inequality in the worlds' national legislatures." *International Journal of Sociology,* 37, 26–51.

Inter-Parliamentary Union. (2017). "Women in national parliaments." *Inter-Parliamentary Union.* http://archive.ipu.org/wmn-e/classif.htm

Kenworthy, L. & Malami, M. (1999). "Gender inequality in political representation: A worldwide comparative analysis." *Social Forces,* 78, 235–269.

McCall, L., & Orloff, A. S. (2017). "The multidimensional politics of inequality: taking stock of identity politics in the U.S. presidential election of 2016." *British Journal of Sociology,* 68, S34–S56.

Payne, L. W. (2013). "Welfare reform in the states: Does the percentage of female legislators in state legislatures affect welfare reform policies?" *Journal of Sociology and Social Welfare,* 40, 53–68.

Schild, V. (2000). "'Gender equity' without social justice: Women's rights in the neoliberal age." *NACLA Report on the Americas,* 34, 25–53.

United Nations. (2007). "Millennium development goals report 2007." http://mdgs.un.org/unsd/mdg/Resources/Static/Products/Progress2007/UNSD%5f_MDG_Report_2007e.pdf

United Nations. (2009). "The Universal Declaration of Human Rights." http://www.un.org/Overview/rights.html

Xydias, C. V. (2007-8). "Inviting more women to the party: Gender quotas and women's substantive representation in Germany." *International Journal of Sociology,* 37, 52-66.

Suggested Reading

Cassese, E., & Holman, M. (2016). "Religious beliefs, gender consciousness, and women's political participation." *Sex Roles,* 75 (9/10), 514–527.

Coffe, H. (2013). "Women stay local, men go national and global? Gender differences in political interest." *Sex Roles,* 69 (5/6), 323–338.

Connell, R. W. (2005). "Change among the gatekeepers: Men, masculinities, and gender equality in the global arena." *Signs: Journal of Women in Culture and Society,* 30, 1801–1825.

Griffin, J. D. & Newman, B. (2005). "Does descriptive representation produce political equality?" Paper prepared for presentation at the *Annual Meeting of the Midwest Political Science Association.* http://americandemocracy.nd.edu/

Kabeer, N. (2005).Gender equality and women's empowerment: A critical analysis of the third Millennium Development Goal. *Gender and Development, 13,* 13–24.

Lees, M. (2000). "Women, work and politics in 2000." *Social Alternatives,* 19, 21–22.

Sandler, J. (2008). "Gender equality is key to achieving the MDGs: Women and girls are central to development." *U.N. Chronicle,* 44, 47–48.

Ruth A. Wienclaw, Ph.D.

Polyamory

ABSTRACT

Polyamory, a neologism that brings together a Greek and a Latin word that together mean "many loves." Polyamory is a lifestyle in which multiple consenting adults agree to establish a domestic arrangement among themselves. The relationship is an intentionally non-monogamous structure in which these members consent to provide each other emotional and financial support, as well as physical intimacy. Presented by its advocates as a viable alternative to traditional sexual dyads, particularly marriage, polyamory creates a broader kind of intimate network wherein adults can more openly address a wider range of emotional matters because the relationship includes a wider range of perspectives.

OVERVIEW

Given the statistics on the failure rate of marriage since the 1970s (more than half of first marriages now end in divorce), interest in the polyamory lifestyle has begun to attract a wider and far more receptive audience. Using the communication tools of the Internet, the movement has provided a significant body of anecdotal research on the benefits of this lifestyle. Hard data on the appeal of polyamory is more difficult to secure, because many who practice the lifestyle prefer to keep the relationship private. Estimates run from a half million Americans who practice the polyamory lifestyle to as many as ten million, or just over 5 percent of adults. When asked whether they would embrace polyamory as a lifestyle, that is, accept it philosophically even if they would not actually practice it, the numbers routinely range closer to 75 percent.

The idea of maintaining a long-term loving relationship with a significant someone with the consent and even encouragement of a significant someone else simultaneously in the same home is a concept radically at odds with centuries of Judeo-Christian tradition, which views exclusive fidelity within monogamous marriage as the ultimate expression of emotional health and well-being between two life partners. The cultural perception of marriage, however, has radically changed since the 1970s. The sexual revolution gave rise to a liberalization of attitudes toward gender roles and expectations between sexual partners, including in marriage. The emergence of relationship counseling and hard research into the actual dynamics of relationships, the extension of marriage to same-sex partners, the exploration of intimate and domestic relationships in movies and television, and the accessibility of the Internet and social media have contributed to a major change in the cultural perception of how best to express romantic love and how best to sustain that commitment across time (Yi, 2013).

Polyamorous households may appear unconventional to outsiders. For example, an educated adult male making a comfortable living shares a house with his long-time partner, who is the mother of their only child, a young boy. Both partners are employed, active in their community, and have good relationships with their more conventional parents. The addition of another adult female has introduced new insights and ideas to their household operations, including in the sexual domain. The arrangement was created by mutual consent and all are committed to the arrangement. The original partners continue to be listed as the owners of the house, with the second female as a renter, though all three contribute to the household finances and have a say in major decisions. They eat together, share all the household chores, provide care for the child, and are mutually sexually engaged.

The question for ethicists is whether three (or more) adults can share intimacy without creating inequitable hierarchies, generating jealousy, or inciting territorial wars? Some ethicists contend that such polygynous relationships simply cannot work. "This central spouse divides him or herself among multiple spouses, but each peripheral spouse remains exclusively devoted to the central spouse. With this hub-and-spoke structure, even a perfectly virtuous central spouse has more rights and fewer obligations than each peripheral spouse" (Strauss, 2012).

Though it may in many ways operate like a conventional marriage, the triad described above is likely a secret arrangement. The partnership comes without religious or governmental sanction and without the legal and tax advantages (or protections) of legal marriage. The second female here, for example, though she contributes financially to the household does not have a legal share of ownership in the house and can be ejected by the others if the relationship were to deteriorate. Each adult may fear repercussions from their employers or the disapproval of their neighbors. Concerns about the reaction of the biological grandparents may include a fear of having the custody of their child challenged on grounds of unfitness or even child abuse.

Although domestic arrangements involving multiple partners are not only common but legal in other countries, experiments in communal marriages within American cultural history have been brief and have been quickly marginalized. Advocates of traditional marriage point to these as inevitable failures—for example, the utopian community of Oneida established in upstate New York just before the Civil War; small remote communities established during the settlement of West when women were relatively scarce; and more recently any of the hundreds of so-called communes established by the more extreme elements of the free-love counterculture movement in the 1960s.

The law, in all jurisdictions in the United States favors monogamous marriage and views it as a basic unit of society worthy of protection against potentially destabilizing alternatives. Regardless of discontent, bickering, frustrations, and simmering resentments (Willoughby, Farero & Busby, 2014), monogamous marriage continues to be the officially preferred expression of committed romantic partnership. Most often pointing out the importance of maintaining a stable and traditional home as a moral environment for raising children, advocates of traditional marriage decry deviations as inevitably a threat to the emotional well-being of children brought up in such nontraditional settings. However, the data is inconclusive. "[C]hildren can thrive in polygamous families where there may be many adults to provide support and attention" (Desar, 2013).

Critics argue that monogamous marriage is merely a social compact, an institutional complex artificially imposed for self-serving reasons by governments and religions solely interested in maintaining their own influence and power. Skeptics of traditional marriage question whether marriage to a single individual, even if that commitment is made in good faith and made with every expectation of making the union succeed, can anticipate the natural personal growth that every adult inevitably experiences? Over time, married partners can slip away from effective and regular communication, which, in turn, impacts virtually every level of satisfaction, most notably in areas of intimacy and sexual relationships. "Poor communication is not the cause of every relational problem, and effective communication is not a panacea for every issue...but any interaction requiring skillful coordination of activity can only reach its full potential when people communicate effectively" (Hess & Coffelt, 2012).

FURTHER INSIGHTS

Advocates of the polyamory lifestyle, which only emerged as a cultural force in the 1980s, are quick to point out—even before delimiting the benefits of this relationship dynamic—what polyamory is not. Because it involves an emotional and even spiritual commitment, polyamory is not "swinging," in which couples, married or otherwise, freely engage in sexual relations with other people, frequently anonymously, as a way to maintain some level of carnal excitement in a marriage. Polyamory is not infidelity, because all partners are consenting. Nor is polyamory a kind of polygyny—in which a person maintains multiple husbands (or wives) simultaneously. There is no prescribed set of legal provisions or protections that necessarily binds any of the adults. Nor is polyamory an open marriage in which partners are permitted by mutual agreement to investigate sexual experiences with others without guilt or consequences. Polyamory upends conventional assumptions about the nature of relationships but is, in fact, a variation on a most conservative and traditional notion of committed sexual and domestically anchored relationship. Within polyamory, relationships are about communication, honesty, above all commitment, elements that have long defined traditional marriage.

Given the widespread disillusion with the premise of monogamy and the expectation that any single person can meet a range of needs and wants, not only sexual but emotional and intellectual as well, for an entire lifetime, polyamory has received a great deal of national attention. Advocates have worked to address the four most prominent objections of skeptics: 1) inevitably within this dynamic jealousy will become a factor, not just over sexual activity, and that will come to shade all decisions and activities; 2) children, either brought into the relationship or a product of the relationship, will be confused over the exact nature of the domestic construct; 3) the commitment to the relationship will not be equally shared and, hence, certain partners will feel compelled to agree to a relationship to which they may actually maintain objections; and 4) the reality is that, as in any relationship, emotions fade, change, lessen, and multiplying the partners simply multiplies the potential for significant problems over time. After all, polyamory relationships face the same possibilities of endings as more traditional marriage. Where, then, is the assurance of stability?

Advocates of polyamory counter that the premise behind each assumption is the fickleness of emotions and the deceptive nature of commitment itself, a cynical view fostered by governments and churches who do not trust individuals to make ethical and moral choices and hence have to be controlled within the conventional construct of a marriage. They argue that conventional marriages give rise to jealousy by creating in individuals a distressing level of attachment experienced as the sense that another person has somehow become a commodity to which they alone have proprietary rights. Polyamory relationships assume that a loved one finding their way to a broadening love from someone else can only enhance the love they have with another. Advocates term this concept "compersion." "[I]f individuals feel that certain needs are met in one relationship, having another partner meet those same needs may have an enhancing effect on both relationships" (Mitchell, Bartholomew & Cobb, 2014).

Proponents of polyamory have been generally apolitical. They have not, as a movement, demanded legal recognition of polyamory for purposes of insurance, home ownership and property rights, inheritance disputes, or income tax filing. There is, however, something of a grassroots movement designed to better define questions of child custody. Nevertheless, the lifestyle has been caught up in one of the most incendiary cultural debates of the Obama Era. When by a narrow 5-4 vote the Supreme Court validated same-sex marriages in 2014, opponents charged that expanding the definition of marriage to include homosexuals opened the door to other domestic arrangements, specifically citing polyamory relationships. Many conservatives view the expansion of marriage as further indication of the demise of Judeo-Christian values at the expense of commitment to a husband/wife home (Yi, 2014).

VIEWPOINTS

Because polyamory arrangements are made ahead of time with the mutual consent of all parties, and because the commitment is made up front to all those involved in the relationship, so-called "polys" accept boundaries in ways that traditional couples never have to. The relationship does not work with ongoing judgmental comparisons ("he's more sensitive than you are"; "she's a better kisser than you are") nor can it work if one partner plays another partner in an effort to gain leverage with the other or others. The boundaries of the relationships are clear and, in the long and short term, necessary. Advocates assert that the only way polyamory works is if there is a true commitment to communication.

According to supporters, one person in a traditional marriage invariably dominates the relationship at the expense of the other, whereas a polyamory household necessarily empowers each person. As such, polyamory advocates see their primary responsibility within the cultural environment is to gift the public with the awareness that there is a significant and workable alternative to marriage. Polys often see traditional marriage as less stable, with husbands or wives more likely to seek out avenues for extramarital sex and as more likely to crash and burn over painful charges of infidelity or irreconcilable differences and/or settle down into unsatisfying routine.

The challenge facing polys is the paucity of data that might measure any long-term impacts of polyamory relationships. Even psychologists, called in to counsel those committed to the polyamory life, have difficulty in grasping the boundaries of this novel relationship dynamic and hence often treat those committed to the lifestyle ineffectively. As Graham (2014) noted, "for optimal therapeutic outcomes, mental health professions need to be trained in and become tolerant of these increasingly common relationship patterns. Failure to do so could result in a poor therapeutic alliance, treatment non-adherence, failure to appreciate the role such relationships play in the patient's stability or wellbeing, and subsequent poor patient outcomes." What is offered now is primarily anecdotal evidence that testifies to the value of the lifestyle or testifies to its negative impact on family, on friendships, on their faith, and on the children involved within such a dynamic. But there is little research. Many of those committed to the lifestyle prefer to keep that lifestyle private. Even those who have "come out" and have advocated the benefits of a relationship, although unconventional, that is based on honesty, transparency, and trust really cannot address long-term impacts as these relationships are still ongoing. Polyamory, its proponents argue, is not an experiment that needs to be researched first—but rather a lifestyle compelled by love and sustained by commitment. "For men and women, it will be possible to have partnerships with various people, who will, in turn, have various partners themselves. At long last, we will recognize that it is human to love different people at the same time" (Attali, 2005).

TERMS & CONCEPTS

Intimate Network: In psychology, a term applied to the widest reach of trust and communication between and among a wide range of adults, rather than the narrower relationship between two adults defined and/or limited by sexual intimacy.

Polygyny: A relationship pattern, usually illegal, in which a person has more than one legally recognized spouse at a same time.

Intentional Community: In sociology, the network created by the voluntary commitment of adults rather than the association among adults because of shared bloodlines (family) or shared geography (neighbors) or shared workplace (co-workers).

Coming Out: In psychology, the decision to make public and/or share with others a controversial lifestyle choice or intimate personal dimension, such as sexual orientation.

Compersion: A term coined by advocates of polyamory that describes the happiness a person feels in response to another's romantic relationship or sexual experience with a mutual partner.

Consanquinity: In psychology, the perception of kinship that expands the family; the broadest possible relationships among all people based on a common bloodline rather than limited by a specific family bloodline.

Monogamy: The practice of maintaining a romantic and/or sexual relationship with a single person.

Bibliography

Attali, J.(2005). "Here today, gone tomorrow: Monogamy." *Foreign Policy*, 150, 44-45.

Desar, L. (2013). "Happily never after." *Psychology Today*, 46(5), 12.

Graham, N. (2014). "Polyamory: A call for increased mental health professional awareness." *Archives of Sexual Behavior*, 43(6), 1031–1034.

Hess, J., and Coffelt, T. (2012). "Verbal communication about sex in marriage: Patterns of language use and its connection with relational outcomes." *Journal of Sex Research*, 49(6), 603–613.

Mitchell, M.., Bartholomew, K., & Cobb, R. (2014). "Need fulfillment in polyamorous relationships." *Journal of Sex Research*, 51(3), 329–339.

Strauss, G. (2012). "Is polygamy inherently unequal?" *Ethics*, 112(3), 516–544.

Willoughby, B., Farero, A., & Busby, D. (2014). "Exploring the effects of sexual desire discrepancy among married couples." *Archives of Sex Research*, 43(2), 551–562.

Yi, J. (2013). "(Re)drawing the lines on marriage and sexuality." *Political Quarterly*, 84(4), 497–505.

Suggested Reading

Barnett, J. (2014). "Polyamory and criminalization of plural conjugal unions in Canada: Competing narratives in the s.293 reference." *Sexuality Research & Social Policy: Journal of NSRC*, 11(1), 63–75.

Johnson, S. M., Giuliano, T. A., Herselman, J. R., & Hutzler, K. T. (2015). "Development of a brief measure of attitudes towards polyamory." *Psychology & Sexuality*, 6(4), 325-339.

Morrison, T. G., Beaulieu, D., Brockman, M., & Beaglaoich, C. Ó. (2013). "A comparison of polyamorous and monoamorous persons: are there differences in indices of relationship well-being and sociosexuality?" *Psychology & Sexuality*, 4(1), 75-91.

Taomino, T. (2008). *Opening up: A guide to creating and sustaining open relationships.* Berkeley, CA.

Veaux, F., & Rickert, E. (2014). *More than two: A practical guide to ethical polyamory.* Portland, OR: Thorntree Press.

Williams, D. J., & Prior, E. E. (2015). "Contemporary polyamory: A call for awareness and sensitivity in social work." *Social Work*, 60(3), 268–270.

Joseph Dewey

Pornography

ABSTRACT

Defined as material, such as writing or pictures, designed to arose sexual desire, pornography has been in existence for centuries and found popularity across every culture The majority of pornography has been directed at heterosexual males, with the audience being primarily white and middle class. There has long been a social stigma, or a non-pecuniary cost, associated with the use of sexually explicit materials (Kendall, 2006). However, social mores have loosened over time and the shame or stigma associated with viewing pornography has also decreased. Pornography is also a "hot button" issue for many feminists -some of whom feel that all pornographic material depicting women degrades and objectifies women. Other opponents of pornography base their views on religious or moral grounds, and see the consumption of pornographic material as a threat to the family and society. Social scientists continue to study the effects of long term exposure to pornography on intimate relationships, as well as the relationship between exposure to pornography and sexually deviant behavior.

OVERVIEW

Defined as material, such as writing or pictures, designed to arose sexual desire, pornography has been in existence for centuries and found popularity across every culture (Hudson, 2008). The majority of pornography is directed at heterosexual males, with the audience being primarily white and middle class (Hudson, 2006).

Opponents of pornography have long argued that pornography has a corrosive effect on individuals, families, and society. Social conservatives view it as capable of undermining monogamous marriages, leading unmarried men into sexual depravity, and corrupting young, impressionable women (Pollard, 1993). Accordingly, there has long been a social stigma, or a non-pecuniary cost, associated with the use of sexually explicit materials (Kendall, 2006). However, social mores have loosened over time and the shame or stigma associated with viewing pornography has also decreased. Historically, as the financial, or pecuniary, costs of accessing pornography have decreased, there have been repeated attempts to increase the non-pecuniary costs associated with pornography (Kendall, 2006). In other words, as sexually explicit materials have become cheaper and more widely available, social forces have shifted in an attempt to control consumption through non-pecuniary means.

The Rising Demand for Pornography

Pornographic materials have been in existence for as long as man created art out of stone and clay. The production and distribution of pornography adapts easily to new media whether they be pictures, print, photography, movies, or computer files. In the US pornographic images gained popularity with GIs during WWII. Twenty years after the war, *Playboy* magazine was first published, and, in a short time, saw its circulation skyrocket. In 1974 the more explicit *Hustler* entered publication and, like *Play- boy,* was well received in the marketplace, showing just how much demand there was for pornography. After Sony introduced the VCR in 1975, pornography began to be sold in the form of x-rated videos tapes, which allowed viewers to watch pornographic movies in the privacy of their homes instead of at public movie houses. When it was created, the Internet and the first graphical browsers represented a "quantum leap in pornography distribution" (Kendall, 2006). It is difficult to ascertain what percentage of Internet sites contain sexually explicit or sexually oriented materials, but estimates are staggering. Some estimates put the growth of sexually oriented web sites at "hundreds" per week, but, with the global reach of pornography, such estimates may be low. Much of the pornography exchanged in digital formats is shared over peer to peer networks. These networks allow creators, distributors, and users to share content directly without having to post it on public sites.

Legislation & Pornography

Some types of pornography are protected under the First Amendment. This protected content depicts adults, and, while adults are free to access it, minors' access may be restricted if the content is deemed "harmful to minors." In 1973 the US Supreme Court decision *Miller v. California* defined what types of sexually explicit materials are and are not excluded from protection under the First Amendment: obscenity and child pornography.

Miller v. California defined basic guidelines for obscenity cases as the following:

- "Whether the average person, applying contemporary community standards, would find that the work, taken as a whole appeals to the prurient interest.
- "Whether the work depicts or describes, in a patently offensive way, sexual conduct specifically defined by the applicable state law.
- "Whether the work taken as a whole, lacks serious literary, artistic, political or scientific value" (Hudson, 2008).

Child pornography was defined by the 1996 Child Pornography Prevention Act as "any visual depiction... [that] is, or appears to be, of a minor engaging in sexually explicit conduct" (Child Pornography Prevention Act, 1996, as quoted in Hudson, 2008, ¶ 20). When minors, including teens, are depicted in pornographic material they are considered "victims" of a crime, and anyone possessing or viewing such material is considered a criminal (Finkelhor & Ormrod, 2004; Hudson, 2008).

Determining what constitutes pornography is both "controversial and confounding" (Hudson, 2008) and, even with the Supreme Court definition, remains the subject of much contentious debate. Pornography is also a "hot button" issue for many feminists—some of whom feel that all pornographic material depicting women degrades and objectifies women. Other opponents of pornography base their views on religious or moral grounds, and see the consumption of pornographic material as a threat to the traditional nuclear family. Social scientists continue to study the effects of long term exposure to pornography on intimate relationships, as well as the relationship between exposure to pornography and sexually deviant behavior. Via the Internet, children and teens have unprecedented access to sexual explicit materials, and researchers have begun to study what effects the accidental and purposeful viewing of pornography has on children and teens.

APPLICATIONS

Pornography & Sexual Violence

A long standing question asked by social scientists concerns the relationship between sexually explicit materials and anti-social behavior (Kendall, 2006). Consider the following public perceptions about exposure to pornography from a survey.

- 49% believe pornography can cause men to rape
- 56% blame it for a breakdown in morals. (Hudson, 2006)

Many researchers have explored the relationship between exposure to pornography and sexually violent behavior. The following examples reveal that research on the question has been largely inconclusive.

In 1979 Neil Malamuth and his colleagues published a study titled *Exposure to Pornography and Reactions to Rape,* the purpose of which was to study the effects of exposure to sexual violence as presented in the mass media on men's and women's attitudes toward rape.

Malamuth's study cited research suggesting that sexually violent depictions can, among other things, perpetuate beliefs about female subservience, lead to assault, and encourage acts of hostility against women (Malamuth, Reisin & Spinner, 1979). However, Malamuth also cited other studies which concluded that there is no evidence that exposure to pornography causes any adverse effects, including aggression towards women. His 1979 study was meant to further understanding of just what effects depictions of sexual violence have on attitudes toward rape.

Malamuth and his colleagues collected a group of 80 male and female students and randomly exposed each of them to one of three different stimuli:

- violent sexually explicit images (*Playboy* magazine images with violent content)
- non-violent sexually explicit images (*Playboy* magazine images without violent content)
- neutral images (*National Geographic* magazine images, primarily landscapes).

After being exposed to the stimuli, all of the students viewed the same video of an interview with a rape victim and then completed a survey about the interview, asking them about their

- "Perceptions of the victim and assailant (e.g., intelligence, attractiveness)
- Perceptions of experience of victim (e.g., pain, trauma, etc.)
- Attitudes toward rape (e.g., responsibility, possible justification, punishment merited, sexual vs. violent motive).
- Subjects' beliefs about their own behavior in such situations (e.g., the possibility of engaging in sexual assault)" (Malamuth, Reisin & Spinner, 1979, p. 5).

Because the researchers were concerned that the experimental environment might skew their results, several weeks after the initial exposure Malamuth and his colleagues asked the same group of students to give their impressions on three stories in the mass media. The stories dealt with the Quebec separatist movement, government regulation of the auto industry, and a story about the dismissal of a rape conviction. Students were tested to see if they connected the two different experiments, and it was found that they did not. Students were then asked to assess their own attitudes about how a variety of factors may contribute to rape acts. The factors that the students were asked to consider in relation to the story about the dismissal of the rape conviction included: mental illness, attitudes of the judicial system, societal attitudes, victim behavior, and pornography (Malamuth, Reisin & Spinner, 1979). The researchers found that "the only effect of exposure to sexual stimuli (violent or non-violent) was a clear reduction in the degree to which pornography was perceived as a cause of rape"(Malamuth, Reisin & Spinner, 1979).

Malamuth (1979) also collected self reported data from male students with regard to their "inclination to rape." When asked to consider if they would commit a rape if they knew they would not be caught, those students who answered affirmatively displayed "a generally callous attitude toward sexual assault" (Malamuth, Reisin & Spinner, 1979, p. 7). They were more likely to believe that the woman in the interview they saw was responsible for her assault, and less likely to believe that her assailant was dangerous. Malamuth and his colleagues believed these findings were consistent with those of other studies. In 1977, Abel, Barlow, Blanchard, & Guild had found a positive correlation between "sexual arousal to the depiction of sexual violence" and "proclivity to rape"(Malamuth, Reisin & Spinner, 1979, p. 8).

As stated previously, researchers are divided on the effects that repeated exposure to pornography may have on a person's proclivity to sexual violence. The following discussion focuses on a study from 2006 that suggests that easy access to pornography actually reduces the number of instances of sexual violence. *Pornography, Rape, and the Internet,* a 2006 article by Todd Kendall of Clemson University set out to investigate the relationship between exposure to pornography and sexual violence. By analyzing statistics on rape and Internet usage from multiple states, Kendall found that "the arrival of the Internet was associated with a reduction in rape incidence" (2006, p. 1).

Kendall's study of pornography and rape is unique because it examines the "global" availability of porn that has resulted from the Internet. Consumers no longer have to deal with the market constraints imposed by geography or age. Barriers to pornography have largely disappeared with the advent of Internet technology.

Kendall states that he finds that because of the major decline in the price of pornographic material, the Internet appears to be acting as a substitute for rape. In fact he states that he found that a 10% increase in Internet access was associated with a 7.3% decline in reported rape victimization (Kendall, 2006). According to Kendall's findings, there is no link between the rise of Internet accessibility and the incidence of other types of crime. Kendall states that his findings are not consistent with many other studies, but are in line with the findings R.A. Posner in his book, *Sex and Reason* (1994). Posner's book outlines his economic theory of sexuality, and, as Kendall paraphrases it, states that "pornography is a complement for masturbation or consensual sex, which are themselves substitutes for rape, making pornography a net substitute for rape" (Kendall, 2006, p. 4).

Social scientists continue to debate the causal relationship between exposure to pornography and sexual violence. Neil Malamuth's research suggests that people may find sexual violence more acceptable when exposed to violent sexual material, while Todd Kendall's implies that pornographic material may actually serve as a substitute for sexual aggression, and even rape. Sociologist on both sides of the debate admit that further research is needed to determine the effects that repeated exposure to pornography has on rates of sexual violence.

Feminist Views of Pornography

Sexual assaults and rape are societal ills that are particularly destructive and damaging, especially to women, who are overwhelmingly the victims. Feminists universally decry rape and violent crime against women, but not all feminists are convinced that pornography leads to sexual violence, or that all pornography is harmful.

Radical Feminism

Radical, or cultural, feminists believe pornography portrays women as "objects merely to serve and submit to male sexual pressure" (Hudson, 2006, p. 72). Radical feminist views during the 1970s and 1980s described sexuality as a form of male violence and saw any act of sexuality as a form of male domination and control over women. In their total condemnation of pornography, these feminists found themselves part of an unlikely coalition. Conservative Christian groups like the Moral Majority agreed with the radical feminist view of pornography and, with them, supported a total ban. Feminist and conservative Christian opposition to pornography failed to make pornography illegal, but their efforts did result in a schism within the feminist movement. More liberal feminists objected to the complete ban on pornographic material: they claimed that many women experience sexual pleasure by viewing pornography, and believe this experience to be liberating.

One of the most vocal of the radical feminists to support a total ban on pornography was attorney Catherine MacKinnon. She equated all sex acts to forcible rape in that, through sex, women are made subordinate to men, and further ratified the idea that all sexuality results in men's control over women (Hudson, 2006). In the ideology of radical feminism, the "personal is political," meaning that the oppression of women through sex has a cascading effect on other issues such as health care, reproductive rights, employment, and politics (Hudson, 2006). In MacKinnon's view, all sexuality is violent and represents subordination, and pornography perpetuates this violence and subordination by portraying women as submissive and "asking for violence" to be inflicted upon them (Hudson, 2006).

Perhaps the most famous example of the radical feminist response to pornography is the anti-porn legislation MacKinnon and Andrea Dworkin proposed in Minneapolis in 1980. Arguing pornography violates women's First Amendment rights by forcing them to speak in such a way as to undermine their dignity, the proposed legislation would have resulted in civil action against the makers, sellers, distributors, and exhibitors of porn. The resulting law was considered "civil rights legislation," and it specifies that pornography does actual harm, and offers "victims of pornography" the right to sue the producers of sexual materials (Pollard, 1994).

Liberal Feminism

Female partners are often consumers of pornography along with their male partners. Women who view some aspects of pornography as positive, "frequently distinguish between 'pornography', which is harmful, and 'erotica', which is not; 'erotica' would be sexual representations 'premised on equality'. However, these women are in wide disagreement about which materials fall into each of these categories" (Pollard, 1994, p. 2). One study of 340 women whose partners use pornography found that greater honesty regarding its use was correlated with higher relationship satisfaction while mutual use lowered levels of distress, though it did not affect satisfaction (Resch & Alderson, 2014).

More liberal feminists believe that the presence of sexual material in society enables women to explore their sexuality and removes guilt about the experience and expression of sexuality (Pollard, 1994). Male and female progressives are more likely to view the suppression of sexual material as a form of censorship that deprives individuals of knowledge about sexuality. Liberal feminists take a similar view: the suppression of pornography is one way of preventing women from learning about sexuality and keeping them under the control of men.

Liberals don't see sex as the dangerous territory that conservatives and radical feminists do. Rather, they tend to oppose strong control over morality and perceive censorship as harmful.

ISSUES

Children & Youths as Consumers of Pornography

Research by the Pew Research Center suggests that the Internet is accessible to 95 percent of twelve- to seventeen-year-olds (Madden et al., 2013)—and this number is certainly growing. With this nearly ubiquitous access, researchers have turned their attentions to exploring how actively this age group seeks out pornography on the Internet, and how exposure to pornography, whether intentional or accidental, affects their development.

While it is clear that computer networks have greatly reduced the barriers to accessing pornographic material, "concerns about the large numbers of young children exposing themselves to pornography may be overstated" (Ybarra & Mitchell, 2005). Because of the ethical and legal consideration that surround research on minors and pornography, most studies on the effects of pornography have been conducted on adult populations. The handful of adolescent surveys that have been done suggest that there is no relationship between pornography and behavior, but, as Ybarra and Mitchell (2005) note, access to pornography through the Internet will logically need to be studied in much greater depth.

Studies of older teens reveal that:

- 59% believe that viewing pornography encourages young people to have sex at an earlier age
- 49% believe that the Internet promotes negative attitudes toward women
- 49% believe that pornographic images may promote the idea that having unprotected sex is "safe" (Ybarra & Mitchell, 2005).

There are gaps in literature regarding the potential effects of pornography on youth. Future studies will need to assess demographic characteristics as well as the specific characteristics of kids who seek out pornography as this data is not widely available. A comparison of those actively seeking porn to their non-porn seeking peers will be necessary to gain greater insights into youth interaction with online and offline pornography. Researchers Ybarra and Mitchell (2005) set out to discover some characteristics of youth who reported that they had sought out pornography. The authors compiled their findings as a result of the Youth Internet Safety Survey. The survey was conducted through telephone interviews with 1501 youths who "self-reported" their pornography seeking experiences.

Demographic characteristics compiled during the survey, suggested the following:

- seekers are far more likely to be male,
- older youth report higher rates of intentional exposure, and
- older youth reported seeking out online sources, while younger youth had more commonly been exposed through magazines or movies. (Ybarra & Mitchell, 2005).

Many of these youths who had sought out pornography also reported instances of delinquency and substance abuse in the prior year. Those who had sought it out online also reported clinical features associated with depression and lower emotional bonding with caregivers (Ybarra & Mitchell, 2005). However, the authors stated that these psychosocial characteristics were unlikely to have been caused by exposure to pornography (Ybarra & Mitchell, 2005). One question that remains unanswered by this research and previous research is whether young people are using the Internet because they are socially isolated, or because they have fewer social demands. Furthermore, neither study explains the factors that spur online users to seek out pornography.

Ybarra and Mitchell (2005) admit, along with many other social scientists, that the relationship between pornography and sexual violence is complex. On the one hand, pornography appears to have no effect on men who have never been convicted of a sexual offense, even when it is viewed frequently. On the other, when men with predispositions toward aggressive sexual behavior are repeatedly exposed to pornography, their level of sexual aggression is four times higher than that of similarly predisposed men who are exposed to less pornography (Ybarra & Mitchell, 2005). Given these findings, it is possible that young people who seek out pornography do so as a symptom of an underlying cause.

CONCLUSION

The sale and distribution of pornographic materials nets billions of dollars across the globe each year. It is a divisive topic, with religious and social conservatives as well as radical feminists favoring its prohibition, and other, liberal groups viewing it as something to be tolerated or enjoyed.

Some research suggests that exposure to sexually violent pornography may increase instances of sexual aggression, particularly toward women. New studies are investigating the impact of the Internet in delivering pornography less expensively and to a much wider audience. The effects of Internet pornography will be the subject of much study for sociologists and other social scientists for many years to come. Of particular interest will be the effects of exposure to pornography on children.

Social scientists, parents, and legislators are all concerned about how many children can access sexually explicit content via the Internet. Data on how many children actively seek out pornography is not well documented. Research suggests that older youth are often "active" seekers of porn, while younger children are often exposed via email solicitations, or by accident. What is of concern to these researchers is the ease with which children may have access to sexually explicit materials. The barriers to access have fallen to all consumers of porn—adults and children alike. The effects of this increased access on young children are not well known.

TERMS & CONCEPTS

Child Online Protection Act (COPA): Legislation passed in 1998 meant to protect children from harmful sexual material on the Internet.

Child Exploitation Pornography: A crime involving the possession or distribution of pornographic material portraying juveniles.

Erotica: Literature or art explicitly portraying sex. Sometimes distinguished from pornography, in that it contains sexual representations "premised on equality."

Non-Pecuniary Costs: Refers to costs or damages that are not monetary.

Peer to Peer Networks: Electronic networks that allow users to connect with one another directly without mediation through a central server. Typically, peer-to-peer (sometimes known as P2P) connections are used for file sharing, in both business and personal environments.

Prurient: Marked by or arousing an immoderate or unwholesome sexual interest or desire.

Social Mores: Established practices and beliefs of a society. They consist of shared understandings about the kinds of behavior likely to evoke approval, disapproval, toleration, or sanction within particular contexts.

Bibliography

Egan, V., & Parmar, R. (2013). "Dirty habits? Online pornography use, personality, obsessionality, and compulsivity." *Journal of Sex & Marital Therapy, 39*(5), 394–409.

Finkelhor, D., & Ormrod, R. (2004). *Child pornography patterns from NIBRS.* Department of Justice Bulletin. http://www.ncjrs.gov/pdffiles1/ojjdp/204911.pdf

Hudson, D. (2008). *Pornography and obscenity.* Firstamendement.org. http://www.firstamendment-center.org/

Hudson, M (2006). "The pornography wars." *Elements, 2* (1), 71–76. http://www.bc.edu/research/elements/issues/2006s/elements-spring06-article8.pdf

Kendall, T, (2006). "Pornography, rape and the Internet." Free Speech Coalition. http://www.freespeechcoalition.com/webdocs/Kendallpaper.pdf

Krause, J. (2008). "The end of the net porn wars." *ABA Journal, 94* (2), 52–56.

Madden, M., Lenhard, A., Duggan, M., Cortesi, S., & Gasser, U. (2013, March 13). *Teens and technology 2013.* Washington, DC: Pew Research Center's Internet & American Life Project. http://www.pewinternet.org/files/old-media//Files/Reports/2013/PIP_TeensandTechnology2013.pdf

Malamuth, N., Reisin, I., & Spinner, B. (1979). "Exposure to pornography and reactions to rape." University of California. http://repositories. cdlib.org/

Owens, E.W., Behun, R.J., Manning, J.C., & Reid, R.C. (2012). "The impact of internet pornography on adolescents: a review of the research." *Sexual Addiction & Compulsivity, 19*(1/2), 99–122.

Pollard, N. (1993). The modern pornography debate. *Media Law and Practice, 14* (4), 1-4. http://www.libertarian.co.uk/lapubs/lapam/ lapam022.pdf

Resch, M. N., & Alderson, K. G. (2014). "Female partners of men who use pornography: Are honesty and mutual use associated with relationship satisfaction?" *Journal of Sex & Marital Therapy, 40*(5), 410–424.

Weber, M., Quiring, O., & Daschmann, G. (2012). "Peers, parents and pornography: Exploring adolescents' exposure to sexually explicit material and its developmental correlates." *Sexuality & Culture, 16*(4), 408–427.

Ybarra, M., & Mitchell, K. (2005). "Exposure to Internet pornography among children and adolescents: A national survey." *Cyberpsychology & Behavior, 8* (5), 473–486. http://www.liebertonline.com/

Suggested Reading

Andrews, D. (2012). "Toward a more valid definition of 'pornography'." *Journal of Popular Culture, 45*(3), 457–477.

Hutson, M. (2008). "Vice or virtue?" *Psychology Today, 41*(1), 18.

Krause, J. (2008). "The end of the net porn wars." *ABA Journal, 94*(2), 52–56.

Johansson, T., & HammarÉn, N. (2007). "Hegemonic masculinity and pornography: Young people's attitudes toward and relations to pornography." *Journal of Men's Studies, 15*(1), 57–70.

Owens, E. W., Behun, R. J., Manning, J. C., & Reid, R. C. (2012). "The impact of internet pornography on adolescents: A review of the research." *Sexual Addiction & Compulsivity, 19*(1/2), 99–122.

Sinković, M., Štulhofer, A., & Božić, J. (2013). "Revisiting the association between pornography use and risky sexual behaviors: The role of early exposure to pornography and sexual sensation seeking." *Journal of Sex Research, 50*(7), 633–641.

"Technology and pornography." (2007). *Brigham Young University Law Review, 6,* 1535–1584.

Wright, P. J. (2013). "U.S. males and pornography, 1973–2010: consumption, predictors, correlates." *Journal Of Sex Research, 50*(1), 60–71.

Carolyn Sprague, MLS

Sex Addiction Disorders

ABSTRACT

Sex addiction is the uncontrollable urge to behave sexually even though negative consequences may occur as a result of that behavior. Various organizations have been created to support sex addicts as well as their families in the treatment community. The Internet is a recent concern for therapists because it allows sex addicts to access pornography in an anonymous way. A study examining the behaviors of sex addicts is reported here as is research conducted, which focuses on the sexual behaviors of college students. Concerns addressing the lives of clergy members and comparisons between behavioral dependencies, like gambling addictions are made to substance dependencies are made here as well.

OVERVIEW

Psychologist Patrick Carnes has spent years devoted to the research of sexual addiction and sexually compulsive behaviors. In 1983, he published a book entitled *The Sexual Addiction.* While many people were suffering from the disorder of sexual dependency at the time, the book did not sell. Once he changed the title to *Out of the Shadows* however, society embraced the possibility that people could become addicted—compulsively seeking out a behavior rather than a substance. In 1987, Carnes and two colleagues founded the organization known as the National Council on Sexual Addiction and Compulsivity (NCSAC). In 2004, NCSAC changed its name to the Society for the Advancement of Sexual Health (SASH), to focus more broadly on sexual health issues. SASH has an international membership and publishes a website focusing on the issues of out-of-control sexual behaviors.

SexHelp.com (2011), a second resource and advocacy organization created by Dr. Carnes, cites the following definition for sexual addiction:

> Sexual addiction is defined as any sexually-related, compulsive behavior that interferes with normal living and causes severe stress on family, friends, loved ones, and one's work environment. Sexual addiction has also been called hypersexuality, sexual dependency and sexual compulsivity. By any name, it is a compulsive behavior that completely dominates the addict's life. Sexual addicts make sex a priority over family, friends, and work. Sex becomes the governing principle of an addict's life. They are willing to sacrifice what they cherish most in order to preserve and continue their unhealthy behavior. No single behavior pattern defines sexual addiction. These behaviors can take control of addicts' lives and become unmanageable. Common behaviors include, but are not limited to compulsive masturbation, compulsive heterosexual and homosexual relationships, pornography, prostitution, exhibitionism, voyeurism, indecent phone calls, and anonymous sexual encounters. ("What is sexual addiction?" 2011).

The SASH website also includes a listing of the following predictable consequences for sexually dependent people.

- **Social:** Addicts become lost in sexual preoccupation, which results in emotional distance from loved ones. Loss of friendship and family relationships may result.
- **Emotional:** Anxiety or extreme stress is common in sex addicts who live with constant fear of discovery. Shame and guilt increase, as the addict's lifestyle is often inconsistent with personal values, beliefs, and spirituality. Boredom, pronounced fatigue, and despair are inevitable as addiction progresses. The ultimate consequence may be suicide.
- **Physical:** Some of the diseases that may occur due to sexual addiction are genital injury, cervical cancer, HIV/ AIDS, herpes, genital warts, and other sexually transmitted diseases. Sex addicts may place themselves in situations of potential harm, resulting in serious physical wounding or even death.
- **Legal:** Many types of sexual addiction result in violation of the law, such as sexual harassment, obscene phone calls, exhibitionism, voyeurism, prostitution, rape, incest, child molestation, and other illegal activities. Loss of professional status and professional licensure may result from sexual addiction.
- **Financial/Occupational:** Indebtedness may arise directly from the cost of prostitutes, cyber-sex, phone sex, and multiple affairs. Indirectly indebtedness can occur from legal fees, the cost of divorce or separation, decreased productivity, or job loss.
- **Spiritual:** Loneliness, resentment, self pity, self blame (www.SASH.net, 2014).

The sex addict, in theory, is no different from the cocaine addict or the alcoholic. He or she wakes up in the morning thinking about sex—finding sex, watching sex, or taking part in sexual acts—and these thoughts consume the addict until they are acted upon. While the cocaine addict or the alcoholic betrays the people in his or her life by lying, spending money the addict may not have, and possibly committing crimes in order to obtain that next fix, the sex addict betrays the people in his or her life in a way that most people can never understand. People have heard of the addictive nature of cocaine and alcohol, but sex as a compulsion? Even with people like Dr. Carnes promoting the reality of the disorder, a wife who has been betrayed may never welcome the psychology of compulsive tendencies. As such, society as a whole was slow to accept the concept.

Theoretical Explanations

The study of sexually compulsive behavior is not new. In fact, there are several theories that have been used to define or describe the disorder. For example, Kaplan's (1995) research identifies sexual desire as the center of the addiction in that the inability to regulate desire is the catalyst for the compulsivity. However, Quadland (1985) notes that much like rape, the condition of sexual addiction is one of control rather than desire. Dr. Carnes believes that the act of orgasm (ejaculation) releases mood-altering endorphins that sex addicts continually chase (1991). This theory is based on the concept of self-medication. Similar to chasing a euphoric high, Milkman and Sunderwirth (1983) identify that the gratifying effect of an orgasm on neurotransmitters (messengers within the brain) is habit-forming because the addict learns to depend on the increase or decrease of brain messages to actually regulate his or her mood (as cited in Guigliamo, 2006, pp. 361–362).

Furthermore, research has looked at early environmental experiences as the cause of sexually addictive behaviors. Creeden (2004) points to trauma theory as a potential explanation. Trauma theory posits that adults who experienced childhood trauma look toward sexual compulsiveness to dissociate with feeling helpless or out-of-control because of earlier experiences. More specifically, Schwartz et al. (1995) looked at adults who had been victimized sexually as children and noted a correlation between their victimization and their resulting compulsive behaviors. Conversely, earlier research identified narcissism as the root of compulsive behavior. In fact, Kohut (1977) noted that a cycle exists for the sex addict who tries to increase his or her self-esteem by gaining the approval of others. Once sex addicts act out, they feel empty and full of shame, which causes them to chase approval again (as cited in Guigliamo, 2006, p. 362).

Characteristics of the Sex Addict

Since sexual addiction is so misunderstood, Guigliamo (2006) conducted a study in order to humanize its effects. The researcher studied 14 men who identified themselves as being sexually addicted (p. 361). In the course of the study, Guigliamo interviewed participants to learn directly about their loss of control over their sexual behavior. Guigliamo's study was limited to participants who were 18 years of age or older and who did not identify themselves as having sex with adolescents or children (p. 363). Each of the interviews lasted between 60 and 90 minutes, and participants gave consent to being audiotaped during the interview. Guigliamo notes that the purpose of the study was to "understand the affective and motivational aspects of repetitive uncontrollable sexual behavior" (p. 364). The behaviors respondents discussed were grouped into the eight categories listed below, with a combination of categories often resulting:

1. **Narcissistic Needs** — To supplement self-esteem, sexual conquests and external validation were employed to meet emotional and psychological needs.
2. **Desire for Human Affection or Connection** — More than half of the informants reported a history of having problems sustaining long-term intimate relationships and about half of the informants expressed an inability to experience any emotional intimacy.
3. **Compensation for Feelings of Low Self-Esteem** — Low self-esteem and self-loathing were also mentioned by nine of the informants.
4. **Avoidance of Disturbing Feelings** — Nine of the informants reported using sexual activities to avoid or escape from negative feelings such as loneliness, boredom, and sadness ... and to escape painful feelings.
5. **Reenactment of Childhood Deficits or Trauma** — Five of the informants believed that they were emotionally abused as children. All but one informant reported parental neglect. Some type of childhood sexual abuse was reported by 9 of the informants. Ten respondents reported incest, six involving sexual activities with siblings.
6. **A Means to Cope with Issues of Sexual Identity/Orientation** — Four of the six gay men in this study reported that their entrance into sexually addictive behaviors was related to coping and understanding their sexual orientation. ... The men described a sense of fear, isolation, and alienation, as well as a lack of guidance and support as they struggled through childhood and adolescence, searching for their identity as sexual people.
7. **Need for Power and Control** — Investigation is essential to assess if the need for control is a result of early feelings of powerlessness that later resulted in habitual sexual aggression or if the feelings of powerlessness progressed over the course of repeated problematic sexual activities.
8. **Libidinal and Sexual Needs** — Only two of the informants explained their problematic

> sexual behaviors in terms of strong libidinal needs (p. 365–367).

Essentially, Guigliamo was able to point toward various theoretical models based on his experiment. What should be clear is that the behaviors resulting from sexual compulsion or sex addiction are not primarily based on issues related to sex itself. The acts of having sex, trying to find sex, or even thinking about sex are means of escape from life, just as having a drink, thinking about drinking, or trying to find the next drink helps the alcoholic escape. What is disturbing is that all but one of the respondents in this study stated that they had been neglected as children and that 9 of the 14 respondents reported childhood sexual abuse. Bancroft & Vukadinovic (2004) identified similar results for 9 out of the 31 study participants they interviewed. Furthermore, Guigliamo notes that "[a]lmost all of the informants in this study who stated that their sexually addictive behaviors began in their early adolescence or teenage years, also reported incest prior to the age of 14" (p. 368).

Guigliamo notes that, while the number of participants here seems low (n = 14), the data retrieved from the study is of a qualitative nature (subjective according to the participants' interview responses), which makes the study valuable regardless of the sample size. Furthermore, five subjects were randomly chosen for follow-up interviews following completion of the study. The purpose of that second interview was for participants to "review and give feedback regarding the accuracy of the recording and interpretation of the data that they gave," thus strengthening the research conclusions (p. 371). In addition, Guigliamo notes the limitation that such a small sample does make the results of the study unavailable for generalization purposes. Indeed, the sexual behaviors of 14 men cannot be representative of the entire population of men, even of those who also view themselves as addicted (p. 369).

FURTHER INSIGHTS

College Students

Dodge, Reece, Cole, and Sandfort (2004) attempted to determine if "an association exists between sexual compulsivity and participation in sexual behaviors that are high risk in terms of HIV/ STD infection" (p. 345). The researchers used a sample of college students for their study because that population had not been a focus for sexual addiction research in previous studies. In addition, they wanted to consider the reliability of the Sexual Compulsivity Scale (SCS) in reference to their participants. Dodge et al. gave the SCS (a questionnaire) to 876 heterosexual college students who responded to questions anonymously (p. 345). Almost half of the study participants were in exclusive relationships. Another fifth were in relationships in which exclusivity was not a condition, and the remaining third of the participants reported not being sexually active at the time the study was conducted (p. 346).

In addition to collecting demographic information, Dodge et al. created subscales of sexual behaviors to determine which participants (if any) were behaving in sexually compulsive ways, and if so, if those same participants were also performing risky sexual acts. The sexual behavior subscales are shown below (p. 345).

- Partner sex activities;
- Solo sex activities;
- Public sex activities; and
- Frequencies of protected and unprotected anal, vaginal, and oral sex (leading to possible HIV/ STD infection) (Dodge et al., 2004, p. 345).

When assessing the SCS scores, Dodge and colleagues determined that the respondents who identified participating in broader ranges of partner sex acts had higher compulsivity scores. Furthermore, a "significant relationship between solo sex activities and sexual compulsivity" was also noted, as was a link between higher compulsivity scores and public sexual activities (p. 346). Looking at gender distribution, more men than women reported being in nonexclusive relationships; that group was also significantly more likely to have higher compulsivity scores when compared to those participants who were in exclusive relationships (primarily women) and those who were not sexually active at the time of the study (p. 347).

Summarizing their findings, Dodge and colleagues noted an additional gender difference:

> Mean scores of sexual compulsivity were higher for men ... than for women ... As age decreased, participants were more likely to have higher mean scores of sexual

> compulsivity ... Sexual compulsivity was positively related to sexual behaviors considered to be risky in terms of HIV/STD infection for both male and female participants ... Men and women who had higher sexual compulsivity scores were more likely to have engaged in unprotected oral, vaginal, and anal sex in the preceding 3 months, respectively (Dodge, et al., 2004, p. 347).

In other words, the male respondents had higher compulsivity scores when compared to women, as did the younger respondents in the group. Higher compulsivity scores were also correlated to risky sexual behaviors for both genders; that is, both men and women who had high SCS scores also participated in risky (unprotected) sexual activity.

Dodge and his colleagues make the following points with regard to limitations within their study. First, "our findings are based on a convenience sample that cannot be considered representative" (p. 348). In other words, any results reported cannot be interpreted as universal for all college students. "Although we found support for construct validity of the SCS in our sample, it is not clear whether the scale distinctly measures sexual compulsivity or taps into other constructs, such as sexual desire and sexual exploration" (Dodge et al., 2004, p. 348). While credit should be given to these researchers for offering limitations, it should be clear what reference they are making with regard to sexual desire and sexual exploration.

It is possible that not all responses provided by the sample were truthful. Furthermore, honest responses may be tied to uncertainty about one's addiction/dependency status. In other words, it is possible that subjects responded to questions about being out of control without realizing that being out of control was atypical. What is clear is that the subjects in this group who behaved in sexually compulsive ways did not protect themselves from sexually transmitted diseases or viruses. It is possible that for this group, the compulsion to have sex was more of a priority than having safe sex. That is the case for heroin addicts who share needles; the need to get high outweighs the need to remain healthy by always using new needles.

The Clergy

According to Frykholm (2007), clergymen may be a population that many people do not consider vulnerable to sexual addiction. To be clear, members of the clergy accused of pedophilia are not necessarily sex addicts. Sex offenders are usually of the mind that controlling their victims is the gain, the "high." Sexual addicts find some other gratification from the experience of searching for and/or having sex. They gain an endorphin rush or the removal of self-loathing for a period of time during or after the chase.

Frykholm discusses a former seminary student, Mark Laaser, who has researched sexual addictions within the field of ministry:

> While a student in seminary and then in a program for pastoral counseling, Laaser was a compulsive user of pornographic material. Gradually his addiction to these materials progressed to encounters with prostitutes and to sexual relationships with several women that he was counseling. In 1986 the women sued him and he had to leave the ministry. Laaser has since devoted himself to research on and treatment of sexual addiction, and he has worked particularly with clergy (Frykholm, 2007, p. 20).

Laaser, author of the book *Healing the Wounds of Sexual Addiction,* is the president of Faithful and True Ministries. Based on his own experiences as well as the research he has conducted since his removal from the ministry, Laaser notes a difference among the sex addicts with whom he works currently when he compares them to those he has served in the past. He blames the difference on pornography and the Internet. For example, Laaser notes that when he first started working in the area of sexual addiction, "nearly all his clients had a history of trauma; for them, sexual addiction was a way of coping with or masking severe emotional pain. Today that is seldom the case: people who have problems with porn look more like the general population" (Frykholm, 2007, p. 20–21).

Laaser identifies three characteristics that are representative of sexual addicts within the clergy: 1) they are lonely; 2) they are angry, and 3) they are bored. These characteristics are those that are fostered by the job itself. For example, Laaser notes that for clergy, "their jobs make high demands, they work in large part independently ... [and] are often isolated and work in contexts where they have few if any peers. Friendships, too, may be rare for pastors. While they are caregivers themselves, pastors may not have care extended to them" (Frykholm, 2007, p. 21). It would be difficult to exhaust emotional support all day when nobody returns the favor. And, anger and other emotions are usually what most addicts try to avoid, thus turning to substances or behaviors instead.

An interesting discovery Laaser made when conducting a study with Delmonico in 2002 is that "sexually addicted clergy were far more likely than the general population to be addicted also to work. Work had become not only a calling but an escape from other life problems" (Frykholm, 2007, p. 21). Indeed, it is rare to find a minister who is not available to his or her congregation at all hours of the night, seven days a week. Laaser believes that the screening process for hiring clergy can become stricter and that warning signs need to be addressed before addictive behaviors take control of those who are trusted the most. For example, potential sex addicts within the clergy tend to work as though nothing else matters (the workaholic). They also appear to be superior to most (rather than being vulnerable like everyone else). While these characteristics tend to define an effective minister, they also define a potential addict (Frykholm, 2007).

The Internet & Pornography

According to Schneider (2004), sexual addiction has changed since the 1990s. "Today an increasing number of sex addicts are caught up in the web of cybersex, devoting endless hours to accessing Internet pornography sites and chat rooms and having real-time sexual encounters online ... For many, the Internet serves as a gateway to live sexual encounters" (p. 5). Furthermore, Hall (2006) points out that the lure of the Internet is twofold: it is easily accessible, and the people using it are anonymous. This makes the hunt for sex easy. People can do it at work, at home, or in cafes while pretending to be productive. The most common online sexual activity is viewing pornography (Hall, 2006), which is both produced and consumed in the United States more than in any other country. This accessibility both promotes and encourages sexual activity. For those who lack the ability to control their sexual impulses, the Internet is a perfect way to feed their addiction.

VIEWPOINTS

According to Dr. Jerome Jaffe (1990), categorizing behaviors like sex, eating, gambling, or shopping addictions together with substance addictions is not an effective way to look at either abusive tendency:

> Any taxonomy that places unwanted repetitive behaviors not involving reinforcing drugs in some super-category along with behaviors which do, does more than suggest that the two subcategories are related; it also tends to minimize any important distinctions that exist between them (Jaffe,1990, p. 1426).

Citing one of the mantras of Alcoholics Anonymous, Jaffe fears that labeling behavioral addictions as such may cause the assumption that a sex (behavior) addict is as powerless over having sex as an alcoholic is of having his next drink (p. 1426). Furthermore, placing together behaviors and dependencies implies that the same treatments should be available to, offered to, and promise relief from all of the above, which is not the case (1427). Twelve-step programs offer treatment for many disorders. However, *abstinence* is not the goal of sex addiction treatment. Behaving appropriately (in thought and action) with regard to sex and intimacy is the goal of treatment, just as the goal of treatment for an eating disorder includes teaching healthy eating habits rather than teaching how to never eat again. Jaffe's point has merit.

So too, does Keane's (2004) counterpoint. Keane posits that while not necessarily neat little packages of dependency,

> ... generalized models of addiction, whether based on neurotransmitters or theories of intimacy, have the potential to be powerful critical resources. They render irrelevant the very distinctions between normal and abnormal, natural and unnatural which give attributions of addiction their moral and political force (Keane, 2004, p. 204).

Indeed, many addicts are viewed as being immoral and weak of will. Having a theoretical model that encompasses the various dependencies may help reduce the assertion that addicts are bad people simply because research and science are behind the assertion.

CONCLUSION

Opinions on this issue are vast. Nevertheless, it is important to look closely at the point Dr. Jaffe tries to make. Being addicted to sex is not the same as being addicted to heroin. For instance, drug addictions change the physiology of the brain as a result of its prolonged exposure to chemicals that were never intended to be ingested. Sexual addiction, on the other hand, may cause an increase of chemical production in the brain during the hunt for sex, the secrecy of that hunt, or even within and after the act of orgasm. That chemical increase in the brain (of endorphins or other neurotransmitters) is not the same as the introduction of an outside source (e.g., heroin) to a brain that does not produce it. The repeated increase of chemicals already produced by the brain may cause brain chemistry to change, but not in the same way that drug dependency does. While the dependent nature of the addictions are the same—the addict "has to have" the substance—the physical damage experienced by the brain from exposure to chemical substances is a complication not found in behavior addictions.

TERMS & CONCEPTS

Abstinence: Restraining from a behavior or activity.

Abuse: Using something in a harmful (often habitual) or illegal way.

Addiction: Physiological or psychological dependence on a drug or behavior.

Compulsion: The inability to resist a desire to do something.

Dependence: The physical, psychological, or physiological need to use a drug or substance or to behave in certain ways despite negative consequences.

Disease: A condition resulting in symptoms that are pathological in nature.

Disorder: A condition that involves a disturbance of the normal mind or body functions.

Predisposition: A susceptibility to an illness, disease or behavior based on genetic factors.

Bibliography

Birchard, T. (2011). "Sexual addiction and the paraphilias." *Sexual Addiction & Compulsivity, 18* (3), 157–187.

Carnes, P. (2011). "What is sexual addiction?" *Important Definitions.* SexHelp.com website: http:// www.sexhelp.com/ addiction%5fdefinitions.cfm

Dodge, B., Reece, M., Cole, S., & Sandfort, T. (2004). "Sexual compulsivity among heterosexual college students." *Journal of Sex Research, 41* (4), 343–350.

Frykholm, A. (2007). "Addictive behavior." *Christian Century, 124* (18), 20–22.

Guigliamo, J. (2006). "Out of control sexual behavior: A qualitative investigation." *Sexual Addiction & Compulsivity, 13* (4), 361–375.

Hall, P. (2013). "A New Classification Model for Sex Addiction." *Sexual Addiction & Compulsivity, 20*(4), 279–91.

Hall, P. (2006). "Understanding sexual addiction." *Therapy Today, 17* (2), 30–34.

Herring, B. (2011). "A 'sex addict' by any other name hurts the same." *Sexual Addiction & Compulsivity, 18* (2), 57–60.

Jaffe, J. H. (1990). "Trivializing dependence." *British Journal of Addiction, 85* (11), 1425–1427.

Jones, K. E., & Hertlein, K. M. (2012). "Four key dimensions for distinguishing Internet infidelity from Internet and sex addiction: Concepts and clinical application." *American Journal of Family Therapy, 40* (2), 115–125.

Keane, H. (2004). "Disorders of desire: Addiction and problems of intimacy." *Journal of Medical Humanities, 25* (3), 189–204.

Rosenberg, K. P., Carnes, P., & O'Connor, S. (2014). "Evaluation and Treatment of Sex Addiction." *Journal of Sex & Marital Therapy, 40*(2), 77–91.

Schneider, J. (2004). "Sexual addiction & compulsivity: Twenty years of the field, ten years of the journal." *Sexual Addiction & Compulsivity, 11* (1/2), 3–5.

Society for the Advancement of Sexual Health (SASH). (2014). "Sexual addiction." SASH website: http://www.ncsac.org/addicts/ papers%5f-sexual%5faddiction.aspx

Woody, J. D. (2011). "Sexual addiction/hyper-sexuality and the DSM: Update and practice guidance for Social workers." *Journal of Social Work Practice in the Addictions, 11* (4), 301–320.

Suggested Reading

About us. (2003). "The Society for the Advancement of Sexual Health (SASH)." SASH website: http://www.ncsac.org

Bancroft, J., & Vukadinovic, Z. (2004). "Sexual addiction, sexual compulsivity, sexual impulsivity, or what? Toward a theoretical model." *Journal of Sex Research, 41* (3), 225– 234.

Barth, R. J. & Kinder, B. N. (1987). "The mislabeling of sexual impulsivity." *Journal of Sex & Marital Therapy, 13,* 15–23.

Benotsch, E. G., Kalichman, S. C. & Pinkerton, S. D. (2001). "Sexual compulsivity in HIV-positive men and women: Prevalence, predictors, and consequences of high-risk behaviors." *Sexual Addiction and Compulsivity 8,* 83–99.

Carnes, P. J., & Adams, K. M. (Eds.). (2002). *Clinical management of sex addiction.* New York: Brunner-Routledge.

Cooper, A., Delmonico, D. L., & Burg, R. (2000). "Cybersex users, abusers, and compulsives: New findings and implications." *Sexual Addiction and Compulsivity, 7,* 5–29.

Delmonico, D. (2005). "Sexual addiction and compulsivity: Watching the field evolve." *Sexual Addiction & Compulsivity, 12* (1), 1–2.

Griffiths, M. D. (2012). "Internet sex addiction: A review of empirical research." *Addiction Research & Theory, 20* (2), 111–124.

Kalichman, S. C., & Rompa, D. (2001). "The sexual compulsivity scale: Further development and use with HIV-positive persons." *Journal of Personality Assessment, 76,* 379–395.

Levine, M. P., & Troiden, R. R. (1988). "The myth of sexual compulsivity." *The Journal of Sex Research, 25,* 347–363.

National Council on Sexual Addiction and Compulsivity. (2004). http://www.ncsac. org/addicts/papers%5fsexual%5faddiction.aspx

Reay, B., Attwood, N., & Gooder, C. (2013). "Inventing Sex: The Short History of Sex Addiction." *Sexuality & Culture, 17*(1), 1–19.

Reece, M., & Dodge, B. (2003). "Exploring the physical, mental, and social well-being among gay and bisexual men who cruise for sex on a college campus." *Journal of Homosexuality, 46* (1/2), 111–136.

Reece, M., & Dodge, B. (2004). "Exploring indicators of sexual compulsivity among men who cruise for sex on campus." *Sexual Addiction & Compulsivity, 11,* 1–27.

Reece, M., Plate, P. L., & Daughtry, M. (2001). "HIV prevention and sexual compulsivity: The need for an integrated strategy of public health and mental health." *Sexual Addiction & Compulsivity, 8,* 157–167.

Zuckerman, M., Kolin, E. A., Price, L., & Zoob, M. (1964). "Development of a sensation seeking scale." *Journal of Consulting and Clinical Psychology, 28,* 477–482.

Zuckerman, M., & Kuhlman, D. M. (2000). "Personality and risk-taking: Common biosocial factors." *Journal of Personality Psychology, 68,* 999–1029.

Maureen McMahon, M.S.

Sex, Gender & Sexuality: Sexually Transmitted Infections

ABSTRACT

Sexually transmitted infections are common and in most instances preventable. Bacterial infections like chlamydia, gonorrhea, and syphilis are discussed below as are the Herpes Simplex Viruses, the human papillomavirus, and the human immunodeficiency virus. Descriptions of symptoms, treatments, current rates of infection, and populations affected are provided. The controversy surrounding the newly recommended vaccination against the human papillomavirus (HPV) is also discussed as is the societal need to combine efforts at prevent infections.

OVERVIEW

Sex is presented in magazines and other media as something everyone should be doing. Teenagers giggle about it; their parents are embarrassed by it, and various cultures treat it like a gift. Underneath the emotion and exhilaration of sexuality hides a reality unique only to sexual activity itself. According to the World Health Organization in 2013 there are 499 million new curable sexually transmitted infections (like syphilis, gonorrhoea, chlamydia and trichomoniasis) every year. That these cases are curable means that with a timely diagnosis and proper treatment, these infections can be eradicated. Those that are not diagnosed early or treated properly make up an entirely different statistic.

Sexually transmitted infections (STIs) can be spread from person to person through anal, oral, or vaginal intercourse or passed from mother to child during pregnancy or delivery. STIs come in the form of bacteria, parasites, or viruses, with the latter remaining in its host indefinitely. While most bacterial forms of STIs (chlamydia, gonorrhea, and syphilis) can be eliminated with a dose of an antibiotic, the lasting effects of an untreated infection can cause pelvic inflammatory disease, infertility, and more serious conditions for infants born to infected mothers. The viral forms of STIs include the human papillomavirus, herpes simplex virus, and human immunodeficiency virus (HIV), which causes the severe complications noted in acquired immunodeficiency syndrome (AIDS). There are antiviral medications that can decrease the effects of viral outbreaks, shortening symptoms and lessoning the number of outbreaks, but there is no cure for the viruses acquired through sexual intercourse.

Many people become infected and never know it. As a result, infections are transmitted without the knowledge of either partner, and those infections do damage in hiding. For most people, however, the symptoms of an STI are acute and obvious. For example, many infected individuals note an unusual discharge, sores known as ulcers on the affected area, genital or lymph node swelling, and pelvic pain. In some cases, fever and cold-like symptoms also appear. Some people experience symptoms right away while others may not note symptoms for weeks, sometimes years, after initial infection.

The only way to avoid acquiring a sexually transmitted infection is to abstain from all types of sexual intercourse or to have monogamous intercourse with an uninfected partner. Male latex condoms are an effective way to avoid an infection (when used consistently and correctly), but they do not guarantee safety, as a condom may not fully cover an affected area.

Prevalence

In 2013 the US Centers for Disease Control and Prevention reported that there are 20 million new STIs annually, with a total of 100 million across the country. The most common STIs are chlamydia, gonorrhea, hepatitis B virus, herpes simplex virus type 2, HIV, human papillomavirus (HPV), syphilis, and trichomoniasis. For example, in the world's poorest countries, where access to condoms, screening, and treatment are limited (or nonexistent), unsafe sex ranks second only to being underweight for causing the population's disease, disability, or death rates (p. 1597). It should be noted that unsafe water and sanitation are ranked third. When one's water supply poses less of a health risk than having sex, the importance of the problem should be clear.

FURTHER INSIGHTS

The Common Infections

Chlamydia

Chlamydia is the most commonly reported sexually transmitted infection, with almost three million Americans infected with it each year. It is probable that this statistic is inaccurate as many people who suffer from the bacterial infection do not appear or feel symptomatic, and therefore, do not get screened for it. If diagnosed early, an antibiotic can clear the infection; if the infection remains undetected, however, Chlamydia can cause infertility in both men and women. It can also cause swelling in the prostate and painful urination in men. In women, the infection can cause pelvic inflammatory disease, chronic pain during intercourse and/or urination, and it can cause eye infections and pneumonia in babies through mother to infant transmission during pregnancy or delivery.

As young adults between the ages of fifteen and twenty-four are the most prolific population to acquire the infection, it is recommended that anyone under the age of twenty-five have a yearly screen as well. In addition, anyone who is pregnant or who is sexually active and experiences pain during intercourse or urination or has an abnormal discharge should be screened as well ("Common STD Risky," 2008).

Human Papillomavirus (HPV)

The human papillomavirus (HPV) is the most common STI in the United States and there is no treatment for it. Once infected with HPV, a person's immune system will clear most HPV within two years, while the disease can still persist in some cases. There are over ten types of high-risk forms of HPV, with types HPV-16 and HPV-18 causing the majority of HPV-caused cancers; most high-risk forms of HPV will not cause cancer. HPV is sexually transmitted through anal, oral, and vaginal intercourse, and it is important to note that no sexual activity is less risky than another.

There is an FDA-approved vaccination for the HPV-16 and HPV-18 viruses. However, as with all vaccines, Gardasil and Cervarix (the brand names of two vaccines) brought some controversy. First, Gardasil was approved for young women, not young men. Therefore, while young women can become vaccinated for the HPV-16 and HPV-18 strains, men cannot, which leaves an entire population of people without protection. Second, the vaccine is recommended for young women prior to becoming sexually active. This means that to be effective, the vaccine should be administered prior to girls becoming teenagers, generally between their tenth and twelfth years. This recommendation comes from the Advisory Committee on Immunization Practices, the American Academy of Pediatrics, and the American Academy of Family Physicians (Iannelli, 2007).

As with most vaccines, a recommendation is not the same as a requirement. In addition, while requiring the vaccine would ensure that young women become protected from cervical cancer, many people could argue that having any defense from a sexually transmitted disease forced upon them is an unconscionable way to offer that protection.

In 2007 it was reported that 47 percent of high school students report having had sexual intercourse, and 34 percent of sexually active students said that they didn't use a condom the last time they had; the CDC also reported that over 14 percent of women who were 18 to 25 with only one lifetime sex partner still had HPV infections (Ianelli, 2007, "Necessity").

In other words, about one in eight young women who have sexual intercourse only once with only one person will still develop an HPV infection; this statistic includes young women who only have oral sex as well. In the chance that HPV develops into cancer, it is possible that someone infected at the age of fifteen would not develop cervical cancer until much later in her life. Yearly gynecological exams (including pap smears) can detect the abnormal cells related to cervical cancer, and early steps like biopsies and excisional procedures (Clifford, Smith, Aguado & Franceschi, 2003, as cited in Cox et al., p. 856) can be taken to halt the development of cancer, but until all young women have easy access to yearly exams and post-diagnosis procedures, the vaccine may be the best option.

Gonorrhea

Much like Chlamydia, Gonorrhea is a bacterial infection that can be treated with an antibiotic. In contrast to the former infection, however, the latter is showing resistance to many antibiotic treatments, making it a potential health hazard in America. According to the CDC in 2012, 820,000 Americans get new gonorrheal infections annually. Gonorrhea can cause no symptoms, making its detection difficult in many cases. When diagnosed, it is usually because symptoms like inflammation in the genitals and reproductive organs, painful urination, or unusual discharge from the vagina or penis are noted (Gonorrhea—CDC Fact Sheet). The infection can be transmitted to infants from their mothers, can cause infertility, and can spread to the blood and joints. In addition, gonorrhea infection raises the risk of acquiring the human immunodeficiency virus (HIV) for anyone who is sexually active (Gonorrhea—CDC Fact Sheet).

Statistically, gonorrhea rates in the United States indicate a higher prevalence in African Americans (than in whites) and in women more than men (CDC Surveillance, 2006). Various antimicrobials (antibiotics) have been used against the gonorrhea bacteria. However, since the early 1930s, the bacteria has changed enough to become resistant to several of these remedies, including Penicillin and other sulfa drugs (Workowski, Berman & Douglas, 2008, p. 606). The regime of cephalosporin treatment works effectively and efficiently; however, as many drugs that have been used in the past fall victim to a stronger bacteria, it is necessary that other options be explored in case resistance occurs for cephalosporin as well (Workowski, Berman & Douglas, 2008, p. 609).

Persons with identifiable risk factors should be screened for gonorrhea, as early detection is the best way to prevent complications from the infection, which decreases the possibility of medicinal resistance. According to the United States Preventive Task Force, women who are pregnant, are younger than 25, who have had a previous gonorrhea or other STD/STI, who have had multiple sex partners, who have used condoms inconsistently, who use drugs, and who are are commercial sex workers should be tested for gonorrhea (U.S. Preventive Services Task Force, 2005). In addition, men who have sex with men should also be tested, especially those with HIV (CDC: CDC: Updated Recommendations). Likewise, anyone in these risk categories should be screened for all other STIs and STDs as well (CDC: Updated Recommendations).

Herpes Simplex Virus

According to Associate Professor of Nursing, Janelle Gardner (2006), the "strongest predictor" of genital herpes is "multiple sexual partners" (p. 26). In other words, contracting the herpes simplex virus (HSV) can be predicted based on whether or not a person has more than one sexual partner in his or her lifetime. Having sex with only one person is risky; that risk increases with every additional sex partner because each new person brings in a risk from someone else, and the numbers multiply quickly, whether the intercourse is oral, anal, or vaginal across partners. By 2013 approximately 776,000 Americans get new herpes infections annually—with approximately 16 percent, of one out of six, of people between the ages of 14 to 49 affected.

Gardner also notes that while some people will become infected with the virus and only have one initial outbreak of symptoms "about 90% of those infected have at least one recurrence during the first year and most have multiple recurrences-6 to 12 outbreaks per year on average" (p. 46); the World Health Organization (WHO) cites 4-5 recurrences as average (Herpes Simplex Type 2). Like other viruses, HSV is incurable. There are antiviral medications that hinder the length of an outbreak and lessen the severity of the symptoms, but the virus remains in its host indefinitely.

In addition, HSV causes a risk of encephalitis to infants born to mothers who carry the virus (Herpes Simplex Type 2), and it poses a constant risk of transmission through sexual activity, even if a condom is used correctly, as the condom may not completely cover all of the HSV infected areas (Gardner, p. 27). According to WHO, "the same independent factors of HSV-2 infection were identified in both genders: older age [between 30-40], higher lifetime number of sexual partners, positive HIV serology and positive syphilis serology" (Herpes Simplex Type 2). WHO also notes that there is "ample evidence that HSV-2 infection is a major cofactor of HIV infection" (Herpes Simplex Type 2). In other words, "people infected with HSV-2 are at increased risk of acquiring HIV" (HIV/AIDS and STD Updates, 2008).

Human Immunodeficiency Virus (HIV) & AIDS

By 2013 HIV/AIDS remained fourth biggest killer globally. Again, in areas where access to condoms and effective treatment is limited, people are going to suffer the consequences of their economic disadvantage. HIV is not just an issue in underdeveloped countries, however. According to the New York City Department of Health and Mental Hygiene in 2009, almost one in five NYC adults are at risk for contracting HIV due to having multiple sex partners, inconsistently using condoms, or because of they use injected drugs; yet, more than ninety percent of the people involved in the survey (who fell into those categories) indicated that they believed they were not at risk (HIV/AIDS and STD Updates, p. 259).

AIDS is the final stage of the HIV infection, which was first identified in the U.S. in 1981. Within a ten-year period the virus was studied, and measures to treat complications from the virus were created, reducing the death rates from AIDS by more than thirty percent annually. The CDC estimates that one million people are infected with the HIV virus, with one in four of those people not knowing they have the infection (Centers for Disease Control and Prevention, 2007a). HIV is only found in bodily fluids—blood, semen, vaginal excretions—and can be transmitted by having anal, oral, or vaginal intercourse, sharing needles with an infected person, or via mother to infant transmission during pregnancy, delivery, or breastfeeding. While previous cases have been identified of people acquiring HIV from blood transfusions, blood donations have been screened for the virus since 1985 (Centers for Disease Control and Prevention, 2007a).

The only way to know for sure if HIV is present in someone is for that person to be tested. There are currently over-the-counter tests available in most pharmacies, and most doctor's offices, health care clinics, and Planned Parenthood offices provide testing as well. Anyone who has already had an STI diagnosis is at greater risk of acquiring HIV than someone who has not had a sexually transmitted infection. Also, the CDC notes that anyone "receiving a blood transfusion or clotting factor during 1978-1985," anyone who has shared injection materials (needles, syringes, etc.) with someone who is HIV positive, anyone who has had anal, oral, or vaginal sex without using a condom, or someone who has exchanged sex for drugs or money is also at risk for HIV infection (Centers for Disease Control and Prevention, 2007a).

Syphilis

In 1999, a campaign was established to eradicate syphilis. The *National Plan to Eliminate Syphilis* combined the efforts of the CDC with federal, state, local, and non-governmental agencies to expand responses to an outbreak, increase screening and treatment of those infected, expand lab services, and enhance the promotion of healthy sex practices (Centers for Disease Control and Prevention, 2007b). For the most part, the plan worked. However, the demographic of people with syphilis has changed, and so has the response. Currently, more than half of new syphilis infections are diagnosed in men who have male sex partners. As such, problematic social issues have made it difficult to identify and treat those infected. "The social contexts of poverty, racism, homophobia, and socio-economic discrimination continue to drive the concentration of the disease in those with high-risk sexual behaviors, poor access to care, or both" (Centers for Disease Control and Prevention, 2007b, par. 3).

While the demographics have changed, the signs and symptoms have not. There are three distinct stages to a syphilis infection. A primary infection is noted by the appearance of one or multiple sores possibly ten to ninety days following infection. If treatment is not provided, secondary syphilis presents a rash that does not itch. Additional symptoms include fatigue, fever, headache, sore throat, swollen lymph glands, and patchy hair. Again, secondary symptoms will resolve without treatment but carry a risk of latent infection if not treated (Centers for Disease Control and Prevention, 2008b).

Latent syphilis infection can appear ten to twenty years after infection was first transmitted. About 15% of people who are not treated in the early stages of syphilis will develop this life-threatening illness and can transmit the infection never knowing they are ill. Latent syphilis causes damage to internal organs including the heart, the liver, the eyes, nerves, blood vessels, joints, and the brain—people actually become mentally ill because of this disease. The deterioration in health is marked by coordination problems, gradual blindness, numbness, paralysis, and dementia. In some cases, irreversible damage is severe enough to cause death (Centers for Disease Control and Prevention, 2008b).

VIEWPOINTS

Global Prevention Program Required

Hook and Leone (2006) offer suggestions for controlling the spread of Herpes Simplex Virus:

> We believe that available tools (serological testing, condom promotion, long-term suppressive antiviral therapy, and disclosure of infection status to sex partners) provide the means for developing a comprehensive national program to control the spread of genital herpes (Hook & Leone, 2006, p. 7).

In addition to Hook and Leone's (2006) view and the CDC's effort to thwart syphilis it seems likely that all sexually transmitted infections could one day be as insignificant as the common cold. That day is a long way away, though. With young people being the most at risk, making that population understand the severity of this problem is just one way to step toward an improvement in statistics.

To diminish certain health problems, developed societies created laws to ban smoking, to admonish drunk driving, and to promote healthy eating. These same societies even integrate sex education in many school systems to deter teenage pregnancy. Yet, these same societies do not band together to encourage safer sex practices for the health of its future; a task as easy as purchasing media time, encouraging family discussions, and requiring yearly screenings. This is the case with regard to sexually transmitted infections. If global activism embraced the issues surrounding sexually transmitted infections the way it has with smoking and recycling, transmission could be controlled in less than a decade.

TERMS & CONCEPTS

Acquired Immunodeficiency Disease (AIDS)™: Various conditions (and often, diseases) caused by complications from the human immunodeficiency virus (HIV).

Chlamydia: A bacterial infection acquired through various sexual contact (oral, anal, and penile/vaginal intercourse), often producing no symptoms but causing serious effects (like infertility and chronic pain) if left untreated.

Gonorrhea: A bacterial infection acquired through sexual contact such as oral, anal, and vaginal intercourse; generally causes inflammation and pain during urination.

Herpes Simplex Viruses (HSV): A viral infection spread through sexual contact (such as oral, anal, and vaginal intercourse) that causes small blisters and swelling where mucous membranes and skin tissue connect in the nose, genitals, or mouth.

Human Immunodeficiency Virus (HIV): A retrovirus passed through body fluids (semen, blood, vaginal secretions) which destroys immune system defenses.

Human Papillomavirus (HPV): A retrovirus that is spread through sexual intercourse that can cause genital warts, cervical cancer, and throat cancers.

Sexuality: Being involved in or interested by sexual activity; sexual orientation.

Sexually Transmitted Diseases: Signs and symptoms of infections acquired through sexual contact (i.e.: symptoms of AIDS (nausea, fatigue, suppressed immune system, are caused by HIV).

Sexually Transmitted Infection: A bacterial or viral infection that passes from one person to another through (oral, anal, or vaginal) sexual activity.

Syphilis: A bacterial infection passed by (anal, oral, or vaginal) sexual intercourse or from mother to child; can result in infections of the brain, the skin, nervous tissue, and genitalia.

BIBLIOGRAPHY

Centers for Disease Control and Prevention. (2007a). "HIV/ AIDS: Basic Information." CDC website: http://www.cdc.gov/hiv/topics/basic/index.htm

Centers for Disease Control and Prevention. (2007b). "Syphilis Elimination Effort (SEE): The National Plan to Eliminate Syphilis from the United States - Executive Summary." CDC website: http://www.cdc.gov/stopsyphilis/SEEexec2006.htm

Centers for Disease Control and Prevention. (2007c). *Sexually Transmitted Disease Surveillance, 2006.* Atlanta, GA: U.S. Department of Health and Human Services. CDC website: http://www. cdc.gov/std/stats/default.htm

Centers for Disease Control and Prevention. (2007d). "Updated recommended treatment regimens for gonococcal infections and associated conditions - United States, April 2007." CDC website: http://www.cdc.gov/std/treatment/2006/updated-regimens.htm

Centers for Disease Control and Prevention. (2008a). "Sexually Transmitted Diseases: Gonorrhea - CDC Fact Sheet." Atlanta, GA: U.S. Department of Health and Human Services. CDC website: http://

www.cdc.gov/std/Gonorrhea/STDFact-gonorrhea.htm

Centers for Disease Control and Prevention. (2008b). "Sexually Transmitted Diseases: Syphilis - CDC Fact Sheet." Atlanta, GA: U.S. Department of Health and Human Services CDC website: http://www.cdc.gov/ std/syphilis/STDFact-Syphilis.htm

"CDC: One in four teens has an STI." (2008). *Contemporary Sexuality, 42* (5), 11-12.

"Common STD risky to young and old." (2008). *Consumer Reports on Health, 20* (5), 6.

Cox, J. T., Mahoney, M. C, Saslow, D. & Moscicki, A. (2008). "ACS releases guidelines for HPV Vaccination." *American Family Physician,* 77 (6), 852-863.

Darrow, W. W. & Biersteker, S. (2008). "Short-term impact evaluation of social marketing campaign to prevent syphilis among men who have sex with men." *American Journal of Public Health, 98* (2), 337-343.

Foster, L. R., & Byers, E. (2013). "Stigmatization of individuals with sexually transmitted infections: effects of illness and observer characteristics." *Journal Of Applied Social Psychology, 43*E141–E152.

Gardner, J. (2006). "What you need to know about genital herpes." *Nursing, 36* (10), 26-27.

Glasier, A., Gulmezoglu, A. M., Schmid, G. P., Moreno, C. G. & Van Look, P. F. A. (2006). "Sexual and reproductive health: A matter of life and death." *Lancet, 368* (9547), 1595-1607.

Healy, B. (2008). "Clueless about risks of oral sex." *U.S. News & World Report, 144* (7), 60.

"HIV/AIDS and STD Updates." (2008). *AIDS Patient Care & STDs, 22* (3), 259-262.

Hook, E. W. & Leone, P. (2006). "Time to translate new knowledge into practice: A call for a national genital herpes control program." *Journal of Infectious Diseases, 194* (1), 6-7.

Iannelli, V., M.D. (2007). "HPV Controversy." About. com: *Pediatrics.* About. com: http://pediatrics.about.com

Lepusic, D., & Radovic-Radovcic, S. (2013). "Risk factors for sexually transmitted infections among young adolescents." *Collegium Antropologicum, 37*(2), 455–458.

Rodriguez, H. P., Chen, J., Owusu-Edusei, K., Suh, A., & Bekemeier, B. (2012). "Local public health systems and the incidence of sexually transmitted diseases." *American Journal Of Public Health, 102*(9), 1773–1781.

U.S. Preventive Services Task Force. (2005). "Screening for gonorrhea: recommendation statement." *American Family Physicians, 72* (9). website: http://www.aafp.org/afp/20051101/us.html

World Health Organization. (2007). "Sexually Transmitted Infections: Infections and transmission." WHO website: http://www.who.int/mediacentre/factsheets/fs110/en/index.html

World Health Organization. (2008). "Sexually Transmitted Diseases: Herpes simplex type 2." WHO website: http://www.who.int/

World Health Organization. (2008). "Sexually Transmitted Diseases: HIV/AIDS." WHO website: http://www.who.int/

Workowski, K., Berman, S. M. & Douglas, J. M. (2008). "Emerging antimicrobial resistance in neisseria gonorrhoeae: Urgent need to strengthen prevention strategies." *Annals of Internal Medicine, 14* (8), 606-W124

Suggested Reading

Abelson, M. B. & Leung, S. (2008). "The many faces of chlamydial infection." *Review of Ophthalmology, 15* (4), 84-87.

Adams, J., Moody, J., & Morris, M. (2013). "Sex, drugs, and race: How behaviors differentially contribute to the sexually transmitted infection risk network structure." *American Journal Of Public Health, 103*(2), 322–329.

Alan Guttmacher Institute. (1999). *Sharing responsibility: Women, society & abortion.* New York: Alan Guttmacher Institute.

Beauman , J. G. (2005). "Genital herpes: A review." *American Academy of Family Physicians,* 72 (8), 1527-1534.

Brown, Z. A., Selke, S., Zeh, J., et al. (1997). "The acquisition of herpes simplex virus during pregnancy." *New England Journal of Medicine, 337,* 509-15.

CDC. "Youth Risk Behavior Surveillance-United States, 2005. (2006)." CDC. *Morbidity & Mortality Weekly Report, 55* (1), 108.

Centers for Disease Control and Prevention. (2003). "Internet use and early syphilis infection among men who have sex with men-San Francisco, California, 1999-2003." MMWR *Morbidity & Mortality Weekly Report, 52* (50), 1229-1232.

Clifford, G. M., Smith, J. S., Aguado, T. & Franceschi, S. (2003). "Comparison of HPV type distribution in highgrade cervical lesions and cervical cancer: A meta-analysis." *British Journal of Cancer, 89* (1), 101-105.

Corey, L., Wald, A., Patel, R., et al. (2004). "Once daily valacyclovir to reduce the risk of transmission of genital herpes." *New England Journal of Medicine, 350,* 11-20.

Darville, T. (2005). "Chlamydia trachomatis infections in neonates and young children." *Seminars in Pediatric*

Infectious Diseases, 16 (4), p. 235-44.

Datta, S. D., Koutsky, L. A., Ratelle, S., Unger, E. R., Shlay, J., McClain, T., Weaver, B., Kerndt, P., Zenilman, J., Hagensee, M., Suhr, C. J. & Weinstock, H. (2008). "Human papillomavirus infection and cervical cytology in women screened for cervical cancer in the United States, 2003- 2005." *Annals of Internal Medicine, 148* (7), 493-501.

"Doctors, Legislators Differ On HPV Vaccine Mandates." (2007). *Pediatric News, 4* (2), 1.

Ezzati, M., Lopez, A. D., Rodgers, A., Vander Hoorn, S., Murray, C. J. L., and the Comparative Risk Assessment Collaborating Group. (2002). "Selected major risk factors and global and regional burden of disease." *Lancet, 360,* 1347-60.

Fleming, D. T. & Wasserheit, J. N. (1999). "From epidemiologic synergy to public health policy and practice: the contribution of other sexually transmitted diseases to sexual transmission of HIV infection." *Sexually Transmitted Infections, 75,* 3-17.

Freeman, E. E., et al. (2006). "Herpes simples virus 2 infection increases HIV acquisition in men and women: systematic review and meta-analysis of longitudinal studies." *AIDS, 20* (1), 73-83.

FUTURE II Study Group. (2007). "Quadrivalent vaccine against human papillomavirus to prevent high-grade cervical lesions." *New England Journal of Medicine, 356* (19), 1915-1927.

Gostin, L. O. & DeAngelis, C. D. (2007). "Mandatory HPV Vaccination: Public Health vs Private Wealth." *JAMA, 297,* 1921-1923.

Harper, D. M., Franco, E. L., Wheeler, C., et al., for the Glaxo- SmithKline HPV Vaccine Study Group. (2004). "Efficacy of a bivalent L1 virus-like particle vaccine in prevention of infection with human papillomavirus types 16 and 18 in young women: a randomized controlled trial." *Lancet, 364* (9447), 1757-1765.

Kalayoglu, M. V. (2002). "Ocular chlamydial infections: Pathogenesis and emerging treatment strategies." *Current Drug Targets: Infectious Disorders, 2* (1), 85-91.

Klausner, J. D., Wolf, W., Fischer-Ponce, L., Zolt, I. & Kate, M. H. (2000). "Tracing a syphilis outbreak through Cyberspace." *JAMA, 284,* 447-449.

McFarlane, M., Bull, S. S. & Rietmeijer, C. A. (2000). "The internet as a newly emerging risk environment for sexually transmitted diseases." *JAMA, 284,* 443-446.

Owusu-Edusei Jr, K., Chesson, H. W., Leichliter, J. S., Kent, C. K., & Aral, S. O. (2013). "The association between racial disparity in income and reported sexually transmitted infections." *American Journal Of Public Health, 103*(5), 910–916.

Paavonen, J., Jenkins, D., Bosch, F. X., et al., for the HPV PATRICIA Study Group. (2007) "Efficacy of a prophylactic adjuvanted bivalent L1 virus-like-particle vaccine against infection with human papillomavirus types 16 and 18 in young women: an interim analysis of a phase III double-blind, randomized controlled trial." *Lancet, 369* (9580), 2161-2170.

Ross, J. A. & Winfrey, W. L. (2002). "Unmet need for contraception in the developing world and the former Soviet Union: an updated estimate." *International Family Planning Perspectives, 28* (3), 138-43.

RØttingen, J. A., Cameron, D.W. & Garnett, G. P. (2001). "A systematic review of the epidemiologic interactions between classic sexually transmitted diseases and HIV: how much really is known?" *Sexually Transmitted Diseases 28* (10), 579-97.

Saslow, D., Runowicz, C. D., Solomon, D., et al. (2002). "American Cancer Society guideline for the early detection of cervical neoplasia and cancer." *CA: A Cancer Journal for Clinicians, 52* (6), 342-362.

Schiffman, M. & Castle, P. E. (2005). "The promise of global cervical cancer prevention." *New England Journal of Medicine, 353* (20), 2101-2104.

U.S. Preventive Services Task Force. (2005). "Screening for genital herpes: Recommendations and rationale." *American Family Physicians,* 72(8), 1557-1561.

Wald, A., Langenberg, A. G., Link, K., et al. (2001). "Effect of condoms on reducing the transmission of herpes simplex virus type 2 from men to women." *JAMA, 285,* 3100-6.

Weinstock, H., Berman, S. & Cates J. W. (2004). "Sexually transmitted diseases among American youth: incidence and prevalence estimates, 2000." *Perspectives on Sex and Reproductive Health, 36* (1), 6-10.

WHO. (2001). *Global prevalence and incidence of selected curable sexually transmitted infections: Overview and estimates.* Geneva: World Health Organization.

WHO. (2004). *Unsafe abortion: Global and regional estimates of the incidence of unsafe abortion and associated mortality in 2000,* (4th ed.). Fourth edition. Geneva: World Health Organization.

WHO. (2004). *Maternal mortality in 2000: estimates developed by WHO, UNICEF and UNFPA.* Geneva: World Health Organization.

Maureen McMahon, M.S.

Sexual Assault and Rape

ABSTRACT

Sexual assault and rape are serious social and public health issues in the United States. Women are overwhelmingly the victims of sexual assault and rape, while men are nearly always the perpetrators. According to a 2010–12 survey conducted by the US Centers for Disease Control and Prevention, in the United States approximately one in three women has experienced a form of contact sexual violence (Smith et al., 2017). The vast majority of women are sexually assaulted by men with whom they are acquainted. Women are far less likely to report a rape or assault when they know their assailant, thus instance of sexual assaults are greatly under-reported. This essay examines a number of reasons why women fail to report an assault to formal support agencies and examines some of the ways in which social services agencies can reach women in need of support. This article also discusses rape prevention programs that are effective in reducing instances of sexual assault, including programs that educate college students on the dangers of alcohol and its association with assault. In addition, the gender role beliefs that play a role in how rape is perceived by men and women, particularly when there is a relationship between the victim and the perpetrator are investigated. A look into the continued study and research regarding rape is also included, specifically the ability of such research to identify risk populations and risk factors as well as the type and format of education required to counter the effects of sexual assault.

OVERVIEW

Sexual violence is a major social and public health problem in the United States. According to the National Intimate Partner and Sexual Violence Survey, nearly one in three women and one in six men report having experienced sexual violence (Smith et al., 2017). The overwhelming majority of victims, however, are women who have been victimized by men (Franiuk, 2007).

Rape is defined as penetration or attempted penetration, but the definition of sexual assault is broader. According to the Center for Disease Control (CDC), sexual assault encompasses the following (2008):

- Completed or attempted penetration;
- Abusive sexual contact without penetration; and
- Non-contact sexual abuse (harassment and voyeurism).

The definition also extends to acts of rape perpetrated during war, sex trafficking, and female genital mutilation (Basile et al., 2005). This essay is limited to a discussion of the three bulleted points above.

In most states, the legal definition of first- or second-degree sexual assault involves non-consensual sexual contact and/or intercourse (Franiuk, 2007). Consent is a critical factor when determining if sexual assault has occurred. If a victim doesn't consent to engaging in sexual activity with another individual, then the act is legally defined as sexual assault. Non-consent or ambiguous consent cannot be construed as affirmative consent. Victims of sexual assault may not be able to give consent due to age, illness, or impairment or may be intimidated through physical violence or threats (Basile et al., 2005) and therefore afraid to refuse.

Historically, rapes and sexual assaults were believed to be perpetrated against women by strangers, but current data shows that women are much more likely to be sexually assaulted by men with whom they are acquainted. In fact, estimates suggest that 82 percent of all victims of sexual assault know their assailant (Basile et al., 2005).

At-Risk Populations. The majority of first-time rape victims are young; 71 percent of all rapes occur before the victim reaches the age of eighteen. Young women between the ages of sixteen and twenty-four are the most at risk for being raped (Feminist Majority Foundation, 2005).

Although women are susceptible in almost any situation, a college campus has unique elements that contribute to higher rates of sexual assault (Franiuk, 2007). College women report they "often feel emotionally and psychologically coerced into sex" (Feminist Majority Foundation, 2005).

A 1987 study of 3,000 college women surveyed indicated that more than 50 percent reported being sexually victimized and 15 percent were victims of rape. The statistics were re-affirmed by subsequent 1997 and 2006 studies (Franiuk, 2007).

Colleges have higher rates of sexual assault than non-college settings because of the prevalence of (Franiuk, 2007):

- Alcohol;
- Men and women living in close proximity;
- Increased exposure to others having sex;
- Many trends are apparent and disturbing when it comes to sexual assault;
- Women are far less likely to report instances of assault if the assailant is known to them. Since only 15 percent of rapes are committed by strangers, this statistic is likely to indicate that only a small number of sexual assaults actually get reported;
- Intoxication clouds judgment and causes uncertainty about what has actually happened;
- Women and men have different ideas about what constitutes "consent;"
- Women may subscribe to sexual scripts that suggest women are prey while men are predators "this is how sex is supposed to be-maybe it wasn't assault;" and
- College students lack knowledge about sexual assault and its prevalence on campus (Franiuk, 2007).

Responding to Sexual Assault through Education

Researchers and sociologist believe that heightened awareness and education for both men and women can reduce the instances of sexual assault at colleges and universities. One such study provided students with a number of different scenarios and asked them to decide which of the situations constituted sexual assault. Student perceptions revealed that many young people do not have an accurate picture (or definition) of what constitutes sexual assault. In a large number of cases, incidents that met the legal definition of rape or sexual assault went unreported simply because the young women involved did not perceive the incident as a sexual assault.

Knowing that the instances are likely to be significantly under-reported, it is imperative to be able to identify which scenarios are actually sexual assault and discuss the factors that make the situations less clear (Franiuk, 2007).

"Discussing and Defining Sexual Assault: A Classroom Activity" used the following methodology to help raise awareness of sexual assault and clarify its definition. Students were required to complete the following steps (Franiuk, 2007):

- Define sexual assault (student's perception);
- Read scenarios and determine if they constitute sexual assault;
- Discuss with classmates and instructor;
- Define sexual assault post discussion with the understanding of what defines "sexual assault" and "consent;"
- After students read and evaluated eight scenarios about what constitutes sexual assault, they discussed the scenarios with others. Students did not accurately label some of the situations as sexual assault for the following reasons (Franiuk, 2007);
- The victim didn't explicitly give consent, but was ambiguous "I don't know if I want to have sex";
- Intimidation and pressure were misconstrued by students and needed to be clarified;

- One victim drank too much and so was labeled by students as "responsible" for the assault: "She should have been more responsible"; and
- Gender of the aggressor confused some students—woman pressured boyfriend to have sex.

Alcohol & Sexual Assault. A report from the United Kingdom documents the role that alcohol plays in increasing the chance of sexual assault and rape. While this study didn't focus specifically on college students, it pointed to the overall link between alcohol use and sexual assault. Eighty-one percent of reported sexual assaults involved alcohol and amounts were significant enough to cause disorientation, memory loss, and loss of consciousness. In 60 percent of cases, the amount of alcohol was significant enough to "make it questionable whether the victim would have been able to even give consent" (French, Beynon,& Delaforce, 2007).

The voluntary use of alcohol is linked to an increased risk of being victimized by sexual assault by reducing inhibitions that affect judgment decisions and generally put the potential victim at greater risk for assault. There is also increased concern about drug facilitated sexual assault (DFSA), but the clandestine use of these drugs is not well documented. One challenge to reporting is that the drugs may cause memory loss or amnesia, which prevents or delays reporting of assault, which puts at risk the collection of evidence and makes confirmation and prosecution of assault more difficult (French et al., 2007).

In the United States, men are being informed of the legal definition of rape as part of rape prevention programs. "It is a felony for a man to have sex with a woman who's too intoxicated to give consent" (Choate, 2003,) but in many cases neither men nor women define this scenario as rape. Prevention needs to focus on sex and relationship education to inform both men and women of what their responsibilities are while participating in healthy relationships (French et al., 2007).

Sexual assault and rape are enormous social and public health problems in the United States and the United Kingdom. In 1994, Congress passed the Violence Against Women Act (VAWA) to draw attention to the impact that sexual violence has on society and to emphasize prevention. Successful prevention and education programs designed to reduce sexual assault provide several benefits, including providing individuals with support and reducing the burden on community social services, health care, and law enforcement agencies (Basile et al., 2005).

APPLICATIONS

Gender Role Perceptions. Gender role perceptions and behaviors are formed from developmental processes and social prescriptions (Simonson & Sublich, 1999). When men and women interact on a sexual level, there are certain attributes that are viewed as traditional gender traits. On a societal level, men are viewed favorably when they act dominant, powerful, and sexually aggressive. When it comes to sexual interactions, society prefers to envision women as passive, fragile, and submissive (Simonson & Sublich, 1999). Substantial research has focused on how gender role affects perceptions of different sexual assault and rape scenarios.

Sociologists are studying how gender role and sex role learning influence the perceptions that men and women have about different rape scenarios. Of particular interest to sociologists is the "relationship" that exists between the victim and perpetrator in a sexual assault and how that relationship affects rape perceptions.

Research supports the theory that men and women view sexual expectations within social interactions in very different ways. Researchers surveyed men and women regarding how they felt about different scenarios between the sexes. The outcome of each scenario was sexual intercourse; what differed was the type and level of relationship that the victim and perpetrator had in each scenario. Relationships were classified as stranger, acquaintance, dating, or marital (Simonson & Sublich, 1999). Observers were asked to rate their perception of the interaction using the four relationship types. Researchers found that perceptions of what constituted rape was highly dependent on how the observer perceived the relationship between the victim and perpetrator. The closer the relationship, the less likely observers were to see the sex act as rape.

Women who were surveyed for the study tended to view the world through a more egalitarian lens and thus were less likely to minimize the severity of the rape. Women's more liberal view on gender roles was largely aligned with their egalitarian attitudes. Because women are traditionally in less powerful roles than men, they may have more to gain from an egalitarian society than men do. When confronted with a rape scenario, women were more likely to consider a rape a rape (Ben-David & Schneider, 2005). Men were seen as having greater self-interest in defining rape more narrowly than women; they were also quicker to minimize the severity of a rape, the affect on the victim, and how severe the punishment should be (Ben-David & Schneider, 2005).

Research studies also concluded that those who hold less traditional gender-role stereotypes saw rape scenarios (overall) as more serious and were less likely to ascribe blame to the victim. These views belonged to individuals who hold more traditional gender-role stereotypes (Simonsen & Sublich, 1999). Gender roles are the behaviors and attitudes that are expected from individuals based on their sex and the learned socialization process (Ben-David & Schneider, 2005). Society has prescribed beliefs about the way that men and women should act in given roles. The role that will be discussed in this context is the one that involves sexual interaction between men and women.

One theory about rape that has gained some credence views rape as an extreme extension of traditional gender roles and associated male-female sexual interaction rather than as a result of deviant or pathological behavior (Brownmiller, 1975; Simonsen & Sublich, 1999; Ben-David & Schneider, 2005). "Rape [can be seen] as a mechanism of social control, [which has an] intimidating effect on all women, not just on victims, and the threat of rape [reinforces] traditional attitudes concerning gender roles and women's rights" (Ben-David & Schneider, 2005).

The more intimate the association between the victim and the assailant, the less responsibility was attributed to the perpetrator, and the less he was seen as responsible for violating the victim's rights. Marital rape was seen as the least serious and was often not viewed as rape at all.

Judicial systems only add to the ambivalence within our society toward victims of sexual assault. Leniency is given to perpetrators who have a known prior relationship with the victim (Ben-David & Schneider, 2005). In other words, when the victim knows her assailant, her claims of rape are diminished. Sociologists question these perceptions by suggesting that a violent assault by a person close to the victim might be considered more heinous because of the "betrayal of trust." Another perception, often referred to as "rape myth," purports that sexually experienced women aren't really damaged by rape—particularly if the victim has had prior sexual relations with the assailant. These perceptions essentially view "rape and consensual sex as the same" (Ben-David & Schneider, 2005). Rape victims do not see rape and consensual sex as equal.

Disclosure of Assault. Community sensitivity around the topic of sexual violence is a significant barrier to implementing rape prevention education (RPE) programs (Basile et al., 2005). Most women who are sexually assaulted do not report the attack to the police or other formal agencies, but statistics show that over 50 percent do reveal the incident to someone (usually a friend or family member). Many women don't tell anyone about their ordeal because they are afraid that no one will believe them, they want to protect their privacy, or they are afraid that they will be blamed for the assault (Feminist Majority Foundation, 2005).

Rape survivors suffer increased psychological symptoms including: Anxiety, PTSD, depression, and low self-esteem; these symptoms may last for years. While statistics vary, it is well documented that many women (50–75 percent) eventually disclose experiences of sexual assault and relatively few (3–10 percent) reveal sexual assault to formal support sources (Starzynski, Ullman, Townsend, Long, & Long, 2007).

There is also evidence that women who received initial positive support reactions from a source (formal or informal) are more likely to disclose sexual assaults to a formal support network. Negative reactions from any support source generally cause women to stop talking (Starzynski et.al, 2007). Many women report that they are hesitant to report their ordeal because they anticipate negative reactions from formal support networks. "Lack of sensitivity and education among clinicians . . . can result in a "second rape" . . . [and] failure to receive adequate support when it is finally sought can be devastating" (Russell & Davis, 2007).

Victims of rape committed by a stranger are more likely to report sexual assaults and seek professional help and seek help sooner. Research also shows that women who experience other stereotypical sexual assaults are more likely to report the assault to formal support services. Besides rape by strangers, women are also more likely to report an assault that involves violence, bodily injury, assault with a weapon (Starzynski et.al, 2007).

It is well documented that women who are assaulted by acquaintances are not as likely to report the incident. However, "acquaintance rape victims still experience similar psychological distress as those who are victims of stranger rape" (Starzynski et.al, 2007). When compared to other crime victims, rape survivors appear to suffer more negative psychological outcomes, which include depression, sexual dysfunction, substance abuse, and PTSD (post-traumatic stress disorder) (Russell & Davis, 2007).

Early intervention can have a significant impact on the long-term stress and negative effects that women suffer from sexual assault. The large number of women who never report sexual assault to formal support networks are at greater risk of suffering long-term psychological consequences. The reasons that women don't access formal support networks for sexual assault are many and varied. Some women simply lack basic knowledge about what services are available, while others have negative attitudes toward seeking help. Women without health insurance, the uneducated, and the young are least likely to seek formal support. Researchers and sociologists suggest that educational materials and information should be given to informal support networks because so many more women rely on such informal networks.

Educating Men. Social learning affects attitudes, knowledge, and behavior regarding date rape. Studying the effects of sex-role learning is helping sociologists design and implement prevention programs for men. Studies show that socialization focused treatment is as effective as traditional rape education programs in reducing rape. Blame and shame are just not effective methods for preventing rape (NASPA, 2007).

Campus rape is a significant problem and accounts for the majority of sexual assault instances. Therefore, reducing the number of sexual assaults on college campuses would significantly reduce the overall instances of sexual assault and rape. Most college rape prevention programs target women and include:

- Risk reduction strategies;
- Self defense classes;
- Increasing campus safety;
- Victim advocacy.

Sex-role learning and gender-role behaviors contribute to men's perceptions, beliefs, and biases about sexual assault. College men are more likely to view sexually coercive behavior as acceptable and rape myths are thought to be widely accepted on college campuses (Choate, 2003). Rape myths are rampant and support false information about rape, rape victims, and rapists in a way that marginalizes the damage of the act (Crider, 2008).

Socio-cultural theories support the idea that gender roles are taught and then reinforced. Among the messages that men receive are that they should be "sexual aggressors or competitors and women are the gatekeepers" (Choate, 2003). This type of social message reinforces the idea that women are to blame for their own victimization. Making an association between gender-role socialization and rape, participants are less accepting of rape myths and receive a strong message that they need to obtain positive consent for sexual activity (Choate, 2003).

Dr. Tracy Davis, assistant professor at Western Illinois University, has studied the effectiveness of rape prevention programs for college fraternity men. Davis's research focuses on social-learning-shaped perceptions and not just the biological differences between men and women.

Davis states that men are seen as "victims of harmful sex-related social learning." As such, it is suggested that researchers "scrutinize the negative impact that some messages can have, explore alternatives, and make new choices." This approach might shed light on why men might, for example, be prone to perpetrating sexual assault. By specifically exploring socialized messages (e.g., real men don't cry or express sensitive emotions), men can begin to better understand themselves and take responsibility for the choices they make (NASPA, 2007).

TERMS & CONCEPTS

Consent: To give assent or approval (Consent, 2009). In terms of sexual activity, consent is often contested; the legal definition of rape or sexual assault requires that both parties consent to engaging in sexual intercourse-free of coercion, ambiguity, or the influence of alcohol.

Egalitarian Attitudes: General beliefs that men and women should enjoy the same rights and privileges. Egalitarian views eschew gender stereotypes.

Gender Roles: Social, cultural, and psychological aspects that distinguish between the sexes in a given social context.

Post Traumatic Stress Disorder (PTSD): After experiencing a severe trauma, victims may suffer long-term effects from an event. The effects inhibit recovery, productivity, and lead to a number of other outcomes such as substance abuse and depression.

Rape Myths: "Prejudicial, stereotyped, or false beliefs about rape, rape victims, and rapists" (Crider, 2008).

Sexual Violence: Non-consensual sexual contact or sexual intercourse that results in a trauma (physical or psychological) to the victim.

Token Resistance: A rape myth that holds that women offer token resistance to sexual advances from men; when she says no to sex, she really means yes.

Bibliography

Abbey, A., & Ross, L. (1996). "Alcohol and dating risk factors for sexual assault among..." *Psychology of Women Quarterly, 20,* 147.

Alderden, M., & Long, L. (2016). "Sexual assault victim participation in police investigations and prosecution." *Violence & Victims, 31*(5), 819–836.

Basile, K., Lang, K., Bartenfeld, T., & Clinton-Sherrod, A. (2005). "Evaluability assessment of the Rape Prevention and Education Program: Summary of findings and recommendations." *Journal of Women's Health, 14,* 201-207.

Ben-David, S., & Schneider, O. (2005). "Rape perceptions, gender role attitudes, and victim-perpetrator acquaintance." *Sex Roles, 53*(5/6), 385-399.

Center for Disease Control and Violence. (2008). "Introduction: The problem of sexual violence." *Sexual Violence Prevention.* http://www.cdc.gov/

Choate, L. (2003). "Sexual assault prevention programs for college men: An exploratory evaluation of the men against violence model." *Journal of College Counseling, 6,* 166.

"Consent." (2015). In Merriam-Webster Online Dictionary. http://unabridged.merriam-webster.com/collegiate

Crider, S. (2008). "Social network and rape myth adherence." *Society for Social Work and Research.* http://sswr.confex.com

Feminist Majority Foundation. (2005). "Violence against women on college campuses." http://www.feministcampus.org/fmla/printable-materials/v-day05/violence%5f_against_women.pdf

Franiuk, R. (2007). "Discussing and defining sexual assault: A classroom activity." *College Teaching, 55,* 104-107.

French, K., Beynon, C., & Delaforce, J. (2007). "Alcohol is the true 'rape drug'." *Nursing Standard, 21,* 26-27. Retrieved May 29, 2008, from EBSCO Online Database Academic Search Complete.

Jordan, C. E., Combs, J. L., & Smith, G. T. (2014). "An Exploration of Sexual Victimization and Academic Performance among College Women." *Trauma, Violence & Abuse, 15,* 191–200.

Littleton, H., & Ullman, S. E. (2013). "PTSD symptomatology and hazardous drinking as risk factors for sexual assault revictimization: Examination in European American and African American women." *Journal of Traumatic Stress, 26,* 345-353.

Maier, S. L. (2013). "Sexual assault nurse examiners' perceptions of the influence of race and ethnicity on victims' responses to rape." *Feminist Criminology, 8,* 67-86.

Mouilso, E. R., Fischer, S., & Calhoun, K. S. (2012). "A prospective study of sexual assault and alcohol use among first-year college women." *Violence & Victims, 27,* 78-94.

National Association of Student Personnel Administrators (NASPA). (2007). "Moral development in practice: Educating college men about rape." *Journal of College and Character.*

Rabin, R. C. (2011, Dec 14) "Nearly 1 in 5 Women in U.S. Survey Say They Have Been Sexually Assaulted." *New York Times* http://www.nytimes.com/2011/12/15/

Russell, P., & Davis, C. (2007). "Twenty-five years of empirical research on treatment following sexual assault." *Best Practice in Mental Health: An International Journal, 3,* 21-37.

Simonson, K., & Subich, L. (1999). "Rape perceptions as a function of gender-role traditionality and victim-perpetrator association." *Sex Roles, 40*(7/8), 617-634.

Smith, S.G., Chen, J., Basile, K.C., Gilbert, L.K., Merrick, M.T., Patel, N., Walling, M., & Jain, A. (2017). *The National Intimate Partner and Sexual Violence Survey (NISVS): 2010–2012 State Report.* National Center for Injury Prevention and Control, Centers for Disease Control and Prevention. https://www.cdc.gov

Starzynski, L., Ullman, S., Townsend, S., Long, L., & Long, S. (2007). "What factors predict women's disclosure of sexual assault to mental health professionals?" *Journal of Community Psychology, 35,* 619-638.

Suggested Reading

Imbesi, R. (2007). "Engaging young people in leadership roles in the prevention of sexual assault: The CASA House Peer Educator Project." *Primary & Middle Years Educator, 5,* 21-25.

Lehavot, K., Molina, Y., & Simoni, J. (2012). "Childhood trauma, adult sexual assault, and adult gender expression among lesbian and bisexual women." *Sex Roles, 67*(5/6), 272-284.

Marquand, I. (1999). "Crime on campus." *Quill, 87,* 38-40.

"Rape & Sexual Assault." (2014). *Georgetown Journal of Gender & the Law, 15,* 155–93.

Tambling, R. (2012). "Solution-oriented therapy for survivors of sexual assault and their partners." *Contemporary Family Therapy: An International Journal, 34,* 391-401.

Walton, G., & Beaudrow, J. (2016). "Tipping the iceberg: Positionality and male privilege in addressing sexual violence against women." *Culture, Society & Masculinities, 8*(2), 140–154.

Yassen, J. & Glass, L. (1984). "Sexual assault survivors groups: A feminist practice perspective." *Social Work, 29,* 252-257.

Carolyn Sprague, MLS

Sexual Development Across the Lifespan

ABSTRACT

The sexual lifespan includes childhood sexual development, adolescent sexual development, adult sexual development, and sex in older adults. Impacts include puberty, menarche, and adolescent issues such as teen pregnancy, use of birth control, and statistical applications. Marriage and sexual activity is also presented. Applications related to the roots of sexual development theory are also given. Issues concerning homosexual sexual development indicate relevant themes from research and implications for extended research.

OVERVIEW

Human Sexual Development

According to DeLamater and Friedrich (2002), human sexuality might be described as a developmental process manifesting different characteristics throughout the human lifespan resulting in stages and milestones consisting of biological and behavioral components. Four stages of development can be identified and characterized in accordance with resulting biological and behavioral manifestations:

- Childhood sexual development;
- Adolescent sexual development;
- Adult sexual development; and
- Sex among older adults.

In his model of sexual development, Bancroft (1989) distinguished three different strands of sexual development, which can be identified as "gender identity, sexual response and the capacity for close, dyadic relationships" (p. 149). Jannsen (2007) added to the conversation regarding human sexual development by arguing that cultural aspects affect human sexuality in multiple ways. All of these factors create the context for better understanding the different stages of human sexuality and provide a framework for understanding not only the biological and behavioral attributes of human sexuality, but may also contribute to the cultural interplay as well.

APPLICATIONS

Childhood Sexual Development

De Graaf and Rademakers (2006) indicated that developing an improved insight into the sexual behavior and feelings of children has become increasingly important. In Western society, parents and educators find it difficult to decide how to react to children's sexual behaviors or questions about sexuality asked by children due to a growing societal fear regarding the risks of sexual victimization by adult predators. According to research that is available on child sexual development and a general consensus of empirical evidence, many opportunities for enhanced understanding regarding increased knowledge of childhood sexual developmental stages exist that seems to point out "which sexual behaviors and feelings should be considered 'normal' for children of certain ages, genders, or cultural backgrounds" (p. 2).

According to Masters, Johnson, and Kolodny (1982), sexual response in infants was found to be evident from birth. For example, vaginal lubrication has been identified in female infants within 24 hours after birth, and in male infants, erections have also been triggered and documented. Moreover, Martinson (1994) indicated that infants have been identified fondling their genitalia and digitally manipulating their genitalia from 2 ½ to 3 years of age. Moreover, the touching of genital parts has been documented in early childhood and even before birth (Brenot & Broussin, 1996). "After birth boys of 6 to 8 months of age and girls of 8 to 11 months of age reportedly discover their genitals by unintentionally touching them" (De Graaf & Rademakers, 2006, p. 4). Masturbation can be identified as a behavior that is solitary in nature and occurs when an individual touches or stimulates his or her own genitals typically for the purpose of stimulating sexual arousal (Bancroft, Herbenick, & Reynolds, 2003; Goldman & Goldman, 1988). Friedrich, Fisher, Broughton, Houston, and Shafran (1998) indicated that masturbatory behaviors are normal and can be observed and indicated by the sexual play of young children, and becomes more clandestine in children aged 6 to 9 after children become more aware of cultural norms attributed to sexual behavior (Reynolds, Herbenick, & Brancroft, 2003). Other sexual expressions might be rooted in pervasive sucking behaviors, cuddling, and other kinds of stimulation (De Lamater & Friedrich, 2002, p. 10).

Bowlby (1965) indicated that attachments form between infants and their parents that affect the quality and capability of relationships and form the basis for a child's sexual and emotional attachments and relationships throughout the lifespan. Goldberg, Muir, and Kerr (1995) argued that appropriate and positive physical contact offers the opportunity to provide stable and fulfilling emotional attachments in adulthood. Moreover, the role of gender identity typically forms around the age of 3 and can be described as an individual's sense of "maleness" or "femaleness." At the same time biological identity forms, a behavioral manifestation of gender-role identity is being socialized by others in relationship to the child (Bussey & Bandura, 1999). Goldman and Goldman (1982) further identified that children from ages 3 to 7 demonstrate an increased level of sexual interest, practiced by playing house or assuming other adult roles tending toward gender specificity. Moreover, children might engage in "playing doctor" and demonstrate an increased interest in the genitals of other children or adults (Okami, Olmstead, & Abramson, 1997).

Indicated by multiple researchers, the showing and touching of genitals can also be part of mutual sexual experiences between children in which both children play an active role (Goldman & Goldman, 1988; Haugaard, 1996; Lamb & Coakley, 1993; Larsson & Svedin, 2002; Reynolds, Herbenick, & Bancroft, 2003). As a result of increased sexual interest, parents may restrict the information they provide their children, and children may resort to gaining information from their peers (Martinson, 1994), leading to potential misinformation resulting in misinterpretation and misidentification. It should be noted that experiences with no direct genital contact, such as talking about sex, kissing and hugging, and exposure of genitals are most common in children up to 12 years. Finally, experiences with oral-genital contact, vaginal or anal insertion with an object or finger, and vaginal or anal intercourse are highly unusual between children 12 years old and younger (de Graaf & Rademakers, 2006, p. 11).

Adolescent Sexual Development

Thome (1993) indicated that during the stage of preadolescent sexual development, children organize themselves into homosocial groups, which can be described as a social division of males and females. One theory as to why this occurs is due to the sexual exploration and learning that occurs in homosocial groups involving individuals of the same gender. Children at this stage gain experience with masturbation as identified by a study indicating that 38 percent of men surveyed and 40 percent of women surveyed recalled masturbating before the onset of puberty (Bancroft, Herbenick, & Reynolds, 2003, p. 161). Furthermore, preadolescents at the ages of 10 to 12 years begin to experience sexual attraction followed by sexual fantasies occurring from several months to one year later (Bancroft et al, 2003; Rosario, Meyer-Bahlburg, Hunter, Exner, Gwadz, & Keller, 1996). Indicatively, homosocial interactions and subsequent exposures from these relationships may initiate the capacity for sustained intimate relationships (Thome, 1993). Simultaneously, behavioral changes are accompanied by biological changes associated with puberty, which begins from 10 years of age to 14 years of age. From a physiological perspective, gonads, genitalia, and secondary sexual characteristics enlarge and mature during this time (Tanner, 1967), all leading to an increased sexual interest and rising levels of sexual hormones and accompanying sexual fantasies.

During adolescence, bodily changes stimulate physical growth, increases in genital size and female breast size, combined with the onset of facial and pubic hair. Reportedly, these changes signal to the adolescent and to others that sexual maturity is occurring. In addition to increased testosterone and estrogen levels and other biological factors, behavioral manifestations create opportunities for sexual interactions that facilitate or inhibit sexual expression (Udry, 1988). Bancroft et al. (2003) reported that males typically begin masturbating between the ages of 13 to 15, and girls somewhat later. However, precipitating factors for increased masturbation and heterosexual intercourse may be attributed to father absence and permissive attitudes regarding sexual behavior, contrasted by regular "church attendance and long-range educational and career plans," both of which may delay female sexual activity (de Lamater & Friedrich, 2002, p. 11).

According to researchers, adolescents are having heterosexual and homosexual intercourse at earlier ages than in the past, which can be attributed to several factors. First, the age at which females have their first period has been falling since the beginning of the twentieth century. The average Caucasian female has her menarche (or first period) at about 150 months (or 12.5 years) of age and the average African American female has her first period at 144 months (12 years) of age, according to a 2012 study published in *Social Science & Medicine.* Additionally, young men and women are increasingly delaying marriage. In 1960, women, on average, married for the first time at 20.8 years of age, while men, on average, married for the first time at 22.8 years of age. In 2009, the median age of first marriage was 26.5 years of age for women and 28.4 years of age for men (Elliott & Simmons, 2011). Additionally, since increasing numbers of individuals are marrying later, there has been a substantial gap between biological readiness and age of marriage of typically 14 to 16 years. Finally, that the rate of teen pregnancies increased between the 1970s and 1991 would appear to indicate that teens used birth control only sporadically during these years; however, the teen pregnancy rate declined by 44 percent between 1991 and 2010 (Hamilton & Ventura, 2012), potentially reflecting an increased access to birth control by teens, increased attention in society to the importance of preventing pregnancy for adolescents, and increased economic opportunities for teenagers (Ventura, Mosher, Curtin, Abma, & Henshaw, 1998). Additional research should be conducted in the areas of sexual education, STDs, and teenagers, and birth control and consistent teen use.

A National Health Statistics Report released in March 2011 indicated that from 2006 to 2008, 2 percent of adolescent males had had sexual encounters with other males, while 10 percent of adolescent females had had sexual encounters with other females. The adolescents participating in studies on teen homosexual behavior generally reported that these encounters were with a peer; some of the participants also indicated that these encounters were initiated out of curiosity and that the behavior was not ongoing (Bancroft et al., 2003; Turner, Rogers, Lindberg, Pleck, Sonenstein, & Turner, 1998).

According to findings from the national High School Youth Risk Behavior Survey, 47.4 percent of U.S. high school students had had sexual intercourse at least once (2011). Adolescence is certainly a pivotal time in human sexual development (de Lamater & Friedrich, 2002, p. 11).

Adulthood & Sexual Development

Factors regarding sexual maturity continue into adulthood. Several factors play a role in adult sexual development and include effective communication between partners engaged in intimate relationships, making informed decisions regarding reproduction and the prevention of sexually transmitted infections (such as HIV) as well as decisions regarding sexual lifestyles, sexual satisfaction, and relationship factors.

In the twenty-first century, adults may choose among many relationship choices and lifestyles. Lifestyle choices include living single; remaining celibate; participating in a single, long-term monogamous relationship; participating in sexual relationships with several individuals; or engaging in serial monogamous relationships involving fidelity with one partner at a time for the duration of each relationship. African American men and women more often remain single than Caucasians. Between the years 2006 and 2010, 56 percent of African American males and 55 percent of African American females were never married in contrast with 44 percent of Caucasian men and 34 percent of Caucasian females (Copen, Daniels, Vespa & Mosher, 2012). Among reporting singles, 8 percent of the men aged eighteen to twenty-four, and 8.2 percent of the women in that age group usually had sex at least twice a week, while 56.9 percent of the men and 50.8 percent of the women in that age group had not had sex for at least one year, according to the 2010 National Survey of Sexual Health and Behavior (cited by Kinsey Institute, 2012).

Despite relationship alternatives, as of 2010, marriage was still categorized as the most prevalent sexual lifestyle choice in the United States. In 2010, 72 percent of American adults had been married at least once, and 61 percent of those never married wished to marry at some point (Cohn, Passel, Wang & Livingston, 2011). The 2010 National Survey of Sexual Health and Behavior found that most American couples, either married or unmarried, engage in sexual intercourse between two to three times a week to a few times a month (Kinsey Institute, 2012). Marriage continues to present the most legitimate social context for sexual expression, despite gradual changes in attitudes toward premarital sex and cohabitation. In the context of marriages in the United States, monogamy has been a widely accepted so practice (Wiederman & Allgeier, 1996), and extramarital sex among marital couples are significantly disapproved within the societal context (Johnson, Stanley, Glenn, Amato, Nock, & Markman, 2002); however, 12.8 percent of General Social Survey respondents between 1972 and 2006 reported having engaging in extramarital sex at some point in their lives (NORC, 2006).

Amos (2006) stated, "Our view of marriage, its goals and its purposes have undergone a seismic shift during the last 50 years" (p. 270). Amos (2006) indicated that during the 1960s and 1970s "a time of radical change began," theoretically constituted by an increased availability of contraception which offered different alternatives to women than was available in previous eras (p. 270). As a result of changing female roles and other contributing factors, cohabitation or "living together" is an increasing option, which can be characterized as a public statement regarding commitment and sexual relationship. While cohabitation may be temporary, according to the United States Census Bureau estimates for 2010, 6.8 million unmarried heterosexual couples and 646,000 unmarried same-sex couples were cohabitating.

Sex & Older Adults

In addition to the changing context of coupling in America, other factors play a role in adult sexual development as well. For example, Smith (1994) reported a decline in the frequency of sexual intercourse with age. Additionally, biological factors that include physical changes and illness may be contributors to diminished sexual expression. DeLamater and Carpenter (2012) indicate that menopause occurs in the late forties to early fifties and hormonal changes marking the menopausal transition can begin as many as ten years prior and continue for a number of years after. Gallicchio, Schilling, Tomic, Miller, Zacur, and Flaws (2007) note a reported decline in sexual activity during the menopausal transition (pp. 132–133). This occurrence might indicate that sexual frequency is tied directly to biological as well as relationship factors. The relationship between the menopausal transition and decreased sexual function has been observed in women despite relationship variables. These relationship variables include "general well-being, physical and mental health, the occurrence of menopausal symptoms, and life situation (p. 133). Moreover, a "hallmark of the menopausal transition is a decline in ovarian function, resulting in dramatic changes in hormone levels" (p. 133). Additional studies should be considered on the impacts of biological, physical, relationship, emotional, and mental health impacts of aging and sexual development.

In contrast with women, men experience andropause (Lamberts, van den Beld, & van der Lely, 1997), which can be described as a ADAM-androgen decline that occurs as men age. This results in a gradual decline in testosterone production, which can occur as early as age 40 (Morales, Heaton, & Carson, 2000). During this time, erections may occur more slowly, and men may experience increased control over their sexual response. According to AARP, older, healthy humans 74 years and older may continue to have regular opportunities for satisfying sexual expression in all forms including masturbation and homosexual behavior (De Lamater & Friedrich, 2002, p. 13). It would seem that much more research exists in terms of female menopause as opposed to male andropause. Additional research should be considered in this area.

VIEWPOINTS

Sigmund Freud

From a developmental application, the study of childhood sexuality is rooted in the work of Sigmund Freud. According to Galatzer-Levy & Cohler (1993), Freud approached theories related to childhood sexuality from the viewpoint of a male child. Indicatively, Freud postulated that life could best be understood from the viewpoint of a child, and he believed post-adolescent development was nonexistent. Moreover, Freud viewed sexuality as "a generalization of the pleasures associated with mucous membrane stimulation, and as the central motive for relating to other people" (p. 5). Anzieu (1975) indicated that much of Freud's beliefs regarding sexual development were rooted in his own experiences, postulating that Freud was jealous of his own father and had formed an erotic attachment to his mother.

Moreover, many of Freud's theories toward childhood sexuality and fascination could be exemplified by Shakespeare's character Hamlet, who similarly possessed an incestuous desire toward his mother and possessed ambivalence toward his dead father, later displaced by a burgeoning hatred toward his stepfather (pp. 235–236). Anzieu (1975) argued that Freud's work was greatly influenced by his treatment of a man who suffered from an obsessive neurosis and homicidal thoughts, ailments that Freud identified in himself (Cohler & Galatzer-Levy, 2008). While seemingly a potentially strange application, Freud's work is considered a key developmental aspect of human sexuality and deserves additional research into the foundations of developmental psychology and sexuality.

Homosexuality

Significant issues related to human sexual development are those related to gay and bisexual men (Berger, 1996; Grossman, D'Augelli, & Hershberger, 2000; Lee, 1989; Vacha, 1985). Murry and Adam (2001) researched and identified several themes regarding homosexuality and human sexual development. Some of the themes included public image as represented by the media, relationships between younger and older men and the orientation of youthfulness in gay culture, a search for intimacy at all ages, and the impact of an entire generation marked by HIV/AIDS. All of these issues were indicated to have played a significant role in the human sexual development of homosexual men.

As of late 2013, the little to no scholarly attention had been paid to the development of lesbian, bisexual, transsexual, or transgender sexualities, as distinct from gay male sexuality and from one another. Findings for combined LGBT populations indicate that sexual minorities experience different levels of psychosocial adjustment depending on when sexual identity formation occurs (Rosario, Schrimshaw & Hunter, 2011) and that although social stigma and discrimination continue to be hurdles for LGBT youth, most are as healthy as their heterosexual peers (Saewyc, 2011). Additional research into these areas of combined interest, as well as the sexual development of lesbian, bisexual, transsexual, and transgendered people, is needed.

Elderly Sexual Activity

Another important issue regarding human sexuality and development relates to attitudes, especially those which define specific behaviors as appropriate or inappropriate. According to DeLamater & Friedrich (2002), sexual attitudes especially relate to age factors and sexual expression and the elderly. Sexual attitudes and prejudice are perpetuated by the unacceptable notion that individuals over 75 should not engage in sexual activity, especially masturbation. A derivative of these attitudes is directly linked to negative attitudes in elder care facilities and nursing homes. Often times, sexual behavior between aged individuals in these kinds of facilities are prohibited. "These attitudes affect the way the elderly are treated, and the elderly may hold such attitudes themselves. These attitudes may be a more important reason why many elderly people are not sexually active than the biological changes they experience" (p. 13). Additional work should be considered in creating a "system of diversity" for all individuals regardless of age or sexual orientation.

CONCLUSION

Human sexual development across the lifespan is a dynamic phenomenon with multiple facets. According to researchers, studies of childhood sexuality are difficult to obtain, because of the potential victimization of children. However, studies that do exist demonstrate that children of all ages display behaviors or have feelings that could be identified as sexual in nature. DeLamater & Friedrich (2002) indicated that human sexual development begins in infancy and certainly extends across the lifespan of humans. Conclusively, human sexuality integrates both behavioral and biological factors manifested in aging, child development, adolescence and puberty, adulthood, and old age. Development at all of these stages shapes sexual attitudes and sexual identity and directly impact sexual behavior. While humans certainly share similarities in their sexual progression, it is further indicated that differences are also present (p. 13). Additional research should be considered in all areas of human sexual development in order to shed light on this area of continued interest and importance in sociological studies and society.

TERMS & CONCEPTS

Childhood Sexual Development: Childhood sexual developmental can be described as stages that take place throughout childhood that seem to point out which sexual behaviors and feelings should be considered "normal" for children of certain ages, genders, or cultural backgrounds.

Cohabitation: Cohabitation can be described "living together," which can be characterized as a public statement regarding commitment and sexual relationship as an alternative to marriage.

Gender Identity: Gender identity can be described as a process that begins to develop typically around the age of 3 and can be described as an individual's sense of "maleness" or "femaleness."

Homosocial Groups: Homosocial groups can be described as a social division of males and females in group settings.

Human Sexuality: Freud believed that human sexuality is a driving force in people's relations with one another.

Bibliography

Amos, C. (2006). "Marriage—and its alternatives: An Anglican perspective, yesterday, and today." *Islam & Christian—Muslim Relations,* 17, 269–279.

Anzieu, D. (1975). *Freud's self-analysis.* P. Graham, trans. Madison, CT: International Universities Press, 1986.

Bancroft, J. (1989). *Human sexuality and its problems.* Edinburgh, Scotland: Churchill Livingstone.

Bancroft, J., Herbenick, D., & Reynolds, M. (2003). "Masturbation as a marker of sexual development." In J.

Bancroft (Ed.), *Sexual development in childhood.* Bloomington, IN: Indiana University Press.

Berger, R. (1996). *Gay and gray.* New York: Haworth Press.

Bowlby, J. (1965). "Maternal care and mental health." In J. Bowlby (Ed.). *Child care and the growth of love.* London: Penguin.

Brenot, P., & Broussin, B. (1996). "Orgasme in utero?" *Sexologies,* 5, 15–16.

Bussey, K., & Bandura, A. (1999). "Social cognitive theory of gender development and differentiation." *Psychological Review,* 106, 676–713.

Cohler, B. J. & Galatzer-Levy, R. M. (2008). "Freud, Anna, and the problem of female sexuality." *Psychoanalytic Inquiry,* 28, 3–26.

Cohn, D., Passel, J. S., Wang, W., & Livingston, G. (2011, December 14). "Barely half of U.S. adults are married—A record low." *PewResearch Social & Demographic Trends* website: http://www.pewsocialtrends.org/2011/12/14/barely-half-of-u-s-adults-are-married-a-record-low/

Copen, C. E., Daniels, K., Vespa, J., & Mosher, W. D. (2012, March 22). "First marriages in the United States: Data from the 2006–2010 National Survey of Family Growth." *National Health Statistics Reports,* 49, 1–22. http://www.cdc.gov/nchs/data/nhsr/nhsr049.pdf

De Graaf, H., & Rademaker, J. (2006). "Sexual behavior of prepubertal children." *Journal of Psychology & Human Sexuality,* 18, 1–21.

DeLamater, J. D., & Carpenter, L. M. (2012). *Sex for life: From virginity to Viagra, how sexuality changes throughout our lives.* New York: New York University Press.

DeLamater, J., & Friedrich, W. N. (2002). "Human sexual development." *Journal of Sex Research,* 39, 10–14.

Eaton, D. K., Kann, L., Kinchen, S., Shanklin, S., Flint, K. H., Hawkins, J. Wechsler, H. (2012, June 8). *Youth risk behavior surveillance—United States, 2011.* Washington, DC: Government Printing Office. http://www.cdc.gov/mmwr/pdf/ss/ss6104.pdf.

Elliott, D. B., & Simmons, T. (2011). "Marital events of Americans: 2009." http://www.census.gov/prod/2011pubs/acs-13.pdf

Friedrich, W. N., Fisher, J., Broughton, D., Houston, M., & Shafran, C. R. (1998). "Normative sexual behavior in children: A contemporary sample." *Pediatrics,* 101. 693–697.

Galatzer-Levy, R. M., & Cohler, B. J. (1993). *The essential other.* NewYork: Persus Books/Basic Books.

Gallicchio, L., Schilling, C., Tomic, D., Miller, S. R., Zacur, H., Flaws, J. A. (2007). "Correlates of sexual functioning among mid-life women." *Climacteric,* 10, 132–142.

Goldberg, S., Muir, R., & Kerr, J. (1995). *Attachment theory: Social, developmental, and clinical perspectives.* Hillsdale, NJ: Analytic Press.

Goldman, R. J., & Goldman, J. D. G. (1982). *Children's sexual thinking.* London: Routledge and Kegan Paul.

Goldman, R., & Goldman, J. (1988). *Show me yours: What children think about sex.* Victoria, Australia: Penguin Books.

Grossman, A., D'Augelli, A., & Hershberger, S. (2000). "Social support networks of lesbian, gay, and bisexual adults 60 years of age and older." *Journals of Gerontology: Series B,* 55B, 171–179.

Hamilton, B. E., & Ventura, S. J. (2012). "Birth rates for U.S. teenagers reach historic lows for all age and ethnic groups." *NCHS data brief, no. 89.* Hyattsville, MD: National Center for Health Statistics.

Haugaard, J. J. (1996). "Sexual behaviors between children: Professionals' opinions and undergraduates' recollections." *Families in Society: The Journal of Contemporary Human Services,* 77, 81–89.

Hofferth, S. L. (1990). "Trends in adolescent sexual activity, contraception, and pregnancy in the United States."

In J. Bancroft & J. Reinisch (Eds.), *Adolescence and puberty* (pp. 217–233). New York: Oxford University Press.

Janssen, D. F. (2007). "First stirrings: Cultural notes on orgasm, ejaculation, and wet dreams." *Journal of Sex Research,* 44, 122–134.

Johnson, C. A., Stanley, S. M., Glenn, N. D., Amato, P. A., Nock, S. L., & Markman, H. J. (2002). *Marriage in Oklahoma: 2001 baseline statewide survey on marriage and divorce (S02096 OKDHS).* Oklahoma City, OK: Oklahoma Department of Human Services.

Kinsey Institute. (2012). "Frequently asked sexuality questions to the Kinsey Institute: Frequency of sex." http://www.iub.edu/~kinsey/resources/FAQ.html#frequency

Lamb, S., & Coakley, M. (1993). "'Normal' childhood sexual play and games: Differentiating play from abuse." *Child Abuse & Neglect,* 17, 515–526.

Lamberts, S. W. J., Van den Beld, A., & Van der Lely, A. J. (1997). "The endocrinology of aging." *Science,* 278, 419–424.

Larsson, I., & Svedin, C. G. (2002). "Sexual experiences in childhood: Young adults' recollections." *Archives of Sexual Behavior,* 31, 263–273.

Laumann, E. O., Gagnon, J. H., Michael, R. T., & Michaels, S. (1994). *The social organization of sexuality: Sexual practices in the United States.* Chicago: The University of Chicago Press.

Lee, J. (1989). "Invisible men." *Canadian Journal on Aging*, 8, 79–97.

Martinson, F. M. (1994). *The sexual life of children.* Westport, CT: Bergin and Garvey.

Masters, W. H., Johnson, V. E., & Kolodny, R. C. (1982). *Human sexuality.* Boston: Little, Brown.

Morales, A., Heaton, J. P. W., & Carson, C. C. (2000). "Andropause: A misnomer for a true clinical entity." *Journal of Urology*, 163, 705–712.

Murry, J., & Adam, B. D. (2001). "Aging, sexuality, and HIV issues among older gay men." *Canadian Journal of Human Sexuality, 10* (3/4), 75–91.

NORC. (2006). "Have sex other than spouse while married." *General Social Surveys, 1972–2006.* http://www3.norc.org

Okami, P., Olmstead, R., & Abramson, R. (1997). "Sexual experiences in early childhood: 18-year longitudinal data from the UCLA Family Lifestyles Project." *Journal of Sex Research*, 34, 339–347.

Reynolds, M. A., Herbenick, D. L., & Bancroft, J. H. (2003). "The nature of childhood sexual experiences: Two studies 50 years apart." In J. Bancroft (Ed.), *Sexual development in childhood.* Bloomington, IN: Indiana University Press.

Rosario, M., Meyer-Bahlburg, H., Hunter, J., Exner, T., Gwadz, M., & Keller, A. (1996). "The psychosexual development of urban lesbian, gay and bisexual youths." *Journal of Sex Research*, 33, 113–126.

Rosario, M., Schrimshaw, E. W., & Hunter, J. (2011). "Different patterns of sexual identity development over time: Implications for the psychological adjustment of lesbian, gay, and bisexual youths." *Journal of Sex Research, 48,* 3–15.

Saewyc, E. M. (2011). "Research on adolescent sexual orientation: Development, health disparities, stigma, and resilience." *Journal of Research on Adolescence, 21,* 256–272.

Smith, T. W. (1994). *The demography of sexual behavior.* Menlo Park, CA: Kaiser Family Foundation.

Tanner, J. M. (1967). "Puberty." In A. McLaren (Ed.), *Advances in reproductive physiology* (Vol. II). New York: Academic Press.

Thome, B. (1993). *Gender play: Girls and boys in school.* New Brunswick, NJ: Rutgers University Press.

Thompson, W. K., Charo, L., Vahia, I. V., Depp, C., Allison, M., & Jeste, D. V. (2011). "Association between higher levels of sexual function, activity, and satisfaction and self-rated successful aging in older postmenopausal women." *Journal of the American Geriatrics Society, 59,* 1503–1508.

Turner, C. F., Ku, L., Rogers, S. M., Lindberg, L. D., Pleck, J. H. & Sonenstein, F. L. (1998). "Adolescent sexual behavior, drug use, and violence: Increased reporting with computer survey technology." *Science*, 280, 867–868.

Udry, J. R. (1988). "Biological predispositions and social control in adolescent sexual behavior." *American Sociological Review*, 53, 709–722.

U.S. Bureau of the Census. (1999). *Statistical abstract of the United States, 1999.* Washington, DC: Author. http://www.census.gov/

U.S. Bureau of the Census. (2000), *Statistical abstract of the United States, 2000.* Washington, DC: Author. http://www.census.gov/main/www/cen2000.html

U.S. Bureau of the Census. (2010). "Increase in opposite-sex cohabiting couples from 2009 to 2010 in Annual Social and Economic Supplement (ASEC) to the Current Population Survey (CPS)." http://www.census.gov

Vacha, K. (1985). *Quite fire.* Trumansburg, NY: Crossing Press.

Ventura, S. J., Mosher, W. D., Curtin, S. A, Abma, J. C, & Henshaw, S. (2001). "Trends in pregnancy rates for the United States, 1976–1997." *National Vital Statistics Reports*, 49.

Wiederman, M.W., & Allgeier, E.R. (1996). "Expectations and attributions regarding extramarital sex among young married individuals." *Journal of Psychology and Human Sexuality*, 8, 21–35.

"Youth Risk Behavior Survey (2007)." Available at http://www.cdc.gov/

SUGGESTED READING

Chodorow, N. (1999). *The power of feelings.* New Haven, CT: Yale University Press.

De Graaf, H., & Rademakers, J. (2011). "The psychological measurement of childhood sexual development in western societies: Methodological challenges." *Journal of Sex Research*, 48 (2/3), 118–129.

Friedman, R. C. (1988). *Male homosexuality: A contemporary psychoanalytic perspective.* New Haven, CT: Yale University Press.

Gay, P. (1988). *Freud: A life for our time.* New York, NY: W. W. Norton.

Martinson, F. M. (1994). *The sexual life of the child.* Westport, CT: Bergin & Garvey.

Sandfort, T. (2012). *Childhood sexuality: Normal behavior and development.* New York, NY: Routledge.

Schur, M. (1972). *Freud living and dying.* New York, NY: International Universities Press.

Thatcher, A. (1999). *Marriage after modernity: Christian marriage in postmodern times.* Sheffield, England: Sheffield Academic Press.

Sharon Link, Ph.D.

Sexual Harassment

ABSTRACT

Noted legal scholar and feminist Catherine MacKinnon defined sexual harassment as "the unwanted imposition of sexual requirement in the context of a relationship of unequal power" (MacKinnon, 1979). Sexual harassment generally falls under two categories: quid pro quo harassment and hostile environment. The majority of victims reporting instances of sexual harassment are women, and the vast majority of reported aggressors are men. Title VII of the Civil Rights Act of 1964 and the Equal Employment Opportunity Commission provide legal recourse for victims of sexual harassment. Some sociologists associate the full integration of women into the modern workforce with an increase in instances of sexual harassment. Social scientists are somewhat critical of common approaches to dealing with sexual harassment—particularly in the workforce. Many organizations have made concerted efforts to heighten awareness of issues related to sexual harassment, though social scientist recommend shifting the focus from identifying instances of sexual harassment to pinpointing factors that contribute to instances of sexual harassment with the ultimate aim of lessening future occurrences.

OVERVIEW

Sexual harassment remains a common occurrence in society. According to the US Equal Employment Opportunity Commission, 7,256 sexual harassment charges were filed in 2013, and a 2011 Washington Post-ABC News poll found that as many as 25 percent of women reported having experienced sexual harassment in the workplace. However, the challenge of defining exactly what constitutes sexual harassment remains. According to Kingsley Browne (2006) of Wayne State University Law School:

> Courts have declared that all of the following kinds of conduct may constitute sexual harassment: forcible rape; extorting sex for job benefits; sexual or romantic overtures; sexual jokes; sexually suggestive pictures or cartoons; sexist comments; vulgar language; harassing actions of a non-sexual form; and even "well intended compliments" (p. 145).

Sexual harassment is defined as a form of sex discrimination under Title VII Federal Law Civil Rights Act of 1964, which prohibits employment discrimination based on race, color, religion, sex, or national origin (U.S. Equal Opportunity Commission, 2002).

Feminist attorney Catherine MacKinnon argued for the legal recognition of sexual harassment as sex discrimination in her 1979 book *Sexual Harassment of Working Women.* In the book, MacKinnon states that because of the traditional gender roles of our society, women disproportionately occupy inferior positions in the workplace. One psychologist writing on the subject concurred with MacKinnon, seeing sexual harassment, "as a form of sex discrimination that keeps the sexes separate and unequal at work" (Berdahl, 2007, p. 435).

MacKinnon (1979) argues that "intimate violations" of women by men were "sufficiently pervasive" as to make the practice nearly invisible (p.1). She also states that internalized power structures within the workplace kept anyone from discussing sexual harassment, making it "inaudible" (p. 1). In her words, the abuse was both acceptable for men to perpetuate and a taboo that women could not confront either publicly or privately. MacKinnon states that the "social failure" to address these pervasive intimate violations hurt women in terms of the economic status, opportunity, mental health, and self-esteem (p. 1).

Many believe that sexual harassment is about the abuse of power, others believe it is about access to sexual favors, and still others believe that sexual harassment is about access to power and sex. In legal terms, sexual harassment is divided into two main categories.

Quid Pro Quo

Quid pro quo harassment occurs when an employee is made to submit to some form of sexual advance in order to obtain a benefit (e.g., a promotion) or to avoid a burden (e.g., being fired). In such cases, sexual harassment is considered sex discrimination because presumably the demand would not have been made if the employee were of the opposite sex (Browne, 2006). Initially, researchers and courts believed that this type of harassment was motivated by sexual desire, but research has subsequently suggested that it is instead meant to assert dominance over or derogate the target (Berdahl, 2007).

Hostile Environment

Hostile environment harassment occurs when a work environment is "permeated with sexuality" or "discriminatory intimidation, ridicule, and insult" (Smith, Craver & Turner, 2011). Within this type of harassment, the victim does not claim specific harassment, but rather that the general work environment is discriminatory. Generally, it is believed that this type of harassment seeks to undermine and humiliate its target and is likely to be motivated by sexual hostility rather than sexual desire (Berdahl, 2007).

Men & Women in the Workplace

As women gain greater equity in the workplace, it might be assumed that the instances of sexual harassment in the workplace would diminish. However, the causes of sexual harassment are complex and hard to identify, and sexual harassment remains prevalent in modern society. Women's increasing presence in the workforce has meant that men and women work together more closely in the twenty-first century than at any other time in history. In fact, there are fewer and fewer "male only" professions as women become much more fully integrated into all corners of the workforce. According to one researcher, "one effect of the breakdown of the sexual division of labor is the expansion of opportunities for sexual conflict in the workplace" (Browne, 2006, p. 145). One outgrowth of this conflict may be sexual harassment.

Wayne State University law professor Kingsley Brown (2006) analyzed data from numerous studies to argue that sexual harassment is rooted in sociocultural causes, as well as biological and psychological causes. Sociocultural theories of sexual harassment, he says, hold that harassment is a means for the harasser to gain power over his target. Biological and psychological theories, on the other hand, hold that men are biologically and psychologically predisposed to be sexually aggressive and that sexual harassment is an outgrowth of these predispositions (Browne, 2006).

Further, Browne (2006) argues that men tend to interpret female interest as sexual, while women are more likely to interpret male attention as mere friendliness. According to Browne, these differing perspectives may oftentimes lead to miscommunication and unintentional harassment. In other words a man, perceiving a woman's friendliness to indicate sexual interest, may escalate his attention to a level that the woman sees as threatening (Browne, 2006).

Token Resistance to Sexual Harassment

Token resistance is a concept that originated in date rape literature and describes the belief that women may ostensibly discourage sexual attention when in fact they wish it to continue (Osman, 2004). In other words, a woman may say "no" when what she really means is "yes."

Research suggests that a sexual aggression continuum exists with nonviolent sexual aggression at one end and rape at the other (Figure 1). Researchers believe that sexual harassment could fall at the less extreme end, a belief that, if correct, could offer insight into the perceptions of aggressors who partake in similar behaviors (Begany & Milburn, 2002). The implications for studying token resistance and sexual harassment could be promising: men who have a strong belief in token resistance on one end of the spectrum may hold similar beliefs at the less extreme end.

Research suggests that men who have a strong belief in token resistance have difficulty determining when their advances are unwanted. They may need stronger signals (verbal resistance, physical

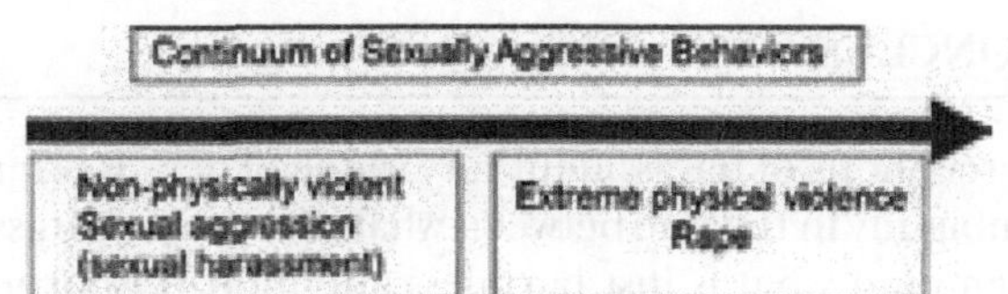

Figure 1: Continuum of Sexual Aggressive Behaviors.

resistance, or both) to convince them that their actions are being rejected.

The study of token resistance and sexual harassment may reveal not only why men may see attention as harmless, but also why women may see it as threatening. As one researcher found, women are more likely than men to identify less severe instances of harassment as harassment. However, this difference tends to disappear as harassment becomes more severe and the target's resistance becomes stronger (Osman, 2007). Osman also points out that most women do not offer direct resistance to unwanted sexual attention, which may fail to dissuade men who have a strong belief in token resistance. Although verbal resistance may be enough to alert most men that their attentions are not wanted, Osman argues that women should also know that in some cases simultaneous verbal and physical resistance is needed to get their message across.

What Motivates Sexual Harassment?

Much contemporary research focuses on the "indirect evidence" that illuminates the causes of sexual harassment. This investigation includes determining the targets of sexual harassment as well as the motives of the harasser (Berdahl, 2007). Psychologists Joseph J. Begany and Michael A. Milburn examined the personality characteristic of authoritarianism to see if there was a correlation between it and sexual harassment. According to Adorno, Frenekl-Brunswik, Levinson, and Sanford (1950), an authoritarian personality can develop as "a result of harsh, punitive child rearing and the consequential displacement of negative emotions into the public realm" (Begany & Milburn, 2002, p. 119). These theorists suggested that authoritarian personalities displace the anger they experienced during childhood onto those who are weaker than themselves and unlikely to retaliate. Additionally, highly authoritarian personalities are likely to "exhibit signs of underlying resentful disrespect for women generally" (Adorno et al., 1950, p. 107, as quoted in Begany & Milburn, 2002, p. 119).

These people may exhibit "fear of a dangerous world, self righteous attitudes and vindictive envy" (Begany & Milburn, 2002, p. 119) and, as a result, may be predisposed to sexually harass others. Men with authoritarian traits may also exhibit a tendency toward hypermasculinity and adhere strictly to traditional culture norms. Authoritarianism has been found to be predictive of sexual and physical aggression as well as battering (Begany & Milburn, 2002).

Begany and Milburn identified two types of sexism that are mediating factors in between authoritarianism and sexual harassment: hostile and benevolent sexism, both of which serve to rationalize men's dominance over women. Men who exhibit benevolent sexism see themselves as protectors of women and have favorable attitudes toward women in traditional gender roles, such as those of a wife, mother, or homemaker. Hostile sexism espouses that men are superior to women and ought to sexually dominate them. The authors found that "authoritarianism... predicts the likelihood that a man will report a greater likelihood of engaging in sexual harassment" (Begany & Milburn, 2002, p. 126). Men with sexist attitudes tend to endorse gender role distinctions that in turn may serve to enhance their own sense of male identity (Berdahl, 2007).

Begany and Milburn's findings support those of psychologist Jennifer Berdahl (2007), who found that women who violate gender ideals are likely to be subjected to sexual harassment. Men who exhibit either benevolent or hostile sexism are likely to view women who possess masculine personality traits as a threat, which can increase the likelihood that they will harass them. According to Berdahl (2007), while sexual harassment of women who exhibit feminine ideals may be more common in the quid pro quo scenario, women who violate feminine gender ideals are much more likely to be subjected to hostile environments. As Berdahl put it, "this suggests that sexual harassment is driven not out of desire for women who meet feminine ideals but out of a desire to punish those who violate them" (2007, p. 434). As a result, having masculine traits may not help women fit into male-dominated fields and may even hurt them.

APPLICATIONS

Gender Ideals in the Workplace

One should not assume that women who conform to archetypal feminine ideals fare better than those who exhibit personality traits traditionally considered masculine. In many cases for women in the workforce, a double bind exists: women who exhibit traditional feminine traits are dismissed and disrespected, while those who have more masculine traits are scorned and disliked (Berdahl, 2007).

Research on the topic of sexual harassment proposes many theories as to why sexual harassment occurs. Harassment that is motivated by sexual desire may or may not be contingent upon a condition (quid pro quo), but at least some harassment does appear to be directed toward women with archetypal feminine traits. Harassment that targets gender-role deviants (those who violate feminine ideals) is more likely to fall into the category of hostile environment (Berdahl, 2007).

Sexual Harassment as Hazing

There appear to be many factors that contribute to sexual harassment, and social scientists and others continue to question how often sex is a motive. If sexual harassment is not really about sex, but power, then the term is a bit of a misnomer. Kingsley Browne (2006) asked whether "abuse that takes a sexual form… is necessarily directed at the target 'because of the sex?'" (p. 147).

Browne suggests that the answer may be no and that sexual harassment may be just another form of hazing—which occurs between men as well as between men and women. Hazing was common in the workplace long before women entered the workforce. Browne's theory is that people who wish to offend deliver messages to which their targets will be especially sensitive. Men might use one message to harass other men (possibly sexual in nature) and a different message to harass women (very often sexual). In the majority of cases, Browne argued, harassment against women will contain sexual overtones because it is a type of harassment to which they are especially sensitive. However, the harassment may not be specifically about sex (Browne, 2006). If some sexual harassment is indeed a form of hazing— particularly in the workplace—it is possible to conclude that some harassment is about demonstrating power over others.

CONCLUSION

Perceptions of harassment vary widely. There is often ambiguity in the line between what constitutes harassment and what is just harmless attention (Osborne, 2007).

The goal of sexual harassment training is to increase employee awareness and sensitivity. However, some sociologists argue that awareness is not enough, employees need to be taught to avoid the miscommunications and attitudes that can contribute to harassment.

Sexual harassment training tends to focus on teaching employees to identify what harassment is and not very much on the underlying attitudes that contribute to harassment. It is extremely common for sexual harassment training programs to be judged upon an employee's ability to recognize sexual harassment as opposed to recognizing the actions and emotions that lead to it (Browne, 2006). In other words, employees are given many examples of what behaviors might be construed as sexual harassment, but far less information about why harassment occurs (Berdahl, 2007).

Sociologists understand that there are many theories about why sexual harassment occurs; research continues to examine the psychological and social factors that contribute to the phenomenon. Much of the literature about sexual harassment focuses on the perspective of the target rather than the harasser; however, some sociologists argue that research needs to be conducted on harassers in order to understand how to address their behavior (Browne, 2006).

TERMS & CONCEPTS

Authoritarian Personality: Types of individuals who seek to dominate others by requiring unquestioning obedience to their authority.

Benevolent Sexism: A type of sexism that, when directed against women, casts them in traditional gender roles, such as wife, mother, or homemaker, with men as their protectors.

Gender Harassment: A form of hostile environment harassment that is directed toward individuals on the basis of their gender.

Gender Ideals: Characteristics a society associates with a "model" male or female. In Western societies, male gender ideals might include independence or assertiveness, while female gender ideals might include compassion or beauty.

Hostile Environment: A form of harassment in which an atmosphere or environment intimidates, belittles, or discriminates against an individual or individuals on the basis of their gender, race, religion, national origin, age, or disability.

Hostile Sexism: A type of sexism that, when directed against women, casts them in inferior roles with men needing to control them through intimidation, threats, or violence.

Quid Pro Quo: Literally, this for that; in the context of sexual harassment law, describes cases of harassment in which granting a sexual favor is a condition for receiving a reward (e.g., being promoted) or avoiding a punishment (e.g., being fired).

Sexual Aggression: Behavior that seeks to coerce or force another into engaging in sexual behavior. On a continuum, sexually aggressive behavior can constitute nonviolent actions, such as verbal pressure, or extremely violent action, such as rape.

Token Resistance: Resistance to sexual advances that offered when the advances are actually welcome. The concept was introduced in date rape literature to explain the belief that when a woman says "no" to sex she is not actually rejecting the man's advances.

Bibliography

Begany, J. ,& Milburn, M. (2002). "Psychological predictors of sexual harassment: Authoritarianism, hostile sexism, and rape myths." University of Massachusetts. http://psych.umb.edu/faculty/milburn/Begany%20and%20Milburn.pdf

Berdahl, J. (2007) "The sexual harassment of uppity women." *Journal of Applied Psychology, 92*(2), 425–427. http://www.rotman.utoronto.ca/

Browne, K. (2006). "Sex, power and dominance, the evolutionary psychology of sexual harassment." *Managerial and Decision Economics, 27,* 145–158. http://www.law.wayne.edu

Galdi, S., Maass, A., & Cadinu, M. (2014). "Objectifying media: Their effect on gender role norms and sexual harassment of women." *Psychology of Women Quarterly, 38*(3), 398–413.

Holland, K. J., & Cortina, L. M. (2013). "When sexism and feminism collide: The sexual harassment of feminist working women." *Psychology of Women Quarterly, 37*(2), 192–208.

Leskinen, E., Cortina, L., & Kabat, D. (2011). "Gender harassment: Broadening our understanding of sex-based harassment at work." *Law & Human Behavior, 35*(1), 25–39.

MacKinnon, C. A. (1979). *Sexual harassment of working women: A case of sex discrimination.* New Haven, CT: Yale University Press. http://books.google.com/

McLaughlin, H., Uggen, C., & Blackstone, A. (2012). "Sexual harassment, workplace authority, and the paradox of power." *American Sociological Review, 77*(4), 625–647.

Nye, C. D., Brummel, B. J., & Drasgow, F. (2014). "Understanding sexual harassment using aggregate construct models." *Journal of Applied Psychology, 99*(6), 1204–1221.

Osman, S. (2004). "Victim resistance: Theory and data on understanding perceptions of sexual harassment." *Sex Roles: A Journal of Research, 50*(3/4), 267–275.

Osman, S. (2007). "Predicting perceptions of sexual harassment based on type of resistance and belief in token resistance." *Journal of Sex Research, 44*(4), 340–346.

Smith, A. B., Craver, C. B., & Turner, R. (2011). *Employment discrimination law: Cases and materials* (7th ed.). New Providence, NJ: LexisNexis.

U.S. Equal Opportunity Commission. (2002). "Federal laws prohibiting job discrimination: Questions and answers." www.eeoc.gov/facts/qanda.html

Suggested Reading

Bursik, K., & Gefter, J. (2011). "Still stable after all these years: Perceptions of sexual harassment in academic contexts." *Journal of Social Psychology, 151*(3), 331–349.

Key, C. W., & Ridge, R. D. (2011). "Guys like us: The link between sexual harassment proclivity and blame. *Journal of Social & Personal Relationships, 28*(8), 1093–1103."

McLaughlin, H., Uggen, C., & Blackstone, A. (2012). "Sexual harassment, workplace authority, and the paradox of power." *American Sociological Review,* 77(4), 625–647.

Nelson, J. (2008). "Out of bounds." *Essence, 38*(12), 160–163.

"Prevention of sexual harassment in the workplace and education setting." (2000). American Academy of Pediatrics. http://aappolicy.aappublications. org

"Sexual harassment in the workplace." (2004). Sexual Violence Justice Institute. http:// www.mncasa.org/documents/svji_fact_sheets/Sexual%20 Harassment.pdf

Carolyn Sprague, MLS

Sexual Orientation and Youth

ABSTRACT

This article explores the developmental and interpersonal experiences by young people as they pertain to gender and sexual orientation. Cognitive isolation from self is one of the unique characteristics of youth struggling with their sexual orientation or identifying as part of a minority sexual orientation group. Sexual orientation outside heterosexuality is referred to as; lesbian, gay, bisexual, transgendered, queer/questioning, intersex and asexual (LBGTQQIA). More commonly this acronym is known as, LBGTQQ and will be referred to as that hereafter. As LBGTQ individuals gain self-knowledge, they are challenged by the choices of invisibility versus self-disclosure and safety versus self-respect. By focusing on shifting American views of LBGTQ issues in relation to adolescent gender and sexual orientation development, this article explores the challenges facing LBGTQ youth and adults.

OVERVIEW

On February 12, 2008, 15-year-old Lawrence King was shot twice in the head as he sat in his Oxnard, California, junior high school computer lab working on a paper. King had been teased by his peers since he had started elementary school because of his effeminate mannerisms. By the age of 10, he had confirmed their accusations, stating that he was gay and sometimes dressing in women's clothing. With Valentine's Day approaching, female friends of King started asking male classmates to be their Valentines. King asked a 14-year-old male student to be his Valentine, and the next day that student brought a handgun to school and killed him (Setoodeh, 2008). According to Katherine Newman's study on school shootings, youth affected by another junior high school shooting in Westside, Arkansas, reported that being called "gay" was a "catastrophic" epithet that would destroy their standing with their peers (Newman, 2004, p. 38). Throughout Newman's analyses of school shootings nationwide, anxiety about sexual orientation played a major role in these murderous confrontations. Thus, despite the profound advancements made in social equality in terms of sexual orientation nationwide, at this time there are also real risks and threats that confront lesbian, gay, bisexual, and transgendered (LBGTQ) individuals every day in our society.

Sexual orientation can be defined in many ways, but the most familiar definitions are the legal ones: heterosexuality, homosexuality and bisexuality. Heterosexuality is a sexual attraction to individuals of the opposite gender, and homosexuality is an attraction to individuals of the same gender. Bisexuality is an attraction to both men and women, although some individuals choose to use the word "polysexual" to avoid the assumption that only two genders exist. Asexuality is a lack of sexual interest altogether. Individuals also might define themselves as pansexual, which means that they express their sexuality in many forms.

Transgender is an umbrella term that includes transvestites and transsexuals. Transvestites are individuals who wear the clothing normally worn by members of the opposite gender in a given society and adopt the stereotypical attributes or mannerisms associated with that gender. Transvestites can be heterosexual, homosexual or bisexual, since their pleasure in wearing the clothing of the opposite gender does not necessarily have anything to do with their sexual orientation. Transsexuals are individuals who feel that their gender identity is different from the one that they were assigned at birth. They may choose to ignore these feelings or, alternately, choose to pass as the opposite gender. Some may choose to undergo gender reassignment through hormone therapy or surgery. Some advocates for transgender individuals are today questioning the requirement for hormone therapy and surgery for an individual to change his or her legally recognized gender, arguing that this process enhances traditional, distorted views of gender in our society rather than supports diversity in gender existence. In terms of their sexual orientation, transgendered individuals who are attracted to women express gynephilia, while individuals attracted to men express androphilia. Queer is an umbrella term used to express sexual flexibility, not conforming to one definition or sexual identity. We also see the Q at times meaning, questioning, which can be used to express that a person is still exploring their sexual orientation. Estimates number of individuals who are gay or lesbian in our culture vary. Some polls indicate a nationwide average of between 3.5 and 4 percent. Since, however, surveys require self-identification, it is difficult to get a fully accurate count—self-identifying as LBGTQ can depend on personal comfort with being out, with the region of the world the respondent lives in, and with how an individual sees himself or herself.

Determining Sexual Orientation

Scholars continue to debate how to determine an individual's sexual orientation, with some relying solely on self-identification and others also taking into account the individual's sexual behavior. For example, if a man has been married to a woman for 30 years and then comes out as gay, understanding his sexuality can be complex. People may choose to identify with a certain sexuality but never have any sexual experiences to confirm their chosen identification. Complicating the matter is the fact some individuals identify with a different sexual orientations at various times in their lives, depending upon their relationships and their state of mind. Conversely, other individuals adhere to one sexual orientation even in the face of numerous sexual encounters that would seem to indicate a different orientation (e.g. a man who identifies himself as heterosexual yet also engages in homosexual encounters). Further, genital sex is not considered a prerequisite for a homosexual or heterosexual identity, meaning that an individual may consider him or herself homosexual without having ever engaged in homosexual intercourse. Part of the LGBTQ movement is the push for open self-identification, since sexuality is truly a internalized experience.

Youth, Social & Sexual Identity

At this time in our society, given the increased visibility of variations on sexual orientation, young people are announcing their sexual identity at a younger age. In the 1970s, it was typical for gay and lesbian individuals to solidify their sexual orientation identity in their mid-to-late twenties. Now, young people are beginning to express their identities in middle and high school, in part because of the greater visibility of LBGTQ issues in our society as well as the increased support for these young people in our schools, religious institutions, and families.

Like other forms of oppression and discrimination, hostility toward LBGTQ individuals (also called "homophobia" or, in the case of transgender individuals, "transphobia") takes a great toll on the individual's sense of being a whole, good, and acceptable person. These negative feelings toward self are called internalized homophobia. Thus, this discussion will start with the individual and early childhood experiences.

Most children are born into family settings that mirror their social identities. In these families, race, gender, ethnicity, linguistic expression, religious orientation, and most of the social categories that define one in relation to family, community, church, and country are cohesive. There are some exceptions, such as children born with mental or physical challenges and interracial adoptions. In general, however, the child reflects the parental social identity, and, ideally, he or she is treasured within the family even if social oppression, such as racism, devalues the child in the wider world. Further, family and supportive community members can prepare the child to face social oppression and can convey to the child their own experiences and a sense of pride in his or her cultural identity. But, even with the best intentioned of parents, LBGTQ children usually grow up in a very different context (Harbeck, 2007).

Often very early in their development, LBGTQ individuals realize that they are different. Until relatively recently, though, there was little accurate information available in our culture on LBGTQ issues to help these individuals form a positive identity. Negative stereotypes and abusive comments abound, even within the close confines of home, church, and community. In fact, LBGTQ youth face high rates of child abuse and neglect as parents, sensing that a LBGTQ child is different, may react hostilely in order to change the child or punish him or her. LBGTQ youth also lack positive role models and mentors, especially when they are young and beginning to realize that they are different. Many of the development processes and rites of passage of our society, which is predominately heterosexual and androcentric, only add to the torment.

As LBGTQ children gain in self-knowledge, they quickly realize that expressing their questions and feelings could be profoundly harmful. Parents and friends may understand, but LBGTQ youth also face a high risk of being shamed, teased, bullied, abused, or even thrown out of their homes by disapproving parents. Their cognitive confusion can increase, though, if they try to hide their identity by lying or isolating themselves from similar individuals or engage in risky behaviors. Some LBGTQ individuals manage their identity by trying to be perfect within all the other realms of their lives. Others drop out of school or are frequently truant in order to avoid gym class, public restrooms, lockers, and other situations that might lead to greater exposure to or harm from others.

With LBGTQ individuals becoming more visible and with politicians and church leaders becoming more vocal on LBGTQ issues, children now learn of their sexual or gender orientation at a much earlier age. Instead of spending twenty-five or more years processing this identity and the developing the skills they needed to manage it in our society, young people are now declaring their sexual orientation to their peers as teenagers. One can see why LBGTQ issues have taken on a whole new dimension in our nation's schools, which often lack the ability to provide positive, safe, interpersonal discussions about these socially and politically fraught issues.

FURTHER INSIGHTS

"Coming Out"

By telling a few close peers that one may be gay, lesbian, bisexual or transgender, children often unknowingly "come out" to most of the other children in their schools and communities. In this age of digital communications, stories abound of young people broadcasting a child's orientation throughout the school community within minutes of its disclosure. Such an act can heighten an already physically and emotionally risky situation by confirming rumors that may have circulated about the child. Harbeck has argued that this is a critical point for the welfare of all the children involved, and that adult's actions and role modeling can play a key role in determining outcomes (2007).

Parents, teachers, and administrators can use such a situation to reinforce the priority of making sure that all children are physically and emotionally safe in the school by helping children learn about LBGTQ issues in a positive manner as well as how to deal with their differences peaceably. But if parents and school personnel ignore the issues or make derogatory jokes or comments, they can signal to other students at the school that bullying or violence against LBGTQ youth is acceptable. Thus, LBGTQ and questioning youth can be subjected to unchecked emotional and physical abuse at their schools, traveling to and from school, and whenever they are out within the community (Harbeck, 2007).

Some LBGTQ youth, like Lawrence King, flaunt their sexual and gender orientation in order to cope with crisis of identity and conflicts it can impose. Other LBGTQ youth and adults internalize homophobia and develop a sense of self-hatred. This can lead to self-destructive behaviors, such as drinking, drugs, and engaging in unprotected sex. LBGTQ youth rejected by their parents can face homelessness and may engage in sex with older adults for money or housing. More often than not, these sexual acts occur with substance abuse and unprotected sex, exposing the youth to HIV and other sexually transmitted diseases.

Youth Suicide

Probably the most often cited concern for LBGTQ youth is the high rate of suicide, suicide attempts, and suicidal ideation. The risk of suicide for LBGTQ youth is higher than for the rest of the population. Parents fear it when they find out their child is LBGTQ; social conservatives employ it to demonstrate that being LBGTQ is deviant and wrong; and well-meaning but poorly informed individuals quote it as if there were an inexorable link between being LBGTQ and committing suicide.

When one reviews the literature on childhood suicide, though, one discovers that the indicating conditions for an at-risk child are isolation, low self-esteem, alcohol abuse, and depression. A catalyst for a suicide attempt under these conditions, then, is often rejection by a peer or parent. Additionally, the issue of cyberbullying in the 2000s has been an increasingly important factor in harassment and youth suicide. Placed within this larger empirical analysis of youth suicide, then, it is clear that LBGTQ youth, under the circumstances set forth above, are more likely to experience the indicators for suicide risk.

As in all youth suicide prevention efforts, we need to identify and reduce the risks faced by all children, but not label their identity as the causal factor of those risks. Studies do suggest that the earlier children become aware of their sexual orientations, and the earlier they disclose their sexual orientation to peers, the higher their risk of attempting suicide. Many of these same youth reported greater loss of friends because of their sexual orientation as well as a higher frequency of going to bars and drinking, despite being underage.

In the early 2000s there was a string of high-profile LBGTQ teen suicides, including those of thirteen-year-old Ryan Halligan in 2003, Rutgers student Tyler Clementi in 2010, and fourteen-year-old Jamey Rodemeyer in 2011, who had himself tried to help victims of bullying. In response, projects such as the It Gets Better Project spread messages that the difficult lives of LBGTQ teens will improve; the project started with video messages from gay adults and some celebrities, and by 2013 included tens of thousands of videos from a diverse body of contributors. Additionally, policies and programs have been developed in communities and schools to protect LBGTQ youth from bullying and offer support and resources.

Rejection

Many LBGTQ youth and adults face rejection from their parents, siblings, teachers, employers, church leaders, peers, and others. They can experience physical and emotion abuse, neglect, and homelessness. A 2012 study by the Williams Institute suggests that as many as 40 percent of all homeless youth are LBGTQ. Interpersonal development is hindered because LBGTQ individuals may not fit in with their heterosexual counterparts and lack the support of other LBGTQ individuals. Not surprisingly, many LBGTQ adults conceal their sexual orientation or are afraid that if they work with LBGTQ youth, they will be accused of pedophilia. Thus, LBGTQ youth are one of the few minority groups that face a lack of leadership and mentoring by like-identified individuals. Similarly, because their social bonds with parents, peers, and others may be disrupted, LBGTQ youth and adults may develop difficulties forming close personal or intimate relationships that are in concert with their LBGTQ identities. Like the individuals described above in the public restroom studies, some LBGTQ individuals may remain in the closet and pass as heterosexual or turn to anonymous homosexual sex.

People of Color (POC)

Another intersection that is important to address is LGBTQ youth who also belong to the POC community. Belonging to both a sexual minority and a racial minority group has its own unique and complex challenges for youth. Growing up as a racial minority youth face oppression, prejudice, racism and less societal opportunity. These youth learn at a young age how the world views them and have to develop strategies to deal with these inherent disadvantages. For example, a young black boy may be told by his mother that the police are going to always view him differently and that he must engage in extremely respectful behavior to not be received with violence. Adding the next layer of being a sexual minority, this person now has the increased challenges of being discriminated against all over again. POC youth may have an increased difficult time "coming out" or may choose to never come out at all due to the potential lack of acceptance or increased societal disapproval. In the example above a black youth may be outwardly told that being gay is going to make his life much harder and encouraged to change his identification. The intersection of the LGBT and POC minorities put youth at risk for higher levels of rejection, struggles "coming out", suicide and other societal disadvantages.

Other Risks

Studies of LBGTQ youth sexuality suggest that factors like low self-esteem, self-hatred, denial, substance abuse, and a lack of financial resources and access to condoms can increase a sexually active LBGTQ youth's likelihood of being raped or contracting a sexually transmitted disease. Knowing the risks of their behavior, these young people can experience a cycle of despair in which they can feel that they have little hope for the future. Throughout their lives, LBGTQ individuals must balance invisibility and disclosure, safety and self-respect. Like all individuals, but with added challenges, LBGTQ individuals must work to develop close interpersonal relationships and loving same-sex intimate bonds.

ISSUES

Besides schools, families, religious organizations and communities, all too often the professionals who provide physical and mental health services do not recognize LBGTQ issues or know how to address them. Heterosexual professionals may fear that if they demonstrate concern for these issues, their colleagues may label them LBGTQ too. And while this prejudice can hurt emotionally, it can also be paired with acts of discrimination, such as a loss of credibility, being overlooked for promotions, or job loss.

Studies on attitudinal change as it relates to interpersonal prejudice suggest that positive, repeated, and sustained interactions with individuals who are different from oneself enhances feelings of acceptance, while short, stereotypical interactions exacerbate prejudices. Taking Lawrence King's story as an example, the extreme, sexualized advances by an out, gay, cross-dressing student may cause some to dismiss the murder, just as they may have exacerbated the cause of the murder. What is missed in many discussions of LBGTQ issues, though, is the realization that hundreds of thousands of young people deal with issues of sexual orientation in their everyday lives and that many face rejection and physical and emotional abuse if they don't adhere to our society's heterosexual and gender norms.

TERMS & CONCEPTS

Androphilia: Having a sexual attraction to males.

Asexual: A person having no sexual attraction to others.

Gynephilia: Having a sexual attraction to females.

Heterosexism: A culturally embedded ideology which privileges heterosexual behavior, relationships, and communities over homosexual behavior, relationships, and communities. A heterosexist society may openly denigrate or stigmatize homosexuality, or seek to simply make it invisible.

Homophobia: An aversion to homosexual people or culture.

Intersex: An individual born with sex characteristics of both sex or unable to be determined.

Pansexual: A term adopted by individuals who believe that human sexuality is a continuum of genders and are attracted to all of these genders.

POC: People of color.

Polysexual: A term adopted by individuals who believe that human sexuality is a continuum of genders and are attracted to some, but not all, of these genders.

Queer: A person not wanting to identify with one sexuality. An umbrella term for sexual minorities to express sexual fluidity or sexual freedom.

Questioning: A person who is continuing to determine their sexuality.

Bibliography

Datta, V., Bialer, P. A., McIntosh, C. A. (2017). Queer invisible: OLGBTQ people of color and mental health. *United Kingdom: Taylor & Francis.*

Dragowski, E. A., Halkitis, P. N., Grossman, A. H., & D'Augelli, A. R. (2011). "Sexual orientation victimization and posttraumatic stress symptoms among lesbian, gay, and bisexual youth." *Journal of Gay & Lesbian Social Services,* 23, 226–249.

Frankowski, B., Kaplan, D., Diaz, A., Feinstein, R., Fisher, M., Klein, J., Yancy, S., et al. (2004). "Sexual orientation and adolescents." *Pediatrics,* 113, 1827-1832.

Grzanka, P. R., & Mann, E. S. (2014). "Queer youth suicide and the psychopolitics of 'It Gets Better.'" *Sexualities,* 17, 369–393.

Harbeck, K. (2007). *Gay, lesbian, bisexual, and transgender youth in American schools and colleges.* Malden, MA: Amethyst Press.

Harbeck, K. (2007). *The legal rights of gay, lesbian, bisexual, and transgendered youth and adults in educational settings.* Malden, MA: Amethyst Press.

Harbeck, K. (2001). *Invisible no more: Addressing the needs of gay, lesbian, bisexual and transgender youth in schools and their advocates.* Malden, MA: Amethyst Press.

Harbeck, K. (1997). *Gay and lesbian educators: Personal freedoms/Public constraints.* Malden, MA: Amethyst Press.

Harbeck, K. (Ed.), (1991). *Coming out of the classroom closet: Gay and lesbian students, teachers, and curricula.* New York: Haworth.

Higa, D., Hoppe, M. J., Lindhorst, T., Mincer, S., Beadnell, B., Morrison, D. M., Wells, E. A., Todd, A., & Mountz, S. (2014). "Negative and positive factors associated with the well-being of lesbian, gay, bisexual, transgender, queer, and questioning (LBGTQQ) youth." *Youth & Society,* 46, 663–687.

Humphreys, L. (1970). *Tearoom trade: Impersonal sex in public places.* Chicago: Aldine-Atherton.

Jimenez, L. M. (2018). Poc, lgbtq, and gender: The intersectionality of America Chavez. *United Kingdom: Taylor & Francis.*

Newman, K. (2004). *Rampage: The social roots of school shootings.* New York: Basic Books.

Priebe, G., & Svedin, C. (2013). "Operationalization of three dimensions of sexual orientation in a national survey of late adolescents." *Journal of Sex Research,* 50, 727–738.

Reitman, D. (2006). Sexuality: Sexual orientation. eMedicine, http://www.emedicine.com/ped/TOPIC2773.htm.

Robertson, M. (2014). "'How do I know I am gay?': Understanding sexual orientation, identity and behavior among adolescents in an LBGTQ youth center." *Sexuality & Culture,* 18 (2), 385-404.

Saewyc, E. M. (2011). "Research on adolescent sexual orientation: Development, health disparities, stigma, and resilience." *Journal of Research on Adolescence,* 21, 256–272.

Setoodeh, R. (2008, July 28). "Young, gay and murdered." *Newsweek,* 152, 40-46.

Suggested Reading

Blackless, M., Charwastra, A., & Derrych, A., Fausto-Sterling, A., Lavzabbem K., & Lee, E. (2000). "How sexually dimorphic are we? Review and synthesis." *American Journal of Human Biology,* 12, 151-166.

Blumenfeld, W. (Ed.), (1992). *Homophobia: How we all pay the price.* Boston, MA: Beacon.

Blumenfeld, W., & Raymond, D. (1993). *Looking at gay and lesbian life.* Boston, MA: Beacon.

Conley, C. L. (2011). "Learning about a child's gay or lesbian sexual orientation: Parental concerns about societal rejection, loss of loved ones, and child well being." *Journal of Homosexuality,* 58, 1022–1040.

DeHaan, S., Kuper, L. E., Magee, J. C., Bigelow, L., & Mustanski, B. S. (2013). "The interplay between online and offline explorations of identity, relationships, and sex: A mixed-methods study with LBGTQ youth." *Journal of Sex Research,* 50, 421–434.

Diamant, L. & McAnulty, R. (Eds.). (1995). *The psychology of sexual orientation, behavior, and identity: A handbook.* Westport, CT: Greenwood.

Dreger, A. (1998). Ambiguous sex—or ambivalent medicine? Ethical issues in the treatment of intersexuality. *Hastings Center Report, 28,* 24-35. http://www.isna.org/articles/ambivalent%5fmedicine

Hurst, C. (1992). *Social inequality: Forms, causes, and consequences.* Needham, MA: Allyn and Bacon.

Orne, J. (2013). "Queers in the line of fire: Goffman's *Stigma* revisited." *Sociological Quarterly,* 54, 229–253.

Remafedi, G. (1999). "Sexual orientation and youth suicide." *Journal of the American Medical Association,* 282, 1291-1292.

Remafedi, G., Resnick, M., Blum, R., & Harris, L. (1992, April). "Demography of sexual orientation in adolescents." *Pediatrics,* 89, 714-721.

Stone, D. M., Feijun, L., Lijing, O., Lippy, C., Hertz, M. F., & Crosby, A. E. (2014). "Sexual orientation and suicide ideation, plans, attempts, and medically serious attempts: Evidence from local youth risk behavior surveys, 2001-2009." *American Journal of Public Health,* 104 (2), 262-271.

Karen M. Harbeck, Ph.D., J.D., and Kimberly Ortiz-Hartman, Psy.D., LMFT

Sexual Orientation in the United States

ABSTRACT

This article explores issues of discrimination and institutional social inequality as they pertain to sexual orientation and gender identity. Lesbian, gay, bisexual, transgender, and queer (LGBTQ) individuals face numerous social inequities that affect their employment, health, welfare, and families. Court challenges and legislative action over the past twenty-five years have radically expanded the rights of LGBTQ individuals.

OVERVIEW

Margaret was married to a man for seventeen years and has three grown children. She is employed as a radiologist, makes a reasonable salary, and worries about her retirement funds. Mark is a former Navy officer who now writes articles for national newspapers. He is happily married and is thinking of buying a summer home with his spouse. Jodie adopted a daughter late in life and faces the joys and challenges of raising a child as an older parent. These identity descriptions may or may not be of people who identify also as lesbian, gay, bisexual, and transgender (LGBTQ) because individuals do not define themselves solely on the basis of their sexual orientation. However, to a large degree, society does define them as such. Each of these individuals has faced job losses, threats to child custody, the inability to marry their partners, acts of hostility from family and strangers, and the loss of financial entitlements, which their heterosexual counterparts take for granted. Sometimes the prejudice and discrimination is deadly.

On February 12, 2008, fifteen-year-old Lawrence King was shot twice in the head as he sat in his Oxnard, California, junior high school computer lab working on a paper. King had been teased by his peers since he had started elementary school because of his effeminate mannerisms. By the age of ten, he had confirmed their accusations, stating that he was gay and sometimes dressing in women's clothing. In 2008, with Valentine's Day approaching and his female friends asking male classmates to be their valentines, King approached a fourteen-year-old male student to be his Valentine. The next day that student brought a handgun to school and killed him (Setoodeh, 2008). According to Katherine Newman's study on school shootings, youth reported that being called "gay" was a "catastrophic" epithet that would destroy their standing with their peers (Newman, 2004, p.38). Throughout Newman's analyses of school shootings nationwide, anxiety about sexual orientation played a major role in some of these murderous confrontations. Thus, despite the profound nationwide advancements made in social equality in terms of sexual orientation, real risks and threats still confront LGBTQ individuals every day.

Sexual orientation can be defined in many ways but the most familiar definitions are heterosexuality, homosexuality, and bisexuality. Heterosexuality is a physical, romantic, and/or emotional attraction to individuals of the opposite gender, while homosexuality is an attraction to individuals of the same gender. Bisexuality is an attraction to both men and women, although some individuals choose to use the word "polysexual" to avoid the assumption that only two genders exist. Transgender is an umbrella term for people whose gender identity (a person's internal, deeply held sense of their gender) or gender expression (external manifestations of gender, such as clothing, haircut, or body characteristics) is different from what is typically associated with the sex they were assigned at birth. Some transgender individuals choose to alter their birth sex through hormone therapy and sex reassignment surgery. In addition to the medical procedures of hormone therapy and surgery, this transition also involves personal and legal steps such as change one's name and sex on legal documents and telling one's friends, family members, and coworkers. Queer is an umbrella term for people who identify as a sexual minority, however might not feel that they fit into any of the other labels.

Whatever the developmental or physiological processes that play a role in sexual orientation, it is individuals' self-knowledge, self-acceptance, and identity that ultimately defines their sexual orientation. If fact, a person need not have engaged in genital sex, either heterosexual or homosexual, in order to define his or her sexual orientation. Similarly, some individuals identify with a specific sexual orientation at various times in their lives, depending upon their relationships. Conversely, some individuals adhere to a heterosexual identity even in the face of numerous homosexual encounters. Homophobia, or hostility towards LGBTQ individuals, has been codified in English, French, and Spanish law for centuries, so it is not surprising that since the founding of the American colonies, US laws have contained sanctions against same-sex relationships. Changes in contemporary attitudes toward privacy, self-expression, and individual and minority rights have lead to many changes in the laws governing the lives of LGBTQ individuals. The balance of this article will look at those institutional and legislative changes and the continuing discrimination faced by LGBTQ individuals in American society.

VIEWPOINTS

One of the most contentious issues surrounding sexual orientation in the United States has been sodomy laws. Sodomy is legally defined as any anal or oral contact during a sexual act with another person or any sexual act that does not lead to procreation. Although it is likely that most heterosexual individuals have violated sodomy laws, in reality the majority of individuals prosecuted under sodomy laws have been LGBTQ. The laws were still in place in fourteen states until 2003 when the Supreme Court, in *Lawrence v. Texas,* struck down the selective application of sodomy laws to LGBTQ individuals, ruling that the due process clause protects adults' freedom to engage in private, consensual sexual acts. In the majority opinion, Justice Anthony M. Kennedy wrote that "the Texas statute furthers no legitimate state interest which can justify its intrusion into the personal and private life of the individual." Thus, LGBTQ individuals, like heterosexual individuals, are now free to engage in sexual activity without fear of being arrested or labeled sex offenders for engaging in same-sex intercourse. However, more than ten years after *Lawrence v. Texas,* only two states that had sodomy laws prior to the ruling—Montana and Virginia—repealed their sodomy laws. In 2014, sodomy laws remained on the books in Alabama, Florida, Idaho, Kansas, Louisiana, Michigan, Mississippi, North Carolina, Oklahoma, South Carolina, Texas, and Utah.

The inclusion of LGBTQ individuals in the military has also been a significant issue throughout recent decades. Hundreds of thousands of LGBTQ individuals have served in the US military over the centuries, but their service became a major issue during the 1940s and 1950s as Senator Joseph McCarthy led a campaign to blacklist and dishonorably discharge known homosexual service members from the military (Harbeck, 1997). After the Clinton administration, the official governmental policy toward LGBTQ individuals serving in the military was "Don't Ask, Don't Tell" (DADT). A significant number of current and former service members supported the policy, but advocates for the policy's repeal claimed that it left LGBTQ military personnel exposed to blackmail, resulted in the dismissal of thousands of otherwise qualified servicemen and servicewomen, and stood as an example of state-sanctioned discrimination. The Don't Ask, Don't Tell Repeal Act was enacted in 2010, and the DADT policy officially ended on September 20, 2011, after receiving certification from President Barack Obama, Secretary of Defense Leon Panetta, and Chair of the Joint Chiefs of Staff Admiral Mike Mullen.

Similarly to the DADT policy, many LGBTQ civilians have faced job loss when their sexual orientation was discovered. This began to change in 1982 when Wisconsin became the first state to prohibit sexual orientation discrimination in employment, including hiring, promotions, job assignments, termination, compensation, and harassment. As of 2016, only nineteen states have employment nondiscrimination laws that cover sexual orientation and gender identity; an additional three states have laws that bar employment discrimination based on sexual orientation but not gender identity. Some states offer protection against discrimination in public employment. In 1998, President Bill Clinton signed Executive Order 13087 to prohibit sexual orientation discrimination in the competitive service of the federal civilian workforce. The administration of President Obama began to include gender identity as a class protected against discrimination as part of the Equal Employment Opportunity Commission (EEOC) in 2010. Two years later, in April 2012, the EEOC added gender identity as a protected class under the ban on sex discrimination in the Civil Rights Act. In 2015, the EEOC concluded that Title

VII of the Civil Rights Act of 1964 prohibits employment discrimination based on an individual's sexual orientation because it is a form of sex discrimination; however, this ruling may not be legally binding in court.

Federal and state legislators have worked to expand hate crime laws to include sexual orientation and gender identity. The Hate Crimes Statistics Act was passed in 1990 and required the Justice Department to collect data on "crimes that manifest evidence of prejudice based on race, religion, disability, sexual orientation, or ethnicity," but sexual orientation is not listed as a protected class in the 1969 federal hate crime law (Federal Bureau of Investigation, 2004, ¶ 2). However, Public Law 103-322A, which was enacted in 1994 to provide stiffer penalties for hate crimes, does list sexual orientation as a class against which a hate crime can be committed. In 2009 the Hate Crimes Statistics Act was modified by the Matthew Shepard and James Byrd, Jr. Hate Crime Prevention Act.

The Matthew Shepard and James Byrd, Jr. Hate Crime Prevention Act (known more commonly as the Matthew Shepard Act or the Hate Crime Prevention Act) was introduced in Congress in honor of a gay college student, Matthew Shepard, who was murdered in Laramie, Wyoming, in 1998. The act was signed into law in October 2009 and amended the 1969 United States federal hate crimes law to include crimes motivated by a victim's real or perceived sexual orientation, gender identity, or disability. Among other aspects, the bill also expands the scope and funding for investigations and prosecutions. It also extended protection for transgender individuals.

One of the major milestones in the fight for LGBTQ civil rights has been same-sex marriage. Opponents of same-sex marriage argued that, if legalized, it would undermine the stability of the family and society by radically redefining marriage and give legal precedent for the legalization of other prohibited marital practices such as polygamy. Advocates, on the other hand, argued that state and federal constitutions should be amended to ban discrimination on the basis of gender. One major factor behind this demand for recognition was that over two hundred entitlements granted to married, heterosexual couples were denied to LGBTQ couples who were not allowed to marry. Many of those entitlements pertain to employment issues, including but not limited to "medical, dental, and vision insurance, disability and life insurance, pension benefits, family and bereavement leave, adoption assistance, education and tuition assistance, credit union membership, relocation and travel expenses and inclusion of parties at company events" (Human Rights Campaign, 2008, ¶ 5). Reductions in taxes, increases in deductions and entitlements, probate protections, child custody, health care assurances, and medical authority over one's partner are just a few of the additional entitlements granted to married couples.

The 1996 Defense of Marriage Act (DOMA) prohibited the federal government from recognizing same-sex marriages, civil unions, and domestic partnerships and allowed states to refuse to recognize them as well, even if the marriages, unions, and partnerships were recognized in other states. In the landmark case *United States v. Windsor* (2013), the Supreme Court deemed that DOMA was unconstitutional because it violated the due process clause of the Fifth Amendment. The ruling allowed LGBTQ couples who were legally married in their own states to receive federal benefits and protections that they had previously been denied. In *Obergefell v. Hodges*, another landmark case, the Supreme Court ruled on June 26, 2015, that the right to marry is a fundamental liberty protected by the due process clause of the Fourteenth Amendment, thereby making same-sex marriage legal in all fifty states.

Worldwide, same-sex marriage was legal in twenty-one countries as of January 2016 (2015 and came into effect on March 1, 2017.) The Netherlands (2000), Belgium (2003), Canada (2005), Spain (2005), South Africa (2006), Norway (2009), Sweden (2009), Argentina (2010), Iceland (2010), Portugal (2010), Denmark (2012), Brazil (2013), England and Wales (2013), France (2013), New Zealand (2013), Uruguay (2013), Luxembourg (2014), Scotland (2014), Ireland (2015), the United States (2015), and Finland (2017) all have recognized same-sex marriages under their national laws. However, LGBTQ couples still face barriers in adoption in several states in the United States and in most countries worldwide.

Thus, while LGBTQ individuals are not so different from their heterosexual counterparts, the legal and social reality is that many do not enjoy the same opportunities, protections, and benefits as heterosexual individuals. While many advances have been made, it also is the case that LGBTQ individuals are still subject to violence, discrimination, prejudice, prohibitions because of their sexual orientation.

TERMS AND CONCEPTS

Civil Union: A form of legal union which allows same sex couples to receive the state rights and benefits conferred upon heterosexual couples. Same-sex couples in civil unions are not eligible for the federal benefits conferred upon heterosexual couples, and states are not required to recognize civil unions that are recognized in other states.

Codified: To arrange things, especially laws and principles, into an organized system.

Domestic Partnership: A form of legal union similar to civil unions in that it grants same-sex couples the state rights and benefits conferred upon heterosexual couples. However, same-sex couples in domestic partnerships generally receive fewer rights and benefits than same-sex couples in civil unions. Same-sex couples in domestic partnerships are not eligible for federal benefits conferred upon heterosexual couples, and states are not required to recognize domestic partnerships that are recognized in other states.

Don't Ask, Don't Tell: A federal policy toward the question of LGBTQ individuals serving in the military that was in effect from 1994 to 2011. In it, the government did not ask recruits about their sexual orientation or gender identity, and LGBTQ military personnel were obliged to keep their orientations and identities private if they wished to serve.

Homophobia: An indiscriminate fear, condemnation, or hatred of homosexual individuals or homosexual culture.

Polysexual: A term used by individuals who are attracted to both men and women, but who chose not to use the term bisexual because they do not believe that there are only two genders, biologically speaking.

Protected Class: Groups of people defined within anti-discrimination law as being protected from discrimination and harassment. At the federal level, race, religion, color, national origin, age, sex, disability status, and veteran status are all protected classes. Some states have also chosen to include sexual orientation as a protected class within their anti-discrimination laws.

BIBLIOGRAPHY

Baunach, D. (2012). "Changing same-sex marriage attitudes in America from 1988 through 2010." *Public Opinion Quarterly,* 76, 364–378.

Bernstein, M. (2015). "Same-sex marriage and the future of the LGBTQ movement." *Gender and Society,* 29 (3), 321–337.

Craney, R. S., Watson, L. B., Brownfield, J., & Flores, M. J. (2018). Bisexual women's discriminatory experiences and psychological distress: Exploring the roles of coping and LGBTQ community connectedness. *Psychology of Sexual Orientation and Gender Diversity, 5,* (3), 324-337.

Frank, N. (2013). "The president's pleasant surprise: How LGBTQ advocates ended Don't Ask, Don't Tell." *Journal of Homosexuality,* 60 (2/3), 159–213.

Frankowski, B. (2004). "Sexual orientation and adolescents." *Pediatrics,* 113, 1827-1832.

Federal Bureau of Investigation. (2004). Appendix A. http://www.fbi.gov

Gates, G. J. (2015). "Marriage and family: LGBTQ individuals and same-sex couples." *Future of Children,* 25 (2), 67–87.

Harbeck, K. (1997). "Gay and lesbian educators: Personal freedoms/ Public constraints." Malden, MA: Amethyst Press.

Human Rights Campaign. (2008). "Domestic partner benefits." www.hrc.org/issues/workplace/benefits/4814.htm

"Legal recognition of same-sex relationships." (2013). *Georgetown Journal of Gender & the Law,* 14, 517–551.

Matthew Shepard Foundation. (2007). "Hate crimes legislation." http://www.matthewshepard.org/

National Gay and Lesbian Task Force. (2008a). "Adoption laws in the United States." http://www.thetaskforce.org/

National Gay and Lesbian Task Force. (2008b). "Hate crime laws in the U.S." http://www.thetaskforce.org/

National Gay and Lesbian Task Force. (2008c). "Relationship recognition for same-sex couples in the U.S." http://www.thetaskforce.org/

Newman, K. (2004). *Rampage: The social roots of school shootings.* New York: Basic.
Reitman, D. (2006). "Sexuality: Sexual orientation." http://www.emedicine.com/ped/TOPIC2773.htm.
Setoodeh, R. (2008, July 28). "Young, gay and murdered." *Newsweek,* 152, 40-46.

Suggested Reading

Axel-Lute, P. "Same-sex marriage: A selective bibliography of the legal literature." http://law-library.rutgers.edu/SSM.html.
Baunach, D., & Burgess, E. O. (2013). "Sexual identity in the American deep south: The concordance and discordance of sexual activity, relationships, and identities." *Journal of Homosexuality,* 60, 1315–1335.
Blumenfeld, W. (Ed.). (1992). *Homophobia: How we all pay the price.* Boston, MA: Beacon.
Blumenfeld, W., & Raymond, D. (1993). *Looking at gay and lesbian life.* Boston, MA: Beacon.
Diamant, L. & McAnulty, R. (Eds.), (1995). *The psychology of sexual orientation, behavior, and identity: A handbook.* Westport, CT: Greenwood.
"End of 'Don't Ask, Don't Tell' and Defense of Marriage Act collide." (2011). *Contemporary Sexuality,* 45, 6.
Eskridge, Jr., W. (2008). *Dishonorable passions: Sodomy laws in America, 1861–2003.* New York: Viking.
Eskridge, Jr., W. (2006). *Gay marriage: For better or for worse? What we've learned from the evidence.* New York: Oxford University Press.
Faderman, L. (2015). *The gay revolution: The story of the struggle.* New York: Simon and Schuster.
Harbeck, K. (Ed.), (1991). *Coming out of the classroom closet: Gay and lesbian students, teachers, and curricula.* New York: Haworth.
Harbeck, K. (2007). *The legal rights of gay, lesbian, bisexual, and transgendered youth and adults in educational settings.* Malden, MA: Amethyst Press.
Hunter, N.; Joslin, C.; & McGowan, S. (2004) *The rights of lesbians, gay men, bisexuals, and transgender people: The authoritative ACLU Guide.* (4th ed.) New York: New York University Press.
Hurst, C. (1992). *Social inequality: Forms, causes, and consequences.* Needham, MA: Allyn and Bacon.
Pierceson, J. (2005). *Courts, liberalism and rights: Gay law and politics in the United States and Canada.* Philadelphia, PA: Temple University Press.
Pinello, D. (2006). *America's struggle for same-sex marriage.* New York: Cambridge University Press.
McWhorter, B. (2006). *Gay and lesbian rights.* (2nd ed.). Naperville, IL: Sphinx.

Karen M. Harbeck, Ph.D., J.D., and
Kimberly Ortiz-Hartman, Psy.D., LMFT

Sexuality and the Media

ABSTRACT

Sexuality—a person's ability to be sexual—is a concept that has changed over the years. So, too, has America's response to it. Explicit sexual references are common in various media sources and are viewed as normal by the public. This may result in young girls behaving in unhealthy sexual ways. Research studies focusing on the influences of some of those media sources are described here. *Seventeen, Cosmopolitan,* and *Cleo* magazines are discussed, as are hip-hop music videos and the internet site MySpace. In contrast, other media sources have been shown to send positive messages, including those concentrating on safe sex, pregnancy prevention, and other healthy behaviors. Some of those sources are discussed here as well.

OVERVIEW

"In the early 1960s the word pregnant was not allowed on television, and movies and television did not show married couples in the same bed" (Kammayer, Ritzer & Yetman, 1994, p. 209). In the twenty-first century, a person is lucky to experience a two-hour time span that avoids either concept. The media did not change overnight, nor did it change in a vacuum. As such, it cannot take full responsibility for the misunderstanding or misrepresentation of sexuality. Indeed, magazine covers, various advertisements, websites, and television programs are viewed by the millions, resulting in representations that are expected by consumers. Yet, they do not necessarily depict reality; only soap opera stars have sex with their husband's sons, becoming pregnant with twins by both men in some bizarre yet plausible way. In addition, the average woman is not a size four like every model in the pages of a magazine. Nor does everyone discuss sex as liberally or as frequently as radio shock jocks. Nevertheless, the television and radio remain turned on, and the magazines sell.

It is possible that audiences live vicariously through these sexual mediums, knowing their lives will never be like those in soap operas; but in living that way, they are promoting those mediums as acceptable, and in many instances, as normal. Normalcy, however, does have standards. In a perfect world, a person would not become involved in sexual activity until he or she was mentally, emotionally, and physically prepared to do so. However, life as a teenager is rarely perfect, and peer pressure, outside influences like the media, and curiosity about changing bodies create an inherent mystique about sex. When the media continuously references sex as fun, popular, and normal, anyone who is not sexually active feels left out and, oftentimes, abnormal.

Sexuality-Based Media

Some media outlets use a variety of tactics to teach responsibility and confidence, but most do not. Indeed, the media that many children are exposed to encourage behaviors that degrade women, suggest provocative displays of physical interaction, and belittle the confidence required to "just say no." Kammayer, et al. (1994) identify three ways that sexual activities are characterized by American culture:

Depersonalized: Sexual acts and sexual partners are treated as though they are unimportant (Schur, 1988, as cited in Kammayer, et al., 1994, p. 200)

Commercialized: Sex is bought and sold, just like any other commodity in the marketplace

- Americans are accustomed to purchasing their recreation and sex is seen by many as a form of recreation
- Includes the sale of sexually oriented clothing and other sexual paraphernalia that are widely advertised and displayed
- In dating situations, when men pay for meals and entertainment, there is often the implicit assumption that the women owe something in return (p. 200-201)

Coercive and aggressive: According to the Centers for Disease Control and Prevention (CDC), as of 2012, one in five women and one in seventy-one men reported experiencing rape at some point in their lives (Centers for Disease Control and Prevention, 2012).

- It is unclear what came first in the formation of sexuality-based media. Did society become used to sexual references and the media opted to make it a marketing tool? Or, did the media slowly introduce images of sexuality and audiences became conditioned to it? It may be that the conditioning toward and the promotion of sexuality as mainstream happened concurrently. Regardless, the consequences of the conditioning remain the same. If sex is seen as purely physical—promoted by sexy pictures in magazines, steamy plots on television shows, and scantily clad women in music videos—rather than emotional—in real-life relationships—young men and women may mature accustomed to sex being a minor detail in their lives.

Teenagers & the Media

Some adolescents will talk to their parents. However, many will turn to their peers. Some may even depend on books, but most will gather information from various media sources. According to a Kaiser Family Foundation survey released in 2010, American children ages 8 to 18 spend, on average, approximately seven and a half hours every day using electronic devices such as smartphones (Kaiser, 2010). Given that American children and adolescents tend to multitask their use of media content, an average of 11 hours of media content is packed into that timeframe (Lewin, 2010).

Considering the breakdown of a twenty-four hour day for an average teenager (eight hours for sleep; seven hours in school; eight hours of media influence), there may not be much time for conversations with parents. What is more important than the lack of time to talk with parents should be the enormous power media sources have on the average teen.

According to Girls Incorporated, teens may rely on the media for information because what insights they do get from adults are not necessarily helpful:

"Two-thirds (64 percent) believe that adults tell teenagers things 'when it's too late.' More than half (57 percent) indicate that adults discuss things that fail to address the situations teenagers actually face. More than one in four girls (27 percent) says she wants more information on how girls get pregnant. About one in three wants more information about where to get (35 percent) and how to use (40 percent) different kinds of birth control methods. Half (50 percent) want more information on how to prevent AIDS or other STDs" (Girls Incorporated, "Girls' Bill of Rights," accessed July 2, 2008).

It is not clear here what is told to teens "too late," but it is possible those criteria may be directed toward physical development, which, especially for young girls, happens earlier than most people want to think. These changes by nature instill curiosity about sexuality. Without honest input from parents, though, adolescents will find information in other ways that may be inaccurate or biased.

Further Insights: The Media

Magazines & Teens

One way to settle that curiosity is to read magazines that specialize in the sexual matters of teenagers such as *Seventeen*. "Adolescent girls cite magazines as significant sources of sexual information that are as meaningful a source as their parents" (Treise & Gotthoffer 2002; Walsh-Childers et al. 2002, as cited in Medley-Rath, 2007, p. 25). Medley-Rath examined the advice column of *Seventeen* for almost ten years trying to determine if teens reading the magazine would gain clear-cut information about sexuality based on the contents of the column. As the column's format is anonymous, based on letters sent by readers, it may be easier for teens to ask *Seventeen* rather than their parents when questions about sex arise, especially those of an explicit nature.

For example, the following question and response were printed in *Seventeen* in December 1995 (p. 46).

Reader: Questions losing her virginity as her boyfriend's penis was "partially inside her vagina."

Seventeen: "There's no textbook definition of sex ... You are right that, technically speaking, penetration pretty much equals sex. For your boyfriend, though, it may not qualify unless he has an orgasm" (Medley-Rath, 2007, p 39).

Medley-Rath notes that in this exchange, "sex is defined [for girls] based on penetration but for boys it might only count if he orgasms" (p. 30). An anxious teen trying to determine one of the most important questions of her life might find this response confusing. If initial ejaculation represents the epic moment for boys, do they lose their virginity through masturbation (self or mutual) or though oral sex? This was not addressed during the nine-year research study conducted by Medley-Rath; the researcher notes that the lack of such information suggests that boys get to decide when they lose their virginity while girls have that decision made for them (p. 39).

Likewise, if an adolescent inquires about gay, lesbian, or alternative sexual acts, Medley-Rath found that he or she was provided the same information that was provided to heterosexual inquiries: virginity (for girls) is lost when a penis penetrates a vagina. This communicates to readers that the important event of losing one's virginity can only happen to girls who have intercourse with boys. It also communicates that intercourse (vaginal penetration with a penis) is normal. According to Medley-Rath,

"Teen magazines present heterosexual sexual behaviors as normative (Carpenter 1998; Currie 1999; Jackson 1999, as cited in Medley-Rath, p. 25) ... Heteronormative virginity loss is placed on a pedestal compared to non-heteronormative virginity loss, even though individuals may have other sexual experiences they consider as important as intercourse" (Medley-Rath, p. 27).

Adolescence is difficult enough. To have feelings that are not discussed by a magazine that is supposed to support teen girls may have a devastating effect. Yet, in the culture of *Seventeen,* that has not seemed to be a concern; heteronormative ideals have continued to be espoused by the magazine in the twenty-first century. On the other hand, Medley-Rath did note that *Seventeen* was clear to stress that abstinence is the only way to avoid sexually transmitted infections (August 1989, p. 172). Conversely, *Seventeen* never supplied an official definition of abstinence for its readers (p. 34). Nor did the magazine discuss the medical determination of a broken hymen with regard to virginity loss in girls within the nine years Medley-Rath studied its column.

Magazines & Adults

Seventeen was created to reach females ages 13 to 18; *Cosmopolitan* and its Australian contemporary, *Cleo,* were created for female readers ages 18 to 34. *Cosmo* is the most widely read women's lifestyle magazine globally (McCleneghan, 2003, as cited in Farvid & Braun, 2006, p. 298), and therefore the information within the magazine reaches (and influences) millions of people. Farvid & Braun (2006) conducted an examination much like Medley-Rath's to determine how sexuality has been approached in these two adult magazines. Farvid & Braun looked at the portrayal of male sexuality and how it conditions female sexuality (both overtly and covertly) from issue to issue (p. 296). They conclude:

> "The focus on men is particularly relevant because, in a heteronormative world, male and female sexualities are constructed simultaneously. Therefore, although previous examinations of constructions of femininity/ female sexuality in magazines have been useful, they are only partially complete, as female (hetero) sexuality is also constructed through the magazines' accounts of male (hetero) sexuality" (Farvid & Braun, 2006, p. 298).

The research was based on six issues of both magazines from January to June 2002 (p. 298), and the data is consistent with that of the *Seventeen* study. Sexuality (for both men and women) was portrayed exclusively as heterosexual (Jackson, 1996; McLoughlin, 2000, as cited in Farvid & Braun, p. 299). Furthermore, while there were a number of incidences in which women were portrayed as being confident and independent,

> "...women were overwhelmingly represented as wanting/ needing men in their lives and ultimately seeking (monogamous) long-term relationships with men; this was often situated as the desired outcome from a new date/sexual encounter...[Furthermore, w]omen were constantly depicted as ultimately looking for their 'Mr Right' (who was presumed to exist for all women)... [and] men were implicitly located as the underlying source of women's fulfilment, security, and happiness. The magazines rarely considered a woman's life without a man ... Men were rarely represented as 'needing' women in the same manner, and their presumed full autonomy and independence was something women implicitly still do not possess, nor should they desire it" (p. 299-300).

As a publication created for women, what men want in and outside of the bedroom was the focus from month to month. In addition, women "giving" men what they want was also the focus in that advice (sometimes from men), provided for readers to best meet the (primarily sexual) needs of the men in their lives. This information was provided based on the assumption that women did not already have it—or could not figure it out on their own. Furthermore, it was clear within the magazines that what men want was their primary concern and should also be the primary concern for women (Farvid & Braun, 2006, p. 300). Of concern is the fact that interviews from men were expanded upon by the magazine editors as though what the men said was gospel. One man described being controlled by his "groin" as though the biology of his body was responsible for his actions; he could not help being a creature of sexual desire (p. 301). Farvid & Braun note how dangerous this concept can be as it "can function to represent male sexuality as not only needy/driven, but also as uncontrollable, which potentially shifts the responsibility of certain sexual actions (such as infidelity/cheating [or sexual assaults]) away from the man" (p. 301).

When articles entitled "Guy talk: Is there any man totally cheat-proof?," which include quotes from men, are juxtaposed to one advertisement after another selling products to hamper the aging process, it should not be a mystery what message women are supposed to take from these publications (*Cosmopolitan*, January 2002, as cited in Farvid & Braun, 2007, p. 302).

However, it should be noted that while magazines like *Cosmopolitan* are very popular, many women enjoy reading them not for the value (or lack of value) of the magazines' advice, but simply for their entertainment value. In addition, a study conducted by Kim and Ward (2012) found that women's lifestyle magazines provide a very strong message about sexual liberation, one that can have both positive and negative consequences. For example, frequent readers were found less likely to view sex as a potentially risky activity. Frequent readers were also more approving of sexual assertion in women for the sake of their own pleasure, and were less likely to support the idea of sexual submissiveness. Conversely, women exposed to *Cosmopolitan* articles who were not as familiar with the type of content were more likely to support sexual submissiveness. Kim and Ward thus concluded that magazines like *Cosmo* can "potentially have both empowering and problematic effects on women's developing sexual identities." Overall, the researchers found that the social position and personal experiences of each woman in the study strongly influenced how they absorbed the magazine's messages.

Hip-Hop Music Videos. Peterson, Wingood, DiClemente, Harrington, and Davies (2007) conducted one of the first studies to examine the relationship between images of sexual stereotypes in rap and hip-hop music videos to negative health consequences for African American female adolescents (p. 1158). To gather the appropriate data, Peterson et al. created a survey and interview questions about participants' "rap music video viewing habits" (p. 1157). Over five-hundred African American female teens aged 14 to 18 (p. 1158) participated in the study by completing the written surveys, taking part in oral interviews, and providing urine for a marijuana screening (p. 1157).

In a summary of their findings, Peterson and colleagues note that teenagers who regularly viewed the stereotypical sexual behaviors often portrayed by rap music were more likely (by their own admission) to,

- Engage in binge drinking,
- Test positive for marijuana,
- Have multiple sexual partners, and
- Have a negative body image (p. 1161).

Furthermore, Peterson et al. note that within the history of rap music videos, "African American women are often portrayed as hypersexual, materialistic, and amoral … their depiction often overemphasizes their sexualized, physical appearance and places them as decorative objects rather than active agents, in the videos" (Emerson, 2002; Stephens & Phillips, 2003; Ward, Hansbrough & Walker, 2005, as cited in Peterson, et al., 2007, p. 1158). It could be argued, however, that women in general (regardless of race) are portrayed the same way in videos representing a variety of musical genres. Consider Madonna, Shakira, Jennifer Lopez, Shania Twain, or Carrie Underwood, who touts a Louisville Slugger proudly as she bashes the headlights out of her cheating boyfriend's truck.

Regardless of how these women behave when the camera is not rolling on them, their videos show them as being amoral, materialistic, and hypersexual. The problem with those depictions is that because they are displayed so frequently, young women may think they represent normal behavior. When those teen bodies, faces, and "attitudes" do not simulate the ones seen on television, youthful audiences may be left to feel abnormal and inadequate, and in many instances, eager to please, possibly before they truly understand the consequences of pleasing behaviors.

The internet. In a matter of seconds, a person can access the internet and read random pieces of information, view images, and watch videos based on a variety of topics. The topics discussed above—music videos, magazines, television, etc.—can all be found online and can all influence one's perception of sexuality, whether an individual is viewing an advertisement or porn. In addition to absorbing all of this media, individuals can interact via many social media platforms, such as Facebook, Tumblr, Twitter, and Reddit. These sites allow individuals to upload pictures of themselves, share specific personal information such as age and location, and discuss their lives in great detail to the general public, on topics ranging in subject from sexual preferences to God to teen pregnancy and abortion. Depending on one's Internet and specific website security settings, almost anyone can view user profiles and current and past discussions on such topics.

In addition, creating a topic or post may also set an author up for criticism. In one instance on MySpace (2008), for example, a teenager wrote in about being pregnant. She was asking anyone who wanted to respond about their opinions regarding her not having an abortion. The girl was ridiculed, heckled, and supported by people she did not even know. Furthermore, her post created a series of discussions on the general topics of teen pregnancy and abortion. After several posts listing various opinions, the author posted a short note (again, to anyone who wanted to read it) stating that she had had a miscarriage. This, in turn, set off further discussions.

Positive Influences: Sexuality Education & the Media

Girls Incorporated is a nonprofit organization dedicated to "inspiring all girls to be strong, smart, and bold" (http://www.girlsinc.org/). The organization focuses educational programming toward high-risk female youth in the United States and Canada. The various programs include "... math and science education, pregnancy and drug abuse prevention, media literacy, economic literacy, adolescent health, violence prevention, and sports participation ... [Participants learn to] confront subtle societal messages about their value and potential, and prepare them to lead successful, independent, and fulfilling lives" (http://www.girlsinc.org/)

What is especially appealing about this resource is that if someone's community does not have a Girls Incorporated organization, most of the programming can be acquired online, through the website. Information about internet safety, friendships, sexuality, violence, and education can be found within seconds when touring this site. In addition, women who lead successful lives—running companies, demonstrating effective parenting skills, participating in political activism—are celebrated every day within the site so that young girls can see the possibilities of thinking positively about themselves.

An article entitled "All he talks about is sex" is sure to raise eyebrows. However, it describes Jairo Bouer, a Brazilian psychiatrist for adolescents who has talked openly about sex—pregnancy prevention, sexually transmitted infections, and HIV—over the Brazilian airwaves to help youth learn the truth about sexuality (Tabakman, 2005).

> "[H]e has two radio programs, appears on television ("I reach the rich by cable and the poor by parabolic antenna"), writes books, participates in conferences (including some organized by the Pan American Health Organization), serves as a government consultant on HIV/AIDS and drug and alcohol prevention, and has his own website–you guessed it–on sex" (Tabakman, 2005, p. 17-18).

Much like Dr. Ruth Westheimer in the United States, Bouer has used humor to reach his audience, many times by seeking out adolescents on their turf; he appeared on MTV Brazil for a four-hour program on sex in 1998. When unable to go to them, Bouer has encouraged youth to use the radio or internet when they need information. He has noted that the call-in format of his talk shows and Q&A section on his website create anonymity for people who simply want accurate information, like one caller who asked, "Can any fluid from the penis make you pregnant?" (Tabakman, 2005, p. 18).

Encouraging the development of positive sexual behaviors is not a concept restricted to the Internet or radio talk shows. The more consistently the message is promoted, the more seriously it will be taken by its audience.

> "When messages appear in different media simultaneously, their effect is intensified. Various partners in the field of reproductive health, such as governmental and non-governmental agencies, industry and trade, and women's and youth groups, can take a lead in mass media work. Schools can facilitate or develop partnerships with mass media representatives to coordinate and collaborate on efforts that address family life, reproductive health, and population issues and to ensure consistent messages" ("Family Life," 2003, p. 47).

According to Dr. Gunta Lazdane, regional advisor of Reproductive Health and Research at the WHO Regional Office for Europe, the goal of any sexuality education collaboration should be all-encompassing:

> "Sexuality education is not just about providing information. It helps young people develop values, attitudes, and skills so that they can make appropriate choices about their sexual behaviour. Having respect for oneself and others, making considered choices about sexual activity and acquiring emotional intelligence are key learning outcomes" (cited in "New Study," 2006, par. 7).

Girls Incorporated, Jairo Bouer, and the World Health Organization encourage a holistic approach to sexuality education delivered via the media. Any young woman who understands that the different pieces of her body are connected to real emotions, a developing intellect, and a future without limits will also understand that she has a responsibility to make the best possible choices.

VIEWPOINTS

Sexuality beyond Adolescence

Clearly, the concept of sexuality is one that focuses on young men and women in the midst of pubescence. Yet, it affects everyone, and oftentimes, the media loses sight of that fact, avoiding older populations in advertisements, in television programming, and in films. The idea of valuing, or classifying one cohort of people over the other based on their age is called age-grading. According to González (2007), age grading is a practice demonstrated regularly by the media (p. 35). Indeed, without advertisements for Viagra, the concept of older people having sex may not be considered. The problem with this is that power relationships are formed through the differences in people who are considered sexually attractive and those who are not, namely the elderly (p. 31).

For example, Simon (1996) notes that when either a child or an elderly woman are raped, communities become enraged, while when a forty-year old woman is raped, communities tend to be less outraged (p. 52–54, as cited in González, 2007, p. 34). This is age-grading: children and the elderly are not sexual creatures and, therefore, when sex is forced upon them, it is despicable; however, when a woman who is expected to be sexually active is raped, it might not be such a big deal. The very young and the very old are seen as more vulnerable; their ages are classified as more important in this situation than the forty-year old. Additionally, an elderly person who is mugged ranks much higher with regard to media coverage than a middle-aged person.

This is a common phenomenon within the media. Middle-aged women are constantly seen in advertisements for products to help them look younger, as younger is classified as a societal value. It is common also to note a distinguished older man, as if the effects of the aging process have not taken their toll on men as they have on older women. This is stereotypical and creates a societal norm that women have to fight the process, while men simply let it happen.

"Consequently, age-graded sexualities are those arenas where our bodies are in constant struggle against their own ageing bodily boundaries while sexually expressing themselves ... Because age-grading configures complex and contested forms of interaction and ways of experiencing sexuality, understanding these aspects requires establishing connections with sociological issues that affect and mediate our society and sexualities. In consequence, age-graded sexualities are certainly not just about sex, but diverse meanings which change through time and space" (González, 2007, p. 43). Indeed, the implication from the media that women need to hide the effects of aging implies that there is something wrong with the aging process, that it needs to be concealed from society. It also creates inconsistency with regard to sexuality in that if those effects are not hidden, mature women are less attractive sexually, while the same standard is not given to men.

CONCLUSION

In America, sexuality is commonly seen through media images, but its realities are not so commonly discussed. The lack of discussion can lead teens to utilize the media for information about sex, even when that information may be inaccurate or misleading. When parents do not discuss sex with their children, the implication is that it is a topic that is better left to other sources, when, in fact, it may be left out of conversation because parents do not realize their children are curious about it. In addition, American culture promotes sex through the media by not enforcing diligent standards against images that commonly degrade women. Finally, music videos, the internet, television programming, and magazines are easily accessible to youth and may lead young girls to believe that sex is something they should use to gain the attention of the opposite sex, even if a homosexual relationship is a girl's primary concern.

TERMS & CONCEPTS

Abstinence: Restraint from sexual intercourse.

Age Grading: Classifying/ranking people based on their ages.

Heteronormative: Basing what is normal on the behaviors of heterosexuals.

Sexual Intercourse: Phrase used to define the act of sexual penetration.

Sexuality: The state of being sexual; involvement or interest in sexual activity; sexual orientation.

Bibliography

Aubrey, J., & Frisby, C. M. (2011). "Sexual objectification in music videos: A content analysis comparing gender and genre." *Mass Communication & Society,* 14, 475–501.

Callister, M., Stern, L. A., Coyne, S. M., Robinson, T., & Bennion, E. (2011). "Evaluation of sexual content in teen-centered films from 1980 to 2007." *Mass Communication & Society,* 14, 454–474.

Centers for Disease Control and Prevention (2012). *Sexual violence: Facts at a glance.* https://www.cdc.gov/violenceprevention/pdf/sv-datasheet-a.pdf

Collins, R. (2011). "Content analysis of gender roles in media: Where are we now and where should we go?" *Sex Roles,* 64 (3/4), 290–298.

Girls Incorporated. (2008). "Girls' bill of rights fact sheet." Girls Incorporated website: http://www.girlsinc.org/takeaction/bill-of-rights-facts.html

Girls Incorporated. (2008). "Homepage: Programs." Girls Incorporated website: http://www.girlsinc.org/

Girls and Sexuality. (2008). "Girls Incorporated." Girls Incorporated website: http://www.girlsinc.org/

González, C. (2007). "Age-graded sexualities: The struggles of our ageing body." *Sexuality & Culture,* 11, p. 31–47.

"Family Life, Reproductive Health, and Population Education: Key Elements of a Health-Promoting School." (2003). http://www.who.int/

Farvid, P. & Braun, V. (2006). "Most of us guys are raring to go anytime, anyplace, anywhere: Male and female sexuality in Cleo and Cosmo." *Sex Roles,* 55 (5/6), p. 295–310.

Kaiser Family Foundation. (2010, January 20). "Daily media use among children and teens up dramatically from five years ago." *Henry J. Kaiser Family Foundation.* http://kff.org/disparities-policy /press-release/daily-media-use-among-children-and-teens-up-dramatically-from-five-years-ago/

Kammayer, K. C. W., Ritzer, G. & Yetman, N. R. (1994). *Sociology: Experiencing Changing Societies* (6th ed.). Needham Heights: Allyn and Bacon.

Lamb, S., Farmer, K. M., Kosterina, E., Lambe Sariñana, S., Plocha, A., & Randazzo, R. (2016). "What's sexy? Adolescent girls discuss confidence, danger, and media influence." *Gender & Education,* 28 (4), 527–545.

Lewin, T. (2010, January 20). "If your kids are awake, they're probably online." *New York Times.* A1. http://www.nytimes.com/2010/01/20/education/20wired.html

Lombard, M., & Jones, M. T. (2013). "Telepresence and sexuality: A review and a call to scholars." *Human Technology,* 9, 22–55.

Medley-Rath, S. R. (2007). "'Am I still a virgin?': What counts as sex in 20 years of *Seventeen.*" *Sexuality and Culture,* 11, p. 24–38.

"New study launched on sexuality education for young people." (2006). *World Health Organization*

Regional Office for Europe. http://www.euro.who.int/mediacentre /PR/2006/20061212_1

Peterson, S. H., Wingood, G. M., DiClemente, R. J., Harrington, K. & Davies, S. (2007). "Images of sexual stereotypes in rap videos and the health of African American female adolescents." *Journal of Women's Health,* 16, p. 1157–1164.

Tabakman, R. (2005). "All he talks about is sex." *Perspectives in Health,* 10. 17–19. http://www.paho.org/

Kim, J. L., & Ward, M. (2012, August 23). "Striving for pleasure without fear: Short-term effects of reading a women's magazine on women's sexual attitudes." *Psychology of Women Quarterly.* http://pwq.sagepub.com

SUGGESTED READING

Baker, C. N. (2005). "Images of women's sexuality in advertisements: A content analysis of Black- and White-oriented women's and men's magazines." *Sex Roles,* 52 (1/2), 13–27.

Ballaster, R., Beetham, M., Frazer, E., & Hebron, S. (1991). *Woman's worlds: Ideology, femininity, and the woman's magazine.* Houndmills, UK: Macmillian.

Bleakley, A., Hennessy, M., & Fishbein, M. (2011). "A model of adolescents' seeking of sexual content in their media choices." *Journal of Sex Research,* 48, 309–315.

Bordo, S. (1993). *Unbearable weight: Feminism, Western culture, and the body.* Berkeley, California: University of California Press.

Boynton, P. M. (1999). "'Is that supposed to be sexy?' Women discuss 'top shelf' magazines." *Journal of Community & Applied Social Psychology,* 9, 449–461.

Bufkin, J. & Eschholz, S. (2000). "Images of sex and rape: A content analysis of popular film." *Violence Against Women,* 6, p. 1317–1344.

Burt, M. (1980). "Cultural myths and support for rape." *Journal of Personality and Social Psychology,* 38, 217–230.

Butler, M., & Paisley, W. (1980). *Women and the mass media. Sourcebook for research and action.* New York: Human Sciences Press.

Calderone, M.S. & Johnson, E.W. (1981). *The family book about sexuality.* New York, NY: Harper and Row.

Campbell, J. C. (2002). "Health consequences of intimate partner violence." *Lancet, 359,* 1331–1336.

Campbell, J. C. & Lewandowski, L. A. (1997). "Mental and physical health effects of intimate partner violence on women and children." *Psychiatric Clinics of North America,* 20 (2), 353–374.

Chester, B., Robin, R., Koss, M. & Goodman, D. (1994). "Grandmother dishonored: Violence against women by male partners in American Indian communities. Special Issue: Violence against women of color." *Violence and Victims,* 9, 249–258.

Coker, A. L., Davis, K. E., Arian, I., Desai, S., Sanderson, M., Brandt, H. M. & Smith, P. H. (2002). "Physical and mental health effects of intimate partner violence for men and women." *American Journal of Preventive Medicine,* 23, 260–268.

Coker, A. L., Smith, P. H., Bethea, L., King, M. & McKeown, R. E. (2000). "Physical health consequences of physical and psychological intimate partner violence." *Archives of Family Medicine,* 9, 451–457.

Cole, J. & Guy-Sheftall, B. (2003). *Gender talk: The struggle for women's equality in African American communities.* New York: Ballantine Publishing Group.

Collins, P. (2000). *Black feminist thought: Knowledge, consciousness, and the politics of empowerment.* New York: Routledge.

Comstock, G. (1980). *Television in America.* Beverly Hills, CA: Sage Publications.

Emerson, R. A. (2002). *Where my girls at? Negotiating black womanhood in music videos.* Gender & Society, 16, p. 115.

Fisher, G. (1989). "Mass media effects on sex role attitudes of incarcerated men." *Sex Roles,* 20 (3/4), p. 191–203.

Gerson, W. M. (1966). "Mass media socialization behavior: Negro-white differences." *Social Forces,* 45, P. 40–50.

Gray, J. (1995). *Mars and Venus in the bedroom: A guide to lasting romance and passion.* New York: HarperCollins.

He, M. (2002). "How much is known about gender difference?" *Chinese Education & Society,* 35, 53.

Henry J. Kaiser Family Foundation. (1996). *The 1996 Kaiser Family Foundation survey on teens and sex: What they say teens today need to know and who they listen to.* Conducted for the foundation by Princeton Survey Research Associates. Menlo Park, CA: Author.

Herman-Giddens, M.E. (1997). "Secondary sexual characteristics and menses in young girls seen in office practice: A study from the pediatric research in office settings network." *Pediatrics,* 99, 505–512.

Hermes, J. (1995). *Reading women's magazines: An analysis of everyday media use.* Cambridge, Massachusetts: Polity.

Hochschild, A. (1983). *The managed heart.* Berkeley, California: University of California Press.

Holland, J., Ramazanoglu, C., Sharpe, S., & Thompson, R. (1992). *Pressured pleasure: Young women and the negotiation of boundaries.* London: Tufnell.

Holland, J., Ramazanoglu, C., Sharpe, S., & Thompson, R. (1998). *The male in the head: Young people, heterosexuality, and power.* London: Tufnell.

Hubbard, J. C., DeFleur, M. L. & DeFleur, L. B. (1975). "Mass media influences on public conceptions of social problems." *Social Problems,* 23, 22–34.

Jackson, S. (2005). "'I'm 15 and desperate for sex': 'Doing' and 'undoing' desire in letters to a teenage magazine." *Feminism & Psychology,* 15, 295–313.

Janus, S. S., & Janus, C. L. (1993). *The Janus report on sexual behavior.* New York: John Wiley & Sons.

Kingsbury, K. (2008). "Pregnancy boom at Gloucester High." *Time.* Time Magazine website: http://www.time.com/

Klapper, J. T. (1960). *The effects of mass communications.* New York: The Free Press.

Laws, J. L., & Schwartz, P. (1977). *Sexual scripts: The social construction of female sexuality.* Hinsdale, IL: The Dryden Press.

Liau, A., DiClemente, R. J., Wingood, G. M., et al. (2002). "Associations between biologically confirmed marijuana use and laboratory-confirmed sexually transmitted diseases among African American adolescent females." *Sexually Transmitted Diseases,* 29, p. 387.

Masters, W. H., Johnson, V. E., & Kolodny, R. C. (1988). *Masters and Johnson on sex and human loving.* Boston, MA: Little, Brown and Company.

McPhillips, K., Braun, V., & Gavey, N. (2001). "Defining (hetero)sex: How imperative is the 'coital imperative'?" *Women's Studies International Forum,* 24, 229–240.

McRobbie, A. (2000). *Feminism and youth culture* (2nd ed.). New York: Routledge.

Mellor, P. A. & Shilling, C. (1997). *Re-forming the body.* London-Thousand Oaks: Sage.

Michaels, S., & Giami, A. (1999). "Review: Sexual acts and sexual relationships: Asking about sex in surveys." *Public Opinion Quarterly,* 63, 401–420.

Milkie, M. A. (1999). "Social comparisons, reflected appraisals, and mass media: The impact of pervasive beauty images on black and white girls' self-concepts." *Social Psychology Quarterly,* 62, 190–210.

Mohler, M. (2000). *Homosexual rites of passage. A road to visibility and validation.* New York-Oxford: Harrington Park Press.

Neugarten, B. (1981). "Age distinctions and their social functions." *Chicago Kent Law Review,* 57, 809–825.

Nicholas, K. B., McCarter, R. E., & Hecket, R. V. (1971). "The effects of race and sex on the imitation of television models." *Journal of Social Psychology,* 85, 315–316.

Presser, H. B. (1975). "Age differences between spouses." *American Behavioural Scientist,* 19, 190–205.

Rivera, R. (2004). "Contraception: Issues in adolescent health and development." *World Health Organization.* WHO website: http://whqlibdoc.who.int/

Rosenfeld, B. (2004). *Assisted suicide and the right to die.* Washington, DC: American Psychological Association.

Ross, K. (Ed.) (2012). *The handbook of gender, sex, and media.* Malden, MA: Wiley-Blackwell.

Russo, N. F. & Pirlott, A. (2006). "Gender-based violence." *Annals of the New York Academy of Sciences,* 1087, p. 178–205.

Seggar, J. F. (1977). "Television's portrayal of minorities and women, 1971–1975." *Journal of Broadcasting,* 2, p. 435–446,

Seggar, J. F. & Wheeler, P. (1973). "World of work on TV: Ethnic and sex representation in TV drama." *Journal of Broadcasting,* 17, p. 201–214,

Smith, C., & Attwood, F. (2018). *The Routledge companion to media, sex and sexuality.* New York: Routledge.

Sprecher, S., Harris, G. & Meyers, A. (2008). "Perceptions of sources of sex education and targets of communication: Sociodemographic and cohort effects." *Journal of Sex Research,* 45, p. 17.

Steele, J. & Brown, J. D. (1995). "Adolescent room culture: Studying media in the context of everyday life." *Journal of Youth & Adolescence,* 24, p. 551.

Williams, T. M., (Ed). (1986). *The impact of television: A natural experiment m three communities.* Orlando, FL: Academic Press.

Wingood, G., DiClemente, R. J., Bernhardt, J. M., et al. (2003). "A longitudinal study of exposure to rap music videos and female adolescents' health." *American Journal of Public Health,* 93, p. 437.

Wingood, G., DiClemente, R.J., Harrington, K. & Davies, S. L. (2002). "Body image and African American females' sexual health." *Journal of Womens' Health and Gender Based Medicine,* 11, p. 433.

Stephens, D. P. & Phillips, L. D. (2003). "Freaks, gold diggers, divas, and dykes: The sociohistorical development of adolescent African American women's sexual script." *Sexuality Culture,* 7, p. 3.

Ward, L., Hansbrough, E. & Walker, E. (2005). "Contributions of music video exposure to black adolescents' gender and sexual schemas." *Journal of Adolescent Research,* 20, p. 143.

Maureen McMahon, M.S.

SOCIOLOGY OF CONTRACEPTION

ABSTRACT

Modern contraception has caused a social revolution in the history of humankind. This article discusses sociology and the sociology of contraception. It focuses on the expressed global need for contraception and its social, health and economic benefits. Also covered are issues surrounding a culture of contraception including sexism of the medical profession, teenage contraception, morality, male contraception, iatrogenic medicine, and long-term contraception including sterilization.

OVERVIEW

Sociology is the study of human behavior in society, including its social institutions and how they develop and change over time. The sociology of contraception then, is the study of how people behave in their sexual and reproductive lives and how contraception has altered that behavior. Sociologists are interested in emerging trends in population growth and the impact of the advent of contraception. Sociologists also study how contraception changes the lives of individuals and the structure of the family. They research the differences in attitudes between men and women regarding contraception.

Global Population

Historically, large families were desirable: the more children in a family, the more chances for the family line to continue. With much higher death rates at an earlier age, people tried to have as many children as possible. A large family meant more helping hands on family homesteads and farms. But things began changing in the twentieth century with the world population exceeding six billion, and with an estimated 8.2 billion expected by 2025 (United Nations Population Fund, 2013). Sociologists worldwide are studying the effects of the global population explosion (Macionis, 2007).

US Population Trends

When the United States was an agrarian society, children had economic value, and birth rates American cities trended lower. In the nineteenth century, birth rates began to go down throughout the country due largely to urbanization. With farmlands diminishing, there was not a need for the extra help on the homestead that having many children provided. By 1930, because of the Great Depression, the US birth rate had fallen to about a third of that recorded in 1800. At the time, the most widely used methods of contraception, limited as they were in success, were coitus interruptus, douching, and the use of condoms.

Following World War II, a baby boom exploded, almost in reaction to the low birth rates of the Depression era. Some researchers argue that with good wages, a strong home construction market, and fathers home from the war fronts, Americans felt they could afford to have children like never before. But others point to inadequate contraception and a high failure rate of 18 to 23 percent for condoms and other devices, notably the diaphragm.

Reliable contraception did not become available until 1960 with the birth control pill. With that powerful method, the US birth rate dropped in the 1960s and 1970s, even if economically people felt that their lifestyles were comfortable. It is unlikely, according to researchers, another baby boom will occur in the United States. Modern contraceptive devices offer success rates in preventing pregnancies up to 99.8 percent (Centers for Disease Control and Prevention, 2014).

The Sexual Revolution

Modern contraception has caused a social revolution. The search for methods to control fertility while still enjoying sexual contact has perhaps been ongoing, but a necessary and workable solution was not found until the twentieth century. To solve the problem of overpopulation, family planning has become necessary worldwide. A side effect of family planning to stem the tide of overpopulation has been the ability for people to have sex without worrying about pregnancy (Benagiano, Bastianelli & Farris, 2007).

Global Need for Better Contraception

Because the worldwide average number of children born to each woman, known as the fertility rate, has declined steadily over the decades, some believe that the overpopulation problem has been resolved. But the global population is still increasing by about eighty million people each year. And many countries have very young populations. So, while highly effective contraception is widely available to women in the United States and other high-income countries, women and men in many developing countries still lack adequate access to contraceptives, which can create severe social and health problems (Potts, 2000).

In some parts of the world, almost all of it in developing countries, rapid population growth is expected to continue for many years. These are the same countries where family-planning services are wanted but highly controversial at the same time. Many countries lack safe food and water supplies as well as medical, financial, and educational institutions, which affect the quality of life of their people.

Contraceptive use has slowly begun to take effect, but often, contraceptives are too expensive or not available to those who need them. The World Health Organization (2014) estimates that each day there are 800 deaths related to pregnancy complications and childbirth could be avoided if all women worldwide had access to contraceptive services, as well as adequate pre- and postnatal care. Maternal mortality rates are particularly high for poor women, who have the least access to contraceptives. Unintended pregnancies increase the risk of suboptimal prenatal care and leave new mothers feeling overwhelmed and underprepared. In some countries, women are forbidden to have access to the contraceptive pill. Even in Ireland, condoms could not be legally obtained until the 1990s.

Poor countries either cannot afford the cost of manufacturing, distributing, and promoting contraceptives, or their governments do not see family planning as a priority. Sometimes, the only way that the people who live in these countries can receive help with family planning is by receiving donations from foreign countries (Potts, 2000).

Positive Social, Health, & Economic Effects of Contraception

Population Control

If large families were necessary to ensure lineage, then contraception was not desirable and the prohibition was emphasized by social institutions. Members of certain religious groups were historically discouraged from using contraception or even from having sexual contact without the desire for conception. Infanticide, or the killing of newborn children, occurs at higher rates in countries with extremely high rates of poverty and overpopulation. Female infants are more likely to be victims of infanticide, due to certain cultural values that make male children more desirable and less of an economic burden. With overpopulation as a concern, humanistic groups and even religious institutions themselves are beginning to change attitudes about contraception. Because people are now living longer thanks to modern technology, the world's population has exploded and population control has become important.

Health

There are other positive benefits for using contraception than controlling population growth. Some people want to plan having families around educational goals and financial concerns. Some women are not physically healthy enough to bear children and contraception helps protect their safety as well as the safety of an unborn child. Older women, as well as very young pregnant girls, risk complications such as birth defects and even death of the infant or the mother (Macionis, 2007). Contraception, therefore, has had positive health benefits by also reducing the need for abortions. And some forms of contraception, such as the condom, have contributed to the reduction of sexually transmitted diseases (Benagiano, Bastianelli & Farris, 2007).

Economics

Contraception has had several positive effects on the economic lives of women. Effective and affordable contraception has given women the opportunity to choose whether and when to conceive and bear children. This, in turn, has allowed women to attain better educations and employment training.

APPLICATIONS

While contraception methods have responded well to concerns about overpopulation as well as to the social, health, and economic well-being of people, there are several issues surrounding the culture of contraception. Conflict over the issue of contraception has existed at least since 1916, when Margaret Sanger, the founder of Planned Parenthood, was jailed for offering advice and contraceptives to married women in Brooklyn. Modern controversies include issues such as sexism in the medical field, teenagers' access to contraceptives, and contraception access in prisons.

Sexism

Women often experience the health care system as paternalistic, in which their own experiences and knowledge are ignored or downgraded. Historically this has been true especially in the areas of pregnancy, childbirth, and contraception.

Because motherhood is considered a natural role for women, abortion of unwanted pregnancy is often seen as unnatural and even terrible. Contraceptive use is relatively widespread in most Western societies, but in developing societies, such as Central and Eastern Europe and sub-Saharan and West Africa, access to contraception is limited. Abortion rates are the highest in the world in these societies and, in the early 1990s, the number of abortions equaled or was higher than the number of live births in some countries. During the 1990s, as contraceptive methods became more easily available, the number of abortions decreased. In fact, the global abortion rate has been gradually decreasing since the late twentieth century. The abortion rate is typically lower in regions with liberal abortion laws; restrictive abortion and contraception laws are not associated with lower abortion rates (Sedgh, et al., 2012).

Teen Sex & Contraception

In an attempt to reduce teenage pregnancies, many governments promote and distribute contraceptive pills to students, even without the parents' permission. This situation brings up two issues: morality and health safety. Some critics argue that it is the parents' place to monitor and regulate their children's sexual activity. Others argue that a strong hormonal drug being given to young girls could have long-term negative effects on her health and development. Even contraceptive devices such as intrauterine devices (IUDs) can have complications or side effects, and there is no contraceptive, except the condom, that will protect young people from sexually transmitted diseases.

If governments, including the US government, are not handing out contraceptives, they are at least attempting to educate children about contraception and safe sex. For example, in India, parents and teachers are angered about sex education in schools that includes information about contraceptives and about sexually transmitted diseases, claiming that it goes against Indian cultural values and is an attempt to impose Western cultural values on Indian society. But in India alone, 88.7 percent of the HIV/AIDS cases occur among young people aged fifteen to twenty-nine years old (National AIDS Control Organization, 2015).

Religious Moral Teaching

Some parents, whether for religious or personal reasons, are not talking with their children about sex, family planning, and birth control. According to Mark Regnerus (2005), African American families belonging to Protestant denominations talk more openly with their children about sex and birth control than do families from other Christian denominations and Jewish families, although these families will talk about the morality of sex with their children.

Moreover, all parents talk about sex and birth control more with their female children than with male children.

While religious institutions once took an active role in church members' sexual lives by prohibiting contraception and encouraging sexual relations for the purpose of procreation, many contemporary religious parents are not discussing sex and birth control with their children productively (Regnerus, 2005). Often another social institution, the school, has taken on the role of sex educator, but with resistance from parents who believe it is their duty to provide such counseling.

Male Contraception or Fatherless Children?

Researchers at the University of Massachusetts Medical School and Spermatech, a Norwegian biotechnology company, are working on developing a male contraceptive pill. But social scientists argue that there must be a change in the attitudes and identities of men and women in many societies for the male contraceptive pill to be widely accepted. For the most part, avoiding an unwanted pregnancy is considered to be the duty of the woman. Women, in turn, are not sure they are willing to turn the responsibility for contraception over to their male partners. If there is a mistake, the women would bear the brunt of the responsibility for an unwanted pregnancy (Roots, 2007).

Iatrogenic Medicine

Some medical intervention is iatrogenic; it causes more harm than good with the effects of the treatment worse than the original illness. There have been certain types of contraceptives that have caused iatrogenic injury, such as the contraceptive pill sold under than brand name Yaz, which significantly increased women's risk for developing blood clots. However, the rate of iatrogenic injury from the use of contraceptive pills is extremely low (less than 0.02 percent), with women over the age of thirtyfive years facing the highest level of risk. Women who smoke and take an oral contraceptive are at even greater risk for cardiovascular complications. According to a 2012 study published in the New England Journal of Medicine, some formulations of oral contraceptives have been found to increase women's risk of having a heart attack or stroke, but in absolute terms the risk remains extremely low because women under the age of fifty years (of reproductive age) rarely have heart attacks or strokes (Lidegaard, et al., 2012). A number of health benefits of oral contraceptives have been identified, including reductions in dysmenorrhea and menorrhagia, iron-deficiency anemia, ectopic pregnancy, and ovarian and endometrial cancer. Some women may experience side effects while taking an oral contraceptive, such as bloating, lowered libido, and nausea. While women deal with the side effects of and responsibility for contraceptive devices, there has been little attempt to develop and market oral contraceptives for men. Therefore, a woman, rather than rely on her partner or risk pregnancy, will choose contraceptive methods that are available.

Women must also rely on doctors for information about what is available. However, Abbot, Wallace, and Tyler (2005) indicated that doctors resent it if patients question their advice or seem to know more than the doctors themselves. Women are also restricted by their partner's preferences. Many men do not like to use condoms, believing it spoils the pleasure of the sexual act, while the contraceptive pill is less intrusive, at least for men. While contraception allows women to make choices about pregnancy, some critics argue that contraception has also maintained medical and social control over women by placing the onus of responsibility largely on women (Abbot, Wallace & Tyler, 2005).

Several medications and devices are available to provide long-term contraception for women. These options offer from one month to five years of contraceptive protection. Some women are voluntarily opting for long-term contraception rather than the more permanent solution to pregnancy prevention of sterilization.

Contraception as Punishment

Three weeks after one of the first long-term contraceptive implants was approved by the US Food and Drug Administration, it was used as part of the sentence imposed on a woman convicted of child abuse. This creates a form of punishment, changing the purpose of the device from something to give women more reproductive freedom to something that will control them with governmental power. Laws have since been enacted to prohibit contraceptive sentencing, and the contraceptive in question, Norplant, was discontinued in the United States in 2000. However, the practice of contraception as punishment could become a reality elsewhere and recalls the forced sterilizations of patients with mental illness that occurred in the early twentieth century. Both the American Medical Association and the American Bar Association oppose all forms of contraceptive punishment on the grounds of a person's fundamental right to refuse medical treatment, the US Constitution's protections against cruel and unusual punishment, and the fact that coerced or forced contraception does not prevent a woman from committing child abuse, therefore making such punishment arbitrary. The developer of Norplant, Dr. Sheldon Segal, condemned the medication's use as punishment, arguing that Norplant "was developed to improve reproductive freedom, not to restrict it" (American Civil Liberties Union, 1994).

Voluntary Sterilization

The most effective and permanent method of birth control, sterilization has been historically used as an involuntary procedure performed on individuals with disabilities and criminal histories in a grave violation of human rights that occurred in the United States and worldwide in the early twentieth century as part of the eugenics movement. But for hundreds of thousands of men and women, sterilization is a voluntary procedure with a number of benefits.

Sterilization for a man or a woman involves blocking the path of the woman's egg or the man's sperm, from reaching the crucial place where conception can occur. No organs are removed, and sexual intercourse is still possible after sterilization. For women, the fallopian tubes are tied off so that no egg can enter the uterus from an ovary in a procedure known as tubal ligation. For men, a piece of the tube known as the vas deferens is cut and tied off in a procedure known as a vasectomy. If a person decides later on to have children, these procedures can be reversed with a 40 to 85 percent success rate, depending on the patient's age, the length of time between the initial procedure and its reversal, and the skill of the surgeons performing the initial procedure and its reversal. These procedures are extremely beneficial for individuals who do not want to have children and need a permanent form of birth control, older women for whom pregnancy would be a significant health risk, and for individuals with a genetic disorder or a partner with a genetic disorder who have decided they do not want to risk passing the genetic risk to a child.

CONCLUSION

In the United States, more than 99 percent of women aged fifteen to forty-four years who have ever had sexual intercourse have used a least one form of contraception. In 2013, more than 60 percent of American women of reproductive age were using a contraceptive method. Approximately two-thirds of women who use contraceptives rely on non-permanent, primarily hormonal methods, such as the pill, patch, or vaginal ring. Among all contraception users in the United States (men and women), 27.5 percent use oral contraceptives, 26.6 percent rely on female sterilization, 16.3 percent use male condoms, 10 percent rely on male sterilization, and 5.6 percent use an intrauterine device, or IUD (Guttmacher Institute, 2013).

The Global Issue of Health & Overpopulation

The proportion of married women who use contraception rose from 55 percent to 63 percent between 1990 and 2011. The proportion of married women with an unmet need for family planning declined from 15 to 12 percent worldwide but remained about 25 percent in forty-two countries, most of them in Africa (Alkema et al., 2013). In an age of rapid population growth, overpopulation, and dwindling natural resources, many people want fewer children and, thus, smaller families. But the size of one's family often depends on available contraceptive options. This is the challenge for an estimated 143 million couples in developing countries who want family planning but had no reliable access to methods of obtaining it (United Nations, 2013). The solution, however, is not only ensuring that those who want contraceptives have the education and the income to pay for it.

Contraception, then, needs to be freely available and less costly. Men and women must be educated and informed so that they do not believe untruths such as that the contraceptive pill causes cancer. The world's population is young and therefore, the global population will continue to increase, even with contraceptive use and family planning. But the health and safety of women can be protected by keeping them and their infant children safe from an unnecessary death (Potts & Campbell, 1994). Further, sociologists Nicholas J. Hill, Mxolisi Siwatu, and Maury Granger (2012) have identified widespread societal benefits of increased rates of contraceptive use, namely a significant reduction in the rate of violent crime since the 1970s, when the use of oral contraceptives was widely adopted; they posit that increased access to contraception has significantly reduced the number of unwanted children born to unprepared or apathetic parents, thereby reducing the number of individuals with high potentials for engaging in criminal activity and contributing to the dramatic reductions in the crime rate witnessed in the 1990s.

TERMS & CONCEPTS

Contraception: A device or drug for the prevention of conception, or pregnancy.

Feminist: One who believes in the social, political, and economic equality of both sexes.

Iatrogenic Medicine: Drugs or procedures with side effects that cause more harm than the condition for which they are used to cure or treat.

Long-Term Contraceptives: Methods of birth control that can be effective for up to five years at a time.

Sexism: Prejudice or discrimination based on a person's sex.

Sexual Revolution: A period during the 1960s and 1970s during which sexual attitudes and behavior changed dramatically in Western cultures, particularly relating to premarital sex and the use of contraceptives.

Sexually Transmitted Disease: An infection that is spread through sexual contact.

Social Institutions: Interrelated social groups or arrangements that teach and uphold a society's cultural values and beliefs; education is a social institution, for example.

Sociology: The study of human social behavior, particularly in groups, or categorizations.

Sterilization: A surgical procedure on a man or a woman that prevents conception; voluntary sterilization is intended to be permanent.

Bibliography

Abbott, P., Wallace, C., & Tyler, M. (2005). *Introduction to sociology* (3rd ed). New York: Routledge.

Alkema, L., et al. (2013). "National, regional, and global rates and trends in contraceptive prevalence and unmet need for family planning between 1990 and 2015: A systematic and comprehensive analysis." *Lancet, 381*(9878), 1642–1652.

American Civil Liberties Union. (1994, January 31). "Norplant: a new contraceptive with the potential for abuse." https://www.aclu.org/ reproductive-freedom/norplant-new-contraceptive-potential- abuse

Benagiano, G., Bastianelli, C., Farris, M. (2007). "Contraception: A social revolution." *European Journal of Contraception & Reproductive Health Care, 12,* (1), 3–12.

Bourbonais, N. (2012). "Class, colour and contraception: The politics of birth control in Jamaica, 1938–1967." *Social and Economic Studies, 61*(3), 7–37.

Centers for Disease Control and Prevention. (2014, December 8). "Contraception." http:// www.cdc.gov/reproductivehealth/UnintendedPregnancy/Contraception.htm#How-effective-are-birth-controlmethods

Davis, K. C., Stappenbeck, C. A., Norris, J., George, W. H., Jacques-Tiura, A. J., Schraufnagel, T. J., & Kajumulo, K. F. (2014). "Young Men's condom use resistance tactics: a latent profile analysis." *Journal of Sex Research, 51*(4), 454–465.

Doyle, R. (2003). "Fertility volatility." *Scientific American, 289* (3), 38.

Dresser, R. (1995). "Long-term contraceptives in the criminal justice system." *Hastings Center Report 25* (1), S15.

Economist, (2007). "The birds, the bees and the taboos." *The Economist, 384* (8546), 54.

Gress-Wright, J. (1993, Fall). "The contraception paradox." *Public Interest* (113), 15–25.

Guttmacher Institute. (2013, August). "Contraceptive use in the United States." http:// www.guttmacher.org/

Hill, N. J., Siwatu, M., & Granger, M. (2012). "Safe sex, safe communities: analyzing the link between contraceptive usage and crime rates." *Southwestern Economic Review, 39*(1), 89.

Lidegaard, O., Lokkegaard, E., Jensen, A., Wessel Skovlund, C., & Keiding, N. (2012). "Thrombotic stroke and myocardial infarction with hormonal contraception." *New England Journal of Medicine, 366,* 2257–2266. http://www.nejm.org/

Mayhew, S., Osei, I., &Bajos, N. (2013). "Sexuality, contraception, unplanned pregnancies and abortion in West Africa and Morocco: the ECAF survey." *Population, 68*(1), 7–14.

National AIDS Control Organisation. (2015, January 5). "HIV data." Department of Health & Family Welfare, Ministry of Health & Family Welfare, Government of India: http://naco.gov.in/NACO/Quick_Links/HIV_Data

Osuafor, G. N., & Mturi, A. J. (2013). "Do religious beliefs influence use of contraception among currently married women in Nigeria?" *Journal of Social Development in Africa, 28*(1), 187–212.

Physicians for Life. (2008). "More contraceptives targeted at teens." http://www.physiciansforlife.org/content/view/161/27/

Potts, M. (2000). "The unmet need for family planning." *Scientific American, 282* (1), 88.

Potts, M., & Campbell, M. (1994). "The philosopher's stone." *Harvard International Review, 16* (4), 22.

Regnerus, M. (2005). "Talking about sex: Religion and patterns of parent-child communication about sex and contraception." *Sociological Quarterly 46,* 79–105.

Roots, K. (2007). "A bitter pill to swallow?" *Science & Spirit, 16* (4), 15–17.

Rose, S. B., Cooper, A. J., Baker, N. K., & Lawton, B. (2011). "Attitudes toward long-acting reversible contraception among young women seeking abortion." *Journal of Women's Health, 20*(11), 1729–1735.

Sedgh, G., Singh, S., Shah, I. H., Ahman, E., Henshaw, S. K., & Bankole, A. "Induced abortion: incidence and trends worldwide from 1995 to 2008." *Lancet, 379*(9816), 625–632. http://www.thelancet.com/journals/lancet/article/PIIS0140-6736%2811%2961786-8/fulltext

United Nations. (2013, October). "World contraceptive patterns 2013." United Nations, Department of Economic and Social Affairs, Population Division: http://www.un.org/en/development/desa/population/ publications/pdf/family/worldContraceptivePatternsWallChart2013. pdf

United Nations Population Fund. (2013, June 13). "World population to increase by one billion by 2025." http://www.unfpa.org/

"Voluntary sterilization." (1965, February 15). *Time.*: http://www.time.com/

Wilcox, B. (2005). "The facts of marriage: Social science and the vindication of Christian moral teaching." [Electronic version]. Reprinted from *Touchstone Magazine, Jan/Feb 2005.* http://www.noroomforcontraception.com/

World Health Organization. (2014, May). "Maternal mortality." http://www.who.int/ mediacentre/factsheets/fs348/en

Zain, M. (2007). "Prohibiting female infanticide." suite101: http://islamic-law. suite101.com/article.cfm/prohibiting_female_infanticide

SUGGESTED READING

Guttmacher, A. (1995). *Hopes and realities: Closing the gap between women's aspirations and their reproductive experiences.* New York, NY: Alan Guttmacher Institute.

Harvey, P. (1999). *Let every child be wanted: How social marketing is revolutionizing contraceptive use around the world.* Westport, CT: Greenwood.

Schoen, J. (2005). *Choice and coercion: Birth control, sterilization, and abortion in public health and welfare (Gender and American Culture).* Chapel Hill, NC: University of North Carolina Press.

Tone, A. (2012). "Medicalizing reproduction: The pill and home pregnancy tests." *Journal of Sex Research, 49*(4), 319–327.

Waltermaurer, E., et al. (2013). "Emergency contraception considerations and use among college women." *Journal of Women's Health, 22*(2), 141–146.

Geraldine Wagner, M.S.

SOCIOLOGY OF PROSTITUTION

ABSTRACT

Prostitution, often called the world's oldest profession, has also been described as the oldest form of oppression. It is widely vilified, but remains an active and thriving market across the globe. The social implications of prostitution are far-reaching and debate surrounding the issue has expanded to moral, ethical, economic, political, and public health forums. Prostitution affords unskilled women one of the best opportunities to make a living wage. While there are economic benefits of prostitution, the less tangible costs are high. Sex workers suffer inordinately from addiction, low self-esteem, and violence. In the eyes of many, prostitution is immoral, degrades women, and contributes to the spread of disease.

OVERVIEW

There are few subjects that draw a wider range of reactions than prostitution. Like its close relative pornography, prostitution is a polarizing issue. By definition, prostitution is the act of engaging in sex acts in exchange for some form of compensation, usually money. It is not entered into with the intent of procreation. As such, one could also consider prostitution "the act of rendering… non- reproductive sex against payment" (Edlund & Korn, 2002, p. 183). The terms "prostitution" and "prostitute" are controversial. Some groups, regarding these terms as stigmatizing and pejorative, prefer the terms "sex work" and "sex worker" (Masenior & Beyrer, 2007).

The sex acts prostitutes perform and the contexts in which they work and survive are far from homogenous. Table 1 illustrates the different types of prostitution and the varying and general conditions and contexts for each.

Is Prostitution Really Lucrative?

Representative data on how much prostitutes earn is not easy to obtain: transactions are mostly made on a cash basis and subject to tax evasion and under-reporting. However, overwhelming evidence shows that prostitution is a lucrative profession, especially when compared to the wages that unskilled women command in the other professions available to them. In general, women who become sex workers would likely be relegated to low-wage service sector jobs if they were to enter the traditional work force.

Research on wages earned from the early twentieth century determined that "no practicable rise in the rate of wages paid to women in ordinary industries can possibly compete with the wages which fairly attractive women of quite ordinary ability can earn by prostitution" (Ellis, 1936, p. 263, quoted in Edlund & Korn, 2002). At the time, prostitution was viewed as easier and less oppressive work than other forms of income available to women. Modern studies—including one of welfare mothers in the late 1990s—showed that prostitutes earned a higher income than

Table 1: Types of Prostitution

Street Level Prostitution	Brothels-Clubs	Escort or Call Girl Services	Mistress
Very large number of clients	Large number of clients	Fewer clients, client list is screened	One client
Work on street, in cars, or motels – not secure.	Work inside a brothel or club – workplace is monitored and more secure	Work independently or with an agency – conditions are fairly safe and clean	Likely works from her home
Very high rate of sexually transmitted diseases (STDs) – condom use is rare	High rate of STDs – condom use is optional	Lower rate of STDs – condom use more frequent to protect client and worker	Low rate of STDs – condom use is likely
Workers less healthy, tend to be older	Workers not as healthy, tend to be older	Workers are healthier and younger	Workers may be younger and more educated
Services less expensive	Services moderately expensive	Service can be very expensive	Client may contribute to living expenses or rent

other women of comparable levels of skill and education. Some researchers have hypothesized that prostitutes earn higher wages because of the inherent risk of their work. However, though not all types of prostitution carry the same risk, the pay premium remains the same across all types of prostitution (Edlund & Korn, 2002).

Career Longevity

Prostitutes earn more when they are young, an inverse of the usual career progression, which typically rewards experience and tenure. Since earning potential declines with age, prostitution is usually a short-term career when compared to other career choices. However, short-term opportunities in prostitution put women at risk of never acquiring skills that pay a living wage outside of sex work (Edlund & Korn, 2002).

FURTHER INSIGHTS

Entering & Exiting Sex Work

Prostitution is a multibillion-dollar business that employs millions of women worldwide. The profession is low skill, labor intensive, predominantly female, and well paid (Edlund & Korn, 2002). One of the major challenges for sociologists when studying prostitutes is the difficulty reaching such a "hard to access" population. Nevertheless, researchers have taken some steps toward better understand why and how women enter into sex work.

The overwhelming reason that women enter sex work is for economic gain. Prostitution is much more lucrative than the other types of work for which unskilled women are qualified. However, this factor also means that most sex workers will exit the profession when they find alternative means to financial security. For most women, leaving prostitution is rarely ever the result of a single decision. Rather, leaving sex work is usually a process that unfolds over time. The cycle of entry, exit, and re-entry is not an uncommon path for women struggling to overcome many of the factors that have precipitated their entry into prostitution (Dalla, 2006).

Globally, economic conditions and lack of opportunity for women are major factors contributing to women's entering into and remaining in prostitution. Even the threat of disease, such as HIV/AIDS, is not sufficient to keep women out of this work (Dalla, 2006). Violence is also endemic in the sex industry regardless of the type of venue: massage parlors, strip clubs, dance clubs, or escort services all carry risks. The visibility of violent acts is greater at street-level prostitution, but the violence is pervasive throughout the industry. Drug addiction and unemployment are, again, a recurring theme that continues to surface in the lives of these women (Patterson, 2007).

Street-level prostitution poses a different set of challenges for women wishing to exit sex work. Street-level prostitutes contend more often with the following factors:

- Lack of treatment for substance abuse and mental health problems;
- Fewer opportunities to secure legal work that pays a living wage;
- Fewer educational opportunities; and
- A higher risk of re-entry due to a lack of treatment, educational, and employment opportunities (Dalla, 2006).

It is difficult to obtain accurate data about the entry-exit process, but numerous cycles of exit and re-entry appear to be common. Rochelle Dalla's research regarding the exit/entry process of street-level prostitute found that:

- Residential treatment centers were shown to provide a means for sex workers to exit the profession and treat substance abuse issues in a safe, supportive environment.
- Counseling sessions from therapists or parole officers were credited with providing information and direction for women.
- The support received from significant relationships with parents, siblings, and spouses was key to a successful exit, too, as was the studied women's desire to raise their children in a positive environment.
- Achieving distance from destructive influences was also key, as was finding employment that pays a living wage.
- Affiliation with a religious institution (church) emerged as a prominent and positive influence in helping prostitutes leave the profession. As their time out of the sex industry increased, reliance on their church communities for inspiration and support increased and use of formal services slowly diminished (Dalla, 2006).

Dalla's research focused on street-level prostitutes, whose experiences can be very different from those of women engaged in other types of prostitution. Additionally, her research is complicated by the fact that her sample size was relatively small. Because of this, her findings cannot be said to represent the experiences of all street-level prostitutes. Further research on the factors influencing street-level prostitutes' desire to leave sex work will require larger sample sizes and more frequent collection of follow-up data.

The Economics of Prostitution

At the annual meeting of the American Economic Association in New Orleans in January 2008, preliminary results of a study of the economics of street prostitution were discussed. The study, titled *An Empirical Analysis of Street-Level Prostitution*, was authored by Steven Levitt, an economics professor at the University of Chicago, and Sudhir Venkatesh, a sociologist at Columbia University. Their research combined official arrest records with data on 2,200 transactions that Venkatesh collected in cooperation with sex workers in three Chicago districts. The findings offer a contemporary view of the paid sex market in a major US city:

- Nearly 50% of all transactions happened on 0.3% of street corners. The authors contended that because sex workers and clients need to be able to find each other easily, geographic concentration is likely more important for sex work than for other services where traditional marketing channels are used.
- Sex workers earned $25–30 per hour, or four times what they could expect to earn in a "legal" job.
- A 10% increase in the number of families on public assistance in a given neighborhood increased the number of prostitutes in that neighborhood by 50%.
- Prostitutes were more likely to have sex with a police officer than to be arrested by one. The authors estimated at 3% of the transactions prostitutes engaged in were done for free in order to avoid arrest (Levitt & Venkatesh, 2007).

The average work week for a sex worker was 13 hours and netted her $340.00 on average (Levitt & Venkatesh, 2007). In one Chicago neighborhood, pimps received 25% of the prostitutes' earnings regardless of whether or not they set up the transaction (Levitt & Venkatesh, 2007). Findings revealed that many workers under-reported their number of transactions and overall earnings in order to keep more money for themselves.

In the case of prostitution, indications are that as population clusters increase, business also increases. Levitt and Venkatesh (2007) found that over the July 4th holiday, business increased by 60% with only a 30% increase in prices. A flexible supply chain accommodated the increase in demand in the following ways:

- Regular prostitutes worked longer hours.
- Prostitutes were recruited from outside the area.
- Temporary sex workers took advantage of the increased business and higher wages.

One controversial finding was that prostitutes do better with pimps—they work fewer hours and are less likely to be arrested by the police or preyed on by gang members. The drawback from an economic standpoint is that pimps are limited in their ability to find customers and therefore operate on a smaller scale (Levitt & Venkatesh, 2007). The overall findings by the authors indicate that the paid sex industry is much like other business: pricing strategies are mirrored by other industries and not unique to the paid sex industry (Levitt & Venkatesh, 2007).

VIEWPOINTS

Politics & Public Health

In 2003, President George W. Bush used his State of the Union address to outline his intention to tackle the global HIV/AIDS epidemic with a $15 billion–spending plan called the President's Emergency Plan for AIDS Relief (PEPFAR). Later that year, Congress passed the United States Leadership Against Global HIV/AIDS, Tuberculosis, and Malaria Act, also known as the Leadership Act or the Global AIDS Act. Linking prostitution and sex trafficking to the spread of HIV, the act called for a worldwide effort to stamp out prostitution.

With passage of the Global AIDS Act, Congress designated seven US government agencies as "primary" implementing agencies with oversight of the government funding. Among the agencies was the US

Agency for International Development (USAID) and the US Department of Health and Human Services (HHS). Under the Global AIDS Act, grant recipients then had to meet two requirements (often called the Anti-Prostitution Pledge) in order to qualify for federal funds:

- Grantees had to publicly endorse policies that explicitly opposed prostitution and sex trafficking, and
- Exhibit certification of compliance with the "Prohibition on the Promotion and Advocacy of the Legalization or Practice of Prostitution or Sex Trafficking" (Masenior & Beyrer, 2007).

Put simply, the US Global AIDS Act barred the use of federal funds to "promote, support, or advocate the legalization or practice of prostitution." Organizations receiving US Global HIV/ AIDS funding also had to adopt specific organization-wide positions opposing prostitution ("Legal and Policy Restrictions on U.S. Global AIDS and Trafficking Funding," 2005). A 2005 directive issued by USAID required that funding for AIDS programs be given only to those organizations—both American and foreign—with policies explicitly opposing prostitution and sex trafficking ("Legal and Policy Restrictions on U.S. Global AIDS and Trafficking Funding," 2005).

Many nongovernmental agencies (NGOs) that relied on federal funding saw the US restrictions as a groundless ideological attempt to control public health policies (Masenior & Beyrer, 2007). The Center for Health and Gender Equity (CHANGE) mirrored these NGOs' opinions by declaring that "such funding restrictions follow other similar—and increasing—efforts to force organizations working in public health to comply with ideological litmus tests that often run counter to both public health practice and human rights standards" ("Legal and Policy Restrictions on U.S. Global AIDS and Trafficking Funding," 2005)

On behalf of one grantee, the Center for Public Health and Human Rights at Johns Hopkins University was asked to undertake an independent review of the scientific evidence on strategies that effectively reduce rates of HIV among sex workers (Masenior & Beyrer, 2007). One finding was that the "merging of the terms "prostitution" and "sex trafficking" in the Global AIDS Act is not accepted as standard language or practice by the scientific literature on HIV/AIDS or by international agencies with HIV prevention programs" (Masenior & Beyrer, 2007, p. 1159). The Johns Hopkins review found no grantee that did not explicitly oppose "sex trafficking" as well as unilateral condemn child prostitution (Masenior & Beyrer, 2007). From a human rights standpoint, trafficking of persons for any reason is a criminal offense with sex trafficking considered to be one of the most damaging aspects of human trafficking. However, many agencies receiving grants recognized sex workers as consenting adults who sell sex of their own volition. Some of these agencies even supported sex workers' demand for workers rights (Masenior & Beyrer, 2007).

These agencies argue that sex workers benefit from education, contraception, and basic health services, and stand to suffer from the "conflation" of sex trafficking and prostitution. They see the Global AIDS Act as a threat to public health initiatives as it forbids grantees from providing any of these services to sex workers (Masenior & Beyrer, 2007).

Five organizations filed suit over the law's restrictions in 2005, and the case eventually went before the Supreme Court, which in June 2013 overturned the Anti-Prostitution Pledge requirement. The court agreed with the plaintiffs that the law violated their First Amendment right to free speech with respect to sex work.

Morality

Like CHANGE, many agencies and advocates consider the antiprostitution pledge to be just another example of the "legislation of morality." Federal funding restrictions for HIV/AIDS are viewed by some as a way to curtail what is perceived as immoral behavior. In the view of sociologist Ron Weitzer (2006) of George Washington University, these efforts amount to "moral crusades." Weitzer explains,

> "Moral crusades arise in reaction to a perceived social problem, which they [the perceived problem's opponents] define as an unqualified evil; participants see their mission as a righteous enterprise whose goals are both symbolic (attempting to redraw or reinforce normative boundaries) and practical (aiming to crack down on evildoers and/or provide relief to victims" (2006, p. 33).

Table 2: Radical & Liberal Feminist Views of Prostitution

Radical Feminist View of Prostitution	Liberal Feminist View of Prostitution
Prostitution degrades all women as they are exploited by male hegemony and cultural norms.	Prostitution helps women earn money, and prostitutes conduct their business under their own volition.
Prostitution is inexorably linked to sex abuse and violence.	Some aspects of prostitution are positive and life affirming
Prostitution is not a victimless crime. It enables men to reduce women to sex objects and is an extension of power politics.	Prostitution is a personal right that trumps concerns for the social good.
Prostitution should be unequivocally condemned on ethical and political grounds.	Prostitution should be tolerated as a legitimate source of income. Sex workers ought to be considered independent contractors.
Critics argue that the radical view fails to consider the diversity of reasons that cause women to enter sex work.	Critics argue that the liberal view's focus on prostitutes as a socioeconomic group shortchanges examination of sex workers' diverse values and beliefs.

(Bromberg, 1997)

On the topic of prostitution, a surprising alliance has formed between conservative Christian groups and radical feminist groups. Both groups are vehemently opposed to all forms of prostitution—though for very different reasons. For religious conservatives, prostitution is a sign of moral decay and family breakdown (Weitzer, 2006). For radical feminists, prostitution is a symptom of male domination, exploitation, and violence against women, whether or not women willingly enter into the profession. As one organization, the Coalition Against Trafficking in Women, proclaimed on its website, "All prostitution exploits women, regardless of women's consent. Prostitution affects all women, justifies the sale of any woman, and reduces all women to sex" (Weitzer, 2006).

Feminist Perspectives

However, not all feminists agree with this view. While radical feminists tend to see prostitution as necessarily exploitative, liberal feminists tend adopt a more laissez-faire attitude. Table 2 provides a rough overview of how radical and liberal feminists approach the topic.

The Economics of Prostitution

A review of the sociological aspects of prostitution would not be complete without looking at the demand for the services. In 2002, economists Lena Edlund and Evelyn Korn published a controversial study called "A Theory of Prostitution."

In the study, Edlund and Korn (2002) argued that women enter prostitution as an alternative way to gain the economic rewards and security that are primarily provided to women through marriage. For the purposes of their paper, Edlund and Korn (2002) argued a prostitute sells nonreproductive sex, or "commercial sex," whereas a wife sells reproductive sex (i.e., sex plus children). According to Edlund and Korn (2002), "prostitution has an unusual feature: it is well paid despite being low skill, labor intensive, and, one might add, female dominated. Earnings even in the worst-paid type, may be several multiples of full-time earnings in professions with comparable skill requirements" (p. 182). The authors suggested that these high earnings may be due to the fact that because prostitutes cannot be wives and wives cannot be prostitutes, prostitutes need to earn a higher wage than they would through other work to compensate for the loss of the earnings that are afforded to other women through marriage (Edlund & Korn, 2002).

Marriage and prostitution are largely incompatible for a woman, Edlund and Korn (2002) argued, because men prefer wives to be faithful. This faithfulness, the authors argue, guarantees that any children born into the marriage are the husband's and also guarantees the husband's parental rights. While some prostitutes are married, the terms of marriage are likely to be less favorable than they would be for other women, Edlund and Korn (2002) claimed.

Married men constitute a small number of clients but represent a large "bulk" of demand for prostitutes, Edlund and Korn (2002) argued. However, even though married men have access to lowcost, nonreproductive sex through their wives, they still seek out prostitutes for paid sex. The fact that many men will pay for sex when they can presumable have it at "no cost" is not well understood, though Edlund and Korn (2002) offer a few theories:

- That women may be as equally inclined as men to seek out sex partners, but the opportunities they lose through social stigma dissuade them from actively pursing extramarital sex.
- Men prefer to marry younger women, but since there are more older men than there are younger women, there are limited opportunities for them to marry a younger woman. If a man cannot marry a younger woman, he may marry an older woman but seek out younger women for sex.
- Since fidelity is expected from young married women and a strong social stigma is attached to prostitution, men will seek out young prostitutes even at a high cost.

The study touched off a major controversy in academic circles. One critic especially took issue with how the authors' work implicitly assumed women and sex to be commercial goods. "The paper [A Theory of Prostitution] was remarkable....because it considered wives and whores as economic 'goods' that can be substituted for each other. Men buy, women sell," Noer (2006, para. 3) stated. Additionally, the authors assumed that all women were, or would become, either wives or prostitutes. Noer (2006) again took issue with the study, writing that "the assumption that there is no 'third way' between wife and whore is problematic, if not outright offensive" (para. 15).

But while controversial, Edlund's and Korn's assumptions are not new among economists. As Noer (2006) notes, "Economists have been equating money and marriage ever since Nobel Prizewinning economist Gary Becker published his seminal paper "A Theory of Marriage"...[which concluded that] mate selection is a market, and marriages occur only if they are profitable for both parties involved" (Noer, 2006).

CONCLUSION

Attitudes about prostitution have long vacillated between condemnation and laissez-faire (Edlund & Korn, 2002). Women enter prostitution for a number of reasons, but for most, financial necessity plays a large role. Despite its risks, sex work pays well compared to the other work for which unskilled women are qualified and, once entered into, can be difficult to exit. Billions of dollars are spent on prostitution across the globe annually, and demand for commercial sex does not appear to be waning. One may expect that until women have better economic options, they will continue to sell sex on the commercial market where demand is very strong.

TERMS & CONCEPTS

Anti-Prostitution Pledge: Conditions built into the Global AIDS Act that require grant recipients to publicly oppose prostitution and sex trafficking in order to be eligible for federal funds.

Christian Fundamentalism: A branch of evangelical Christianity that, among other beliefs, affirms the Bible's inerrancy and endorses conservative social attitudes.

Commercial Sex: The sale of sex for money. This term does not make a distinction between trafficked sex workers and voluntary sex workers.

Patriarchal Family: A type of social organization in which families are headed by a male and title is typically traced through the male line.

The President's Emergency Plan for AIDS Relief (PEPFAR): Announced in 2003, President George W. Bush's plan to tackle the global HIV/AIDS epidemic with a $15 billion–spending package.

Pimp: A man who manages a prostitute's sex transactions for a percentage of the take of the transaction.

Radical Feminism: A branch of feminism that opposes the patriarchal family system as one that leads to the oppression of women under male domination.

Street-Level Prostitution: A type of prostitution in which prostitutes solicit clients on the street. Sex workers at this level are subject to the lowest wages, highest rate of disease, and most dangerous working conditions.

Trafficking: Refers to the buying, selling, and moving people or goods in an illegal manner.

Bibliography

Bromberg, S. (1997). "Feminist issues in prostitution." http://www.feministissues.com

Clarke, R. J., Clarke, E. A., Roe-Sepowitz, D., & Fey, R. (2012). "Age at entry into prostitution: Relationship to drug use, race, suicide, education level, childhood abuse, and family experiences." *Journal of Human Behavior in the Social Environment, 22*(3), 270–289.

Cobbina, J. E., & Oselin, S. S. (2011). "It's not only for the money: An analysis of adolescent versus adult entry into street prostitution." *Sociological Inquiry, 81*(3), 310–332.

Dalla, R. (2006). "You can't hustle all your life: An exploratory investigation of the exit process among street-level prostituted women." *Psychology of Women Quarterly, 30*(3), 276–290.

Edlund, L., & Korn, E. (2002). "A theory of Prostitution." *Journal of Political Theory, 110*(11), 181–214. http://the-idea-shop.com/papers/ prostitution.pdf

Hubbard, P., & Prior, J. (2013). "Out of sight, out of mind? Prostitution policy and the health, well-being and safety of home-based sex workers." *Critical Social Policy, 33*(1), 140–159.

"Legal and policy restrictions on US Global AIDS and Trafficking funding." (2005). Center for Health and Gender Equity. http://www. healthgap.org/

Levitt, S., & Venkatesh, S. (2007). "An empirical analysis of street level prostitution." University of Chicago. http://economics.uchicago.edu/pdf/ Prostitution%205.pdf

Masenior, N., & Beyrer, C. (2007). "The US anti-prostitution pledge: First Amendment challenges and public health priorities." *PLoS Medicine, 4*(7), 1158–1161.

McCray, K., Wesely, J. K., & Rasche, C. E. (2011). "Rehab retrospect: Former prostitutes and the (re)construction of deviance." *Deviant Behavior, 32*(8), 743–768.

Noer, M. (2006, February 14). "The economics of prostitution." Forbes magazine: http:// www. forbes.com/2006/02/11/

Patterson, Margot. "Hard truths about prostitution." (2007). *National Catholic Reporter, 43*(17), 12–13.

Rosen, R., & Goldman, M. (1984). "Lost sisterhood: Prostitution in America, 1900–1918 (1982)." *Signs: Journal of Women in Culture and Society, 9*(3), 504–506.

"Selling sex." (2008, January 19). *Economist*.

Vanwesenbeeck, I. (2013). "Prostitution push and pull: Male and female perspectives." *Journal of Sex Research, 50*(1), 11–16.

Weitzer, R. (2006). "Moral crusade against prostitution." *Society, 43*(3), 33–38.

Williamson, C., & Folaron, G. (2003). "Understanding the experiences of street level prostitutes." *Qualitative Social Work, 2*(3), 271–287.

Suggested Reading

Brewer, D., Dudek, J., Potterat, J., Muth, S., Roberts, J., & Woodhouse, D. (2006). "Extent, trends, and perpetrators of prostitution-related homicide in the United States." *Journal of Forensic Sciences, 51*(5), 1101–1108.

Minichiello, V., Scott, J., & Callander, D. (2013). "New pleasures and old dangers: Reinventing male sex work." *Journal of Sex Research, 50*(3/4), 263–275.

"Morality gets a massage." (2007, May 28). *Nation, 284*(21), 3.

"Sex isn't a spectator sport." (2006). *Christianity Today, 50*(7), 20–21.

Smith, M., Grov, C., Seal, D., & McCall, P. (2013). "A socialcognitive analysis of how young men become involved in male escorting." *Journal of Sex Research, 50* (1), 1–10.

Carolyn Sprague, MLS

Structural Functionalist Theories of Gender Inequality

ABSTRACT

Structural functionalists posit that gender roles arise from the need to establish a division of labor that will help maintain the smooth running of the family and concomitantly contribute to the stability of society. In this view, girls and boys are taught different approaches to life. Boys are taught instrumentality—that is, to be goal oriented, to focus on tasks, and to be concerned for the relationship of the family to outside societal structures. Girls, on the other hand, are taught to be expressive—that is, to express their emotions and to look for and react to the emotions of others. In many ways, the functionalist perspective of gender equality is a product of its times, describing the realities of gender roles and inequalities of the 1950s but not explaining them. However, the functionalist perspective is less useful for describing the realities of gender in the postindustrial age, in which many women work outside the home, men can stay at home with the children, and everyone helps with the housework. More research is needed in order to gain a better understanding of the role of gender in twenty-first-century society and how the changing requirements of the postindustrial age affect these roles and the stability they enforce on society.

OVERVIEW

Gender inequality can be defined as the existence of disparities among individuals based solely on their gender rather than objective differences in skills, abilities, or other characteristics. Gender inequality may be obvious (e.g., not receiving the same pay for the same job) or subtle (e.g., not being given the same subjective opportunities for advancement). Although there are US federal laws in place that prohibit discrimination on the basis of sex and that require equal pay for equal work regardless of one's gender, on average, men continue to be paid more money than women in the United States. Women are also often victims of gender stratification, or the hierarchical organization of a society in such a way that members of one gender have more access to wealth, prestige, and power than do the members of the other gender. However, gender inequality is not an issue confined to the United States or other developed countries: It occurs in societies and cultures around the world. Gender inequality is a matter of social justice and human rights wherever it occurs. However, in many developing countries, it is even more so as women are marginalized and thought of as second-class citizens. In fact, gender inequality is so important that it is included in the Millennium Development Goals developed by the United Nations. While it is known that gender inequality exists, why it exists is not completely understood. As a complex issue with many underlying determinants, there are a number of different perspectives on why it occurs. It is important to investigate these differing perspectives as each provides different suggestions for solving the gender inequality problem. The structural functionalist perspective is one such view that highlights some theories as to why gender inequality occurs; these are discussed in the following paragraphs.

Structural Functionalism & Gender Inequality

Structural functionalists attempt to explain the nature of social order and the relationship between the various parts (structures) in society by examining the functionality of each to determine how it contributes to the stability of society as a whole. Although theorists using other perspectives argue that gender differentiation is bad for society in general and women in particular because it keeps women from reaching their potential and contributing fully to society, from the functionalist perspective, gender differentiation contributes to the stability of a society. Gender roles, in this view, arise from the need to establish a division of labor within the family. Because of their biological role in childbirth and breastfeeding, women in virtually every culture and society around the planet have the primary responsibility for child care. Similarly, men have traditionally had the responsibilities for hunting and waging war because of their relatively greater size and strength.

Socialization

Through the socialization process, these roles are taught to succeeding generations. Although in modern times there are other options for feeding an infant and many jobs require brain power more than muscle power, this differentiation between gender roles has become ingrained to a great degree. Through socialization, individuals learn to differentiate between what the society regards as acceptable versus unacceptable behavior and act in a manner that is appropriate for the needs of the society. The family (and, later, the larger society) begins teaching gender roles almost immediately after birth. For example, most infant girls are held more gently and treated more tenderly than are infant boys. As the child grows older, both mothers and fathers usually play more roughly with little boys than with little girls. As children, little boys are typically also allowed to roam a wider territory without permission than are little girls, and boys are typically expected to run errands earlier than are girls.

Worldview

In addition, through the socialization process, boys and girls are frequently taught different worldviews. For example, sons are typically told that "real boys don't cry" and encouraged to control their softer emotions, while girls are taught not to fight and not to show anger or aggression. Functionalists refer to these different worldviews as instrumentality and expressiveness.

- Instrumentality is a worldview that includes an emphasis on tasks, a focus on long-term goals, and concern for the relationship between one's family and other social institutions. To teach this attitude, for example, boys may be taught to be goal-oriented by encouraging them to participate in team sports in which they compete and strive to win or to build models or other long-term projects where gratification is not immediate.
- Expressiveness, on the other hand, is a worldview that includes a concern for maintaining harmony and emotional affairs internal to the family. Girls are typically taught to be more emotion-oriented (as opposed to emotional) than boys. For example, girls are often taught how to express their emotions and to look for and react to the emotions of others.

The socialization process of gender roles can be so subtle that when the disparity between the way they teach and treat their daughters and sons is pointed out to many parents, they often respond that the sexes are naturally different not only biologically but behaviorally as well. According to the functionalist perspective, these divergent ways of interacting with the world are mutually supportive. For example, by being expressive and maintaining a harmonious home and family life, women free men from such responsibilities, thereby enabling them to go out into the world and focus on long-term tasks and goals. Similarly, by men having an instrumental outlook and interacting with the larger society, women are freed to focus on creating a harmonious home and family life. Although functionalists do not suggest that such traditional gender roles are the only way in which to bring about a stable society, they posit that traditional roles do have this result.

Parsons & Bales

The functionalist perspective of gender roles with its view of expressive females and instrumental males is based on the work of Parsons and Bales in traditional societies. Part of the concern of these theorists was that if both partners in a marriage worked outside the home, competition could arise and the marriage could be threatened. As a result, they did separate spheres for men and women as a way to preserve the institution of marriage, which they believed was not well supported in urban, industrialized societies. Further, this theory arose during a time in which theories of social stratification assumed that the status of a woman was determined by the status of her husband. Postmodern, postindustrial society no longer accepts this assumption as a given.

APPLICATIONS

The Functionalist Approach within a Twenty-First-Century Framework

The functionalist perspective of division of labor concerned with instrumental and expressive gender roles was situated in 1950s America, where such traditional roles were de rigueur. In many ways, this perspective of gender roles is a product of its time and, perhaps, less appropriate in the twenty-first-century context, where girls are taught to be goal oriented and participate in sports and boys are taught that it is acceptable to express their emotions. Further, if the functionalist perspective of gender role differentiation were correct, it would be reasonable to expect that all girls and women would be interested in babies and either want to be mothers or to work with children. However, as increasing numbers of women who choose to remain single and childless shows, this is not true.

Similarly, boys and men can lack interest in hard-driving, high-powered roles as executives in the workplace and prefer to work in more expressive endeavors and spend time with their children. If the structural functionalist perspective were followed to its logical conclusion, such a common class of individuals would be forced into roles for which they were not well-suited, thereby negatively affecting their emotional and psychological well-being. Further, although the functionalist perspective attempts to explain the pervasiveness of traditional gender roles, it does not well explain why males should be instrumental and females should be expressive. Similarly, the functionalist perspective does not take into account other cultures in which females are instrumental and males are expressive.

Changing Family Structure & Gender Roles

Hare-Mustin (1988) underscores one of the weaknesses of the functionalist perspective of gender in her discussion of family change and gender differences. She points out that the functionalist view of gender continues to emphasize the separate roles for men and women despite the changing nature of the family in Western society in the late twentieth and early twenty-first centuries. Traditionally, most families were patriarchal in nature with a hierarchical structure in which the husband was the head of the household. In such traditional settings, the value of women to the family was their ability to bear and nurture children; the primary value of the children was for their contribution to the family production and, eventually, as caregivers to their aging parents. Family organization was based on specialization by age and gender, predicated on the belief that different types of family members (e.g., males vs. females; young vs. old) were better suited for different kinds of work. In many ways, this specialization was self-sustaining: Men typically disliked doing traditional "women's work" (e.g., housecleaning, doing the dishes, cooking) and women disliked doing traditional "men's work" (e.g., mowing the lawn, fixing the car, paying the bills). However, with the advent of modernization, traditional gender roles began to change. With industrialization, many people sought work in offices, factories, and other organizations, and the home became no longer the center of production. As women began to become an increasingly significant part of the workforce, many women found themselves in a position of either having to renegotiate gender roles or find themselves working a "second shift" as career women in the office and housewives in the home.

Developed vs. Developing Societies

Further, although the historical norms regarding the division of labor between the sexes are similar across cultures, they are based on the needs and realities of less developed societies. To a great extent, these norms are changing in more developed societies. Women are no longer confined by their biology to be physically present with an infant to feed it and ensure its survival. Not only can this task be taken on by other women (e.g., nannies, preschool teachers), but by men as well. Similarly, many of the jobs in industrial and postindustrial societies do not require the physical strength necessary in hunter-gather societies in order to successfully provide for one's family. Jobs in information and service industries, for example, require little more physical strength than the ability to sit up in front of a computer and rely on brain power, not physical power.

Gender Equality at Work & Home

As women earn more gender equality in the workplace, they also tend to look for more gender equality in the home as well. This attitude frequently affects the division of labor for domestic responsibilities. Many postmodern men no longer see housework as "women's work" and have no problem vacuuming the living room or doing the dishes, while the wife pays the bills or finishes writing a document for work. In both cases, the jobs needed for the smooth running of the home get accomplished. Although functionalists posit that traditional gender roles are important for the stability of society, it can be argued that the stability of society depends on the tasks of the various roles being accomplished, not on who accomplishes them. As more women participate in the workforce not only in traditional support roles but in those roles that were once thought to be the sole domain of men, they find that they need different skills and attitudes than are needed for the care of hearth and home. To be a high-level executive in a major corporation, for example, does not require a woman to be expressive. Rather, it requires a goal-oriented, instrumental orientation.

Further, not every woman is married. For some, this is a choice: An increasing number of women are choosing to not get married but to focus on their careers instead. In addition, the high rate of divorce—approximately half of marriages end in separation, divorce, or annulment in the United States—means that a high number of women voluntarily or involuntarily no longer have a man to take the instrumentalist role in the household. Further, increasingly, neither group of women is tending to return to their parents to live but are instead setting up their own households as female head. In these situations, when a woman finds herself in the situation where she is responsible for both the goal-oriented tasks as well as the emotional ones, the gender role is expanded to include both expressiveness and instrumentality so that both the household tasks and the child care tasks are accomplished.

CONCLUSION

The functionalist perspective of gender roles with its expressive females and instrumental males is a product of its times and its assumptions. Certainly, traditional gender roles in most societies are based on a division of labor in which women stay home and attend to hearth and family, while men go out (whether it be to the hunting ground, agricultural fields, or modern office) and earn a living. However, both for the sake of society and for the sake of the individual and family, it is important that gender roles be flexible so that they can be adapted to changing times of a society, different needs of a family or families, and individual variations in personality and proclivities. It can be argued that the functionalist perspective of gender roles and the concomitant gender inequality that it yields is a description rather than an explanation. Although functionalists do not necessarily imply that traditional gender role paradigms are the only—or even the best—way to ensure the stability of society, they also do not offer alternatives nor do they well consider the changing needs of postindustrial societies. The functionalist perspective was good as far as it went, describing the reality of most families in the United States of the 1950s and reflecting the assumptions of stratification theorists of that time and place. However, the times have changed and the functionalist perspective no longer adequately describes—let alone explains—the realities of contemporary gender roles and gender inequality. More research is needed in order to gain a better understanding of the role of gender in postmodern society and how the changing requirements of the postindustrial age affect these roles and the stability they affect on society.

TERMS & CONCEPTS

Economic Development: The sustainable increase in living standards for a nation, region, or society. More than mere economic growth (i.e., a rise in output), economic development is sustainable and positively affects the well-being of all members of the group through such things as increased per capita income, education, health, and environmental protection. Economic development is progressive in nature and positively affects the socioeconomic structure of a society.

Expressiveness: A worldview that includes a concern for maintaining harmony and emotional affairs internal to the family.

Functionalism: A theoretical framework used in sociology that attempts to explain the nature of social order and the relationship between the various parts (structures) in society by examining the functionality of each to determine how it contributes to the stability of society as a whole. Also referred to as structural functionalism.

Gender: Psychological, social, cultural, and behavioral characteristics associated with being female or male. Gender is defined by one's gender identity and learned gender role.

Gender Inequality: Disparities among individuals based solely on their gender rather than objective differences in skills, abilities, or other characteristics. Gender inequalities may be obvious (e.g., not receiving the same pay for the same job) or subtle (e.g., not being given the same subjective opportunities for advancement).

Gender Role: Separate patterns of personality traits, mannerisms, interests, attitudes, and behaviors that are regarded as "male" and "female" by one's culture. Gender role is largely a product of the way in which one was socialized and may not be in conformance with one's gender identity.

Gender Stratification: The hierarchical organization of a society in such a way that members of one gender have more access to wealth, prestige, and power than do the members of the other gender.

Industrialization: The use of mechanization to produce the economic goods and services within a society. Historically, industrialization is a society's transition between farm production and manufacturing production. Industrialization is associated with factory production, division of labor, and the concentration of industries and populations within certain geographical areas and concomitant urbanization.

Instrumentality: A worldview that includes an emphasis on tasks, a focus on long-term goals, and concern for the relationship between one's family and other social institutions.

Patriarchy: A social system (e.g., society or group) in which the male is the head of the family, descent may be traced through the father's side of the family, and men have power over women.

Postindustrial: The nature of a society whose economy is no longer dependent on the manufacture of goods (i.e., industrial) but is primarily based upon the processing and control of information and the provision of services.

Social Stratification: A relatively fixed hierarchical organization of a society in which entire subgroups are ranked according to social class. These divisions are marked by differences in economic rewards and power within the society and different access to resources, power, and perceived social worth. Social stratification is a system of structured social inequality.

Socialization: The process by which individuals learn to differentiate between what the society regards as acceptable versus unacceptable behavior and act in a manner that is appropriate for the needs of the society.

Society: A distinct group of people who live within the same territory, share a common culture and way of life, and are relatively independent from people outside the group. Society includes systems of social interactions that govern both culture and social organization.

Worldview: Broad framework of ideas and beliefs used by an individual, class, or culture to interpret the data received from the world and determine the appropriate way of interacting with the world.

BIBLIOGRAPHY

Baker, J. K., Fenning, R. M., & Crnic, K. A. (2011). "Emotion socialization by mothers and fathers: Coherence among behaviors and associations with parent attitudes and children's social competence." *Social Development,* 20, 412–430.

Flather, A. J. (2013). "Space, place, and gender: The sexual and spatial division of labor in the early modern household." *History & Theory,* 52, 344–360.

Hare-Mustin, R. T. (1988). "Family change and gender differences: Implications for theory and practice." *Family Relations,* 37, 36–41.

Schaefer, R. T. (2002). *Sociology: A brief introduction* (4th ed.). Boston: McGraw-Hill.

Zalta, A. K., & Chambless, D. L. (2012). "Understanding gender differences in anxiety: The mediating effects of instrumentality and mastery." *Psychology of Women Quarterly,* 36, 488–499.

SUGGESTED READING

Fulcher, J., & Scott, J. (2003). "Theories and theorizing: Sociology moves on." In *Sociology* (2nd ed.; pp. 63–71). New York: Oxford University Press.

Hall, M. A. (1988). "The discourse of gender and sport: From femininity to feminism." *Sociology of Sport Journal,* 5, 330–340.

Lorber, J. (2011). *Gender inequality: Feminist theories and politics.* Oxford, England: Oxford University Press.

Rice, J. K. (1994). "Reconsidering research on divorce, family life cycle, and the meaning of family." *Psychology of Women Quarterly, 18*, 559–584.

Sperling, S. (1991). "Baboons with briefcases: Feminism, functionalism, and sociobiology in the evolution of primate gender." *Signs,* 17, 1–27.

Stanworth, C. (2000). "Women and work in the information age." *Gender, Work and Organizations,* 7, 20–32.

Szelényi, S., & Olvera, J. (1996)."The declining significance of class: Does gender complicate the story? Comments." *Theory and Society,* 25, 725–530.

Wharton, A. S. (2012). *The sociology of gender: An introduction to theory and research* (2nd ed.). Malden, MA: Wiley.

Ruth A. Wienclaw, Ph.D.

Teen Pregnancy

ABSTRACT

Teen pregnancy and resulting births pose many societal challenges, and as a result require the collective efforts of many to provide solutions. Teen pregnancy has been considered a "social ill" for centuries in the United States and has always challenged moral and ethical sensibilities. The economic costs of teens giving birth are significant, and there are many compelling reasons to reduce the teen pregnancy. Research shows that reducing the number of births to teens and increasing the age at which a women gives birth yields significant cost savings for the public sector. Efforts to reduce teen pregnancy are mainly focused on prevention and sex education is a large part of the effort. Current sex education programs focus on two main strategies, they are: abstinence only education and abstinence plus education. Abstinence only teaches that abstaining from sexual activity is the only truly effective way to prevent unintended pregnancy. Abstinence plus education focuses on delaying the initiation of sexual activity and recommends the use of contraception if a teen is sexually active. The success of abstinence only education has been exaggerated according to many sociologists and researchers. Scientific research indicates that abstinence plus education is actually much more effective in preventing teen pregnancy. Solving the problem of teen pregnancy has largely been relegating to treating the symptoms of the problem and employing prevention strategies aimed at young women. Sociologists believe that reducing the rate of teen pregnancy will require developing more comprehensive and holistic solutions in the future. Researchers, teachers, parents and community leaders are recommending and developing programs that focus on the role of boys and young men in the teen pregnancy puzzle. Current research indicates that involving boys and young men in "male only" sex education may help to significantly reduce the rate of teen pregnancy over the coming years. The effectiveness of approaching the teen pregnancy problem from holistic or system-wide view will be documented in future research.

OVERVIEW

Teen pregnancy is largely regarded as a societal problem that is most effectively dealt with through prevention strategies. However, some researchers argue that the discrepancies between the realities of teen pregnancy and the strategies for its prevention hinder the issue from being adequately addressed on a holistic level (Kohili & Nyberg, 1995). Cultural and political attitudes toward sexuality may also hinder the formulation of a concerted effort toward confronting the problem of teen pregnancy. Instead, policy makers, educators, researchers, and parents have generally focused on preventing teen pregnancy itself rather than on addressing the societal influences that may encourage teen pregnancy. Variables such as the age at which a teen first engages in sexual intercourse and the use or non-use of contraception can all predict the likelihood of a teen becoming pregnant. However, both of these variables are in turn influenced by a number of societal indicators such as peer pressure, pro-social values, parent-child communication, and self esteem (Kohili & Nyberg, 1995).

Young, unwed women have been giving birth for centuries. The "objective conditions" around teen births have not changed significantly over time. However, changes in the language associated with the issue illustrate significant shifts in the subjective perception of "teen pregnancy" throughout history (Luker, 1997).

In the Colonial era, women who gave birth outside of wedlock were called "fallen women" and considered to be sinners. The children born out of wedlock were "bastards" or "illegitimate." The economic impact of these children and their mothers were a pressing social concern: without a husband's support, unwed mothers and their children might need to become wards of the state. During the Progressive era of the early 1900s a more compassionate attitude toward unwed women and their children evolved. Unplanned pregnancies were no longer considered a moral or economic problem, but rather "a societal problem, an index of what was wrong with society" (Luker, 1997, p. 20). A stigma has long been associated with giving birth out of wedlock, and the fear and shame that went along with bearing illegitimate children kept the number of unmarried births low until relatively recent decades. Today, many sociologists admit that the stigma is largely gone, and that its disappearance has had at least some relation to the increase in teen sexual activity and pregnancy. (Kohili & Nyberg, 1995)

The Economic Cost of Teen Pregnancy

Though teen pregnancy rates declined by 36 percent from 1990–2002 and by 33 percent among girls aged fifteen to nineteen from 1991–2004; as of 2013 the teen pregnancy rate in the United States is still the highest of all the industrialized nations. Children born to teens are very likely to grow up in single parent households, and poverty in households that are headed by single women is between four and five times more severe than in households headed by married couples (Haskins & Sawhill, 2007). According the Haskins & Sawhill, "reversing the trend toward single-parent families would have an immediate effect in reducing poverty rates. But perhaps more important, it would also have a long-term effect on children's growth and development" (p. 4).

The age of a woman when she has her first child has a significant impact on the public sector costs associated with the birth. The younger the mother is, the higher the net cost of the birth (Hoffman, 2006). A 2006 report, *By the Numbers: The Public Costs of Teen Childbearing*, and a 2013 report, *Counting It Up: The Public Costs of Teen Childbearing* (both released by the National Campaign to Prevent Teen and Unplanned Pregnancy), both attempted to calculate the relative costs associated with births to teens. The former report describes the methodology which both use:

> The cost estimates provided in this report are based on a very conservative research approach that only includes costs that can be *confidently* attributed to teen childbearing itself rather than to other traits or disadvantages that often accompany teen childbearing (such as poverty) (Hoffman, 2006, p. 3).

By the Numbers calculated the costs in two areas: costs associated with the mother and her partner and costs associated with the children of teen mothers. Public sector costs associated with teen mothers and partners are calculated primarily as loss of tax revenue due to lower lifetime earnings. Public sector costs associated with children of teens include publicly provided healthcare, foster care, and child welfare services. The more indirect costs incurred by children who are born to teens often show up as incarceration costs and lost tax revenue due to the children's lower earnings (Hoffman, 2006).

Sociologist's goals in reviewing these net costs associated with teen births is to "make apparent the economic value of preventing early pregnancy" (Hoffman, 2006, p. 3) Delaying the age of first birth saves significant money in the public sector because teens who have children frequently rely on social services for support and, over their lifetimes, pay lower taxes (Hoffman, 2006) The primary goal is to measure the costs that could be averted if today's mothers delay their first birth until their early 20s (Hoffman, 2006).

The total cost as estimated in the 2013 report was $9.4 billion, with an average annual cost to taxpayers of $1,682 per child until the age of fifteen. While this number is still quite high, it is lower than the amount estimated in the previous report due to the continuing decline in teen pregnancies.

Teen pregnancy declined by about one-third between 1991 and 2009, consequently reducing the number of children in poverty; by 2013 the rate of teen pregnancy was still declining. Trends in teen sexual activity and contraceptive use suggest that a combination of existing policies and changes in the larger culture have produced reductions since the early 1990s (Haskins & Sawhill, 2007).

Between 2010 and 2011 there was an additional drop of 8 percent for babies born to mothers between the ages of fifteen and nineteen. Birth rates fell by 11 percent for mothers between the ages of fifteen and seventeen.

Sociologists are eager to identify programs and policies that successfully reduce the number of teen pregnancies. A great many programs focus on preventing teen pregnancy; however, this essay will not attempt to provide a comprehensive review of all of them. Instead, it will discuss research surrounding sex education, namely abstinence only education and abstinence plus education. The discussion surrounding sex education will focus not only on current research findings, but also on the veracity of the research that has produced different and often conflicting results. Finally, this essay will discuss programs that focus on the role of boys and young men in teen pregnancy prevention. Research reveals that involving boys and young men in the decision making process surrounding teen sex, contraception, and the responsibility of parenthood are serving to address teen pregnancy from a more holistic view.

APPLICATIONS

Prevention Programs

Prevention of teen pregnancy through sex education has largely focused on two strategies: the first concentrates on teaching teens abstinence only, while the second encourages teens to both delay sexual activity and, if they do choose to become sexually active, to use contraception.

Researchers are still exploring the effectiveness of abstinence only programs. In 2001 the National Campaign to Prevent Teen Pregnancy published a study titled *Emerging Answers: Research Findings on Programs to Reduce Teen Pregnancy* . The report, which reviewed a number of programs designed to reduce teen pregnancy by delaying the initiation of sex and increasing use of contraception, stated that "the evidence is not conclusive about the impact of abstinence-only programs," and that "there do not currently exist any abstinence-only programs with reasonably strong evidence that they actually delay the initiation of sex or reduce its frequency." (Kirby, 2002a, p. 8)

A year after *Emerging Answers* was published, Robert Rector, a Senior Research Fellow at the Heritage Foundation, published *The Effectiveness of Abstinence Education Programs in Reducing Sexual Activity Among Youth* . Rector's study pointed to 10 studies of abstinence only programs found to be effective in reducing teen pregnancy and concluded that "abstinence education programs for youth have been proven to be effective in reducing early sexual activity," (Rector, as quoted in Kirby, 2002b, p. 1).

The different conclusions reached by the two studies prompted sociologist Doug Kirby to embark on his own review of the 10 studies from the Heritage study. Kirby teamed with The Effective Programs and Research Task Force (EPR) of the National Campaign to Prevent Teen Pregnancy to established criteria by which research could be objectively reviewed. Kirby (2002b) and his team determined that in order for the programs to be considered scientifically valid, they needed to meet the following criteria:

- "The study must have used an appropriate and valid experimental or quasi-experimental design" (p. 2)
- "Post-intervention data must have been collected for a minimum number of months after the intervention"
- "Have a sample size of at least 100 and must measure actual behavior"
- "The study must have employed proper statistical analysis" (Kirby, 2002, p. 2)

These same criteria were used to determine if a study qualified for inclusion in Kirby's *Emerging Answers* report.

Results & Validity of Abstinence Only Research

According to Kirby, 9 of the 10 programs identified as "successful" by the Heritage study failed to provide "credible evidence" that the programs caused teens to delay sexual activity or reduce their sexual activity (Kirby, 2002b). Further, Kirby argued that the 10 studies in the Heritage report were not representative of all the studies on abstinence only programs. Rather, he claimed, they were selected because they showed positive outcomes whereas many other studies were inconclusive or showed negative outcomes (Kirby, 2002b). Kirby concluded that, "It seems likely... that sooner or later studies will produce strong evidence that some abstinence-only programs are effective at delaying sex and that others are not. However, until needed research is completed, we won't know which programs delay the initiation of sex, nor will we know whether they affect contraceptive use and teen pregnancy" (Kirby, 2002, p. 6). Other research concurs with Kirby's findings. According to AbstinencePlus, abstinence only programs have not yet been proven in preventing teen pregnancy and may in fact provide teens with misleading information (2005).

Abstinence Plus or Comprehensive Sex Education

Abstinence Plus programs encourage abstinence as the first and best choice, yet also encourage young people to use contraception if they do have sex. Sometimes called comprehensive sexuality education, Abstinence Plus programs outline a hierarchical approach to reducing teen pregnancy which includes abstinence or delay of sex, and information about contraception, HIV, and STDs.

Research on these programs has shown that, overall, their outcomes are positive. One 2008 report by the National Campaign to Prevent Teen and Unplanned Pregnancy indicated that 66 percent of the studied abstinence programs positively affected teens' sexual behavior ("Sex Ed Programs Actually Can Work"). They were shown to help teens delay sexual activity as well as use contraception; additionally, there was little evidence demonstrating that the programs caused teens to become sexually active sooner or engage in sexual activity more often ("Sex Ed Programs Actually Can Work", 2008).

The Need for Prevention Programs

Though policy makers, parents, and researchers may continue to debate which prevention programs ought to be implemented, they are all in agreement that some type of program is needed. Amato and Maynard claimed in 2007 that

- If teens aged 12 to 19 were to delay their first intercourse by an average of one year, it would lower their risk of pregnancy by 9%
- This delay would in turn lower the number of teen births by 24%
- If half of the teens not using contraception were to begin doing so, the number of births to teen parents would decline by 14% (Haskins & Sawhill, 2007).

They advise that, "ideally, the federal government would provide districts with tested curriculum models that emphasize both abstinence and the use of contraception" (Haskins & Sawhill, 2007, p. 11). Further, they recommend the following guidelines to support comprehensive sex education:

- Start sex education in middle school and enforce a message about the challenges of parenthood for unmarried teens and young adults.
- Enlist school systems, parents, and community groups to help educate teens about all methods to prevent unintended pregnancies.
- Ensure that young people understand that pregnancy is preventable, and that it has significant costs for the mother, the father, and the child, as well as society in general. (Haskins & Sawhill, 2007)

ISSUES

Role of Boys in Preventing Teen Pregnancy

Efforts to reduce teen pregnancy have traditionally focused on girls, but researchers are speculating that targeting teen boys and young men can have significant effects on preventing teen pregnancy as well. Boys and young men have for too long been a "neglected piece of the teen pregnancy puzzle" argues Hutchins (1999, p. 59). Involving boys and young men as the "other half" of the issue may prove to be a key part of effective pregnancy prevention.

In 1999 study *Involving Teen Boys and Young Men in Teen Pregnancy Prevention,* was one of the studies to examine what types of male-only programs are most successful reaching young men and boys with a consistent and effective message about their role in teen pregnancy. The study recommended a number of programs and strategies that were showing success in educating and involving boys in teen pregnancy prevention:

- Developing education modules to teach young men and boys about responsible fatherhood
- Implementing community based programs that are led by male staff.

- Having health clinics target men with information about contraception.
- Casting a wider net to reach boys who may be in nontraditional schools, be dropouts, or be incarcerated (Hutchins, 1999).

A 2006 study *It's a Guy Thing: Boys, Young Men, and Teen Pregnancy Prevention* found that many of the strategies recommended in Hutchins' report have proved to be effective in helping to reduce unwanted teen pregnancies. *It's a Guy Thing* looked back at nearly a decade of research and statistics to identify best practices for involving boys and young men in further reducing instances of teen pregnancy. A number of emerging trends were revealed in the 2006 study which indicated that "there have been dramatic shifts in the sexual behavior of boys" (Marsiglio, Ries, Sonenstein, Troccoli, & Whitehead, 2006, p. 1). The report found that fewer boys are having sex, that condom use has increased, and that boys are reporting having had fewer sexual partners. However, the researchers admitted that they know much more about how girls' attitudes and behaviors affect trends related to sex than they do about boys'. They concluded that further research is needed to prove that boy's attitudes and behaviors are responsible for the positive trends found in the study (Marsiglio, Ries, Sonenstein, Troccoli, & Whitehead, 2006).

Still, the suggested positive outcomes of these programs have lead to an increased interest in implementing them. The authors of *It's a Guy Thing* encourage the following approaches when creating "male only" programs.

- Make initiatives welcoming and engaging for young men; have male only services and employ male staff.
- Establish a trusting environment and foster rapport with young men and boys.
- Make the messages about teen pregnancy positive rather than punitive. Focus on the overall meaning of fatherhood through discussions of the emotional support and parental involvement it requires rather than just the financial aspect.
- Tailor programs to specific populations by age, ethnicity, and socio-economic background.
- Making connections between pregnancy and other issues is important. Emphasize the importance of education and the future attainments that boys can achieve by delaying fatherhood.
- Involve parents—both mothers and fathers—in prevention programs. Help parents communicate with their children and give them consistent messages.
- Creative outreach programs work best. One size doesn't fit all, and success can come from a variety of outreach methods. (Marsiglio, Ries, Sonenstein, Troccoli, & Whitehead, 2006)

CONCLUSION

In 2011 teenage pregnancy cost approximately $10.9 billion in such areas as child health care, foster care, public assistance, lost tax revenue, and even involvement in the criminal justice system; in 2013, it cost approxminately $9.4 billion. Total cost to society resulting from teen births puts costs at double the figures given above-and can be attributed to loss of tax revenue associated with lower earning potential, lower educational attainment and increase chance of contact with the criminal justice system. Teens who give birth make up a large proportion of single parent households. Research shows that "reversing the rate of single parent households would have a very positive effect on children by reducing poverty rates (Haskins & Sawhill, 2007).

Research regarding the success of abstinence only programs claims that many of these programs are effective in reducing teen pregnancy. However, claims about the success of these programs have not been substantiated when rigorous scientific research principals are applied. Abstinence Plus programs encourage teens to delay of initiation of sex and provide teens and young adults with comprehensive information regarding contraception and other pregnancy and disease prevention techniques. Abstinence Plus programs have been proven to be successful in reducing teen pregnancies.

Many of the social programs highlighted throughout this article have shown sound statistical evidence that when implemented correctly, can reduce the rate of teen pregnancy. The costs of the social programs outlined are expensive, but "poverty is expensive too: it drains resources from the nation while simultaneously depriving it of human capital that would increase productivity and reduce social problems" (Haskins & Sawhill, 2007).

TERMS & CONCEPTS

Abstinence Only: Refer to sex education that teaches that abstaining from sex is the only reliable means to prevent unintended pregnancies.

Abstinence Plus: These programs encourage teens to delay initiation of sexual activity, but also provide information about contraception if a teen is sexually active.

Comprehensive Sexuality Education: See also Abstinence Plus.

Non-Marital Births: Refer to all births to single mothers and not just to teenage mothers.

Public Sector Costs: Refers to costs associated with federal, state, local agencies-as well as taxpayers.

Punitive: Refer to actions that denote punishment.

Teen Childbearing: In the literature refers to teens 17 or under or those who have not completed their primary education (high school).

Bibliography

"Abstinence Plus Basic Information." (2005) http://www.abstinenceplus.info/resources_ basicinformation.php Teen births cost U.S. taxpayers $10 billion. (2011).

Contemporary Sexuality, 45(8), 7.

Grose, R. G., Grabe, S., & Kohfeldt, D. (2014). "Sexual education, gender ideology, and youth sexual empowerment." *Journal of Sex Research, 51*(7), 742–753.

Haskins, R, & Sawhill, I (2007) "Introducing the Issue." *Future of Children.* http://www. futureofchildren.org/usr_doc/7_01_Intro.pdf

Hoffman, S. (2006). *By the Numbers: The Public Costs of Teen Childbearing.* Washington, DC: National Campaign to Prevent Teen Pregnancy. http://www. teenpregnancy.org/

Huang, C., Costeines, J., Kaufman, J., & Ayala, C. (2014). "Parenting stress, social support, and depression for ethnic minority adolescent mothers: Impact on child development." *Journal of Child and Family Studies, 23*(2), 255–262.

Hutchins, J. (1999) *Involving Teen Boys and Young Men in Teen Pregnancy Prevention.* U.S. Department of Health and Human Services. http://aspe.hhs.gov/

Kirby, D. (2002). *Do Abstinence-Only Programs Delay the Initiation of Sex Among Young People and Reduce Teen Pregnancy?* Washington, DC: National Campaign to Prevent Teen Pregnancy. http://www. teenpregnancy.org/resources/research/reports.asp

Kohili, V, & Nyberg, K (1995) "Teen Pregnancy Prevention Through Education." CSU.edu: http://www.csus.edu/calst/government_affairs/reports/Teen_Pregnancy_Prevention_Through_Education. pdf

Luker, K. (1997) *Dubious Conceptions: The Politics of Teenage Pregnancy.* Cambridge, Mass.: Harvard University Press, 1966.

Marsiglio,W., Ries, A., Sonenstein, F., Troccoli, K. & Whitehead,W. (2006). *It's a Guy Thing: Boys, Young Men, and Teen Pregnancy Prevention* . Washington, DC: National Campaign to Prevent Teen Pregnancy: http://www.teenpregnancy.org/

Sex Ed Programs Actually Can Work. (2008). *USA Today Magazine.*

Sisson, G. (2012). "Finding a way to offer something more: Reframing teen pregnancy prevention." *Sexuality Research & Social Policy: Journal Of NSRC, 9*(1), 57–69.

Weber, J. (2012). "Becoming teen fathers: Stories of teen pregnancy, responsibility, and masculinity." *Gender & Society, 26*(6), 900–921.

Suggested Reading

Ayadi, M., Kuo, T., Adams, E., & Gavin, N. I. (2012). "Contraceptive use among medicaid-covered teens and risk of teen conception: A longitudinal study." *Journal Of Women's Health (15409996), 21*(2), 146–153.

Chen, C., Yamada, T., & Walker, E. M. (2011). "Estimating the cost-effectiveness of a classroom-based abstinence and pregnancy avoidance program targeting preadolescent sexual risk behaviors." *Journal Of Children & Poverty, 17*(1), 87–109.

Girma, S., & Paton, D. (2013). "Does parental consent for birth control affect underage pregnancy rates? The case of Texas." *Demography, 50*(6), 2105–2128.

Kotz, D. (2007). "A Debate About Teaching Abstinence." *U.S. News & World Report, 142* (23), 28-28.

McCave, E. (2007). "Comprehensive Sexuality Education vs. Abstinence-Only Sexuality Education: The Need for Evidence-Based Research and Practice." *School Social Work Journal, 32* (1), 14-28.

Samuels, C. (2006). A"bstinence Programs Lack Factual Reviews, GAO Study Concludes." *Education Week, 26* (13), 11-11.

Carolyn Sprague, MLS

Index